# BUSINESS FINANCE
## SIXTH EDITION

# BUSINESS FINANCE

## SIXTH EDITION

**GRAHAM PEIRSON** *Monash University*
**RON BIRD** *Westpac Investment Services*
**ROB BROWN** *Monash University*
**PETER HOWARD** *Monash University*

**McGRAW-HILL BOOK COMPANY** Sydney
New York San Francisco Auckland Bogotá
Caracas Lisbon London Madrid Mexico City
Milan Montreal New Delhi San Juan
Singapore Tokyo Toronto

First published 1972
Second edition 1977
Reprinted 1979 (twice)
Third edition 1981
Reprinted 1981, 1982, 1983 (twice)
Fourth edition 1985
Reprinted 1986, 1987 (twice), 1989
Fifth edition 1990
Reprinted 1991, 1992 (three times), 1993

Copyright © 1995 Graham Peirson, Rob Brown, Peter Howard, McGraw-Hill Book Company

Apart from any fair dealing for the purposes of study, research, criticism or review, as permitted under the *Copyright Act*, no part may be reproduced by any process without written permission. Enquiries should be made to the publisher, marked for the attention of the Permissions Editor, at the address below.

**Copying for educational purposes**
Under the copying provisions of the *Copyright Act*, copies of parts of this book may be made by an educational institution. An agreement exists between the Copyright Agency Limited (CAL) and the relevant educational authority (Department of Education, university, TAFE, etc.) to pay a licence fee for such copying. It is not necessary to keep records of copying except where the relevant educational authority has undertaken to do so by arrangement with the Copyright Agency Limited.

For further information on the CAL licence agreements with educational institutions, contact the Copyright Agency Limited, Level 19, 157 Liverpool Street, Sydney NSW 2000. Where no such agreement exists, the copyright owner is entitled to claim payment in respect of any copies made.

Enquiries concerning copyright in McGraw-Hill publications should be directed to the Permissions Editor at the address below.

---

**National Library of Australia Cataloguing-in-Publication data:**

Business finance.

   6th ed.
   Includes index.
   ISBN 0 07 470108 8.

   1. Business enterprises—Finance. 2. Cash management. 3. Corporations—Finance. I. Peirson, Graham, Date

658.15

---

Published in Australia by
**McGraw-Hill Book Company Australia Pty Limited**
**4 Barcoo Street, Roseville NSW 2069, Australia**
Typeset in Australia by Midland Typesetters Pty Ltd
Printed in Australia by McPherson's Printing Group

Sponsoring Editor:   Andrew Stammer
Supervising Editor:   Caroline Hunter
Designer:   Peter Hargreave
Cover Illustrator:   Robin Board

# CONTENTS

About the authors ........................................................... v
Preface to the Sixth Edition .............................................. vii
Chapter 1 INTRODUCTION ............................................. 1
Chapter 2 CONSUMPTION, INVESTMENT AND THE CAPITAL MARKET ........................................ 13
Chapter 3 THE TIME VALUE OF MONEY: AN INTRODUCTION TO FINANCIAL MATHEMATICS ............... 29
    *Appendix 3.1* The use of calculators with $Y^x$ function .... 73
Chapter 4 APPLYING THE TIME VALUE OF MONEY TO SECURITY VALUATION ................................. 76
    *Appendix 4.1* Duration and immunisation ...................... 98
Chapter 5 PROJECT EVALUATION: PRINCIPLES AND METHODS .................................................. 107
Chapter 6 PORTFOLIO THEORY AND ASSET PRICING ........... 134
Chapter 7 THE CAPITAL MARKET ..................................... 172
    *Appendix 7.1* Australian banks ....................................... 189
    *Appendix 7.2* Regulation of Australian banks ................. 191
    *Appendix 7.3* Authorised short-term money market dealers ......................................................... 194
Chapter 8 SOURCES OF SHORT-TERM DEBT .......................... 195
Chapter 9 SOURCES OF LONG-TERM FINANCE: EQUITY ....... 213
Chapter 10 SOURCES OF LONG-TERM FINANCE: DEBT ........... 232

| | Chapter 11 | DIVIDEND DECISIONS | 255 |
|---|---|---|---|
| | | *Appendix 11.1* The dividend imputation tax system | 286 |
| | Chapter 12 | CAPITAL STRUCTURE DECISIONS: THEORY | 292 |
| | | *Appendix 12.1* Capital structure and taxes: the effects of the imputation system | 330 |
| | Chapter 13 | CAPITAL STRUCTURE DECISIONS: PRACTICE | 335 |
| | Chapter 14 | CAPITAL MARKET EFFICIENCY | 361 |
| | Chapter 15 | FUTURES CONTRACTS | 408 |
| | Chapter 16 | OPTIONS AND CONTINGENT CLAIMS | 454 |
| Wk 8,9 | Chapter 17 | THE COST OF CAPITAL | 502 |
| | | *Appendix 17.1* The cost of capital under alternative tax systems | 533 |
| Wk 4,5 | Chapter 18 | THE APPLICATION OF PROJECT EVALUATION METHODS | 543 |
| Wk 10 | Chapter 19 | LEASING AND EQUIPMENT FINANCE | 603 |
| | Chapter 20 | ANALYSIS OF TAKEOVERS | 633 |
| | Chapter 21 | INTERNATIONAL FINANCE MANAGEMENT | 670 |
| Wk 11 | Chapter 22 | MANAGEMENT OF SHORT-TERM ASSETS: AN INTRODUCTION | 720 |
| Wk 11 | Chapter 23 | INVENTORY MANAGEMENT | 726 |
| Wk 12 | Chapter 24 | LIQUIDITY MANAGEMENT | 744 |
| Wk 13 | Chapter 25 | ACCOUNTS RECEIVABLE MANAGEMENT | 771 |
| | | *Appendix 25.1* Financial statement analysis | 791 |
| | | *Appendix A* Numerical tables | 802 |
| | | Glossary | 812 |
| | | Author index | 825 |
| | | Subject index | 829 |

# ABOUT THE AUTHORS

GRAHAM PEIRSON
Graham Peirson is Director of the Centre for Research in Accounting and Finance at Monash University (Clayton Campus). He is a member of the Public Sector Accounting Standards Board and Chairman of the Australian Society of CPAs External Reporting Centre of Excellence. He is co-author of *Issues in Financial Accounting* and *Financial Accounting Theory*. A graduate of the University of Adelaide, he has taught at the University of Adelaide, University of California, Berkeley, University of Illinois, the University of Florida and the University of Washington.

ROB BROWN
Rob Brown is National Australia Bank Professor of Finance at Monash University (Clayton Campus). He is Associate Editor of *Accounting and Finance*, the journal of the Accounting Association of Australia and New Zealand, and a Founding Member of the Asia Pacific Finance Association. He is co-author of *Financial Accounting Theory* and has had articles accepted for publication in many journals including *Accounting and Finance, Economica, The Australian Journal of Management* and *The Journal of Banking and Finance*. He has taught at the University of Sydney and at Lancaster University. His current research interests are option pricing and banking.

PETER HOWARD
Peter Howard is Lecturer in Accounting and Finance at Monash University (Clayton Campus). For eight years he worked as an engineer in the petrochemical and mining industries. He has extensive experience in project evaluation and operations planning as well as staff training courses. He has published in the journal *Accounting and Finance* on lease evaluation and the effects of imputation on dividend and financing decisions. He has fifteen years' teaching experience at both postgraduate and undergraduate levels. His current research interests include capital structure and dividend policy, particularly in the context of the imputation tax system.

## RON BIRD

Ron Bird is a Director of Westpac Investment Management where he heads Investment Technology and Product Development. He manages the largest research team within any Australian funds management operation. After a teaching career that spanned more than twenty years he was made an Emeritus Professor at the Australian National University. He has taught at Monash University (Clayton Campus), ANU, Macquarie University, University of Washington and University of California, Berkeley. He was a Principal of Towers Perrin before joining Westpac. His current research interests include investment protection strategies and forecasting risk and returns across various markets.

# PREFACE TO THE SIXTH EDITION

As with previous editions of this book, the Sixth Edition is designed primarily for use in a first subject in business finance. Our objective is to introduce readers to finance theory and to the tools of financial decision making in the context of the Australian institutional environment.

Since the Fifth Edition there have been many changes in both finance theory and practice which have necessitated changes that have marginally increased the scope and size of the book. A major change is the restructuring of the book so that in our view the chapter order follows more logically than in previous editions. For example, while the principles of valuing securities and other assets continue to be discussed in the early chapters, the application of the net present value method to project evaluation is now discussed in Chapter 18, after the effects of taxes on corporate financing and dividend decisions have been considered.

Most chapters have been rewritten and all have been updated where necessary. In particular the chapter on financial mathematics has been rewritten in a way that assumes the use of electronic calculators rather than financial mathematics tables. Also the effects of the imputation system on dividend decisions, capital structure decisions, the calculation of the cost of capital and project evaluation have been integrated into the relevant chapters.

As with previous editions, we have received assistance from a number of sources. In particular, we would like to highlight the contribution of Kathy Avram who drafted Chapters 7 and 8. Rayna Brown also provided valuable input by commenting on various sections of the manuscript and, in particular, Chapters 8 and 21.

We have also received valuable assistance from Bill Volum (BHP Ltd), Ron Hardaker (Australian Equipment Lessors Association) and our colleagues Steve Easton, Les Nethercott and Margaret Webb. We are also indebted to Allison Sarkies and Merrilyn Sorensen for their care and patience in word processing numerous drafts of each chapter. Finally, and most importantly, we thank Chris, Carrie, Rayna and Dawn for their continued support for this project.

GRAHAM PEIRSON
RON BIRD
ROB BROWN
PETER HOWARD

**CHAPTER 1**

# INTRODUCTION

## 1.1 THE NATURE OF BUSINESS FINANCE

This book is concerned with business finance. Finance in this context is the financial resources available to a business entity. In most cases the management of these resources is delegated by the owners to employee managers. The managers are concerned with acquiring, managing and financing the business entity's resources or assets, which may be either tangible assets such as inventory and plant and equipment, or intangible assets such as research and development and patents. Of course the business entity's assets have to be paid for and to do this the managers may raise funds by selling shares to the public, issuing debt securities, borrowing from banks, leasing assets or retaining cash from operations.

The book considers the investment and financing decisions made by the managers of a business.

## 1.2 FINANCIAL DECISIONS

The financial decisions made by the managers of a business are either investment decisions or financing decisions.

In **investment decisions**, managers consider the amount invested in the assets of the business and the composition of that investment. Managers are therefore involved in the task of choosing, usually from a long list of available projects, those which are to be undertaken. In addition to considering new investments, managers also review past investments and make decisions about the composition of the business entity's assets. Managers must also ensure that the business entity's investments in current assets, including cash, inventories and debtors, are at appropriate levels throughout the year. For example, a major function of the financial manager is to ensure that the business has sufficient cash to enable payment of its obligations as they become due.

In addition to decisions about the amount and composition of investments, managers have to decide how to finance them—**financing decisions**. This will involve generating funds internally or from sources external to the business. Financial decisions also involve **dividend decisions** because payment of dividends reduces the internally generated funds that are available. When formulating financial policy, managers also have to consider the appropriate balance between short-term and long-term finance and the appropriate mix of sources of finance.

Table 1.1 shows some of the assets in which businesses invest and how those assets are financed.

**Table 1.1** *Financial decisions made by managers*

| Investment decisions | Financing decisions |
|---|---|
| Assets | Liabilities and equity |
| Current assets | Current liabilities |
|    Cash |    Accounts payable |
|    Accounts receivable |    Short-term debt |
|    Inventory |    Income tax payable |
| Non-current assets | Non-current liabilities |
|    Investments |    Long-term debt |
|    Land and buildings |    Leases |
|    Plant and equipment |    Employee entitlements |
|    Brand names | Equity |
|    Patents |    Paid-up capital |
| |    Retained profits |
| |    Reserves |

The ultimate objective of investment and financing decisions is to maximise the shareholders' wealth. This means that managers need to make investment and financing decisions that add the maximum amount of value to the business. It also needs to be recognised that all of a business entity's activities affect its value. Therefore, a knowledge and understanding of the ideas discussed in this book are as relevant for those involved in, say, the marketing and distribution functions as they are for those involved in the finance function.

## 1.3 TYPES OF ENTITY

In this book, financial decisions by the managers of business entities are considered. Most business entities are sole proprietorships, partnerships or companies.

A **sole proprietorship** is a business owned by one person. Many small service businesses, retail stores and professional practices are operated as sole proprietorships. Although the owner of a sole proprietorship is legally liable for its debts, the business should be regarded by the proprietor as a separate entity.

A **partnership** is a business owned by two or more people acting as partners.

There are no legal requirements that need to be met to form a partnership. All that is necessary is an agreement, preferably in writing to avoid future disagreements, by the persons forming the partnership.

Partnerships are not separate legal entities and the partners are therefore personally liable for the debts of the partnership. From a management viewpoint, however, a partnership is treated as an entity separate from the partners. Many small service businesses, retail stores and professional practices are operated as partnerships.

A **company** is a separate legal entity formed under the Corporations Law. The owners of a company are called **shareholders** because their ownership interests are represented by shares in the company's capital. The shareholders of most companies have limited liability, which means that their liability to contribute to the assets of the company is limited to any amount unpaid on the shares held in the company. When shares are fully paid there is no obligation for shareholders to make further contributions.

Separate legal entity status enables a company to conduct its operations in its own name as a legal person. A company can buy, own, and sell property; it can sue or be sued in its own name; and it can enter into contracts with other entities. Therefore a company is treated as a legal person with all the rights, duties and responsibilities of a person.

Companies vary greatly in size and objectives. They may range from large companies listed on the stock exchange with many thousands of shareholders, to small family companies carrying on a relatively small scale business. The Corporations Law distinguishes between public companies which may invite members of the public to invest in them, and proprietary companies which have no such intention.

This book focuses on financial decision making by managers of a public company whose shares are listed on the Australian Stock Exchange. However, most of the concepts in this book can also be applied to the other forms of business entity referred to in this section. There will, of course, be differences in the details of financial decision making depending on the entity's size and the nature of its business. In addition, many of the ideas considered in this book can be applied to public sector entities.

## 1.4 THE FINANCIAL MANAGER

The financial manager has a major role in a company's management. This role is essentially the same in all companies, that is, to acquire the necessary funds and to ensure that they are used effectively. In many companies the financial manager may not be an independently identifiable employee; this is particularly the case for small companies where financial management is often in the hands of the secretary–accountant. Frequently, the executive responsible for the financial management of a company is also responsible for its accounting functions. This is true even of large companies as the organisation chart of The Broken Hill Proprietary Company Ltd (BHP) in Figure 1.1 shows.

# 4 BUSINESS FINANCE

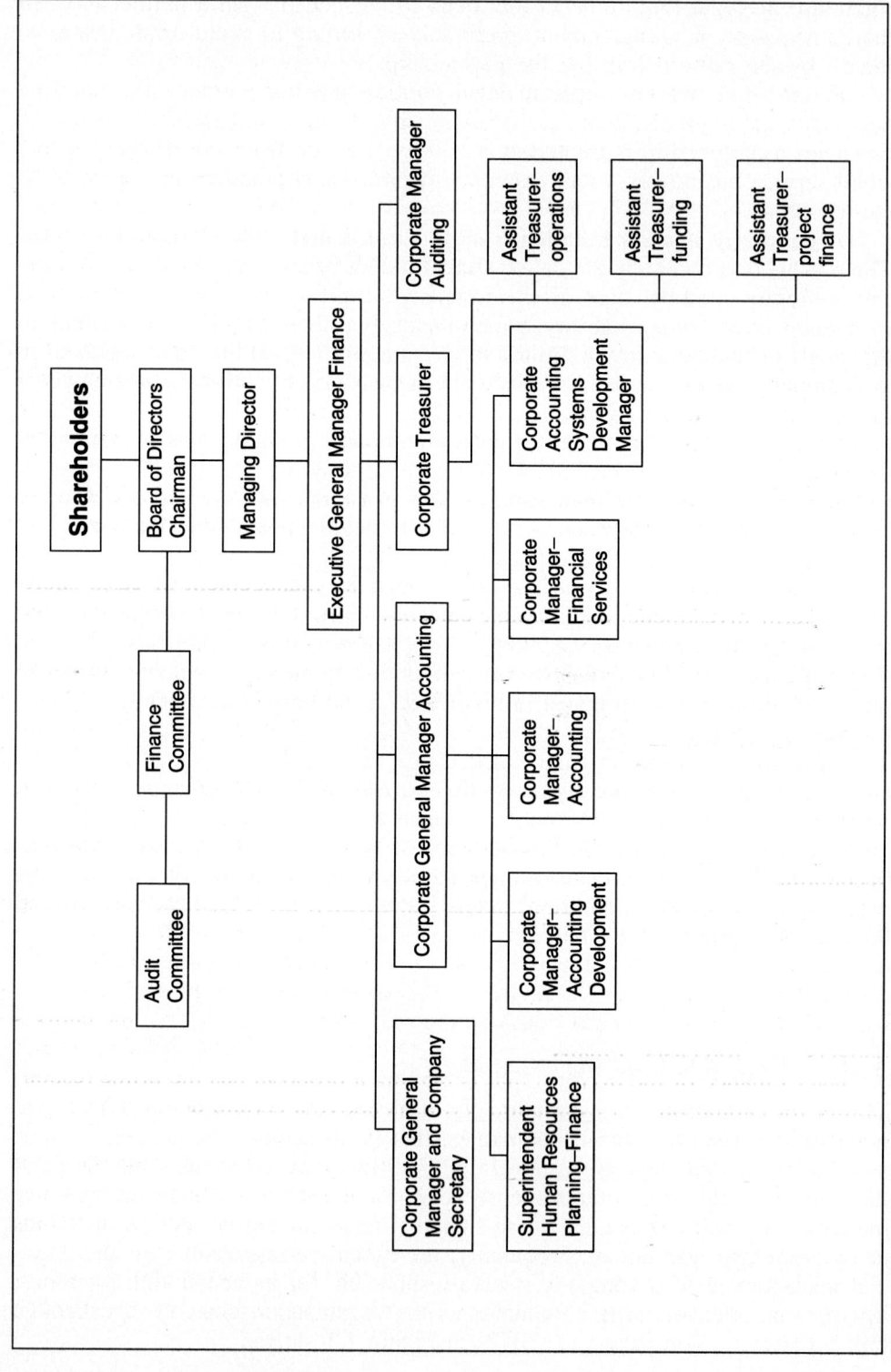

**Fig. 1.1** Organisation chart: The Broken Hill Proprietary Company Ltd, February 1993

The organisation of the finance function at BHP is fairly typical of most large companies. The financial manager is a key member of the top management team. At BHP, the Executive General Manager Finance is responsible to the Managing Director for all financial matters throughout the group of companies and is a member of both the Board of Directors and the Finance Committee. The main functions of the Finance Committee are to review financial policies and plans before they are submitted to the Board of Directors and to act for the Board in matters delegated to it. The Executive General Manager Finance supervises and coordinates the work of the Corporate Treasurer, the Corporate General Manager Accounting, the Corporate Manager Auditing and the Corporate General Manager and Company Secretary. The Corporate Treasurer is responsible for the acquisition and custody of funds; the Corporate General Manager Accounting is responsible for accounting, reporting and control; the Corporate Manager Auditing is responsible for the internal audit function; and the Corporate General Manager and Company Secretary is responsible for the functions of company secretary, investor relations, and tax planning and compliance.

As can be seen from the organisation chart in Figure 1.1, the Corporate Treasurer supervises and coordinates the work of the Assistant Treasurers. The Assistant Treasurers have responsibility for the following functions:
1. **operations**, which involves controlling the management of cash, short-term investments and foreign currency of the group of companies, and the management and servicing of borrowed funds;
2. **funding**, which relates to the non-specific raising of debt or equity to meet the requirements of the group of companies; and
3. **project financing**, which involves the negotiation of finance for specific projects such as joint ventures.

The Corporate General Manager Accounting supervises and coordinates the work of the Corporate Manager–Accounting Development (responsible for accounting policies both in Australia and offshore), the Corporate Manager–Accounting (responsible for financial and management accounting services, including the preparation of the financial statements), the Corporate Accounting Systems Development Manager (responsible for the introduction and maintenance of accounting systems), the Superintendent Human Resources Planning–Finance and the Corporate Manager–Financial Services. The prime function of the Corporate Manager–Financial Services is to prepare and review the entity's budgets and forecasts. Finally, in the BHP group of companies the General Manager Finance of the division that is making a proposal has the prime responsibility for capital project evaluation. Projects above a certain dollar amount are reviewed by members of the Corporate Treasurer's staff.

The Corporate General Manager and Company Secretary is responsible for all company secretarial matters as well as administering the investor relations program associated with the listing of BHP shares on Australian and overseas stock exchanges, and with tax planning and compliance.

It can be concluded from this outline of the BHP finance function that major investment and financing decisions are made at senior levels in such organisations.

## 1.5 The Company's Financial Objective

Rational solutions to investment and financing problems can only be achieved if the company's objective[1] is clearly specified. In microeconomics it is usually assumed that managers seek to maximise economic profit. Where there are no contributions by owners, or distributions to owners, during a period, economic profit is measured by the change in the market value of the company. As economic profit is measured by changes in the market value of the company, an objective expressed in terms of maximising the value of the company is equivalent to one expressed in terms of maximising economic profit. The objective assumed in this book is that management seeks to maximise the market value of the company's ordinary shares. Because an alternative term for *shares* is *equity*, this objective is often expressed as the maximisation of the market value of shareholders' equity. Given that shareholders derive utility (satisfaction) from wealth, a policy of maximising shareholders' wealth must maximise shareholders' utility.

## 1.6 Basic Concepts of Finance

For a financial manager to make decisions that will achieve the company's objective it is necessary for the manager to understand the material in this book. In the first instance this requires an understanding of some basic concepts of financial economics. In this section the concepts of value, time and uncertainty, nominal and real amounts, market efficiency, and agency relationships will be outlined.

### 1.6.1 Value

In Section 1.5 it was noted that investment and financing decisions should be made with the objective of maximising the market value of shareholders' equity. The financial manager has, therefore, to make investment and financing decisions which add value to shareholders' equity. To achieve this objective, the financial manager must understand how financial markets work. This is because to finance a company's investments the financial manager will generally need to issue securities such as shares and debt securities. The actions of buyers and sellers of those securities in financial markets will determine the price of the securities and therefore the value of the company on those markets.

Individuals may use their wealth either for consumption or investment. One way for individuals to increase their wealth is to defer consumption, and increase the amount invested. Individuals who are relatively risk averse may choose to invest in debt securities for which they receive interest and repayment of the amount invested at a future date. Individuals who are prepared to be exposed to

---

[1] As discussed in Section 1.6.5, a complex organisation such as a company involves relationships between shareholders, managers, lenders and other groups. The company is simply a legal structure which serves as a nexus for the contractual relationships between these parties. Therefore, the company does not have any personal qualities, and cannot set any objectives: this is done by people such as the company's directors. However, for ease of exposition, we use the term *company's objective*.

greater risk may instead prefer to invest in a company's shares, which represents a partial ownership interest in the company. As partial owners, shareholders are entitled to a share of the company's profits in proportion to their ownership interest. The profits of a company may be paid to shareholders in the form of dividends or may be retained for further investment.

The value of the company $V$ on the financial markets may therefore be expressed as: $V = D + E$,
where:  $D$ = the value of debt and
        $E$ = the value of equity

The value that the financial markets place on the debt and equity securities will depend on the risk and return from investments in those securities. This, in turn, will depend on the success of the investments in assets made by the company. In finance the success of an investment will be judged by its ability to generate more cash than originally outlaid on the investment. This will enable the company to make the fixed interest payments to debtholders, and repay the principal, and to pay dividends to shareholders.

### 1.6.2 TIME AND UNCERTAINTY

The value of an investment made by a company depends on the amount and timing of the cash flows generated by the investment. Similarly, the value of debt securities or shares depends on the amount and timing of the cash flows to debtholders and shareholders. This gives rise to a fundamental principle of finance that individuals prefer to receive a dollar today rather than a dollar in a year's time. This is referred to as the **time value of money** and is discussed in Chapter 3.

In addition, the amount and timing of cash flows are not usually known with certainty. It is assumed in this book that investors are averse to risk. The relationship between risk and return is discussed in Section 1.6.4 and in Chapter 6.

### 1.6.3 NOMINAL AND REAL AMOUNTS

The cash flows from investment and financing decisions are measured in money terms. For example, the cost of an asset is expressed as the number of dollars sacrificed to acquire the asset. The price at which this exchange takes place is the **nominal** price of the asset. However, the purchasing power of money changes as a result of price increases (inflation) and decreases (deflation). During a period of inflation there is an increase in the general level of prices, with a consequent decrease in the general purchasing power of money. The increase in the general level of prices is equivalent to a decrease in the value of money. By contrast, during a period of deflation there is a decrease in the general level of prices, with a consequent increase in the general purchasing power of money. The decrease in the general level of prices is equivalent to an increase in the value of money.

It is necessary, therefore, to distinguish between the nominal or face value of money and the **real** or inflation-adjusted value of money. For example, if the annual rate of inflation is 3 per cent, the real value of a dollar is decreasing annually by 3 per cent. That is, relative to the purchasing power of a dollar today, a dollar next year will be worth only 97 cents in real terms.[2] This means that an increase in cash flows must be at a rate greater than the rate of inflation if it is to increase shareholders' purchasing power.

Interest rates can also be expressed in nominal or real terms. The nominal interest rate is the rate quoted in financial markets for borrowing and lending transactions. The interest rate may also be expressed in inflation-adjusted or real terms. However, as the observed market rates are in nominal terms, for consistency it is usual to use nominal cash flows.

### 1.6.4 MARKET EFFICIENCY AND CAPITAL ASSET PRICING

In Section 1.6.1 it was noted that a financial manager will have to finance investments by issuing securities on financial markets. At least as a first approximation it is generally assumed that these markets are efficient. This means that financial markets are composed of numerous well-informed individuals whose trading activities cause prices to adjust instantaneously and without bias in response to new information. Price changes are therefore caused by the availability of new information and are independent of past price changes.

The concept of market efficiency means that we should expect securities and other assets to be fairly priced, given their expected risks and returns.

It is generally agreed that investors require a higher return on those investments which are perceived to be more risky. The return that investors in debt receive can be in the form of interest and an increase in the price of the debt security. The return that investors in shares receive can be in the form of dividends and an increase in the price of the shares. However, shares are normally more risky than debt and investors expect to be compensated for the greater risk by a higher rate of return.

A difficulty for the financial manager is to measure the riskiness of an investment and to establish the trade-off between risk and expected return. A model that has been developed to assist the manager in this task is the **capital asset pricing model (CAPM)**. Risk can be attributed to two sources:

1. market-wide factors such as interest rates and foreign exchange rates— this is called **systematic risk** (and also referred to as **non-diversifiable** or **market risk**); and
2. factors that are specific to a particular company, such as the discovery of a new mineral deposit by a mining company—this is called **unsystematic risk** (and also referred to as **diversifiable** or **unique risk**).

While unsystematic risk can be largely eliminated for an investor who holds a well diversified portfolio, systematic risk cannot be eliminated. Another model that has been developed to measure the riskiness of an investment and to establish

---

2 This is an approximation. With a rate of inflation of 3 per cent per annum. $1 today is equivalent to $1.03 next year and it follows that a dollar next year is worth $1 ÷ $1.03 = $0.970 874 today. This is discussed further in Chapter 3.

the trade-off between risk and expected return is **arbitrage pricing theory** (APT). These models are discussed in Chapter 6.

According to the CAPM and the APT, risk-averse investors would diversify their investments to eliminate unsystematic risk. Consequently the market will only reward investors for bearing systematic or market risk, and the financial manager should therefore focus on this type of risk when deciding on the required rate of return for a proposed investment.

In the following chapters, we will explain the basic concepts of finance we have outlined in this chapter. The basic concepts may be summarised as follows:

- the company's objective is to maximise shareholders' wealth;
- a dollar received today is preferred to a dollar received later; and
- investors prefer less risk to more risk, other things being equal, that is, they are risk averse.

### 1.6.5 AGENCY RELATIONSHIPS

In an agency relationship, one party known as the *principal* delegates decision making authority to another party, the *agent*. The principal and the agent enter into a contract which defines the relationship. In negotiating such a contract both the principal and the agent recognise that the other party is a self-interested individual. Examples of such relationships are those between a company's shareholders and its managers, and between shareholders and debtholders.

It was noted in Section 1.5 that a company's objective should be the maximisation of shareholders' wealth. That is, managers should take decisions that result in the maximisation of shareholders' wealth. This objective is consistent with the view that the company involves a set of contractual relationships among individuals. Under this view, the company is regarded as a collection of self-interested individuals who have agreed to cooperate by entering into contracts which provide sufficient incentives to gain their cooperation. The relationship between shareholders and managers is seen as a principal–agent relationship. The managers of the company are the agents and the shareholders are the principals.

The principal–agent relationship gives rise to *agency costs*. One component of these costs is the reduction in the value of the company directly attributable to managers acting in their own best interest. Managers do this by making decisions which are inconsistent with the maximisation of shareholders' wealth and by directly diverting the company's resources to maximise their own utility; acquiring expensive company cars, taking business trips to exotic locations, and so on. As shareholders are aware of the possibility that managers may transfer wealth by such practices, they have an incentive to limit the extent of this behaviour. To this end, shareholders attempt to *monitor* the behaviour of managers in the hope of discouraging practices inconsistent with the maximisation of shareholders' wealth and to institute contracts so as to *bond* the interests of managers and shareholders. The total agency costs are the sum of the costs of monitoring and bonding, plus the loss to shareholders from managers acting in their own interest. The shareholders and managers bear the agency costs and therefore have incentives to structure contracts to reduce these costs.

## THE EVIDENCE

The separation of ownership and control in the modern corporation gives rise to the question of whether companies are managed solely in the interests of shareholders. A number of theories have been advanced suggesting that managers place the major emphasis on maximising their own satisfaction. However, it has been recognised that there are reasons to suggest that managers and shareholders are drawn towards a common objective of maximising the market value of the company's shares. The extent to which managers might depart from this objective remains an empirical question.

A number of American studies have examined the relationship between the degree of management control of an organisation and the behaviour of management. The results are somewhat inconclusive. For example, Larner found that the risk-taking attitudes of management and the level of profitability of a company were independent of the extent of management control of the firm.[3] In contrast, Monsen, Chiu and Cooley found that owner-controlled companies were more profitable than manager-controlled companies.[4]

A United Kingdom study evaluated, among other things, the priority that managers claimed to give to particular groups when making decisions, and managers' views as to the important objectives for the company.[5] By a considerable margin, most respondents claimed that the top priority was either shareholders' interests or 'the company as a whole'. Most respondents indicated that multiple objectives rather than a single objective were pursued. A total of 95 per cent of respondents indicated that profit was either their primary objective (77.1 per cent) or secondary objective (17.9 per cent). The other goals that assumed a much smaller significance were growth, risk and liquidity. The results of this study suggest that the prime objective of management when making financial decisions is the welfare of shareholders and, although multiple goals are considered when evaluating financial decisions, these goals are largely proxies for a single objective of maximising the market value of the company's shares.

The evidence suggests that the objective of maximising the market value of shares is a good approximation of reality. However, it should not be expected that all managers will pursue this objective on all occasions. There are incentives for managers to depart occasionally from the pursuit of this objective. However, the objective does have the advantage of enabling a consistent development of the topics addressed in this book and allows us to draw on the wealth of academic writing on the subject. Further, it has the advantage of highlighting both what a

---

3 R. Larner, *Management Control and the Large Corporation*, Donellan, New York, 1970.
4 R. Monsen, J. Chiu & D. Cooley, 'The Effect of Separation of Ownership and Control on the Performance of the Large Firm', *Quarterly Journal of Economics*, August 1968, pp. 435–51.
5 K. Bhaskar & P. McNamee, 'Multiple Objectives in Accounting and Finance', *Journal of Business Finance and Accounting*, Winter 1983, pp. 595–621.

management should do if it adopts this objective, and the 'costs' to shareholders where managers make decisions inconsistent with it.

Agency cost analysis has been employed to examine the determinants of a company's dividend policy, capital structure and leasing decisions. Application of agency cost analysis to these decisions will be discussed in Chapters 11, 12 and 19 respectively.

## 1.7 OUTLINE OF THE BOOK

The concepts introduced in this chapter are developed in the remainder of the book. In Chapters 2 to 6, some fundamental concepts underlying finance theory are developed. Chapters 7 to 10 consider the institutional framework in which financing decisions are made. In Chapters 11, 12 and 13, dividend decisions and capital structure decisions are discussed. Chapter 14 reviews the literature on market efficiency, while Chapters 15 and 16 consider futures contracts and options and contingent claims respectively. In Chapter 17, the discount rate to be used in project evaluation is developed, and Chapter 18 considers the application of project evaluation methods. Chapters 19 and 20 involve specific applications of the net present value method of project evaluation. In Chapter 21, the application of the principles outlined earlier in the book to international financial management is explored, while Chapters 22 to 25 apply those principles to short-term asset management, including inventory, cash and accounts receivable.

## SELECTED REFERENCES

Bhaskar, K. & McNamee, P., 'Multiple Objectives in Accounting and Finance', *Journal of Business Finance and Accounting*, Winter 1983, pp. 595–621.

Jensen, M. & Meckling, W., 'Theory of the Firm: Managerial Behaviour, Agency Costs and Ownership Structure', *Journal of Financial Economics*, October 1976, pp. 306–60.

Monsen, R., Chiu J., & Cooley, D., 'The Effect of Separation of Ownership and Control on the Performance of the Large Firm', *Quarterly Journal of Economics*, August 1968, pp. 435–51.

## QUESTIONS

1. Distinguish between investment and financing decisions.
2. Explain the following:
   (a) a sole proprietorship;
   (b) a partnership; and
   (c) a company.
3. What are the main functions of financial managers?
4. Maximisation of the value of the firm is equivalent to the maximisation of economic profit, but it is not equivalent to the maximisation of accounting profit. Discuss.
5. Why do people usually prefer to receive $1 today instead of in a year's time?
6. Comment on the statement that:
   A company should borrow during times of high inflation because it can repay the loan in cheaper dollars.

7. What is the relationship between diversifiable and non-diversifiable risk? How does this distinction affect the reward that investors demand for bearing risk?
8. What is meant by the terms *agency relationships* and *agency costs*?

# CHAPTER 2

# CONSUMPTION, INVESTMENT AND THE CAPITAL MARKET

## 2.1 INTRODUCTION

In Chapter 1 we described briefly the major features of the finance function. In this chapter we present a theoretical framework that shows important relationships between firms, their shareholders and the capital market. We use this framework to make some observations on investment decisions, financing decisions and dividend policy. Although the framework we present is simple and rather abstract, it provides important insights into some fundamental issues in finance.

## 2.2 THE FIRM'S OBJECTIVE

Rational solutions to investment and financing problems can be achieved only if the objective of the firm is clearly specified. In microeconomics it is usually assumed that managers seek to maximise a firm's economic profit. If, during a period, the firm's owners (the shareholders) neither contribute more resources to the firm, nor take any resources from the firm, the firm's *economic profit* in the period is measured by the change in its market value.[1]

As economic profit is measured by changes in the market value of the firm, an objective expressed in terms of maximising the value of the firm is equivalent to one expressed in terms of maximising economic profit. As noted in Chapter 1, the objective assumed throughout this book is that a firm's managers seek to maximise the market value of the firm's ordinary shares. Because an alternative

---

[1] For a more detailed discussion see D. Solomons, 'Economic and Accounting Concepts of Income', *The Accounting Review*, July 1961, pp. 374–83.

term for *shares* is *equity*, this objective is often expressed as the maximisation of the market value of equity.[2] Given that shareholders derive utility (satisfaction) from wealth, a policy of maximising wealth must also maximise shareholders' utility.

## 2.3 FISHER'S ANALYSIS

The assumed objective of a firm is to maximise the market value of its ordinary shares. A firm's managers, therefore, have to make investment, financing and dividend decisions consistent with that objective. The managers' job would be easier if there were a consistent set of decision rules that could be employed in making investment, financing and dividend decisions. The work of Irving Fisher provides a framework in which such rules can be developed.[3] Initially these decision rules are developed in a very simplified setting. However, the decision rules are applicable even where more realistic assumptions are made.

The assumptions in Fisher's analysis are:
1. There are only two points in time: the present time (Time 1) and a later time (Time 2).
2. There is no uncertainty, and hence the outcome of all decisions is known to everybody.
3. There are no imperfections in the capital market.

The analysis involves three participants: the firm, the shareholders and the capital market. The characteristics of each participant are described in turn and the major implications of the analysis for financial decision making are presented.

### 2.3.1 THE FIRM

It is assumed that the firm's managers wish to use the firm's resources according to the wishes of the shareholders. The firm is assumed to be endowed with a fixed amount of resources at Time 1 and the managers have to decide how much of these resources should be invested and how much should be paid out as dividends. Any resources not paid out at Time 1 are invested, and the level of this investment determines the resources available to pay dividends at Time 2.

The investment opportunities available to the firm are summarised in a **production possibilities curve** (PPC) as illustrated in Figure 2.1. The horizontal axis measures resources available to the firm at Time 1. Assume that the firm has 200 units of resources available to it. It could pay this amount as a dividend at Time 1. In this case, investment would be zero and dividends at Time 2 would also be zero. The point (200, 0) represents this extreme decision. At the other extreme, the firm could pay no dividend at Time 1 and invest the whole of the

---

[2] At this stage it is assumed there is no debt, and therefore the market value of the firm equals the market value of its ordinary shares. However, where debt has been issued there is the possibility of conflict between debtholders and shareholders. For example, a decision may simultaneously increase the market value of debt, decrease the market value of equity, and yet increase the market value of the firm.

[3] I. Fisher, *The Theory of Interest*, Macmillan Company, New York, 1930. See also J. Hirshleifer, *Investment, Interest and Capital*, Prentice–Hall, Englewood Cliffs, New Jersey, 1970.

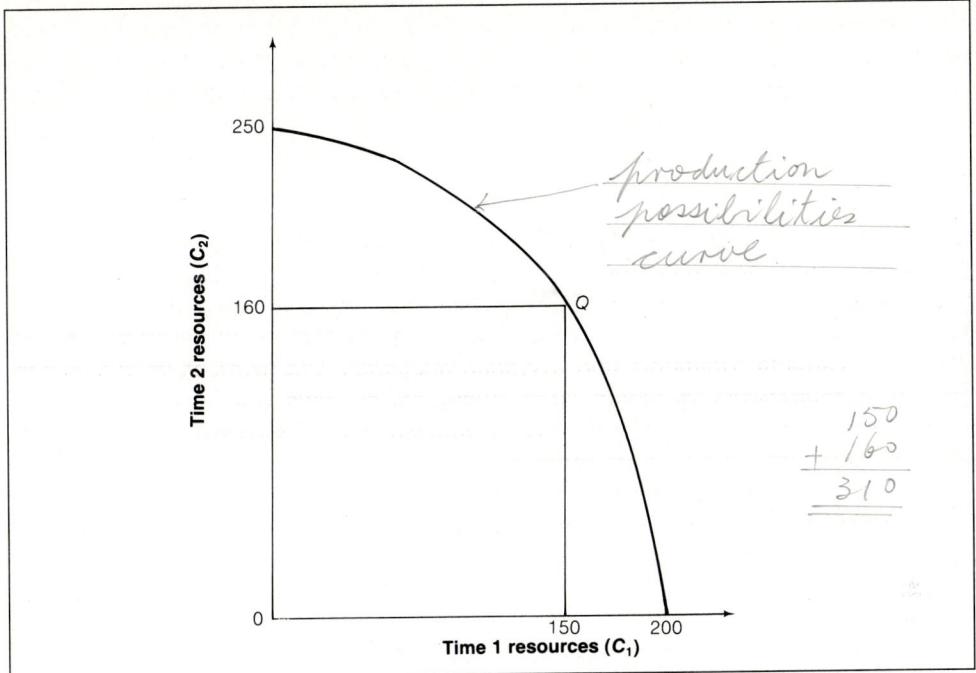

**Fig. 2.1** *Production possibilities curve*

firm's resources. This decision would result in 250 units being available for distribution as a dividend at Time 2 and is represented by the point (0, 250). Point $Q$ is an intermediate case in which a dividend of 150 units is paid at Time 1, leaving 50 units to be invested. The PPC shows that an investment of 50 units can be transformed into 160 units of resources at Time 2. Therefore the dividend at Time 2 is 160 units.

### 2.3.2 THE SHAREHOLDERS

Shareholders forego current consumption by investing in a firm at Time 1 in order to receive a return which then increases their consumption opportunities at Time 2. A person's preference for consumption at Time 1 ($C_1$) or at Time 2 ($C_2$) is represented by **indifference curves** as depicted in Figure 2.2. The term *indifference* indicates that the person derives equal utility from the bundles of $C_1$ and $C_2$ represented by all points on a single curve; for example, equal utility is derived from points $X$ and $Y$ in Figure 2.2. However, any point on a higher indifference curve is preferred to all points on lower curves; for example, $Z$ is preferred to $X$ and $Y$.

The slope of an indifference curve at any point shows the consumer's willingness to trade off $C_1$ for $C_2$. It can be seen from Figure 2.2 that the indifference curves are convex, and approach the horizontal as the level of $C_1$ increases, and approach the vertical as the level of $C_2$ increases. The implication is that a consumer's desire to increase consumption further at a given time decreases as the level of consumption at that time increases.

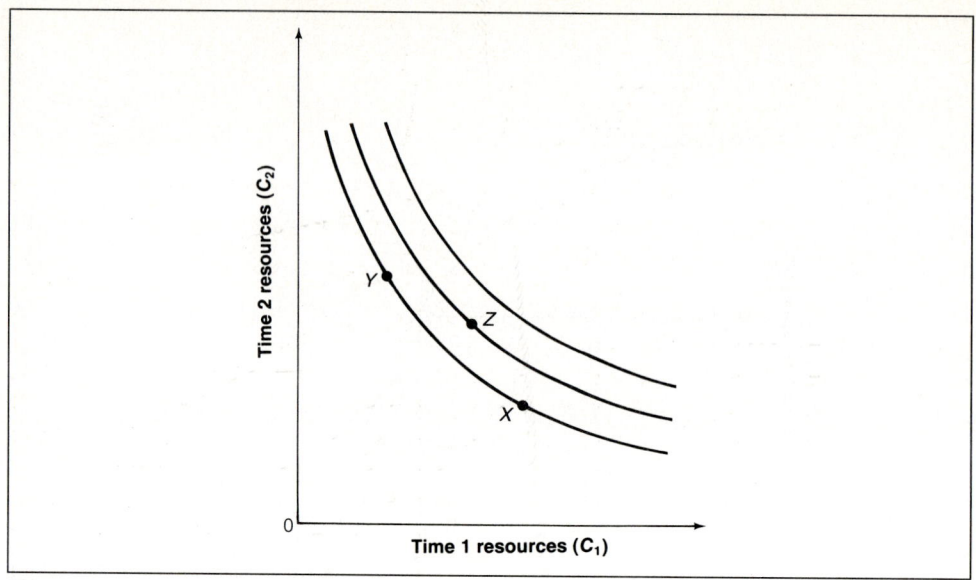

**Fig. 2.2**  *Indifference curves*

### 2.3.3 THE FIRM'S DECISION[4]

We now bring together the firm and the shareholders in an attempt to identify the decision the firm should make. We assume that there are only two shareholders, A and B. In Figure 2.3, indifference curves for shareholder A are labelled $A_1$, $A_2$ and $A_3$, and indifference curves for shareholder B are labelled $B_1$, $B_2$ and $B_3$. If the firm chooses point A, that is, a current dividend of 90 and investment of 110, yielding a dividend of 228 at time 2, then shareholder A's utility is maximised. However, shareholder B's utility is not maximised at this point; it is maximised only if the firm chooses point B. This requires a current dividend of 160 and investment of 40, yielding a dividend of 144 at Time 2. In short, the firm is unable to reach a decision which will lead simultaneously to maximum utility for both shareholders. This situation poses a severe dilemma for the firm because it means that the firm must consider the preferences of each of its shareholders when making investment decisions. In other words, there is no simple decision rule which will satisfy all shareholders. Such a rule does exist, however, if there is a capital market.

### 2.3.4 THE CAPITAL MARKET

In this simple model the capital market can be thought of as a place where current resources may be transformed into future resources and vice versa at a constant rate, $i$ per period. In effect, $i$ is an interest rate. For example, if $i$ is 10 per cent

---

[4] In fact, decisions are made by managers rather than by an inanimate 'firm' but for ease of expression we frequently refer to a firm making a decision. We have assumed that managers will seek to maximise the interests of the shareholders.

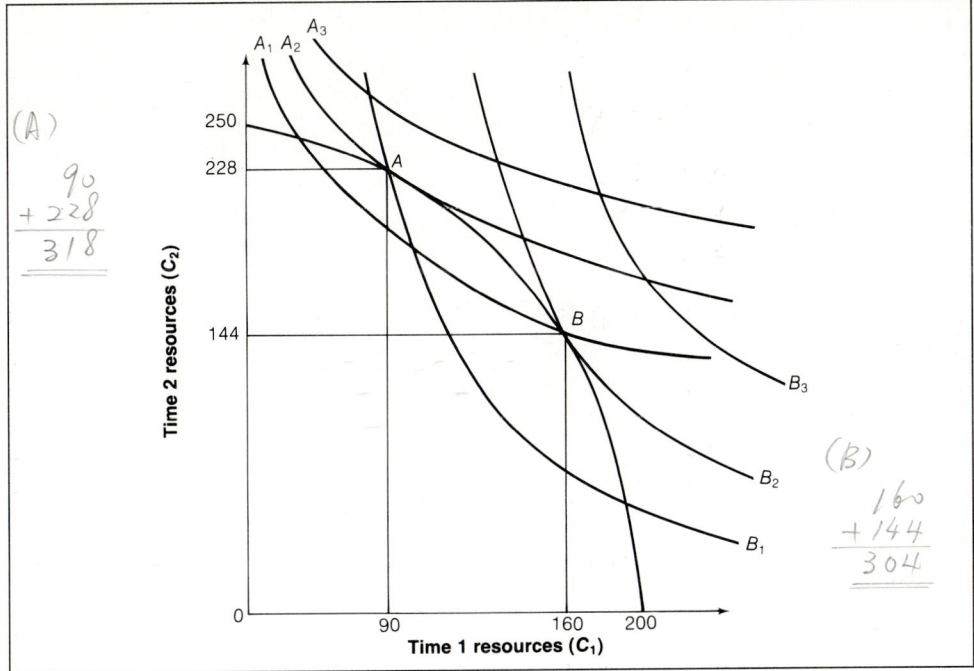

Fig.2.3

per period, and 100 units of current resources are placed with the capital market for one period, then 100 × 1.1 = 110 units of resources become available at Time 2. In effect, this is lending to the capital market. Similarly, if a person has a claim to receive 110 units of resources at Time 2, the capital market may be used to transform this claim into 110/1.1 = 100 units of resources at Time 1. This transaction corresponds to a person borrowing 100 units at Time 1 and repaying the loan with a payment of 110 units at Time 2.

Suppose that a person has claims on resources in both periods. For example, a person may have an income of 100 units at Time 1 and an income of 165 units at Time 2. What consumption opportunities are available if the interest rate is 10 per cent per period? If the person chooses to consume only at Time 2, the consumption at Time 1 is zero and consumption at Time 2 is 165 + 100(1.1) = 275 units. If, however, the person chooses to consume only at Time 1, then consumption at Time 1 is (165/1.1) + 100 = 250 units. Therefore this person's claim on current resources is 250 units. In short, *wealth* at Time 1 is 250 units. Figure 2.4 illustrates this case.

The line joining these two extreme positions is shown in Figure 2.4 and may be called a **market opportunity line** as it defines all combinations of consumption possibilities at the two times consistent with an initial wealth level of 250 units. If a person can reach any one point on this line, then by borrowing or lending, all other points on the line are also available to the person. For example, if a person can reach point A (100 units at Time 1 and 165 units at

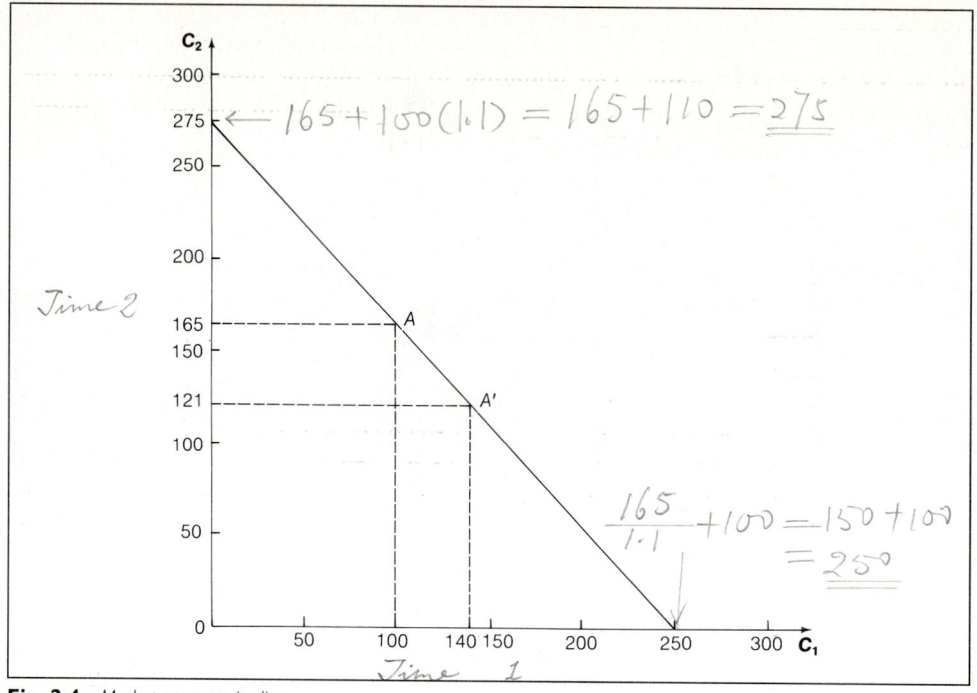

**Fig. 2.4** Market opportunity line

Time 2), then the person can also reach point A' (140 units at Time 1 and 121 units at Time 2), by borrowing 40 units today and repaying 44 units at Time 2.

The equation of a market opportunity line can be derived as follows. If a person's income at Time 1 is $C_1$ and at Time 2 is $C_2$, and the market interest rate is $i$ per period, then the person's wealth $W_1$ at Time 1 is:

$$W_1 = C_1 + \frac{C_2}{1+i} \qquad (2.1)$$

Equivalently, this can be written:

$$W_1(1+i) = C_1(1+i) + C_2$$

or
$$C_2 = -(1+i)C_1 + W_1(1+i) \qquad (2.2)$$

This is a linear equation with slope $-(1+i)$ and intercept $W_1(1+i)$. With a current wealth level of 250 and an interest rate of 10 per cent per period the equation is:

$$C_2 = -(1+0.1)C_1 + 250(1.1)$$

therefore
$$C_2 = -1.1C_1 + 275$$

To illustrate further the interpretation of market opportunity lines, suppose that the person is offered a choice of two income streams, A or B. Stream A consists of 100 units at Time 1 and 165 units at Time 2, while Stream B consists of 120 units at Time 1 and 55 units at Time 2. It has already been shown that at an interest rate of 10 per cent, Stream A corresponds to a wealth level of 250 units at Time 1 and the equation of the market opportunity line is $C_2 = -1.1\,C_1 + 275$. The wealth level corresponding to Stream B is $120 + 55/1.1 = 170$ units. The equation of the market opportunity line for Stream B is $C_2 = -1.1C_1 + 187$. These lines, together with the person's indifference curves, are shown in Figure 2.5.

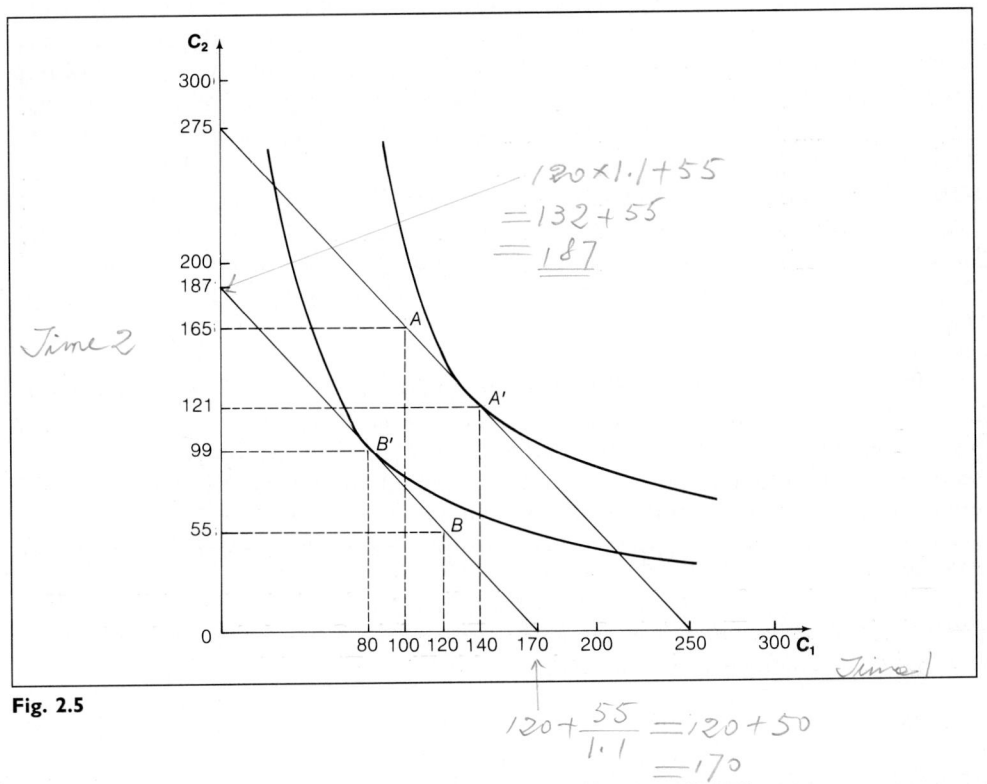

**Fig. 2.5**

Figure 2.5 shows that this person will maximise utility by accepting income Stream A and then converting Stream A to Stream A' by means of a capital market transaction. As we have seen, Stream A provides an income of 100 units at Time 1 and 165 units at Time 2, and a wealth level of 250 units. The person then enters the capital market and borrows 40 units at Time 1, achieving a consumption level of 140 units at Time 1. In return, the claim on Time 2 resources is reduced by 44 units (from 165 units to 121 units). The loan repayment required at Time 2 is, of course, 44 units (since $40 \times 1.1 = 44$). Had Stream B been accepted, the optimum point would have been B' which could have been achieved by lending $120 - 80 = 40$ units at Time 1 and consuming $55 + (40)(1.1) = 99$ units at Time 2. However, point B' is on a lower indifference curve than point A' and therefore yields lower utility. To summarise: Stream A should be chosen because it corresponds to a higher wealth level, which, in turn, ensures that higher utility can be achieved, given access to a capital market.

### 2.3.5 FISHER'S SEPARATION THEOREM

Fisher's separation theorem combines all three elements: the firm, the shareholders and the capital market.

Suppose that the firm has $E$ units of resources and is considering three investment/dividend policies, shown in Figure 2.6 as points $P_1$, $P_2$ and $P$. A market opportunity line with slope $-(1 + i)$ has been drawn through each of the three points. The line through $P_1$ shows that if policy $P_1$ were adopted, the shareholders' wealth would increase from $E$ to $W_1$. Similarly, if policy $P_2$ were adopted, the shareholders' wealth would increase to $W_2$, and if policy $P$ were adopted, the shareholders' wealth would be $W$. Because the utility of shareholders depends directly on their wealth, they will unanimously prefer policy $P$ because the resulting wealth level $W$ is the maximum achievable. Relative to policy $P$, it is clear that $P_1$ represents too little investment by the firm, whereas $P_2$ represents too much investment by the firm. Policy $P$, which occurs at the point of tangency between the production possibilities curve and the market opportunity line, is the optimum policy for the firm and will receive the support of all shareholders. This result may be shown more formally by superimposing representative indifference curves for shareholders $A$ and $B$ on Figure 2.6. This is shown in Figure 2.7.

The firm chooses policy $P$; that is, it invests $(E - C_1^*)$ and pays dividends of $C_1^*$ at Time 1 and $C_2^*$ at Time 2. Shareholder $A$ enters the capital market and lends resources so that the shareholder's *personal* optimum point $P^A$ is reached. Shareholder $B$ borrows from the capital market in order to reach $P^B$ which is $B$'s *personal* optimum point. Any policy other than $P$ will result in lower utility for *both* shareholders. For example, if the firm were to choose policy

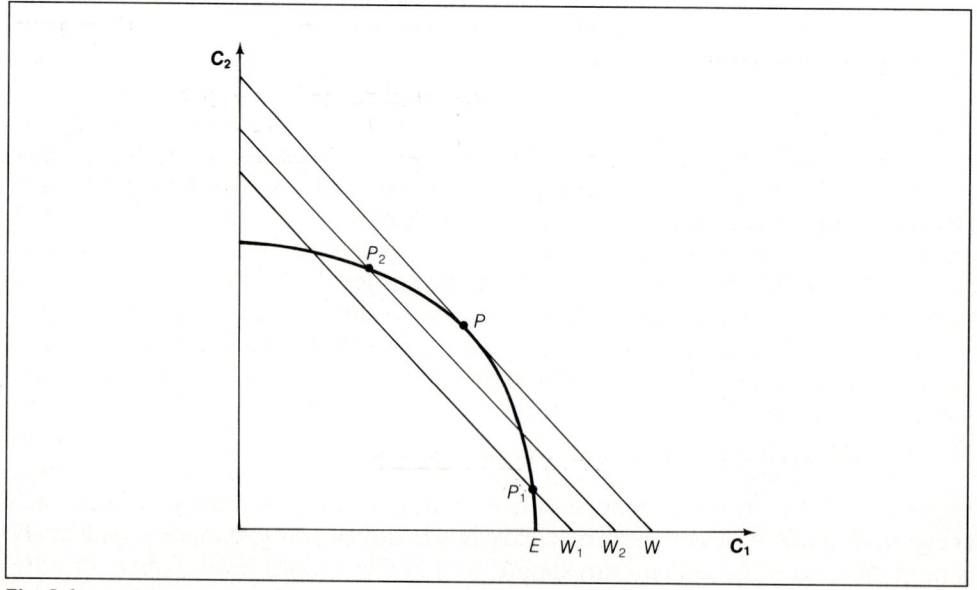

Fig. 2.6

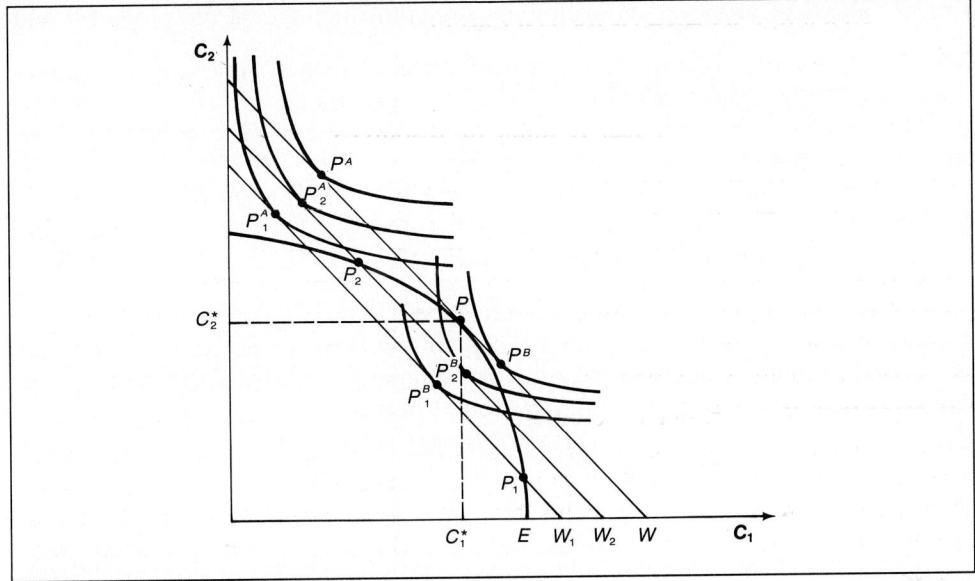

**Fig. 2.7**

$P_1$, then shareholder $A$'s maximum utility would occur at point $P_1^A$ which is on a lower indifference curve than point $P^A$ and shareholder $B$'s maximum utility would occur at point $P_1^B$ which is on a lower indifference curve than point $P^B$. The same conclusion holds if the firm were to choose policy $P_2$.

There is, therefore, just one policy $P$ which will maximise the utility of all shareholders simultaneously. Regardless of differences in their utility functions, all shareholders will support the firm's decision to choose policy $P$. In this sense, the firm and its shareholders are *separate*. The firm does *not* need to consult each shareholder before it makes its decision because it knows in advance that *all* shareholders, regardless of differences in their personal preferences, will support the choice of policy $P$. Since policy $P$ does not require knowledge of any shareholder's utility function (preferences), it follows that $P$ might be identifiable using data directly available to the firm. That this is in fact the case is proved in the following section.

### 2.3.6 IDENTIFYING THE OPTIMUM POLICY

Suppose that a firm is endowed with $E$ units of current resources and is considering a number of *small* investment projects, each requiring an outlay of $\Delta$ units of resources. It has ranked these projects from the highest rate of return to the lowest. The project with the highest rate of return will return $C'_2$ units at

Time 2. <u>The firm proposes the following decision rule: accept the project if and only if:</u>

$$\frac{\text{Return at Time 2}}{1+i} - \Delta > 0$$

This is illustrated in Figure 2.8.

It is clear from Figure 2.8 that $C'_2 > \Delta(1 + i)$ and therefore:

$$\frac{C'_2}{1+i} - \Delta > 0$$

Under the proposed rule, the project is accepted. Fisher's separation theorem also recommends acceptance since policy $P$ has not yet been achieved. Now consider the second project, which also requires an outlay of $\Delta$ and which returns $C''_2$ at Time 2. Reading from Figure 2.8, it is found that:

$$C'_2 + C''_2 > C'_2 + \Delta(1 + i)$$

therefore
$$\frac{C''_2}{1+i} - \Delta > 0$$

Again, both Fisher's separation theorem and the rule recommend acceptance of this project. This will continue to be the case until policy $P$ is reached. Beyond that point, both the theorem and the rule recommend rejection. This is shown in Figure 2.9.

Reading from Figure 2.9 it is found that:

$$C^*_2 + \Delta(1 + i) > C^*_2 + C'''_2$$

therefore
$$\frac{C'''_2}{1+i} - \Delta < 0$$

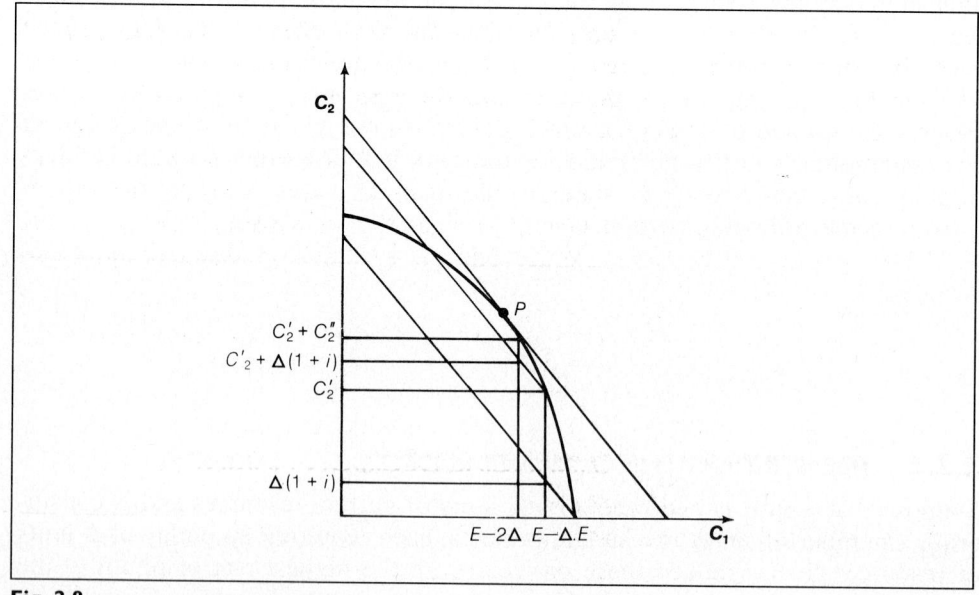

Fig. 2.8

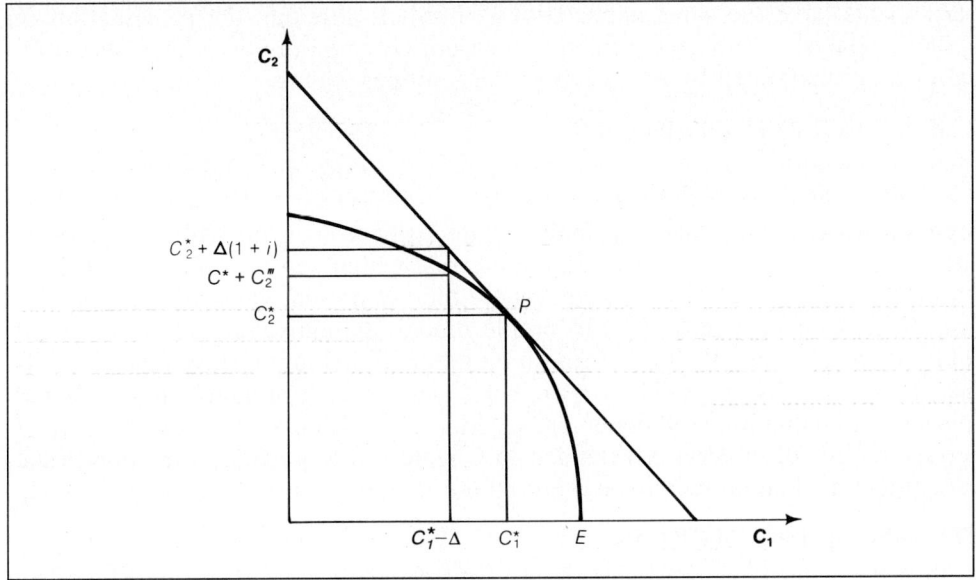

**Fig. 2.9**

Therefore, both the proposed rule and the theorem recommend rejection of this project.

The proposed rule and the theorem are completely consistent. All projects which are acceptable according to the theorem are also acceptable according to the rule. All projects rejected by the theorem are also rejected by the rule. Therefore, a firm which always applies this rule to its investment decisions will be able to locate the optimum investment/dividend policy and will maximise the wealth of its shareholders. In turn, the shareholders can use the capital market to achieve their preferred consumption patterns and thereby maximise utility.

The name given to this rule is the **net present value rule**. The return next period is discounted by the factor $(1 + i)$ to convert the future return into a present value. The investment outlay is then subtracted from the present value to give the net present value (NPV). If the NPV is positive, the project will increase the wealth of the shareholders and should therefore be accepted. If the NPV is negative, the reverse is true. The NPV rule is considered further in Chapter 5.

## 2.3.7 IMPLICATIONS FOR FINANCIAL DECISION MAKING

A number of implications for investment, financing and dividend decisions can be drawn from Fisher's analysis. These implications will hold where there are perfect markets for both capital and information. However, Fisher's analysis is unaffected by the introduction of uncertainty, provided it is assumed that all participants have the same expectations.[5] Further, although the presentation of Fisher's analysis has been confined to a case involving only two times, its implications are unaffected by extension to the multiperiod case.[6]

## THE INVESTMENT DECISION

Fisher's separation theorem means that a firm can make investment decisions in the interests of every shareholder, regardless of differences between shareholders' preferences; that is, a firm can make an investment decision with which every shareholder will agree. Moreover, there is a rule which will identify that decision: a firm should invest up to the point where the net present value of the marginal unit of investment is zero. In this simple model, an equivalent rule is to invest up to the point where the rate of return on the marginal unit of investment equals the market interest rate. These two rules and other commonly implemented investment evaluation techniques are considered in Chapter 5 in the context of certainty. This discussion is extended in Chapter 18 to consider the appropriate investment evaluation technique where there is uncertainty.

## THE FINANCING DECISION

In Fisher's analysis there is a single market rate of interest. In effect, there is no distinction between debt and equity securities, and the cost to the firm of acquiring funds is independent of the type of security issued. It follows that the value of the firm and the wealth of its shareholders are independent of the firm's capital structure. As a result, the financing decision can be described as 'irrelevant'. When the financing decision is discussed in Chapter 12 this result is confirmed in a less restrictive framework.

## THE DIVIDEND DECISION

In Fisher's analysis, all resources not invested at Time 1 are distributed to shareholders as dividends, and all returns at Time 2 are also distributed as dividends. That is, it is assumed that the firm itself does not borrow or lend in the capital market, although its shareholders may do so. Suppose, however, that the firm is permitted to borrow or lend in the capital market. In that case, the firm has greater choice in its dividend policy, while maintaining the same level of investment. For example, the firm could pay a higher dividend at Time 1 and borrow the resources needed to maintain investment at the optimum level given by the point of tangency between the PPC and the market opportunity line. This is illustrated in Figure 2.10.

Compared with the basic Fisher analysis (Fig. 2.7), the firm in Figure 2.10 pays a larger dividend at Time 1 and a smaller dividend at Time 2. To maintain the firm's investment level at $E - C_1^*$, the firm borrows $C_1^{**} - C_1^*$ from the capital market. At Time 2 the firm's gross return is $C_2^*$ but the loan repayment reduces the net return at Time 2 to $C_2^{**}$. In short, the firm's investment decision is unchanged but its dividend decision is different. The important point to note

---

[5] E. Fama & M. Miller, *The Theory of Finance*, Holt, Rinehart & Winston, New York, 1972, pp. 301–4.
[6] Ibid., pp. 64–7.

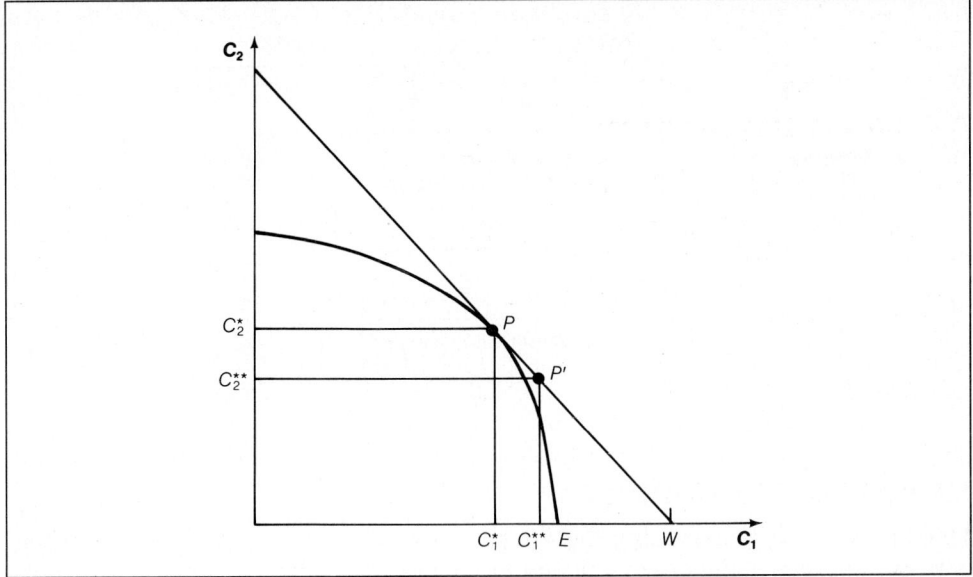

**Fig. 2.10**

is that the new policy $P'$ lies on the same market opportunity line as the original 'Fisher policy' $P$ and therefore the wealth of shareholders is unchanged. The ability of shareholders to maximise their utility is also unchanged. As explained previously, if any one point on a market opportunity line is attainable, then by borrowing or lending, all other points on the line are also attainable. From the shareholders' point of view, therefore, point $P'$ is no better or worse than point $P$.

In summary, provided that the firm does not alter its investment decision, the dividend decision does not affect shareholders' wealth. In this sense dividend policy is irrelevant. This is discussed further in Chapter 11.

## 2.4 INVESTORS' REACTIONS TO MANAGERS' DECISIONS

The link between decisions made by a firm and the resultant actions by investors is illustrated in Figure 2.11. A firm's managers may, on behalf of the firm, make an investment decision, a financing decision or a dividend decision. Information about this decision is transmitted to investors. On the basis of this information, investors may adjust their expectations of future returns from an investment in the firm, and revise their valuation of the firm's shares. Investors will then compare the current market price of the firm's shares with their revised valuation and either buy or sell shares in the firm. Investors' actions in the share market will determine the new market price of the firm's shares.

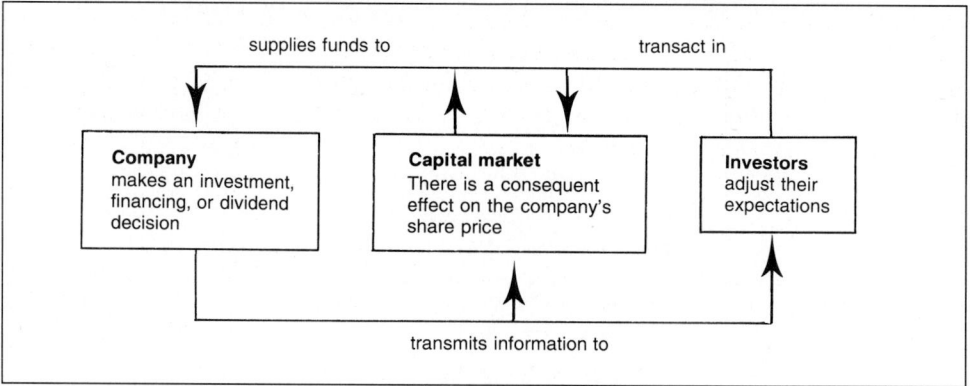

Fig. 2.11

### 2.4.1 Perfect certainty

Pursuing a goal of maximising the market value of a firm's equity is easy when there are no market imperfections and no uncertainty. Managers know with certainty an investment's cash flows and its net present value. Therefore, they will know whether acceptance of the investment will increase the market value of the firm's equity. As all investors also know the investment's net present value, there will be an immediate increase in the price of the firm's shares to reflect the resulting increase in the wealth of the firm. Further, managers and investors know that financing and dividend decisions are irrelevant and therefore these decisions will have no effect on the market value of the firm's equity.

### 2.4.2 The introduction of uncertainty

In practice there *is* uncertainty. What effect will the acceptance of an investment proposal have on the market value of a firm's shares? As is illustrated in Figure 2.11, any change in the firm's share price will depend on the reaction of investors to the decisions made by the managers. Obviously there can be no reaction unless investors obtain information about that decision. When there is uncertainty, the effect on the share price of decisions made by managers is no longer perfectly predictable. A simplification is to assume that everyone agrees about the probability distribution of the outcomes of all decisions. This means that although there is uncertainty, the exact nature of that uncertainty is agreed upon by all. In this case, when investors obtain information, the share price will adjust immediately to reflect the best estimate of the 'true' value of the firm.

Sufficient conditions for this to arise are:

'. . . a market in which (i) there are no transactions costs in trading securities, (ii) all available information is costlessly available to all market participants and (iii) all agree on the implications of current information for the current price and distributions of future prices of each security.'[7]

---

[7] E. Fama, 'Efficient Capital Markets: A Review of Theory and Empirical Work', *Journal of Finance*, May 1970, p. 387.

As these conditions are not satisfied in existing capital markets, it is fortunate that they are sufficient but *not* necessary conditions.[8] For example, decisions may still have an impact on share prices even though there are transaction costs and/or there are only a limited number of investors who have access to information about managers' decisions.

It is true that departures from the sufficient conditions give rise to the problem that managers are unable to predict with certainty the impact that a particular decision will have on a firm's share price. Fortunately there is a great deal of empirical evidence on the reaction of share prices to the release of information. This evidence is reviewed in Chapter 14. At this point we simply note that there is evidence in well-developed capital markets (such as the Australian capital market) that there are investors who react quickly to the receipt of new information, with the result that this information will be reflected in security prices. In general, therefore, managers should not depart from a course that they expect will increase the value of the firm's shares.

## SELECTED REFERENCES

Copeland, T., & Weston, J, *Financial Theory and Corporate Policy*, 3rd edn, Addison Wesley, Reading, Massachusetts, 1988.
Fama, E., & Miller, M., *The Theory of Finance*, Holt, Rinehart & Winston, New York, 1972.
Fisher, I., *The Theory of Interest*, Macmillan Company, New York, 1930.
Hirshleifer, J., *Investment, Interest and Capital*, Prentice–Hall, Englewood Cliffs, New Jersey, 1970.
Neave, E., & Wiginton, J., *Financial Management: Theory and Strategies*, Prentice–Hall, Englewood Cliffs, New Jersey, 1981.
Solomon, E., *The Theory of Financial Management*, Columbia University Press, New York, 1963.
Solomons, D., 'Economic and Accounting Concepts of Income', *The Accounting Review*, July 1961, pp. 374–83.

## QUESTIONS

1. Outline the roles played by firms, shareholders and the capital market in Fisher's analysis.
2. Consider the following situation:
   (a) A firm starts with $12 million in cash.
   (b) The rate of interest is 15 per cent.
   (c) The optimum policy for the firm is to invest $6 million in assets.
   (d) The net present value of this investment is $2 million.
   Answer the following questions:
   (i) In 1 year's time, how much will the firm receive from the investment?
   (ii) Draw, to scale, the Fisher diagram that represents this case.
   (iii) What are the marginal and average rates of return on the investment?
   (iv) What is the total wealth of the firm's shareholders immediately after the investment plan is announced?
3. Resketch your diagram for Question 2 to show the effect of a decrease in interest rates on the firm's investment plan. Show the net present value of the revised investment plan. Would all investors be made better off by the decrease in interest rates and the consequential revision in the investment plan? Give reasons for your answer.

---

[8] Ibid., pp. 387–8.

4. Return to the diagram you have drawn for Question 2. Suppose that the firm decides to invest $7.5 million, that is, $1.5 million more than before. Redraw the market opportunity line consistent with this new level of investment. What effect has the increased level of investment had on the firm's shareholders?

5. Assume a three-date model in which a rational economic agent has an endowment of $200 now, $100 in Year 1 and $50 in Year 2. If the agent wishes to consume $40 now and $120 in Year 2, what could she consume in Year 1 if:
   (a) no capital market opportunities exist?
   (b) capital markets exist and $i = 5$ per cent?

6. A sole proprietor has an initial endowment (wealth level) of $32 000. His firm has a production possibilities curve which conforms to the equation:
$$(C_1 + 10)^2 + (C_2 + 5)^2 = 1789, \text{ for } C_1, C_2 \geq 0$$
   where $C_1$ is present consumption (dividend) measured in thousands of dollars and $C_2$ is future output measured in thousands of dollars. (Graphically, this is part of a circle with centre at $(-10, -5)$ and a radius of $\sqrt{1789}$.) The sole proprietor has a utility function given by:
$$U = 40C_1^2 + 100C_1C_2$$
   where $C_1$ is his present consumption (in thousands of dollars) and $C_2$ is his future consumption (in thousands of dollars). It may be shown that this implies that along an indifference curve:
$$\frac{dC_2}{dC_1} = -0.8 - \frac{C_2}{C_1}$$
   Borrowing and lending may be undertaken at an interest rate of 20 per cent per period.
   (a) Graph the production possibilities curve and plot several *market opportunity lines*.
   (b) Using the graph, estimate the optimum levels of investment, current dividend and future output.
   (c) Find the exact values for the optimum levels of investment, current dividend and future output.
   (d) Calculate the net present value of the investment.
   (e) Find the exact values for present and future consumption which will maximise the sole proprietor's utility.
   (f) Show that the sole proprietor's planned consumption levels are financially feasible.

7. *Fisher's separation theorem ties together many of the basic notions which underlie much of modern finance theory: wealth maximisation, utility maximisation and net present value.* Discuss.

8. What is Fisher's separation theorem? What are its major implications for financial decision making?

9. *Financial decision making is a trivial task in a world of perfect certainty.* Discuss.

10. What are the implications for financial decision making when the interest rate on borrowing is greater than the interest rate on lending?

# CHAPTER 3

# THE TIME VALUE OF MONEY: AN INTRODUCTION TO FINANCIAL MATHEMATICS

Financial mathematics is an area of study that provides the finance specialist with some extremely useful tools to solve financial problems. In this chapter we present the major tools of financial mathematics and indicate some of their applications to financial problems. A thorough understanding of these tools, and how they may be used, will be very valuable when the material in later chapters is studied. Although you will find a large number of formulae in this chapter, you will not master financial mathematics if you simply try to memorise the formulae. It is preferable to understand the approach and the logic that is embodied in them. Our presentation emphasises these aspects.

## 3.1 FUNDAMENTAL CONCEPTS

In this section we explain four fundamental concepts in financial mathematics: cash flows, rate of return, interest rate, and time value of money.

*Cash flows*: financial mathematics concerns the treatment of cash flows between parties to a financial contract.[1] For example, when money is borrowed

---

[1] We use the term *contract* broadly. For example, we include depositing money in a bank as an act carried out as part of the contract between the depositor and the bank.

there is an initial flow of cash from the lender to the borrower, and subsequently one (or more) cash (re)payments from the borrower to the lender. In financial mathematics, as in finance generally, we are concerned with the cash flow consequences of a decision or a contract. How much cash will flow between the parties? When will these cash flows occur? These are the basic questions that must first be answered when analysing a financial contract using the tools of financial mathematics. We are not concerned with the possible non-cash consequences of a contract, such as effects on reported profit; nor are we concerned with effects on parties outside the contract.

*Rate of return*: financial decision makers usually find it convenient to relate the cash inflows that result from a contract to the cash outflows that the contract requires. Typically, this information is presented as a rate of return. Where there are only two cash flows in a financial contract—one at the start of the contract and another at the end—the rate of return is usually measured by[2]:

$$r = \frac{C_1 - C_0}{C_0} \tag{3.1}$$

where $C_1$ = cash inflow at Time 1
$C_0$ = cash outflow at Time 0
$r$ = rate of return per period

The value of $C_1 - C_0$ measures the dollar return to the investor; dividing the dollar return by $C_0$, which is the investment outlay, measures the rate of return.

### Example 3.1

On 1 January 1994, Paul buys an antique clock for $20 000. On 1 January 1995 the clock is sold for $24 000. What rate of return has been achieved?

Using Equation 3.1, the rate of return is:

$$r = \frac{C_1 - C_0}{C_0}$$

$$= \frac{\$24\ 000 - \$20\ 000}{\$20\ 000}$$

$$= \frac{\$4\ 000}{\$20\ 000}$$

$$= \frac{1}{5}$$

$$= 20 \text{ per cent per annum}$$

Note that a rate of return is always measured over a time period. In Example 3.1 the time period is one year. It is meaningless to state that an investment has returned, say, 20 per cent, without also specifying the time period involved.

*Interest rate*: the term *interest rate* is an important special case of the more general term *rate of return* and is used when the financial contract is in the form of debt. Although a precise definition of *debt* is difficult, the general principle

---

[2] There are other measures. For example, under some circumstances it is convenient to measure the rate of return by $\ell n\ (C_1/C_0)$. This is discussed further in Section 3.3.4.

involved is that <u>one party (the borrower) provides a specific promise</u> regarding the cash flow(s) payable to the other party (the lender). This may be contrasted with an investment where no particular promise exists as to the future cash flows. For example, Paul's investment in a real asset in Example 3.1 did not promise any particular cash inflow. Similarly, where an investment is made in ordinary shares, the shareholder is not promised any particular cash inflows from the investment.

*Time value of money:* One of the most important principles of finance is that <u>money has a time value.</u> This means that a given sum of money (say, a cash flow of $100) should be valued differently, depending on **when** the cash flow is to occur.

Suppose you have the choice of receiving $100 either today, or in one year's time. As a rational person you will choose to take the money today. Even if you do not plan to spend the money until one year later, you will still choose to take the money today rather than in one year's time because you will be able to earn interest on the money during the coming year. In that event, because of the interest you will earn you will have more than $100 in one year's time. Obviously, from your point of view this is better than receiving only $100 in one year's time. By your choice of taking the $100 today, rather than $100 in one year's time, you are in effect saying that $100 received today is more valuable to you than the promise of $100 to be received in one year's time. In short you have said that the value of a cash flow depends on when the cash flow is to occur: money has a time value.³

An important consequence of the time value of money is that we cannot simply add cash flows that will occur on different dates. Suppose you are offered $100 today *and* $100 in one year's time. How much is this worth to you? At this stage we cannot answer this question, except to say that the value today is **less than** $200. The value today of the cash flow of $100 in one year's time is less than $100, so the total value of the two cash flows must be less than $200. In financial mathematics it is extremely important <u>never to attempt to add cash flows from different dates</u>.

## 3.2 SIMPLE INTEREST
### 3.2.1 THE BASIC IDEA

Many financial contracts specify the interest rate to be paid, rather than specifying explicitly the cash payment(s) required. Simple interest is typically used when there is only a single time period involved; that is, money borrowed on

---

3 Other reasons for taking the money today rather than later are *risk* (you are not certain that the future cash flow will be paid) and *expected inflation* (you fear that in a year's time the purchasing power of $100 will be lower than it is today). While these reasons are valid, note that <u>money has a time value, even in the absence of these reasons</u>. That is, <u>even if the risk is zero</u> (you are certain that the future cash flow will be paid) and <u>you expect that the inflation rate next year will be zero or negative</u> (purchasing power either will not change or will increase) you will *still* take the $100 today, in preference to $100 later, <u>simply because interest rates are positive</u>.

one date is repaid in a lump sum payment made on a later date. Suppose, for example, that you borrow $1000, and agree to repay the loan by making a lump sum payment in one year's time at an interest rate of 12 per cent per annum.

Then: interest owed = 0.12 × $1000
= $120
Lump sum payment = $1000 + $120
= $1120

This example is, of course, very straightforward. Only one time period is involved—in this case it happens to be one year—and the interest rate is quoted on a matching (annual) basis. There is not much scope for confusion in this case. But suppose the contract had specified payment after six months, but still quoted the interest rate as 12 per cent *per annum*. How do we apply an annual rate to a period that is not equal to one year?

To answer this question we need a rule or convention to enable us to *translate* an annual interest rate into a semi-annual payment. There are several ways in which this can be done, one of which is *simple interest*. The distinguishing feature of using simple interest is that in *translating* from one time measurement to another, a simple ratio is taken. Thus, under simple interest, a contract that specifies an interest rate of '12 per cent per annum payable after half a year' means that in fact interest will be paid at the rate of 6 per cent per half-year. Similarly, '12 per cent per annum, payable after one quarter' means that, in fact, interest will be paid at 3 per cent per quarter.

*Example 3.2*

Molly's Bakeries Ltd borrows $10 000 and agrees to repay the loan in a lump sum payment in six months' time. The interest rate is 8 per cent per annum. Calculate the lump sum payment.

$$\text{Interest rate per half year} = \frac{1}{2} \times 8 \text{ per cent}$$
$$= 4 \text{ per cent}$$
$$\text{Interest payable} = \$10\,000 \times 0.04$$
$$= \$400$$
$$\text{Lump sum payable} = \$10\,000 + \$400$$
$$= \$10\,400$$

### 3.2.2 FORMULA DEVELOPMENT: FUTURE SUM

Suppose a principal sum $P$ is borrowed and will be repaid in a lump sum. The interest rate is $r$ per period (for example, per annum) and repayment is required after $t$ periods. The required future sum $S$, necessary to repay the amount borrowed, is given by:

$$S = \text{principal and interest}$$
$$= P + Prt$$
$$S = P(1 + rt) \tag{3.2}$$

## Example 3.3

(a) Use Equation 3.2 to calculate Molly's repayment of a loan of $10 000 after six months if the interest rate is 8 per cent per annum.
(b) What would be the repayment if the lump sum repayment were instead required after 15 months?

(a) $S = P(1 + rt)$

$= \$10\,000 \left[1 + (0.08)\left(\frac{6}{12}\right)\right]$

$= \$10\,000 \times 1.04$

$= \$10\,400$

(b) $S = P(1 + rt)$
$= \$10\,000 \left[1 + (0.08)(15/12)\right]$
$= \$10\,000 \times 1.1$
$= \$11\,000$

### 3.2.3 FORMULA DEVELOPMENT: PRESENT VALUE

In many practical cases, we know the future repayment $S$, the interest rate $r$, and the time period $t$, and our problem is to find the principal $P$ (or present value) that results. In this case we simply rearrange Equation 3.2 to find:

$$P = \frac{S}{1 + rt} \qquad (3.3)$$

The present value $P$ is the sum of money that corresponds to today's value of the future sum promised. The fact that $P$ is not equal to $S$ accords with the fact that money has a time value. Importantly, $P$ in Equation 3.3 can also be thought of as a *price*. Thus if a prospective borrower offers to pay a sum $S$ in $t$ years' time, then given today's interest rate $r$, we can calculate the price (value) of the borrower's promised repayment of $S$. In other words, viewing the loan from the lender's perspective, the principal represents the price (or present value) paid by the lender to secure from the borrower the promise to pay the future cash flow required by the contract. Looked at from the borrower's viewpoint, the promised future cash flow has been sold by the borrower to the lender for its present value, which is the loan principal.

### 3.2.4 SIMPLE INTEREST APPLICATIONS

There are many commercial applications of simple interest. For example, simple interest is used for Treasury notes, bills of exchange and many bank deposits. Because large sums of money are often involved, it is important that there be clear rules used in applying simple interest. These rules involve conventions that can differ between countries. Using bills of exchange as an example, the Australian conventions are:

(a) Interest rates are quoted on an annual basis.
(b) The time period $t$ is calculated as the exact number of days divided by 365.

(c) In a leap year, February 29 is included in the number of days, but the year is still assumed to consist of 365 days.
(d) Calculations are made to the nearest cent.

Bills of exchange are discussed in detail in Section 8.3.2.

*Example 3.4*
Stars Ltd borrows $100 000 on 20 January 1992, repaying in a lump sum on 2 March 1992. The interest rate is 8.75 per cent per annum. Calculate the lump sum repayment.

The time period involved is 42 days, consisting of 11 days in January, 29 days in February and 2 days in March; note that we do not count *both* 20 January and 2 March but we *do* count 29 February as 1992 was a leap year. Thus, in Equation 3.2, $r = 0.0875$ and $t = 11 + 29 + 2 = 42$ days.

Using this equation and the conventions explained in this section:

$$\begin{aligned} S &= P(1 + rt) \\ &= \$100\,000\,[1 + (0.0875)(42/365)] \\ &= \$100\,000 \times 1.010\,068\,493 \\ &= \$101\,006.85 \end{aligned}$$

*Example 3.5*
Moon Ltd promises to pay $500 000 in 60 days' time. For a company with Moon's credit standing the market interest rate for a loan period of 60 days is 14.4 per cent per annum. How much can Moon borrow?

Using Equation 3.3 and the conventions explained in this section, Moon can borrow the sum of:

$$\begin{aligned} P &= \frac{S}{1 + rt} \\ &= \frac{\$500\,000}{1 + (0.144)(60/365)} \\ &= \frac{\$500\,000}{1.023\,671\,232} \\ &= \$488\,438.07 \end{aligned}$$

## 3.3 COMPOUND INTEREST
### 3.3.1 THE BASIC IDEA

When interest is received by a lender, the interest can then itself be lent and, in due course, will earn further interest. The basic idea of compound interest is that interest generates further interest, which then generates still more interest, and so on. This is illustrated in Example 3.6.

## Example 3.6

On 31 December 1990, Kee Saw deposited $100 000 in a bank account that pays interest at the rate of 5 per cent per annum. How much will be in the account after four years?

The history of Kee Saw's account is as follows:

| Date | | Balance |
|---|---|---|
| 31 December 1990 | Account opened | $100 000.00 |
| 31 December 1991 | Interest 0.05 × $100 000.00 = $5000.00 | $105 000.00 |
| 31 December 1992 | Interest 0.05 × $105 000.00 = $5250.00 | $110 250.00 |
| 31 December 1993 | Interest 0.05 × $110 250.00 = $5512.50 | $115 762.50 |
| 31 December 1994 | Interest 0.05 × $115 762.50 = $5788.13 | $121 550.63 |

As the growth in Kee Saw's account makes clear, with compound interest, the amount of interest each year increases. In the first year the interest received is $5000; in the fourth year the interest received is $5788.13. After four years, Kee Saw's account balance is $121 550.63 but had the account been paid interest at the rate of $5000 per annum—that is, if Kee Saw had not been able to reinvest interest to earn further interest—the balance would have been only $120 000. Therefore, in four years Kee Saw has earned $1550.63 of 'interest on interest'.

### 3.3.2 FORMULA DEVELOPMENT

Assume that a principal of $P$ dollars is deposited (or lent) for a term of $n$ periods, with interest paid at the rate $i$ per period at the end of each period. Our task is to develop a formula for the future sum $S$ that will be accumulated after $n$ periods, allowing for compound interest.

After one period the interest earned is $iP$, so the account balance at the end of the first period is $P + iP = P(1+i)$. In fact the balance (or accumulated sum) at the end of any given period is simply the balance at the start of that period multiplied by $(1+i)$. During the second period interest will be earned on the amount $P(1+i)$.

So:

Balance at end of Period 2 = (balance at start of Period 2) × (1 + $i$)
= (balance at end of Period 1) × (1 + $i$)
= $P(1 + i) \times (1 + i)$
= $P(1 + i)^2$

Similarly:

Balance at end of Period 3 = (balance at start of Period 3) × (1 + $i$)
= (balance at end of Period 2) × (1 + $i$)
= $P(1 + i)^2 \times (1 + i)$
= $P(1 + i)^3$

Generalising from this discussion, the sum accumulated after $n$ periods is given by $P(1 + i)^n$,

so the formula is:
$$S = P(1 + i)^n \tag{3.4}$$

The corresponding formula to find the present value $P$ of a future sum $S$ is:
$$P = \frac{S}{(1 + i)^n} \tag{3.5}$$

where $S$ = future sum after $n$ periods
$P$ = principal (or present value)
$i$ = interest rate per period
$n$ = number of periods

To illustrate Equation 3.4 we use the information in Example 3.6. The value of Kee Saw's deposit after selected terms is shown in Table 3.1.

**Table 3.1** *Accumulated sum (future value) of $100 000 at 5 per cent per annum*

| Date | Number of years completed | Calculation | Accumulated sum ($) |
|---|---|---|---|
| 31 December 1991 | 1  | $100 000 (1.05) | 105 000.00 |
| 31 December 1992 | 2  | $100 000 (1.05)$^2$ | 110 250.00 |
| 31 December 1993 | 3  | $100 000 (1.05)$^3$ | 115 762.50 |
| 31 December 1994 | 4  | $100 000 (1.05)$^4$ | 121 550.63 |
| 31 December 1995 | 5  | $100 000 (1.05)$^5$ | 127 628.16 |
| 31 December 2000 | 10 | $100 000 (1.05)$^{10}$ | 162 889.46 |
| 31 December 2010 | 20 | $100 000 (1.05)$^{20}$ | 265 329.77 |
| 31 December 2040 | 50 | $100 000 (1.05)$^{50}$ | 1 146 739.98 |

The effect of compound interest becomes more pronounced as the number of periods becomes large. For example, after 50 years, the value of Kee Saw's account is nearly $1.15 million, or more than 10 times the amount with which he opened the account.

To illustrate Equation 3.5, which gives the present value of a future sum promised, suppose that an individual is offered the sum of $100 000 to be received after 5 years. If the relevant interest rate is 5 per cent per annum, compounded annually, the present value of this promised sum is:

$$\begin{aligned} P &= \frac{S}{(1 + i)^n} \\ &= \frac{\$100\,000}{(1.05)^5} \\ &= \frac{\$100\,000}{1.276\,281\,563} \\ &= \$78\,352.62 \end{aligned}$$

That is, looking ahead five years to this promised sum, it is worth, in today's terms, only $78 352.62. The logic is that if one wished to set aside money today to accumulate a sum of $100 000 in five years' time, the amount needed to be set aside today is $78 352.62. After five years, this sum will accumulate to $78 352.62 $(1.05)^5$ = $100 000. Clearly, all other things being equal, the present value is lower, the longer the waiting period. That is, the later the promised sum is to be received, the lower is its value today. This is illustrated in Table 3.2 which shows the present value of $100 000 to be received at selected future dates, using an interest rate of 5 per cent per annum.

**Table 3.2**  *Present value of $100 000 at 5 per cent per annum*

| Number of years to wait | Calculation | Present value ($) |
|---|---|---|
| 1 | $100 000/1.05 | 95 238.10 |
| 2 | $100 000/(1.05)$^2$ | 90 702.95 |
| 3 | $100 000/(1.05)$^3$ | 86 383.76 |
| 4 | $100 000/(1.05)$^4$ | 82 270.25 |
| 5 | $100 000/(1.05)$^5$ | 78 352.62 |
| 10 | $100 000/(1.05)$^{10}$ | 61 391.33 |
| 20 | $100 000/(1.05)$^{20}$ | 37 688.95 |
| 50 | $100 000/(1.05)$^{50}$ | 8 720.37 |

Again, the effect of the compound interest factor becomes more pronounced when the number of periods is large. Thus a promise to be paid $100 000 in 50 years' time is worth only $8720.37 in today's terms if the interest rate is 5 per cent per annum.

### 3.3.3  NOMINAL AND EFFECTIVE INTEREST RATES

Many financial contracts specify that a loan shall be repaid over more than one time period, rather than by a lump sum at the end of a single time period. For example, so called 'interest-only' loans require the payment of interest at regular intervals and the repayment of the principal in a lump sum on the maturity date.

In most loans the interest rate specified is a *nominal* interest rate, which is defined as an interest rate where the frequency of payment does *not* match the time period specified by the interest rate. Examples of nominal interest rates are: 15 per cent per annum with quarterly payments, and 4.5 per cent per quarter with monthly payments.[4] Where a nominal interest rate is used in a loan contract a rule is needed to decide how an interest rate quoted for one time period will be applied to a different time period. The convention adopted is to take a simple ratio. So, for example, '15 per cent per annum payable quarterly', means that interest will be charged each quarter at the rate of 3.75 per cent per quarter. That is, the annual rate of 15 per cent is simply scaled down to one-quarter of this rate because there are four quarters in a year. Similarly, '4.5 per cent per quarter payable monthly' means that interest will be charged each month at 1.5 per cent per month because one-third of 4.5 is 1.5.

Conversely, an *effective* interest rate is one where the frequency of payment does match the time period specified by the interest rate. Examples of effective interest rates are: 15 per cent per annum with annual payments, and 1 per cent per month with monthly payments. While few financial contracts specify an

---

4 To simplify matters, we assume that interest is charged (and therefore compounded) on the same dates as payments are to be made. This assumption is relaxed in Section 3.8.

effective interest rate, it is an important concept because it provides a consistent basis on which to compare interest rates. This use is illustrated in Example 3.8.

From the lender's viewpoint it is preferable to have interest paid more frequently, all other things being equal. To illustrate this fact, suppose that a bank is willing to lend $100 000 for one year at 15 per cent per annum but has the choice of receiving either annual or quarterly interest payments. Thus, the bank faces a choice between the cash inflows shown in Table 3.3:

**Table 3.3** Cash inflows at 15 per cent per annum

| | Cash inflow at time t | | | |
|---|---|---|---|---|
| | At t = 1 quarter | At t = 2 quarters | At t = 3 quarters | At t = 4 quarters |
| Annual interest | $0 | $0 | $0 | $115 000 |
| Quarterly interest | $3750 | $3750 | $3750 | $103 750 |

If we simply add up the cash flows of Table 3.3 we would, of course, find that both total $115 000. But as we explained earlier, this procedure is not valid because it involves adding cash flows that occur at different dates. Because earlier cash inflows are preferred to later cash inflows, the quarterly interest stream is worth more to the bank. It is worth more because the 'early' cash inflows of $3750 can themselves be re-lent to earn further interest later in the year.

Exactly how much more valuable the quarterly stream will prove to be will depend on the level of interest rates during the year, but provided interest rates are always positive, the bank cannot lose by accepting quarterly payments rather than an annual payment. An important special case can be developed by assuming that during the coming year the bank can continue to lend money at 3.75 per cent per quarter. Thus the first quarterly inflow of $3750 can be re-lent for the remaining three quarters, generating further quarterly interest payments of $0.0375 \times \$3750 = \$140.63$, together with the repayment of $3750 at the end of the fourth quarter. A quarter-by-quarter analysis is shown in Figure 3.1:

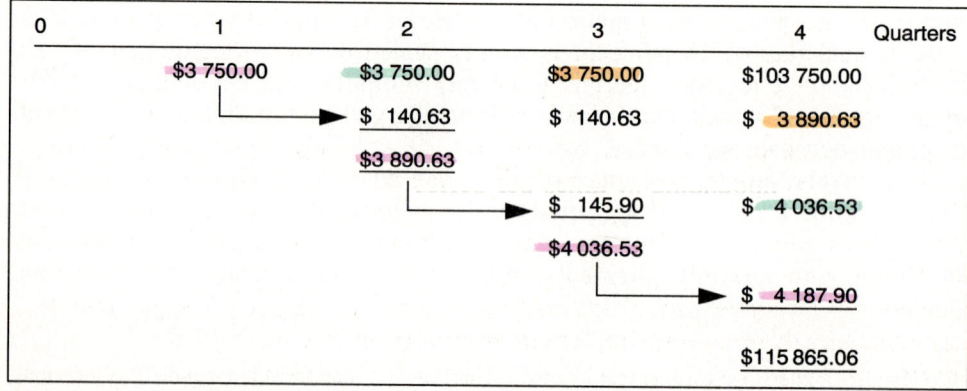

**Fig. 3.1** Cash flows re-lent at 3.75 per cent per quarter

As shown in Figure 3.1, taking into account opportunities for re-lending, the bank can secure a total cash inflow, at the end of the fourth quarter, of $115 865.04 which is clearly preferable to a cash inflow (at the same date) of only $115 000. In effect, with interest paid quarterly, the bank has earned at an annual rate of return given by:

$$\frac{\$115\,865.04 - \$100\,000}{\$100\,000}$$
$$\approx 15.865 \text{ per cent}$$

With an annual interest payment the bank would have had to specify an interest rate of 15.865 per cent per annum to equal this return. Therefore this example has established a sense in which the nominal interest rate of 15 per cent per annum, payable quarterly, is equivalent to an effective interest rate of 15.865 per cent per annum, payable annually. The sum of $115 865 is simply the future sum, equivalent to earning compound interest at the rate of 3.75 per cent per quarter for four quarters. This is easily seen by noting that:

$$\$100\,000 \times (1.0375)^4 \approx \$100\,000 \times 1.158\,65 = \$115\,865$$

Generalising from this example, if a lender advances a principal of $P$ and specifies a nominal interest rate of $j$ per period, with payments required every subperiod, and there are $m$ subperiods in every period, the future sum at the end of one period is given by:

$$S = P\left(1 + \frac{j}{m}\right)^m$$

The effective rate of interest per period is:

$$i = \frac{S - P}{P}$$

$$= \frac{P\left(1 + \frac{j}{m}\right)^m - P}{P}$$

therefore
$$i = \left(1 + \frac{j}{m}\right)^m - 1 \qquad (3.6)$$

Equation 3.6 is the formula for the effective interest rate $i$ for a nominal interest rate $j$, compounding $m$ times per period.

## Example 3.7
Calculate the effective annual interest rates corresponding to 12% per annum, compounding: (a) semi-annually, (b) quarterly, (c) monthly, (d) daily.
Solution
Using Equation 3.6, the calculations are as follows:

| Compounding frequency | Calculation | Effective annual interest rate |
|---|---|---|
| (a) Semi-annually | $(1.06)^2 - 1$ | 12.3600 per cent |
| (b) Quarterly | $(1.03)^4 - 1$ | 12.5509 per cent |
| (c) Monthly | $(1.01)^{12} - 1$ | 12.6825 per cent |
| (d) Daily | $(1.000\,328\,767)^{365} - 1$ | 12.7475 per cent |

These calculations illustrate very clearly the fact that, all other things being equal, more frequent compounding produces a higher effective interest rate.

### Example 3.8

Lake Developments Ltd is offered its choice of loan funds at the following nominal interest rates:

(a) 15.00 per cent per annum, payable annually;
(b) 14.50 per cent per annum, payable semi-annually;
(c) 14.00 per cent per annum, payable quarterly; and
(d) 13.92 per cent per annum, payable monthly.

Which of these nominal interest rates provides the lowest cost of finance in terms of the corresponding effective annual interest rate?

### Solution

Using Equation 3.6, the effective annual interest rates are:

(a) $i = 15$ per cent per annum;
(b) $i = (1.0725)^2 - 1 = 15.026$ per cent per annum;
(c) $i = (1.035)^4 - 1 = 14.752$ per cent per annum;
(d) $i = (1.0116)^{12} - 1 = 14.843$ per cent per annum.

Thus option (c), which is a nominal rate of 14.00 per cent per annum with quarterly compounding, provides the lowest effective annual interest rate.

### 3.3.4 COMPOUND INTEREST: TWO SPECIAL CASES AND A GENERALISATION

In this section we discuss real interest rates, continuous interest rates and geometric rates of return. To understand the remainder of the chapter, knowledge of these issues is *not* required, so some readers may wish to omit this section.

### SPECIAL CASE NO. 1: THE REAL INTEREST RATE

The word 'real' in this context is used in the same sense as it is used in phrases such as 'real GNP' and 'real wages'. The real interest rate is the interest rate *after* taking out the effects of inflation. The interest rate *before* taking out the effects of inflation is usually referred to as the 'nominal interest rate'. This should not be confused with using the same term, 'nominal interest rate', to mean an interest rate where the frequency of payment or compounding does not match the basis on which the interest rate is quoted.

Suppose that a representative basket of consumption goods costs $500. If the inflation rate in the coming year is expected to be 20 per cent per annum, the price of a basket at the end of the year is expected to be $600. Suppose also that a lender currently has $2000 that will be lent at a nominal interest rate for one year. By lending this sum the lender foregoes the consumption now of four representative baskets of goods. If a *real* interest rate of 5 per cent per annum is to be achieved, then the lender requires that at the end of the year the sum generated will be sufficient to purchase 4.2 baskets of goods. That is, the sum required in one year is:

$$4.2 \text{ baskets} \times \$600 \text{ per basket} = \$2520$$

Therefore, the nominal annual interest rate required is:

$$\frac{\$2520 - \$2000}{\$2000} = 26 \text{ per cent}$$

Generalising from this example, let:
$B$ = the price today of a representative basket of goods
$P$ = principal
$p$ = expected inflation rate
$i^*$ = required real interest rate
$i$ = nominal interest rate

Thus the lender foregoes consumption of $\frac{P}{B}$ baskets today, to be able to consume $\frac{P}{B}(1 + i^*)$ baskets in a year's time. The expected price of one basket in a year's time is $B(1 + p)$. Therefore, the nominal interest rate required is:

$$i = \frac{\frac{P}{B}(1 + i^*) B (1 + p) - P}{P}$$

On simplifying, this gives:

$$i = (1 + i^*)(1 + p) - 1 \tag{3.7}$$

Equation 3.7 shows the link with the idea of compounding: the nominal interest rate is not simply the sum of the real interest rate and the expected inflation rate, but rather is in the form of the real interest rate 'compounded' by the expected inflation rate. Rearranging Equation 3.7:

$$i^* = \frac{1 + i}{1 + p} - 1 \tag{3.8}$$

Equation 3.8 gives the real interest rate, $i^*$, corresponding to a nominal interest rate $i$ if the expected inflation rate is $p$. Expansion of Equation 3.8 gives the result:

$$i^* = i - p - pi^*$$
$$\neq i - p$$

That is, the real interest rate is *not* simply the difference between the nominal rate and the inflation rate. However, where the rates are 'small', $pi^*$ will also be small and the approximation $i^* = i - p$ will be close.

## Example 3.9

If the inflation rate is expected to be 20 per cent per annum and the nominal interest rate is 30 per cent per annum, calculate the corresponding real interest rate.

Using Equation 3.8:

$$i^* = \frac{1 + i}{1 + p} - 1$$
$$= \frac{1.30}{1.20} - 1$$
$$= 8.33 \text{ per cent per annum}$$

## SPECIAL CASE NO 2: CONTINUOUS INTEREST RATES

As we showed in Section 3.3.3, the more frequently compounding occurs, the higher the effective interest rate is, other things being equal. In the limiting case, compounding becomes so frequent that the time period between each interest payment approaches zero. This is known as 'continuous interest' and it can be shown that continuous interest is an example of exponential growth:

$$S = Pe^{jn} \qquad (3.9)$$

where $S$ = future sum
$P$ = principal
$j$ = continuously compounding interest rate per period
$n$ = number of periods
$e \approx 2.718\ 281\ 828\ 46$

## Example 3.10

If the interest rate is 12 per cent per annum, compounding continuously, how much will a principal of $100 000 be worth after one year? After two years?

Using Equation 3.9, the future sum after one year is:

$$S = Pe^{jn}$$
$$= \$100\ 000 \times e^{(0.12)(1)}$$
$$= \$100\ 000 \times 1.127\ 496\ 852$$
$$= \$112\ 749.69$$

Again using Equation 3.9, the future sum after two years is:

$$S = Pe^{jn}$$
$$= \$100\ 000\ e^{(0.12)(2)}$$
$$= \$100\ 000\ e^{0.24}$$
$$= \$127\ 124.92$$

The effective interest rate that results from continuous compounding is found by setting $n$ equal to 1 period and solving:

$$i = \frac{S - P}{P}$$
$$= \frac{Pe^j - P}{P}$$
$$i = e^j - 1 \qquad (3.10)$$

where $i$ = effective interest rate per period
$j$ = continuously compounding interest rate per period

## Example 3.11
What is the effective annual interest rate corresponding to a nominal interest rate of 12 per cent per annum, compounding continuously?

Using Equation 3.10, the effective annual interest rate $i$ is given by:

$$i = e^j - 1$$
$$= e^{0.12} - 1$$
$$\approx 12.749\,69 \text{ per cent per annum}$$

This of course, is the interest rate implicit in Example 3.10.

Although continuous compounding is rarely used in loan contracts, it is frequently used in other contexts. In particular, academic studies of security prices often assume that returns compound continuously between the dates on which the prices are observed. Consider the security prices $P_0$, $P_1$ and $P_2$ observed at dates 0, 1 and 2. These dates are assumed to be equally spaced. For example, the prices may be observed at weekly intervals. Assuming that returns accrue continuously through time, we can apply Equation 3.10 to assert that:

in the first week:  $P_1 = P_0 e^{r_1}$ and
in the second week: $P_2 = P_1 e^{r_2}$

where $r_1$ is the continuously compounding weekly rate of return in the first week and $r_2$ is the continuously compounding weekly rate of return in the second week.

Solving for $r_1$ and $r_2$:

$$r_1 = \ln(P_1/P_0)$$
$$r_2 = \ln(P_2/P_1)$$

where $\ln$ means logarithm to the base $e$ (usually referred to as the natural logarithm).

More generally, we can write that the rate of return in period $t$ is:

$$r_t = \ln(P_t/P_{t-1}) \tag{3.11}$$

Expressions of the form $\ln(P_t/P_{t-1})$ are called 'log price relatives' and $r_t$ is called a 'logarithmic rate of return' or a 'continuous rate of return'.

There are two reasons for choosing to measure rates of return in this way. First, the correct way to compound logarithmic rates of return is simply to add them. Thus, for example:

$$P_2 = P_1 e^{r_2}$$
$$\text{But } P_1 = P_0 e^{r_1}$$

Substituting:

$$P_2 = P_0 e^{r_1} e^{r_2}$$
$$\text{that is, } P_2 = P_0 e^{r_1 + r_2}$$

The total rate of return over the two time periods is simply the sum of the rates of return in each of the two constituent periods. Thus calculations such as finding an average rate of return are simpler when using logarithmic rates of return. As discussed later in this section, it is *not* valid to add rates of return if they are measured using the simple 'arithmetic' definition that:

$$r_t = (P_t - P_{t-1})/P_{t-1}$$

The second reason for measuring rates of return in this way is a statistical one. The greatest loss an investor can suffer is when the security price falls to zero. Using the simple arithmetic definition, the rate of return associated with this event is $-1$; that is, the rate of return is $-100$ per cent. Using logarithmic rates of return, the same event will register as a rate of return of $-\infty$. Given that there is no upper limit to the rate of return that might be achieved, it follows that while arithmetic rates of return fall in the range $-1$ to $+\infty$, logarithmic rates of return fall in the range $-\infty$ to $+\infty$. Thus, while the statistical distribution that describes logarithmic rates of return *might* have the convenient property of symmetry, and thus could (perhaps) follow the normal distribution, this *cannot* be true of arithmetic rates of return.

## A GENERALISATION: GEOMETRIC RATES OF RETURN

Compound interest is a special case of geometric rates of return. In the case of compound interest, the interest rate is the same in each period. Imagine, however, the more general case of geometric rates of return in which the rate of interest (or rate of return) is different in each period. In this case, the sum invested is still subject to the compounding process but the *rate* at which compounding occurs will differ from period to period.

As an example, suppose that $1000 is invested for four years and earns interest as follows:

In Year 1: 10 per cent per annum
In Year 2: 5 per cent per annum
In Year 3: 8 per cent per annum
In Year 4: 15 per cent per annum.

The value of this investment therefore grows as follows:

After Year 1: $1000.00 (1.10) = $1100.00
After Year 2: $1100.00 (1.05) = $1155.00
After Year 3: $1155.00 (1.08) = $1247.40
After Year 4: $1247.40 (1.15) = $1434.51

Of course, this result could have been found more quickly and conveniently by calculating, in one step:

$1000 (1.10) (1.05) (1.08) (1.15) = $1434.51

Writing the calculation in this way emphasises the similarity between compound interest and the more general case of geometric rates of return.

It is natural to ask: What compound interest rate would have produced the same result? In other words, what single rate of return per period would need to be earned in *each* of the four periods, to produce the same future sum? To answer this question we need to solve:

$$\$1000\,(1.10)\,(1.05)\,(1.08)\,(1.15) = \$1\,000\,(1+i)^4$$

that is, $i = [(1.10)\,(1.05)\,(1.08)\,(1.15)]^{\frac{1}{4}} - 1$

$\qquad = (1.434\,51)^{0.25} - 1$

$\qquad = 9.440$ per cent per annum

In fact, $i$ in this calculation is the mean (or average) geometric rate of return. It is that rate of return which, if earned in every period, and allowing for the effects of compounding, would produce the same outcome as that actually observed. In the general case, the mean geometric rate of return is:

$$i = [(1 + r_1)\,(1 + r_2)\,\ldots\,(1 + r_n)]^{\frac{1}{n}} - 1 \qquad (3.12)$$

where $r_k$ = the rate of return in period $k$
$\qquad k = 1, 2, \ldots, n$
$\qquad n$ = the number of completed periods

If the rate of return is calculated each period from security prices $P_0, P_1, \ldots, P_n$ then:

$$r_k = \frac{P_k - P_{k-1}}{P_{k-1}}$$

$$\quad = \frac{P_k}{P_{k-1}} - 1$$

Substituting in Equation 3.12:

$$i = \left[\left(1 + \frac{P_1 - P_0}{P_0}\right)\left(1 + \frac{P_2 - P_1}{P_1}\right)\ldots\left(1 + \frac{P_n - P_{n-1}}{P_{n-1}}\right)\right]^{\frac{1}{n}} - 1$$

$$\quad = \left[\left(\frac{P_1}{P_0}\right)\left(\frac{P_2}{P_1}\right)\ldots\left(\frac{P_n}{P_{n-1}}\right)\right]^{\frac{1}{n}} - 1$$

$$\quad = \left(\frac{P_n}{P_0}\right)^{\frac{1}{n}} - 1 \qquad (3.13)$$

It is important to understand that the mean rate of return is *not* $(r_1 + r_2 + \ldots + r_n)/n$. That is, it is *not* correct simply to sum the rates of return and divide by the number of periods.

*Example 3.12*

An investment of $100\,000$ produces rates of return as follows:
$\qquad$In Year 1: a gain of 10 per cent
$\qquad$In Year 2: a loss of 5 per cent
$\qquad$In Year 3: a loss of 8 per cent
$\qquad$In Year 4: a gain of 3 per cent.

Calculate the value of the investment at the end of the fourth year and the mean annual rate of return.
$\qquad$The value of the investment at the end of the fourth year is:

$$\$100\,000\,(1.10)\,(0.95)\,(0.92)\,(1.03)$$
$$= \$99\,024.20$$

Using Equation 3.13, the mean annual rate of return is:

$$i = \left(\frac{P_n}{P_0}\right)^{\frac{1}{n}} - 1$$

$$= \left(\frac{\$99\,024.20}{\$100\,000}\right)^{\frac{1}{4}} - 1$$

$$= -0.002\,448$$

$$= -0.2448 \text{ per cent}$$

This small negative mean rate of return is consistent with the outcome that the final value ($99 024.20) is less than the sum invested ($100 000). Note that the *incorrect* calculation of the mean as:

$$\frac{10\% - 5\% - 8\% + 3\%}{4}$$

$$= 0\%$$

clearly gives a nonsensical answer because the mean rate of return must be negative.

## 3.4 VALUATION OF MULTIPLE CASH FLOWS

### 3.4.1 INTRODUCTION

Many loan contracts stipulate that more than one cash flow is required to repay the loan. For example, a housing loan may require monthly repayments over a period of twenty years—a total of 240 repayments. In this section we consider the valuation of multiple cash flows. We do not assume that the cash flows conform to any particular pattern as regards amount or timing. Some important special cases involving equal amounts at equally spaced time intervals are considered in Section 3.5.

### 3.4.2 VALUE ADDITIVITY

While cash flows occurring at *different* times *cannot* be added, it *is* valid to add cash flows that occur at the *same* time. Therefore, if a contract requires cash payments to be made on, say, 1 April and 1 May, we cannot simply add these cash flows. However, if we first value the 1 April cash flow *as if* it were to occur on 1 May, we could then add the two cash flows, since one is actually a May cash flow and the other has, so to speak, been converted to the equivalent of a May cash flow. Alternatively, we could first value the 1 May cash flow *as if* it were to occur on 1 April; summation of these two cash flows then provides the total value of the two cash flows as at 1 April. For that matter we could choose any date at all, value the two cash flows as if they were to occur at that date, and thus produce a valuation as at that date.

## THE TIME VALUE OF MONEY

To implement this approach we need only to specify how a 1 April cash flow is to be valued as at 1 May. The answer is provided by the interest rate. Using our knowledge of compound interest we can easily use Equation 3.4 to carry forward in time (accumulate) the value of any cash flow, provided we know the interest rate to use. Similarly, we can just as easily use Equation 3.5 to carry backward in time (discount) the value of any cash flow if we know the interest rate to use.

### Example 3.13

On 1 February 1994 you sign a contract that entitles you to receive two future cash flows, as follows:

    On 1 February 1996:     $10 000
    On 1 August 1998:     $ 6 000

Assuming that the relevant interest rate is 5 per cent per annum (effective), value this contract as at: (a) 1 August 1998, (b) 1 February 1996, (c) 1 February 1994.

| $t = 0$ years | $t = 2$ years | $t = 3.5$ years |
|---|---|---|
| 1 February 1994 | 1 February 1996 | 1 August 1998 |
|  | $10 000 | $6 000 |

#### (a) VALUATION AS AT 1 AUGUST 1998

The cash flow of $10 000 on 1 February 1996 must be accumulated for $1\frac{1}{2}$ years to calculate an equivalent amount as at 1 August 1998. Therefore, the valuation as at 1 August 1998 is:

$$V_a = \$10\,000\,(1.05)^{1.5} + \$6000$$
$$= \$10\,759.30 + \$6000$$
$$= \$16\,759.30$$

Because 1 August 1998 is the date of the final cash flow of the contract, $V_a$ is known as the *terminal value* of the contract.

#### (b) VALUATION AS AT 1 FEBRUARY 1996

The cash flow of $6000 on 1 August 1998 must be discounted for $1\frac{1}{2}$ years to calculate an equivalent amount as at 1 February 1996. Therefore the valuation as at 1 February 1996 is:

$$V_b = \$10\,000 + \frac{\$6000}{(1.05)^{1.5}}$$
$$= \$10\,000 + \$5576.57$$
$$= \$15\,576.57$$

### (c) VALUATION AS AT 1 FEBRUARY 1994

Both cash flows must be discounted to 1 February 1994. This requires that the $10 000 to be received on 1 February 1996 be discounted for 2 years and the $6000 to be received on 1 August 1998 be discounted for $3\frac{1}{2}$ years. Therefore, the valuation as at 1 February 1994 is:

$$V_c = \frac{\$10\,000}{(1.05)^2} + \frac{\$6000}{(1.05)^{3.5}}$$

$$= \$9070.2948 + \$5058.1151$$

$$= \$14\,128.41$$

If this valuation is undertaken on 1 February 1994, then $V_c$ is the *present value of the contract*.

In Example 3.13, the three valuations $V_a$, $V_b$ and $V_c$ are all valuations of the same financial contract. They differ because the implied date of valuation differs. There should, therefore, be logical connections between the three valuations. For example, $V_c$ (the valuation as at 1 February 1994) should be the same as taking $V_a$ (the valuation as at 1 August 1998) and discounting for $3\frac{1}{2}$ years. In fact, the mathematics underlying the valuation process guarantees this result as the following calculation confirms:

$$\frac{V_a}{(1.05)^{3.5}}$$

$$= \frac{\$16\,759.30}{(1.05)^{3.5}}$$

$$= \$14\,128.41$$

$$= V_c$$

In effect, the valuation process uses compound interest to discount and accumulate cash flows to calculate value equivalents at a common point in time. The valuation as at that date is then found simply by adding the value equivalents for that date.

### 3.4.3 FORMULA DEVELOPMENT

Where a cash flow of $C$ dollars occurs at a time $t$, the value of that cash flow at a valuation date $t^*$ is given by:

$$V_{t^*} = C_t\,(1 + i)^{t^* - t} \tag{3.14}$$

In Equation 3.14, if $t^*$ is less than $t$, then the power $(t^* - t)$ is negative and a discounting of $C_t$ is indicated.

If there is more than one cash flow to be valued, the total value of the contract is the sum of the values of each cash flow.

## Example 3.14

Confirm that Equation 3.14 is correct by using it to make the valuations required in Example 3.13. In each case, $i = 5$ per cent per annum, $C_2 = \$10\,000$ and $C_{3.5} = \$6000$. The value of $t^*$, however, differs in each case.

### (a) VALUATION AS AT 1 AUGUST 1998

In this case, $t^* = 3.5$
Using Equation 3.14:

$$\begin{aligned}
V_{3.5} &= \$10\,000\,(1.05)^{3.5-2} + \$6000\,(1.05)^{3.5-3.5} \\
&= \$10\,000\,(1.05)^{1.5} + \$6000\,(1.05)^0 \\
&= (\$10\,000 \times 1.075\,929\,83) + \$6000 \\
&= \$16\,759.30 \\
&= V_a \text{ as calculated in Example 3.13}
\end{aligned}$$

### (b) VALUATION AS AT 1 FEBRUARY 1996

In this case, $t^* = 2$
Using Equation 3.14:

$$\begin{aligned}
V_2 &= \$10\,000\,(1.05)^{2-2} + \$6000\,(1.05)^{2-3.5} \\
&= \$10\,000\,(1.05)^0 + \$6000\,(1.05)^{-1.5} \\
&= \$10\,000 + \frac{\$6000}{(1.05)^{1.5}} \\
&= \$10\,000 + \$5576.57 \\
&= \$15\,576.57 \\
&= V_b \text{ as calculated in Example 3.13}
\end{aligned}$$

### (c) VALUATION AS AT 1 FEBRUARY 1994

In this case, $t^* = 0$
Using Equation 3.14:

$$\begin{aligned}
V_0 &= \$10\,000\,(1.05)^{0-2} + \$6000\,(1.05)^{0-3.5} \\
&= \$10\,000\,(1.05)^{-2} + \$6000\,(1.05)^{-3.5} \\
&= \frac{\$10\,000}{(1.05)^2} + \frac{\$6000}{(1.05)^{3.5}} \\
&= \$9070.2948 + \$5058.1151 \\
&= \$14\,128.41 \\
&= V_c \text{ as calculated in Example 3.13}
\end{aligned}$$

### 3.4.4 MEASURING THE RATE OF RETURN

When there are multiple cash flows in an investment there are also multiple time periods. Inevitably the question arises: For a given set of cash flows extending over two or more time periods, how can we measure the rate of return per period?

There are a number of different answers to this question but the answer most frequently offered is to employ a measure known as the 'internal rate of return'. In this section we outline this method. It is discussed in greater detail in Section 5.4.2.

First, however, we review the measurement of the rate of return over a *single* period. Consider a one-period investment that costs $1000 and produces a cash inflow of $1120 one year later. Such an investment would usually be described simply as a one-year loan of $1000 at an interest rate of 12 per cent per annum. We would calculate the interest rate by noting that the interest component of the cash flow after one year is $120, so the interest rate is $120/$1000 = 12 per cent. This is, of course, the result given by the simple definition of 'rate of return' in Equation 3.1. Equally we could have said that the rate of return is the value of $r$ that solves the following equation:

$$\frac{\$1120}{1+r} - \$1000 = 0$$

The calculation $1120/(1+r)$ is the present value of $1120 using a discount rate of $r$. On solving this equation we would, of course, find that $r = 0.12$, or 12 per cent.

The advantage of thinking about the rate of return in this way is that we can readily see how to extend this approach to the case of many cash flows and time periods. Consider the following investment. An initial investment of $1000 is made and, as before, a cash flow of $1120 is to be received after one year but, in addition, a further cash flow of $25 is to be received two years after making the initial investment. In tabular form, the cash flows of this investment are:

| Year | Cash flow ($) |
|------|---------------|
| 0    | −1000         |
| 1    | +1120         |
| 2    | + 25          |

Obviously this investment promises a rate of return of more than 12 per cent per annum, since the first cash inflow alone is sufficient to produce a rate of return of 12 per cent per annum. As an investor, however, we would prefer the $25 inflow to have been promised for Year 1 rather than Year 2. Had this occurred, the cash inflow after one year would be $1145, representing a rate of return of 14.5 per cent per annum. Putting these observations together, the investment's annual rate of return must be more than 12 per cent, but less than 14.5 per cent.

The internal rate of return measure proposes that the rate of return in this case is the value of $r$ that satisfies the following equation:

$$\frac{\$1120}{1+r} + \frac{\$25}{(1+r)^2} - \$1000 = 0$$

The term $\$25/(1 + r)^2$ can be thought of as the present value of $\$25$, discounted for two years at the rate $r$ per annum. Solving this equation[5], we find $r = 14.19$ per cent per annum. We can confirm this by noting that:

$$\frac{\$1120}{1.1419} + \frac{\$25}{(1.1419)^2} - \$1000$$
$$= \$980.821\,438 + \$19.172\,725\,87 - \$1000.00$$
$$= -\$0.005\,836\,178$$
$$\approx 0$$

The figure of 14.19 per cent falls within the bounds of 12 to 14.5 per cent, as suggested by our earlier intuitive reasoning.

Where there are $n$ cash inflows $C_t$ ($t = 1, ..., n$), following an initial cash outflow of $C_0$, the internal rate of return is that value (or values) of $r$ that solves the equation,[6]

$$\frac{C_1}{1+r} + \frac{C_2}{(1+r)^2} + \ldots + \frac{C_n}{(1+r)^n} - C_0 = 0,$$

or

$$\sum_{t=1}^{n} \frac{C_t}{(1+r)^t} - C_0 = 0 \qquad (3.15)$$

## 3.5 ANNUITIES

### 3.5.1 DEFINITION AND TYPES OF ANNUITY

In Section 3.4 we explained how to analyse contracts that require more than one repayment. We dealt with a general case that can be used to deal with a wide range of contracts. There is, however, a special case that is found in a large number of financial contracts and hence requires further discussion. This is the case of the *annuity*.

An *annuity* is a series of cash flows of equal amount, equally spaced in time. Thus, for example, a contract that requires $500 to be paid each month for a year is an annuity. Similarly, $600 per week for twelve weeks is an annuity; so is $20 000 per annum for 10 years. Annuities are involved in many types of personal loans, as well as in some commercial loans and certain kinds of financial instruments such as bonds.

Initially we consider four types of annuity:

### (a) THE ORDINARY ANNUITY

Like all annuities, the cash flow pattern of the ordinary annuity consists of equal amounts, equally spaced in time. The distinguishing characteristic of the ordinary annuity is that the time period from the date of valuation to the first payment is equal to the time period between each subsequent cash flow.

---

[5] In this particular case, $r$ can be found by solving the resulting quadratic equation. In more general cases, involving three or more periods, some iterative (trial-and-error) procedure is usually required.

[6] If the cash flows are produced by a bond, it is conventional to call the internal rate of return the bond's *yield-to-maturity* (or *yield* for short). For further discussion, see Section 4.4.

Diagrammatically, the cash flow pattern of the ordinary annuity, using six cash flows as an example, is:

| 0 | 1 | 2 | 3 | 4 | 5 | 6 |
|---|---|---|---|---|---|---|
|   | $C | $C | $C | $C | $C | $C |

### (b) THE ANNUITY-DUE

The distinguishing feature of the annuity-due is that <u>the first cash flow is to occur *immediately*.</u>

Diagrammatically, the cash flow pattern of the annuity-due, using six cash flows as an example, is:

| 0 | 1 | 2 | 3 | 4 | 5 |
|---|---|---|---|---|---|
| $C | $C | $C | $C | $C | $C |

### (c) THE DEFERRED ANNUITY

The distinguishing feature of the deferred annuity is that <u>the first cash flow will not occur until a time period has passed</u> *longer than* <u>the time period between subsequent cash flows.</u>

Diagrammatically, the cash flow pattern of the deferred annuity, using as an example six cash flows, the first to occur after three time periods, is:

| 0 | 1 | 2 | 3 | 4 | 5 | 6 | 7 | 8 |
|---|---|---|---|---|---|---|---|---|
|   |   |   | $C | $C | $C | $C | $C | $C |

### (d) THE ORDINARY PERPETUITY

The ordinary perpetuity is simply <u>an ordinary annuity</u> with the special feature that <u>the cash flows are to continue forever</u>.[7]

Diagrammatically the cash flow pattern of the ordinary perpetuity is:

| 0 | 1 | 2 | 3 | 4 | → |
|---|---|---|---|---|---|
|   | $C | $C | $C | $C | → |

where the arrows indicate continuing forever.

## 3.5.2 FORMULA DEVELOPMENT: PRESENT VALUE OF AN ORDINARY ANNUITY

The formula for the present value of an ordinary annuity is one that we will use frequently. This formula can then be adapted to apply to the other types of annuities.

The cash flow pattern of an ordinary annuity of $n$ cash flows, of $C$ dollars each, is shown below:

| 0 | 1 | 2 | 3 | ...... | $n-1$ | $n$ |
|---|---|---|---|--------|-------|-----|
|   | $C | $C | $C |        | $C    | $C  |

---

[7] We could, of course, also consider the categories *perpetuity-due* and *deferred perpetuity* but have not done so because the purpose at this stage is simply to introduce the idea of a perpetuity, as distinct from an annuity of finite life.

The present value $P$ of this stream of cash flows is given by the sum of the present values of the individual cash flows:

$$P = \frac{C}{1+i} + \frac{C}{(1+i)^2} + \frac{C}{(1+i)^3} + \ldots + \frac{C}{(1+i)^{n-1}} + \frac{C}{(1+i)^n} \quad (3.16)$$

where $i$ = the interest rate per period.

Multiplying both sides of Equation 3.16 by $(1+i)$:

$$P(1+i) = C + \frac{C}{1+i} + \frac{C}{(1+i)^2} + \ldots + \frac{C}{(1+i)^{n-2}} + \frac{C}{(1+i)^{n-1}} \quad (3.17)$$

Subtracting Equation 3.16 from Equation 3.17, we find that all terms on the right-hand side cancel out, except the last term of Equation 3.16 and the first term of Equation 3.17:

$$P(1+i) - P = C - \frac{C}{(1+i)^n}$$

or

$$Pi = C - \frac{C}{(1+i)^n}$$

which, on rearrangement gives:

$$\boxed{P = \frac{C}{i}\left[1 - \frac{1}{(1+i)^n}\right]} \quad (3.18)$$

It is often convenient to consider an annuity of $1 per period. That is, we set $C = 1$ and Equation 3.18 becomes:

$$\boxed{P = A_{\overline{n}|i} = \frac{1}{i}\left[1 - \frac{1}{(1+i)^n}\right]} \quad (3.19)$$

Equation 3.19 is thus the formula for the present value of an ordinary annuity consisting of $n$ payments, each of $1 per period. It is conventional to use the notation $A_{\overline{n}|i}$, sometimes read as 'A angle n at rate i', to indicate this value. There is no special significance in this notation: it is simply a convention. Mathematically, the functional notation $P(n, i)$ would serve equally well. Values of $A_{\overline{n}|i}$ for different values of $n$ and $i$ are provided in Table 4 of Appendix A.

**Example 3.15**
Find the present value of an ordinary annuity of $5000 per annum for four years if the interest rate is 8 per cent per annum by (a) using a calculator to discount each individual cash flow, (b) using a calculator to evaluate the formula given in Equation 3.18, and (c) using Table 4 of Appendix A to evaluate the formula given by Equation 3.19.

**Solution**
(a) Discounting each cash flow:

$$\text{(a)} \quad \frac{\$5000}{(1+0.08)} + \frac{\$5000}{(1+0.08)^2} + \frac{\$5000}{(1+0.08)^3} + \frac{\$5000}{(1+0.08)^4} = \$16,560.63$$

$$\text{(b)} \quad P = \frac{5000}{0.08}\left[1 - \frac{1}{(1+0.08)^4}\right] = \$16,560.63$$

$$\text{(c)} \quad P = A_{\overline{n}|i} = 5000 \times 3.3121 = \$16,560.5$$

**54** BUSINESS FINANCE

$$P = \frac{C}{1+i} + \frac{C}{(1+i)^2} + \frac{C}{(1+i)^3} + \frac{C}{(1+i)^4}$$

$$= \frac{\$5000}{1.08} + \frac{\$5000}{(1.08)^2} + \frac{\$5000}{(1.08)^3} + \frac{\$5000}{(1.08)^4}$$

$$= \$4629.6296 + \$4286.6941 + \$3969.1612 + \$3675.1493$$

$$= \$16\,560.63$$

(b) Using Equation 3.18:

$$P = \frac{C}{i}\left[1 - \frac{1}{(1+i)^n}\right]$$

$$= \frac{\$5000}{0.08}\left[1 - \frac{1}{(1.08)^4}\right]$$

$$= \$5000 \times 3.312\,126\,84$$

$$= \$16\,560.63$$

(c) Using Table 4 of Appendix A:

$$P = C\,A_{\overline{n}|i}$$

$$= \$5000 \times 3.3121$$

$$= \$16\,560.50$$

Except for the relatively small rounding error when using Table 4, the three answers are identical.

### 3.5.3 FURTHER FORMULA DEVELOPMENT: PRESENT VALUES OF ANNUITIES-DUE, DEFERRED ANNUITIES AND ORDINARY PERPETUITIES

The cash flow pattern of an *annuity-due* with $n$ cash flows of $C$ dollars each is shown below:

```
   0      1      2      3            n - 2    n - 1
  $C     $C     $C     $C  ......     $C       $C
```

It is important to be aware that, with $n$ cash flows in an annuity-due, there are only $(n - 1)$ time periods involved.[8]

Inspecting the annuity-due diagram, it is clear that an annuity-due of $n$ cash flows is simply an ordinary annuity of $(n - 1)$ cash flows, plus an immediate cash flow. The present value is therefore:

---

[8] This is frequently a source of confusion. For an ordinary annuity it makes no difference whether $n$ is defined as the number of cash flows or the number of time periods, since these are equal. For an annuity-due, we must choose whether to define $n$ in terms of the number of cash flows or the number of time periods. We have chosen to develop the formula with $n$ representing the number of cash flows.

$$P = C + \frac{C}{i}\left[1 - \frac{1}{(1+i)^{n-1}}\right] \qquad (3.20)$$

$$\text{or } P = C(1 + A_{\overline{n-1}|i}) \qquad (3.21)$$

where  $P$ = present value
$C$ = periodic cash flow
$i$ = interest rate per period
$n$ = number of cash flows

### Example 3.16

Kathy's rich uncle promises her an allowance of $1000 per month, starting today, with a final payment to be made 6 months from today. If the interest rate is 0.5 per cent per month, what is the present value of the promised allowance?

Kathy has been promised *seven* payments of $1000 with the first being due immediately. Thus she has been promised $1000 today, plus an *ordinary* annuity of *six* payments. This is the logic embodied in Equation 3.20. Using this equation with $n$ set equal to 7:

$$P = C + \frac{C}{i}\left[1 - \frac{1}{(1+i)^{n-1}}\right]$$

$$= \$1000 + \frac{\$1000}{0.005}\left[1 - \frac{1}{(1.005)^{7-1}}\right]$$

$$= \$1000 + \frac{\$1000}{0.005}\left[1 - \frac{1}{(1.005)^{6}}\right]$$

$$= \$1000 + \$5896.38$$

$$= \$6896.38$$

*[handwritten: $P = \$1000(1 + A_{\overline{6}|0.5})$*
*$= \$1000(1 + 5.89638)$*
*$= \$1000 \times 6.89638$*
*$= \$6,896.38$ ]*

The cash flow pattern of a *deferred annuity* is as follows:

| 0 | 1 | 2 | ... | $k-1$ | $k$ | $k+1$ | ... | $k+n-2$ | $k+n-1$ |
|---|---|---|---|---|---|---|---|---|---|
|   |   |   |   |   | $C | $C |   | $C | $C |

In this case, there are $n$ cash flows and the first cash flow occurs after $k$ periods.

To find the present value of this series of cash flows, imagine that the valuation was to be made at date $(k-1)$ instead of date zero. Looking ahead from date $(k-1)$, the cash flow pattern is that of an ordinary annuity of $n$ cash flows. Thus, at date $(k-1)$, the present value is given by the present value of an ordinary annuity:

$$P_{k-1} = \frac{C}{i}\left[1 - \frac{1}{(1+i)^n}\right] \qquad (3.22)$$

where $P_{k-1}$ means the present value at date $(k-1)$.

To shift the valuation date back from date $(k-1)$ to date zero, we simply discount the value given by Equation 3.22 for $(k-1)$ periods. Thus the required formula is:

$$P = \frac{1}{(1+i)^{k-1}} \frac{C}{i}\left[1 - \frac{1}{(1+i)^n}\right] \quad (3.23)$$

or

$$P = \frac{C}{(1+i)^{k-1}} A_{\overline{n}|i} \quad (3.24)$$

where  $C$ = cash flow per period
$\quad\quad i$ = interest rate per period
$\quad\quad n$ = number of cash flows
$\quad\quad k$ = number of time periods until the first cash flow

Alternatively, the present value of a deferred annuity can be found by first imagining that cash flows are to occur at *all* $(k + n - 1)$ dates. The present value of such a stream is, of course, given by the present value of an ordinary annuity consisting of $(k + n - 1)$ cash flows. The effect of the deferral period is accounted for by subtracting the present value of the first $(k - 1)$ 'missing' cash flows, because these cash flows will not occur. That is:

$$P = \left[\begin{array}{c}\text{Present value of an}\\ \text{ordinary annuity of}\\ (k+n-1) \text{ cash}\\ \text{flows}\end{array}\right] \text{ less } \left[\begin{array}{c}\text{Present value of an}\\ \text{ordinary annuity of}\\ (k-1) \text{ cash flows}\end{array}\right]$$

That is

$$P = \frac{C}{i}\left[1 - \frac{1}{(1+i)^{k+n-1}}\right] - \frac{C}{i}\left[1 - \frac{1}{(1+i)^{k-1}}\right]$$

$$= C\left[A_{\overline{k+n-1}|i} - A_{\overline{k-1}|i}\right] \quad (3.25)$$

### Example 3.17

Jason will be starting a 9 month live-in training course in 5 months' time. His father, Sam, has promised him a living allowance of $200 per month to help support him during this time. If the simple interest rate is 9 per cent per annum, payable monthly, how much money will Sam need to set aside today to finance Jason's allowance?

### Solution

Sam needs to set aside the present value of the promised allowance. The allowance is an annuity of 9 payments, the first payment to be made 5 months from today. Diagrammatically, the cash flows are:

```
0    1    2    3    4    5    6    7    8    9    10   11   12   13
                              $200 $200 $200 $200 $200 $200 $200 $200 $200
                               1    2    3    4    5    6    7    8    9  months
```

Using the logic we have developed in this section, we can approach this problem in two stages. First, *when viewed from the standpoint of date 4*, the cash flows form an ordinary annuity of 9 payments. We therefore value this stream, as at date 4, using Equation 3.18 which gives the present value of an ordinary annuity. Secondly, we find the value as at date zero by discounting for 4 periods. The calculations are shown below. Note that the interest rate is $0.09/12 = 0.75$ per cent per month.

As at date 4 the value is:

$$P = \frac{C}{i}\left[1 - \frac{1}{(1+i)^n}\right]$$

$$= \frac{\$200}{0.0075}\left[1 - \frac{1}{(1.0075)^9}\right]$$

$$= \$1734.315\ 285$$

As at date zero, the value is thus:

$$P = \frac{\$1734.315\ 285}{(1.0075)^4}$$

$$= \$1683.25$$

This is, of course, the logic embodied in Equation 3.23, as we now show. In this case, $n = 9$, $k = 5$ and $i = 0.09/12 = 0.75$ per cent per month. Using Equation 3.23:

$$P = \frac{1}{(1+i)^{k-1}} \frac{C}{i}\left[1 - \frac{1}{(1+i)^n}\right]$$

$$= \frac{1}{(1.0075)^4} \frac{\$200}{0.0075}\left[1 - \frac{1}{(1.0075)^9}\right]$$

$$= \frac{1}{1.030\ 339\ 191} \times \$200 \times 8.671\ 576\ 423$$

$$= \frac{\$1734.315\ 285}{1.030\ 339\ 191}$$

$$= \$1683.25$$

Alternatively, using Equation 3.25, and again using $n = 9$, $k = 5$ and $i = 0.75$ per cent per month, the required sum is:

$$P = \frac{C}{i}\left[1 - \frac{1}{(1+i)^{k+n-1}}\right] - \frac{C}{i}\left[1 - \frac{1}{(1+i)^{k-1}}\right]$$

$$= \frac{\$200}{0.0075}\left[1 - \frac{1}{(1.0075)^{13}}\right] - \frac{\$200}{0.0075}\left[1 - \frac{1}{(1.0075)^4}\right]$$

$$= \$200\ (12.342\ 345\ 08 - 3.926\ 110\ 409)$$

$$= \$200 \times 8.416\ 234\ 676$$

$$= \$1683.25$$

The cash flow pattern of an *ordinary perpetuity* of $C$ dollars per period, is shown below:

```
 0      1      2      3      4      5
 |------|------|------|------|------|------>
        $C     $C     $C     $C     $C------>
```

The ordinary perpetuity is simply an ordinary annuity where the number of cash flows $n$ becomes indefinitely large. Therefore, to find its present value we need to consider the formula for the present value of an ordinary annuity and allow $n$ to approach $\infty$. Thus the problem is to value:

$$P = \lim_{n \to \infty} \frac{C}{i}\left[1 - \frac{1}{(1+i)^n}\right]$$

Because the interest rate $i$ is positive, $(1+i)^n$ becomes indefinitely large as $n$ becomes indefinitely large. This means that $\frac{1}{(1+i)^n}$ becomes very small because the denominator of this fraction becomes very large. In the limit, the value of this fraction approaches zero and thus the present value of an ordinary[9] perpetuity is:

$$P = \frac{C}{i} \quad (3.26)$$

where $C$ = the cash flow per period
$i$ = the interest rate per period

*Example 3.18*
A government security promises to pay $3 per annum forever. If the interest rate is 8 per cent per annum and a payment of $3 has just been made, how much is the security worth?
*Solution*
Using Equation 3.26:

$$P = \frac{C}{i}$$

$$= \frac{\$3}{0.08}$$

$$= \$37.50$$

The value of the security is $37.50.

## 3.6 FUTURE VALUE OF ANNUITIES

It is frequently necessary to calculate the value of an annuity as at the date of the final cash flow. Such a calculation is required if, for example, regular savings are being made towards a target future sum.

To derive the formula for the future value of an ordinary annuity, we use a two-stage process. First, the *present* value of the annuity is calculated. Secondly, the *future* value is calculated by accumulating the present value for the $n$ periods

---

[9] Similarly, it is a simple matter to show that the present value of a perpetuity-due is $C + \frac{C}{i}$, and the present value of a deferred perpetuity, where the first cash flow occurs after $k$ periods, is $\frac{1}{(1+i)^{k-1}} \times \frac{C}{i}$.

from the valuation date to the date of the final cash flow. In effect we use the compound interest formula $S = P(1 + 1)^n$, where, in this case, $P$ is given by the present value of an ordinary annuity. That is:

$$S = \frac{C}{i}\left[1 - \frac{1}{(1+i)^n}\right](1+i)^n$$
$$= \frac{C}{i}[(1+i)^n - 1] \qquad (3.27)$$

If $C = \$1$, Equation 3.27 is normally written as:

$$S_{\overline{n}|i} = \frac{(1+i)^n - 1}{i} \qquad (3.28)$$

Values of $S_{\overline{n}|i}$ for different values of $n$ and $i$ are given in Table 3 of Appendix A.

### Example 3.19
Starting with his next monthly salary payment, Harold intends to save $200 each month. If the interest rate is 8.4 per cent per annum, payable monthly, how much will Harold have saved after two years?
*Solution*
The monthly interest rate is 0.7 per cent. Using Equation 3.27, Harold's savings will amount to:

$$S = \frac{C}{i}[(1+i)^n - 1]$$
$$= \frac{\$200}{0.007}[(1.007)^{24} - 1]$$
$$= \$200 \times 26.034\ 925\ 07$$
$$= \$5206.99$$

We could use this two-stage approach to derive formulae for the future values of annuities-due and deferred annuities. In practice, however, it is usually just as easy to apply this approach using the particular numbers of the problem. As we said at the start of this chapter, rather than learning a list of *formulae*, it is preferable to learn the *approach* and then apply this approach to the particular problem. This is illustrated in Example 3.20.

### Example 3.20
Harold's sister Janice can also save $200 per month, but intends to start saving today. With an interest rate of 0.7 per cent per month, how much will she have in two years' time? Reconcile this with the savings achieved by Harold in the previous example.
*Solution*
This problem requires the future value of an annuity-due. We first calculate the present value, then accumulate this amount for 24 months:

*Step 1*
$$P = C + \frac{C}{i}\left[1 - \frac{1}{(1+i)^n}\right]$$
$$= \$200 + \frac{\$200}{0.007}\left[1 - \frac{1}{(1.007)^{24}}\right]$$
$$= \$4604.321\ 714$$

*Step 2*
$$S = P(1+i)^n$$
$$= \$4604.321\ 714\ (1.007)^{24}$$
$$= \$5443.43$$

Janice is thus able to save $\$5443.43$ after two years, compared to Harold's savings of $\$5206.99$. That is, Janice will save $\$236.44$ more than Harold. Logically, this amount should equal the future value of the extra $\$200$ saved by Janice, accumulated for 24 months at 0.7 per cent per month. This is in fact the case, because $\$200\ (1.007)^{24} = \$236.44$.

## 3.7 PRINCIPAL-AND-INTEREST LOAN CONTRACTS

### 3.7.1 THE BASIC STRUCTURE OF THE CONTRACT

An important application of annuities is to loan contracts where the principal is gradually reduced by a series of equal repayments. These loans are often called *principal-and-interest* or *credit foncier* loans. Many commercial loans, consumer loans and housing loans are in this category. The promised repayments form an annuity and the present value of the repayments is equal to the loan principal. Therefore, if the promised future repayments are made on time the debt should reduce gradually during the loan term; and when the final promised repayment is made the debt should be extinguished. This pattern is illustrated in Example 3.21.

### Example 3.21

On 31 December, 19X0, Pennant Ltd borrows $\$100\ 000$ from ZNA Bank. Annual repayments are required over five years at a fixed interest rate of 11.5 per cent per annum. How much is each annual repayment? Show the year-by-year record of the loan account for the five years ended 31 December 19X5.

*Solution*

The annual repayments of $C$ dollars form an ordinary annuity with a present value of $\$100\ 000$. Using Equation 3.18:

$$\$100\ 000 = \frac{C}{0.115}\left[1 - \frac{1}{(1.115)^5}\right]$$
$$= C \times 3.649\ 877\ 847$$
$$\text{Thus } C = \frac{\$100\ 000}{3.649\ 877\ 847}$$
$$= \$27\ 398.18$$

The annual repayment required is $\$27\ 398.18$.

The year-by-year record of the loan account is:

| Date | Entry | Balance owing |
|---|---|---|
| 31 Dec 19X0 | Principal borrowed | $100 000.00 |
| 31 Dec 19X1 | Add interest 0.115 × $100 000.00 = $11 500.00 | $111 500.00 |
| | Less repayment $27 398.18 | $ 84 101.82 |
| 31 Dec 19X2 | Add interest 0.115 × $84 101.82 = $9671.71 | $ 93 773.53 |
| | Less repayment $27 398.18 | $ 66 375.35 |
| 31 Dec 19X3 | Add interest 0.115 × $66 375.35 = $7633.17 | $ 74 008.52 |
| | Less repayment $27 398.18 | $ 46 610.34 |
| 31 Dec 19X4 | Add interest 0.115 × $46 610.34 = $5360.19 | $ 51 970.53 |
| | Less repayment $27 398.18 | $ 24 572.35 |
| 31 Dec 19X5 | Add interest 0.115 × $24 572.35 = $2825.83 | $ 27 398.18 |
| | Less repayment $27 398.18 | $         0.00 |

The year-by-year record shows that annual repayments of $27 398.18 are just sufficient to repay the loan over the five-year term.

### 3.7.2 PRINCIPAL AND INTEREST COMPONENTS

As shown by the loan account in Example 3.21, the required repayments are just sufficient to extinguish the debt at the required date. This is achieved by a series of repayments, each of which is sufficient to cover interest accrued at that date and to reduce the principal. As the principal decreases, so also does the interest accruing and thus, as time passes, a larger proportion of each repayment goes to reducing the principal. The principal and interest components of the repayments in Example 3.21 are shown below.

| | A | B = C − A | C |
|---|---|---|---|
| Year ended 31 December | Interest component | Principal component | Repayment |
| 19X1 | $11 500.00 | $15 898.18 | $27 398.18 |
| 19X2 | $ 9 671.71 | $17 726.47 | $27 398.18 |
| 19X3 | $ 7 633.17 | $19 765.01 | $27 398.18 |
| 19X4 | $ 5 360.19 | $22 037.99 | $27 398.18 |
| 19X5 | $ 2 825.83 | $24 572.35 | $27 398.18 |

This pattern is more marked where the number of repayments to be made is large. This is shown in Example 3.22.

### Example 3.22

Phantom Ltd borrows $100 000 at an interest rate of 11.5 per cent per annum, repayable by equal monthly instalments over 20 years. Calculate the principal and interest components of the first and last repayments.
*Solution*
In this example, the monthly interest rate is 0.115/12 = 0.009 583 333 and the loan term is 240 months. Therefore, using Equation 3.18:

$$\$100\,000 = \frac{C}{0.009\,583\,333}\left[1 - \frac{1}{(1.009\,583\,333)^{240}}\right]$$

$$= C \times 93.770\,840\,22$$

$$\text{Thus } C = \frac{\$100\,000}{93.770\,840\,22}$$

$$= \$1066.43$$

The interest accrued during the first month of the loan is $0.009\,583\,333 \times \$100\,000 = \$958.33$. Therefore, when the first monthly repayment of $1066.43 is made, $958.33 (or nearly 90 per cent of the repayment) is required to meet the interest accrued during the first month and only $108.10 (just over 10 per cent of the repayment) is available to be used to reduce the principal. At the end of the loan term this pattern is reversed. Only a small amount of interest will accrue during the last month, so almost the whole of the final monthly repayment will be available to reduce the principal. The component of principal in the final repayment is $\$1066.43/1.009\,583\,333 = \$1056.31$; therefore, the interest component is only $10.12. One aspect of this pattern is that the balance owing decreases slowly in the early stages of the loan, but decreases rapidly as the maturity date is approached. This is considered in more detail in the next section.

### 3.7.3 BALANCE OWING AT ANY GIVEN DATE

The balance owing at any given date is the present value of the then remaining repayments. We explained earlier how the principal is the present value of *all* promised repayments. Of course, the principal is simply the balance owing at the time the loan is made. Similarly, the balance owing at any given date is the present value of the repayments still to be made as at that date.

*Example 3.23*
Consider again Phantom Ltd's loan of $100 000 at an interest rate of 11.5 per cent per annum, repayable by equal monthly instalments over 20 years. As shown in Example 3.22, the required monthly repayment is $1066.43. What is the balance owing when (a) one-third of the loan term has expired, and (b) two-thirds of the loan term has expired?
*Solution*
(a) The loan term is 240 months. Therefore, when one-third (or 80 months) of this term has expired 160 monthly repayments still have to be made. The balance owing at the end of month 80 is the present value of the then remaining 160 repayments:

$$P_{80} = \frac{\$1066.43}{0.009\,583\,333}\left[1 - \frac{1}{(1.009\,583\,333)^{160}}\right]$$

$$= \$87\,087.85$$

(b) When two-thirds (or 160 months) of the loan term has expired, 80 monthly repayments still have to be made. Therefore, the balance owing at the end of month 160 is:

$$P_{160} = \frac{\$1066.43}{0.009\,583\,333}\left[1 - \frac{1}{(1.009\,583\,333)^{80}}\right]$$
$$= \$59\,394.64$$

In the previous section we explained that, in these types of loans, the balance owing reduces slowly at first and more rapidly towards the end of the loan term. This is clearly evident in Example 3.23. When one-third of the loan term has expired, the balance owing is still more than $87 000 out of an original loan of $100 000. One-third of the loan term has seen the principal fall by less than 13 per cent. When two-thirds of the loan term has expired, only about 40 per cent of the debt has been repaid. A more detailed presentation of this effect is provided in Figure 3.2.

### 3.7.4 LOAN TERM REQUIRED

In some applications it is necessary to solve for the required loan term $n$ given the principal, interest rate and repayment schedule. For example, in order to plan future expenditure, a borrower may wish to know when an existing loan will be repaid. Solving for the loan term requires us to rearrange Equation 3.18 so that $n$ appears on the left-hand side:

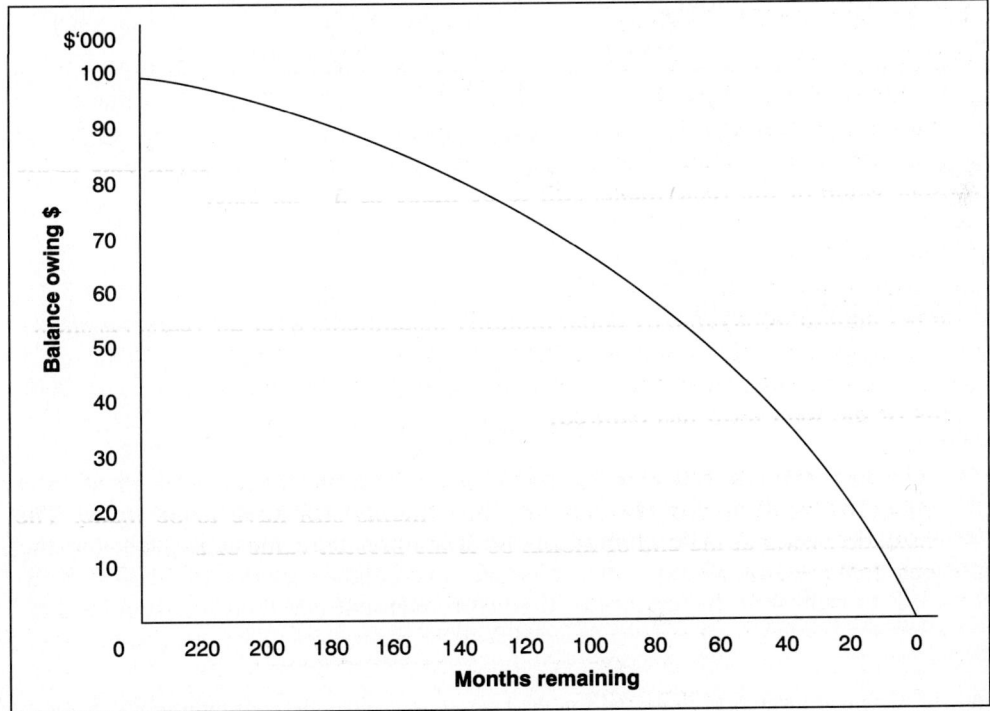

**Fig. 3.2** *Balance owing as loan is repaid*

Thus
$$P = \frac{C}{i}\left[1 - \frac{1}{(1+i)^n}\right]$$

$$\frac{1}{(1+i)^n} = 1 - \frac{Pi}{C}$$

$$(1+i)^n = \frac{C}{C - Pi}$$

and
$$n = \frac{\log[C/(C - Pi)]}{\log(1+i)} \qquad (3.29)$$

Logarithms to any base (such as base 10 or base $e$) will give the correct answer.

### Example 3.24

One year ago, Canberra Fruit Ltd borrowed $750 000 at an interest rate of 12 per cent per annum. The loan is being repaid by monthly instalments of $16 683.34 over five years. As a result of making the promised repayments over the past year, the balance owing is now $633 532.48. The company can now afford repayments of $20 000 per month and wishes to know when the loan will be repaid if repayments are increased to that level.

### Solution

Using Equation 3.29:

$$n = \frac{\log[C/(C - Pi)]}{\log(1+i)}$$

$$= \frac{\log[\$20\,000/\{\$20\,000 - (\$633\,532.48)(0.01)\}]}{\log(1.01)}$$

$$= \frac{\log[\$20\,000/\{\$13\,664.6752\}]}{\log(1.01)}$$

$$= \frac{\log[1.463\,627\,91]}{\log(1.01)}$$

Using 'common' logarithms (logarithms to the base 10)[10]:

$$n = \frac{0.165\,430\,682}{0.004\,321\,373}$$

$$= 38.282 \text{ months}$$

The loan will be repaid after a further 39 months; for the first 38 months the repayment will be $20 000 per month, while the last (39th) repayment will be a smaller amount. The amount of the last repayment must be such that the present value of all 39 repayments equals the balance owing of $633 532.48. Using $R$ to represent the amount of the last repayment, we therefore require that:

---

[10] Use of natural logarithms (logarithms to the base $e$), must give the same answer: $n = (0.380\,918\,223)/(0.009\,950\,33) = 38.282$.

$$\$633\,532.48 = \frac{\$20\,000}{0.01}\left[1 - \frac{1}{(1.01)^{38}}\right] + \frac{R}{(1.01)^{39}}$$

$$\$3839.2139 = \frac{R}{(1.01)^{39}}$$

Thus $\quad R = \$5659.47$

The amount of the last (39th) repayment is thus $5659.47.

### 3.7.5 Changing the interest rate

In some loan contracts, the interest rate can be changed at any time by the lender, although in practice, changes are normally made only when there has been a change in the general level of interest rates in the economy. In Australia, most housing loan contracts, and many commercial loans, are in this category. Typically, the parties to the contract will at the outset agree on a notional loan term—say 15 years for a housing loan—and the lender will then require a regular repayment that is calculated *as if* the current interest rate is fixed for 15 years. If, as is usually the case, the general level of interest rates changes, the interest rate charged on the loan will be changed. The lender will then calculate the new required repayment. Alternatively, the lender may allow the borrower to continue making the same repayment and, instead, alter the loan term to reflect the new interest rate.[11] Of course, a combination of both responses is also a possibility. These choices are illustrated in Example 3.25.

### Example 3.25

Three years ago Claude and Janet borrowed $80 000, repayable by equal monthly instalments over 15 years. At the time they borrowed the money the interest rate was 9.6 per cent per annum. Following standard procedures the lender correctly calculated the required monthly payment to be $840.21. Claude and Janet have made all repayments on time and the balance owing is now $71 685.05. Interest rates have been rising and the lender has now decided to increase the interest rate to 10.8 per cent per annum. What will be the new monthly repayment if the loan term is to remain unchanged? If, instead, the monthly repayment is left at $840.21, by how many months will the loan term increase?

### Solution

The new monthly repayment $C$ must be set so that the present value, calculated using the new interest rate, of the remaining 144 repayments equals the balance outstanding of $71 685.05. The new interest rate is 10.8 per cent per annum or 0.9 per cent per month. Therefore, using Equation 3.18:

---

[11] Note, however, that if the interest rate is increased to a level where the monthly repayment is less than the monthly interest accruing (that is, $C < Pi$) the loan term becomes infinite. In these circumstances lenders will usually require a higher monthly repayment.

$$\$71\,685.05 = \frac{C}{0.009}\left[1 - \frac{1}{(1.009)^{144}}\right]$$

$$= 80.531\,669\,39\,C$$

Thus  $C = \$890.15$

The new repayment is $890.15 per month.

Alternatively, if the loan term is extended, the new loan term may be found using Equation 3.28:

$$n = \frac{\log\left[C/(C - Pi)\right]}{\log(1 + i)}$$

$$= \frac{\log\left[\$840.21/\{\$840.21 - (\$71\,685.05)(0.009)\}\right]}{\log(1.009)}$$

$$= \frac{\log(4.307\,785\,068)}{\log(1.009)}$$

$$= 162.998 \text{ months}$$

$$\approx 163 \text{ months}$$

The remaining loan term is now 163 months, which is 19 months longer than the 144 'expected' at the time of the interest rate increase.

## 3.8  GENERAL ANNUITIES

In our discussion of annuities, the frequency of compounding has coincided with the frequency of payments. For example, we have considered cases where interest is calculated and charged annually, and the borrower is required to make annual repayments. In practice, however, this is not always the case. Situations arise where loan repayments are required more frequently, or less frequently than interest is compounded. Annuities with this feature are called *general annuities*.

In a general annuity, the frequency of compounding does not match the frequency of repayment. There are thus two cases to consider:

1. *The frequency of compounding is greater than the frequency of repayment.* For example, a loan contract may specify an interest rate of 20 per cent per annum, compounding quarterly, but repayments are made annually.
2. *The frequency of compounding is less than the frequency of repayment.* For example, a loan contract may specify an interest rate of 20 per cent per annum, compounding quarterly, but repayments are made monthly.

In both cases, the problem is solved by adjusting the interest rate to a rate where the compounding frequency matches the payment frequency[12]. This adjustment is made using the concept of the effective interest rate that we discussed in Section 3.3.3. This concept was summarised in Equation 3.6:

---

[12] Alternatively, an adjustment can be made to the repayment amount. However, when using a calculator it is generally easier to adjust the interest rate.

## THE TIME VALUE OF MONEY

$$i = \left(1 + \frac{j}{m}\right)^m - 1$$

where $i$ = the effective interest rate per period
$j$ = the nominal interest rate, compounding $m$ times per period

Note that the time dimension of $i$ is for a longer period than the time dimension of $j/m$. For example, $i$ might be an interest rate per annum while $j/m$ might be an interest rate per quarter. Thus it is easier to restate Equation 3.6 in terms of an interest rate $i_s$, for the shorter time period, and an interest rate, $i_l$, for the longer time period. That is, Equation 3.6 is rewritten as:

$$i_l = (1 + i_s)^m - 1 \qquad (3.30)$$

where $m$ = the number of 'short' periods in one 'long' period

### Example 3.26
Use Equation 3.30 to express 20 per cent per annum, compounding quarterly, as (a) an effective annual interest rate, and (b) an effective monthly interest rate.

### Solution
(a) In this case, interest is compounding quarterly and we wish to calculate an equivalent interest rate in which compounding occurs annually. Thus $i_l$ is to be calculated, where $i_s = 0.20/4 = 0.05$, and $m = 4$.

Using Equation 3.30:

$$i_l = (1 + i_s)^m - 1$$
$$= (1.05)^4 - 1$$
$$= 0.215\,506\,25$$
$$\approx 21.55 \text{ per cent per annum}$$

(b) In this case, interest is compounding quarterly and we wish to calculate an equivalent interest rate in which compounding occurs monthly. Thus $i_s$ is to be calculated, where $i_l = 0.20/4 = 0.05$ and $m = 3$.

Using Equation 3.30:

$$i_l = (1 + i_s)^m - 1$$
$$0.05 = (1 + i_s)^3 - 1$$
$$i_s = (1.05)^{\frac{1}{3}} - 1$$
$$= 0.016\,396\,357$$
$$\approx 1.64 \text{ per cent per month}$$

### Example 3.27
A loan is currently being repaid by repayments of $406.80 at the end of each quarter. The interest rate is 20 per cent per annum. The borrower wishes to change to a monthly repayment schedule that will pay off the loan by the same date. Calculate the amount of each monthly repayment.

*Solution*
The repayment schedule for a typical quarter is shown in Figure 3.3.

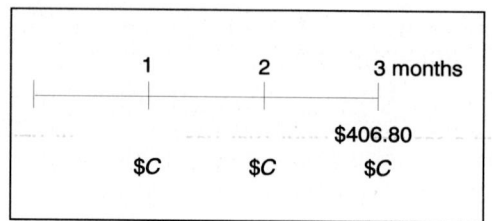

**Fig. 3.3** *Monthly and quarterly repayments*

As shown in Figure 3.3, it is proposed to replace each end-of-quarter cash flow of $406.80 with three end-of-month cash flows of $C each. Interest is charged quarterly at a nominal rate of 20 per cent per annum. That is, the effective *quarterly* interest rate is 5 per cent. As shown in Example 3.26 (b), the equivalent effective *monthly* interest rate is 1.639 6357 per cent. Equating the present values of the quarterly and monthly cash-flow streams gives:

$$\frac{\$406.80}{1.05} = \frac{\$C}{0.016\ 396\ 357}\left[1 - \frac{1}{(1.016\ 396\ 357)^3}\right]$$

Note, however, that though we have included the calculation of $(1.016\ 396\ 357)^3$ in this expression, this calculation should by definition equal 1.05 (see the calculation in Example 3.26 (b) for clarification). Therefore, we need to solve:

$$\frac{\$406.80}{1.05} = \frac{\$C}{0.016\ 396\ 357}\left[1 - \frac{1}{1.05}\right]$$

which gives $C = \$133.40$.

Therefore, monthly repayments of $133.40 will pay the loan off at the same date as making quarterly repayments of $406.80. Note that $3 \times \$133.40 = \$400.20$, which is slightly less than the quarterly repayment of $406.80. This difference reflects the present-value effect of making monthly repayments earlier than the quarterly repayments they replace.

## SELECTED REFERENCES

Crapp, H. & Marshall, J. *Money Market Maths*, Allen and Unwin, Sydney, 1986.
Hart, W. L., *Mathematics of Investment*, 5th edn, Heath, Lexington, 1975.
Martin, P. & Burrow, M., *Applied Financial Mathematics*, Prentice–Hall, Sydney, 1991.

## QUESTIONS

1. Albert deposits $2000 in a bank fixed deposit for six months at an interest rate of 13.25 per cent per annum. How much interest will he earn?

2. If Albert reinvests the $2000, *plus* the interest earned (see Question 1), for a further six months, again at 13.25 per cent per annum, how much interest will he earn in this second six-month period?
3. Jane borrowed $10 000 and repaid the loan 30 days later by a single payment of $10 400. What is the implied annual simple interest rate?
4. Mary borrowed $7250 at an annual simple interest rate of 15.50 per cent. She repaid the loan by paying a lump sum of $7394.70. What was the loan term?
5. (a) What will be the accumulated value, at the end of 10 years, of $1000 invested in a savings account that pays 8 per cent per annum? Assume that no withdrawals are made from the savings account until the end of the tenth year. What is the interest element of the accumulated value?
   (b) Assume that interest is withdrawn every year. What will be the total interest earnings at the end of the tenth year? Why does this amount differ from the interest earned in (a)?
6. If you invest $65 000 for 3 years at 14.7 per cent per annum (interest payable annually), how much will you have at the end of the 3 years?
7. Frank has invested $10 000 for 10 years at 12.4 per cent per annum. He has to pay tax on the interest income each year. Calculate the value of the investment at the end of the tenth year if his tax rate is :
   (a) 47 per cent per annum;
   (b) 39 per cent per annum;
   (c) 20 per cent per annum;
   (d) zero per annum.
   (e) Rework your answer to (a), if, instead of having to pay tax each year, Frank must pay in tax 47 per cent of the accumulated interest at the end of the tenth year. Which tax system is better for him? Why?
8. Philip invests $17 200 at an interest rate of 2.5 per cent per quarter. How much is the investment worth after 2 years?
9. Calculate the following present values:
   (a) $1000 payable in 5 years if the interest rate is 12 per cent per annum.
   (b) $1000 payable in 10 years if the interest rate is 12 per cent per annum.
   (c) $1000 payable in 5 years if the interest rate is 6 per cent per annum.
   (d) $16 205 payable in 1 year if the interest rate is 1.5 per cent per month.
   (e) $1 million payable in 40 years if the interest rate is 15 per cent per annum.
   (f) $1 million payable in 100 years if the interest rate is 15 per cent per annum.
10. Sam borrows $8000 repayable in a lump sum after 1 year. The interest rate he agrees to is described as '15.0 per cent per annum, calculated monthly'. How much is the repayment?
11. Matthew bought a house for $182 000. After four years he estimates that its value has changed as follows:
    In the first year: an increase of 7 per cent.
    In the second year: an increase of 27 per cent.
    In the third year: a decrease of 5 per cent.
    In the fourth year: an increase of 11 per cent.
    How much is it worth now? What is the average annual rate of return?
12. If the real interest rate is 10 per cent per annum, and the expected inflation rate is 25 per cent per annum, what should be the nominal interest rate?

13. In Xanadu, the consumer price index (CPI) stood at 147.6 on 1 January 19X0. On that date, SBF Ltd invested $50 000 for four years at an interest rate of 11.4 per cent per annum (compound). On 1 January 19X4 the CPI stood at 193.8. What real annual rate of return has SBF earned?

14. What is the annual interest rate (compound) implied by each of the following future values, present values and terms:
    (a) FV = $92 000;    PV = $82 000;    $t = 2$ years
    (b) $1 604 600;      $1 500 000;      $t = 4$ years
    (c) $2 million;      $1 307 600;      $t = 3$ years
    (d) $10 million;     $6 000 000;      $t = 6$ years
    (e) $10 million;     $6 000 000;      $t = 5.5$ years.

15. What is the corresponding effective annual interest rate for each of the following nominal interest rates:
    (a) 18 per cent per annum, payable half-yearly.
    (b) 18 per cent per annum, payable monthly.
    (c) 18 per cent per annum, payable fortnightly.
    (d) 18 per cent per annum, payable daily.
    (e) 18 per cent per annum, payable continuously.

16. A bank bill is bought for $91 107 and is sold 54 days later for $93 323. What is the effective annual interest rate?

17. Rock Solid Ltd sells, on credit, goods to the value of $8465.95 to University Garden Supplies Ltd. Rock Solid offers a discount of half of 1 per cent for payment within 7 days; otherwise, payment must be made on the thirtieth day. What is the effective annual interest rate implicit in the discount being offered? State any assumptions you make.

18. Since 1 August 19X2, Wing Yin's investment policy has been to lodge fixed (term) deposits at her local bank. The bank pays interest on the maturity date of a deposit and the interest rate is expressed as an annual simple interest rate. When a deposit matures, Wing Yin's policy is to relodge the whole sum (principal and interest) immediately for a further period. She chooses the term of each deposit according to her assessment of the interest rates available at that time. Wing Yin's decisions to date are as follows:

    | Date | Decision |
    | --- | --- |
    | 1 August 19X2 | 8 month deposit at 9.15 per cent per annum |
    | 1 April 19X3 | 6 month deposit at 8.45 per cent per annum |
    | 1 October 19X3 | 10 month deposit at 8.16 per cent per annum. |

    Calculate, as at 1 August 19X4, the effective annual interest rate Wing Yin has earned since she began this policy. (In doing so, assume that all months are of equal length.) Briefly explain each step.

19. What is the present value (at 7 per cent per annum) of a contract which provides for the following three payments to be made:
    After 6 months:        $ 7601, and
    After $2\frac{1}{2}$ years:    $ 9900, and
    After 7 years:         $18 522.

20. Luke borrows $200 000 from a bank to set up a medical practice. He agrees to pay a fixed interest rate of 18.48 per cent per annum (calculated monthly) and to repay by equal monthly instalments over 10 years. Calculate the monthly repayment. By how much does Luke's *first* repayment

reduce the principal? If the loan is paid off as planned, by how much will the *last* repayment reduce the principal?

21. After 21 monthly repayments, Luke inherits a large sum of money and decides to repay the (remaining) loan. When he arrives at the bank to make the 22nd repayment he asks for the payout figure. How much should it be?

22. John decides that he desperately needs a new Italian suit priced at $1999. He borrows the money and agrees to pay $71.07 each month at an interest rate of 16.8 per cent per annum, payable monthly. How long will he be paying?

23. What is the approximate annual rate of return on an investment with an initial cash outlay of $10 000, and net cash inflows of $2770 per year for 5 years?

24. Warren Cameron buys a motorboat for $6000, paying $1000 deposit. The remainder is borrowed from the Goodfriend Loan Co. to be repaid by 15 monthly payments of $405.50 each. What is the monthly interest rate being charged? What is the nominal annual interest rate? What is the effective annual interest rate?

25. Anne Hopewell has just borrowed $70 000 to be repaid by monthly repayments over 20 years at an interest rate of 18 per cent per annum. Based on this information, the monthly repayment is approximately $1080 but Anne intends to make higher monthly repayments. She asks you how long it will take to repay the loan if the amount paid per month is:
    (a) $1100
    (b) $1200
    (c) $1500

26. Stanley turns 55 today. He plans to retire on his 65th birthday and wants to put aside the same sum of money every birthday (starting today) up to and including his 65th birthday. He then wants to be able to withdraw $10 000 every birthday (starting with his 66th) up to and including his 85th birthday. He believes that an interest rate of 10 per cent per annum is a reasonable estimate. How much does he need to put aside each birthday?

27. Layla borrows $50 000, repayable in monthly instalments over 10 years. The nominal interest rate is 12 per cent per annum. What is the monthly repayment? After 3 years have passed, the lender increases the interest rate to 13.5 per cent per annum and Layla is given the choice of either increasing the monthly repayment or extending the term of the loan. What would be the new monthly repayment? What would be the new loan term?

28. Don and Jenny wish to borrow $80 000, to be repaid over a period of twenty years by monthly instalments. The interest rate (nominal) is 14.7 per cent per annum. The first payment is due at the end of the first month.
    (a) Calculate the effective annual interest rate.
    (b) Calculate the amount of the monthly repayment if the same amount is to be repaid every month for the period of the loan.
    (c) Suppose, instead, that Don and Jenny are to repay $800 per month for the first twelve months, then $900 per month for the twelve months after that, then $x per month thereafter. Assuming that the term is to stay at 20 years, how much is $x?

(d) Alternatively, suppose that Don and Jenny decide to repay $2000 per month from the time the money is borrowed until it is repaid. How long would it take to repay the loan? What would be the amount of the final payment?

29. Peter borrowed $800 000 to refit his fishing trawler. The loan requires monthly repayments over 15 years. When he borrowed the money the interest rate was 13.5 per cent per annum, but eighteen months later the bank decided to increase the interest rate to 15.0 per cent per annum, in line with market rates. The bank tells Peter he can increase his monthly repayment (so as to pay off the loan by the originally agreed date) or he can extend the term of the loan (and keep making the same monthly repayment). Calculate:
    (a) the new monthly repayment if Peter accepts the first option; and
    (b) the extra period added to the loan term if Peter accepts the second option.

30. How much money would be needed to establish a permanent scholarship paying $1000 at the end of each year if money can be invested at 8 per cent per annum?

31. A pine plantation returns nothing to its owner in the first 2 years. In the following 2 years, the returns are $1000 and $1500, respectively, and after that the return is $2000 per year in perpetuity. All returns are in cash and occur at year end.
    (a) What is the present value of the constant return stream at the beginning of the fifth year if the returns can be invested at 8 per cent per annum?
    (b) What is the current present value of the whole return stream at the same required rate of return?

32. An ordinary annuity of $300 per quarter is to be replaced by annual payments (the payments to be made at the end of each year). What will be the annual payments if the interest rate is 6 per cent per annum?

33. What is the present value of a perpetual cash inflow of $100 received at the end of each year, the first inflow occurring 2 years from now, if the interest rate is 5 per cent per annum? This cash flow can be produced by investing $1000 in a business this year and $600 next year. What is the present value of the investment? Is it profitable?

## APPENDIX 3.1

# THE USE OF CALCULATORS WITH $Y^x$ FUNCTION

Apart from the standard arithmetic functions (addition, subtraction, multiplication and division), financial mathematics explained in Chapter 3 requires only one specialised function: the $Y^x$ function. Today, most calculators provide this facility. The $Y^x$ function raises any number, $Y$, to any power, $x$. Suppose, for example, that we wish to calculate $8^2$ (eight squared). The steps are:

$$\boxed{8}\ \boxed{Y^x}\ \boxed{2}\ \boxed{=}$$

and the answer appearing is 64. Of course, in this case it would have been just as easy to perform:[13]

$$\boxed{8}\ \boxed{\times}\ \boxed{8}\ \boxed{=}$$

The real usefulness of the $\boxed{Y^x}$ function becomes apparent with more complex problems. Suppose that we wish to calculate 8 raised to the power of 50. The steps are:

$$\boxed{8}\ \boxed{Y^x}\ \boxed{5}\ \boxed{0}\ \boxed{=}$$

and the answer ($1.427\,246\,8 \times 10^{45}$) appears. This is much easier than performing each of the fifty multiplications.

This alone is an impressive time saver but there are still further uses for the $\boxed{Y^x}$ function. Suppose we wish to find the $n$th root of a number. We note that:

$$\sqrt[n]{Y} = Y^{\frac{1}{n}}$$

---

[13] On some calculators, it is easier this way since $\boxed{8}\ \boxed{\times}\ \boxed{=}$ will give the correct answer.

Therefore, to find a square root, we use $x = \frac{1}{n} = \frac{1}{2} = 0.5$; to find a tenth root we use $x = \frac{1}{n} = \frac{1}{10} = 0.1$, and so on. For example, suppose that we wish to calculate the tenth root of 56. Then:

$$\boxed{5}\,\boxed{6}\,\boxed{Y^x}\,\boxed{.}\,\boxed{1}\,\boxed{=}$$

and the answer (1.495 611 5) appears.

Finally, if we wish to find the inverse of a number raised to any power $\left(\text{for example, } \frac{1}{7^6} = \frac{1}{7 \times 7 \times 7 \times 7 \times 7 \times 7}\right)$ we can use negative powers. This is because $\frac{1}{Y^x} = Y^{-x}$. So to calculate $\frac{1}{7^6}$ we perform:[14]

$$\boxed{7}\,\boxed{Y^x}\,\boxed{6}\,\boxed{+/-}\,\boxed{=}$$

and the answer ($8.499\,85 \times 10^{-6}$) appears. Similarly, $\frac{1}{\sqrt[4]{19}}$ can be calculated by performing:

$$\boxed{1}\,\boxed{9}\,\boxed{Y^x}\,\boxed{.}\,\boxed{2}\,\boxed{5}\,\boxed{+/-}\,\boxed{=}$$

The answer is 0.478 973 6.

## THE USE OF $Y^x$ IN FINANCIAL MATHEMATICS

To a very great extent, financial mathematics is concerned with compounding and discounting over $n$ time periods. Compounding involves terms of the form:

$$(1 + i)^n$$

where $i$ is the interest rate per period. Discounting involves terms of the form:

$$\frac{1}{(1 + i)^n} \quad \text{or} \quad (1 + i)^{-n}$$

Therefore, a $Y^x$ function is extremely useful in solving these problems. We simply use $Y = (1 + i)$ and $x = n$ (or $x = -n$).

For example, what is the accumulated value ($S$) if $100 is invested for 22 years at 11.3 per cent per annum? To find the answer, we need to calculate $100(1.113)^{22}$. So we perform:

$$\boxed{1}\,\boxed{.}\,\boxed{1}\,\boxed{1}\,\boxed{3}\,\boxed{Y^x}\,\boxed{2}\,\boxed{2}\,\boxed{=}\,\boxed{\times}\,\boxed{1}\,\boxed{0}\,\boxed{0}\,\boxed{=}$$

The answer is $1054.13.

---

[14] With a calculator with a reciprocal $\left(\frac{1}{X}\right)$ function, we could perform:

$$\boxed{7}\,\boxed{Y^x}\,\boxed{6}\,\boxed{=}\,\boxed{\tfrac{1}{X}}$$

and get the same answer.

Suppose we need to calculate the present value of $1000 payable in 6 years' time if the interest rate is 12 per cent per annum. We need to calculate:

$$\frac{\$1000}{(1.12)^6}$$
$$= \$1000(1.12)^{-6}$$

We perform:

$\boxed{1}\ \boxed{.}\ \boxed{1}\ \boxed{2}\ \boxed{Y^x}\ \boxed{6}\ \boxed{+/-}\ \boxed{=}\ \boxed{\times}\ \boxed{1}\ \boxed{0}\ \boxed{0}\ \boxed{0}\ \boxed{=}$

The answer is $506.63.

As a final example, suppose that we need to calculate the price (present value) of a 15-year bond with a face value of $100 paying annual interest of $12 if the required yield is 13 per cent per annum. In other words, we wish to calculate:

$$\frac{\$12}{0.13}\left[1 - \frac{1}{(1.13)^{15}}\right] + \frac{\$100}{(1.13)^{15}}$$

Using a calculator with one memory cell we can calculate the price without resort to pen and paper. Without a memory cell we would need to record one number by hand. The steps are:

$\boxed{1}\ \boxed{.}\ \boxed{1}\ \boxed{3}\ \boxed{Y^x}\ \boxed{1}\ \boxed{5}\ \boxed{+/-}\ \boxed{=}\ \boxed{+/-}\ \boxed{+}\ \boxed{1}\ \boxed{=}$
$\boxed{\times}\ \boxed{1}\ \boxed{2}\ \boxed{=}\ \boxed{\div}\ \boxed{.}\ \boxed{1}\ \boxed{3}\ \boxed{=}$

So far we have the present value of the stream of interest payments (77.548 546). We now record this number or store it in the memory cell, if available. The present value of the face value is found by performing:[15]

$\boxed{1}\ \boxed{.}\ \boxed{1}\ \boxed{3}\ \boxed{Y^x}\ \boxed{1}\ \boxed{5}\ \boxed{+/-}\ \boxed{=}\ \boxed{\times}\ \boxed{1}\ \boxed{0}\ \boxed{0}\ \boxed{=}$

The answer is 15.989 08.

We now recall the present value of the interest payments and sum the two present values:

$\boxed{+}\ \boxed{M_C^R}\ \boxed{=}$

to give the final answer, 93.537 621, or $93.54 to the nearest cent.

This procedure required the use of about forty button pushes. This may seem a little frightening at first, but with practice, the calculation can take less than half a minute.

---

[15] If we had two memory cells, we could have recalled the value of $(1.13)^{-15}$ and avoided the need to calculate this number twice.

# CHAPTER 4

# APPLYING THE TIME VALUE OF MONEY TO SECURITY VALUATION

## 4.1 INTRODUCTION

In Chapter 1 we discussed briefly the important concept of the time value of money. In Chapter 3 we presented some mathematical tools useful in analysing problems involving the time value of money. In particular, we showed how promised streams of future cash flows can be valued, provided that the required rate of return is known.

In this chapter we apply these tools to the valuation of debt and equity securities. Initially we assume that the security's future cash flows are known with perfect certainty. Later in the chapter we introduce uncertainty, but only in a limited way. A more formal and detailed treatment of uncertainty is given in Chapter 6.

## 4.2 FINANCIAL ASSET VALUATION UNDER CERTAINTY[1]

The benefits from owning an asset are the present and future consumption opportunities attributable to it. For a financial asset, these benefits are in the form of cash. For example, an investor who holds a government bond until maturity receives cash in the form of coupon interest during the bond's life, and, at maturity, further cash from the payment of the face value. In the case of shares, the investor receives cash in the form of dividends, and on sale of the shares in the form of the price obtained for the shares.

---

[1] In this section we review some of the results explained in Chapter 3. Readers familiar with this material may safely omit this section.

# APPLYING THE TIME VALUE OF MONEY TO SECURITY VALUATION

A decision to invest implies a simultaneous decision to forego current consumption. It is assumed that at any time, investors prefer more consumption to less consumption, other things being equal. Application of this principle between two points in time implies that, other things being equal, earlier cash inflows are preferred to later cash inflows. As explained in Chapter 3, these observations may be summarised by the phrase 'money has a time value'.

To review this principle, suppose that a person is given a choice between receiving $100 now or $100 in 1 year's time. A rational person will always choose to receive the cash immediately, even if there is no desire to consume immediately. The reason, of course, is that the earlier cash flow can be invested. This will enable even greater consumption later. If the interest rate is 12 per cent per annum, the investor (consumer) in this example can invest for 1 year the immediate cash flow of $100, and at the end of the year have $112 available for consumption. Clearly $112 of consumption is preferable to $100 of consumption. In this example the cash flows were, in effect, a gift. Suppose, however, that the investor is offered the chance to *buy* the right to receive $100 in 1 year's time. What is the maximum price the investor should offer for this right? We have just seen that $100 is 'worth' $100 × 1.12 = $112 in 1 year's time. The right to receive $100 in 1 year's time is therefore worth at present:

$$P_0 = \frac{\$100}{1.12}$$
$$= \$89.29$$

The amount $89.29 is referred to as the *present value* of $100 to be received in 1 year's time if the *discount rate* is 12 per cent per annum. Therefore the interest rate has two functions: it is the rate at which present sums can be converted to equivalent future sums, and it is also the rate at which promised future sums can be converted to equivalent present values. This implies that the value of a financial asset is *not* simply the sum of the cash that it generates in future periods. For example, a financial asset that generates returns of $100 at the end of each of the next 5 years is not worth $500 today. It is not valid to add together cash flows of different years. However, adding together present values is valid because each value relates to the same time, the present.

Where there are many cash flows from the same asset, the present value is the sum of the present values of every future cash flow. The present value is calculated using the relevant interest rate. Thus:

$$P_0 = \frac{C_1}{1+i} + \frac{C_2}{(1+i)^2} + \ldots + \frac{C_n}{(1+i)^n}$$

or

$$P_0 = \sum_{t=1}^{n} \frac{C_t}{(1+i)^t} \qquad (4.1)$$

where: $P_0$ = current market price of the asset
$C_t$ = dollar return (cash flow) at time $t$
$n$ = term of the investment
$i$ = interest rate per time period
$t$ = 1, 2, ..., $n$

Assume that an investor is prepared to pay $450 for an asset that returns $100 per annum for 5 years. As shown in the following calculation, this implies that the investor requires an annual interest rate of 3.62 per cent as compensation for foregoing current consumption. Substituting in Equation 4.1 we find that:

$$\$450 = \frac{\$100}{1+i} + \frac{\$100}{(1+i)^2} + \ldots + \frac{\$100}{(1+i)^5}$$

This equation cannot be solved directly for $i$ and the use of either tables (Appendix A, Table 4) or numerical methods (trial and error) is necessary. Using either method, we find that $i$ is equal to 0.0362 or 3.62 per cent. The fact that this value solves the equation is now shown:

$$\begin{aligned}P_0 &= \frac{\$100}{1.0362} + \frac{\$100}{(1.0362)^2} + \frac{\$100}{(1.0362)^3} + \frac{\$100}{(1.0362)^4} + \frac{\$100}{(1.0362)^5} \\ &= \$96.506 + \$93.135 + \$89.881 + \$86.741 + \$83.711 \\ &= \$449.974 \\ &\approx \$450\end{aligned}$$

In summary, a financial asset is valued under certainty by discounting the known future cash flows at the market interest rate, thus compensating investors for their preference for current consumption.

## 4.3 VALUATION OF SHARES

### 4.3.1 VALUATION OF SHARES ASSUMING PERFECT CERTAINTY

In a world of perfect certainty, Equation 4.1 can be used to value shares.[2] The periodic cash flows from an investment in shares are called *dividends*. Unless liquidation of the company is contemplated, the dividends are assumed to continue indefinitely. Therefore, Equation 4.1 may be rewritten as:

$$P_0 = \sum_{t=1}^{\infty} \frac{D_t}{(1+i)^t} \qquad (4.2)$$

where $D_t$ = dividend per share in period $t$.

It can be seen that the market interest rate is the discount rate that equates future dividends with the current market price of the shares. The appropriate discount rate remains the market interest rate, because under conditions of perfect certainty investors require the same rate of return on all assets.

It might be thought that Equation 4.2 ignores a second potential source of return from an investment in shares, that is, the capital gain from selling the shares at a price greater than the price at which they were purchased. Suppose that an individual purchases shares with the intention of selling them in 5 years' time. Equation 4.2 may be expanded as follows:

---

[2] The discussion that follows is directed towards the valuation of ordinary shares. Preference shares are another form of equity capital. The valuation of preference shares is discussed in Chapter 17 and the distinction between ordinary shares and preference shares is discussed in detail in Chapter 10.

$$P_0 = \sum_{t=1}^{5} \frac{D_t}{(1+i)^t} + \frac{P_5}{(1+i)^5} \qquad (4.3)$$

where $P_5$ = share price at the end of year 5.

The capital gain (or loss) is the difference between $P_5$ and $P_0$. The price of the shares when they are sold is:

$$P_5 = \sum_{t=6}^{\infty} \frac{D_t}{(1+i)^{t-5}} \qquad (4.4)$$

Substituting Equation 4.4 into Equation 4.3:

$$P_0 = \sum_{t=1}^{5} \frac{D_t}{(1+i)^t} + \sum_{t=6}^{\infty} \frac{D_t}{(1+i)^t}$$

$$= \sum_{t=1}^{\infty} \frac{D_t}{(1+i)^t}$$

which, of course, is Equation 4.2.

Therefore, where a company is assumed to have an infinite life, the current market price of its shares can be expressed as the present value of an infinite stream of dividends. Even in a market where investors are seeking capital gains, the valuation formula remains the same.

### 4.3.2 THE INTRODUCTION OF UNCERTAINTY

Valuing a security under uncertainty is very difficult and, in general, few (if any) people can consistently expect to reach a better valuation than that given by the current market price. This statement is discussed fully in Chapter 14. However, the statement is not helpful if the company is not traded on a stock exchange, because there is then no current market price to observe. Moreover, to say that the best estimate of a share's 'true' value is its current market price provides no insight into the factors that give a share its value. In this section, some of the fundamental factors determining a share's value are considered.

Where there is uncertainty, investors require compensation in the form of a higher promised rate of return. Equation 4.2 becomes:

$$P_0 = \sum_{t=1}^{\infty} \frac{E(D_t)}{(1+k_e)^t} \qquad (4.5)$$

where $E(D_t)$ = expected dividend per share in period $t$
$k_e$ = required rate of return on the shares

The appropriate value of $k_e$ is determined using the concept of the opportunity cost of capital. The 'true' or economic cost of investing in a particular security is the return foregone on the next best alternative. For a risky security, this is clearly *at least* the return on the risk-free security. In short, $k_e > i$. The amount by which $k_e$ exceeds $i$ is often referred to as the security's risk premium. Further, the riskier the security being considered, the higher will be the risk premium and the higher will be $k_e$. Determination of exactly how much higher $k_e$ should be requires a measurement of 'risk' and a theory linking that measure to required rates of return. Two such theories are the **capital asset pricing model** and the **arbitrage pricing theory** which are developed in some detail in Chapter 6.

At this point, however, we avoid the issue by assuming that all investors reach the same assessment of risk, and therefore apply the same opportunity cost of capital (discount rate) to the same expected dividend stream, therefore arriving at the same price for the company's shares. It may seem unrealistic to assume that everyone has the same expectations. However, in an *ex ante* sense, it may be reasonable for the company's management to assume that its assessment of the likely impact of a financial decision on the company's share price will prove to be correct. If this is so, then management should act *as if* an assumption of homogeneous expectations is realistic.

The simplest assumption to make when estimating a share's value is that the company will maintain in perpetuity the current dividend per share, $D_0$. In this case the estimate is:[3]

$$P_0 = \frac{D_0}{k_e} \qquad (4.6)$$

Assume that the Rankine Company is currently paying a dividend of 90 cents per share. If investors expect this dividend to be maintained, and require a rate of return of 15 per cent on the investment, the value of the shares is $0.90/0.15 = $6.00.

It is usually more realistic to assume that a company's dividend per share will change. For example, it may be assumed that the dividend per share will grow at a constant rate. In this case, the estimate is:

$$P_0 = \sum_{t=1}^{\infty} \frac{D_0(1+g)^t}{(1+k_e)^t} \qquad (4.7)$$

where $g$ = expected growth rate in dividend per share.

Where $k_e$ is greater than $g$, Equation 4.7 can be written:[4]

---

[3] This formula treats the dividends as an ordinary perpetuity. For further details, see Section 3.5.
[4] The terms in Equation 4.7 form an infinite geometric series, with a common factor (or ratio) between each term of $\frac{1+g}{1+k_e}$. Provided that $-1 < \frac{1+g}{1+k_e} < 1$, there will be a limiting sum equal to the first term of the series, divided by (1 − the common ratio). That is:

$$P_0 = \frac{D_0(1+g)}{1+k_e} \bigg/ \left(1 - \frac{1+g}{1+k_e}\right)$$

$$= \frac{D_0(1+g)}{1+k_e} \bigg/ \frac{k_e - g}{1+k_e}$$

$$= \frac{D_0(1+g)}{k_e - g}$$

If $k_e < g$, the model breaks down. Under these circumstances:

$\frac{1+g}{1+k_e} > 1$, and there is no limiting sum ($P_0 \to \infty$).

# Applying the Time Value of Money to Security Valuation

$$P_0 = \frac{D_0(1 + g)}{k_e - g} \qquad (4.8)$$

One approach to estimating $g$ is to calculate the past growth rate in dividend per share and use this as the estimate of the expected growth rate.

### Example 4.1

Assume that for the past 10 years the growth rate in the Rankine Company's dividend per share has been 10 per cent per annum. Assume further that this growth rate is expected to be maintained indefinitely. The latest dividend per share was $0.90 and was paid yesterday. Using Equation 4.8, the company's value per share is:

$$\begin{aligned} P_0 &= \frac{D_0(1 + g)}{k_e - g} \\ &= \frac{\$0.90(1.10)}{0.15 - 0.10} \\ &= \$19.80 \end{aligned}$$

A second approach to estimating $g$ is to assume that the growth in dividend per share is related to the company's retained earnings and to the rate of return on those earnings. If the company retains a constant proportion $b$ of its earnings each year, and reinvests those earnings at a constant rate $r$ then $g = br$, and Equation 4.8 can be rewritten:

$$P_0 = \frac{D_0(1 + br)}{k_e - br} \qquad (4.9)$$

### Example 4.2

If the Rankine Company retains 40 per cent of its earnings each year ($b = 0.4$), and these earnings are reinvested to earn a 25 per cent rate of return ($r = 0.25$), the price of Rankine's shares using Equation 4.9 is:

$$\begin{aligned} P_0 &= \frac{0.90[1 + 0.4(0.25)]}{0.15 - 0.4(0.25)} \\ &= \$19.80 \end{aligned}$$

The assumption that the past growth rate is expected to be maintained indefinitely is unlikely to be realistic, particularly where the company has been experiencing a relatively high growth rate. We might therefore assume that the current growth rate will be maintained for several years before falling to a level expected to be sustained indefinitely. This is shown in Example 4.3.

### Example 4.3

Assume that the current growth rate of 10 per cent per annum is expected to be maintained for only a further 3 years, and is then expected to fall to 6 per cent per annum and remain at that level indefinitely. This complication is easily handled by using Equation 4.8 to estimate the value of the shares as at the end of the third year. The value of the shares today is then given by the present value of this estimate, plus the present value of the dividends to be paid in the first three years. Given these expectations, the price of Rankine's shares is calculated as follows:

$$P_0 = \frac{D_1}{(1+k_e)} + \frac{D_2}{(1+k_e)^2} + \frac{D_3}{(1+k_e)^3} + \frac{1}{(1+k_e)^3}\frac{D_4}{(k_e-g)}$$

$$= \frac{\$0.90(1.10)}{1.15} + \frac{\$0.90(1.10)^2}{(1.15)^2} + \frac{\$0.90(1.10)^3}{(1.15)^3}$$

$$+ \frac{1}{(1.15)^3}\frac{\$0.90(1.10)^3(1.06)}{(0.15-0.06)}$$

$$= \$11.75$$

Comparing the previous two examples, the reduction in the expected dividend growth rate has resulted in a reduction in the value of the shares from $19.80 to $11.75. This highlights the sensitivity of the share value to estimates of the future growth rate in dividend per share.

The formulae used to estimate a share value may also be used to estimate the required rate of return on a company's shares, given their current market price. This aspect is discussed further in Chapter 17.

### 4.3.3 SHARE VALUATION AND THE PRICE–EARNINGS RATIO

The ratio of a company's share price to its earnings per share (that is, its price–earnings ratio) is often used by security analysts to estimate the value of the company's shares.[5] To illustrate this method of valuation, we again use the example of the Rankine Company, and assume that Rankine's current earnings per share is $2.25. Assume also that an analyst estimates that the appropriate price–earnings ratio for the company is 9.0. Therefore, the value of each share is estimated at $20.25 (that is, $2.25 × 9.0). This estimate would then be compared with the current market price to determine whether the shares should be purchased.

However, this leaves unanswered the question: How does an analyst estimate the appropriate price–earnings ratio? In most cases where analysts use this method of valuation the appropriate price–earnings ratio is determined in a way that can best be described as a judgement, that is, no formal model is used but the analyst tries to take into account the factors considered to be relevant.

Two important factors are risk and growth opportunities. The riskier the analyst believes the investment to be, the lower the appropriate price–earnings ratio. Therefore, even if two companies have the same earnings level, the lower-risk company would be assigned a higher price–earnings ratio, all other things being equal.

To see this, imagine that an analyst is trying to value two companies that are equivalent in all respects, including the expected earnings pattern, except that

---

[5] A detailed discussion of the use of the price–earnings ratio to value shares is contained in most texts on investments. (See, for example, W.F. Sharpe & G.J. Alexander, *Investments*, 4th edn, Prentice–Hall, Englewood Cliffs, 1990, pp. 474–8.)

one company is riskier than the other. Because investors dislike risk (other things being equal), the riskier company will be less attractive to investors and will thus have a lower value. Since both companies have the same earnings, the ratio of price to earnings will be lower for the riskier company.

The other important factor is growth opportunities. If an analyst believes a company has substantial opportunities for growth, a high price–earnings ratio will be assigned. In this case the current earnings level is likely to be surpassed in future, thereby justifying a price today that appears 'high' relative to current earnings. Other factors likely to be considered include the price–earnings ratios of companies in the same industry and prospects for the industry and the economy as a whole.

## 4.4 VALUATION OF DEBT SECURITIES

As we saw in Section 4.3, the returns on an investment in shares are **dividends**. In the case of an investment in debt securities (frequently called **bonds** or **debentures**), the returns are usually in the form of **interest payments** and the repayment of **face value** or **principal**. As explained for shares, if all securities offer perfectly certain returns, each security's opportunity cost of capital is the risk-free market interest rate (or yield) $i$. Therefore, under perfect certainty, $i$ is the appropriate discount rate to apply. Equation 4.1 is rewritten for bonds as follows:

$$P_0 = \sum_{t=1}^{n} \frac{I_t}{(1+i)^t} + \frac{P_n}{(1+i)^n} \qquad (4.10)$$

where $I_t$ = interest payment at time $t$
$P_n$ = face value (principal repayment) at maturity
$n$ = number of periods to maturity
$i$ = market interest rate (yield)

*Example 4.4*
Consider the case of a bond with a face value of $100, and offering 10 per cent interest per year for 3 years, followed by payment of $100 at the end of the third year. If the required rate of return is also 10 per cent per year, we would expect such a bond to be worth exactly $100 today. This is indeed the valuation given by Equation 4.10:

$$P_0 = \frac{\$10}{1.1} + \frac{\$10}{(1.1)^2} + \frac{\$10}{(1.1)^3} + \frac{\$100}{(1.1)^3}$$
$$= \$9.091 + \$8.264 + \$7.513 + \$75.131$$
$$= \$100.00$$

Once a bond has been issued—that is, sold by the borrower to the lender—its promised future cash flows are fixed. Ownership of the bond entitles the owner to receive from the issuer a fixed schedule of future cash flows. If the market interest rate changes, it will affect the attractiveness of the bond to potential investors. If market interest rates decrease, the bond will become more attractive; if market interest rates increase, the bond will be less attractive. This, of course, will cause bond prices to change. A decrease (increase) in market interest rates will cause an increase (decrease) in bond prices. This is illustrated in Example 4.5.

### Example 4.5
Suppose that immediately after Rankine's debt contract is agreed to, conditions in the debt market change and the required rate of return falls to 8 per cent per annum. The borrower must still make interest payments of $10 each year, but investors now require a return of 8 per cent per annum. Again applying Equation 4.10, the security is now valued more highly:

$$P_0 = \frac{\$10}{1.08} + \frac{\$10}{(1.08)^2} + \frac{\$10}{(1.08)^3} + \frac{\$100}{(1.08)^3}$$
$$= \$105.15$$

Similarly, if the required rate had risen from 10 per cent to 12 per cent, the price would have fallen:

$$P_0 = \frac{\$10}{1.12} + \frac{\$10}{(1.12)^2} + \frac{\$10}{(1.12)^3} + \frac{\$100}{(1.12)^3}$$
$$= \$95.20$$

## 4.5 INTEREST RATE RISK

Example 4.5 shows that when interest rates change, so also do bond prices. The possibility of unforeseen price changes means that the bond is risky because its future value is uncertain. Thus, even if a bond is *risk free* in the sense that the borrower will certainly make the promised cash payments, it *is* risky in the sense that the bond holder (lender) can suffer unforeseen losses if interest rates change. This is known as *interest rate risk*.

When interest rates increase, bond prices fall. For the investor in bonds this is a capital loss, and therefore in this respect the increase in interest rates is undesirable. Against that loss must be set a benefit: the interest receipts can be reinvested at the new, higher rate of interest. The opposite occurs when interest rates fall. Investors make capital gains but interest receipts can be reinvested only at the new lower rate. These effects are known as the *price effect* and the *reinvestment effect* and are always of opposite sign for a given change in market interest rate. The net effect for the investor depends on the size of the interest rate change and on the period for which the bond is held. Appendix 4.1 outlines a possible method that an investor may use to obtain some protection against interest rate risk.

At any given time, the market-determined interest rate (or yield) on a bond will depend on the features of that bond. Two features usually particularly important to market participants are the term of the security and the risk of the borrower defaulting on the promised payments. The connection between term and interest rates is called the *term structure of interest rates*, while the connection between default risk and interest rates is called the *default risk structure of interest rates*. These are now considered.

## 4.6 THE TERM STRUCTURE OF INTEREST RATES

### 4.6.1 WHAT IS THE TERM STRUCTURE?

To consider the effect of a bond's term on its interest rate, we need to hold all other factors constant. Thus, to eliminate the effect of differences in default risk, the term structure of interest rates is usually studied by focusing on the interest rates offered by Commonwealth Government bonds since all such bonds have the same risk of default (zero).

The least complicated measure of interest rate is the market yield on a government bond which pays no interest during its life, but, like a bill of exchange, pays a fixed sum at maturity. In practice, such bonds are relatively rare, except for very-short-term securities such as Treasury Notes. Therefore, in practice it is usual to use bond yields, which are really internal rates of return. (For further details, see Sections 3.4.4 and 5.4.2). The pattern of yield against term is called the *yield curve*. Data for the Australian yield curve at eight different dates are given in Table 4.1.

**Table 4.1** *Australian yield curve data*

| Date of yield curve | Term to maturity | | | | |
| --- | --- | --- | --- | --- | --- |
| | 3 months | 6 months | 2 years | 5 years | 10 years |
| June 1986 | 12.38 | 12.79 | 12.80 | 12.80 | 12.95 |
| June 1987 | 12.23 | 12.95 | 13.00 | 13.10 | 12.80 |
| June 1988 | 11.31 | 11.54 | 11.70 | 11.95 | 11.95 |
| June 1989 | 17.17 | 17.27 | 15.40 | 14.20 | 13.50 |
| June 1990 | 14.75 | – | 14.05 | 13.80 | 13.40 |
| June 1991 | 10.11 | 10.19 | 10.55 | 11.05 | 11.15 |
| June 1992 | 6.17 | 6.01 | 6.35 | 7.85 | 8.90 |
| June 1993 | 5.08 | 5.06 | 5.20 | 6.15 | 6.65 |

*Source: Reserve Bank of Australia Bulletin*, December 1991 and September 1993. Yields for 3(6) months are issue yields for 13(26) week Treasury Notes. Yields for 2, 5 and 10 years are bond yields.

Yield curves can have a wide range of shapes, but they are typically either downward sloping, flat or upward sloping. For example, as shown in Table 4.1, the Australian yield curve was essentially downward sloping in June 1989, almost flat in June 1986, and upward sloping in June 1992. These shapes are illustrated in Figure 4.1.

### 4.6.2 TERM STRUCTURE THEORIES: EXPECTATIONS AND LIQUIDITY (RISK) PREMIUM

Obviously the term structure at any given time is no accident. Presumably, participants in the debt markets do not set the interest rate for, say, a term of 2 years without in some way considering the 1-year and 3-year interest rates. In

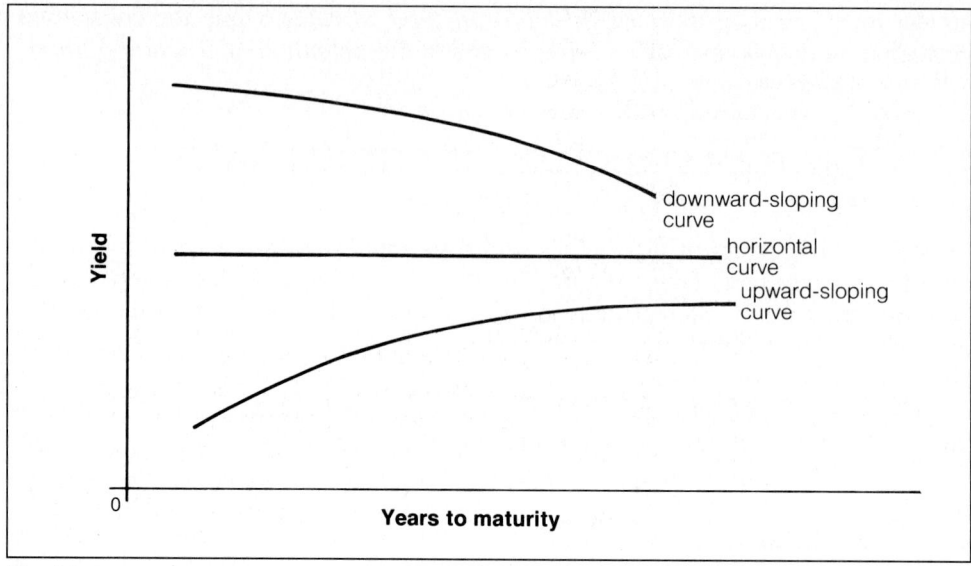

**Fig. 4.1**

other words, the interest rate for a particular term will be determined by the market *in the context of* interest rates for other terms. If this were not so, what would explain the smooth, regular shapes nearly always displayed by yield curves? The exact identity of the factors that explain the term structure is controversial, with different theories proposing different mechanisms. There is, however, broad agreement that expectations of the future course of interest rates are central to explaining the term structure.

The core of the **expectations theory of the term structure** is that interest rates are set by the market, so investors in bonds or other debt securities can expect, on average, to achieve the same return over any future period, regardless of the security in which they invest. For example, suppose that in the current term structure the interest rate for a zero-coupon bond with a two-year term to maturity is 8 per cent per annum, while the interest rate on a three-year zero-coupon bond is 9 per cent per annum. Suppose, further, that an investor pays $1000 for the three-year bond. In three years the investor will have $1000 $(1.09)^3$ = $1295.03. Alternatively, suppose the same investor pays $1000 for the two-year bond. After two years, the investor will have $1000 $(1.08)^2$ = $1166.40. If the investor can re-lend this sum for the third year at an interest rate of 11.028 per cent per annum, then, at the end of the third year the investor will have $1166.40 × 1.110 28 = $1295.03, which is the same as the return from buying the three-year bond to cover the whole period. This is shown in Figure 4.2.

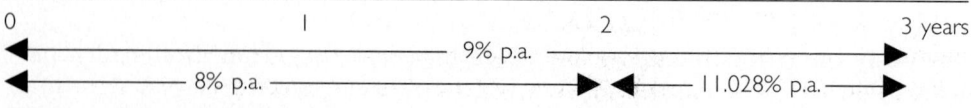

**Fig. 4.2** *Current and expected interest rates*

As shown in Figure 4.2, the current term structure is 8 per cent per annum for a term of 2 years and 9 per cent per annum for a term of 3 years. According to the expectations theory, the factor that explains the current term structure is the market's expectation that the one-year interest rate on the day two years from now will be 11.028 per cent per annum. In that case investors will earn 9 per cent per annum over the coming three years, regardless of whether they invest for three years by:

(a) buying the three-year bond today; or
(b) buying the two-year bond today, *and* buying a one-year bond in two years' time.

Therefore, the expectation of the future interest rate determines today's term structure.

This process is extended in Figure 4.3.

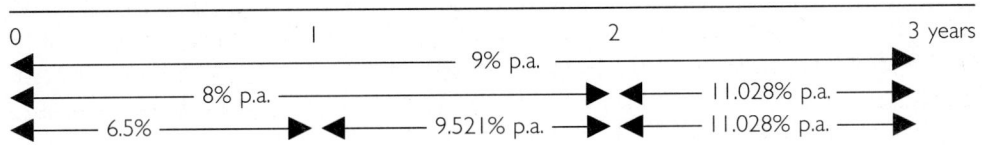

**Fig. 4.3** *Current and expected interest rates*

Suppose the market expects next year's one-year interest rate to be 9.521 per cent per annum. Then today's one-year interest rate must be 6.5 per cent per annum, because $(1.08)^2 = 1.065 \times 1.09521 = 1.1664$. The economic interpretation is that the same return is expected over the next two years, regardless of whether an investor:

(a) buys the two-year bond today; or
(b) buys a one-year bond today *and* buys a further one-year bond in one year's time.

As a final illustration of the expectations mechanism, consider again the information shown in Figure 4.3, and imagine that there is an investor who intends to lend $1000 for a two-year period. Consider the following three ways in which such an investment could be made:

1. Buy the two-year bond now, and hold it until it matures. At the end of the two-year period this investment will have accumulated to $1000 (1.08)^2 = \$1166.40$.
2. Buy a one-year bond now, and after one year, reinvest in a further one-year bond, which is then held until maturity. At the end of the two-year period the investment is expected to have accumulated to $1000 (1.065) (1.09521) = \$1166.40$.
3. Buy the three-year bond now, and sell it after two years. At the end of the two-year period the investment is expected to be worth: $1000 (1.09)^3/1.11028 = \$1166.40$.

As these calculations show, it is expected that the outcome will be the same, regardless of the route taken. The market has set today's term structure in such a way that it reflects the market's expectations of the future course of interest rates.

To formalise our discussion of the expectations theory we make the following assumptions.[6]
- Future short-term interest rates are known with perfect certainty.
- There are no transaction costs.

Given these assumptions, competition in the capital market will result in a yield curve that ensures that the sum to which a dollar accumulates over $n$ years at a long-term interest rate $r_n$ must equal the sum to which it accumulates over $n$ years when invested at present and future short-term interest rates $i_1, i_2, \ldots, i_n$. As a consequence, an investor who wants to invest for, say, 10 years is indifferent between the purchase of a 10-year government security or the purchase of a 1-year security in each of the next 10 years. The expectations theory is therefore represented by the following relationship between short-term and long-term interest rates:

$$1 + r_1 = 1 + i_1$$
$$(1 + r_2)^2 = (1 + i_1)(1 + i_2)$$
$$\vdots$$
$$(1 + r_n)^n = (1 + i_1)(1 + i_2) \ldots (1 + i_n)$$

From these relationships we can derive the appropriate formula for the long-term rate. For example, because investors must expect to receive the same capital sum by accumulating for two periods at the rate $r_2$, or for one period at $i_1$ followed by a second period at $i_2$, the long-term rate is equal to the geometric mean of the current one-period rate and the forward one-period rate for the next period.

Generalising this result:

$$r_1 = (1 + i_1) - 1$$
$$r_2 = \sqrt{(1 + i_1)(1 + i_2)} - 1$$
$$\vdots$$
$$r_n = \sqrt[n]{(1 + i_1)(1 + i_2) \ldots (1 + i_n)} - 1$$

Thus, in our earlier discussion, the two-year interest rate is:

$$r_2 = \sqrt[2]{(1.065)(1.09521)} - 1$$
$$= 8.0 \text{ per cent per annum}$$

and the three-year interest rate is:

---

[6] These are the assumptions set out in F. Lutz, 'The Structure of Interest Rates', *Quarterly Journal of Economics*, November 1940, pp. 29–63. Four versions of the theory are identified in J.C. Cox, J. E. Ingersoll & S.A. Ross, 'A Re-examination of Traditional Hypotheses about the Term Structure of Interest Rates', *Journal of Finance*, September 1981, pp. 769–99. These versions differ (and in fact are inconsistent) in the presence of uncertainty. See also the response in J.Y. Campbell, 'A Defense of the Traditional Hypotheses about the Term Structure of Interest Rates', *Journal of Finance*, March 1986, pp. 183–95.

$$r_3 = \sqrt[3]{(1.065)(1.09521)(1.11028)} - 1$$
$$= 9.0 \text{ per cent per annum}$$

The essence of the expectations theory is that the shape of the yield curve is determined by investors' expectations of short-term rates within the maturity of the competing long-term security.[7] The expectations theory can help to reconcile the existence of the differing shapes of the yield curve shown in Figure 4.1. In general, an upward-sloping yield curve implies that investors expect future short-term interest rates to increase.[8] In that case, investors are not prepared to invest in long-term securities unless the yield is greater than that on short-term securities, because the investors would be better off investing in short-term securities and re-investing the proceeds at maturity. In general, a downward-sloping yield curve implies that investors expect future short-term interest rates to decrease. That is, investors are prepared to purchase long-term securities yielding less than short-term securities because they expect their return to be no larger if they adopted an investment strategy requiring continual reinvestment in short-term securities. In short, if expectations about the level of future short-term rates change, then actual long-term yields on existing securities will tend to adjust in the same direction. A flat yield curve means that investors expect future short-term interest rates to be the same as the current short-term rate. Consequently, the long-term rates will equal the short-term rates.

Commentators on the expectations theory of the term structure have suggested that interest rates are not formed solely on the basis of expectations. For example, the **liquidity premium (risk premium) theory** suggests that although expectations are a foundation for the term structure, there is in addition a premium due to uncertainty about the future level of interest rates. This causes an upward bias in the yield curve because interest rate risk increases with the term to maturity of the debt security.[9]

Our earlier discussion of interest rate risk suggested that the holder of a bond may, in the end, either benefit or lose as the result of a change in the general level of interest rates. For example, if interest rates increase, the market value of the bond will fall, but the interest receipts could be reinvested at a

---

[7] It is convenient to think of short-term rates as determining long-term rates, but in fact the market determines all rates simultaneously.

[8] That this is not always the case may be seen from the following example. If the current term structure is:
   1 year   6%;
   2 years  10%;
   3 years  11%;
the 1-year interest rate, 1 year hence, is expected to be:
$$\frac{(1.1)^2}{1.06} - 1 = 14.15\%$$
while the 1-year interest rate, 2 years hence, is expected to be:
$$\frac{(1.11)^3}{(1.10)^2} - 1 = 13.03\%$$

[9] The liquidity premium theory was first developed by J. Hicks, *Value and Capital*, 2nd edn, Clarendon Press, Oxford, 1946.

higher rate of return. The proponents of the liquidity premium theory concentrate on the market value effect and point out that for a given change in interest rate, the effect is greater for long-term bonds than for short-term bonds. This is illustrated in Example 4.6.

### Example 4.6

Assume that there is a flat yield curve where the current interest rate on all government bonds is 10 per cent per annum. The Government has just issued 1-year, 2-year, 5-year, and 10-year bonds, all offering an interest rate of 10 per cent, a face value of $100, and paying interest once per annum. Table 4.2 shows the market price for each of these bonds, assuming that immediately following purchase of the bonds at $100 there is either a parallel upward movement in the yield curve to 12 per cent per annum, or a parallel downward movement in the yield curve to 8 per cent per annum.[10]

**Table 4.2** Market price of government bonds

|  | If interest rate (required yield) is 12% | Change in price (%) | If interest rate (required yield) is 8% | Change in price (%) |
|---|---|---|---|---|
| 1-year bond | $98.214 | −1.786 | $101.852 | +1.852 |
| 2-year bond | $96.620 | −3.380 | $103.567 | +3.567 |
| 5-year bond | $92.790 | −7.210 | $107.985 | +7.985 |
| 10-year bond | $88.700 | −11.300 | $113.420 | +13.420 |

Thus the price of long-term debt is more volatile. It is true that the holders of a 10-year government bond benefit most from a fall in interest rates, but they also lose most if rates increase. In this sense, long-term bonds are 'riskier'. The liquidity premium theory suggests that investors would require a higher rate of return to compensate for this higher risk. Therefore there is a natural tendency for the yields on long-term bonds to be greater than those on short-term bonds. Consequently there will be a bias towards an upward-sloping yield curve. This means that compared with the yield curves that would be observed if only expectations mattered, an upward-sloping yield curve will become steeper, a downward-sloping yield curve will become less steep, and a flat yield curve will become slightly upward sloping.

### 4.6.3 EMPIRICAL EVIDENCE

The empirical evidence on the theories we have discussed presents a rather complex picture. In Australia, the early studies by Bloch and Juttner et al. found that, while a version of the expectations theory appeared to fit the data for shorter-term bonds, this was not true in tests involving both short-term and long-

---

[10] Market prices are calculated using Equation 4.10.

term bonds.[11] In any event, the yields used in these studies were probably heavily influenced by the Reserve Bank's activities. It is therefore difficult to know the extent to which the yields were the result of market forces or of regulation by the authorities. In the US, the results have tended to be contrary to the expectations theory and there is some evidence of a premium for longer terms.[12] However, while Fama found evidence supporting the existence of a premium, he also concluded that the premium does not increase for terms beyond 8 or 9 months.[13] This is inconsistent with both the pure expectations model and the liquidity premium model. More recent evidence in Australia is not in line with this US evidence. In a test at the short end of the term structure (90-day interest rates, compared with 180-day interest rates), Tease found that the data quite strongly supported the expectations theory in various forms.[14]

### 4.6.4 INFLATION AND THE TERM STRUCTURE

One issue yet to be considered is the relationship between the inflation rate and the term structure of interest rates. In general we would expect lenders to require the nominal interest rate to compensate them for expected inflation.[15] Therefore, the higher the expected inflation rate, the higher will be the observed nominal interest rate. As a consequence, if the inflation rate is expected to increase over time, the nominal interest rate on short-term bonds will also be expected to increase over time. According to the expectations theory we will therefore see an upward-sloping yield curve. In addition, unexpected changes in the inflation rate are also likely to have an impact on the term structure.[16] Such unexpected changes will cause a change in the level of interest rates. As explained earlier, the possibility of such changes gives rise to interest rate risk, and the liquidity premium theory suggests that this in turn will give rise to the tendency for interest rates on long-term bonds to be higher than those on short-term bonds.

### 4.6.5 SEGMENTED MARKETS AND THE TERM STRUCTURE

Another factor sometimes claimed to play an important role in the determination of the term structure is the existence of **segmented markets** for bonds and other

---

11 See F. Bloch, 'The Term Structure of Interest Rates in Australia: A Test Using the Error–Learning Model', *The Economic Record*, March 1974, pp. 77–93; and D. J. Juttner, G. Madden & R. Tuckwell, 'Time Series Analysis of the Term Structure of Australian Interest Rates', *The Economic Record*, March 1975, pp. 19–30.
12 See B.J. Friedman, 'Interest Rate Expectations Versus Forward Rates: Evidence from an Expectations Survey', *Journal of Finance*, September 1979, pp. 965–73; and D. S. Jones & V. V. Roley, 'Rational Expectations and the Expectations Model of the Term Structure: A Test Using Weekly Data', *Journal of Monetary Economics*, October 1983, pp. 453–65.
13 E. F. Fama, 'Term Premiums in Bond Returns', *Journal of Financial Economics*, December 1984, pp. 529–46.
14 W. J. Tease, 'The Expectations Theory of the Term Structure of Interest Rates in Australia', *The Economic Record*, June 1988, pp. 120–7.
15 See Equation 3.7 and the discussion in Section 3.3.4.
16 See R. Brealey & S. Schaefer, 'Term Structure and Uncertain Inflation', *Journal of Finance*, May 1977, pp. 277–89.

forms of debt.[17] Lenders are regarded as having 'preferred habitats' over the maturity range of securities. It is suggested that these 'preferred habitats' are determined solely by the structure of the liabilities of the particular lenders. As a result it is argued that certain financial institutions traditionally maintain a fairly rigid structure in their bond portfolios and do not move freely from one maturity range to another to take advantage of interest rate differentials. For example, life insurance companies are predominantly long-term lenders because of the long-term nature of their obligations to policy holders.

Supporters of the segmented markets approach suggest that the capital market is to a large extent segmented and that, as a result, the interest rates for different maturity ranges are determined more or less independently. That is, the interest rate in each maturity range is determined by the supply of loanable funds in that maturity range and the demand for loanable funds in that maturity range.[18] For example, if the supply of funds offered by long-term lenders is high relative to the demand for long-term loans while the reverse is the case for short-term lenders, a downward-sloping yield curve results. However, the various segments of the capital market are not completely insulated from one another. While relatively small yield differentials may not be sufficient to induce lenders with traditionally rigid portfolio structures to shift their 'preferred habitats', there are always other suppliers of loanable funds whose positions are more flexible. In addition, if the differentials widen considerably, even those institutions that traditionally hold a relatively rigid portfolio may find it feasible to move at least a portion of their funds into investments with more attractive maturities. Finally, even if all investors are completely inflexible in their choice of 'habitat', the segmented markets theory will still fail if these 'habitats' overlap. The available empirical evidence does not lend much support to the market segmentation approach to the term structure.[19]

## 4.7 THE DEFAULT RISK STRUCTURE OF INTEREST RATES

As explained in Section 4.3.2, the presence of uncertainty causes the opportunity cost of capital for securities to exceed the risk-free interest rate. In the case of debt, this is because borrowers may default on their promised payments. For debt of a given term, the higher the market's assessment of the probability of default, the higher will be $k_d$, the required rate of return (or yield) on the debt. However, because debtholders rank ahead of shareholders, it is expected that the required rate of return on a company's debt will be less than the required rate of return on its shares. In short, for any given company, $i < k_d < k_e$.

Example 4.7 shows the effect that default risk has on a bond's yield to maturity.

---

[17] See J. Culbertson, 'The Term Structure of Interest Rates', *Quarterly Journal of Economics*, November 1957, pp. 485–517.
[18] This is in contrast to the expectations theory which implies that interest rates are independent of the relative supply of the bonds across the range of maturities.
[19] See J. Dodds & J. Ford, *Expectations, Uncertainty and the Term Structure of Interest Rates*, Chapter 6, Martin Robertson, London, 1974.

## Example 4.7

Bonds issued by the Red Vines Company mature in 1 year's time with a maturity value of $110. There is no cash flow during the year. The market believes that there is a 90 per cent chance that the full payment of $110 will be made and a 10 per cent chance that no payment will be made. Therefore the expected payment at the end of the year is 0.90($110) + 0.10($0) = $99. Assuming that the market requires an expected rate of return of 10 per cent on these bonds, they will have a price of:

$$P_0 = \frac{\$99}{1.10}$$
$$= \$90$$

The yield is therefore found by solving:

$$\$90 = \frac{\$110}{1 + k_d}$$

Therefore
$$k_d = \frac{\$110}{\$90} - 1$$
$$= 22.22 \text{ per cent}$$

That is, an investor who purchases the bonds for $90 will earn a rate of return of 22.22 per cent per annum if Red Vines does not default.

## Example 4.8

Suppose that Red Vines restructures its activities, and as a result, the market reduces its assessment of the probability of default from 10 per cent to 5 per cent. What will be the new yield on Red Vines' debt?

The expected payment is 0.95($110) + 0.05($0) = $104.50. Therefore the price is:

$$P_0 = \frac{\$104.50}{1.10}$$
$$= \$95$$

and the new yield is found by solving:

$$\$95 = \frac{\$110}{1 + k_d}$$

Therefore
$$k_d = 15.79 \text{ per cent}$$

Comparing this yield with the yield in Example 4.7 it is clear that as the probability of default decreases, so also does the required yield.

In the US, services have existed for many years that supply ratings on the 'quality' of debt securities issued by both public and private sector borrowers. There is evidence to suggest that there is a high correlation between these ratings and the probability of default and it is not surprising, therefore, that the promised yields are related to the quality rating.

In Australia, ratings are supplied by S & P–Australian Ratings, a member of the Standard & Poor's Rating Group and by Moody's Investors Service. Long-term debt is rated by S & P–Australian Ratings on a 20-point scale, ranging from AAA (extremely strong capacity to pay interest and repay principal) down to C (high risk of default, or reliant on third party arrangements to prevent default). A D–rating indicates that default has already occurred.[20] The information in Table 4.3 is indicative of the ratings supplied.

## 4.8 OTHER FACTORS AFFECTING INTEREST RATE STRUCTURES

Yield differentials on securities may also result from differences in marketability, that is, ability to convert the securities into cash without a price penalty. All other things being equal, an investor will buy a security of low marketability only if the yield is greater than that on a security of high marketability. For example, a life insurance company would usually require a higher interest rate to lend mortgage funds to a company than to lend the same amount by purchasing the company's debentures, which are listed on a stock exchange. Similarly, it is conceivable that tax effects will give rise to differences in yields on bonds. For example, a tax rebate of 10 cents is allowable for each dollar of interest included in taxable income on certain Commonwealth, State or semi-government bonds. The rebate applies only to bonds issued before 1 November 1968.

Finally, we refer briefly to the relationship between the yield on bonds and the required rate of return on ordinary shares. In Section 4.3 we suggested that the required rate of return on ordinary shares may be expressed as the rate of discount that equates the present value of the expected future dividends with the current market price of the shares. Clearly, if dividends are expected to grow over time, the required rate of return on an investment in ordinary shares will be greater than the current dividend yield ($D_0/P_0$). Therefore, it is not valid to compare the yields on debt securities with the dividend yields on ordinary shares. Not surprisingly, the evidence suggests that the required returns on ordinary shares exceed those on debt securities.[21] This evidence is consistent with the idea that investors require a higher expected rate of return to invest in ordinary shares than to invest in, say, debentures because ordinary shareholders are exposed to greater risk. Their risk exposure is greater because ordinary shareholders are the residual claimants on the cash flows of the company. Therefore, their returns are the first to be affected by a downturn in the company's prospects and, in the event of the company being wound up, ordinary shareholders have the last claim on its assets.

---

[20] Moody's rates long-term debt on a 19-point scale ranging from Aaa (interest payments are protected by a large, or by an exceptionally stable, margin and principal is secure) to C (regarded as having extremely poor prospects of ever attaining any real investment standing). Both Moody's and S & P provide ratings of short-term debt on a four-point scale.

[21] For Australian data see R.R. Officer, 'Rates of Return to Shares, Bond Yields and Inflation Rates, An Historical Perspective', in *Share Markets and Portfolio Theory*, Eds R. Ball et al., 2nd edn, University of Queensland Press, St Lucia, 1989, pp. 207–11.

**Table 4.3** *Australian corporate and government ratings*

|  | Rating | | A$ Senior implied long-term | |
|---|---|---|---|---|
| Extremely strong capacity to pay | AAA | Australian Wheat Board | NSW Treasury Corporation (Guar. State of NSW) Queensland Treasury (Guar. State of Qld) | Telstra (formerly AOTC) Commonwealth Bank (Guar. Commonwealth of Aust.) |
| Very strong capacity to pay | AA+ | ACT Government | Nestlé Australia | Shell Australia |
| | AA | Lend Lease | National Australia Bank | SEC Vic. (Guar. State of Vic.) |
| | AA− | Coca-Cola Amatil | Coles Myer | Tascorp (Guar. State of Tas.) |
| Strong capacity to pay | A+ | BTR Nylex | CRA | ANZ Banking Group |
| | A | BHP | CSR | Pacific Dunlop |
| | A− | Caltex Australia | Ford Motor | St George Bank |
| Adequate capacity to pay | BBB+ | ANI | Pioneer International | Qantas Airways |
| | BBB | Burns Philp | Challenge Bank | Renison |
| | BBB− | News Corporation | Pasminco | |
| Uncertainties or adverse conditions could lead to inadequate capacity to pay | BB+ | Foster's | | |
| | BB | | | |
| | BB− | | | |
| Adverse conditions likely to impair capacity to pay | B+ | | | |
| | B | | | |
| | B− | Ansett | TNT | |
| Vulnerable to default | CCC | Ariadne | | |
| High risk of default | C | | | |
| Default | D | | | |

*Source*: Monthly Bulletin: Australia & New Zealand, S & P–Australian Ratings, 1 August 1993.

## SELECTED REFERENCES

Campbell, J. Y., 'A Defense of the Traditional Hypotheses about the Term Structure of Interest Rates', *Journal of Finance*, March 1986, pp. 183–95.
Cox, J. C., Ingersoll, J. E. & Ross, S. A., 'A Re-examination of Traditional Hypotheses about the Term Structure of Interest Rates', *Journal of Finance*, September 1981, pp. 769–99.
Dodds, J. & Ford, J., *Expectations, Uncertainty and the Term Structure of Interest Rates*, Martin Robertson, London, 1974.
Fama, E., 'Short-Term Interest Rates as Predictors of Inflation', *American Economic Review*, June 1975, pp. 269–82.
Fisher, I., *The Theory of Interest*, Macmillan Company, New York, 1930.
Fisher, L., 'Determinants of Risk Premiums on Corporate Bonds', *Journal of Political Economy*, June 1959, pp. 217–37.
Gordon, M. & Shapiro, E., 'Capital Equipment Analysis: The Required Rate Profit', *Management Science*, October 1956, pp. 102–10.
Hicks, J., *Value and Capital*, 2nd edn, Clarendon Press, Oxford, 1946.
Hirshleifer, J., *Investment, Interest and Capital*, Prentice–Hall, Englewood Cliffs, New Jersey, 1970.
Juttner, D. J., 'The Risk Structure of Interest Rates', *Economic Papers*, December 1986, pp. 73–91.
Lutz, F., 'The Structure of Interest Rates', *Quarterly Journal of Economics*, November 1940, pp. 29–63.
Officer, R.R., 'Rates of Return to Shares, Bond Yields and Inflation Rates, An Historical Perspective', in *Share Markets and Portfolio Theory*, Eds R. Ball et al., 2nd edn, University of Queensland Press, St Lucia, 1989, pp. 207–11.
Tease, W.J., 'The Expectations Theory of the Term Structure of Interest Rates in Australia: *The Economic Record*, June 1988, pp. 120–7.

## QUESTIONS

1. *Assuming perfect certainty, the rates of return on all financial assets will be identical.* Outline why this statement is correct and indicate the factors on which this market rate of return depends.
2. *A company's share price reflects the discounted value of either its future dividends or its future earnings.* Discuss.
3. The required rate of return on the shares in the companies identified in (a) to (c) below is 15 per cent per annum. Calculate the current share price in each case.
   (a) The current earnings per share of Zero Ltd are $1.50. The company does not reinvest any of its earnings, which are expected to remain constant.
   (b) Speedy Ltd's current dividend per share is 80 cents. This dividend is expected to grow at 5 per cent per annum.
   (c) Reduction Ltd's current dividend per share is 60 cents. The dividend of the company has been growing at 12 per cent per annum in recent years, a rate expected to be maintained for a further 3 years. It is then envisaged that the growth rate will decline to 5 per cent per annum and remain at that level indefinitely.
4. *Differences between the current yields on different bonds can be explained by their relative riskiness and different terms to maturity.* Discuss.
5. *Government bonds are not riskless.* Do you agree with this statement? Why?
6. *Although the market price of long-term bonds is much more sensitive to changes in market interest rates than the market price of short-term bonds is, it is not obvious that an individual wishing to invest for a fixed period should choose to invest in a series of shorter-term bonds.* Discuss the rationale for this statement.

7. What is the term structure of interest rates? Discuss the various theories that try to explain the term structure of interest rates.
8. *Given an upward-sloping yield curve, it is preferable for a company to raise debt by issuing short-term debt securities.* Discuss.
9. A 10 per cent $100 government bond which pays interest annually, and currently is 5 years from maturity, is selling for $103.29.
   (a) What is the required rate of return on this bond?
   (b) What is the implied real interest rate if the expected inflation rate is 5 per cent per annum?
10. A 12 per cent $100 government bond pays interest twice yearly and matures in 5 years. The current market yield on the bond is 10 per cent per annum. If an interest payment has just been made, what is the current price of the bond?
11. Consider two 12 per cent $100 government bonds that differ only in that one matures in 2 years' time and the other in 5 years' time. Both bonds are currently selling for $100 and pay interest annually.
    (a) What will be the price of each bond, given an immediate fall in the required yield to 10 per cent per annum?
    (b) What will be the price of each bond, given an immediate increase in the required yield to 14 per cent per annum?
    (c) Explain the relative price movements in response to interest rate changes as evidenced by parts (a) and (b).
12. The current interest rates on government bonds are as follows:

| Years to maturity | Interest rate (% p.a.) |
|---|---|
| 1 | 6.00 |
| 2 | 6.50 |
| 3 | 6.90 |
| 4 | 7.20 |
| 5 | 7.40 |

   (a) Assume that the term structure can be explained purely by expectations of future interest rates, and therefore there is no liquidity or risk premium. Calculate the expected 1-year interest rates for the next 4 years.
   (b) Explain why it is not possible in this market for the interest rate on a government bond with 6 years to maturity to be 6 per cent per annum.
13. What is 'immunisation'? (See Appendix 4.1.) How can duration matching help? What are the problems of duration matching?
14. An investor is considering the purchase of a 10-year bond that pays a single annual coupon at the rate of 10 per cent. The bond's face value is $1000 and its current price is $1134.19. Determine whether the investor can ensure a particular rate of return over a 7-year time horizon.

# APPENDIX 4.1

# DURATION AND IMMUNISATION

In Section 4.5 it was shown that holders of bonds are subject to interest-rate risk. A change in the level of interest rates affects both the market price of an existing bond and the interest rate at which interest receipts can be reinvested. For example, an increase in interest rates means an immediate capital loss to holders of bonds because the price of their securities will fall. However, there is then the opportunity to reinvest interest receipts at the higher interest rate. The reverse applies if interest rates fall.

The possibility of changing interest rates presents difficulties for investors. Suppose, for example, that an investor wishes to have a target sum of money in 3 years' time. The challenge is to choose a bond investment that will achieve this target, regardless of interest rate changes during the 3 years. Such an objective is called **immunisation**. If possible, the investor should buy a 3-year bond that makes no interest payments (known as **coupons**) during its life. Such securities are usually called **zero-coupon bonds**.[22] The investor knows with certainty the price of the bond at the end of the 3 years because the bond will then be worth exactly its face value, as it matures at that time. Since there are no coupon interest payments, the investor also has no doubts arising from uncertainty about the interest rate that will be earned on reinvested coupons. Therefore, the investor knows precisely what the investment will be worth at the end of the 3 years, and thus achievement of the target is guaranteed. The problem is that although zero-coupon bonds exist, bonds with non-zero coupons are more usual. Immunisation using coupon-paying bonds is more difficult to achieve.

---

[22] With zero-coupon bonds, an investor receives no regular interest payments during the bond's life. A zero-coupon bond is purchased at a discount from its face value and it is either held to maturity, when the investor receives the face value, or sold before maturity at a price determined in the marketplace.

A technique certain to immunise an investment in coupon-paying bonds against all possible changes in interest rates has never been achieved. However, there is a technique that will immunise a bond investment in a relatively simple environment in which the yield curve is flat, but may make a parallel shift up or down.[23] This technique is based on the concept of **bond duration** and its origins can be traced to research undertaken in the 1930s by Macaulay.[24]

## BOND DURATION

Macaulay realised that a bond paying a low coupon rate is in a sense a 'longer' investment than a higher coupon bond with the same term to maturity. For example, consider two 5-year bonds, both of which have a face value of $1000, pay interest annually, and are currently priced to yield 10 per cent per annum. They differ, however, in that one has a coupon rate of 5 per cent per annum and the other a coupon rate of 15 per cent per annum.

The cash flows and their present values are shown in Table A4.1.1.

**Table A4.1.1**

| Year | 5% coupon | | 15% coupon | |
|---|---|---|---|---|
| | Cash flow ($) | Present value ($) | Cash flow ($) | Present value ($) |
| 1 | 50 | 45.45 | 150 | 136.36 |
| 2 | 50 | 41.32 | 150 | 123.97 |
| 3 | 50 | 37.57 | 150 | 112.70 |
| 4 | 50 | 34.15 | 150 | 102.45 |
| 5 | 50 | 31.05 | 150 | 93.14 |
| | 1000 | 620.92 | 1000 | 620.92 |
| Total | | 810.46 | | 1189.54 |

Therefore, the price of the 5 per cent coupon bond is $810.46 and the price of the 15 per cent coupon bond is $1189.54. For the low-coupon bond, the face value payment ($1000) represents about 77 per cent of its price (because $620.92/$810.46 ≈ 0.77). For the high-coupon bond, the face value represents only about 52 per cent of its price ($620.92/$1189.54 ≈ 0.52). Conversely, if we concentrate on the first interest payment, this contributes only about 5.6 per cent to the value of the low-coupon bond ($45.45/$810.46 ≈ 0.056) but contributes nearly 11.5 per cent to the value of the high-coupon bond ($136.36/$1189.54 ≈ 0.115). It is clear that the low-coupon bond brings returns to the

---

[23] For a discussion of techniques appropriate to several more complex environments, see E. J. Elton & M. J. Gruber, *Modern Portfolio Theory and Investment Analysis*, 3rd edn, John Wiley and Sons, New York, 1987, pp. 500–503.

[24] F. Macaulay, *Some Theoretical Problems Suggested by the Movements of Interest Rates, Bond Yields and Stock Prices in the U.S. since 1856*, National Bureau of Economic Research, New York, 1938.

investor later in its life, relative to the high-coupon bond. In this sense, the low-coupon bond is 'longer'.

Macaulay proposed that this timing feature could be incorporated into a duration measure by weighting the number of periods that will elapse before a cash flow is received by the fraction of the bond's price that the present value of that cash flow represents. In this way the time period is weighted by the 'relative importance' of the cash flow that will occur at that time.

Table A4.1.2 shows the calculation of duration for the two bonds discussed above.

**Table A4.1.2**

|  | 5% coupon | | 15% coupon | |
| --- | --- | --- | --- | --- |
| Time | Weight | Weight × time | Weight | Weight × time |
| 1 | 45.45/810.46 = 0.056 08 | 0.056 08 | 136.36/1189.54 = 0.114 63 | 0.114 63 |
| 2 | 41.32/810.46 = 0.050 98 | 0.101 96 | 123.97/1189.54 = 0.104 22 | 0.208 44 |
| 3 | 37.57/810.46 = 0.046 36 | 0.139 08 | 112.70/1189.54 = 0.094 74 | 0.284 22 |
| 4 | 34.15/810.46 = 0.042 14 | 0.168 56 | 102.45/1189.54 = 0.086 13 | 0.344 52 |
| 5 | 31.05/810.46 = 0.038 31 | 0.191 55 | 93.14/1189.54 = 0.078 30 | 0.391 50 |
|  | 620.92/810.46 = 0.766 13 | 3.830 65 | 620.92/1189.54 = 0.521 98 | 2.609 90 |
| Total = duration |  | 4.487 88 |  | 3.953 21 |

As suggested earlier, the duration of the low-coupon bond (4.488 years) is longer than the duration of the high-coupon bond (3.953 years).

Duration and term to maturity are equal only for a zero-coupon bond. The duration of a bond with a positive coupon interest rate is always less than its term to maturity. For a bond whose current market price is above its face value, duration increases with term to maturity, but at a decreasing rate. For a bond whose current market price is below its face value, duration increases with term to maturity up to a point that is less than the term to maturity, and thereafter duration declines.

The steps used to calculate duration $D$ are summarised in the formula:

$$D = \sum_{t=1}^{n} \left[ \frac{PV(C_t)}{P_0} \right] t \qquad \textbf{(A4.1.1)}$$

where
$C_t$ = cash flow (coupon interest or principal) at time $t$
$PV(C_t)$ = present value of $C_t$
$$= \frac{C_t}{(1+i)^t}$$

Now $P_0$ = price of the bond
$$= \sum_{t=1}^{n} \frac{I_t}{(1+i)^t} + \frac{P_n}{(1+i)^n}$$

where $I_t$ = coupon interest at time $t$
$P_n$ = face value payment at maturity
$i$ = required yield per period
$n$ = number of periods to maturity

Equation A4.1.1 can be rewritten in its more usual form:

$$D = \frac{\sum_{t=1}^{n} \frac{C_t \times t}{(1+i)^t}}{\sum_{t=1}^{n} \frac{C_t}{(1+i)^t}} \qquad \text{(A4.1.2)}$$

Example A4.1.2 (see later in this appendix) includes a duration calculation which follows Equation A4.1.2. First, however, we provide a brief mathematical analysis to highlight the importance of the duration measure. Readers uninterested in this analysis can omit this section.

## DURATION AND INTEREST ELASTICITY

As explained in Section 4.4, if interest rates increase (decrease) then bond prices decrease (increase). When there is a change in interest rates, all bond prices respond in the opposite direction, but they do not all respond to the same extent. In other words, different bonds have different **interest elasticities**. It is important for a bond investor to know the interest elasticity of the bond because this will be a good indicator of the interest rate risk being borne.

The notion of elasticity is prominent in economics. Perhaps the best known example is the price elasticity of demand for a particular good. This is expressed as follows:

$$\eta = \frac{P}{Q} \frac{dQ}{dP}$$

where $\eta$ = price elasticity of demand
$P$ = price of the good
$Q$ = quantity of the good demanded
$\frac{dQ}{dP}$ = derivative of quantity demanded with respect to price

Price elasticity indicates the response of the quantity demanded to a change in price.

What matters for a bond investor is the interest elasticity of the bond price; in other words, what matters is the response of the bond price to a change in the interest rate. The elasticity $E$ is given by:

$$E = \frac{i}{P_0} \frac{dP_0}{di} \qquad \text{(A4.1.3)}$$

Writing out the formula for bond price:

$$P_0 = \frac{I_1}{1+i} + \frac{I_2}{(1+i)^2} + \ldots + \frac{I_n}{(1+i)^n} + \frac{P_n}{(1+i)^n}$$

and therefore:

$$\frac{dP_0}{di} = -\frac{I_1}{(1+i)^2} - \frac{2I_2}{(1+i)^3} - \ldots - \frac{nI_n}{(1+i)^{n+1}} - \frac{nP_n}{(1+i)^{n+1}}$$

$$= \left(\frac{-1}{1+i}\right)\left(\frac{I_1}{1+i} + \frac{2I_2}{(1+i)^2} + \ldots + \frac{nI_n}{(1+i)^n} + \frac{nP_n}{(1+i)^n}\right)$$

Substituting into Equation A4.1.3:

$$E = -\left(\frac{i}{P_0}\right)\left(\frac{1}{1+i}\right)\left(\frac{I_1}{1+i} + \frac{2I_2}{(1+i)^2} + \ldots + \frac{nI_n}{(1+i)^n} + \frac{nP_n}{(1+i)^n}\right)$$

or
$$E = -\left(\frac{i}{1+i}\right)D \qquad (A4.1.4)$$

where $D$ is as defined in Equation A4.1.1.

This shows that the interest elasticity of a bond's price is proportional to its duration. The longer the duration, the greater (in the sense of being more negative) is the interest elasticity. For example, if the interest rate is 10 per cent and the duration is 4.5, the interest elasticity is:

$$E = -\left(\frac{0.10}{1.10}\right)(4.5)$$
$$= -0.409$$

If the duration is 9, the interest elasticity is:

$$E = -\left(\frac{0.10}{1.10}\right)(9)$$
$$= -0.818$$

## DURATION AND BOND PRICE CHANGES

Given that duration can be related to interest elasticity, it follows that it is possible to use duration to work out the approximate percentage price change that will occur for a given change in interest rate. Using Equations A4.1.3 and A4.1.4:

$$\frac{i}{P_0}\left(\frac{dP_0}{di}\right) = -\left(\frac{i}{1+i}\right)D$$

It follows that:

$$\frac{dP_0}{P_0} = -\left(\frac{1}{1+i}\right)D\,di$$

Therefore, for 'small' discrete changes in interest rates and bond prices we have the following approximation:

$$\frac{\Delta P_0}{P_0} \approx -\left(\frac{1}{1+i}\right)D\Delta i \qquad (A4.1.5)$$

## Example A4.1.1

Consider the 5-year 15 per cent coupon bond priced to yield 10 per cent per annum. As shown in Table A4.1.1, the price of this bond is $1189.54 (per $1000 face value) and its duration is 3.953 years. What is the percentage price change if the interest rate falls to 9.5 per cent per annum?

In this case the interest rate change is $-0.5$ per cent $= -0.005$. Equation A4.1.5 gives the approximate answer as:

$$-\left(\frac{1}{1.10}\right)(3.953)(-0.005)$$

$$= 0.017\,97$$

In other words, the result will be a capital gain of approximately 1.8 per cent. (The exact answer is close to 1.819 per cent.)

## DURATION AND IMMUNISATION

Suppose that the yield curve is flat, but it may make a parallel shift up or down. If at the time of a parallel shift an investor is holding a bond whose duration matches the remaining investment period, the investment is immunised against the shift. That is, the investment will achieve at least the target yield, notwithstanding the yield shift. This can be seen in the following example.

## Example A4.1.2

Suppose that there is a flat yield curve at an interest rate of 10 per cent per annum. An investor wishes to 'lock in' this yield for a 3-year investment period. Bond A has a term of 3.4 years, a face value of $1000, a coupon rate of 7 per cent and pays interest annually. Table A4.1.3 shows the calculation of Bond A's duration, using Equation A4.1.2.

**Table A4.1.3** Bond A

| Time (years) | Cash flow ($) | Present value of cash flow ($) | Time × present value ($) |
|---|---|---|---|
| 0.4 | 70 | 67.382 | 26.953 |
| 1.4 | 70 | 61.256 | 85.758 |
| 2.4 | 70 | 55.687 | 133.649 |
| 3.4 | 1070 | 773.836 | 2631.042 |
| Total | | 958.161 | 2877.402 |

$$\text{Duration} = \frac{\$2877.402}{\$958.161}$$

$$= 3.003 \text{ years}$$

According to the immunisation strategy, Bond A should provide an immunised investment because its duration matches the investment period. That is, an investment of $958.161 in Bond A will be worth at least $958.161 × (1.1)³ = $1275.312

in 3 years' time, regardless of an interest rate shift. To demonstrate this, it is assumed that:
1. immediately after buying Bond A, the yield curve makes a parallel shift from 10 per cent to 8 per cent, and remains at that level for the next 3 years;
2. as each coupon interest payment is received, the investor reinvests in (that is, buys more of) the same bond;
3. bonds and dollars are infinitely divisible, thereby allowing the investor to purchase or sell any fraction of Bond A.

After 0.4 years have passed, the investor receives a coupon payment of $70. The bond is now a 3-year bond. The yield curve has shifted down to 8 per cent, so the price of one bond is then:

$$\frac{\$70}{1.08} + \frac{\$70}{(1.08)^2} + \frac{\$1070}{(1.08)^3}$$
$$= \$974.229$$

Therefore, the investor can purchase the fraction 70.00/974.229 of one bond. This fraction is 0.071 852, so the investor now holds 1.071 852 bonds. After 1.4 years, the investor receives a further coupon payment of $70 per bond; therefore the cash received is $70 × 1.071 852 = $75.0296. The bond is now a 2-year bond and its price is:

$$\frac{\$70}{1.08} + \frac{\$1070}{(1.08)^2}$$
$$= \$982.167$$

The investor can now purchase a further 75.0296/982.167 = 0.076 39 of a bond. This type of cycle is repeated after 2.4 years and the investment in bonds is then sold after 3 years. Table A4.1.4 summarises the progress of the investment.

### Table A4.1.4

| | \multicolumn{5}{c}{Date = investment period expired (years)} | | | | |
|---|---|---|---|---|---|
| Item | 0.0 | 0.4 | 1.4 | 2.4 | 3.0 |
| Bond term remaining (years) | 3.4 | 3.0 | 2.0 | 1.0 | 0.4 |
| Coupon interest received ($) | nil | 70.0000 | 75.0296 | 80.3770 | nil |
| Price of one bond ($)[a] | 958.161 | 974.229 | 982.167 | 990.741 | 1037.563 |
| Bonds purchased (No.) | 1.000 00 | 0.071 85 | 0.076 39 | 0.081 13 | nil |
| No. of bonds held | 1.000 00 | 1.071 85 | 1.148 24 | 1.229 37 | 1.229 37 |
| Value of bonds held ($) | 958.161 | 1044.227 | 1127.764 | 1217.987 | 1275.549 |

(a) Present value of remaining cash flows per $1000 face value. Yield used is 10 per cent per annum for the price at date zero. Yield used is 8 per cent per annum for prices calculated after date zero.

As can be seen in the bottom right-hand corner of the table, the sum received from the sale after 3 years is $1275.549 and the investment has therefore achieved the target rate of return of at least 10 per cent per annum.

What if the interest rate had risen to 12 per cent (instead of falling to 8 per cent)? In that case, the progress of the investment would be as shown in Table A4.1.5.

**Table A4.1.5**

| Item | Date = investment period expired (years) | | | | |
|---|---|---|---|---|---|
| | 0.0 | 0.4 | 1.4 | 2.4 | 3.0 |
| Bond term remaining (years) | 3.4 | 3.0 | 2.0 | 1.0 | 0.4 |
| Coupon interest received ($) | nil | 70.0000 | 75.5688 | 81.3468 | nil |
| Price of one bond ($)[a] | 958.161 | 879.908 | 915.497 | 955.357 | 1022.578 |
| Bonds purchased (No.) | 1.000 00 | 0.079 55 | 0.082 55 | 0.085 15 | nil |
| No. of bonds held | 1.000 00 | 1.079 55 | 1.162 10 | 1.247 25 | 1.247 25 |
| Value of bonds held ($) | 958.161 | 949.905 | 1063.897 | 1191.565 | 1275.406 |

[a] Present value of remaining cash flows per $1000 face value. Yield used is 10 per cent per annum for the price at date zero. Yield used is 12 per cent per annum for prices calculated after date zero.

Again, therefore, the investment has achieved the target yield of 10 per cent per annum, notwithstanding the shift in yield after the investment was made.

Managing risk by matching Macaulay's duration to the investment horizon is an important idea but the procedure we have described has a number of limitations. In particular, it is important to investigate what happens if there is more than one yield shift during the investment period. Consider again Example A4.1.2 and suppose that the yield had shifted down to 8 per cent immediately after date 0.0, but then shifted up to 12 per cent just before date 3.0 (the end of the investment period). In that case, the investor will hold 1.229 37 bonds after 3 years have passed, but the price will be only $1022.578 per bond, which gives a value of $1.229\ 37 \times \$1022.578 = \$1257.127$. This falls short of the target of having at least $1275.312. In principle this problem can be solved easily. When the yield changes, so too does the duration of the bond held. When the yield shifts on the first occasion, the investor should change the bond holding so that, once again, duration matches the investment period. The investor is then immunised against the *next* yield shift. This is simple in principle but in practice there are difficulties because it implies that a rebalancing of the investment—buying and selling bonds—is needed every time the duration of the investment changes. Because duration is a function of the current yield and future coupon payments, this means that a bond transaction is needed every time the yield shifts, and every time a coupon payment is received. This can be costly and cumbersome.

Only a flat yield curve subject to parallel shifts has been considered. What if a sloped yield curve shifts in parallel fashion? What if a sloped yield curve shifts in some non-parallel way? The answers to these questions are beyond the scope of this book but we offer a few brief comments. A solution to the first problem has been provided in the article by Fisher and Weil (1971). Essentially, the investor still matches duration and investment period, but the duration formula is slightly more complex. There is no single answer to the second question. It depends on the type of non-parallel shift assumed to occur. For an example, see the article by Cox, Ingersoll and Ross (1979).

## SELECTED REFERENCES

Bierwag, G. O. & Kaufman, G. C., 'Coping with the Risk of Interest Rate Fluctuations: A Note', *Journal of Business*, July 1977, pp. 364–70.

Cox, J. C., Ingersoll, J. E. & Ross, S. A., 'Duration and the Measurement of Basis Risk', *Journal of Business*, January 1979, pp. 51–61.

Fisher, L. & Weil, R. L., 'Coping with the Risk of Interest Rate Fluctuations: Returns to Bondholders from Naive and Optimal Strategies', *Journal of Business*, October 1971, pp. 408–31.

Granito, M. R., *Bond Portfolio Immunisation*, Lexington Books, Lexington, 1984.

Gushee, C., 'How to Hedge a Bond Investment', *Financial Analysts Journal*, March–April 1981, pp. 44–51.

Macaulay, F., *Some Theoretical Problems Suggested by the Movements of Interest Rates, Bond Yields and Stock Prices in the U.S. since 1856*, National Bureau of Economic Research, New York, 1938.

# CHAPTER 5

# PROJECT EVALUATION: PRINCIPLES AND METHODS

## 5.1 INTRODUCTION

In Chapter 1 we described the primary financial functions of the financial manager as raising funds and allocating them to investment projects so as to maximise shareholders' wealth. In this chapter, we consider how such projects should be selected to ensure the maximisation of shareholders' wealth. The term *investment project* is interpreted very broadly to include any proposal to outlay cash in the expectation that cash inflows will result. There is, therefore, a wide range of projects, including proposals for the replacement of plant and equipment, a new advertising campaign, proposals for research and development activities, proposals to take over competing firms, and so on.

In this book, investment and financial decisions are discussed in the order in which they are generally considered in practice. In general, management will first examine the alternative investment projects available to it. After the acceptability of these projects has been determined, management will, if necessary, set about raising the funds to implement them. It is logical, therefore, to discuss the evaluation and selection of proposed investment projects before discussing the methods of financing them. In this chapter, we examine the basic principles and methods of project evaluation. In Chapter 18, the application of these principles and methods is discussed.

The evaluation and selection of investment projects is only one element of the capital-expenditure process. Therefore, before discussing the methods of project evaluation, the capital-expenditure process is outlined.

## 5.2 Capital-expenditure Process

Capital-expenditure management involves the planning and control of expenditures incurred in the expectation of deriving future economic benefits in the form of cash inflows. Consider the following cases: a manufacturer is considering building a new plant; an airline is considering the replacement of several of its aircraft; a company is considering a new research and development program. Each proposal involves making current outlays in the expectation of future cash inflows and, therefore, each can be analysed as a capital-expenditure proposal. This is the case even though, for example, the costs of research and development are usually recognised for accounting purposes as expenses in the period in which they are incurred.

Capital expenditures are important for a company because frequently the amounts of money involved are large and their effects extend well into the future. After capital expenditures have been made it is likely that their effects will have to be endured for some time as many projects are not easily modified. Where there is either no second-hand market or, at best, only a 'thin' market for capital assets, management may have to abandon a project if it proves to be unprofitable. Because of the longevity and frequent irreversibility of many investments they are likely to commit a company to a particular technology and to have a considerable influence on the pattern of its future operating cash flows. The importance of these decisions, therefore, is not confined to the period when the initial capital outlay is made.

Broadly speaking, the capital-expenditure process involves the following steps:

(a) the generation of investment proposals;
(b) the evaluation and selection of those proposals;
(c) the approval and control of capital expenditures; and
(d) the post-completion audit of investment projects.

### 1. Generation of Investment Proposals

The first step in the capital-expenditure process is the generation of investment proposals. Investment proposals can originate from any level in the company, from employees on the shop floor to top management. Many ideas for investment proposals are generated at lower levels in the company where any waste or inefficiency in its operations is likely to be readily apparent. For example, employees on the shop floor may be aware of equipment that needs to be replaced, or they may have ideas for improving the company's operations. In contrast, top management is more likely to have ideas for plant expansion, new product development, diversification, corporate takeovers, and other large capital expenditures. The generation of good ideas for capital expenditure will be facilitated if there is a systematic means of searching for them. In some companies, for example, the search for investment opportunities is assigned to a corporate planning department.

## 2. THE EVALUATION AND SELECTION OF INVESTMENT PROPOSALS

After the generation of investment proposals it is necessary to assemble the data required to evaluate them. Many companies use standard evaluation forms and procedures so that all proposals are assessed on a uniform basis. The data for a proposal should include:

(a) a brief description of the proposal;
(b) a statement indicating why it is desirable or necessary;
(c) an estimate of the amount and timing of the cash outlays;
(d) an estimate of the amount and timing of the cash inflows;
(e) an estimate of when the proposal will come into operation; and
(f) an estimate of its economic life.

Using these data, an economic evaluation of the proposal is made. The methods of evaluation are discussed in Section 5.3. Because many of the financial variables are estimates, and because investors are assumed to be risk averse, an economic evaluation of a proposal should take its riskiness into account. The methods of including risk in the analysis are discussed in Chapters 17 and 18. After the investment proposals have been evaluated quantitatively, management will select the projects to be included in the capital budget, taking into account any relevant qualitative factors.[1]

## 3. APPROVAL AND CONTROL OF CAPITAL EXPENDITURES

After selection of the investment projects, a capital-expenditure budget which details the estimated capital expenditure on new and continuing projects for each of the next few years should be prepared. In a survey of Australian capital budgeting practices it was found that 87 per cent of the ninety-eight organisations responding to the survey prepared capital-expenditure budgets, with 55 per cent preparing both long-range and short-range capital budgets each year.[2] Short-range budgets are generally prepared for periods of from 6 months to 2 years, and long-range budgets for periods of from 2 years to 5 years. The main reason for developing a capital-expenditure budget is to ensure that expenditures are kept within the authorised limits, so that the timing of the expenditures, particularly for major items, is consistent with other demands on the company's resources and with the company's overall financial plan.

After an investment project has been approved and the spending of a sum of money authorised, the company needs appropriate administrative procedures to implement it. As a first step, a project manager will be appointed to be responsible for the implementation of each project. Implementation will include the adoption of a realistic timetable for the project's completion, and procedures for controlling costs.[3]

---

1 Qualitative factors are discussed in Chapter 18.
2 P.G. Lilleyman, 'Capital Budgeting: Current Practices of Australian Organizations', *The Australian Accountant*, March 1984, p. 131.
3 For a discussion of techniques, such as PERT (Program Evaluation and Review Technique) and CPM (Critical Path Method), which may be used to plan and schedule investment projects, see H.W.A. Sweeney & R. Rachlin, *Handbook of Budgeting*, John Wiley & Sons, New York, 1981, pp. 557–67.

The time taken to complete a project is important as any delay in its completion is likely to result in foregoing cash inflows. Even a short delay in a project's implementation may cause it to be unprofitable. To assist in controlling costs, a separate account may be established for each project. This account will be charged with the outlays as the invoices are received. Control over expenditure will be facilitated by the submission of progress reports to management. These reports compare the amount spent on the project, and its expected date of completion, with the forecasts. Where the expenditures are significantly above budget, or the project has fallen well behind schedule, the project should be reassessed as it may no longer be desirable to proceed with it.[4]

## 4. POST-COMPLETION AUDIT OF INVESTMENT PROJECTS

After a project has been in operation for a reasonable period, it is important to consider whether it is performing to expectations. Such an assessment is referred to as a **post-completion audit**. It is an essential part of the capital-expenditure process. The audit report should highlight any cash flows that have deviated significantly from budget and, where possible, provide explanations for those deviations. There are three potential benefits from conducting a post-completion audit:

(a) It may provide valuable information to enable implementation of improvements in the project's operating performance.
(b) It may improve the quality of investment decisions. Those responsible for the initial evaluation are likely to be more careful if they know that their estimates will later be compared with the results.
(c) It may lead to the re-evaluation and possible abandonment of an unsuccessful project.

As the time taken for each project to become fully operational will vary, the precise timing of the post-completion audit will vary from project to project. In addition, selection of the projects to be audited will vary from company to company. In most companies it is unlikely that all projects will be audited and, therefore, criteria for determining a project's eligibility for post-completion audit will have to be devised.

Who should perform the audit? The person who made the initial evaluation of the project is probably in the best position to review its operating performance because he or she will have the greatest familiarity with the original estimates and the factors that influence the project's operation. However, there may be serious doubt about the objectivity of such a review and, because of their independence, the accounting department or internal audit department may be asked to conduct the audit.

---

[4] In situations where initial assumptions about a project prove to be incorrect, or where additional new investment opportunities arise, failure to abandon projects which are no longer desirable could be very costly. Abandonment of projects is discussed in Chapter 18.

## 5.3 METHODS OF PROJECT EVALUATION

In this section we consider the evaluation and selection of investment projects. First, we consider the net present value and the internal rate of return methods which were developed in a one-period setting in Chapter 2. We then consider other methods that have been employed in project evaluation.

Many methods are used to evaluate and compare investment projects. The methods outlined in this section are the ones that surveys of business practice suggest are used most frequently. They are of two basic types: first, the discounted cash flow methods, such as the internal rate of return and net present value methods, which discount the estimated cash flows to allow for the magnitude, timing and risk of the cash flows and secondly the non-discounted cash flow methods, such as the accounting rate of return and pay-back period methods. Table 5.1 shows the results of a survey of project evaluation methods adopted by Australian companies in 1989.

**Table 5.1** *Project evaluation methods used by entities surveyed*

| Method | Percentage* |
|---|---|
| Accounting rate of return | 33% |
| Discounted Cash Flow profitability index | 23% |
| Internal rate of return | 72% |
| Net present value | 75% |
| Pay-back period | 44% |
| Other | 49% |

\* The aggregate percentage exceeds 100 per cent because most respondents used more than one method of project evaluation.
Source: Freeman, M. & Hobbes, G. 'Capital Budgeting: Theory versus Practice', *Australian Accountant*, September 1991, p. 38.

In this chapter it is initially assumed that investment projects are independent. Two projects are said to be **independent** if the acceptance of one project does not affect the acceptance of the other project. Two conditions are necessary for projects to be independent:
    (a) It must be technically feasible to undertake one project, irrespective of the decision made concerning the other project.
    (b) The net cash flows from each project must be unaffected by the acceptance or rejection of the other project.

For example, an entity may be considering whether to purchase new machinery for its factory, and whether to commission a new advertising campaign. These investments are independent. Consequently, management can make an accept/reject decision on each investment without considering its relationship to other investments. Problems caused by the presence of mutually exclusive projects are considered in Section 5.4.4.

### 5.3.1 Discounted Cash Flow Methods

It can be seen from Table 5.1 that the two most frequently employed discounted cash flow (DCF) methods are the net present value and internal rate of return methods.

The **net present value** is equal to the difference between the present value of the net cash flows generated by a project and the initial cash outlay.[5] Assuming a cash outlay at the beginning of the project's life, and a series of net cash flows in the following periods, the net present value (NPV) of a project is calculated as follows:

$$\text{NPV} = \frac{C_1}{(1+k)} + \frac{C_2}{(1+k)^2} + \ldots + \frac{C_n}{(1+k)^n} - C_0 \tag{5.1}$$

which can be written more conveniently as:

$$\text{NPV} = \sum_{t=1}^{n} \frac{C_t}{(1+k)^t} - C_0 \tag{5.2}$$

where  $C_0$ = the initial cash outlay on the project
 $C_t$ = net cash flow generated by the project at time $t$
 $n$ = the life of the project
 $k$ = required rate of return

The required rate of return used to discount the cash flows is the minimum acceptable rate of return on investments of similar risk. For the time being the required rate of return is assumed to be given. Its derivation is considered in Chapter 17.

The **internal rate of return** is the rate of return that equates the present value of the net cash flows generated by a project with its initial cash outlay.[6] The internal rate of return is found by solving for $r$ in the following equation:

$$C_0 = \frac{C_1}{(1+r)} + \frac{C_2}{(1+r)^2} + \ldots + \frac{C_n}{(1+r)^n} \tag{5.3}$$

This can be written more conveniently as:

$$C_0 = \sum_{t=1}^{n} \frac{C_t}{(1+r)^t} \tag{5.4}$$

where  $C_0$ = the initial cash outlay on the project
 $C_t$ = net cash flow generated by the project at time $t$
 $n$ = the life of the project
 $r$ = the internal rate of return

---

[5] The cash flows could be discounted to equivalent values at any point in time. It is usual to discount the cash flows to the present; hence the use of the term *net present value*. An alternative would be to calculate a *net terminal value*. This is equal to the difference between the accumulated value of the net cash flows generated by a project, and the accumulated value of the initial cash outlay. Use of the net terminal value method gives the same decision as for the net present value method.

[6] Other terms used to describe the same concept include 'the DCF return on investment', 'yield', and 'the marginal efficiency of capital'.

## 5.4 THE DISCOUNTED CASH FLOW METHODS COMPARED

The assumed objective of a company is to maximise shareholders' wealth. Consistent with this objective, projects should be accepted only if they are expected to result in an increase in shareholders' wealth. Therefore, the method of project evaluation must be consistent with maximising shareholders' wealth. Other things being equal, this will occur where a project generates more cash, rather than less cash, and generates cash sooner, rather than later. The ability of the net present value and internal rate of return methods to result in decisions consistent with this objective is considered in the following sections.

### 5.4.1 NET PRESENT VALUE

The net present value (NPV) of a project is found by discounting the project's future net cash flows at the required rate of return and deducting from the resulting present value the initial cash outlay on the project. Therefore:

$$\text{NPV} = \sum_{t=1}^{n} \frac{C_t}{(1 + k)^t} - C_0 \qquad (5.5)$$

Where the investment outlays occur over more than one period, $C_0$ in Equation 5.5 refers only to the initial cash outlay. All subsequent outlays are included in the calculation of the net cash flows of future periods. Of course, this may result in subsequent negative net cash flows in addition to the initial cash outlay.

Management should select projects with a positive net present value and reject projects with a negative net present value. The amount of any positive net present value represents the immediate increase in the company's wealth that will result from accepting the project. It is equivalent to an unrealised accretion in value.

The magnitude of a project's net present value depends on the project's cash flows and the rate used to discount those cash flows. The correct discount rate to apply is the opportunity cost of capital.[7] This is the rate of return required on the next best (that is, foregone) alternative investment. If the net cash flows have been estimated on an after-tax basis then, to be consistent, the appropriate required rate of return is the after-tax rate. As noted in Section 5.3.1, calculation of the required rate of return is considered in Chapter 17.

---

7 Estimation of the required rate of return, or discount rate, is discussed in Chapter 17. It is sufficient at this stage to point out that the required rate of return is simply the rate of return that a project must generate in order to justify raising funds to undertake it. Where there is perfect certainty about the outcome of an investment, the risk-free rate, such as the current yield on government securities of the same maturity as the investment, is the appropriate discount rate. However, where there is uncertainty about the outcome of the investment, a risk-adjusted required rate of return must be used. For a detailed discussion of the theoretical justification for this assertion, see C.W. Haley & L.D. Schall, *The Theory of Financial Decisions*, 2nd edn, McGraw-Hill, New York, 1979. Throughout the remainder of this part of the book we will use the term *required rate of return* to indicate the discount rate used in discounted cash flow calculations.

## Example 5.1

Management is considering an investment of $9000 in a project that will return net cash flows of $5090, $4500 and $4000 at the end of Years 1, 2 and 3 respectively. Assuming a discount rate of 10 per cent, the net present value may be calculated as shown in Table 5.2.

**Table 5.2** *Calculating a project's net present value (NPV)*

| Year | Net cash flows ($) | Discount factor at 10% | Present value ($) |
|---|---|---|---|
| 0 | (9000)[a] |  | (9000) |
| 1 | 5090 | 0.909 09 | 4627[b] |
| 2 | 4500 | 0.826 45 | 3719[b] |
| 3 | 4000 | 0.751 31 | 3005[b] |
| NPV ($) |  |  | 2351 |

(a) The amount in brackets represents the initial cash outlay.
(b) The sum $4627 + $3719 + $3005 = $11 351 is the maximum amount the company would be prepared to pay for the project if the required rate of return is 10 per cent.

At a discount rate of 10 per cent, the project has a positive NPV and is therefore acceptable.

This method is consistent with the company's objective of maximising shareholders' wealth. If a company implements a project that has a positive net present value, the company will be better off than before it undertook the project, and therefore, other things being equal, the total market value of the company's shares should increase by the same amount as the net present value of the new project. In other words, the company is undertaking a project that has a net present value in excess of that necessary to leave its share price unchanged. This was shown formally in Chapter 2 using Fisher's separation theorem.

### 5.4.2 INTERNAL RATE OF RETURN

A project's internal rate of return (IRR) is that rate of return which equates the present value of its net cash flows with its initial cash outlay. This means that Equation 5.4 can be rewritten as follows:

$$\sum_{t=1}^{n} \frac{C_t}{(1+r)^t} - C_0 = 0 \qquad (5.6)$$

From Equation 5.6 the internal rate of return is the discount rate that results in a zero net present value. However, the internal rate of return is not only the discount rate that causes the net present value of the project's cash flows to be zero, but also represents:

> ... the highest rate of interest an investor could afford to pay, without losing money, if all the funds to finance the investment were borrowed, and the

loan (principal and accrued interest) was repaid by application of the cash proceeds from the investment as they were earned.[8]

In other words, the internal rate of return is akin to a rate of interest which results from the recovery of the investment outlay, plus a return on the investment project during its life.

Even if the investment outlays occur in more than one period, $C_0$ in Equation 5.6 refers only to the initial cash outlay. Any subsequent investment outlays are subtracted from the cash flows of future periods, which suggests that some of the net cash flows in Equation 5.6 may be negative. The effect on the internal rate of return of negative net cash flows in subsequent periods is discussed later in this section.

If, as is usual in practice, the project's net cash flows in each period are not equal, the internal rate of return can be found only by trial and error, that is, by varying the discount rate until the present value of the cash flows is equal to the investment outlay.[9] If it is found by this process that the present value of the net cash flows is greater than the initial cash outlay, some higher discount rate should make them equal, and vice versa.

After the internal rate of return has been calculated, the acceptability of an investment project is determined by comparing the internal rate of return $r$ with the required rate of return $k$. Any project with $r > k$ should be accepted, while any project with $r < k$ should be rejected.

*Example 5.2*

If we take the cash flows of Example 5.1, the project's internal rate of return may be calculated as follows:

$$C_0 = \frac{C_1}{(1+r)} + \frac{C_2}{(1+r)^2} + \frac{C_3}{(1+r)^3}$$

Thus

$$\$9000 = \frac{\$5090}{(1+r)} + \frac{\$4500}{(1+r)^2} + \frac{\$4000}{(1+r)^3}$$

By trial and error, $r = 25$ per cent. If the required rate of return is, say, 15 per cent, the project's internal rate of return of 25 per cent exceeds the required rate of return and the project is acceptable.

Use of this method therefore appears to be consistent with the company's objective of maximising shareholders' wealth. If the required rate of return is the minimum return that investors demand on investments, then, other things being equal, accepting a project with an internal rate of return greater than the required rate should result in an increase in the price of the company's shares. This expectation of an increase in the company's share price will result whenever the company accepts a project with an internal rate of return exceeding the rate of return necessary to maintain the shares' current market price.

---

[8] Harold Bierman Jr & Seymour Smidt, *The Capital Budgeting Decision*, 7th edn, Macmillan Company, New York, 1988, p. 69.

[9] In practice a programmable calculator may be used to calculate the internal rate of return and eliminate the time consuming computations involved in the trial and error process.

## MULTIPLE AND INDETERMINATE INTERNAL RATES OF RETURN

In Example 5.2 the investment's cash flows consisted of an initial cash outlay, followed by a series of positive net cash flows. In such cases a unique positive internal rate of return will usually exist.

In certain circumstances, however, it is possible for the present value of the future net cash flows to be equal to the initial cash outlay at more than one discount rate. That is, a project may have more than one internal rate of return. This is of concern because it is possible that after the analyst has calculated an internal rate of return a decision may be made by management based on that result. The fact that there may be more than one internal rate of return could be overlooked. It is important, therefore, to know when multiple internal rates of return on a project might be found.

A **necessary** condition for multiple internal rates of return is that one or more of the net cash flows in the later years of the project's life must be negative. The presence of negative net cash flows in the later years of a project's life is not a **sufficient** condition for multiple internal rates of return. In many cases, negative cash flows in the later years of a project's life are consistent with there being only one internal rate of return.[10] While, in practice, there is little likelihood of the occurrence of multiple internal rates of return, it is important to recognise that there are circumstances where multiple internal rates do occur.[11]

### Example 5.3

Consider an investment project with the cash flows shown in Table 5.3:

**Table 5.3**

| Year | 0 | 1 | 2 |
|---|---|---|---|
| Cash flow ($'000) | −14 545 | 34 182 | −20 000 |

Such a cash flow pattern may occur where a mining company is obliged, after completion of its mining operations, to restore the mine site to its original condition. If we solve for the internal rate of return of this project we find that its net present value is zero at both 10 per cent and 25 per cent; that is, the

---

10 Descartes' rule of signs states that there can be as many positive roots for $1 + r$ as there are changes in the sign of the cash flows. Therefore, if after the initial cash outlay the net cash flows are always positive, there will be at most one positive root for $1 + r$, and consequently only one for $r$ itself. However, two sign changes in the cash flow can result in two positive values for $1 + r$, so there may also be two positive values for $r$. For example, if the two positive values for $1 + r$ are $+1.1$ and $+1.3$, there will be two positive values for $r$: 10 per cent and 30 per cent. In the remainder of this section we use the term *internal rate of return* to mean **positive** internal rate of return.

11 Merrett & Sykes (1973) point out that in this case the internal rate of return method may be adapted to remove the possibility of obtaining multiple positive internal rates of return. The resulting method is referred to as the 'extended internal rate of return method'. See A.J. Merrett & Allen Sykes, *The Finance and Analysis of Capital Projects*, 2nd edn, Longman, London, 1973, pp. 135–7, and Robert Dorfman, 'The Meaning of Internal Rates of Return', *Journal of Finance*, December 1981, pp. 1011–21.

project has two internal rates of return. The net present value profile of this project is shown in Figure 5.1.

The number of internal rates of return is limited to the number of sign reversals in the cash-flow stream. In this case there are two sign reversals, which is a necessary, though not sufficient, condition for two internal rates of return. Three sign reversals is a necessary condition for three rates, and so on.

It may be argued that multiple rates do not constitute a problem because the project may be abandoned at the beginning of Year 2, thereby avoiding the subsequent negative cash flow, and also the multiple internal rate of return problem. If the project is terminable and has a positive residual value, a unique internal rate of return may be calculated. However, in some cases, abandonment of the project may not be possible; it may involve substantial abandonment costs in the early years of operation, or there may be a legal obligation to continue the project for a number of years.[12]

In addition to the problem of multiple internal rates of return, it is possible for an investment project to have no internal rate of return. For example, a project with a pattern of cash flows of $-\$80$, $+\$100$, $-\$50$, has no internal rate of return.

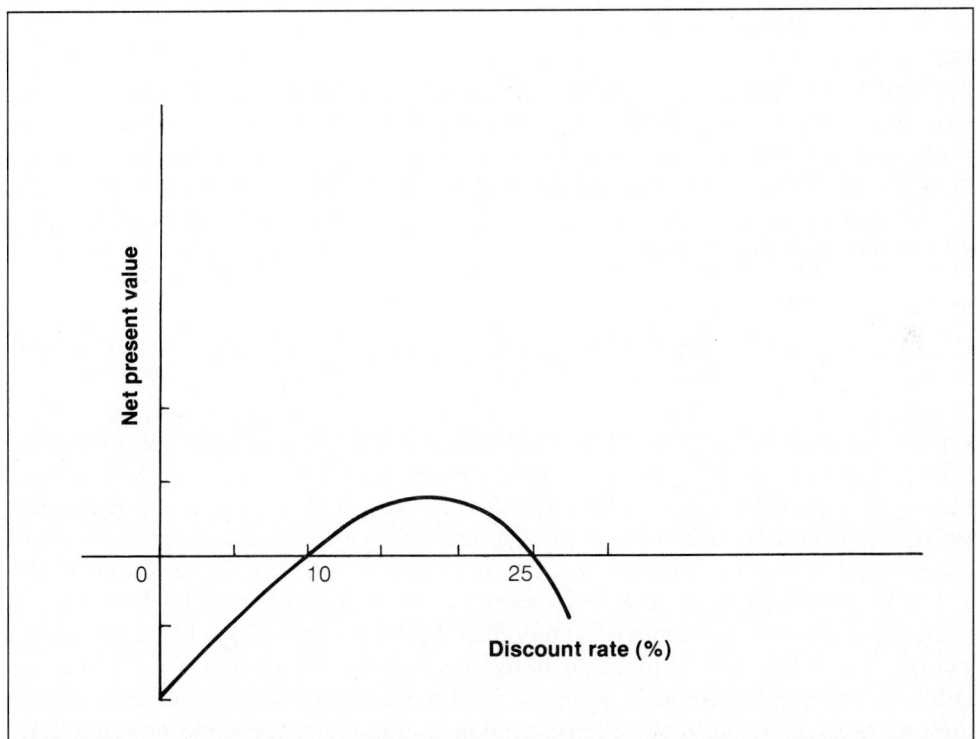

**Fig. 5.1** *Relationship between discount rates and net present value, showing two internal rates of return*

---

12 See P.H. Karmel, 'The Marginal Efficiency of Capital', *The Economic Record*, December 1959, pp. 429–32.

Projects with a cash-flow stream that results in either multiple internal rates of return, or no internal rate of return, are likely to be rare in practice, but the possibility of such occurrences does exist.

### 5.4.3 CHOOSING BETWEEN THE DISCOUNTED CASH FLOW METHODS

#### INDEPENDENT INVESTMENTS

For independent investments, both the IRR and NPV methods of investment evaluation lead to the same accept/reject decision, except for those investments where the cash flow patterns result in either multiple internal rates of return, or no internal rate of return. In other words, if a project has an internal rate of return greater than the required rate of return, the project will also have a positive net present value when its cash flows are discounted at the required rate of return. That is, NPV $\lesseqgtr$ 0 when $r \lesseqgtr k$, and NPV = 0 when $r = k$. This is always true, provided that the projects' cash flows consist of one or more periods of cash outlay followed only by positive net cash flows. This is illustrated in Figure 5.2 where the net present value of such an investment project is plotted as a function of the required rate of return. The figure shows that the higher the discount rate, the lower is the net present value. The intercept with the horizontal axis at $k = r$ is the internal rate of return as it is the discount rate at which the net present value is zero.

Figure 5.2 shows that at a required rate of return of $k_1$ the net present value is positive and $r > k_1$, while at a required rate of return of $k_2$ the net present value is negative and $r < k_2$. Where management has to decide whether to accept or reject an independent investment project, both the internal rate of return method and the net present value method will give results consistent with maximising shareholders' wealth.

#### MUTUALLY EXCLUSIVE INVESTMENTS

So far it has been assumed that investment projects are independent, which means that management can make an accept/reject decision about each project without considering its relationship with other projects. In this section, we allow for the fact that investment projects may be interdependent. In this case, the expected benefits from one project are affected by the decision to accept or reject another project. In the extreme case where the expected cash flows from a project will completely disappear if another project is accepted, or it is technically impossible to undertake the proposed project if another project is accepted, the projects are said to be **mutually exclusive**. For example, if a company owns land on which it can build either a factory or a warehouse, then these two projects are mutually exclusive. If a decision is made to build the factory, the company is unable to build the warehouse. Another example of mutually exclusive projects is where different types of equipment may be used to manufacture the same product. The choice of one type of equipment automatically leads to the rejection of the other.

In the remainder of this section the discounted cash flow methods will be evaluated, assuming that investment projects are mutually exclusive. Where management has to select from mutually exclusive projects it is necessary to rank

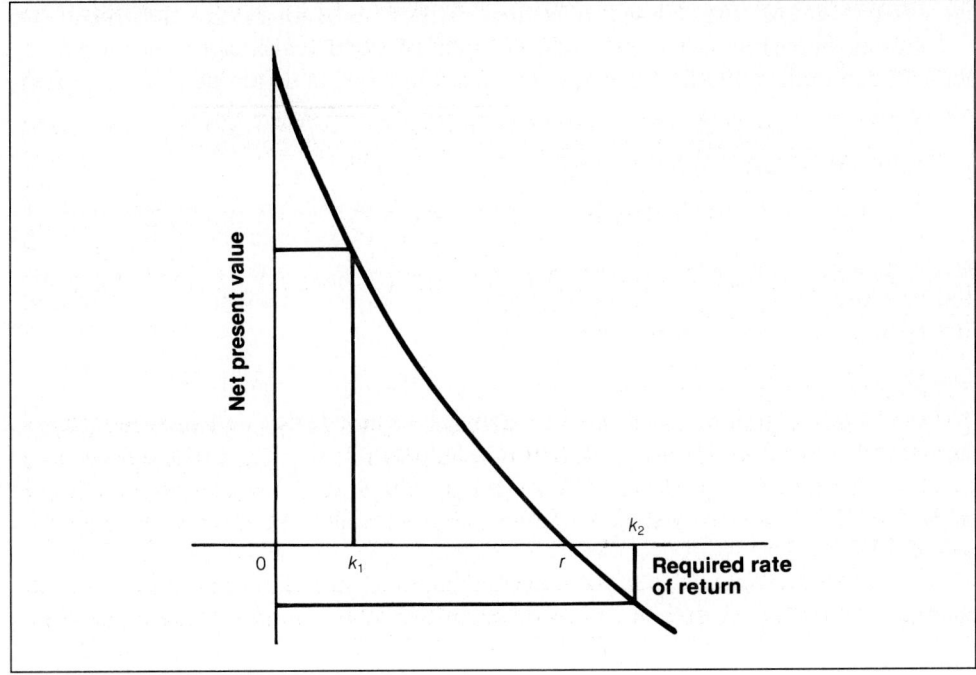

**Fig. 5.2** *Relationship between the discount rate and net present value*

the projects in order of acceptability. This means that it is necessary to determine whether it makes any difference to project selection if projects are ranked according to their internal rates of return or their net present values.

First we consider whether the internal rate of return or net present value methods should be used to evaluate mutually exclusive investments.

### Example 5.4

Consider the mutually exclusive investments, A and B, in Table 5.4:

**Table 5.4**

| Project | Cash outlay ($) | Net cash flow one year after the year of outlay ($) | r (%) | NPV @10% ($) |
|---|---|---|---|---|
| A | −1 | +10 | 900 | 8.09 |
| B | −100 000 | +200 000 | 100 | 81 820 |

The internal rate of return method ranks a 900 per cent return on $1 ahead of a 100 per cent return on $100 000. At a required rate of return of 10 per cent, both investments are worth undertaking, but where a choice has to be made between the two investments, investment B with the larger absolute return is to be preferred. This is because B adds more to the company's value than A. The net present value method will ensure that the value of the company is maximised, whereas use of the internal rate of return method will not ensure that result. It is apparent, therefore, that the internal rate of return and net present value methods can rank mutually exclusive investment projects differently. This is now explained.

## RANKING MUTUALLY EXCLUSIVE INVESTMENTS

Although both projects in Example 5.4 had the same life, the initial cash outlays were different. However, even if the initial cash outlays and the projects' lives had been the same, it is still possible that the internal rate of return and net present value methods would rank mutually exclusive investments differently. This is illustrated by Example 5.5.

### Example 5.5

Two projects, A and B, have the same initial cash outlays and the same lives but different net cash flows, as shown in Table 5.5.

**Table 5.5**

| Project | Net cash flows ($) | | |
|---|---|---|---|
| | Year 0 | Year 1 | Year 2 |
| A | −20 000 | 2 000 | 36 400 |
| B | −20 000 | 20 000 | 15 000 |

Table 5.6 shows the internal rates of return and the net present values at a required rate of return of 10 per cent for projects A and B.

**Table 5.6**

| Project | Internal rate of return (%) | Net present value ($) |
|---|---|---|
| A | 40 | 11 901 |
| B | 50 | 10 579 |

Both projects have a positive net present value and an internal rate of return greater than the required rate of return and are therefore acceptable in their own right. Once again it is because the projects are mutually exclusive that the problem occurs. Using the net present value method, A is preferred to B, while using the internal rate of return method, B is preferred to A.

In Example 5.5, the difference in ranking is caused by differences in the magnitude of the net cash flows. In addition to differences in ranking caused by differences in the cash flow streams, the internal rate of return and net present value methods may give a different ranking where the investment projects have unequal lives.

It may be concluded, therefore, that **any difference in the magnitude or timing of the cash flows may cause a difference in the ranking of investment projects using the internal rate of return and net present value methods.**

This is illustrated in Figure 5.3 which shows net present value as a function of a range of discount rates for two projects, A and B. Assume, as in Example 5.5, that the two projects have the same cash outlay and lives, and that the pattern of net cash flows results in the net present value profiles shown in Figure 5.3. In this case, the net present value profiles of the two projects intersect. At a discount rate of $r_1$, or at any other discount rate less than $r_2$, the net present value of A is greater than the net present value of B, while at a discount rate of $r_3$, or at any other discount rate greater than $r_2$, the net present value of B is greater than the net present value of A.[13]

On the other hand, it has already been shown that the internal rate of return is found where the net present value is zero and, using this rule, project B is ranked ahead of project A because its internal rate of return, $r_5$, is greater than

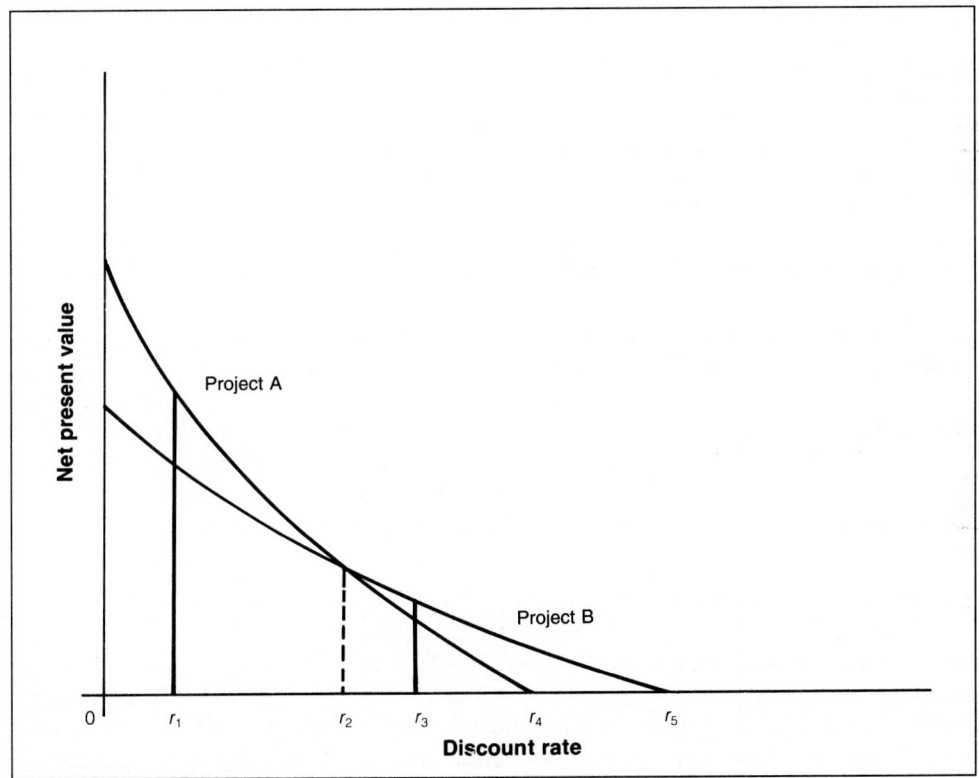

**Fig. 5.3** *Relationship between discount rates and net present values for projects A and B*

---

[13] For projects such as those in Table 5.5 with the same initial cash outlay, $r_2$ is found by equating the present values of projects A and B as follows:

$$\text{PV}_\text{A} = \sum_{t=1}^{n} \frac{C_{At}}{(1 + r_2)^t} = \sum_{t=1}^{n} \frac{C_{Bt}}{(1 + r_2)^t}$$

In this instance, $r_2 = 18.89$ per cent. This means that if the required rate of return is less than 18.89 per cent, the internal rate of return and net present value methods result in conflicting rankings.

$r_4$ which is the internal rate of return of A.[14] In this instance, the two rules provide management with different rankings of projects of A and B.

Like Example 5.5, Figure 5.3 shows that even where two mutually exclusive projects have the same capital costs and the same lives, a difference in the projects' rankings may still occur as a result of the projects' different time patterns of net cash flows. Therefore, for mutually exclusive investment projects the net present value method is superior to the internal rate of return method, because it always gives a wealth-maximising decision.

Even where the projects are mutually exclusive the two methods could yield consistent rankings if the patterns of the projects' net cash flows result in net present value profiles that do not intersect. This is illustrated in Figure 5.4. In this case, the net present value of project C at a discount rate of $r_1$ is greater than the net present value of project D. This is consistent with the internal rate

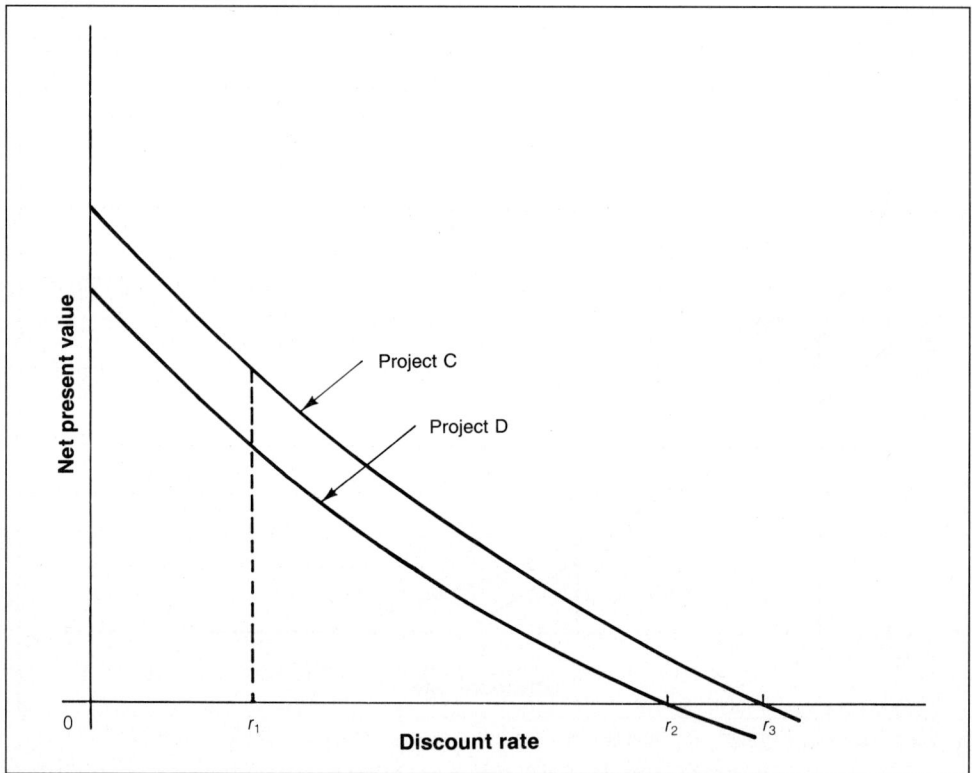

**Fig. 5.4** *Relationship between discount rates and net present values for projects C and D*

---

14 Remember that discounting of the net cash flows at the internal rate of return will result in a net present value of zero. Therefore:

$$0 = \sum_{t=1}^{n} \frac{C_t}{(1+r)^t} - C_0$$

of return method as $r_3$, the internal rate of return of project C, is greater than $r_2$, the internal rate of return of project D.

However, because of the possibility that the internal rate of return method may give an incorrect ranking of mutually exclusive investment projects, the net present value method is preferred.[15]

## THE INCREMENTAL INTERNAL RATE OF RETURN APPROACH TO RANKING MUTUALLY EXCLUSIVE INVESTMENTS

The internal rate of return method can be adapted so that it does not result in an incorrect ranking of mutually exclusive projects. This is shown in Example 5.6.

### Example 5.6
The cash flows for two projects, A and B, are as shown in Table 5.7.

**Table 5.7**

| Project | Cash flows ($) | | | | | |
|---|---|---|---|---|---|---|
| | Year 0 | Year 1 | Year 2 | Year 3 | Year 4 | Year 5 |
| A | −4500 | 1350 | 1350 | 1350 | 1350 | 1350 |
| B | −3000 | 915 | 915 | 915 | 915 | 915 |

If the required rate of return is 8 per cent per annum, both projects are acceptable using either the net present value or the internal rate of return methods, as shown in Table 5.8.

**Table 5.8**

| Project | Internal rate of return (%) | Net present value ($) |
|---|---|---|
| A | 15.2 | 890 |
| B | 16.0 | 653 |

If the two projects are mutually exclusive, then using the net present value method, A is preferred to B, while using the internal rate of return method, B is preferred to A.

Consider a company which has $4500 to invest and uses the internal rate of return method. Suppose that this company is considering projects A, B, and C. The cash flows for A and B are as already given, while the cash flows for project C are as shown in Table 5.9.

---

[15] See J. Hirshleifer, 'On the Theory of Optimal Investment Decisions', *Journal of Political Economy*, August 1958, pp. 329–52; and James H. Lorie & Leonard J. Savage, 'Three Problems in Rationing Capital', *Journal of Business*, October 1955, pp. 229–39.

**Table 5.9**

| Year | 0 | 1 | 2 | 3 | 4 | 5 |
|---|---|---|---|---|---|---|
| Cash flows for project C ($) | −1500 | 435 | 435 | 435 | 435 | 435 |

Project C has an internal rate of return of 13.8 per cent. With $4500 to invest, the company may invest either in A only, or in both B and C.

Using the internal rate of return method, project B is accepted first because it has the highest internal rate of return. However, the company can also afford to accept project C which also has an internal rate of return (13.8 per cent) greater than the required rate of return (8 per cent). Therefore, C is also acceptable. Observe, however, that the cash flows of C are equivalent to the cash flows of a notional project 'A minus B'. Acceptance of both B and C is therefore equivalent to accepting B plus 'A minus B', or A. The incremental internal rate of return method indicates that A should be chosen. Therefore A, and not B, should be ranked first. This is the ranking given by the net present value method.

The possibility of conflict between the internal rate of return and net present value methods may therefore be avoided by the use of this 'incremental internal rate of return' approach. It results in a ranking of mutually exclusive projects, which is consistent with the net present value method. However, the net present value method is simpler and is more obviously consistent with the objective of wealth maximisation, which is expressed in absolute dollar terms rather than in percentage terms.

### 5.4.4 BENEFIT–COST RATIO (PROFITABILITY INDEX)

In Table 5.1 it was noted that the discounted cash flow profitability index was employed by a number of the surveyed companies. In this method, instead of showing the net present value as an absolute amount, the present value of the net cash flows is related to the initial cash outlay and presented in the form of a benefit–cost ratio or profitability index.

A benefit–cost ratio for the project in Table 5.2 is calculated as follows:

$$\text{Benefit–cost ratio} = \frac{\text{present value of net cash flows}}{\text{initial cash outlay}} \quad (5.7)$$

$$= \frac{\$11\,351}{\$9\,000}$$

$$= 1.26$$

Using the benefit–cost ratio, the decision rule is to accept projects with a benefit–cost ratio greater than 1, and to reject projects with a benefit–cost ratio less than 1. Clearly, projects with benefit–cost ratios greater than 1 will have positive net present values, and those with benefit–cost ratios less than 1 will have negative net present values. In the above example, the net present value is $2351 and the benefit–cost ratio is 1.26. Both methods therefore indicate that the project is acceptable and in general, both methods will give the same accept-reject decision for independent projects.

However, the benefit–cost ratio provides no information additional to that already provided by the NPV method. Thus there is little point in using this method. In addition, it can be shown that, in common with the internal rate of return method, the use of the benefit–cost ratio can result in a ranking of mutually exclusive projects which differs from the ranking that would result from using the NPV method.[16]

### Example 5.7
Consider the mutually exclusive investment projects in Table 5.10.

**Table 5.10**

|  | Project E | Project F |
| --- | --- | --- |
| Present value of net cash flows ($) | 26 000 | 10 000 |
| Initial cash outlay ($) | 18 000 | 5 000 |
| Net present value ($) | 8 000 | 5 000 |
| Benefit–cost ratio | $\frac{26\,000}{18\,000} = 1.44$ | $\frac{10\,000}{5\,000} = 2.0$ |

In this case, although the net present value of project F is less than the net present value of project E, the benefit–cost ratio of F is greater than that of E. Therefore, if the benefit–cost ratio is used it may result in management preferring projects with lower net present values. The benefit–cost ratio must therefore be rejected as a ranking technique because it can provide incorrect rankings of mutually exclusive projects.

## 5.5 OTHER METHODS OF PROJECT EVALUATION

In Table 5.1, there were two major non-discounted cash flow methods employed by the companies surveyed. They are the accounting rate of return and the payback period methods. These methods are frequently employed in conjunction with DCF methods of project evaluation.

### THE ACCOUNTING RATE OF RETURN

There are many ways to calculate the accounting rate of return or return on investment. The most popular methods are those which express a project's average annual earnings as a percentage of either the initial investment, or the average investment in the project. That is:

---

16 See H. Martin Weingartner, 'The Excess Present Value Index—A Theoretical Basis and Critique', *Journal of Accounting Research*, Autumn 1963, pp. 213–24; Bernhard Schwab & Peter Lusztig, 'A Comparative Analysis of the Net Present Value and the Benefit–Cost Ratio as Measures of the Economic Desirability of Investments', *Journal of Finance*, June 1969, pp. 507–16.

$$r_a = \frac{\text{average annual earnings}}{\text{initial investment in a project}} \times \frac{100}{1}\% \quad (5.8)$$

or

$$r_a = \frac{\text{average annual earnings}}{\text{average investment in a project}} \times \frac{100}{1}\% \quad (5.9)$$

## PAY-BACK PERIOD

The pay-back period is the length of time it takes for an entity to recover a project's initial cash outlay. For example, the pay-back period of a machine that costs $3000 and has net cash flows of $1000 per annum is 3 years.

In Sections 5.5.1 and 5.5.2 it is shown that the accounting rate of return and pay-back methods are inferior to the net present value method.

### 5.5.1 ACCOUNTING RATE OF RETURN

Essentially, the accounting rate of return is the earnings from a project, usually after deducting both depreciation and income tax, expressed as a percentage of the investment outlay. It is compared with a required rate of return or cut-off rate to determine a project's acceptability. If the accounting rate of return is greater than the required rate of return the project is acceptable; if it is less than the required rate of return the project is unacceptable.

The accounting rate of return has many variants, of which we will calculate only three. Each variant yields a different rate of return. For example, if a company calculates the rate of return by dividing average annual earnings by the **average** investment outlay, the project's rate of return would be much higher than if it had calculated the project's rate of return by dividing average annual earnings by the **initial** investment outlay.

To calculate these variants of the accounting rate of return, management must first estimate:

(a) The average annual earnings to be generated by the project. This is calculated by dividing the total net profit from the project by the number of years during which the profit is expected to be received.

(b) The investment outlay on the project. This is equal to either its initial investment outlay, including additional and permanent working capital requirements, or the average capital employed in the project. The average capital employed in a project is calculated either as the average book value of the investment, or more frequently as the average of the capital invested in the project at the beginning and the end of its life.

The methods of calculating the accounting rate of return are illustrated in Example 5.8.

### Example 5.8

Assume that a company is considering an investment project that costs $10 000 and generates returns in Years 1, 2 and 3 as shown in Table 5.11.

**Table 5.11** Data for calculating the accounting rate of return

| Item | Year 1 | Year 2 | Year 3 | Average |
|---|---|---|---|---|
| Earnings (after depreciation and income tax) ($) | 2 000 | 3 000 | 4 000 | 3 000 |
| Book value ($)(a): | | | | |
| 1 January | 10 000 | 7 000 | 4 900 | |
| 31 December | 7 000 | 4 900 | 3 430 | |
| Average | 8 500 | 5 950 | 4 165 | 6 205 |

(a) Assuming that depreciation is calculated at 30 per cent on the reducing balance.

Using these data, the following accounting rates of return may be calculated:
(a) Accounting rate of return based on the initial investment is:

$$\frac{\$3\,000}{\$10\,000} = 30\%$$

(b) Accounting rate of return based on the average book value is:

$$\frac{\$3000}{\$6205} = 48.35\%$$

(c) Accounting rate of return based on average investment as measured by the average of the capital invested at the beginning and the end of the project's life is:

$$\frac{3\,000}{\frac{\$10\,000 + \$3\,340}{2}} = \frac{\$3000}{\$6715} = 44.68\%$$

If the initial investment, instead of average investment, is used in calculating the accounting rate of return, the capital employed in the project is overstated and the rate of return is understated. This is because the progressive recovery of the amount invested and the consequent reduction in the investment over the project's life is ignored.

There are two fundamental problems with using the accounting rate of return, irrespective of the way it is defined. Of importance is that it is arbitrary. This is because it is based on accounting earnings rather than cash flows. As a result, factors such as the depreciation method employed, and the method of valuing inventories, will have a substantial bearing on the measurement of earnings and therefore on the accounting rate of return. The other main problem is that it ignores the timing of the earnings stream. Equal weight is given to the earnings in each year of the project's life. This problem is illustrated in Example 5.9.

### Example 5.9

A company is considering two projects, A and B. Both projects cost $1000 at the beginning of the first year and have a life of 5 years. The residual value of each project at the end of the fifth year is zero. The earnings for each project are shown in Table 5.12.

**Table 5.12**

| Project | Outlay ($) | Annual earnings ($) | | | | | Total |
|---|---|---|---|---|---|---|---|
| | | Year 1 | Year 2 | Year 3 | Year 4 | Year 5 | |
| A | 1000 | 25 | 50 | 100 | 150 | 175 | 500 |
| B | 1000 | 175 | 150 | 100 | 50 | 25 | 500 |

The average rate of return for projects A and B is:

$$\frac{\$500/5}{\$1000/2} = \frac{\$100}{\$500} \times \frac{100\%}{1} = 20\%$$

Project A has increasing earnings while project B has decreasing earnings. However, both result in the same total earnings, and therefore the same average annual earnings. Consequently both projects are regarded as equally acceptable if the accounting rate of return method is used. However, the two projects are not equally acceptable because the earnings from project B are received earlier than the earnings from project A. Intuition would suggest, therefore, that project B is preferable to project A. The accounting rate of return fails to reflect the advantages that earlier returns have over later returns. As a result, this method ranks projects with the same capital cost, life and total earnings equally, even though the projects' patterns of earnings streams may be different. In addition, if projects with the same capital cost and total earnings have different lives, the accounting rate of return method will automatically favour projects with short lives. However, there is no reason why such projects should necessarily prove to be the most profitable projects.

Because of its significant shortcomings, the accounting rate of return method should not be used to evaluate investment projects. However, as we observed earlier, in practice the accounting rate of return is often used in conjunction with the discounted cash flow methods. Because external financial analysts use earnings (profit) to assess a company's performance, management may wish to ensure that projects are acceptable according to both accounting and discounted cash flow criteria.

### 5.5.2 PAY-BACK PERIOD

The pay-back period is the time it takes for the initial cash outlay on a project to be recovered from the project's after-tax net cash flows. It is calculated by summing the after-tax net cash flows from a project in successive years until the total is equal to the initial cash outlay. This is illustrated in Table 5.13.

**Table 5.13**

| Year | Project A | | Project B | |
|---|---|---|---|---|
| | Initial cash outlay ($) | After-tax net cash flow ($) | Initial cash outlay ($) | After-tax net cash flow ($) |
| 0 | 10 000 | | 10 000 | |
| 1 | | 2 000 | | 2 000 |
| 2 | | 3 000 | | 4 000 |
| 3 | | 3 000 | | 4 000 |
| 4 | | 2 000 | | 2 000 |
| 5 | | 4 000 | | 2 000 |
| Total | | 14 000 | | 14 000 |
| Pay-back period | | 4 years | | 3 years |

In order to decide whether a project is acceptable, its pay-back period is compared with some maximum acceptable pay-back period. A project with a pay-back period shorter than the maximum will be accepted, while a project with a pay-back period longer than the maximum will be rejected.

An important question is: What length of time represents the 'correct' pay-back period as a standard against which to measure the acceptability of a particular project? In practice a maximum pay-back period is set which is inevitably arbitrary and may be from, say, 2 to 5 years. All projects with a pay-back period greater than this maximum are rejected.

Calculation of the pay-back period takes into account only the net cash flows up to the point where they equal the investment outlay. The calculation of the pay-back period ignores any net cash flows after that point. As a result, the pay-back method of evaluation discriminates against projects with long gestation periods and large cash flows late in their lives.

The pay-back period is not a measure of a project's profitability. If the most profitable projects were always those that recovered the investment outlay in the shortest period of time, then current assets such as inventory and accounts receivable would yield higher returns than non-current assets, and non-current assets with short lives would yield higher returns than non-current assets with long lives. Mere recovery of the outlay on a project yields no profit at all. If there is a profit on the project it must be due to additional cash flows after the investment outlay has been recovered. Therefore the major weakness of the pay-back method is its failure to take account of the magnitude and timing of all of a project's cash inflows and outflows.

Why then is pay-back popular as a method of investment evaluation? To a large extent its apparent simplicity accounts for its widespread popularity. In addition the pay-back method has some merit where the liquidity of a project is important in assessing its attractiveness. Calculation of projects' pay-back periods helps management to assess the company's future cash position, which is particularly important for companies that tend to experience liquidity problems.

However, liquidity is not a virtue in its own right. It is merely a constraint in achieving the objective of maximising shareholders' wealth. If a company has a liquidity problem it is best solved directly through its cash management program; for example, a company may borrow cash against the security of its assets. This is likely to be a better approach to the problem than if a company's management insists on, say, a 3-year pay-back period.

## 5.6 Summary

Of the two discounted cash flow methods of investment evaluation, we recommend the net present value method because it is consistent with the objective of maximising shareholders' wealth. It is also simple to use and gives rise to fewer problems than the internal rate of return method. We have shown that where mutually exclusive projects are being considered the internal rate of return method may result in rankings that conflict with those provided by the net present value method. In addition, we have shown that even if investment projects are independent it is possible that a project's pattern of cash flows may give rise to multiple internal rates of return, or to no internal rate of return at all.

If the net present value method is adopted, the rules necessary for making correct investment decisions seem to be straightforward:
 (a) Calculate each project's net present value, using the required rate of return as the appropriate discount rate.
 (b) If the projects are independent, accept a project if its net present value is greater than zero, and reject it if its net present value is less than zero.
 (c) If the projects are mutually exclusive, accept the project with the highest net present value, provided that it is greater than zero.

In practice, companies often use one method of project evaluation in conjunction with other methods. For example, one of the discounted cash flow methods may be used to measure a project's profitability, but the pay-back period may also be used either as a check on liquidity effects, or as a means of monitoring the project's cash flows against expectations. Numerous qualitative factors may also have an important role in project selection.

## Selected References

Bailey, Martin J., 'Formal Criteria for Investment Decisions', *Journal of Political Economy*, October 1959, reprinted in *Foundations for Financial Management*, Ed. James Van Horne, Richard D. Irwin, Homewood, Illinois, 1966.

Bierman, Harold Jr, & Smidt, Seymour, *The Capital Budgeting Decision: Economic Analysis of Investment Projects*, 7th edn, Macmillan Company, New York, 1988.

Dorfman, Robert, 'The Meaning of Internal Rates of Return', *Journal of Finance*, December 1981, pp. 1011–21.

Freeman, M. & Hobbes, G., 'Capital Budgeting: Theory versus Practice', *Australian Accountant*, September 1991, pp. 36–41.

Gordon, Myron, J., 'The Payoff Period and the Rate of Profit', *Journal of Business*, October 1955, reprinted in *The Management of Corporate Capital*, Ed. Ezra Solomon, The Free Press of Glencoe, Illinois, 1959, pp. 48–55.

Hirshleifer, J., 'On the Theory of Optimal Investment Decisions', *Journal of Political Economy*, August 1958, reprinted in Solomon (Ed.), op. cit., pp. 205–28.

Hoskins, C. G., 'Benefit–Cost Ratios versus Net Present Value: Revisited', *Journal of Business Finance and Accounting*, Summer 1974, pp. 249–65.

Karmel, P. H., 'The Marginal Efficiency of Capital', *The Economic Record*, December 1959, pp. 429–32.

Lerner, Eugene M. & Rappaport, Alfred, 'Limit DCF in Capital Budgeting', *Harvard Business Review*, September–October 1968, pp. 133–9.
Levy, H. & Sarnat, M., *Capital Investment & Financial Decisions*. 4th edn, Prentice–Hall International, Englewood Cliffs, New Jersey, 1990.
Lorie, James H. & Savage, Leonard J., 'Three Problems in Rationing Capital', *Journal of Business*, October 1955, pp. 229–39.
McConnell, John J. & Muscarella, Chris J., 'Corporate Capital Expenditure Decisions and the Market Value of the Firm', *Journal of Financial Economics*, September 1985, pp. 399–422.
Narayanan, M.P., 'Observability and the Payback Criterion', *Journal of Business*, July 1985, pp. 309–23.
Pinches, George E., 'Myopia, Capital Budgeting and Decision Making', *Financial Management*, Autumn 1982, pp. 6–19.
Schall, Lawrence D., Sundem, Gary L. & Geijsbeek, William R. Jr, 'Survey and Analysis of Capital Budgeting Methods', *Journal of Finance*, March 1978, pp. 281–7.
Weingartner, H. Martin, 'Some New Views on the Payback Period and Capital Budgeting Decisions', *Management Science*, August 1969, B594–B607.
Weingartner, H. Martin, 'The Excess Present Value Index—A Theoretical Basis and Critique', *Journal of Accounting Research*, Autumn 1963, pp. 213–24.

# QUESTIONS

1. Outline the four steps in the capital-expenditure process.
2. Compare the internal rate of return and net present value methods of project evaluation. Do these methods always lead to comparable recommendations? If not, why not?
3. Assume that you are asked to analyse the following three projects:

| Project | Cash flow ($) | | | | | |
|---|---|---|---|---|---|---|
| | Year 0 | Year 1 | Year 2 | Year 3 | Year 4 | Year 5 |
| A | −2000 | 200 | 200 | 200 | 200 | 2200 |
| B | −2000 | 527.60 | 527.60 | 527.60 | 527.60 | 527.60 |
| C | −2000 | – | – | – | – | 3221 |

   (a) Assuming a 10 per cent discount rate, calculate the net present value of each of these projects, then rank them.
   (b) Calculate the internal rate of return for each of the projects, then rank them.
   (c) Assuming a 6 per cent discount rate, calculate the net present value of each of the projects, then rank them.
   (d) Assuming a 15 per cent discount rate, calculate the net present value of each of the projects, then rank them.
   (e) Which of these methods would you recommend? Give reasons.
4. Each of the following mutually exclusive investment projects involves an initial cash outlay of $240 000. The estimated net cash flows for the projects are as follows:

| Year | Project A | Project B |
|---|---|---|
| 1 | $140 000 | $20 000 |
| 2 | 80 000 | 40 000 |
| 3 | 60 000 | 60 000 |
| 4 | 20 000 | 100 000 |
| 5 | 20 000 | 180 000 |

The company's required rate of return is 11 per cent. Calculate the NPV and IRR for both projects. Which project should be chosen? Why?

5. Evidence suggests that financial managers use more than one method to evaluate investment projects. Comment.

6. The internal rate of return method of project evaluation is easier to use because it avoids the need to calculate a required rate of return. Comment.

7. Even where projects are independent, the uncritical use of the internal rate of return method can seriously mislead management. Discuss.

8. Distinguish between independent and mutually exclusive investment projects.

9. The following investment proposals are independent. Assuming a required rate of return of 10 per cent, and using both the internal rate of return and net present value methods, which of the proposals are acceptable?

| | | Cash Flow ($) | |
|---|---|---|---|
| Proposal | Year 0 | Year 1 | Year 2 |
| A | −40 000 | 8 000 | 48 000 |
| B | −40 000 | 42 000 | – |
| C | −40 000 | 48 000 | – |

10. A company wishes to evaluate the following mutually exclusive investment proposals:

| | | | Cash flow ($) | | | |
|---|---|---|---|---|---|---|
| Proposal | Year 0 | Year 1 | Year 2 | Year 3 | Year 4 | Year 5 |
| A | −97 400 | 34 000 | 34 000 | 34 000 | 34 000 | 34 000 |
| B | −63 200 | 24 000 | 24 000 | 24 000 | 24 000 | 24 000 |

(a) Calculate each proposal's net present value and internal rate of return. Assume the required rate of return is 8 per cent.
(b) How would you explain the different rankings given by the net present value and internal rate of return methods?

11. Demonstrate, for independent investment projects, that the internal rate of return and net present value methods of evaluation yield identical decisions.

12. You have been asked to evaluate the following investment proposals:

|  | Cash flow ($) | | |
| --- | --- | --- | --- |
| Proposal | Year 0 | Year 1 | Year 2 |
| A | 1000 | −1400 | 600 |
| B | −120 | 240 | −200 |

Calculate the net present value (assuming a required rate of return of 12 per cent) and the internal rate of return for each project. Explain your results.

13. What problems are associated with the use of the accounting rate of return and pay-back period methods for the evaluation of investment proposals?

14. Using the following data, calculate:
    (a) the accounting rate of return; and
    (b) pay-back period.

    | | |
    |---|---|
    | Project cost | $40 000 |
    | Estimated project life | 5 years |
    | Estimated residual value | $8000 |
    | Annual accounting profit (equal to annual net cash inflow) | $12 000 |

    How would your answers to (a) and (b) differ if the estimated dollar returns were:

    | | |
    |---|---|
    | Year 1 | $12 000 |
    | Year 2 | $16 000 |
    | Year 3 | $24 000 |
    | Year 4 | $20 000 |
    | Year 5 | $8 000 |

15. Using the following data, calculate the:
    (a) accounting rate of return;
    (b) pay-back period;
    (c) internal rate of return; and
    (d) net present value.

    | | |
    |---|---|
    | Project cost | $10 000 |
    | Estimated life | 5 years |
    | Estimated residual value | $2000 |
    | Annual net cash flow | $3000 |
    | Required rate of return | 10% |

    How would your answers differ if the net cash flows were as follows?

    | | |
    |---|---|
    | Year 1 | $3000 |
    | Year 2 | $4000 |
    | Year 3 | $6000 |
    | Year 4 | $2000 |
    | Year 5 | $5000 |

**CHAPTER 6**

# PORTFOLIO THEORY AND ASSET PRICING

## 6.1 INTRODUCTION

A financial decision typically involves risk. For example, a company that borrows money faces the risk that interest rates may change, and a company that builds a new factory faces the risk that product sales may be lower than expected. These and many other decisions involve future cash flows that are risky. Investors generally dislike risk, but they are also unable to avoid it. The valuation formulae for shares and debt securities outlined in Chapter 4 showed that the price of a risky asset depends on its expected future cash flows, the time value of money, and risk. However, little attention was paid to the causes of risk or to how risk should be defined and measured.

To make effective financial decisions, managers need to understand what causes risk, how it should be measured, and the effect of risk on the rate of return required by investors. These issues are discussed in this chapter using the framework of portfolio theory, which shows how investors can maximise the expected return on a portfolio of risky assets for a given level of risk. The relationship between risk and expected return is described by two models for valuing assets under uncertainty: the capital asset pricing model (CAPM), and one based on arbitrage pricing theory.

To understand the material in this chapter it is necessary to understand what is meant by *return* and *risk*. Therefore we begin by discussing these concepts.

## 6.2 RETURN AND RISK

The return on an investment and the risk of an investment are basic concepts in finance. Return on an investment is the financial outcome for the investor. For example, if someone invests $100 in an asset and subsequently sells that asset for $111, the **dollar return** is $11. Usually an investment's dollar return is converted to a **rate of return** by calculating the proportion or percentage represented by the dollar return. For example, a dollar return of $11 on an investment of $100 is a rate of return of $11/$100, which is 0.11, or 11 per cent. In the remainder of this chapter the word *return* is used to mean *rate of return*.

Risk is present whenever investors are not certain about the outcomes an investment will produce. Suppose, however, that investors can attach a probability to each possible dollar return that may occur.[1] For example, assume that the probability distribution in Table 6.1 is an investor's assessment of the dollar returns $R_i$ that may be received from holding a share in a company for 1 year.

**Table 6.1**

| Dollar return, $R_i$ ($) | Probability, $P_i$ |
|---|---|
| 9  | 0.1 |
| 10 | 0.2 |
| 11 | 0.4 |
| 12 | 0.2 |
| 13 | 0.1 |

Suppose the investor wishes to summarise this distribution by calculating two measures, one to represent the size of the dollar returns, and the other to represent the risk involved. The obvious measure to represent the size of the dollar returns is the expected value of the distribution. The expected value $E(R)$ of the dollar returns is given by the weighted average of all the possible dollar returns, using the probabilities as weights. That is:

$$E(R) = \sum_{i=1}^{n} R_i P_i$$

$$= (\$9)(0.1) + (\$10)(0.2) + (\$11)(0.4) + (\$12)(0.2) + (\$13)(0.1)$$

$$= \$11$$

The choice of a measure for risk is less obvious. In this example, risk is present because any one of five outcomes ($9, $10, $11, $12 or $13) might result from the investment. If the investor had perfect foresight, then only one possible outcome would be involved, and there would not be a probability distribution to be considered. This suggests that risk is related to the dispersion of the distribution. The more disperse or widespread the distribution, the greater is the risk involved. Statisticians have developed a number of measures to represent

---

[1] Sometimes a distinction is drawn between *risk* and *uncertainty*. Where this is done, *risk* refers to situations where a probability can be assigned to each of the possible outcomes, whereas *uncertainty* refers to situations where so little is known that the assignment of probabilities is impossible. However, we do not draw this distinction, and the words *risk* and *uncertainty* are used synonymously.

dispersion. These measures include the range, the mean absolute deviation, and the variance. However, it is generally accepted that in most instances the **variance** (or its square root, the **standard deviation** σ) is the most useful. Accordingly, this measure of dispersion is the one we will adopt to represent the risk of a single investment. The variance of a distribution of dollar returns is the weighted average of the square of each dollar return's deviation from the expected dollar return, again using the probabilities as the weights. That is:

$$\sigma^2 = \sum_{i=1}^{n} (R_i - E(R))^2 \, P_i$$

$$= (9 - 11)^2(0.1) + (10 - 11)^2(0.2) + (11 - 11)^2(0.4)$$
$$+ (12 - 11)^2(0.2) + (13 - 11)^2(0.1)$$
$$= 1.20$$

The standard deviation is therefore:

$$\sigma = \sqrt{1.20}$$
$$\approx \$1.095$$

In these calculations we have used dollar returns rather than returns measured in the form of a rate. This is because it is generally easier to visualise dollars than rates, and because it avoids calculations with a large number of zeros following the decimal point. However, there is no difference in substance, as may be seen from reworking the example using returns in rate form. If it is assumed that the sum invested is $100, then a dollar return of $9, for example, is a return of 0.09 when expressed as a rate.

**Table 6.2**

| Return, $R_i$ | Probability, $P_i$ |
|---|---|
| 0.09 | 0.1 |
| 0.10 | 0.2 |
| 0.11 | 0.4 |
| 0.12 | 0.2 |
| 0.13 | 0.1 |

Using rates, the expected return $E(R)$, is:
$$E(R) = (0.09)(0.1) + (0.10)(0.2) + (0.11)(0.4) + (0.12)(0.2) + (0.13)(0.1)$$
$$= 0.11$$
$$= 11\%$$

The variance of returns is:
$$\sigma^2 = (0.09 - 0.11)^2(0.1) + (0.10 - 0.11)^2(0.2)$$
$$+ (0.11 - 0.11)^2(0.4) + (0.12 - 0.11)^2(0.2)$$
$$+ (0.13 - 0.11)^2(0.1)$$
$$= 0.000\,12$$

The standard deviation of returns is therefore:

$$\sigma = \sqrt{0.000\,12}$$
$$\approx 0.010\,95$$
$$= 1.095\%$$

It is often assumed that an investment's distribution of returns follows a normal distribution. This is a convenient assumption because a normal distribution can be fully described by its expected value and standard deviation. Therefore an investment's distribution of returns can be fully described by its expected return and risk. Assuming that returns follow a normal probability distribution, the table of areas under the standard normal curve (see Table 5 of Appendix A) can be used to calculate the probability that the investment will generate a return greater than or less than any specified return. For example, suppose that the returns on an investment in Company A are normally distributed, with an expected return of 13 per cent and a standard deviation of 10 per cent, and an investor in the company wishes to calculate the probability of a loss. That is, the investor wishes to calculate the probability of a return of less than zero per cent. A return of zero per cent is 1.3 standard deviations below the expected return (because 0.13/0.10 = 1.3). Figure 6.1 illustrates this case. The shaded area represents the probability of a loss. The table of areas under the standard normal curve (Table 5, Appendix A) indicates that the probability of a loss occurring is 0.0968 or slightly less than 10 per cent.

To highlight the importance of the standard deviation of the return distribution, assume that the same investor has the opportunity of investing in Company B with an expected return of 13 per cent and a standard deviation of 6.91 per cent. The probability distributions of the returns on investments in companies A and B are shown in Figure 6.2.

On the basis of the dispersion of the returns, an investment in Company A (with a standard deviation of 10 per cent) is more risky than an investment in Company B (with a standard deviation of 6.91 per cent).

Suppose that the investor selects a return of zero per cent as representative of an unsatisfactory result. A return of zero per cent on an investment in Company B is 1.88 standard deviations below the expected return (because 0.13/0.0691 = 1.88). The probability of this occurring is 0.03. Therefore the

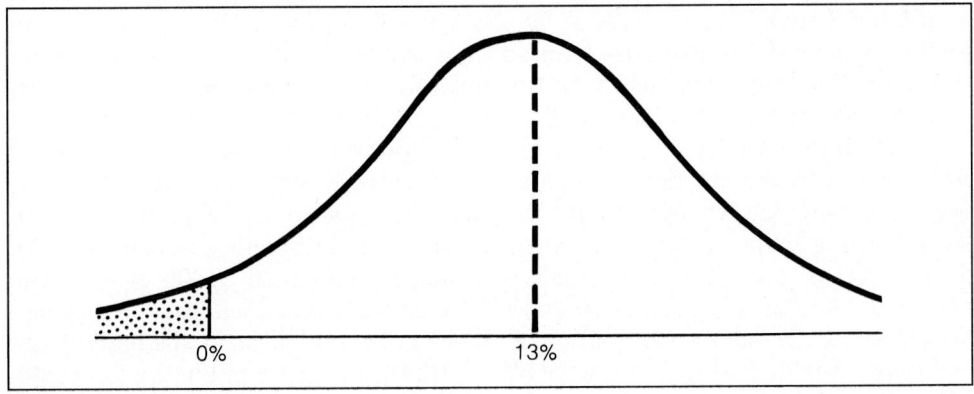

Fig. 6.1

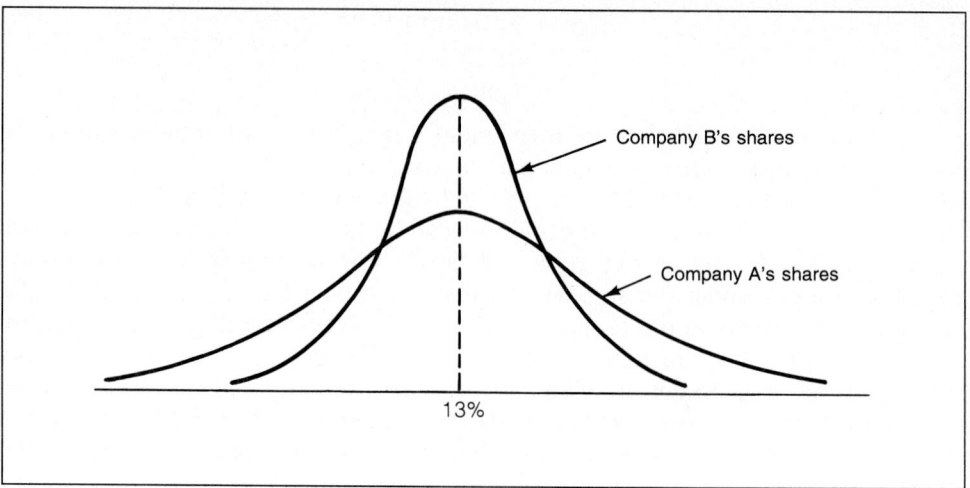

**Fig. 6.2**

probability that an investment in Company B will generate a negative return is 3 per cent compared with 10 per cent for an investment in Company A. However, when the investor considers returns at the upper end of the distributions it is found that an investment in Company A offers a 10 per cent chance of a return in excess of 26 per cent, compared with only a 3 per cent chance for an investment in Company B. The fact that the investor is more uncertain about the return from an investment in Company A does not mean that the investor will necessarily prefer to invest in Company B. The choice depends on the investor's attitude to risk. This is considered in the next section.

## 6.3 THE INVESTOR'S UTILITY FUNCTION

A preference for investing in either Company A or Company B will depend on the investor's attitude to risk. An investor may be **risk averse, risk neutral** or **risk seeking**. A risk-averse investor attaches decreasing utility to each increment in wealth; a risk-neutral investor attaches equal utility to each increment in wealth; while a risk-seeking investor attaches increasing utility to each increment in wealth. Typical utility-to-wealth functions for each type of investor are illustrated in Figure 6.3.

The characteristics of a risk-averse investor warrant closer examination as risk aversion is the standard assumption in finance theory. Assume that a risk-averse investor has wealth of $\$W^*$ and has the opportunity of participating in the following game: a fair coin is tossed and if it falls tails (probability 0.5), then $1000 is won; if it falls heads (probability 0.5), then $1000 is lost. The expected value of the game is $0 and it is, therefore, described as a 'fair game'. Would a risk-averse investor participate in such a game? If he or she participates and wins, wealth will increase to $\$(W^* + 1000)$, but if he or she loses, wealth will fall to $\$(W^* - 1000)$. The results of this game are shown in Figure 6.4.

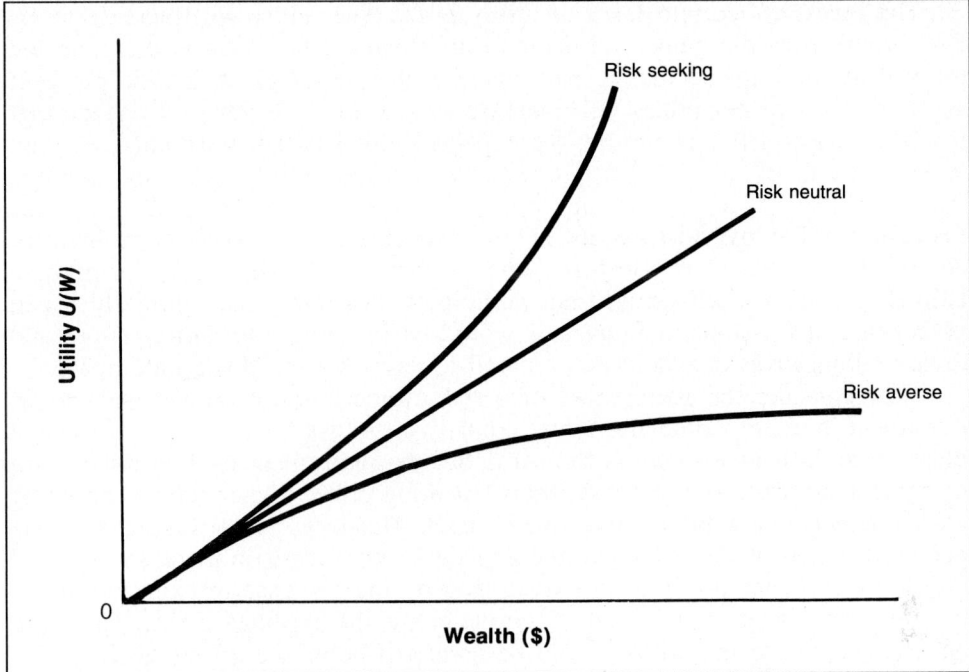

**Fig. 6.3** *Utility-to-wealth functions for differtent types of investors*

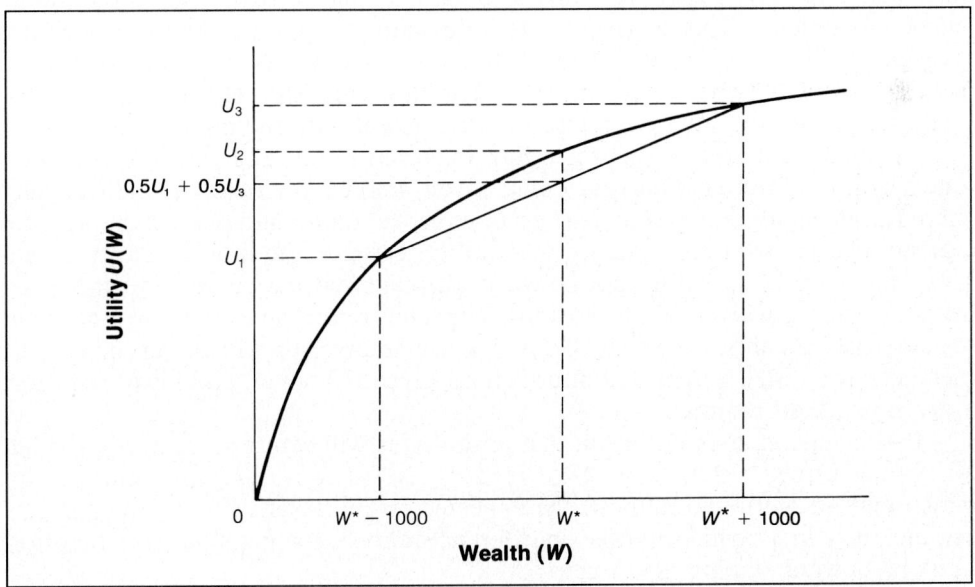

**Fig. 6.4**

The investor's current level of utility is $U_2$. The utility will increase to $U_3$ if he or she wins the game and decrease to $U_1$ in a loss. What is the expected utility if the investor decides to participate in the game? There is a 50 per cent chance that his or her utility will increase to $U_3$, and a 50 per cent chance that it will decrease to $U_1$. Therefore, the expected utility is $0.5U_1 + 0.5U_3$. As can be seen from Figure 6.4, the investor's expected utility with the gamble $(0.5U_1 + 0.5U_3)$ is lower than the utility obtained without the gamble $(U_2)$. As it is assumed that investors maximise their expected utility, a risk-averse investor would refuse to participate in this game. In fact, a risk-averse investor may be defined as someone who would not participate in a fair game. Similarly it can be shown that a risk-neutral investor would be indifferent to participation, and a risk-seeking investor would be prepared to pay for the right to participate.

Now consider the preferences of a risk-averse investor with respect to an investment in either Company A or Company B. As we have seen, the expected return from each investment is the same but the investment in A is riskier. An investment in A offers the possibility of making either higher returns or lower returns, compared with an investment in B. However, from Figure 6.2, the increased spread of returns above the expected return tends to increase expected utility, but this increase will be outweighed by the decrease in expected utility resulting from the greater spread of returns below the expected return. Therefore the investor's expected utility would be greater if he or she invests in B.

As both investments offer the same expected return, the risk-averse investor's choice implies that the increased dispersion of returns makes it riskier. This suggests that the standard deviation of the return distribution may be a useful measure of risk for a risk-averse investor. Similarly it can be argued that the risk-neutral investor would be indifferent between these two investments. For any given amount to be invested, such an investor will always choose the investment that offers the higher return, irrespective of the relative risk of the alternative investments. That is, the standard deviation is ignored. The risk-seeking investor would choose to invest in A. If a given amount is to be invested, and there are on offer two investments that offer the same expected return, the risk-seeking investor will always choose the investment with the higher risk.

An investor's preferences regarding expected return and risk can be illustrated using indifference curves. For a given amount invested, an indifference curve traces out all those combinations of expected return and risk which provide a given investor with the same level of utility. Because the level of utility is the same, the investor is indifferent between all points on the curve. A risk-averse investor has a positive attitude towards expected return and a negative attitude towards risk. By this, we mean that a risk-averse investor will prefer an investment to have a higher expected return (for a given risk level) and lower risk (for a given expected return).

Risk aversion does *not* mean that an investor will refuse to bear any risk at all. Rather it means that an investor regards risk as something undesirable, but which may be worth tolerating if the expected return is sufficient to compensate for the risk. In graphical terms, indifference curves for a risk-averse investor must be upward sloping (see Figure 6.5).

# PORTFOLIO THEORY AND ASSET PRICING

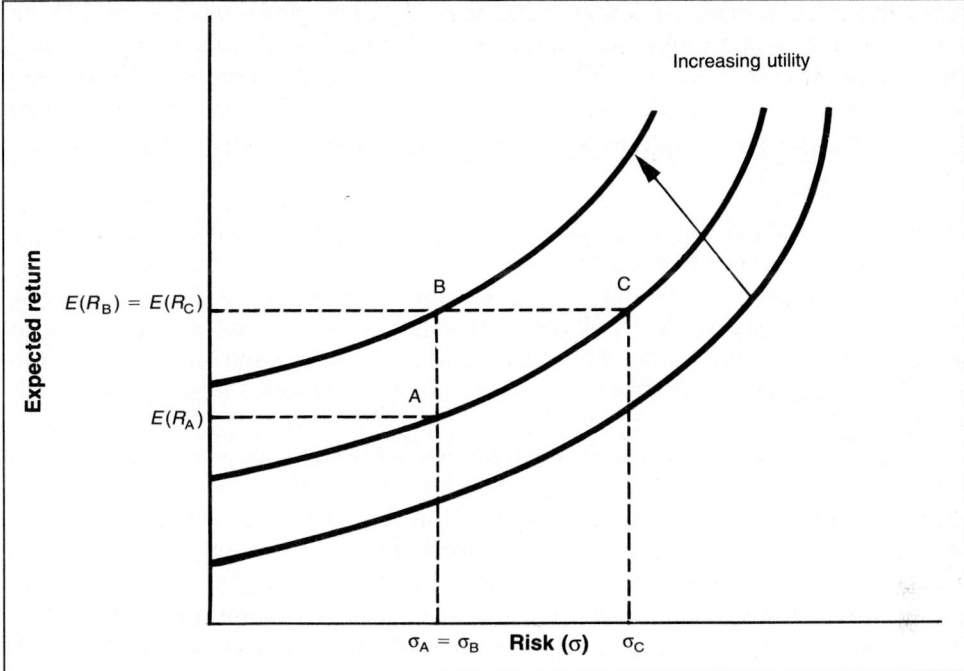

**Fig. 6.5** *Indifference curves for a risk-averse investor*

The risk–return coordinates for a risk-averse investor are shown in Figure 6.5 for three investments, A, B and C. It is apparent that this investor would prefer investment B to investment A, and would also prefer investment B to investment C. This investor prefers a higher expected return at any given level of risk (compare investments B and A) and a lower level of risk at any given expected return (compare investments B and C). However, this investor would be indifferent between investments A and C. The higher expected return on investment C compensates this investor exactly for the higher risk. In addition, for a given expected return the expected utility of a risk-averse investor falls at an increasing rate as the dispersion of the distribution of returns increases. As a result, the rate of increase in expected return required to compensate for every increment in the standard deviation increases faster as the risk becomes larger, and indifference curves for a risk-averse investor are not only upward sloping, but also convex, as shown in Figure 6.5.

So far we have concentrated on the characteristics and behaviour of a risk-averse investor. However, there are instances where individuals behave in a way contrary to risk aversion. For example, a risk-averse person will never purchase a lottery ticket as the expected value of the gamble is less than the price of the ticket. However, many individuals whose current level of wealth is quite low relative to the lottery prize are prepared to purchase lottery tickets because, while only a small outlay is required, there is the chance (though small) of achieving a relatively large increase in wealth. In decisions that involve larger outlays, risk aversion is much more likely. As the financial decisions considered in this book generally involve large investments and small rates of return (at least relative to winning a lottery prize), it is assumed throughout that investors behave as if they are risk averse.

## 6.4 THE STANDARD DEVIATION AS THE MEASURE OF RISK

So far it has been assumed that investors' expectations of the returns from an investment can be represented by a normal probability distribution. In such circumstances the standard deviation is a relevant measure of risk for a risk-averse investor. Further, it has been shown that a risk-averse investor is prepared to accept higher risk for higher expected return, with the result that the required return on a particular investment increases with the investor's perception of its risk.

However, if the returns are not normally distributed the standard deviation may not be an adequate measure of risk. Figure 6.6 illustrates the case where the probability distribution of the returns from an investment in Company C's shares is skewed to the right, while the distribution for Company D's shares is skewed to the left, but both offer the same expected return and standard deviation of return. An investment in C offers a greater chance of generating a return much *higher* than the expected return, while an investment in D offers a greater chance of generating a return much *lower* than the expected return. This means that although both investments offer the same expected return and standard deviation, an investment in C would be preferred. This indicates that the standard deviation may not be an adequate measure of risk where the probability distributions are skewed.

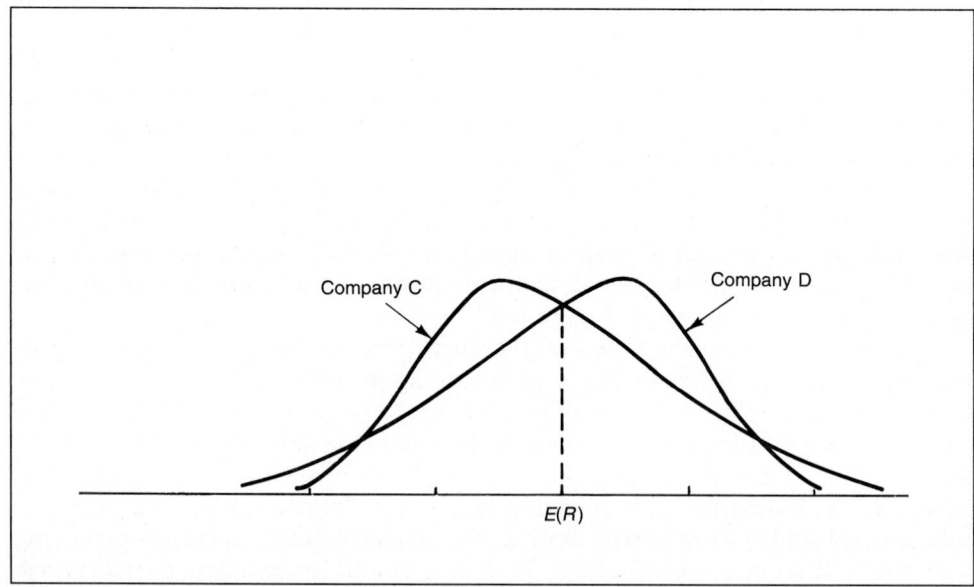

**Fig. 6.6** *Skewed probability density functions*

However, to simplify the discussion it is assumed that investors' risk–return preferences can be fully described by two parameters: the expected return and the standard deviation of returns.

We have suggested that the standard deviation of the return from a single investment is a relevant measure of its riskiness. This is true where an individual is considering the investment of all available funds in one asset. However, it is exceptional to limit investments in this way. Most people invest in a number of assets; they may invest in a house, a car, their human capital, and numerous other assets. In addition, where they hold shares, it is likely that they are in a number of companies. Typically, therefore, people invest their wealth in a portfolio of assets. The relevant measure of the risk of a single asset is the standard deviation of the returns on that asset. The relevant measure of the risk of a portfolio is the standard deviation of the returns on the portfolio. However, this tells us nothing about the relevant measure of the risk of an asset as a *component* of a portfolio of assets. What we need to know is how individual portfolio components (assets) contribute to the risk of the portfolio as a whole. As the next section shows, an apparently plausible guess that the contribution is proportional to the single asset standard deviation turns out to be almost always incorrect.

## 6.5 PORTFOLIO THEORY

Portfolio theory was initially developed by Markowitz (1959) as a normative approach to investment choice under uncertainty.[2] Two important assumptions of portfolio theory have already been discussed. These are:

(a) The returns from investments are normally distributed. Therefore two parameters, the expected return and the standard deviation, are sufficient to describe the distribution of returns.[3]

(b) Investors are risk averse. Therefore investors prefer the highest expected return for a given standard deviation and the lowest standard deviation for a given expected return.

Given these assumptions, it can be shown that it is rational for a utility-maximising investor to hold a well-diversified portfolio of investments. Suppose that an investor holds a number of securities. Let $E(R_i)$ be the expected return on the $i$th security, and $E(R_p)$ the expected return on a portfolio of securities. Then:

$$E(R_p) = \sum_{i=1}^{n} w_i E(R_i) \qquad (6.1)$$

---

[2] H.M. Markowitz, *Portfolio Selection: Efficient Diversification of Investments*, John Wiley & Sons, New York, 1959.

[3] As stated earlier, other parameters may exist if the distribution is non-normal. In this case it is assumed that investors base decisions on expected return and standard deviation and ignore other features such as skewness.

where $w_i$ = the proportion of the total current market value of the portfolio constituted by the current market value of the $i$th security; it is the 'weight' attached to the security
$n$ = the number of securities in the portfolio

### Example 6.1
Assume that there are only two securities (1 and 2) in a portfolio and $E(R_1) = 0.08$ and $E(R_2) = 0.12$. Also assume that the current market value of security 1 is 60 per cent of the total current market value of the portfolio (that is, $w_1 = 0.6$ and $w_2 = 0.4$). Then:

$$E(R_p) = (0.60)(0.08) + (0.4)(0.12)$$
$$= 0.096$$

The expected return on a portfolio is therefore simply the weighted average of the expected returns on the securities constituting the portfolio. However, the standard deviation of the return on the portfolio ($\sigma_p$) is not as simple to measure. This is because it depends not only on the riskiness of the individual securities but also on the relationship between the returns on those securities. The variance of the return on a portfolio is given by:

$$\sigma_p^2 = \sum_{i=1}^{n} \sum_{j=1}^{n} w_i w_j \rho_{ij} \sigma_i \sigma_j \tag{6.2}$$

where $w_i$ = the proportion of the current market value of the portfolio constituted by the $i$th security
$w_j$ = the proportion of the current market value of the portfolio constituted by the $j$th security
$\rho_{ij}$ = the correlation coefficient between the returns on securities $i$ and $j$, and by definition, $\rho_{ij} = \rho_{ji}$ and $\rho_{ii} = 1$
$\sigma_i$ = the standard deviation of the possible returns on the $i$th security
$\sigma_j$ = the standard deviation of the possible returns on the $j$th security
$n$ = the number of securities in the portfolio

The correlation coefficient $\rho_{ij}$ depends on the relationship *between* returns on two securities, $i$ and $j$. A correlation coefficient can have a value between $+1$ and $-1$. If the correlation coefficient between the returns on two securities is $+1$, the returns are said to be **perfectly positively correlated**. This means that if the return on security $i$ is 'high' (compared with its expected level), then the return on security $j$ will, unfailingly, also be 'high' (compared with *its* expected level) to precisely the same degree. If the correlation coefficient is $-1$, the returns are **perfectly negatively correlated**; high (low) returns on security $i$ will always be paired with low (high) returns on security $j$. A correlation coefficient of zero indicates the absence of a systematic relationship between the returns on the two securities. The term $\rho_{ij}\sigma_i\sigma_j$, where $i \neq j$, is known as the **covariance** between the returns on security $i$ and security $j$, often written as $\sigma_{ij}$.

As may be seen from Equation 6.2, the variance of a portfolio depends on:
(a) the proportion of the current market value of the portfolio constituted by each security;
(b) the standard deviation of the possible returns for each security;

(c) the correlation between the possible returns on the securities held in the portfolio.

## Example 6.2

An investor wishes to construct a portfolio consisting of securities 1 and 2. The expected returns on the two securities are $E(R_1) = 0.08$ and $E(R_2) = 0.12$, and the standard deviations are $\sigma_1 = 0.04$ and $\sigma_2 = 0.06$. The correlation coefficient between their returns is $\rho_{1,2} = -0.5$. The investor is free to choose the investment proportions $w_1$ and $w_2$, subject only to the requirements that $w_1 + w_2 = 1$ and that both $w_1$ and $w_2$ are positive.[4] Obviously there is no limit to the number of portfolios that meet these requirements, since there is no limit to the number of proportions that sum to one. Therefore a representative selection of values is considered for $w_1$: 0, 0.2, 0.4, 0.6, 0.8 and 1.

Using Equation 6.1, the expected return on a two-security portfolio is:

$$E(R_p) = w_1 E(R_1) + w_2 E(R_2)$$

In this example:

$$E(R_p) = (0.08)w_1 + (0.12)w_2$$

Using Equation 6.2, the variance of the return on a two-security portfolio can be expressed as:

$$\sigma_p^2 = w_1^2 \sigma_1^2 + w_2^2 \sigma_2^2 + 2w_1 w_2 \rho_{1,2} \sigma_1 \sigma_2 \qquad (6.3)$$

In this example:

$$\sigma_p^2 = (0.04)^2 w_1^2 + (0.06)^2 w_2^2 + 2w_1 w_2(-0.5)(0.04)(0.06)$$
$$\therefore \quad \sigma_p^2 = 0.0016 w_1^2 + 0.0036 w_2^2 - 0.0024 w_1 w_2$$

The standard deviation is found by taking the square root of $\sigma_p^2$. Each pair of proportions is now considered in turn:

(i)      $w_1 = 0$ and $w_2 = 1$
$$E(R_p) = (0.08)(0) + (0.12)(1)$$
$$= 0.12$$
$$\sigma_p^2 = (0.0016)(0)^2 + (0.0036)(1)^2 - (0.0024)(0)(1)$$
$$\sigma_p^2 = 0.0036$$
$$\therefore \quad \sigma_p = 0.06$$

(ii)      $w_1 = 0.2$ and $w_2 = 0.8$
$$E(R_p) = (0.08)(0.2) + (0.12)(0.8)$$
$$= 0.112$$
$$\sigma_p^2 = (0.0016)(0.2)^2 + (0.0036)(0.8)^2 - (0.0024)(0.2)(0.8)$$
$$= 0.001\,984$$
$$\therefore \quad \sigma_p = 0.0445$$

---

[4] Negative investment proportions would indicate a 'short sale' which means that the asset is first sold and later purchased. Therefore a short-seller benefits from price decreases.

(iii)      $w_1 = 0.4$ and $w_2 = 0.6$
$$E(R_p) = (0.08)(0.4) + (0.12)(0.6)$$
$$= 0.104$$
$$\sigma_p^2 = (0.0016)(0.4)^2 + (0.0036)(0.6)^2 - (0.0024)(0.4)(0.6)$$
$$= 0.000\,976$$
$\therefore$      $\sigma_p = 0.0312$

(iv)      $w_1 = 0.6$ and $w_2 = 0.4$
$$E(R_p) = (0.08)(0.6) + (0.12)(0.4)$$
$$= 0.096$$
$$\sigma_p^2 = (0.0016)(0.6)^2 + (0.0036)(0.4)^2 - (0.0024)(0.6)(0.4)$$
$$= 0.000\,576$$
$\therefore$      $\sigma_p = 0.024$

(v)      $w_1 = 0.8$ and $w_2 = 0.2$
$$E(R_p) = (0.08)(0.8) + (0.12)(0.2)$$
$$= 0.088$$
$$\sigma_p^2 = (0.0016)(0.8)^2 + (0.0036)(0.2)^2 - (0.0024)(0.8)(0.2)$$
$$= 0.000\,784$$
$\therefore$      $\sigma_p = 0.028$

(vi)      $w_1 = 1.0$ and $w_2 = 0$
$$E(R_p) = (0.08)(1) + (0.12)(0)$$
$$= 0.08$$
$$\sigma_p^2 = (0.0016)(1)^2 + (0.0036)(0)^2 - (0.0024)(1)(0)$$
$$= 0.0016$$
$\therefore$      $\sigma_p = 0.04$

These results are summarised in Table 6.3.

**Table 6.3**

|  | Portfolio | | | | | |
| --- | --- | --- | --- | --- | --- | --- |
|  | (i) | (ii) | (iii) | (iv) | (v) | (vi) |
| Proportion in 1 ($w_1$) | 0.0 | 0.2 | 0.4 | 0.6 | 0.8 | 1.0 |
| Proportion in 2 ($w_2$) | 1.0 | 0.8 | 0.6 | 0.4 | 0.2 | 0.0 |
| Expected return $E(R_p)$ | 0.1200 | 0.1120 | 0.1040 | 0.0960 | 0.0880 | 0.0800 |
| Standard deviation $\sigma$ | 0.0600 | 0.0445 | 0.0312 | 0.0240 | 0.0280 | 0.0400 |

Reading across Table 6.3, the investor places more wealth in the low-return security 1 and less in the high-return security 2. Consequently, the expected return on the portfolio declines with each step. The behaviour of the standard deviation is more complicated. It declines over the first four portfolios, reaching a minimum value[5] of 0.0240 when $w_1 = 0.6$, but then rises to 0.0400 at the sixth

---

[5] The minimum value of the standard deviation actually occurs slightly beyond portfolio (iv) at proportions $w_1 = 12/19 \approx 0.6316$, and $w_2 = 7/19 \approx 0.3684$. The standard deviation for this portfolio is 0.0238 and its expected return is 0.0947.

portfolio which consists entirely of security 1. This is an important finding as it implies that some portfolios would never be held by risk-averse investors. For example, no risk-averse investor would choose portfolio (v) because portfolio (iv) offers both a higher expected return and a lower risk than portfolio (v). An 'efficient' portfolio is one that offers the highest expected return at a given level of risk. The data in Table 6.3 are plotted in Figure 6.7. As can be seen from Figure 6.7, portfolios (v) and (vi) are not efficient.

### 6.5.1 GAINS FROM DIVERSIFICATION

Example 6.2 shows that some portfolios enable an investor to achieve simultaneously higher expected return and lower risk; for example, compare portfolios (iv) and (vi) in Figure 6.7. It should be noted that portfolio (iv) consists of both securities, whereas portfolio (vi) consists only of security 1, that is, portfolio (iv) is diversified, whereas portfolio (vi) is not.

The magnitude of the gain from diversification is closely related to the value of the correlation coefficient, $\rho_{ij}$. To show the importance of the correlation coefficient, securities 1 and 2 are again considered. This time, however, the investment proportions are held constant at $w_1 = 0.6$ and $w_2 = 0.4$ and different values of the correlation coefficient are considered. Portfolio variance is given by:

$$\sigma_p^2 = w_1^2\sigma_1^2 + w_2^2\sigma_2^2 + 2w_1w_2\rho_{1,2}\sigma_1\sigma_2$$
$$= (0.6)^2(0.04)^2 + (0.4)^2(0.06)^2 + 2(0.6)(0.4)\rho_{1,2}(0.04)(0.06)$$
$$= 0.001\ 152 + 0.001\ 152\rho_{1,2}$$

$$\therefore \quad \sigma_p = \sqrt{0.001\ 152 + 0.001\ 152\rho_{1,2}}$$

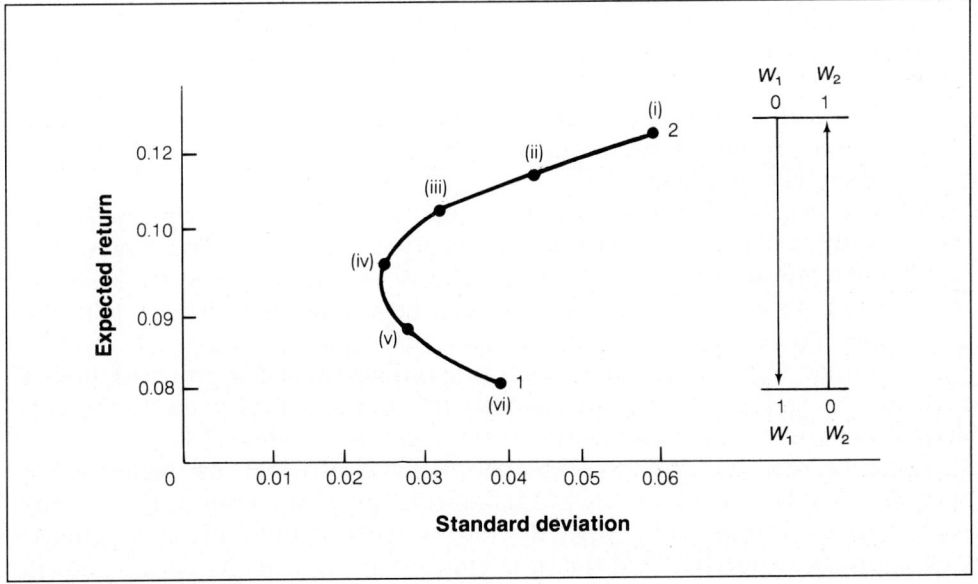

**Fig. 6.7**

(i) 
$$\rho_{1,2} = +1.00$$
$$\sigma_p = \sqrt{0.001\ 152 + 0.001\ 152(1)}$$
$$= 0.0480$$

(ii)
$$\rho_{1,2} = +0.50$$
$$\sigma_p = \sqrt{0.001\ 152 + 0.001\ 152(0.5)}$$
$$= 0.0416$$

(iii)
$$\rho_{1,2} = 0.00$$
$$\sigma_p = \sqrt{0.001\ 152 + 0.001\ 152(0)}$$
$$= 0.0339$$

(iv)
$$\rho_{1,2} = -0.50$$
$$\sigma_p = \sqrt{0.001\ 152 + (0.001\ 152)(-0.5)}$$
$$= 0.0240$$

(v)
$$\rho_{1,2} = -1.00$$
$$\sigma_p = \sqrt{0.001\ 152 + (0.001\ 152)(-1)}$$
$$= 0$$

These results are summarised in Table 6.4.

**Table 6.4** *Effect of correlation coefficient on portfolio standard deviation*

| Correlation coefficient | $\rho_{1,2} = +1.00$ | $\rho_{1,2} = +0.50$ | $\rho_{1,2} = 0.00$ | $\rho_{1,2} = -0.50$ | $\rho_{1,2} = -1.00$ |
|---|---|---|---|---|---|
| Standard deviation | 0.0480 | 0.0416 | 0.0339 | 0.0240 | 0.0000 |

Table 6.4 shows three important facts about portfolio construction:
(a) Combining two securities whose returns are perfectly positively correlated (that is, the correlation coefficient is +1) results only in risk averaging, and does not provide any risk reduction. The weighted average of the two standard deviations is $(0.6)(0.04) + (0.4)(0.06) = 0.0480$.
(b) The real advantages of diversification result from the risk reduction caused by combining securities whose returns are less than perfectly positively correlated.
(c) The degree of risk reduction increases as the correlation coefficient between the returns on the two securities decreases. The largest risk reduction available is where the returns are perfectly negatively correlated, so the two risky securities can be combined to form a portfolio that has zero risk ($\sigma_p = 0$).

By considering different investment proportions $w_1$ and $w_2$, a curve similar to that shown in Figure 6.7 can be plotted for each assumed value of the correlation coefficient. These curves are shown together in Figure 6.8.

It can be seen that the lower the correlation coefficient, the higher is the expected return for any given level of risk (or the lower the level of risk for any given expected return). This shows that the benefits of diversification increase as the correlation coefficient decreases. The significance of the dotted lines in Figure 6.8 is that a risk-averse investor would never hold combinations of the

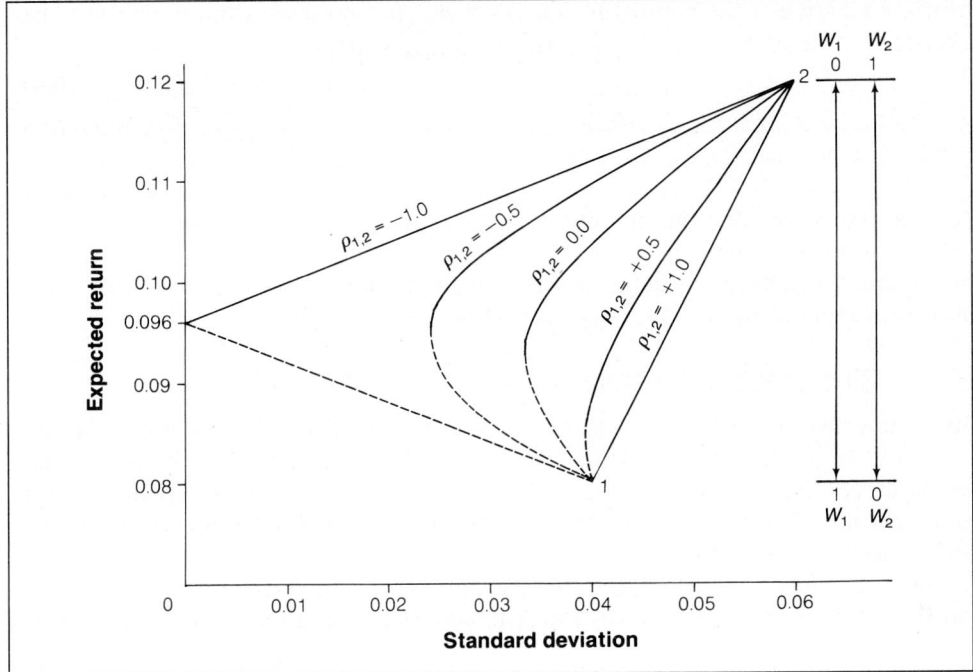

**Fig. 6.8**

two securities represented by points on the dotted lines. At any given level of correlation these combinations of the two securities are always dominated by other combinations which offer a higher expected return for the same level of risk.

While the above discussion relates to the two-security case, even stronger conclusions can be drawn for larger portfolios. Suppose that an investor holds a portfolio of fifty assets and is considering the addition of an extra asset to the portfolio. The investor is concerned with the effect that this extra asset will have on the standard deviation of the portfolio. The effect is determined by the portfolio proportions, the extra asset's variance, and the fifty covariances between the extra asset and the assets already in the portfolio. Not surprisingly the covariance terms are the dominant influence. For example, Fama (1976) found that in an equally weighted portfolio of fifty randomly selected securities, 90 per cent of the portfolio standard deviation was due to the covariance terms.[6] That is, to the holder of a large portfolio the risk of an asset is largely determined by the covariance between the return on that asset and the return on the holder's existing portfolio. The variance of the return on the extra asset is of little importance, notwithstanding that this variance would probably be of paramount importance to investors who held only one or two assets in their portfolios. Therefore the risk of an asset when that asset is held in a large portfolio is determined by the

---

6 E.F. Fama, *Foundations of Finance*, Basic Books, New York, 1976, pp. 245–52. See also Footnote 15.

covariance between the return on the asset and the return on the portfolio. The covariance of a security $i$ with a portfolio $p$ is given by:

$$\sigma_{ip} = \rho_{ip}\sigma_i\sigma_p \qquad (6.4)$$

The holders of large portfolios of securities can still achieve risk reduction by adding a new security to their portfolios, provided that the returns on the new security are not perfectly positively correlated with the returns on the existing portfolio. However, the incremental risk reduction due to adding a new security to a portfolio decreases as the size of the portfolio increases, and it has been shown that the additional benefits from diversification are very small for portfolios that include more than fifty securities.[7]

### 6.5.2 THE EFFICIENT FRONTIER

The simple two-security case can be extended to include all risky assets. There is no limit to the number of portfolios that can be formed from risky assets and the expected return and standard deviation of the return can be calculated for each portfolio. The coordinates for all possible portfolios are represented by the shaded area in Figure 6.9.

Only portfolios on the curve between points $A$ and $B$ are relevant since all portfolios below this curve yield lower expected return and/or greater risk. The

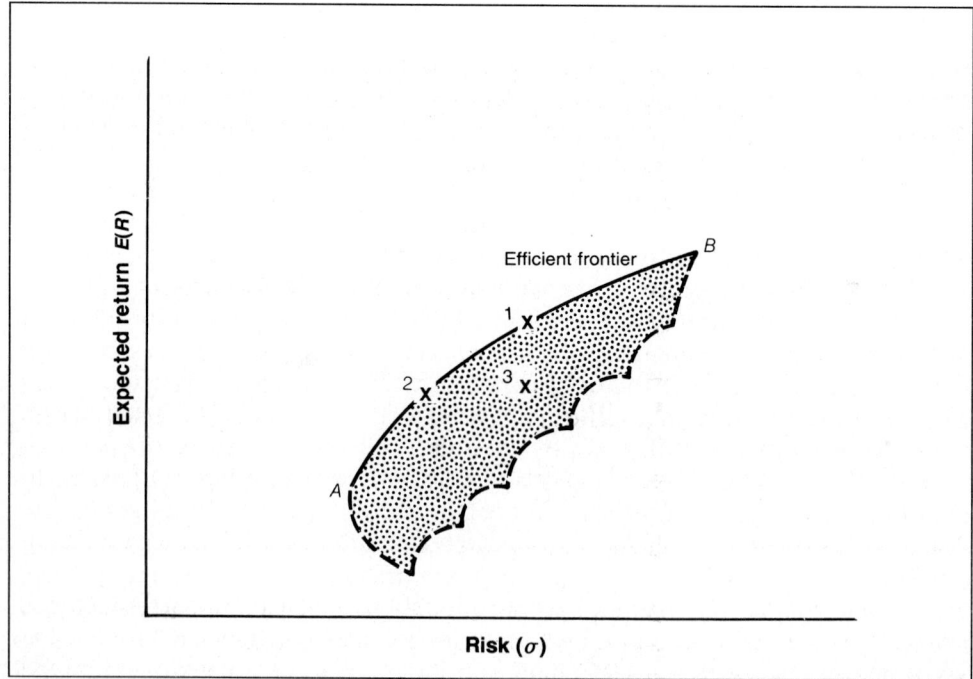

**Fig. 6.9**

---

[7] E.F. Fama, *Foundations of Finance*, Basic Books, New York, 1976, pp. 252–6.

curve *AB* is referred to as the **efficient frontier** and it includes those portfolios that offer the maximum expected return for a given level of risk. For example, portfolio 1 is preferred to an internal point such as portfolio 3 because portfolio 1 offers a higher expected return for the same level of risk. Similarly, portfolio 2 is preferred to portfolio 3 because it offers the same expected return for a lower level of risk. No such 'dominance' relationship exists between efficient portfolios, that is, between portfolios whose risk–return coordinates plot on the efficient frontier.

Investors' preferences can now be combined with the efficient frontier to illustrate an investor's choice of an optimum portfolio. This is shown for a representative investor in Figure 6.10.

Given risk aversion, the investor will want to hold a portfolio on the efficient frontier. Risk-averse investors will choose the portfolio at the point of tangency between their indifference curve and the efficient frontier. For the representative investor of Figure 6.10, this is the point *Q*. As investors are a diverse group there is no reason to believe that they will have identical utility functions. Each investor may therefore prefer a different point (portfolio) along the efficient frontier. As companies have many shareholders, all with different utility functions, it may seem that portfolio theory will not be of much use in explaining the valuation of shares, because, presumably, different investors will place a different value on the same shares depending on their utility function. It is shown later that this problem may be overcome.

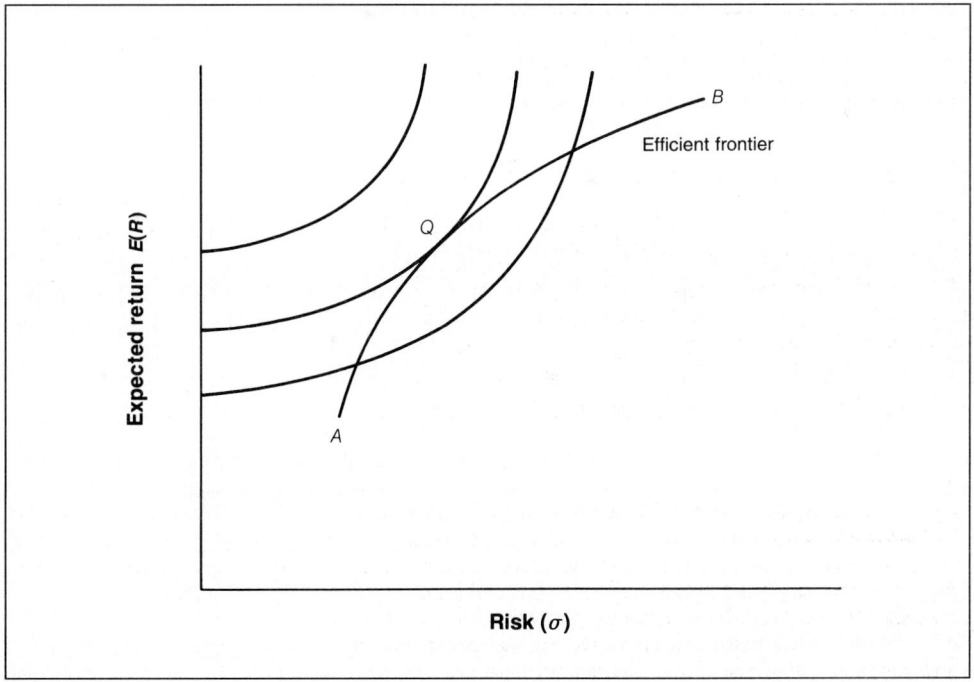

**Fig. 6.10**

In summary, the essential conclusions of portfolio theory are that diversification reduces risk, and that its effectiveness in doing so depends on the correlation or covariance between returns on the individual assets combined into a portfolio. The principles of portfolio theory as developed by Markowitz are not complex but use of his theory can involve significant practical complexities. Preparation of a graph of the efficient frontier such as Figure 6.10 requires estimates of the expected return and variance for each possible asset. Also needed are estimates of the covariance between the returns of each pair of assets. As the number of assets increases, the number of estimates required dramatically increases. For a portfolio of $n$ assets there are $\dfrac{n(n-1)}{2}$ individual covariances to be estimated. Therefore, if 20 assets are considered, 190 covariances have to be estimated; with 100 assets, the number increases to 4950! This problem, together with the high cost of computer time when Markowitz developed his theory, meant that few people used it. However, several authors tried to simplify the required procedures, and in doing so, extended portfolio theory to model the relationship between risk and expected return for individual risky assets. This work is discussed in Section 6.6.

## 6.6 THE PRICING OF RISKY ASSETS

Portfolio theory deals with investment decision making by individuals. We now shift the focus from the behaviour of individuals to the pricing of risky assets and we introduce the assumption that investors can borrow and lend unlimited amounts of cash at the risk-free rate of interest, $R_f$. Typically this is regarded as the rate of interest on a government security, such as Treasury Notes.

Purchase of the risk-free asset is equivalent to lending at the risk-free rate, while selling (or issuing) of the risk-free asset is equivalent to borrowing at the risk-free rate. Lending involves investing a positive amount in the risk-free asset, while borrowing involves 'investing' a negative amount in the risk-free asset. We continue to assume that all investors in a particular market behave according to portfolio theory, and ask: How would prices of individual securities in that market be determined? The work of Sharpe (1964), Lintner (1965) and others provides an answer to this question.[8] In addition to the assumptions of portfolio theory and the assumption of risk-free borrowing and lending, three further assumptions are needed:

---

[8] W.F. Sharpe, 'Capital Asset Prices: A Theory of Market Equilibrium under Conditions of Risk', *Journal of Finance*, September 1964, pp. 425–42; J. Lintner, 'The Valuation of Risk Assets and the Selection of Risky Investments in Stock Portfolios and Capital Budgets', *Review of Economics and Statistics*, February 1965, pp. 13–37. See also J. Mossin, 'Security Pricing and Investment Criteria in Competitive Markets,' *American Economic Review*, December 1969, pp. 749–56; and E.F. Fama, 'Risk, Return and Equilibrium: Some Clarifying Comments', *Journal of Finance*, March 1968, pp. 29–40.

Although we have referred to the 'pricing' of assets, much of this work deals with expected returns, rather than asset prices. However, there is a simple relationship between expected return and price. This is discussed in Section 6.8.

(a) All investors have the same estimates of the expected return on each asset, the variance of return for each asset, and also the covariance between returns for each pair of assets.
(b) All investors have a common single-period time horizon for investment decision making.
(c) All assets are traded in perfect markets; that is, all assets are marketable, there are no transaction costs or taxes, and all investors are price takers.

### 6.6.1 THE CAPITAL MARKET LINE

With the opportunity to borrow and lend at the risk-free rate an investor is no longer restricted to holding a portfolio which is on the efficient frontier $AB$. Investors can now invest in combinations of risky assets and the risk-free asset in accordance with their risk preferences. This is illustrated in Figure 6.11.

The line $R_f MN$ is tangential at the point $M$ to the efficient frontier ($AB$) of portfolios of risky assets. This line represents portfolios which consist of an investment in portfolio $M$ and an investment in the risk-free asset. Points on the line to the left of $M$ require a positive amount to be invested in the risk-free asset; that is, they require the investor to lend at the risk-free rate. Points on the line to the right of $M$ require a negative amount to be invested in the risk-free asset; that is, they require the investor to borrow at the risk-free rate.

It is apparent that the line $R_f MN$ dominates the efficient frontier $AB$ since at any given level of risk a portfolio on the line offers an expected return at least

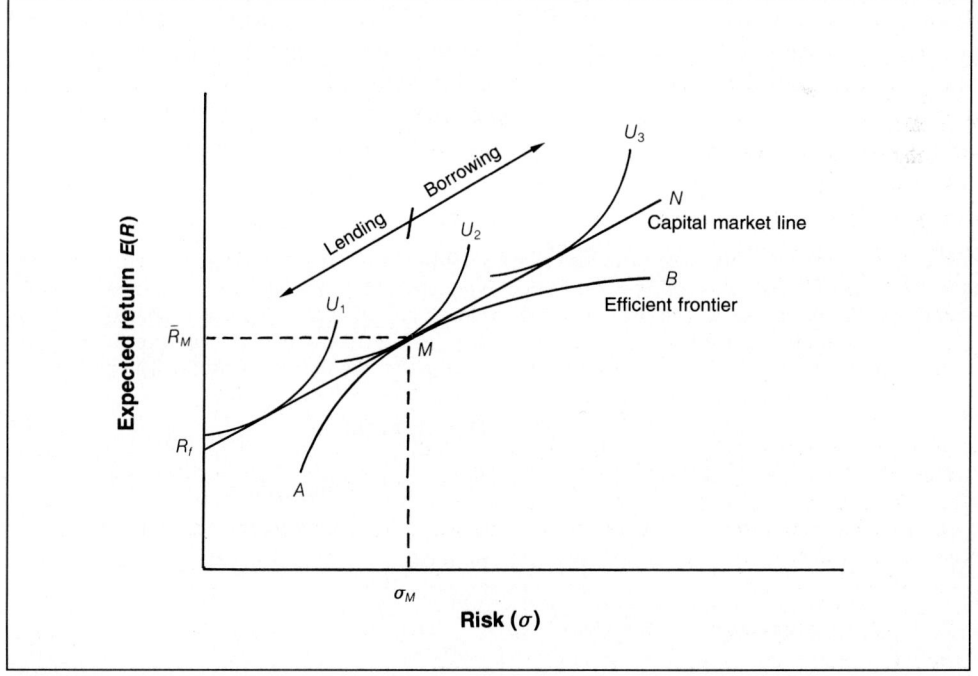

Fig. 6.11

as great as that available from the efficient frontier (curve *AB*). Risk-averse investors will therefore choose a portfolio on the line; that is, some combination of the risk-free asset and portfolio *M*. This is true for all risk-averse investors who conform to the assumptions of portfolio theory. We show this by including in Figure 6.11 the relevant indifference curve for three representative investors: 1, 2 and 3. Having chosen to invest in portfolio *M*, each investor combines this risky investment with a position in the risk-free asset. In Figure 6.11, investor 1 will invest partly in portfolio *M* and partly in the risk-free asset, investor 2 will invest all funds in portfolio *M*, while investor 3 will borrow at the risk-free rate and invest his or her own funds, plus the borrowed funds, in portfolio *M*. A fourth strategy, not shown in Figure 6.11, is to invest only in the risk-free asset. This is the least risky strategy, whereas the strategy pursued by investor 3 is the most risky.

If all investors in a particular market behave according to portfolio theory, *all investors hold portfolio M* as at least a part of their total portfolio.[9] In turn this implies that portfolio *M* must consist of all risky assets. In other words, under these assumptions, a given risky asset *X* is either held by all investors as part of portfolio *M* or it is not held by any investor. In the latter case, asset *X* does not exist. Therefore, portfolio *M* is often called the **market portfolio** because it comprises all risky assets available in the market. For example, if the total market value of all shares in company *X* represents 1 per cent of the total market value of all assets, then shares in company *X* will represent 1 per cent of every investor's total investment in risky assets.

The line $R_f MN$ is called the **capital market line** because it shows all the total portfolios in which investors in the capital market might choose to invest. Since investors will choose only efficient portfolios, it follows that the market portfolio is predicted to be 'efficient' in the sense that it will provide the maximum expected return for that particular level of risk. The capital market line therefore shows the trade-off between expected return and risk for all efficient portfolios. The equation of the capital market line is given by:[10]

---

[9] This ignores the extreme case of investors who hold only the risk-free asset.

[10] Equation 6.5 is derived as follows: Let portfolio *p* consist of an investment in the risk-free asset and the market portfolio. The investment proportions are $w_f$ in the risk-free asset and $w_M = 1 - w_f$ in the market portfolio. Therefore portfolio *p* is, in effect, a two-security portfolio where one security is the risk-free asset and the other 'security' is the market portfolio. The portfolio's expected return, $E(R_p)$, is given by:

$$E(R_p) = w_f R_f + (1 - w_f) E(R_M)$$

and the variance of its return is:

$$\sigma_p^2 = w_f^2 \sigma_f^2 + (1 - w_f)^2 \sigma_M^2 + 2 w_f (1 - w_f) \rho_{fM} \sigma_f \sigma_M$$

By definition, $\sigma_f^2 = 0$, and therefore $\sigma_f = 0$ and $\rho_{fM} = 0$. Making these substitutions:

$$\sigma_p^2 = (1 - w_f)^2 \sigma_M^2$$

Therefore $\sigma_p = (1 - w_f) \sigma_M$

Rearranging this expression we have:

$$w_f = 1 - \frac{\sigma_p}{\sigma_M}$$

$$E(R_p) = R_f + \left(\frac{E(R_M) - R_f}{\sigma_M}\right)\sigma_p \qquad (6.5)$$

where $\sigma_M$ is the standard deviation of the return on the market portfolio M.

The slope of this line is $\dfrac{E(R_M) - R_f}{\sigma_M}$, and this measures the market price of risk. It represents the additional expected return that investors would require to compensate them for incurring additional risk, as measured by the standard deviation of the portfolio.

### 6.6.2 THE CAPITAL ASSET PRICING MODEL (CAPM) AND THE SECURITY MARKET LINE

Although the capital market line holds for efficient portfolios, it does not describe the relationship between expected return and risk for individual assets or inefficient portfolios. In equilibrium, the expected return on a risky asset (or inefficient portfolio), $i$, can be shown to be:[11]

$$E(R_i) = R_f + \left(\frac{E(R_M) - R_f}{\sigma_M^2}\right)\sigma_{iM} \qquad (6.6)$$

where $E(R_i)$ = the expected return on the $i$th risky asset and
$\sigma_{iM}$ = the covariance between the returns on the $i$th risky asset and the market portfolio

Equation 6.6 is often called the **CAPM equation**. An equivalent version is given in Equation 6.8. The CAPM equation shows that the expected return demanded by investors on a risky asset depends on the risk-free rate of interest, the expected return on the market portfolio, the variance of the return on the market portfolio, and the *covariance* of the return on the risky asset with the return on the market portfolio.

The covariance term $\sigma_{iM}$ is the only explanatory factor in the CAPM equation that is specific to asset $i$. The other explanatory factors ($R_f$, $E(R_M)$, and $\sigma_M^2$) are the same, regardless of which asset $i$ is being considered. Therefore, according to the CAPM equation, if two assets have different expected returns, this must be due to their having different covariances with the market portfolio. In other words, the measure of risk relevant to pricing a risky asset is $\sigma_{iM}$, the covariance of its returns with returns on the market portfolio, as this measures

---

Substituting into the expression for $E(R_p)$:
$$E(R_p) = \left(1 - \frac{\sigma_p}{\sigma_M}\right)R_f + \frac{\sigma_p}{\sigma_M}E(R_M)$$
that is,
$$E(R_p) = R_f + \left(\frac{E(R_M) - R_f}{\sigma_M}\right)\sigma_p$$
which is Equation 6.5. This is a linear equation with intercept $R_f$ and slope $\dfrac{E(R_M) - R_f}{\sigma_M}$.

[11] This is a purely mathematical problem. For a derivation see H. Levy & M. Sarnat, *Capital Investment and Financial Decisions*, 4th edn, Prentice–Hall, New Jersey, 1990, pp. 319–22, or T. Brailsford & R. Faff, 'A Derivation of the CAPM for Pedagogical Use', *Accounting and Finance*, May 1993, pp. 53–60.

the *contribution* of the risky asset to the riskiness of an efficient portfolio. In contrast, for the efficient portfolio itself the standard deviation of the portfolio's return is the relevant measure of risk (see Figure 6.11).

The measure of risk associated with an investment in a risky asset $i$ is often referred to as its **beta factor**, $\beta_i$, where:

$$\beta_i = \frac{\sigma_{iM}}{\sigma_M^2} \tag{6.7}$$

Because $\sigma_{iM}$ is the risk of an asset held *as part of* the market portfolio, while $\sigma_M^2$ is the risk (in terms of variance) of the market portfolio, it follows that $\beta_i$ measures the risk of $i$ relative to the risk of the market as a whole. Using beta as the measure of risk the CAPM equation can be rewritten:

$$E(R_i) = R_f + \beta_i(E(R_M) - R_f) \tag{6.8}$$

When graphed, Equation 6.8 is called the **security market line** and is illustrated in Figure 6.12.

The constant term is the risk-free rate $R_f$ and the slope of the line is equal to the risk premium $E(R_M) - R_f$. The beta value of the market portfolio is 1.[12] A risky asset with a beta value greater than 1 (that is, higher risk) will have an expected return greater than $E(R_M)$ while the expected return on a risky asset

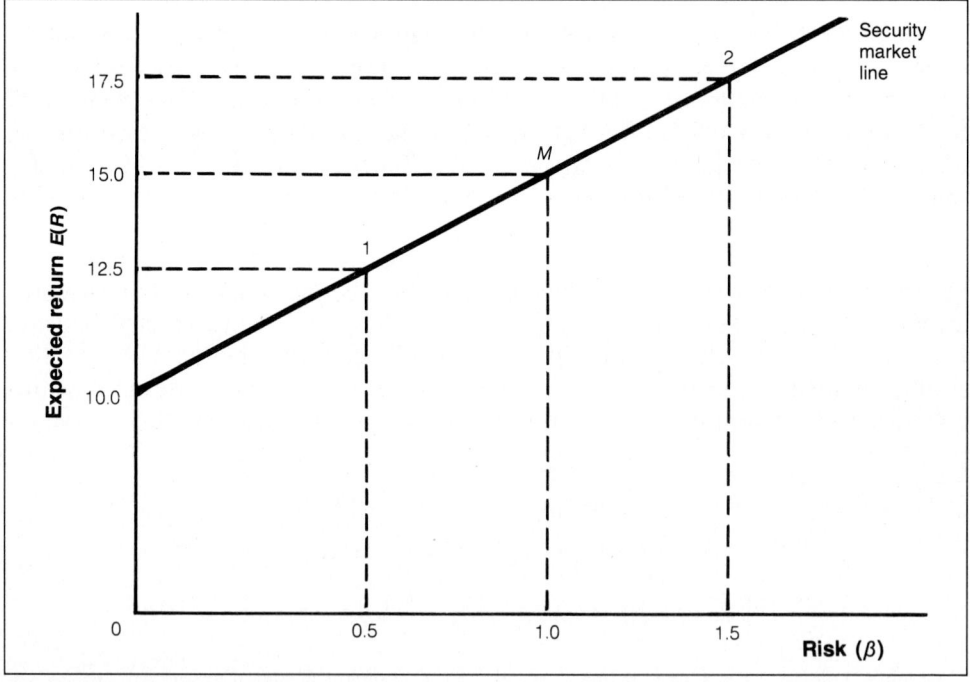

**Fig. 6.12** *Security market line*

---

[12] Since $\beta_i = \dfrac{\sigma_{iM}}{\sigma_M^2}$, we have $\beta_M = \dfrac{\sigma_{MM}}{\sigma_M^2} = \dfrac{\sigma_M^2}{\sigma_M^2} = 1$

with a beta value of less than 1 (that is, lower risk) will be less than $E(R_M)$. Assuming that the risk-free rate is 10 per cent and the risk premium $(E(R_M) - R_f)$ is 5 per cent, the expected return on risky asset 1 with a beta value of 0.5 will be 12.5 per cent, while the expected return on risky asset 2 with a beta value of 1.5 will be 17.5 per cent.

The capital asset pricing model applies to individual assets and to portfolios. The beta factor for a portfolio $p$ is simply:

$$\beta_p = \frac{\sigma_{pM}}{\sigma_M^2} \tag{6.9}$$

where $\sigma_{pM}$ = the covariance between the returns on portfolio $p$ and the market portfolio

Equation 6.9 is simply Equation 6.7 rewritten in terms of a portfolio $p$, instead of a particular asset $i$. Fortunately there is a simple relationship between a portfolio's beta $(\beta_p)$ and the betas of the individual assets that make up the portfolio. This relationship is:

$$\beta_p = \sum_{i=1}^{n} w_i \beta_i \tag{6.10}$$

where $n$ = the number of assets in the portfolio and
$w_i$ = the proportion of the current market value of portfolio $p$ constituted by the $i$th asset

Equation 6.10 states that the beta factor for a portfolio is simply a weighted average of the betas of the assets in the portfolio.[13] One useful application of Equation 6.10 is to guide investors in choosing the investment proportions $w_i$ to achieve some target portfolio beta, $\beta_p^*$. An important special case is to construct such a portfolio using only the market portfolio $(\beta = 1)$ and a position in the risk-free asset $(\beta = 0)$. In this case, investors place a proportion $w_M$ of their total

---

13 Our discussion has omitted the steps between Equations 6.9 and 6.10. For the interested reader, these steps are as follows:

Since $R_p = \sum_{i=1}^{n} w_i R_i$, it follows that:

$$\sigma_{pM} = \text{Cov}(R_p, R_M)$$
$$= \text{Cov}\left(\sum_{i=1}^{n} w_i R_i, R_M\right)$$
$$= \sum_{i=1}^{n} w_i \text{Cov}(R_i, R_M)$$

Substituting in Equation 6.9:

$$\beta_p = \frac{\sum_{i=1}^{n} w_i \text{Cov}(R_i, R_M)}{\sigma_M^2}$$
$$= \sum_{i=1}^{n} w_i \beta_i$$

funds in the market portfolio, and a proportion $w_f = 1 - w_M$ in the risk-free asset. Using Equation 6.10, the target beta is given by:

$$\beta^*_p = w_f\beta_f + w_M\beta_M$$

Substituting $\beta_f = 0$ and $\beta_M = 1$ gives:

$$w_M = \beta^*_p$$

and

$$w_f = 1 - \beta^*_p$$

For example, if $\beta^*_p = 0.75$, investors should invest 75 per cent of their funds in the market portfolio and lend 25 per cent of their funds at the risk-free rate. If $\beta^*_p = 1.3$, investors should borrow an amount equal to 30 per cent of their own investment funds and invest the total amount (130 per cent) in the market portfolio.

### 6.6.3 THE MARKET MODEL

If it is assumed that, on average, the expected return on an asset is equal to its realised return, then provided certain statistical conditions are met we could apply regression analysis to estimate the following equation from time series data:

$$R_{it} = \alpha_i + \beta_i R_{Mt} + e_{it} \qquad (6.11)$$

where $\alpha_i$ = a constant, specific to asset $i$ and

$e_{it}$ is an error term

Equation 6.11 is generally called the **market model**. Its relationship to the security market line can be readily seen by rewriting Equation 6.8 as follows:

$$E(R_i) = R_f + \beta_i E(R_M) - \beta_i R_f$$

$$\therefore \quad E(R_i) = R_f(1 - \beta_i) + \beta_i E(R_M) \qquad (6.12)$$

Therefore the market model is a counterpart (or analogue) of Equation 6.12. The magnitude of the betas that result from using this model when it is applied to returns on shares is illustrated in Table 6.5 which contains a sample of betas for Australian industry groups and for the shares of companies in the building materials industry. The values are calculated using ordinary least squares (OLS) regression.

**Table 6.5** *Betas of industry groups and shares, calculated using OLS regression from monthly data for the period 1990–1993*

| Name of industry | Beta | Name of company | Beta |
| --- | --- | --- | --- |
| Gold | 1.09 | Adelaide Brighton | 0.35 |
| Oil and gas | 0.64 | Boral | 1.23 |
| Diversified resources | 1.13 | CSR | 0.98 |
| Building materials | 0.98 | Hardie (James) Industries | 0.79 |
| Alcohol and tobacco | 0.74 | Pioneer International | 1.16 |
| Media | 2.19 | Wattyl Ltd | 0.29 |
| Property trusts | 0.43 | Whittakers Ltd | 2.47 |

Source: *Risk Measurement Service*, June 1993 edn, Centre for Research in Finance, Australian Graduate School of Management.

### 6.6.4 SYSTEMATIC AND UNSYSTEMATIC RISK

Suppose that we assume that Equation 6.11—the market model—is valid. Taking the variance of both sides of this equation:

$$\text{Var}(R_{it}) = \text{Var}(\alpha_i + \beta_i R_{Mt} + e_{it})$$

As $\alpha_i$ is a constant, it has no effect on the variance, and hence can be omitted. Therefore:

$$\text{Var}(R_{it}) = \text{Var}(\beta_i R_{Mt} + e_{it})$$

The right-hand side of this equation is the variance of the sum of two variables. As we saw when we considered the variance of the return on a portfolio of two assets, this involves a covariance term:

$$\text{Var}(R_{it}) = \text{Var}(\beta_i R_{Mt}) + \text{Var}(e_{it}) + 2\,\text{Cov}(\beta_i R_{Mt}, e_{it})$$
$$= \beta_i^2 \text{Var}(R_{Mt}) + \text{Var}(e_{it}) + 2\beta_i \,\text{Cov}(R_{Mt}, e_{it})$$

However, it is normally assumed that $\text{Cov}(R_{Mt}, e_{it})$ is zero. This means that the error term $e_{it}$ is independent of the return on the market portfolio. For example, this rules out a tendency for the error term to be larger when the return on the market portfolio is very high. Therefore:

$$\text{Var}(R_{it}) = \beta_i^2 \text{Var}(R_{Mt}) + \text{Var}(e_{it}) \qquad (6.13)$$

Equation 6.13 states that the variance (total risk) of asset $i$ can be divided into two components, both of which also involve variances. The first component is $\beta_i^2 \text{Var}(R_{Mt})$. It is determined by the variance of the return on the market portfolio and the beta of the particular asset. In other words, it depends on the risk of the market as a whole, and on the sensitivity ($\beta$) of the particular asset to that risk. This type of risk is unavoidable and is sometimes called **systematic risk**.[14] As it is always present, and no amount of diversification can eliminate it, it is also called **non-diversifiable risk**. The second component is $\text{Var}(e_{it})$. Since this is also a variance, it makes sense to interpret it as a 'risk'. Unlike the first component, it has no systematic relationship with the market as a whole. Hence it is called **unsystematic risk**.

To understand further the nature of this risk, suppose that 'asset' $i$ is thought of as a portfolio to which more and more assets are added. At the extreme where an individual holds the market portfolio, the error term (and hence its variance) is zero. As assets are added to a portfolio it becomes more diversified and there is a tendency for $\text{Var}(e_{it})$ to fall. Accordingly, this component is also known as **diversifiable risk**. However, as each new asset is added to the portfolio the incremental amount of risk reduction achieved tends to fall. Figure 6.13 is a

---

[14] $\text{Var}(R_{Mt})$ is the same for all assets as it relates to the market as a whole. Therefore, treating $\text{Var}(R_{Mt})$ as given, the systematic risk of any particular asset $i$ depends only on the value of its beta ($\beta$). For this reason, $\beta$ is sometimes described as the measure of systematic risk.

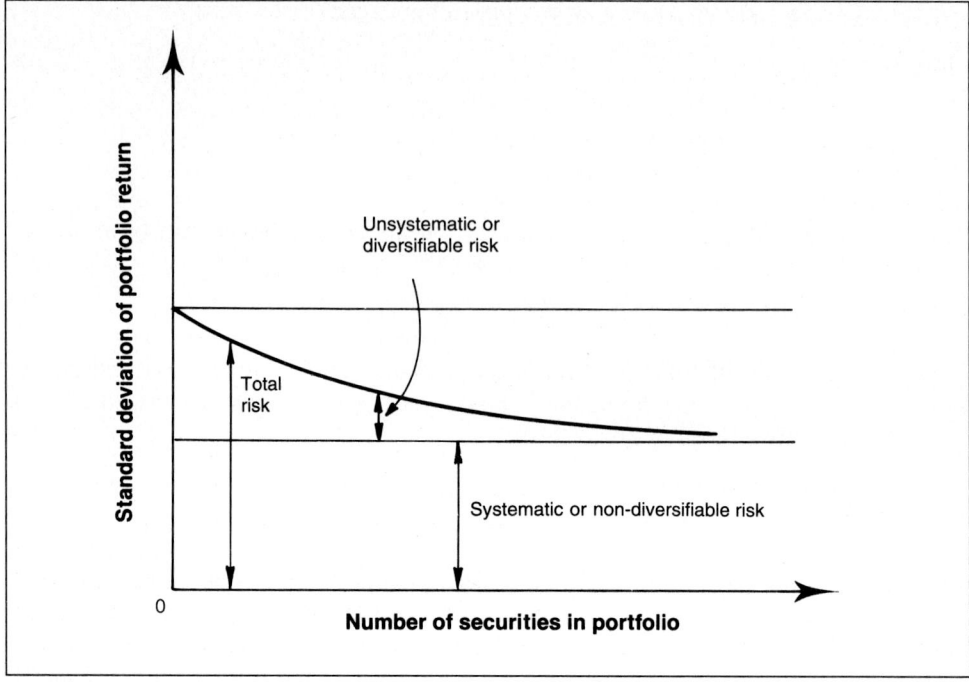

**Fig. 6.13**

representation of this effect. In fact, most of the advantages of diversification are achieved by holding a randomly selected portfolio of, say, fifty assets.[15]

### 6.6.5 RISK AND THE CAPM

The distinction between systematic and unsystematic risk is important in explaining why the CAPM should represent the risk–return relationship for assets such as shares. The returns on a company's shares can vary for many reasons: for example, interest rates may change, or the company may develop a new product, attract important new customers, or change its chief executive. These factors can be divided into two categories: those related only to an individual company (company-specific factors) and those which affect all companies (market-wide factors). As the shares of different companies are combined in a portfolio, the effects of the company-specific factors will tend to cancel each other out; this is how diversification reduces risk. However, the effects of the market-wide factors will remain, no matter how many different shares are included in the portfolio. Therefore, systematic risk reflects the influence of market-wide factors, while unsystematic risk reflects the influence of company-specific factors.

---

[15] See E. Elton & M. Gruber, 'Risk Reduction and Portfolio Size: An Analytical Solution', *Journal of Business*, October 1977, pp. 415–37; E. Elton & M. Gruber, *Modern Portfolio Theory and Investment Analysis*, 3rd edn, John Wiley and Sons, New York, 1987, pp. 30–3; and R. Bird & M. Tippett, 'Naive Diversification and Portfolio Risk—A Note', *Management Science*, February 1986, pp. 244–51.

Because unsystematic risk can be eliminated by diversification, the capital market will not reward investors for bearing this type of risk. The capital market will only reward investors for bearing risk that cannot be eliminated by diversification: the risk inherent in the market portfolio. There are cases when, with hindsight, we can identify investors who have reaped large rewards from taking on unsystematic risk. These cases do not imply that the CAPM is invalid: the model simply says that such rewards cannot be *expected* in a competitive market. The reward for bearing systematic risk is a higher expected return and, according to the CAPM, there is a simple linear relationship between expected return and systematic risk as measured by beta.

## 6.7 CAPM: EMPIRICAL EVIDENCE

Equation 6.8, the CAPM equation or the security market line, is one of the best known results in the theory of finance. Not surprisingly a number of researchers have tried to test it empirically.[16] Typically, these studies used stock market data and generally concluded that, with some reservations, the CAPM gave useful insights into asset pricing. Much of this type of work ended when an important article by Richard Roll was published.[17] He pointed out that the security market line follows purely as a matter of mathematics from the capital market line. In other words, the primary prediction made by the theory is that the market portfolio is 'efficient'. If that prediction is true, then the other results follow automatically. So, if the market portfolio is efficient, there will be a perfect linear relationship between beta and expected return. Even more importantly, he showed that the converse is *not* true. An empirical test is likely to produce an apparently linear relationship between beta and returns, even if the market portfolio is not efficient. In short, the security market line will appear to be valid even when it is not.

In effect, Roll said that researchers had been testing the wrong thing. The fundamental prediction of the theory is that the market portfolio is efficient. Why not test that prediction directly? In principle this is a good idea and it has been tried on a number of occasions, using returns on shares to represent returns on the market portfolio. Two Australian studies of this kind report mixed results. While some of the evidence is consistent with the mean–variance efficiency of a stock market index, this is not always the case.[18] While such tests provide some

---

16 For example, F. Black, M. Jensen & M. Scholes, 'The Capital Asset Pricing Model: Some Empirical Tests', in *Studies in the Theory of Capital Markets*, Ed. M. Jensen, Praeger, New York, 1972, pp. 47–78; and E. Fama & J. MacBeth, 'Risk Return and Equilibrium: Empirical Tests', *Journal of Political Economy*, May–June 1973, pp. 607–36. For an Australian study in a similar vein, see R. Ball, P. Brown & R. Officer, 'Asset Pricing in the Australian Industrial Equity Market', *Australian Journal of Management*, April 1976, pp. 1–31.
17 R. Roll, 'A Critique of the Asset Pricing Theory's Tests; Part 1: On the Past and Potential Testability of the Theory', *Journal of Financial Economics*, March 1977, pp. 129–76
18 See R.W. Faff, 'A Likelihood Ratio Test of the Zero-beta CAPM in Australian Equity Returns', *Accounting and Finance*, November 1991, pp. 88–95 and J. Wood, 'A Cross-sectional Regression Test of the Mean–Variance Efficiency of an Australian Value-weighted Market Portfolio', *Accounting and Finance*, November 1991, pp. 96–109.

reassurance that the CAPM is a useful model, their results can never be definitive because, as Roll also pointed out, the market portfolio is a portfolio of *all* assets, not just shares. It also includes bonds, land, buildings and much else, and there is no chance that anyone will ever be able to measure returns on all these assets.

For practical purposes, it therefore seems that the CAPM is untestable. Needless to say, this is a severe problem for any theory. However, this alone does not mean that the CAPM is 'wrong', nor does it mean that it is not a useful aid in thinking about financial problems; it also does not mean that the CAPM ought to be abandoned—at least not until something better comes along.[19]

Even if Roll had not written his critique, the CAPM would still have been subjected to criticism because of the emerging evidence on empirical regularities in asset prices. Whereas the CAPM implies that *only* systematic risk should be important in explaining returns, a number of researchers have discovered *other* factors that seem to explain returns. For example, compared with what the CAPM would predict, it has been found that returns on the shares of small companies are too high. Similarly, share returns seem to be related to the month of the year and the day of the week.[20] The evidence on regularities is discussed in more detail in Chapter 14. In assessing the role of the CAPM we should remember that any model involves some simplification of real-world complexities; therefore no model is perfect but they can be very useful in providing insights into complex phenomena. In the case of the CAPM there are two underlying ideas. First, because investors are risk averse they require compensation, in the form of a higher expected rate of return, for investing in risky assets. Secondly, investors require compensation only for risk which cannot be eliminated by diversification. The first idea is hardly controversial and was widely accepted long before the CAPM was developed. The second idea is not a complete description of the risk–return relationship but the evidence suggests that systematic risk is an important determinant of returns. In summary, the CAPM provides important insights but it is by no means perfect. Therefore, the search for better asset pricing models continues.

---

[19] One of Roll's criticisms was that the statistical tests of the CAPM had low 'power'. This means that the tests are unlikely to reject the CAPM, even if it is false. Gibbons used multivariate tests which rejected the CAPM. However, as these tests did not specify an alternative hypothesis, they cannot suggest a replacement for the CAPM. See M.R. Gibbons, 'Multivariate Tests of Financial Models: A New Approach', *Journal of Financial Economics*, March 1982, pp. 3–27. Gibbons' conclusions have also been questioned on statistical grounds; see J. Shanken, 'Multivariate Tests of the Zero-beta CAPM', *Journal of Financial Economics*, December 1985, pp. 327–48.

[20] There is considerable evidence on these issues. For an overview see D.B. Keim, 'Stock Market Regularities: A Synthesis of the Evidence and Explanations', in *Stock Market Anomalies*, Ed. E. Dimson, Cambridge University Press, Cambridge, 1988, pp. 16–39. For a survey from an Australian perspective, see R. Faff, 'Capital Market Anomalies: A Survey of the Evidence', *Accounting Research Journal*, Spring 1992, pp. 3–22.

## 6.8 Valuation Formula for Risky Assets

The CAPM provides estimates of expected returns rather than values of risky assets. This is Equation 6.8:

$$E(R_i) = R_f + \beta_i (E(R_M) - R_f)$$

To obtain estimates of asset values it is necessary to link expected returns and prices. Assume that a risky asset is expected to produce a cash flow of $E(P_1)$ at the end of a time period. For example, if the risky asset is a share, then $E(P_1)$ equals the expected price of the share at the end of the period, plus any dividend received at that time. If the price of an asset $i$ at the beginning of a period is $P_0$, then the expected return $E(R_i)$ for the period is:

$$E(R_i) = \frac{E(P_1) - P_0}{P_0} \qquad (6.14)$$

Equating Equations 6.8 and 6.14, and rearranging the resulting expression, the following equation for the equilibrium price of a risky asset can be obtained:

$$P_0 = \frac{E(P_1)}{1 + R_f + \beta_i (E(R_M) - R_f)} \qquad (6.15)$$

The numerator in Equation 6.15 is the expected cash flow at the end of the period and the denominator is 1 plus the risk-adjusted discount rate, as given by the CAPM.

## 6.9 The Arbitrage Pricing Model

The arbitrage pricing model was formulated by Ross (1976) as an alternative to the CAPM. Much of this work is very mathematical but many of the insights can be explained in simple terms.[21] It is assumed that investors can short sell assets; this means that assets can be sold first and purchased later. If short selling is undertaken, the investor obtains a cash inflow at the start of the investment period and experiences an outflow at the end of the investment period. It is also assumed that 'arbitrage' is not possible. Essentially this means that it is not possible to make something out of nothing; there are no 'free lunches'.

Consider the following situation. Suppose that an investor short sells a share in company X for $1 and simultaneously buys a share in Company Y for $1. The net investment outlay is therefore zero. Suppose further that there is no change in the risk of the investor's portfolio. What return would this operation be expected to yield? If there are no opportunities for arbitrage, the answer to this question must be zero. If both the net additional investment and risk are zero, the expected return should be zero.

---

[21] The seminal article is S. Ross, 'The Arbitrage Theory of Capital Asset Pricing,' *Journal of Economic Theory*, December 1976, pp. 341–60. A very readable discussion can be found in D. Bower, R. Bower & D. Logue, 'A Primer on Arbitrage Pricing Theory', in *The Revolution in Corporate Finance*, Eds J.M. Stern & D.H. Chew, 2nd edn, Basil Blackwell, Oxford 1992, pp. 98–106.

In the simplest case, the model is derived from the assumption that the return on a particular security $i$ can be described by the following equation:[22]

$$R_i = \alpha_i + \beta_i(F - E(F)) + e_i \qquad (6.16)$$

where $\alpha_i$ = a constant, specific to asset $i$
$\beta_i$ = a measure of the 'sensitivity' of returns on asset $i$ to 'factor' $F$
$F$ = a risk 'factor' which explains returns
$E(F)$ = the expected value of $F$
$e_i$ = an error term which has an expected value of zero, and is specific to asset $i$

Equation 6.16 asserts that the returns on each security depend on some risk 'factor' $F$, and on an error term $e$. The effects of events specific to the security will be reflected in the error term. In principle the risk factor $F$ might be almost anything, but realistically it is likely to be a macroeconomic variable that has a pervasive influence. For example, it could be the inflation rate or the level of industrial production. Whatever $F$ is, Equation 6.16 specifies that unanticipated variations in $F$ will cause returns to change. So, for example, returns will change if there is an unexpected increase in the inflation rate. Returns will also change owing to company-specific events, but the effects of these events can be eliminated by diversification. Therefore company-specific risks will not affect expected returns but factor risk cannot be removed by diversification and will affect expected returns. If, as 'expected', $F = E(F)$ and $e_i = 0$, we have $\alpha_i = d_i$. Therefore $\alpha_i$ is the expected return on asset $i$ and will be directly related to the asset's sensitivity to changes in factor $F$.

For example, suppose that Equation 6.16 is true, and a well-diversified investor observes three shares (1, 2 and 3) with sensitivity measures (betas) of 0.5, 1.5, and 4.0 respectively. Suppose further that the expected returns are 14 per cent, 18 per cent, and 30 per cent respectively. If this is the case, arbitrage is possible. Imagine that the investor buys $1 worth of shares in company 1. He or she can then select investments in shares 2 and 3 in such a way that the net additional investment and risk are both zero, but the expected return is higher; in other words, there is a 'free lunch'. The investor's problem is to solve simultaneously the following equations:

Net investment = $\$1.00 + \$X_2 + \$X_3 = 0$, and
risk = $(0.5)(\$1.00) + (1.5)(\$X_2) + (4.0)(\$X_3) = 0$

where $X_2$ and $X_3$ are, of course, the amounts to be invested in shares 2 and 3 respectively.[23]

The problem is quite simple: there are two equations and two unknowns. The solutions are:

---

[22] Typically the more complex situation of more than one factor is assumed. This is discussed later in the section.
[23] In calculating the risk, we have included only the betas and the amounts invested. We have ignored the error terms $e_i$. We justify this by our assumption that the investor is well-diversified and hence not concerned with events specific to any single asset $i$. Therefore the influence of the error terms is negligible.

$X_2 = -\$1.40$ (that is, a short sale of company 2 shares to the value of $1.40)

$X_3 = \$0.40$ (that is, a purchase of $0.40 worth of company 3 shares)

We can check that the solution is correct as follows:

Net investment = $1.00 − $1.40 + $0.40 = 0

Risk = (0.5)($1.00) + (1.5)(−$1.40) + (4.0)($0.40) = 0

According to arbitrage pricing assumptions the return on such an operation should be zero, but using the numbers in this example, and again ignoring the error terms, the outcome is:

(0.14)($1.00) − (0.18)($1.40) + (0.30)($0.40)
= $0.14 − $0.252 + $0.12
= $0.008

Therefore $0.008 is earned for every dollar invested in shares in company 1. The single dollar is, of course, just a scaling factor and if it is interpreted as, say, $1 million, then the dollar return is $8000—an excellent outcome when there is no additional investment or risk!

In well-functioning markets it should not be possible to undertake arbitrage. Competition should eliminate it. So prices (and therefore returns) should be set by the market in such a way that arbitrage is not possible. For example, one possible set of returns that would eliminate the arbitrage described in the above example is if the return on company 3 shares is 28 per cent instead of 30 per cent. The dollar return is then:

(0.14)($1.00) − (0.18)($1.40) + (0.28)($0.40)
= $0.14 − $0.252 + $0.112
= $0

To this point it has been shown that if returns can be described by an equation like Equation 6.16, some sets of expected returns will not be possible if arbitrage is to be prevented. For example, the set of expected returns of 14 per cent, 18 per cent, and 30 per cent for shares 1, 2, and 3 respectively is *not* possible, whereas the set 14 per cent, 18 per cent, and 28 per cent *is* possible. What general rule can be used to distinguish the sets of expected returns that are possible from those that are not? Ross (1976) shows that a solution is that the expected return on every share (or, more generally, every asset) $i$ is given by:

a constant + (another constant) × ($\beta$ of $i$)

This can be written more formally as:

$$E(R_i) = \lambda_0 + \lambda_1 \beta_i \tag{6.17}$$

where $\lambda_0$ and $\lambda_1$ are constants.

To construct the example, we used 12 per cent for $\lambda_0$ and 4 per cent for $\lambda_1$ to get expected returns of:

$E(R_1) = 0.12 + (0.04)(0.5) = 0.14 = 14\%$
$E(R_2) = 0.12 + (0.04)(1.5) = 0.18 = 18\%$
$E(R_3) = 0.12 + (0.04)(4.0) = 0.28 = 28\%$

The economic interpretations of the two constants are as follows: The first constant $\lambda_0$ is a risk-free return in the sense that it is the return expected if the risk sensitivity measure $\beta$ is zero. If there is a zero-variance asset, then $\lambda_0$ is $R_f$, the interest rate on the zero-variance asset. The second constant $\lambda_1$ is the risk premium for the risk factor $F$. It is the additional expected return required for each unit of the risk involved.[24]

To this point in the discussion the arbitrage pricing model looks very like the CAPM. Both models are based on the principles that investors require compensation for taking on risk, and that the market will only reward investors for bearing risks that cannot be eliminated by diversification. The major difference is that in the CAPM, the market portfolio is identified as ultimately the single source of risk, whereas in the discussion of the arbitrage pricing model, the single risk factor $F$ was not identified. However, while it is true that arbitrage pricing theory (unlike the CAPM) does not identify a risk factor, it does permit there to be more than one factor. So far only one has been considered, purely to keep the discussion simple. In fact, however, one of the distinctive features of the arbitrage pricing model is that several (or indeed, many) risk factors are possible. For example, if there are two risk factors $F_1$ and $F_2$, each asset $i$ will have two sensitivity measures (betas). The first, $\beta_{i_1}$, measures the sensitivity of the return on asset $i$ to variations in factor $F_1$ while the second, $\beta_{i_2}$ measures the sensitivity of the return on asset $i$ to variations in factor $F_2$. Therefore, in place of Equation 6.16 we have the following equation:

$$R_i = \alpha_i + \beta_{i_1}(F_1 - E(F_1)) + \beta_{i_2}(F_2 - E(F_2)) + e_i \tag{6.18}$$

The same arbitrage-based arguments can again be applied, and in this case, to prevent arbitrage, the equation in place of Equation 6.17 is:

$$E(R_i) = \lambda_0 + \lambda_1 \beta_{i_1} + \lambda_2 \beta_{i_2} \tag{6.19}$$

As discussed earlier, $\lambda_0$ is interpreted as a risk-free return, while $\lambda_1$ and $\lambda_2$ are the risk premiums for the first and second risk factors respectively.

As explained earlier, if there is a zero-variance asset, then $\lambda_0 = R_f$. Making this assumption, and generalising from two factors to $k$ factors, the expected return on asset $i$ according to arbitrage pricing theory is given by:

$$E(R_i) = R_f + \lambda_1 \beta_{i_1} + \lambda_2 \beta_{i_2} + \ldots + \lambda_k \beta_{i_k} \tag{6.20}$$

where $E(R_i)$ = expected return on asset $i$
$R_f$ = the risk-free rate of interest
$\lambda_j$ = the risk premium for the $j$th factor; $j = 1, \ldots, k$
$\beta_{i_j}$ = the sensitivity measure of asset $i$ for the $j$th risk factor
$j$ = $1, \ldots, k$

The CAPM equation (6.8) is a special case of the arbitrage pricing equation (6.20). A single-factor arbitrage pricing equation, where the single factor is returns on the market portfolio, is indistinguishable from the CAPM. In practice, therefore, it is important to turn to the empirical evidence. Unfortunately the

---

[24] If it is believed that $F$ is the return on the market portfolio, then, with appropriate statistical assumptions, the CAPM equation becomes a special case of Equation 6.17.

empirical research is complex and in some respects contradictory.[25] The three distinct questions on which evidence is sought are:
  (a) Do share returns appear to have an implicit factor structure, and if so, how many factors might there be?
  (b) How well do sensitivities to factors explain asset prices (returns)?
  (c) What might be the economic identities of the risk factors?

In brief, these three questions refer to testing the assumed *existence* of factors, testing the pricing *performance* of the factors, and establishing the *identity* of the factors. Answers to these questions are important to anyone who attempts to use the arbitrage pricing model to estimate the expected return on an asset because to do so requires identification of a manageable number of factors, estimation of the risk premium for each factor, and estimation of the asset's sensitivity to each factor. The evidence, in brief, is as follows:

# EXISTENCE

Share returns seem to have a factor structure but the number of factors is uncertain. For example, using Australian data Sinclair (1977) found *prima facie* evidence of the existence of perhaps three factors but the evidence for the existence of the second and third factors was much weaker than that for the first.[26] Using Australian data from a later period, Faff (1988) concluded that while the data set 'conforms best to the existence of an approximate one-factor structure, additional factors cannot be categorically rejected'.[27]

# PERFORMANCE

Using US data, Roll and Ross (1980) found that at least three, and possibly four, factors were 'priced' (that is, helped to 'explain' returns).[28] Chen (1983) supported a five-factor model;[29] Cho, Elton and Gruber (1984) found five or six priced factors.[30] In Australia, Faff (1988) found that up to three factors seemed to be priced, but, in a direct comparison between arbitrage pricing and the CAPM, found results that were generally inconclusive.[31]

---

[25] For partial summaries covering both US and Australian evidence, see N.A. Sinclair, 'Multifactor Asset Pricing Models', *Accounting and Finance*, May 1987, pp. 17–36; and R.W. Faff, 'An Empirical Test of the Arbitrage Pricing Theory on Australian Stock Returns 1974–85', *Accounting and Finance*, November 1988, pp. 23–43.
[26] N.A. Sinclair, 'Aspects of the Factor Structure Implicit in the Australian Industrial Equity Market: February 1958 to August 1977', *Australian Journal of Management*, June 1984, pp. 23–36.
[27] R.W. Faff, 'An Empirical Test of the Arbitrage Pricing Theory on Australian Stock Returns 1974–85', *Accounting and Finance*, November 1988, p. 33.
[28] R. Roll & S. Ross, 'An Empirical Investigation of the Arbitrage Pricing Theory', *Journal of Finance*, December 1980, pp. 1073–104.
[29] N.F. Chen, 'Some Empirical Tests of the Theory of Arbitrage Pricing', *Journal of Finance*, December 1983, pp. 1393–414.
[30] D.C. Cho, E.J. Elton & M.J. Gruber, 'On the Robustness of the Roll and Ross Arbitrage Pricing Theory', *Journal of Financial and Quantitative Analysis*, March 1984, pp. 1–10.
[31] R.W. Faff, 'An Empirical Test of the Arbitrage Pricing Theory on Australian Stock Returns 1974–85', *Accounting and Finance*, November 1988, pp. 23–43.

## IDENTITY

There is little or no theory to specify the identity of the factors. However Chen, Roll and Ross (1986) suggest that important influences in the US are unanticipated changes in the following variables: inflation, the term structure of interest rates, the growth rate of industrial production, and the yield premium on corporate bonds compared with Treasury bonds.[32]

## SELECTED REFERENCES

Ball, R., Brown, P. & Officer, R., 'Asset Pricing in the Australian Industrial Equity Market', *Australian Journal of Management*, April 1976, pp. 1–31.
Chen, N. F., Roll, R. & Ross, S. A., 'Economic Forces and the Stock Market: Testing the APT and Alternative Asset Pricing Theories', *Journal of Business*, July 1986, pp. 383–403.
Faff, R. W., 'An Empirical Test of the Arbitrage Pricing Theory on Australian Stock Returns 1974–85', *Accounting and Finance*, November 1988, pp. 23–43.
Fama, E. F., *Foundations of Finance*, Basic Books, New York, 1976.
Jensen, M., 'Capital Markets: Theory and Evidence', *Bell Journal of Economics and Management Science*, Autumn 1972, pp. 357–98.
Keim, D. B., 'Stock Market Regularities: A Synthesis of the Evidence and Explanations', in *Stock Market Anomalies*, Ed. E. Dimson, Cambridge University Press, Cambridge, 1988, pp. 16–39.
Markowitz, H. M., *Portfolio Selection: Efficient Diversification of Investments*, John Wiley & Sons, New York, 1959.
Roll, R., 'A Critique of the Asset Pricing Theory's Tests; Part I: On the Past and Potential Testability of the Theory', *Journal of Financial Economics*, March 1977, pp. 126–76.
Ross, S., 'The Arbitrage Theory of Capital Asset Pricing', *Journal of Economic Theory*, December 1976, pp. 343–60.
Ross, S., 'The Current Status of the Capital Asset Pricing Model (CAPM)', *Journal of Finance*, June 1978, pp. 885–901.
Sinclair, N. A., 'Multifactor Asset Pricing Models', *Accounting and Finance*, May 1987, pp. 17–36.

## QUESTIONS

1. Is risk aversion a reasonable assumption? What is the relevant measure of risk for a risk-averse investor?
2. Mr Barlin is considering a 1-year investment in shares in one of the following three companies:
    Company X: expected return = 15% with a standard deviation of 15%.
    Company Y: expected return = 15% with a standard deviation of 20%.
    Company Z: expected return = 20% with a standard deviation of 20%.
    Rank the investments in order of preference for each of the cases where it is assumed that Mr Barlin is:
    (a) risk averse;
    (b) risk neutral;
    (c) risk seeking.
    Give reasons.
3. What are the benefits to an investor of diversification? What is the key factor determining the extent of these benefits?
4. *Risky assets can be combined to form a riskless asset.* Discuss.
5. Explain each of the following:
    (a) the efficient frontier;

---

[32] N.F. Chen, R. Roll & S.A. Ross, 'Economic Forces and the Stock Market: Testing the APT and Alternative Asset Pricing Theories', *Journal of Business*, July 1986, pp. 383–403.

(b) the capital market line;
(c) the security market line.

6. *Total risk can be decomposed into systematic and unsystematic risk.* Explain each component of risk, and how each is affected by increasing the number of securities in the portfolio.

7. An investor places 40 per cent of her funds in company A's shares and the remainder in company B's shares. The standard deviation of the returns on A is 20 per cent and on B is 10 per cent. Calculate the variance of return on the portfolio, assuming that the correlation between the returns on the two securities is:
   (a) +1.0
   (b) +0.5
   (c) 0
   (d) −0.5.

8. The standard deviations of returns on assets A and B are 8 per cent and 12 per cent respectively. A portfolio is constructed consisting of 40 per cent in asset A and 60 per cent in asset B. Calculate the portfolio standard deviation if the correlation of returns between the two assets is:
   (a) 1
   (b) 0.4
   (c) 0
   (d) −1
   Comment on your answers.

9. You believe that there is a 50 per cent chance that the share price of company L will decrease by 12 per cent and a 50 per cent chance that it will increase by 24 per cent. Further, there is a 40 per cent chance that the share price of company M will decrease by 12 per cent, and a 60 per cent chance that it will increase by 24 per cent. The correlation coefficient of the returns on shares in the two companies is 0.75. Calculate:
   (a) the expected return, variance, and standard deviation for each company's shares;
   (b) the covariance between their returns.

10. Harry Jones has invested one-third of his funds in share 1 and two-thirds of his funds in share 2. His assessment of each investment is as follows:

| Item | Share 1 | Share 2 |
| --- | --- | --- |
| Expected return (%) | 15 | 21 |
| Standard deviation (%) | 18 | 25 |
| Correlation between the returns | | 0.5 |

   (a) What is the expected return and the standard deviation of return on Harry's portfolio?
   (b) Recalculate the expected return and the standard deviation where the correlation between the returns is 0 and 1.0.
   (c) Is Harry better off or worse off as a result of investing in two securities rather than in one security?

11. The table gives information on three risky assets A, B, and C.

|   | Expected return | Standard deviation of return | Correlations | | |
|---|---|---|---|---|---|
|   |   |   | A | B | C |
| A | 12.5 | 40 | 1.00 | 0.20 | 0.35 |
| B | 16.0 | 45 | 0.20 | 1.00 | 0.10 |
| C | 20.0 | 60 | 0.35 | 0.10 | 1.00 |

There is also a risk-free asset F whose expected return is 9.9.
(a) Portfolio 1 consists of 40 per cent asset A and 60 per cent asset B. Calculate its expected return and standard deviation.
(b) Portfolio 2 consists of 60 per cent asset A, 22.5 per cent asset B and 17.5 per cent asset C. Calculate its expected return and standard deviation. Compare your answers to (a) and (b) and comment.
(c) Portfolio 3 consists of 4.8 per cent asset A, 75 per cent asset B, and 20.2 per cent in the risk-free asset. Calculate its expected return and standard deviation. Compare your answers to (a), (b), and (c) and comment.
(d) Portfolio 4 is an equally-weighted portfolio of the three risky assets A, B, and C. Calculate its expected return and standard deviation. Comment.
(e) Portfolio 5 is an equally-weighted portfolio of all four assets. Calculate its expected return and standard deviation. Comment.

12. The expected return on the $i$th asset is given by:

$$E(R_i) = R_f + \beta_i (E(R_M) - R_f)$$

(a) What is the expected return on the $i$th asset where $R_f = 0.08$, $\beta_i = 1.25$ and $E(R_M) = 0.14$?
(b) What is the expected return on the market portfolio where $E(R_i) = 0.11$, $R_f = 0.08$ and $\beta_i = 0.75$?
(c) What is the systematic risk of the $i$th asset where $E(R_i) = 0.14$, $R_f = 0.10$ and $E(R_M) = 0.15$?

13. The table provides data on two risky assets, A and B, the market portfolio M and the risk-free asset F.

|   | Expected return | Variances and covariances | | | |
|---|---|---|---|---|---|
|   |   | A | B | M | F |
| A | 10.8 | 324 | 60 | 48 | 0 |
| B | 15.6 | 60 | 289 | 96 | 0 |
| M | 14.0 | 48 | 96 | 80 | 0 |
| F | 6.0 | 0 | 0 | 0 | 0 |

An investor wishes to achieve an expected return of 12 and is considering three ways this may be done:
(a) invest in A and B;
(b) invest in B and F;
(c) invest in M and F.

For each of these options, calculate the portfolio weights required and the portfolio standard deviation. Show that assets A and B are priced according to the capital asset pricing model and, in the light of this result, comment on your findings.

14. *An important conclusion of the CAPM is that the relevant measure of an asset's risk is its systematic risk.* Outline the significance of this conclusion for a manager making financial decisions.
15. Compare and contrast the CAPM and the arbitrage pricing model.
16. For investors who aim to diversify, shares with negative betas would be very useful investments, but such shares are very rare. Explain why few shares have negative betas.
17. Diversification is certainly good for investors. Therefore investors should be prepared to pay a premium for the shares of companies that operate in several lines of business. Explain why this statement is true or false.
18. Minco Ltd, a large mining company, provides a superannuation fund for its employees. The fund's manager says: 'We know the mining industry well, so we feel comfortable investing most of the fund in a portfolio of mining company shares'. Advise Minco's employees on whether to endorse the fund's investment policy.
19. Farmers can insure their crops against damage by hailstorms at reasonable rates. However, the same insurance companies refuse to provide flood insurance at any price. Explain why this situation exists.

# CHAPTER 7

# THE CAPITAL MARKET

## 7.1 INTRODUCTION

In Chapter 5 the methods used to select a company's investments were discussed. Management also has to decide on the methods of financing those assets. In this chapter we discuss the benefits of having a capital market. We then consider the major features of the Australian capital market, paying particular attention to the characteristics of the important institutions that participate in the market.

### 7.1.1 THE FLOW OF FUNDS

Over a given period of time an economic entity will be either a 'savings-deficit unit' or a 'savings-surplus unit'. A savings-deficit unit is one whose expenditure exceeds its revenue during a particular period, whereas a savings-surplus unit is one whose revenue exceeds its expenditure during a particular period. The financing process involves a flow of funds from the savings-surplus units to the savings-deficit units.

If a company wishes to expand but does not generate sufficient funds internally[1] to finance an increase in its assets (that is, the company is a savings-deficit unit), it will need to finance the difference by drawing on the funds held by the savings-surplus units. Savings-surplus units may be households, other businesses, governments or the overseas sector.

This flow of funds may be direct or indirect. A direct flow of funds from a savings-surplus unit to a savings-deficit unit may result solely from negotiation between the parties, or a financial institution may be involved as an adviser or underwriter.[2] For example, when a company raises funds by issuing debentures, a broking firm may advise on and/or underwrite the issue.

---

[1] Internally generated sources of funds are discussed in Section 9.7.
[2] Underwriting is discussed further in Section 7.2.1.

However, the funds will flow from the purchaser of the debentures to the issuing company. Direct funding is more commonly used where the borrower has a recognised credit rating and wishes to raise relatively large amounts over a relatively long period.

Alternatively, the flow of funds may be indirect, that is, it occurs through financial intermediaries such as banks and finance companies. In this case the savings-deficit unit obtains funds from a financial intermediary that has borrowed the funds from a savings-surplus unit. Intermediated funding is more commonly used where the credit risk of the savings-deficit unit (the borrower) needs to be assessed, and where the amounts for both borrowers and lenders are relatively small. The role of financial intermediaries is therefore to facilitate the flow of funds from savings-surplus units to savings-deficit units. Collectively, financial intermediaries are a very important segment of the capital market.

### 7.1.2 THE CAPITAL MARKET

The capital market enables the suppliers of funds (the savings-surplus units) and the users of funds (the savings-deficit units) to negotiate the conditions on which the funds will be transferred. Equity or share markets involve an essentially permanent transfer of funds, with returns to shareholders contingent on the future profitability of the company raising the funds. Debt markets usually involve a temporary transfer of funds with predetermined returns to debtholders. In the finance literature, equity and debt markets together form the capital market.[3]

### 7.1.3 PRIMARY AND SECONDARY MARKETS

Markets for financial assets may be either **primary** markets where assets are first sold by their originators, or **secondary** markets where existing financial assets are traded. Primary markets are important because it is in these markets that savings-deficit units raise capital to finance their physical investment plans.

A transaction in the secondary market does not raise any new funds for the company. All that happens is a change of ownership; the seller of the security transfers, for a price, ownership of the security to the buyer. However, secondary markets are important because they provide liquidity. This enables borrowers to raise long-term funds, even though individual suppliers of funds may be willing to provide funds only for much shorter terms. In this way the existence of an active secondary market facilitates capital raising in the primary market. Without an active secondary market, many investors would not participate in primary markets because they require the flexibility to redeploy their funds. The secondary market provides this flexibility.

### 7.1.4 DEREGULATION IN THE 1980s

During the 1980s the Australian capital market changed fundamentally. Many of these changes began with the establishment by the Commonwealth Government

---

[3] In practice, participants in the financial markets usually refer to the direct short-term debt market, that is where loans are for twelve months or less, as the *money market*, and the term *capital market* is used to describe the direct long-term debt market.

of the Committee of Inquiry into the Australian Financial System (the Campbell Committee) in 1979. In 1981 the Final Report[4] of the Campbell Committee was published. In 1983, the newly elected Commonwealth Government established the Martin Group to review the Campbell Committee Report; the report of this group was published in 1984.[5] Both reports supported the deregulation of the Australian financial system.

The Campbell Committee Report concluded that deregulation would improve the efficiency of the Australian financial system. It suggested that the efficiency with which a capital market allocates funds from savings-surplus units to savings-deficit units may be judged using three criteria. The first is the market's *allocative efficiency*, which is the extent to which funds are directed to their most productive use. The second is the market's *operational efficiency*, which is the extent to which the costs of providing the service are minimised. The third is the market's *dynamic efficiency*, which is its capacity to adopt new technology and techniques in pursuit of productivity gains and to respond to changing needs by product innovation.[6]

The process of deregulation continued throughout the 1980s.[7] Major elements of this process included:

1. Lifting of controls over the interest rates paid by banks in December 1980.
2. Removal of quantitative controls over bank lending in June 1982.
3. Floating of the Australian dollar in December 1983.
4. Removal of restrictions on the terms of bank deposits in August 1984.
5. Reducing the barriers to entry to the banking industry by allowing access to banking licences for suitable building societies and foreign banks. This commenced in February 1985 when sixteen foreign banks were invited to take up banking licences.
6. Removal of the remaining bank interest rate ceilings, with the exception of owner-occupied housing loans under $100 000, in April 1985. The interest rate ceiling on new housing loans was subsequently removed in April 1986.

### 7.1.5 BUSINESS FUNDING

This chapter outlines the major financial institutions in the Australian capital market involved in providing funds to companies. Institutions such as building societies and credit unions, whose main function is consumer lending, are not discussed.[8]

---

4 Committee of Inquiry into the Australian Financial System, (J.K. Campbell, Chairman), *Final Report*, AGPS, Canberra, 1981.
5 Committee of Inquiry into the Australian Financial System, (V. Martin, Chairman), *Report of the Review Group*, AGPS, Canberra, 1984.
6 Committee of Inquiry into the Australian Financial System, (J.K. Campbell, Chairman), *Final Report*, AGPS, Canberra, 1981, p. 2.
7 For a summary see *Reserve Bank of Australia Bulletin*, March, 1990, pp. 40–1.
8 For a discussion of these institutions see O'Brien, K.P., 'The Thrift Institutions: Building Societies, Credit Unions and Friendly Societies', in M.K. Lewis & R.H. Wallace, Eds, *The Australian Financial System*, Longman Cheshire, Sydney, 1993, pp. 83–135.

A distinction should be drawn between a **financial agency institution**, which arranges or facilitates the direct transfer of funds from lenders to borrowers and a **financial intermediary**, which provides funds as a principal. For example, it is usual for companies to use either a broking house (stockbroker) or a merchant bank when they wish to raise debt or equity. Broking houses function solely as agency institutions. In contrast, merchant banks may function as both financial intermediaries and agency institutions. Banks function as financial intermediaries.

Companies with large funding requirements and high credit ratings are well placed to access funds directly. Such companies can therefore raise most or all of their funding requirements without the services of an intermediary. However, the process of intermediation offers significant benefits where there are large numbers of relatively small deposits and loans to be handled. Frequently, savings-surplus units have relatively small amounts that they wish to lend for relatively short periods, while savings-deficit units wish to borrow relatively large amounts for relatively long periods. Further, savings-surplus units often desire a lower level of default risk than can be offered by many savings-deficit units. By accepting deposits and repackaging the funds into loans, financial intermediaries can cater for these different preferences. Thus the process of intermediation can harmonise the differences in size, maturity and risk preferences between savings-surplus units and savings-deficit units. In addition, economies of scale are generated by the specialist skills that financial intermediaries acquire in credit assessment and monitoring of the performance of borrowers. Financial intermediaries can also pool the risks associated with a portfolio of loans.[9]

## 7.2 FINANCIAL AGENCY INSTITUTIONS

Financial agency institutions are financial institutions that facilitate direct funding but do not themselves provide the funds. These institutions operate in the primary markets to bring together savings-surplus units and savings-deficit units and assist with the design of appropriate contracts. They also operate in the secondary markets.

### 7.2.1 BROKING HOUSES AND THE STOCK EXCHANGE[10]

The traditional function of the stock exchange (and of stockbrokers) is to provide facilities for the trading of shares, bonds and other securities such as convertible notes, options and preference shares. As a result, a stock exchange performs three functions. First, it mobilises savings. The stock exchange allows companies to issue debt or equity in relatively small units, and each savings-surplus unit can then invest its desired amount. Because there are large numbers of investors, issues of securities can be for large sums. Secondly, it allocates resources. A stock exchange facilitates the allocation of resources (savings) among a large

---

9 See Chapter 6 for a discussion of how diversification of a portfolio can reduce risk.
10 For a more detailed discussion, see P. Marshman, & P. Davies, 'The Role of the Stock Exchange and the Financial Characteristics of Australian Companies', in R. Bruce, et al., Eds, *Handbook of Australian Corporate Finance*, 4th edition, Butterworths, Sydney, 1991, pp. 78–115.

number of competing investment opportunities. Thirdly, it allows investments to be realised through the sale of securities. That is, it provides investors with liquidity, and therefore the opportunity to adjust their portfolios. As explained earlier, the existence of a liquid secondary market encourages investment in the primary market.

## DEVELOPMENT OF THE AUSTRALIAN STOCK EXCHANGE

The Australian Stock Exchange Ltd (ASX) was preceded by the Australian Associated Stock Exchanges (AASE) which was incorporated in 1937 as a national body representing the six capital city stock exchanges. Although each stock exchange was autonomous, the Council of the AASE was the national policy-making body for the stock exchanges and was responsible for ensuring uniformity on important matters. For example, it ensured that uniform listing requirements were adopted by each exchange.

It was not until April 1987 that the ASX commenced business as a truly national stock exchange. The members of the independent exchanges became members of the ASX. The ASX is the parent company of a group of companies consisting of the ASX and its six state subsidiaries. The Board of Directors of the ASX has authority over the group but delegates responsibility for operational and disciplinary matters to the state subsidiaries.

## SECOND BOARD MARKETS

In the early 1980s it was recognised that there were many unlisted companies that would benefit from listing on a stock exchange but were unable to meet all the requirements imposed on listed companies. As a result, second board markets were created, with listing requirements that were less demanding than those for companies on the so-called main board. The first of these markets was established in 1984 by the Stock Exchange of Perth and the other exchanges quickly followed suit.

Initially, trading in shares listed on the second boards flourished but turnover dropped substantially after a stock market crash in October 1987. As a result of the crash, investors became more risk averse and the ensuing 'flight to quality' saw investment funds directed away from the more risky second board shares. This effect was exacerbated by declining company performance in the recessionary economic environment of the early 1990s. By June 1992, all the second boards had been closed.

## AUTOMATION OF TRADING

In the past, the focal point of the stock exchange was the trading floor where brokers met to buy and sell shares for their clients. The ASX no longer uses trading floors. Since October 1990, all shares have been traded on the Stock Exchange Automated Trading System (SEATS). This electronic system enables stockbrokers to trade from terminals in their offices. Visitors to the stock exchanges can now view share prices and other information on video screens in the visitor's gallery. Table 7.1 provides some ASX market statistics for the period 1981 to 1992.

**Table 7.1** ASX Market Statistics as at end of December, 1981–1992

|      | All Ordinaries Share Price Index | Market capitalisation A$m (equities & fixed interest securities) | Number of issues listed (equities and fixed interest securities) |
|------|------|---------|------|
| 1981 | 596  | 48 680  | 3909 |
| 1982 | 485  | 42 620  | 3885 |
| 1983 | 775  | 66 793  | 3809 |
| 1984 | 726  | 67 046  | 3830 |
| 1985 | 1004 | 103 679 | 3858 |
| 1986 | 1473 | 180 470 | 3961 |
| 1987 | 1319 | 190 985 | 4290 |
| 1988 | 1487 | 214 565 | 3940 |
| 1989 | 1650 | 229 625 | 3543 |
| 1990 | 1280 | 196 520 | 3244 |
| 1991 | 1651 | 261 271 | 3117 |
| 1992 | 1550 | 389 455 | 2924 |

Source: Australian Stock Exchange Limited, *Fact Book 1993*, pp. 33–34.

## THE ROLE OF THE STOCKBROKER

Traditionally, the member firms (broking houses) of the ASX have played the leading role in the new-issues market. A company may maintain a continuing relationship with a broking house which advises it on the most appropriate means of raising funds and the terms of a new issue of securities. It is also usual for the same broker or an associated company to underwrite the issue, which means that the broker or associated company agrees to take up any portion of the issue that is not taken up by other investors during a given period. In addition, a broker may undertake to sell the issue, mainly to the broker's clients and institutional investors. The larger broking houses also frequently advise companies considering a takeover or merger, and may assist with negotiations if the takeover or merger proceeds.

Many brokers have extended their services beyond those traditionally offered and now also provide a complete service in the short-term money market.[11] This includes accepting short-term deposits and relending them, and operating in the commercial bill market.[12] Although some brokers provide these services directly, most provide them through associated merchant banks.

### 7.2.2 MERCHANT BANKS

Merchant banks are classified under the (Commonwealth) *Financial Corporations Act* 1974 as money market corporations.[13] They are not authorised by the Reserve Bank of Australia and therefore are not permitted to use the word 'bank' in their business names.

---

[11] For a comprehensive discussion of the services provided by brokers and the impact of deregulation of the broking industry which occurred in 1984, see ibid, pp. 78–89.
[12] These methods of obtaining finance are discussed in Chapter 8.
[13] See Appendix 7.1 for a list of money market corporations.

## FUNCTIONS OF MERCHANT BANKS

Merchant banks have been involved in financial markets both as financial agents and as financial intermediaries. Those that provide a complete range of services have four main functions:

1. **The money market operation** provides a service to companies that wish to deposit temporarily idle cash balances, or to borrow funds for a short to medium period.
2. **The investment management function** involves managing the portfolios of institutional investors and a merchant bank's own unit trusts. Part of this function is to direct funds to the new issues of Australian companies.
3. **The corporate financial advisory (or investment banking) function** involves providing advice to companies about raising additional capital, or a merger or takeover, and the provision of underwriting facilities and marketing services for new issues. The underwriter will frequently purchase the entire issue and then arrange for it to be sold to the public at a higher price, thereby earning a profit. The underwriter's skills and knowledge of the capital market are expected to result in a higher price than if the issuer attempted to market the securities itself. In addition, the marketing risk is assumed by the underwriter. If the issue is accurately priced, the supply of securities will exactly match the demand. If the issue is over-priced, the underwriter will be left holding the unsold securities.
4. **Making a market in foreign exchange and derivative securities**[14] involves being willing to quote both a price to buy, and a price to sell, in these markets. That is, this function requires the merchant bank to be willing to deal on both sides of the market at all times.

## TRENDS IN AUSTRALIAN MERCHANT BANKING

The first merchant bank in Australia (the Australian United Corporation) was established in 1948. Its background is similar to that of a number of other merchant banks in that it was closely associated with a broking house (Potter Partners). Its purpose was to expand the activities of the broking house beyond its traditional role as an agency institution into the field of financial intermediation.

The other major shareholders of merchant banks are Australian and overseas banks. An important reason for this ownership structure was the restrictive regulations to which banks were subject in the past. Banks were not permitted to pay interest on deposits accepted for periods of less than 30 days and one way for a bank to gain access to this part of the market was through an ownership interest in a merchant bank. This was particularly attractive to banks because merchant banks were not subject to bank regulations and their associated costs. Overseas banks, which were unable to acquire banking licences, were able to gain access to the Australian market by acquiring an interest in an Australian merchant bank.

---

[14] Derivatives include futures contracts, which are discussed in Chapter 15, options, which are discussed in Chapter 16, swaps, which are discussed in Section 10.5 and Section 21.8.5, and forward rate agreements (FRAs), which are discussed in Section 15.10.

In the 1980s, merchant banks expanded their lending operations to include bill acceptance or discount facilities with terms of up to five years and, for large amounts, loan syndications.[15] Merchant banks were also involved, usually on an agency basis, in arranging foreign currency loans or bond issues for Australian borrowers. This was an important source of business for merchant banks with strong links overseas. In addition, most merchant banks were licensed foreign exchange dealers and were active in the rapidly evolving markets for options, futures and swaps.

Merchant banks fared well in the financial conditions of the 1980s but towards the end of the decade a number of factors had an adverse impact. The high level of bad debts associated with the recession of the late 1980s led to the withdrawal of some merchant banks, and initiated rationalisation in many others.

This trend was further strengthened by the removal of the regulation-driven advantages that had stimulated much of the merchant banks' earlier expansion. First, limits on access by overseas financial institutions to the Australian financial market were reduced.[16] Secondly, since 1984, banks have been allowed to pay interest on all deposits, including those lodged for less than 30 days. Thirdly, bank capital adequacy regulations (introduced in 1988) had two major implications for merchant banks: the capital requirements for a parent bank were extended to cover its merchant bank subsidiary, and loans from banks to merchant banks required more capital backing than interbank lending. As a result, bank ownership of a merchant bank subsidiary became less attractive. Fourthly, the Liquid Assets and Government Securities (LGS) convention and the Statutory Reserve Deposit (SRD) requirement imposed on banks under the old banking regulations were replaced by the less onerous Prime Assets Requirement and Non-callable Deposit respectively.[17] This effectively reduced the banks' cost of funds, thereby eroding the merchant banks' competitiveness in the lending market. In many cases merchant banks which were subsidiaries of banks found that their intermediation function was transferred to the parent bank, leaving them with the remaining agency function. Merchant banks which were not bank subsidiaries followed a similar strategy since they also found that their competitive advantage lay in those areas.

To summarise, initially the major role of merchant banks was as financial intermediaries taking short-term deposits and lending either by cash advance or by discounting commercial bills. However, in response to market demand this role broadened considerably to include a large range of fee-based 'agency' services and longer-term lending. By 1988 there were more than two hundred money market corporations with total assets of approximately $50 billion.[18] These

---

15 For a more detailed discussion of these funding methods, see Chapter 8 for a discussion of commercial bills, and Chapter 10 for a discussion of how these instruments are used for longer-term funding.
16 In 1985 the entry of sixteen new foreign banks was approved, but only as subsidiaries domiciled in Australia. In 1992 it was announced that foreign banks would be permitted to establish branches in Australia.
17 These regulations are discussed in more detail in Appendix 7.2.
18 *Reserve Bank of Australia Bulletin*, October, 1988.

institutions varied from small specialised institutions to large financial corporations providing a full range of services.

Following the 1988 changes in bank regulation the merchant banking sector underwent substantial rationalisation. By September 1992 there were 183 money market corporations with total assets of only $44 billion.[19] The focus of their operations had generally narrowed to money market operations and the financial agency services related to corporate advice, derivative securities and investment functions. In the 1990s, many money market corporations prefer to describe themselves as investment banks.

### 7.2.3 SECONDARY MORTGAGE MARKET

Most mortgage loans are private contracts between a borrower and a lender. They are not marketable securities. For example, the typical housing loan is based on a mortgage and is a contract between the mortgagor (the home owner who is the borrower) and the mortgagee (the lender, who is usually a bank or other financial institution). From the lender's viewpoint, this arrangement has a significant disadvantage: the lender must commit funds for the period of the loan. This may be a very long period of up to 20 years or more. This considerably reduces the lender's freedom to manage its assets. Private contracts may be contrasted with securities such as bonds and debentures. A security can usually be traded in a secondary market. Thus, compared with a private contract a security offers the lender flexibility in the management of its assets because it can be sold in the secondary market.

As the name implies, a secondary mortgage market is an attempt to provide a mechanism whereby mortgage loans can be traded, thus providing mortgage lenders with the same kind of flexibility offered by bonds and other securities. However, mortgages cannot be simply traded. Instead, in a process known as *securitisation*, a parcel of mortgages is sold to a trust and the trust then issues securities. It is the trust's securities that may be traded. Thus while the mortgages themselves are not traded, securities *representing* those mortgages are traded.

The trust holding the mortgages may choose to issue securities that resemble equity or debt. The equity-like security is known as a 'pass-through', because the cash flows paid by the borrowers simply pass through the trust on their way to the new ultimate investors. At the other extreme the trust may issue debt—for example, promissory notes—and its portfolio of mortgages is used as security for the debt. Between these two extremes are various intermediate solutions. For example, the trust may issue debt, but also attach a guarantee from the original mortgage lender. Thus the security for the debt issued by the trust rests not only on the quality of the mortgages but also on the credit rating of the original lender. In practice the success of a securitisation program depends heavily on the trust's securities being awarded a high credit rating. A range of techniques, including mortgage insurance, lines of credit, letters of credit and letters of comfort, are used to ensure this result. This process is generally known as *credit enhancement*.

---

[19] For a list of money market corporations see *Reserve Bank of Australia Bulletin*, December, 1992.

In the US, interest in establishing a secondary mortgage market dates from the 1930s with the establishment of the Federal National Mortgage Association.[20] Interest in Australia is more recent. In 1984 the National Mortgage Market Corporation (NMMC) was established to encourage an active secondary market in mortgages in Australia. It commenced with an authorised capital of $5 million, 26 per cent of which was held by the Victorian Government, and the remainder issued to approved mortgage managers such as building societies and banks.

The NMMC initiated operations in the secondary mortgage market in 1985. Essentially the NMMC coordinates the entire process of securitisation—the mortgage origination by its approved group of building societies and banks, transfer of the mortgages to a trust, creation and credit enhancement of mortgage-backed securities, and finally issue of these securities. In 1992 it managed five mortgage origination and mortgage securitisation programs,[21] including the Aussie Mac program where promissory notes with a maturity of 185 days are issued against the security of a pool of mortgages on real estate originated by an approved mortgage manager–shareholder of the NMMC. As at 30 June 1992, NMMC had $1560 million in outstanding securities.

Other organisations have also entered the market. These include the First Australian National Mortgage Corporation Limited (FANMAC) established by the New South Wales Government, and the Mortgage Guaranties Insurance Corporation of Australia Ltd (MGICA) established by the AMP Society. Mortgage securities now include short-term securities and longer-term notes and bonds.

A major advantage of securitisation is that it allows institutions to specialise. Lending institutions with expertise in credit assessment and loan establishment can use these skills in making the original lending decisions. Such institutions are best placed to be mortgage originators, but are not necessarily in the best position to be long-term investors in mortgages. When these assets are securitised, investing institutions, such as superannuation funds, can indirectly invest in mortgages by taking up securities issued by the trust holding the mortgages. Because these securities can be traded, the investing institutions have the flexibility they require, while the mortgage originators can use funds obtained from the sale of the mortgages to finance further loans. In effect, therefore, the credit assessment function is separated from the function of providing the funds to be lent.

At this stage, however, the secondary mortgage market is still relatively undeveloped. This is largely due to the difficulty of obtaining suitable mortgages. Australian mortgages usually pay interest rates that vary with the general level of interest rates in the economy. Thus the interest earned on these mortgages is variable, whereas the interest payable on a debt security is usually fixed. As a result, fixed-rate mortgages are more suited to securitisation, but in Australia these are relatively uncommon.

---

20 For more detail, see F.J. Fabozzi & F. Modigliani, *Capital Markets: Institutions and Instruments*, Prentice–Hall, Englewood Cliffs, 1992, pp. 570–1.
21 According to the corporate profile of the National Mortgage Market Corporation 1992, these were: Aussie Mac Certificates, National Mortgage Bonds, National Housing Securities, Home Opportunity Loans/Victorian Housing Bonds and Keystart Loans.

## 7.3 FINANCIAL INTERMEDIARIES

Financial intermediaries are financial institutions that borrow funds on their own behalf and then lend the funds to another party.

### 7.3.1 BANKS

Banks are primarily financial intermediaries borrowing from depositors and lending to a wide range of borrowers, including governments, businesses and consumers. In addition, banks are also usually involved in 'off balance sheet' areas such as providing guarantees, letters of credit, bill endorsements, and market-related activities such as forward rate agreements, foreign currency hedges, and dealing in other derivative products. As can be seen from Table 7.2, banks are the largest group of financial institutions in Australia, with their assets accounting directly for almost 50 per cent of the assets held by all financial institutions (December 1992).[22] However this understates their overall importance because many banks also have interests in other financial institutions such as merchant banks, finance companies, insurance companies, and stockbrokers.[23]

**Table 7.2** *Total assets of selected financial institutions as at December 1992*

|  | $'000 million |
|---|---|
| Banks | 319.2 |
| Non-bank deposit-taking institutions | 112.0 |
| Life offices and superannuation funds | 175.5 |
| Other financial institutions | 83.3 |

Source: Australian Bureau of Statistics, *Australian National Accounts, Financial Accounts*, Catalogue 5232.0.
Note: Non-bank deposit-taking institutions include institutions whose liabilities are included in the calculation of *broad money*, that is, permanent building societies, credit co-operatives, finance companies, authorised money market dealers, pastoral finance companies, money market corporations, general financiers and cash management trusts.

In December 1993 there were thirty-nine authorised banks operating in Australia, eight of which were subsidiaries of other Australian banks. In total, there are effectively thirty-three banking groups.[24] They are listed in Appendix 7.1. The approval of the Reserve Bank of Australia (RBA) is required before a bank is permitted to operate in Australia. The RBA also imposes a number of other controls over banks, including minimum capital requirements, asset requirements, and the provision of extensive data on bank activities and management systems. More details on these controls are given in Appendix 7.2.

---

22 *Source*: Australian Bureau of Statistics, *Australian National Accounts, Financial Accounts*, Catalogue Number 5232.0.
23 In the 1980s these other interests grew rapidly as banks responded to financial innovation, globalisation of financial markets, and the entry of new foreign banks, which posed a threat to their domination of the Australian market. After about 1988, banks tended to rationalise their activities and fold into the parent bank most core banking activities relating to intermediation. This was in response to capital adequacy requirements and an economic recession.
24 *Source*: *Reserve Bank of Australia Bulletin*, June 1993, Table B.9.

As a result of the close relationship between banks and the RBA, the market generally regards bank deposits as being implicitly guaranteed by the RBA.[25] This gives banks an advantage in raising deposit funds. Banks also have a unique role in the payments system in that the settlement of cheques is conducted through exchange settlement accounts at the RBA which are held only by banks.[26] Bank assets include a range of loans, the most distinctive being the overdraft facility, which involves an arrangement whereby the borrower may draw funds, at his discretion, up to a specified limit.

The Australian banking sector is dominated by four major banks, the ANZ Banking Group, the National Australia Bank, the Commonwealth Bank of Australia, and Westpac Banking Corporation. These major banks accounted for approximately 70 per cent of the total assets of the Australian banking sector as at June 1993.[27] Each has a nationwide branch network and provides a full range of banking services for private as well as business customers. Other banks are smaller and usually more focused. For example, the Bank of Melbourne is largely a Victorian bank which concentrates on retail services such as housing and personal loans, while Macquarie Bank has its head office in New South Wales and concentrates on corporate banking.

### 7.3.2 Authorised dealers in the short-term money market[28]

The Australian system of authorised dealers in the short-term money market was set up to encourage the growth of trading in short-term deposits and securities. Four authorised dealers were accredited by the Reserve Bank of Australia in 1959. The number has varied since then and at April 1993 there were eight authorised dealers (see Appendix 7.3). Ownership of the companies operating as authorised dealers is largely in the hands of stockbrokers, life insurance companies, merchant banks, and foreign banks.

The short-term money market is extremely active, with major participation from banks and merchant banks, as well as authorised dealers. The distinguishing feature of the authorised dealers is their relationship with the RBA. The authorised dealers benefit from this relationship in a number of ways, including a lender-of-last-resort arrangement[29] and direct same-day payments to and from

---

25 The *Banking Act* 1959 charges the RBA with the protection of depositors of banks which are subject to the Act. However, the RBA does not interpret this as an explicit guarantee of bank deposits. The Commonwealth Bank of Australia (CBA) is different in this respect in that the Commonwealth Government does guarantee deposits with the CBA.
26 There are presently moves to open up the payments system to other financial institutions. However, at the time of writing (1994), the banks retain this long-standing monopoly. Other cheque-issuing institutions operate through a bank which acts as its agent to effect cheque settlements.
27 *Source*: Reserve Bank of Australia Bulletin, August 1993, Table B.9.
28 For a more detailed discussion of these institutions, see Reserve Bank of Australia, 'Authorised Short-Term Money Market Dealers', *Reserve Bank of Australia Bulletin*, June 1991, pp. 19–25.
29 These are the only institutions to receive lender-of-last-resort assistance from the RBA. In the past, lender-of-last-resort facilities were available to banks, but this ceased in 1985.

the RBA (that is, they do not need to go through the overnight cheque-clearing system).

In addition, when the RBA buys or sells Commonwealth Government securities of less than one year to maturity it nearly always conducts its trading with authorised dealers. These open-market operations are the main method by which the RBA implements monetary policy. Essentially, RBA sales of securities reduce the money supply and tend to force interest rates up, while RBA purchases of securities increase the money supply and tend to allow interest rates to fall. The RBA also uses these transactions to stabilise interest rates in the face of potential interest rate volatility stemming from seasonal variations in money demand and supply.

However, authorised dealers are also subject to a range of guidelines imposed by the RBA, including minimum capital adequacy requirements, limitations on ownership, and restrictions on portfolio composition. Dealers are restricted to holding assets such as Commonwealth Government securities, which are highly liquid and have low credit risk. Table 7.3 shows the major assets held by authorised dealers.

**Table 7.3** Authorised money market dealers selected assets as at June 1993

| Assets | ($ million) |
| --- | --- |
| Cash and bank deposits | 440 |
| Commonwealth Government securities | 4024 |
| Local, semi-government and other public authority securities | 877 |
| Bills of exchange | 496 |
| Promissory notes | — |
| **Total Assets** | 5887 |

Source: Reserve Bank of Australia Bulletin, October 1993, Table C.3.

The dealers accept deposits overnight at call, or for fixed periods (which are rarely longer than six months). The minimum deposit is $50 000 but most deposits are significantly larger. Banks are the largest single group of lenders to dealers, supplying more than 70 per cent of dealers' funds.[30]

Banks must pay net cheque settlement amounts through their exchange settlement accounts at the RBA on a daily basis. Their deposits with authorised dealers are the most cost effective and accessible source of liquid funds for this purpose. Consequently, banks maintain substantial deposits with the authorised dealers as part of their liquidity management processes.

Although the authorised dealers are not a major source of corporate finance, they have a pivotal role, through their trading with the RBA, in the delivery of monetary policy. They also play an important part in the payments system and provide an outlet for the investment of a company's temporarily idle cash balances.

---

[30] *Reserve Bank of Australia Bulletin*, March 1993, Table C.3.

## 7.3.3 Finance Companies

Initially, finance companies were primarily concerned with lending to individuals by providing instalment credit for retail sales. In 1954 this accounted for 85 per cent of finance company lending but by 1992, lending to individuals accounted for less than 20 per cent of the total assets of finance companies. The majority of finance companies' funds are raised by public debenture issues, which typically are taken up by the general public, but also have some institutional support.

Finance companies grew rapidly in the 1970s. They offered a wide range of financial services for companies, including instalment credit, lease financing, inventory financing, factoring, mortgages, and other commercial loans. Their success was due largely to the regulatory constraints on their natural competitors, the banks. In fact, each of the major banks acquired a finance company subsidiary in order to gain access to markets denied them by bank regulations.

The deregulation of the banking sector in the 1980s removed much of the competitive advantage hitherto enjoyed by finance companies. Moreover, capital adequacy requirements imposed on banks in 1988 provided cost incentives for the banks to transfer much of the lending activities of their finance company subsidiaries to the parent bank. As can be seen from Table 7.4, the falling rate of asset growth of finance companies turned into an absolute decline in 1991. In the 1990s, finance companies have become specialised institutions focusing on specific areas such as motor vehicle finance.[31]

**Table 7.4** *Finance companies: Total assets*

| June | $ million |
|---|---|
| 1988 | 27 360 |
| 1989 | 36 485 |
| 1990 | 40 732 |
| 1991 | 35 806 |
| 1992 | 30 446 |
| 1993 | 30 186 |

Source: *Reserve Bank of Australia Bulletin*, Table C.6.

## 7.3.4 Insurance and Superannuation Companies

Life insurance and general insurance companies, and superannuation funds, are major sources of company finance. These institutions raise large amounts as premiums and contributions which are largely long-term commitments, and accordingly, such institutions tend to acquire long-term assets such as shares issued by public companies, and bonds and other forms of debt issued by governments and companies. The institutions are regulated by the Commonwealth Government's Insurance and Superannuation Commission.

---

[31] For more detail on finance companies see the *Annual Report of the Australian Finance Conference*.

Australia's superannuation industry is expected to grow rapidly in the 1990s in response to the Commonwealth Government's superannuation guarantee charge policy which aims to promote universal superannuation coverage.[32] Table 7.5 shows the recent growth in assets of life insurance companies and superannuation funds.

**Table 7.5** *Selected assets held in Australia by life insurance companies and assets of superannuation funds*

| June | Life insurance $ million | Superannuation $ million | Total $ million |
|---|---|---|---|
| 1988 | 54 558 | 59 866 | 114 424 |
| 1989 | 66 263 | 65 052 | 131 315 |
| 1990 | 76 325 | 72 820 | 149 145 |
| 1991 | 82 513 | 76 438 | 158 951 |
| 1992 | 89 961 | 85 845 | 175 806 |
| 1993 | 92 268 | 94 878 | 187 146 |

*Source: Reserve Bank of Australia Bulletin, Tables C.15 and C.17.*

### 7.3.5 OTHER

In addition to the institutions discussed in the preceding pages there are a number of other sources of company finance. Some of them are now considered:

#### UNIT TRUSTS AND INVESTMENT COMPANIES

Investors place their money in such institutions to obtain a spread of risk over a wide range of securities. Many of these institutions invest most of their funds in shares and commercial bills, although there are also a large number of trusts that specialise in investments in real property such as shops, offices and other rental properties.

#### AUSTRALIAN INDUSTRY DEVELOPMENT CORPORATION (AIDC)

Originally established by the Commonwealth Government as a statutory corporation, the AIDC was partially privatised in July 1989. However, the Commonwealth Government retains control. The objectives of the AIDC are to finance greater Australian participation in, and ownership of, Australian industry, particularly in the mining and manufacturing sectors.

The AIDC provides a range of long-term, short-term and medium-term finance, including some equity funding. It also guarantees loans, underwrites securities, and provides corporate financial advice. Its funding is largely achieved through the issue of securities both domestically and in the European debt markets.

---

[32] For a discussion of the pattern of investment of superannuation and approved deposit funds, see D. Knox, 'An Analysis of the Equity Investments of Australian Superannuation Funds', *The Australian Banker*, October 1993, pp. 233–9.

## COMMONWEALTH DEVELOPMENT BANK (CDB)

The CDB is a wholly-owned subsidiary of the Commonwealth Bank of Australia. It is charged with providing finance to small business (including primary production businesses) where the project is judged worthwhile, but unlikely to attract finance from normal commercial channels. The CDB provides a range of long-term, short-term and medium-term finance. It raises most of its funds by domestic issues of securities.

## OVERSEAS SOURCES

In recent years there has been a sizeable flow of funds from overseas for investment in Australian companies. This has comprised mainly equity contributions and fixed-term lending from overseas companies, overseas portfolio investment and eurodollar loans, and other forms of fixed-term borrowing. Some of these sources of funds are discussed in more detail in Chapter 21.

## SELECTED REFERENCES

Bruce, R., McKern, B., Pollard, I. & Skully, M., Eds, *Handbook of Australian Corporate Finance*, 4th edition, Butterworths, Sydney, 1991.
Carew, E., *Fast Money 3*, George Allen & Unwin, Sydney, 1991.
Committee of Inquiry into the Australian Financial System, (J.K. Campbell, Chairman), *Final Report*, Australian Government Publishing Service (AGPS), Canberra, 1981.
Committee of Inquiry into the Australian Financial System, (V. Martin, Chairman), *Report of the Review Group*, Australian Government Publishing Service (AGPS), Canberra, 1984.
Lewis, M.K. & Wallace, R.H., Eds, *The Australian Financial System*, Longman Cheshire, Melbourne, 1993.
McGrath, M., *Financial Institutions, Instruments and Markets in Australia*, McGraw-Hill, Sydney, 1994.
*Reserve Bank of Australia Bulletin*, various issues.
*Reserve Bank of Australia Functions and Operations*, Reserve Bank of Australia, Sydney, 1987.
Weerasooria, W.S., *Banking Law and the Financial System in Australia*, 3rd edition, Butterworths, Sydney, 1993.

## QUESTIONS

1. Distinguish between direct finance and intermediated finance. Discuss why some borrowers might prefer direct finance, while others might prefer intermediated finance.
2. Why is the existence of a secondary market expected to increase the demand for securities issued in the corresponding primary market?
3. Discuss the relative importance of the following institutions as providers of company finance:
   - stockbrokers
   - merchant banks
   - banks
   - finance companies
   - superannuation funds
4. Outline the services provided by financial institutions, such as stockbrokers and merchant banks, to companies wishing to raise funds direct from the market.
5. Define *securitisation*.
6. *Institutional investors have always been major suppliers of company finance.* Discuss this statement and explain how this flow of funds occurs.

7. Distinguish between monetary policy and prudential regulation of banks. Explain how these two activities were linked in the past, but are now separate.
8. *The authorised short-term money market dealers are not a major source of corporate finance but they play an important role nonetheless in Australian financial markets. Discuss.*

**APPENDIX 7.1**

# AUSTRALIAN BANKS

As at 31 December 1993, the following banks were licensed to operate in Australia:
Advance Bank Australia Limited
Australia and New Zealand Banking Group Limited
Bank of America Australia Limited
Bank of China
Bank of Melbourne Limited
Bank of New Zealand
Bank of Queensland Limited
Bank of Queensland Savings Bank Limited
Bank of Singapore (Australia) Limited
Bank of Tokyo Australia Limited
Bankers Trust Australia Limited
Banque Nationale de Paris
Barclays Bank Australia Limited
Challenge Bank Limited
Citibank Limited
Citibank Savings Limited
Commonwealth Bank of Australia
Commonwealth Development Bank of Australia
Deutsche Bank Australia Limited
HongkongBank of Australia Limited
IBJ Australia Bank Limited
Lloyds Bank NZA Limited
Macquarie Bank Limited
Metway Bank Limited
Mitsubishi Bank of Australia Limited
National Australia Bank Limited
NatWest Australia Bank Limited
Overseas Union Bank Limited

Primary Industry Bank of Australia Limited
St George Bank Limited
Standard Chartered Bank Australia Limited
The Chase Manhattan Bank Australia Limited
Town & Country Bank Limited
Trust Bank Tasmania
Westpac Banking Corporation
State Bank of New South Wales Limited
State Bank of South Australia
R & I Bank of Western Australia Limited
United Overseas Bank Limited

Source: *Reserve Bank of Australia Bulletin*, July 1993, pp. 39–40 and January 1994, p. 36.

# APPENDIX 7.2

# REGULATION OF AUSTRALIAN BANKS

The primary regulator of Australia's banks is the Reserve Bank of Australia (RBA). The *Banking Act* 1959 gives the RBA extensive powers over almost all aspects of banking operations. Other relevant legislation is the *Banks (Shareholdings) Act* 1972 and the *Banking Legislation Amendment Act* 1989.

In the past, these powers have been used to implement monetary policy, in that the RBA has managed interest rates and the money supply by seeking to control the amount and the price (interest rate) of bank lending and deposits. Because this focused bank lending on low-risk borrowers, it reduced the need for prudential supervision of banks' activities.

However, in the 1980s the implementation of monetary policy was reoriented so that the RBA now relies almost exclusively on open market operations to implement monetary policy. For example, if the RBA wishes to pursue a contractionary policy it will sell bonds to the public rather than issue directives to banks to reduce their lending. This approach increases the banks' freedom to lend to higher-risk borrowers, and, accordingly, greater emphasis is now placed on having a system of prudential supervision of banks.[33]

## NON-CALLABLE DEPOSITS (NCDs)[34]

A non-callable deposit (NCD) is a deposit that all banks are required to lodge with the RBA. The required NCD (1994) is 1 per cent of a bank's total liabilities less shareholders' funds. The balance is adjusted monthly. Funds in the NCD earn interest at the same rate as Treasury Notes.

---

[33] For a comprehensive discussion of prudential supervision of Australian banks see W.P. Hogan, & I.G. Sharpe, 'Prudential Supervision of Australian Banks', *The Economic Record*, June 1990, pp. 127–45.

[34] The NCD replaced the Statutory Reserve Deposit in August 1988.

## PRIME ASSETS REQUIREMENT (PAR)[35]

The prime assets requirement (PAR) specifies that banks must hold at least 6 per cent of their total liabilities, less shareholders' funds, in prime assets. Prime assets are defined to include notes and coin, Commonwealth Government Securities (CGS), and deposits with the authorised short-term money market dealers which are secured against CGS. The effect of PAR is to ensure that banks hold a minimum level of highly liquid assets. In fact they must also hold a buffer of free liquidity for day-to-day requirements since the minimum 6 per cent is required to satisfy PAR.[36]

## CAPITAL ADEQUACY REQUIREMENT

In August 1988, the RBA introduced a risk-weighted capital adequacy requirement for banks. This is based on the recommendations of the Bank for International Settlements. All banks are required to maintain capital of at least 8 per cent of total risk-weighted assets. Briefly, the system involves the following calculations:

1. A bank's capital is calculated. Capital is categorised into two tiers: *tier 1 capital* (*core capital*), comprising paid-up capital, non-cumulative irredeemable preference shares, minority interests in subsidiaries, and reserves including general reserves, retained profits and share premium reserves. *Tier 2 capital* (*supplementary capital*) comprises general reserves for doubtful debts, asset revaluation reserves, other preference shares, mandatory convertible notes, perpetual subordinated debt and some categories of term subordinated debt.[37] For calculation of the ratio, tier 2 capital may not exceed tier 1 capital, and there are also restrictions on the maximum amounts of some of the elements of tier 2 capital.
2. Every asset is assigned a risk weight which largely reflects the credit risk of the counter-party; the lower the risk, the lower the weight, and effectively, therefore, the less capital the bank is required to hold. There are five categories of risk weights: 0, 10, 20, 50 and 100 per cent. Low risk assets such as notes and coin, gold, deposits with the RBA, and Commonwealth Government securities not exceeding maturities of twelve months, are assigned a risk weight of zero. Assets such as Commonwealth Government securities with maturities exceeding twelve months, and State Government securities, are given a 10 per cent weight; assets such as claims on other banks are given a 20 per cent weight; mortgages on residential properties are given a 50 per cent weight; and assets such as bank premises and loans to companies are given a 100 per cent weight.

---

[35] PAR replaced the Liquid Assets and Government Securities Convention in May 1985.
[36] In the past, banks had access to a lender-of-last-resort facility from the RBA. If a bank fell below its minimum liquidity ratio it could draw on this facility. However, this was withdrawn when the PAR was introduced. As a result, if a bank is in danger of breaching the PAR it must acquire the requisite prime assets in the market at market rates.
[37] Subordinated debt has a lower ranking for payment in the event of the issuer being placed in liquidation.

In addition to assets, off-balance-sheet items are also brought into the calculation of risk-weighted assets. These items include standby letters of credit, guarantees, and derivative instruments. Each such item is converted to an on-balance-sheet equivalent, risk-weighted accordingly, and then included in the calculation of total risk-weighted assets.
3. The capital adequacy ratios are calculated as follows:
   (a) tier 1 capital/total risk-weighted assets;
   (b) total capital/total risk-weighted assets.

## OTHER ASPECTS OF RBA PRUDENTIAL SUPERVISION OF BANKS

The RBA imposes a range of other prudential controls on banks. This includes limits on ownership of banks. In general a single shareholding should not exceed 10 per cent of a bank's equity. Banks are also constrained in that their subsidiaries should generally be in the finance industry and should not be large relative to the parent bank.

Banks are also subject to exposure limits on large loans and on foreign exchange transactions. In addition, banks are required to provide the RBA with extensive data on their activities and on their management systems. Moreover, each bank's external auditor provides an annual report to the RBA on the quality of the bank's financial systems.

These controls are typically less precise than the ratio-based controls discussed earlier and banks may apply to the RBA to modify the requirements if circumstances warrant. However, if a bank does not comply with the RBA's decisions, penalties including a higher capital adequacy ratio could be applied.

**APPENDIX 7.3**

# AUTHORISED SHORT-TERM MONEY MARKET DEALERS

The authorised short-term money market dealers as at April 1993 were as follows:
Australian Gilt Discount Limited, NSW
Colonial Mutual Discount Company Limited, NSW
CS First Boston Australia Discount Limited, Victoria
F.R. Australian Discount Limited, ACT
Potter Warburg Discount Limited, Victoria
Rothschild Australia Discount Limited, NSW
Schroders Australia Discount Limited, NSW
Short Term Discount Limited, NSW

Source: *Reserve Bank of Australia Press Release*, Authorised Money Market Dealers, 20 April 1993

# CHAPTER 8

# SOURCES OF SHORT-TERM DEBT

## 8.1 INTRODUCTION

In this chapter and in Chapters 9 and 10, we discuss the methods by which a company may finance its assets. In this chapter we discuss short-term debt. Chapter 9 covers equity and Chapter 10 covers long-term debt. Leasing is considered in more detail in Chapter 19 and foreign currency loans are considered in Chapter 21.

Short-term debt is defined as debt due for repayment within a period of 12 months. Australian companies may borrow for short periods through trade credit or through the short-term money market; alternatively, intermediaries such as banks and finance companies also provide short-term debt.

## 8.2 TRADE CREDIT

When a company sells goods or services on credit it acquires an asset generally referred to as either *accounts receivable* or *debtors*. Similarly, when a company purchases goods or services on credit, it incurs a debt, generally referred to as either *accounts payable* or *creditors*. By allowing the purchaser time to pay, the seller in effect lends the purchase price to the purchaser. There are no direct charges for this service and trade credit therefore provides a readily available source of finance that, from the viewpoint of the purchasing company, will normally appear to be cheap—perhaps even 'free'.

In Australia, trade credit provides about 50 per cent of companies' short-term financial needs.[1] However, there is a fairly wide variation between industries in the use of trade credit. At one extreme, accounts payable provide less

---

[1] All percentages in this paragraph were calculated from information contained in *Reserve Bank of Australia Bulletin*, April 1988.

than 10 per cent of total liabilities and shareholders' funds of companies in the mining industry. At the other extreme, in the retail trade industry, accounts payable provide about 20 per cent of total liabilities and shareholders' funds of companies.

An important characteristic of trade credit as a source of funds is its ready availability. As a company's credit purchases increase, the amount of trade credit also increases. For example, a company that sells a product with a peak demand in December will need to plan for this peak by building up its inventory of that product beforehand. As a result, the company will require more short-term funds to finance this temporary increase in its inventory. As the company increases its purchases of supplies, it receives more trade credit which, in turn, reduces the amount of short-term debt it needs to obtain elsewhere. Nevertheless, the amount of trade credit a company can obtain is limited because each of the company's suppliers will normally place a limit on the maximum amount of trade credit to be granted to each customer.

A particular company will generally be offered trade credit on the same terms as other companies with a similar credit rating. For example, companies may be allowed one month to pay their accounts. However, there are instances where the bargaining power of the purchaser outweighs that of the supplier to such an extent that the purchasing company can influence the credit terms it receives.

Although a purchasing company cannot control the *amount* of trade credit it is offered by its suppliers, it does have considerable control over the *timing* of the payment of its accounts. For example, management of the purchasing company may delay paying accounts until after the due date, in order to avoid the use of other, more expensive, forms of short-term finance. Companies that do this when cash is short are said to be 'stretching' their accounts payable. However, the practice of stretching accounts payable may involve some costs for a company. First, direct costs may be incurred if creditors impose 'book-keeping charges' when accounts are paid after the due date. Secondly, payment after the due date may damage the company's credit rating and consequently may make finance more difficult and/or more expensive to obtain in the future. Thirdly, where the credit terms include a discount, there is an opportunity cost for failure to pay within the discount period. In some cases this cost can be very high, as the following example illustrates.

## Example 8.1

Consider the case where company A sells goods for $1000 to company B and offers credit terms of 2/10, $n/30$ (that is, a 2 per cent discount for payment within 10 days, otherwise full payment is required within 30 days). Assuming that it does not wish to stretch its accounts payable, B has two options:
1. it can pay $980 within 10 days of receiving an invoice of its account from A; or
2. it can choose to wait 30 days and then pay $1000.

If B takes the second option it will incur a cost of $20 to extend the use of trade credit for a further 20 days. This is equivalent to an effective annual interest rate of:

$$\left(1 + \frac{20}{980}\right)^{\frac{365}{20}} - 1 = 44.6 \text{ per cent}$$

This calculation implies that B should take the discount unless it can earn at an annual rate of at least 44.6 per cent on an alternative use of its funds. Forgoing the discount for early payment is, therefore, an expensive form of finance. However, if B's management decides to stretch its accounts payable, the cost is lower because it is spreading the discount forgone over a longer period.[2]

## 8.3 THE SHORT-TERM MONEY MARKET AS A SOURCE OF SHORT-TERM DEBT

### 8.3.1 MAIN FEATURES OF THE MARKET

In the short-term money market, large companies, financial institutions, government bodies and others borrow and lend for short periods. The sums involved in each transaction are large and the competition intense. The short-term money market is not a physical place. Participants trade from their own offices and keep in touch by electronic means. Some of the lending in this market is 'direct' in that companies with excess funds may lend to companies seeking funds. Transactions of this kind occur in the intercompany market, which is part of the short-term money market. Loans available from this market are discussed in Section 8.3.2. Much of the lending in the short-term money market is, however, 'indirect' in that the funds are lent by financial intermediaries who have obtained the funds by accepting deposits from companies and others with excess funds.

The links between companies with a short-term cash surplus and companies with a short-term cash requirement are shown in Figure 8.1.

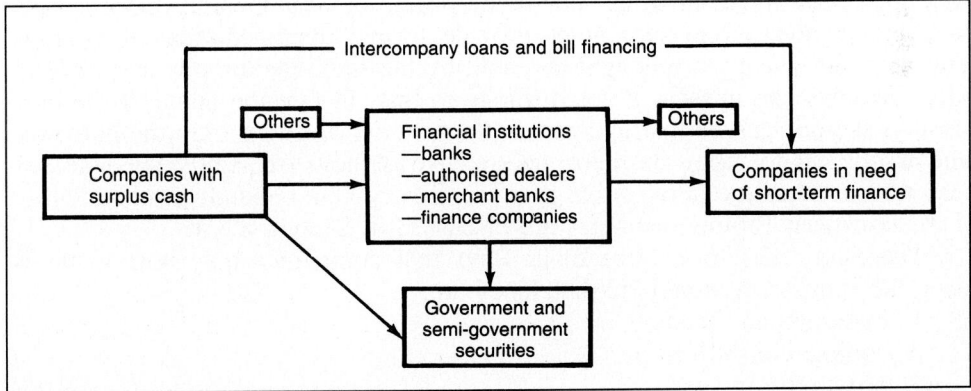

**Fig. 8.1** *The short-term money market*

---

2 For example, if a company is offered credit terms of 2/10, n/30, and chooses not to pay until 1 month after the end of the credit period, the equivalent annual cost of the cash discount forgone is 15.9 per cent, rather than the 44.6 per cent if the account is paid at the end of the credit period.

As shown in the figure, an investment by companies in government or semi-government securities does not result in a cash flow to other companies. However, it can be seen that other investments by companies with a cash surplus will flow, in large measure, to companies that require cash. For example, banks and finance companies accept short-term funds *from* companies and make short-term loans *to* companies. For banks, a major form of lending is the provision of overdrafts, while for finance companies it is the provision of more specialised financial services such as leases and instalment credit.

Financial institutions do not deal solely with companies. A further aspect of Figure 8.1 is the importance of the 'others' who either supply funds *to*, or obtain funds *from*, the financial institutions that form part of the short-term money market. For example, the banks rely on deposits from individuals for a large proportion of their funds, while individuals, as well as companies, borrow from the banks. Finance companies obtain most of their funds by issuing debentures and unsecured notes to which the public subscribes, while they provide credit to consumers and business by means of instalment credit, leasing, and the provision of other financial services. The authorised dealers receive a large proportion of their funds from banks and lend only a small proportion of their funds to companies. Authorised dealers lend mostly to government. By comparison, merchant banks receive a much greater proportion of their funds from companies, almost all of which is also lent to companies.

Trading in commercial bills is an important activity in the short-term money market. A company requiring short-term funds can issue (sell) a bill of exchange. The lending institution that discounts (buys) the bill can subsequently rediscount it with other institutions and/or companies. As the number of bills outstanding has grown, an active market in these bills has also grown. The process of bill financing is discussed in Section 8.3.3.

As an alternative to issuing commercial bills, companies can issue promissory notes (also referred to as 'one-name paper' or 'commercial paper'). Like commercial bills, promissory notes provide formal documentation of a short-term debt and usually are bought and sold by the same institutions that trade in bills. However, promissory notes differ from bills in that the name of the borrower is the only name that appears on the security and it is only the borrower who is obliged to repay the debt, irrespective of how frequently the note has been traded. Thus the default risk of a promissory note depends on the identity of the borrower. Promissory notes are discussed in Section 8.3.4.

There are, therefore, three main ways that companies may borrow funds using the short-term money market. They are:
1. intercompany loans;
2. commercial bills;
3. promissory notes.

### 8.3.2 INTERCOMPANY LOANS

The intercompany market, which involves a direct loan from one company to another, commenced in the period just before World War 2. However, the market was not very active until the early 1950s. The intercompany market became firmly established during 1960–61 when a credit squeeze caused financial managers to look beyond their traditional sources of finance. More recently, intercompany lending has grown from $8.5 billion in June 1989 to $10.4 billion in December 1992.[3]

All companies with idle cash balances may lend on the intercompany market. It has been suggested that the major lenders in the market are insurance offices, finance companies, and major retailers.[4] As most intercompany loans are unsecured, lending companies are usually prepared to lend only to large, profitable and financially secure companies. Lenders usually have a list of companies to whom they will lend. Finance companies and merchant banks also participate in this market.

An intercompany loan may be overnight, at 24-hour call, or for a fixed period. Overnight loans are also called 11.00 a.m. money as these loans are provided on the understanding that either the borrower or the lender may terminate the loan by giving notice by 11.00 a.m. on the following day. Alternatively, the loan may continue, but the interest rate is renegotiated each day.

The second category of intercompany loans is 24-hour loans, so named because after the first seven days these loans may be terminated or renegotiated on 24 hours' notice by either the borrower or the lender.

Intercompany fixed-term loans are rarely for terms of more than three months. Some loans for a fixed period may be allowed to continue at call after their due date.

The interest rate on an intercompany loan is generally higher than the yield on a Treasury Note, but lower than the overdraft rate. This is because Treasury Note yields are relatively low because of their status as risk-free securities, while the overdraft interest rate exceeds the intercompany rate because otherwise companies would find it profitable to use their overdraft to lend to other companies.

It is rare for security to be taken on an intercompany loan as the standing of the borrower is such that the risk of default is low. However, when security is required it usually is a direct charge over real assets or shares, a parent company guarantee, or a guarantee from a bank.

## 8.3.3 COMMERCIAL BILLS[5]

Before 1965 the provision of short-term finance via bills of exchange was largely confined to a number of finance companies. In January 1965 the Reserve Bank took steps to encourage the development of an active bills market. By 1970 this

---

3 *Source: Australian National Accounts, Financial Accounts*, December Quarter 1992, Table 15, Catalogue No. 5232.0.
4 *Australia's Financial and Economic Structure*, 4th edn, National Australia Bank, Melbourne, 1984.
5 For a detailed discussion of the Australian commercial bill market, see R.W. Peters, *The Commercial Bill Market in Australia*, Longman Cheshire, Melbourne, 1987.

objective had been largely achieved with trading banks,[6] authorised dealers, merchant banks and finance companies all playing important roles. The market continued to grow strongly but the size of the market began to level out in 1988 when there were important changes in bank regulation. Before 1988, bill finance did not attract Statutory Reserve Deposits (SRDs) [see Appendix 7.3] but in that year the SRD was replaced by the non-callable deposit (NCD), which is levied on a new base that includes bank-accepted bills. In addition, the new capital adequacy requirements for banks, also introduced in August 1988, were extended to apply to off-balance-sheet business, including bill endorsements by banks. Both of these changes reduced the benefits to the banks of lending through bill finance.

There are two basic types of bills of exchange, sometimes called the *trade bill* and the *accommodation bill*. A trade bill is normally created where there is an underlying trade debt. The purchaser will accept the trade bill, thereby allowing the issuer to discount the trade bill and receive immediate cash from the sale of goods, without waiting for payment by the purchaser. In an accommodation bill there is no underlying transaction in goods; it is purely a means of providing short-term finance. In this chapter, only accommodation bills are discussed. The trade bill is discussed again in Chapter 25. Both accommodation bills and trade bills can be traded in the bills market.

There may be up to three parties involved in the creation of a bill. They are referred to as the drawer, the acceptor (or drawee), and the discounter. The roles of the drawer and acceptor are explained later. The role of the discounter is to provide (lend) the funds. In principle the discounter could be any entity with funds to lend, but in practice it is usually a financial intermediary or some other financial institution. The discounter has the choice of either holding the bill until maturity, when payment will be received from the acceptor, or selling (rediscounting) the bill. However, if the bill is sold, the seller normally endorses the bill at the time of sale. This means that if the acceptor is unable to pay on the maturity date, an endorser may be obliged to pay a subsequent holder of the bill. Consequently, when a seller endorses a bill the seller has a contingent liability until the bill matures.

There are two ways of creating an accommodation bill:
1. A company wishing to borrow draws up a bill suitable to its needs.[7] The company (the drawer) first has to find an acceptor for the bill. The acceptor's role is to repay the face value of the debt at maturity. From the drawer's viewpoint, the acceptor is, in effect, guaranteeing the drawer's ability to repay the debt. After the bill has been accepted, the drawer has to find a discounter who, in exchange for the bill, will lend money to the

---

6 Prior to 1988, Australian banks were designated as either *trading* banks or *savings* banks. Essentially, trading banks provided financial services for business, while savings banks provided financial services for individuals. This distinction is no longer made.

7 These 'needs' refer to the funds it requires and the period for which it requires the funds. If the company wishes to raise, say, $1 million, it is often preferable for it to draw up smaller bills (for example, two of $500 000 rather than one with a face value of $1 million) because it may be easier to find parties willing to discount bills with a lower face value.

drawer. The acceptor and the discounter may be the same entity.

Figure 8.2 shows the steps in the creation of a bill where the acceptor and the discounter are different entities.

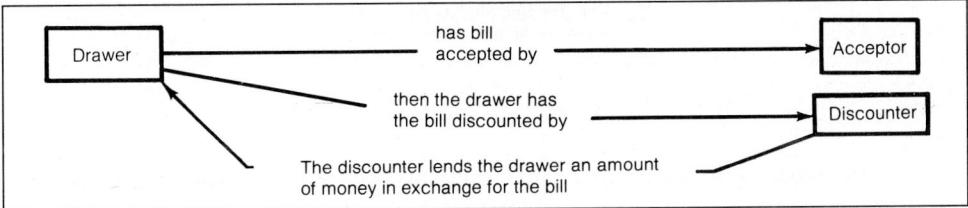

**Fig. 8.2**

The amount the drawer receives from the discounter depends on the face value of a bill and the rate at which it is discounted. For example, in exchange for a 90-day bill with a face value of $100 000 and a discount rate of 2 per cent per 90-day period, the drawer will receive $98 000 from the discounter. The yield is slightly more than 2 per cent, as it costs $2000 to borrow $98 000, which represents a yield of approximately 2.0408 per cent per 90-day period. The simple annualised yield is $(2000/98\,000) \times (365/90) = 8.277$ per cent per annum. For further details on calculating bill prices and yields (interest rates) see Section 3.2.4.

When the bill matures, the holder of the bill at that time will be repaid by the acceptor. The bill itself does not formally oblige the drawer to repay the acceptor. Therefore, when an entity agrees to accept a bill it will require an undertaking in writing from the drawer that the drawer will reimburse the acceptor for paying the bill on the maturity date. The normal process of repayment is illustrated in Figure 8.3.

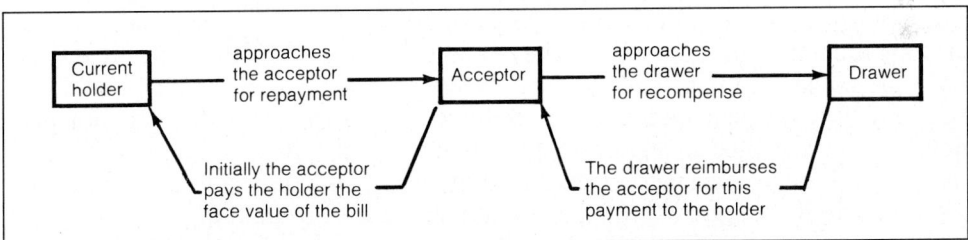

**Fig. 8.3**

2. Occasionally a bill is created by having a bill drawn and discounted by the entity lending the funds. In this case the borrower acts as acceptor, and hence is responsible for making the payment on the maturity date. Therefore the borrower has no 'guarantor' in this case. The drawer therefore lends funds to the acceptor and holds the bill as documentation of the debt. Figure 8.4 shows how such a bill is created.

When the bill reaches maturity, the acceptor pays the face value of the bill to the holder. An advantage of this form of bill is that no secondary

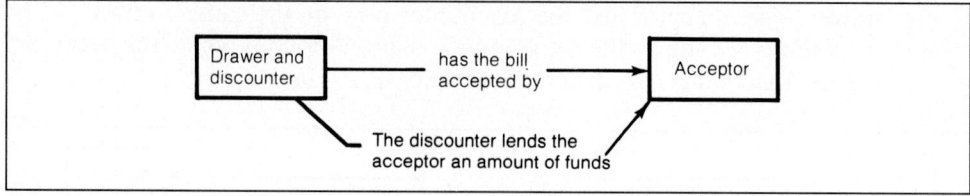

**Fig. 8.4**

agreement is required to ensure that the acceptor is reimbursed because the acceptor is the original borrower. The disadvantage is that there is no 'guarantor', whereas the bill form of contract is often used specifically to bring in a party to fill the role of guarantor.

Assuming that the bill does not change hands during its life, its repayment at maturity is as illustrated in Figure 8.5.

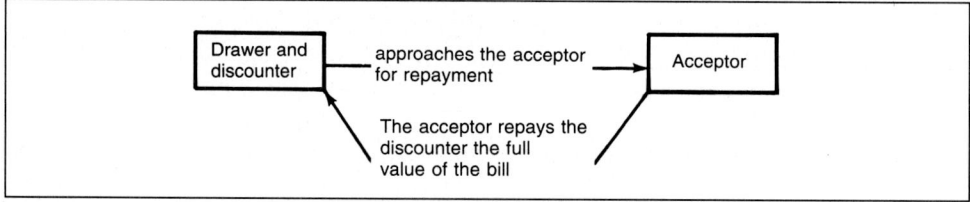

**Fig. 8.5**

The roles of the various institutions in the commercial bills market warrant further discussion. It has already been stated that banks act as acceptors and discounters. When a bank accepts a bill it is obliged to repay the bill at maturity. Banks also endorse commercial bills, which means that they 'put their name' to a bill already accepted by another party.[8] (For example, this is the normal procedure when a bill is sold in the secondary market.) In this case, the bank has an obligation to repay the bill if the acceptor, and in turn the drawer, do not repay the holder of the bill at maturity. While such a chain of events is unlikely, bank endorsement can increase the creditworthiness of a bill that has not previously been accepted or endorsed by a bank or other party with a high credit rating. A bill either accepted or endorsed by a bank is referred to as a bank bill. Table 8.1 shows the growth of the Australian bank bill market.

A typical bank bill usually takes the form shown in Figure 8.6. This type of bill is equivalent to the first type of bill discussed earlier.

Authorised dealers, merchant banks, bill acceptance companies and finance companies also accept and discount bills. Such bills are called non-bank bills because they have neither bank acceptance nor endorsement. A typical non-bank bill takes the form shown in Figure 8.7.

---

[8] At one time this was done physically. That is, the seller would sign the paper document that was the bill. Most transactions now occur through Austraclear which is a computerised central clearing house for bank bills, promissory notes, and other money market securities.

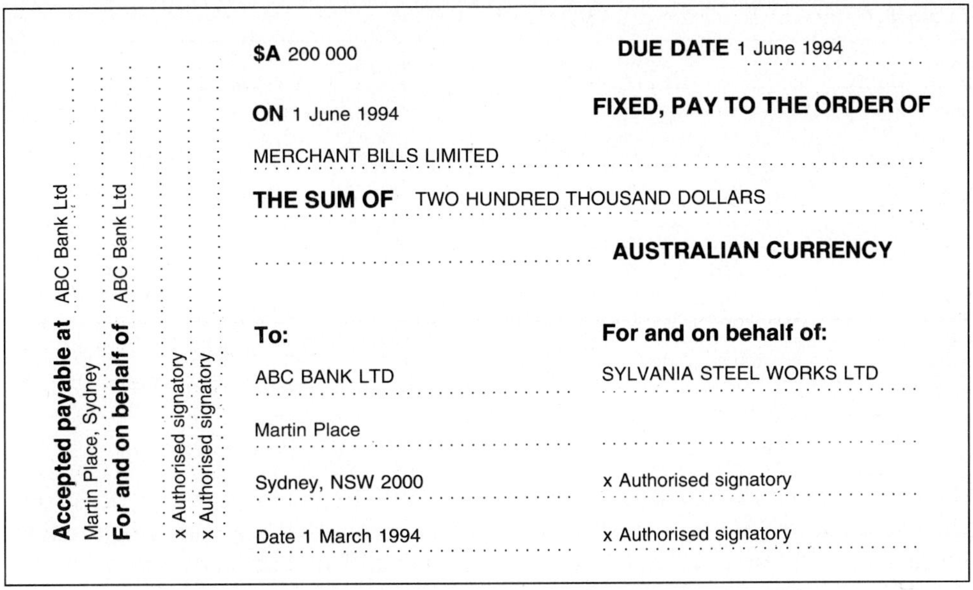

# SOURCES OF SHORT-TERM DEBT

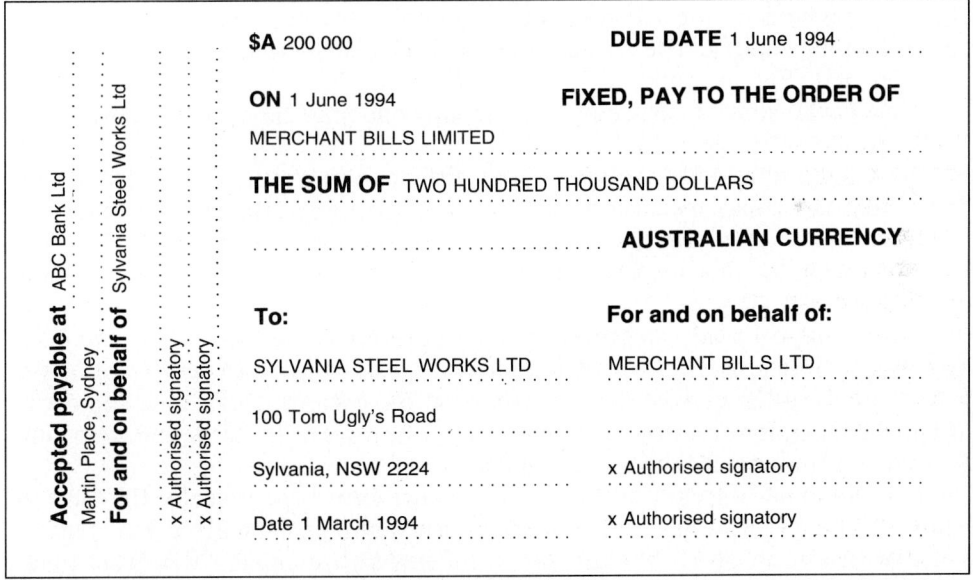

**Fig. 8.6** *Bank bill drawn by company, accepted by a bank and discounted by a merchant bank*

**Fig. 8.7** *A non-bank bill with a merchant bank as drawer and discounter*

A non-bank bill may be more difficult to discount in the bills market than a bank bill because it is generally regarded as an inferior quality bill. 'Quality' means the likelihood that the holder will be repaid when the bill matures, which largely depends on the financial stature of the drawer and the acceptor of the bill. In practice most bills have been accepted or endorsed by a bank.

**Table 8.1** *Bank bills outstanding ($m)*

| Date | Acceptances | Endorsements | Total |
|---|---|---|---|
| June 1986 | na | na | 28 396 |
| June 1987 | na | na | 36 609 |
| June 1988 | na | na | 61 403 |
| June 1989 | 58 846 | 8 257 | 67 103 |
| June 1990(a) | 60 893 | 7 372 | 68 265 |
| June 1991 | 60 988 | 5 289 | 66 277 |
| June 1992 | 59 302 | 3 766 | 63 068 |
| June 1993 | 58 758 | 2 677 | 61 435 |

*Source: Reserve Bank of Australia Bulletin*, Table C.7., September 1989 and Table B.12, September 1993.
(a) Break due to introduction of new data source for bank bills on issue.

Many companies do not restrict their use of bill financing to those occasions when they require funds to meet their immediate needs, but maintain a continuing bill facility with either a bank or a merchant bank. This bill facility may be one of two basic types:
1. A fully drawn facility, which provides a company with a specified amount for a specified period. In this case the company has to borrow the full amount, which is provided by issuing a series of bills. New bills are issued as the existing bills mature, until the agreed period of the facility expires. The interest rate is recalculated each time a new bill is issued. For example, a 3-year facility may be covered by six 180-day bills. In some instances partial repayment may be required during the period of the loan.
2. A revolving credit facility, which differs from a fully drawn facility, in that the company is permitted to draw on the facility as the funds are required, provided that it does not borrow more than the total agreed amount. In this respect a revolving credit facility is similar to a bank overdraft.

Within these broad categories, many variations are possible. For example, some bill facilities fix in advance the interest cost to the borrower, while others provide funds at the current market rate, or at the current market rate subject to an agreed maximum rate or 'cap'. Generally, however, the term and cost conditions for commercial bills are as follows:

*Term:* A company issues a bill to obtain a short-term loan. Usually the term of a bill is 90 days, 120 days, or 180 days, although occasionally a bill may be issued with a term of 12 months. Often, however, a company will want guaranteed access to short-term funding, and will seek a bill facility for, say, 3 years.
*Costs:* The costs of a bill facility include the fees for establishing and maintaining the facility, the charge for discounting the bill, and the acceptance fee. The establishment and maintenance fees reimburse the lender for the cost incurred in establishing and administering the facility. Typically these fees are expressed as a percentage of the amount of the facility. In addition the company incurs the cost of discounting the bill. As explained earlier, the effective cost to the

company is slightly higher than the discount rate.[9] At any given time, there is a market-determined discount rate (expressed as a yield) applicable to bills with the same term to maturity and creditworthiness. Although all bills that have been accepted and/or endorsed by a bank are normally called bank bills, there can be slight differences in yield, depending on the credit rating of the bank involved. Yields indicative of those applying to bank bills are shown in Table 8.2.

**Table 8.2** Yields for 90-day bank accepted bills[(a)]

| Date | % pa |
| --- | --- |
| June 1985 | 16.45 |
| June 1986 | 14.80 |
| June 1987 | 13.35 |
| June 1988 | 13.15 |
| June 1989 | 18.30 |
| June 1990 | 15.10 |
| June 1991 | 10.50 |
| June 1992 | 6.40 |
| June 1993 | 5.25 |

Source: Reserve Bank of Australia Bulletin, Table J1, August 1988 and Table F1, September 1993.
[(a)] Rates are an average of assessed daily market yields for the week ended last Wednesday of the month.

The third element of the cost of a bill facility is the acceptance fee. This fee is the acceptor's return for taking on the risks associated with the bill facility. The main risk is that the company will default on its obligations under the facility. The margin charged by the lender depends on the amount and term of the facility and the security given by the borrower.

For a borrowing company there are a number of advantages in choosing bill finance over other forms of short-term debt. The major advantage is access to funding sources that, without the creditworthiness provided by acceptance, would not be available. Another important advantage is the variety of bill facilities available, which means that bill funding provides flexibility for the borrower.

### 8.3.4 PROMISSORY NOTES

A promissory note market has existed in Australia for many years, although it has been an active market only since 1977. As mentioned earlier, promissory notes are negotiable instruments that differ from commercial bills in that only the borrowing company's name appears on the paper. Although the note is negotiable, it is not endorsed by anyone selling the note, so the borrower is the only party with an obligation to pay the face value at maturity. Therefore, as is the case in the intercompany market, only 'blue chip' companies (that is, large, reputable companies with a high credit rating) and government instrumentalities

---

[9] See Section 8.3.3 for a brief discussion. For more detail see Section 3.2.4.

are able to raise funds by issuing promissory notes. Issuers of promissory notes have included Shell Australia, BHP Finance, James Hardie Industries, and the Australian Wheat Board.

Promissory notes usually have short-term maturities within the range 30 days to 180 days, although other maturities are also possible. Promissory notes enable a company to tailor the period of the loan to suit its needs. However, if a company finds that it does not require the funds for the full period of the loan, it can repurchase the promissory notes by buying them at the market price.

Promissory note issues may be underwritten, and this may involve the use of both an underwriting syndicate and a tender panel. Banks, merchant banks, and other financial institutions are usually involved in these arrangements. The tender panel is given the first opportunity to purchase the promissory notes. If there is a shortfall in the amount of the issue purchased by the tender panel the balance is bought by the underwriting syndicate. Each member of the syndicate agrees that, if required by the issuer, it will purchase promissory notes up to a specified amount.

Promissory notes also offer certain advantages to both borrowers and lenders when compared with other forms of lending. For the lender, they have advantages over ordinary loans in that they are marketable. Also, they have the previously mentioned advantage over commercial bills that an entity selling a promissory note does not incur a contingent liability. For a borrower with a credit rating equal to that of a bank there may be few if any benefits associated with obtaining bank acceptance. Thus, for these borrowers, promissory notes may be an attractive alternative to bank bills. Because of the advantages that promissory notes offer both borrowers and lenders they have become very popular in recent years. At the end of December 1992 there was $20.5 billion in outstanding promissory notes held in Australia.[10]

## 8.4 BORROWING FROM BANKS

Banks are the most important institutions that lend to Australian companies. A bank will often provide a company with a funding package which includes more than one of the sources of finance discussed in this chapter. For example, a package may include an overdraft, a fully drawn advance, a bill acceptance and/or discount facility, foreign currency loans, and a promissory note underwriting facility. The major forms of short-term finance provided by banks are discussed in this chapter. Borrowing from finance companies is discussed in Section 8.5 and borrowing from merchant banks is discussed in Section 8.6.

### 8.4.1 BANK OVERDRAFT

An overdraft permits a company to run its current (cheque) account into deficit up to an agreed limit. The overdraft limit specifies the amount by which the company can overdraw its account. Strictly speaking the amount by which the

---

[10] *Source: Australian National Accounts, Financial Accounts,* December Quarter 1992, Table 17, Catalogue No. 5232.0.

company's current account is overdrawn is usually at call. This means that the bank can withdraw the overdraft facility at any time, and require repayment of the overdrawn amount. However, banks rarely exercise this right.

The cost of a bank overdraft includes the interest cost and fees. Interest rates are negotiated between the bank and the company and will depend on factors such as the company's creditworthiness and the purposes for which the overdraft is sought. The interest rate charged is normally on the basis of a margin above an indicator rate published from time to time by the bank. The Reserve Bank has the power to set maximum interest rates on bank overdrafts but, in practice, overdraft interest rates have been determined by market forces, following successive deregulation initiatives in the period 1976–85.

A company that borrows by bank overdraft has to pay interest only on the amount by which its account is overdrawn, not on the amount of the overdraft limit. The interest on an overdraft is calculated by applying the interest rate to the daily amount by which the account is overdrawn and is charged monthly in arrears. Fees will usually include an establishment fee and an account service fee to cover the bank's transaction costs. In addition a fee is charged on any unused portion of the overdraft limit. This fee reflects the costs to the bank of having to maintain liquid funds in case the borrower decides to draw extra funds. It can also be seen as a charge that reflects the value to the borrower of having the option to increase the amount borrowed.

The two major variables in an overdraft agreement are the overdraft limit and the interest rate. These are subject to negotiation between a bank and a company and the result will depend on factors such as the following:

### 1. THE BARGAINING POWER OF THE COMPANY

Since deregulation, there has been more competition between banks, and a company dissatisfied with its bankers is now more likely than in the past to change banks. In negotiating an overdraft agreement, both the bank and the company will be aware of what competing banks are likely to offer.

### 2. THE CURRENT AND FUTURE PROFITABILITY AND FINANCIAL POSITION OF THE COMPANY

A bank can obtain an indication of a company's profitability and financial position from its financial statements. In addition, a bank will usually require a cash budget to assist it in assessing the company's ability to service an overdraft. The bank will be particularly interested in the reasons for an overdraft application and the likely effects that providing an overdraft will have on the company's future profitability and financial position. Generally speaking, banks regard an overdraft as suitable for funding short-term assets.

### 3. THE SECURITY FOR AN OVERDRAFT

Although some companies may be granted an overdraft without any security, in most cases a bank will request security for an overdraft. Indeed, the terms of the overdraft may depend on the security a company can offer. In addition the bank may place other restrictions on the company. For example, in an effort to ensure that the company does not encounter short-term liquidity problems, the bank may require it to maintain some minimum current ratio.

After an overdraft has been granted, a company can draw on its current account until the overdraft limit is reached. The overdraft limit is reviewed by the bank at regular intervals. In general the company will be able to maintain the same overdraft limit from year to year unless its profitability or financial position has markedly deteriorated.

Traditionally banks have regarded an overdraft as a short-term loan available to finance a company's monthly or seasonal short-term asset requirements. In practice an overdraft may be used to finance temporarily the acquisition of longer-term assets while alternative methods of financing those assets are arranged. Therefore a profitable company can regard a significant proportion of its overdraft as a relatively long-term source of funds, even though the overdraft is theoretically at call. Although statistics on the percentage of overdraft limits used by companies are not published, it is likely that, on average, companies use approximately 70 per cent of their overdraft limits. As a result a considerable reduction in overdraft limits is required before the limits would be lower than the current level of most companies' overdrafts. For example, if a company has an overdraft limit of $100 000 and it is currently using only 55 per cent of its overdraft, that is, $55 000, a reduction in the limit by 20 per cent to $80 000 will not seriously affect the company's finance arrangements.

As a result, companies regard a large proportion of their overdrafts as a permanent source of funds and therefore suitable for financing the acquisition of long-term assets. There are several reasons why companies maintain unused overdraft limits. Companies require ready access to cash as a precaution against contingencies. An unused overdraft provides the necessary access. A second and related reason for companies maintaining unused overdraft limits developed with the growth in the intercompany market. Funds obtained on the intercompany market are generally at call. Consequently, if the lending company suddenly requires repayment, the borrowing company could be financially embarrassed. The risk of financial embarrassment is removed if the borrowing company has an adequate unused overdraft limit. In this case the unused portion of the overdraft acts as 'security' for the intercompany loan.

While overdrafts are an important form of short-term bank lending, there are a number of other forms of bank lending available to companies, including fully drawn advances, commercial bill finance, short-term mortgages, and lease finance.

### 8.4.2 FULLY DRAWN ADVANCES

Where a company needs medium-term or long-term debt finance, a bank will lend by making a fully drawn advance rather than an overdraft. With a fully drawn advance a bank lends funds for a fixed period. Generally the length of this period is between 3 and 10 years. However, early repayment can normally be arranged which means that fully drawn advances may be used to provide short-term funding. The full amount of the loan is usually borrowed immediately it is approved[11] and it is repaid by regular instalments over the agreed term of the advance. The regular instalments may be interest only with the principal repayable at the end of the loan period, or the instalments may include both interest and principal repayments. The timing of instalments will usually be at equal intervals but this may be modified to reflect the borrower's cash flows.

The interest rate on a fully drawn advance may be fixed for the full life of the loan but is usually linked to the bank's indicator rate, and thus will vary from time to time.

### 8.4.3 Bills of Exchange[12]

A bank may also provide a company with a bill discount or acceptance facility. With a bill discount facility a bank undertakes to discount (buy) bills of exchange drawn by the company up to a specified amount. That is, the bank promises to lend up to the specified amount. From the bank's point of view the advantage of this method of lending is that it holds a marketable security in the form of the bill, which it can later sell if it wishes. Thus, while the bank is committed to providing the funds initially, it is not committed to providing the funds for the full term of the bill. With a bank acceptance facility the bank agrees to act as an acceptor of bills issued by a company up to a specified amount. In effect the bank guarantees borrowing by a company up to that amount. This makes it relatively easy for the company to borrow elsewhere in the capital market by selling bills.

The use of bills of exchange has become a popular method of short-term borrowing by companies. However, this was not always the case. Until the early 1970s bank lending was mostly by overdraft. However, since then the banks have reduced their emphasis on overdrafts and have substantially increased their lending in other forms, including lending by way of bills. Since 1988 this trend has steadied. The growth in bank bill finance was shown in Table 8.1.

### 8.4.4 Finance Leases

In economic terms a finance lease is a loan made to enable the acquisition of a particular asset, usually a piece of equipment such as a car, truck, or machine. The term of a typical finance lease is four or five years and thus a finance lease has a term that exceeds the definition of 'short'. An important feature of a finance lease is that, in legal terms, ownership of the asset remains with the lender, who then allows the borrower to use the asset on a long-term basis in return for lease payments. Responsibility for the operation, maintenance, and insurance of the asset falls on the borrower. Thus, while the legal form of the contract is that of a lease, the economic substance is that of a loan. During the past 25 years there has been rapid growth in leasing. In addition to providing funds via traditional finance leases, banks have also participated as equity partners in leveraged leases and partnership leases. Finance leases are discussed in detail in Chapter 19.

---

[11] If funds are not borrowed immediately, an additional commitment fee will usually be charged.
[12] The characteristics of bills of exchange were discussed in Section 8.3.3.

## 8.5 Borrowing from finance companies

Finance companies are important lenders to Australian businesses. A brief survey is now given of the sources of short-term finance they provide.

### 8.5.1 Loans through the short-term money market

In discussion of the short-term money market we noted that finance companies lend on short term to companies, and also provide funds through the commercial bills market. However, this form of lending by finance companies is relatively minor.

### 8.5.2 Factoring and accounts receivable finance

Factoring allows a company to raise funds by selling its accounts receivable to a financier, called a *factor*, who is then responsible for collecting the debts. If the debts are factored *without* recourse, the factor bears the cost of any defaults. If the debts are factored *with* recourse, the factor can claim reimbursement from the selling company if a debtor defaults. The benefits of factoring include both the access to finance and the reduction in the cost of debt collection.

Alternatively, a company may raise funds by borrowing against the security of its accounts receivable. In this case the company gains funding but retains the role of debt collection and bears the costs of defaults.

### 8.5.3 Inventory loans

An inventory loan is another form of finance provided by finance companies. Although the inventory of any durable item may be financed by this means, the bulk of this form of lending has been used to finance the inventory of motor vehicle retailers.[13] This form of lending is known as floor-plan or wholesale finance and it makes up a significant proportion of finance company lending. The interest rate charged on inventory loans is based on the 180-day bank bill rate plus a margin, with the size of the margin varying with the size of the loan. For small loans of, say, $100 000, the rate of interest will generally be 1 per cent higher than on large loans in excess of $500 000.

### 8.5.4 Short-term mortgages or bridging finance

Bridging finance refers to a short-term loan, usually in the form of a mortgage, used to 'bridge' a short period of time. Often this need arises from the timing of a series of transactions. For example, a property investor may wish to sell one building and use the sale proceeds to buy another building but, unfortunately, the timing of the transactions is such that the payment for the second building must be made, say, a month before the sale proceeds from the first are available.

---

[13] For a detailed discussion of inventory loans, see B. Mellare & R. Willoughby, 'Finance Company Finance', in R. Bruce et al. (Eds), *Handbook of Australian Corporate Finance*, 4th edn, Butterworths, Sydney, 1991.

Thus a loan is required to bridge this gap of one month. During this period the investor will own both properties, and if necessary both may therefore be mortgaged to secure the bridging loan.

### 8.5.5 INSTALMENT CREDIT

Instalment credit is the traditional form of lending by finance companies. Although instalment credit is best known as a form of consumer finance it is also used by some companies to finance the purchase of plant and machinery. Instalment credit as a form of company finance is commonly known as commercial hire purchase, and is discussed in Chapter 19.

### 8.5.6 FINANCE LEASES

Lease financing is mentioned at this stage only to emphasise that finance companies are the institutions most actively involved in providing this form of lending. Finance leases are discussed in detail in Chapter 19.

## 8.6 BORROWING FROM MERCHANT BANKS

Merchant banks may lend to companies requiring short-term finance. This lending may be at call or for a fixed period. In addition the loan agreement may provide for the interest rate on a loan to vary with other short-term interest rates. It is also usual for a merchant bank to require inclusion of a clause in the loan agreement giving it the right to convert its cash loan to a commercial bill arrangement. This permits the merchant bank, in the event that it requires cash, to convert the loan into a commercial bill, which it can discount to raise funds.

Short-term loans from merchant banks may be unsecured. However, companies may be required to provide security in the form of a charge over assets, or a guarantee by a bank or overseas parent company.

## SELECTED REFERENCES

Hunt, B. & Terry, C., *Financial Instruments and Markets*, Thomas Nelson, South Melbourne, Australia, 1993.
Lewis, M.K. & Wallace, R.H., Eds, *The Australian Financial System*, Longman Cheshire, Melbourne, 1993.
McGrath, M., *Financial Institutions, Instruments and Markets in Australia*, McGraw-Hill, Sydney, 1994.
Peters, R.W., *The Commercial Bill Market in Australia*, Longman Cheshire, Melbourne, 1987.

## QUESTIONS

1. *Trade credit is a spontaneous source of funds that is largely beyond the control of the purchasing company.* Discuss.
2. Define an *intercompany loan*. What are the normal terms of such loans?
3. Discuss recent developments in the commercial bills market in Australia and evaluate its importance as a source of short-term finance.
4. Describe the roles of the drawer, acceptor, and discounter of a commercial bill.
5. What is an *accommodation bill*? Describe how such a bill is created and subsequently traded.

6. *A bank bill is considered to be a much better quality paper than a non-bank bill.* Discuss the significance of this statement for both the borrower and the lender.
7. Distinguish between a bank-accepted bill and a bank-endorsed bill.
8. To raise $97 000, a company decides to draw up a commercial bill with a face value of $100 000, payable in 180 days. What is the implicit simple interest rate (yield) on the bill? What is the implicit effective annual interest rate on the bill?
9. How does a promissory note differ from a commercial bill?
10. What are the advantages of borrowing by means of a promissory note?
11. Discuss the factors that affect the terms of a bank overdraft negotiated by a company.
12. *A bank overdraft provides a company with a flexible source of funds.* Discuss the significance of this flexibility for the financial manager and the difficulties it causes the banks.
13. Describe the major types of bank lending other than overdraft.

**CHAPTER 9**

# SOURCES OF LONG-TERM FINANCE: EQUITY

## 9.1 INTRODUCTION

Sources of long-term finance are discussed in this chapter (equity finance) and in Chapter 10 (long-term debt). In this chapter, several ways of issuing shares are considered, giving most attention to public issues, 'rights' issues, and private issues. In addition, retained profits as a form of equity finance is discussed. Consideration of preference shares and convertible securities is deferred to Section 10.6 because an understanding of these sources of finance can be achieved more easily after the characteristics of equity and debt are understood.

## 9.2 GENERAL CHARACTERISTICS OF ORDINARY SHARES

A limited liability company is incorporated with an authorised share capital divided into ordinary shares. An ordinary share gives the holder ownership of a proportion of the equity of the company. If a company has 100 000 issued shares and an investor has purchased 1000, the investor owns 1 per cent of the net assets of the company. This does not mean that the investor can exercise ownership rights with respect to specific assets of the company. However, when dividends are paid, or if the company is placed into liquidation, the investor has the right to receive 1 per cent of the payments made to ordinary shareholders.

Shares also have a *par value*. For example, a company's authorised share capital may be $10 million, comprising ten million shares, each having a par value of $1.[1] In this case, no more than ten million shares can be issued, although, if necessary, the company's authorised capital can later be increased with the

---

[1] P. Lipton & A. Herzberg, *Understanding Company Law*, 5th edn, Law Book Company, Sydney, 1993, pp. 77 and 179. See also Section 117(1)(b) of the *Corporations Law*.

213

approval of its shareholders. The par value of $1 means that the company cannot issue shares at a price less than $1 without the approval of its shareholders and the Courts.[2] However, it is free to issue shares at a price greater than $1. In this case, the shares are said to be issued at a **premium**. For example, it may offer shares with a par value of $1 at an issue price of $2.50 fully paid on subscription. In this case the shares are fully paid and issued at a premium of $1.50. The company may also issue shares which are partly paid. In this case the shares may be issued with $1 payable on application, to be followed by two calls of 75 cents each, payable on dates which may be specified. In this case, the shares remain partly paid until the two calls have been paid.

The term **limited liability** means that the liability of a shareholder is limited to any amount unpaid on the shares held.[3] For example, if an investor purchases shares with an issue price of $2.50 per share and $1.75 has been paid on each share, the investor's liability for future payments is limited to 75 cents per share. Consequently, if the company is placed into liquidation and has insufficient cash to pay its creditors, holders of its partly-paid shares can be required to contribute up to 75 cents per share towards the payment of creditors.

If a company is placed into liquidation, ordinary shareholders have a residual claim on the proceeds from the sale of the company's assets. As a result they are more likely than other investors to lose their investment if the company fails and they are therefore said to provide the company's risk capital. To compensate for this risk, investors in ordinary shares expect a rate of return which is greater than they could obtain by lending to the company.

As part owners of the company, ordinary shareholders exert a degree of control over its management through their right to elect members of the Board of Directors. The Board, which is usually elected at the Annual General Meeting, has ultimate control over the day-to-day operations of the company. Usually, shareholders have one vote for each share held.[4] The right of shareholders to elect the Board of Directors gives them some control over the company's operations. However, in practice their control is limited because the Board of Directors is generally able to muster sufficient votes, including proxies, to ensure that its members are re-elected at the Annual General Meeting.[5] Therefore when a new issue of ordinary shares is being considered, the Board of Directors will take into account the possible effects of the issue on control.

The majority of companies listed on the Australian Stock Exchange (ASX) are limited liability companies. However, because of their high rate of failure, many exploration and mining companies are likely to have difficulty in raising

---

[2] See Section 190 of the *Corporations Law*. However, under Section 194, a company may apply for a court order validating an issue of shares that has been made improperly.

[3] Lipton & Herzberg, op cit, p. 248. See also section 516 of the *Corporations Law*.

[4] The voting rights of a company's shareholders must be specified in its Articles of Association—see 3rd Schedule, Table A of the *Corporations Law*, especially Clause 2. For companies listed on the Australian Stock Exchange, the form of the voting rights is specified in Section K of the Exchange's *Listing Rules*.

[5] As many shareholders do not attend the Annual General Meeting, the right to vote by proxy is provided. Voting by proxy involves a shareholder assigning to another person the right to vote on resolutions at the Annual General Meeting.

share capital if they have limited liability. Potential investors may not be prepared to subscribe for partly-paid shares which require them to make subsequent payments in the event of the company's failure. An alternative is for such companies to be formed as no-liability companies which means that shareholders have no obligation for unpaid calls.

### 9.2.1 THE CONCEPT OF *PAR VALUE*

It has already been mentioned that every share issued by an Australian company must have a stated par value. There has been much criticism of the par value concept and there is very little evidence to suggest that it serves any useful purpose.[6] A major criticism of par value relates to its use as the basis for many financial calculations. Its use in this way is likely to cause confusion. For example, a company's dividend rate is often expressed as a percentage of the par value of each share. Therefore, a 5 cent dividend on a 50 cent par value share is often expressed as a dividend rate of 10 per cent. However, if the current market price of the shares is $5, the dividend yield is only 1 per cent. Therefore, a dividend rate expressed as a percentage of par value is misleading. Similarly, other measures such as the rate of return on paid-up capital and the ratio of debt to equity based on paid-up capital, are also misleading.

## 9.3 THE FLOTATION OF A PUBLIC COMPANY

When a company first invites the public to subscribe for shares it is usual to refer to this as *floating* the company. A company undertaking a float may be either a new company or an existing private company. There are several reasons why a private company may be floated, including the owners' wish to realise a capital gain.

A company making its first issue of ordinary shares to the public will usually apply for stock exchange listing, which means that shareholders in the company can sell their shares on the exchange.[7] To obtain listing, the company must ensure that its proposed capital structure satisfies the requirements for listing on the ASX. The most important requirements are that the issue price of the shares must be at least 20 cents and there must be a minimum of 500 shareholders, each subscribing for shares with a value of at least $2000.[8] The ASX sets these conditions in an effort to ensure that there will be an active market in the company's shares after they are listed.

An alternative to making a public issue of ordinary shares is for the company to issue shares to institutional investors. This is known as a **private issue**. It is not likely that a company undertaking a float will make a private issue, because

---

[6] The Companies and Securities Law Review Committee Report, 'Shares of No Par Value and Partly-Paid Shares', issued in 1990, recommended amendment of legislation to allow any company to issue no-par-value shares.

[7] An alternative way to become a listed public company is by a 'back-door listing'. This involves an unlisted company taking over a company that is listed on the stock exchange.

[8] These listing requirements relate to an industrial company. They are set out in detail in Section 1 of the *Listing Rules*, Australian Stock Exchange.

it is unlikely either to receive institutional support, or to attract the number of shareholders required for it to be listed on the stock exchange.[9] Therefore the flotation of a company generally involves a public issue of ordinary shares.

## 9.4 INITIAL PUBLIC OFFERING OF ORDINARY SHARES

When a company is to 'go public' it is usual for its promoters to seek the assistance of a financial institution that specialises in arranging company flotations. Typically this has been the function of the larger broking houses, although merchant banks have also established departments which provide this service. Both types of institution can advise on the price of the issue, underwrite the issue, and handle the sale of the shares.

### 9.4.1 PRICING A NEW ISSUE

Deciding on the price of a new issue is a very difficult task. The issuer faces potential problems if the offer price is set too high or too low. If the price is set too high, few investors will want to subscribe and the underwriter will have to meet the shortfall. In turn, this outcome will have a negative effect on the market price of the shares after they are listed. If the price is set too low the owners will suffer an opportunity loss because they would have received a higher payment if the new issue had been made at a higher price. The available evidence suggests that, on average, new issues trade initially at a price above the issue price. In this sense they are 'underpriced'. However, the extent of the underpricing varies considerably from case to case.[10]

The task of setting the issue price is particularly difficult when the company has just been formed as there is no earnings record. Where the company has previously operated as a private company the task is not as difficult because past earnings may be a guide to future earnings. The most common approach to pricing used by advisers is to use historic earnings as the basis for estimating future earnings per share. The adviser will also examine the price/earnings ratio (the market price divided by the earnings per share) of existing companies in the same or similar industries. Forecasts of future earnings per share and the information on price/earnings ratios will then be used to provide the adviser with a possible range of issue prices for the company's shares. For example, if a company is expected to earn 10 cents per share and the price/earnings ratios of similar companies are between 9 and 14, this suggests an issue price of between 90 cents and $1.40. If institutions are enthusiastic about the proposed issue, the issue price may be set close to $1.40. In contrast, if there is little interest in the

---

[9] Institutional investors are generally reluctant to purchase shares in a company unless there is evidence of past profitability. Companies that have operated successfully as private companies for a number of years are in a better position to attract the necessary institutional support to make a private issue feasible.

[10] For further discussion of underpricing, see K. Rock, 'Why New Issues are Underpriced', *Journal of Financial Economics*, 1986, pp. 187–212; and for Australian evidence, see F.J. Finn & R. Higham, 'The Performance of Unseasoned New Equity Issues-cum-stock Exchange Listings in Australia,' *Journal of Banking and Finance*, September 1988, pp. 333–51.

issue, the issue price may be set closer to the lower end of the range. As is evident from the above description, use of this approach to set the issue price involves considerable judgement.[11]

A typical fixed price offer is open for several weeks and consequently the success of the offer is subject to general movements in share prices during that period. For example, if the general level of share prices increases significantly during that period, it is likely that the fixed price will be too low. However, if share prices decrease significantly during that period, investors may regard the fixed price as being too high, and the issue will close under-subscribed.

In some countries it is common practice when pricing a new issue to use techniques that seek the views of market participants. These techniques are known as *pre-marketing*. In the United States it is common to issue a document, popularly referred to as a 'red herring' prospectus, which provides an indicative price range rather than a single fixed price and includes indicative dates for closing the offer and issuing the shares. Over a period of three to four weeks the adviser collects bids at various prices and these bids are then used to set the issue price. Once the price is set, the shares are sold immediately to those who have already indicated a willingness to purchase at this or a higher price. Therefore, trading in the shares can commence almost immediately. In the United Kingdom, a similar approach is frequently used, with the final price being set on the basis of the market's response to what in the UK is referred to as a 'pathfinder' prospectus.

Techniques of this kind were first used in Australia by the New South Wales Government when it sold the Government Insurance Office (GIO) in 1992. In this case an offer was made to the general public at a provisional price of $2.40 per share. However, at the same time institutions were invited to bid for shares at prices between $2.10 and $2.40. The final price for all the shares was to be set at the level at which all the shares offered to the institutions would be sold (that is, the market clearing price for the institutional shares). If this price was less than $2.40, the price at which the public had been invited to subscribe, subscribers would have received a rebate. In fact, there was a high demand for GIO shares and the final price was the original maximum of $2.40. Since the GIO issue, the Woolworths float and the second issue of shares in the Commonwealth Bank have been made on a similar basis. It seems likely that this type of technique will be used more frequently, particularly in the case of very large issues.

With a fixed price offer, once the terms have been set the adviser usually ensures that the proposed offer satisfies all relevant legal requirements and assists in preparing the offer document (usually a prospectus),[12] ensures that stock exchange listing requirements are met, registers the prospectus with the Australian Securities Commission (ASC), and markets the shares to institutional and private investors. The costs of preparing the prospectus include legal fees,

---

11 See also Chapter 12, where the effect of alternative methods of financing on share price is discussed in greater detail.
12 All persons involved in preparing a prospectus, including experts and advisers, are liable for any false or misleading statements attributable to them.

accounting fees and the cost of printing. The total costs of the advisory services, including the costs of preparing a prospectus and obtaining stock exchange listing, can vary widely and usually represent between 3 and 5 per cent of the amount raised. If the promoters agree with the adviser's recommendations on the terms of the float the same adviser will be appointed to underwrite and handle the sale of the shares.

### 9.4.2 UNDERWRITING A NEW ISSUE

As previously indicated, with a fixed price offer the issuer is subject to the vagaries of the market during the period when the issue is being marketed. Typically the issuer will pass this risk on to an underwriter, although the need for an underwriter is significantly reduced if the issue has been pre-marketed. The obligations of the company and the underwriter are contained in the underwriting agreement. An underwriter is typically a broking house or merchant bank. The underwriter contracts to purchase all shares for which applications have not been received by the closing date of the issue.[13] In return, the underwriter charges a fee based on a fixed percentage of the amount to be raised by the issue. The fee is negotiated and is usually fixed at somewhere between 1 and 6 per cent of the issue price, with the average being about 3 per cent. The percentage charged will reflect the underwriter's perception of the difficulty of selling the issue and this in turn will be determined by factors such as the company's stature in the market, the price of the issue and general market conditions. The underwriting agreement is likely to include escape clauses that specify the circumstances under which the underwriter will be released from its obligations.[14]

An underwriter will frequently attempt to limit exposure to the risk of undersubscription by inviting other institutions to act as sub-underwriters. These institutions may include life and general insurance companies, banks, and superannuation funds. The role of the sub-underwriter is to take up a proportion of any undersubscription in return for a fee, paid by the underwriter, that is based on a fixed proportion of the issue price.[15]

### 9.4.3 BROKER TO A NEW ISSUE

If a broking house underwrites an issue of shares it will usually act as a selling agent for the issue. By promoting an issue, a broking house protects its interests as underwriter and also earns brokerage fees. Brokerage fees are negotiable and depend on factors such as the size of the issue, the status of the issuing company, and the period for which the issue is to remain open.

---

13 As a prospectus is operative for only 6 months, this is the maximum period of time before the closing date.
14 The escape clauses in an underwriting agreement relate to factors that would seriously affect demand for the shares, such as the outbreak of war.
15 The sub-underwriting fee is usually only slightly less than the underwriting fee. For example, if the underwriting fee was 3 per cent of the issue price, the sub-underwriting fee would usually be about 2.5 per cent of the issue price.

Brokerage fees are usually set between 1 and 2 per cent of the issue price. The larger broking houses are major underwriters, primarily because they have an established clientele prepared to subscribe for the issues they underwrite. In recent years the amount of underwriting by merchant banks has increased considerably. However, merchant banks have generally been at some disadvantage in selling the shares, as they may not have access to as many clients as the broking houses.[16] Therefore, where a merchant bank acts as the underwriter to an issue, it is frequently necessary for it to appoint brokers to assist in marketing the shares. In return the broker receives a commission which is subject to negotiation but is likely to be about 1 per cent of the issue price of the shares sold by the broker.

A typical feature of most Australian public issues is that they are generally open to all investors, the only requirement being that each application must be for a minimum number of shares. In some of the larger share issues, such as those by Woolworths and the Commonwealth Bank, quotas have been set for various categories of investors such as individuals, broking houses, Australian institutions and overseas institutions. In each case there has been a 'clawback' provision which has allowed for an increase in the allocation to individuals at the expense of institutions in the event of a sizeable oversubscription for the quota initially allocated to individuals. There are two reasons for having a clawback provision. The first is to encourage greater participation by individual investors. Another way in which this may be achieved is to set the issue price to individuals at a level below that set for institutions, subject to approval from the ASC and/or the ASX. The second is to encourage institutions to buy shares in the secondary market.

## 9.5 Subsequent Issues of Ordinary Shares

After a company has been floated, additional external finance will usually be required at some future date to finance expansion. Management has the choice of issuing more shares and/or borrowing. If it is decided to issue more shares, the issue will usually take the form of either a rights issue or a private issue.

### 9.5.1 Rights Issue

A rights issue is an issue of new shares to existing shareholders. Under the terms of a rights issue, shareholders receive the right to subscribe for additional shares in a fixed ratio to the number of shares already held. Provided that each shareholder accepts the offer, there is no dilution of any shareholder's ownership percentage in the company.

To illustrate the elements of a rights issue, assume that an investor holds 1000 shares which represent 1 per cent of a company's issued capital of 100 000 shares. If the company makes a rights issue that entitles each shareholder to

---

[16] Since deregulation of the broking industry in 1984, a number of merchant banks have bought into broking houses. For these merchant banks, at least, this problem can be avoided.

purchase one additional share for every four shares held, the shareholder is entitled to buy an extra 250 shares, thus increasing the shareholding to 1250. The percentage ownership of the shareholder in the company remains unchanged at 1 per cent because 1250/125 000 = 1 per cent.

With a rights issue, shareholders buy additional shares. The company, therefore has to set a **subscription price**. Traditionally the subscription price for a rights issue was set well below the current market price of the shares. Supposedly this was to ensure that shareholders exercised their rights. However, in recent years, companies have made rights issues with subscription prices much closer to (but, of course, still below) current market prices. Because the subscription price is below the current market price of the shares, the rights have a value. A shareholder usually has the opportunity to realise the value of the rights to the new shares by selling them on the stock exchange; that is, the rights are renounceable.

There is a formula, known as the *theoretical rights price* that can be used to estimate the value of a right. To develop this formula, suppose that a company makes a 1-for-$N$ renounceable rights issue at a subscription price of $S$ dollars per share. That is, each shareholder obtains the right to purchase one new share for every $N$ shares currently held and will pay $S$ dollars for each new share. All rights issues specify a date, called the **ex-rights date**. If an investor purchases shares in the company before the ex-rights date, the purchase is said to be **cum rights** and the investor *will* participate in the rights issue. The rights themselves may be sold separately from the shares on or after the ex-rights date. If an investor purchases shares on or after the ex-rights date the purchase is said to be **ex rights** and the investor *will not* participate in the rights issue.

Now assume that an investor purchases $N$ shares just before the ex-rights date. The cost of this purchase is therefore $NM$ where $M$ is the market price of a share cum rights. This investor is entitled to the right to purchase one new share. Exactly the same investment can be achieved by entering the market just after the shares begin trading ex rights and purchasing $N$ shares ex rights and also purchasing the right to one new share. This will cost $NX + R$, where $X$ is the market price of a share ex rights and $R$ is the market price of the right to purchase one new share. In the absence of any new information which causes prices to change, both investment strategies should cost the same. That is:

$$NM = NX + R \qquad (9.1)$$

If the subscription price is payable immediately, then the right to one new share can be converted to a new share by payment of the subscription price. Therefore, when the shares begin trading ex rights an investor could obtain a share either by buying the right to one new share at a cost of $R$ and then paying the subscription price of $S$, or by buying a share directly at a price of $X$. To prevent arbitrage, both investment strategies must cost the same. That is:

$$R + S = X \qquad (9.2)$$

Substituting Equation 9.2 into Equation 9.1, and rearranging, gives:

# SOURCES OF LONG-TERM FINANCE: EQUITY

$$R = \frac{N(M - S)}{N + 1} \quad (9.3)$$

Substituting Equation 9.3 into Equation 9.2, and rearranging, gives:

$$X = \frac{NM + S}{N + 1} \quad (9.4)$$

The prices that result from using Equations 9.3 and 9.4 are often referred to as the **'theoretical' rights price** and the **'theoretical' ex-rights share price**, respectively.

What is the effect of a rights issue on the value of an investment in shares? To answer this question, suppose that an investor holds $qN$ shares in a company which makes a rights issue. Before the ex-rights date the value of the investment is $qNM$. After the ex-rights date the investor has $qN$ shares each worth $X$, and $q$ rights each worth $R$. The ex-rights value of the investment $I$ is therefore:

$$I = qNX + qR \quad (9.5)$$

Substituting Equations 9.3 and 9.4 into Equation 9.5, the value of the investment is now:

$$I = qN \left[ \frac{NM + S}{N + 1} \right] + q \left[ \frac{N(M - S)}{N + 1} \right]$$

$$= \frac{qNM(N + 1) + qNS - qNS}{N + 1}$$

$$= qNM$$

According to this analysis the total value of the investment is unaffected. Because each shareholder now owns both shares and rights, the market value of the investment in shares must decrease: $qNX < qNM$. Of course this implies that $X < M$; that is, the ex-rights price per share is less than the cum-rights price per share. The value of the rights ($qR$ in this case) is therefore equivalent to a return of $qR$ dollars of capital to the shareholder. To make the same point in a slightly different way, the value of the rights just offsets the decline in the value of the shares. This is illustrated in Example 9.1.

### Example 9.1

Athol owns 1000 shares in Raven Enterprises Ltd (REL) whose current share price (cum rights) is $2 per share. REL makes a 1-for-4 rights issue with a subscription price of $1.40 per share. Athol wishes to calculate:
  (a) the value $R$ of the right to one new share;
  (b) the ex-rights share price $X$;
  (c) the value of his investment cum rights and ex rights.
In this case, $N = 4$, $M = \$2.00$ and $S = \$1.40$.
  (a) Using Equation 9.3, the value of the right to one new share is:

$$R = \frac{N(M-S)}{N+1}$$

$$= \frac{4(\$2.00 - \$1.40)}{4+1}$$

$$= 48 \text{ cents}$$

(b) Using Equation 9.4 the ex-rights share price is:

$$X = \frac{NM + S}{N+1}$$

$$= \frac{4(\$2.00 + \$1.40)}{4+1}$$

$$= \$1.88$$

(c) Cum rights, the investment is worth:

(1000)($2)
= $2000

Ex rights, the investment is worth:

(1000)($1.88) + (250)($0.48)
= $2000

This analysis relates to the value of an investment made at the time of the ex-rights date. It suggests that shareholders' wealth is not affected by the mere fact of a share beginning to trade on an ex-rights basis. In turn, this suggests that, of itself, a rights issue has no value to shareholders. This should not be a surprise. If a rights issue increased (decreased) shareholders' wealth we would expect rights issues to occur much more (less) frequently than they do.

However, this does not imply that the *announcement* of a rights issue may not affect shareholders' wealth. The major reason for the effect on shareholders' wealth is that the announcement of a rights issue can have information content. For example, US evidence suggests that the market interprets the announcement of a rights issue as 'bad' news.[17] This implies that the market considers a rights issue to be an unfavourable indication of the company's future net operating cash flows, with the result that the announcement of a rights issue will decrease shareholders' wealth.

However, even on the ex-rights date the price of a share may not decrease to its so called theoretical value. The reason is that the model from which the theoretical value was derived relies on some simplifying assumptions. For example, the model assumes that the subscription price is payable on the ex-rights date, whereas, in fact, it is usually not payable until several weeks or months later. This gives rise to the further point that the holder of a right is permitted to purchase shares at the subscription price, but is not obliged to do so. If the share price on the subscription date is less than the subscription price,

---

[17] See Clifford W. Smith, Jr, 'Raising Capital: Theory and Evidence', *Midland Corporate Finance Journal*, Spring 1986, pp. 6–22.

the holder of the right does not have to purchase the shares. This type of agreement is known as an **option** but the theoretical model ignores the option-like features of a right and is therefore likely to understate the value of a right.[18]

Where a company sets the subscription price on a rights issue substantially below the current market price of its shares, there is a high probability that shareholders will exercise their entitlement, or sell their rights to others who will subscribe for the shares. In this case it is usually unnecessary for the company to have the issue underwritten. The closer the subscription price on the rights issue is set to the market price of shares, the greater is the need to have the issue underwritten, and the higher the underwriting fee. The underwriting fee will usually be between 0.25 and 0.50 per cent of the subscription price.

A company making a rights issue is required to issue a prospectus. The costs of preparing a prospectus will be lowest when the company has just issued its annual report or its half-yearly report. In these cases the financial statements included in the report can also be used in the prospectus. In addition, because of the lower underwriting fee for a rights issue the total issue costs are usually much lower than for a public issue. Further, provided that shareholders take up their entitlement, a rights issue will have no effect on the control of the company as there is no change in shareholders' relative voting strengths. For these reasons a rights issue may appeal to a financial manager as a means of raising finance. However, against these advantages must be set the fact that because the announcement of a rights issue typically causes a company's share price to fall, current shareholders may benefit if the need for such issues is minimised. This subject is discussed in Chapter 13.

While most companies making rights issues permit the rights to be traded on a stock exchange, sometimes a rights issue will be non-renounceable. This means that shareholders cannot sell their rights. The only choice available to them is to exercise their rights entitlement or permit it to lapse.[19] If investors take the latter choice the issue will be under-subscribed. For this reason non-renounceable rights issues are frequently underwritten and the fee will be larger than for a similar renounceable issue. As a result the costs of making a non-renounceable rights issue may exceed those of an equivalent renounceable rights issue.

## 9.5.2 Private Issue (Placement)

A placement of ordinary shares is one restricted to a limited number of potential investors. These issues are typically made to the larger institutions such as life insurance companies and investment funds. Such organisations (and to a lesser extent, overseas investors) began to replace individual investors as the major holders of Australian company shares in the mid-1950s.[20] These institutions have

---

18 The valuation of rights as a type of option is discussed further in Chapter 16.
19 Ignoring transaction costs, the choices available to shareholders are not reduced by a non-renounceable rights issue. Shareholders can take up the rights and then realise their value by selling the shares.
20 P. Marshman & P. Davies, 'The role of the stock exchange and the financial characteristics of Australian Companies' in *Handbook of Australian Corporate Finance*, 4th edn, R. Bruce et al, Eds, Butterworths, Sydney, 1991.

therefore become the prime targets for placements because they have large sums to invest. This means that a significant amount of capital can be raised quickly by making a placement to a small number of institutions. The Board of Directors can also try to ensure that only parties sympathetic to the Board are offered the opportunity to participate in the placement. A further advantage is that the issuing company is not required to issue a prospectus if the minimum investor subscription is set at $500 000 or more, or the shares are offered to fewer than 20 offerees per year.[21]

It is unusual for a private issue to be underwritten, although it is usual for the company making the issue to use the services of, say, a broker, to assist in placing the shares with institutions. The broker is not obliged to dispose of all the shares and the broker's task is best described as undertaking the placement of the shares on a 'best-efforts' basis. The fee for this service will depend on the size of the placement, the discount on market price and the broker's judgement as to the institutional investors' interest in the issue. The total issue costs associated with a placement of shares can be quite small.

There has been considerable opposition from shareholders to companies making placements of shares and the ASX has placed a limit of 10 per cent on the amount of capital that a company can issue privately in any one year without the prior approval of its shareholders.[22] Opposition by shareholders to placements is not difficult to understand. First, some shareholders may believe that they are being deprived of a possible profit from the sale of the rights. However, we have already shown that the return that shareholders receive from the sale of rights represents, in effect, a return of a portion of their investment in the company. More importantly, if the placement is made to institutions at a price below current market price, there is a reduction in the value of each shareholder's investment. While placements are usually made at prices below the current market price, the price discount is generally very small and therefore any harm to existing shareholders is likely to be small. Secondly, shareholders oppose placements because they reduce the percentage ownership and voting power of existing shareholders.

## 9.6 ALTERNATIVE ORDINARY SHARE ISSUES

We have outlined the methods of issuing shares that are most frequently employed. Less frequently employed methods include bonus issues, options, and deferred shares. These are now considered.

### 9.6.1 BONUS ISSUES

A bonus issue is a 'free' issue of shares made to existing shareholders in proportion to their current investment. It is equivalent to a rights issue with a zero subscription price. A company can make a bonus issue by using the balances of reserves (such as a share premium reserve) and/or retained profits.

---

[21] See Section 66 of the *Corporations Law*.
[22] See Section 3E(6) of the Australian Stock Exchange *Listing Rules*, which provides that, in general, only 10 per cent of a company's issued share capital may be issued to non-shareholders without the prior approval of shareholders at a general meeting.

## Example 9.2

Assume that a company which has an issued capital of 100 000 one-dollar shares makes a 1-for-1 bonus issue to its shareholders. If management chooses to 'finance' the issue from accumulated reserves, the effect on the shareholders' funds section of the company's balance sheet may be as shown in Table 9.1.

**Table 9.1** *Effect of a bonus issue on the balance sheet*

| Item | Before bonus issue ($) | After bonus issue ($) |
|---|---|---|
| Paid-up capital | 100 000 | 200 000 |
| Share premium reserve | 100 000 | nil |
| Retained profits | 100 000 | 100 000 |
| Total | 300 000 | 300 000 |

The company receives no cash as a result of the issue. A bonus issue requires a book entry to adjust the shareholders' funds section of the company's balance sheet. Its financial position remains the same, except that it has doubled the number of shares on issue. Therefore, the market price of the company's shares should decrease by half—in this case from $2 to $1—and the total market value of the shares held by each investor should remain unchanged.

More generally, if the market price is $M$ dollars per share and there is a 1-for-$N$ bonus issue, what price per share is expected after the bonus? As a bonus issue raises no new funds, it is expected that the *value* of a holding of $N$ shares will be worth, in total, the same amount after the bonus issue as before it. However, the *number* of shares in such a holding will increase to $(N + 1)$. Therefore:

$$MN = X(N + 1)$$

where $X$ is the ex-bonus price per share. Therefore:

$$X = \left(\frac{N}{N + 1}\right)M \qquad (9.6)$$

In Example 9.2, $N$ was 1 and $M$ was $2. Application of Equation 9.6 confirms that the ex-bonus price should be $1/2 \times \$2 = \$1$. Comparing Equation 9.6 with Equation 9.4, which is the rights issue counterpart, it is readily seen that, in fact, Equation 9.6 is simply Equation 9.4 with the subscription price $S$ set equal to zero. This follows from the earlier observation that a bonus issue is equivalent to a rights issue with a zero subscription price. The Australian evidence is consistent with Equation 9.6.[23] In other words, the evidence indicates that bonus issues do not affect shareholders' wealth.

---

23 See Richard G. Sloan, 'Bonus Issues, Share Splits and Ex-day Share Price Behaviour: Australian Evidence', *Australian Journal of Management*, December 1987, pp. 277–91. This evidence contrasts with the US evidence which has found positive abnormal returns on the ex-day for US stock dividends (bonus issues); see J. Lakonishok & T. Vermaelen, 'Tax Induced Trading Around Ex-dividend Days', *Journal of Financial Economics*, 1986, pp. 287–319.

However, in practice there may be an increase in the share price following the *announcement* by a company of a forthcoming bonus issue. This increase can occur because such an announcement may have information content. Investors are aware that, following a bonus issue, companies usually do not reduce dividends per share to the extent necessary to maintain the same total dividend payout. For example, after a 1-for-1 bonus issue, a company currently paying a dividend of 10 cents per share would need to pay a dividend of only 5 cents per share to maintain its dividend payout. However, companies will often not reduce their dividend per share to that extent. For example, the company may end up paying a dividend of, say, 7.5 cents per share after the bonus issue has been made. If the behaviour of most companies after a bonus issue follows this pattern, the market will be confident that a company making a bonus issue will probably increase its total dividend payout.[24] This, in turn, indicates the confidence of management in the company's future. Consequently, the share price may increase in response to this new information.

In addition to providing the market with information, a bonus issue also enables management to justify reducing what may be perceived to be an exceedingly high dividend per share without reducing the total dividend payout. This may lead to a reduction in pressures from those who believe that a high dividend per share indicates excessive profitability. Also, a bonus issue may be made by a company with a 'thin' market for its shares. Management may believe that reducing the market price per share will increase the demand for the company's shares. If this were true, the market value of the company's equity would increase. A share split, which represents a reduction in the par value of the shares from say $1 to 50 cents, is usually made with the same aim in mind. The essential difference between a bonus issue and a share split is that a split does not increase the company's paid-up capital.

Following the introduction of the dividend imputation tax system in 1987, the amount of a bonus issue is treated as dividend income in the hands of shareholders for taxation purposes unless the issue is made on a pro rata basis to all shareholders out of a share premium reserve. As a result, there has been a reduction in the number of bonus issues made by companies.

### 9.6.2 SHARE OPTIONS[25]

An option to purchase the shares of a company gives the holder of that option the right to take up shares in the company by a specified date on predetermined terms. For example, a company may issue, at no cost, 10 000 options which may be exercised by the payment of $1 per option during the next 5 years. Consequently an investor can purchase a maximum of 10 000 shares for $1 each at any time during the next five years, regardless of their market price at the time. The recipient of the option therefore obtains the opportunity to benefit from an

---

24 R. Ball, P. Brown & F.J. Finn, 'Share Capitalisation Changes, Information and the Australian Equity Market', *Australian Journal of Management*, October 1977, pp. 105–25.
25 The nature and valuation of options are discussed in Chapter 16.

increase in the market price of the company's shares. So if the company's share price increases to $1.20, the investor can purchase 10 000 shares for $10 000, which is $2000 below their current market value.

There are therefore three major provisions included in an option agreement: the exercise price of the option, the period during which the options may be exercised, and the rights of option holders in the event of new issues by the company. In general, it is usual for the exercise price of an option to be set near the share price at the time the option is issued. The period during which the option may be exercised is restricted to a maximum of 5 years by Section 216 of the *Corporations Law*. In addition, it is usual for a company to prevent the option holder from exercising the option for a certain period after it has been granted. If a company makes an issue of shares during the option's life, it is possible for the value of the option to be reduced to almost zero. For example, if a company makes a 1-for-1 bonus issue, other things being equal, the price per share will be halved. In turn, this will result in a corresponding reduction in the possibility that the option holder will benefit from any subsequent increase in the share price. As a result, option agreements usually provide holders with the right to participate in rights or bonus issues by the company during the life of the option.

Options may be issued as follows:

### 1. To employees
The objective when making option issues is to reward employees in a way that is likely to encourage them to work towards improving the company's profitability. Such issues are typically made with an exercise price equal to the current share price, which does not expose the employee to any immediate tax obligation. If the company becomes more profitable, it is likely to command a higher share price. This will flow through to the price of the option and thus the employee benefits through an increase in the value of the option.

### 2. As a sweetener to an equity issue
Many exploration and mining companies issue both ordinary shares and options to subscribe for additional shares. For example, an investor purchasing 1000 shares in a new issue may also receive 1000 options, each of which entitles the investor to buy one additional share at par before a specified date. Frequently these options are listed separately on the stock exchange. Therefore an investor obtains the opportunity to make an additional gain from an increase in the company's share price. A company that issues shares accompanied by options hopes to encourage investors to participate in the issue, thereby reducing the possibility of under-subscription.

### 3. As a sweetener to a private debt issue
On occasions, a company seeking debt finance will offer share options to an institution on the understanding that the institution provides the required amount of debt finance. The company benefits either by obtaining debt finance that it would not otherwise have received, or by obtaining the funds on better terms, for example, at a lower interest rate. However, neither party

to an agreement of this type can make the options conditional upon the granting of the loan because this may jeopardise the tax deductibility of interest on the debt.[26]

In the cases outlined above, it is evident that options are not issued primarily as a means of raising finance, although they are often issued as part of a finance package. Nevertheless, options have been used by companies as a means of raising finance. For example, in 1986, TNT raised almost $60 million by a 1 for 5 issue of options at an issue price of $1.

### 9.6.3 DEFERRED SHARES

A deferred share has the characteristics of an ordinary share, except that the deferred shareholders' entitlement to dividends is delayed for a specified period. During this period, the company can declare and pay a dividend on its ordinary shares, but it is not obliged to pay an equivalent dividend on its deferred shares. This type of share is ideally suited to the financing of projects where a cash flow will not be generated for a number of years. The company can use the funds obtained from an issue of deferred shares to develop the project, and not have to pay dividends until after the project has begun to generate a cash flow.

## 9.7 SHARE BUY-BACKS/REPURCHASES

In many countries, companies are permitted to purchase their own shares on the stock market and then proceed either to cancel them or to retain them as **treasury stock**. The ability to repurchase shares allows a company to manage its capital structure more effectively.

In Australia, Section 205(1)(b) of the *Corporations Law* generally precludes a company from purchasing its own shares. However, there are exceptions to this general prohibition and these are set out in Sections 206AA to 206UF of the *Corporations Law*. In particular, public companies are allowed to repurchase and then cancel up to 10 per cent of their shares in a 12-month period. These repurchases may be made on the stock market. A number of controls over share repurchases are included in the legislation, including a requirement that directors sign **solvency declarations**. These declarations, in effect, make the directors personally liable for any amount paid by a company to repurchase shares if the company becomes insolvent in the 12 months following the repurchase. While the legislation on share repurchases relaxes a longstanding prohibition, the stringent requirements for share repurchases seem likely to discourage such activity.

## 9.8 INTERNAL EQUITY FINANCE

So far we have discussed external sources of equity finance. However, a major source of equity finance for Australian companies is equity finance which is 'internal' to the company, in the sense that it results from the positive net cash

---

[26] The tax implications of the ownership and discharge of options are set out in Section 26AAC of the *Income Tax Assessment Act* 1936.

flows that a successful company generates. A measure of internal equity finance is **funds from operations** which is calculated by subtracting from revenues those expenses which require the use of funds. Therefore:

Funds from operations = revenue − expenses requiring the use of funds.

A company's accounting profit is calculated after deducting total expenses, including both fund-using and non-fund-using expenses, from revenue. Therefore, an alternative method of calculating a company's funds from operations is to add back to its profit those expenses not requiring the use of funds. Several expenses do not require the use of funds but the major expense of this type is depreciation.[27] Therefore, another way of calculating funds from operations is as follows:

Funds from operations = operating profit before tax + depreciation charges.

However, part of the funds from operations will generally have to be used to pay company income tax and dividends. Therefore:

$$\text{Total internal equity finance} = \text{Funds from operations} - \text{Income tax paid} - \text{Dividend payments}$$

Clearly, other things being equal, higher dividend payments mean that a company will have lower internal equity finance.

The relative importance of internal equity finance in providing a company's total financial requirements has varied widely over the years. In the late 1970s, internal equity provided about 60 per cent of all funds raised, but by the mid-1980s this proportion had fallen to about 50 per cent.[28] In more recent years this proportion appears to have fallen even further, owing to the dividend imputation tax system which has caused companies to increase significantly their dividend payout ratios. The effect of this reduction has been offset by the introduction of dividend reinvestment plans, which are discussed in Section 9.8.3.

## 9.8.1 DEPRECIATION CHARGES

Depreciation charges are not a source of finance for a company. It is the company's revenue that is the primary source of funds from operations. However, the practice of depreciating assets has the effect of reducing a company's accounting profit. A company is restricted by law to paying dividends out of the current year's profit, or the accumulated retained profit of previous years. As a result, a profitable company will be forced to retain funds at least equivalent to the total accumulated depreciation charges.[29]

---

[27] Examples of other non-fund-using expenses include the allowance for doubtful debts and the annual amortisation of a lump-sum payment made to obtain a long-term lease.
[28] See: *Bulletin Supplement, Company Finance*, Reserve Bank of Australia, August 1986, Table 2.2.
[29] See Section 201 of the *Corporations Law*.

## 9.8.2 Retained Profits

Management can directly influence the level of retained profits by its dividend policy. For example, a company with a profit after tax of $3 million that pays a dividend of $2 million will have a retained profit of $1 million. The relationship between the dividend decision and other financing decisions is discussed in Chapter 11.

Retained profits are not a free source of finance for a company. The profit of a company belongs to its shareholders and therefore any retained profits are reinvested by the company on its shareholders' behalf. It follows that the retention of profit by a company has an opportunity cost. This is discussed in more detail in Chapter 17.

The use of retained profits as a source of finance also has advantages. Retention of profits does not affect the control of the company as it does not involve the company in issuing any additional shares. In addition, the retention of profits does not commit the company to increased dividend payments in the future, with the result that no additional strain is placed on the company's cash resources. A further advantage of the use of retained profits as a source of finance is that, unlike a new issue of shares, the retention of profits involves no issue costs such as brokerage and fees paid to advisers, lawyers and accountants.

## 9.8.3 Dividend Reinvestment Plans

The first dividend reinvestment plans were introduced by Australian companies in the early 1980s.[30] Within ten years, most of Australia's largest companies were offering such plans. The introduction of the dividend imputation tax system caused investors to demand high dividend payouts. A dividend reinvestment plan allows a company to meet the demand for high dividends without straining its cash resources. Technically, investors receive the dividends and therefore obtain the tax benefits of imputation, and then reinvest the cash in the company. Achievement of a high level of reinvestment was very important for many of these companies who, at the time, were attempting to reduce very high debt–equity ratios.

## Selected References

Bailleau, E. L & C., *The Structure of Substantial Public Offerings*, Sydney, 1993.
Bruce, R., et al, Eds, *Handbook of Australian Corporate Finance*, 4th edn, Butterworths, Sydney, 1991, Chs 4 and 5.
Peacock, R. W. & Jones, M. D, 'Company-issued Options', *Professional Administrator*, December 1982, pp. 243–7.
Pilioussis, T. A. & Woods, I. R., 'Bonus Share Issues in Australia'. *JASSA*, April 1983, pp. 19–23.
Smith, Clifford W. Jr, 'Raising Capital: Theory and Evidence', *Midland Corporate Finance Journal*, Spring 1986, pp. 6–22.

---

[30] Dividend reinvestment plans are discussed in more detail in Chapter 11.

# QUESTIONS

1. A company is floated by making a public issue of ordinary shares. Outline the procedures involved in floating a company.
2. A company usually seeks the assistance of a financial institution before undertaking any large capital raising. Explain why this is so. Describe fully the relevant services that a financial institution provides.
3. Distinguish between limited liability and no-liability companies. Why are no-liability companies confined to exploration and mining companies?
4. Explain why company promoters might prefer to pre-market an equity issue.
5. Company A has 4 000 000 shares on issue and wishes to raise $4 million by a 1-for-4 rights issue.
   (a) What is the theoretical value of one right if the market price of one share (cum rights) is $5?
   (b) What is the theoretical share price (ex rights)?
   (c) Does an investor gain through a rights issue?
6. Although most companies permit rights to be traded on the stock exchange, a number of companies have made non-renounceable rights issues. Why would companies wish to make their rights issues non-renounceable?
7. There has been resistance to companies raising funds by a private placement of shares. Describe the advantages and disadvantages to existing shareholders of a private placement.
8. What is a bonus issue? Why might the directors of a company wish to make such an issue?
9. Explain briefly why the share price of a company may increase when it announces a bonus issue.
10. Choose a company, and trace the major changes in its capital structure during the past 10 years. Outline the economic factors that you consider have contributed to the major changes in its financing policy during this period.
11. Australian companies are required by law to attach a par value to their shares. What purpose does par value serve and what reasons are usually presented for discarding the par value concept?
12. Options are often used as an incentive to various groups or individuals. Describe how options can be used to the advantage of a company and its shareholders.
13. Depreciation charges account for about 30 per cent of new fund raisings by Australian companies. Discuss this statement, indicating your view on the classification of depreciation as a source of funds.
14. What are retained profits? Why are they highly regarded by management as a source of funds?
15. Outline the impact that the introduction of the dividend imputation system has had on companies in terms of their raisings of equity capital.

# CHAPTER 10

# SOURCES OF LONG-TERM FINANCE: DEBT

## 10.1 Introduction

In this chapter, we consider long-term debt, that is, debt with a term to maturity in excess of 12 months. On average, long-term debt typically comprises 75 to 80 per cent of the total debt of listed Australian companies.[1]

Term loans from Australian banks and non-bank financial intermediaries, and debenture issues, have traditionally been the major domestic sources of long-term debt. In recent years the growth in bank lending has switched to variable interest rate loans. The interest rates on these loans are based on short-term rates, and companies that require long-term, fixed-rate borrowing can obtain a fixed rate by swap transactions. In addition, non-finance companies have almost completely withdrawn from making debenture issues, with the total amount outstanding from such issues now declining. Companies' needs for long-term, fixed-rate debt finance are now met in part by issuing other securities, including some that are convertible into equity.

In the next section we outline the main characteristics of long-term debt and the main effects of using long-term debt. This is followed by discussion of the major types of long-term debt used by Australian companies and a discussion of interest rate swaps. The chapter concludes by considering preference shares and convertible notes which are hybrids of debt and equity securities.

## 10.2 General Characteristics of Long-Term Debt

The various types of long-term debt can be classified into two general categories: marketable and non-marketable debt. Marketable debt takes the form of securities

---

[1] See Stock Exchange Financial and Profitability Survey, 1993.

such as notes, bonds, or debentures which are issued direct to investors and can then be traded in a secondary market. Non-marketable debt takes the form of loans arranged privately between two parties where the lender is usually a bank or other financial intermediary. These types of long-term debt are discussed in more detail in Sections 10.3 and 10.4. However, both these types of debt have some common characteristics that we now discuss.

## 10.2.1 The interest cost of debt

When a company borrows, it is committed to the payment of interest and to the repayment of the principal when the debt matures. In Chapter 4, the setting of interest rates in the Australian capital market was discussed. It was pointed out that, given the general structure of interest rates at a point in time, the rate of interest that a company will have to pay to borrow funds for a specified period will depend on the risk characteristics of that company. For example, at a time when the Commonwealth Government has to pay an interest rate of 6 per cent per annum to borrow funds for 5 years, a secure industrial company may have to pay 7.5 per cent, while a less secure industrial company may have to pay 10 per cent.

The cost of raising funds by borrowing is reflected by the interest rate that the company is required to offer to obtain the funds. In most cases, marketable long-term debt securities have a **fixed interest rate**, which does not vary over the life of the security. Non-marketable debt can also have a fixed interest rate. Where a variable interest rate applies, the rate will generally consist of a base rate plus a margin that depends on the risk of the borrower. The interest rate will therefore change whenever the base rate or indicator lending rate changes.

Debtholders rank ahead of shareholders in that dividends cannot be paid unless all accrued interest payments to debtholders have been met. Further, in the event of liquidation of a company, all obligations to debtholders have priority and shareholders have only a residual claim to any cash raised from the sale of the company's assets. As a consequence, debtholders are subject to less risk than are shareholders and they are therefore prepared to accept a lower expected rate of return. However, not all debtholders rank equally in terms of their claims when it comes to interest and principal repayments. In other words, debt can be **subordinated** to other debt and, as a consequence, the holders of subordinated debt will demand a higher interest rate than do the holders of **unsubordinated** debt. Where borrowed funds are used to generate taxable income, interest on the debt is tax deductible. However, interest income is taxable in the hands of debtholders and this increases the interest rate that investors require. Therefore the fact that interest is tax deductible does not necessarily give debt a cost advantage over equity finance. Under the imputation system the impact of taxes is fairly neutral in terms of its impact on the costs of debt and equity finance. This is discussed further in Chapters 12 and 13.

As noted earlier, a feature that distinguishes the various types of debt securities is the extent to which they are **marketable**. Marketability is the ease with which the holder is able to trade the security. Investors favour being able to sell securities at short notice. In other words, they favour securities that are traded actively in a liquid market. Therefore marketable securities tend to be issued at a lower interest rate than other securities, provided the other characteristics of the securities are equivalent.

### 10.2.2 EFFECT OF DEBT ON RISK

While the rate of return required by lenders is less than the rate of return that shareholders expect, increasing the amount of debt also increases the company's financial risk. The effects of financial risk include effects on the rate of return expected by shareholders. A company financed solely by ordinary shares is not required to pay dividends and therefore has no financial risk. Borrowing introduces financial risk, which involves two separate but related effects. First, because the returns to lenders are 'fixed', the use of debt rather than equity has a leverage effect. That is, it increases the variability of returns to shareholders and increases the rate of return they expect. Secondly, the more a company borrows, the greater the interest and principal repayments to which it is committed, and therefore the greater is the risk of financial distress. In the extreme case, where a company has insufficient cash to meet its contractual obligations, the consequences can be far reaching and may even result in the company being wound up. In such a situation the shareholders will usually receive little or no return from the sale of the company's assets because the company's lenders have a prior claim to the proceeds. However, financial distress is costly and many of the costs fall on lenders. Therefore lenders will require a margin to compensate for the expected level of these costs and this will be reflected in higher interest rates on loans to borrowers with higher default risk. Also, to limit their exposure or risk, lenders will generally set an upper limit on the financial leverage of borrowers.

### 10.2.3 EFFECT OF DEBT ON CONTROL

Another important feature of debt is that, provided the company meets its obligations, debtholders have no control over the company's operations. Unlike shareholders, debtholders have no voting rights. However, if a company fails to meet its obligations, debtholders can exert, either directly or indirectly, significant influence over the operations of the company. In this case the debtholders, or frequently a trustee acting on their behalf, can seek to protect their interests. This may be achieved by taking control of the security for the loan, appointing an administrator, having the company placed into receivership, or having the company placed into liquidation. In recent years some Australian companies that were unable to repay large loans have, in effect, been run by committees of bankers while assets were sold and operations restructured. Therefore, while debtholders usually exert no control over a company, they have a large degree of potential control, which they can exert if the company breaches a loan agreement.

### 10.2.4 OTHER CHARACTERISTICS OF DEBT

A company may borrow on either a secured or an unsecured basis. Where borrowing is secured, the security is typically a claim over some of the company's assets. If no security is provided by the company it will usually have to pay a slightly higher interest rate. The better the quality of the assets pledged as security, the easier it is for the company to borrow and the lower the interest rate it has to pay. The importance of security will be seen when the restrictions (covenants) imposed on a company under a trust deed attached to a debenture issue are considered in Section 10.3.1.

Also, a company issuing debt can choose the period for which it wishes to borrow. Frequently a company's financial manager will construct a cash budget to estimate its future needs for cash and will issue debt with maturities that match those requirements. This is discussed in Chapter 22.

## 10.3 TYPES OF MARKETABLE LONG-TERM DEBT
### 10.3.1 DEBENTURES AND UNSECURED NOTES

Debentures and unsecured notes are identical, except that a debenture holder is a secured creditor whereas an unsecured note holder is an unsecured creditor. Debentures and unsecured notes involve the payment of a specified amount of interest at a regular interval[2] and repayment at maturity of the amount borrowed.[3] In the case of a debenture or unsecured-note issue, a company divides the amount it wishes to borrow into small denominations (typically $1000) which it sells to individuals and institutions. For example, a company that wishes to borrow $2 million may do so by accepting subscriptions for debenture stock with a minimum subscription of $3000 and multiples of $1000 thereafter.

The security for debenture issues will be one of two types. One secures the loan by a fixed charge over specified assets, and the other secures the loan by a floating charge over all of the company's assets that have not been pledged to other lenders. Most debenture issues involve a floating charge because a fixed charge impedes the company's freedom to deal in its own assets.

If a company fails to meet its financial obligations on a fixed-charge debenture, the debenture holders may obtain payment by forcing the sale of the pledged assets. In the event that the sale fails to realise an amount sufficient to repay the debenture holders, they rank as unsecured creditors for the unpaid balance. In the case of a floating-charge debenture the debenture holders have no claim to the cash generated by selling assets pledged to other lenders, although they rank ahead of unsecured creditors for cash generated by the sale of unpledged assets.

The order of priority for the repayment of different classes of creditors in the event of the company being wound up is quite a complicated matter covered by various Acts of Parliament. However, for our purposes, the most important

---

[2] The interest payments are usually half-yearly or quarterly.
[3] In some cases, early repayment options are included in the contract, although this is not a usual feature in Australia.

point to note is that secured creditors rank in order of priority for repayment of debt ahead of unsecured creditors.

From the holders' point of view, therefore, debentures are a less risky investment than unsecured notes because debenture holders have a prior claim over the company's assets in the event of it being wound up. To compensate for the greater risk of unsecured notes, a company usually offers a higher rate of interest on unsecured notes than on debentures. A company may also issue debentures that rank differently with respect to principal repayment in the event of the company being wound up. In this case a first-charge debenture will require a lower interest rate than a second-charge debenture.

After a company has decided on the form that the debenture issue should take, it must decide on the terms to maturity and the interest rates to be attached to the issue. It is usual for debentures issued as a result of a **public** issue to have terms to maturity that range from 2 years to 5 years.[4]

The terms to maturity of new issues of debentures have shortened considerably since the early 1970s. At that time an industrial company would rarely offer a term to maturity of less than 5 years. It is now unusual for a company to offer a term to maturity greater than 5 years. The main reason for this change was the presence of high rates of inflation in the early 1970s and the uncertainty that this engendered in the minds of lenders. As lenders were uncertain about future interest rates and their future financial requirements they were inclined to lend for much shorter periods than was previously the case.

The interest rates attached to a debenture issue will depend mainly on the general level of interest rates at the time, and on the riskiness of the company. First, a company has to compete with government and semi-government entities, financial institutions, and other companies for funds. Therefore, when there is an increase in the general level of interest rates a company will have to offer higher interest rates to attract subscriptions to its debenture issue. Secondly, a profitable and financially stable company that can offer good security will be able to raise funds at a lower interest rate than a company lacking those attributes.

The interest rate will also be affected by the term to maturity of the debentures and their marketability. The liquidity preference of investors means that they require a higher interest rate on longer-term borrowing[5] and on debentures that are not readily marketable. Generally the interest rates attached to a debenture issue remain unchanged for the life of that issue. The interest rates that a finance company would need to offer in order to raise debenture funds on the Australian capital market in mid-1994 are shown in Table 10.1.

Although interest rates on debentures generally remain fixed until the debentures mature, a few companies have issued debentures with variable interest rates. The rates are recalculated regularly on the basis of movements in other interest rates, such as the banks' fixed-deposit rates and/or movements in the consumer

---

[4] A company will set maturity dates within these maturity ranges to suit its future financial requirements.

[5] There are times when interest rates on short-term borrowings exceed those on longer-term borrowings. For a discussion of the reasons why this may occur, see Section 4.6.

**Table 10.1** *Typical rates of interest on a public issue of debentures, mid-1994*

| Term | Rate of interest (% p.a.) |
|---|---|
| 2 years | 5.0–6.0 |
| 3 years | 6.0–7.0 |
| 5 years + | 7.0–8.0 |

price index. Attaching variable interest rates to an issue protects investors, if only partially, from the effects of inflation.

The *Corporations Law* contains general requirements designed to protect the interests of holders of debentures and unsecured notes. One such requirement is that the issuing company shall execute a trust deed.

## TRUST DEED

A company that issues debentures or unsecured notes is required to draw up a trust deed for the issue and appoint a trustee for the holders. The trust deed sets out the nature of the security for the issue and specifies where the security ranks in terms of any claim against the company's assets. The trust deed also specifies restrictions on the company's total borrowings, which are usually expressed in terms of some proportion of the company's total tangible assets. For example, an industrial company's debenture trust deed will typically include restrictions on:

(a) senior debt that has priority over debenture holders (senior debt is usually limited to about 10 per cent of total tangible assets);
(b) total secured liabilities (usually limited to 40 per cent of total tangible assets); and
(c) total liabilities (usually limited to 60 per cent of total tangible assets).

If the debentures or notes are to be listed on the Australian Stock Exchange (ASX), the trust deed must also conform to the ASX *Listing Rules* which impose some additional restrictions. For example, the trust deed must require that the company insure its assets.

The role of the trustee is to hold the security on behalf of the debenture holders and to ensure that the borrower does not breach any of the covenants contained in the trust deed. In the event of any breach the trustee has to act to protect the debenture holders. Possible actions include making application to the Court for the appointment of a receiver. To assist the trustee in carrying out these duties, the borrowing company has to provide specified information to the trustee, including a quarterly report that specifies whether there has been any breach of the trust deed and whether the security for the amount borrowed has been endangered.

## DEBENTURES AND FINANCIAL DISTRESS

If a company is in financial distress, the existence of debentures and the associated trust deed can compound the difficulties because:

(a) the company is required to meet the interest payments on the debentures;

(b) a decline in the carrying amount of its total tangible assets may mean that its total tangible assets do not provide sufficient coverage for the amount borrowed and it is therefore in breach of the liability restrictions in the trust deed;
(c) the borrowing restrictions may prevent the company from raising the funds necessary to overcome its financial difficulties;
(d) the publicity resulting from any actions taken by the trustee may make other parties wary of trading with, or assisting, the company; and
(e) the existence of the trustee to protect debenture holders will increase the probability that the company will be placed in receivership and possibly liquidated.

The greater a company's financial commitments resulting from its use of debentures (or other forms of long-term debt), the more likely is it to face serious financial difficulties in the event of a decline in the profitability of its operations. While some of the above factors are also applicable to other types of debt, the restrictions imposed by a debenture trust deed can nevertheless be costly and involve delays. For example, proposals to change the relationship between the company and the debenture holders may require approval by a meeting of debenture holders. Other forms of debt are likely to be less restrictive and provide greater flexibility in the event of financial distress, or breaches of restrictive covenants.

## 10.3.2 CORPORATE BONDS

As noted in Section 10.1, debentures were traditionally an important source of long-term debt finance for Australian companies. Their place has been largely taken by other forms of debt such as loans from banks, and bonds or marketable securities issued in offshore markets. However, in the late 1980s, long-term corporate debt securities re-emerged in the domestic market when some large companies began to issue corporate bonds. The main differences between these bonds and debentures are as follows:
- corporate bonds are typically issued as unsecured notes;
- the trust deed is less restrictive than a debenture trust deed;
- corporate bonds are placed privately with institutional investors rather than issued publicly; and
- because only institutional investors are involved, there may be no need for a prospectus. If a prospectus is required, it will be less costly to prepare than a prospectus for a public issue.

The market for corporate bonds grew rapidly in the late 1980s when borrowing by the public sector declined. This reduction, which occurred when the Commonwealth Government's budgetary position changed from a deficit to a surplus, reduced the supply of new government bonds and left life offices and superannuation funds with long-term funds to invest elsewhere. Some of these funds flowed into the corporate bond market, which reportedly grew to about $19 billion by early 1990. However, the majority of these securities were issued by banks and other financial institutions rather than industrial companies and subsequent growth in the market has been limited.

Companies issuing corporate bonds require high credit ratings and the securities are usually placed with the assistance of a panel of investment banks. Institutional demand for a company's bonds will be greater in cases where these banks are also committed to acting as market makers to ensure a liquid secondary market.

### 10.3.3 AUSTRALIAN DOLLAR EUROBONDS

An Australian dollar eurobond is a debt security denominated in Australian dollars but issued outside Australia with a view to attracting non-Australian investors.

The first Australian dollar eurobond issue was made by the Australian Industry Development Corporation in 1976. Although this way of raising long-term debt was slow to develop, by the late 1980s it was well established.

Eurobonds are purchased primarily by international fund managers. As a result, only well-known Australian companies are able to issue Australian dollar eurobonds. The size of such issues has usually been between $A50 million and $A100 million. Issues of Australian dollar eurobonds have generally been made by the borrower negotiating an underwriting arrangement with a merchant bank, which takes responsibility for arranging a syndicate to underwrite and market the issue.

Australian dollar eurobonds have a number of advantages for Australian borrowers. First, the borrower will have access to a wider group of investors. Secondly, these issues can avoid Australian prospectus requirements because they are not sold to Australian residents. Thirdly, issuing bonds in offshore markets provides borrowers with flexibility in terms of the currency, terms to maturity, and innovative characteristics such as zero coupon issues. For some Australian companies the benefit of the Australian dollar eurobond market lies in the possibility of reducing the costs of borrowing by cross-currency interest rate swap transactions. Interest rate swaps are discussed in Section 10.5.

## 10.4 TYPES OF NON-MARKETABLE LONG-TERM DEBT

The Australian domestic long-term corporate debt market is not well developed and most companies rely instead on non-marketable debt such as loans from banks. In the discussion that follows, we consider some major types of non-marketable long-term debt.

### 10.4.1 TERM LOANS FROM BANKS

The one element common to all term loans is that they are entered into for a fixed period, which typically ranges from 3 to 10 years. The loan agreement will specify whether the full amount of the loan must be borrowed at once, or whether it can be drawn down by instalments prior to a specified date. The repayment schedule is structured to suit the borrower's requirements.

Frequently the first repayment is postponed for a certain period, called a **'holiday'**, to permit the project financed by the loan to generate a cash flow from which repayments can be made. For example, a company that negotiates a term loan in June 1994 may be permitted to borrow in instalments until the full amount of the loan has been borrowed, say by June 1995. The term loan may also permit the first repayment to be postponed until June 1997, with the total amount to be repaid by June 2001.[6]

The interest rate on a term loan is usually slightly higher than that on a bank overdraft. The interest rate may be fixed or it may be changed in line with changes in the general level of interest rates. Banks are prepared to lend for longer terms when the interest rate on the loan is variable rather than fixed. For example, variable interest loans may be available for up to 10 years, but fixed interest loans are generally available for no more than 5 to 7 years. The usual establishment fees and loan service fees apply and a commitment fee is usually charged on any undrawn balance of the loan. Usually banks also require security for term loans. The security may take the form of a charge over property or other assets, or the guarantee of an overseas bank or parent company.

Banks first offered term loans in the early 1960s when a Term Loan Fund was established with the assistance of the Reserve Bank. The banks subsequently augmented the funds available for this form of financing when they contributed equity funds to establish the Australian Resources Development Bank (ARDB). Term loans from the banks gradually grew in importance as a source of funds for capital expenditure for rural, industrial, and commercial borrowers. They peaked as a source of finance in early 1986 when the banks' term loans reached nearly $5.5 billion. By the early 1990s they had stabilised at around $5 billion. The use of the Term Loan Fund and the ARDB has now ceased and all term loans are currently funded by each bank in the same way as other bank loans.

### 10.4.2 LONG-TERM LOANS FROM SPECIALISED INTERMEDIARIES— THE AUSTRALIAN INDUSTRY DEVELOPMENT CORPORATION (AIDC) AND THE COMMONWEALTH DEVELOPMENT BANK (CDB)

The Australian Industry Development Corporation (AIDC) was established by the Australian government under an Act of Parliament 'to assist in the provision of financial resources required by Australian companies engaging or proposing to engage in industries in Australia concerned with manufacture, processing or treatment of goods or with the recovery of minerals for the purpose of facilitating and encouraging the establishment, development and advancement of these industries.'[7] The AIDC is an active development lender and investor. It focuses its lending on proposals that involve the development and restructuring of Australian industry. Requests for funding are judged not only on the usual commercial criteria but also on whether the proposal is in the national interest.

Finance provided by the AIDC can be in various forms, including the provision of long-term debt, either by a term loan or by standby credit, the provision of lease finance or equity funds, loan guarantees, or the underwriting of share

---

[6] The term of the loan commences from the date at which it is due to be fully drawn (that is, June 1995). Therefore, the loan in this example is classified as a 6-year term loan.
[7] *Australian Industry Development Corporation Act*, 1970, section 6(i).

issues. Most funds have been provided in the form of term loans, typically for periods of less than 7 years at interest rates similar to those charged by banks. The interest rates are reviewed annually.

When the Commonwealth Bank of Australia was restructured in 1959 the Commonwealth Development Bank (CDB) was formed to provide finance either to primary producers or to manufacturers, particularly small ones, in cases where the applicants had worthwhile projects that could not be financed suitably elsewhere. Since that date its powers have been widened so that the CDB may provide funds to applicants from any sector of the Australian economy to assist either with the purchase of capital equipment or with their working capital needs.

The CDB undertakes two forms of lending. The majority of its funds are lent in the form of term loans for periods of between 3 and 20 years with the repayments tailored to meet the needs of the borrower. In addition the CDB provides commercial hire-purchase and other instalment finance for plant and equipment. The interest rate charged on hire-purchase finance is generally lower than that charged by finance companies.

### 10.4.3 SYNDICATED LOANS

One of the major financing developments of the 1970s was the provision of syndicated loans by merchant banks in cases where a creditworthy borrower required more funds than could easily be provided by a single lender. The main feature of these loans was that a number of merchant banks would join together effectively to provide term loans for amounts up to $50 million, with each lender having identical rights. Features of these loans were that they were generally unsecured and had a variable interest rate, usually based on the bank-bill rate. Like the term loans offered by the banks, this means of providing term loans had also become much less important by the 1990s.

### 10.4.4 EURODOLLAR LOANS

In the early 1970s a shortage of funds and high interest rates in the domestic capital market forced some Australian companies to seek long-term debt at lower cost offshore.[8] Even though these conditions no longer exist, Australian companies still seek to borrow overseas when the cost of such borrowing is less than in Australia. Although borrowing in many other currencies may be achieved at a lower interest rate, this has to be balanced against the exchange risk associated with borrowing in these currencies. Further discussion of overseas borrowing is deferred to Chapter 21.

### 10.4.5 SECURITY FOR LOANS

Long-term lenders generally require that the borrower enter into a loan agreement which includes various restrictions designed to protect the lender against possible loss. These restrictions are commonly referred to as 'security' arrangements,

---

[8] See G. Mizon & K. Sue, 'Funding from Offshore Sources' in *Handbook of Australian Corporate Finance*, R. Bruce, et al., Eds, 4th edn, Butterworths, Sydney 1991, Chapter 14.

although strictly speaking a loan is secured only if it involves a mortgage or other charge over assets. Unsecured loan agreements typically impose limits on the borrowers' liabilities, and restrictions on the levels of working capital and shareholders' funds. This approach to lending emphasises the importance of cash flow generated by the borrowers' business rather than the need to have tangible assets that can be pledged as security.

In this section, we discuss mortgage loans and negative pledge lending as examples of secured and unsecured loans.

## MORTGAGE LOANS

A mortgage requires a borrower to pledge property as security for a loan. Traditionally, the major source of mortgage finance for companies has been life insurance companies, with superannuation funds and trustee companies also providing some mortgage finance. In Chapter 8 it was noted that banks and finance companies provide short-term mortgage finance. The discussion in this section will therefore consider only long-term mortgage finance.

Mortgage finance is used largely by borrowers who wish to finance their own offices, shops, and factories, and by developers who wish to undertake activities such as the construction of buildings and the subdivision of land.

In the early 1970s, insurance companies began to restrict the term of their mortgage lending and switched towards taking equity participation in property developments rather than supplying long-term debt. To illustrate this point, the value of properties owned by the life insurance companies in the early 1970s was approximately equal to the amount outstanding in mortgage loans, but by the early 1990s their property holdings were almost seven times their mortgage loans. This growth in equity participation is shown in Table 10.2. However, the substantial decline in the property market during the 1990s may cause the life insurance companies to reassess the way in which they finance property development.

**Table 10.2** *Life insurance companies—property holdings and mortgage loans, 1987–92*

| As at June: | Property holdings ($m) | Mortgage loans ($m) |
|---|---|---|
| 1987 | 7 827 | 1 402 |
| 1988 | 9 778 | 1 377 |
| 1989 | 13 279 | 1 980 |
| 1990 | 14 749 | 2 295 |
| 1991 | 14 271 | 2 191 |
| 1992 | 11 709 | 1 941 |

Source: Reserve Bank of Australia, *Bulletin*, July 1993

Most life insurance companies specify a minimum amount for mortgage finance, usually upwards of $200 000. Of course the majority of mortgage loans involve much larger amounts. An insurance company will usually lend from 65 to 85 per cent of its valuation of the property. For example, if an insurance company values a property at $1 million, it would be prepared to lend the owner a maximum amount of from $650 000 to $850 000, with the property as security for the loan.

Typically, mortgage loans are made on a **credit foncier** basis, which means that the principal is repaid over the term of the loan. However, if funds are borrowed to finance the development of a property, the initial repayment of principal is often delayed for some time until the project generates a cash flow from which repayments can be made. Frequently the periodic repayments will be insufficient to repay the principal during the term of the loan, so a 'balloon' payment will be necessary at maturity. For example, the repayment schedule for a 10-year $1 million mortgage loan may result in the repayment of only $600 000 of the principal during the term of the loan. At the loan's maturity, therefore, there will be a balloon payment which includes $400 000 of principal.

For a secure industrial company the interest rate on mortgage loans in early 1994 was approximately 8.5 per cent per annum. This rate will be reviewed annually to take account of changes in the general level of interest rates.

## NEGATIVE PLEDGE LENDING

Institutions may be prepared to lend on an unsecured basis where a negative pledge provision is included in the loan agreement. The principle of a negative pledge is that the borrower undertakes not to pledge existing or future assets of the company or group to anyone else without the consent of the lender. Borrowing on this basis initially became popular in Australia among companies that found debenture trust deeds unduly restrictive. The lender may not require the borrower to pay out all secured loans before lending on an unsecured basis with a negative pledge. However, the company is not permitted to undertake any additional secured borrowing without the lender invoking the negative pledge, unless the lender agrees to waive this requirement.

Apart from agreeing not to borrow additional funds on a secured basis, the loan agreement usually places other restrictions on the company. The company may be restricted from increasing its borrowing and total external liabilities beyond a specified proportion of total tangible assets, including overseas assets. Other covenants in the loan agreement may restrict the payment of dividends to a specified percentage of each period's profit, require the company to maintain various financial ratios such as the current ratio at specified levels, and so on. The aim of such covenants is to provide protection for lenders, while also allowing the company to be managed in ways that maximise profits for shareholders.

However, experience has shown that negative pledges have provided less than the expected protection for lenders when covenants are breached. For example, because there is no charge over assets, the lender is unable to appoint a receiver to control and sell the borrower's assets. Because of the problems experienced by lenders to some large borrowers who encountered financial distress it is unlikely that negative pledge lending will continue on a large scale.

## 10.5 INTEREST RATE SWAPS

In recent years interest rate swaps have become the major mechanism by which Australian companies raise long-term debt at a fixed interest rate.[9] A swap is an arrangement between two or more parties to exchange a set of cash flows over a specified period of time. The parties that agree to the swap are known as counterparties. The first interest rate swap occurred in the early 1980s, and since that time the volume of interest rate swaps has grown rapidly. Figures prepared by the International Swap Dealers Association indicate that total outstanding swaps worldwide stood at almost $US700 billion at the end of 1987, and in excess of $US3000 billion at the end of 1993.

In a 'plain vanilla' interest rate swap, counterparty A makes a series of payments to counterparty B that are based on the future course of interest rates. For example, each quarter for the next four quarters, A may pay B an amount calculated according to that quarter's 90-day bank-bill rate. In return, B agrees to pay A an amount each quarter that is calculated on the basis of a fixed interest rate agreed to today. The amount payable will depend on the notional principal involved (say, $10 million) and, in practice, instead of A paying B *and* B paying A, only the *net* amount is paid each quarter. Note that no exchange of principal is involved; only interest flows are exchanged. These features are illustrated in Example 10.1.

*Example 10.1*

On 1 April 19X1, counterparties A and B enter into an interest rate swap. The notional principal is $10 million and cash flows are to occur quarterly, in arrears, for one year. Counterparty A agrees to pay B floating-rate payments based on the bank-bill rate. Counterparty B agrees to pay A fixed-rate payments at 9 per cent per annum. A year later the agreement has ended and A's financial manager calls for a report on the cash flows that were made in the swap. On 1 April 19X1, when the swap was entered into, the bank-bill rate was 7.60 per cent per annum. Subsequently, it was:

|   |   |
|---|---|
| on 1 July 19X1, | 8.70 per cent; |
| on 1 October 19X1, | 9.35 per cent; and |
| on 1 January 19X2, | 9.25 per cent. |

The report appears on page 245.

As shown in the table, each quarter a swap payment was made with interest calculated in arrears. When the bank-bill rate exceeded the fixed rate of 9 per cent, A paid B; when the bank-bill rate was less than 9 per cent, B paid A. The risk exposure of both parties was limited to the net interest flows shown in the final column. This exposure is, of course, much less than the exposure involved in making a $10 million loan.

While Example 10.1 sets out the mechanics of an interest rate swap, it does not make clear the motivations behind them. Australian companies have largely used interest rate swaps to exchange floating interest rate obligations for long-term fixed interest rate obligations. This typically involves the company first borrowing

---

[9] For a full discussion of swap markets, see T. Dixon, T. McFayden & B. Montague, 'Swaps', in R. Bruce, et al., (Footnote 8) Chapter 13, or B. Hunt & C. Terry, *Financial Instruments and Markets*, Nelson, 1993, Chapter 12.

## Company A: Report on interest rate swap

| Date | Days in period ended | Bank bill swap rate % p.a. | Floating rate swap payment (A pays B) | Fixed rate swap payment (B pays A) | Swap payment made |
|---|---|---|---|---|---|
| 1 April 19X1 | — | 7.60 | — | — | — |
| 1 July 19X1 | 91 | 8.70 | (0.076)(91/365)($10m) = $189 479.45 | (0.09)(91/365)($10m) = $224 383.56 | $34 904.11 (B paid A) |
| 1 October 19X1 | 92 | 9.35 | (0.0870)(92/365)($10m) = $219 287.67 | (0.09)(92/365)($10m) = $226 849.32 | $7561.65 (B paid A) |
| 1 January 19X2 | 92 | 9.25 | (0.0935)(92/365)($10m) = $235 671.23 | (0.09)(92/365)($10m) = $226 849.32 | $8821.91 (A paid B) |
| 1 April 19X2 | 90 | — | (0.0925)(90/365)($10m) = $228 082.19 | (0.09)(90/365)($10m) = $221 917.81 | $6164.38 (A paid B) |

from a bank on a floating-interest-rate basis. For example, it may negotiate a continuing bill facility with a bank where the bank agrees to provide the company with a loan (say, $1 million) over a specified period (say, 5 years) with interest payments calculated at a floating rate (say, 2% above the bank-bill rate).

What the company wants is a $1 million 5-year loan at a **fixed rate of interest**, similar to what it could obtain by issuing debentures. To achieve this it enters into an interest rate swap under which it **receives** floating rate cash flows (thus offsetting its floating rate payments to the bank) and **pays** fixed-rate cash flows. Fortunately there are investment banks willing to be counterparties in such swap arrangements and so provide Australian companies with the fixed-rate borrowings that many of them require.

This is perhaps the most attractive feature of the swaps market to many companies. It enables them to borrow fixed-rate funds which otherwise would not be available and/or would be available only at higher interest rates. The main reason for this is that many companies are assessed by institutional lenders as being too risky to lend to on a long-term fixed-interest-rate basis. However, the banks are willing to lend to them at a floating interest rate. It is an easy process to swap this floating rate for a fixed rate as the other party to the swap is taking on very limited risk exposure. The potential cost savings associated with using swap arrangements are illustrated in Example 10.2.

### Example 10.2
Assume that the floating-rate and fixed-rate borrowing costs in Table 10.3 apply to a company with a BBB credit rating and an investment bank with an AAA credit rating.

**Table 10.3** *Interest rates for Example 10.2*

|  | Interest rate | |
|---|---|---|
|  | Floating rate[a] | Fixed rate |
| Company (BBB) | Bank-bill rate + 1% | 10% |
| Bank (AAA) | Bank-bill rate + 0.5% | 8% |
| Difference in rates | 0.5% | 2% |

[a] The floating rates are based on the yield on bank bills, plus a margin.

Compared with the company, the bank faces lower interest rates for both fixed-rate and floating-rate borrowings. However, the bank has a relatively greater advantage in the fixed-rate market than in the floating-rate market: its borrowings are 2 per cent cheaper in the fixed-rate market, but only 0.5 per cent cheaper in the floating-rate market. Despite the fact that the bank has an absolute cost advantage in both markets, both the bank and the company can gain if they enter into an interest-rate swap agreement.[10] Under this agreement, the bank will borrow funds at a fixed rate of interest of 8 per cent, while the company will borrow funds at a floating rate of interest which is 1 per cent above the bank-bill rate. Under the swap agreement the bank makes floating-rate payments to the company, while the company makes fixed-rate payments to the bank. These 'swap payments' can be set at levels that produce a net saving of interest costs for *both* parties.

To understand how and why this is possible, suppose that the company paid the bank at a fixed rate of 8 per cent, and the bank paid the company at a floating rate of bank-bill rate plus 1 per cent. This is equivalent to a straight swap of debt and the net costs are a fixed rate of 8 per cent for the company and a floating rate of bank-bill rate plus 1.5 per cent for the bank. This would save the company 2 per cent (since its 'direct' fixed rate is 10 per cent) but would **cost** the bank 0.5 per cent (since its 'direct' floating rate is bank bill rate plus 0.5 per cent). The total savings available are therefore 2.0 per cent minus 0.5 per cent = 1.5 per cent.

Of course the bank would not agree to these swap payments but the calculations show that a total saving of 1.5 per cent is achievable. The only thing wrong with the straight swap is that the division of this saving between the two parties is unequal; in fact it is so unequal that the bank would lose. To make the swap attractive to both parties requires that more of the total saving available flows to the bank. This can be achieved by requiring the company to make higher swap payments to the bank and/or requiring the bank to make lower swap payments to the company. Adopting the first solution, suppose that the company's swap payments to the bank are set at 9.2 per cent. The resulting costs and savings are shown in Table 10.4.

---

[10] Note that in the same way that banks do not generally 'link together' particular borrowers and depositors, they do not necessarily link together particular swap partners.

**Table 10.4** *Interest rate swaps and borrowing costs*

| | Borrowing interest rate | + | Interest rate swap payments | − | Interest rate swap receipt | = | Net borrowing cost | Cost saving |
|---|---|---|---|---|---|---|---|---|
| Company | (Bank-bill + 1%) | + | 9.2% | − | (Bank-bill + 1%) | = | 9.2% | 0.8% |
| Bank | 8% | + | (Bank-bill + 1%) | − | 9.2% | = | (Bank-bill − 0.2%) | 0.7% |
| Total saving | | | | | | | | 1.5% |

The swap results in a saving of 0.8 per cent for the company because had it borrowed 'directly' at a fixed rate of interest it would have had to pay 10 per cent. The bank borrows from the public at a fixed rate of interest of 8 per cent, while it has to make payments to the company at a rate which is 1 per cent above the ruling bank-bill rate, but it receives 9.2 per cent from the company. The interest-rate swap therefore reduces the bank's borrowing costs to 0.2 per cent below the yield on bank bills, which is a saving of 0.7 per cent compared with the 'direct' floating-rate borrowing. Therefore, as a result of the swap transaction the 1.5 per cent cost saving is divided fairly evenly between the two parties.[11]

The form of swap arrangement described above is a simple arrangement. Variations include providing an option to reverse the swap where a specified event occurs, such as where the bank-bill rate rises above a certain level. Another form of interest-rate swap involves a cross-currency transaction. For example, a company may swap an Australian dollar loan for a US dollar loan. Of course this will involve a currency risk but it is possible to obtain cover for the currency risk, which may still make it cheaper to borrow using a cross-currency swap. A discussion of how a currency exposure might be hedged is contained in Chapter 21.

In contrast to the market for debentures the swap market offers a high level of liquidity. As a result, a swap counterparty can, in effect, reverse its commitment, simply by entering into a further swap. Often the new counterparty takes over the obligations of the existing counterparty. A highly liquid swap market benefits both borrowers and lenders. For example, a borrower can use swaps to try to keep its interest costs down by paying on a floating-rate basis when interest rates fall, and on a fixed-rate basis when interest rates rise.

A further advantage of having a swaps market relates to credit assessment. Before a bank makes a floating-rate loan, it assesses the creditworthiness of the borrower. On the basis of this assessment it may advance the loan principal to the borrower. If, subsequently, the borrower enters into an interest rate swap, the

---

[11] This example makes clear a motivation for swaps. However, note that, in practice, swaps are now standardised in format so that the variable rate flow is always based on the bill rate, while the fixed rate is determined by market forces.

swap counterparty in effect converts this to a fixed-rate loan. However, the principal of the loan is undisturbed: only the interest-rate basis has changed. In effect, where the equivalent of a fixed-rate loan is created via an interest rate swap, its 'fixed-rate' feature is provided by the swap counterparty but the 'loan' itself stays with the original floating-rate lender. Typically the original lender is a bank. Thus, interest rate swaps allow the important task of credit assessment to remain largely in the hands of the banks, which are usually seen as having more experience and better access to information than many other potential lenders.

## 10.6 Hybrids of Debt and Equity Finance

In this section we consider two forms of finance that have characteristics common to both debt and equity. The first is preference shares. These are legally regarded as equity, although investors frequently regard them as a form of debt. The second is convertible securities. These securities are debt, but they may be converted into equity at the option of the security holders.

### 10.6.1 Preference Shares

A preference share is a form of equity finance that gives the holders preference over ordinary shareholders with respect to the payment of dividends, and usually with respect to capital repayment in the event of the company's liquidation. As a result, dividends cannot be paid to ordinary shareholders until preference dividends have been paid. In most instances the dividend is fixed for the life of the preference share. With respect to capital repayment the preference shareholders may be entitled to full repayment of the amount subscribed before any payment is made to ordinary shareholders, but they will rank after lenders and other creditors.

Both the *Corporations Law* and the Australian Stock Exchange's *Listing Rules* require that the rights of preference shareholders be stated fully in the company's Articles of Association. Therefore, a company that issues preference shares must abide by the provisions specified in its Articles with respect to those shares. Preference shares may have various characteristics as follows:

1. **Cumulative or non-cumulative**

   A company that issues cumulative preference shares is required to pay any accumulated preference dividends before a distribution may be made to ordinary shareholders. For example, if a company which has issued 1 million 10 per cent preference shares with a par value of $1 fails to pay preference dividends for 2 years, it has accumulated an obligation to pay $200 000 in preference dividends. Non-cumulative preference shares do not oblige the company to pay any past accumulation of unpaid preference dividends.

2. **Redeemable, irredeemable, converting or convertible**

   A redeemable preference share is very similar to a debenture, but, as is the case with all preference shares, the dividends on redeemable preference shares are not deductible for income tax purposes. An irredeemable preference share, in contrast, is similar to an ordinary share in that the amount subscribed does not have to be repaid. A converting preference share automatically converts to ordinary shares at some specified time in the future. A convertible preference share can be converted to ordinary shares at the option of the holder. These are discussed in the next section.

3  **Participating or non-participating**
   If the company grants preference shareholders the right to participate in the distribution of profit available to ordinary shareholders, preference shareholders may be entitled to a return in excess of the stated preference dividend rate. For example, a company may issue participating preference shares which allow shareholders to share in any profit earned in excess of a certain amount. As a result, preference shareholders can obtain a dividend in excess of the preference dividend rate if the company has a very profitable year. A non-participating preference shareholder is not entitled to a dividend in excess of the stated dividend rate. Traditionally, most preference share issues were cumulative, irredeemable, and non-participating. However, the popularity of different types of preference shares has varied considerably over time, due largely to changes in taxation provisions.

Two advantages of preference shares are as follows:

## LEVERAGE EFFECT

An issue of preference shares may be desirable for a company that is prevented from issuing additional debt because of the borrowing restrictions imposed by loan agreements, or by the trust deed to an earlier debenture issue. The company may be able to use preference shares to achieve what is, in effect, additional 'fixed interest' borrowing. In addition the use of preference shares will increase the equity base of the company, enabling the company to increase its borrowing in the future.

## FINANCIAL RISK

The financial risk associated with debt does not apply to irredeemable preference shares because the company is not committed to a dividend payment and the amount invested does not have to be repaid. Therefore the lower financial risk of preference shares compared with debt may cause preference shares to be regarded as a desirable fundraising method, especially for a company with high financial leverage. However, managers usually regard preference dividends in much the same light as interest payments on debt. It is likely that the omission of a preference dividend would be taken as a sign of serious financial weakness, which would have adverse effects on future attempts to borrow or raise capital in other ways.

## 10.6.2  CONVERTIBLE SECURITIES

Convertible securities take a number of forms but basically they provide a holder with the right to convert them into ordinary shares at some future date or dates. If the security holder chooses not to exercise the right to convert, the security will be redeemed at maturity.[12] Convertible securities have usually taken the form of convertible unsecured notes, or convertible preference shares. Convertible notes have traditionally been the most frequently issued form of convertible security in Australia but converting preference shares are a new type of security which have been issued by several companies in the early 1990s.

## CONVERTIBLE NOTES

A convertible note is usually unsecured debt that is issued for a fixed term at a fixed rate of interest, with the additional feature that the holder has the right to convert the note to an ordinary share at certain specified dates.

In effect, the purchaser of a convertible note acquires a fixed-interest security plus an option to purchase ordinary shares in the company at a specified price. As a result, note holders gain from an increase in the company's share price. Assume that a company issues 10-year, 8 per cent, convertible notes with a face value of $10 that at maturity can be converted to shares at a conversion ratio of one to one. The holder of 100 notes receives $80 interest per year and the repayment of $1000 at maturity. Alternatively, each note may be converted to one ordinary share in the company. The note holder will convert if the price of the company's shares at the note's maturity is above $10 because the value of a share exceeds the face value of the note. For example, if the share price is $11, the holder will make a gain of $1 per note by converting, rather than allowing the notes to be redeemed. It is usual for convertible note holders to be able to participate in new issues, such as rights issues and bonus issues, in the same ratio as if the notes had already been converted. It is also usual for the holders to be given the opportunity by the issuer to convert the notes into shares immediately, if there is a takeover offer for the issuing company.

Investors accept lower interest rates on convertible notes than they do on straight unsecured notes because the option inherent in convertible notes is valuable. The conversion price can be set at an amount which is greater than the current market price of the company's shares because the option to convert will have a value, provided that there is some chance that the share price may eventually exceed the conversion price.

Convertible notes typically have terms of up to ten years, which makes them attractive to issuers requiring long-term, fixed-rate debt finance. Because the notes are unsecured they can be issued by companies whose existing assets are pledged as security for other loans. As a long-term security, convertible notes are a natural investment for life offices and superannuation funds which have long-term liabilities.

---

12 Another equity-related debt security that has gained increasing acceptance overseas is the **warrant bond**. The warrant bond is a low-coupon bond with an option to purchase shares. The option to purchase shares can be traded separately from the bond; in contrast to convertible notes, the bond component remains, even if the option to purchase shares is exercised. For a more detailed discussion of warrant bonds, see J. Aldersley, 'Developments in Corporate Financing Techniques', *The Chartered Accountant in Australia*, June 1984, p.26.

Convertible notes can be issued by a rights issue to existing shareholders or by a placement to institutions. Placements of convertible notes by listed companies are restricted under ASX listing rule 3E(6), the '10% rule'. Some Australian companies have issued convertible notes on offshore markets, in which case they may be described as 'convertible bonds'. The convertible note framework allows scope for innovative security design and some recent issues by Australian companies have been undated and/or subordinated. Undated notes can usually be converted to ordinary shares at any time during a specified period, which may be several years. If a holder does not exercise the right of conversion by the final date, the notes become irredeemable or 'perpetual' debt. Therefore, such notes will generally be treated as equity for the purpose of calculating balance sheet ratios used in loan agreements, but they will be treated as debt for tax purposes. The tax treatment of convertible notes is discussed in Section 10.6.3.

## CONVERTING PREFERENCE SHARES

A converting preference share offers a guaranteed dividend prior to a specified conversion date, at which time the preference shares automatically convert to ordinary shares in the company at a conversion ratio. The conversion ratio is usually expressed in terms of some discount applied to the price of the ordinary shares **at the time of the conversion**. This means that the holder is effectively protected against a fall in the price of the ordinary shares prior to conversion. Such issues have become popular in recent years and have been made by several companies including Coles Myer, News Corporation, and Westpac. The conversion date for such shares is typically 5 years from the date of issue, with the issuer often having the option to enforce early conversion. The conversion price has generally been set at a discount of between 5 per cent and 10 per cent of the market price of the ordinary shares at the time of conversion. The effect of arranging the conversion in this way is shown in Example 10.3.

*Example 10.3*
ABC Ltd issues converting preference shares with a face value of $20 which convert to ordinary shares on 30 October 1998. The conversion ratio will be determined by dividing $20 by:
- an amount equal to the price of ABC's ordinary shares on 30 October 1998, less 10 per cent; or
- $20, whichever yields the greater number of shares.

This means that if the price of the ordinary shares on 30 October 1998 is less than $22.22, the conversion ratio will vary inversely with the ordinary share price. Alternatively, if the price of the ordinary shares is greater than $22.22, the conversion ratio will be one.

Suppose that on 30 October 1998 the price of one ABC share is $8.23. The conversion ratio will be: $\frac{\$20}{\$8.23 \times 0.9}$ = 2.7. In this case, each preference share will convert to ordinary shares with a value of 2.7 × $8.23 = $22.22.

Alternatively, if the ordinary share price is greater than $22.22, each preference share will convert to one ordinary share. Therefore the holder of each preference share is assured of receiving ordinary shares worth at least $22.22 at the time of conversion.

Converting preference share dividends can be franked, and the issuing company has usually promised that they will be fully franked. Of course where the dividends are unfranked the yield on the shares will have to be much greater than if the dividends are franked. The tax treatment of converting preference shares is discussed in the next section.

### 10.6.3 Hybrid Securities and the Tax System

The Australian tax system involves fundamental differences between the tax treatment of debt and equity. Where a company uses debt finance, interest on the debt is tax deductible for the company and taxable in the hands of investors. In the case of equity finance, dividends are not tax deductible, but can be franked, in which case resident investors will benefit if they are able to use tax credits. Where a tax system relies on making a distinction between debt and equity, there is potential for difficulties in dealing with hybrid securities. For example, when a convertible note is converted to an ordinary share, is any gain taxable? If so, is it taxable as ordinary income or as a capital gain? Similarly, should preference shares be classified as equity or debt for tax purposes? Clearly, the answers to these and other questions are important to issuers and investors. Therefore, we outline some of the tax rules currently applicable to convertible notes and preference shares, and some of the changes in these rules.

#### Convertible Notes

A company that issues convertible notes can claim the interest paid as a tax deduction, provided that the notes conform to criteria specified in Section 82SA of the *Income Tax Assessment Act*. Some of these criteria are as follows:
1. The decision to convert must be made by the holder, not the issuer, and the notes must not be callable by the issuer.
2. For notes issued in the domestic market, the interest rate must be fixed for the term of the note.
3. The rights and obligations of the holder must be independent of whether the conversion option is exercised.

The tax rules are also important for investors because for notes purchased after 10 May 1989 the conversion to shares is treated as a sale and any gain is taxable. The market value of the note at the time of conversion then becomes the cost base for the purpose of assessing capital gains tax on shares acquired by conversion.

#### Preference Shares

The tax treatment of preference shares can be complex because in some cases they are treated as debt, while in others they are treated as equity. Also, the inter-company tax rebate on dividends under s.46 of the *Income Tax Assessment Act* does not apply to some preference share dividends. Traditionally, preference shares have been treated as equity for tax purposes. However, the traditional approach was changed on more than one occasion during the 1980s. These

changes focused mainly on redeemable preference shares, which became popular during the 1980s, initially as part of tax-effective financing arrangements for companies with carry-forward tax losses. Later, they were used to transfer imputation credits between companies. These strategies were attacked by amendments to the *Income Tax Assessment Act*. These amendments provide that:
- preference share dividends will be classified as 'debt dividends' in cases where payment of the dividend may reasonably be regarded as equivalent to the payment of interest on a loan;
- the inter-company tax rebate will apply only to dividends that are franked; and
- 'debt dividends' cannot be franked.

The effect of these provisions is that dividends on redeemable preference shares will be deemed to be 'debt dividends'. Therefore redeemable preference shares are no longer a viable form of financing in Australia. Dividends on other preference shares could also be classified as debt dividends unless the Commissioner of Taxation is satisfied that the returns to investors are related to the performance of the company, rather than to interest rates.

Most issues of converting preference shares carry franked dividends and are treated as equity, which is consistent with the fact that they will automatically convert to ordinary shares. The Commissioner of Taxation has confirmed that for converting preference shares:
- the dividends will be treated as equity dividends rather than debt dividends; and
- the conversion to ordinary shares will not be regarded as a sale and will not trigger any tax liability.

## SELECTED REFERENCES

Bruce, R., et al., Eds, *Handbook of Australian Corporate Finance*, 4th edn, Butterworths, Sydney, 1991, Chapter 5.
Carew, E., *Fast Money 3*, Allen and Unwin, Sydney, 1992.
CCH Corporation Law Editors, *Australian Corporations and Securities Law Reporter*, CCH Australia Limited, Sydney, 1993.
Donaldson, G., 'In Defence of Preferred Stock', *Harvard Business Review*, July–August 1962, pp. 123–36.
Kelly, B. W, 'Corporate Trust Deeds: The Quiet Revolution', *The Australian Accountant*, September 1984, pp. 627–31.
Kolb, R.W, *Financial Derivatives*, New York Institute of Finance, New York, 1993, Chapters 1 and 4.

## QUESTIONS

1. The amount of debt that a company should use in its capital structure should be determined by comparing the associated costs and benefits. Discuss these costs and benefits.
2. The establishment of the trading banks' Term Loan Fund helped to fill a gap in the Australian capital market. Discuss.
3. What are the terms of the typical mortgage agreement?
4. Discuss the term *security* as it relates to the difference between debentures and unsecured notes.

5. What are the functions of the trustee and the trust deed to a debenture issue?
6. Explain the twofold effect that the borrowing restrictions contained in the trust deed have upon the operations of a company.
7. *The borrowing restrictions contained in trust deeds to debenture issues have proved very restrictive for some Australian companies. Discuss.*
8. Explain the technique of *negative pledge lending*.
9. Explain why interest swaps are popular with corporate borrowers and also many traditional lenders.
10. *Most companies regard preference shares as a form of long-term debt.* What causes them to hold such a view? How does this affect their use of preference shares to raise funds?
11. *Convertible notes have not proved a popular form of borrowing for Australian companies. Discuss this statement.*
12. A number of large Australian companies used converting preference shares to raise capital in the early 1990s. What are converting preference shares, and why did these companies find them appropriate to their needs?

# CHAPTER 11

# DIVIDEND DECISIONS

## 11.1 INTRODUCTION

This chapter considers a company's dividend decisions. An important aspect of these decisions is dividend policy. We define dividend policy in some detail in Section 11.2, but in general terms a company's dividend policy determines how much of its profit will be paid to shareholders as dividends and how much will be retained.[1] The return on a shareholder's investment consists of the dividends received and the increase or decrease in the share price during the period the shares are held. Therefore, it might seem obvious that shareholders would prefer dividends to be as large as possible. However, this is not necessarily the case because shareholders can also benefit from the company retaining cash and investing it in additional assets, or using it to repay debt. That is, dividend decisions are often related to other financial decisions, and to analyse dividend policy we need to hold constant both investment decisions and other financing decisions. When this is done, we find that, from the shareholders' viewpoint, dividend policy involves a trade-off between dividends and capital gains.

When we ask whether there is an optimum dividend policy that maximises shareholders' wealth, we find that there are three possible answers. First, it can be shown that in a perfect capital market, dividend policy is irrelevant, in the sense that it has no effect on shareholders' wealth. When we introduce capital market imperfections such as taxes, agency costs, and transaction costs, there are two other possible answers. Some factors favour a policy of paying high dividends, while others favour a policy of paying low dividends. Thus there are three views on this controversy: (a) dividend policy does not matter, (b) a high dividend policy is best, and (c) a low dividend policy is best. Analysis of these three views is central to this chapter, but before presenting that analysis we describe briefly some institutional features of dividends.

---

1 See section 6(1) of the *Income Tax Assessment Act* 1936 for a definition of what constitutes a dividend under the Act.

## 11.1.1 LEGAL CONSIDERATIONS

Legally, a company's dividend may be paid only out of profits, and is not to be paid out of capital.[2] Profits in this context include accumulated retained profits as well as the current year's profit. Capital can be returned to shareholders only if the company follows strict legal procedures. Dividends may also be restricted by covenants in trust deeds and other loan agreements.

## 11.1.2 DIVIDEND DECLARATION PROCEDURES

In Australia, companies generally pay dividends twice a year. A company's Board of Directors, when announcing a dividend, will specify a date on which the 'books' will close. To qualify for a dividend, a shareholder's name must be entered in the shareholders' register (books) by that date. For shares listed on the Australian Stock Exchange, the rules of the exchange specify an ex-dividend date which is 7 business days before the date on which the books close. Investors who purchase shares before the ex-dividend date are entitled to receive the dividend. Those who purchase shares after the ex-dividend date are not entitled to receive the dividend. Provided that the legal requirements and the stock exchange listing requirements are met, a company's dividend decisions are at the discretion of its directors.

## 11.1.3 TYPES OF DIVIDENDS

Dividends are normally paid in cash, but many Australian companies have adopted dividend reinvestment plans which give shareholders the option of applying all or part of their dividend to purchase additional newly issued shares from the company. These plans are discussed in Section 11.5.3. Dividends are sometimes given a designation such as 'special' to indicate that shareholders should not expect them to be repeated. The significance of these 'special' dividends is discussed in Section 11.4.1.

The remainder of this chapter consists of four main sections. First, we analyse the primary question: is dividend policy important? After showing that it is irrelevant to shareholders' wealth in a perfect capital market, we next discuss possible reasons for the relevance of dividend policy, and review the empirical evidence. Finally, we discuss factors that may be important in establishing a company's dividend policy, with emphasis on the effects of taxation.

---

2 See section 201, *Corporations Law*. For a detailed discussion of the interpretation of this section, see P. Lipton & A. Herzberg, *Understanding Company Law*, 5th edn, Law Book Company, 1993, Ch.10.

## 11.2 IS DIVIDEND POLICY IMPORTANT TO SHAREHOLDERS?

### 11.2.1 ALTERNATIVE DIVIDEND POLICIES

Before discussing reasons why dividend policy may or may not be important to shareholders we outline some of the dividend policies a company's directors might adopt. One possibility is simply to treat dividends as a residual. A company that adopts this policy would pay out as dividends any profits which, in the opinion of management, cannot be profitably invested. Alternatively, if the company's investment needs are greater than its profit, dividends would be omitted and extra finance would be raised externally. This **pure residual** dividend policy can result in dividends fluctuating significantly from year to year. A more popular policy is the **stable** or 'smoothed' dividend policy. Under this policy, management sets a target dividend payout ratio, that is, a target proportion of annual profits to be paid out as dividends so that dividends are equal to the long-run difference between expected profits and expected investment needs. The amount of each dividend is then changed only when this long-run difference changes. For example, the dividend per share will be increased if there is an increase in profit which is regarded as sustainable, but it will not be changed in response to fluctuations in profit which are believed to be only temporary. Similarly, if profit falls, the dividend per share will be maintained unless the outlook for profits is so poor that the current dividend level is considered to be unsustainable.

Two consequences of a stable dividend policy are: changes in dividends tend to lag changes in profits, and dividends are much less variable than profits. Another consequence is that the dividend payout ratio may fluctuate dramatically. For example, if profit is unexpectedly high in a particular year, the dividend payout ratio will fall. If management is concerned to avoid these fluctuations in payout ratio, it could adopt a **constant payout** policy, whereby the dividend payout ratio remains essentially the same each year. Clearly for a company following this policy the variability of dividends and profits will be very similar.

### 11.2.2 MANAGERS AND DIVIDEND DECISIONS

There is abundant empirical evidence that managers regard dividend decisions as important. In an important early study, Lintner interviewed the managers of 28 US companies and found that in most cases dividends were an 'active decision variable', and were seldom regarded purely as a residual, or influenced significantly by financing requirements.[3]

Lintner's findings have been summarised as follows:[4]

1. Most companies have a long-term target dividend–payout ratio.

---

[3] J. Lintner, 'Distribution of Incomes of Corporations Among Dividends, Retained Earnings and Taxes', *American Economic Review*, May 1956, pp. 97–113.

[4] This four point summary was provided by T. Marsh & R. Merton, 'Dividend Behavior for the Aggregate Stock Market', *Journal of Business*, January 1987, pp. 1–40. The wording they used has been modified here.

2. In determining dividends, managers focus more on the change in payout than on the absolute level of payout.
3. Dividends are 'smoothed' relative to profits and are typically changed in response to a sustainable change in profits. Dividends are unlikely to be affected by temporary fluctuations in profits.
4. Most managers are reluctant to make changes in dividends that are likely to have to be reversed in the near future.

Therefore, managers treat dividend decisions as being important and most companies adopt an identifiable dividend policy. However, this does not necessarily mean that dividend policy influences shareholders' wealth. In fact, a thorough analysis by Miller and Modigliani proved that under certain restrictive assumptions, dividend policy has no effect on shareholders' wealth.

### 11.2.3 THE IRRELEVANCE OF DIVIDEND POLICY

The proposition that a company's dividend policy has no effect on shareholders' wealth was first advanced by Miller and Modigliani (MM).[5] Their analysis demonstrates the irrelevance of dividend policy under the following assumptions:

1. The company has a given investment plan which is not affected by changes in dividend policy.
2. There is a perfectly competitive capital market, with no transaction costs, flotation costs or information costs.
3. There are no taxes, so investors are indifferent between receiving dividends or capital gains.

To define dividend policy we consider the major sources and uses of funds for a company, assuming no change in items such as inventory and accounts receivable. For an all-equity company there are two sources of funds and two uses of funds, as follows:

| Sources | Notation |
|---|---|
| Cash from operations | $X$ |
| Cash raised from new share issues | $\Delta S$ |
| Uses | Notation |
| Investment | $I$ |
| Dividends (where $n$ = number of issued shares and $D$ = dividend per share). | $nD$ |

Since sources and uses of funds must be equal:

$$X + \Delta S = I + nD \tag{11.1}$$

If the dividend per share $D$ is increased, then under the MM assumptions the funds used to pay the dividend can be replaced from only one source: a new share issue. Therefore dividend policy is a trade-off between: retaining profit; and paying dividends and making new share issues to replace the cash paid out.

---

[5] M. Miller & F. Modigliani, 'Dividend Policy, Growth and the Valuation of Shares', *Journal of Business*, October 1961, pp. 411–33.

Suppose a company decides to pay a cash dividend. To maintain the resources necessary to finance its given investment plan it will need at the same time to make a new share issue (at the current market price) of the same amount. This company has changed its dividend policy but nothing else. Under these circumstances, shareholders would be indifferent to the payment of dividends compared to the retention of profits. This is hardly surprising: it says that a shareholder paid an increased dividend, but then immediately asked to return the extra cash in exchange for new shares, feels no better or worse off. In other words, on reflection, the irrelevance of dividend policy, under the MM assumptions, is obvious.

MM's argument is now outlined more formally. The market price per share at time zero is equal to the present value of the dividend that investors will receive on each share at the end of a period, plus the present value of the market price per share at the end of the period. Therefore:

$$P_0 = \frac{1}{1 + k_e} [D_1 + P_1] \qquad (11.2)$$

where $P_0$ = market price per share at time zero
$k_e$ = rate of return required by investors on the company's equity capital
$D_1$ = dividend per share at time 1
$P_1$ = market price per share at time 1, after payment of the dividend

If $n$ is equal to the number of shares outstanding at time zero, Equation 11.2 can be rewritten to reflect the total market value of the company $V_0$, which is equal to $nP_0$:

$$nP_0 = V_0 = \frac{1}{1 + k_e} [nD_1 + nP_1] \qquad (11.3)$$

If the company pays a dividend at time 1 and then issues $\Delta n$ new shares priced at $P_1$ each to replace the cash paid out, Equation 11.1 becomes:

$$X + \Delta n P_1 = I + nD_1$$

which on rearrangement becomes:

$$nD_1 = X - I + \Delta n P_1 \qquad (11.4)$$

Substituting from Equation 11.4 for the $nD_1$ term in Equation 11.3 gives:

$$V_0 = \frac{1}{1 + k_e} [X - I + \Delta n P_1 + nP_1]$$

Since $(n + \Delta n) P_1$ equals $V_1$, the value of the company at time 1, the final result is:

$$V_0 = \frac{1}{1 + k_e} [X - I + V_1] \qquad (11.5)$$

As the $nD_1$ term has cancelled out, the next dividend $D_1$ does not appear in Equation 11.5. Therefore, the company value is independent of the next dividend. Future dividends could affect $V_0$ only through $V_1$ which, using Equation 11.3, can be expressed in terms of $P_2$ and $D_2$. However, we could then repeat the above procedure to eliminate $D_2$. Obviously this elimination of successive future dividends could be repeated indefinitely, leading to MM's conclusion that company value is not related to the company's dividend policy. In a perfect capital market, dividend policy has no effect on shareholders' wealth because any cash paid out as dividends can be costlessly replaced by issuing additional shares. While Equation 11.5 shows that dividend policy does *not* affect shareholders' wealth, it also shows what *does* determine shareholders' wealth: $(X - I)$, which represents the company's net cash flows. Therefore the important issue for the financial manager is the company's investment decisions, and they need have no connection with its dividend policy. In other words, the company can pay any future dividends that management chooses without affecting its value now, provided the cash paid out is replaced by a new share issue to maintain the same investment program.

Example 11.1 illustrates the irrelevance of dividend policy.

### Example 11.1

The ABC company has 10 000 shares on issue, with a market price of $11 each. Its balance sheet in market values is:

**Table 11.1** ABC Company market value balance sheet $

| | | | |
|---|---|---|---|
| Cash | 15 000 | Debt | 10 000 |
| Fixed assets | 100 000 | | |
| Investment opportunity | 5 000 | Equity | 110 000 |
| Total assets | 120 000 | Value of company | 120 000 |

The $15 000 cash has been reserved for the investment opportunity which has not yet been taken up, and is therefore shown at its estimated NPV of $5000. Suppose that management decides instead to use the cash to pay a dividend of $15 000, and then issues more shares to replace the cash and proceed with the new investment. After these transactions the company still has the same assets, so its value should still be $120 000. The new shares should be worth the amount paid for them, $15 000, so the value of the original shares is:

$$\begin{aligned}\text{Value of original shares} &= \text{value of company} - \text{value of debt} - \text{value of new shares} \\ &= \$120\,000 - \$10\,000 - \$15\,000 \\ &= \$95\,000\end{aligned}$$

Therefore, the original shareholders have suffered a capital loss of $15 000, exactly offsetting the dividend of $15 000 which is now cash in their hands. By having the ABC Company pay a dividend, its original shareholders have converted part of their stake in the company into cash of $15 000. Since the stake transferred to the new shareholders is also worth $15 000, the net change in the wealth of the original shareholders is zero. Suppose the company had not paid the dividend, but the original shareholders wished to obtain cash. In this case the shareholders could have generated the $15 000 directly by selling some of their shares to other investors. After this sale their remaining shares would again be worth $95 000, exactly as they were after ABC paid the dividend. Therefore, dividend policy is irrelevant, because whether ABC shareholders receive a cash dividend of $15 000 or generate $15 000 cash by selling some of their shares, their wealth, that is, the sum of the cash plus the market value of their remaining stake in the company, remains exactly the same. In other words, for each dollar they receive in dividends, the original shareholders give up future dividends with a present value of one dollar, which reduces the value of their shares by one dollar.

Our discussion shows that the MM dividend irrelevance proposition is valid in a perfect capital market with no taxes. Therefore, if dividend policy is important in practice, the reasons for its importance must relate to factors that MM's assumptions excluded from their analysis. These factors include taxes, transaction costs, information costs, and agency costs. Before examining these factors we examine a persistent argument for paying dividends which does not rely on market imperfections.

## 11.2.4 Resolution of uncertainty

An argument which has been expressed in various ways is that investors prefer a high dividend policy because it resolves uncertainty. This argument, known as the 'bird-in-the-hand argument', was advanced in its most sophisticated form by Gordon.[6] He argued that dividends expected in the near future are less risky than those expected in the more distant future. Because shareholders are risk averse, dividends expected in the more distant future will be discounted at a higher rate per period to compensate for the extra risk. According to this argument a company's share price will decrease if dividends are reduced now in order to increase the growth in future profits and dividends. In other words, Gordon suggests that investors are not indifferent to a dollar of dividends compared to the capital gains expected from a dollar of retained profits. The expected capital gains are seen as uncertain because their eventual realisation depends on the returns from risky future investments. Because investors prefer the early resolution of uncertainty, they will be prepared to pay a premium for the shares of companies with higher current dividends. Such shares are less risky, in Gordon's view, than shares with lower dividends and higher retained profits.

Careful analysis of his argument has shown that it is flawed because it confuses dividend decisions with investment decisions.[7] Essentially, he argues that if profits are retained and invested in risky assets, future profits should be discounted at a risk-adjusted rate related to the risk of those assets. The problem with Gordon's argument is that this relationship between asset risk and discount rate holds true, regardless of dividend policy. The reason can be seen by considering a company which follows Gordon's advice and pays out all its profits as dividends. Provided the company's investment decisions are unchanged, adoption of this extreme dividend policy cannot increase company value because the risk of future dividends must be exactly the same as the risk of future profits.

---

6 See M. Gordon, *The Investment, Financing and Valuation of the Corporation*, Richard D. Irwin, Homewood, Illinois, 1962, Ch.5.
7 M. Brennan, 'A Note on Dividend Irrelevance and the Gordon Valuation Model', *Journal of Finance*, December 1971, pp. 1115–21 and R. Higgins, 'Dividend Policy and Increasing Discount Rates: A Clarification', *Journal of Financial and Quantitative Analysis*, June 1972, pp. 1757–62.

Therefore there is no reason to discount dividends at a lower rate than profits, and no reason for investors to value dividends more highly than retained profits.

The fallacy inherent in Gordon's argument can also be highlighted in the following way.[8] As discussed earlier, cash paid out as dividends must be replaced by issuing new shares if the company's investment plans are to remain unchanged. Therefore, unless there is a change in investment policy, payment of dividends does not cause any change in a company's stock of risky assets. The old shareholders receive cash in hand but suffer an offsetting capital loss. The new shareholders outlay cash to buy a claim to a future dividend stream. In a competitive market the new shares should be priced so that these transactions have a net present value of zero to both parties. To argue that the old shareholders gain from higher dividends is to argue that the new shareholders lose by paying more than the shares are worth. Moreover the 'new' shareholders may well be the same as the 'old' ones. A shareholder who receives a dividend and then subscribes for shares issued by the company is exposed to the same risk as if there had been no dividend. In summary, if the company maintains the same investment policy, there can be no bird-in-the-hand effect.

## 11.3 REASONS FOR THE RELEVANCE OF DIVIDEND POLICY

Miller and Modigliani's conclusion that dividend policy is irrelevant is logically true under their assumptions. In practice their assumptions are violated in ways that may mean that dividend policy is important. For example:

- dividends and capital gains may be taxed at different rates;
- investors do not have costless access to the same information as managers;
- there can be conflicts of interest between shareholders and managers;
- investors and companies incur transaction costs in selling and issuing shares.

If these and other market imperfections alter the MM dividend irrelevance conclusion, then shareholders will want the company's managers to adopt the policy that maximises shareholders' wealth.

### 11.3.1 TAXATION[9]

The existence of taxes can either favour or penalise payment of dividends, depending on whether the tax burden on profits distributed as dividends is greater or less than the tax burden on capital gains arising from retained profits. For example, under the classical tax system which applied in Australia before 1 July 1987, individual investors were taxed on dividends at their full marginal tax rate, whereas capital gains were either tax free or taxed at lower rates than dividends.

---

[8] The discussion in this paragraph relies on F. Easterbrook, 'Two Agency-cost Explanations of Dividends', *American Economic Review*, September 1984, p. 651.

[9] Readers who are not familiar with the dividend imputation tax system should refer to Appendix 11.1 before reading this section.

Since dividends were paid from profits that were subject to company income tax, the classical tax system involved double taxation of dividends. Under those conditions it could be argued that investors were disadvantaged by payment of dividends and would have preferred that companies retain profits, thus allowing investors to realise returns as tax-advantaged capital gains. Despite this apparent tax disadvantage of paying dividends, many Australian companies did pay out a significant percentage of their profits as dividends.

A similar situation existed in the US. Black and Scholes suggested that in these circumstances, particular classes of investors may be attracted to companies with different dividend policies.[10] That is, a company may attract a 'clientele' of investors who find that its dividend policy suits their tax position. Individual investors subject to high personal tax rates would prefer the shares of companies that pay low dividends or no dividends. Other investors who are taxed more heavily on capital gains than on dividends would prefer the shares of companies which pay high dividends, while tax exempt investors would find all dividend policies equally attractive. Black and Scholes argued that the amount of dividends paid by companies may change until there is an equilibrium in which the needs of investors in all three clienteles are satisfied by the range of available dividend policies. If this equilibrium were achieved, there would be no incentive for a company to change its dividend policy. That is, in terms of the value of the company, one clientele is as good as another, and dividend policy would be irrelevant for any particular company. In other words, Black and Scholes argued for an equilibrium in which competition among companies ensures that the supply of dividends matches the demand for dividends, and no company could increase its share price by changing its dividend policy.

While the dividend clientele argument has considerable appeal, it also has the weakness that it is difficult to explain why so many investors would have demanded dividends. Under the classical tax system, high dividends meant high taxes for many investors. However, differential taxation of dividends and capital gains may not be important if investors use **tax arbitrage** schemes to convert dividends into capital gains. These schemes typically involve borrowing by the investor so that, for tax purposes, interest can be claimed as a deduction against dividend income. Miller and Scholes showed how such schemes could operate in the US when dividends were taxed more heavily than capital gains.[11] Although Miller and Scholes maintained that their proposed tax arbitrage method was practical, it is complicated and may involve non-trivial transaction costs. Further, it is now of limited relevance to Australia where the taxation of company profits was changed fundamentally by the introduction of the imputation tax system on 1 July 1987.

Under the imputation system, the impact of income tax on different classes of investors is not uniform but, for Australian resident investors, the system

---

10 F. Black & M. Scholes, 'The Effects of Dividend Yield and Dividend Policy on Common Stock Prices and Returns', *Journal of Financial Economics*, May 1974, pp. 1–22. Note that the existence of dividend clienteles was first suggested by Miller & Modigliani, see Footnote 5, p. 431.
11 M. Miller & M. Scholes, 'Dividends and Taxes', *Journal of Financial Economics*, December 1978, pp. 333–64.

generally favours payment of dividends out of profits which have been subject to Australian company income tax. These dividends, known as **franked dividends**, carry tax credits related to the income tax paid by the company. Individual investors are taxed on dividends received but personal income tax for Australian investors is reduced by tax credits to the extent that dividends are franked. Individual investors also pay tax on realised capital gains in excess of the rate of inflation, unless the shares were purchased prior to 20 September 1985. In the case of investors that are public companies, Section 46 of the *Income Tax Assessment Act* 1936 provides for such investors to be allowed a tax rebate equal to the amount of dividends included in taxable income, multiplied by the average rate of tax payable on their taxable income. This means that under most circumstances dividends received by public companies are not taxed.[12] The same rebate on dividends received applies to insurance companies. However, the tax treatment of capital gains for companies is not uniform. For companies such as insurance companies which the Commissioner of Taxation regards as share traders, realised capital gains are included in assessable income with no adjustment for inflation. For the vast majority of public companies, only real capital gains on assets acquired on or after 20 September 1985 are taxed. Since 1 July 1988, superannuation funds have been taxed at a rate of 15 per cent on dividends but can benefit from tax credits on franked dividends.

As discussed above, it seems likely that a company will tend to attract a clientele of investors who are suited by its dividend policy. For example, most resident individual investors and superannuation funds probably would favour investing in companies with a high payout of franked dividends. Non-resident investors are likely to prefer capital gains, since they are unable to benefit directly from tax credits on franked dividends, and are exempt from Australian capital gains tax, provided they hold less than 10 per cent of the shares issued by an Australian company.

The nature of the imputation system is such that the overall tax burden on returns to investors depends critically on the dividend policies adopted by companies. Under the imputation system, it is only by payment of franked dividends that credits for company tax paid can be transferred to investors, who can then use the credits to offset their personal tax liabilities. Because of the time value of money, investors generally prefer to receive tax credits sooner rather than later. Therefore, it has been argued that there is an optimum dividend policy for Australian companies whose shares are held by resident investors. This optimum dividend policy is simply that the company should pay the maximum franked dividends that it can, given the balance in its franking account.[13]

---

12 The intercorporate dividend rebate is subject to various anti-avoidance provisions. For example, dividends on redeemable preference shares are regarded as 'debt dividends,' which means that they are not rebatable and cannot be franked unless the shares were issued before 16 August 1989.

13 P. Howard & R. Brown, 'Dividend Policy and Capital Structure Under the Imputation Tax System: Some Clarifying Comments', *Accounting and Finance*, May 1992, pp. 51–61 and D. Hamson & P. Ziegler, 'The Impact of Dividend Imputation on Firms' Financial Decisions', *Accounting and Finance*, November 1990, pp. 29–53. It has also been argued that under imputation, this policy will be optimal for all Australian companies, irrespective of the tax status of

## 11.3.2 INFORMATION EFFECTS AND SIGNALLING TO INVESTORS

There is empirical evidence that share price changes around the time of the announcement of dividend changes are positively related to the change in dividend. For example, it is clear that announcements of large increases in dividends are often followed immediately by increases in share price, and that reductions in dividend can result in decreases in share prices.[14] Does this fact invalidate the dividend irrelevance theorem? MM argued that it is not the dividend payments *per se* that determine the value of a company but the present and future cash flows from the company's investments.[15] A change in dividends is one way that management's 'inside' information about future cash flows is conveyed to the market. Thus the announcement of a change in dividends provides the *occasion* for a change in share price, but the change in dividends is not itself the *cause* of the price change. In summary, MM's response is that the information effect of dividends can be consistent with their irrelevance theorem and the share price response to a change in dividends tells us nothing about investors' preferences for dividends and capital gains.

If dividend announcements convey information, it is possible that management deliberately uses dividend policy to signal information to investors.[16] This argument relies on the existence of information asymmetry, whereby management has valuable inside information that it is unable to release direct to investors. The greater uncertainty for investors that results may cause a company's share price to be lower than it would be if investors were fully informed. It is argued that the adverse effects of information asymmetry can be reduced in a cost-effective way through dividend policy. Dividends have the potential to provide a credible signal because the payment of dividends is some proof of management's ability to ensure that the company generates sufficient cash to be able to pay dividends, and also provides information on management's expectations as to the company's future profitability. It is unlikely, for example, that management will increase a company's dividend payout unless it expects to be able to maintain that payout in the future.[17] By paying dividends and increasing them regularly, management is effectively committing itself to making a series of future payments to shareholders. This commitment reduces uncertainty for investors and assures them that management is not concealing important adverse information. It is clear that dividend changes have information effects and that the potential exists for signalling via dividends. However, it is less clear why payment of dividends should be the most efficient way of conveying information

---

their shareholders; see R. Nicol, 'The Dividend Puzzle: An Australian Solution?', *Australian Accounting Review*, November 1992, pp. 42–55.
14 Studies that formally document these effects are discussed in Section 11.4.1.
15 M. Miller & F. Modigliani, see Footnote 5, pp. 415–21.
16 Theories based on dividends as signals to investors are presented by S. Bhattacharya, 'Imperfect Information, Dividend Policy, and "The Bird in the Hand" Fallacy', *Bell Journal of Economics*, Spring 1979, pp. 259–70; and M. Miller & K. Rock, 'Dividend Policy Under Asymmetric Information', *Journal of Finance*, September 1985, pp. 1031–51.
17 J. Lintner, see Footnote 3, p. 99.

to investors, particularly if dividends are taxed more heavily than capital gains.[18] The next section discusses a related but somewhat different role for dividend policy under conditions of information asymmetry.

### 11.3.3 AGENCY COSTS

We saw in Chapter 1 that, given the separation of ownership and control of companies, agency costs may be incurred as a result of shareholders' fears that managers may attempt to increase their personal wealth at the expense of shareholders' wealth. Because of this uncertainty, monitoring and bonding arrangements will evolve, with the objective of minimising agency costs.

It is argued that the incentive to minimise agency costs will influence managers to pay higher dividends.[19] Higher dividends will force a company to raise capital externally more frequently than it would otherwise need to. Capital raising is accompanied by the provision of information to investors, underwriters, and other capital market agents, particularly potential new investors. As a result, investors will have the opportunity to scrutinise the company closely at a relatively low cost. The capital raising process provides an efficient mechanism for contributors of new capital to monitor the performance of the managers. Existing shareholders also benefit from this process because managers who are subject to regular monitoring are more likely to act in shareholders' interests than managers subject to less scrutiny.

The potential for agency costs to be important is probably greatest when a company generates large free cash flows, which are defined as cash flows in excess of those required to fund all available projects that have positive net present values. Managers have incentives to achieve growth because it is likely that the larger the company, the more power and higher remuneration there will be for the managers. Therefore, managers may retain cash and invest it in new projects, even though they have negative net present values, or they may waste resources by allowing inefficiencies to develop. It follows that shareholders' wealth will be increased if managers commit themselves to paying out this cash as dividends rather than retaining it within the company.[20] In summary, dividend policy can have a role in reducing agency costs by disciplining managers to act in the best interests of shareholders.

---

[18] Signalling models are discussed by M. Miller, 'The Informational Content of Dividends', in J. Bosons, R. Dornbusch & S. Fischer, Eds, *Macroeconomics: Essays in Honor of Franco Modigliani*, MIT Press, Boston, 1986, and critically reviewed by J. Crockett & I. Friend, 'Dividend Policy in Perspective: Can Theory Explain Behaviour?', *Review of Economics and Statistics*, November 1988, pp. 603–13.

[19] M. Rozeff, 'Growth, Beta and Agency Costs as Determinants of Dividend Payout Ratios', *Journal of Financial Research*, Fall 1982, pp. 249–59. For further discussion of the relevance of agency costs, see: F. Easterbrook, Footnote 8, pp. 650–9.

[20] M. Jensen, 'Agency Costs of Free Cash Flow, Corporate Finance and Takeovers', *American Economic Review*, May 1986, pp. 323–9. Jensen argues that use of debt finance will be particularly effective in reducing these agency costs because severe penalties are associated with failure to meet obligations to lenders. Commitments to pay regular dividends may have a similar, but less pronounced, effect because of the well known reluctance of managers to reduce dividends.

### 11.3.4 Shareholders' preference for current income

Another reason proposed for the relevance of dividends is that some shareholders may require their shares to yield current income. The contrary position taken by MM is that shareholders who require current income can always sell a portion of their share portfolio. Although MM are correct, investors pursuing such a policy will be subject to transaction costs such as brokerage fees and stamp duty. Also, such investors will lose proportionate voting power, which may concern some (larger) shareholders. Therefore, a company's dividend policy may be attractive to particular investors.

### 11.3.5 Issue and transaction costs

If a company pays dividends and its retained earnings are insufficient to meet its investment needs, it will need to raise funds externally and the company will incur issue costs which could have been avoided by reducing its dividends. Therefore companies may restrict dividends and may be discouraged from paying a higher dividend, even where there appears to be an excess demand for companies with such a dividend policy.

If a company seeks to reduce its dividend payout, some shareholders may need to sell some of their shares, thus creating 'home-made' dividends to maintain their current consumption. However, as explained in Section 11.3.4, these shareholders will incur transaction costs. Shareholders may therefore resist a change in dividend policy. Again, the existence of transaction costs discourages a company from changing its dividend policy to take advantage of a perceived excess demand for the shares of companies which follow a particular dividend policy.

### 11.3.6 Dividend–clientele effect

As discussed in Section 11.3.1, the fact that different classes of investors are taxed differently on dividends and capital gains is likely to give rise to a clientele effect. That is, a company will tend to attract a clientele of investors who are suited by its dividend policy. Similarly a clientele effect could also develop owing to different preferences for current income. Companies that pay high dividends would attract investors who require income from their share portfolio to meet consumption needs. Conversely, companies that pay low or zero dividends would attract investors with adequate income from other sources. Such investors would reinvest any dividends they receive, but can avoid the transaction costs of doing so by investing in companies that retain most or all of their profits, or by investing in companies that have dividend reinvestment plans.

Even if dividend clienteles exist, it does not necessarily follow that a company can influence the market value of its shares by altering its dividend policy. Where the supply of companies with a particular dividend payout is equal to the demand for companies with that payout, the price of each company's shares will be independent of its dividend policy. That is, there will be no incentive for one more company to adopt a different payout policy. However, if clienteles exist, management should consider carefully whether any suggested change in dividend policy is justified. If a company changes its dividend policy it may decrease its appeal to existing shareholders, so some of them will sell their shares and switch their investment to other companies. Shareholders who switch companies will be disadvantaged because of the transaction costs. Therefore the existence of investor clienteles and transaction costs suggests that companies should follow a stable dividend policy. Managers who instead allow dividends to fluctuate may find that their companies' shares do not appeal to any clientele of investors.

### 11.3.7 SUMMARY

The arguments considered in Section 11.2 and Sections 11.3.1 to 11.3.6 indicate that there are three schools of thought on dividend policy. First, MM maintain that dividend policy cannot affect shareholders' wealth in a perfect capital market. The dividend–clientele effect suggests that the MM conclusion may still hold when market imperfections exist. Secondly, arguments for low dividends are based on the existence of issue and transaction costs, and on the effect of taxes when dividends are taxed more heavily than capital gains. Thirdly, arguments for high dividends are based on the existence of agency costs, shareholders' preference for current income, and, under the imputation system, taxes.

In addition to these varied views on the importance of dividend policy the argument that dividend announcements convey information to investors suggests that *changes* in dividends are important even if the *level* of dividends is not. Whether the effects of taxes and other imperfections are sufficient, in practice, to invalidate the MM view is an issue for empirical research. However, the likelihood of there being information effects indicates that unambiguous evidence about the importance of dividend policy may be difficult to obtain. Section 11.4 reviews some of the extensive empirical evidence.

## 11.4 EMPIRICAL EVIDENCE

The theories discussed in Sections 11.2 and 11.3 suggest that dividend decisions may be influenced by many factors including:

- information effects;
- agency costs;
- clientele effects; and
- taxes.

Also it is likely that dividend decisions will be influenced by competing uses of funds such as the need to acquire additional assets. We now review empirical evidence on each of these issues.

### 11.4.1 INFORMATION EFFECTS

As discussed in Section 11.3.2, MM suggested that the share price changes that accompany announcements of changes in dividends may be due to information effects. Early studies, which attempted to identify the information content of dividends, were inconclusive because it is often difficult to distinguish between the effects on share prices of dividends and new information about other variables, particularly earnings. Also, in some cases a change in dividend may not convey information to the market because investors expected the company to make the change.

Asquith and Mullins minimised these problems by studying cases where companies were either paying their first dividend or resuming payment of dividends after a break of at least 10 years.[21] Over a two-day announcement period the average return associated with these dividend initiations exceeded the market return for the same level of risk by a highly significant 3.7 per cent. This finding is consistent with the view that dividends convey valuable information to the market. Similarly, Richardson, Sefcik and Thompson studied dividend initiations and found a five-day average 'excess' return of +4.0 per cent.[22] Healy and Palepu studied the earnings performance of companies that initiated dividends, and companies that omitted dividends.[23] They found that these extreme changes in dividend policy were related to changes in earnings in the year prior to, and the year of, the dividend change. This relationship meant that the changes in dividend policy could, in part, be predicted by changes in earnings. However, consistent with the previous studies there was a significant market reaction to the dividend policy changes. Moreover, companies that initiated (omitted) dividends experienced significant increases (decreases) in earnings for at least one year after the change of dividend policy. These findings are consistent with the propositions that dividend initiations and omissions convey information to the market, and that this information is related to future earnings.

The results of the three studies discussed so far are convincing but they examined only extreme changes in dividend policy. Therefore they do not necessarily mean that all dividend increases (decreases) simply convey good (bad) news about future earnings. For example, dividends are sometimes labelled by management as 'extra', 'special' or 'year-end' to indicate that investors should not expect them to be repeated. Therefore, these labelled dividends may not convey information to the market. Brickley studied the US market response to labelled dividends in comparison to increases in regular dividends.[24] He found that labelled dividends conveyed information to the market but, on a per dollar basis, their information content was less than that of regular dividends.

Another complication is that the true meaning of a change in dividends can vary, depending on the reason for the change. For example, a higher dividend could mean that a company's investment opportunities have declined, and management believes that shareholders can benefit by investing the cash elsewhere.

---

[21] P. Asquith & D. Mullins, 'The Impact of Initiating Dividend Payments on Shareholders' Wealth', *Journal of Business*, January 1983, pp. 77–96.
[22] G. Richardson, S. Sefcik & R. Thompson, 'A Test of Dividend Irrelevance Using Volume Reactions to a Change in Dividend Policy', *Journal of Financial Economics*, December 1986, pp. 313–33.
[23] P. Healy & K. Palepu, 'Earnings Information Conveyed by Dividend Initiations and Omissions', *Journal of Financial Economics*, September 1988, pp. 149–75.
[24] J. Brickley, 'Shareholder Wealth, Information Signalling and the Specially Designated Dividend', *Journal of Financial Economics*, August 1983, pp. 187–209.

Conversely, a lower dividend could mean that the company has attractive investment opportunities, or growth prospects which can be financed more cheaply by retaining cash, rather than maintaining the dividend and raising funds externally. Therefore there is the possibility of ambiguity: an increase in dividends could be either good or bad news, as could a decrease in dividends. Woolridge and Ghosh discuss this alternative information hypothesis and examine returns on the shares of a sample of US companies that reduced or omitted dividends.[25] As expected, share prices fell on average during the three-day period centred on the announcement, but the fall in share price was smaller where the dividend reduction was associated with the announcement of either higher earnings or significant future investment or growth opportunities. Clearly the positive effects of the announced growth prospects were not sufficient to offset fully the usual negative response to a dividend reduction. However, it appeared that the lost share value was recouped fairly quickly. Over the next three months, companies that had made 'growth-induced' dividend reductions outperformed the market by almost nine per cent on average.

The results of the studies discussed so far can be used to infer that changes in dividends cause market participants to revise their expectations, but they do not provide direct evidence of such revisions. Direct evidence of the effects on expectations of unexpected dividend changes is provided by Ofer and Siegel who analyse both share price movements and analysts' earnings forecasts.[26] They find that after an unexpected dividend change, analysts' revisions of previous earnings forecasts are positively related to the size of the unexpected dividend change. The forecast revisions are also related positively to the change in share prices surrounding the announcement, and their results are consistent with dividend changes conveying information about the expected level of cash flows. Thus Ofer and Siegel provide direct evidence that, as proposed by various dividend-signalling models, market participants revise their expectations following announcements of dividend changes.

Brown, Finn and Hancock analysed the information content of dividend and profit announcements by Australian companies.[27] In Australia, it is difficult to distinguish the relative importance of each of these announcements as they are usually made simultaneously. They found that where the information signals of dividends and profit announcements are not in conflict there is an immediate and significant effect on share prices. Where the signals conflict, the combined effect on share prices is considerably reduced. Although this evidence might be interpreted as suggesting that dividend announcements have information content, Brown, Finn and Hancock were unable to isolate the impact of dividend announcements from the impact of profit announcements.

---

25 J. Woolridge & C. Ghosh, 'Dividend cuts: Do they always signal bad news?', in *The Revolution in Corporate Finance*, Eds J. Stern & D. Chew, 2nd edn, Blackwell, Oxford 1992, pp. 462–73.
26 A. Ofer & D. Siegel, 'Corporate Financial Policy, Information, and Market Expectations: An Empirical Investigation of Dividends', *Journal of Finance*, September 1989, pp. 889–911.
27 P. Brown, F. Finn & P. Hancock, 'Dividend Changes, Earnings Reports and Share Prices: Some Australian Findings', *Australian Journal of Management*, October 1977, pp. 127–47.

A subsequent study using Australian data by Easton and Sinclair improved the methodology used by Brown, Finn and Hancock to unravel the information content of simultaneous dividend and profit announcements.[28] They found that dividend announcements provided information over and above the more significant information provided by profit announcements. A further study by Easton found that there is an interaction effect between the information conveyed by earnings and dividend announcements.[29] This suggests that investors evaluate earnings and dividend announcements in relation to each other and take into account the extent to which the two announcements provide consistent signals. In summary, there is ample evidence that dividend announcements do have information content and that they convey information primarily about the expected level of a company's cash flows.

## 11.4.2 Agency costs

Evidence supporting the role of dividends in reducing the agency costs of equity was found by Rozeff.[30] He found a significant negative relationship between dividend payout ratio and the fraction of the company's shares held by insiders such as managers and directors. If insiders owned a high proportion of the shares, dividends tended to be lower. He also found that the dividend payout ratio was positively related to the number of shareholders in the company—a measure of the dispersion of ownership. These findings are consistent with the proposition that ownership of equity by insiders and payment of dividends are complementary measures, both of which can reduce agency costs. When a higher proportion of a company's shares is owned by managers and directors, their interests will be more closely aligned with those of outside shareholders. When 'inside' ownership is lower there will be a greater need for other measures to ensure that this alignment of interests is maintained. Rozeff's results suggest that the payment of dividends has a role in this process. It appears that outside shareholders demand higher dividends if they own a higher fraction of the company's equity and if their ownership is widely dispersed. More recent evidence, which supports Rozeff's finding of a negative relationship between dividend payments and insider ownership, is reported by Crutchley and Hansen and by Jensen, Solberg and Zorn.[31]

---

[28] S. Easton & N. Sinclair, 'The Impact of Unexpected Earnings and Dividends on Abnormal Returns to Equity', *Accounting and Finance*, May 1989, pp. 1–19.
[29] S. Easton, 'Earnings and Dividends: Is There an Interaction Effect?', *Journal of Business Finance and Accounting*, January 1991, pp. 255–66.
[30] M. Rozeff, see Footnote 19, p. 250.
[31] C. Crutchley & R. Hansen, 'A Test of the Agency Theory of Managerial Ownership, Corporate Leverage, and Corporate Dividends', *Financial Management*, Winter 1989, pp. 36–46 and G. Jensen, D. Solberg & T. Zorn, 'Simultaneous Determination of Insider Ownership, Debt, and Dividend Policies', *Journal of Financial and Quantitative Analysis*, June 1992, pp. 247–63. It should be noted that while this finding is consistent with the agency cost explanation, it is also consistent with a tax-based explanation. If 'insiders' face higher taxes on dividends than on capital gains, dividend payments are likely to be restricted.

The role of dividends in controlling agency costs is also supported by the findings of Smith and Watts.[32] They predict and find that dividend yield is negatively related to the use of stock-option plans. The argument linking these variables is that both are related to a company's growth opportunities. Companies with greater growth opportunities will have lower free cash flow and pay lower dividends. Greater growth opportunities mean that managers' actions are harder to observe, thus making monitoring by outside shareholders less effective. In turn, this increases the incentive to link manager's remuneration to the effects of their actions on company value. This link is achieved by the stock-option plans. Smith and Watts also expect regulated companies, such as utilities, to pay higher dividends because the resultant increase in the frequency of fund raising in the capital market provides evidence about the companies' cost of capital. This information is valuable because it can be used to justify the companies' rates of return. This prediction is also supported by their results. These findings are also interesting in that they do not support information signalling models of dividend policy. For example, Bhattacharya's model predicts that companies of high quality will pay high dividends to signal their superior quality. Presumably, the need for such signalling increases with the degree of information asymmetry between managers and investors. Therefore companies with greater information asymmetry—generally unregulated companies with more growth opportunities—should pay higher dividends.[33] The fact that Smith and Watts' results are the reverse of the signalling model's prediction does not necessarily mean that signalling models are invalid. It does, though, suggest that agency costs may be more important than signalling motives in influencing dividend policies.

### 11.4.3 CLIENTELE EFFECTS

The dividend–clientele effect was first suggested by MM in 1961 but there is little empirical evidence of its importance. Pettit evaluated investors' preferences for current income and the impact of taxation as factors that may contribute to a clientele effect.[34] On the basis of evidence from other studies he used investors' age and income as surrogates for their need to consume out of current income. The hypothesis is that the older an investor and the lower his current income, the higher is his preference for current consumption. Pettit found a positive relationship between the age of investors and the dividend yield of the companies in which they invest, and a negative relationship between the income of shareholders and the companies' dividend yield. He also examined whether the dividend yields of different companies are explained by the tax circumstances of their shareholders. He found that investors whose tax rate on dividends was greater than (less than) the tax rate on capital gains tended to invest in companies with a low (high) dividend yield. In summary, Pettit's results tend to support the existence of a dividend–clientele effect.

---

32 C. Smith & R. Watts, 'The Investment Opportunity Set and Corporate Financing, Dividend, and Compensation Policies', *Journal of Financial Economics*, December 1992, pp. 263–92.
33 See Footnote 32, p. 273.
34 R. Pettit, 'Taxes, Transaction Costs and the Clientele Effect on Dividends', *Journal of Financial Economics*, December 1977, pp. 419–36.

A study by Lewellen, Stanley, Lease and Schlarbaum also found some evidence to suggest that investors are influenced by taxes, in that there was a weak inverse relationship between dividend yield and investors' marginal tax rates.[35] In a regression model relating the dividend yields of investors' portfolios to various investor characteristics the tax rate variable was statistically significant but economically unimportant.

A different approach was used by Richardson, Sefcik and Thompson.[36] They argued that if dividend clienteles exist, a change in dividend policy should be followed by a substantial increase in trading volume as existing shareholders sell to other investors who are better suited by the new policy. They found that for companies announcing an initial cash dividend there was a significant increase in trading volume around the announcement date. However, analysis suggested that the increased trading was largely related to the information about future earnings conveyed by the announcement, and trading for dividend–clientele reasons was relatively minor.

In summary, evidence for the existence of tax-related dividend clienteles is weak. This is consistent with models proposed by both Long and Modigliani, in which investors making portfolio choices face a trade-off between minimising risk by diversification and minimising the impact of taxes.[37] A portfolio chosen only on the basis of tax considerations is likely to be poorly diversified, and Modigliani concluded that the composition of portfolios will differ only modestly between investors with high and low marginal tax rates.

## 11.4.4 DIVIDENDS, TAXES AND SHARE VALUATION

The fact that different tax rates apply to dividend income and capital gains has been suggested as a major factor explaining why a company's share price may not be independent of its dividend policy. Numerous empirical studies have attempted to test this proposition. Two main approaches have been used.

First, many studies, commencing with one by Black and Scholes in 1974, use adjusted forms of the CAPM to test for the existence of a relationship between the expected rate of return on shares and the level of dividends paid on those shares.[38] A similar methodology was used in Australia by Ball, Brown, Finn and Officer.[39] However it has been argued that the CAPM-based studies

---

[35] W. Lewellen, K. Stanley, R. Lease & G. Schlarbaum, 'Some Direct Evidence on the Dividend Clientele Phenomenon', *Journal of Finance*, December 1978, pp. 1385–99.

[36] G. Richardson, S. Sefcik & R. Thompson, see Footnote 22.

[37] J. Long, 'Efficient Portfolio Choice with Differential Taxation of Dividends and Capital Gains', *Journal of Financial Economics*, August 1977, pp. 25–53 & F. Modigliani, 'Debt, Dividend Policy, Taxes, Inflation and Market Valuation', *Journal of Finance*, May 1982, pp. 255–73.

[38] F. Black & M. Scholes, 'The Effects of Dividend Yield and Dividend Policy on Common Stock Prices and Returns', *Journal of Financial Economics*, May 1974, pp. 1–22. The CAPM is discussed in Section 6.6.

[39] R. Ball, P. Brown, F. Finn & R. Officer, 'Dividends and the Value of the Firm: Evidence From the Australian Equity Market', *Australian Journal of Management*, April 1979, pp. 13–26.

are subject to methodological weaknesses which are likely to make their results unreliable. Therefore, we do not review the results of these studies.[40]

Secondly, several authors have studied the price decline that occurs when shares are quoted ex dividend. In the absence of income taxes, arbitrage opportunities would exist unless, on the ex-dividend day, the share price decreases by an amount equal to the dividend per share. When dividend income is taxed more heavily than capital gains, the share price should decline by an amount that is less than the dividend. This issue has been studied by observing rates of return on shares on the ex-dividend day and by observing the dividend **drop-off ratio**, which is the ratio of the decline in share price on the ex-dividend day to the dividend per share. Some authors have also used observed drop-off ratios to estimate the marginal tax rates of shareholders and have sought evidence for the existence of investor clienteles by examining whether the drop-off ratio is related to dividend yield.[41] However, Kalay has argued that share price behaviour around ex-dividend dates may be influenced by short-term traders whose tax rates differ from those of average investors.[42] The activities of such traders mean that observed drop-off ratios will also be influenced by transaction costs. Therefore such tests are unreliable as a means of estimating the tax rates of shareholders, or of providing evidence on the existence of investor clienteles. Despite this limitation, drop-off ratios can be used to measure the value of dividends and, where applicable, the value of any accompanying tax credit.[43] Example 11.2 illustrates the effect of imputation tax credits on the ex-dividend drop-off.

### Example 11.2

Norfolk Ltd shares have a closing price of $10.85 on 3 November 1993. On the next day they will begin trading on an ex-dividend basis. The dividend is 25 cents per share, fully franked at the company tax rate of 33 per cent. What is the expected ex-dividend share price?

Investors who buy Norfolk shares on 4 November are paying for an interest in the company's future net cash flows. Investors who bought the shares on 3 November were buying essentially the same interest in future net cash flows, *plus* the dividend. Since the dividend is fully franked, it carries a tax credit which, as shown in Appendix 11.1 (Equation A11.1.3) is equal to DIV $t_c/(1 - t_c)$ = 25(0.33)/0.67 = 12.31 cents. Therefore, if expectations of Norfolk's future cash flows remain unchanged, and if both the dividend and the tax credit are fully

---

40 A review of the CAPM-based studies is provided by T. Copeland & J. Weston, *Financial Theory and Corporate Policy*, 3rd edn, Addison-Wesley, 1988, pp. 588–94. See also M. Miller, 'Behavioral Rationality in Finance: The Case of Dividends', *Journal of Business Supplement* 1986, pp. S459–62 and J. Crockett & I. Friend, see Footnote 18, pp. 605–7.
41 See, for example, E. Elton & M. Gruber, 'Marginal Stockholders' Tax Rates and the Clientele Effect', *Review of Economics and Statistics*, February 1970, pp. 68–74 who reported evidence of a tax-induced clientele effect in the US.
42 A. Kalay, 'The Ex-dividend Day Behaviour of Stock Prices: A Re-examination of the Clientele Effect', *Journal of Finance*, September 1982, pp. 1059–70.
43 N. Hathaway & R. Officer, 'The value of imputation tax credits', Unpublished paper, Graduate School of Management, University of Melbourne, November 1992.

valued by investors, the ex-dividend drop-off should be 25 + 12.31 = 37.31 cents, giving an expected ex-dividend share price of approximately $10.48.

Drop-off ratios can also be used to assess the effects of changes in the tax system on the relative values of dividends and capital gains. Empirical evidence in the US shows that the dividend drop-off ratio is generally less than one. Barclay examined ex-dividend day share prices in the US prior to the introduction of income tax in 1910.[44] As suggested above, the dividend drop-off ratio was not significantly different from one, but during a later 'post-tax' period, the ratio was less than one.

Three Australian studies of the ex-dividend day behaviour of share prices have provided mixed results. Brown and Walter found clear evidence that over the period 1974–85, the dividend drop-off ratio was less than one.[45] They estimated the average drop-off ratio to be 0.75 to 0.80, but they were not prepared to attribute this result to the effects of taxes.

Subsequently, Brown and Clarke studied an extended time period in order to examine the effects of three changes in the Australian tax system.[46] These changes were: (a) the introduction of capital gains tax from 19 September 1985, (b) the introduction of imputation on 1 July 1987, and (c) the extension of imputation to superannuation funds, approved deposit funds and friendly societies on 1 July 1988. All of these changes favoured dividends relative to capital gains. Therefore, if the magnitude of the drop-off ratio is determined primarily by taxes, the ratio would be expected to increase after each of the tax changes. Contrary to this prediction, Brown and Clarke found that the average drop-off ratio decreased after the introduction of capital gains tax. After the introduction of imputation, the average drop-off ratio increased, but the increase was not statistically significant. In contrast, after July 1988 the increase in the drop-off ratio was significant, but it remained significantly less than one.[47] Brown and Clarke concluded that the tax laws alone cannot explain the ex-dividend day trade-off between dividends and capital gains.

Hathaway and Officer studied the drop-off ratio in order to estimate the value of imputation tax credits in the Australian market.[48] Their only clear conclusion was that the market does place a positive value on such credits, but they found a wide range of estimated values. This divergence of values is consistent with the possibility that the marginal shareholders in some companies are Australian taxpayers able to get full value from tax credits, while in other companies the marginal shareholders may be non-residents, who cannot get full value from tax credits. Hathaway and Officer expected that over time a clientele effect would

---

[44] M. Barclay, 'Dividends, Taxes and Common Stock Prices', *Journal of Financial Economics*, September 1987, pp. 31–44.
[45] P. Brown & T. Walter, 'Ex-dividend Day Behaviour of Australian Share Prices', *Australian Journal of Management*, December 1986, pp. 139–52.
[46] P. Brown & A. Clarke, 'The Ex-dividend Day Behaviour of Australian Share Prices Before and After Dividend Imputation', *Australian Journal of Management*, June 1993, pp. 1–40.
[47] After the introduction of imputation, dividend drop-off ratios were reported on a grossed-up basis to reflect tax credits associated with franked dividends.
[48] N. Hathaway & R. Officer, see Footnote 43, pp. 22–4.

develop where companies paying fully franked dividends would attract shareholders who receive the greatest value from tax credits. The development of such shareholder clienteles should be reflected in a consistent value for tax credits, but their data set covers a time span which is too short to demonstrate these effects.

Given the mixed nature of the evidence, it seems reasonable to accept Miller's view that empirical studies have yet to show there is any significant difference between the market value of a dollar of dividends and the market value of a dollar of capital gains.[49]

While there is a lack of clear evidence about the relative *market values* of dividends and capital gains, there is evidence that the *quantity* of dividends is sensitive to changes in the tax burden on dividends relative to capital gains.[50] These changes are most likely to be detectable when there is a major change in the tax regime. In Australia, the change in 1987 from the classical tax system to the imputation system was followed by significant increases in the dividend payout ratios of companies able to pay franked dividends.[51] Similarly, Khoury and Smith reported that Canadian companies significantly increased their dividend payout ratios after capital gains tax and partial dividend imputation were introduced in 1973.[52] Further evidence consistent with these findings is provided by Poterba and Summers, who studied the effects of several post-1950 changes in the UK tax system.[53]

## 11.4.5 Dividends, Company Attributes and Corporate Policies

Most empirical studies that seek to explain variations in dividend policy between companies examine dividend policy in isolation from other policies such as debt policy. For example, Rozeff used regression analysis with the dividend payout ratio as the dependent variable, and several explanatory variables chosen only as proxies for 'real' company attributes such as growth, risk and agency costs.[54] One finding was that the dividend payout ratio was negatively related to both past and expected future growth in sales revenue. To achieve growth in sales, companies will generally need to make higher investment expenditures. For example, additional fixed assets may be needed to increase production capacity. Therefore his results showed that investment policy influences dividend policy 'in the sense that, holding other factors constant',[55] greater investment is associated with a lower dividend payout. The other factors held constant included financial leverage, insider ownership, and compensation policy. However, in

---

[49] M. Miller, see Footnote 40, pp. S460–2.
[50] Ibid.
[51] R. Nicol, see Footnote 13, pp. 47–50.
[52] N. Khoury & K. Smith, 'Dividend Policy and the Capital Gains Tax in Canada', *Journal of Business Administration*, Spring 1977, pp. 19–32.
[53] J. Poterba & L. Summers, 'The economic effects of dividend taxation', in E. Altman & M. Subrahmanyam, Eds, *Recent Advances in Corporate Finance*, Irwin, 1985, pp. 227–84.
[54] M. Rozeff, see Footnote 19, pp. 253–8.
[55] Ibid. p. 258.

practice, these policies may be related to each other, both directly, and indirectly through their relationship to real or operating company attributes such as business risk.

In a study which incorporated both real attributes and corporate policies, Jensen, Solberg and Zorn (JSZ) used a system of equations to examine simultaneously the determinants of dividend, leverage, and insider ownership policies.[56] They found that in relation to real attributes, the dividend payout ratio was negatively related to investment and growth, and positively related to profitability. In relation to other corporate policies, dividend payout was found to be negatively related to both financial leverage and the level of insider ownership. In other words, JSZ found that more profitable companies tend to pay out a higher proportion of profits as dividends, but management sets the payout ratio so that the equity portion of expected investment can be financed internally. Their results also showed that if a company has high fixed financial costs through debt, managers are unwilling also to commit the company to high dividend payouts. Finally, as noted in the previous section, their results suggest that the need to control agency costs by high dividend payout decreases as insider ownership of equity increases.

## 11.5 ESTABLISHING A DIVIDEND POLICY
### 11.5.1 THE ROLES OF THEORY AND EVIDENCE

The choice of a dividend policy is not important unless a company's value can be affected by its dividend policy. We have seen that in a perfect capital market with no taxes, company value depends only on the company's investment decisions, and is not affected by its dividend policy. When we allow for the imperfections that exist in practice, dividend decisions may be important because of taxes, information effects, agency costs, and transaction costs. Three decades of debate and empirical research have yielded many theoretical models and supported the relevance of some of these factors, particularly information effects. While this shows that *changes* in dividends are important, the research has not demonstrated conclusively the effects, if any, of dividend *policy* on company value. Therefore, in making recommendations on dividend policy it is necessary to rely, to a considerable extent, on theoretical analysis.

The most important imperfection is likely to be taxes or, more precisely, differential taxation of dividends and capital gains. However, one view holds that differential taxation may be neutralised by the formation of dividend clienteles and, under the classical taxation system, by the ability of investors to shelter dividends from extra taxation through schemes such as the one suggested by Miller and Scholes.[57] Another view is that payment of dividends does involve an extra tax burden, but this burden is offset by the benefits of dividends, such as reducing agency costs and conveying information to investors. As discussed

---

[56] G. Jensen, D. Solberg & T. Zorn, 'Simultaneous Determination of Insider Ownership, Debt, and Dividend Policies', *Journal of Financial and Quantitative Analysis*, June 1992, pp. 247–63.
[57] M. Miller & M. Scholes, 'Dividends and Taxes', *Journal of Financial Economics*, December 1978, pp. 333–64.

earlier, the empirical evidence does not support rejection of one view in favour of the other. If Australia still used the classical tax system we would suggest that companies should adopt a stable or smoothed dividend policy with a target payout ratio set low enough to minimise the need for share issues. However, now that Australia uses an imputation tax system we suggest that the dividend policies of Australian companies should be driven largely by tax-related considerations. The effects of taxes are discussed in the next section.

### 11.5.2 Dividend decisions and taxes

The effect of taxes on dividend policy depends on the tax system employed. Under the classical tax system, where dividends are taxed more heavily than capital gains, it can be argued that low dividends should be preferred. That is, it makes good sense to set a target payout ratio which is low enough to minimise the need for new share issues. Some observers would go further and argue that under these circumstances, companies should not pay any dividends at all. However, as discussed in Section 11.3.1, many large investors in the Australian market did not pay tax on dividends before 1 July 1987 because they were either tax-exempt (superannuation funds) or received the inter-company tax rebate (companies and life offices).

The imputation tax system which replaced the classical system in Australia on 1 July 1987 provides resident investors, particularly superannuation funds, with reason to prefer dividends rather than capital gains. Essentially this is because company profits distributed as franked dividends offer a tax advantage to many resident investors. On the other hand, retained company profits are subject to company income tax and the resultant capital gains may be taxed when they are realised by investors. Therefore, the change to the imputation tax system means that double taxation of profits paid out as dividends has been replaced by double taxation of retained profits. Not surprisingly, this change has had significant effects on the dividend practices of many Australian companies. These effects are now discussed.

As shown in Appendix 11.1 (Equation A11.1.5), the after-tax income of shareholders $\pi_{ps}$ under the imputation system, but ignoring capital gains tax, is:

$$\pi_{ps} = \delta Y (1 - t_{pe}) + (1 - \delta) Y (1 - t_c)$$

where $\delta$ is the dividend payout ratio defined as dividends paid divided by company profit after payment of company income tax, $Y$ is the company's profit before company income tax, $t_{pe}$ is the shareholders' personal income tax rate and $t_c$ is the company income tax rate. To illustrate the effect of dividend policy under the imputation tax system, assume that $Y = \$100$, $t_c = 0.33$, and $t_{pe} = 0.15$. We have chosen a personal tax rate of 15 per cent because this is the income tax rate applicable to superannuation funds. If the company pays no dividend ($\delta = 0$) then all income to shareholders will be in the form of capital gains. In this case, Equation A11.1.5 becomes:

$$\pi_{ps} = Y(1 - t_c)$$
$$= \$100\,(1 - 0.33)$$
$$= \$67$$

Thus, company income tax of $33 will be paid and shareholders receive $67 after tax.

Alternatively, if all company profit is paid out as dividends ($\delta = 1$), then Equation A11.1.5 becomes:

$$\pi_{ps} = Y(1 - t_{pe})$$
$$= \$100\,(1 - 0.15)$$
$$= \$85$$

Comparing these two extreme cases, an increase in the dividend payout ratio $\delta$ from zero to 100 per cent increases shareholders' after-tax income from $67 to $85. This is because payment of the franked dividend allows shareholders to benefit from a credit for tax paid by the company. As discussed in Appendix 11.1, distributed company profit is effectively taxed at the shareholders' personal income tax rate, whereas undistributed profit is taxed at the company income tax rate. Because, in this example, the company income tax rate (33 per cent) exceeds the personal income tax rate (15 per cent), shareholders benefit from a high dividend payout.

It can also be seen that the dividend policies adopted by companies are critical in determining the after-tax benefits received by investors because shareholders are unable to use tax credits until franked dividends are paid. We would therefore expect the dividend payout ratios of companies able to pay franked dividends to have increased since 1 July 1987. There is strong evidence that this has occurred. Nicol found that for a sample of over 400 of the largest listed companies in Australia, the median dividend payout ratio increased from 31 per cent in 1986 to 50 per cent in 1990.[58] For some subsets the median payout ratio in 1990 was higher; 63 per cent for the top 100 companies ranked by market capitalisation and approximately 70 per cent for companies with dividend reinvestment plans or dividend election schemes. While dividend payouts have increased substantially, it is difficult to assess whether companies are distributing all the franking credits potentially available to shareholders. The payout ratios mentioned above would suggest that on average they are not, but this is uncertain because these ratios are based on accounting profit, not taxable income.

While the demand for franked dividends is high, simply maximising the payout of franked cash dividends is unlikely to be an optimum dividend policy for all companies. One reason is that many companies have large numbers of non-resident and tax-exempt shareholders who do not benefit directly from tax credits. A second reason is that companies that pay substantially increased dividends may be in danger of running short of cash to finance new investments. This problem has been addressed through dividend reinvestment plans. These plans and dividend election schemes are discussed in the next section.

---

[58] R. Nicol, see Footnote 13, pp. 47–8.

### 11.5.3 DIVIDEND REINVESTMENT PLANS AND DIVIDEND ELECTION SCHEMES

Dividend reinvestment plans were introduced in Australia in the early 1980s.[59] They offer shareholders the option to apply all or part of their dividends to the purchase of additional newly-issued shares. While shareholders have always been able to use dividend income to purchase additional shares, these plans enable shareholders to purchase additional shares without incurring transaction costs. In addition, the shares can normally be obtained at a discount of 5 to 10 per cent from the current market price. This discount benefits shareholders taking up the new shares at the expense of those who do not. As a result, there is an incentive for shareholders to join a dividend reinvestment plan.

The number of listed companies operating dividend reinvestment plans has increased from only five in late 1982 to more than one hundred and fifty by 30 June 1993. The incentive to increase payouts under the imputation system has undoubtedly contributed to this increased popularity. Clearly, a company that responds to the demand for franked dividends by increasing its payout may run short of cash. Management could respond by making additional rights issues or share placements to replace the extra cash paid out as dividends. However, these measures can be slow and involve significant transaction costs. Adoption of a dividend reinvestment plan can be a more attractive and less costly solution. Where a shareholder chooses to reinvest a franked dividend, no cash is paid out by the company but tax credits are still transferred to the shareholder. The evidence suggests that dividend reinvestment plans are well received by shareholders. Figures reported by Nicol on shareholder participation for 10 companies show that on average about 44 per cent of dividends were reinvested.[60] Examination of daily share returns has shown that, prior to imputation, there was little market reaction when a company announced that it was introducing a dividend reinvestment plan. However, after introduction of imputation, such announcements were associated with a significant positive market response, but this response was confined to the period after 1 July 1988 when imputation was extended to superannuation funds.[61]

Dividend reinvestment plans are the most popular of the various dividend-related plans in the Australian market. Some companies also operate dividend election schemes (DES) which offer shareholders the option of receiving their dividends in one or more of a number of forms. The popularity of DES increased considerably following introduction of the imputation system, although subsequent legal changes have reduced their tax effectiveness. As well as fully franked

---

[59] A. Wills, 'A Decade of Dividend Reinvestment', *The Australian Accountant*, August 1989, pp. 65–73.
[60] R. Nicol, see Footnote 13, p. 52. Note that a 44 per cent reinvestment rate would allow a company to increase its dividend payout ratio by a multiple of $1/(1 - 0.44) = 1.786$, without increasing the cash paid out. As an example, the payout ratio could increase from 50% to almost 90%.
[61] K. Chan, D. McColough & M. Skully, 'Australian Tax Changes and Dividend Reinvestment Announcement Effects: A Pre- and Post-imputation Study', *Australian Journal of Management*, June 1993, pp. 41–62.

dividends, the options could include unfranked dividends (at a higher rate than the franked dividends), dividends paid by an overseas subsidiary, or bonus shares issued from the share premium account in lieu of dividends. These schemes were designed to make a company's shares attractive to different classes of shareholders and to enable imputation tax credits to be 'streamed' to those shareholders who could use them most effectively. For example, fully franked dividends appeal to superannuation funds and resident individuals in low personal income tax brackets. Higher unfranked dividends appeal to non-residents and tax exempt investors who cannot use imputation tax credits. Finally, bonus shares are likely to appeal to investors holding shares purchased before the introduction of capital gains tax on 20 September 1985 because these holdings are not subject to capital gains tax and any additions to them through bonus issues also inherit their tax-free status.

The use of DES to 'stream' imputation tax credits to particular classes of investors has now been restricted.[62] Despite the restrictions, many companies have retained their DES but typically the choice of dividend substitutes is now confined to bonus shares and dividends paid by an overseas subsidiary. These choices are offered through separate plans, typically called bonus share plans and overseas dividend plans. Overseas dividend plans can be attractive to non-resident shareholders in Australian companies with overseas subsidiaries. For example, a shareholder who resides in the UK might elect to receive a dividend paid by a UK subsidiary of an Australian company in lieu of a dividend from the Australian parent company. The dividend could then carry a tax credit related to company tax paid in the UK. Finally, it should be noted that the restrictions on dividend streaming from 1 July 1990 are confined to schemes which allow shareholders to *choose* between dividends and various dividend substitutes. However, these restrictions do not prevent companies from streaming tax credits through issuing more than one class of securities with different *rights* attached to them.

## 11.5.4 DIVIDEND POLICY UNDER IMPUTATION

Under the imputation tax system, there are strong incentives for tax-paying companies to pay franked dividends, and the benefits of doing so are greatest for resident shareholders subject to marginal tax rates which are lower than the company tax rate. On the other hand, shareholders with marginal tax rates higher than the company tax rate may prefer that companies retain profits, although this conclusion is subject to the magnitude of the capital gains tax rate. Therefore, if the company tax rate and the top personal marginal tax rate were equal, the situation would be straightforward. In that case there would not be any resident shareholders with a tax-based preference for retention of profits. Consequently,

---

62 The schemes are still allowed, but, for most shareholders, their tax effectiveness has been eliminated. From 1 July 1990, companies must debit their franking accounts in respect of all dividends paid under a DES. Also, bonus shares paid from a share premium account are deemed to be dividends, unless the bonus shares are distributed pro rata to all shareholders on a non-renounceable basis. This means that a company offering bonus shares in lieu of dividends under a DES must debit its franking account in respect of the bonus shares.

the optimum dividend policy for Australian companies owned by resident shareholders would be simple: pay the maximum possible franked dividends and adopt a dividend reinvestment plan.

In practice, the situation is more complex for three main reasons. First, many companies have both resident shareholders who can use imputation tax credits and overseas shareholders who cannot use them. Secondly, the equality that once existed between the company income tax rate and the top personal income tax rate no longer exists. The company tax rate has been reduced from 49 per cent to 39 per cent and then to 33 per cent, while personal tax rates continue to be as high as 47 per cent. This has increased the number of resident shareholders who are likely to prefer the retention of profits. Thirdly, there are factors other than taxes that can still be important. For example, a company operating a dividend reinvestment plan may find that the level of reinvestment is such that the company has free cash flow which it cannot invest profitably.[63] Also, changes in dividends can still have information effects, although we might expect them to be less important than they were in the pre-imputation period.[64]

Problems associated with a company having both resident and overseas shareholders, or resident shareholders with disparate tax rates, can be approached in two ways. One is to adopt a policy that suits the tax position of one type of shareholder with the aim of attracting more of that type as a dominant clientele. Given that superannuation funds with a tax rate of 15 per cent are already large shareholders in most major companies, it is logical for such companies to adopt the high payout/dividend reinvestment plan combination. The other approach is to issue different classes of shares, designed to appeal to different types of investors. Some types of preference shares have been used in this way. Finally, while the information content of dividends may have diminished, managers are still likely to be concerned about the traditional adverse effect of a reduction in dividends. This concern may well be the main reason why the median post-imputation dividend payout ratio of major companies is 65 to 70 per cent, rather than, say, 95 to 100 per cent. Another reason may be the desire to avoid the transaction costs involved in making share issues to replace cash paid out.

## SELECTED REFERENCES

Ball, R., Brown, P., Finn, F. & Officer, R., 'Dividends and the Value of the Firm: Evidence from the Australian Equity Market', *Australian Journal of Management*, April 1979, pp. 13–26.

Black, F. & Scholes, M., 'The Effect of Dividend Yield and Dividend Policy on Common Stock Prices and Returns', *Journal of Financial Economics*, May 1974, pp. 1–22.

Brown, P. & Clark, A., 'The Ex-dividend Day Behaviour of Australian Share Prices Before and After Dividend Imputation', *Australian Journal of Management*, June 1993, pp. 1–40.

Brown, P. & Walter, T., 'The Ex-dividend Day Behaviour of Australian Share Prices', *Australian Journal of Management*, December 1986, pp. 139–52.

---

[63] Companies operating successful dividend reinvestment plans can suspend them if this occurs.

[64] The reason for this expectation is that if companies distributed all or most of their available tax credits each year, it follows that dividends would vary from year to year in line with variations in profit. Thus, a dividend increase (decrease) would indicate only that profit had increased (decreased) in that year; it would not necessarily indicate anything about the longer-term prospects of the company.

Easterbrook, F., 'Two Agency-cost Explanations of Dividends', *American Economic Review*, September 1984, pp. 650–9.
Hamson, D. & Ziegler, P., 'The Impact of Dividend Imputation on Firms' Financial Decisions', *Accounting and Finance*, November 1990, pp. 29–53.
Howard, P. & Brown, R., 'Dividend Policy and Capital Structure Under the Imputation Tax System: Some Clarifying Comments', *Accounting and Finance*, May 1992, pp. 51–61.
Lintner, J., 'Distribution of Incomes of Corporations Among Dividends, Retained Earnings and Taxes', *American Economic Review*, May 1956, pp. 97–113.
Miller, M., 'The informational content of dividends', in *Macroeconomics: Essays in Honor of Franco Modigliani*, Eds. J. Bosons, R. Dornbusch & . Fischer, MIT Press, Boston, 1986.
Miller, M., & Modigliani, F., 'Dividend Policy, Growth and the Valuation of Shares', *Journal of Business*, October 1961, pp. 411–33.
Nicol, R., 'The Dividend Puzzle: An Australian Solution?', *Australian Accounting Review*, November 1992, pp. 42–55.
Rozeff, M., 'Growth, Beta and Agency Costs as Determinants of Dividend Payout Ratios', *Journal of Financial Research*, Fall 1982, pp. 249–59.
Woolridge J., & Ghosh, C., 'Dividend cuts: Do they always signal bad news?', in *The Revolution in Corporate Finance*, Eds. J. Stern and D. Chew, 2nd edn, Blackwell, Oxford, 1992, pp. 462–73.

## QUESTIONS

1. Define the following terms:
   Ex-dividend date
   Franked dividend
   Dividend reinvestment plan
   Dividend drop-off ratio
   Overseas dividend plan
   Franking account.
2. Are the following statements true or false?
   (a) A company can pay a dividend only if it is currently earning profits.
   (b) In Australia, dividends and capital gains are taxed at the same rate for individual investors.
   (c) The pure residual dividend policy is used by most companies.
   (d) The imputation system involves personal tax being collected at the company level.
   (e) To Australian resident investors, a dollar of franked dividends is worth more than a dollar of unfranked dividends.
3. What reasons are there to suppose that a company's dividend payout ratio is a relevant variable in assessing the value of its ordinary shares?
4. The payment of dividends is said to have information content. Outline the evidence supporting the presence of information content.
5. *Dividends are taxed at a lower rate than capital gains. This suggests that companies should have high dividend payout ratios.* Discuss this statement, giving special attention to its appropriateness in the Australian tax environment.
6. What reasons are there to suppose that there is a dividend–clientele effect? Does the empirical evidence support the existence of such an effect? If such an effect exists, does this mean that a company can influence its market value by changing its dividend policy? Why/why not?
7. *Even though companies have investment opportunities well in excess of the earnings available to finance them, they still insist on paying dividends.* Why?
8. *Some people have pointed out that high dividend payout companies tend to have high price–earnings ratios.* Does this evidence necessarily provide a rationale for high dividend payout ratios? Why/why not?

9. There is evidence to suggest that dividends have a more stable pattern than earnings. What reasons can you suggest for management adopting a policy of paying a stable dividend in the face of fluctuating earnings?
10. When dividends are taxed more heavily than capital gains and there are transaction costs, a company that pays dividends and subsequently makes a rights issue is behaving illogically. Discuss.
11. Usually the Board of Directors increases dividend per share only slowly in response to rising profits, and is even more reluctant to decrease dividend per share than to increase it. Give reasons for this behaviour pattern. Is this behaviour likely to change under the imputation tax system?
12. The Dromana Dredging Company has asked your advice on its dividend policy. There has been only a small change in earnings and dividends over the years and the company's share price has also been relatively stable during the same period. It has been suggested that the company should expand its activities from dredging into providing services for off-shore oil exploration companies. To undertake the proposed expansion activity the company intends to make a rights issue. As the expansion is expected to average approximately 25 per cent return on investment each year, it is not expected that there will be any difficulty in convincing shareholders to take up their rights. Below are data on earnings, dividends and share prices for the years 1990–93 and the expected figures for 1994.

*Dromana Dredging Company—Data for 1990–93*

|  | 1990 | 1991 | 1992 | 1993 | Expected 1994 |
|---|---|---|---|---|---|
| Earnings per share | 40c | 42c | 44c | 43c | 44c |
| Cash available per share | 60c | 67c | 67c | 66c | 66c |
| Dividend per share | 20c | 20c | 22c | 22c | ? |
| Average market price of ordinary shares | $4.00 | $4.10 | $4.40 | $4.35 | $4.40 |

Make a recommendation on the dividend payment for 1994. Give your reasons.
13. The Wrex Manufacturing Company has a history of rapid growth, with a rate of return on assets of about 20 per cent per annum. For the past five years its dividend payout ratio has been approximately 60 per cent. A high payout has been justified on the grounds that the company is operated in the shareholders' interests and dividends paid by the company have a beneficial effect on the company's share price. What factors would you take into consideration when deciding on the appropriate dividend policy for the company? Is the above dividend policy justified?
14. Examine the daily share price behaviour of any company in the four-week period before and after its most recent change in cash dividends. What conclusions can you draw from the movements in the share price?
15. Under the imputation tax system, there is an optimum dividend policy for all Australian companies: always pay the maximum possible franked dividend, given the balance in the franking account. Discuss.

16. *The imputation system encourages payment of high dividends. Companies that do so may be left short of cash.* Comment.
17. Explain how the following circumstances could affect a company's dividend policy:
    (a) The company issues cumulative preference shares carrying an entitlement to fully franked dividends.
    (b) The company receives a large unexpected fully franked dividend from another company.
    (c) Owing to continued losses, retained profits have been reduced to almost zero.
    (d) A large US investor recently acquired 40 per cent of the company's shares.
    (e) The exploration division of the company has confirmed that several ore deposits are economically viable and ready for development into mines.
18. Dribnor Ltd has announced a fully franked dividend of $1 per share. The company tax rate is 33 per cent. By how much should the share price fall on the ex-dividend date if:
    (a) Imputation tax credits are of no value?
    (b) Imputation tax credits are fully valued?
19. *The MM dividend irrelevance hypothesis appears to be quite inconsistent with the model which relies on discounting future dividends to value a share.* Do you agree? Explain.
20. Explain the likely effects on dividend payout ratios of each of the following:
    (a) The imputation tax system is modified to allow investors only partial (50 per cent) credit for company tax paid.
    (b) Personal income (but not capital gains) tax rates are increased.
    (c) Capital gains tax is abolished.
    (d) Interest rates increase substantially.
    (e) Company profitability increases.
    (f) Prospectus regulations are tightened, increasing the costs of share issues.

# APPENDIX 11.1

# THE DIVIDEND IMPUTATION TAX SYSTEM

A tax 'reform' package announced on 19 September 1985 included the adoption in Australia of an imputation system of company taxation and the introduction of a capital gains tax. These are logically separate measures and this appendix is restricted to describing the operation of the imputation system and illustrating its major effects on shareholders. Analysis of its effects on dividend and financing decisions is contained in Chapters 11, 12 and 13.

The imputation system commenced in the 1987–88 tax year and originally applied only to resident individual shareholders. Extension of the system to include superannuation funds took effect on 1 July 1988, coinciding with the imposition of a tax at the rate of 15 per cent on the earnings of such funds. Overseas investors are not intended to receive the benefits of imputation and in this appendix, the term 'shareholders' refers only to Australian resident shareholders.

The basic intention of the imputation system is to eliminate the double taxation of dividends which is inherent in the so-called classical system previously used in Australia, and still used in many countries, including the United States. This intention is achieved by giving shareholders a credit for the income tax paid by a company on its taxable income. The overall effect is that the profit of a company distributed as dividends is effectively *taxed* only at the personal level, but the tax is *collected* primarily at the company level. It is worth noting that the tax treatment of debt remains the same as it was under the classical system. That is, interest paid on debt is deductible at the company level, but is taxable in the hands of investors receiving the interest. Therefore, under both systems, a company's operating profit paid out as interest to debtholders is taxed only once—at the personal level. Hence the change to an imputation system has direct effects only on the taxation of company profit attributable to shareholders, which is the meaning we attach to 'company profit' in this appendix.

Imputation tax systems are not new; Canada, the United Kingdom and many European countries have operated partial imputation systems for many years. The Australian version is a full imputation system, in that shareholders receive a credit for the full amount of company income tax related to dividends. New Zealand also has a full imputation system. In Australia the system operates as follows:

1. Company income tax is assessed in the normal way at the company tax rate $t_c$.
2. Dividends paid out of a company's after-tax profit are referred to as **franked dividends**. For each dollar of franked dividends received, a shareholder's taxable income is increased by the 'grossed-up' amount of $\$1/(1 - t_c)$. It is **as if** the shareholder is assumed to have earned, personally, the company income that required the payment of company income tax.
3. For each dollar of this grossed-up amount, the shareholder is allowed a tax credit of $\$t_c$ against any tax assessed on the shareholder's taxable income from all sources.

The imputation system requires a franking account to be kept by each company. Credits to a company's franking account arise from two sources: payment of company income tax and receipt of franked dividends from other companies. For each dollar of company income tax paid, the credit to the franking account is:

$$\$\left(\frac{1 - t_c}{t_c}\right)$$

In the case of franked dividends received, the credit is equal to the dividend. Similarly, when a franked dividend is paid, the debit to the franking account is equal to the dividend paid. Thus the balance in a company's franking account at any time shows the maximum amount that it can pay as a franked dividend.

Dividends passing between resident companies continue to be exempt from company income tax (unless classed as 'debt dividends'). In addition, where such dividends are franked, the recipient company will receive an imputation tax credit which can only be used when passed on to its shareholders by payment of a franked dividend. Similarly, imputation tax credits can be passed through partnerships and trusts.

## EFFECTS ON SHAREHOLDERS

Since the tax credit allowed to shareholders offsets the company income tax previously paid, the net effect is that the company's profit distributed as dividends is effectively taxed at the shareholders' marginal income tax rate. More formally, let:

$Y$ = company profit before tax [65]
$t_c$ = company income tax rate
$t_{pe}$ = shareholders' marginal income tax rate
DIV = franked dividend paid
$\delta$ = dividend payout ratio (after company tax)
   = DIV/$Y(1 - t_c)$
$\pi_{ps}$ = shareholders' income after all taxes

First, note that:
$$\text{DIV} = \delta Y (1 - t_c), \text{ and} \qquad (A11.1.1)$$
$$\text{Retained profit} = (1 - \delta) Y (1 - t_c) \qquad (A11.1.2)$$

To pay a dividend DIV out of the current period's profit, the company has to earn, before company tax, an amount DIV/$(1 - t_c)$. The implicit company income tax related to the dividend is referred to as the imputation credit. The imputation credit $I_c$ is:

$$I_c = \frac{t_c \, \text{DIV}}{(1 - t_c)} \qquad (A11.1.3)$$

Personal tax is then assessed as if the shareholder received as income both the dividend and the imputation credit. However, the shareholder also receives a tax credit (not a tax deduction) equal to the imputation credit. Therefore:

Net personal tax = gross personal tax *less* imputation credit

$$= t_{pe} \left[ \text{DIV} + \frac{t_c \, \text{DIV}}{(1 - t_c)} \right] - \frac{t_c \, \text{DIV}}{(1 - t_c)} \qquad (A11.1.4)$$

Retained company profits are assumed to be invested to earn the opportunity cost of capital and will therefore give rise to capital gains. While these capital gains are not realised until the shares are sold, the shareholders' after-tax income is defined here as the sum of dividends and capital gains attributable to the company's profit. Therefore:

$\pi_{ps}$ = DIV *less* net personal tax *plus* capital gain

$$\pi_{ps} = \text{DIV} - t_{pe} \left[ \text{DIV} + \frac{t_c \, \text{DIV}}{(1 - t_c)} \right] + \frac{t_c \, \text{DIV}}{(1 - t_c)} + (1 - \delta) Y (1 - t_c)$$

Substituting for DIV from Equation A11.1.1, this equation simplifies to:

$$\pi_{ps} = \delta Y (1 - t_{pe}) + (1 - \delta) Y (1 - t_c) \qquad (A11.1.5)$$

Equation A11.1.5 is useful in that it demonstrates three important features of the imputation system. These are:

1. If all of a company's after-tax profit is paid out as dividends ($\delta = 1$), the equation becomes: $\pi_{ps} = Y (1 - t_{pe})$, which shows that under these

---

[65] In this appendix, company taxable income is assumed to be equal to company profit before tax. Generally, these amounts will not in practice be equal because the *Income Tax Assessment Act 1936* allows companies to claim deductions for items which are not cash outflows. Examples include: depreciation rates for tax purposes are generally greater than the rate of economic depreciation; also, at times, a deduction has been allowed for 150 per cent of research and development expenditure.

circumstances, a company's profit $Y$ is effectively taxed only at the personal rate $t_{pe}$. In this case, the equation implies that the company income tax rate is irrelevant[66] and company income tax can be regarded as a withholding tax against the personal tax liabilities of shareholders.

2. If no dividend is paid ($\delta = 0$), then Equation A11.1.5 becomes:
$$\pi_{ps} = Y(1 - t_c)$$
which shows that under these circumstances, a company's profit is taxed only at the company tax rate $t_c$.

3. If the company and personal tax rates are equal ($t_c = t_{pe}$), then Equation A11.1.5 becomes:
$$\pi_{ps} = \delta Y(1 - t_{pe}) + (1 - \delta)Y(1 - t_{pe})$$
$$= Y(1 - t_{pe})$$
which shows that under these circumstances, the overall incidence of tax is not affected by the dividend payout ratio.

The effect of the imputation system on resident shareholders is illustrated by the numerical example in Table A11.1.1. The after-tax returns from $100 of company profit are shown under three circumstances. These are:

1. the *classical* system, with a company income tax rate of 46 per cent and a personal income tax rate of 47 per cent, the rate for individuals in the top tax bracket from 1 January 1990;
2. the *imputation system*, with a company income tax rate of 33 per cent and a personal income tax rate of 47 per cent; and

**Table A11.1.1**  Comparison of the classical and imputation tax systems

| | Tax system | | |
|---|---|---|---|
| Item | Classical | Imputation | Imputation |
| Shareholder's tax rate | 47% | 47% | 15% |
| Company tax rate | 46% | 33% | 33% |
| (1) Company profit before tax | $100 | $100 | $100 |
| (2) Company income tax | 46 | 33 | 33 |
| (3) Company profit after tax | 54 | 67 | 67 |
| (4) Dividend (if payout ratio is 60%) | 32.4 | 40.2 | 40.2 |
| (5) Imputation credit, (4) × $\frac{0.33}{1 - 0.33}$ | — | 19.8 | 19.8 |
| (6) Grossed-up dividend (4) + (5) | 32.4 | 60 | 60 |
| (7) Tax on dividend | 15.2 | 28.2 | 9.0 |
| (8) Tax credit, equals (5) | — | 19.8 | 19.8 |
| (9) Net income tax, (7) − (8) | 15.2 | 8.4 | −10.8 |
| (10) Dividend income after tax, (4) − (9) | 17.2 | 31.8 | 51.0 |
| (11) Retained profit | 21.6 | 26.8 | 26.8 |
| (12) Shareholders' income (10) + (11) | 38.8 | 58.6 | 77.8 |
| (13) Total tax paid (2) and (9) | 61.2 | 41.4 | 22.2 |

---

[66] In practice, the company income tax rate retains some relevance because there will be a time delay between the payment of company income tax and recovery of that tax by shareholders.

3. the *imputation* system, with a company income tax rate of 33 per cent and a personal income tax rate of 15 per cent, the rate applicable to superannuation funds since 1 July 1988.

In all three cases, a dividend payout ratio of 60 per cent is assumed, and the Medicare levy is ignored.

The shareholders' income under the imputation system, shown in line 12 (columns 3 and 4) of Table A11.1.1, can of course be calculated using Equation A11.1.5. For example, for the individual shareholder with a personal tax rate of 47 per cent, the equation gives:

$$\pi_{ps} = 0.6 \times \$100\,(1 - 0.47) + 0.4 \times \$100\,(1 - 0.33)$$
$$= \$58.60$$

The overall tax rate is shown at line 13 of the table. The heavy, 'double' taxation of the classical system is seen in the overall tax rate, 61.2 per cent in this example, under the classical tax system. This may be compared with the overall tax rate of 41.4 per cent in this example (under imputation) for the individual shareholder. This is a weighted average of the personal and company tax rates. The weights are based on the company's dividend payout ratio. In this case, the overall tax rate equals:

$$47\% \times 0.6 + 33\% \times 0.4$$
$$= 41.4\%$$

This occurs because the distributed company profit is taxed at the shareholder's marginal tax rate of 47 per cent, while the company's retained profit is taxed at the company tax rate of 33 per cent.

Similarly, for the superannuation fund, the overall tax rate of 22.2 per cent is a weighted average of the company and personal tax rates of 33 per cent and 15 per cent respectively. It is clear that the superannuation fund would benefit from an increase in dividend payout to 100 per cent of the company's after-tax profit. Total tax paid would then be reduced to $15, provided that the fund can utilise the surplus tax credit ($18) to offset tax on other income. However, for the individual shareholder whose tax rate exceeds the company tax rate, tax considerations favour retention of profits rather than payment of dividends. Therefore, while the imputation system has, as shown in Table A11.1.1, substantially reduced the incidence of taxes on company profit, it has not eliminated the tax-based bias towards retention of profits, rather than payment of dividends. This bias was inherent in the classical system, and still exists for shareholders whose marginal income tax rates are greater than the company income tax rate.[67]

## IMPUTATION AND FINANCIAL DECISIONS

The imputation system eliminates double taxation of dividends by effectively taxing distributed company profit at the shareholder's personal marginal tax rate. Therefore, as noted above, from the viewpoint of Australian resident shareholders, company tax is essentially a withholding tax rather than a separate tax. It

---

[67] In practice, the capital gains tax works against this bias in the income tax system.

follows that the system can eliminate distortions that were inherent in the classical system. In particular, taxes should no longer be an important factor in deciding whether to incorporate a business. Also, for businesses that are incorporated, imputation ensures greater neutrality in the tax treatment of different sources of finance. Where equity is used, profits distributed as dividends are taxed only once at the shareholder's tax rate. Similarly, where debt is used, interest is taxed only once at the lender's tax rate.

Elimination of the previous distortions is generally seen as an advantage of the imputation system. However, this property of the imputation system also means that it is difficult for the Government to use the tax system to favour activities such as investment. For example, tax concessions such as investment allowances and accelerated depreciation allowances granted to companies are likely to be of little benefit to resident shareholders: the reduction in company tax is 'washed out' because distributed profits are taxed at personal rates.[68] Therefore, the main beneficiaries of tax concessions are likely to be foreign shareholders because, as they are excluded from the imputation system, company tax is to them a separate tax. So, while imputation has eliminated some distortions, it has introduced others. Another distortion in the system as it has been employed in Australia is that franking credits arise only from payment of Australian company tax. Therefore, the system favours the shareholders of Australian companies that invest locally rather than abroad.

---

[68] For a detailed analysis of the 'washout' phenomenon, see Bureau of Industry Economics, *Research Report 44, Tax Concessions and Dividend Imputation*, AGPS, Canberra, 1993.

# CHAPTER 12

# CAPITAL STRUCTURE DECISIONS: THEORY

## 12.1 INTRODUCTION

In Chapters 8 to 10, the sources of funds that may be used to finance a company's operations were outlined. The mix of finance sources used by a company is called its **capital structure**. This chapter considers the effect of capital structure on the market value of a company and on its shareholders' wealth.

The fundamental source of a company's value is the stream of net cash flows generated by its assets. This stream is usually referred to as the company's 'net operating cash flows' or 'earnings before interest and tax'.[1] The capital structure adopted by a company divides this stream between different classes of investors. If a company is financed entirely by equity, all of this stream is available to provide income to shareholders. Where a company borrows funds as well as issuing shares, the debtholders have first claim on the net operating cash flows, and shareholders are entitled to the riskier, residual cash flows that remain after the debtholders have been paid. Therefore, asking whether there is an optimum capital structure for a company amounts to asking whether the value of the stream of net operating cash flows depends on how it is divided between payments to debtholders and shareholders.

---

1 Company net operating cash flows are also often referred to as 'net operating income' but in general we reserve the term income for cash flows to investors. In the examples in this chapter, before-tax net operating cash flows are assumed to remain constant in perpetuity. This assumption implies that the company keeps the same assets in place at all times. Therefore the before-tax net operating cash flows must be net of the investment required each year to replace assets that deteriorate through use or obsolescence. Deducting this investment is the same, in principle, as deducting depreciation to determine 'earnings' or 'profit' which can be distributed while maintaining capital intact. Therefore we use the terms 'net operating cash flows' and 'earnings before interest and tax' interchangeably.

While this question sounds simple, the answer to it is neither simple, nor generally agreed. There are two basic schools of thought. One holds that capital structure is not important. According to this school, a company's value depends on the value of its assets, and cannot be changed by altering the way in which its net operating cash flows are divided between different classes of investors. The other school argues that an optimum capital structure exists, owing to the effects of factors such as taxes, agency costs, costs of financial distress, and the incentive effects of debt. In other words, value can be created by judicious use of debt finance.

Decisions on capital structure involve more than choosing a ratio of debt to equity. In addition to borrowing funds and issuing ordinary shares, there are sources of finance such as preference shares, leases, and hire purchase contracts. Also, debt may be short term or long term and some types of debt and preference shares can be convertible into ordinary shares. In summary, financing decisions involve two main issues: the mix of different types of finance and the mix of short-term and long-term sources of funds. In this chapter we discuss the first issue: the mix of long-term sources of finance. The second issue is discussed in Chapter 24. In Section 12.2 we examine the effects of financial leverage, and this is followed in Section 12.3 by the theory of capital structure in the context of a perfect capital market. In Sections 12.4 to 12.6 we examine the effects of taxes and other factors that can influence financing decisions such as agency costs, incentive effects of debt, costs of financial distress, and information asymmetry.

## 12.2   THE EFFECTS OF FINANCIAL LEVERAGE

All companies are subject to **business risk**. When the management of a company decides to enter a particular line of business, it knows that there are risks involved. For example, new competitors may emerge, technology may change in unexpected ways, new government regulations may be introduced, or consumers' tastes may change. These and other factors contribute to a company's business risk. As a result, a company's net operating cash flows will fluctuate over time. If a company is financed entirely by equity, variations in the return to shareholders are attributable only to business risk. When a company also uses 'fixed-charge' finance such as debt, preference shares, or lease finance, the returns to ordinary shareholders will also be affected by financial leverage. The term financial leverage, or gearing, refers to the use of fixed-charge finance to increase the expected rate of return to ordinary shareholders. An important effect of financial leverage is that ordinary shareholders are exposed to increased variability in the rate of return on their investment. Financial leverage therefore exposes shareholders to **financial risk**. This results from the fact that the payments to lenders and providers of other similar forms of finance are 'fixed'.[2] These payments must be made, even if the company suffers a serious decline in its net operating cash flows.[3] Therefore a company's financial risk is directly related to the proportion of debt in its capital structure.

---

[2] For ease of exposition, we will use the term 'debt' to refer to all forms of fixed-charge finance.
[3] If a company is unable to meet its obligations to debtholders, they can take control of the company, and this can result in its liquidation.

It is assumed in this section that a company's set of assets is fixed, so the company's business risk is assumed to be constant. This enables us to concentrate on the effects of financial leverage. The effects on shareholders of leverage are illustrated by the following example.

### Example 12.1

Dribnor Ltd is currently unlevered (that is, it has not borrowed) and has issued capital of 1 000 000 ordinary shares with a market price of $2 each. The company's financial manager is considering a proposal to repurchase half of the shares by borrowing $1 000 000 at an interest rate of 12 per cent per annum. This will not affect the company's assets or business risk, but it will change its capital structure. It is assumed that there are no taxes and that the company's expected earnings before interest are $300 000 per annum. Earnings available to ordinary shareholders are assumed to be paid out as dividends. However, it is not certain that these earnings will be achieved and the financial manager wishes to analyse the effects of earnings increasing to $400 000 or decreasing to $200 000 per annum. He also wishes to analyse the effects of earnings being $240 000 per annum, because, in that event, the rate of return on assets would be 12 per cent per annum, which is the same as the interest rate on debt. The results of the financial manager's calculations are shown in Table 12.1.

### Table 12.1

| | | | | |
|---|---|---|---|---|
| Earnings before interest ($) | 200 000 | 240 000 | 300 000 | 400 000 |
| Rate of return on assets (%) | 10 | 12 | 15 | 20 |
| **Existing capital structure (100% equity)** | | | | |
| Number of shares (million) | 1.0 | 1.0 | 1.0 | 1.0 |
| Earnings per share (cents) | 20 | 24 | 30 | 40 |
| Rate of return on equity (%) | 10 | 12 | 15 | 20 |
| **Proposed capital structure (50% equity, 50% debt)** | | | | |
| Number of shares (million) | 0.5 | 0.5 | 0.5 | 0.5 |
| Interest on debt ($) | 120 000 | 120 000 | 120 000 | 120 000 |
| Earnings available to ordinary shareholders ($) | 80 000 | 120 000 | 180 000 | 280 000 |
| Earnings per share (cents) | 16 | 24 | 36 | 56 |
| Rate of return on equity (%) | 8 | 12 | 18 | 28 |

Example 12.1 illustrates two important effects of financial leverage. First it shows that when a company borrows, the expected rate of return to ordinary shareholders is increased. If the expected earnings before interest of $300 000 per annum are maintained, the proposed capital structure results in an increase in the expected rate of return on equity from 15 per cent to 18 per cent per annum. Similarly, the expected earnings per share (EPS) increases from 30 cents to 36 cents. Secondly, financial leverage increases the variability of returns to shareholders. If earnings before interest are $400 000 per annum, the levered structure increases the rate of return on equity from 20 per cent to 28 per cent per annum, but if earnings before interest are only $200 000 per annum, the levered structure *decreases* the rate of return to shareholders from 10 per cent

to 8 per cent per annum. The effects of the alternative capital structures on the returns to shareholders are shown in Figure 12.1.

With the existing all-equity capital structure, the rate of return earned by shareholders is always equal to the rate of return on Dribnor's assets. Under the proposed structure, this remains true only when the rate of return on Dribnor's assets is equal to the interest rate paid on its debt, which is 12 per cent. If the rate of return on assets is greater than 12 per cent, the levered structure results in a higher rate of return on equity than the all-equity structure. If the rate of return on assets is less than 12 per cent, the levered structure results in a lower rate of return on equity. In other words, the effect of leverage works in *both* directions and the expected favourable effect on the rate of return to Dribnor's ordinary shareholders cannot be achieved without incurring the risk that the effects may turn out to be unfavourable. The effect of leverage in creating financial risk is shown clearly by the different slopes of the two lines in Figure 12.1.

In summary, the choice of capital structure for Dribnor involves a trade-off between risk and expected return. Clearly, any valid analysis of the choice must consider *both* factors: the financial manager should not determine a target debt–equity ratio based only on the expected level of EPS or the rate of return on equity. Provided that the expected rate of return on assets is greater than the interest rate on debt, increasing the debt–equity ratio will always increase

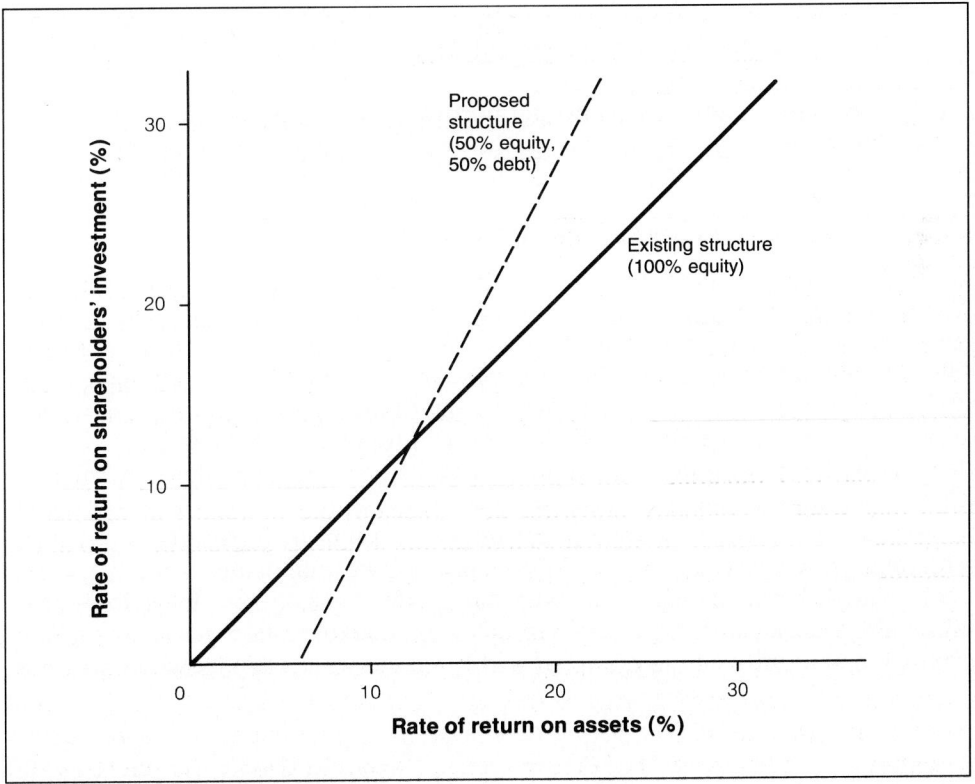

**Fig. 12.1** *The effect of leverage on returns*

expected EPS and the expected rate of return on equity. Inevitably these expected benefits come at a price: increased financial risk. Thus, in years when business conditions are either normal or buoyant, financial leverage will be advantageous, in that the rate of return to ordinary shareholders will be higher. However, in poor years, when business profitability falls, they will feel the adverse effects of leverage: their rate of return will be lower than it would have been with all-equity finance.

We have shown that financial leverage has important effects. However, we have not yet considered the most important question: does changing a company's capital structure change the value of the company, and therefore affect shareholders' wealth? The first rigorous analysis of this question was provided by Modigliani and Miller and showed that in a perfect capital market with no taxes, capital structure is irrelevant to company value and shareholders' wealth. Their analysis is considered in the next section.

## 12.3 THE MODIGLIANI AND MILLER ANALYSIS

Modigliani and Miller (MM) analysed the effect of capital structure on company value based on a set of restrictive assumptions.[4] The assumptions sufficient for their analysis are:

1. Securities issued by companies are traded in a perfect capital market; this is a frictionless market in which there are no transaction costs and no barriers to the free flow of information.
2. There are no taxes.
3. Companies and individuals can borrow at the same rate of interest.
4. There are no costs associated with the liquidation of a company.

### 12.3.1 MODIGLIANI AND MILLER'S PROPOSITION 1

Given the preceding assumptions, MM proved that the value of a company is independent of its capital structure. In effect, this means that changing a company's debt–equity ratio will change the way in which its net operating cash flows are divided between debtholders and shareholders, but will not change the total value of the cash flows. This is their now famous Proposition 1 and it can be proved in many different ways. The proof provided by MM is based on the idea that perfect substitutes should not sell at different prices in the same market at the same time. If this were not the case, an instantaneous excess profit could be earned. The process of taking advantage of such an opportunity is called **arbitrage**. In the context of the MM analysis, two companies with the same assets, but different capital structures, are perfect substitutes. If their market values are not the same, investors will enter the market to take advantage of the arbitrage opportunity and in doing so will force the values of the two companies

---

[4] F. Modigliani & M. Miller, 'The Cost of Capital, Corporation Finance and the Theory of Investment', *American Economic Review*, June 1958, pp. 261–97.

## Example 12.2

Table 12.2 sets out data for two companies, one of which has borrowed (a levered company L) and the other has not borrowed (an unlevered company U). Both companies have the same assets, which generate net operating cash flows of $90 000 per annum. These cash flows are assumed to remain constant in perpetuity. Company L's debt has a market value of $200 000 and it pays interest of 15 per cent per annum. Earnings after interest are available to ordinary shareholders and are assumed to be paid to them as dividends. There are no taxes.

**Table 12.2**

|  | Item | Company U | Company L |
|---|---|---|---|
|  | Earnings ($) before interest | 90 000 | 90 000 |
| less | Interest ($) on debt (at 15%) | 0 | 30 000 |
| equals | Income available to ordinary shareholders ($) | 90 000 | 60 000 |
| divided by | Cost of equity capital | 0.19 | 0.20 |
| equals | Market value of shares $E$ ($) | 473 684 | 300 000 |
| plus | Market value of debt $D$ ($) | 0 | 200 000 |
| equals | Total market value $V = E + D$ ($) | 473 684 | 500 000 |

Based on data in Table 12.2, L has a higher total market value than U. If this situation occurred, an investor could earn an arbitrage profit by selling shares in L, borrowing on personal account and investing in the shares of U. For example, consider an investor who owns 1 per cent of the shares in L; the market value of these shares is therefore $3000. Recognising the arbitrage opportunity, this investor could sell the shares for $3000 and replicate the leverage of L ($200 000/$300 000) by borrowing $2000 on personal account. Given the assumptions, the interest rate on the amount borrowed is 15 per cent. The investor can now use the total funds of $5000 to purchase shares in U.

Originally the investor's annual income from the investment in L was 20 per cent of $3000 = $600. The annual net income from the levered investment in U is:

Income from investment in U:
$5000 × 0.19        $950
less Interest on borrowing:
$2000 × 0.15        $300
equals Net income:  $650

The investor can therefore increase annual income by $50, with no change in risk. Should such an opportunity arise, many investors will quickly exploit it. Using MM's approach, investors will be selling shares in L, then borrowing and buying shares in U. Their actions will drive down the price of L's shares and/or drive up the price of U's shares until there is no further opportunity to earn arbitrage profits. Proposition 1 will then hold. Essentially, leverage does not add value to L because by borrowing, L is not doing anything that its shareholders cannot do for themselves. Therefore there is no reason for investors to pay a premium for the shares of levered companies.

It is sometimes argued that the arbitrage process employed by MM is unrealistic because company leverage and personal leverage are not perfect substitutes. For example, individual investors who borrow are likely to face higher interest rates and transaction costs than companies that borrow. Although true, this observation has little substance as a criticism because the particular arbitrage procedure used by MM is not the only way to prove their proposition. Another way, which uses a more realistic arbitrage procedure, is shown in the following example.

*Example 12.3*

This example again compares Company L and Company U using the information provided in Example 12.2.

Consider an investor who owns 1 per cent of L, that is, 1 per cent of its shares *and* 1 per cent of its debt. Referring again to Table 12.2, the market value of this investment will be $3000 in shares, plus $2000 in debt, giving a total value of $5000. The annual income from the investment will be:

$$\begin{array}{lll} \text{Shares:} & 0.20 \times \$3000 = & \$600 \\ \text{Debt:} & 0.15 \times \$2000 = & \underline{\$300} \\ & & \underline{\$900} \end{array}$$

Of course $900 is 1 per cent of L's net operating cash flow of $90 000 per annum, since the investor owns 1 per cent of both the shares and the debt issued by L.

In this case the arbitrage transaction involves selling L's securities and buying 1 per cent of the shares issued by U. The sale proceeds will be $5000, but only $4736.84 has to be invested in U's shares to yield the same income stream of $900 per annum. Therefore the investor can achieve the same annual income as that provided by the investment in L and have $5000 − $4736.84 = $263.16 remaining.

Clearly the difference between the values of the two companies could not persist and the actions of investors selling L's securities and buying U's shares would quickly establish an equilibrium in which their values would be exactly the same.

This example shows that Proposition 1 does not depend on the particular arbitrage process that MM originally used in their proof. Proposition 1 will hold, provided that investors are able to trade in both debt securities and shares and it is not necessary for arbitrage transactions to involve personal borrowing.

Proposition 1 is a **law of conservation of value** and states that the value of an asset remains the same, regardless of how the net operating cash flows generated by the asset are divided between different classes of investors. Companies, of course, hold many assets, but the logic remains the same. If the company's set of assets is taken as given, a change in the company's capital structure simply changes the way in which the net operating cash flows generated by those assets are divided between shareholders and debtholders. Regardless of how these flows are divided, their size remains the same. Therefore the value of the company's assets remains the same. Similarly, because the company's securities represent claims against those assets, the total market value of the securities also remains the same. To illustrate this with an everyday analogy, we cannot change the size of a cake simply by cutting it into a different number of slices!

## 12.3.2 MODIGLIANI AND MILLER'S PROPOSITION 2

Our discussion of Proposition 1 focused on the effect of capital structure decisions on shareholders' wealth and company value. Proposition 2 is discussed more readily in terms of the effect of capital structure on a company's **cost of capital**.[5] The cost of capital for a company is the minimum rate of return the company needs to earn in order to maintain its value.

If a company's net operating cash flows are constant in perpetuity, the company's cost of capital $k$ is simply the annual net operating cash flow divided by the market value of the company $V$. That is:

$$k = \frac{\text{annual net operating cash flow}}{V} \qquad (12.1)$$

In a perfect capital market, the annual net operating cash flow depends only on the profitability of the company's assets and is not affected by the company's capital structure. Proposition 1 shows that the value of the company will also not be affected by the company's capital structure. Therefore it follows that the choice of capital structure does not affect the company's cost of capital. Consequently, the company's cost of capital will be equal to the rate of return $k_e^*$ that would be required on the company's shares if it were financed solely by equity. This rate will depend on the company's business risk. A company's cost of capital is equal to a weighted average of the costs of each of the individual sources of finance used by the company. With no taxes, and two sources of finance, equity and debt, it follows that:

$$k = k_e^* = k_e \left(\frac{E}{V}\right) + k_d \left(\frac{D}{V}\right) \qquad (12.2)$$

where  $k$ = company cost of capital
$k_e^*$ = cost of capital with all equity finance
$k_e$ = cost of equity capital
$k_d$ = cost of debt capital
$E$ = the market value of the company's equity capital
$D$ = the market value of the company's debt capital
$V = E + D$ = the total market value of the company

Equation 12.2 can be rearranged to show how the cost of equity capital $k_e$ is affected by the use of debt finance. This gives:

---

[5] The cost-of-capital approach is consistent with the company-value approach because if there is a capital structure which maximises the value of the company, then under the assumptions used here, this same structure will also minimise the company's cost of capital.

$$k_e = k_e^* + (k_e^* - k_d)\frac{D}{E} \qquad (12.3)$$

Equation 12.3 is MM's Proposition 2, which shows that for a levered company the cost of equity capital consists of two components. The first is $k_e^*$, the rate of return that shareholders require, based on the company's business risk. The second component is an increment for financial risk and is proportional to the company's debt–equity ratio $D/E$, and also depends on the difference between $k_e^*$ and $k_d$.

If a company can always issue debt with no risk of default, the cost of debt $k_d$ will remain constant as the company's debt–equity ratio increases and the relationship between the cost of equity capital and the debt–equity ratio will be linear. Proposition 2 for the case of risk-free debt is shown in Figure 12.2.

Propositions 1 and 2 may appear contradictory. How is it possible for shareholders to be indifferent to borrowing by a company when, as Proposition 2 shows, this increases their expected rate of return? The answer is that because of the financial risk associated with borrowing, the shareholders' *required* rate of return also increases in a way that exactly offsets the effect of the increase in their *expected* return. Therefore, borrowing by a company has no effect on its shareholders' wealth. While Proposition 1 is a law of conservation of value, Proposition 2 is based on the **natural conservation of risk**. Assume that a company is able to issue risk-free debt. When the company borrows, it transfers a risk-free cash flow stream to debtholders. The business risk associated with the company's assets, and therefore with its net cash flows, remains the same regardless of its capital structure. Under the assumption of risk-free debt, this

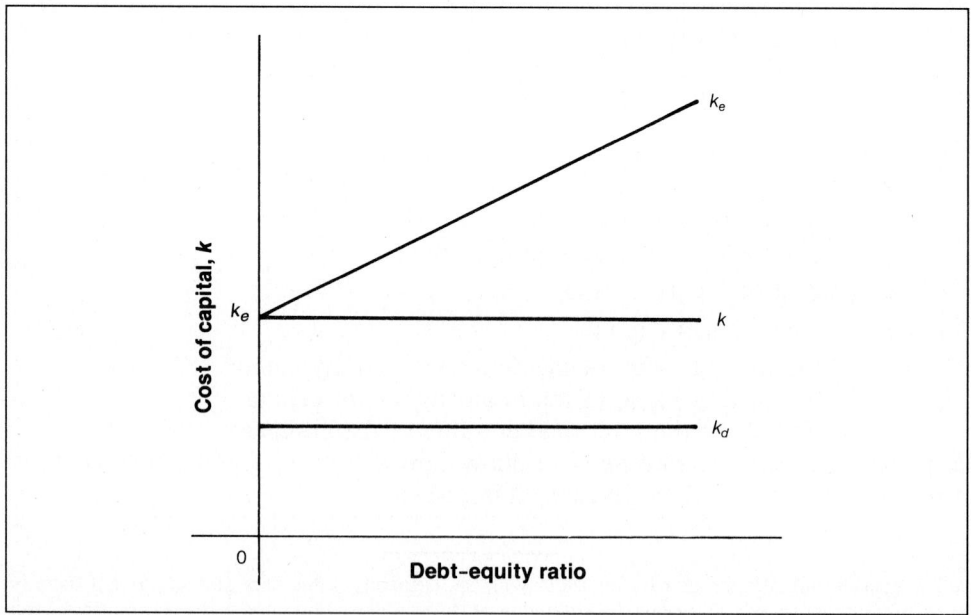

**Fig. 12.2** *Modigliani and Miller's Proposition 2 (no tax)*

risk will affect only shareholders. While changing the capital structure does not change the total risk to which shareholders are exposed, it does concentrate that risk on a smaller amount of equity capital. Therefore, borrowing increases the risk *per dollar* of equity and, as shown in Example 12.1, it increases the variability of the shareholders' rate of return. Being risk averse, shareholders respond by requiring a higher rate of return and Proposition 2 shows the precise relationship between the company's debt–equity ratio and the rate of return required by shareholders.

Up to this point it has been assumed that all debt is risk free. In practice, corporate debt is not risk free because with any non-government borrower, there is always some risk of default. Other things being equal, the higher a company's debt–equity ratio, the greater is the risk of default. Therefore, as a company borrows more, it will have to pay higher rates of interest. Proposition 2 for both risk-free and risky debt is illustrated in Figure 12.3.

As shown in Figure 12.2, if debt is risk free, the relationship between the debt–equity ratio and the cost of equity capital is linear. When debt becomes risky, the rate of return required by shareholders will continue to increase, but at a decreasing rate. Therefore, as the debt–equity ratio increases, both $k_d$ and $k_e$ increase, but the company's overall cost of capital $k$ remains constant. This may at first appear to be mathematically impossible, since as shown in Equation 12.2, $k$ is a weighted average of $k_e$ and $k_d$. However, there is no mathematical problem: as the debt–equity ratio increases, debtholders are bearing more of the company's business risk. Consequently, shareholders bear proportionately less risk and the

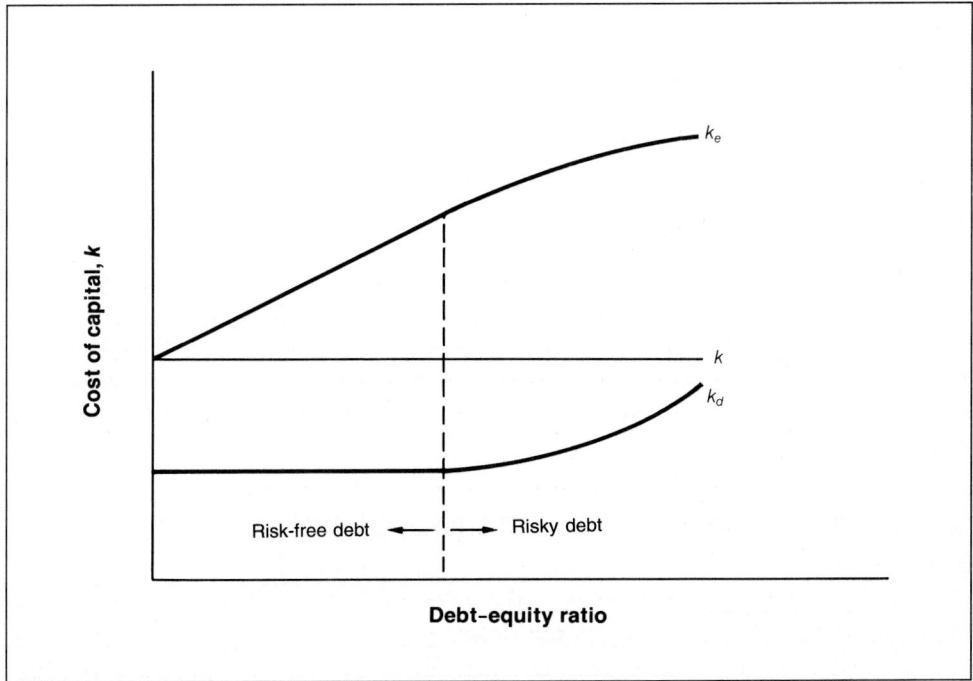

**Figure 12.3**

rate of increase in $k_e$ diminishes. Moreover, the proportion of equity is decreasing and the combined effect of these changes is that the overall cost of capital remains constant.

Proposition 2 highlights the error in the belief that debt is 'cheaper' than equity. A simple comparison of rates certainly suggests that debt is cheaper than equity but the error inherent in such a comparison is shown in the following example.

*Example 12.4*

Consider again Example 12.1, in which Dribnor Ltd is financed solely by equity and its shareholders require a rate of return of 15 per cent per annum. This rate reflects the business risk of Dribnor's assets. Dribnor can borrow at an interest rate of 12 per cent. Suppose that Dribnor borrows $1 000 000 and uses these funds to repurchase shares. What will be the effects on the cost of equity capital and the company's overall cost of capital?

We can answer the first question using Proposition 2 as shown in Equation 12.3:

$$k_e = k_e^* + (k_e^* - k_d)\frac{D}{E}$$

$$= 0.15 + (0.15 - 0.12)\frac{1}{1}$$

$$= 0.18 \text{ or } 18\% \text{ p.a.}$$

Dribnor's overall cost of capital can be calculated using Equation 12.2:

$$k = k_e\left(\frac{E}{V}\right) + k_d\left(\frac{D}{V}\right)$$

$$= 0.18 \times 0.5 + 0.12 \times 0.5$$

$$= 0.15 \text{ or } 15\% \text{ p.a.}$$

Introduction of debt finance has not changed Dribnor's overall cost of capital of 15 per cent, despite the fact that the interest rate on debt is only 12 per cent. The reason is that the borrowing caused the cost of equity capital to increase to a level that exactly offsets the effect of the apparently cheaper debt. In other words, the interest cost of debt is only its *explicit* cost. The financial risk created by borrowing increases the cost of equity capital, and this increase is an *implicit* cost associated with the debt. The true cost of the debt to Dribnor is its weighted average cost of capital, 15 per cent, which is not affected by capital structure decisions.

### 12.3.3 MODIGLIANI AND MILLER'S PROPOSITION 3

MM's Proposition 3 is that the appropriate discount rate for a particular investment proposal is independent of how the proposal is to be financed. The appropriate discount rate depends on the features of the investment proposal, in particular, its riskiness. Whether the investing company obtains the funds by borrowing, or by issuing shares, or both, has no effect on the appropriate discount rate. This is consistent with the irrelevance of the financing decision as shown by Proposition 1.

Taken together, the MM propositions maintain that in a perfect capital market with no taxes, it is only the investment decision that is important in the pursuit of wealth maximisation. The financing decision is of no consequence.

### 12.3.4 THE ROLE OF MM'S ANALYSIS

We have given considerable space to an explanation of the MM analysis. This should not be taken to imply that we regard the MM analysis as providing a complete description of the effects of real-world financing decisions. Clearly, it cannot do so because important factors such as taxes have so far been ignored. However, it cannot be denied that, given their assumptions, the logic of the MM analysis is unassailable. If there is a problem, it is that, as with many economic models, the underlying assumptions are unrealistic. Nevertheless there is considerable value in having a thorough understanding of the MM analysis and the significance of its underlying assumptions. One reason is that such an understanding is helpful in framing the right questions to ask about financing decisions. Another reason is that an understanding of the MM propositions helps in distinguishing between logical and illogical reasons that may be suggested for particular financing decisions. For example, it may be suggested that companies should use at least some debt finance because debt is 'cheaper' than equity. This suggestion is consistent with the **traditional view** of capital structure.

The traditionalists argue that a company can undertake a moderate level of borrowing without its cost of equity capital increasing to the degree shown by Proposition 2. Thus, according to this approach a company's overall cost of capital can be reduced by financial leverage, provided that the degree of leverage is not too great. Beyond some degree of leverage, investors will realise the risks to which they are exposed and the costs of both debt and equity will increase, as will the company's overall cost of capital. The traditional view suggests that there is some 'magic' in financial leverage because investors are supposed to ignore important information. In contrast to the traditional view, the essential message of the MM analysis is that *there is no magic in financial leverage.*

In summary, the MM analysis shows that under their assumptions the financing decision has no effect on company value or shareholders' wealth. To extend the analysis, we need to consider the effects of factors excluded by their assumptions. In particular, we need to focus on factors that will cause the net cash flows available to investors to be affected by a company's capital structure. These factors, which include taxes, agency costs and the costs of financial distress, are discussed in the following sections.

## 12.4 THE EFFECTS OF TAXES

Most analysis of the effects of taxes on capital structure is based on the classical tax system which applied in Australia before the introduction of the imputation system on 1 July 1987. The two systems differ in the taxation treatment of dividends paid to shareholders. Under both systems, company profits are subject to company income tax and dividends are taxed in the hands of shareholders.

Under the classical system, shareholders are taxed on the dividends they receive, with no account being taken of the fact that the company has already paid company tax on the profit that gave rise to the dividend. In this sense, shareholders are taxed twice—once at the company level (on company profit) and again at the personal level (on dividends paid out of profit). Under the imputation system, dividends paid out of profit on which Australian company tax has been paid are called **franked dividends** and such dividends carry credits for the income tax already paid by the company. These credits can be used by Australian resident shareholders to offset tax on their income. In effect, resident shareholders who receive franked dividends can recover the tax paid at the company level. Therefore a fundamental difference between the systems is that under imputation, company and personal taxes on equity are, in a sense, integrated, whereas under the classical system, these two taxes are separate.

An important consequence for investors under an imputation system is that dividends are no longer subject to the 'double taxation' that occurs under the classical system. Under imputation, company profits paid out as dividends are effectively taxed only once, at the personal level. The treatment of interest on debt is the same under both systems: interest is tax deductible at the company level and taxable as income at the personal level. Thus, under the imputation system the overall tax rates on dividend income and interest income will be equal for a given investor. This property of the system is often described as neutrality and, as we later show formally, it means that the system may not have any tax-related bias towards use of debt finance.

To understand the role of taxes, it is useful to begin by separately analysing the effects of company income tax and personal income tax. In Section 12.4.5 the effects of taxes under the imputation system are discussed.

### 12.4.1 COMPANY INCOME TAX

MM extended their original no-tax analysis to incorporate the effect of company income tax under the classical system.[6] When company profit is taxed after allowing a deduction for interest on debt, borrowing causes a significant reduction in company tax and a corresponding increase in the after-tax net cash flows to investors. The tax savings associated with debt are shown in Example 12.5 which is based on the same data as Example 12.1.

*Example 12.5*

The two capital structures proposed for Dribnor Ltd are compared in Table 12.3, assuming that earnings before interest and tax are $300 000 per annum.

---

[6] The original MM article (see Footnote 3) included the effect of tax savings on interest but valued the savings incorrectly. The error was rectified in F. Modigliani & M. Miller, 'Corporate Income Taxes and the Cost of Capital: A Correction', *American Economic Review*, June 1963, pp. 433–43.

## Table 12.3

| Capital structure | 100% equity | 50% equity 50% debt |
|---|---|---|
| Earnings before interest and tax ($) | 300 000 | 300 000 |
| Interest on debt ($) | — | 120 000 |
| Taxable income ($) | 300 000 | 180 000 |
| Company income tax ($) | | |
| (tax rate, $t_c = 0.33$) | 99 000 | 59 400 |
| After-tax company income ($) | 201 000 | 120 600 |
| After-tax cash flows available to investors | | |
| (shareholders and debtholders) ($) | 201 000 | 240 600 |
| Increase in after-tax cash flow ($) | — | 39 600 |

Example 12.5 shows that by borrowing $1 000 000, Dribnor increases its after-tax net cash flow by $39 600 per annum. This increase is equal to the tax savings on interest, which is calculated by multiplying the annual interest payment $I$ by the company income tax rate $t_c$. Therefore:

Tax savings on interest = $t_c \times I$
$= 0.33 \times \$120\ 000$
$= \$39\ 600$ p.a.

What is the effect of the tax savings on the value of the company? Since the annual after-tax net cash flows increase by an amount equal to the annual tax savings on interest, it follows that the market value of a levered company, $V_L$, must be equal to the value of an equivalent unlevered company, $V_U$, plus the present value of the tax savings on interest. Therefore:

$$V_L = V_U + \text{(PV of tax savings on interest)} \quad (12.4)$$

What is the appropriate risk-adjusted discount rate to apply to the tax savings? Assuming that the tax savings are just as risky as the interest payments on debt, the appropriate discount rate is simply the cost of debt $k_d$.

If the annual interest payment remains constant in perpetuity, Equation 12.4 becomes:

$$V_L + V_U + \frac{t_c(I)}{k_d} \quad (12.5)$$

In this case the annual interest payment $I$ is equal to the cost of debt $k_d$, multiplied by the value of debt $D$. Making these substitutions, Equation 12.5 can be rewritten as follows:

$$V_L = V_U + \frac{t_c\ (k_d)\ (D)}{k_d}$$
$$= V_U + t_c\ D \quad (12.6)$$

Equations 12.4 to 12.6 express MM's Proposition 1, modified to incorporate the effects of company income tax. Equation 12.6 implies that a levered company is always worth more than an equivalent unlevered company. Moreover, the more it borrows, the more its value increases. The implication for capital structure policy is clear but extreme: all companies should have 100 per cent debt! In practice, of course, it is only possible to have 100 per cent debt in a state of insolvency, a fate that all sensible managers strive to avoid. While most public companies borrowed to some extent when the classical tax system was in use, few of them even approached such extreme levels of debt. This indicates that while debt must have some advantages, there must also be other factors that offset the tax advantages of debt finance. One important factor that can do so is personal taxes which are generally larger on returns to debt than equity.

### 12.4.2 PERSONAL TAXES

The term *personal taxes* is widely used in the finance literature to refer to taxes paid at the investor level. Such taxes include the income tax paid by superannuation funds as well as that paid by individual investors, but to be consistent with the literature we will use the term *personal taxes*. The significance of personal taxes was highlighted by Miller who pointed out that the personal tax rate $t_{pd}$ on income to debtholders is generally greater than the personal tax rate $t_{ps}$ on income to shareholders.[7] For example, under the US classical tax system discussed by Miller, $t_{pd}$ is the debtholder's marginal income tax rate, while $t_{ps}$ is an average of the shareholder's income tax rates on dividends and capital gains. Capital gains were taxed at a lower rate than ordinary income (interest and dividends), so $t_{ps}$ was lower than $t_{pd}$.[8] Miller suggested that the differential taxation of income to debtholders and shareholders was the most important factor offsetting the company tax advantages of debt. Further, he argued that the effects of company and personal taxes could be exactly offsetting. In this case the original MM Proposition 1 would still hold.

The combined effects of company and personal taxes are illustrated in Table 12.4 which traces the fate of $100 of company earnings before interest and tax. Depending on the company's capital structure, this $100 can be paid out as interest to debtholders or it can provide income to shareholders.

The value of a company should be maximised if its capital structure can be arranged to maximise the income to investors after all taxes, where 'all taxes' includes personal tax paid by investors, as well as company income tax. The bottom line of Table 12.4 shows that the preferred source of finance depends on a comparison between $(1 - t_{pd})$ and $(1 - t_c)(1 - t_{ps})$. In making this comparison it is essential to recognise that the personal tax rates on debt and equity are generally different. Interest on debt is treated as income for tax purposes and

---

7 M. Miller, 'Debt and Taxes', *Journal of Finance*, May 1977, pp. 261–75.
8 Note that $t_{ps}$ is a composite personal tax rate which is a weighted average of the personal tax rates applicable to dividends, $t_{pe}$, and to capital gains, $t_g$. Weighting these tax rates in accordance with the company's dividend payout ratio δ gives: $t_{ps} = δt_{pe} + (1 - δ)t_g$. Also, note that $t_{pe}$ is the investor's marginal income tax rate, so, for a given investor, $t_{pe} = t_{pd}$. Miller's argument was based on the classical tax system, which has been replaced in Australia by the imputation system. Therefore in applying Miller's argument to Australia we confine the discussion at this stage to the pre-imputation context. The effects of taxes under imputation are discussed in Section 12.4.5.

## CAPITAL STRUCTURE DECISIONS: THEORY

**Table 12.4** *Effect of taxes on income to holders of debt and equity*

| Source of finance | Debt | Equity |
|---|---|---|
| Earnings before interest and tax ($) | 100 | 100 |
| Company tax ($) | nil | $100 \times t_c$ |
| Earnings after company tax ($) | 100 | $100(1 - t_c)$ |
| Personal tax ($) | $100 \times t_{pd}$ | $100(1 - t_c) \times t_{ps}$ |
| Net income after all taxes ($) | $100(1 - t_{pd})$ | $100(1 - t_c)(1 - t_{ps})$ |

$t_c$ = company income tax rate
$t_{pd}$ and $t_{ps}$ are personal tax rates as defined at the start of this section.

will be taxed at the investor's marginal income tax rate. Therefore, based on the tax rates that applied under the classical system in Australia during the 1980s, $t_{pd}$ could be as high as 0.49. Under that system, dividends were taxed as income, but capital gains were either tax-free for most individual investors, or taxed at a relatively low rate, because the capital gains tax introduced in 1985 applies only to realised gains in excess of the rate of inflation. Since $t_{ps}$ is a weighted average of the investor's marginal tax rates on dividends and capital gains, it would generally be significantly lower than $t_{pd}$. Consequently, $(1 - t_{pd})$ could be less than, greater than, or equal to $(1 - t_c)(1 - t_{ps})$. The combined effects of these taxes and their implications for capital structure decisions were analysed formally by Miller.[9] This analysis is presented in the next section.

### 12.4.3 MILLER'S ANALYSIS

Our discussion of Miller's analysis under the classical tax system relies on the following assumptions:[10]

1. The personal tax rate on income from shares, $t_{ps}$, is zero. Miller later relaxed this assumption but pointed out that $t_{ps}$ can be zero if, for example, all the income to shareholders is in the form of unrealised capital gains.
2. All debt is riskless, and investors are risk-neutral, and they will therefore be indifferent between equal after-tax income from debt and equity. Miller's analysis is illustrated in Figure 12.4.

The $r_d(D)$ curve represents the demand for corporate debt, which is explained as follows:

- The rate $r_0$ is the interest rate on tax-exempt government securities.[11]
- The flat section of the curve represents the demand for corporate debt from tax-exempt investors. To understand this, suppose that all companies were financed entirely by equity. That situation cannot persist

---

[9] M. Miller, see Footnote 7.
[10] These assumptions are employed to simplify the presentation of Miller's analysis but his conclusions do not necessarily depend on their validity.
[11] While such securities do not exist in Australia, they do in some other countries. In the Australian context, $r_0$ can be interpreted as the minimum rate of return that tax exempt investors would require on risk-free assets. Many charities, and public bodies such as universities and non-profit hospitals, are tax-exempt.

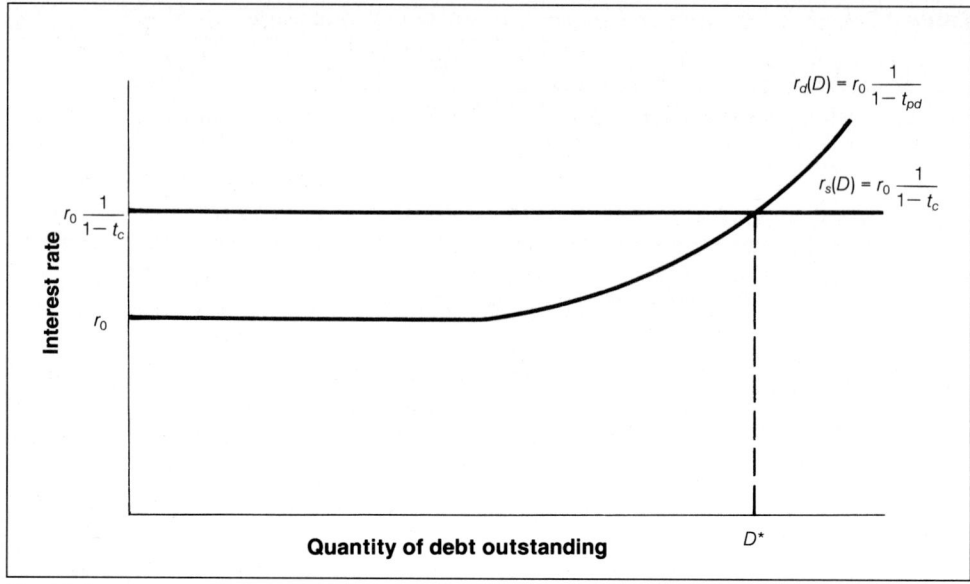

**Fig. 12.4**

because there would be a strong incentive for companies to reduce company tax by borrowing. Tax-exempt investors should readily move from holding equity to holding debt because they would pay no tax in either case. Further, under the assumption that corporate debt is risk free, such investors would accept the rate $r_0$. The initial impact of the change from all-equity financing would be to reduce total taxes, because company taxes are being reduced without any increase in personal taxes.

- When tax-exempt investors have been satisfied, companies will have to persuade investors who pay tax on their debt income to purchase debt. The rate of interest offered to potential debtholders must therefore increase, in order to attract investors with higher and higher marginal personal income tax rates $t_{pd}$. Therefore, the demand curve in Figure 12.4 is upward sloping. Companies can afford to persuade investors to switch from holding equity to holding debt, provided that the company tax saved by issuing the additional debt is greater than the personal tax payable by the debtholder (remember that $t_{ps} = 0$). Therefore the process should stop when, for the marginal investor, $t_{pd}$ equals $t_c$.

- The horizontal supply curve $r_s(D)$ is consistent with all companies being prepared to issue debt at a rate of interest equal to $r_0/(1 - t_c)$. If the rate of interest were lower than this, there would be an incentive for companies to reduce overall taxes by issuing more debt. Therefore the supply and demand curves intersect at the point where there is no incentive for companies to issue more debt.

Miller's analysis has several implications. These include:

(a) There is an optimum quantity of debt $D^*$, *for the corporate sector as a whole*, and therefore an optimum debt–equity ratio for the corporate sector as a whole. This optimum debt–equity ratio will depend on the company income tax rate and on the funds available to investors who are subject to different tax rates.

(b) The securities issued by different companies will appeal to different clienteles of investors. For example, tax-exempt investors should invest only in debt securities, while investors subject to marginal personal income tax rates greater than the company income tax rate should invest only in shares. Therefore companies with different capital structures will attract different clienteles of investors, but according to Miller, 'one clientele is as good as the other'.[12] Consequently, in equilibrium there is no optimum debt–equity ratio *for an individual company*.

(c) The shareholders of levered companies end up receiving no benefit from the company tax savings on debt because the saving is passed on to debtholders in the form of a higher interest rate on debt. That is, companies are effectively required to compensate the debtholders for personal tax payable on interest income. The compensation is paid in the form of an interest rate that is higher than it would be if personal income tax did not exist. The main beneficiaries of the company tax savings on debt are therefore tax-exempt investors. They would be prepared to hold debt paying an interest rate $r_0$, but will receive, in Miller's equilibrium, the higher 'grossed up' rate, $r_0/(1 - t_c)$.

(d) When the assumption that $t_{ps} = 0$ was relaxed, Miller showed that the value of a levered company could be expressed as:

$$V_L = V_U + \left[1 - \frac{(1 - t_c)(1 - t_{ps})}{1 - t_{pd}}\right] D \qquad (12.7)$$

where $D$ = the market value of debt.

The second term on the right-hand side of Equation 12.7 is often referred to as the gain from leverage $G_L$ and is derived in Appendix 12.1.

All the previous relationships between leverage and company value can be viewed as special cases of Equation 12.7. When there are no taxes (that is, $t_c = t_{ps} = t_{pd} = 0$), then $V_L = V_U$ as in MM's Proposition 1. Where there is company income tax but no personal income tax (that is, $t_c > 0$ but $t_{ps} = t_{pd} = 0$), then $V_L = V_U + t_c D$ which is, of course, the result obtained by MM when only company income tax is included. This result still holds when there are both company and personal income taxes, provided that the personal tax rates applied to income from shares and debt are equal (that is, $t_{ps} = t_{pd}$).

Where, as discussed earlier, $t_{ps}$ is less than $t_{pd}$, the tax benefits from using debt are less than $t_c D$. Miller argues that in equilibrium the marginal investor will be indifferent between holding either debt or equity. This occurs when the following relationship holds:

$$(1 - t_{pd}) = (1 - t_c)(1 - t_{ps}) \qquad (12.8)$$

Comparing Equation 12.8 with the after-tax income from debt and equity in Table 12.4, it can be seen that if $(1 - t_{pd})$ is greater than $(1 - t_c)(1 - t_{ps})$,

---

[12] M. Miller, 'Debt and Taxes', *Journal of Finance*, May 1977, p. 269.

income to investors can be increased by increasing the debt–equity ratio. Conversely, if $(1 - t_{pd})$ is less than $(1 - t_c)(1 - t_{ps})$, income to investors can be increased by reducing the debt–equity ratio. Finally, when $(1 - t_{pd})$ is equal to $(1 - t_c)(1 - t_{ps})$ the marginal investor's income after all taxes cannot be increased by changing the proportions of debt and equity in the capital structure. Therefore the capital structure is optimum at this point. In addition, when Equation 12.8 holds, $G_L$ will be zero and $V_L = V_U$. In other words, MM's Proposition 1 would still hold because the effects of company and personal taxes exactly offset each other.

Miller's analysis is valuable in explaining empirical observations such as the fact that the average debt–equity ratio of US companies did not increase substantially from the 1920s to the 1970s, despite an almost fivefold increase in the company income tax rate during that period. Miller's explanation is that personal income tax rates increased in a similar manner, thereby offsetting what would otherwise have been a strong incentive for companies to issue more debt. On the other hand, some empirical observations are inconsistent with Miller's argument. In particular there is no evidence that the investor clienteles suggested by Miller's argument actually exist. It appears, therefore, that the combined effects of corporate and personal taxes are more complex than Miller suggested. Some reasons for this are discussed in the next section.

### 12.4.4 AN INTERMEDIATE APPROACH

The preceding sections have discussed two different theories of the effects of taxes on capital structure decisions. First, the MM analysis with company income tax predicts that company value will be maximised by adopting an all-debt capital structure. Secondly, Miller proposes that the effects of personal and company taxes can exactly offset each other so that an *individual* company's value is independent of its capital structure, even though there is an optimum debt–equity ratio for the corporate sector *taken as a whole*. This section considers a third, intermediate approach with conclusions between those of MM and Miller. Essentially this approach is based on relaxing some of the assumptions that underlie Miller's argument.

So far it has been assumed that the effective company income tax rate for all companies equals the statutory rate, which was typically 46 per cent under the Australian classical system. This implies that companies are certain to generate sufficient profits to ensure that their taxable income is positive. Hence they are certain to save 46 cents of company tax for every dollar of interest paid. In practice, this will not always be the case, for two reasons. First, if a company incurs a loss, it is carried forward as a deduction against later years' taxable income and the present value of the tax savings on an additional dollar of interest will be less than 46 cents. In practice, few, if any, companies are certain always to be profitable, and, other things being equal, the higher the level of debt, the lower will be a company's effective tax rate. Secondly, De Angelo and Masulis have pointed out that borrowing is not the only way for companies to save tax.[13] For example, depreciation on many assets can be claimed as a tax deduction, and the higher a company's deductions for depreciation and other non-debt items, the less is its need to save company income tax by borrowing.

With uncertain future interest tax savings and non-debt tax deductions the Miller equilibrium no longer applies. Instead there will be an optimum capital structure for each company and the companies whose shareholders will benefit from corporate borrowing will be those best able to use the tax deductions generated by the interest paid on debt.[14] In other words, borrowing can add value for companies with high effective tax rates because the company tax saved by borrowing is greater than the additional personal tax paid. Conversely, for companies with low effective tax rates, borrowing can reduce company value and shareholders' wealth because borrowing increases total taxes.

It should also be noted that in relaxing some of Miller's assumptions we have not yet allowed for the fact that companies that borrow can incur various leverage-related costs. Miller recognised that these costs, which are discussed in Section 12.5, are relevant to capital structure decisions. However, he argued that these costs were too small for them to have a significant effect on company value. In summary, his argument is important in that it shows that both personal and corporate taxes must be taken into account. It also shows that the effects of the two taxes tend to be offsetting, but it does not show conclusively that their effects exactly offset each other.

### 12.4.5 THE EFFECTS OF TAXES: THE IMPUTATION TAX SYSTEM

Under the imputation system, company income tax and personal income tax are integrated in a way that makes it impossible to discuss them separately. For example, if a company reduces its debt–equity ratio and as a result pays more company income tax, the full effects cannot be assessed without considering the fact that such a change will increase the company's capacity to pay franked dividends. This is important because resident shareholders receiving franked dividends can recover some or all of the income tax paid by the company.

Appendix 12.1 provides a derivation, consistent with Miller's approach, of the gain from leverage under the imputation system $G_{LI}$. The general result, Equation A12.1.16, is:

$$G_{LI} = D \left[ 1 - \frac{\delta(1 - t_{pe}) + (1 - \delta)(1 - t_c)(1 - t_g)}{1 - t_{pd}} \right]$$

It is important to note that in discussing the imputation system, we treat separately the dividend and capital gains components of income to shareholders. Therefore we now use the separate tax rates $t_{pe}$ and $t_g$ rather than the composite

---

13 H. De Angelo & R. Masulis, 'Optimal Capital Structure Under Corporate and Personal Taxation', *Journal of Financial Economics*, March 1980, pp. 3–29.
14 For US evidence that the marginal effective tax advantage of debt differs between companies, see J. Cordes & S. Sheffrin, 'Estimating the Tax Advantage of Corporate Debt', *Journal of Finance*, March 1983, pp. 95–105.

rate $t_{ps}$ which was defined in Footnote 8. In using Equation A12.1.16, it is necessary to specify a value for the **dividend payout ratio** $\delta$, which is the ratio of dividends paid to company profit after payment of company income tax. If the value of $\delta$ does not represent the company's optimum dividend policy, misleading results can be obtained. The significance of dividend policy and its interaction with financing decisions is shown in the following example.

### Example 12.6

Suppose that a company's shares and debt are both held by superannuation funds, so that the personal tax rates $t_{pe}$ and $t_{pd}$ both equal 0.15. Assume also that the company income tax rate $t_c$ is 0.33, and assume, for simplicity, that there is no capital gains tax ($t_g = 0$). Also suppose that the company pays no dividends, so $\delta = 0$.

Substitution of these values into Equation A12.1.16 shows that the gain from leverage per dollar of debt is $[1 - 0.67/0.85] = 0.2118$. This result suggests that by borrowing and saving company income tax the company's value should increase by 21.18 cents per dollar of additional debt.

Given the data, this result is 'correct', but it is also very misleading because the calculation ignores an even simpler way to increase the value of the company: by changing its dividend policy. As shown in Appendix 12.1, distributed company profit is effectively taxed at the shareholder's personal income tax rate, whereas retained profit is taxed at the company income tax rate. Thus in this case the company should distribute as much profit as possible, so the optimum dividend policy will be to set $\delta = 1$. Making this change, the gain from leverage per dollar of debt becomes $[1 - 0.85/0.85] = 0$. The correct interpretation of these two calculations may not be obvious. Initially the company's dividend policy was non-optimal and this *reduced* the company's value below its potential level. The value reduction could be eliminated by borrowing, or could be reversed by simply adopting the optimum dividend policy. The second calculation shows that once the optimum dividend policy has been adopted there is no scope for any further increase in value by borrowing.

Example 12.6 illustrates three points which are relevant to the choice of capital structure under the imputation system. First, any calculations which suggest that a company's value can be increased by changing its debt–equity ratio should be checked to determine whether similar benefits can be achieved by a change in dividend policy. Secondly, dividend decisions are probably more important, relative to capital structure decisions, than they were under the classical tax system. Thirdly, under imputation it is difficult to devise a sensible combination of dividend and capital structure policies which results in a non-zero gain from leverage. Some combinations of these policies are now considered.

If a company pays the maximum possible franked dividends, that is, $\delta = 1$, then as shown in Appendix 12.1, Equation A12.1.16 simplifies to Equation A12.1.17:

$$G_{LI} = D \left[ \frac{t_{pe} - t_{pd}}{1 - t_{pd}} \right]$$

For any given investor, $t_{pe}$ is equal to $t_{pd}$ so for the gain from leverage to be non-zero, equity and debt must be held by investors with different marginal income tax rates. For example, the gain from leverage would be positive if all of a company's shares were held by individuals taxed at the maximum personal income tax rate ($t_{pe}$ = 0.47) and if all of the company's debt were held by superannuation funds ($t_{pd}$ = 0.15). However, as discussed in Section 12.4.3, companies would then have an incentive to issue more debt and both the interest rate on debt and the tax rate of marginal debtholders should increase until an equilibrium is reached. This equilibrium occurs when marginal investors are indifferent between holding shares and holding debt but, for any such investor, $t_{pe}$ and $t_{pd}$ are equal. Equation A12.1.17 shows that the gain from leverage is then zero. Therefore, if the optimum dividend policy is to set $\delta = 1$, then for companies following this policy the substantial bias towards debt finance suggested by the MM analysis with company income tax can no longer exist under the imputation system.

Now consider the other extreme dividend policy: zero dividends. In this case $\delta = 0$ and Equation A12.1.16 simplifies to Equation A12.1.18:

$$G_{LI} = D \left[ 1 - \frac{(1 - t_c)(1 - t_g)}{1 - t_{pd}} \right]$$

For simplicity, again assume that $t_g$ is zero. In this case the gain from leverage depends on the magnitude of $t_{pd}$ relative to $t_c$.

First, suppose that $t_{pd}$ is less than $t_c$. This is the case considered in Example 12.6. As shown in that example, company value can be increased by changing the dividend payout ratio from zero to one. However, after that has been done, changing the debt–equity ratio will have no effect on company value.

Secondly, suppose that $t_{pd}$ is greater than $t_c$. The gain from leverage will be non-zero, but it will be negative rather than positive. This result simply reflects the fact that investors on marginal income tax rates greater than the company income tax rate should hold shares rather than debt. In other words, for such investors the imputation system is biased towards equity as a source of company finance.

In summary, the imputation tax system has the potential to be neutral between debt and equity. In this context, 'neutral' means that the overall tax burden is the same for each source of finance. If neutrality is achieved, we are back to MM's Proposition 1 in the original no-tax case: the choice of capital structure does not affect a company's value. In practice, the imputation system is neutral for some investors, but not for others. Specifically, the system is not neutral for investors with personal income tax rates greater than the company income tax rate. However, for these investors the system is biased towards equity rather than debt. We have not been able to identify any conditions under which the imputation system favours the use of debt finance by companies.

The approach we have used to analyse the effects of the imputation system is analogous to Miller's approach and we have reached a similar conclusion: the effects of company tax and personal taxes are potentially offsetting. However, there is an important difference between the two cases. Miller's argument is based on the classical tax system and his conclusion relies on the existence of a *market equilibrium*. In the case of the imputation system, our conclusion is based on the *structure* of the system. That is, the designers of the imputation system had as one of their main objectives the removal of any tax-related bias towards the use of debt finance by companies. Our analysis indicates that this objective should be achieved in the case of companies which are wholly owned by Australian resident investors. However, taxes can still be an important influence on financing decisions for many companies. For example, overseas investors in Australian companies are outside the imputation system. Such investors are effectively still operating under the classical tax system. Financing strategies which can be tax effective when a company's shares are owned by both resident and non-resident investors are discussed in Chapter 13.

## 12.5 AGENCY COSTS AND THE COSTS OF FINANCIAL DISTRESS

The non-tax factors that can cause a company's value to depend on its capital structure include agency costs and costs of financial distress. We first outline the nature of financial distress and then discuss the effects of direct bankruptcy costs. The effects of agency costs are discussed in Section 12.5.2.

A company is said to be in a state of financial distress when it incurs problems in meeting its commitments to debtholders. In serious cases these problems may lead to the liquidation of the company. Alternatively a receiver–manager may be appointed by the debtholders; this may lead either to eventual liquidation or to control reverting to shareholders if the company trades out of its difficulties. In less serious cases of financial distress a company may trade out of its difficulties without resort to formal measures such as receivership. In other even less serious cases, the mere possibility of financial difficulties can create incentives for management and other stakeholders such as customers and suppliers to act in ways which decrease company value. Therefore we can distinguish between costs associated with a formal transfer of control to debtholders, that is, **bankruptcy costs**,[15] and costs of financial distress which can affect companies whose problems are less serious. The latter costs include those associated with conflicts of interest between debtholders and shareholders, and costs associated with the incentive effects of debt, both of which are agency costs.[16]

---

15 Technically, the term 'bankruptcy' in Australia applies only to the insolvency of individuals. When a company fails to meet its financial obligations its creditors have a number of options such as seeking the appointment of a receiver, a receiver–manager or a liquidator. We use the term 'bankruptcy' to describe the status of such companies because of its widespread use in the finance literature.
16 For a detailed discussion of agency theory, see M. Jensen & W. Meckling, 'The Theory of the Firm: Managerial Behaviour, Agency Costs and Ownership Structure', *Journal of Financial Economics*, October 1976, pp. 305–60; or A. Barnea, R. Haugen & L. Senbet, 'Market Imperfections, Agency Problems, and Capital Structure: A Review', *Financial Management*, Summer 1981, pp. 7–22.

## 12.5.1 BANKRUPTCY COSTS

In Section 12.2 we explained that any borrowing by a company creates financial risk. This is true even if the debt–equity ratio is so low that there is no risk of default, that is, the debt is risk free. MM's analysis shows that financial risk increases the cost of equity capital but has no effect on a company's overall cost of capital or on its market value.

Increasing a company's debt–equity ratio increases financial risk and also increases a separate but related risk: the risk that the company will default on its debt. When there is some probability of default, debt is described as 'risky'. However, the MM analysis shows that even if debt is risky, with no taxes, a company's market value is not affected by its debt–equity ratio. This conclusion also relies on the assumption that, while default is possible, there are no costs associated with default.[17] That is, bankruptcy costs are assumed to be zero.

In practice there are both direct and indirect costs associated with bankruptcy and these costs will affect companies that issue risky debt. The direct costs are out-of-pocket costs associated with receivership or liquidation and consist mainly of fees paid to lawyers, accountants and other professionals. Indirect costs relate to factors such as the effect of lost sales, and managerial time devoted to attempts to avert failure and, as noted above, they also include some types of agency costs.

The effect of bankruptcy costs on company value is easily seen in the case of direct bankruptcy costs. When a company issues risky debt there is some probability that the company will subsequently default, in which case direct bankruptcy costs will be incurred. Therefore by issuing risky debt, a company gives outsiders (liquidators and other insolvency specialists) a potential claim against its assets, which must decrease the value of the company to its shareholders and/or its debtholders. Where there are both benefits, such as tax savings, and costs, in the form of bankruptcy costs, associated with debt finance, the value of a company can be written as follows:

$$\text{Value of company} = \text{value of equivalent all-equity financed company} + \text{present value of benefits of debt} - \text{Present value of expected bankruptcy costs}$$

The present value of expected bankruptcy costs is calculated as follows:

$$\text{Present value of expected bankruptcy costs} = \text{probability of bankruptcy} \times \text{present value of costs incurred if bankruptcy occurs}$$

The probability of bankruptcy will depend on both the company's business

---

[17] The assumption of no costs associated with default does not mean that there are no losses incurred by investors. Typically, both debtholders and shareholders will incur losses because the value of the company's assets has declined. This decline *causes* the company to default but if there are no costs associated with default, the total, albeit reduced, value of the assets is available for distribution to investors. Therefore investors do not suffer additional losses as a *result* of default.

risk and its financial risk, but at any given level of business risk, the higher the company's financial risk, the higher will be the probability of bankruptcy. Therefore, the present value of expected bankruptcy costs will increase as a company's debt–equity ratio increases.

Bankruptcy costs would not concern shareholders if they were borne entirely by other parties such as debtholders. It is therefore necessary to consider whether bankruptcy costs will be borne by shareholders, debtholders, or both shareholders and debtholders. When a company is liquidated it is rare for shareholders to receive any return. The costs incurred in administering the liquidation therefore reduce the pool of funds available for distribution to debtholders. However, before they lend money, potential debtholders should realise that they will suffer in the event of liquidation and respond by demanding a higher interest rate on their loans. Consequently, while debtholders will bear *realised* liquidation costs, the *expected* costs are likely to be borne by shareholders. Therefore, expected bankruptcy costs decrease both company value and shareholders' wealth. In addition to the fairly obvious direct costs of bankruptcy there are other less obvious indirect costs of financial distress associated with the use of debt. Many of these indirect costs are agency costs, which are discussed in the next section.

## 12.5.2 AGENCY COSTS

As discussed in Chapter 1, operation of companies involves a set of contractual or agency relationships between various parties including managers, shareholders, debtholders, customers, and suppliers. These relationships involve agency costs, which arise from the potential for conflicts of interest between the parties. In this section we discuss the major ways in which agency costs can affect financing decisions. The relevant costs include those associated with conflicts of interest between investors, and the incentive effects of debt. Equity finance also has agency costs because there can be conflicts of interest between shareholders and managers.

### CONFLICTS OF INTEREST BETWEEN INVESTORS

When a company issues debt, debtholders may fear that management will make decisions which will transfer wealth from debtholders to shareholders. This conflict of interest is one type of agency problem. The following examples illustrate the potential for such conflicts of interest.[18]

1. *Claim dilution*—A company may issue new debt which ranks equal with, or has a higher ranking than, its existing debt. If the proceeds from the issue are used to pay dividends, the total assets of the company are maintained and the only change is in the company's debt–equity ratio. However, the holders of the old debt now have a less secure claim on the company's assets and therefore their investment has become more risky. Accordingly the market value of their securities decreases. The

---

[18] S. Myers, 'Determinants of Corporate Borrowing', *Journal of Financial Economics,* November 1977, pp. 147–75; C. Smith & J. Warner, 'On Financial Contracting: An Analysis of Bond Covenants', *Journal of Financial Economics,* June 1979, pp. 117–61.

value of the company is unchanged by the new debt and therefore wealth is transferred from the holders of the old debt to shareholders.
2. *Dividend payout*—A company may significantly increase its dividend payout. By doing so, it decreases the company's assets and increases the riskiness of its debt. Again this results in a wealth transfer from debtholders to shareholders. Further, the incentives for management to increase a company's dividends become greater when the company is facing financial distress. In this case the dividend payout provides a means for the shareholders to receive returns that otherwise are likely to go to the debtholders on liquidation.
3. *Asset substitution*—A company's incentive to undertake risky investments increases because of the use of debt. This is particularly the case if the market value of its shares is relatively low. In these circumstances a company may undertake a high-risk investment even if it has a negative net present value. The reason is that if the investment proves successful, most of the benefits will flow to shareholders, but if the investment fails, most of the costs will be borne by debtholders. Therefore, at the time the investment is undertaken, the total value of the company will decrease (given that the investment has a negative net present value) but the value of the shares will increase and the value of the debt will fall. Again there is a transfer of wealth from debtholders to shareholders.
4. *Underinvestment*—A company may reject proposed low-risk investments which have a positive net present value. If a company's debt is very risky it may not be in the interest of shareholders to contribute additional capital to finance profitable new investments. While undertaking the investments would increase company value, shareholders can still lose because the risk of the debt will fall and its value will increase. The amount of this increase can be greater than the net present value of the investments.

Debtholders should realise that their wealth may be eroded by managers' decisions made in the best interests of the company's shareholders. Debtholders would be expected to attempt to protect themselves against such behaviour by managers; the need for them to seek such protection seems likely to increase with increases in the company's debt–equity ratio. One response by lenders is to require a higher rate of interest on debt than would otherwise be the case, in order to compensate them for the losses they may suffer. This imposes costs on the company which will be borne largely by shareholders. In addition, lenders may require covenants to be inserted in loan agreements. Such covenants could include restrictions on issuing additional debt, particularly debt that has a higher ranking, a restriction on the disposal of assets, a limitation on the payment of dividends, limitations on the types of investments the company can undertake, and requirements that the company maintain specific financial ratios.[19] The fact that these types of covenants have been in existence for many years suggests

---

[19] Smith & Warner, see Footnote 18. In addition, note that the law may limit the behaviour of managers. For example, by law, dividends can be paid only out of 'profits'.

that lenders are well aware of their need for protection. The costs of such covenants have an impact on the value of the company and shareholders' wealth in two ways:

1. Costly monitoring will be required to ensure that the covenants are not breached.
2. There may be opportunity costs in cases where the restrictive covenants prevent managers from implementing value-maximising decisions. For example, covenants designed to prevent the company undertaking high-risk projects with negative net present values may also result in some profitable, high-risk projects being foregone.

Therefore, it can be seen that there are costs that will be borne by the shareholders of levered companies as a direct result of conflicts of interest between them and debtholders. The magnitude of these costs will increase with the debt–equity ratio of the company. Together with bankruptcy costs, these conflict-of-interest costs are part of the costs of financial distress. The next section outlines some of the costs that can result from the incentive effects of debt.

## ADVERSE INCENTIVE EFFECTS OF DEBT

Shapiro and Titman discuss another type of agency problem of debt: the adverse incentive effects of debt finance.[20] The basic problem is that the threat of corporate bankruptcy provides incentives for managers and other stakeholders such as customers, suppliers, and employees to behave in ways which can disrupt a company's operating activities and thus decrease its value. For example, if a company is experiencing financial difficulties, managers are likely to pay less attention to issues such as product quality and employee safety.

Clearly, if product quality falls and this fall is easily noticed by customers, sales and revenue will be lost. Also there are cases where product quality is important, but difficult to assess. In these cases, the mere perception that a company's product quality is likely to suffer because of financial difficulties can deter customers. For example, travellers are likely to be wary of financially insecure airlines because of fears that safety may be impaired by inadequate maintenance. Therefore it can be important for companies to maintain an image of low risk because loss of sales and customers will exacerbate any financial difficulties that exist. Restricting the level of debt is one way of restricting a company's overall risk.

Titman discusses these issues, with emphasis on the nature of a company's products and the effect this can have on liquidation decisions and company value.[21] He points out that shareholders and debtholders are not the only parties who can suffer if a company liquidates or withdraws voluntarily from a particular line of business. Titman argues that expected future costs imposed on parties such as employees and customers will affect shareholders' wealth. For example,

---

[20] A. Shapiro & S. Titman, 'An integrated approach to corporate risk management' in *The Revolution in Corporate Finance*, Eds J. Stern & D. Chew, 2nd edn, Blackwell, Oxford, 1992, pp. 331–45.

[21] S. Titman, 'The Effect of Capital Structure on a Firm's Liquidation Decision', *Journal of Financial Economics*, March 1984, pp. 137–51.

suppose that a machinery manufacturer is considered likely to liquidate. Customers will expect problems in obtaining spare parts and service, so the price they are prepared to pay for the company's products will fall. Sales, profits, and share price would be greater if the company could in some way guarantee not to liquidate, except under restricted conditions.

Achievement of such a guarantee through explicit contracts may be costly and encounters the problem that companies have an incentive to cheat. After transacting with customers and employees on terms which reflect the guarantee not to liquidate, they may decide to do so as soon as the liquidation value of the company's assets exceeds their value as a going concern. Titman suggests that the choice of capital structure can, in effect, tie the company to a liquidation policy without any explicit constraints. Since debtholders have a higher priority claim to liquidation proceeds than shareholders, they are more likely than shareholders to favour liquidation. Therefore, adopting a higher debt–equity ratio will increase the probability of liquidation and worsen the company's current terms of trade with customers and other associates. The adverse effect on the company's current terms of trade is part of the cost of borrowing.

Titman's model has the testable implication that companies such as car manufacturers and computer manufacturers, whose liquidation would impose large costs on customers and other associates, will adopt capital structures with relatively low levels of debt. Empirical evidence on this issue is presented in Chapter 13. In addition to its adverse effects on sales, a company's risk of financial distress can also increase its operating costs and its financing costs. For example, a greater risk of financial distress will mean that it is harder to attract and retain skilled employees. Similarly, it can impair a company's ability to borrow and to obtain trade credit.

## CONFLICTS OF INTEREST BETWEEN SHAREHOLDERS AND MANAGERS

The agency costs discussed above relate only to debt but there can also be agency costs associated with equity. These costs arise when a company's shares are owned by 'outside' investors rather than by 'insiders' such as top-level managers. To see this, consider a company owned entirely by an entrepreneur who also manages its operations. In this case there are no agency costs of equity because one person both owns and controls the company. Many companies are clearly too large to be structured in this way and equity capital is provided by shareholders who have little or no involvement in its operations, which are controlled on a day-to-day basis by employee managers. With this separation of ownership and control there can be conflicts of interest between shareholders and managers. For example, employee managers are unlikely to be as motivated as an entrepreneur to work hard, strive for maximum efficiency, and search actively for profitable investment opportunities.

The agency costs of equity can be reduced by measures which align the objectives of managers with those of shareholders. These measures include employee share ownership schemes and inclusion of options on the company's shares as part of the remuneration for top-level managers. If these measures are effective, this prompts the question: would it be efficient to eliminate the costs associated with the separation of ownership and control by having a company's equity capital provided only by its managers? The answer is generally no, for two main reasons. First, while the owner/manager structure is preferred for many small businesses, there are few individuals who have the combination of wealth and skills to both own and manage a company involved in activities such as large scale industrial operations. Secondly, while uniting the functions of management and provision of capital has advantages in terms of agency costs, it has disadvantages in terms of risk bearing.

As discussed in Chapter 6, investors can reduce risk by diversification and it is easy for them to diversify by simply combining the shares of many companies in a portfolio. Diversification can eliminate firm-specific or unsystematic risk, and investors will require compensation only for bearing systematic risk which cannot be removed by diversification. In other words, the existence of a stock market allows companies to raise equity capital on terms that reflect the benefits of diversification. But these benefits are not available where a company's manager also becomes one of its shareholders. As an employee, the manager's wealth is linked to some extent to the fortunes of the individual company. For example, managers generally develop skills and knowledge which are firm-specific. That is, they have skills and knowledge that are valuable in their current employment, but of less value elsewhere. Even if this is not the case, managers, particularly at the top level, have a large stake in the prosperity of the company because association with a corporate failure will harm their employment prospects. In summary, managers inevitably bear some firm-specific risks which they are unable to remove by diversification. Managers who buy shares in the company that provides their employment are taking on more of the *same* risks. Clearly it would not be attractive for managers to do so unless they could expect compensation for these risks. This implies that managers would require a higher rate of return on their investment than 'outside' investors. In other words, managers would 'charge' more for bearing risk than outside investors who can diversify. Essentially, the ownership of a company's shares involves a trade-off between agency costs and efficient risk bearing. This trade-off illustrates the point that capital structure involves issues other than the debt–equity ratio. Issues such as *who provides* a company's equity capital can also be important because of agency costs and costs associated with risk bearing.

## THE COMBINED EFFECTS OF AGENCY COSTS

As discussed above, there are agency costs associated with both debt and equity. Jensen and Meckling argue that the agency costs of debt will increase as the fraction of debt in a company's capital structure increases.[22] Similarly the agency costs of equity will increase as the fraction of equity owned by outside shareholders increases. This means that there can be an optimum capital structure which minimises total agency costs. To appreciate this, consider an all-equity financed company where managers own a small proportion of the shares, so the agency costs of equity are relatively large. If some of the outside equity is replaced by a moderate proportion of debt the agency costs of equity will fall because the proportion of equity owned by managers will increase. While the

---

22 M. Jensen & W. Meckling, see Footnote 16.

debt will involve some agency costs, these should be small, given that the level of debt is moderate. Therefore, with the introduction of debt, total agency costs should fall, and there will be an optimum capital structure at the point where the marginal agency costs of debt and equity are equal.

The role of debt in reducing the agency costs of equity may be clearest in the case of the free cash flow problems discussed by Jensen.[23] He argues that the agency costs of equity can be considerable when a company generates large free cash flows. While it would be best for investors for this cash to be paid out, managers have incentives to use cash in ways that benefit them. For example, they may invest cash in new projects or takeovers which increase their command over resources, even though these investments have negative net present values. Also, cash may be wasted through allowing inefficiencies to develop. This can occur through failure to take hard decisions such as retrenching surplus employees and failure to adapt to changes in technology.

As discussed in Chapter 11, these agency costs can be reduced by paying out free cash flow as dividends, but this may not be very effective because dividends are largely at the discretion of managers. Borrowing should be much more effective because there are serious penalties if obligations to debtholders are not met. Therefore, in cases where free cash flow is large, agency costs can be reduced by borrowing heavily and using the borrowed money to pay a large dividend, or return capital to shareholders, possibly through buying back some of their shares. In this way the present value of future cash flows is paid to shareholders now, and managers are committed to operating efficiently in the future because the company must generate cash flows that are sufficient to repay the debtholders.

The sequence of transactions we have just described may sound unusual, but it does occur. Essentially this is what happens in some corporate restructuring transactions, such as leveraged buyouts, which are discussed in Chapter 20. One obvious question is: Why would the managers of a company with severe agency problems decide to borrow heavily, eliminate unprofitable expansion plans, return cash to shareholders, and increase efficiency? The answer is that such companies are often prime targets for takeover by other, better managed, companies.

## 12.6 OPTIMUM CAPITAL STRUCTURE: THE TRADE-OFF THEORY

The possibility of a trade-off between the opposing effects of the benefits of debt finance and the costs of financial distress may mean that an optimum capital structure exists.[24] An investor in a company with a low debt–equity ratio is likely to attach a low probability to that company encountering the severe financial

---

[23] M. Jensen, 'Agency Costs of Free Cash Flow, Corporate Finance and Takeovers', *American Economic Review*, May 1986, pp. 323–9.

[24] Several authors have discussed optimum capital structure theories of this type. See, for example, J. Scott, 'A Theory of Optimal Capital Structure', *Bell Journal of Economics*, Spring 1976, pp. 33–54.

difficulties that we call financial distress. Therefore if such a company issues a small amount of additional debt, then under the classical tax system the resulting tax savings are likely to outweigh the very small increase in expected costs of financial distress. Consequently the value of the company will increase. However, as the proportion of debt increases still further, so also does the probability of financial distress, and the expected costs of financial distress. These higher expected costs will offset the effect of the additional tax savings and eventually a point will be reached beyond which the value of the company starts to decrease. This is illustrated in Figure 12.5.

The trade-off theory outlined here was popular as a way of reconciling observed capital structures with the MM analysis (with company income tax). There are several reasons for suggesting that the trade-off theory provides an over-simplified view of the relationship between capital structure and company value. These include:

- Miller has argued that when both corporate and personal taxes are considered, the net effect of taxes on company value can be zero.
- The imputation system has the potential to be neutral between debt and equity as sources of company finance. In cases where it is not neutral the system is biased towards equity, not debt.
- There is evidence that the direct costs of bankruptcy are small relative to company value.[25]

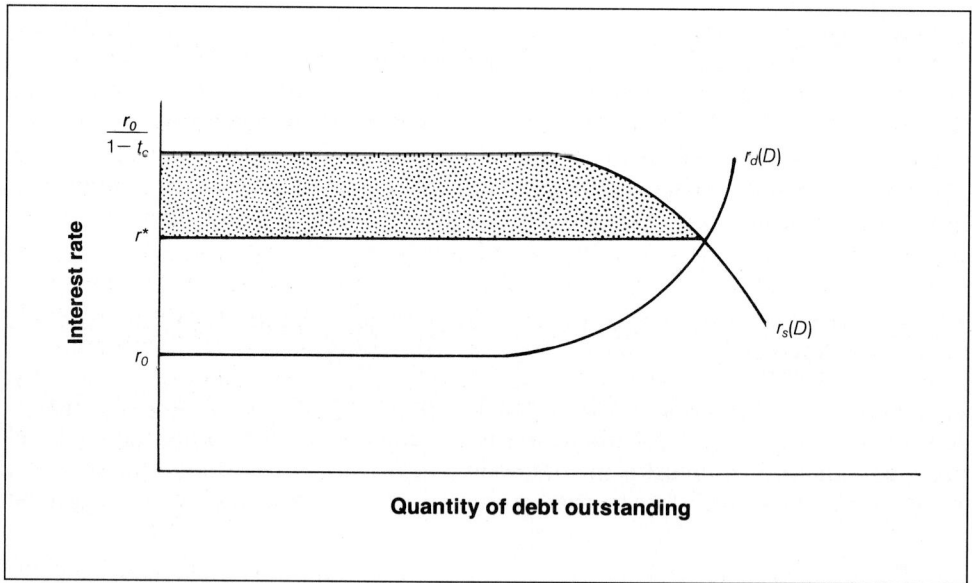

**Fig. 12.5**

---

[25] J. Warner, 'Bankruptcy Costs: Some Evidence', *Journal of Finance*, May 1977, pp. 337–47.

- While the theory predicts that an optimum capital structure exists, it does not provide any practical method of calculating the preferred debt–equity ratio for a company.
- It has been noted that companies in the US used debt finance long before the introduction of income taxes, which suggests that whether or not the tax advantages of debt are real, there must be other non-tax advantages of debt.[26] The main such advantage probably involves agency costs. As discussed in Section 12.5.2, debt can be valuable in reducing the agency costs of equity.

While the trade-off theory has significant limitations, its central message may still be valid: there are both advantages and disadvantages of debt which can give rise to an optimum capital structure consisting of a combination of different types of finance. Therefore, despite its limitations, the trade-off theory is useful in that it can help managers to focus their attention on some of the factors that can be important in making financing decisions.

It is worth emphasising that acceptance of the trade-off theory does not mean acceptance of the traditional view of capital structure. While these two approaches share a common conclusion, the routes by which that conclusion is reached are quite different. The traditional view is based on assumed market inefficiency and irrational behaviour, while the trade-off theory starts from the sound foundation of the MM analysis. That analysis is then modified to allow for some of the factors that MM excluded by their assumptions: taxes, bankruptcy costs, and agency costs. Another factor that MM also excluded, information asymmetry, is discussed in Section 12.7.

## 12.7 CAPITAL STRUCTURE, INFORMATION ASYMMETRY, AND SIGNALLING

Several authors have proposed models in which financing decisions are used by managers to convey information to investors. These models assume that managers have 'inside' information about the company's prospects which is superior to the information available to investors outside the company.

The actions of managers can influence investors' expectations of a company's future cash flows and therefore can influence the value of the company. For example, after receiving good news of some kind, management may decide to increase the company's debt–equity ratio. Investors treat this decision as a signal that management expects increased cash flows, and they respond to this good news about the company's prospects by increasing the company's share price. If investors respond in this way to such signals, surely it would be expected that the managers of less successful companies would attempt to increase the share prices of those companies by copying the actions of more successful companies.

The counter argument relies on two main points. First, companies will be able to increase their borrowing only if lenders are convinced of their ability to

---

[26] T. Copeland & J. Weston, *Financial theory and corporate policy*, 3rd edn. Addison-Wesley, Reading, 1988, p. 509.

repay the additional debt. Therefore, positive signals cannot be copied by the managers of unsuccessful companies because these companies do not have the cash flows to support such signals. Secondly, increased leverage means an increased risk of financial distress and most managers are likely to be unemployed for a time if the company fails. Consequently, managers are unlikely to increase the company's debt–equity ratio unless there are sound reasons to believe that the outlook is good.[27]

Myers and Majluf also present a model which explains financing choices based on information asymmetry and signalling.[28] Managers are again assumed to have inside information about the true value of the company and proposed new projects. They are also assumed to act in the best interests of the existing ('old') shareholders. Suppose that a company needs to issue shares to finance a new project which management knows has a positive net present value. If the shares are issued at a price equal to their true value, the NPV to the 'new' shareholders is zero and the 'old' shareholders will receive the full benefit of the profitable new project.

However, suppose that management knows that the company's shares are undervalued in the market. Consequently, new shares can be sold only for less than their true value and the net present value of the new project must be shared between the old and new shareholders. If the degree of undervaluation is sufficiently large, the combination of issuing shares and undertaking the project can decrease the wealth of the old shareholders, even though the project's net present value is positive. In such a case, management would decide not to make the share issue. Conversely, if management knows that the shares are overvalued, it will always issue more shares and invest, even if the investment has only a zero net present value.

If managers behave in this way, the decision to issue new shares will signal bad news to investors and the announcement of an issue will cause the share price to fall. This is illustrated in Example 12.7.

### Example 12.7

Pinrose Ltd has two million shares on issue with a market price of $5 each, giving a market capitalisation of $10 million. The company has plans to introduce a new production process which will reduce the cost of manufacturing one of its products. Management estimates that the net present value of the project is $2 million, which is equal to $1 per share. Therefore, after its plans are announced the share price should increase to $6. The project requires an investment of $5 million, which could be raised by issuing one million shares at $5 each.

After the share issue and the release of the information about the value of the project, Pinrose's share price, $P_1$, will be:

---

[27] For formal development of a model which incorporates signalling and managerial incentives, see S. Ross, 'The Determination of Financial Structure: The Incentive Signalling Approach', *Bell Journal of Economics*, Spring 1977, pp. 23–40.

[28] S. Myers & N. Majluf, 'Corporate Financing and Investment Decisions When Firms have Information that Investors do not Have', *Journal of Financial Economics*, June 1984, pp. 187–221.

$$P_1 = \frac{\text{old market value} + \text{NPV of project} + \text{cash raised}}{\text{number of shares on issue}}$$

$$= \frac{\$10 \text{ million} + \$2 \text{ million} + \$5 \text{ million}}{3 \text{ million}}$$

$$= \$5.67$$

While the new share price of $5.67 is more than the current price, the critical point is that it is less than the $6 that management believes the old shares are worth. Is there a solution that enables the company to undertake the project and simultaneously ensures that the old shareholders obtain the true value of their shares? Myers and Majluf point out that the answer is yes, if the $5 million required can be borrowed, or better still, can be provided from internal funds. Therefore they suggest that in raising funds, companies will tend to follow a 'pecking order' in which internal funds are the first choice.[29] Myers suggests that managers will set target dividend payout ratios based on the investment opportunities available to companies.[30] However, dividends tend to be 'sticky' and target payout ratios are only gradually adjusted to changes in investment opportunities. With sticky dividend policies and unexpected changes in both profitability and investment opportunities, internally generated cash flow may be either more or less than investment outlays. If it is less, the company will first draw down its cash balance or sell marketable securities. If external funds are required, management will prefer to issue debt first, followed by hybrid securities and then an issue of ordinary shares as a last resort.

An important difference between this pecking order theory and the trade-off theory is that the pecking order theory does not rely on the concept of a target debt–equity ratio.[31] Instead, a company's observed capital structure will simply reflect its history in terms of capital requirements. For example, suppose that a company enjoys exceptional profitability, which results in a substantial increase in its share price. Therefore, in market value terms the company's debt–equity ratio will have decreased. According to the trade-off theory the company's next capital raising should be debt, to move back towards the target debt–equity ratio. However, the pecking order theory suggests otherwise. In fact, because of the company's exceptional profitability, it may not need to raise external funds at all. Therefore, profitable companies will tend to have low debt–equity ratios because of the availability of internal funds. Less profitable companies in the same industry will have higher debt–equity ratios because they generate fewer funds internally and because debt is first on the pecking order of external sources of funds.

---

[29] For a discussion of the 'pecking order' approach and a comparison with the trade-off theory, see S. Myers, 'The Capital Structure Puzzle', *Journal of Finance*, July 1984, pp. 575–92.
[30] See Footnote 29, p. 581.
[31] Note that there are two forms of equity finance, internal and external equity, and these are at opposite ends of the pecking order.

## 12.8 Conclusions

Financial leverage increases the expected rate of return to shareholders, but also increases the risk of their returns. However these effects are offsetting, and in a perfect capital market with no taxes, changing a company's capital structure does not change company value or shareholders' wealth. Under these conditions, capital structure is irrelevant because changing it simply changes the way in which the stream of net operating cash flows is divided between different classes of investors. In a perfect capital market, dividing this cash flow stream is costless and cannot change its total value.

When the perfect market assumptions are relaxed, the factors that could make capital structure important include taxes, agency costs, costs of financial distress, and information asymmetry. When there are income taxes, debt finance can increase company value only if the company tax saved by borrowing is greater than the extra personal tax paid. While this is possible for at least some companies under the classical tax system, the imputation system is designed to remove any tax advantages of debt.

Debt issued by companies is risky in that there is some probability of default, which can lead to receivership or liquidation. These outcomes involve direct bankruptcy costs, largely in the form of fees paid to insolvency specialists. Therefore any company that borrows is giving outsiders a claim against its assets, which reduces the value of the company to investors. Direct bankruptcy costs appear to be small as a proportion of company value but financial distress can also involve various indirect costs which include agency costs of debt. Equity can also have agency costs so there can be an optimum capital structure which maximises company value, based on a trade-off between the benefits and costs of debt. The trade-off theory suggests that management should aim to maintain a target debt–equity ratio. An alternative approach proposes that, in raising finance, managers follow a pecking order in which internal funds are preferred, followed by debt, hybrid securities, and then as a last resort, a new issue of ordinary shares. The pecking order approach does not rely on the existence of a target debt–equity ratio. Rather a company's actual debt–equity ratio will vary over time, depending on its needs for external finance. Chapter 13 reviews empirical evidence on the validity of these two theories and discusses the factors that can influence financing decisions.

## Selected References

De Angelo, H. & Masulis, R., 'Optimal Capital Structure under Corporate and Personal Taxation', *Journal of Financial Economics*, March 1980, pp. 3–29.
Harris, M. & Raviv, R., 'The Theory of Capital Structure', *Journal of Finance*, March 1991, pp. 297–355.
Miller, M., 'Debt and Taxes', *Journal of Finance*, May 1977, pp. 261–75.
Modigliani, F. & Miller, M., 'The Cost of Capital, Corporation Finance and the Theory of Investment'. *American Economic Review*, June 1958, pp. 261–97.
Modigliani, F. & Miller, M., 'Corporate Income Taxes and the Cost of Capital: A Correction', *American Economic Review*, June 1963, pp. 433–43.
Myers, S., 'Determinants of Corporate Borrowing', *Journal of Financial Economics*, November 1977, pp. 147–75.
Myers, S., 'The Capital Structure Puzzle', *Journal of Finance*, July 1984, pp. 575–92.
Myers, S. & Majluf, N., 'Corporate Financing and Investment Decisions When Firms Have Information that Investors do not Have'. *Journal of Financial Economics*, June 1984, pp. 187–221.

Shapiro, A. & Titman, S., 'An Integrated Approach to Corporate Risk Management' in *The Revolution in Corporate Finance*, Eds J. Stern & D. Chew, 2nd edn, Blackwell, Oxford, 1992, pp. 331–45.

Smith, C. & Warner, J., 'On Financial Contracting: An Analysis of Bond Covenants', *Journal of Financial Economics*, June 1979, pp. 117–61.

Titman, S., 'The Effect of Capital Structure on a Firm's Liquidation Decision', *Journal of Financial Economics*, March 1984, pp. 137–51.

Warner, J., 'Bankruptcy Costs: Some Evidence', *Journal of Finance*, May 1977, pp. 337–47.

## QUESTIONS

1. What are the potential advantages and disadvantages to a company's shareholders if the company increases the proportion of debt in its capital structure?
2. Distinguish between: business risk, financial risk, and default risk.
3. (a) Outline the Modigliani & Miller valuation propositions. Specify the assumptions on which their propositions are based.
   (b) Modigliani & Miller's Propositions 1 and 2 are contradictory. Shareholders cannot be indifferent to the use of debt when it increases the expected rate of return on their investment. Comment.
4. Alternative proofs of the MM propositions show that it is not necessary to assume the operation of arbitrage involving personal borrowing for the propositions to hold. Discuss.
5. Company A and Company B, which are in the same risk class, are identical in every respect except that A has no debt while B has $2 million in 8 per cent debentures outstanding. Assume that the valuation of the two companies is as follows:

| | Item | Company A | Company B |
|---|---|---|---|
| | Earnings ($) before interest | 700 000 | 700 000 |
| less | Interest on debentures ($) | – | 160 000 |
| equals | Income available to ordinary shareholders ($) | 700 000 | 540 000 |
| divided by | Cost of equity ($k_e$) | 0.14 | 0.16 |
| equals | Market value of equity ($) | 5 000 000 | 3 375 000 |
| plus | Market value of debt ($) | – | 2 000 000 |
| equals | Total market value ($) | 5 000 000 | 5 375 000 |

Assume that an investor owns $10 000 worth of Company B's shares. Show the process and the amount by which the investor could increase her income by the use of arbitrage.

6. The following information relates to two companies with the same business risk:

| Item | Company A | Company B |
|---|---|---|
| Earnings before interest ($) | 10 000 | 10 000 |
| Market value of debt ($) | 50 000 | – |
| $k_d$ (%) | 4 | – |
| $k_e$ (%) | 12 | 10 |
| Market value of equity ($) | 66 666 | 100 000 |
| Total market value ($) | 116 666 | 100 000 |

According to Modigliani and Miller, the total market value of the two companies should be the same, irrespective of the methods used to finance their investments.

Suppose you hold one per cent of the shares in A. Show the process and the amount by which you could increase your income by the use of arbitrage.

7. The following information relates to the market valuation of Ceel Ltd, assuming two different capital structures and using the MM (no-tax) approach.

|  | Item | All equity | Financed by Equity and 10% debentures |
|---|---|---|---|
|  | Earnings before interest ($) | 600 000 | 600 000 |
| less | Interest on debentures ($) | — | 150 000 |
| equals | Earnings available to ordinary shareholders ($) | 600 000 | 450 000 |
| divided by | Cost of equity ($k_e$) | 0.15 | 0.18 |
| equals | Market value of equity ($) | 4 000 000 | 2 500 000 |
| plus | Market value of debentures ($) | — | 1 500 000 |
| equals | Total market value of company ($) | 4 000 000 | 4 000 000 |

Assuming that there are no personal taxes, calculate the total market value of the company for both capital structures, where the company income tax rate is 33 cents in the dollar.

8. Outline Miller's argument that the tax advantages of debt are reduced or completely offset once personal taxes are included in the analysis. How appropriate is Miller's analysis, given the Australian tax system?
9. Miller's analysis assumes that a company can fully utilise the tax deductions generated by interest payments on debt. Is this assumption likely to be true for all companies? Give reasons.
10. An investor will wish to invest in a company because of its capital structure. Discuss.
11. Outline the significance of bankruptcy costs in the capital structure debate.
12. Management, when pursuing the objective of maximising the value of the company to its shareholders, may make decisions which are not in its debtholders' best interest. Explain why this statement may be true, and give examples of decisions that may lead to a transfer of wealth from debtholders to shareholders.
13. What are *agency costs*? Of what significance are they in capital structure decisions?
14. Comment on the following statements:
    (a) Under imputation, the Australian tax system is neutral in the sense that there is no bias towards the use of either debt or equity.
    (b) Costs of financial distress will be borne entirely by debtholders.

(c) Evidence such as that produced by Warner indicates that the costs of financial distress are too small to have any effect on capital structure decisions.

15. Miller Pty Ltd and Modigliani Pty Ltd are two identical companies with expected earnings (before interest and taxes) of $1 500 000 per annum. The only difference between the two companies is that Miller Pty Ltd has issued debt securities to finance the identical activities that Modigliani Pty Ltd has financed with equity securities alone. Details of the two companies are as follows:

| Item | Miller Pty Ltd | Modigliani Pty Ltd |
|---|---|---|
| Market value of equity ($) | 6 000 000 | 8 000 000 |
| Market value of debt ($) | 4 000 000 | nil |
| Number of shares issued | 6 000 000 | 5 000 000 |
| Cost of debt ($k_d$) | 0.08 | nil |

An investor owns 600 000 shares in Miller Pty Ltd.
   (a) What is the current market value of the investor's shares, and what is his or her income from Miller Pty Ltd?
   (b) Show how the investor can obtain an identical income with a lower net outlay.

16. (a) Calculate the rate of return available to shareholders for a company financing $1 million of assets with the following three arrangements:
      (i) all equity;
      (ii) 50 per cent equity, and 50 per cent debt at an interest rate of 10 per cent per annum;
      (iii) 25 per cent equity, and 75 per cent debt at an interest rate of 12 per cent per annum.
      The assets are expected to generate earnings before interest of $150 000 per annum in perpetuity.
   (b) Interpret your answer, and explain what effect a change in the perpetual earnings stream might have on the rate of return available to shareholders.

17. Critically evaluate the following statements:
   (a) It is obvious that companies should use as much debt as possible. It is cheaper than equity and the interest is tax deductible as well.
   (b) The probability of financial distress should be negligible for companies with a low proportion of debt. Therefore, a low proportion of debt should not have any noticeable effect on the cost of equity.

# APPENDIX 12.1

# CAPITAL STRUCTURE AND TAXES: THE EFFECTS OF THE IMPUTATION SYSTEM

The main purpose of this appendix is to consider the relationship between company value and financial leverage under the imputation tax system. The notation used is as follows:

$\Pi_{ps}$ = income of shareholders after all taxes
$\Pi_{pd}$ = income of debtholders after tax
$X$ = company net operating cash flow before tax
$Y$ = company profit before tax[32]
$\delta$ = dividend payout ratio on an after-company-tax basis
$\phantom{\delta} = \dfrac{\text{total dividend paid}}{Y(1 - t_c)}$
$t_c$ = company income tax rate
$t_{pe}$ = shareholders' personal income tax rate
$t_{pd}$ = debtholders' personal income tax rate
$t_g$ = capital gains tax rate on an accruals basis[33]

---

[32] As in Appendix 11.1, company taxable income is assumed to be equal to company profit before tax.

[33] Capital gains are taxed only when realised, which may be after several years. The Australian capital gains tax system is so complex that precise mathematical modelling is virtually impossible. Therefore we employ the fiction that capital gains tax can be represented by the rate $t_g$ on an 'accruals' basis. Where $t_g$ appears in any formulae, this should be interpreted as meaning that the related income is potentially subject to capital gains tax.

$t_{ps}$ = effective personal tax rate on income to shareholders, which will be a weighted average of $t_{pe}$ and $t_g$
$D$ = market value of debt
$k_d$ = interest rate on debt
$V_U$ = value of an unlevered company
$V_L$ = value of an equivalent levered company
$G_L$ = gain from leverage due to taxes under the classical tax system
$G_{LI}$ = gain from leverage due to taxes under the imputation tax system

To provide a basis for comparison between the classical and imputation tax systems, the first step is to derive the expression for the gain from leverage proposed by Miller. The net operating cash flow before tax, $X$, is assumed to remain constant in perpetuity and must therefore be net of the annual investment required to keep the same assets in place. Therefore when all cash flows are constant in perpetuity, $X$ can also be described as earnings before interest and tax. After-company-tax earnings (profit) may be paid out as dividends to shareholders or retained. Provided that the retained profit is invested to earn the opportunity cost of capital, shareholders will receive capital gains. While these capital gains are not realised until the shares are sold, the shareholders' 'income' after all taxes, $\Pi_{ps}$, is defined as the sum of dividends and capital gains attributable to the company's operating profit.

Under the classical tax system, after-company-tax profit, $Y(1 - t_c)$ will be divided between dividends and capital gains in accordance with the dividend payout ratio, $\delta$. Therefore dividends paid will equal $\delta Y(1 - t_c)$ before personal tax, and $\delta Y(1 - t_c)(1 - t_{pe})$ after personal tax. Similarly, retained profits of $(1 - \delta)Y(1 - t_c)$ will provide income (after capital gains tax) of $(1 - \delta)Y(1 - t_c)(1 - t_g)$. Therefore, under the classical tax system the income of shareholders after all taxes is:

$$\Pi_{ps} = \text{dividends after taxes} + \text{capital gains after taxes}$$
$$= \delta Y(1 - t_c)(1 - t_{pe}) + (1 - \delta)Y(1 - t_c)(1 - t_g) \quad \text{(A12.1.1)}$$

In Appendix 11.1 it was shown that under the imputation system, profit paid out as franked dividends is taxed only once at the shareholder's personal income tax rate $t_{pe}$. Therefore, the dividend income after all taxes is $\delta Y(1 - t_{pe})$. Comparing this with the first term in Equation A12.1.1 shows that the $(1 - t_c)$ factor drops out under the imputation system. This is consistent with the fact that franked dividends provide shareholders with a credit for company income tax paid. Since the classical and imputation systems differ only in relation to the taxation of dividends, the second term in Equation A12.1.1 remains unchanged.

Therefore, under the imputation system used in Australia the income of shareholders after all taxes is:

$$\Pi_{ps} = \delta Y(1 - t_{pe}) + (1 - \delta)Y(1 - t_c)(1 - t_g) \quad \text{(A12.1.2)}$$

## THE CLASSICAL TAX SYSTEM

In this section we derive the equation for the gain from leverage $G_L$ under the classical tax system. This result is due to Miller.[34] For an unlevered company, interest payments are zero, so $Y = X$. Therefore the value of the company $V_U$, will be the present value of the after-tax income stream shown in Equation A12.1.1 with $Y$ replaced by $X$. Therefore:

$$V_U = PV[\delta X(1 - t_c)(1 - t_{pe}) + (1 - \delta)X(1 - t_c)(1 - t_g)] \quad (A12.1.3)$$

For a levered company with tax-deductible interest payments, taxable income $Y$ is:

$$Y = X - k_d D \quad (A12.1.4)$$

Substituting from Equation A12.1.4 for $Y$ in Equation A12.1.1 gives:

$$\Pi_{ps} = \delta(X - k_d D)(1 - t_c)(1 - t_{pe}) + (1 - \delta)(X - k_d D)(1 - t_c)(1 - t_g) \quad (A12.1.5)$$

The after-personal-tax income of debtholders is:

$$\Pi_{pd} = k_d D(1 - t_{pd}) \quad (A12.1.6)$$

The value of a levered company, $V_L$, is the sum of the present values of the two after-tax income streams shown in Equations A12.1.5 and A12.1.6:

$$V_L = PV(\Pi_{ps} + \Pi_{pd}) \quad (A12.1.7)$$

Substituting Equations A12.1.5 and A12.1.6 into Equation A12.1.7, multiplying out brackets, and rearranging, gives:

$$V_L = PV[\delta X(1 - t_c)(1 - t_{pe}) + (1 - \delta)X(1 - t_c)(1 - t_g)$$
$$+ k_d D(1 - t_{pd}) - \delta k_d D(1 - t_c)(1 - t_{pe})$$
$$- (1 - \delta)k_d D(1 - t_c)(1 - t_g)] \quad (A12.1.8)$$

Comparing Equations A12.1.8 and A12.1.3, it is found that the first two terms on the right-hand side of Equation A12.1.8 are equal to the value of an unlevered company as shown in Equation A12.1.3. Therefore:

$$V_L = V_U + PV[k_d D(1 - t_{pd}) - \delta k_d D(1 - t_c)(1 - t_{pe})$$
$$- (1 - \delta)k_d D(1 - t_c)(1 - t_g)] \quad (A12.1.9)$$

Therefore the gain from leverage, $G_L$, is the present value of the terms in square brackets in Equation A12.1.9. These terms represent interest payments and the associated tax savings after personal taxes. Assuming that the tax savings are just as risky as the company's debt, the appropriate discount rate is the rate of return that debtholders require after personal taxes. This rate is $k_d(1 - t_{pd})$. Therefore the gain from leverage is:

---

[34] See M. Miller, 'Debt and Taxes', *Journal of Finance*, May 1977, pp. 261–75.

$$G_L = \frac{k_d D[(1 - t_{pd}) - \delta(1 - t_c)(1 - t_{pe}) - (1 - \delta)(1 - t_c)(1 - t_g)]}{k_d(1 - t_{pd})}$$

$$= \frac{D\{(1 - t_{pd}) - (1 - t_c)[\delta(1 - t_{pe}) + (1 - \delta)(1 - t_g)]\}}{1 - t_{pd}}$$

$$= D\left\{1 - \frac{(1 - t_c)[\delta(1 - t_{pe}) + (1 - \delta)(1 - t_g)]}{1 - t_{pd}}\right\} \quad \text{(A12.1.10)}$$

The gain from leverage in Equation A12.1.10 is not in the same form as Miller's result because he used a composite personal tax rate $t_{ps}$, which is a weighted average of the personal tax rates applicable to dividends $t_{pe}$, and to capital gains, $t_g$. Weighting these tax rates in accordance with the company's dividend payout ratio gives:

$$t_{ps} = \delta t_{pe} + (1 - \delta)t_g. \quad \text{(A12.1.11)}$$

Substituting from Equation A12.1.11 in Equation A12.1.10 we obtain the gain from leverage under the classical system:

$$G_L = D\left[1 - \frac{(1 - t_c)(1 - t_{ps})}{1 - t_{pd}}\right] \quad \text{(A12.1.12)}$$

which is Miller's result.

## THE IMPUTATION TAX SYSTEM

In this section we derive expressions for the gain from leverage under imputation, $G_{LI}$. The basis for the analysis is Equation A12.1.2. For an unlevered company, $Y = X$, so the value of the company will be:

$$V_U = PV[\delta X(1 - t_{pe}) + (1 - \delta)X(1 - t_c)(1 - t_g)] \quad \text{(A12.1.13)}$$

Debt is treated in the same way under both tax systems. Therefore, again we have:

$$Y = X - k_d D$$

so Equation A12.1.2 becomes:

$$\Pi_{ps} = \delta(X - k_d D)(1 - t_{pe}) + (1 - \delta)(X - k_d D)(1 - t_c)(1 - t_g) \quad \text{(A12.1.14)}$$

The after-personal-tax income of debtholders remains as shown in Equation A12.1.6. Substituting Equations A12.1.14 and A12.1.6 into Equation A12.1.7, multiplying out brackets, and rearranging, gives:

$$V_L = PV[\delta X(1 - t_{pe}) + (1 - \delta)X(1 - t_c)(1 - t_g)$$
$$+ k_d D(1 - t_{pd}) - \delta k_d D(1 - t_{pe})$$
$$- (1 - \delta)k_d D(1 - t_c)(1 - t_g)] \quad \text{(A12.1.15)}$$

Comparing Equations A12.1.15 and A12.1.13, it is found that the first two terms on the right-hand side of Equation A12.1.15 are equal to the value of an unlevered company as shown in Equation A12.1.13. Therefore:

$$V_L = V_U + PV[k_dD(1 - t_{pd}) - \delta k_dD(1 - t_{pe})$$
$$- (1 - \delta)k_dD(1 - t_c)(1 - t_g)].$$

Again, the appropriate discount rate for the terms in the square brackets is assumed to be $k_d(1 - t_{pd})$. Therefore the gain from leverage under the imputation system is:

$$G_{LI} = \frac{k_dD[(1 - t_{pd}) - \delta(1 - t_{pe}) - (1 - \delta)(1 - t_c)(1 - t_g)]}{k_d(1 - t_{pd})}$$

$$= \frac{D\{(1 - t_{pd}) - [\delta(1 - t_{pe}) + (1 - \delta)(1 - t_c)(1 - t_g)]\}}{1 - t_{pd}}$$

$$= D\left\{1 - \frac{\delta(1 - t_{pe}) + (1 - \delta)(1 - t_c)(1 - t_g)}{1 - t_{pd}}\right\} \qquad \text{(A12.1.16)}$$

The gain from leverage under imputation shown in Equation A12.1.16 could also be rewritten in the same form as Equation A12.1.12 but $t_{ps}$ would no longer be a simple weighted average of $t_{pe}$ and $t_g$. Therefore, that approach will not be pursued.

Equation A12.1.16 can be simplified in cases where the company adopts an extreme dividend policy, that is, when $\delta = 1$ or 0. If $\delta = 1$ and all after-tax profit is paid out as franked dividends,[35] Equation A12.1.16 simplifies to:

$$G_{LI} = D\left[\frac{t_{pe} - t_{pd}}{1 - t_{pd}}\right] \qquad \text{(A12.1.17)}$$

In the other limiting case, when $\delta = 0$ and all 'income' to shareholders is in the form of capital gains, the result is:

$$G_{LI} = D\left[1 - \frac{(1 - t_c)(1 - t_g)}{1 - t_{pd}}\right] \qquad \text{(A12.1.18)}$$

The significance of these results is discussed in Chapter 12.

---

[35] The situation where $\delta = 1$ does not imply that all shareholders' income will be in the form of dividends with no capital gains. While retained earnings should give rise to capital gains for shareholders, capital gains can also arise from other sources such as unexpected increases in asset values. Similarly, capital losses can arise from unexpected declines in asset values. Such gains (and losses) are outside the framework adopted in this appendix.

**CHAPTER 13**

# CAPITAL STRUCTURE DECISIONS: PRACTICE

## 13.1 INTRODUCTION

Chapter 12 outlined the Modigliani and Miller (MM) analysis which showed that, under their restrictive assumptions, financial leverage is irrelevant and does not affect company value. It follows from the MM analysis that in a perfect capital market *all* capital structure decisions are unimportant. In other words, while MM showed that company value is not affected by the choice between debt and equity finance, their analysis implies that company value is not affected by *any other* financing decision, such as the choice between short-term and long-term debt. While that conclusion is valid under their assumptions, the significant practical message of the MM analysis is that if capital structure is in fact important, then the reasons for its importance must relate to factors that MM excluded by their assumptions. These factors include taxes and market imperfections such as costs of financial distress, agency costs and information asymmetry.

The proposed effects of these factors have been combined to yield two theories of capital structure which were outlined in Sections 12.6 and 12.7. First, the **trade-off theory** suggests that there is an optimum capital structure which maximises the market value of a company. The trade-off is between the benefits of debt and various leverage-related costs. Many of these costs are costs of financial distress, which include bankruptcy costs and some agency costs of debt.[1] Secondly, the **pecking order theory**, which is based on the effects of financing decisions under information asymmetry, suggests that capital structures are determined largely by companies' past needs for external finance rather than by attempts to adhere to a target debt–equity ratio. A basic distinction between these two theories is that the trade-off theory is essentially a static approach, whereas the pecking order theory is dynamic in that it attempts to explain financing decisions over time.

The trade-off and pecking order theories are not necessarily mutually exclusive and both may be useful in explaining observed capital structures. The practical significance of the two theories is an empirical issue. We therefore review recent empirical evidence on capital structure, beginning with a description of capital structures in Australia and in some major overseas countries.

## 13.2 Capital Structures in Australia and Overseas

If the MM leverage irrelevance theorem holds in practice, we might expect the leverage of companies to be distributed randomly over the whole range of possible levels from zero debt to almost all debt. On the other hand, if leverage is important, there should be observable regularities such as differences in leverage between industries and, perhaps, significant trends in the leverage of the corporate sector over time. To determine whether such regularities exist we examine recent evidence on capital structure in Australia and make some comparisons between countries. This type of evidence is of interest because of recent controversial phenomena such as the much publicised growth in borrowing, particularly by some 'entrepreneurial' companies in Australia during the 1980s and the popularity of junk bonds in the US. Table 13.1 shows debt as a percentage of total assets in various industrial sectors in Australia.

Leverage measures are often based on only interest-bearing debt but the data in Table 13.1 are based on all liabilities, which gives a more comprehensive measure of leverage. These data show that capital structure exhibits noticeable differences between industries which tend to remain stable over time. For example, if the industries are ranked by leverage, both the transport and paper and packaging industries are in the top five in all four years. Similarly, the investment and financial services industry has the lowest leverage in all four years. This suggests that capital structure decisions are influenced by factors which are similar for all companies in an industry. For example, all companies in an industry will have similar assets and be exposed to similar business risk. The data also show that in some cases the average leverage of an industry changes greatly over time.

---

1 Originally the benefits of debt were attributed to company tax savings. However the imputation tax system does not allow any tax-based gain from leverage. Other theories propose that borrowing can increase company value through factors such as agency costs and signalling. Therefore, we use the term *trade-off theory* as a general one to refer to all theories which propose that there is an optimum capital structure based on balancing the costs of debt against its benefits.

**Table 13.1** Debt as a percentage of total assets: industry averages for Australian listed companies

| Industry | 1989 | 1990 | 1991 | 1992 |
|---|---|---|---|---|
| Gold | 40.3 | 36.7 | 40.7 | 43.0 |
| Other metals | 44.0 | 42.6 | 41.1 | 43.5 |
| Solid fuels | 49.4 | 45.7 | 48.3 | 49.3 |
| Oil and gas | 53.9 | 51.7 | 51.2 | 52.7 |
| Diversified resources | 63.9 | 62.6 | 65.5 | 64.0 |
| Developers and contractors | 54.5 | 52.7 | 51.9 | 55.4 |
| Building materials | 52.0 | 56.9 | 51.7 | 50.4 |
| Alcohol and tobacco | 58.2 | 72.2 | 71.8 | 83.2 |
| Food and household | 58.6 | 60.8 | 57.3 | 57.3 |
| Chemicals | 55.0 | 54.3 | 50.9 | 50.1 |
| Engineering | 56.9 | 53.6 | 54.9 | 54.8 |
| Paper and packaging | 62.8 | 63.9 | 68.1 | 67.1 |
| Retail | 57.0 | 55.3 | 64.8 | 75.6 |
| Transport | 68.4 | 67.2 | 69.7 | 64.4 |
| Media | 61.2 | 62.7 | 65.4 | 59.3 |
| Entrepreneurial investors | 49.3 | 50.9 | 61.9 | 76.5 |
| Investment and financial services | 31.1 | 36.4 | 39.2 | 38.3 |
| Miscellaneous services | 51.7 | 49.6 | 51.7 | 49.6 |
| Miscellaneous industrial | 45.4 | 47.4 | 49.2 | 49.6 |
| Diversified industrials | 61.0 | 59.9 | 55.3 | 57.7 |

*Source*: Stock Exchange Financial and Profitability Study, 1993

Changes in the capital structure of the Australian corporate sector over the period 1973 to 1990 have been documented by Lowe and Shuetrim.[2] Using the book value debt–asset ratio, they found that leverage remained fairly stable during the 1970s but increased strongly during the 1980s and this increase was widespread, at least until 1987. From 1987 to 1990 some companies, typically ones that were already highly levered, continued to borrow heavily, but the majority of companies either reduced or maintained their leverage. The general increase in leverage was also reflected in the aggregate interest cover ratio which averaged 6.7 between 1973 and 1980 but fell to 4.1 in 1982 and then declined slowly to reach 3.0 by 1990. More recent data show that the trend to increased corporate leverage during the 1980s was reversed during the early 1990s, so that by 1992 many companies had reduced their leverage to levels around, or below, those of the early 1980s.[3]

While increased corporate leverage was widespread in Australia and the US during the 1980s, it was not a universal phenomenon. Remolona examined the leverage of the corporate sectors in France, Germany, Italy, Japan, the Netherlands, the UK and the US.[4] Over the 1982–87 period the US was the only one

---

[2] P. Lowe & G. Shuetrim, 'The Evolution of Corporate Financial Structure: 1973–1990', *Research Discussion Paper* 9216, Reserve Bank of Australia, December 1992.
[3] K. Mills, S. Morling & W. Tease, 'Balance Sheet Restructuring and Investment', *Research Discussion Paper* 9308, Reserve Bank of Australia, June 1993.
[4] E. Remolona, 'Understanding International Differences in Leverage Trends', *FRBNY Quarterly Review*, Spring 1990, pp. 31–42.

of these countries with consistently rising leverage, and in some of the others leverage fell significantly. Using aggregate data for listed industrial companies in six countries including Australia, Remolona also examined changes in the use of short-term and long-term debt between 1983 and 1987–88. The data show that in countries where leverage fell, much of the decrease was due to a lower proportion of short-term debt, but in the US and Australia, overall increases in leverage were associated with higher long-term debt. His study also revealed persistent differences in leverage between countries. For example, during the 1980s, France, Germany, Italy and Japan all had relatively high leverage, while the UK and the US had lower leverage, with the Netherlands between these two groups. In summary, corporate leverage has noticeable patterns, in that it differs between countries and between industries, changes over time within countries, and in the case of Australia, increased significantly, but temporarily, during the 1980s.

These observations suggest that capital structure decisions are important but, as Myers points out, none of the patterns disproves the MM leverage irrelevance theorem which was based on a perfect capital market with no taxes.[5] The important implication of the MM 'no magic in leverage' principle is that if there is an optimum capital structure, it should be due to the effects of taxes or some identifiable market imperfection. Therefore we must turn to the results of empirical research on the effects of factors which are predicted to influence capital structure decisions when the MM assumptions are relaxed.

## 13.3 Empirical evidence

The empirical studies that we review examine capital structure in several ways. First, we consider evidence on the significance of several variables which have been proposed as determinants of capital structure. Most of this evidence is provided by studies whose objective is to explain the observed leverage of companies as a function of variables such as tax rates, business risk, asset type and agency costs. These studies focus on differences between companies at a particular time, and therefore many of their findings relate to the trade-off theory. Some of these studies also examine changes in capital structure over time by including macroeconomic measures, such as asset price indices, as additional explanatory variables.

Secondly, evidence on whether the costs of financial distress are large enough to have a significant effect on company value is examined. Also there are studies of the effects of exchange offers and recapitalisations. These transactions provide an insight into capital structure decisions because they are transactions in which one type of security is issued in exchange for another, with no simultaneous change in asset structure. Essentially, these studies focus on the effects of changes over time in the capital structures of individual companies.

---

[5] S. Myers, 'Still Searching for Optimal Capital Structure', *Journal of Applied Corporate Finance*, Spring 1993, p. 4.

Finally, some studies specifically designed as tests of the pecking order theory are reviewed. Before discussing the empirical studies, some of the testable implications of the trade-off and pecking order theories are reviewed.

## 13.3.1 IMPLICATIONS OF THE TRADE-OFF THEORY

If each company has an optimum capital structure as proposed by the trade-off theory, then most companies should have a preferred debt–equity ratio or leverage target. Unexpected changes in cash flows and investment opportunities could cause a company's leverage at any particular time to deviate from the target. However, if the company has a leverage target, its average leverage over time should be approximately equal to the target. Each company's leverage target would be influenced by various determinants of capital structure, which can vary between companies. For example, if as predicted by the theory, costs of financial distress are important, there should be an inverse relationship between business risk and leverage. This is one testable implication of the theory.

Further, the costs of financial distress are likely to be most serious for companies with large growth opportunities (profitable new investments) and other intangible assets. These assets typically have value only as part of a going concern and cannot be sold separately to raise cash. Also, intangible assets such as human capital may simply 'evaporate' in times of financial difficulty. For example, when there are signs of financial difficulty, key employees may leave, reducing a company's ability to operate effectively. A related argument is that growth opportunities provide greater scope for asset substitution than tangible assets which can be readily observed by lenders. Therefore, another testable implication of the trade-off theory is that companies with mostly intangible assets should borrow less, other things being equal, than companies with mostly tangible assets.

Tax effects are also emphasised by the trade-off theory, at least in the context of the classical tax system. When future interest tax savings are uncertain, then, as discussed in Section 12.4.4, borrowing may add value for companies with high effective tax rates. This argument has two testable implications. First, there should be a positive relationship between leverage and profitability because companies with larger income streams should have a greater incentive to save company income tax by borrowing. Moreover the expected costs of financial distress should be relatively low for such companies. Secondly, as suggested by De Angelo and Masulis, companies with large non-debt tax shields such as deductions for depreciation should have less incentive to save company tax by borrowing.[6] If this is the case, there should be a negative relationship between leverage and non-debt tax shields.

In summary, the essence of the trade-off theory is that each company has an optimum capital structure based on balancing the tax and other advantages of debt against the expected costs of financial distress. It follows that leverage should be related to observable company characteristics such as business risk and asset type.

---

6 See Section 12.4.4.

## 13.3.2 Implications of the pecking order theory

If companies follow a hierarchy of fund sources as proposed by the pecking order theory, then observed capital structures will be influenced largely by the relationship between companies' internally-generated funds and their investment needs. Therefore, for any given level of investment, less profitable companies will need more external finance and will borrow more than companies with higher profitability, because debt is first on the pecking order of external sources of funds. In other words, the pecking order theory implies a negative relationship between leverage and profitability, which is the exact opposite of the relationship implied by the trade-off theory. Some other less obvious implications of the pecking order theory are discussed in Section 13.3.6. The next section reviews studies which examine some of the testable implications of the two theories.

## 13.3.3 Evidence on determinants of capital structure

The studies discussed in this section generally use models that express the observed leverage of companies as a function of several variables that are predicted by one or more theories to influence capital structure decisions. In broad terms, these explanatory variables, which we refer to as determinants of capital structure, can be divided into two groups. These are first, measures of tax effects, and secondly, measures of agency, bankruptcy, transaction or information costs. Measures of tax effects include companies' effective tax rates and non-debt tax shields. Variables in the second group include measures of profitability, growth, size and earnings volatility. In some cases the nature of the expected relationship is clear. For example, higher earnings volatility indicates higher business risk, which implies higher expected bankruptcy costs. Therefore, leverage should be negatively related to earnings volatility.

In other cases the direction of the relationship is uncertain. Growth provides a good example. A company in an industry with low or moderate current profitability, but large growth opportunities, will need large amounts of external finance. According to the pecking order theory, such a company will, whenever possible, raise new funds by borrowing, rather than by issuing new shares. This suggests a positive relationship between leverage and growth in assets. On the other hand, growth opportunities are a type of intangible asset. A higher proportion of intangible assets implies higher costs of financial distress and greater opportunities for asset substitution, which implies higher agency costs of debt. Clearly, these factors suggest a negative relationship between leverage and growth opportunities.

### Evidence from the US

Bradley, Jarrell and Kim developed and tested a model based on the trade-off theory of capital structure.[7] The model incorporated personal and company income taxes, costs of financial distress and the existence of non-debt tax shields such as depreciation.

---

[7] M. Bradley, G. Jarrell & E. H. Kim, 'On the Existence of an Optimal Capital Structure: Theory and Evidence', *Journal of Finance*, July 1984, pp. 857–78.

In testing the model, the authors regressed companies' average debt–total value ratios over a 20-year period against three variables:
1. a measure of earnings volatility, which was used as a proxy for the variability of company value; therefore, it is a measure of the risk of financial distress;
2. the ratio of annual depreciation charges and investment tax credits to earnings, which was used as a measure of non-debt tax shields; and
3. the ratio of advertising and research and development (R & D) expenses to sales, which was used as a measure of intangible assets.

As expected, the authors found strong negative relationships between leverage and earnings volatility and between leverage and the level of advertising and R & D expenses. However, the relationship between leverage and non-debt tax shields was positive, which raises doubts about the validity of the argument that non-debt tax shields act as substitutes for interest deductions associated with debt. A possible explanation is that companies with large non-debt tax shields (as measured by depreciation charges and investment tax credits) will typically be companies with significant tangible assets. Such assets are suitable for use as security for debt and may enable companies to borrow at lower cost. Another possible explanation is that the measure of non-debt tax shields used in the study may have been inadequate. In particular, advertising and R & D expenses could also be included in a measure of non-debt tax shields because they are investments which are tax deductible immediately. However, the fact that these expenses are negatively related to leverage, while the depreciation-based measure used by Bradley et al. is positively related to leverage, suggests that these variables capture other important factors. Therefore, their results concerning non-debt tax shields are, at best, inconclusive.

Long and Malitz used a similar approach, but included additional explanatory variables chosen mainly to test the effects on capital structure decisions of the type of assets used by companies.[8] In particular, they focused on the arguments outlined in Section 13.3.1 that intangible assets cannot support as much debt as tangible assets because they generally lose more of their value in the event of financial distress and provide greater scope for asset substitution. Their results were consistent with this argument in that advertising and R & D expenses were negatively related to leverage. They concluded that the type of assets a company acquires is a very important factor that influences leverage. Long and Malitz also found that there was a strong negative relationship between leverage and operating cash flow. This finding runs counter to the trade-off theory, but supports the pecking order theory. Therefore, their results provide support for some aspects of both theories. They suggest that the availability of internal funds may be the most important factor in determining whether a company seeks external funds. Then if external funds are needed, the nature of its assets is important in determining the choice of debt or equity.

---

[8] M. Long & I. Malitz, 'Investment patterns and financial leverage', in *Corporate Capital Structures in the United States*, Ed. B. Friedman, University of Chicago Press, 1985, pp. 325–51.

Titman and Wessels used a newer two-stage technique to investigate the effects of several company attributes on leverage.[9] To outline the main difference between this technique and conventional regression, suppose that the researcher wishes to investigate the effects on leverage of various company attributes which are not directly observable. Using regression, two or more observable variables chosen as proxies for each attribute might be included as explanatory variables. This approach involves statistical problems when the observable variables are imperfect proxies for the attributes they represent. The newer technique is designed to overcome these problems by first using each group of observable variables to extract an estimate of an underlying factor which more accurately represents the chosen attribute. The factors extracted in this first stage are then used as explanatory variables in the second-stage analysis.

Titman and Wessels extracted measures of seven factors: growth, uniqueness, non-debt tax shields, tangible assets, size, profitability and volatility and examined their relationships with six measures of leverage. These measures were the ratios of long-term, short-term and convertible debt to the book value of equity and the market value of equity. They found that the measures of growth, non-debt tax shields, tangible assets and volatility did not appear to be related to leverage. The strongest results were significant negative relationships between leverage, and both uniqueness and profitability. This evidence is consistent with Titman's theory that low levels of debt will be preferred by companies in cases where their liquidation would impose high costs on customers and other associates, and it supports the pecking order theory.[10]

The technique used by Titman and Wessels has statistical advantages but it also has an important limitation in that the researcher has considerable discretion in choosing the variables used to develop each extracted factor and these choices may involve some ambiguity. For example, Titman and Wessels extracted their uniqueness factor from several variables, including advertising and R & D expenses. They note that these two variables could also be used as measures of non-debt tax shields, or of intangible assets.

Balakrishnan and Fox extended previous research on capital structure using a different two-stage approach.[11] In the first stage, they investigated the relative importance of unique company-specific characteristics and industry characteristics as determinants of capital structure. Using data on a sample of single industry companies they found that company-specific effects contributed far more than industry effects to the total variation in leverage. In the second stage they used regression to identify which company characteristics were important determinants of leverage. The explanatory variables were chosen to measure risk, growth, and asset characteristics such as intangibility and the extent to which assets are

---

[9] S. Titman & R. Wessels, 'The Determinants of Capital Structure Choice', *Journal of Finance*, March 1988, pp. 1–19. The same methodology has been applied to Australian data by C. Chiarella, T. Pham, A. Sim & M. Tan, 'Determinants of corporate capital structure: Australian evidence', in *Pacific-Basin Capital Markets Research*, Volume III, Eds S. G. Rhee & R. P. Chang, Elsevier Science Publishers, 1992, pp. 139–58.

[10] See Section 12.5.2.

[11] S. Balakrishnan & I. Fox, 'Asset Specificity, Firm Heterogeneity and Capital Structure', *Strategic Management Journal*, January 1993, pp. 3–16.

company specific. The authors' main proposition was that company-specific assets, particularly if they are also intangible, will support less debt than assets that can readily be redeployed. Company-specific assets are, by definition, worth much more in their current use than in alternative uses. In other words, the costs of financial distress will be high for such assets. The authors used as explanatory variables measures similar to, or the same as, those used by Bradley et al. and Titman and Wessels. However, some of these measures were interpreted differently. In particular they use depreciation and investment tax credits as a proxy for redeployable assets, rather than as a measure of non-debt tax shields.

Balakrishnan and Fox's results support their main proposition. They found that leverage was positively related to redeployable assets and negatively related to both R & D and growth. Contrary to expectations, leverage was positively related to advertising expense. A suggested explanation is that advertising contributes to assets such as 'brand name' which, while intangible, can be bought and sold. Therefore it is important not to assume that all intangible assets are company specific and unable to support debt.

## AUSTRALIAN EVIDENCE

Gatward and Sharpe studied the capital structures of 164 listed companies over the period 1967 to 1985.[12] They used book value data and divided capital structure into three components: equity, long-term debt and short-term debt. Four variables were found to be significant in explaining the ratios of these components to total assets as follows:

- High profitability was associated with low levels of both types of debt.
- Companies with high growth opportunities had relatively high debt ratios.
- Large companies had relatively high debt ratios, particularly for long-term debt.
- Companies that were relatively liquid had higher short-term debt and lower long-term debt than less liquid companies.

Measures designed to reflect both tax effects and the level of tangible assets were not statistically significant.

A study by Shuetrim, Lowe and Morling used more recent data to examine 209 Australian companies between 1973 and 1991 using a model which incorporates both company-specific factors and macroeconomic factors.[13] Results are provided for the whole period and also for two subperiods: 1974 to 1981 and 1982 to 1990. During the first of these subperiods the Australian financial system was subject to significant regulation such as controls on interest rates and on the volume of bank lending. These controls were largely removed during the early 1980s and the two subperiods used in the study can therefore be regarded as pre- and post-deregulation. The company-specific factors show that leverage is negatively related to cash flow and positively related to growth, size and the

---

12 P. Gatward & S. Sharpe, 'Capital structure dynamics with interrelated adjustment: Australian evidence', University of New South Wales, School of Banking and Finance, *Working Paper* No. 53, 1993.
13 G. Shuetrim, P. Lowe & S. Morling, 'The determinants of corporate leverage: A panel data analysis', *Research Discussion Paper* 9313, Reserve Bank of Australia, December 1993.

level of tangible assets. No significant relationship was found between leverage and a measure of the potential tax savings associated with borrowing. However, the authors did find an industry effect in that mining and manufacturing companies tended to have lower leverage than companies in other industry groups. These differences between industries persisted after controlling for the effects of other relevant variables, but within each industry group there was considerable variation in leverage between companies, which was not explained by the model.

The overall results suggested that the macroeconomic variables used were generally not important in explaining leverage. However the subperiod results revealed a significant positive relationship between leverage and an index of real asset prices during the post-deregulation period. Also the relationship between leverage and size was much stronger before deregulation than after it. Taken together, these two findings suggest that financial deregulation had important effects on the availability of debt finance for Australian companies and that these effects were related to company size. It appears that under regulation, large companies had substantially better access to debt finance than small companies. Deregulation resulted in improved access to debt finance and the improvement was relatively greater for smaller companies.

## EVIDENCE ON TAXES

The studies outlined so far in this section provide evidence that capital structures are related to various company attributes, particularly size, profitability, and proxies for both agency costs and bankruptcy costs. However, evidence of any significant relationship between leverage and taxes is sparse. As MacKie-Mason notes, this is somewhat surprising because 'nearly everyone believes' that taxes must be important in financing decisions.[14] He suggests that taxes are important but have failed to show up in most previous studies because they were designed to test for average rather than marginal effects. To see this point, consider the De Angelo and Masulis argument that the incentive to save tax by borrowing is less when a company has non-debt tax shields. The underlying logic of this argument is that higher non-debt tax shields will lower a company's *expected* marginal tax rate, thus reducing the expected tax savings on additional debt. While this logic is sound, non-debt tax shields will lower a company's *actual* marginal tax rate only if they are large enough to reduce its taxable income to zero—a condition known as 'tax exhaustion'.

MacKie-Mason argues that in most cases, non-debt tax shields will cause only a small change in the probability of tax exhaustion and a similarly small change in a company's expected marginal tax rate. Therefore, cross-sectional differences in expected marginal tax rates will be small and difficult to measure. Another problem is that previous studies have typically measured the leverage of companies using balance-sheet ratios, which reflect the cumulative results of many separate financing decisions made over several years. To overcome these problems it is necessary to examine individual financing decisions on a marginal

---

14 G. MacKie-Mason, 'Do Taxes Affect Corporate Financing Decisions?', *Journal of Finance*, December 1990, pp. 1471–93.

basis for companies that are at, or near, the point of tax exhaustion. Using this approach, MacKie-Mason finds strong evidence that taxes do influence financing decisions.

## SUMMARY

There is evidence that capital structure decisions are made systematically. Generally this evidence comes from regression models which find statistically significant relationships between measures of leverage and several determinants of capital structure. This type of evidence is useful but it has two important limitations. First, the evidence is indirect in that it relates to effects on *leverage* rather than to effects on company *value*. Secondly, it is possible that some of the determinants are *statistically* significant but *economically* unimportant. Some indication of the economic significance of the various determinants is given by their coefficients in the regression models.

Using this approach, Shuetrim, Lowe and Morling estimate that to change a typical company's leverage ratio by one percentage point would require the ratio of cash flow to total assets to change by 5 percentage points, growth to change by 33 percentage points, and the ratio of tangible assets to total assets to change by 10 percentage points.[15] Therefore cash flow and tangible assets may be regarded as economically significant, but given that growth rates of 5 to 10 per cent are 'normal' the effects of growth on leverage are, in most cases, minimal. To focus more directly on the possible effects of capital structure on company *value*, we examine further evidence, first on the size of financial distress costs and then on the effects of changes in capital structure through exchange offers and recapitalisations.

### 13.3.4 Evidence on the costs of financial distress

The trade-off theory proposes that each company has an optimum capital structure based on a trade-off between the benefits of debt on the one hand and the adverse effects of financial distress costs on the other. While few would dispute the argument that the costs associated with financial distress can reduce company value, there is some dispute about whether these costs are large enough to have an economically significant effect. First, there is evidence that suggests that direct bankruptcy costs are too small to have a significant effect on company value. For example, Warner estimated that the bankruptcy costs incurred by 'failed' US railroad companies averaged only 5.3 per cent of the market value of their assets at the date of bankruptcy.[16] This figure falls to 1 per cent if company value is measured 7 years before bankruptcy. Similarly, Pham and Chow reported direct bankruptcy costs averaging 3.6 per cent of company value at the date of bankruptcy for a sample of Australian companies.[17] The cost figures quoted in this paragraph are *realised* bankruptcy costs. Expected costs would be even smaller as the realised costs have to be multiplied by the probability of bankruptcy. For

---

15 Shuetrim, Lowe & Morling, see Footnote 13, pp. 23–6.
16 J. Warner, 'Bankruptcy Costs: Some Evidence', *Journal of Finance*, May 1977, pp. 337–47.
17 T. Pham & D. Chow, 'Some Estimates of Direct and Indirect Bankruptcy Costs in Australia: September 1978–May 1983', *Australian Journal of Management*, June 1987, pp. 75–95.

most companies, it seems that expected direct bankruptcy costs would be minuscule.

While expected direct bankruptcy costs appear to be very small, companies considered likely to fail may incur significant indirect bankruptcy costs. For example, sales may be lost because customers change to more reliable suppliers, and efficiency is likely to suffer because management's efforts are directed towards attempts to avert failure. There is empirical evidence indicating that indirect bankruptcy costs can be a significant proportion of a company's value. Altman has estimated *both* direct and indirect bankruptcy costs for a sample of twenty-six bankrupt US companies.[18] He found that in many cases the aggregate bankruptcy costs exceeded 20 per cent of the value of the company just before bankruptcy. Using a revised version of Altman's methodology, Pham and Chow found that, for a sample of fourteen failed Australian companies, aggregate bankruptcy costs averaged 22.4 per cent of company value just before failure.[19] These results are much greater than the level of direct bankruptcy costs reported by Warner. Altman also examined the trade-off between expected tax benefits and expected bankruptcy costs for fourteen bankrupt companies in his sample. He found that the expected bankruptcy costs exceeded the expected tax benefits for eight of the fourteen companies two years before bankruptcy, and for thirteen of the fourteen companies one year before bankruptcy. Pham and Chow found that expected bankruptcy costs exceeded the expected tax benefits for thirteen of their fourteen companies two years before bankruptcy. The results of both studies suggest that bankruptcy costs can be large enough to have a significant effect on company value when financial leverage is high.

### 13.3.5 Exchange offers and recapitalisations

Exchange offers are transactions in which one type of security is issued in exchange for another. For example, ordinary shares may be issued to retire debt. While such transactions are rare in Australia, they occur to a greater extent in the US. Participation in exchange offers is voluntary. Recapitalisations also involve the retirement of shares or debt, but differ in that they generally involve the participation of all holders of the relevant securities. Exchange offers and recapitalisations involve a change in capital structure with no simultaneous change in asset structure. Such transactions therefore appear ideal for studying the relationship between capital structure and company value.

Several authors have studied the effects of exchange offers and other similar transactions, using the event study method discussed in Chapter 14. In this case they generally measured the returns on the companies' shares and other listed securities on a daily basis over a period surrounding the announcement of the transaction. The evidence is summarised by Smith, who identifies two clear findings:[20]

---

[18] E. Altman, 'A Further Empirical Investigation of the Bankruptcy Cost Question', *Journal of Finance*, September 1984, pp. 1067–89.
[19] T. Pham & D. Chow, see Footnote 17.
[20] C. W. Smith, 'Raising Capital: Theory and Evidence', *Midland Corporate Finance Journal*, Spring 1986, pp. 6–22.

1. The share market responds positively to leverage-increasing transactions, and negatively to leverage-decreasing transactions. For example, Masulis found an average 2-day announcement period return on ordinary shares of 14.0 per cent where offers are made to issue debt and retire ordinary shares.[21] For exchanges in which ordinary shares were issued and debt was retired, the share return was minus 9.9 per cent over the 2-day announcement period.
2. The larger the change in leverage, the greater was the reaction of the ordinary share price.

The latter conclusion is supported by the observation that 'debt for ordinary share' offers have larger positive share price reactions than 'preference share for ordinary share' offers. Similarly 'ordinary share for debt' offers have larger negative price reactions than 'ordinary share for preference share' offers.

While the positive share price effects associated with debt-for-equity transactions could be explained by company tax advantages associated with additional debt, a tax-based argument is not relevant to 'preference share for ordinary share' exchanges. Also, the negative share price effects associated with leverage-decreasing transactions seem puzzling. Why do managers voluntarily undertake such transactions if they may be expected to decrease shareholders' wealth?

A possible explanation is that the announcement of these transactions can have information content. For example, management's decision to decrease a company's leverage may follow receipt by management of bad economic news which has negative implications for future cash flows. Based on this revised outlook, a decrease in leverage may in fact be optimal, but announcement of the proposed decrease also conveys the bad news to the market. Another possible explanation is that changes in capital structure cause wealth transfers between different classes of security holders. For example, an increase in leverage could increase the risk of existing debt, thereby lowering its value and transferring wealth from debtholders to shareholders. The evidence for such wealth transfers is mixed.

Surprisingly, perhaps, the evidence for tax effects is also mixed. For example, Masulis reported a significant tax effect but pointed out that the tax variable may have been a proxy for an information effect.[22] Cornett and Travlos studied exchange offers and tested for tax effects, wealth transfers and information effects.[23] The variables used to capture information effects were based on unexpected earnings for two years subsequent to the exchange offer, and the effect of the exchange on the fraction of shares held by managers. The reasoning behind the use of unexpected earnings is that in deciding to make an exchange offer management may use inside information about the company's prospects. For example, the decision to increase leverage through a debt-for-equity exchange may reflect management's belief that earnings are about to increase

---

21 R. Masulis, 'The Impact of Capital Structure Change on Firm Value: Some Estimates', *Journal of Finance*, March 1983, pp. 107–26.
22 See Footnote 21.
23 M. Cornett & N. Travlos, 'Information Effects Associated with Debt-for-equity and Equity-for-debt Exchange Offers', *Journal of Finance*, June 1989, pp. 451–68.

significantly. Consequently, announcement of such an exchange offer would act as a positive signal to investors and should be associated with positive abnormal returns on a company's shares. Similarly, a debt-for-equity exchange in which managers do not participate increases the fraction of shares owned by managers and should also be perceived by investors as a positive signal. The results supported the hypothesis that exchange offers convey information about the company's earnings prospects, and did not support explanations based on tax effects or wealth transfer effects. In other words, the studies on exchange offers suggest that they can be important signals to the market. However, the results serve mainly to reaffirm the importance of cash flows, rather than providing evidence of the significance of tax effects on capital structure.

### 13.3.6 Tests of the pecking order theory

Many of the studies outlined in previous sections report a significant negative relationship between leverage and profitability. This consistent empirical result supports the pecking order theory. Other testable implications can also be developed by examining the concepts on which the theory is based. The pecking order theory can be outlined in four steps:[24]

1. Managers prefer internal finance.
2. Managers adapt target dividend payout ratios to their companies' investment opportunities, but dividends are 'sticky' and payouts are adjusted only gradually to shifts in available investment opportunities.
3. Sticky dividend policies plus unpredictable changes in profitability and investment opportunities mean that internally generated cash flows may be inadequate to meet investment needs. If this occurs, the company draws first on its cash and marketable securities.
4. If external finance is required, companies issue the safest security first. They start with debt, then hybrids, and finally equity as a last resort.

The concept of a financing pecking order is not new: it can be found in a study by Donaldson more than 30 years ago.[25] However, for much of that time it lacked an explanation consistent with rational, wealth-maximising behaviour. Myers and Majluf provided such an explanation for the pecking order approach, based on information asymmetry, although other explanations are also possible.[26] These include explanations based on minimising transaction costs, or on managers' desire to avoid the need to justify the raising of additional equity capital. Therefore, while the negative relationship between leverage and profitability provides general support for the concept of a financing pecking order, this evidence does not necessarily mean that any particular explanation should be preferred.

---

24 See S. Myers, 'The Capital Structure Puzzle', *Journal of Finance*, May 1984, pp. 575–92.
25 G. Donaldson, *Corporate Debt Capacity*, Division of Research, Harvard Business School, Boston, 1961.
26 S. Myers & N. Majluf, 'Corporate Financing and Investment Decisions When Firms have Information That Investors Do Not Have', *Journal of Financial Economics*, June 1984, pp. 187–221.

Baskin points out that confidence in the Myers and Majluf explanation would be increased if predictions that are more specific could also be substantiated.[27] These predictions can be developed by recognising that the Myers and Majluf explanation is based on sticky dividend policies as well as on information asymmetry. First, sticky dividend policies mean that there are restrictions on the use of retained profits to finance investments. For example, suppose a company has a profitable project which could be financed internally if its dividend payout were reduced substantially. It is well known that dividend reductions are generally viewed by investors as bad news and are typically followed by a fall in share price. If the company proceeded with the project it would probably borrow and at least maintain its previous dividend payout. Therefore, another implication of the Myers and Majluf explanation is that for a given level of profitability there should be a positive relationship between the level of previous dividends and current leverage. Baskin tested this hypothesis in the US and found a significant positive relationship between companies' dividend payouts in 1965 and their leverage in 1972. Using Australian data, Allen also found a significant relationship but it was negative rather than positive.[28] He argued that this conflicting evidence may reflect the influence of high correlation between profitability and dividends. Therefore, while his results reject the hypothesis that he tested, they should not necessarily be seen as rejecting the pecking order theory.

Another implication of information asymmetry in financial markets is that investment decisions will be influenced by the availability of internal funds. The pecking order theory proposes that companies will mainly use debt finance to bridge any gap between desired investment and the available supply of retained profits. Additional retained profits will tend to lower the level of debt, which reduces the probability of financial distress. Lower expected costs of financial distress should lower the company's marginal cost of capital and increase its investment. This argument implies that investment should be positively related to profitability but negatively related to dividends, because more generous payouts will reduce the funds available for investment. Baskin in the US, and Allen in Australia, have tested the hypothesis that payment of relatively high dividends will result in lower investment. On this point the US and Australian evidence is generally consistent. Baskin found that past dividends have a highly significant negative effect on subsequent investment. Allen's results were not as strong but he also concluded that there was a significant negative relationship between growth in investment and previous dividend levels.

The negative relationship between dividends and subsequent investment is important because it indicates that the availability of internal funds can influence investment decisions. In perfect financial markets this should not be the case: companies would be able to raise sufficient funds externally to finance any profitable projects that cannot be financed internally. However, the evidence suggests otherwise and it appears that the level of investment by companies is sensitive

---

[27] J. Baskin, 'An Empirical Investigation of the Pecking Order Hypothesis', *Financial Management*, Spring 1989, pp. 26–36.
[28] D. Allen, 'The Pecking Order Hypothesis: Australian Evidence', *Applied Financial Economics*, June 1993, pp. 101–12.

to the availability of internally-generated funds. This is consistent with information asymmetry acting as a type of barrier between companies and financial markets. This barrier operates in two ways. First, companies do not have free access to retained profits because they are constrained by the information effects of dividend changes to follow sticky dividend policies. Secondly, as discussed in Section 12.7 they are reluctant to raise external equity because of the adverse information that announcement of a share issue can convey to the market.

## SHARE PRICE RESPONSE TO NEW FINANCING

An important prediction of the pecking order theory is that announcement of a new share issue will cause the company's share price to fall. When debt or hybrid security issues are announced, the fall in share price should be smaller. The empirical studies reviewed by Smith report findings that are consistent with these predictions.[29] Various proposed explanations were investigated but the only consistent result was that the price response was related to the type of security issued. However, it seems likely that the market response should also depend on the company's growth prospects. For example, Jensen argues that free cash flow is likely to be invested unprofitably, or wasted by allowing inefficiencies to develop.[30] When a company announces that it intends to raise new funds, the market will assess the company's ability to invest the funds profitably. If the company is mature, with few growth opportunities, the market is likely to perceive that the new funds will create free cash flow and the company's share price will fall. On the other hand, if the company is growing rapidly, the market will expect the new funds to be invested in positive net present value (NPV) projects and its share price is likely to rise.

The effect of growth opportunities on the share price response to new security issues was studied by Pilotte.[31] He found that for share issues, the average share price response was negative, but the average price fall was much larger for mature companies than for growth companies. For issues of debt, the share prices of mature companies fell significantly, but for growth companies, there was no significant price change. Therefore, Pilotte's results show that the share price response to new financing depends on the company's growth opportunities and on the riskiness of the new security.

### 13.3.7 DISCUSSION AND FURTHER EMPIRICAL EVIDENCE

The evidence outlined in Section 13.2, and the results of the studies on determinants of capital structure outlined in Section 13.3.3, suggest that capital structures are chosen systematically. There is evidence that differences in leverage between industries tend to persist over time. There is also evidence of statistically significant relationships between leverage and various company characteristics such as growth, size and asset type. These findings suggest that companies do

---

[29] C. W. Smith, see Footnote 20.
[30] M. Jensen, 'Agency Costs of Free Cash Flow, Corporate Finance and Takeovers', *American Economic Review*, May 1986, pp. 323–9.
[31] E. Pilotte, 'Growth Opportunities and the Stock Price Response to New Financing', *Journal of Business*, July 1992, pp. 371–94.

have leverage targets, and they suggest that capital structure decisions are influenced by factors such as costs of financial distress. However, there is little evidence to suggest that the effects of these factors on company value are particularly large. For example, according to the trade-off theory, corporate borrowing is limited by costs of financial distress, but the available evidence suggests that expected direct costs of this type are very small as a proportion of company value. In other words, while there is indirect evidence for the existence of an optimum capital structure for each company, as proposed by the trade-off theory, empirical support for the theory is certainly not conclusive. Indeed, one finding to emerge clearly from all relevant studies is that leverage is negatively related to profitability. As noted earlier, this finding is the opposite of the trade-off theory's prediction, and instead supports the pecking order theory.

Exchange offers and recapitalisations potentially enable the researcher to focus directly on the effects of changes in capital structure on the values of shares and other marketable securities. Studies of these transactions indicate that their effects, particularly on the prices of ordinary shares, are both statistically and economically significant. However, the findings provide only weak support for the existence of a tax-based gain from leverage. They also provide only weak support for the concept that exchange offers are a mechanism for transferring wealth from debtholders to shareholders.

The evidence provided by exchange offers is strongly consistent with the explanation that these transactions are important in conveying management's superior information to investors. The positive share market response to leverage-increasing transactions indicates that these transactions convey good news to investors. This positive response could also be explained by a tax-based gain from leverage which is consistent with the trade-off theory. However, if the trade-off theory is entirely valid, and exchange offers are motivated by the desire to move towards an optimum debt–equity ratio, there should also be a positive share market response to leverage-decreasing transactions. The evidence is that the market response to these transactions is negative. This is, of course, consistent with the information-based explanation, which basically says that the market is reacting to information about future cash flows.

Therefore, while the trade-off theory explains some of the observed features of capital structures it cannot explain all of them; that is, some features are contrary to the theory. In particular, the theory predicts that companies with above-average profitability should have above-average leverage because of their ability to repay debt, and, under the classical tax system, the incentive to save company tax by borrowing. However, as mentioned earlier, empirical studies consistently report a negative relationship between leverage and profitability. This relationship is consistent with the pecking order theory of Myers and Majluf.[32] Therefore, companies with high profitability may use less debt than other companies, simply because they have less need to raise funds externally and because debt is first on the pecking order of external fund sources.

Some researchers have studied capital structure by surveying and interviewing managers to study the factors they take into account in making financing

---

[32] S. Myers & N. Majluf, see Footnote 26. See also Section 12.7.

decisions. Three findings consistently emerge from these studies.[33] First, managers prefer internal finance to external finance, and are generally reluctant to issue new ordinary shares.[34] Secondly, managers' reluctance to issue new ordinary shares appears to vary over time, depending on the recent behaviour of the company's share price. In particular, a new issue of shares is more likely after a sustained rise in the price of the company's shares. Third, managers prefer to retain some reserve borrowing capacity.

These findings are consistent with Myers and Majluf's pecking order theory. Of course this is to be expected, since these findings represent the behaviour they set out to explain. While their explanation is not the only possible one,[35] the trade-off theory cannot explain these findings. For example, a rise in share price means that, other things being equal, the company's debt–equity ratio has decreased in market value terms. If management is concerned to maintain a target debt–equity ratio, it should respond by borrowing more, not by raising more equity. Therefore, in this case, the trade-off theory's prediction is the *opposite* of what appears to occur in practice. On the other hand, as Myers acknowledges, the pecking order theory also cannot fully explain financing practices because it is not unknown for companies to raise external equity when they could have issued low risk debt securities.[36]

Clearly there is, as yet, no single theory that is a complete guide to capital structure decisions in practice. Some aspects of both the trade-off and pecking order theories are supported by empirical evidence. As we suggested in Section 13.1, the two theories are not mutually exclusive and each may have a useful role in explaining capital structure decisions. Evidence to support this contention is provided by Remolona who analysed data from four countries: Germany, Japan, the UK and the US.[37] He tested for the existence of leverage targets using a model which attempted to explain company leverage in terms of the costs of debt and equity and the ratio of fixed assets to total assets. The model was more successful when the leverage measure was based on long-term debt rather than total debt. Remolona concluded that companies have leverage targets and manage their *long-term* debt to achieve an optimum capital structure, but adjust *short-term* debt in response to unexpected changes in cash flow.

In summary it appears that the financing practices of companies are well illustrated in general terms by the following scenario. Companies have a leverage

---

[33] See, for example, G. Donaldson, *Corporate Debt Capacity*, Division of Research, Harvard Business School, Boston, 1961. For recent Australian evidence, see D. E. Allen, 'The Determinants of the Capital Structure of Listed Australian Companies: The Financial Manager's Perspective', *Australian Journal of Management*, December 1991, pp. 103–27.

[34] This statement should not be seen as inconsistent with the regular issue of new shares through dividend reinvestment plans. In setting dividends, managers will be guided by the net payout that is likely to result after allowing for the fact that a known proportion of shareholders reinvest their dividends. In other words, equity raised through such plans is essentially internal equity that has been 'relabelled'.

[35] For example, managers' reluctance to issue new shares might stem from a desire to avoid publicity and the scrutiny of the capital market.

[36] S. Myers, 1993, see Footnote 5. p. 8.

[37] E. Remolona, see Footnote 4.

target which they seek to maintain. However, their leverage varies over time, owing in part to unexpected changes in operating cash flows.

An *unexpected decrease in net cash inflows* would increase leverage, possibly to a level well above the target. Management would then have an incentive to reduce leverage for two reasons. First, the risk of financial distress may be unacceptably high. Second, managers prefer to maintain spare borrowing capacity. The reduction in leverage could be achieved by postponing planned investments (and thereby postponing borrowing) or, if necessary, by issuing more shares.

Conversely, *unexpectedly high net cash inflows* would decrease leverage and put the company below its target. If management decides to return to its target, it might do so by planning additional investments that can be financed largely by borrowing. However, in this case there is no real need to return to the target: while high leverage can cause problems that require urgent attention, low leverage does not. Therefore, observed leverage ratios will reflect both company profitability and any leverage targets that are set. Before discussing the factors that management should consider in making capital structure decisions, we consider the view that the financing decision is basically a marketing problem.

## 13.4 FINANCING AS A MARKETING PROBLEM

Companies raise external finance by borrowing, by issuing preference shares, and by issuing ordinary shares. The differences between these three methods are significant in terms of risk, required rate of return, tax treatment, voting rights attached (if any), and priority for repayment in the event of liquidation. Less obvious perhaps are the differences that can exist within these categories, particularly debt. For example, companies can borrow in different currencies, for different periods of time, and the interest rate may be fixed or variable. In addition, the repayment terms can differ, in that the principal may be repayable in instalments or in a lump sum. Also, the priority of the lender's claim can differ and some debt is convertible to ordinary shares. The reason for outlining all these differences is to show that in choosing a capital structure a company is essentially choosing a particular package of financial services which it supplies to investors. That is, in raising different forms of finance a company provides financial assets that offer investors different combinations of risk, return, liquidity and voting power. Further, the return can consist of different proportions of capital gains, compared to ordinary income, and in turn this will have taxation consequences.

Shapiro points out that to a person skilled in marketing, the reason for these different combinations is obvious.[38] Different securities coexist for the same reason that different makes and models of cars coexist: individuals have different

---

[38] A. C. Shapiro, 'Guidelines for corporate financing strategy, in *The Revolution in Corporate Finance*, 2nd edn., Eds J. Stern & D. Chew, Blackwell, Oxford, 1992, pp. 217–30. Shapiro is not the only author to emphasise that the financing decision can be viewed as a marketing problem. See also R. Brealey & S. Myers, *Principles of Corporate Finance*, 4th edn, McGraw-Hill, New York, 1991, Chapter 17.

tastes, preferences and levels of wealth. The sales of a given model of car will depend on the demand for the package of features it offers, the cost of manufacturing that package, and the competition from suppliers of similar vehicles. Similarly, the capital structure decisions of companies will be influenced by the demand for different financial services, the costs of providing each package of financial services, and the level of competition from financial institutions that provide similar services.

The marketing approach suggests another way in which MM's Proposition 1 can be violated. Cars and other products will sell at a higher price if they are well designed and have characteristics tailored to the preferences of potential buyers. The same principle can be applied to security issues. If a company's financial manager can design a security that appeals to a particular clientele of investors, such that these investors are prepared to pay a higher price for it, the company can raise funds at a lower cost than would otherwise be the case. That is, the required rate of return on the security is less than the market's required rate of return on other securities of the same risk. In other words, the marketing approach focuses on the *disequilibrium* that can exist when there is some mismatch between the demands of investors and the available supply of securities.

In a competitive market, a disequilibrium of this type will generally be short lived but can certainly occur. For example, increased inflation could increase the demand for indexed bonds. When the unsatisfied demand for a particular type of security becomes evident, innovative financial managers will move to exploit the opportunity and the supply of suitable securities is likely to increase substantially. Therefore, while there are rewards for financial innovation, the benefits are likely to go only to the companies whose financial managers are the genuine innovators. As the supply of new securities increases, the price investors are prepared to pay for them will decrease, and therefore the required rate of return will increase. Once the clientele's needs have been met, those managers who follow the innovators cannot expect to sell their companies' securities at a premium.

## 13.5 DETERMINING A FINANCING STRATEGY

The evidence discussed in this chapter shows that financing decisions are important and can be influenced by many factors. There is no single model or theory that can be used to specify the best financing strategy for any particular company. Such a strategy could include adoption of a long-term leverage target. However, any leverage target chosen need not be adhered to precisely. Also, a leverage target should be seen as only one part of an overall strategy because financing decisions involve choices between many alternatives. For example, suppose a company needs to raise external funds and its financial manager has decided to do so by borrowing. There are then many more decisions to be made. Should the company borrow from banks or should it issue marketable debt securities direct to lenders? What should be the term of the loan? Should the interest rate be fixed or variable? Are there opportunities to add value by adding some new features to the security? Clearly, there are no simple solutions that will always be the best, but by drawing on both theory and evidence, it is possible to specify some general principles and guidelines that can be used by financial managers to determine a company's financing strategy.

An important principle that should guide the financial manager is that it is not as easy to add value by making good financing decisions as it is by making good investment decisions. While a company may be able to find investment projects with positive net present values, the highly competitive nature of financial markets means that it is much more difficult to make financing decisions which have positive net present values. For example, as discussed in Section 13.4 any marketing advantage associated with issuing a security that is in high demand will generally be short lived.

Investment decisions are important because the primary source of a company's value is the cash flows generated by its assets. By comparison, the financing decision is less important because it involves how the company's cash flows are divided between different classes of investors. Therefore, it seems sensible to suggest that a company's financing strategy should be designed to complement and support its investment strategy. In particular, factors such as business risk and asset type, which are discussed below, can have important effects.

A second important principle is that while it is not easy to add value by making *good* financing decisions, it is certainly possible to reduce value by making *bad* financing decisions. For example, a high proportion of debt can reduce shareholders' wealth because the expected costs of financial distress become significant.

Some of the more important factors to be taken into account in setting a leverage target and making other capital structure decisions are now discussed.

## BUSINESS RISK

In Section 12.5 we pointed out that a company's expected bankruptcy costs reduce its market value. The expected bankruptcy costs are equal to the product of the present value of bankruptcy costs and the probability of bankruptcy occurring. Bankruptcy costs are largely beyond a company's control. However, the probability of bankruptcy depends partly on the company's ability to meet its fixed financial commitments. By issuing debt, the company increases these financial commitments, and hence also increases its probability of bankruptcy.

In order to gauge the bankruptcy cost implications of issuing (more) debt, a financial manager has to consider the variability of the company's future net cash flows. The greater the variability, the greater is the probability that, at some future time, the company will be unable to meet its financial commitments. The variability of the net cash flows from a company's assets is typically taken as a measure of its business risk. Therefore, the greater a company's business risk, the less the company can borrow before its probability of bankruptcy is increased. As a result, the optimum capital structure for a company will be affected by its business risk. Therefore, some similarities may be expected between the capital structures of companies in the same industry. However, the evidence discussed in Section 13.3 indicated that industry factors are much less important than company-specific factors in explaining differences in leverage. These company-specific factors include the characteristics of the company's assets.

## ASSET CHARACTERISTICS

Most companies have both tangible assets and intangible assets. Also, some assets, referred to as 'general purpose assets' can easily be redeployed to alternative uses, while other assets, referred to as 'company-specific assets', are worth much more in their current use than in any alternative uses. For example, a motor vehicle is a general purpose asset, while a specialised item of equipment may be company specific. Many company-specific assets are also intangible. These asset characteristics are important in determining how much a company can borrow. This is the case because a lender's risk is lower if the company's value is largely attributable to assets which can be sold with low transaction costs and little or no loss of value.

Tangible assets are usually easier to sell than intangible assets; indeed, many intangible assets cannot be sold separately from the business as a whole. This suggests that companies with a high proportion of tangible assets would be able to borrow more than companies which have a high proportion of intangible assets. For example, companies in many service industries, such as advertising agencies and consulting firms, have a high proportion of intangible assets and are largely financed by equity capital. Similarly, general purpose assets can support more debt than company-specific assets. Lenders recognise that company-specific assets will lose much of their value if the borrower defaults and is liquidated. In other words, expected bankruptcy costs will be high and this will be reflected in the interest rate charged.

A related argument is that the agency costs of debt are high for companies with a high proportion of intangible assets. For example, if a company relies heavily on R & D activities, problems such as asset substitution will be difficult for lenders to detect. Therefore, borrowing would involve high monitoring costs which would also be passed on to borrowers in the form of higher interest rates. Rather than incur the higher interest cost, such companies will tend to operate on relatively low debt–equity ratios.

## TAX POSITION

The effects of taxes on financing decisions will depend to a large extent on the nature of the country's tax system. However, under *any* tax system it should not be assumed that debt has a tax advantage just because interest is tax deductible. Such an assumption is unwarranted because it ignores personal taxes. As discussed in Section 12.4.3, Miller has shown that under the classical system, the effects of corporate and personal taxes can be exactly offsetting. If there is, in practice, any net tax advantage of corporate borrowing under the classical system this advantage is likely to go only to companies with high and stable earnings. For companies which are unable to make immediate use of interest deductions (because, for example they have tax losses being carried forward) borrowing will increase personal taxes but there will be no immediate reduction in company tax. Therefore, in this case, borrowing is likely to have a net tax disadvantage.

Under a pure imputation tax system, company income tax is, as discussed in Appendix 11.1, effectively a withholding tax and can therefore be largely ignored in making capital structure decisions. If all company tax paid is effectively recovered by shareholders through receipt of franked dividends, any advantage from reducing company tax would be due only to differences in the timing of tax payments. However, in practice, managers are unlikely to ignore the effects of company tax. One reason for this is the fact that many Australian companies have both resident and non-resident shareholders. While Australian residents can use imputation credits, non-residents cannot use them and are therefore effectively still operating under the classical system. In other words, if a company pays franked dividends and some of its shares are held by non-residents some tax credits will be 'wasted'. One way to reduce this waste is to issue a further class of shares which allows a higher proportion of the tax credits to be transferred to resident investors. Some companies have achieved this by issuing converting preference shares which typically carry an entitlement to fully franked dividends at a fixed rate. If these shares are issued to ordinary shareholders via a rights issue, non-resident shareholders can sell their rights to residents. The price residents are prepared to pay for the rights will reflect the value, to them, of the tax credits. Therefore, reduction of the wastage of tax credits means that all shareholders are able to benefit, either directly or indirectly.

As discussed in Section 12.4.5, the imputation system has the potential to be neutral between debt and equity, but, in its Australian version, it tends to be biased towards equity. Thus the conclusion is that under the imputation system, simply changing a company's debt–equity *ratio* is unlikely to have any significant tax-based effect on company value. However, the above discussion shows that changing the *type* of equity securities that a company issues can have important tax effects.

## MAINTAINING RESERVE BORROWING CAPACITY

As discussed in Section 12.7, when there is information asymmetry between managers and investors, announcement of a new share issue is likely to cause the company's share price to fall. Therefore, if a company needs to issue new shares to finance a new project the overall effect can be a reduction in shareholders' wealth, even though the project has a positive net present value. This problem does not occur if the project can be financed internally, or financed by borrowing. In other words, information asymmetry can effectively force companies to follow a financing pecking order in which internal funds are the first choice and external equity is the last choice. The evidence discussed in Section 13.3 provides strong support for the pecking order approach.

It was also noted in Section 13.3 that there is evidence that the announcement of a share issue causes the company's share price to fall. The problem of being forced to choose between foregoing a positive NPV project and seeing the share price fall because of a share issue, can be overcome by maintaining reserve borrowing capacity. In this way additional finance can always be raised at short notice to take advantage of profitable investments. Clearly, the value of maintaining reserve borrowing capacity will be greatest for companies that operate in industries where there are significant growth opportunities.

A survey of financial managers by Allen found that the vast majority of Australian companies have a policy of maintaining a substantial 'cushion' of reserve borrowing capacity, typically in the form of unused credit facilities established with banks and other financial intermediaries.[39] However, while reserve borrowing capacity or 'financial slack' can be valuable for companies with significant growth opportunities, this does not necessarily mean that financial slack is valuable for all companies. Suppose that a company is currently very profitable but operates in an industry with few growth opportunities. If, as is likely, this company has a low debt–equity ratio, it will have considerable financial slack. However, such a company will also have a large free cash flow and there is a danger that resources may be squandered on takeovers or diversification projects which benefit managers, but harm shareholders. In other words, as discussed in Section 12.5.2, the agency costs of equity can be large when a company has large free cash flow and one solution to this problem is to increase debt.

## OTHER FACTORS

In discussing the effects of business risk we referred to the variability of cash flows as a measure of risk. It is important to recognise that a company's cash flows can vary for many reasons, and financial managers should not assume that business risk will be much the same for all companies in a given industry. To illustrate some of the many risk factors that can influence financing decisions we consider political risk and inflation risk.

*Political risk*  Many multinational companies have operations in developing countries which can be politically unstable. There is the risk that a sudden change of government may be followed by expropriation of foreign-owned assets. Also it is typically much more difficult to take dividends out of such countries than it is to move investment capital into them. Multinational companies will therefore structure the financing of foreign operations and projects to minimise the impact of political risk. For example, they may invest as little of their own funds as possible, and raise most of the finance within the foreign country.

*Inflation risk*  Financial managers should consider the effects of inflation when deciding whether to borrow at fixed or floating interest rates. If the rate of inflation increases, nominal interest rates will increase, with the result that floating-rate borrowers will incur higher loan repayments. This may not be a significant problem if operating cash inflows also increase in line with inflation. For example, companies that provide services are generally able to increase their prices in line with inflation, or they may have contracts with their customers that provide for regular rate reviews in accordance with a general price index. On the other hand, capital-intensive industries are likely to suffer reductions in real cash flows under inflationary conditions. One reason for this is that the cost of replacing productive assets as they wear out will increase, but for tax purposes companies can only claim depreciation based on the historical cost of their assets. For a company in this situation, borrowing at fixed interest rates may be preferred because borrowing at floating rates will tend to increase the variability of its net cash flows.

---

[39] D. E. Allen, 1991, see Footnote 33.

## Selected References

Allen, D. E., 'The Determinants of the Capital Structure of Listed Australian Companies: The Financial Manager's Perspective', *Australian Journal of Management*, December 1991, pp. 103–27.
Bradley, M., Jarrell, G. & Kim, E. H., 'On the Existence of an Optimal Capital Structure: Theory and Evidence', *Journal of Finance*, July 1984, pp. 857–78.
Masulis, R., 'The Impact of Capital Structure Change on Firm Value: Some Estimates', *Journal of Finance*, March 1983, pp. 107–26.
Myers, S., 'Still Searching for Optimal Capital Structure', *Journal of Applied Corporate Finance*, Spring 1993, pp. 4–14.
Myers, S. & Majluf, N., 'Corporate Financing and Investment Decisions When Firms Have Information that Investors do not Have', *Journal of Financial Economics*, June 1984, pp. 187–221.
Shapiro, A. C., 'Guidelines for Corporate Financing Strategy', in *The Revolution in Corporate Finance*, 2nd edn, J. Stern & D. Chew, Eds, Basil Blackwell, Oxford, 1992, pp. 217–30.
Smith, C. W., 'Raising Capital: Theory and Evidence', *Midland Corporate Finance Journal*, Spring 1986, pp. 6–22.
Titman, S. & Wessels, R., 'The Determinants of Capital Structure Choice', *Journal of Finance*, March 1988, pp. 1–19.

## QUESTIONS

1. Outline the characteristics you would expect a company to have if it had:
   (a) a very low debt–equity ratio;
   (b) a very high debt–equity ratio.
2. Empirical evidence suggests that management takes account of market conditions and recent security prices when determining whether to make a debt or an equity issue. Discuss the relevance of these factors for management's decision.
3. Would you expect companies in the same industry necessarily to have similar debt–equity ratios? Give reasons.
4. The company income tax rate was reduced from 49 per cent to 39 per cent during 1988. Assume that the classical tax system applied.
   (a) What would the MM (with company tax) approach suggest about the effect of this change on the capital structures of companies?
   (b) What would Miller's model predict about the effect on:
      (i) the quantity of debt for the corporate sector as a whole?
      (ii) the capital structures of individual companies?
5. The costs of financial distress are likely to be high for some types of companies, and low for others. Outline the types of companies for which these costs are likely to be:
   (a) high;
   (b) low.
6. *The empirical observation that there is a negative relationship between profitability and leverage is embarrassing for the trade-off theory of capital structure.* Explain why.
7. *If the trade-off theory is correct, then those exchange offers which increase leverage and those which decrease leverage should both be associated with increases in share price.* Discuss this statement in the light of the empirical evidence on exchange offers.
8. (a) The trade-off theory of capital structure can explain some of the debt–equity ratio differences *between* industries, but cannot explain such differences between companies *within* a given industry. Explain why this is correct or incorrect.
   (b) Briefly outline another theory which can explain differences in capital structures between companies in the same industry.

9. Study the capital structures of a bank, a finance company, a retailer, and a manufacturer. Are there discernible differences in the capital structures of the companies chosen? Give reasons for any differences you find.
10. Choose a company, and trace the major changes in its capital structure over the past 10 years. Outline the economic factors you consider have contributed to the major changes in its financing policy during this period.
11. Examination of capital structures shows that most of the variation in leverage between companies is related to company-specific effects and that such factors are more important than industry effects. Outline possible explanations for these observations.
12. The MM analysis of capital structure assumes that the company's net operating cash flows are given. Capital structure is irrelevant under the MM assumptions because, in a perfect capital market with no taxes, the value of this cash flow stream is unaffected by capital structure decisions. One reason why capital structure decisions may be important in practice is that cash flows are *not* independent of these decisions. Explain how this could occur for:
    (a) a company which generates large free cash flow; and
    (b) a company which is highly levered.
13. An executive of a mining company explains that it has a policy of maintaining a portfolio of projects at various stages of development. In this way the need for external finance is minimised because the cash flow generated by operating mines can be used to finance development of new ones. Also the company's net cash flows can be smoothed by adjusting production plans to suit the timing of new projects. For example, if there are delays in bringing a new mine into production, the life of an old mine might be extended by mining low-grade ore that would not normally be considered economic. Critically evaluate the company's strategy from the viewpoint of shareholders.
14. The chief executive of Planets Ltd, a young company which has just set up a manufacturing operation, says: We decided to borrow most of the funds needed to establish our operations because high leverage would signal to the markets that we were confident and fully committed to making this business succeed. Evaluate this strategy, assuming that Planets manufactures:
    (a) computers;
    (b) household detergents.

# CHAPTER 14

# CAPITAL MARKET EFFICIENCY

## 14.1 INTRODUCTION

In Chapter 1, the objective of a company was assumed to be the maximisation of the market value of its shares. In the chapters that followed, we discussed the investment, financing and dividend decisions consistent with that objective. Throughout those chapters it was implicitly assumed that investors would react quickly to such decisions, and accordingly the market price of the company's shares would adjust quickly to reflect the impact of each decision on the company's value. In other words it was assumed that the shares were traded in a market that was 'efficient' in the sense that share prices accurately reflect available information.

The **efficient market hypothesis** is a statement about how an asset's price should react to new information concerning the asset. It has been tested empirically many times. Most of these tests have used share prices, but in principle the market for any asset could be tested for its degree of efficiency.[1] Many types of information may be relevant to pricing an asset, including, in the case of shares, decisions made by the management of the company. This chapter considers the efficient market hypothesis and its implications for financial decision making.

---

1 Other assets include, for example, bonds, options and foreign currency. For examples, see M. J. Brennan & E. S. Schwartz, 'An Equilibrium Model of Bond Pricing and a Test of Market Efficiency', *Journal of Financial and Quantitative Analysis*, September 1982, pp. 301–29; and R. E. Whaley & J. K. Cheung, 'Anticipation of Quarterly Earnings Announcements: A Test of Option Market Efficiency', *Journal of Accounting and Economics*, October 1982, pp. 57–83. Tests using foreign currency exchange rates are discussed in Section 21.4.

## 14.2 THE EFFICIENT MARKET HYPOTHESIS (EMH)

In 1978, Lorie and Brealey wrote: 'One of the most important ideas in the field of investments is that capital markets are 'efficient' . . . The idea was considered bizarre in 1960 but by 1970 was very generally accepted'.[2] Starting around the late 1970s, this 'general acceptance' began to fracture. By 1990, while the idea had certainly not reverted to the status of the bizarre, it was proving to be rather more complex, and subject to rather more qualification, than ever before. One reviewer has written that it is now 'open season on the efficient markets hypothesis'.[3] In Section 14.6 we indicate how and why this happened. Nevertheless, the concept of market efficiency remains one of considerable academic and practical significance.

We begin by discussing the principle of an efficient market and reviewing some of the evidence that has been used to support it.

Fama has defined an **efficient capital market** as one in which security prices 'fully reflect' all available information. Security prices change when new information becomes available. If the market processes new information efficiently, the reaction of market prices to new information will be *instantaneous* and *unbiased*.[4] To gain an intuitive understanding of these requirements it is useful to examine a hypothetical example of a non-instantaneous price reaction and a hypothetical example of a biased price reaction.

### 14.2.1 A NON-INSTANTANEOUS PRICE REACTION

Efficiency requires that the price react instantaneously. In practice this means that after new information becomes available it should be fully reflected in the next price established in the market. Suppose that the market in Copperama NL shares is open for trading between 10.00 a.m. and 1.00 p.m. On a particular day, the first trade in Copperama shares occurs at 10.45 a.m. and the price established in the market is $1. At 11.00 a.m., Copperama makes a completely unexpected announcement: a large deposit of gold has been discovered in one of its copper mines. Naturally this is good news. Suppose that this news warrants an increase in Copperama's share price from $1 to $1.50. At 11.15 a.m., a shareholder in Copperama wishes to sell his shares. However, he has not heard the news of the gold discovery and asks only $1 per share for his shares. The sale is made at $1. At 11.30 a.m., a Copperama shareholder who *has* heard the news wishes to sell her shares. Her asking price is $1.50 per share and the sale is made at $1.50.

---

[2] J. Lorie & R. Brealey (Eds), *Modern Developments in Investment Management*, 2nd edn, Dryden Press, Hinsdale, Illinois, 1978, p. 101.

[3] B. N. Lehmann, 'Asset Pricing and Intrinsic Values: A Review Essay', *Journal of Monetary Economics*, 1991, p. 485.

[4] E. Fama, 'Efficient Capital Markets: A Review of Theory and Empirical Work', *Journal of Finance*, May 1970, pp. 383–417. There are alternative definitions; for example, a market may be said to be efficient in relation to a piece of information if equilibrium prices and portfolios would remain unchanged even if that piece of information were revealed to all market participants. See M. Latham, 'Informational Efficiency and Information Subsets', *Journal of Finance*, March 1986, pp. 39–52.

The market is inefficient. The price established at 11.15 a.m. did not reflect the 11.00 a.m. announcement. Eventually at 11.30 a.m. the market price reacted to the news. However, this reaction was not instantaneous because it should have occurred at the 11.15 a.m. trade. Competition between informed potential buyers should have set the 11.15 a.m. price at $1.50, notwithstanding the fact that the seller was uninformed.

This simple example also illustrates the importance of 'excess' or 'abnormal' profits in efficiency tests. The *buyer* at 11.15 a.m. has made an excess profit of 50 cents per share because he has obtained his shares at a price 50 cents below the price that should have been established, given the information available to the market at 11.15 a.m. Note, however, that although the buyer at 10.45 a.m. has also made a profit of 50 cents on the day, his profit *cannot* be described as excess. Given the information available to the market at 10.45 a.m., the price he paid was 'correct' at that time.

This example also illustrates the role of trading strategies. If the market often fails to react instantaneously, share traders can develop simple rules to generate excess profits. In this case, the rule would be: purchase shares immediately a company makes an unanticipated announcement of good news. The market will not react instantaneously and the shares will increase in price when the reaction does eventually occur.

## 14.2.2  A BIASED PRICE REACTION

Suppose the market in the shares of Mortlake Ltd is open for trading between 10.00 a.m. and 1.00 p.m. On a particular day, the first trade in Mortlake's shares occurs at 10.45 a.m. and the price established is $1. At 11.00 a.m., the company makes a completely unexpected announcement: an uncontrollable fire has destroyed its major factory, and Mortlake's management has discovered that owing to an error by a junior employee the company is not insured against fire. Investors panic and the next sale of Mortlake's shares at 11.15 a.m. is at 5 cents per share. Shortly after, however, cooler heads prevail and it is remembered that Mortlake also has a number of smaller factories and substantial investments in securities. At 11.30 a.m. the market price of Mortlake's shares is 35 cents.

The market is inefficient. The price established at 11.15 a.m. was an **overreaction** to the news, and, given the information available to the market at 11.15 a.m., it should have been recognised at that time as an overreaction. Competition between informed potential buyers should have prevented such a low price occurring, notwithstanding the fact that poorly informed sellers had panicked.

As in the previous example, this example can be interpreted in terms of excess profits and trading strategies. The buyer at 11.15 a.m. has made an excess profit of 30 cents per share. The buyer at 10.45 a.m. has made a loss on the day of 65 cents per share, but this loss cannot be called excess. If the market often overreacts to bad news, the following trading rule will be successful: purchase shares immediately a company makes an unanticipated announcement of bad news. The market will at first overreact, and the shares will rise in price when the market reappraises the information in a more rational fashion.

A second kind of biased reaction is an **underreaction**. In this case the market responds gradually to a piece of new information, moving towards the equilibrium price in a series of steps. This will create observable price trends. The trading strategy in this case would be to buy immediately, if the news is good, and to sell immediately if the news is bad.

### 14.2.3 INFORMATION EFFICIENCY

As suggested earlier, the EMH implies that investors cannot earn abnormal returns by using information that is already available. This implication has been the basis for most empirical tests of the hypothesis. The concept of efficiency inherent in this definition may be described as **information efficiency** as it relates to the impounding of information into market prices. It does not directly address questions concerning the allocative or operational efficiency of capital markets.

Fama provides a useful classification of market efficiency. He points out that the market may be efficient with respect to some sources of information but not with respect to others.[5] Fama classifies the EMH as follows:

1. **Weak-form efficiency**, which implies that the information contained in the past sequence of prices of a security is fully reflected in the current market price of that security.
2. **Semi-strong-form efficiency**, which implies that all publicly available information is fully reflected in a security's current market price.
3. **Strong-form efficiency**, which implies that all information, whether public or private, is fully reflected in a security's current market price.

The information content of each successive classification is cumulative. Therefore the second classification includes all previous price information, as well as all other publicly available information, while the third classification includes all publicly available information and all privately held information. The implication of strong-form efficiency is that an investor cannot earn abnormal returns from having inside information. If this were true, and everybody believed it to be true, investors would have no incentive to seek information, as they could expect no rewards for their efforts. It has been pointed out that this leads to an obvious paradox: the capital market can be efficient only if at least some investors believe it to be inefficient.[6] However, if the capital market is less than strong-form efficient, there are incentives for investors to seek information.

In Sections 14.3 to 14.5 we review some of the empirical evidence which, except for strong-form efficiency, has generally been interpreted as supporting the EMH. In these sections we emphasise the available Australian evidence. In Sections 14.6 and 14.7 we consider some of the more recent evidence which

---

[5] This classification was used by Fama in his famous 1970 article (see Footnote 4). Fama has since revised this classification in a follow-up article (see E. Fama, 'Efficient Capital Markets: II', *Journal of Finance*, December 1991, pp. 1575–1617). We continue to use the old classification because it is so well known and because we think it will be more readily understood by readers unfamiliar with the concept of market efficiency.

[6] J. Lorie, P. Dodd & M. H. Kimpton, *The Stock Market: Theories and Evidence*, 2nd edn, Richard D. Irwin. Homewood, Illinois, 1985, p. 80.

challenges the view that share markets are efficient. Most, though not all, of this evidence relates to US share markets. Finally, in Section 14.8 some conclusions are drawn.

## 14.3 WEAK-FORM MARKET EFFICIENCY

The forerunner of weak-form efficiency was the hypothesis that the time sequence of returns on shares is random. Evidence in support of this so-called **random-walk hypothesis** was later interpreted as support for weak-form market efficiency, although it is now clear that a random walk does not imply, nor is it implied by, weak-form market efficiency. The random-walk model assumes that successive percentage price changes are independent and are identically distributed over time. Neither assumption is necessary for a market to be weak-form efficient. The weak form of the EMH requires only that an analysis of past prices cannot be used as the basis for earning abnormal returns. The random-walk tests of efficiency assume that the *expected* return on the asset is constant from period to period, and therefore that the fluctuations in *actual* returns around this constant expected return should be random. If they are not random, they are to some degree predictable, and therefore abnormal returns are achievable.

Empirical studies of weak-form efficiency can be divided into two broad types:

1. *Statistical tests designed to detect the presence of patterns in price movements over time.* The implication is that if a pattern exists, an investor could formulate a profitable strategy based on knowledge of it. Most studies of this type are really tests of the random-walk hypothesis but if they fail to reject the hypothesis, they are generally interpreted as support for weak-form efficiency.[7]
2. *Tests of trading strategies that try to determine directly whether trading strategies based on past price movements can earn abnormal returns.* If markets are weak-form efficient, the strategies would not generate abnormal returns. A problem with these tests is that it is impossible to replicate all possible trading strategies, with the result that one can never be certain that profitable strategies do not exist. Nevertheless, evidence in support of weak-form efficiency is accumulated if more and more strategies are shown not to generate abnormal returns.

Before turning to the formal statistical tests it is instructive to consider the two price charts shown in Figures 14.1 and 14.2.[8]
Figure 14.1 charts simulated prices, beginning at a price of $1, which are constructed to conform to the random-walk hypothesis. Figure 14.2 charts actual

---

[7] How could an efficient market produce prices that have distinct patterns? Imagine a share whose equilibrium expected return changes as time passes. This means its price *should* display patterns. The random-walk hypothesis would be rejected, but the market could still be efficient. See E. F. Fama, *Foundations of Finance: Portfolio Decisions and Security Prices*, Basic Books, New York, 1976, pp. 149–51. This issue is considered further in Section 14.6.3.

[8] These are taken from a set of eleven similar charts in R. Ball & R. Officer, 'Try This on Your Chartist', *Superfunds*, June 1978.

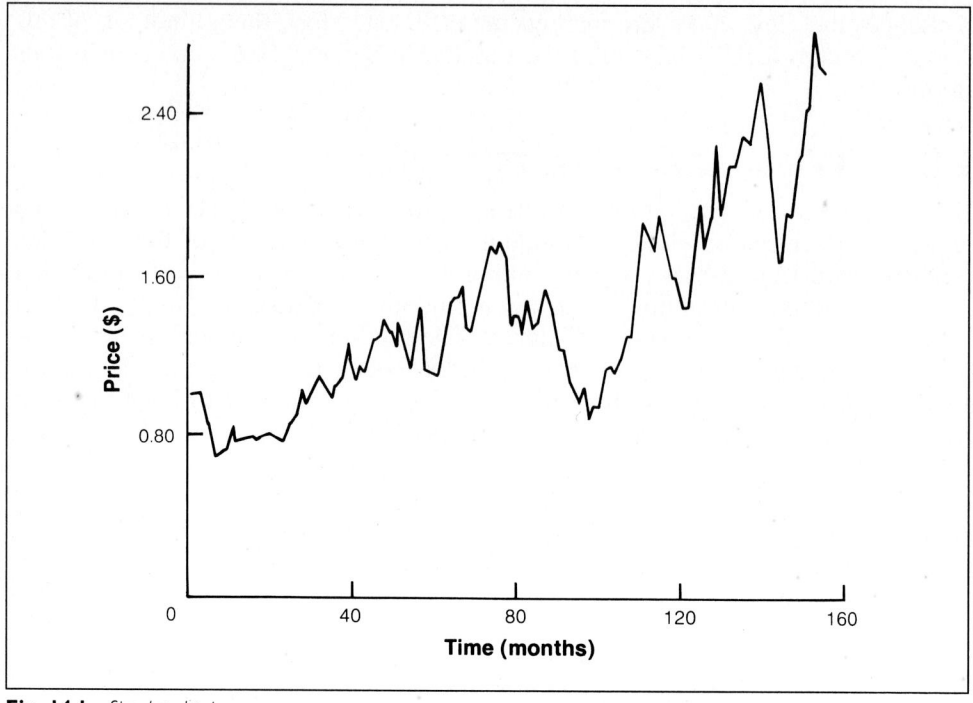

**Fig. 14.1** *Simulated prices*

monthly prices on the Melbourne Stock Exchange for Danks Holdings Limited, adjusted for dividends and changes in capital, for the period 1958–1970.

To make the two figures comparable, the opening price of Danks Holdings Limited was scaled to equal $1. Comparing Figures 14.1 and 14.2, it would be impossible to decide which represented the real prices, and which represented the simulated prices. This illustrates the random-walk hypothesis but is not, of course, an adequate test of it. Careful statistical tests should be used.

### 14.3.1 STATISTICAL TESTS FOR PATTERNS

The most frequently used tests to study whether there is any pattern in share price movements over time are as follows:

#### SERIAL CORRELATION TESTS

Serial correlation tests measure the correlation between successive price changes or, more frequently, the correlation between yields in one period and yields in a prior period. Positive correlation indicates that there are trends in price movements, while negative correlation indicates a tendency towards reversals in price movements. Either result would indicate the possible existence of potentially profitable trading strategies. Zero correlation is consistent with the random-walk hypothesis.

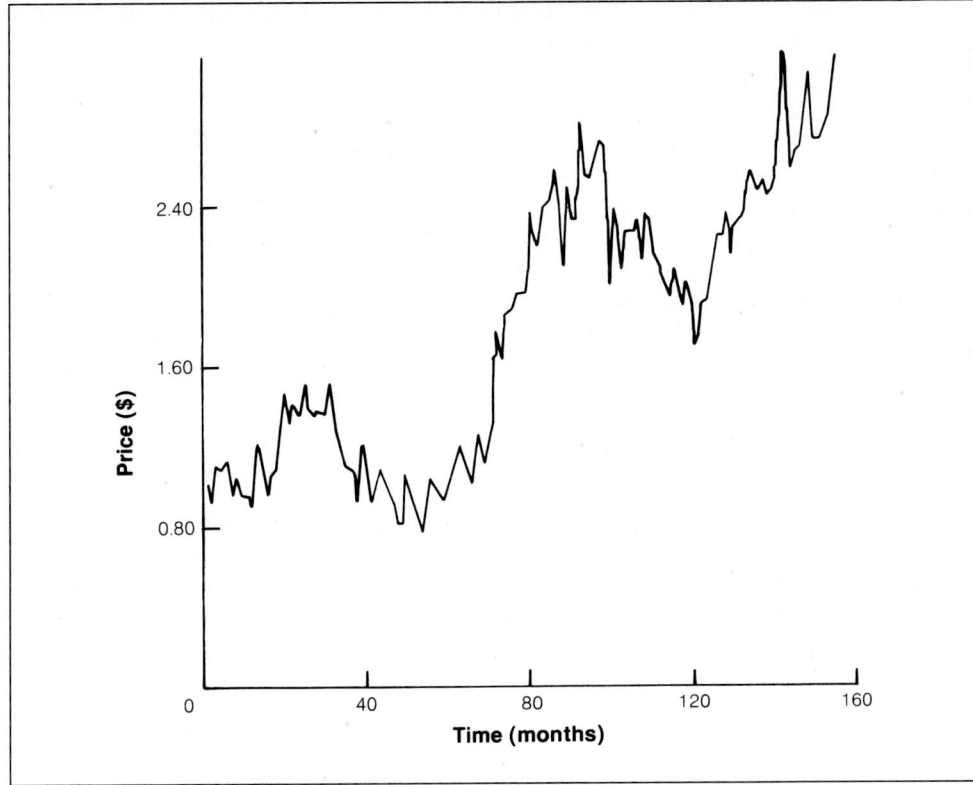

**Fig. 14.2** *Real prices*

## RUNS TESTS[9]

Runs tests provide an alternative way to test for independence. Runs tests examine the sign of price changes, or yields, during a specified sample period. All positive price changes are designated as a '+', all negative changes are designated as a '−', while no price change is designated as '0'. For example, the following sequence of end-of-week prices would have the representations shown:

$1.05   $1.10   $1.15   $1.12   $1.08   $1.10   $1.05   $1.03   $1.00   $1.00   $1.03
       +      +      −      −      +      −      −      −      0      +

This sequence contains six runs: one run of three, two runs of two, and three runs of one. Assuming that price changes are independent, the expected number of runs, and the expected number of runs of a particular length, for a particular price series can be calculated. The actual number of runs exhibited by a price series can then be compared with the expected number of runs, in order to determine whether there is any evidence of dependence in price changes. For

---

[9] Some studies using spectral analysis have also been published. For example, see C. Granger & O. Morgenstern, *Predictability of Stock Market Prices*, Heath, Boston, 1970; and P. Praetz, 'A Spectral Analysis of Australian Share Prices', *Australian Economic Papers*, June 1973, pp. 70–8.

example, positive (negative) correlation is associated with a smaller (larger) than expected number of runs, and more (fewer) longer runs than expected.

A number of studies have employed serial correlation and runs tests. In general, they suggest that successive price changes (yields) are uncorrelated.[10]

The results of studies using Australian data are consistent with those of overseas studies. Praetz conducted serial correlation and runs tests on twenty companies' shares, and sixteen share price indices.[11] For nine of the twenty shares, he found evidence of significant negative correlation at lag one. That is, the returns from holding the shares for 1 week were negatively correlated with the returns in the previous week. However, on average, the returns in 1 week explained less than 1.5 per cent of the variation in returns in the following week. This suggests insufficient dependence between returns in successive periods for a profitable trading strategy to be employed, once transaction costs such as brokerage charges are taken into account. The runs tests were consistent with this finding.

Officer calculated serial correlation coefficients for the returns on 126 companies using monthly data.[12] His study confirmed Praetz's result of slight negative correlation at lag one. However, the average correlation coefficient at this lag was $-0.063$, which indicates that the return in 1 month explains only $(-0.063)^2 = 0.4$ per cent of the return in the subsequent month.

### 14.3.2 Tests of trading strategies

An alternative approach to testing for weak-form efficiency is to replicate investment strategies based on past prices, in order to determine whether these strategies can earn abnormal returns. This approach has the advantage that it is a direct test of weak-form efficiency but it has the disadvantage that it is open ended in that there is no limit to the number of strategies that can be put forward for evaluation.

As an example of a trading strategy, consider the **filter rule** which is usually stated in the following way:

> If the price of a security moves up at least $y$ per cent, buy and hold the security until its price moves down at least $y$ per cent from a subsequent high, at which time simultaneously sell, and go short. The short position is maintained until the price rises at least $y$ per cent above a subsequent low, at which time one covers the short position, and goes long. Moves less than $y$

---

[10] However, there is a tendency for estimated first-order serial correlation coefficients to be non-zero. Australian findings are discussed in the next paragraph. For a review of non-Australian findings, see S. Taylor, *Modelling Financial Time Series*, John Wiley and Sons, Chichester, 1986, pp. 49–52. However, it is often asserted that the value of the typical first-order coefficient is too small for the returns from any trading strategy based on it to offset the transaction costs that would be incurred.

[11] P. Praetz, 'Australian Share Prices and the Random-Walk Hypothesis', *Australian Journal of Statistics*, 1969, pp. 121–39.

[12] R. Officer, 'Seasonality in Australian Capital Markets: Market Efficiency and Empirical Issues', *Journal of Financial Economics*, January 1975, pp. 29–52.

per cent in either direction are ignored. Such a system is called a *y* per cent filter.[13]

An investor might adopt such a strategy if prices are believed to react slowly to new information, so an increase in price of *y* per cent is indicative of a further increase to a new equilibrium price, while a decrease in price of *y* per cent is indicative of a further decrease to a new equilibrium price. It is envisaged, therefore, that an investor using such a filter rule can profit without having access to the information that is causing the price to move.

An early test of filter rules was performed by Fama and Blume who tested filters ranging from 0.5 per cent to 50 per cent for the thirty American companies included in the Dow–Jones index.[14] Returns from the filter were compared with the strategy of buying and holding shares in the same companies. The 0.5 per cent filter generated much higher returns than those generated by the buy-and-hold strategy. This result is consistent with a small positive serial correlation between successive price movements. However, the use of such a small filter results in numerous transactions, so when transaction costs are deducted, the buy-and-hold strategy outperforms the filter-rule strategy.

In Australia, Ball conducted a filter rule test on 128 shares listed on the Melbourne Stock Exchange.[15] He contended that there were two problems with earlier filter-rule tests such as those conducted by Fama and Blume. First, they failed to match the filter-rule portfolio and the buy-and-hold portfolio for risk. Secondly, they were concerned only with finding a filter rule which outperformed the buy-and-hold strategy. Ball pointed out that an unsuccessful trading strategy can be converted into a successful strategy simply by doing the opposite of what the rule indicates. After allowing for both these factors, Ball's results are consistent with weak-form efficiency.[16]

Other trading strategies that have been investigated include a moving-average variation on the filter rule and strategies based on relative-strength ratios.[17] In general, trading strategies are not found to generate large abnormal returns after taking account of risk and transaction costs. This should not be surprising. If a successful strategy is discovered and published, market participants can be expected to exploit the strategy and to continue to do so until its success is eliminated. There is, therefore, an incentive not to publish results that identify successful trading strategies. Alternatively, it may simply be that there are very few such strategies in existence.

---

13 Fama, *Foundations of Finance*, see Footnote 7, pp. 140–1.
14 E. Fama & M. Blume, 'Filter Rules and Stock-Market Trading', *Journal of Business*, January 1966, pp. 226–41.
15 R. Ball, 'Filter Rules: Interpretation of Market Efficiency, Experimental Problems and Australian Evidence', *Accounting Education*, November 1978, pp. 1–17.
16 Ball's test design automatically allows for transaction costs, which means that there is no need to suggest transaction costs as an explanation for apparent trading profits.
17 See A. Seelenfreund, G. Porter & J. Van Horne, 'Stock Price Behavior and Trading', *Journal of Financial and Quantitative Analysis*, September 1968, pp. 263–81; R. Levy, 'Relative Strength as a Criterion for Investment Selection', *Journal of Finance*, December 1967, pp. 595–610 and M. Jensen & G. Benington, 'Random Walks and Technical Theories: Some Additional Evidence', *Journal of Finance*, May 1970, pp. 469–82.

## 14.4 SEMI-STRONG-FORM MARKET EFFICIENCY

Whereas the weak form of the EMH considers only the information content of past movements in security prices, the semi-strong form considers the market response to *all* publicly available information. Semi-strong-form market efficiency requires that security prices adjust instantaneously and without bias to the public announcement of information. It follows that abnormal returns should not be earned from a subsequent analysis of this information.

The tests of the semi-strong form of the EMH analyse whether there are any post-announcement abnormal returns associated with the public release of information. These same tests are frequently used to evaluate the information content of particular types of information such as profit announcements and dividend announcements. The information content is measured by the presence of abnormal returns both prior to, and at the time of, the announcement. These tests are generally called **event studies**. If markets are efficient, the price change measures as accurately as possible the 'true value' of the information to investors. Many people believe that event studies are among the clearest and most reliable tests of market efficiency. An information release ('event') is identified and the price response at that time is then studied to test its consistency with the hypothesis of market efficiency.[18]

### 14.4.1 THE METHODOLOGY OF EVENT STUDIES

There are many variants of event study methodology. Rather than provide details of each variant, we illustrate the major issues involved by using the announcement of annual profit as an example of an 'event'. For each announcement the following three questions need to be answered:

1. What is the (new) information?
2. When was it announced?
3. Were there abnormal returns associated with its announcement?

We now consider each question. First, an annual profit figure provides information only if the announced or reported profit differs from the profit expected by investors. This is because, in an efficient market, the effects of the *expected* profit will already be reflected in the share price before the announcement. Only the unexpected part of the reported profit should cause the share price to react. It is therefore necessary to estimate the expected annual profit so that we can derive an estimate of the unexpected component. For example, it could be assumed that the expected annual profit is equal to the previous year's profit. If the reported profit is greater than expected, the unexpected component is positive, the event is classified as good news, and the market's response should also be positive. The reverse applies if reported profit is less than expected.

Secondly, it is important to identify the event date accurately, in this case the exact date on which the annual profit became public knowledge. This is important because the market may react in anticipation of the announcement as investors revise their expectations. The market should also react at the time of the announcement to any unanticipated information. However, the market should

---

[18] See Fama (1991), see Footnote 5, especially pp. 1601–2, for further discussion.

not continue to react after the date of the announcement because its response should be instantaneous and unbiased.

Thirdly, it is necessary to calculate the response of the market to the announcement. In essence, this response is the percentage change in share price in excess of (or below) the percentage change that would normally be expected. Therefore, some model of 'normal' security price movement is needed. Inevitably, tests of market efficiency are simultaneously tests of the pricing model used to estimate what is 'normal'.

Most studies use some variant of the market model as a basis for estimating the normal rate of return on a security.[19] The standard market model is specified as follows:

$$R_{it} = \alpha_i + \beta_i R_{mt} + u_{it} \tag{14.1}$$

where $R_{it}$ = rate of return on security $i$ in period $t$
$R_{mt}$ = rate of return on the market index in period $t$
$\alpha_i$ = constant in regression equation
$\beta_i$ = slope of regression equation (that is, beta value of security $i$)
$u_{it}$ = disturbance term

Factors that affect the whole market, such as war, drought, monetary policy and exchange rate changes, are captured by the term $R_{mt}$. The remaining (that is, abnormal) return is therefore attributed to company-specific factors such as the public release of information relating to the company.

Suppose that Equation 14.1 is estimated using monthly data and the following estimate is obtained:

$$R_{it} = 0.005 + 1.25 R_{mt} + e_{it}$$

Abnormal returns $AR$ on security $i$ in a later month $t$ are measured by:

$$AR_{it} = R_{it} - 0.005 - 1.25 R_{mt}$$

Suppose that in the month of the profit announcement for company $i$ the return on the shares of $i$ was 8 per cent and the return on the market index that month was 2 per cent. Then the abnormal return in month zero, the announcement month, is:

$$AR_0 = 0.08 - 0.005 - (1.25)(0.02)$$
$$= 0.05$$

This may be interpreted as follows: During the month, this security returned 8 per cent to investors, of which 5 percentage points were due to company-specific events such as the profit announcement. However, as mentioned earlier, part of the test involves estimating and examining abnormal returns before and after the announcement, as well as the abnormal returns at the time of the announcement.

---

[19] For a discussion of the alternative models used to estimate normal and abnormal rates of return, see S. J. Brown & J. B. Warner, 'Measuring Security Price Performance', *Journal of Financial Economics*, September 1980, pp. 205–58; and T. J. Shevlin, 'Measuring Abnormal Performance on the Australian Securities Market', *Australian Journal of Management*, June 1981, pp. 67–107.

Typically this involves estimating and examining abnormal returns for, say, each of the 12 months before the event, and for each of the 6 months after the event.

This completes the procedure for one company's announcement date. The total sample will consist of a large number of companies and announcement dates. For each announcement date the procedure is repeated for the company announcing on that date. Each announcement date in the sample is labelled time zero; points in time *before* the announcement are labelled $-1, -2, -3, \ldots, -12$, and points in time *after* the announcement are labelled $+1, +2, \ldots, +6$. This is known as **event time**. At each point in event time the abnormal returns are calculated. For example, at time zero a large positive abnormal return would be expected for companies announcing profits classified as 'good news'. At each point in event time the average abnormal return across companies is calculated. The average abnormal returns are then summed over event time. The procedures are illustrated in the following simplified example.

*Example 14.1*

Companies A, B and C announced, at different dates, profits which were higher than expected (see Table 14.1).[20]

**Table 14.1**

| Month relative to announcement date | Abnormal returns | | | | |
|---|---|---|---|---|---|
| | A (%) | B (%) | C (%) | Average (%) | Cumulative average (%) |
| −12 | 1.0 | −1.4 | 2.1 | 0.57 | 0.57 |
| −11 | 4.2 | 0.9 | −1.2 | 1.30 | 1.87 |
| −10 | −0.2 | −3.6 | 0.4 | −1.13 | 0.74 |
| −9 | 1.2 | −2.2 | 4.4 | 1.13 | 1.87 |
| −8 | 0.6 | −2.2 | 2.1 | 0.17 | 2.04 |
| −7 | 1.8 | 1.1 | 3.1 | 0.80 | 2.84 |
| −6 | 0.0 | 1.9 | 0.4 | 0.77 | 3.61 |
| −5 | 0.4 | −0.4 | −0.9 | −0.30 | 3.31 |
| −4 | 1.0 | 7.6 | −1.2 | 2.47 | 5.78 |
| −3 | −0.2 | 2.6 | 3.1 | 1.83 | 7.61 |
| −2 | −0.3 | −0.7 | 1.1 | 0.03 | 7.64 |
| −1 | 0.9 | 2.1 | −0.6 | 0.80 | 8.44 |
| 0 | 5.1 | 7.9 | 4.2 | 5.73 | 14.17 |
| +1 | −0.2 | 1.4 | −0.6 | 0.20 | 14.37 |
| +2 | 0.6 | −3.2 | 1.9 | −0.23 | 14.14 |
| +3 | 1.2 | 0.1 | −0.5 | 0.27 | 14.41 |
| +4 | −0.8 | 0.4 | −0.9 | −0.43 | 13.98 |
| +5 | 0.0 | −1.2 | 1.1 | −0.03 | 13.95 |
| +6 | 0.5 | −1.9 | 3.0 | 0.53 | 14.48 |

This explains the high abnormal returns for each company at time zero. For A, B and C, the abnormal returns averaged 5.73 per cent at time zero. It is likely

---

[20] This hypothetical example is very simple in that with a sample size of only three companies, the results, in reality, are unlikely to be so well behaved.

that the market was anticipating good news. The evidence of this anticipation is the predominance of positive average abnormal returns in the 12 months before the announcement. However, following the announcement the average abnormal returns are close to zero, but do not have a detectable trend. This pattern is typical of an 'efficient' market in that there is an instantaneous reaction at the announcement date to the unanticipated component of the information and no subsequent drift in the average abnormal returns. The final column in Table 14.1 shows the cumulative average abnormal returns, which are plotted in Figure 14.3.

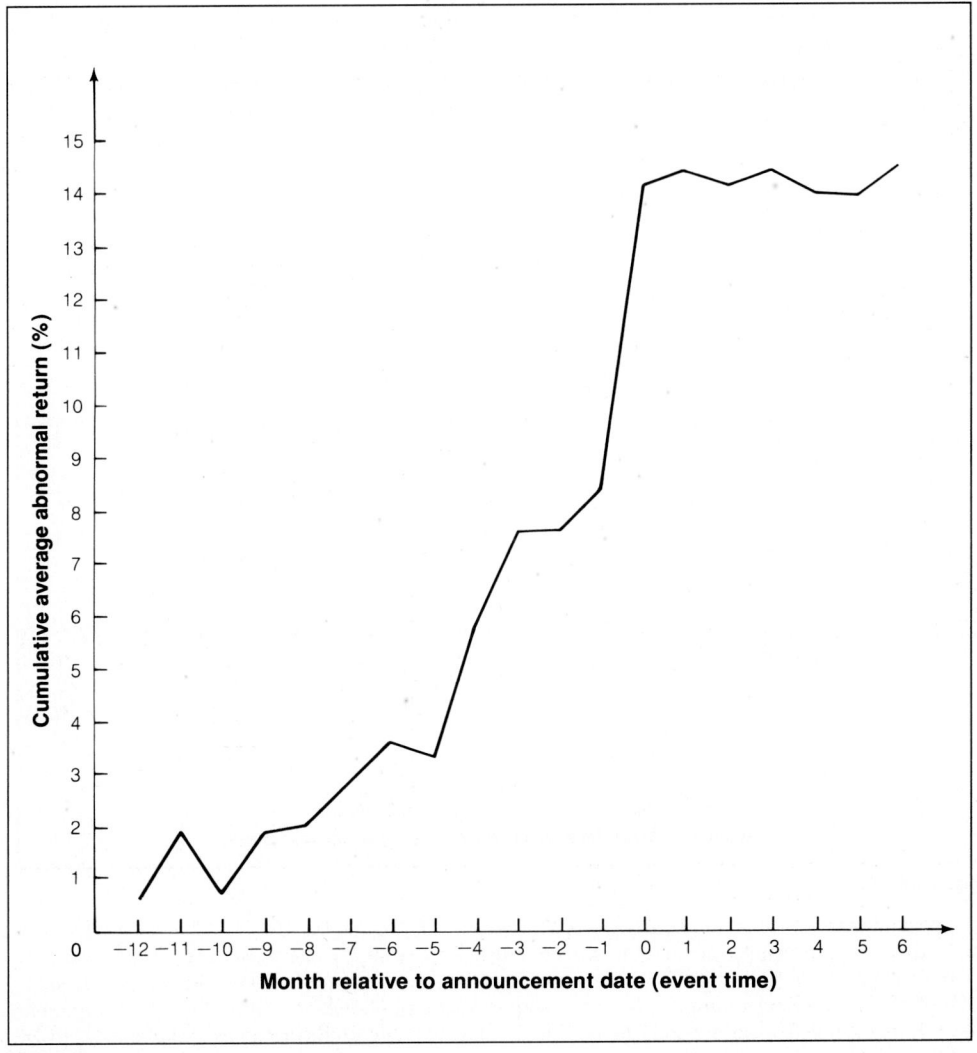

**Fig. 14.3** *Cumulative average abnormal returns*

### 14.4.2 EVIDENCE: PROFIT ANNOUNCEMENTS IN AUSTRALIA

To illustrate the empirical evidence found in event studies we consider the evidence on the reaction of share prices in Australia to profit announcements. In Australia the first test of the impact on share prices of the announcement of the annual profit figure was that conducted by Brown.[21] He used earnings per share (EPS) for a sample of 118 companies for the period 1959–1968. The methodology is similar to that explained earlier. Figure 14.4 shows the abnormal performance index associated with the good news announcements, the bad news announcements, and the total sample of announcements.

Analysis of the results shows the following:

1. At time zero, the index values were 1.054 for the good news group and 0.905 for the bad news group. This indicates that information contained in profit figures was important for determining share prices.
2. Abnormal returns were larger around the time of the half-yearly and annual profit announcements. In month zero, the average abnormal return for the good news group was 1.2 per cent, and for the bad news group, −2.0 per cent. This suggests that much of the information contained in

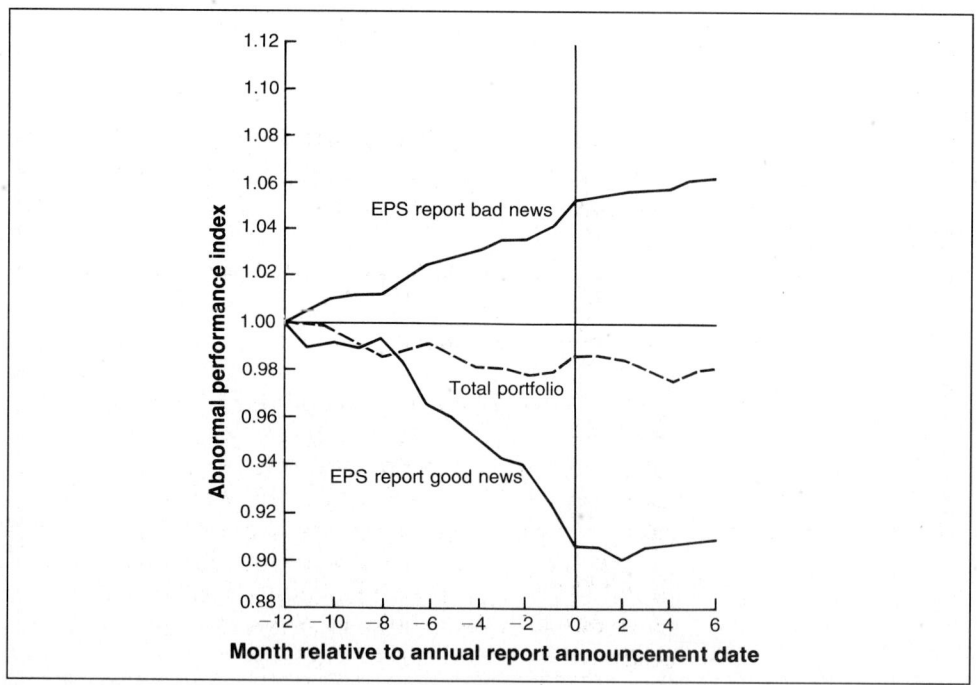

**Fig. 14.4** *Abnormal performance index*

---

21 P. Brown, 'The Impact of the Annual Net Profit Report on the Stock Market', *The Australian Accountant*, July 1970, pp. 272–82. Brown uses the 'abnormal performance index' which accumulates (multiplies) returns rather than adding them as shown in Table 14.1. The abnormal performance index corresponds to the cumulative average abnormal return explained earlier. However, for simplicity we continue to use the term 'abnormal return'.

the annual profit figure had already been impounded into share prices by the time of the profit announcements. Investors had obtained information from other sources such as press reports.
3. The abnormal returns for each group in the months after the announcement date were close to zero. This is consistent with an instantaneous and unbiased reaction to new information and is therefore consistent with efficiency.

In a subsequent study, Brown evaluated the impact of the release of half-yearly reports on share prices.[22] The methodology used in this study was similar to that illustrated in Table 14.1. However, as half-yearly reports were being studied, abnormal returns were measured only from 6 months before the release of the half-yearly report to 3 months after its release. The results are presented in Figure 14.5 and indicate that the market anticipated the announcement, and share prices reacted rapidly to the unanticipated component of the announcement. However, there was evidence that could be interpreted as implying that the market's reaction to reports covering the first half of the financial year was not instantaneous. Early studies of the market's response to the release of quarterly profit figures for American companies found similar evidence.[23]

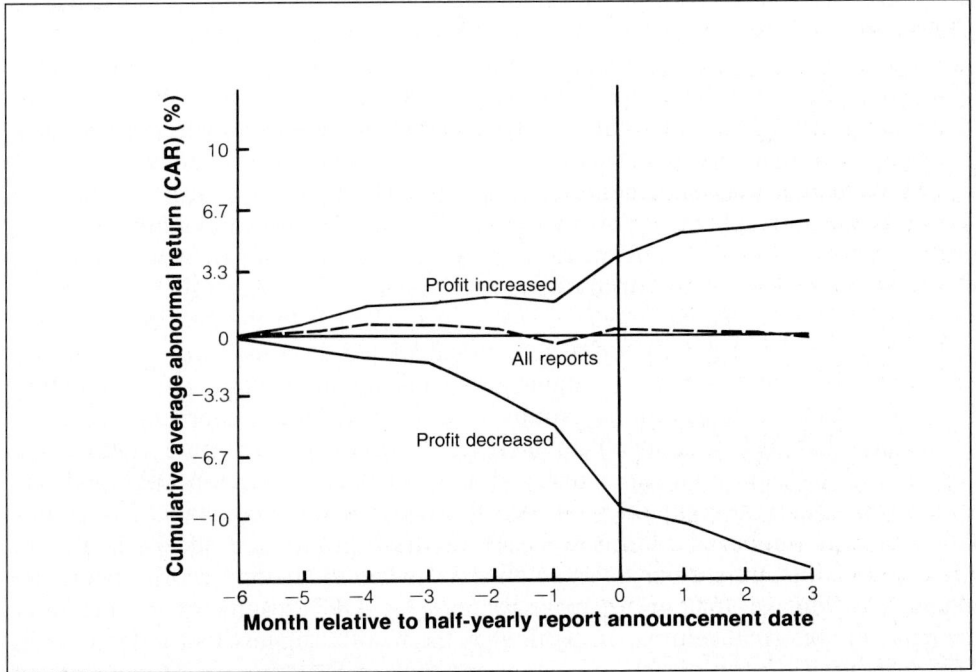

**Fig. 14.5** *Cumulative average abnormal returns*

---

22 P. Brown, 'Those Half-yearly Reports', *Society Bulletin* No. 13, Australian Society of Accountants, Melbourne, 1972.
23 See, for example, C. Jones & R. Litzenberger, 'Quarterly Earnings Reports and Intermediate Stock Price Trends', *Journal of Finance*, March 1970, pp. 143–8. This issue is discussed further in Section 14.6.

Brown's 1970 and 1972 studies used monthly data. Brown and Hancock examined the effect of the half-yearly and annual profit announcements on security prices using daily data.[24] Their sample consisted of the 118 companies included in Brown's 1970 study, and the period covered was the 7 years commencing in January 1964. Returns were calculated for the 4 days before the announcement date and the 6 days after the announcement date. Two groups were formed, one comprising companies which announced increased profit, and the other comprising companies which announced decreased profit. To avoid confusing the effects of any dividend announcements with those of profit announcements, only profit announcements not associated with a change in dividend per share were included in the groups. Because of difficulties in determining the exact day on which the profit announcement became public knowledge, the effective announcement period for the study extended over 2 days.

The cumulative average returns for the two groups are shown in Figure 14.6. The results suggest that the profit announcements contain new information as evidenced by the relatively large returns occurring within the announcement period. They also suggest that information indicating increased profit is immediately impounded into share prices. It is not possible to conclude that the market is efficient with respect to announcements of decreased profit, as the negative returns appeared to persist for a few days after the announcement.

The evidence provided by these three studies has not established conclusively that the Australian capital market had semi-strong-form efficiency with respect to profit (specifically half-yearly) announcements. However, these studies produced little evidence that was inconsistent with market efficiency.

In Australia, announcements of profit are nearly always accompanied by simultaneous announcements of dividends. Thus it is useful to examine both the profit and the dividend information in an empirical test. Brown, Finn and Hancock conducted a study of dividend announcements by Australian companies for the period from January 1963 to December 1969.[25] In the first part of their study they examined the abnormal returns calculated on a monthly basis for the 12 months on each side of an annual dividend announcement. After adjusting for capitalisation changes, three groups were formed: one comprising shares in companies that had announced an increase in dividend per share (DPS), one comprising shares in companies that had announced a decrease in DPS, and one comprising shares in companies whose DPS had remained constant. The cumulative average abnormal returns for each of these groups are shown in Figure 14.7. The results are similar to those obtained when evaluating profit announcements and suggest that an increase/decrease in DPS results in an increase/decrease in abnormal returns. In particular, the results suggest that a decrease in DPS had significant information content and that, on average, investors expected

---

[24] P. Brown & P. Hancock, 'Profit reports and the stockmarket', in *Capital, Income and Decision-making: Introductory Readings in Accounting*, Eds L. Tilley & P. Jubb, Holt, Reinhart & Winston, Sydney, 1977.

[25] P. Brown, F. Finn & P. Hancock, 'Dividend Changes, Earnings Reports and Share Prices: Some Australian Findings', *Australian Journal of Management*, October 1977, pp. 127–47.

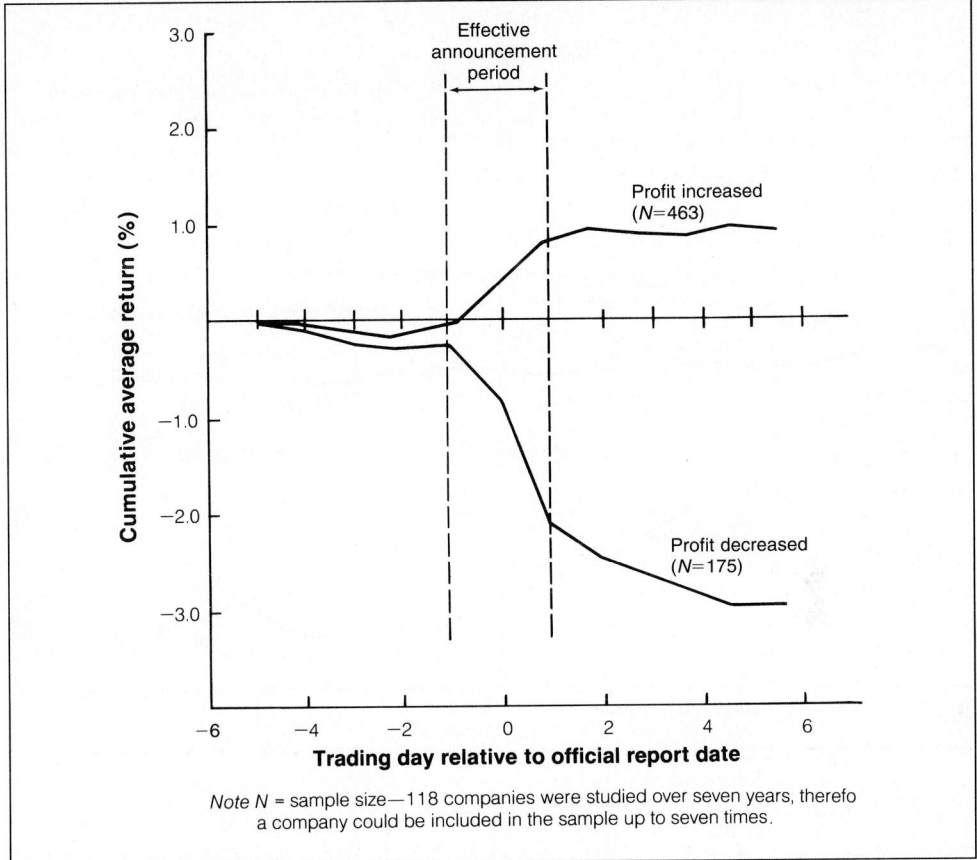

**Fig. 14.6** *Cumulative average returns*

an increase in DPS. As with profit announcements, much of the information content of dividend announcements had been obtained earlier from other sources. Overall, these results are consistent with market efficiency.

Recognising that dividend and profit announcements usually occur simultaneously, Brown, Finn and Hancock divided each of the three groups into two subgroups, depending on whether profits increased or decreased. The cumulative average abnormal returns (CAR) associated with each subgroup are shown in Figure 14.8. The evidence suggests that the information content of the two sources of information is increased when they are in agreement. The highest positive abnormal returns are associated with the simultaneous announcement of profit and DPS increases. Similarly, the lowest (most negative) abnormal returns are associated with the simultaneous announcement of profit and DPS decreases. Where the signals are mixed, for example, profit increase with DPS decrease, abnormal returns fall between these two extremes. In general, these results support market efficiency.

In the second part of their study, Brown, Finn and Hancock examined the effect of dividend announcements using daily return data. This facilitates the

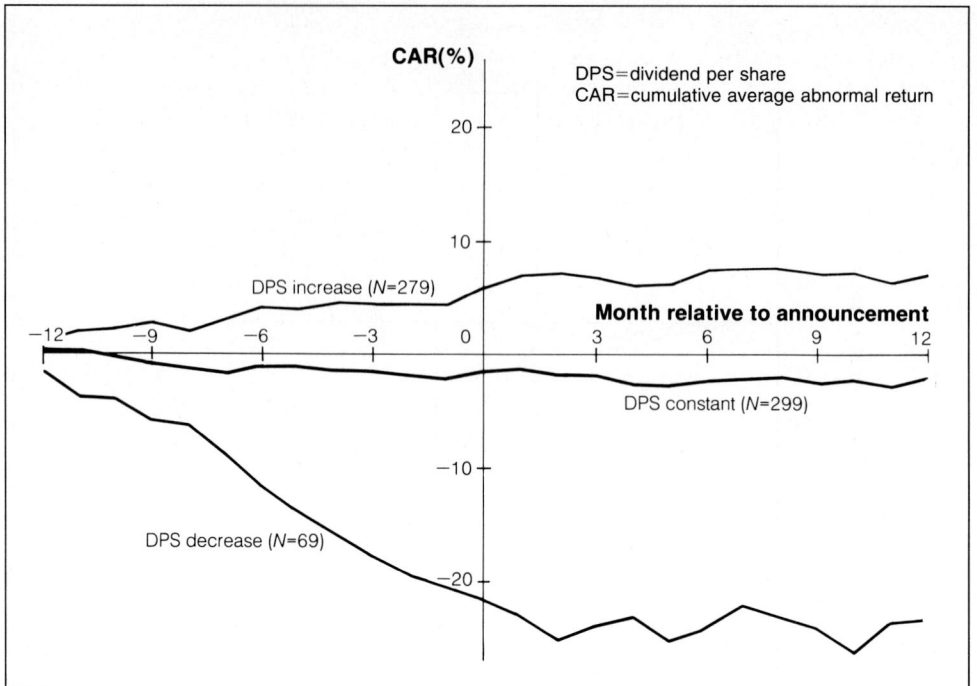

**Fig. 14.7** Cumulative average abnormal returns

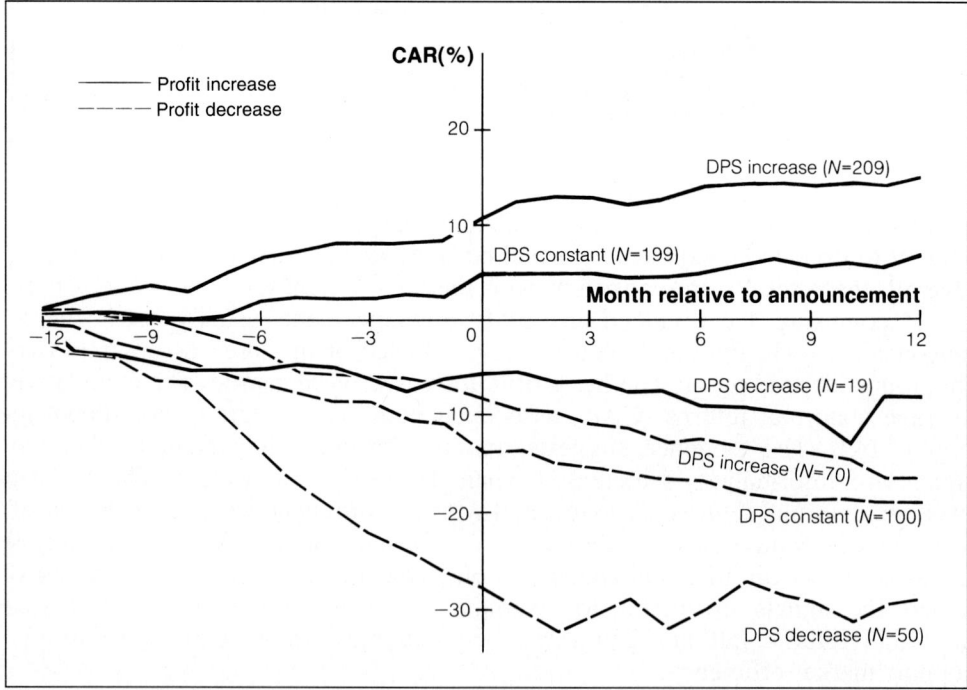

**Fig. 14.8** Cumulative average abnormal returns for each of the six subgroups

evaluation of the speed with which information is impounded in share prices. The sample differed from that used in the first part of the study and covered the period from January 1964 to December 1972. Average returns were calculated for the period from 4 days before each announcement to 6 days after each announcement. Owing to problems in identifying the exact time at which the announcement became public, the effective announcement period covered 2 days. Five groups were formed, each containing different combinations of profit and dividend changes. The cumulative average returns associated with each group are shown in Figure 14.9. The evidence suggests that the announcements contained new information and that investors reacted quickly.

The share price reaction to simultaneous profit and dividend announcements was investigated further by Easton and Sinclair.[26] Using nearly 900 half-yearly

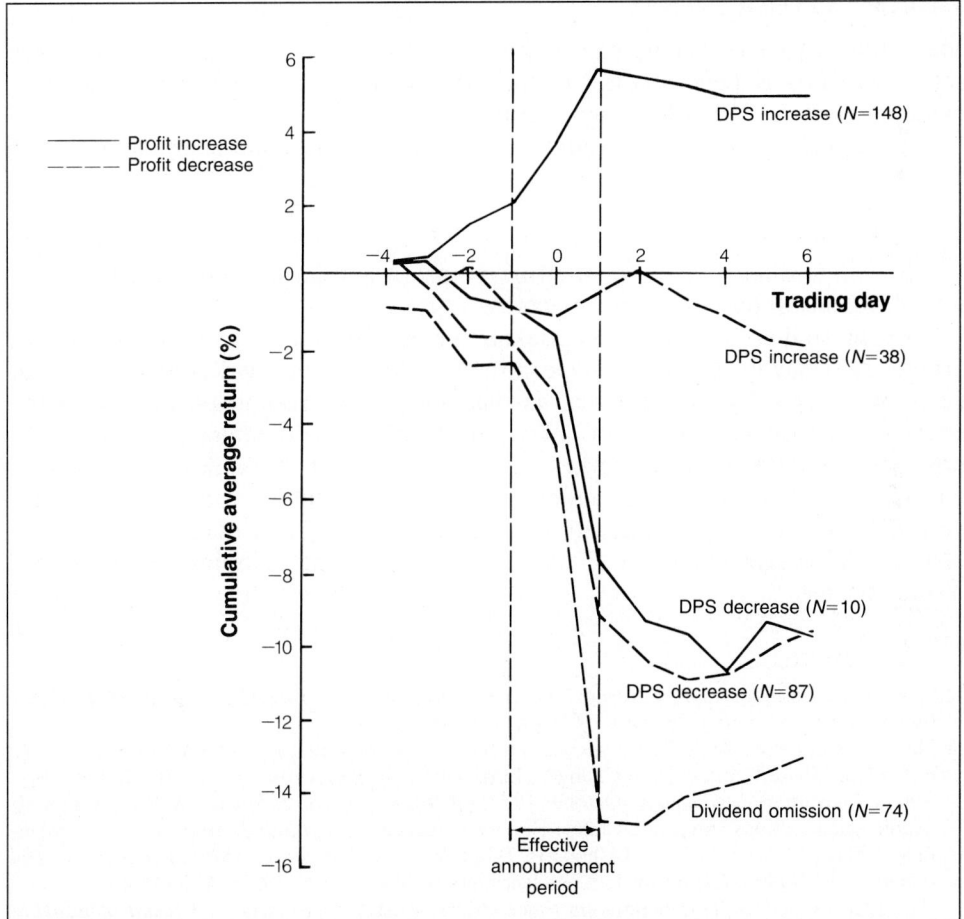

**Fig. 14.9** *Cumulative average returns associated with each of the five groups*

---

26 S. Easton & N. Sinclair, 'The Impact of Unexpected Earnings and Dividends on Abnormal Returns to Equity', *Accounting and Finance*, May 1989, pp. 1–14.

announcements by Australian companies in the period 1978–1980, they applied a technique which, in a statistical sense, can isolate the market's reaction to the profit announcement from the market's reaction to the dividend announcement. They found that both types of announcement caused a reaction, but that the reaction to dividends was weaker than the reaction to profits. In a subsequent study using the same sample, Easton conducted a more formal examination of the reaction to dividend and profit announcements and found that the share price response depends not only on the separate dividend and profit signals but also on the interaction between the signals.[27] In other words, the market appears to take account of the interrelation of the profit and dividend information.

### 14.4.3 OTHER EVENTS

Many other types of events have been studied in Australia, and an even larger set of events has been studied in the US and other markets. The Australian evidence includes the following 'events':

1. capitalisation changes (bonus issues, rights issues and share splits);
2. audit qualifications;
3. takeovers;
4. block trades;
5. extraordinary items reported in the profit and loss statement; and
6. money supply announcements.[28]

Event studies are often undertaken for reasons other than to test market efficiency. Usually, however, some inference concerning market efficiency can be drawn. Typically the inference is that prices have responded rapidly to the event studied. Indeed, as Fama notes, this 'result is so common that this work now devotes little space to market efficiency. The fact that quick adjustment is consistent with efficiency is noted, and then the studies move on to other issues.'[29] This, of course, does not mean that the event study evidence is entirely clear-cut. However, we defer discussion of some of the complexities until later in the chapter.

---

[27] S. Easton, 'Earnings and Dividends: Is There an Interaction Effect?', *Journal of Business Finance and Accounting*, January 1991, pp. 255–66.

[28] This list is not exhaustive. The evidence referred to may be found in: (1) R. Ball, P. Brown & F. J. Finn, 'Share Capitalization Changes, Information and the Australian Equity Market', *Australian Journal of Management*, October 1977, pp. 105–26; (2) T. J. Shevlin & G. P. Whittred, 'Audit Qualifications and Share Prices: Further Evidence', *Australian Journal of Management*, June 1984, pp. 37–52; (3) S. Bishop, P. Dodd & R. R. Officer, *Australian takeovers: The evidence 1972–1985*, Centre for Independent Studies, St Leonards, 1987; (4) R. Ball & F. Finn, 'The Effect of Block Transactions on Share Prices: Australian Evidence', *Journal of Banking and Finance*, July 1989, pp. 397–419; (5) S. Easton, 'The Impact of the Disclosure of Extraordinary Accounting Items on Returns to Equity', *Accounting and Finance*, November 1990, pp. 1–14; and (6) R. A. Singh, 'Response of Stock Prices to Money Supply Announcements: Australian Evidence', *Accounting and Finance*, November 1993, pp. 43–60.

[29] Fama (1991), see Footnote 5, pp. 1601–2.

## 14.5 STRONG-FORM MARKET EFFICIENCY

Strong-form market efficiency requires that abnormal returns be not available even to investors who have private (inside) information about a company. However, by definition it is usually impossible to identify the date on which private information becomes available, and therefore the methodology used to test semi-strong-form efficiency cannot be applied directly to studies of strong-form efficiency. Therefore, less direct tests have to be used. For example, one test involves identifying those investors who might be assumed to have access to private information, and then determining whether they earn abnormal returns. Typically, investors who may have access to private information include corporate insiders and professional fund managers.

In Australia there have been no tests of the investment performance of corporate insiders as details of their investment transactions are not available. In the US, the Securities and Exchange Commission (SEC) requires that all investors who hold more than a certain percentage of the shares in a company, or who hold a senior management position in a company, must report any purchases or sales of that company's shares. The SEC subsequently publishes this information. If these investors have access to private information they would be able to time the purchase/sale of their shares before a future increase/decrease in the share price. Lorie and Niederhoffer[30] and Jaffe[31] found evidence that insiders purchased before price increases, and sold before price decreases, and were able to earn positive abnormal returns. These results are not consistent with strong-form efficiency because they imply that insiders have information that is not reflected in market prices. Another strand of the literature has evaluated the performance of fund managers and other 'professional investors' on the principle that if they have access to information that is not reflected in prices, they should display superior investment performance. The US evidence presents a mixed picture, with some studies suggesting that professional investors have access to private information—but only at a cost—and others finding no evidence of such access.[32]

A number of Australian studies have examined the performance of mutual funds, unit trusts, and superannuation funds.[33] None of these studies concluded that funds in general were able to earn abnormal returns. These studies could be interpreted as supporting strong-form efficiency if it is assumed that the fund

---

[30] J. Lorie & V. Niederhoffer, 'Predictive and Statistical Properties of Insider Trading', *Journal of Law and Economics*, April 1968, pp. 35–53.

[31] J. Jaffe, 'Special Information and Insider Trading', *Journal of Business*, July 1974, pp. 410–28.

[32] For a review, see Footnote 5, Fama (1991), pp. 1603–8. Fama concludes that the mixed findings may be due to the difficulty of finding a suitable model of 'normal' returns. This is difficult because investment performance needs to be measured over a long period, so model error will accumulate and the results may look like inefficiency.

[33] See, for example, P. Praetz, 'The Measurement of MutualFund Performance in Australia', *JASSA*, September 1976, p. 10; R. Bird, H. Chin & M. McCrae, 'Australian Superannuation Fund Managers—How Do They Rate?', *JASSA*, December 1982, pp. 9–11; and G.N. Robson, 'The Investment Performance of Unit Trusts and Mutual Funds in Australia for the Period 1969 to 1978', *Accounting and Finance*, November 1986, pp. 55–79.

managers have access to private information but cannot use it to earn abnormal returns. However, in the light of other evidence an alternative interpretation is that this evidence has little bearing on strong-form efficiency. This interpretation would deny that managers have access to private information, or, if they do have such access, they do not use it to advantage.

Two other Australian studies have evaluated the performance of investment analysts. Brown and Walter analysed confidential buy-and-sell recommendations made by analysts.[34] On a risk-adjusted basis, these recommendations outperformed the market. If the analysts employed private information when making their recommendations, then these results are contrary to strong-form efficiency. Finn evaluated the performance of recommendations made by analysts employed by a large institutional investor.[35] He found that, if acted on, these recommendations would have resulted in abnormal returns. This result is consistent with that of Brown and Walter. Both studies found that the analysts' ability to identify shares that should be sold exceeded their ability to identify shares that should be purchased. Interestingly, the institutional investor studied by Finn earned negative abnormal returns, which is consistent with much of the previous evidence on the performance of fund managers. Finn's results suggest that analysts employed by the institutional investor may have had access to private information but that the institution failed to act quickly enough to benefit from the information. This suggests that it is inappropriate to use the evidence provided by studies of the performance of fund managers to make assertions about strong-form efficiency.

The evidence relating to Australian and American share markets supports the conclusion that neither market is strong-form efficient. It appears that market prices do not adjust instantaneously to new private information. Therefore investors with access to such information can earn abnormal returns, unless the costs of gathering or acting on the information are high enough to offset this advantage.

## 14.6 REAPPRAISAL OF THE EFFICIENT MARKET HYPOTHESIS

For many years the dominant view among researchers was that stock markets were efficient. Study after study produced empirical results which were interpreted as being consistent with the EMH. But beginning around the mid- to late-1970s, researchers began to find results that seemed incompatible with the EMH. Rather than rejecting the EMH outright, these results were labelled 'anomalies', leaving open the possibility that at some later stage they could be explained in a way compatible with the EMH, or with some revised version of the EMH. Enough anomalies have been found to fill whole issues of a leading journal and an entire conference has been organised around the theme, the conference papers

---

[34] P. Brown & T. Walter, 'Sharemarket Efficiency and the Experts: Some Australian Evidence', *Australian Journal of Management*, June 1982, pp. 13–32.
[35] F. J. Finn, *Evaluation of the Internal Processes of Managed Investment Funds*, JAI Press, Greenwich, Connecticut, 1984.

being subsequently published as proceedings in book form.[36] Obviously the material is by now voluminous so a detailed review cannot be given here.[37]

At about the same time, there developed another body of work that is much less sympathetic to the EMH and has been seen as an attempt to build an alternative view of how asset markets operate. This work implies, for example, that a share price can deviate significantly from the value justified by the 'fundamentals' and that share prices fluctuate more than they should, perhaps because of the transactions of uninformed traders. This work, also, is voluminous and will not be covered in detail here.[38]

In the following sections we provide an overview of the EMH reappraisal, emphasising, where possible, the available Australian evidence. We also briefly mention some of the explanations that have been suggested. The material is not presented chronologically; rather, it is presented in an order that we believe will promote understanding of the issues involved. It is also important to recall, at the outset, that a test of market efficiency must simultaneously be a test of some model or other of how an efficient market ought to price securities. That is, an efficiency test is also a test of the asset pricing model used by the researcher. Therefore an empirical test interpreted as a rejection of market efficiency could instead be interpreted as a rejection of whatever asset pricing model is used in the test. However, to present the evidence as clearly as possible we emphasise in this section the 'inefficient market' interpretation of the evidence. In Section 14.7 we return to the important issue of alternative interpretations. Finally, to simplify the presentation further, we also defer most discussion of the interrelations of anomalies until Section 14.7.

## 14.6.1 REGULARITIES IN PRICE SEQUENCES

A 'regularity' is a characteristic that appears consistently in the phenomenon being studied. Although the terms 'anomaly' and 'regularity' are sometimes used interchangeably, we draw the following distinction. When the term 'anomaly' is used, it connotes failure on the part of the accepted theory to explain the observed phenomenon. When the term 'regularity' is used, it connotes more caution on the part of the user; perhaps with further thought and research, the characteristic will be seen to conform with the accepted theory or with some more elaborate version of the accepted theory. Thus the distinction is clearly a matter of judgement.

---

36 See the June/September 1978 and the June 1983 issues of the *Journal of Financial Economics* and E. Dimson (Ed.), *Stock Market Anomalies*, Cambridge University Press, Cambridge, 1988.
37 Fortunately, there are excellent articles that review much of this work. See, for example, Fama (1991), see Footnote 5, and D. B. Keim, 'Stock market regularities: A synthesis of the evidence and explanations' in Dimson, see Footnote 36, pp. 16–39. For a review emphasising Australian evidence, see R. Faff, 'Capital Market Anomalies: A Survey of the Evidence', *Accounting Research Journal*, Spring 1992, pp. 3–22.
38 For reviews, see, for example, J. H. Cochrane, 'Volatility Tests and Efficient Markets: A Review Essay', *Journal of Monetary Economics*, 1991, pp. 463–85; A. Shleifer & L. H. Summers, 'The Noise Trader Approach to Finance', *Journal of Economic Perspectives*, Spring 1990, pp. 19–34, and S. F. LeRoy, 'Capital Market Efficiency: An Update', Federal Reserve Bank of San Francisco *Economic Review*, Spring 1990, pp. 29–38.

## DISCOVERY OF SHORT-TERM PATTERNS

It has long been recognised that the standard serial correlation and runs tests could not *prove* the *presence* of a random walk, but rather could only provide evidence that certain alternatives to a random walk were *not* present in the data. In other words, it is possible that a time series of share prices could have patterns too subtle (or too complicated) for detection by these tests. As long ago as 1970, Fama constructed an example of such a pattern.[39] Some researchers have claimed to find evidence of such patterns in actual share prices.[40] It is also well known that results inconsistent with a random walk are more likely to be found using returns measured over short time intervals. In other words, while it is very difficult to reject a random walk using weekly or monthly data, small but statistically significant departures from a random walk are generally present in daily data.[41]

If transactions data are used, that is, every price change is included even if the prices are only seconds apart, the random-walk model can be soundly rejected. For example, while Patell and Wolfson report evidence of small positive first-order serial correlation using daily data, they find using transactions data for the same sample of companies that the typical correlation coefficient is significantly negative (typically, approximately $-0.4$).[42]

One interpretation of these results is that there may be some forms of anomaly or pricing inefficiency that are not instantaneously corrected; the process may require two or three transactions, or, in calendar time, perhaps a trading day. However, the pricing 'error' envisaged is presumably small in absolute terms and, taking into account transaction costs, may be too small to permit a profitable trading rule to be developed. This does not, of course, mean that it is unimportant. But it does leave virtually undisturbed the notion that stock markets can correctly value shares; when the stock market is asked to value a share, it gives the right answer, but it may take a day or so. This is well short of instantaneous, but seems unlikely to lead to a serious systematic misallocation of resources!

## DISCOVERY OF LONG-TERM PATTERNS

At the opposite extreme, another group of researchers has suggested that there may be other kinds of inefficiency that will be detected only by taking a long-term view. It is suggested that there could be pricing errors that are eliminated

---

39 E. Fama, 'Efficient Capital Markets: A Review of Theory and Empirical Work', *Journal of Finance*, 1970, Footnote 10, p. 392.
40 J. A. Scheinkman & B. LeBaron, 'Nonlinear Dynamics and Stock Returns', *Journal of Business*, July 1989, pp. 311–37.
41 This is so, particularly if a long time series is used. See, for example, K. French & R. Roll, 'Stock Return Variances: The Arrival of Information and the Reaction of Traders', *Journal of Financial Economics*, September 1986, pp. 5–26. This phenomenon appears to be pervasive. Using 40 years of nineteenth century daily data, Brown and Easton report a statistically significant first-order serial correlation of 0.05. See R. L. Brown & S. A. Easton, 'Weak Form Efficiency in the Nineteenth Century: A Study of Daily Prices in the London Market for 3 per cent Consols 1821–60', *Economica*, February 1989, pp. 61–70.
42 J. M. Patell & M. A. Wolfson, 'The Intraday Speed of Adjustment of Stock Prices to Earnings and Dividend Announcements', *Journal of Financial Economics*, June 1984, pp. 223–52.

so slowly that it could take *years* for the market to eliminate the error. Summers has proposed one such model.[43] Reduced to its simplest terms, Summers' argument is as follows. Suppose that the stock market has wrongly priced a company's shares and, for whatever reason, the market corrects this error very slowly over perhaps a period of years. While the correction process is proceeding, there are, of course, many new pieces of information released about the company, and possibly many other events too, all of which cause the share price to change from day to day. Because the error correction process is so slow, its influence will be very difficult to isolate from the thousands of other impacts on the share price.

Summers provides a mathematical model in which the share's true value is known to Summers, but the market behaves in the manner just outlined. The result is very like the behaviour of real share prices: serial correlations are so close to zero that few statistical tests would find them statistically different from zero.[44] Moreover, the share price in Summers' market would still respond to any 'event', such as a profit announcement, by a sudden increase or decrease. All this could occur, despite the share being undervalued or overvalued by 30 per cent or more!

Imagine that a researcher reports a near-zero serial correlation coefficient in a random-walk test, or an apparently instantaneous price response in an event study. The traditional interpretation has been 'no evidence of inefficiency', to which has often been added, either explicitly or implicitly, 'which suggests that the market is efficient'. However, using Summers' argument the same research findings could be interpreted this way: 'no evidence of inefficiency, but the market could still be grossly inefficient'. Other interpretations are also possible.

In a market that behaved like Summers' market, the price of a share could deviate from its fundamental value for a long time, but would eventually return to its fundamental value. Therefore, long-period returns would exhibit *negative* serial correlation, while the short-period returns on the same shares would exhibit *near-zero* serial correlation. Fama and French, using 60 years of US data and 3- to 5-year periods to measure long-period returns, found serial correlations consistent with this pattern.[45] Market inefficiency is, of course, only one possible interpretation of these findings. In addition, the results were clearest in the period 1926–1941, therefore weakening the relevance of their results to today's markets.

What type of stock market would be consistent with the evidence and ideas of Summers and Fama/French? An obvious candidate is an overreactive market. Having mispriced a share, perhaps by being overly pessimistic or optimistic, the market then takes a lengthy period to eliminate its mistake. De Bondt and Thaler

---

[43] L. H. Summers, 'Does the Stock Market Rationally Reflect Fundamental Values?', *Journal of Finance*, July 1986, pp. 591–601.

[44] But note that the true correlation was *not* zero. In reality, of course, the researcher cannot *know* this, but it was known to Summers because this 'market' was entirely his own creation.

[45] E. Fama & K. French, 'Permanent and Temporary Components of Stock Prices', *Journal of Political Economy*, April 1988, pp. 246–73.

provide evidence which is in this tradition.[46] De Bondt and Thaler identify better-performing shares (the winners) and poorer-performing shares (the losers) over a period of several years. They then track the performance of these shares in the following years. On average, the winners turn into losers and the losers turn into winners. The Australian evidence is partially consistent with the US evidence. In Australia, while there is a tendency for winners to become losers, the reverse does not seem to occur.[47] The implied trading rules are clear. In the US and Australia, sell the winners; in the US, buy the losers as well.

## PRICE 'BUBBLES'

A related issue is the hypothesis that share prices (and the prices of other assets) might display 'bubbles'. Various definitions of a 'bubble' have been proposed but it is usually suggested that the following two features would constitute a bubble.[48] First, prices show a strong tendency to rise for a period, possibly followed by a decrease, which may be quite sudden. Secondly, as a result, the price departs from the true, fundamental value of the asset. While the first of these features seems to be readily observable in stock markets (for example, in the crashes of October 1929 and October 1987), the mere presence of the first does *not*, of course, imply the presence of the second. Prices following a random walk will occasionally produce, purely by chance, episodes displaying the first feature. These episodes would probably *appear* to be bubbles, but they may not in reality be bubbles in the sense that we have suggested. A bubble could, of course, arise where market participants behave irrationally. Suppose, however, that a share price depends in part on its expected rate of change. It becomes a 'high' price because it is expected to go higher still. In the presence of such self-fulfilling prophecy, prices may increase, even though there is no change in the 'fundamentals'. However, even these prices may be 'rational' in the sense that market participants form unbiased expectations. This situation is sometimes referred to as a **rational bubble**.

Whether price bubbles occur is a controversial issue. In principle, bubbles will not arise if there are enough traders whose time horizon is infinite (and hence they 'look beyond' the term of the bubble). Of course, no-one lives forever but inheritance rules might produce much the same effect. Ultimately, this becomes an empirical issue, but the empirical testing of bubbles is a complex area beyond the scope of this book. At least one reviewer is sceptical: 'It is our contention that no econometric test has yet demonstrated that bubbles are present

---

[46] W. De Bondt & R. Thaler, 'Does the Stock Market Overreact?', *Journal of Finance*, July 1985, pp. 793–805; and 'Further Evidence on Investor Overreaction and Stock Market Seasonality', *Journal of Finance*, July 1987, pp. 557–81.
[47] T. J. Brailsford, 'A Test for the Winner–loser Anomaly in the Australian Equity Market 1958–87', *Journal of Business Finance and Accounting*, 1992, pp. 225–42.
[48] See R. P. Flood & P. M. Garber, 'Market Fundamentals Versus Price-level Bubbles: The First Tests', *Journal of Political Economy*, August 1980, pp. 745–70; and O. J. Blanchard, 'Speculative Bubbles, Crashes and Rational Expectations', *Economics Letters*, 1979, pp. 387–9.

in the data. In each case, misspecification of the model or alternative market fundamentals seems the likely explanation of the findings'.[49]

## THE STOCK MARKET CRASH OF 1987

On 19 and 20 October 1987, share prices around the world fell suddenly and steeply. In New York the fall was about 20 per cent; in Australia, more than 30 per cent. The size of the fall comfortably exceeded the famous 1929 stock market crash. What this episode can teach us about market efficiency depends on one's interpretation of the evidence.

One interpretation that appeals to many people is that of the bursting bubble. In the months before the crash, share prices had climbed steadily. So, one view is that during this 'bull run' in prices, the market lost sight of the fundamentals. Eventually the gap between market prices and 'true values' became unsustainable and the resulting correction came suddenly and, perhaps, efficiently. But it is difficult under this interpretation to explain why different markets crashed at the same time, and by roughly similar percentages, despite wide differences in their pre-crash experience. In short, why should different bubbles burst in the same way at the same time? Nevertheless, this interpretation seems to fit many of the facts. But, unfortunately, so also does its exact opposite: maybe the bull run was a correct reflection of the good economic news of the time and was brought, inefficiently, to a sudden end by a short period of senseless panic.

Others have sought to blame the crash on institutional changes such as the spread of computer-based trading and portfolio insurance. But while prices did indeed crash in markets with these features, it is noteworthy that prices also crashed in markets where those features were *not* widespread. Other commentators have emphasised that a sudden downward movement in prices does not necessarily indicate inefficiency. If the news is bad enough the resulting price fall can be large and sudden. For example, in the US at the time of the 1987 crash there were rumours that interest rates might be increased. Many analysts, while admitting that this scenario is technically possible, think it is highly implausible. LeRoy, for example, states his view that 'no economic information of an even mildly unusual nature was made public that day'.[50] Unfortunately we are left with no generally agreed explanation for the crash, and few unambiguous implications for market efficiency.[51]

## EXCESS PRICE VOLATILITY

Finally, mention should be made of the so-called 'excess volatility' debate, which began around 1980 and is still unresolved. The origin of the debate is readily

---

[49] This view is expressed in R. P. Flood & R. J. Hodrick, 'On Testing for Speculative Bubbles', *Journal of Economic Perspectives*, Spring 1990, p. 87.
[50] LeRoy, see Footnote 38, p. 30.
[51] There is now a large literature that has considered alternative explanations of the crash. See, for example, R. Kamphuis et al. (Eds), *Black Monday and the Future of Financial Markets*, Irwin, Homewood, Illinois, 1989.

understood.[52] Finance theory holds that the share price today, $P_t$, should equal the expected value of $P_t^*$, the 'true' present value of actual future (but currently unknown) dividends. We can therefore state that:

$$P_t^* = P_t + u_t$$

where $u_t$ is a forecast error. Taking the variance of both expressions:

$$\text{Var}(P_t^*) = \text{Var}(P_t) + \text{Var}(u_t) + 2\,\text{Cov}(P_t, u_t)$$

However, as $u_t$ is a forecast error, the covariance term should be zero.

Therefore: $\text{Var}(P_t^*) = \text{Var}(P_t) + \text{Var}(u_t)$

and therefore: $\text{Var}(P_t^*) \geq \text{Var}(P_t)$

In words, this loosely translates to a statement that observed share prices $P_t$ should be *less* variable than the true present value of future dividends $P_t^*$. However, in fact, dividends do *not* vary very much from year to year. If one is willing to make the rather heroic assumption of a constant discount rate for dividends, it is no surprise that share prices then appear to vary much more than the present value of dividends. In short, share prices are 'too volatile'. However, the statistical issues turned out to be complex and a lengthy debate ensued.[53] At first, excess volatility tests were interpreted as tests of efficiency: if prices are 'too volatile', the market must be inefficient. More recently this interpretation has been revised and the focus has shifted to asking what might *cause* excess volatility. If, for example, the causes of excess volatility are fads or 'crowd psychology', there is a clear role for inefficiency.[54]

### 14.6.2 REGULARITIES FOLLOWING ANNOUNCEMENTS

In Section 14.4, we reviewed the major characteristics of 'event studies'. We considered in some detail the 'event' of a company announcing its profit. From an information efficiency viewpoint it is expected that at the date of the event the share price should respond instantaneously and without bias. In an event study this behaviour would manifest itself as a sharp change in the cumulative abnormal return (CAR) immediately following the event. But thereafter the CAR measure should have no pattern because there should be no further abnormal returns associated with the event.

Although there are many event studies that produce such CAR patterns, a significant number do not. In fact one of the first anomalies to be well documented was the tendency of the CAR measure to 'drift' in the period after the announcement of company profit.[55] An example of **post-announcement drift**,

---

[52] Two early and influential papers are: R. J. Shiller, 'Do Stock Prices Move too Much to be Justified by Subsequent Changes in Dividends?', *American Economic Review*, June 1981, pp. 421–36; and S. F. LeRoy & R. D. Porter, 'The Present-value Relation: Tests Based on Implied Variance Bounds', *Econometrica*, May 1981, pp. 555–74.

[53] For a review, see Cochrane, see Footnote 38, pp. 465–8.

[54] See, for example, R. J. Shiller, 'Stock Prices and Social Dynamics', *Brookings Papers on Economic Activity*, December 1984, pp. 457–510.

[55] For a survey which, though now somewhat dated, is still very useful, see R. Ball, 'Anomalies in Relationships Between Securities Yields and Yield-Surrogates', *Journal of Financial Economics*, June/September 1978.

as it is sometimes called, can probably be seen in Figure 14.5.[56] In that figure, the CAR graph for the 'profit decreased' group continues to decline after the announcement.

The best documented examples of post-announcement drift concern the reaction of share prices to profit announcements. In the earliest event studies the sample of announcements was split into two groups corresponding to 'good news' and 'bad news'. Many later studies use five or ten groups. For example, in a study using US data, Rendleman, Jones and Latane used ten groups, with Group 1 corresponding to the 'worst news' group, Group 2 the next worst, and so on, up to Group 10, the 'best news' group.[57] They then calculated a CAR measure for each group for the 3 months post-announcement. If drift is present, it would be expected that the 'worst news' group would show the lowest returns (most negative CAR) after 3 months, the 'best news' group would show the highest returns (most positive CAR) after 3 months, and the other groups would be between these extremes. A simple test is thus to observe whether the ten groups have preserved their rankings after 3 months. It was found that the ranking was almost perfectly preserved; the only exception was that Groups 2 and 3 had exchanged ranks. Similar evidence of drift was also found by Foster, Olsen and Shevlin.[58] In Australia, Easton and Sinclair used five groups and found that the ranking was perfectly preserved 3 months after the profit announcement.[59] However, this did not occur in the groups formed on the basis of dividends.

### 14.6.3 CALENDAR-BASED PRICE REGULARITIES

The early random-walk/weak-form-efficiency literature was loosely based on the notion that, if share returns displayed any patterns, arbitragers would quickly move to exploit those patterns and would continue to exploit them until the patterns were no longer present. However, strictly speaking, the EMH asserts that only *abnormal* returns should not display exploitable patterns. Essentially, a random-walk test using daily returns assumes that the expected (or normal) daily return on any given share is a constant. Typically this constant is likely to be a small, positive number. The random-walk test is whether there are predictable patterns in returns which exceed (or fall short of) this assumed constant daily expected return.

Is it reasonable to assume that the expected daily return, on any given day, is a constant? Suppose that, at the start of the year, shares in Nurk Ltd are priced at $9 per share, and after 1 year's share trading the price is $11.55 per share. If

---

[56] We cautiously use the word 'probably' because there is always a chance that sampling error can produce a spurious pattern.
[57] R. J. Rendleman, C. P. Jones & H. A. Latane, 'Empirical Anomalies Based on Unexpected Earnings and the Importance of Risk Adjustment', *Journal of Financial Economics*, November 1982, pp. 269–87.
[58] G. Foster, C. Olsen & T. Shevlin, 'Earnings Releases, Anomalies and the Behavior of Security Returns', *The Accounting Review*, October 1984, pp. 574–603.
[59] S. Easton & N. Sinclair, 'The Impact of Unexpected Earnings and Dividends on Abnormal Returns to Equity', *Accounting and Finance*, May 1989, Table 5.

there are 250 trading days in the year, the average price change per day has been 0.1 per cent, or roughly 1 cent per day. This is a realistic example, in that shares do, on average, return approximately zero per day. Perhaps it was this observation that encouraged some researchers to assume that the *expected* return on a share was a constant—presumably a small, positive constant. But in fact there may be a difference between the observation and the assumption. For example, the *expected* return per day for Nurk shares could have been −0.1 per cent on Tuesdays and +0.15 per cent on all other days. Over a long period, the *observed* average return on Nurk shares would be steady at 0.1 per cent per day (that is, a number close to zero) but the *expected* return per day is different on different days of the week. But that isn't likely . . . or is it?

## DAILY SHARE PRICE REGULARITIES

In 1980, French published a paper in which he reported that a daily index of US share prices over the period 1953–1977 showed that average returns on Mondays were negative, while average returns on Fridays were positive.[60] If this were true, why would anyone buy shares on a Friday afternoon? Why not wait until late Monday when, on average, the price will be lower? The result was puzzling and the mystery deepened in the following years. Lakonishok and Smidt studied 90 years of US data (from 1897 to 1987) and found negative average Monday returns over the period as a whole, and in all ten subperiods that they studied.[61]

What could explain these findings? A number of suggestions have been made but there is as yet no definitive answer. One possibility is settlement procedures. Suppose, for example, that a share buyer must pay for the shares on the next trading day. On Fridays, payment is not required until Monday, therefore giving the buyer a slight advantage. For example, the buyer could earn interest for 3 days on the money owed to the seller, when normally only 1 day's interest is available. If this advantage is built into prices, then on Friday, prices will be 'high', but on the following Monday, prices will revert to normal. Thus, on average, the return from Friday night to Monday morning is expected to be negative. Lakonishok and Levi find that settlement procedures can explain some, but not all, of the observed pattern in the US.[62]

Nor is the phenomenon purely American. The results for the Australian stock market over the period 1974–1984 are as shown in Table 14.2.[63]

---

[60] K. French, 'Stock Returns and the Weekend Effect', *Journal of Financial Economics*, March 1980, pp. 55–69. There had been earlier, less detailed studies published in the professional literature. The returns reported by French were statistically significant. Throughout this section we omit most references to statistical significance.

[61] J. Lakonishok & S. Smidt, 'Are Seasonal Anomalies Real? A Ninety-year Perspective', *Review of Financial Studies*, 1988, pp. 403–25.

[62] J. Lakonishok & M. Levi, 'Weekend Effects in Stock Returns: A Note', *Journal of Finance*, June 1982, pp. 883–9.

[63] R. Ball & J. Bowers, 'Daily seasonals in equity and fixed-interest returns: Australian evidence and tests of plausible hypotheses', in E. Dimson (Ed.), *Stock Market Anomalies*, Cambridge University Press, Cambridge, 1988, p. 79. The statistical reliability of these results has been supported by tests reported in S. Easton & R. Faff, 'An Investigation of the Robustness of the Day-of-the-week Effect in Australia', *Applied Financial Economics*, 1994, forthcoming.

**Table 14.2**

| Day | Monday | Tuesday | Wednesday | Thursday | Friday |
|---|---|---|---|---|---|
| Mean return (%) | −0.007 | −0.152 | 0.053 | 0.191 | 0.161 |

Note: Returns exclude days following holidays.

Australia appears to have a 'negative Tuesday'. Is it coincidence that when it is Tuesday in Australia, it is Monday in America? Moreover, daily interest rates in Australia show a very similar pattern: high on Thursday and low on Tuesday.[64] Other international comparisons turned up further results:[65] Canada's pattern is very like that of the US; the UK has a negative Monday, but its Friday is only marginally positive; France, Japan and Singapore have negative Tuesdays. A common thread is that every country has some kind of daily pattern, but not necessarily the same pattern as that found in other countries.

A second daily regularity relates to public holidays. In the study referred to earlier, Lakonishok and Smidt found that the average return on the day before a holiday was twenty-three times larger than the average returns on all other days.[66] Half the average annual capital gains occurred on approximately ten pre-holiday trading days per year. This is a regularity of astonishing proportions. Moreover, like the other regularities, it is not confined to the US. In Australia, the average pre-holiday return is perhaps eight or ten times larger than the average return on other days.[67] Cadsby and Ratner confirm the pre-holiday effect in the US and Australia and also find such an effect in Canada, Japan and Hong Kong—but, curiously, not in any of the five European markets they investigated.[68]

There are also patterns *within* days. Harris reports that prices on the New York Stock Exchange tend to rise in the last 15 minutes of trading and, except for Mondays, also tend to rise in the first 45 minutes of trading.[69] However, on Monday mornings there is a tendency for prices to fall.

## MONTHLY SHARE PRICE REGULARITIES

An article by Officer, published in 1975, investigated the possibility of there being a monthly seasonal effect in Australian share prices.[70] Although the effect did not appear to be large, its presence seemed clear and his conclusion was:

---

[64] See F. J. Finn, A. Lynch & S. Moore, 'Intra-week Regularities in Security Returns: Further Australian Evidence', *Australian Journal of Management*, December 1991, pp. 129–44.

[65] L. Condoyanni, J. O'Hanlon & C. W. R. Ward, 'Weekend effects in stock market returns: International evidence', in Dimson, see Footnote 36, p. 54. See also J. Jaffe & R. Westerfield 'The Weekend Effect in Common Stock Returns: The International Evidence', *Journal of Finance*, June 1985, pp. 433–54.

[66] Lakonishok & Smidt, see Footnote 61.

[67] S. Easton, 'Returns to Equity Before and After Holidays: Australian Evidence and Tests of Plausible Hypotheses', *Australian Journal of Management*, December 1990, pp. 281–96.

[68] C. Cadsby & M. Ratner, 'Turn-of-the-month and Pre-holiday Effects in Stock Prices: Some International Evidence', *Journal of Banking and Finance*, 1992, pp. 497–509.

[69] L. Harris, 'Intra-day stock return patterns', in Dimson, see Footnote 36, pp. 91–108.

[70] R. Officer, 'Seasonality in Australian Capital Markets: Market Efficiency and Empirical Issues', *Journal of Financial Economics*, January 1975, pp. 29–51.

'there appears to be a seasonal in the Australian share market'.[71] Investigating the same question, but using US data and a different method of analysis, Rozeff and Kinney reported a remarkable fact:[72] the average return in January was more than five times larger than the average of returns in the other 11 months. Why didn't a lot of investors buy in December to benefit from this regularity? In doing so, of course, they would increase the December price level and eventually eliminate the high January return.

As with the daily share price regularities, this effect was also found in other countries. One study of stock markets in seventeen different countries (including the US) found that January was the highest return month in fourteen countries.[73] Using Australian market-wide data for the period 1958–1981 the monthly percentage rates of return areas are as shown in Table 14.3.[74]

**Table 14.3**

| Month | Jan | Feb | Mar | Apr | May | Jun | Jul | Aug | Sep | Oct | Nov | Dec |
|---|---|---|---|---|---|---|---|---|---|---|---|---|
| Rates of return (%) | 3.14 | −0.08 | 0.17 | 1.24 | 0.98 | 0.95 | 1.24 | 0.34 | −1.07 | 2.23 | 0.28 | 3.45 |

In Australia during this period the strongest monthly seasonal effects for the market as a whole were for December and January. Together, these 2 months contributed, on average, 6.59 percentage points, while the other 10 months contributed a total of only 6.28 percentage points. In other words, 2 months contributed more than half of the total return for the year for the market as a whole.

It is not clear why January should be different to other months. One possible explanation investigated thoroughly is **tax loss selling**. The end of a tax year could induce heavy selling pressure in the last month, causing lower prices, followed by a rebound in prices in the first month of the new tax year. As the US has a tax year ending in December, this might explain the US January effect. In Australia, tax loss selling by domestic investors would produce high returns in July, while in the UK, high returns would occur in April. Although high returns are indeed observed at these times, Australia and the UK also have strong

---

[71] See Footnote 70, p. 49.
[72] M. Rozeff & W. Kinney, 'Capital Market Seasonality: The Case of Stock Returns', *Journal of Financial Economics*, November 1976, pp. 379–402.
[73] M. Gultekin & B. Gultekin, 'Stock Market Seasonality: International Evidence', *Journal of Financial Economics*, December 1983, pp. 469–82. In the other three cases, January ranked 2nd, 3rd and 5th.
[74] P. Brown, D. Keim, A. Kleidon & T. Marsh, 'Stock Return Seasonalities and the Tax-loss Selling Hypothesis: Analysis of the Arguments and Australian Evidence', *Journal of Financial Economics*, June 1983, pp. 105–27. The high January return also occurred in Australia in the earlier time period of 1936 to 1957; see T. Brailsford & S. Easton, 'Seasonality in Australian Share Price Indices Between 1936 and 1957', *Accounting and Finance*, November 1991, pp. 69–85.

January effects which are not predicted by the tax-loss selling hypothesis. Therefore, tax effects provide, at best, a partial explanation.[75] The January effect is also closely related to the 'size effect' discussed in the next section.

A second monthly pattern relates to time periods within each month. Specifically, in the US, the last day and the first three days of each month are, on average, days of high return. This is sometimes referred to as the 'turn-of-the-month' effect. One US estimate is that the average daily return at the turn of the month is more than seven times larger than the average daily return calculated using all days.[76] The turn-of-the-month effect has also been found for stock markets in Australia, Canada, the UK, Switzerland, and West Germany, but not in Japan, Hong Kong, Italy, or France.[77] A related phenomenon is reported by Ariel.[78] Using US data for the period 1963–1981, Ariel found that the average return in the second half of calendar months is virtually zero. This regularity, also, has been found in Australia,[79] although the high returns appear to begin a day earlier, that is, on the second-last day of the month. If the last 2 days of the month are excluded, returns in the second half of the month are, on average, negative.

### 14.6.4 OTHER REGULARITIES IN PRICES

If the capital asset pricing model is correct, and if the stock market is efficient, then once 'beta risk' has been taken into account, no other variable should be able to explain returns. Although empirical studies have not usually reported a strong relationship between beta and returns,[80] it was not until the mid-1970s that researchers began to report finding other variables that add to the explanation of returns. An early and influential study by Basu found that the price–earnings ratio was, for many companies, related to returns even after taking account of beta risk.[81] Since then there have been a number of studies reporting similar findings. Some of these studies are reviewed in this section.

---

75 For a detailed and entertaining review, see R. Haugen & J. Lakonishok, *The Incredible January Effect: The Stock Market's Unsolved Mystery*, Dow-Jones-Irwin, Homewood, Illinois, 1988. Faff (1992, pp. 11–13) (see Footnote 37) provides a concise review of the evidence on tax-loss selling.
76 Lakonishok & Smidt, see Footnote 61, p. 26.
77 Cadsby & Ratner, see Footnote 68.
78 R. A. Ariel, 'Evidence on intra-month seasonality in stock returns', in Dimson, see Footnote 36, pp. 109–14.
79 P. Brown & T. Walter, 'Erratum: Ex-dividend Day Behaviour of Australian Share Prices', *Australian Journal of Management*, June 1987, pp. 147–8. The effect is weak in Canada and the UK, while Japan has the opposite pattern; see J. Jaffe & R. Westerfield, 'Is There a Monthly Effect in Stock Market Returns? Evidence from Foreign Countries', *Journal of Banking and Finance*, May 1989, pp. 237–44.
80 This may be an overly cautious understatement. Schwert, for example, believes that the 'statistical evidence supporting the positive relation between risk and expected return is surprisingly weak'. See G. W. Schwert, 'Size and Stock Returns, and Other Empirical Regularities', *Journal of Financial Economics*, June 1983, p. 4.
81 S. Basu, 'The Investment Performance of Common Stocks in Relation to Their Price–earnings Ratios: A Test of the Efficient Market Hypothesis', *Journal of Finance*, June 1977, pp. 663–82.

## THE SIZE EFFECT OR SMALL-FIRM EFFECT

One of the most intensively studied of all the empirical regularities concerns the effect of company 'size' as measured by the total market value of a company's shares. The size effect in share returns is the observation that returns on the shares of small companies exceed the returns on the shares of larger companies both before and after adjusting for beta risk. Put simply, returns on small-company shares are 'too high'. This effect was first documented for US companies[82] and it has since been observed in the share prices of Australian, Canadian, Japanese, and UK companies.[83] As an example, we present the findings of Brown et al. using Australian share returns, not adjusted for beta risk.[84] Portfolios were formed according to deciles; that is, the smallest 10 per cent of companies were placed in portfolio 1, the next smallest 10 per cent in portfolio 2, and so on, with the largest 10 per cent in portfolio 10. Therefore, each portfolio contained an equal number of shares. The average monthly return on portfolio 1 was 6.75 per cent, while portfolio 2 returned 2.23 per cent per month. The other eight portfolios all returned between 1 and 2 per cent per month. Portfolio 10 (the largest companies) returned just 1.02 per cent per month. The high returns on small companies are not due merely to the small companies having higher betas. After taking account of this factor, the *excess* monthly return on portfolio 1 (the smallest companies) was still 5.66 per cent, and for portfolio 2 the excess monthly return was 1.27 per cent.

The size effect in Australia has also been investigated by Beedles, Dodd and Officer, who found that the effect is still clearly present in the data, even when different measurement techniques are used.[85] However, they did identify several factors that may partly explain the size effect. In particular, they report that shares in small companies trade less frequently than shares in larger companies. This is consistent with shareholders in small companies requiring a higher expected return, to compensate for the illiquidity of their investment.

While the cause of the size effect is unclear, the relationship between the size effect and the January effect is well documented. In the US, this relationship is strong, with approximately half the difference in the returns on the shares of small and large companies being due to returns in January.[86] Loosely speaking, if just 1 month (January) is ignored, half the size effect disappears. In Australia the relationship is not so pronounced.[87] In fact, the Australian smallest-company

---

[82] Among the earliest studies are R. W. Banz, 'The Relationship Between Return and Market Value of Common Stock', *Journal of Financial Economics*, March 1981, pp. 3–18 and M. Reinganum, 'Misspecification of Capital Asset Pricing: Empirical Anomalies Based on Earnings' Yields and Market Values', *Journal of Financial Economics*, March 1981, pp. 19–46.

[83] For a survey, see D. B. Keim, 'Stock market regularities: A synthesis of the evidence and explanations' in Dimson, see Footnote 36, pp. 20–4.

[84] Brown, Keim, Kleidon & Marsh, see Footnote 74.

[85] W. Beedles, P. Dodd & R. Officer, 'Regularities in Australian Share Returns', *Australian Journal of Management*, June 1988, pp. 1–29.

[86] D.B. Keim, 'Size-related Anomalies and Stock Return Seasonality: Further Empirical Evidence', *Journal of Financial Economics*, March 1983, pp. 13–32. See also M. R. Reinganum, 'The Anomalous Stock Market Behavior of Small Firms in January: Empirical Tests for Tax-loss Selling Effects', *Journal of Financial Economics*, June 1983, pp. 89–104.

[87] Brown, Keim, Kleidon & Marsh, see Footnote 74.

portfolio generates higher returns in July and October than in January. That is, January ranks only third among the months (and lower still, sixth, if beta-adjusted returns are used).

## THE DIVIDEND-YIELD EFFECT

A share's **dividend yield** is the value of the dividend (per share) divided by the share price. A number of US studies have found that dividend yield helps to explain returns, even after adjustment for beta risk.[88] Typically these studies find that beta-adjusted returns are higher, the higher the dividend yield. That is, there appears to be a relationship between returns and dividend yields which cannot be explained by the capital asset pricing model. A similar result has been found using Australian data for the period 1960–1969.[89]

The dividend-yield effect may be due, in part, to taxation. If dividends are taxed more heavily than capital gains, investors will prefer a dollar of before-tax capital gains to a dollar of before-tax dividends. Putting this another way, investors will require high before-tax returns on shares that pay high dividends in order to compensate them for the higher tax burden that the high dividends will impose. However, there are two reasons why taxation is at best a partial explanation. First, there is evidence that shares which pay *no* dividends have higher returns than shares which pay low dividends.[90] That is, the dividend-yield effect changes character when the dividend yield is zero. But the taxation explanation is not consistent with this finding as it predicts that shares with a zero dividend yield should require lower returns than shares with a low dividend yield. Secondly, in Australia at least, the size of the dividend-yield effect appears to be too large to be explained by taxation effects. Ball et al. estimated that, to be a complete explanation, the tax rate on dividends would have to be 146 per cent, whereas the maximum tax rate payable by any investor at the time of the study was only 67 per cent.[91]

## THE PRICE-EARNINGS EFFECT

The share price, divided by earnings per share, is usually called the 'price–earnings ratio', or the 'P/E ratio', and has for many years been used in decision making by investment analysts. In 1977 Basu reported that the P/E ratio helps to explain returns even after adjustment for beta risk.[92] Specifically, risk-adjusted returns were higher, the lower the P/E ratio. Basu's results were confirmed in a larger and more detailed study of US shares by Reinganum.[93] In Australia, the

---

[88] For a brief survey of nine such studies, see Keim, in Dimson, see Footnote 36, p. 19.
[89] R. Ball, P. Brown, F. Finn & R. R. Officer, 'Dividends and the Value of the Firm: Evidence from the Australian Equity Market', *Australian Journal of Management*, April 1979, pp. 13–26.
[90] M.E. Blume, 'Stock Returns and Dividend Yields: Some More Evidence', *Review of Economics and Statistics*, November 1980, pp. 567–77.
[91] Ball, Brown, Finn & Officer, see Footnote 89, p. 23. Note, however, that this study pre-dates the introduction of the imputation system of dividend taxation.
[92] S. Basu, 'The Investment Performance of Common Stocks in Relation to their Price–earnings Ratios: A Test of the Efficient Market Hypothesis', *Journal of Finance*, June 1977, pp. 663–82.
[93] M. R. Reinganum, see Footnote 86.

P/E effect appears to be weaker and has been documented only for larger companies.[94] Therefore, there appears to be a relationship between returns and P/E ratios which cannot be explained by the capital asset pricing model.

### 14.6.5 Successful investment strategies

If share markets are semi-strong-form efficient, it should not be possible to earn consistent, risk-adjusted profits using only public information. That is, there should be no successful investment strategies, other than those which use inside information. On this definition, probably, most investment strategies are unsuccessful, but the investment recommendations made by the Value Line investor survey do appear, on average, to produce positive beta-adjusted returns. This result has been reported in several independent studies, beginning with an article by Black.[95]

How is Value Line able to do this? In Australia there is no direct parallel to the Value Line case. Certainly there is no evidence of excess profitability in the investment recommendations studied by Ball, Brown and Finn.[96] There is, however, mixed evidence that investment recommendations made on two occasions by Potter Partners earned excess returns in the 12 months following the release of the recommendations.[97]

## 14.7 Stock market 'anomalies': discussion

In Section 14.6, our intention for the most part was to present the evidence in a way that facilitated an interpretation of market inefficiency. In this section, we consider other issues and interpretations.

### 14.7.1 Interrelations between regularities

Although we have, for the most part, discussed each regularity separately, it is in fact well known that many regularities are interrelated. For example, as we mentioned in Section 14.6.4, the small-firm effect and the January effect are closely related. This implies that if, say, the January effect can be explained, then much of the mystery of the small-firm effect should disappear. There are many other such interrelations suggested in the literature. Examples include the following:
1. The turn-of-the-month effect is strong in January.
2. Portfolios of losing firms tend to earn high returns in January.

---

[94] D. Anderson, A. Lynch & N. Mathiou, 'Behaviour of CAPM Anomalies in Smaller Firms: Australian Evidence', *Australian Journal of Management*, June 1990, pp. 1–38.
[95] See F. Black, 'Yes, Virginia, There is Hope: Tests of the Value Line Ranking System', *Financial Analysts Journal*, September–October 1972, pp. 10–14. For more recent evidence, see T. E. Copeland & D. Mayers, 'The Value Line Enigma (1965–1978): A Case Study of Performance Evaluation Issues', *Journal of Financial Economics*, November 1982, pp. 289–321.
[96] R. Ball, P. Brown & F. J. Finn, 'Published Investment Recommendations and Share Prices: Are There Free Lunches in Security Analysis?', *JASSA*, June 1978, pp. 5–10.
[97] R. Ma & G. Whittred, 'Ben Graham's Last Will and Testament: An Evaluation', *Australian Journal of Management*, June 1981, pp. 51–65.

3. The P/E ratio is a major factor in Value Line's investment selection methods.

It is useful to know how the various regularities are related, as such knowledge defines more clearly the nature of what needs to be explained. However, this type of work cannot, by itself, provide an *explanation* of what has been observed. An explanation is more than mere description as it requires some kind of theory. This is considered in the next section.

## 14.7.2 EXPLANATIONS

Empirical studies of market efficiency require three inputs. These are:
1. data on returns;
2. a model that specifies expected or normal returns;
3. tests of abnormal returns to determine whether the market is efficient.

Accordingly, when an empirical regularity is observed, there are at least three possible interpretations. These are:
1. There is something wrong with the data.
2. There is something wrong with the asset pricing model used to measure normal returns.
3. There is something wrong with the market—it is inefficient, perhaps due to irrational behaviour by market participants.

All three interpretations appear frequently in the literature and we will provide a few examples to illustrate them.

### DATA PROBLEMS

There are numerous problems in constructing a data base of share prices. We provide three examples. First, the sheer volume of data makes occasional recording errors virtually inevitable. Secondly, share prices are artificially affected by dividend payments, bonus issues, rights issues, and so on. Some means of adjusting for these effects must be found and implemented. Thirdly, trading in shares is never literally continuous, so the most recent price at any given time will nearly always be dated. For example, the end-of-month price for one share may be observed only several minutes before the end of the month, while for others the most recent price at the end of the month may be hours or even days old. This problem is often referred to as the **thin-trading problem**.

Data errors have the potential to invalidate any empirical study and the possibility of there being data errors therefore deserves careful attention. As an example, consider the effect of a wrongly recorded share price on serial correlation calculations. Suppose that the *true* sequence of prices is $1.00, $1.10, and $1.15, but the *recorded* sequence is $1.00, $1.70 and $1.15. The true returns are 10 per cent and 4.5 per cent, but the recorded returns are 70 per cent and −32.4 per cent. The recorded returns are much larger than they should be, and form a price reversal (in this case, an increase followed by a decrease). Price reversals produce negative serial correlation. In short, data errors can produce negative first-order serial correlation when, in fact, none is present.[98]

---

[98] For a detailed mathematical discussion, see S. Taylor, *Modelling Financial Time Series*, John Wiley and Sons, Chichester, 1986, pp. 145–6.

The artificial effects of dividends and capitalisation changes on share prices have to be corrected, but there is no perfect method to do this. Dividends, for example, are usually added into the shareholder's return. Effectively, this assumes that a dividend of $1 is expected to produce a share price decrease of $1. However, in fact the decrease in price is likely to be less than this. One Australian study estimates the decrease to be, on average, only 77 cents per dollar of dividends.[99]

Consider next the effect of a rights issue. As explained in Section 9.5.1, the share price is expected to fall on the ex-rights date. The amount of this fall can be closely approximated using the 'theoretical' rights pricing model given in Section 9.5.1, but an adjustment based on such a model is not likely to be perfect. Therefore there may be small inaccuracies in the data around ex-dividend and ex-rights dates. If these dates tend to cluster on certain days of the week, or in certain months of the year, spurious calendar-based regularities could result. Officer's early study on seasonality suggested that these types of effects may have contributed to the reported seasonal patterns.[100]

Finally, the thin-trading problem means that it is impossible to obtain a set of genuinely *simultaneous* prices for different shares. Accordingly it is not possible to construct a portfolio using simultaneous prices for all the shares in the portfolio. It follows, therefore, that portfolio returns will be measured with error and it can be shown that spurious negative first-order serial correlation can result.[101] It has also been shown that the use of quoted closing prices tends to overstate the returns on small firms because they trade less frequently with wider bid–ask spreads than large firms.[102]

## PROBLEMS WITH ASSET PRICING MODELS

Although the development of modern portfolio theory and the capital asset pricing model contributed significantly to our understanding of asset pricing, it is also true that this level of understanding is still far from perfect. Therefore, empirical studies which produce apparent evidence of market inefficiency may instead produce nothing more than evidence of the researcher's imperfect knowledge of asset pricing. This interpretation is favoured by many researchers, possibly because it does not require any dilution of belief in the virtues of markets, and because it may lead to the development of better models of asset pricing.

First, consider those studies which produce evidence of calendar-based patterns in share returns. These patterns could be interpreted as evidence of inefficiency; that is, by asserting that an efficient market *should* eliminate all patterns, it follows that evidence of patterns counts against market efficiency.

---

[99] P. Brown & T. Walter, 'Ex-dividend Day Behaviour of Australian Share Prices', *Australian Journal of Management*, December 1986, pp. 139–52. Note, however, that this evidence pre-dates the introduction of the imputation system of dividend taxation.

[100] R. Officer, 'Seasonality in Australian Capital Markets: Market Efficiency and Empirical Issues', *Journal of Financial Economics*, January 1975, Footnote 20, p. 51.

[101] M. Scholes & J. Williams, 'Estimating Betas from Non-synchronous Data', *Journal of Financial Economics*, December 1977, pp. 309–27.

[102] M. E. Blume & R. F. Stambaugh, 'Biases in Computed Returns: An Application to the Size Effect', *Journal of Financial Economics*, November 1983, pp. 387–404.

But it is by no means certain that an efficient market should eliminate all patterns. As an aid to understanding, consider the following analogy. The price of turkeys is probably higher in December than in January. Yet few people would suggest that delaying purchase of a turkey until January is an 'arbitrage'. This seasonal pattern in turkey prices does not necessarily mean that the turkey market is inefficient. It could simply mean that consumers of turkeys genuinely value turkeys more highly before Christmas than after Christmas. In the context of asset pricing, if the equilibrium expected return (or opportunity cost of capital) follows a pattern, then so also should observed returns. Patterns do not necessarily imply inefficiency. As an example, Ball and Bowers discuss the possibility that the equilibrium expected return on shares could be different over the weekend because the return on real assets is presumably lower over the weekend when factories are closed.[103]

Secondly, consider those studies which produce evidence of post-announcement drift. After reviewing a number of such studies, Ball concludes that the most likely explanation is that one or more factors have been omitted from the asset pricing models used in the studies.[104] For example, imagine there is some factor X which helps to determine equilibrium returns. Assume that the relationship is positive, so that if X is high (low), the equilibrium return is high (low). However, the X-factor has been omitted from the asset pricing model. Suppose further that the X-factor is positively correlated with earnings, so that shares with high (low) earnings tend also to have high (low) X-factors. A researcher, who does not know of the existence of the X-factor, studies returns following earnings announcements. Naturally the researcher will discover that the high (low) earnings groups produce high (low) returns in the months following the earnings announcement. Clearly it would be wrong (or at least premature) to conclude that the market is inefficient. Of course, similar stories can be invented to deal with other variables which appear to explain returns. Perhaps, for example, dividend yield helps to explain returns because an X-factor has been omitted from the basic version of the asset pricing model used. Liquidity effects and transaction costs might also be considered as variables (or proxies for variables) which have been incorrectly omitted from the asset pricing model.

Thirdly, there has been some limited success in explaining empirical regularities by using different asset pricing models. For example, using arbitrage pricing theory instead of the simpler capital asset pricing model (CAPM), Connor and Korajczyk found they could explain the January/size effect present in US monthly share price data.[105] Alternatively, it may be that the CAPM is an adequate model, but beta varies in systematic ways. If, for example, a share's beta is different on different days of the week, we would *expect* to see a daily pattern

---

103 R. Ball & J. Bowers, 'Daily seasonals in equity and fixed-interest returns: Australian evidence and tests of plausible hypotheses', in E. Dimson (Ed.), *Stock Market Anomalies*, Cambridge University Press, Cambridge, 1988.
104 See Footnote 55. In a later paper, however, Ball is more willing to consider market inefficiency as a likely explanation. See R. Ball, 'The Earnings–price Anomaly', *Journal of Accounting and Economics*, 1992, pp. 319–45.
105 G. Connor & R. Korajczyk, 'Risk and Return in an Equilibrium APT (Application of a New Test Methodology)', *Journal of Financial Economics*, 1988, pp. 255–89.

in share returns. The returns would simply be following the daily variations in beta—as theory would predict—and the observed patterns need not imply inefficiency in the market.

Fourthly, consider the evidence of event studies. Where the timing of an event can be very accurately pinpointed by the researcher—to the hour, or day, for example—the choice of asset pricing model matters very little. No matter how it is modelled, the expected (or normal) return on a one-hour investment is going to be very close to zero. So in these cases the 'joint test' problem is relatively unimportant and the evidence of event studies usually supports market efficiency.

**PROBLEMS WITH MARKETS**

The final interpretation is that markets are, at least to some degree, inefficient. There is no doubt that such an inference can be drawn logically from the evidence, but as discussed earlier, it is not the only possible inference. If it is accepted that markets are inefficient, numerous questions immediately follow. Chief among them is the query: Why? If a market is genuinely inefficient, there is an unexploited profit opportunity. Why would such an opportunity remain unexploited for even a short time? An incomplete list of possible explanations is: institutional constraints; zero marginal utility of wealth; and irrationality. First, the presence of institutional constraints is an argument that investors are aware of the inefficiency, and would like to exploit it, but some external force prevents them from doing so. Ultimately this argument does not really provide an answer because, ideally, such constraints should appear in the asset pricing model. In other words this argument is another variant of the 'problems with the asset pricing model' argument. Secondly, zero marginal utility of wealth is consistent with investors being aware of the inefficiency and able to exploit it, but unwilling to do so. If this is the case, there is too little greed in the world. This seems to us an inherently unlikely prospect. Thirdly, irrationality is, of course, consistent with any behaviour pattern whatsoever. To be accepted as an explanation, the irrationality hypothesis will need to be made testable. For example, restrictions could be developed on the types of irrationality that might be expected. One strand of work has attempted this task by borrowing concepts from social psychology and seeking links between stock market swings and peer pressures, shifts in fashions, fads, and so on.[106]

## 14.8 IMPLICATIONS OF THE EMH

Suppose that, notwithstanding the evidence on anomalies, the stock market is semi-strong-form efficient. Then there are clear implications for investors in securities and for financial managers.

---

[106] For example, R. J. Shiller, 'Stock Prices and Social Dynamics', *Brookings Papers on Economic Activity*, December 1984, pp. 457–510.

### 14.8.1 IMPLICATIONS FOR INVESTORS IN SECURITIES

Notwithstanding the evidence on anomalies, some frequently used techniques to evaluate investments in securities are of doubtful validity. These are discussed in the following subsections 1 to 4. In subsection 5, we offer some comments on trying to beat the market.

### 1. CHARTING, OR TECHNICAL ANALYSIS

Some security analysts plot a share's historical price record on a chart. On the basis of such a chart, predictions are made as to the likely future short-term course of prices. For example, a rising trend may be detected, or perhaps a presumed cycle of peaks and troughs may be predicted to continue. The random-walk evidence suggests that simple short-term repetitive patterns are unlikely to be present. It is possible that more complex patterns are present, but attempts to detect these patterns by judgement and visual inspection are prone to self-delusion. We remain sceptical about the alleged benefits of this type of analysis.[107] Furthermore, although the calendar-based anomalies are of considerable research interest, their implications for short-term investment strategies generally seem to us to be slight.

### 2. FUNDAMENTALS ANALYSIS

Other security analysts believe that the market either ignores some publicly available information, or systematically misinterprets that information. These analysts maintain that sometimes the market is short-sighted and a share price cannot be justified on the basis of the company's 'fundamental' features, such as its earnings record, or its net asset backing, which determine the share's 'true value'. Consequently they believe that a careful analysis of available information may reveal mispriced securities, and therefore excess returns can be made by the skilled fundamentals analyst.

In a market which is efficient in the semi-strong-form sense, all publicly available information is reflected in the market price. Fundamentals are publicly available. On its own, the analysis of such information should not yield excess returns in an efficient market. The evidence on post-announcement drift can be interpreted as a chronic tendency toward underreaction and, on this interpretation, some possibilities to make excess returns could exist.

The evidence that markets have a long-term tendency to overreact, coupled with perhaps a slow but steady elimination of pricing errors, suggests that at present it is possible to defend rationally a claim that an entire stock market may, on average, be overpriced or underpriced at a particular time. If so, this can be used to support the so-called 'top down' investment approach which begins with a broad allocation of investment funds between, say, shares, bonds, and real property. Such an approach is consistent with a claim that, for example,

---

[107] There is at least one exception. Analysts may find the past record of prices useful in trying to assess whether the market has already impounded some private information held by the analyst. See J. L. Treynor & R. Ferguson, 'In Defense of Technical Analysis', *Journal of Finance*, July 1985, pp. 757–73.

the stock market as a whole may be overpriced compared with its longer-term value, even though individual shares within that market may be properly priced *relative to each other*.

## 3. RANDOM SELECTION OF SECURITIES

It is sometimes suggested that acceptance of the EMH implies that investors might as well choose their investments randomly,[108] since the EMH asserts that all securities are 'correctly' priced. It is true that the EMH implies that security prices are 'correct', given the information available. But this does not imply that investors should select their investments randomly. First, returns on a large portfolio of randomly selected securities will be highly correlated with returns on the market portfolio. Therefore, the risk of such a portfolio will be close to the risk of the market portfolio. This may not suit the risk preferences of the investor. Secondly, investors should consider their tax position when selecting investments, which would obviously not be the case if investments were selected randomly.

## 4. BUY-AND-HOLD POLICIES

In similar vein it is sometimes suggested that acceptance of the EMH implies that a buy-and-hold policy is the best investment strategy.[109] It is true that, for many investors, the EMH advises against trying to beat the market, because such an attempt cannot be expected to succeed, and will generate higher transaction costs. However, this does not mean that a buy-and-hold policy is always optimum for all investors. First, as share prices change over time, there will be changes in the proportion of the portfolio that a given shareholding represents. Thus the risk of the portfolio is also likely to have changed. There will be further changes in the portfolio's risk if the risks of individual securities change over time. The result may well be that the portfolio's risk will diverge from the investor's desired risk level. The solution is to rebalance the portfolio and this will usually require the sale of some securities and the purchase of others. An inflexible buy-and-hold policy is not optimum. Secondly, some investors may occasionally come upon private information about a company. It has already been stated that there is evidence suggesting that the market is not efficient in the strong-form sense. Thus there will be private information that is not reflected in prices, and trading on the basis of such information may therefore yield excess returns. The possibility that an investor may discover private information provides a justification for studying public information such as that found in company annual reports. How can private information be identified and evaluated, without some knowledge of the company's characteristics?

## 5. BEATING THE MARKET

In a market which is semi-strong-form efficient, it is not sensible for the average investor to try to beat the market. Obviously, if an investor has private

---

[108] See, for example, L. Bernstein, 'In Defense of Fundamental Investment Analysis', *Financial Analysts Journal*, January–February 1975, pp. 57–61.
[109] See Footnote 108.

information which is not yet reflected in the share price, then beating the market becomes a distinct possibility. But average investors do not often have such information. This suggests that most investors, most of the time, would do well to follow a passive investment approach. By this we mean that most investors should adopt a long-term view, hold a diversified portfolio and trade infrequently. In our view, this remains sound advice. If there are individuals (other than insiders) who can genuinely beat the market, we expect them to be few in number, and we would be surprised if their success could be replicated using simple tools of charting or 'fundamentals' analysis. We would be even more surprised if such individuals were willing to donate any of the rewards to the average investor.

### 14.8.2 IMPLICATIONS FOR FINANCIAL MANAGERS

If the share market can be considered efficient in the semi-strong-form sense, there are significant implications for financial managers. Some of them are considered in the following subsections 1 to 4.[110] In subsection 5, we offer some comments on the significance for financial managers of the anomalies evidence.

### 1. PROJECT SELECTION

If the share market is efficient, a company's share price will reflect all available information concerning the company. This means that the share market will respond instantaneously and without bias to information, including information that is released by company management. If investing in a project really does increase the company's 'true value', the company's share price will reflect this fact when the information becomes available to the market.

### 2. COMMUNICATING WITH THE STOCK MARKET

In an efficient market, prices respond quickly to information, including information released by company management. However, the market's reactions will not be unthinking, mechanical responses, since such responses would be identifiable as underreactions or overreactions. Managers must therefore expect that announcements of factors such as profit, dividends, takeovers, new security issues, and capital reconstructions will elicit a price response that represents the market's collective view of the true situation.[111]

---

[110] The issues raised in these four subsections are similar to some of those identified in S. M. Keane, *Stock Market Efficiency: Theory, Evidence and Implications*, Philip Allan, Oxford, 1983, Ch. 8; and in M. C. Jensen & C. W. Smith, 'The theory of corporate finance', in their volume of readings, *The Modern Theory of Corporate Finance*, McGraw-Hill, New York, 1984.

[111] For further discussion, see G. B. Steward & D. M. Glassman, 'How to Communicate with an Efficient Market', *Midland Corporate Finance Journal*, Spring 1984, pp. 73–79 and P. Healy & K. Palepu, 'How investors interpret changes in corporate financial policy' in J. M. Stern & D. H. Chew (Eds), *The Revolution in Corporate Finance*, 2nd edn, Basil Blackwell, Oxford, 1992, pp. 33–8.

## 3. USING SHARE PRICE AS A MEASURE OF COMPANY PERFORMANCE

In an efficient market, the current share price is the best available estimate of a company's 'true value'. The historical share price record (taking into account the effects of dividends and changes in capital) will be an accurate statement of the record of the company's performance. This is not to say that the company's management is entirely responsible for this record, but presumably it must bear significant responsibility for it.

## 4. ISSUING NEW SECURITIES

If markets are efficient, there are a number of implications for companies intending to issue new securities. These implications affect decisions on the pricing of the security and the timing of the issue.

### (a) Pricing the security

If the market is efficient, securities are 'correctly' priced, given the available information. If the market is inefficient, it is quite likely that a company's shares will be underpriced. In that case, issuing new shares at the market price would be against the interests of existing shareholders because the new shareholders would obtain a stake in the company for less than the true value of that stake. If the market is efficient, and new shareholders are charged the market price, the wealth of existing shareholders is not affected.[112]

### (b) The timing of new issues

It is sometimes proposed that financial managers should take account of existing market conditions when seeking new capital. For example, the fact that a company's share price is at an historical low may be seen as a reason to avoid issuing new shares. Implicitly, this assumes that because a share price is low compared to its past level, it is also likely to be low compared to its future level. That is, it assumes there is a pattern in share prices such that it is possible to identify from publicly available information shares that are currently underpriced. This is inconsistent with the EMH, which suggests that shares will be correctly priced given the current, publicly available information.

The timing of a particular issue is a concern if a company's financial manager has some private information suggesting that the company's shares are mispriced. For example, the manager may have information that suggests that the shares are underpriced. One possibility is to make the information publicly available so that the share price will increase immediately. The new shares can then be issued at the higher price. Clearly, this benefits the current shareholders. Alternatively, the manager may have information suggesting that the shares are overpriced. In this case, there is an incentive to issue shares before the information becomes public knowledge; of course, the market will be aware that this

---

[112] However, the proportionate ownership of each existing shareholder will fall if the shares are sold to outsiders. This could harm existing shareholders and would therefore be a legitimate concern.

incentive exists, and may therefore respond negatively to the announcement of a new share issue, particularly where the market believes that it is relatively poorly informed.[113]

## 5. THE FINANCIAL MANAGER AND THE EVIDENCE ON ANOMALIES

To what extent does the evidence on anomalies require modification of these implications of efficiency for the financial manager? We believe that, at least until further research has clarified the issues, these implications provide a valid guide to financial managers. Whether this belief is correct will ultimately require a personal value judgement, but we offer several reasons for this view.

First, it is clear that markets can be expected to respond positively to good news and negatively to bad news. Therefore, news of successful operations and of wise decisions by management are still expected to increase share prices, while news of losses, mistakes and failure will decrease share prices. The performance of companies and, implicitly, the performance of management, is still ultimately to be judged by the stock market.

Secondly, until there is greater understanding of the causes of anomalies, and of when and how the stock market corrects inefficiencies, there will often be few alternatives to behaving as if the stock market is efficient. For example, if the financial manager of a small company interprets the evidence on the size effect to mean that the company may be undervalued, it is difficult to see exactly how this should guide his or her actions unless there is also some knowledge of what causes the underpricing and of when the underpricing may be expected to cease. If the manager decides not to raise new capital by way of a share issue, is a debt issue necessarily a superior choice? What if debt issued by small companies is even more underpriced than shares issued by small companies?

Thirdly, many of the anomalies are not important so much for their size or practical significance, as for the fact that they appear to be there at all. For example, they may not of themselves have a great capacity to generate excess returns for an investor, but they may give a greater insight into asset pricing, thereby indirectly leading to the development of better pricing models.

Fourthly, it should always be remembered that efficiency tests are joint tests of the assumed asset pricing model and of the efficiency of the market. Most of the asset pricing models that have been used are quite simple and it would not be surprising to learn that they do not work well when applied to 'extreme' cases such as the smallest companies and the first few hours or days of trading for the year.

Fifthly, the idea of an efficient market was only ever intended to be a model of the behaviour of real markets. In pushing the efficient markets model toward, and perhaps beyond, the point at which its validity is impaired, it is easy to forget that 'models are to be used, but not to be believed'.[114] In other words, as

---

113 See T. A. Manuel, L. D. Brooks & F. P. Schadler, 'Common Stock Price Effects of Security Issues Conditioned by Current Earnings and Dividend Announcements', *Journal of Business*, October 1993, pp. 571–93.
114 Henri Theil, quoted in T. H. Wonnacott & R. J. Wonnacott, *Introductory Statistics for Business and Economics*, 2nd edn, John Wiley and Sons, New York, 1977, p. 331.

with asset pricing models, it may be that the model of market efficiency does not work as well in 'extreme' circumstances as it does in more usual circumstances. This does not mean that ordinary investors and financial managers operating in ordinary circumstances should ignore the lessons of an efficient market.

## SELECTED REFERENCES

Ball, R., Brown, P., Finn, F. J., & Officer, R. R., (Eds), *Share Markets and Portfolio Theory*, 2nd edn, University of Queensland Press, St Lucia, 1989.
Cochrane, J. H., 'Volatility Tests and Efficient Markets: A Review Essay', *Journal of Monetary Economics*, 1991, pp. 463–85.
De Bondt, W. F. M., & Thaler, R. H., 'A Mean Reverting Walk Down Wall Street', *Journal of Economic Perspectives*, Winter 1989, pp. 189–202.
Dimson, E., (Ed.), *Stock Market Anomalies*, Cambridge University Press, Cambridge, 1988.
Faff, R. W., 'Capital Market Anomalies: A Survey of the Evidence', *Accounting Research Journal*, Spring 1992, pp. 3–22.
Fama, E., 'Efficient Capital Markets: A Review of Theory and Empirical Work', *Journal of Finance*, May 1970, pp. 383–417.
Fama, E., 'Efficient Capital Markets: II', *Journal of Finance*, December 1991, pp. 1575–1617.
Keane, S. M., *Stock Market Efficiency: Theory, Evidence and Implications*, Philip Allan, Oxford, 1983.

## QUESTIONS

1. What is an 'efficient capital market'? Illustrate your answer with an example.
2. *The EMH implies that all financial assets are always correctly priced. Is this statement correct? Give reasons.*
3. What would cause a capital market to be efficient?
4. What is meant by 'weak-form', 'semi-strong-form' and 'strong-form' market efficiency?
5. Outline the empirical tests of weak-form efficiency. Outline the empirical evidence on weak-form efficiency.
6. Design an empirical test of the effect of companies' dividend announcements on security prices. What are some of the problems in constructing a valid test?
7. Outline the empirical evidence on semi-strong-form efficiency.
8. *As it is impossible to determine when private information becomes available, it is impossible to construct a test of strong-form market efficiency. Discuss.*
9. *Empirical evidence suggests that professional investment managers do not earn positive abnormal returns. Discuss the implications of this evidence, especially as it relates to strong-form market efficiency.*
10. What are the implications of the empirical evidence on market efficiency for:
    (a) technical analysis?
    (b) fundamentals analysis?
11. Assuming that you have $0.5 million to invest, how would you structure your investment?
12. Outline the importance of market efficiency for the assumed objective of maximising the market value of a company's equity.
13. *If capital markets are efficient, it makes no difference which securities a company issues. Discuss.*

14. Interpret the following statements in terms of their implications for the various classifications of market efficiency.
    (a) Shares in risky companies give higher returns than shares in safe companies.
    (b) The shares in a company increase in price in the period before that in which a takeover bid is announced for the company.
    (c) Tax-exempt government bonds are issued at lower interest rates than taxable government bonds.
    (d) Company directors tend to make profits from investments in the shares of companies with which they are associated.
    (e) There is evidence that share prices follow a trend.
15. What are the implications of the evidence on market efficiency for those who support greater regulation of corporate disclosure?
16. *The significance of calendar-based anomalies lies not so much in their size as in the fact that they exist at all.* Discuss.
17. Suppose that Esther McDonald has undertaken a study of the efficiency of the stock market's reaction to the announcement of changes in steel prices. Specifically, she finds that share prices appear to continue reacting for some months after the announcement. Advise Esther on the alternative interpretations her study might be given.

# CHAPTER 15

# FUTURES CONTRACTS

## 15.1 INTRODUCTION

A futures contract is an agreement which provides that something will be sold in the future at a fixed price. In short, the price is decided today, but the transaction is to occur later. Such contracts are traded on various futures exchanges around the world. The largest and most famous futures exchanges are in Chicago but there are also exchanges in many other cities including New York, London, Paris, Singapore, Tokyo, Osaka and Sydney. Much of the material in this chapter relates to futures contracts traded on the Sydney Futures Exchange, although the principles discussed also have application to contracts traded on other futures exchanges.

Trading in futures contracts on a formally organised exchange can be traced back to the middle of last century, when the Chicago Board of Trade introduced a futures contract on corn.[1] Such a contract enables farmers to sell their corn 'in advance' and the farmer therefore knows the price he will receive for his crop before it is harvested and sold. In Australia, the first futures contract was one on greasy wool and was introduced in 1960. Until the early 1970s, virtually all futures contracts traded on the various exchanges around the world were futures contracts on commodities. In 1972, the world's first futures contract on a foreign currency was traded, followed in 1975 by the first futures contract on a debt instrument. In 1982, trading began in a futures contract on an index of stock market prices. Australia did not lag far behind, introducing futures on a debt instrument in 1979, on foreign currency in 1980, and on a share price index in 1983. These **financial futures**, as they are called, have grown very rapidly in importance and nearly all trading on the Sydney Futures Exchange is now in financial futures rather than commodity futures. In this chapter, we focus on

---

[1] For a detailed history, see J. W. Markham, *The History of Commodity Futures Trading and its Regulation*, Praeger, New York, 1987.

financial futures, and, in particular, on the opportunities they provide for financial managers. However, because they are often more readily understood, we use commodity futures to illustrate some of the principles.

Futures contracts can be used for hedging purposes and speculative purposes. **Hedgers** wish to lock in, today, the price of the 'commodity' in which they will need to deal in the future, so that they are not affected by any future changes in the market price of the commodity. For example, a farmer (or a flour miller) could wish to fix, in advance, the price to be received (or paid) for wheat. Similarly, a company planning to lend (or borrow) could wish to fix, in advance, the interest rate to be received (or paid). The goal of the hedger is to control risk and this goal can be at least partly achieved by appropriate trading in a relevant futures contract. **Speculators** have no wish to deal in the 'commodity' itself, but are willing to trade in futures contracts in the hope of profiting from correctly anticipating movements in the futures price. The motive of the speculator is to profit through bearing risks that others do not wish to bear. Successful speculation can be extremely profitable. Of course, unsuccessful speculation can be extremely expensive.

## 15.2 WHAT IS A FUTURES CONTRACT?

### 15.2.1 FORWARD CONTRACTS AND FUTURES CONTRACTS

**Forward contracts** predate **futures contracts** by centuries, but are still common, particularly in foreign exchange.[2] Futures contracts developed out of forward contracts, so we begin by considering a *forward* contract on a commodity. Suppose that I own an ounce of gold which today (1 March) is worth $600. However, I plan to sell my gold some time in the near future. Suppose further that you know (today) that on 1 April you will need to buy an ounce of gold to use in your jewellery-making business. We might therefore agree today to the following contract: on 1 April, I will deliver one ounce of gold to you at your premises and you will pay me, on that date, $610. This is a 1-month forward contract on gold. It has the following features:

1. The forward price ($610) is decided now (1 March) but the transaction is to occur on a nominated future date (1 April).
2. The details of the commodity which is the subject of the contract are spelt out (in this case, one ounce of gold to be delivered to your premises).
3. The contract is a private contract between you and me. I cannot pass on to anyone else my responsibility to deliver an ounce of gold in 1 month's time and likewise you cannot pass on to anyone else your responsibility to accept delivery of the gold and to pay $610 for it.

A *futures* contract on gold will also have features 1 and 2 in this list. That is, the price will be decided now for a transaction to occur at a later date in a commodity (or other item) which has been carefully defined. However, feature 3 is *not* true of a futures contract. A futures contract is not a personalised

---

[2] Forward contracts on foreign currency are discussed in more detail in Chapter 21.

agreement. Futures contracts are always agreed to through an exchange and, most importantly, can be discontinued ('closed out' or 'reversed') at any time through a further transaction on the exchange. Exactly how this is done is explained later. At this stage, the important point to note is that a futures contract is like a forward contract which can be traded on an exchange.[3]

## 15.2.2 How a futures market is organised

Before turning to a description of how the Sydney Futures Exchange is organised, the important points are explained in the mythical example of the Deakin Futures Exchange described here. In other words, the following is a simplified discussion of how futures markets operate.

Suppose that the Deakin Futures Exchange is offering, for the first time, futures contracts on gold. The contract document defines the amount and purity of the gold, who is qualified to certify its purity, the place where it is to be delivered, and other such details. There may be several different contracts, each specifying a different maturity date. Of course, the one important feature *not* specified by the exchange is the futures price. This is determined by market forces. Consider the Deakin gold futures contract which requires that one ounce of gold be delivered on 1 April (today being 1 March). On 1 March, a person named B1 enters the Exchange and offers to buy one ounce of gold for $610 on 1 April. In other words, B1 has offered to enter into one Deakin April gold futures contract to buy at a price of $610. Another person, named S1, is at the Exchange and is willing to enter into one April gold futures contract to sell at a price of $610. Therefore, B1 and S1 agree, and the April gold futures price at the Deakin Futures Exchange is currently $610.

The next step in the procedure is crucial to an understanding of futures markets. A company, Deakin Clearing House Ltd, now interposes itself between B1 and S1. That is, the agreement between B1 and S1 becomes two contracts which, for convenience, we will call *contract 1a* and *contract 1b*.[4] These contracts are as follows.

*Contract 1a* is between B1 and the Clearing House. Under this contract, B1 agrees to pay the Clearing House $610 on 1 April and the Clearing House agrees to deliver one ounce of gold to B1 on 1 April. In short, the Clearing House plays the role of seller in B1's contract to buy.

*Contract 1b* is a contract between S1 and the Clearing House. Under this contract, the Clearing House agrees to pay S1 $610 on 1 April and S1 agrees to

---

[3] For a detailed comparison, and for empirical evidence on price differences between futures and forwards, see J. Cox, J. Ingersoll & S. Ross, 'The Relation Between Forward Prices and Futures Prices', *Journal of Financial Economics*, December 1981, pp. 321–46; B. Cornell & M. Reinganum, 'Forward and Futures Prices: Evidence from the Foreign Exchange Markets', *Journal of Finance*, December 1981, pp. 1035–45, and K. R. French, 'A Comparison of Futures and Forward Prices', *Journal of Financial Economics*, November 1983, pp. 311–42.

[4] This is the easiest way to visualise what occurs. For a detailed description of the strict legal position, see M. Markovic, 'The Legal Status of Futures Market Participants in Australia', *Company and Securities Law Journal*, April 1989, pp. 82–100.

deliver one ounce of gold to the Clearing House on 1 April. In short, the Clearing House plays the role of buyer in S1's contract to sell.

There is no longer any agreement or contract between B1 and S1. Indeed, B1 and S1 need not even know each other's identity. Instead, B1 looks to the Clearing House to deliver the gold and S1 looks to the Clearing House to pay the agreed price. Note that, provided the Clearing House has faith in the financial strength and honesty of B1 and S1, it is in a riskless position. It 'owes' $610 to S1, but is 'owed' $610 by B1. It 'owes' one ounce of gold to B1 but is 'owed' one ounce of gold by S1. The net position of the Clearing House is therefore zero in both money and gold.

A few minutes after B1 and S1 agree on a futures price of $610, a new buyer, B2, and a new seller, S2, meet in the exchange and a new price of, say, $611 is established. The Clearing House follows the same procedure, creating two new contracts, 2a and 2b. It becomes the seller to B2 (*contract 2a*) and the buyer for S2 (*contract 2b*). The net position of the Clearing House is still zero.

New buyers and sellers come and go all day at the Deakin Futures Exchange. If, at the close of business on 1 March, 37 April gold futures contracts have been bought and sold, Deakin Clearing House has 74 obligations: 37 to buy and 37 to sell, with, as always, a net position of zero. During the day, prices have responded to market forces and have ranged between, say, $608 and $615, closing at $614.

As time passes, more contracts are bought and sold. Now suppose that, on 8 March, B1 observes that the then current price for April gold futures is $620. Recall that under the terms of contract 1a, B1 will be entitled to buy gold at $610 per ounce. Sellers are at present entering futures contracts to sell at $620. Therefore, on current indications, B1 has a 'paper' profit of $10. With a futures contract, B1 is able to realise this profit, and, having done so, will be free of all further obligations. The mechanism by which this is achieved is as follows. On 8 March, B1 enters the futures exchange *as a seller*. For example, B1 may become S200, the seller in the 200th April contract traded. In the exchange, S200 and B200 agree on a price of, say, $620. The Clearing House becomes a seller to B200 (*contract 200a*) and a buyer for S200 (*contract 200b*). Therefore, on 8 March, B1's financial position may be summarised as follows:

| | | |
|---|---|---|
| B1 owes the Clearing House | $610 | (*contract 1a*) |
| B1 (who is also S200) is owed by the Clearing House | $620 | (*contract 200b*) |
| Therefore, the Clearing House owes B1 | $ 10 | |

In effect, B1 is able to offset his original contract as a buyer by entering another contract as a seller, taking the profit (or loss) which results. It is this offsetting procedure that permits futures traders to 'close out' (or 'reverse') their contracts before the maturity date. The procedure is feasible only because the two contracts are *identical* (except for the price) and both are with the *same* party, namely the Clearing House. For example, the first April gold contract is the same as the 200th April gold contract, except for the price. There would be little point in the Clearing House delivering the gold to B1 to fulfil the terms of contract 1a, only to have B1 (in his role as S200) re-deliver the same gold to the Clearing House a moment later to fulfil the terms of contract 200b. Instead, B1 is released of all obligations and keeps the $10 profit.

Note the following five points about this procedure:

1. Because the Clearing House becomes the counterparty in every contract, it is not necessary for buyers and sellers to know the identity or creditworthiness of the other buyers and sellers. For example, it is not necessary for B200 to know that S200 is, in fact, an existing buyer (that is, that S200 is also B1) who wants to sell in order to reverse his existing bought position. Similarly, as B200's contract is with the Clearing House, it is not necessary for B200 to know the identity of S200.
2. However, it is necessary for S200 to inform the Clearing House that he (S200) is in fact the same person as B1. Otherwise, instead of the offsetting procedure described earlier, B1 will find that he has *two* ongoing contracts: as the buyer in contract 1a and as the seller in contract 200b. Both will run through to 1 April and then be settled.
3. Even though the contract was not due to be settled until 1 April, B1 has in fact ended his involvement on 8 March. Moreover, no gold was ever delivered to, or by, B1. *No gold changed hands*. This is usual in futures markets. Generally speaking, only about 2 per cent of contracts end in delivery of the 'commodity', the other 98 per cent being closed out by the offsetting procedure.[5]
4. Existing sellers can also reverse out of their positions. For example, B200 could in fact be a former seller (S57 say) seeking to offset his existing sold position with a bought position. In this way, a seller in a futures contract can sell first and buy later and at no time is it necessary for the seller to *own* the item which is the subject of the futures contract. Selling first and buying later is referred to as **short selling** and the ability to short sell is essential for the smooth functioning of futures markets.
5. Each day, the financial press reports the 'volume' of futures contracts traded the previous day, as well as the number of 'open positions'. These terms are often misunderstood, so it is worth explaining their meanings. The 'volume traded' refers to the number of contracts that have been agreed to over a particular period, such as during the previous day. Therefore, volume is a 'flow' concept; it is something measured over an interval of time. The number of 'open positions' is the number of contracts still in force (that is, which are yet to be closed out) at a certain time, such as at the close of business on the previous day. The number of open positions is a 'stock' concept; it is something measured as at a particular point in time. Both measures indicate the level of interest in the contract and the ease with which a trading partner can be found.

The foregoing description of how a futures market functions is much simpler than the reality. For example, in real futures exchanges, ordinary traders are

---

5 K. Jameson & L. Howard, 'The futures markets', in *Handbook of Australian Corporate Finance*, Eds R. Bruce et al., 4th edn, Butterworths, Sydney, 1991, p. 410.

permitted to trade only through brokers. However, this is not central to an understanding of how futures exchanges operate. Of the many other differences between real futures exchanges and the mythical Deakin Futures Exchange, two in particular stand out:
1. Deakin has no system of deposits and margins;
2. Deakin has no mark-to-market rule.

In reality, futures exchanges always have Feature 1 and usually have Feature 2. These two features are explained in the next section.

### 15.2.3 DEPOSITS, MARGINS AND THE MARK-TO-MARKET RULE

In the example in Section 15.2.2, the futures trader B1 made a profit of $10 because the futures price rose by $10 between 1 March and 8 March. Where does the $10 come from? The answer lies in the system of deposits, margins, and the mark-to-market rule.

The Clearing House requires all traders to deposit a certain sum of money with the Clearing House *before* they enter into their first contract. Each intending trader is required to have an account and the first entry in the account is the deposit paid by the intending trader. At the close of each trading day the Clearing House calculates whether the trader has gained or lost since the close of the previous trading day. If a gain has been made, the Clearing House adds the gain to the trader's account balance. If a loss has been made, the Clearing House subtracts the loss from the trader's account balance. This process is called **marking-to-market** because each day the trader's financial position is 'marked' (that is, adjusted) according to the change in the 'market' (that is, the movement in the market price of that futures contract since the previous marking date).[6]

The deposit system just described does not protect the Clearing House if the following situation arises. Suppose that a trader has sold a futures contract and subsequently the futures price has increased steadily. Each day, the trader's account is marked to market. Because the trader is steadily making losses, the deposit is being steadily eroded. If this continues long enough the deposit will vanish and the Clearing House will be in the unhappy position of having to trust the trader to make good any further losses. The same situation could also arise if a trader bought a futures contract and the price subsequently fell significantly.

To protect itself against this situation, a clearing house will have a system of 'margin calls'. For example, the Deakin Clearing House could require that further funds be deposited whenever a trader's account balance is eroded by, say, 25 per cent. That is, if the balance of the account falls below an amount equal to 75 per cent of the required initial deposit, the trader is required to bring the account balance back up to the amount of the initial deposit. The demand that extra funds be deposited is known as a **margin call**. If a trader does not respond to a margin call within, say, two days, the Clearing House will close out the trader's position. The Clearing House faces a slight risk in this case. If

---

[6] There is an obvious exception. Logically, a newly opened position should be adjusted by the difference between the agreed price and the price at the close of trading. Thereafter, the daily adjustment is as described in the text.

the futures price should move very quickly during the two-day response period, the loss sustained by the trader could exceed the remaining funds in the trader's account. The Clearing House is then just an unsecured creditor of the trader.

### 15.2.4 THE PRESENT VALUE OF A FUTURES CONTRACT

A futures contract does not require a payment on initiation so it is clear that the present value of a futures contract must be zero.[7] In other words, the futures price is the price at which both buyer and seller are willing to agree to the terms of the contract, with neither party seeking any immediate payment from the other. For example, if the current futures price is thought to be too low, a prospective buyer would, if necessary, be willing to pay a potential seller to agree to the futures contract at the current futures price. The present value of such a contract would not be zero. However, this is not the way a futures market behaves when the current futures price is thought to be too low. Instead of paying money *today*, buyers bid up the *futures* price until a seller is induced (for zero payment today) to agree to the futures contract at the higher price. Therefore, the present value of the futures contract would again be zero. Accordingly, it is, in a sense, impossible to calculate a rate of return on a futures contract. If the outlay is zero, any subsequent gain is an infinite *percentage* gain and any subsequent loss is an infinite *percentage* loss. In practice, some traders calculate percentage returns relative to the deposit required, but there is no particularly compelling reason to do so.

## 15.3 THE SYDNEY FUTURES EXCHANGE

The Sydney Futures Exchange (SFE) opened for trading in 1960, although it was then known as the Sydney Greasy Wool Futures Exchange.[8] The SFE is a company with three classes of membership of which the most significant is **floor membership**. As the name implies, the floor members are permitted to be on the trading floor of the exchange and can trade on behalf of clients, charging brokerage fees for their services. These fees are negotiable between the floor member and client. Other classes of membership are limited in one way or another, compared with the floor members.

The exchange offered only wool futures contracts until 1979 when a contract on cattle was introduced. A major shift occurred in October 1979 when the exchange introduced a contract on 90-day bank accepted bills (known as 'BABs' for short). This contract has been extremely successful and now trades in large volumes. More than six million such contracts were traded on the SFE in 1993.

The shift away from agricultural commodities towards 'financial commodities' proved to be very important. It introduced to futures trading a wide range of users who had little or no interest in agricultural commodities. These users

---

[7] Recall that the deposit is not the value of the contract; it simply provides a guarantee that the trader's obligations will be met.
[8] For a detailed history, see E. Carew, *Fast Forward: The History of the Sydney Futures Exchange*, Allen & Unwin, St Leonards, 1993.

include banks, merchant banks, building societies, finance companies, and industrial companies. In fact, any party planning to borrow or lend significant sums of money for relatively short periods could find a BAB futures contract useful. In retrospect, it is clear that the introduction of the BAB contract was the first step along the path which led to the SFE being transformed from a market serving mainly rural interests to a market that plays a substantial role in the finance industry. Other financial futures that have proved successful are the All-Ordinaries Share Price Index contract (the 'SPI contract' for short) introduced in 1983, the 10-Year Treasury Bond contract introduced in 1984, and the 3-Year Treasury Bond contract introduced in 1988. The volume of trading in these three contracts totalled more than 12 million in 1993. These financial futures are discussed in detail later in the chapter.

Australia's first option-on-futures contract was introduced at the SFE in 1982. A **call option on futures** gives the option buyer the right (but not the obligation) to assume a bought position in the futures contract. Similarly, a **put option on futures** gives the option buyer the right (but not the obligation) to assume a sold position in the futures contract. Options are currently available only for financial futures contracts and have proved popular with traders.[9]

The SFE operates its own clearing house. The major functions of the clearing house are:
1. to establish and collect deposits;
2. to call in margins as required;
3. to apportion the gains and losses (mark-to-market rule).

The clearing house varies minimum contract deposits, depending on market conditions. For example, the greater the price volatility, the greater is the risk, and therefore the greater the deposit required. To give an indication of the typical sums involved, some of the standard deposits required of members as at 10 January 1994 were as shown in Table 15.1.[10]

**Table 15.1** *Major Sydney Futures Exchange contracts: January 1994*

| Contract type | Deposit per contract ($) | Approximate value underlying one contract ($) |
| --- | --- | --- |
| 90-day BABs | 350 | 493 000 |
| 3-Year Treasury Bonds | 800 | 117 000 |
| 10-Year Treasury Bonds | 2500 | 114 000 |
| All Ordinaries SPI | 2000 | 56 000 |

In addition to operating its trading floor, the SFE has, since 1989, also operated SYCOM—the Sydney Computerised Overnight Market, an automated screen-dealing system. Trades during the day (from 8.30 a.m. to 4.30 p.m. for

---

9 In 1993, more than two million SFE option contracts were traded. These contracts are in fact option contracts, rather than futures contracts. These and other option contracts are discussed in Chapter 16.
10 The members, in turn, require their clients to lodge deposits.

most contracts) are made on the trading floor. From 4.40 p.m. to 6.00 a.m. trades are made through SYCOM. In 1993, SYCOM accounted for about 5 per cent of SFE volume.

## 15.4 DETERMINANTS OF FUTURES PRICES

So far we have not tried to explain (or model) futures prices. It has simply been stated that the futures price is determined by market forces. From a management viewpoint, there is much to recommend this approach. Managers trade in futures contracts in order to control risk, and the only way to undertake the necessary transactions is to agree to buy (or sell) at the futures price determined by the market. Whether this market price does or does not accord with some model of futures pricing is, on this view, largely irrelevant.

Nevertheless, it is beneficial to have some understanding of the determinants of futures prices. A useful insight into some of the forces underlying futures pricing is provided by the following theorem:

> The futures price for a late-delivery contract must be less than (or equal to) the futures price for an equivalent early-delivery contract, plus the carrying cost.

The **carrying cost** is the cost of holding a commodity from one time period to another. It includes an interest factor (opportunity cost of funds used to finance the holding of the commodity) and in the case of physical commodities, the costs of insurance and storage. The logic underlying the theorem can readily be seen in the following example.

### Example 15.1

The January gold futures price is $650 per ounce and the February gold futures price is $660 per ounce. Assume that the carrying cost for gold is $7 per ounce per month, payable at the end of the month. A trader could exploit these prices by buying a January contract and selling a February contract. When the January maturity date arrives, the trader accepts delivery of the gold and pays the agreed price of $650. The trader then stores the gold for 1 month. In February, the trader delivers (sells) the gold at the agreed price of $660 and pays the carrying cost of $7, giving a net cash inflow of $653 in February. The resulting profit of $3 is a 'pure' profit (that is, in excess of the opportunity cost) since the $7 carrying cost covers the opportunity cost of holding gold. Of course other traders will undertake similar activities and will continue to do so until the gap between the January and February futures prices is $7 or less. For example, the market may set a January futures price of $651 and a February futures price of $657. At this point the price of the late-delivery contract ($657) is less than or equal to the price of the early-delivery contract ($651), plus the carrying cost ($7). This is the result stated in the theorem.

A limiting case of this theorem is of special significance. In the limit, the early-delivery contract could be for immediate delivery; in other words, its term to maturity could be zero. The **spot price** is the price paid in a standard commodity purchase; that is, it is the price of the commodity when the buyer pays immediately and the seller delivers immediately. Therefore, to prevent arbitrage, the spot price should be very close to the price of a futures contract which has a term to maturity of zero. Substituting 'the spot price' for 'the futures price for an equivalent early-delivery contract', the theorem becomes:

> A futures price must be less than (or equal to) the current spot price plus the carrying cost.

In this way, the theorem provides a maximum price for the futures contract, given the current spot price and the carrying cost. Algebraically, it can be written as:

$$F \leq S + C \tag{15.1}$$

where $F$ = futures price
$S$ = current spot price
$C$ = carrying cost

We now put futures contracts briefly to one side and direct our attention to the market in the commodity itself. Suppose that the current spot price of gold is $650 per ounce and that, taking into account the expected output of gold mines, the forecast demand for jewellery, the political situation in South Africa (a gold-producing country), and, in principle, any other factor thought to be relevant, a trader forecasts that in 1 month's time, the spot price of gold will be at least equal to today's spot price ($650) and possibly much more. In other words, it is forecast that the spot price of gold will increase. Assume, for example, that the price is forecast to be $680 per ounce in 1 month's time. In this case, it is predicted that a trader could buy gold, hold it for 1 month and then sell it for $680. Net of the carrying cost of $7, the predicted profit is $23. Is this large enough to induce a trader to adopt this strategy? Perhaps so; perhaps not. Unlike the investment strategy underlying the theorem, this is a risky proposition and perhaps $23 is not enough to compensate for the risk involved. However, there will clearly be some level of predicted profit from holding gold which will induce gold purchases; that is, gold will be purchased if:

$$S + C + \text{risk factor} < E(S) \tag{15.2}$$

where $S$ = current spot price
$C$ = carrying cost
$E(S)$ = expected future spot price

Gold will be bought, and the spot price will increase, until Equation 15.2 no longer holds; that is, until:

$$E(S) \leq S + C + \text{risk factor} \tag{15.3}$$

Equation 15.3 therefore provides the maximum value that the expected spot price, $E(S)$, can be, given the current spot price, the carrying cost, and a risk factor. Similarly Equation 15.1 provides the maximum value that the futures price $F$ can be, given the current spot price and the carrying cost.

Finally, can $F$ and $E(S)$ be linked? Suppose, for example, that $F$ was $651 and $E(S)$ was $680. It is likely that, in the hope of profit, someone would be willing to buy a futures contract, possibly with the intention of accepting delivery on the maturity date and then immediately reselling the gold. Again, this is a risky strategy, but a forecast profit of $29 may be enough to induce someone to try it. In fact, there is a group of analysts who believe that futures prices and expected spot prices are very closely related.

This traditional theory can be adapted to financial futures. One way in which this might be done is discussed briefly in Section 15.9. As both a prelude to this discussion, and as a topic of considerable importance in its own right, we first discuss in some detail how futures contracts (especially financial futures contracts) can be used.

## 15.5 FUTURES MARKET STRATEGIES: SPECULATING AND HEDGING

### 15.5.1 INTRODUCTION

Traditionally, participants in futures markets have been divided into two groups: speculators and hedgers.[11] A **speculator** in this context is someone who has traded in a futures contract but who has no direct interest in the 'commodity' underlying the futures contract. For example, if someone trades a gold futures contract but owns no gold and does not intend to buy any, the futures market transaction is purely speculative. A **hedger** is someone who has traded in a futures contract and has a 'genuine' interest in the 'commodity' underlying the futures contract. For example, if a jewellery manufacturer trades a futures contract on gold, the futures market transaction provides a hedge against changes in gold prices.

In short, the distinction between a speculator and a hedger in futures contracts is simply this: a speculator is affected by the futures price (but not the spot price) of the 'commodity', whereas a hedger is affected by *both* the futures price and the spot price of the 'commodity'. By trading in futures contracts the speculator is exposed to the risks of changes in the futures price; this is a risk to which he would not otherwise have been exposed. By trading in futures contracts, the hedger, too, is exposed to the same risks of changes in the futures price but only in an attempt to offset the pre-existing risk of changes in the 'commodity' price itself. The speculator uses futures contracts to increase his exposure to risk, whereas the hedger uses futures contracts to decrease his exposure to risk.

There is a large body of theory (and evidence) relating to speculators and hedgers and to the various influences that have a bearing on spot prices and futures prices. Much of this theory was developed in the context of futures contracts on physical commodities, and, as a result, not all of it is relevant to financial futures. In particular, there is a substantial literature which focuses on such issues as inventories, insurance, storage costs, and production seasonalities, but as these issues are of limited relevance to financial futures, this material will not

---

11 A third group, arbitrageurs, can also be distinguished. An 'arbitrage' is a set of simultaneous transactions in different markets that guarantees a risk-free profit. The transactions in Example 15.1 were an arbitrage involving futures prices, spot prices, and carrying costs. Arbitrage is discussed further in Sections 15.6.3 and 15.9.

be presented.[12] However, the basic features of speculating and hedging are applicable to both types of futures contracts. For ease of exposition we continue to use futures on physical commodities to establish the principles. Detailed applications to financial futures are provided in Sections 15.6, 15.7 and 15.8.

## 15.5.2 SPECULATING

In the simplest case, a speculator hopes to:
1. take a long position (that is, buy) when the futures price is 'low', reversing out (that is, selling later) when the futures price has increased; *and/or*
2. take a short position (that is, sell) when the futures price is 'high', reversing out (that is, buying later) when the futures price has decreased.

In either case, the speculator gains. Of course, if the opposite occurs, the speculator loses. This is shown in Table 15.2.

**Table 15.2**  *Basic speculation outcomes*

| | If futures prices subsequently: | |
|---|---|---|
| If futures contract is held | increase | decrease |
| Long | gain | loss |
| Short | loss | gain |

The time period over which a speculator hopes to gain will vary depending on the type of speculator. It is common to distinguish five kinds of speculation.

### 1 SCALPING

The time period during which a **scalper** holds a futures contract is extremely short and is usually measured in seconds or minutes. For this reason, only traders who are permitted onto the floor of the exchange to trade on their own account can be scalpers. In effect, scalpers try to develop a continuously updated 'feel' for the market, anticipating and exploiting perceived short-term excesses of supply or demand. Scalpers perform the useful function of providing liquidity to the market.

### 2 SPREADING

A **spread** is a long (bought) position in one maturity date, paired with a short (sold) position in another maturity date. An example is a bought March BAB futures contract and a sold June BAB futures contract. Speculators will adopt this spread if they believe that the current difference between the two futures prices is too wide. Speculators will gain if the difference (or 'spread') narrows. It is a simple matter to show this. Let the current (that is, time zero) futures price

---

[12] For surveys, see R. W. Kolb, *Understanding Futures Markets*, 3rd edn, Simon & Schuster/New York Institute of Finance, New York, 1991, Ch. 5; or B. A. Goss & B. S. Yamey (Eds), *The Economics of Futures Trading*, 2nd edn, Macmillan, London, 1978, pp. 1–62.

of the March contract be $F(0, M)$. Similarly, let the current (that is, time zero) futures price of the June contract be $F(0, J)$. The spread at time zero is:

$$F(0, J) - F(0, M)$$

Similarly, the spread at time 1 is:

$$F(1, J) - F(1, M)$$

Between time zero and time 1, the bought position in the March contract will produce a gain of:

$$F(1, M) - F(0, M) \qquad (15.4)$$

Similarly, over the same time period, the sold position in the June contract will produce a gain of:

$$F(0, J) - F(1, J) \qquad (15.5)$$

Note that the 0 and the 1 in Equation 15.5 are reversed, compared to Equation 15.4. This is because Equation 15.4 gives the gain from a bought position, while Equation 15.5 gives the gain from a sold position. A sold position generates a gain if the futures price falls, that is, if $F(1, J) < F(0, J)$.

The spread speculator's total gain $G$ is given by the sum of Equations 15.4 and 15.5:

$$\begin{aligned} G &= F(1, M) - F(0, M) + F(0, J) - F(1, J) \\ &= [F(0, J) - F(0, M)] - [F(1, J) - F(1, M)] \\ &= [\text{spread at time 0}] \text{ less } [\text{spread at time 1}] \\ &> 0 \text{ if } [\text{spread at time 0}] \text{ exceeds } [\text{spread at time 1}] \end{aligned}$$

In this case, then, the spread speculator will gain if the spread at time 1 is narrower than the spread at time zero. The spread speculator performs the useful function of keeping in line the prices of different futures contracts on the same commodity. The spread speculator may hold a futures position for any period, but will often do so for only a matter of hours, or perhaps days.

## 3  STRADDLING

A **straddle** is similar in concept to a spread but refers to positions in futures contracts on different commodities, rather than futures contracts on the same commodity for different months. For example, a trader might buy a March BAB contract and sell a March bond contract. The reasons for straddling are similar to those for spreading.

## 4  DAY TRADING

**Day traders** are prepared to trade as they see fit during a trading day, but regard an overnight position as too risky. Quite simply, too much can happen while the exchange is closed.

## 5  LONG-TERM/OVERNIGHT POSITION TAKING

This is both the simplest and the riskiest type of speculation. Speculators form a view that the current futures price is too low (or too high), trade accordingly, and wait for events to prove them right. It can be a quick way to riches —or rags.

## 15.5.3 HEDGING

The essence of hedging is easily explained. Consider, for example, a grazier who intends to sell his cattle in several months' time. He is affected by movements in the spot price of cattle, gaining if it increases (since his cattle become more valuable) and losing if it decreases (since his cattle become less valuable). If he wishes to be protected against these changes, he can sell cattle futures; that is, he becomes what is known as a **short hedger**. The position of the short hedger is shown in Table 15.3.

**Table 15.3** *Short hedging outcomes*

|  | If prices rise | If prices fall |
|---|---|---|
| Short futures contract | loss | gain |
| Cattle-spot | gain | loss |
| Net result | approx. zero | approx. zero |

The net result is approximately zero. Therefore the hedger achieves his objective, in that whether prices rise or fall, there is little or no effect on the hedger.

Note, though, that the result is shown as only *approximately* zero. Why not *precisely* zero? There are many reasons why a perfect hedge is most unlikely but before looking at some of the reasons, we need to consider hedges achieved by buying futures contracts. Such a hedge is called a long hedge and if the position of a long hedger is simply the exact reverse of the position of the short hedger, the outcomes for the long hedger are as shown in Table 15.4.

**Table 15.4** *Long hedging outcomes*

|  | If prices rise | If prices fall |
|---|---|---|
| Long futures contract | gain | loss |
| Cattle-spot | loss | gain |
| Net result | approx. zero | approx. zero |

However, on close inspection, it should be clear that the long hedger's position is not necessarily simply the reverse of the short hedger's position. For example, compare the position of a long hedger such as a manufacturer of beef sausages with that of a short hedger such as a grazier. There can be no doubt that a grazier gains if spot cattle prices rise. For example, if spot cattle prices rise from $1.00/kg to $1.20/kg, a grazier benefits by $0.20/kg multiplied by the number of kilograms of cattle owned. The grazier's wealth has risen by that amount. Is a sausage manufacturer $0.20/kg poorer? It is not clear that the answer to this question is 'yes'. To a grazier, cattle are obviously assets; but to a sausage manufacturer, cattle are not likely to be liabilities. If a sausage manufacturer has short sold cattle, then cattle might be liabilities, but in practice it is impossible (or at least very difficult) to sell commodities short. However, for simplicity, we will treat long hedging as simply the reverse of short hedging.[13]

## 15.5.4 Some reasons why hedging with futures is imperfect

In this section we discuss three reasons why hedging with futures may be imperfect. These are: imperfect convergence, basis risk, and specification differences.

### I Imperfect convergence

Suppose that a jewellery manufacturer is committed to buying an ounce of gold on 27 March and it so happens that there is a futures contract that precisely matches this need. That is, there is a futures contract that specifies an ounce of gold of the same quality and at the same location as the manufacturer requires, and the maturity date of the futures contract is 27 March. Even in this case a perfect hedge may not be possible because of the problem of imperfect convergence between spot and futures prices.

Logically, the price of a futures contract with zero time to maturity ought to be equal to the spot price. If this were not so, then in principle an instantaneous profit can be made. For example, if the spot price were the lower one, a trader could simultaneously buy in the spot market and sell in the futures market, delivering the commodity purchased in satisfaction of the futures market commitment. However, in reality the futures price at maturity can be slightly different from the spot price on the maturity date. In short, the convergence between the spot price and the futures price as the maturity date approaches can be imperfect. Yet it may not be possible to profit from this difference. For example, transaction costs could prevent the opportunity from being exploited. This will affect the quality of a hedge, but typically the problem should not be very serious because convergence is generally close, even though not perfect.

Consider again the jewellery manufacturer who has bought gold futures. Suppose that she faces the following situation and has closed out her contract:

| | |
|---|---|
| Futures price (when bought) | $600 |
| Futures price (at maturity) | $660 |
| Spot price (on futures maturity date) | $662 |

The jewellery manufacturer will have a futures profit of $60 to add to the price of $600 she knew she would have to pay, but will be $2 short of the $662 needed to buy gold (spot). In other words, the gold ends up costing her $602 instead of $600 as was planned. This, admittedly is imperfect, but the problem is not serious. Certainly it is better to have to find $2 unexpectedly, than to have to find $62 unexpectedly.

---

[13] A slightly different approach to long hedging is to think of the long hedger as gaining or losing on the spot, relative to the *forward* price of the commodity. Of course forward prices may be unobservable. For a discussion, see Goss & Yamey, (see Footnote 12), pp. 24–5.

## 2 BASIS RISK

By definition, a hedger is planning to transact in the spot market at some future time. However, it is unusual for the date of the planned spot transaction to coincide with the maturity date of a futures contract. At any given time a futures exchange will offer only a restricted number of maturity dates—sometimes only four or five. As a result, there is only a small chance that the date of the planned spot transaction will coincide with a futures contract maturity date. When the dates do not coincide, the hedger must reverse out of the futures contract before it matures and, when this action is required, hedgers face a risk known as 'basis risk'. We define the **basis** at any given time as the spot price $S$ at that time of a commodity that matches exactly the commodity defined in the futures contract, minus the futures price $F$ at that time (for delivery of the commodity at some later time).[14] Therefore, the basis $B$ at time zero is:

$$B(0) = S(0) - F(0)$$

Similarly, the basis at some later time, say time 1, is:

$$B(1) = S(1) - F(1)$$

Now consider a short hedger and assume that the 'commodity' held by the short hedger can be stored costlessly. A short hedger makes a gain (loss) on the futures contract if the futures price decreases (increases), and a gain (loss) on holding the commodity if the spot price increases (decreases). Therefore in the interval between time zero and time 1:

$$\begin{aligned}\text{Total gain to short hedger} &= \text{gain made on futures} + \text{gain made on spot} \\ &= [F(0) - F(1)] + [S(1) - S(0)] \\ &= [S(1) - F(1)] - [S(0) - F(0)] \\ &= B(1) - B(0) \\ &= \text{change in basis between time zero and time 1}\end{aligned}$$

The point is simple: the change in the basis over a given time period is not, in general, precisely zero. Yet a perfect hedge is one in which the wealth of the hedger is immune to the movement of prices. It follows that a hedger does not, in fact, eliminate all risk. There remains basis risk.

It is important to appreciate this point. However, it is also important to place basis risk in context. *In general*, futures prices and spot prices tend to move together. Of course this tendency is not perfect and for some agricultural commodities it may not even be close to perfect. For example, if a bumper harvest is expected next season but, simultaneously, unexpected shortages in the spot market develop today, then futures prices might fall at the same time as spot prices rise. But this type of situation is the exception. In general, whatever causes spot prices to increase (or decrease) will also tend to cause futures prices to increase (or decrease).

The following example illustrates basis risk.

---

[14] Conventions vary. We have defined basis as 'spot minus futures', but others define it as 'futures minus spot'. For example, compare Kolb, p. 83 and Goss & Yamey, p. 10 (see Footnote 12).

*Example 15.2*

Suppose that some dramatic event causes a large fall in spot prices, and suppose that this same event causes a similar, but slightly smaller, fall in futures prices, as shown in Table 15.5.

**Table 15.5** *Example of basis risk*

|  | Prices | | |
| --- | --- | --- | --- |
|  | At time zero | At time 1 | Gain (+) or loss (−) |
| Spot (long) | $1026 | $806 | −$220 |
| Futures (short) | $1040 | $825 | +$215 |
| Gain (+) or loss (−) made by short hedger | | | −$5 |

In the table, time zero is the date on which the hedge is set up and time 1 is the date on which the spot transaction is made and the hedge is lifted. As shown in the table, the hedge is not perfect, as there is a net loss of $5, which is equal to the change in the basis:

$$\begin{aligned}\text{Change in basis} &= B(1) - B(0) \\ &= [S(1) - F(1)] - [S(0) - F(0)] \\ &= [\$806 - \$825] - [\$1026 - \$1040] \\ &= -\$19 - [-\$14] \\ &= -\$5\end{aligned}$$

However, a loss of $5 is trivial when compared with the loss of $220 that would have been incurred had no futures contract been entered. Basis risk is much less than price risk. In this example a short hedger faced an initial basis of −$14 that later fell to −$19 and the outcome was a loss of $5. Table 15.6 sets out the full range of possibilities.

**Table 15.6** *Hedging outcomes and basis changes*

|  |  | Outcome if Basis* | |
| --- | --- | --- | --- |
| Description | Positions | increases | decreases |
| Short hedger | Futures (short) Commodity (long) | gain | loss |
| Long hedger | Futures (long) Commodity (short) | loss | gain |

*Basis is defined as spot price less futures price.

## 3 SPECIFICATION DIFFERENCES

'Specification differences' refers to the fact that the specification of the 'commodity' that is the subject of the futures contract may not precisely correspond to the specification of the 'commodity' that is of interest to a hedger. For example, a hedger may be interested in a particular grade of wool that is slightly different to the grade of wool specified in the futures contract. Alternatively, a hedger may be interested in buying wool to be delivered to a certain location. However, this location may be only one of a number of locations acceptable for delivery under a futures contract. Or it may not even be one of the acceptable locations at all. Similar observations are relevant to financial futures. Some examples are as follows:

(a) A borrower may intend to issue 120-day BABs, but the futures contract specifies 90-day BABs.
(b) An investor may own a diversified portfolio which is similar to, but not identical to, the shares in the share price index that the futures contract specifies.
(c) A lender may intend to invest in 5-year company debentures, but the futures contract specifies 3-year government bonds.

In fact, only rarely is a hedger able to find a futures contract whose specification is *precisely* the same as the commodity which is of interest to the hedger. Specification differences introduce a further element of imperfection in the hedging process. This is illustrated in the following example.

## Example 15.3

Assume that a jewellery manufacturer intends to buy one ounce of high grade gold but the futures contract specifies one ounce of premium-grade gold. Nevertheless, as a hedge, he enters into one futures contract to buy premium-grade gold. Suppose that the following prices, shown in Table 15.7, occur.

**Table 15.7** *Prices for Example 15.3*

| | Prices ($) | |
|---|---|---|
| | At time zero | At time 1 |
| High grade—spot | 650 | 693 |
| Premium grade—spot | 680 | 720 |
| Premium grade—futures | 690 | 728 |

'Loss' on spot = $693 − $650 = $43 (loss)
Gain on futures = $728 − $690 = $38 (gain)
Net result: $5 (loss)

Because a small loss has resulted, the hedge is imperfect. Two components of the loss can be identified:

1. *Basis risk*, which caused a loss of $2. At time zero, the basis was $10, and at time 1, $8. In other words, whereas the spot price increased by $40, the futures price increased by only $38.
2. *Specification differences*, which caused a further loss of $3. At time zero, the price gap between the two grades was $30, but at time 1, it was only $27. In other words, the grade sought by the hedger has become *relatively* more expensive.

Again, however, compared with no hedge at all (in which case a loss of $43 would have been incurred), the result is quite good, even though the hedge is imperfect.

### 15.5.5 HEDGING AND REGRETTING

The previous examples have been constructed to show how hedging can reduce losses which would otherwise have been incurred. However, it should not be forgotten that by its very nature, hedging also reduces profits which would otherwise have been made. Consider the following short hedge (Table 15.8).

**Table 15.8** *A short hedge*

|  | Prices ($) | |
| --- | --- | --- |
|  | At time zero | At time 1 |
| Spot price (long) | 430 | 500 |
| Futures price (short) | 440 | 510 |

In this case, there is a gain on the spot of $70 and an offsetting loss on the futures of $70. The hedge has performed perfectly; it produced immunity to price movements. Of course, it is obvious that, *in retrospect*, the hedger would have been better off by $70 not to have hedged. The message is simple: to have protection against losses a hedger must be willing to forego profits which would otherwise have been made.

### 15.5.6 SELECTING THE NUMBER OF FUTURES CONTRACTS

In the examples we have discussed, the number of futures contracts to be used in the hedge was obvious. However, in practice this is not always the case and hedgers need to adopt a systematic approach to deciding how many futures contracts they should buy or sell. If a hedger enters into too few (or too many) futures contracts, the position is riskier than desired.[15]

Suppose that a hedger has an interest in $N_S$ units of a 'commodity'. If this interest is a long (short) position, then $N_S$ is positive (negative). Suppose further that $f$ futures contracts have been entered into, each of which covers $N_F$ units of the commodity. If a long (short) position is held in futures contracts, then $f$ is positive (negative). The gain $G$ to the hedger is:

$$G = N_s \times \begin{pmatrix} \text{change in} \\ \text{spot price} \\ \text{per unit} \end{pmatrix} + f N_F \times \begin{pmatrix} \text{change in} \\ \text{futures price} \\ \text{per unit} \end{pmatrix}$$

$$= N_S (\tilde{S}_1 - S_0) + f N_F (\tilde{F}_1 - F_0) \tag{15.6}$$

---

[15] Note that simply increasing the number of futures contracts in an attempt 'to make sure enough are held' does *not* solve this problem. For example, if buying 9 futures contracts would produce a perfect hedge, but 10 contracts are bought, the hedger is one futures contract long on a net basis. That is, the hedger is in fact a long speculator in relation to one contract, and hence will make a loss if futures prices fall.

where $S_0$ = spot price per unit when the hedge is entered ('today')
$F_0$ = futures price per unit when the hedge is entered ('today')
$\tilde{S}_1$ = spot price per unit when the hedge is lifted
$\tilde{F}_1$ = futures price per unit when the hedge is lifted

The tilde (~) is used to emphasise that the subsequent prices are random variables. That is, their value is uncertain.

Obviously, when the hedge is lifted and the spot transaction is made, the outcomes $S_1$ and $F_1$ will be known with certainty. Therefore, *with hindsight*, the ideal number of futures contracts from a hedging viewpoint will be obvious and can be found by setting $G$ equal to zero and rearranging Equation 15.6. This gives:

$$f = - \frac{N_S (S_1 - S_0)}{N_F (F_1 - F_0)}$$

But in practice, this equation cannot be used because $S_1$ and $F_1$ are not known at the time the hedge is set up. Inevitably, therefore, deciding how many futures contracts should be entered into requires some assumption or forecast that relates changes in the futures price to changes in the spot price. This will usually involve some error.

Using Equation 15.6, the gain per unit of commodity is $g$, where:

$$g = \frac{G}{N_S} = (\tilde{S}_1 - S_0) + \frac{fN_F}{N_S} (\tilde{F}_1 - F_0)$$

Now define $h = f N_F/N_S$, where $h$ is the 'hedge ratio', which is the number of units covered by futures contracts per unit of spot commodity. Therefore:

$$g = (\tilde{S}_1 - S_0) + h(\tilde{F}_1 - F_0)$$

The components of $g$ resemble a two-asset portfolio, and the variance (risk)[16] is given by:

$$\begin{aligned} \text{Var}(g) &= \text{Var}(\tilde{S}_1 - S_0) + \text{Var}[h(\tilde{F}_1 - F_0)] \\ &\quad + 2 \text{Cov}[(\tilde{S}_1 - S_0), h(\tilde{F}_1 - F_0)] \\ &= \text{Var}(\tilde{S}_1) + h^2 \text{Var}(\tilde{F}_1) + 2h \text{Cov}(\tilde{S}_1, \tilde{F}_1) \end{aligned}$$

We assume[17] that the hedger will choose the hedge ratio $h$ so as to minimise the variance of $g$. To find how to achieve this goal we differentiate Var($g$) with respect to $h$, and set the derivative equal to zero:

$$\frac{d \text{Var}(g)}{dh} = 2h \text{Var}(\tilde{F}_1) + 2 \text{Cov}(\tilde{S}_1, \tilde{F}_1) = 0$$

The risk-minimising value of $h$ is thus $h^*$ where:

---

[16] Calculating the risk of a portfolio is explained in detail in Chapter 6.
[17] As we have stated, this is merely as assumption. In general, it is expected that financial markets will price assets so that there is a trade-off between risk and expected return. Depending on the decision maker's preferences as between risk and expected return, a risk-minimising strategy may or may not be optimal.

$$h^* = -\frac{\text{Cov}(\tilde{S}_1, \tilde{F}_1)}{\text{Var}(\tilde{F}_1)} \qquad (15.7)$$

An estimate of $h^*$ can be found from regressing spot prices against futures prices. Using the definition of the hedge ratio $h$ the optimum number of futures contracts to enter into is $f^*$ where:

$$f^* = \frac{N_S}{N_F} h^*$$

Substituting from Equation 15.7 gives:

$$f^* = -\frac{N_S}{N_F} \frac{\text{Cov}(\tilde{S}_1, \tilde{F}_1)}{\text{Var}(\tilde{F}_1)} \qquad (15.8)$$

Equation 15.8 suggests that the number of futures contracts to enter into depends on four factors:

(a) $N_S$, the number of units of the commodity at risk in the spot market;
(b) $N_F$, the number of units of the commodity underlying one futures contract;
(c) $\text{Cov}(\tilde{S}_1, \tilde{F}_1)$, which describes the relationship between spot and futures prices; and
(d) $\text{Var}(\tilde{F}_1)$, which describes the variability of futures prices.

An interesting special case arises if it is assumed that spot and futures prices move equi-proportionately—that is, an $x$ per cent change in the spot price will always be matched by an $x$ per cent change in the futures price. Then:

$$\frac{\tilde{S}_1 - S_0}{S_0} = \frac{\tilde{F}_1 - F_0}{F_0}$$

which on rearrangement gives:

$$\tilde{S}_1 = \left(\frac{S_0}{F_0}\right) \tilde{F}_1$$

and therefore:

$$\text{Cov}(\tilde{S}_1, \tilde{F}_1) = \text{Cov}\left(\frac{S_0}{F_0} \tilde{F}_1, \tilde{F}_1\right)$$
$$= \frac{S_0}{F_0} \text{Cov}(\tilde{F}_1, \tilde{F}_1)$$
$$= \frac{S_0}{F_0} \text{Var}(\tilde{F}_1)$$

Substituting in Equation 15.8, the optimum number of futures contracts $f^*$ is:

$$f^* = -\frac{N_S}{N_F} \frac{S_0/F_0 \ \text{Var}(\tilde{F}_1)}{\text{Var}(\tilde{F}_1)}$$
$$= -\frac{N_S}{N_F} \frac{S_0}{F_0} \qquad (15.9)$$

*Example 15.4*

Goss Gold owns 119 ounces of gold and is committed to selling the gold in three weeks' time. The spot price (today) is $507 per ounce and the futures price for delivery in seven weeks' time is $516 per ounce. One futures contract covers 3 ounces of gold. Goss Gold wants to hedge using futures and needs to decide on the number of futures contracts it should enter. As a first pass at the problem, Goss Gold is willing to assume that a 1 per cent change in the spot price will be matched by a 1 per cent change in the futures price.

Using Equation 15.9, the number of futures contracts is:

$$\begin{aligned} f^* &= -\frac{N_S}{N_F}\frac{S_0}{F_0} \\ &= -\frac{119}{3}\frac{\$507}{\$516} \\ &= -38.97 \\ &\approx -39 \end{aligned}$$

Thus Goss Gold should sell 39 futures contracts.

A variation on this simple approach when applied to bond futures is illustrated in Example 15.10.

## 15.6 FINANCIAL FUTURES ON THE SFE: THE 90-DAY BANK ACCEPTED BILL (BAB) FUTURES CONTRACT

As mentioned in Section 15.3, most contracts traded on the SFE are financial futures, rather than commodity futures. In this and the following two sections, principles that we have developed and explained in terms of commodity futures are applied to SFE financial futures. More space is devoted to bank-accepted bill (BAB) futures than to the others, because there is simply more material to cover and because BAB futures are used to explain the major principles.

### 15.6.1 A BRIEF REVIEW OF BANK BILLS[18]

A **bank bill** is a short-term debt instrument which is readily tradeable. Bank bills are generally issued for standard fixed terms (such as 90 days or 180 days) and at standard face values (such as $100 000 or $500 000). The face value is repaid at maturity. Prior to maturity a bill is priced according to the principles of simple interest. Equation 15.10 shows the bill pricing formula used in this chapter.

$$P = \frac{V}{1 + (i)\,(t/365)} \qquad (15.10)$$

---

[18] For further details, see Sections 3.2.4 and 8.3.3.

where $P$ = bill price
$V$ = face value
$i$ = nominal annual yield (also known as the bill rate)
$t$ = term (in days) remaining to bill's maturity date

*Example 15.5*
A bill with 90 days remaining to maturity, priced to yield 12.88 per cent per annum, and with a face value of $500 000, requires a price of:

$$P = \frac{\$500\,000}{1 + (0.1288)(90/365)} = \$484\,609.34$$

If the yield were to increase by, say, 0.25 per cent per annum to 13.13 per cent per annum, the price decreases. Then:

$$P = \frac{\$500\,000}{1 + (0.1313)(90/365)} = \$484\,319.97$$

This represents a capital loss of $289.37 to the investor (lender). Similarly, if yields decrease, prices increase. An 'equivalent' *fall* in yield of 0.25 per cent per annum, to 12.63 per cent per annum, will produce a price increase. Then:

$$P = \frac{\$500\,000}{1 + (0.1263)(90/365)} = \$484\,899.05$$

This represents a capital gain of $289.71 to the investor (lender). Note that the capital gain is a little larger than the capital loss for the same shift in yield.

For many purposes, a bank bill is the same as any other 'commodity'. It has a market price and this price changes from day to day according to market forces. There is therefore no reason at all why there cannot be a futures contract on 90-day bank bills.

### 15.6.2 SPECIFICATION OF THE BAB FUTURES CONTRACT

The bank-accepted bill (BAB) futures contract has the following major features:

#### 1 CONTRACT UNIT

The contract unit is a 90-day BAB with a face value of $500 000, or five 90-day BABs, each with a face value of $100 000.

#### 2 SETTLEMENT

The contract is deliverable, that is, sellers can deliver BABs in satisfaction of their futures contract responsibilities. Technically, bills that have a term as short as 85 days or as long as 95 days are acceptable. However, bills shorter than 90 days are worth more than 90-day bills because they are discounted with respect to a shorter time period. Therefore, buyers must pay a little more than the stated futures price in that case. Similarly, if sellers deliver a bill longer than 90 days, then buyers pay a little less than they would for a 90-day bill. Also, bank negotiable certificates of deposit can be substituted for bank bills. The settlement date is the second Friday of the maturity (delivery) month.

## 3 QUOTATIONS
One hundred minus the annual percentage yield to two decimal places.

## 4 TERMINATION OF TRADING
Trading ceases at 12 noon on the business day immediately prior to the settlement date.

It is important to realise that a BAB futures contract is not a contract on any presently *existing* 90-day BAB because tomorrow, an existing 90-day BAB will be an 89-day BAB and the next day an 88-day BAB, and so on.

To illustrate the nature of the BAB futures contract, consider the price of 94.96 reported for the June (1994) BAB futures contract in the *Australian Financial Review* of 24 March 1994. The reported price of 94.96 refers to the price in the last trade on 23 March and represents 100 minus the annual percentage yield. In other words, the annual yield is:

$$100 - 94.96$$
$$= 5.04\%$$
$$= 0.0504$$

Using Equation 15.10 the dollar price implicit in this futures contract is therefore:

$$\frac{\$500\,000}{1 + (0.0504)\,(90/365)} = \$493\,862.57$$

The settlement date is the second Friday of June 1994, that is, 10 June 1994. The BAB involved has 90 days to run; this 90-day period is to *begin on 10 June 1994*. Therefore the BAB involved is one that matures on 8 September 1994. The term of the futures contract expires on 10 June 1994 which is 79 days after it was entered into on 23 March 1994.

To clarify this, suppose that a trader bought one such contract on 23 March, held it to settlement day (10 June), accepted delivery of the bill on that day and then held the bill to its maturity date. Ignoring cash flows due to deposits, margins and the mark-to-market rule, the cash flows involved are as shown in Figure 15.1.

The yield earned over the 90-day period from 10 June to 8 September is, as it must be, 5.04 per cent per annum. By entering the futures contract, a particular yield (5.04 per cent per annum) has been locked in on 23 March for the 90-day period that begins on 10 June and ends on 8 September.

Of course most traders do not hold a futures contract until settlement. Typically the buyer in this example would soon reverse out by a sale. If, for example, the reversing sale was made at the closing price on 30 March, the quoted price, according to the *Australian Financial Review* of 31 March, would have been 94.86. The yield indicated is $100 - 94.86 = 5.14$ per cent and again using Equation 15.10, the dollar price is:

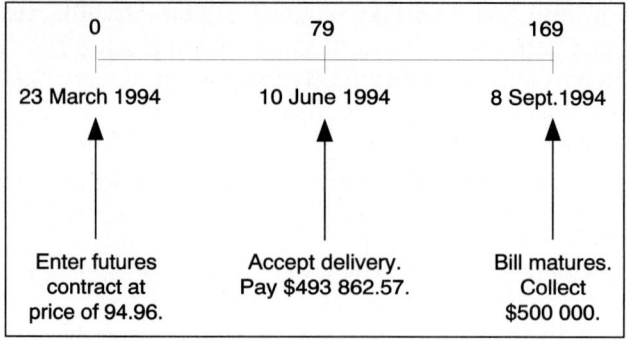

**Fig. 15.1** *Major cash flows in a BAB futures contract*

$$P = \frac{\$500\,000}{1 + (0.0514)(90/365)}$$
$$= \$493\,742.32$$

Ignoring transaction costs, this gives a loss of $120.25.

### 15.6.3 Uses of the BAB contract

The BAB contract can be used in speculation, hedging, and arbitrage.

#### Speculation with BAB futures

All futures contracts lend themselves to speculation. There is nothing special to explain about this. If traders can forecast the subsequent course of the BAB futures price, they can make money simply by buying (selling) when the futures price is low (high).

#### Hedging with BAB futures

As has been explained, simple hedging involves a futures transaction which largely offsets a risk to which the hedger is already exposed. This is illustrated in the following detailed worked examples.

*Example 15.6*

Several weeks ago, the financial controller of Annamay Ltd decided that the company should borrow by issuing a 90-day bank bill with a face value of $500 000. As the funds were not needed for another 2 weeks, it was decided that the issue would not be made until the 2 weeks had passed. In her planning, the financial controller assumed that the 90-day bank bill rate would not change from its then current level of 14.40 per cent per annum. However, she was aware that a risk was involved and therefore decided that Annamay should protect itself against an increase in bill rates by selling one BAB futures contract. This was done at a price of 85.78. During the next 2 weeks the financial controller was amazed to see the 90-day bill rate climb rapidly. Annamay eventually issued a bill at a rate of 16.50 per cent per annum and lifted the hedge by reversing its futures position at a price of 83.70.

The financial controller is asked to provide a report to the Board of Directors on the following matters:
1. the (gross) dollar shortfall that Annamay would have faced if a futures contract had not been entered into;
2. the gain made on the futures contract (ignoring transaction costs);
3. the net dollar shortfall;
4. an explanation of (3) in terms of basis risk; and
5. a brief assessment of the effectiveness of the hedge.

The answers to these questions are as follows:

1.  $$\text{Planned borrowing} = \frac{\$500\,000}{1 + (0.1440)(90/365)}$$
    $$= \$482\,855.33$$
    $$\text{Actual borrowing} = \frac{\$500\,000}{1 + (0.1650)(90/365)}$$
    $$= \$480\,452.81$$
    $$\text{Dollar shortfall (gross)} = \$482\,855.33 - \$480\,452.81$$
    $$= \$2402.52$$

2.  There is a notional sale at 85.78 (that is, at 14.22 per cent per annum) followed by a notional purchase at 83.70 (that is, at 16.30 per cent per annum).
    $$\text{Notional inflow from sale} = \frac{\$500\,000}{1 + (0.1422)(90/365)}$$
    $$= \$483\,062.38$$
    $$\text{Notional outflow from purchase} = \frac{\$500\,000}{1 + (0.1630)(90/365)}$$
    $$= \$480\,680.59$$
    $$\text{Result from futures} = \$483\,062.38 - \$480\,680.59$$
    $$= \$2381.79 \text{ (gain).}$$

3.  Net dollar shortfall = $2402.52 - $2381.79
    = $20.73

4.  Basis is spot price less futures price. When the hedge was entered the basis was:
    (Price at yield of 14.40%) *less* (price at yield of 14.22%)
    = $482 855.33 - $483 062.38
    = -$207.05
    When the hedge was lifted, the basis was:
    (Price at yield of 16.50%) *less* (price at yield of 16.30%)
    = $480 452.81 - $480 680.59
    = -$227.78
    Change in basis = (later basis) *less* (earlier basis)
    = -$227.78 - (-$207.05)
    = -$20.73

As a short hedger's net result is given by the change in the basis,[19] this indicates that the hedger's net result is a loss of $20.73, which is the result calculated in part 3.

5. Without the hedge, the dollar shortfall would have been $2402.52. With the hedge, the net dollar shortfall is only $20.73, a reduction of 99.1 per cent. The result can also (equivalently) be assessed in terms of yields. Annamay's total funds inflow is the amount borrowed plus the net gain on the futures contract. This is:

$$\$480\,452.81 + \$2381.79 = \$482\,834.60$$

The repayment required is $500 000 in 90 days' time. The implied annual nominal yield is:

$$\left(\frac{\$500\,000}{\$482\,834.60} - 1\right) \times \frac{365}{90} = 14.418\%$$

This compares with a planned borrowing rate of 14.400 per cent. Clearly the hedge has been extremely effective.

In Example 15.6, Annamay Ltd intended to issue a security which, with the exception of the intended date of issue, matched precisely the security specified in the futures contract. In other words, both the security of interest to Annamay and the security specified in the futures contract were 90-day bank-accepted bills. A close match between the security of interest to the hedger and the security specified in the futures contract increases the likely quality of the hedge. However, as explained in Section 15.5.4, there are often 'specification differences' between the hedger's needs and the futures contract. This is illustrated in Example 15.7.

### Example 15.7

Suppose that, instead of 90-day bank bills, Annamay Ltd had planned to issue 120-day bank bills. As there is no futures contract on 120-day bank bills, Annamay would still have hedged using the 90-day BAB contract. Assume that all other facts remain the same and the relevant data are as shown in Table 15.9.

**Table 15.9** *Yields for Example 15.7*

|  | Yield when hedge entered (% p.a.) | Yield when hedge lifted (% p.a.) |
|---|---|---|
| 90-day bank bills | 14.40 | 16.50 |
| 120-day bank bills | 14.55 | 16.70 |
| 90-day BAB futures | 14.22 | 16.30 |

---

[19] See Table 15.6. Note that Annamay Ltd has been a little unlucky. Given that, at maturity, a futures price must be very close to the spot price, it follows that, on average, the basis will tend towards zero as time passes and the maturity date becomes closer. However, in this example, the basis has gone from −$207.05 to −$227.78; that is, it has moved further away from zero.

The financial controller is required to report on the following matters:
1. the (gross) dollar shortfall that Annamay would have faced if a futures contract had not been entered into;
2. the gain made on the futures contract (ignoring transaction costs);
3. the net dollar shortfall;
4. an explanation of (3) in terms of basis risk and specification differences;
5. a brief assessment of the effectiveness of the hedge.

The answers to these questions are as follows:

1. $$\text{Planned borrowing} = \frac{\$500\,000}{1 + (0.1455)(120/365)}$$
$$= \$477\,174.08$$
$$\text{Actual borrowing} = \frac{\$500\,000}{1 + (0.1670)(120/365)}$$
$$= \$473\,976.73$$
Dollar shortfall (gross) = $477 174.08 − $473 976.73
= $3197.35

2. As this calculation involves only the futures contract, it is the same as in Example 15.6. That is, the result is a gain of $2381.79.

3. Net dollar shortfall = $3197.35 − $2381.79
= $815.56

4. This net shortfall can be broken into components reflecting basis risk and specification differences. The latter arises because Annamay has risks related to 120-day bills but is using futures on 90-day bills to hedge against these risks. Table 15.10 shows the results in detail. All prices are calculated using Equation 15.10.

**Table 15.10** Basis risk and specification differences in Example 15.7

| Description | Price when hedge entered ($) | Price when hedge lifted ($) | Change ($) |
|---|---|---|---|
| 1. **Basis risk:** | | | |
| 90-day bank bill (spot) | 482 855.33 | 480 452.81 | |
| BAB futures | 483 062.38 | 480 680.59 | |
| | −207.05 | −227.78 | −20.73 |
| 2. **Specification differences:** | | | |
| 120-day bank bill (spot) | 477 174.08 | 473 976.73 | |
| 90-day bank bill (spot) | 482 855.33 | 480 452.81 | |
| | −5 681.25 | −6 476.08 | −794.83 |
| | | | −815.56 |

5. The hedge has reduced the dollar shortfall from $3197.35 to $815.56; this is a reduction of 74.5 per cent. The nominal annual yield is:
$$\left(\frac{\$500\,000}{\$473\,976.73 + \$2381.79} - 1\right) \times \frac{365}{120}$$
$$= 15.096\%$$

This compares with a planned yield of 14.550 per cent. Although the hedge has been quite effective, its performance falls short of the excellent performance in Example 15.6.

In both Example 15.6 and 15.7 the hedger established a short futures position; that is, the hedge was achieved by first entering a futures contract to sell.

Example 15.8 illustrates a hedge which requires that a BAB futures contract be held long; that is, the futures contract is first bought and subsequently sold.

*Example 15.8*

The Chesterheaton Investment Fund chose to hedge when it was told to expect an inflow of around $500 000 in 2 months' time, to be invested in 90-day bank bills. When the hedge was entered, yields per annum were 8.45 per cent (spot) and 8.80 per cent (futures). When the hedge was lifted, yields were 7.15 per cent (spot) and 7.38 per cent (futures). Describe an appropriate hedge, and assess its effectiveness in the light of subsequent yields, ignoring transaction costs.

The Chesterheaton Fund buys a BAB futures contract. The notional purchase price is $489 381.10 and the notional selling price is $491 063.98, giving a gain of $1682.88. When the hedge is lifted, 90-day bank bills offer a yield of 7.15 per cent. This implies a price of $491 337.65. Using its gain from the futures contract, Chesterheaton can buy such a bill for a net outlay of $489 645.77, implying that its annual yield will be:

$$\left(\frac{\$500\,000}{\$489\,654.77} - 1\right) \times \frac{365}{90} = 8.568\%$$

This is in fact slightly *higher* than the planned rate of 8.450 per cent. The fact that this is not equal to the planned rate indicates that not all risks were eliminated by the hedge, but it is clear that this hedge has been very effective.

## ARBITRAGE WITH BAB FUTURES

As we mentioned earlier an 'arbitrage' is a set of simultaneous transactions in different markets that guarantees a risk-free profit. Although the word 'arbitrage' is sometimes used very loosely, it is used in this chapter in its precise sense. For example, if an investor is assured of a positive return, at no risk, from a net investment of zero dollars, then arbitrage has been achieved. Obviously if markets are efficient, arbitrage should not be possible. If there are no transaction costs and investors can borrow or lend at the same market yields, then there will be an arbitrage opportunity present unless:

$$(1 + i_t)(1 + i_{t,T}) = 1 + i_T \tag{15.11}$$

where $t$ = the maturity date of the futures contract
$i_t$ = the (spot) yield on a bill maturing at date $t$

$i_{it,T}$ = the (futures)[20] yield for a futures contract, maturing at date $t$ on a bill maturing at a later date $T$

$i_T$ = the (spot) yield on a bill maturing at date $T$

The logic behind Equation 15.11 is the same as that used in Section 4.6.2 to explain the expectations theory of the term structure of interest rates. Suppose that on date zero, an investor invests \$1 at a yield of $i_t$ for a period of $t$ days and simultaneously buys a futures contract which entitles him to invest, on date $t$, the proceeds of his investment at a yield of $i_{t,T}$. Therefore at date $T$, the investor has an accumulated sum of $\$1(1 + i_t)(1 + i_{t,T})$. This amount is perfectly foreseeable on date zero. Clearly the investor should compare this amount with the accumulated sum if on date zero he instead invests in a bill which matures on date $T$ and offers a yield of $i_T$. On an investment of \$1 this will produce an accumulated sum of $\$1(1 + i_T)$. The investor will choose the alternative that produces the greater sum on date $T$. Because competition between traders should eliminate arbitrage opportunities, it is expected that both alternatives should yield the same accumulated sum. Therefore Equation 15.11 should hold.

Equation 15.11 implies that the futures yield $i_{t,T}$ which will prevent arbitrage is:

$$i_{t,T} = \frac{1 + i_T}{1 + i_t} - 1 \qquad (15.12)$$

If the actual futures yield is less than this yield, an arbitrage operation known as **cash and carry** is feasible. If the opposite is true, then an arbitrage operation known as **reverse cash and carry** is feasible.[21] An important conclusion to draw is that the BAB futures price must be closely related to current bill yields.

## 15.7 FINANCIAL FUTURES ON THE SFE: THE 10-YEAR TREASURY BOND FUTURES CONTRACT[22]

Whereas the BAB contract is suitable for speculation, hedging, and arbitrage in short-term interest rates, the 10-year Treasury bond contract is designed for similar operations involving long-term interest rates.

---

20 Strictly speaking, $i_{t,T}$ should be a *forward* yield, but this difference does not significantly affect the gist of the argument. The forward contract matures on date $t$; the underlying 'commodity' is a bank bill which is delivered on date $t$ and matures on date $T$. In the context of a Sydney BAB futures contract it is required that $T - t = 90$ days.

21 Details of these arbitrages are beyond the scope of this book. Briefly, in a cash-and-carry operation the investor simultaneously (on date zero) issues $t$-day bills, buys $T$-day bills and sells the futures contract. On date $t$, the bills held have become $(T - t)$-day bills and are delivered in order to settle the sold futures position; the sum received will be more than enough to pay out the maturing bills issued. In a reverse cash-and-carry operation the investor simultaneously (on date zero) issues $T$-day bills, buys $t$-day bills, and buys the futures contract. On date $t$, the funds from the maturing bills are used to buy the bills received under the terms of the futures contract. On date $T$, funds from the maturing bills held will be more than sufficient to pay out the maturing bills issued.

22 The 3-year Treasury bond futures contract is similar in concept and may be used in similar fashion to the 10-year contract.

## 15.7.1 A BRIEF REVIEW OF BOND PRICING

A bond pays a series of equal interest payments at equal time intervals throughout its life. These payments are known as **coupons**. At maturity the face value is repaid. In Australia most government bonds pay interest twice each year. Bonds can be bought and sold, and prices rise and fall according to market forces. Given a bond price it is always possible to calculate **the yield to maturity**, which is simply the bond's internal rate of return. Alternatively, given a required yield to maturity a bond price can always be calculated. In Australia it is usual to quote both coupon interest rates and yields on an annual basis, even though all calculations take into account the fact that cash flows are in fact half-yearly. The annual rates are simply double the half-year rates.

A standard bond-pricing formula is:

$$P = \frac{C}{i}\left[1 - \frac{1}{(1+i)^n}\right] + \frac{V}{(1+i)^n} \qquad (15.13)$$

where $P$ = bond price
$C$ = coupon payment per half-year
$i$ = half-yearly yield
$n$ = number of half-years to maturity
$V$ = face value

Equation 15.13 is illustrated in the following example.

*Example 15.9*

Consider a bond with exactly 3 years to maturity, a face value of $100, and a coupon interest rate of 12.6 per cent per annum, payable half-yearly. If the required yield is 14.2 per cent per annum, what is the price of the bond?
The half-yearly coupon payment is:

$$0.5 \times \$100 \times 0.126$$
$$= \$6.30$$

The required yield per half-year is:

$$0.5 \times 0.142$$
$$= 0.071$$

Using Equation 15.13, the price $P$ is:

$$P = \frac{\$6.30}{0.071}\left[1 - \frac{1}{(1.071)^6}\right] + \frac{\$100}{(1.071)^6}$$

$$= \$29.936\,720 + \$66.261\,792$$

$$= \$96.198\,512$$

Obviously, if market interest rates fall, then so do required yields, and consequently bond prices rise. Conversely, if yields rise, then bond prices fall.

## 15.7.2 SPECIFICATION OF THE 10-YEAR BOND FUTURES CONTRACT

The 10-year bond futures contract has the following major features:

## 1  CONTRACT UNIT
The contract unit is a 10-year government bond with a face value of $100 000, offering a coupon rate of 12 per cent per annum (payable half-yearly).

## 2  SETTLEMENT
The contract is settled by cash, not by delivery. All contracts still in existence at the close of trading are closed out by the Clearing House. In effect the Clearing House *assumes* that all traders have closed out. The price used to close out is a proxy market price, which is calculated by obtaining from twelve bond dealers the yield at which they would buy and sell bonds in a basket of maturities set down in advance by the Exchange. The two highest buying yields and the two lowest selling yields are discarded and the remaining yields are averaged. This average yield is then converted to a settlement price using Equation 15.13, the bond-pricing formula.

## 3  QUOTATIONS
Like the BAB contract, the bond contract is quoted as 100 minus the annual percentage yield, but has a minimum fluctuation of 0.005.

## 4  TERMINATION OF TRADING
Trading ceases at 12 noon on the fifteenth day of the cash settlement month, or the next trading day if that is not a business day. Settlement day is the business day following the date on which trading ceases.

To illustrate the pricing of the 10-year bond futures contract, consider the price of 92.500 reported for the June (1994) 10-year bond futures contract in the *Australian Financial Review* of 24 March 1994. The implied yield is $100 - 92.500 = 7.500$ per cent per annum, or 3.750 per cent per half-year. The face value is $100 000. The half-yearly coupon rate is $0.5 \times 12$ per cent = 6 per cent. Therefore each coupon payment is $6000. The term is 10 years, or 20 half-years. Using Equation 15.13, the dollar price $P$ implicit in this futures price is:

$$P = \frac{\$6000}{0.0375}\left[1 - \frac{1}{(1.0375)^{20}}\right] + \frac{\$100\,000}{(1.0375)^{20}}$$

$$= \$83\,377.23 + \$47\,889.23$$

$$= \$131\,266.46$$

It is clear that, when using Equation 15.13 for the 10-year bond futures contract, $C$ is always $6000 and $V$ is always $100 000.

### 15.7.3  USES OF THE 10-YEAR BOND FUTURES CONTRACT
The 10-year bond futures contract can be used in similar ways to those explained for the BAB contract and therefore we do not explain these ways in full detail.

#### SPECULATION WITH 10-YEAR BOND FUTURES
As always, speculators are hoping to profit by correctly anticipating price changes. For example, if a long position is entered into at a futures price of 92.500 and reversed out at 93.500, a gain is made. As shown in the previous

calculations, a futures price of 92.500 corresponds to a dollar price of $131 266.46. A price of 93.500 corresponds to a half-yearly yield of 3.250 per cent and hence to a dollar price of:

$$P = \frac{\$6000}{0.0325}\left[1 - \frac{1}{(1.0325)^{20}}\right] + \frac{\$100\,000}{(1.0325)^{20}}$$
$$= \$139\,983.20$$

The gain is therefore $139 983.20 − $131 266.46 = $8716.74.

## HEDGING WITH 10-YEAR BOND FUTURES

The 10-year bond futures contract can be a useful hedging instrument where there is an exposure to changes in long-term fixed-interest rates. For example, an investor who holds long-term bonds or debentures will suffer a capital loss if yields increase. Such an investor might consider selling bond futures. Similarly, a company that plans to borrow funds in the future on a long-term fixed-interest basis will lose if yields increase before the funds are borrowed. Again, selling bond futures could be considered. Alternatively, an investor who plans to buy bonds, or a company that has issued debentures but is planning to repurchase them, could consider buying bond futures. These are essentially straightforward applications.

*Example 15.10*
Wantdough Ltd is committed to issuing 7-year 16 per cent per annum debentures in 2 months' time and plans to borrow $5 million. The debentures will pay interest twice per annum. Wantdough decides to hedge using futures contracts on 10-year government bonds. These are currently priced at 85.00. Wantdough assumes that an $x$ per cent change in the futures yield will be matched by an $x$ per cent change in the required rate of return on its debentures. The problem is to design a suitable hedge.

Wantdough sells 10-year bond futures. It will still encounter basis risk and it also faces specification differences in that there are important differences between 10-year 12 per cent government bonds and 7-year 16 per cent company debentures. Not much can be done about basis risk, but risks stemming from specification differences can be partly controlled by carefully selecting the number of futures contracts to be sold. Suppose that the futures price falls from 85.00 to 84.00, due to, say, a 1 per cent rise in current yields on government bonds. Using Equation 15.13, the contract value would fall by $4344.55 (from $84 708.26 to $80 363.71). Now suppose that, simultaneously, the required yield on the debentures also rises by 1 per cent from 16 per cent per annum to 17 per cent per annum. Using Equation 15.13, and assuming that the proposed coupon rate of 16 per cent is maintained, the funds raised would be:

$$\frac{\$400\,000}{0.085}\left[1 - \frac{1}{(1.085)^{14}}\right] + \frac{\$5\,000\,000}{(1.085)^{14}} = \$4\,799\,747.58$$

Therefore, there would be a shortfall of $200 252.42. The number of contracts required to hedge this shortfall would therefore be:

$$\frac{\$200\ 252.42}{\$4344.55}$$
$$= 46 \text{ contracts}$$

Therefore, Wantdough should sell 46 futures contracts.

The use of 10-year bond futures contracts for a hedging purpose is illustrated in Example 15.11. This example is a continuation of Example 15.10.

*Example 15.11*

Suppose that Wantdough sells 46 bond futures contracts at the current futures price of 85.00 and that when the debentures are issued the futures price is 84.58 and the required yield on the debentures is 16.50 per cent per annum. The problem is to assess the effectiveness of the hedge.

Using Equation 15.13, the change in the futures price is $1865.89 per contract, giving a profit of $85 831 from 46 contracts. Again, using Equation 15.13, if the required yield is 16.50 per cent per annum (8.25 per cent per half-year), then 7-year debentures with a face value of $5 million offering a coupon rate of 8 per cent per half-year will raise $4 898 427, thereby giving a gross shortfall of $101 573. After taking account of the profit on futures, the net shortfall is $15 742. Therefore the futures hedge has eliminated nearly 85 per cent of the shortfall that otherwise would have occurred. Most of the other 15 per cent is due to the fact that while the futures price changed by 0.42 (from 85.00 to 84.58), the debenture yield changed by 0.50 per cent (from 16.00 per cent to 16.50 per cent). As discussed in Example 15.10, Wantdough's assumption was one for one: if the debenture yield changed by one percentage point the futures yield would also change by one percentage point. Had the required debenture yield changed to 16.42 per cent (instead of to 16.50 per cent) the gross funds shortfall would have been $85 519 and there would then have been a small net gain of $312.

The detail of these calculations is less important than the recognition that it is not correct simply to hedge the face value. Had this been done, 50 futures contracts would have been sold (because $5million/$100 000 = 50). This would have exposed the company to net losses if yields had fallen.

## 15.8 FINANCIAL FUTURES ON THE SFE: THE SHARE PRICE INDEX (SPI) FUTURES CONTRACT

### 15.8.1 A BRIEF REVIEW OF THE SHARE PRICE INDEX (SPI)

The all-ordinaries share price index is calculated by the Australian Stock Exchange (ASX). Essentially the ASX collects data on the market prices of over 250 listed shares, calculates an average, and expresses the result in index form. Movements in the index give a clear indication of movements in the general level of share prices. Consequently the percentage change in the index is likely to approximate closely the percentage change in the value of a well-diversified portfolio of Australian listed shares.

### 15.8.2 SPECIFICATION OF THE SPI FUTURES CONTRACT

The SPI futures contract has the following major features:

#### 1 CONTRACT UNIT

The contract unit is the value of the all-ordinaries SPI, multiplied by $25.

#### 2 SETTLEMENT

The contract is not deliverable. All contracts still in existence at the close of trading are closed out by the Clearing House at the relevant spot SPI value, calculated to one decimal place.

#### 3 QUOTATIONS

The all-ordinaries SPI, to one full index point.

#### 4 TERMINATION OF TRADING

Trading ceases on the last business day of the contract month. Settlement day is the second business day following the cessation of trading.

For example, the *Australian Financial Review* of 9 March 1994 reported the price of the March (1994) SPI contract to be 2176. This means that in dollar terms the contract price on 8 March 1994 was 2176 × $25 = $54 400.

### 15.8.3 USES OF THE SPI CONTRACT

#### SPECULATION WITH SPI FUTURES

Because the SPI futures price is highly correlated with the SPI itself, it is a simple matter to use SPI futures for speculative purposes. This is illustrated in Example 15.12.

*Example 15.12*

On 8 March 1994 the all-ordinaries SPI closed at 2171.7 and the March (1994) SPI futures price was 2176. Suppose that a speculator believes that share prices are likely to fall in the following two weeks and she therefore decides to sell March SPI futures. On 22 March 1994 the speculator finds that the all-ordinaries SPI has fallen to 2140.8 and the March SPI futures price has fallen to 2145. Note that the fall in the all-ordinaries SPI (30.9 points, or 1.423 per cent) is closely matched by the fall in the SPI futures price (31 points, or 1.425 per cent).[23] The position is reversed out by taking a bought position at 2145.

---

[23] The match is frequently not as close as in this example although it is usually in the same direction if the shift is sizeable. For example, over the same period the price of the June futures contract fell from 2200 to 2164—a fall of 36 points, or 1.636 per cent.

Although the speculator's gain has accrued over time by application of the mark-to-market rule, the total gain can be calculated as follows:

| | | |
|---|---|---|
| Notional sale at | 2176 × $25 = | $54 400 (inflow) |
| Notional purchase at | 2145 × $25 = | $53 625 (outflow) |
| Gain (net inflow) | | $775 |

## HEDGING WITH SPI FUTURES

Although speculation is the most obvious application of SPI futures, there are also hedging uses. The following example provides a simple application.[24]

### Example 15.13

Michael Saint manages a portfolio of Australian shares with a current market value of $1 510 700. The portfolio is to be sold in 4 weeks' time. The SPI futures price today is 2162. The following two problems are relevant:
1. Saint requires assistance in designing an appropriate hedge.
2. Later, the portfolio is sold for $1 444 450 and the futures position is reversed at a price of 2054. Saint wishes to assess the effectiveness of the hedge.

Possible solutions to these problems are as follows:
1. The futures price at the initiation of the hedge is 2162 × $25 = $54 050. To design a hedge, some assumption must be made about the relationship between changes in the value of the portfolio and changes in the SPI futures price. For example, it might be assumed that proportionate changes in the portfolio's value will be matched by proportionate changes in the futures price. In other words, in designing this hedge it is assumed that if the portfolio's value decreases by $x$ per cent, then so also will the SPI futures price decrease by $x$ per cent. Using Equation 15.9, the number of futures contracts indicated is:

$$\begin{aligned} f^* &= -\frac{N_S}{N_F}\frac{S_0}{F_0} \\ &= -\frac{\text{Value of spot position}}{\text{Value of one futures contract}} \\ &= -\frac{\$1\,510\,700}{2162 \times \$25} \\ &= -27.95 \\ &\approx -28 \end{aligned}$$

That is, 28 futures contracts should be sold.
2. The effectiveness of the hedge is summarised in Table 15.11.

---

[24] For a more advanced discussion, see S. Figlewski & S. Kon, 'Portfolio Management with Stock Index Futures', *Financial Analysts Journal*, January/February 1982, pp. 52–9.

**Table 15.11** Hedging outcome in Example 15.13

| Date | SPI futures price per contract (index form) | SPI futures price for 28 contracts ($) | Portfolio value ($) |
|---|---|---|---|
| When hedge entered | 2162 (sold) | 1 513 400 | 1 510 700 |
| When hedge lifted | 2054 (bought) | 1 437 800 | 1 444 450 |
| Gain (loss) | | 75 600 | (66 250) |

Therefore the hedge has, in fact, resulted in a net gain of $75 600 − $66 250 = $9350. There are two reasons why the result is not precisely zero. First, the number of contracts sold was 28 not 27.95. However, this is a minor factor in this example. If it had been possible to sell 27.95 contracts the net gain would have been $9215. Secondly, while the portfolio value decreased by 4.39 per cent, the SPI futures price decreased by 5.00 per cent. Therefore the loss on the portfolio was more than offset by the gain on the sold futures contracts. There are two factors that are likely to explain the difference between the futures price fall of 5.00 per cent and the portfolio fall of 4.39 per cent. These are basis risk and specification differences between the composition of the SPI and the composition of Michael Saint's portfolio. Included in the latter is the possibility of dividends being received, whereas the SPI does not include reinvested dividends.

Obviously it is fairly crude to assume that there will be equal proportionate changes in the portfolio's value and the SPI futures price. A slightly more sophisticated approach is to apply Equation 15.7, which gives the risk-minimising hedge ratio, $h^*$:

$$h^* = - \frac{\text{Cov}(\tilde{S}_1, \tilde{F}_1)}{\text{Var}(\tilde{F}_1)}$$

In the case of SPI futures, Equation 15.7 is more recognisable if rewritten as:

$$h^* = - \frac{\text{Cov}(\tilde{R}_P, \tilde{R}_F)}{\text{Var}(\tilde{R}_F)}$$

where $\tilde{R}_P$ = returns on the hedger's portfolio of shares

$\tilde{R}_F$ = returns on the SPI futures contract

An estimate of $h^*$ is found by performing the regression:

$$\tilde{R}_{Pt} = \alpha_P + \beta_P \tilde{R}_{Ft} + u_t \qquad (15.14)$$

The estimate $\hat{\beta}_P$ is an estimate of $h^*$. Note that while $\hat{\beta}_P$ will be of the same order of magnitude as the asset 'betas' we discussed in Chapter 6, the hedging beta in Equation 15.14 is a different concept. A hedging beta is estimated by regressing portfolio returns on SPI futures; an asset beta is estimated by regressing portfolio returns on the SPI itself.

## 15.9 VALUATION OF FINANCIAL FUTURES

In Section 15.4 we analysed some of the determinants of futures prices. That analysis applies to futures contracts on physical commodities and to futures contracts on financial 'commodities'. In this section we build on that analysis, but narrow our focus to BAB futures and SPI futures.

Equation 15.1 provided a restriction on the valuation of a futures contract:

$$F \leq S + C$$

where $F$ = futures price
$S$ = current spot price
$C$ = carrying cost

If the commodity can readily be sold short, and if the opportunity cost of investment is the only form of carrying cost, then it can be shown that Equation 15.1 should hold as an equality:

$$F = S + C \qquad (15.15)$$

### 15.9.1 VALUATION OF BAB FUTURES

If it is assumed that bank bills can be sold short,[25] then Equation 15.15 should apply to bank-bill futures. In this case it is usual to express $C$ in terms of the yield $i_t$ applicable to the term $t$ of the futures contract. That is, the carrying cost is:

$$C = S i_t \qquad (15.16)$$

Substituting Equation 15.16 into Equation 15.15 gives:

$$F = S(1 + i_t) \qquad (15.17)$$

Implicitly, the pricing of bank-bill futures was also considered in the discussion of arbitrage in Section 15.6.3. This concluded with Equation 15.12:

$$i_{t,T} = \frac{1 + i_T}{1 + i_t} - 1$$

where = the maturity date of the futures contract
$i_{t,T}$ = the (futures) yield for a futures contract, maturing at date $t$, on a bill maturing at a later date $T$
$i_T$ = the (spot) yield on a bill maturing at date $T$
$i_t$ = the (spot) yield on a bill maturing at date $t$

Equation 15.12 is consistent with Equation 15.17. If the bill underlying the futures contract has a face value of $V$ dollars, then by definition:

$$F = \frac{V}{1 + i_{t,T}} \qquad (15.18)$$

Substituting Equation 15.12 into Equation 15.18 gives:

$$F = \frac{V(1 + i_t)}{1 + i_T} \qquad (15.19)$$

---

[25] This assumption is not as unreasonable as it may appear. When a bank bill is issued, it is effectively sold at its market price and it is subsequently repurchased at its face value.

The spot price $S$ of a T-day bill that also has a face value of $V$ is by definition:

$$S = \frac{V}{1 + i_T} \quad (15.20)$$

Substituting Equation 15.20 into Equation 15.19 gives:

$$F = S(1 + i_t)$$

This is the result stated in Equation 15.17.

According to this equation the BAB futures price is simply the spot price of the relevant bank bill, accumulated at the yield applicable to the term of the futures contract. The 'relevant bank bill' is *not* usually a 90-day bank bill. For example, if a BAB futures contract matures in 30 days' time, the relevant bank bill currently has a term of 120 days.

### 15.9.2 VALUATION OF SPI FUTURES

The valuation of share price index futures can be approached in a similar manner. This problem is slightly more complex because dividends are paid on many shares in the index but the calculation of the share price index excludes dividends. As in the discussion of bill futures, we continue to ignore the mark-to-market rule, and instead assume that the cash flows occur only on date 1, the maturity of the futures contract. Suppose that on date zero an investor buys all the shares in the index at a total cost of $S_0$, and also borrows a sum of money equal to PV($D$), the present value of the dividends that the shares will generate on date 1. All the shares in the index are subsequently sold on date 1 at their *then* current spot value of $S_1$. On the same date, the loan is repaid and dividends of $D$ are collected. Putting this in tabular form:

**Table 15.12** *Strategy producing a future cash flow of $S_1$*

| | On date zero | | On date 1 | |
|---|---|---|---|---|
| Action | | Cash flow | Action | Cash flow |
| Buy index | | $-S_0$ | Sell index | $+S_1$ |
| Borrow PV(D) | | $+$PV(D) | Repay loan | $-D$ |
| | | | Collect dividends | $+D$ |
| Total | | PV(D) $- S_0$ | Total | $S_1$ |

As an alternative, suppose that on date zero the investor buys SPI futures (price $F_0$) which mature on date 1 and also deposits (lends) the sum of $\frac{F_0}{1+r}$ to earn interest at a rate $r$. On date 1, the futures contract is settled and the deposit (plus interest) is withdrawn. The futures contract is settled by a notional sale at $F_1$, the futures price on date 1. However, as date 1 is the expiry date of the futures contract, convergence between spot prices and futures prices should ensure that

$F_1 = S_1$, the spot price on date 1. The cash flow from the futures contract is therefore $F_1 - F_0 = S_1 - F_0$. Putting this in tabular form:

**Table 15.13** *Alternative strategy producing a future cash flow of $S_1$*

| On date zero | | On date 1 | |
| --- | --- | --- | --- |
| Action | Cash flow | Action | Cash flow |
| Buy SPI futures | 0 | Settle futures | $S_1 - F_0$ |
| Deposit $\dfrac{F_0}{1+r}$ | $\dfrac{-F_0}{1+r}$ | Withdraw deposit plus interest | $+F_0$ |
| Total | $\dfrac{-F_0}{1+r}$ | Total | $S_1$ |

The point to note about Tables 15.12 and 15.13 is that both indicate a net cash inflow of $S_1$ dollars on date 1. Of course it is not known what $S_1$ will be, but it is known that both tables (that is, both investments) will generate the same future cash flow. Therefore both investments should cost the same on date zero:

$$\mathrm{PV}(D) - S_0 = \frac{-F_0}{1+r}$$

Solving for the futures price $F$ and, since they are no longer needed, dropping the subscripts, gives:

$$F = [S - \mathrm{PV}(D)](1 + r) \qquad (15.21)$$

Equation 15.21 and Equation 15.17 have the same form, except that Equation 15.21 has a simple adjustment which takes into account the complication caused by dividends. Equation 15.21 implies that the SPI futures price will generally exceed the current index value, but may not do so if there will be significant dividend payments during the life of the futures contract.

## 15.10 FORWARD-RATE AGREEMENTS (FRAs)

Forward-rate agreements (FRAs) are private agreements between two parties. Usually at least one of the parties is a bank or other financial institution. FRAs are not futures contracts but we discuss them in this chapter because they are often used as an alternative to interest-rate futures contracts.

Loosely speaking an FRA works as follows. Suppose Party A and Party B enter into an FRA. This means that if, on a specified future date, interest rates are 'low', then Party A must pay cash to Party B—and the lower the interest rates have fallen, the more cash A must pay B. However, the reverse also holds. If, on the specified future date, interest rates are 'high', then B must pay cash to A—again, the higher the interest rates have become, the more cash B must pay to A. In effect such a contract provides both parties with a guaranteed interest rate in the future. Thus, for example, Party A might be a company planning to borrow on the expiry date of the FRA. If interest rates rise before the loan is made, the FRA gives A a cash inflow to compensate for the higher interest rate. If, instead, interest rates fall during the period, the FRA requires A to make a cash payment, but this is compensated by the lower interest rate that will be charged on the funds borrowed.

We now turn to an example which provides a detailed explanation of how FRAs work.

*Example 15.14*

Company A intends to borrow $1 million in 3 months' time. This will be repaid (with interest) in a lump sum, 180 days later. That is, repayment will occur approximately 9 months from now. At present the interest rate on a 180-day loan is about 16.4 per cent per annum. Company A fears that in 3 months' time this rate might have risen substantially. Therefore, Company A approaches Bank B to set up a forward-rate agreement (FRA). The bank agrees, setting a contract rate of 16.50 per cent per annum. This means that if, in 3 months' time when the FRA expires, the 180-day bank bill rate exceeds 16.50 per cent, Bank B will pay Company A enough cash to compensate. In return, Company A has agreed that if, at that time, the 180-day bank bill rate is less than 16.50 per cent per annum, Company A will pay enough cash to Bank B to compensate. Note that the cash flow represents only a *difference* in interest payments, not the total interest payment. Further, no payment of principal is involved.

To show how the cash flow in an FRA is calculated, assume that when the FRA expires the market interest rate for a term of 180 days is 17.25 per cent per annum. Notionally, the FRA commits Company A to the following cash flows.

At date of FRA expiry: Inflow of $1m = sum borrowed.
180 days after FRA expiry: Outflow (repayment) of
$1m × [1 + (0.1650)(180/365)]
= $1 081 369.86

However, at the FRA's expiry date, the present value of this outflow is only:

$$\frac{\$1\,081\,369.86}{1 + (0.1725)(180/365)} = \$996\,591.34$$

In other words, the present value of Company A's promised repayment is, at the expiry of the FRA, worth $3408.66 less than $1 million. Under the terms of the FRA, Bank B pays Company A the sum of $3408.66.

The effect of this procedure is that Company A is able to borrow at a net cost of 16.5 per cent per annum, despite the increase in interest rates. Company A can borrow $996 591.36 for 180 days at an interest rate of 17.25 per cent per annum; adding to this amount the inflow of $3408.66 from Bank B, Company A will have funds of $1 million available. The repayment required is:

$996 591.34[1 + (0.1725)(180/365)]
= $1 081 369.86

Of course this is the same as the amount required to repay a loan of $1 million at 16.5 per cent per annum over 180 days, as required by Company A. That is,

Company A has locked in an interest rate of 16.5 per cent on its future borrowings.

A formula for the FRA can be developed as follows. Assume that the notional sum of $P$ dollars is to be borrowed for a period of $t$ days and the interest rate specified in the FRA is $i$ per annum. In Example 15.14, $P$ was $1 million, $t$ was 180 and $i$ was 16.5 per cent. This produces a notional promised future cash flow of $P[1 + (it/365)]$. At the expiry of the FRA the present value of this promised amount is $P[1 + (it/365)]/[1 + (rt/365)]$, where $r$ is the market interest rate for $t$ days at the expiry of the FRA. The prospective borrower receives, under the terms of the FRA, a sum of $Q$ dollars where:

$$Q = P - \frac{P[1 + (it/365)]}{1 + (rt/365)} \tag{15.22}$$

In Example 15.14, $r$ was 17.25 per cent per annum and $Q$ was $3408.66. Of course $Q$ can be negative and, in this case, the prospective borrower pays the other party to the FRA.[26]

Equation 15.22 can be rewritten to show more clearly that the cash flow produced by the FRA is due to the difference between the market interest rate $r$ at the expiry of the FRA, and the interest rate $i$ specified in the FRA. This is shown in Equation 15.23:

$$Q = \frac{(r - i)(t/365)P}{1 + (rt/365)} \tag{15.23}$$

The application of Equation 15.23 can be illustrated using the data of Example 15.14. This is shown in Example 15.15.

*Example 15.15*
In this case, $r = 0.1725$, $i = 0.1650$, $t = 180$, and $P = \$1m$. Therefore $Q$, the payment by the lender (Bank B) to the borrower (Company A), is:

$$Q = \frac{(0.1725 - 0.1650)(180/365)\$1m}{1 + [(0.1725)(180/365)]}$$

$$= \frac{0.003\,698\,630}{1.085\,068\,493}\$1m$$

$$= \$3408.66$$

If interest rates had instead fallen to, say, 15 per cent (that is, $r = 0.15$), then Equation 15.23 gives $Q = -\$6887.76$. Had this occurred, Company A would have been required to pay Bank B $6887.76 at the expiry of the FRA.

Forward-rate agreements are also entered into between banks and depositors. In this case, the bank pays the depositor if interest rates *decrease* during the life of the FRA, and the depositor pays the bank if interest rates *increase* during the life of the FRA. However, in most FRAs the client is a prospective borrower

---

[26] An FRA can also be written in terms of a future (or face) value $F$ instead of a principal sum $P$. The appropriate value of $Q$ can still be found using Equation 15.22, simply by substituting $P = F/(1 + it/365)$ in Equation 15.22.

seeking protection against rising interest rates, rather than a prospective depositor seeking protection against falling interest rates. Finally, many FRAs are agreements between banks, rather than agreements between clients and banks.

Many companies, particularly those which are small or medium in size, prefer to use an FRA rather than a futures contract. This is largely because an FRA can be tailored more closely to their specific needs in relation to amount, timing, and choice of interest rate. In addition, FRAs do not normally impose the same complex deposit and margin requirements as exist in futures contracts. However, larger companies, and particularly companies in the finance industry, may prefer a futures contract because it offers the flexibility of being able to reverse out at any time through a transaction on the futures exchange. Indeed, banks and other financial institutions use futures contracts to hedge the risks they create by entering into FRAs with their clients.

## SELECTED REFERENCES

Cornell, B. & Reinganum, M., 'Forward and Futures Prices: Evidence from the Foreign Exchange Markets', *Journal of Finance*, December 1981, pp. 1035–45.

Cox, J., Ingersoll, J. & Ross, S., 'The Relation between Forward Prices and Futures Prices', *Journal of Financial Economics*, December 1981, pp. 321–46.

Das, S., 'Forward Rate Agreements', *The Australian Banker*, June 1988, pp. 91–7.

Figlewski, S. & Kon, S., 'Portfolio Management with Stock Index Futures', *Financial Analysts Journal*, January/February 1982, pp. 52–9.

Goss, B. A. & Yamey, B. S. (Eds), *The Economics of Futures Trading*, 2nd edn, Macmillan, London, 1978.

Kolb, R. W., *Understanding Futures Markets*, 3rd edn, Simon & Schuster / New York Institute of Finance, New York, 1991.

Jameson, K. & Howard, L., 'The Futures Markets' in *Handbook of Australian Corporate Finance*, Eds R. Bruce et al., 4th edn, Butterworths, Sydney, 1991.

Sydney Futures Exchange publications:
    *Annual Report 1992*
    *90-Day Bank Bill Futures & Options Contracts*
    *Share Price Index (SPI) Futures & Options*
    *10-Year & 3-Year Treasury Bond Futures & Options Contracts*
    *SYCOM: The Sydney Computerised Overnight Market*
    *SFE Bulletin*, January/February 1994

## QUESTIONS

1. What are the major differences between a forward contract and a futures contract?

2. Distinguish between the following, providing in your answer brief examples to illustrate the points you make:
   (a) Deliverable futures contract and non-deliverable futures contract;
   (b) Speculator and hedger;
   (c) Short hedger and long hedger.

3. Obtain a recent copy of the *Australian Financial Review* and locate the table that reports on the Sydney Futures Exchange. List the 'commodities' on which futures contracts are traded. Why is there not a futures contract on wine?

4. *Futures markets are really there for the benefit of speculators, not hedgers. Very few contracts end in delivery, so obviously the futures market traders aren't interested in the actual commodities, and if they're not interested in the actual*

commodities, they can't be hedgers. Many contracts aren't even deliverable. How could anyone hedge with contracts like that? Consider carefully the various claims made in this statement.

5. Suppose that, at a particular time, the June futures price is $1200 and the September futures price is $1260. You are convinced that the spread between the June and September prices will soon widen, but you have no belief as to whether both prices will rise, or both prices will fall. What action(s) should you take? Show that as a result of your action(s) you will make a profit, if, on a subsequent date, the June futures price is $1300 and the September futures price is $1380.

6. On a particular day in the Xanadu Futures Exchange the following gold futures prices were observed:

| Delivery date (months) | Futures price per ounce ($) |
|---|---|
| 1 | 579 |
| 2 | 588 |
| 3 | 602 |
| 6 | 619 |
| 12 | 639 |

In Xanadu the interest rate is 1 per cent per month (compound). It costs $2 per ounce per month (payable for the whole period, in advance) to store and insure gold. Each futures contract covers eight ounces of gold. The current spot price of gold is $573 per ounce.

Identify any arbitrage opportunities. Explain how such opportunities could be exploited and calculate the profit per contract. Ignore transaction costs, taxes, and any interest received or foregone due to deposits or margins.

7. Consider the effects of an overnight share price fall of around 25 per cent on:
   (a) a speculator with a long position in the SPI futures contract; and
   (b) a superannuation fund with a short position in the SPI futures contract.

8. On 2 September the quoted price of the 90-day bank-bill futures contract maturing on 12 December was 82.00. On 8 September the price was 82.50. The face value of the bank bills underlying one contract is $500 000. Suppose that Harold sold fifteen such contracts on 2 September and closed out his position on 8 September. Ignoring transaction costs, how much has Harold made (or lost)?

9. On 2 March 1994 the June 1994 10-year bond futures contract was priced at 92.610. On 16 March 1994 the price was 92.590. If Maude held the contract 'long' over this period, how much has she made (or lost)?

10. You are the finance manager of Play Safe Ltd. On 28 August, Play Safe's Board of Directors decides that, in 7 weeks' time, Play Safe will issue four bank bills, each with a face value of $100 000 and a term of 120 days. In its planning, the Board has assumed that yields will not change from their current levels. On 29 August you are told to arrange a hedge for Play Safe. On that date, you are given the following data:

|  |  |  |
|---|---|---|
| BAB yields: | 90 days | 13.82 per cent per annum |
|  | 120 days | 14.07 per cent per annum |
| BAB futures: | September | 86.10 |
|  | December | 85.85 |

You arrange an appropriate hedge. Several months later you are asked to write a report on your hedging performance, including reasons for any net gain or loss made. Consulting the records, you discover that the bills were issued on time at a rate of 15.37 per cent per annum and the futures contract was reversed at 84.65. At that time the 90-day bill rate was 15.13 per cent per annum. Describe how you would have hedged in this situation. What major points would you make in the report? Include relevant calculations.

11. Jane Hedges has today invested in a 180-day bank bill with a face value of $500 000, priced to yield 14.30 per cent per annum. Simultaneously she has sold a futures contract on a 90-day bank bill with a face value of $500 000. The futures contract will expire in 90 days' time from today. The futures price is 85.55. Jane intends to settle the futures contract by delivery. Ignoring any effects from the mark-to-market rule, what yield (simple interest, in per cent per annum) will Jane achieve on her investment? What, if anything, does this imply about today's 90-day bank bill yield? Why?

12. Today, Hank Ltd issued a 120-day bank bill with a face value of $500 000 at a yield of 8.90 per cent per annum Simultaneously Hank bought a futures contract on a 90-day bank bill at a price of 91.03. The futures contract matures in 30 days' time and is based on a face value of $500 000. Hank intends to allow the futures contract to be settled by delivery. Ignoring any effects from the mark-to-market rule, describe carefully the economic substance of Hank's transactions. Include in your answer details of all cash flows (amount, timing, and whether inflows or outflows). What yield (simple interest, in per cent per annum) will Hank pay? What, if anything, does this imply about today's interest rates? Why?

13. Thurber Ltd is a firm of underwriters that today has had to take up at face value ($7.5 million) 8-year debentures issued by Beetham Properties Ltd. The Beetham debentures offer a coupon rate of 16.5 per cent per annum, payable half-yearly. Thurber is therefore an 'unwilling lender' but, for various reasons, Thurber intends to hold the Beetham debentures until the first coupon date, which is in 6 months' time, and then sell the debentures. Thurber intends to hedge by using the SFE futures contract on 10-year government bonds. The current price of this contract is 85.00.
    (a) How many SFE contracts should be entered into? Show your calculations and explain briefly.
    (b) What risks (if any) do you think Thurber may still face, despite having hedged?

14. On 18 February you observe that the share price index (SPI) stands at 2317.4, while the March SPI futures price is 2353 and the June SPI futures price is 2390. You believe that the difference between the March and June futures prices is too narrow and will soon widen, but you have no views as to whether the SPI or the SPI futures prices will increase or decrease. How can your beliefs be put to the (financial) test? Show that, if your prediction is right, you will profit from trading futures, regardless of whether share prices as a whole increase or decrease.

15. You are the manager of the Dorfman Investment Fund. On 9 March you receive notice that a segment of the fund must be sold on or about 30 March. This segment comprises a broadly-based selection of listed Australian shares and is currently valued at $6 165 000. The risk is hedged using April SPI futures. On 28 March the shares are sold and the futures contract is reversed. Relevant data are as follows:

|  | On 9 March | On 28 March |
|---|---|---|
| Portfolio value | $6 165 000 | $5 840 000 |
| SPI | 1322.6 | 1261.1 |
| SPI futures | 1349 | 1272 |

**Required:**
Bearing in mind that on 9 March you do not know the 28 March outcomes, report on how you would have hedged. Include in your report the number of futures contracts and whether they were bought or sold. Assess the effectiveness of the hedge and explain any imperfections experienced.

16. As at today's date, the value of shares in the Xanadu share price index (SPI) is $126 000. A four-month futures contract on those shares is priced at $125 913. In four months' time, dividends totalling $5203 will be paid on the shares. Of course $S$, the value of shares at that time, is currently not known. In Xanadu the interest rate for both borrowing and lending is 1% per month (compound). There are no transaction costs or taxes in Xanadu.

   (a) Suppose that today you buy the shares in the index and also borrow $5000. After four months you collect the dividends, sell the shares, and repay the loan. Calculate the resulting cash flows for today and after four months.
   (b) Suppose instead that today you buy the futures contract and deposit the sum of $121 000 in an interest-bearing account. After four months you settle on the futures contract and withdraw your deposit (with interest). Calculate the resulting cash flows for today, and after four months.
   (c) Explain in detail why the above calculations show that the futures contract is correctly priced today.
   (d) If today the futures price is $126 913, calculate the current and future cash flows that result if today the following transactions are entered into simultaneously: borrow $126 000, buy shares, and sell the futures contract. Comment.

# CHAPTER 16

# OPTIONS AND CONTINGENT CLAIMS

## 16.1 INTRODUCTION

In this chapter we consider financial contracts known as options. Most of this chapter is concerned with options to buy or sell shares, but other types of options are also considered. An option is a special case of a type of contract called a **contingent claim**. Stated simply, a contingent claim is an asset whose value depends on the value of some other asset. A surprisingly large number of financial arrangements fall into this category. Contingent claims are discussed in Section 16.7. First, however, we consider options and option markets.

## 16.2 OPTIONS AND OPTION MARKETS

### 16.2.1 THE NATURE OF AN OPTION

An option is the right (but not the obligation) to force a transaction to occur at some future time on terms and conditions agreed to now. For example, the buyer of a **call option** on shares obtains the right to buy shares in the future from the seller (or writer) of the call at a price determined now.[1] The buyer of the call can exercise the right to obtain the shares at the predetermined price, regardless of what is then the current market price of the shares. Similarly the buyer of a **put option** has the right to sell shares in the future to the writer of the put at a predetermined price, regardless of what is then the share's current market price.

---

1 Shares are of course not the only assets that can be the subject of an option contract. For example, there are options on stock market indices, on debt instruments, on foreign currencies, and on futures contracts. The last two are discussed in Sections 16.5 and 16.6. Detailed discussion of all four can be found in H. R. Stoll & R. E. Whaley, *Futures and Options: Theory and Applications*, South-Western Publishing, Cincinnati, 1993.

This right to buy (in the case of a call) or to sell (in the case of a put) must be paid for by the option buyer at the time the option is purchased. The amount paid is called the option price and is determined by market forces.

The Australian Options Market provides facilities for the trading of calls and puts on the shares of approximately 45 major companies listed in Australia. The following example, taken from that market, illustrates the nature of a *call option*. On 8 March 1994 the closing price of the 'June 17.00' series of call options on the shares of BHP was $1.32. The closing price of BHP shares on the same date was $17.60. Here, 'June' refers to the month in which the call expires. In this case, the date of expiry is 23 June 1994.[2] The figure '17.00' indicates an **exercise price** (or **strike price**) of $17.00, while the $1.32 is the price of the call. Shares in BHP are the 'underlying shares' in this transaction and like most contracts in the Australian Options Market, each option contract covers 1000 shares. Therefore the call buyer has paid 1000 × $1.32 = $1320 to obtain the right to buy 1000 BHP shares at any time between 8 March 1994 and 23 June 1994 at a predetermined price of $17.00 per share. If the buyer calls on the writer to 'deliver' (sell) the underlying shares, he is said to 'exercise' the option. Because the call buyer is able to exercise *at any time* up to (and including) the expiry date, the option is said to be of the 'American' type; if exercise can occur only on the expiry date (and not before) it is an option of the 'European' type.

The following example, also taken from the Australian Options Market, illustrates the nature of a *put option*. On 8 March 1994 the closing price of the 'April 12.00' series of put options on the shares of the National Australia Bank (NAB) was 45 cents. The closing price of NAB shares on the same date was $11.92. The expiry date is 28 April 1994, the exercise price is $12.00, and the price of the put is 45 cents per share. The put buyer has paid 1000 × $0.45 = $450 to obtain the right to sell 1000 NAB shares at any time between 8 March 1994 and 28 April 1994 at a predetermined price of $12.00 per share. If the put buyer requires the put writer to purchase the underlying shares, he is said to 'exercise' the option. As with calls, puts traded in the Australian Options Market are of the American type.

The value of a call when it expires depends on whether the share price at that time is greater than or less than the exercise price. If the share price at the expiry of the call exceeds the exercise price, the call is worth the difference between the two. However, if the share price at that time is less than the exercise price, the call is worth zero. For example, if the price of BHP shares at the close of trading on 23 June 1994 had been, say, $18.00 per share, the June 17.00 call would have been worth $1 per optioned share. The reason is as follows. If the call were priced at less than $1 (say 90 cents), a riskless arbitrage would exist. An investor could buy the call for 90 cents per share, exercise the call at a cost of $17.00 per share, and then resell, for $18.00 per share, the shares obtained through exercise. The cash inflow from this strategy is $18.00 per share, while

---

2 This is the last day of trading and if an option is to be exercised, this must be done before 5 p.m. on that day. The exchange, however, uses the term 'date of expiry' to refer to the next day. See Australian Options Market, *Understanding Options Trading*, p. 5.

the cash outflow is only $17.90, giving an instantaneous profit of 10 cents per share. Similarly it is easy to show that there will also be an instantaneous profit available if the call were priced at more than $1. Therefore, the call's price would be $1.[3] However, if the closing price of BHP shares on 23 June 1994 had been less than $17.00, there would have been no benefit to be gained from exercise, and no remaining life to give the call a value. The call would therefore have been worth zero. In summary, at expiry a call is worth, and should therefore be priced at:

$$\text{Max}\,[0,\,P^* - C]$$

where $P^*$ = the share price on the call's expiry date[4]
$C$ = the exercise price of the call

Similar reasoning can be applied to determine the value of a put at its expiry. If, when a put expires, the share price is less than the exercise price, the put is worth the difference between the two. However, if the share price is less than the exercise price, the put is worth zero. If, for example, on 28 April 1994 the price of NAB shares had been $11.00, the value of the April 12.00 put on that date would have been $1. A put price of less than $1 would yield an instantaneous profit for an investor undertaking the strategy of buying both the put and the shares and then reselling the shares by exercising the put. Similarly a put price greater than $1 would also permit an instantaneous profit to be made. In summary, at expiry, a put is worth, and should therefore be priced at:

$$\text{Max}\,[0,\,C - P^*]$$

where $P^*$ = the share price on the put's expiry date
$C$ = the exercise price of the put

### 16.2.2 How options are created and traded

Options on shares may be created by the company whose shares underlie the option contract, or by parties who have no association with the company. Options created by the company are nearly always call options and may be created for a number of reasons, of which two are the most common. First, these call options may be issued to investors as a means of raising capital for the company. The sale of the options will raise capital and there will be a further inflow of capital if the options are subsequently exercised. Options of this kind may be listed on the stock exchange and appear in the share lists together with other securities issued by the company. Secondly, the company may issue call options to senior employees or directors of the company. Typically, in the case of listed companies, options of this kind form part of the compensation package for managers and are not a significant source of capital for the company.

Options can also be created by parties who may have no association with the company. For example, two share market observers, A and B, may enter into

---

[3] To make the same point in a different fashion, since expiry brings the call's life to a close, there exist no later opportunities that could otherwise warrant a call price greater than $1.

[4] Throughout this chapter, an asterisk (*) is used to indicate the value of the variable on the option's expiry date. Note also that in the option-pricing literature, $S$ or $X$ is the usual notation for share price. The symbol $P$ is used here to conform with earlier chapters in this book.

a private option contract on the shares of BHP. This will not raise any capital for BHP and does not require any agreement or involvement on the part of BHP. Frequently one or other of the parties will be a shareholder in the company— for example, B may be a shareholder who buys a put on BHP shares to give protection against a fall in BHP's share price. However, it may be that neither party is a shareholder at the time of entering into the option contract. Only if the option is subsequently exercised will it be necessary for shares to be delivered. Shares for this purpose can be purchased if and when the option is exercised. Many of the terms in private option contracts will be subject to negotiation between the parties. After negotiation the contract will specify at least the following: the type and number of shares to be optioned, the exercise price, the expiry date, the adjustment (if any) to be made in the event of a change in capital structure (due to any bonus or rights issue for example), the adjustment (if any) to be made in the event of a dividend payment, and, of course, the price of the option. On payment of the option price the buyer and writer are bound contractually.

While options created by private negotiation have the advantage that the features desired by the parties can be specified precisely, there are three major disadvantages. First, since there is no organised system for bringing together potential parties to the contract it will often be very difficult to find a party with whom to contract. Secondly, even if such a party is found and a contract entered into, it will not be possible to reverse out of the contract before the agreed expiry date. Thirdly, it will be necessary to investigate the creditworthiness of the other party every time an option is created. A solution to all three problems is to establish an organised market, called a listed option market, that provides a standardised form of option contract, a list of options in which trading can be undertaken, and a procedure that avoids the need for repeated checking of creditworthiness. The Australian Options Market is a market of this type.[5]

In a listed option market, traders select the desired underlying share, expiry date, and exercise price from a list of those available. Each contract covers a fixed number of shares, and, although adjustments are made for new share issues during the life of the option, they are not made for dividend payments. The only negotiable term is the option price, which is determined by market forces. An individual buyer in any option series is not bound contractually to an individual writer, but rather the class of buyers (as a whole) is bound contractually to the class of writers (as a whole), with exercise notices being distributed randomly between individual writers. However, exercise is fairly uncommon, as most activity is in the secondary option market, which is relatively easy to organise because of the standardised form of contract. For example, instead of exercising, the holder of a call option can take his profit by selling the call in the secondary market.[6] It is possible in this case that the buyer will be an existing writer who

---

[5] Similar observations were made in Chapter 15 about the development of futures contracts from forward contracts. There are many similarities between the organisation of a listed option market and the organisation of a futures market.

[6] Some reasons for preferring a sale to an exercise are explained in Section 16.2.8. As a consequence, in practice relatively few options are exercised.

wishes to cancel out his position, in order to avoid being exercised against. The organisers of the market check the creditworthiness of all traders and, in a manner similar to the role of futures market authorities, take the role of counterparty in every transaction. A description of this process in the futures markets is provided in Section 15.2.2.

There are numerous option markets around the world organised along these lines. The first such market to be established was the Chicago Board Options Exchange, which opened in 1973. The Australian Options Market has a similar structure and opened in 1976. The vast majority of share options in Australia are traded through the Australian Options Market, although the Sydney Futures Exchange offers options on share price index futures contracts.

### 16.2.3 OPTION CONTRACTS AND FUTURES CONTRACTS

It is important to distinguish between option contracts and futures contracts because it is often mistakenly thought that there are only minor differences between them. Of course there are some notable similarities. For example, both types of contract may involve the delivery of some underlying asset at a future date and at a predetermined price. However, there are very significant differences between them. Most importantly, a futures contract *requires* the delivery of the underlying asset, whereas an option buyer *chooses* whether delivery will occur. Buyers in futures contracts have an *obligation* to buy the underlying asset, whereas buyers of, say, call options have the *right* to buy if they so choose. Therefore, if buyers in futures contracts take no action to cancel their positions, they will be required to buy the underlying asset at the expiry of the contract. If buyers of call or put options take no action to cancel their positions, the options simply expire and there are no subsequent transactions. A related difference concerns payment. When a futures contract is made, the payment of the futures price is not required until the expiry date, but when an option contract is made, the buyer must immediately pay the option price to the writer. If the option is subsequently exercised, there is a further transaction when the exercise price is paid.

### 16.2.4 PAYOFF STRUCTURES FOR CALLS AND PUTS

It is an axiom of finance theory that, ultimately, the prospect of future cash flows is the only source of value. An alternative term for the future cash flows of a contract is its **payoff structure**. The easiest financial contract to value is one which promises (with certainty) a fixed amount to be paid in cash on a fixed future date. That is, the payoff structure is a single cash flow with a probability of 1.0. The payoff structures for options are more complicated because the payoff (cash flow) depends on the share price on the expiry date of the option.

Consider the BHP 17.00 call option discussed in Section 16.2.1. If, on the call's expiry date, the BHP share price is $17.00 or less, the call will be worth nothing on expiry. There will be no payoff at all. If, however, the share price at the expiry of the call is more than $17.00, the payoff per share is the difference before the share price and the exercise price of $17.00. For example, if the share price at the expiry of the call is $17.50, the payoff is $0.50. The payoff structure is shown in more detail in Table 16.1. The information in Table 16.1 is shown in graphical form in Figure 16.1.

**Table 16.1** *Payoff structure for a call with an exercise price of $17.00*

| If the share price ($) on the call's expiration date is | Then the payoff (cash flow) ($) to the call holder is |
|---|---|
| 15.00 | 0 |
| 15.50 | 0 |
| 16.00 | 0 |
| 16.50 | 0 |
| 17.00 | 0 |
| 17.50 | 0.50 |
| 18.00 | 1.00 |
| 18.50 | 1.50 |
| 19.00 | 2.00 |
| 19.50 | 2.50 |

The payoff structure for a put option is illustrated using as an example the NAB 12.00 put option also discussed in Section 16.2.1. If, on the put's expiry date, the NAB share price is $12.00 or more, the put will be worth nothing on expiry. There will be no payoff at all. However, if the share price on the expiry date of the put is less than $12.00, the payoff is the difference between the exercise price of $12.00 and the share price. For example, if the share price at the expiry of the put is $10.50, the payoff is $1.50. The payoff structure is shown in more detail in Table 16.2 and the information in Table 16.2 is shown in graphical form in Figure 16.2.

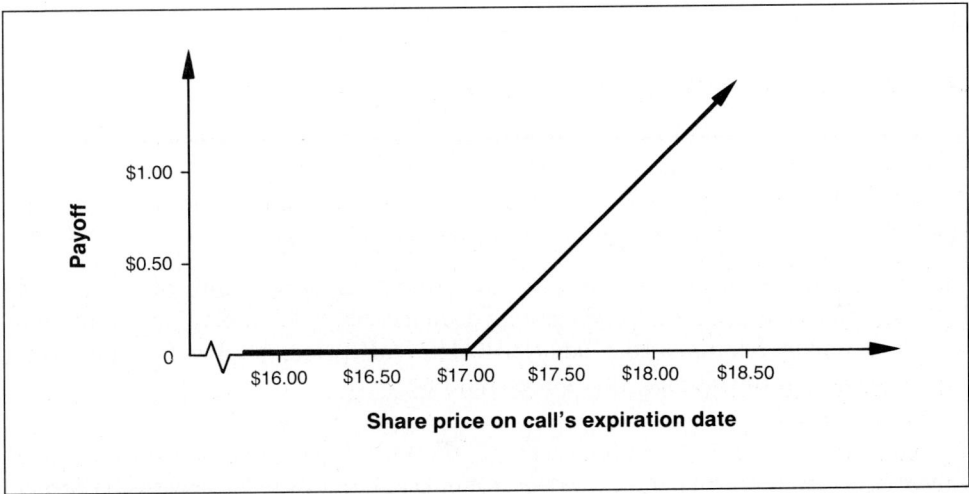

**Fig. 16.1** *Payoff structure: call (bought)*

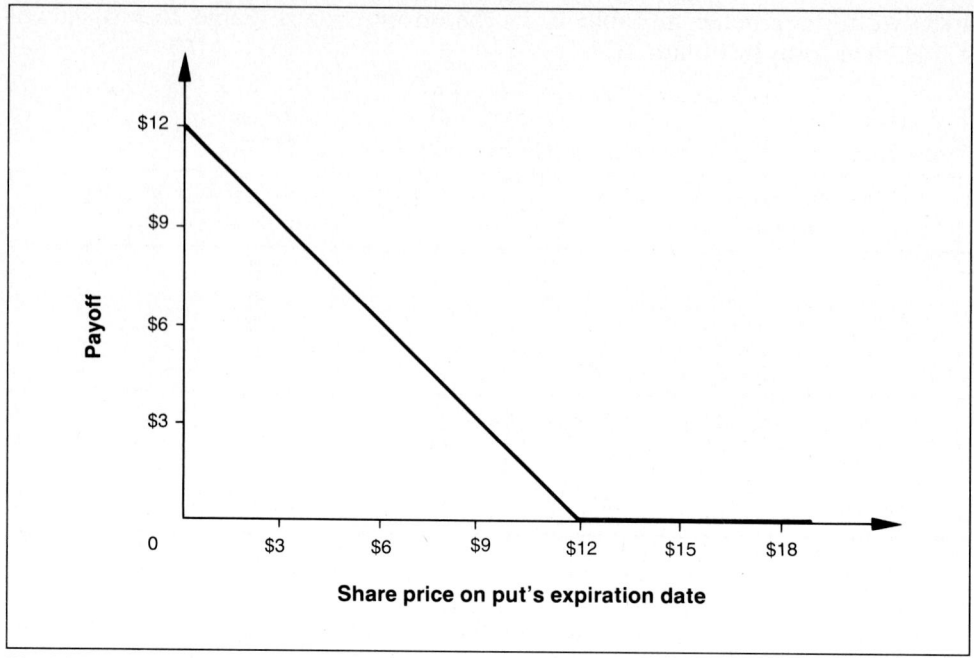

**Fig. 16.2**  *Payoff structure: put (bought)*

**Table 16.2**  *Payoff structure for a put with an exercise price of $12.00*

| If the share price ($) on the put's expiration date is | Then the payoff (cash flow) ($) to the put holder is |
| --- | --- |
| 9.50  | 2.50 |
| 10.00 | 2.00 |
| 10.50 | 1.50 |
| 11.00 | 1.00 |
| 11.50 | 0.50 |
| 12.00 | 0 |
| 12.50 | 0 |
| 13.00 | 0 |
| 13.50 | 0 |

### 16.2.5 FACTORS AFFECTING CALL OPTION PRICES

The aim of this section is to develop an intuitive understanding of the factors that will affect the price of a call option.[7] Discussion of formal valuation models is undertaken in Sections 16.3 and 16.4. The call prices shown in Table 16.3 will be useful in developing this understanding.

---

[7] Similar factors are relevant to the determination of put prices. These are discussed in Section 16.2.6.

**Table 16.3** *Prices of selected call options on BHP shares on 22 and 23 March 1994*

| Expiry date | Exercise price ($) | Call prices[a] on: 22 March 1994 ($) | Call prices[a] on: 23 March 1994 ($) | Percentage increase in price |
|---|---|---|---|---|
| 28 April 1994 | 17.00 | 0.60 | $0.70\frac{1}{2}$ | 17.5 |
| 28 April 1994 | 17.50 | $0.37\frac{1}{2}$ | 0.54 | 44.0 |
| 28 April 1994 | 18.00 | $0.19\frac{1}{2}$ | 0.33 | 69.2 |
| 23 June 1994 | 17.00 | 0.91 | 1.07 | 17.6 |
| 23 June 1994 | 17.50 | $0.65\frac{1}{2}$ | 0.84 | 28.2 |
| 23 June 1994 | 18.00 | 0.47 | $0.63\frac{1}{2}$ | 35.1 |
| Share price ($) | | 17.10 | 17.42 | 1.9 |

Source: *Australian Financial Review*, 23 and 24 March 1994
[a] Note: option prices shown are actually means of closing bid and ask prices.

Options have value because option buyers can exercise the option to their advantage, should the opportunity to do so arise. A fundamental advantage of holding a call option is that it may be possible to obtain the underlying shares more cheaply by exercising the option than by direct share purchase. Intuitively the price paid for the right to exercise should therefore reflect, among other factors, the probability that the share price will rise above the exercise price (or rise further above it, if it has already been exceeded). This probability should, in turn, be related to the following factors.

### 1 THE CURRENT SHARE PRICE

The higher the current share price, the greater is the probability that the share price will increase above the exercise price, and therefore the higher the call price, other things being equal. Ignoring market imperfections, a call whose underlying share price is already above the exercise price must be worth at least the difference between the two. This is referred to as its **intrinsic value**. However, even a call whose exercise price is above the current price of the underlying share must be worth something. It has value as long as there is some chance, however small, that at some point in the call's life the intrinsic value may become positive. In Table 16.3, every call commands a price that is greater than its intrinsic value. For example, on 22 March, the intrinsic value of the June 17.00 is 10 cents, and its price is 91 cents. The dependence of the call price on the current share price can be seen in the fact that all six calls increased in price when there was an increase in the price of the underlying shares. Note also that the percentage increases for the call prices far exceed the percentage increase in the share price. That is, the leverage offered by call options is very high.

### 2 THE EXERCISE PRICE

Clearly, the higher the exercise price, the lower is the probability that the share price will increase above the exercise price, and therefore the lower the call price, other things being equal. This relationship can be seen in the prices given in Table 16.3. For example, on 22 March, the June 17.00 has a price of 91 cents, whereas the June 18.00 has a price of only 47 cents.

## 3 THE TERM TO EXPIRY

The longer the term to expiry, the greater is the probability that the share price will increase above the exercise price. Therefore the longer the term to expiry, the greater is the call price, other things being equal. To make the same point in a slightly different way, consider two American calls which are equivalent in every respect, except that one has a shorter term to expiry than the other. In the period before the expiry of the shorter-term call, both calls provide the option buyer with the same rights. However, the rights conferred by the longer-term call continue for a further period. Therefore, the longer-term call is more valuable. The amount of the call price over and above any intrinsic value is called the **time value**, since with all other factors constant it will be greater, the longer the term to expiry. Note, however, that term to expiry is only one factor determining the time value. It should also be distinguished from the 'time value of money', which is dealt with in (5) below. This effect of term to expiry on call price can be seen in the prices given in Table 16.3. For example, on 22 March, the April 17.00 has a price of 60 cents whereas the longer-term June 17.00 has a price of 91 cents.

## 4 THE VOLATILITY OF THE SHARE

The volatility of a share is the variability of its price over time.[8] The effect of volatility on call price is illustrated in the following simple example. Consider a high volatility share $H$ whose current price is $5, and a low volatility share $L$, whose current price is also $5. Consider call options on $H$ and $L$ at a moment before expiry. The exercise price of both call options is $5. As explained previously, calls at expiry are worth a positive amount if the difference between the share price and the exercise price is positive. Otherwise they are worth zero. Suppose further that the probabilities of various share prices at expiry are known to be those shown in Table 16.4.

**Table 16.4** *Probability distributions for shares H and L*

| Share H | | | Share L | | |
|---|---|---|---|---|---|
| Share price ($) | Probability | Value of call ($) | Share price ($) | Probability | Value of call ($) |
| 4.00 | 0.2 | 0 | 4.00 | 0.04 | 0 |
| 4.50 | 0.2 | 0 | 4.50 | 0.16 | 0 |
| 5.00 | 0.2 | 0 | 5.00 | 0.60 | 0 |
| 5.50 | 0.2 | 0.50 | 5.50 | 0.16 | 0.50 |
| 6.00 | 0.2 | 1.00 | 6.00 | 0.04 | 1.00 |

The expected values of the calls on shares $H$ and $L$ are:

---

[8] Volatility can be measured in various ways. One frequently used measure is the variance of the share's returns over a recent period.

$$E(\text{call on } H) = (0.2)(\$0.50) + (0.2)(\$1.00)$$
$$= \$0.30$$
$$E(\text{call on } L) = (0.16)(\$0.50) + (0.04)(\$1.00)$$
$$= \$0.12$$

The call on the low-volatility share is less valuable than the call on the high-volatility share. This result is not peculiar to this particular example and it may be shown that, other things being equal,[9] calls on high-volatility shares are worth more than calls on low-volatility shares.

The basic reason for this result is the asymmetric nature of the payoffs on a call option. As shown in Table 16.4, at the time of expiry the holder of a call is indifferent between all share prices which are less than or equal to the exercise price. All such share prices are equally disastrous for the call holder because in all such cases the value of the call is zero. However, at expiry, for share prices which exceed the exercise price, the value of the call increases by 1 cent for every 1 cent increase in the share price. At times before expiry this asymmetry is not as sharp, but it remains true that the holder of a call benefits more from, say, a 1 cent increase in share price than is lost from a 1 cent decrease in share price. While a higher share price volatility increases the chance of *both* large increases and large decreases in the share price, the asymmetric features just described mean that the holder of a call gains more from the increased chance of a large increase in share price than is lost from the increased chance of a large decrease in share price. Therefore, on balance the call holder has a favourable view of volatility. Higher volatility increases the price of a call, other things being equal.

## 5   THE RISK-FREE INTEREST RATE

The buyer of a call option can defer paying for the shares. (Of course the call also confers the right not to buy the shares at all, but this is not the point we are making.) Because interest rates are positive, money has a **time value**, so the right to defer payment is valuable. The higher the interest rate, the more valuable is this right. Therefore it is plausible to suggest that the higher the risk-free interest rate, the higher is the price of a call, other things being equal.

## 6   EXPECTED DIVIDENDS

It was explained in Section 11.4.4 that if a company pays a dividend to its ordinary shareholders the share price will fall on the ex-dividend date by approximately the amount of the dividend per share. It has already been explained in this chapter that the price of a call will decrease if the price of the underlying share decreases. It is to be expected, therefore, that a call on a share that will go ex-dividend before the expiry of the call is worth less than if the share either never pays dividends or, if it does pay dividends, will not reach the next ex-dividend date until after the call has expired.[10] In short, calls on shares that pay

---

[9] For a proof, see R. C. Merton, 'Theory of Rational Option Pricing', *Bell Journal of Economics and Management Science*, Spring 1973, p. 149.
[10] For further discussion of this proposition, see Merton, (Footnote 9), pp. 151–4.

high dividends during the life of the call are worth less than calls on shares that pay low dividends during the life of the call, other things being equal.

The effect of dividends on call price may be reduced, though not eliminated, if the option is of the 'American' type.[11] As mentioned in Section 16.2.1, this type of option may be exercised at any time before expiry. By exercising just before an ex-dividend date, the holder of a call becomes a shareholder and is therefore entitled to the dividend. The cost of this strategy is that the call's expiry date is, in effect, shifted to the ex-dividend date, thereby reducing its effective term to expiry. As explained earlier, a shorter term to expiry reduces the time value of a call and hence reduces its price. Therefore, in deciding whether a call should be exercised before an ex-dividend date, the call holder needs to balance carefully the benefit of obtaining the dividend against the cost of forfeiting the option's time value.

To summarise, other things being equal, call prices should be higher (lower):
1. the higher (lower) the current share price;
2. the lower (higher) the exercise price;
3. the longer (shorter) the term to expiry;
4. the more (less) volatile the price of the underlying share;
5. the higher (lower) the risk-free interest rate;
6. the lower (higher) the expected dividend to be paid following an ex-dividend date that occurs during the term of the call.

### 16.2.6 SOME BASIC FEATURES OF PUT OPTION PRICING

The buyer of a put option obtains the right to sell shares at the exercise price. The higher the exercise price, the more the buyer of the put stands to gain. For example, the right to sell a share for $1 is a more valuable right than the right to sell for only 90 cents, other things being equal. Therefore, for put options, the higher the exercise price, the higher is the price of the option. For call options the opposite is true. Similarly the right to sell a share at a fixed price is less valuable, the higher the current share price, other things being equal. For example, suppose that the holder of a put exercised her right to sell a share at the exercise price of $1. If the current share price is 90 cents, the holder of the put gains 10 cents because she has been able to sell the share for 10 cents more than it is currently worth. If the share price had been higher at, say, 95 cents, the gain would have been only 5 cents. Therefore higher share prices imply lower put prices, other things being equal. For call options the opposite is true. The relationship between put price and term to expiry is straightforward in the case of American puts. Consider two American puts, equivalent in all respects except that one has a longer term to expiry. Both puts may be exercised at any time up to (and including) their respective expiry dates. Therefore, the long-term put permits exercise at all of the times permitted by the short-term put, but in addition

---

11 European-type options usually contain a clause that adjusts the contract's terms if there is a dividend. Like the right to exercise early, these 'dividend protection clauses', as they are known, reduce, but do not eliminate, the effects of dividends.

the long-term put permits exercise after the expiry of the short-term put. Therefore, for American puts, a longer term to expiry increases the value of the put, other things being equal.[12] This is also true of call options.

Table 16.5 shows the prices of six NAB put options on 22 March 1994. The closing share price on that date was $11.82.

**Table 16.5** *Prices of selected put options on NAB shares on 22 March 1994*

| Expiry date | Exercise price ($) | Put price[a] ($) |
| --- | --- | --- |
| 28 April 1994 | 11.00 | $0.07\frac{1}{2}$ |
| 28 April 1994 | 12.00 | 0.41 |
| 28 April 1994 | 13.00 | 1.25 |
| 28 July 1994 | 11.00 | 0.33 |
| 28 July 1994 | 12.00 | 0.74 |
| 28 July 1994 | 13.00 | 1.45 |
| Share price ($) | | 11.82 |

Source: *Australian Financial Review*, 23 March 1994.
[a] Note: Option prices shown are actually the means of closing bid and ask prices.

The influences of exercise price and term to expiry can be seen in the put prices given in Table 16.5. For example, the price of the April 13.00 exceeds that of the April 12.00, which in turn exceeds that of the April 11.00; this illustrates that, other things being equal, a higher exercise price implies a higher put price. Comparing puts of different terms, it is also clear that a longer term implies a higher put price, other things being equal. For example, the price of the April 12.00 put is 41 cents, while the price of the July 12.00 put is 74 cents.

Unlike calls, puts have a maximum value. For example, in the case of the April 11.00 put in Table 16.5, even if the price of NAB shares should fall to zero, the payoff to the holder of the put cannot exceed $11.00. Because share prices can never fall below zero, a put can never be worth more than its exercise price.

The buyer of a put option gains if share prices fall. Consequently, puts are especially attractive to shareholders who fear that the share price may decrease, but who nevertheless do not wish to sell their shares. Consider, for example, an investor who on 22 March 1994 buys a NAB share for $11.82 and a NAB July 11.00 put for 33 cents, making a total outlay of $12.15. The put option ensures that, until it expires in July, the investor is guaranteed a price of at least $11.00 per share. Thus if the share price decreased to, say, $8.00, which represents a loss of $3.82 or 32 per cent of the share price of $11.82, this investor will be

---

12 The relationship between term to expiry and the price of a European put is more complex. On the one hand, a short-term European put can be exercised earlier than an otherwise equivalent long-term European put, therefore generating an earlier cash inflow for the holder of the put. This suggests that a short-term European put is more valuable than a long-term European put. On the other hand, a longer term to expiry increases the probability that the share price will fall below the exercise price, and this suggests that a long-term European put is more valuable than an equivalent short-term European put. For any given European put, both factors are relevant and either influence can dominate the other, depending on the put being considered.

able to sell at $11.00 and thus will lose only $1.15 or 9.5 per cent of the total outlay of $12.15. In effect, the purchase of a put is an insurance policy against the share price falling below a given level.

As with call options, higher share price volatility implies a higher option price. Higher volatility implies a greater chance of large increases and large decreases in the share price. From the put holder's viewpoint, share price increases are bad news, while decreases are good news. But a put holder gains more from a share price decrease than is lost from an increase of the same amount. So, on balance, a put holder has a favourable view of share price volatility.

Because a put confers the right to receive a future cash inflow, it is expected that put prices should be negatively related to interest rates. A higher interest rate reduces the present value of whatever future cash inflow may be received. Finally, dividend payments reduce share prices, which benefits put holders, so higher expected dividend payments increase put prices.

The effects for American calls and puts are summarised in Table 16.6. Positive (negative) means the option price responds in the same (opposite) direction to a change in the factor affecting prices.

**Table 16.6** *Factors affecting American option prices*

| Factor | Call prices | Put prices |
| --- | --- | --- |
| Current share price | Positive | Negative |
| Exercise price | Negative | Positive |
| Term to expiry | Positive | Positive |
| Volatility of the share | Positive | Positive |
| Risk-free interest rate | Positive | Negative |
| Expected dividends | Negative | Positive |

## 16.2.7 PUT–CALL PARITY

For European options on shares that do not pay dividends there is an equilibrium relationship between the prices of puts and calls that are written on the same underlying share, are traded simultaneously, and have the same exercise price and term to expiry. This relationship, known as **put–call parity**, was derived by Stoll and was subsequently analysed further by Merton.[13] The relationship is now derived and explained.

It is assumed that options are traded in frictionless markets and that no security (or portfolio) dominates any other security (or portfolio). The meaning of 'dominance' in this context may be illustrated as follows. Suppose that on some future date there can be only three possible sets of market conditions or 'states of the world', and the payoffs on securities (or portfolios) A and B in these states will be as shown in Table 16.7:

---

[13] H. R. Stoll, 'The Relationship Between Put and Call Option Prices', *Journal of Finance*, December 1969, pp. 802–24; Merton (see Footnote 9), pp. 156–60; R. C. Merton, 'The Relationship Between Put and Call Option Prices: Comment', *Journal of Finance*, March 1973, pp. 183–4.

**Table 16.7** *Payoffs showing a dominant portfolio*

| Portfolio | Payoff ($) in: | | |
|---|---|---|---|
| | State 1 | State 2 | State 3 |
| A | 5 | 7 | 11 |
| B | 5 | 7 | 10 |

If A and B sell for the *same* price today, then A dominates B because A pays the same as B in states 1 and 2, but pays more than B in state 3. Therefore, to prevent dominance, the price of A *today* must be *greater* than the price of B. Formally, A dominates B if, on some known date in the future, the payoff on A is greater than the payoff on B in one (or more) of the possible states, and the payoff on A is at least as great as the payoff on B in all other possible states. A special case of the no-dominance requirement arises if A and B have the same payoff in all possible states. In that case A and B must command the same price today. If the market is perfect, a no-dominance requirement is equivalent to a requirement that no arbitrage opportunities exist.

Using these assumptions, it can be shown that the following relationship, known as put–call parity, exists between put and call prices:

$$x = w - P + \frac{C}{1 + r'} \qquad (16.1)$$

where $x$ = the price of the European put
$w$ = the price of the European call
$P$ = the share price
$C$ = the exercise price
$r'$ = the risk-free interest rate for borrowing or lending for a period equal to the term of the put and the call

Expressed in words, put–call parity says that the put price equals the call price, less the share price, plus the present value (at the risk-free interest rate for the term of the option) of the exercise price.

To prove that Equation 16.1 holds, consider two portfolios, A and B. The composition and payoffs of these portfolios are shown in Table 16.8.

**Table 16.8** *Payoffs showing put–call parity*

| Portfolio | Value now | Payoff in State 1 ($P^* \geq C$) | Payoff in State 2 ($P^* < C$) |
|---|---|---|---|
| A | $w + \frac{C}{1 + r'}$ | $(P^* - C) + C = P^*$ | $0 + C = C$ |
| B | $x + P$ | $0 + P^* = P^*$ | $(C - P^*) + P^* = C$ |

Portfolio A consists of the call, plus an investment of $\frac{C}{1 + r'}$ dollars invested at the risk-free rate, to mature on the expiry date of the put and the call. Therefore the cash outflow required to set up portfolio A is $w + \frac{C}{1 + r'}$. Portfolio B consists of the put plus one share. The outflow required is therefore $x + P$. As both options are European, they cannot be exercised before expiry, and the relevant 'states of the world' are the possible payoffs on the expiry date. In particular, State 1 is a share price that is greater than or equal to the exercise price ($P^* \geq C$) and State 2 is a share price that is less than the exercise price ($P^* < C$). If State 1 occurs, the call is worth $P^* - C$ and the put is worth zero. If State 2 occurs, the call is worth zero and the put is worth $C - P^*$. In either state, the risk-free investment will mature with a value of:

$$\left(\frac{C}{1 + r'}\right)(1 + r') = C \text{ dollars}$$

If State 1 occurs, then both A and B have a payoff of $P^*$, but if State 2 occurs, then both A and B have a payoff of $C$. There is therefore no reason to prefer A to B (or vice versa) and to prevent dominance, A and B must command the same price now. That is, the cost of A and B must always be equal. This requires that:

$$w + \frac{C}{1 + r'} = x + P$$

Rearranging this expression gives Equation 16.1.

This theorem has two important implications. First, if a formula can be derived to price, say, a European call, then by using Equation 16.1, a formula can be derived to price the equivalent put. Secondly, Equation 16.1 implies that the expected return on the underlying share is not directly relevant to pricing puts or calls. For example, suppose that an investor believes that the price of the underlying share will increase in the near future. Obviously, such an investor is likely to buy a call, and sell a put. It is tempting to suggest that this action will tend to increase the call price (because the demand for calls has increased) but decrease the put price (because the supply of puts has increased). But if this happened, Equation 16.1 would be violated and a profitable arbitrage would exist. Therefore the expected return on the share is not directly relevant to option pricing. This conclusion may at first seem paradoxical but is in fact quite easy to explain. Investors' expectations of the future direction of a share price are relevant to the determination of the share price itself. That is, the share price will reflect the influence of these expectations. Therefore these expectations *are* relevant to option prices but *only* via their influence on the share price itself. They have no independent role to play. This conclusion has great significance for attempts to construct formulae to price options because it implies that these formulae do not need to include a measure of expectations of the future direction of the share price. Such measurements are notoriously difficult to make.

The put–call parity theorem applies only to European options, whereas, in practice, most options are of the American type. While there is no simple equation linking the values of American puts and calls, the following upper and lower bounds have been established:[14]

---

14 Capital letters, $X$ and $W$, denote *American* options.

$$W - P + \frac{C}{1 + r''} \leq X \leq W - P + C \qquad (16.2)$$

where $X$ = the price of the American put
$W$ = the price of the American call
$P$ = the share price
$C$ = the exercise price
$r''$ = the risk-free interest rate for borrowing

In effect, the lower bound in Equation 16.2 matches the result for European put–call parity, while the upper bound exceeds this lower bound by the difference between the exercise price and the present value of the exercise price. This reflects the fact that an American put can be exercised early, thus producing an earlier cash inflow to the put holder. In many cases the gap between the upper and lower bounds will be quite small.[15]

Klemkosky and Resnick tested a dividend-adjusted version of American put–call parity using prices of exchange-traded options listed on the Chicago market.[16] Although some calls appeared to be overpriced, their overall results supported put–call parity. In Australia, Loudon studied approximately 1300 pairs of prices for BHP puts and calls in 1985 and concluded that although violations of put–call parity were not uncommon, investors facing normal transaction costs would be unable to profit from the violations.[17]

### 16.2.8 THE MINIMUM VALUE OF CALLS AND PUTS

Assuming frictionless markets and the same no-dominance framework used earlier to derive the put–call parity theorem, the minimum value of a European call on a share which does not pay dividends is:

$$\text{Min } w = \text{Max}\left[0, P - \frac{C}{1 + r'}\right] \qquad (16.3)$$

To prove this equation, consider two portfolios, A and B'. Their composition and payoffs are shown in Table 16.9. As in the proof of put–call parity, portfolio A consists of the call and a risk-free investment of $\frac{C}{1 + r'}$ dollars. Portfolio B' consists of only one share. The two relevant states are again State 1 ($P^* \geq C$) and State 2 ($P^* < C$).

---

[15] For a detailed treatment of put–call parity under a range of conditions, see J. Cox & M. Rubinstein, *Options Markets*, Prentice-Hall, Englewood Cliffs, New Jersey, 1985, pp. 39–44 and 150–4.
[16] R. C. Klemkosky & B. G. Resnick, 'Put–call Parity and Market Efficiency', *Journal of Finance*, December 1979, pp. 1141–55.
[17] G. F. Loudon, 'Put–call Parity Theory: Evidence from the Big Australian', *Australian Journal of Management*, June 1988, pp. 53–67.

**Table 16.9** Payoffs showing the minimum value of a call option

| Portfolio | Value now | Payoff in State 1 ($P^* \geq C$) | Payoff in State 2 ($P^* < C$) |
|---|---|---|---|
| A | $w + \dfrac{C}{1 + r'}$ | $(P^* - C) + C = P^*$ | $0 + C = C$ |
| B' | $P$ | $P^*$ | $P^*$ |

The explanation of the entries in the table for Portfolio A is the same as in the proof of put–call parity. Portfolio B', which consists of only the share, pays off $P^*$ regardless of the state that occurs. Therefore, if State 1 occurs, both A and B' have a payoff of $P^*$, but if State 2 occurs, then A pays off more than B' because in that state, $C > P^*$. Invoking the no-dominance assumption, it follows that the value of A must therefore be no less than the value of B' at all times before the call expires. That is:

$$w + \frac{C}{1 + r'} \geq P$$

which implies that:

$$w \geq P - \frac{C}{1 + r'}$$

The right-hand side of this inequality can be negative but, because of limited liability, call prices can never be negative. That is, $w \geq 0$. Combining these two inequalities gives Equation 16.3.

This result has an important implication: in the absence of dividends, American call options should not be exercised before expiry. Clearly the holder of an American call would not even consider exercise unless the share price $P$ exceeded the exercise price $C$. Suppose that $P > C$ and the holder of an American call has decided to dispose of the call. To do so a choice must be made between exercising the call and selling the call. However, this choice is easy. If the call is exercised, the payoff is $P - C$ but if the call is sold, then, by Equation 16.3, the payoff is *at least* $P - \dfrac{C}{1 + r'}$, which will exceed $P - C$ provided only that the interest rate $r'$ is positive. Given that interest rates are always positive, the payoff from selling the call must exceed the payoff from exercising the call. Therefore, at all times before the instant of expiry, selling an American call on a share which does not pay dividends is always preferable to exercising the call. It follows that an American call will never be exercised early and, accordingly, the right to do so is valueless. The call might just as well be European. Under the conditions we have assumed, the distinction between European calls and American calls is irrelevant to their valuation.

At first sight this conclusion may be surprising, but it has an intuitive explanation. If a call is exercised early, two things happen. First, the option's life is cut short, so the call holder forfeits any time value the option had. Secondly, the call holder must pay for the shares earlier than would otherwise have been necessary. Both outcomes are undesirable and both can be avoided simply by selling rather than exercising the call.

The rule against early exercise does not necessarily hold if an *ex-dividend* date will occur during the life of the call. As mentioned in Section 16.2.5, early exercise of an American call can be rational in these circumstances and therefore the right to exercise early has value. However, even in these cases it is rational only if undertaken just before the ex-dividend date. This implies that exercising of options should occur only at times either just before the expiry date or just before an ex-dividend date. By and large the available Australian empirical evidence is consistent with this implication.[18]

The minimum value of a European put can be found by combining put–call parity (Equation 16.1) and the minimum value of a European call (Equation 16.3). The result is:

$$\text{Min } x = \text{Max} \left[ 0, \frac{C}{1 + r'} - P \right] \tag{16.4}$$

However, unlike the case of calls, the expression for the minimum value of a European put cannot be used to show that the distinction between American and European options is irrelevant for puts, even in the absence of dividends. It can be rational to exercise an American put before expiry, and therefore American puts are worth more than their European counterparts. Again there is an intuitive explanation. If a put is exercised, two things happen. First, as with calls, the option's time value is forfeited and this outcome is undesirable. Secondly, the put holder is paid for the shares earlier than would otherwise be the case. Because early cash inflows are preferred to later cash inflows, this outcome is desirable. In some circumstances—for example, if the current share price is very low and interest rates are very high—the second effect outweighs the first, and early exercise is desirable.

## 16.3 THE BLACK–SCHOLES MODEL OF CALL OPTION PRICING[19]

In a famous article, Black and Scholes presented a model that determines the price of a call as a function of five variables: the current price of the underlying share, the exercise price of the call, the call's term to expiry, the volatility of the share price (as measured by the variance of the distribution of returns on the share), and the risk-free interest rate. This article stimulated a great deal of further research into options and, because of its importance, it is presented here in some detail.

### 16.3.1 ASSUMPTIONS

The Black–Scholes model assumes the following:
1. There exists a constant risk-free interest rate at which investors can borrow and lend unlimited amounts.

---

[18] See R. L. Brown & K. A. Rainbow, 'Exercising of Options in the Australian Options Market', *Australian Journal of Management*, June 1981, pp. 1–21.
[19] F. Black & M. Scholes, 'The Pricing of Options and Corporate Liabilities', *Journal of Political Economy*, May–June 1973, pp. 637–54.

2. Share returns follow a random walk in continuous time with a variance rate proportional to the square of the share price. The variance rate is a known constant. This assumption relates to the behaviour of the share price over time. In particular, returns on this share are assumed to follow a random walk and the share is continuously traded in the market. The model is therefore cast in terms of continuous time, as distinct from discrete time, which considers a series of time periods. The distribution of the rate of return on the shares has a known, constant variance, which is a measure of volatility. It can also be shown that this assumption implies that the distribution of possible share prices at the end of any given time period (such as at the end of the option's life) is lognormal. Empirical studies suggest that share markets do not behave in exactly the way assumed here. While trading in many shares is frequent, it is not literally continuous. The variance rate is unlikely to be constant. The random-walk model and the lognormal distribution are not perfect descriptions of their real-world counterparts. Nevertheless the assumed behaviour can be regarded as a close first approximation to actual behaviour.
3. There are no transaction costs, taxes, or other sources of friction.
4. Short selling is allowed with no restrictions or penalties. This assumption means that any number of securities can be sold, regardless of the number actually held. For example, two calls can be written (sold) even if only one share is held, and there is no need to deposit cash to secure such a position.

These four assumptions define conditions in the share and option markets. In addition, Black and Scholes simplify the problem with two further assumptions:

5. There are no dividends, rights issues, or other complicating features.
6. The call is of the European type.

Assumptions 5 and 6 are in fact alternatives, since it was shown in Section 16.2.8 that if assumption 5 holds, the distinction between American and European calls is irrelevant. Therefore, if assumption 5 is made, the pricing formula will be valid for both American and European calls.

With these assumptions, the price $w$ of any given call is a function only of the current share price $P$ and time $t$. The risk-free interest rate $r'$, the variance rate $\sigma^2$, and the exercise price $C$ are known constants in the problem. That is, we have:

$$w = w(P, t)$$

### 16.3.2 RISK-FREE HEDGING

Using shares and calls, it is possible to construct a portfolio that has no risk. The recognition of this possibility was an important factor that led to the development of the model. We illustrate the process of risk-free hedging using a simple example. Suppose that we observe a share price of $1.50 and the price of a call on that share is 40 cents. Suppose we also know that, at this share price and point in time, a 2-cent movement in share price up or down would cause a movement in call price of approximately 1 cent in the same direction. By writing two calls for every share held we can almost eliminate the risk because any change in share price will be almost offset by the change in the value of the calls.[20] This is shown in Example 16.1.

*Example 16.1*
Initially, as described in the preceding paragraph, the position is:
    Asset of one share (current price $1.50):      $1.50
    *less*    liability in respect of two calls written
                 (current price 40 cents):      $0.80
    *equals* equity in portfolio:      $0.70
If the share price rises to $1.52 the position will be:
    Asset of one share (current price $1.52):      $1.52
    *less*    liability in respect of two calls written
                 (current price approximately 41 cents):      $0.82 approx.
    *equals* equity in portfolio:      $0.70 approx.
If the share price falls to $1.48, the position will be:
    Asset of one share (current price $1.48):      $1.48
    *less*    liability in respect of two calls written
                 (current price approximately 39 cents):      $0.78 approx.
    *equals* equity in portfolio:      $0.70 approx.

Therefore, whether the share price rises or falls, the portfolio is approximately risk-free.[21] It can be made perfectly risk-free by continuously adjusting the number of calls in response to the continuous changes occurring in the share price over time.

---

[20] It can also be achieved by the reverse strategy of buying options and short selling shares.

[21] In mathematical terms, hedging requires that we write $\dfrac{1}{\partial w/\partial P}$ calls for every share held.

Initially, equity in the position is:
$$E_1 = P - \frac{1}{\partial w/\partial P} w(P, t)$$

Now consider a small movement in share price from $P$ to $P + \Delta P$. By the definition of a partial derivative:
$$\frac{\partial w}{\partial P} \approx \frac{w(P + \Delta P, t) - w(P, t)}{\Delta P}$$

and therefore:
$$w(P + \Delta P, t) \approx w(P, t) + \frac{\partial w}{\partial P} \Delta P$$

Therefore, equity in the position is now given by:
$$\begin{aligned} E_2 &= P + \Delta P - \frac{1}{\partial w/\partial P} [w(P + \Delta P, t)] \\ &\approx P + \Delta P - \frac{1}{\partial w/\partial P} \left[ w(P, t) + \frac{\partial w}{\partial P} \Delta P \right] \\ &= P + \Delta P - \frac{1}{\partial w/\partial P} w(P, t) - \Delta P \\ &= E_1 \end{aligned}$$

### 16.3.3 THE BLACK–SCHOLES EQUATION

The notion of risk-free hedging is used to provide an equilibrium condition. The return on all risk-free portfolios, including of course one constructed as outlined above, must, in equilibrium, be equal to the risk-free interest rate. This follows from the fact that in a perfect market, perfect substitutes must sell for the same price and therefore must yield the same return. A further condition is that, at expiry, calls must sell for either share price minus exercise price, or zero, whichever is the greater.

It now becomes a purely mathematical problem to derive the Black–Scholes equation, which is:

$$w = P\,N(d_1) - Ce^{-r'T}\,N(d_2) \quad (16.5)$$

$$\text{where } d_1 \equiv \frac{\ln(P/C) + (r' + \tfrac{1}{2}\sigma^2)T}{\sigma\sqrt{T}}$$

$$d_2 \equiv \frac{\ln(P/C) + (r' - \tfrac{1}{2}\sigma^2)T}{\sigma\sqrt{T}}$$

$$\equiv d_1 - \sigma\sqrt{T}$$

$N(d)$ indicates the cumulative standard normal density function with upper integral limit $d$. In other words, $N(d)$ is the area under the standard normal curve from $-\infty$ to $d$. The definitions of $P$, $C$, $r'$ and $\sigma^2$ are as given previously, and $T$ is the term to expiry. $N(d_1)$ and $N(d_2)$ are probabilities and are therefore numbers between zero and one. Values of the function $N$ are given in Table 5 of Appendix A. In continuous time, $e^{-r'T}$ is the appropriate discount factor for $T$ periods at rate $r'$ per period. Therefore $Ce^{-r'T}$ is the present value of $C$.

*Example 16.2*

Suppose that we wish to find the Black–Scholes price for a call with the following characteristics:

$$\begin{aligned}
\text{Current share price} &= P = \$1.76 \\
\text{Exercise price} &= C = \$1.60 \\
\text{Term to expiry} &= T = 3 \text{ months} = 0.25 \text{ years} \\
\text{Volatility (variance)} &= \sigma^2 = 0.09 \text{ per annum} \\
\text{Standard deviation} &= \sigma = 0.3 \text{ per annum} \\
\text{Risk-free interest rate} &= r' = 0.1 \text{ per annum, continuously compounding}
\end{aligned}$$

The first task is to calculate $d_1$ and $d_2$:

$$d_1 = \frac{\ln(\$1.76/\$1.60) + [0.1 + (0.5)(0.09)](0.25)}{0.3\sqrt{0.25}}$$

$$= \frac{\ln(1.1) + 0.036\,25}{0.15}$$

$$\approx 0.877$$
$$d_2 = 0.877 - 0.15$$
$$\approx 0.727$$

Using Table 5 in Appendix A:

$N(0.87)$ is given as $0.5 + 0.3078 = 0.8078$
$N(0.88)$ is given as $0.5 + 0.3106 = 0.8106$

An estimate of $N(0.877)$ that is sufficiently accurate for the present purpose is $N(0.877) = 0.8098$. Similarly $N(0.727) = 0.7664$. The discounting factor $e^{-r'T} = e^{-0.025} = 0.9753$. Substituting into Equation 16.5:

$$w = P N(d_1) - Ce^{-r'T} N(d_2)$$
$$= (\$1.76)(0.8098) - (\$1.60)(0.9753)(0.7664)$$
$$= \$0.2293$$

The Black–Scholes call price is therefore slightly less than 23 cents.

Table 16.10 shows further examples of the call prices that result from the Black–Scholes model if different values of the variables are assumed.[22] Also shown in the table is the greater of $(P - Ce^{-r'T})$ and zero, which is the minimum theoretical price; equivalently, it is the call price under conditions of perfect certainty.

**Table 16.10** *Examples of Black–Scholes call option prices*

| Example | Share price (P) | Exercise price (C) | Term to expiration (T) | Standard deviation rate (σ) | Risk-free interest rate (r') | Model price (w) | Greater of zero and $P - Ce^{-r'T}$ |
|---|---|---|---|---|---|---|---|
| (a) | 1.00 | 1.00 | 0.25 | 0.3 | 0.1 | 7.22 | 2.47 |
| (b) | 1.10 | 1.00 | 0.25 | 0.3 | 0.1 | 14.33 | 12.47 |
| (c) | 1.00 | 1.10 | 0.25 | 0.3 | 0.1 | 3.22 | 0 |
| (d) | 1.00 | 1.00 | 0.5 | 0.3 | 0.1 | 10.91 | 4.88 |
| (e) | 1.00 | 1.00 | 0.25 | 0.4 | 0.1 | 9.17 | 2.47 |
| (f) | 1.00 | 1.00 | 0.25 | 0.3 | 0.15 | 7.89 | 3.68 |

Each of the examples (b) to (f) changes *one* of the values used in Example (a). Therefore the effect of a higher share price—Example (b)—is shown to be a substantial rise in the call price, as discussed in Section 16.2.5. The direction of influence of the other variables is likewise in line with our comments in that section. These conclusions are quite general and do not depend on the particular numbers used in the examples. Similarly the model price is never less than the minimum theoretical price.

The Black–Scholes model (Equation 16.5) is shown graphically in Figure 16.3. For some given variance rate, interest rate, and exercise price, Figure 16.3 plots call price against share price for different values of term to expiry. For a finite, positive value of $T$, the curve approaches asymptotically the broken line

---

[22] An extensive tabulation can be found in F. Black, 'Fact and Fantasy in the Use of Options', *Financial Analysts Journal*, July–August 1975, pp. 36–41 and 61–72.

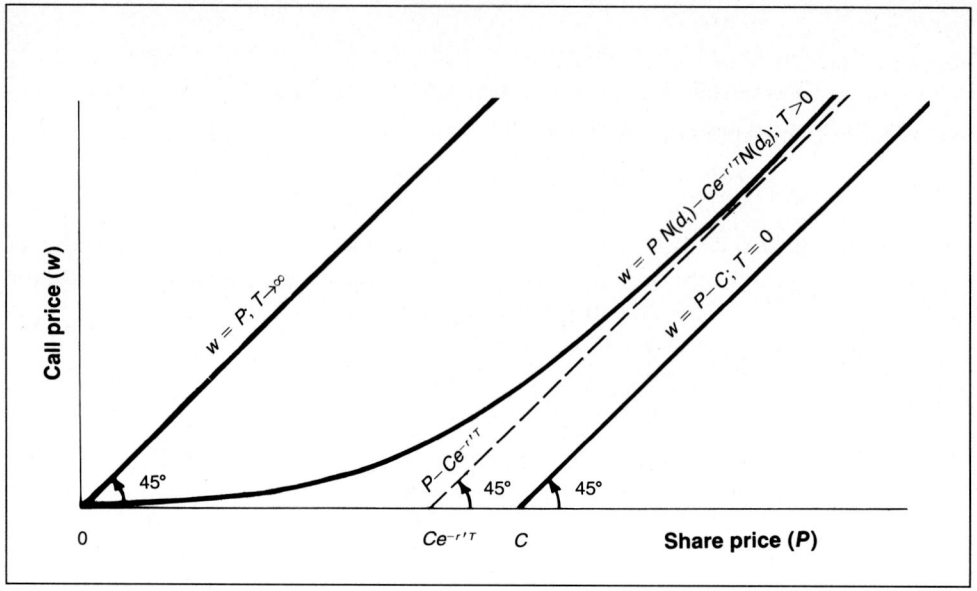

**Fig. 16.3** *Graphical representation of the Black–Scholes equation*

representing $w = P - Ce^{-r'T}$ as $P$ increases. At expiry, $T = 0$, the call is worth $P^* - C$ or zero, whichever is the greater, while a perpetual call ($T \to \infty$) commands a price equal to the share price.

By invoking Equation 16.1, the put–call parity equation, the Black–Scholes analysis also provides an equation to value European puts on shares which do not pay dividends.[23] Converting Equation 16.1 into a continuous time formulation gives:

$$x = w - P + Ce^{-r'T} \qquad (16.6)$$

where $x$ is the price of the put.

Substituting Equation 16.5 into Equation 16.6 and rearranging gives:

$$x = P[N(d_1) - 1] + Ce^{-r'T}[1 - N(d_2)] \qquad (16.7)$$

Equation 16.7 is the **Black–Scholes put pricing model**.[24]

---

[23] Note that it is necessary to assume a European-type put *and* no dividends. This is because, even in the absence of dividends, it can sometimes pay to exercise prematurely an American-type put. This feature makes the pricing of American-type puts more complex than American-type calls. For a more advanced model of put pricing, see R. Geske & H. Johnson, 'The American Put Option Valued Analytically', *Journal of Finance*, December 1984, pp. 1511–24; and E. C. Blomeyer, 'An Analytic Approximation for the American Put Price for Options on Stocks with Dividends', *Journal of Financial and Quantitative Analysis*, June 1986, pp. 229–33. For empirical evidence, see E. C. Blomeyer & H. Johnson, 'An Empirical Examination of the Pricing of American Put Options', *Journal of Financial and Quantitative Analysis*, March 1988, pp. 13–22.

[24] Since $N(d_1) - 1 = -N(-d_1)$ and $1 - N(d_2) = N(-d_2)$, Equation 16.7 can also be written as $x = -P\,N(-d_1) + Ce^{-r'T} N(-d_2)$.

## Example 16.3

Suppose that we wish to find the Black–Scholes price for the put option, which is the counterpart to the call option described in Example 16.2. That is:

Current share price $= P = \$1.76$
Exercise price $= C = \$1.60$
Term to expiry $= T = 3$ months $= 0.25$ years
Volatility (variance) $= \sigma^2 = 0.09$ per annum
Standard deviation $= \sigma = 0.3$ per annum
Risk-free interest rate $= r' = 0.1$ per annum, continuously compounding

The calculations in Example 16.2 showed that with these values, $N(d_1) = 0.8098$, $N(d_2) = 0.7664$ and $e^{-r'T} = 0.9753$. Substituting into Equation 16.7, the Black–Scholes put price is:

$$x = P[N(d_1) - 1] + Ce^{-r'T}[1 - N(d_2)]$$
$$= (\$1.76)(0.8098 - 1) + (\$1.60)(0.9753)(1 - 0.7664)$$
$$\approx \$0.0298$$

The Black-Scholes put price is therefore slightly less than 3 cents.

### 16.3.4 A BRIEF ASSESSMENT OF THE MODEL

An obvious feature of great appeal is that the valuation equation is a neat, closed-form solution. The model specifies a particular functional form linking the variables, rather than simply specifying the direction of each variable's influence. Slightly less obvious, but also a strength of the model, is the number of variables which are *not* present. As suggested earlier, the return that investors expect on the underlying share has no place in the model. No assumption concerning the attitude of investors towards risk is required or implied. Conversely, the variables which *are* present are for the most part observable and have reliable data available. The share price, exercise price, and term to expiry are directly observable, and proxies exist for the risk-free interest rate. The variance rate is less concrete; Black has described it as 'the big unknown in the option formula'.[25] However, if a share's volatility as measured by the variance rate is relatively constant (as the model assumes), then the sequence of past prices may be used to estimate the volatility. Therefore, although investors' expectations of the return on the share have no place in the equation, this is not true of volatility expectations. The model, in effect, sidesteps this problem by assuming that the volatility is a known constant. In practice, users of the model may try a range of values for this variable. In other cases users may take market prices of options and then solve the Black–Scholes equation for the volatility 'implied' by the market price of the option.

The model can also be extended in a number of directions by relaxation of the assumptions. Necessarily, this produces more-complex pricing equations which include the Black–Scholes equation as a special case. An important extension is to incorporate the effect of dividends. Other extensions include a variable

---

25 Black, (see Footnote 22), p. 36.

interest rate, alternative specifications of share price behaviour, transaction costs, taxes, and restrictions on short sales.[26]

A crucial factor in assessing a model is to examine its predictive ability. While a detailed review of the literature on testing the model is beyond the scope of this chapter, some general observations are made.[27] In the first test of the model, Black and Scholes studied option contracts that included a dividend protection clause, and found that, on average, the model was able to price these options successfully.[28] If the model is to be used to price listed options, which never contain a dividend protection clause, the basic model needs to be adjusted to allow for dividends. The empirical evidence suggests that the Black–Scholes model can price exchange-traded call options accurately, provided that a dividend-adjusted model is used. Using data from the Chicago market, Whaley studied over 15 000 call prices, each of which was affected by one dividend, and found that a dividend-adjusted version of the Black–Scholes model could price calls with great accuracy.[29] For example, the average market price of all calls studied was $4.1388, whereas the average model price was $4.1291. The average percentage difference between market and model prices was only 1 per cent. While the model appeared to be able to price all types of calls, it did show a tendency to overprice calls on high-volatility shares and to underprice calls on low-volatility shares.

In Australia, relatively little evidence has been published on the ability of the model to price options, although it is widely known and used by practitioners. Brown and Shevlin tested a dividend-adjusted version of the model using about 1500 prices in the Australian Options Market.[30] They found that the median

---

[26] For a review which, although somewhat dated, remains a valuable paper, see C. W. Smith, 'Option Pricing: A Review', *Journal of Financial Economics*, January–March 1976, pp. 3–51. Alternatively, see J. C. Cox & M. Rubinstein, (Footnote 15), Sections 6.2 and 7.1.

[27] Brief reviews can be found in Cox & Rubinstein, (Footnote 15), pp. 338–42, and in P. Ritchken, *Options: Theory, Strategy, and Applications*, Scott Foresman, Glenview, Illinois, 1987, pp. 225–8. See also D. Galai, 'A Survey of Empirical Tests of Option Pricing Models', in *Option Pricing: Theory and Applications*, Ed. M. Brenner, Lexington Books, Lexington, 1983, pp. 45–80. The performance of various models is compared in M. Rubinstein, 'Nonparametric Tests of Alternative Option Pricing Models Using all Reported Trades and Quotes on the 30 Most Active CBOE Option Classes from August 23, 1976 through August 31, 1978', *Journal of Finance*, June 1985, pp. 455–80.

[28] F. Black & M. Scholes, 'The Valuation of Option Contracts and a Test of Market Efficiency', *Journal of Finance*, May 1972, pp. 399–418. Because the dividend protection clause provides imperfect protection, the effect was only reduced, rather than eliminated. Black and Scholes found that the model tended to overvalue calls on high-variance shares and to undervalue calls on low-variance shares. It has subsequently been shown that this finding is consistent with the effects induced by imperfect protection against dividends. See R. Geske, R. Roll & K. Shastri, 'Over-the-counter Option Market Dividend Protection and "Biases" in the Black–Scholes Model: A Note', *Journal of Finance*, September 1983, pp. 1271–7.

[29] See R. E. Whaley, 'Valuation of American Call Options on Dividend-paying Stocks: Empirical Tests', *Journal of Financial Economics*, March 1982, pp. 29–58. The same model is also tested empirically in E. C. Blomeyer & R. C. Klemkosky, 'Tests of Market Efficiency for American Call Options', in *Option Pricing: Theory and Applications*, Ed. M. Brenner, Lexington Books, Lexington, 1983, pp. 101–21.

[30] See R. L. Brown & T. J. Shevlin, 'Modelling Option Prices in Australia Using the Black–Scholes Model', *Australian Journal of Management*, June 1983, pp. 1–20.

percentage difference between model prices and market prices was of the order of only 1 per cent. However, a study by Castagna and Matolcsy concluded that either the market was inefficient or the model could not price options correctly.[31]

### 16.3.5 MARKET EFFICIENCY[32]

The efficiency of option markets has been studied extensively, mainly by determining whether investors could use an option-pricing model to make excess profits. These studies will not be reviewed in any detail but the major findings can be stated simply. Some of the earlier studies tended to find that excess profits could have been made by some groups of investors (such as brokers) who pay lower transaction costs than the majority of investors.[33] However, several later studies, which have had access both to higher quality data and to more advanced versions of the model, have found in favour of market efficiency.[34]

## 16.4 BINOMIAL OPTION PRICING

Although the Black–Scholes model is justly famous, an alternative approach, known as binomial option pricing, is often easier to apply and is more readily adapted to a range of option pricing problems. Binomial option pricing was first suggested by Sharpe, and developed in an article by Cox, Ross and Rubinstein.[35] The Black–Scholes model is a special case of their binomial model. In this section we present the main features of their model.

### 16.4.1 THE BASIC IDEA: PRICING A SINGLE-PERIOD CALL OPTION USING THE BINOMIAL APPROACH

The distinguishing feature of binomial option pricing is the assumption that, in each time period, the price of the underlying asset can be one of only two numbers, (hence the use of the term 'binomial', which means 'two numbers'). This may sound unrealistic, but it turns out that the approach gives very realistic answers, provided that a large number of short time periods are used in the analysis. However, in this section we restrict ourselves to the single-period case which, although clearly unrealistic, permits a clear illustration of basic principles. We explain these principles using Example 16.4.

---

31 See A. D. Castagna & Z. P. Matolcsy, 'The Evaluation of Traded Options Pricing Models in Australia', *Journal of Business Finance and Accounting*, Summer 1983, pp. 225–33.
32 For a definition and description of market efficiency, see Chapter 14.
33 For American studies, see, for example, D. Galai, 'A Survey of Empirical Tests of Option-pricing Models', in Brenner, (see Footnote 29); D. Chiras & S. Manaster, 'The Information Content of Option Prices and a Test of Market Efficiency', *Journal of Financial Economics*, June–September 1978, pp. 213–34. For an Australian study, see A. D. Castagna & Z. P. Matolcsy, 'A Two Stage Experimental Design to Test the Efficiency of the Market for Traded Stock Options and the Australian Evidence', *Journal of Banking and Finance*, December 1982, pp. 521–32.
34 See Whaley (1982), (Footnote 29); Blomeyer & Klemkosky, (see Footnote 29).
35 J. C. Cox, S. A. Ross & M. Rubinstein, 'Option Pricing: A Simplified Approach', *Journal of Financial Economics*, 1979, pp. 229–63.

## Example 16.4

Consider a one-year call option with a $10.50 exercise price, on a share whose current price is $10. It is known that in one year's time the share price will be either $11.50 or $9.50. No other share price outcome is possible: the share price will be one of these two numbers. The one-year risk-free interest rate is 8 per cent per annum.

Using only this information, together with the standard assumption that arbitrage will not be possible, we can work out what the call price will be. First, however, we calculate the payoffs. If, at the expiry of the call in one year's time, the share price is $11.50, the call's payoff will be $1. If the other share price ($9.50) occurs, the call's payoff will be zero. We now compare the payoffs on portfolios A and B:

*Portfolio* A: Buy two calls, each costing $w$ dollars.
*Portfolio* B: Buy one share ($10.00) and borrow $9.50/1.08 ≈ $8.80, which is the present value of $9.50.

The payoffs to these strategies are shown in Table 16.11.

**Table 16.11**  *Payoffs for a single-period binomial model*

| Portfolio | Cash flow now | Payoff if $P^* = \$9.50$ | Payoff if $P^* = \$11.50$ |
|---|---|---|---|
| A (buy 2 calls) | $-2w$ | 0 | $2.00 |
| B buy 1 share | $-\$10.00$ | $9.50 | $11.50 |
| borrow ($9.50/1.08) | $+ \$8.80$ | $-\$9.50$ | $-\$9.50$ |
| Total (B) | $- \$1.20$ | 0 | $2.00 |

The payoffs shown in Table 16.11 are identical. It doesn't matter whether an investor chooses portfolio A or B: the outcome in both cases is a cash flow of zero if the final share price is $9.50, or a cash flow of $2.00 if the final share price is $11.50. Since A and B are, in effect, the same thing, they should be worth the same today. To prevent arbitrage, the cash flow required today to set up portfolio A should equal the cash flow required today to set up portfolio B. That is:

$$-2w = -\$1.20$$

which, of course, solves to give today's call price $w$ as being $0.60.[36]

Example 16.4 illustrates the fact that buying a call (portfolio A) is like borrowing to buy shares (portfolio B). In Example 16.4, buying two calls was like borrowing to buy one share. We could equally well describe this as 'buying one call is like borrowing to buy half a share'. Of course, the figure of one-half is peculiar to this example. It is found by calculating the ratio of the option spread and the share spread—in this case the calculation is:

---

[36] We have rounded this answer. A more accurate answer is:

$$\frac{1}{2}\left[\$10 - \frac{\$9.50}{1.08}\right] = \$0.60\ 185\ 185$$

$$(\$1 - \$0)/(\$11.50 - \$9.50) = \tfrac{1}{2}$$

In other cases, this ratio could be any number between zero and one. This ratio is called the 'hedge ratio' or 'delta'. Estimates of option 'deltas' are provided in the *Australian Financial Review*. The general principle of risk-free hedging with options was discussed in Section 16.3.2.

## 16.4.2 RISK NEUTRALITY AS A SOLUTION METHOD

Perhaps the most remarkable feature of Example 16.4 is not that we could work out the call price, but that we were able to do so *without making any assumption about risk*. The call in Example 16.4 is worth 60 cents, regardless of the risk preferences of the people who comprise the market. If, for example, everyone in the market was risk averse, they would set the call price at 60 cents. If everyone was risk neutral (or for that matter, risk seeking) they would still set the call price at 60 cents.[37]

We can use this fact to provide an easy solution method. We *pretend* that all investors are risk neutral. This means that they ignore risk in their decision making. In a market comprising only risk-neutral people, all assets are priced so that they are expected to yield the risk-free return. In a risk-neutral world, pricing assets is thus very easy. It is simply a matter of finding out the expected value of a future cash flow and then discounting this value at the risk-free interest rate. We reiterate that our answer does not *depend* on risk neutrality. We would get the same answer for the call price if we assumed, say, risk aversion. We choose risk neutrality only because it is easy. To illustrate how the method works we show in Example 16.5 how the call option in Example 16.4 would be priced if every participant were risk neutral.

### Example 16.5
A share is worth $10 today and promises to pay off either $11.50 or $9.50 in one year's time. We will call the payoff of $11.50 'State U' (for 'up') and the payoff of $9.50 'State D' (for 'down'). Given that this is a risk-neutral world, we can deduce the probabilities of States U and D occurring. This is possible because, under risk neutrality, $10 must equal the expected payoff in one year, discounted for one year at the risk-free interest rate. That is:

$$\$10 = \frac{p\,(\$11.50) + (1 - p)\,(\$9.50)}{1.08}$$

where $p$ is the probability of State U occurring and
$1 - p$ is the probability of State D occurring
Solving this equation gives $p = 0.65$ and $1 - p = 0.35$.[38]

---

[37] How is this possible? Essentially, the reason is that we could redesign portfolios A and B to give two risk-free outcomes. Regardless of individual differences in attitudes to risk, all market participants will agree that risk-free is indeed risk-free and will price the portfolios accordingly.

[38] A warning: These probabilities *do* depend on risk neutrality. They are not the probability of any actual event occurring in the real world.

Turning our attention to the call option, its payoff is $1 in State U and $0 in State D. In a world of risk neutrality, the call price $w$ will also equal its expected payoff, discounted at the risk-free interest rate:

$$w = \frac{(0.65)(\$1) + (0.35)(\$0)}{1.08}$$
$$\approx \$0.601\,851\,85$$
$$\approx \$0.60$$

This, of course, is the same answer as we found in Example 16.4 when we did not pretend that all market participants were risk neutral.

### 16.4.3 BINOMIAL OPTION PRICING WITH MANY TIME PERIODS

The single-period case is not realistic, but the basic principles can be extended to more than one period. In practice it is usual to use, say, one or two hundred time periods. The calculations are readily made using a computer. To explain the procedures, we use three time periods.

The solution to a multi-period binomial option pricing problem has three major stages.

Stage 1: Building up a lattice of share prices.
Stage 2: Calculating the option payoffs at expiry from the expiry share prices.
Stage 3: Calculating option prices by calculating expected values and discounting at the risk-free interest rate.

These stages are explained in Example 16.6.

### Example 16.6

We wish to value a three-month call option with an exercise price of $10.25. The current share price is $10.00 and the risk-free interest rate is 1.5 per cent per month. We use three time periods of one month each. It is assumed that at the end of each month the share price can move to only one of two values.

*Stage 1: The lattice of share prices*

In Stage 1, our objective is to lay out all the future share prices that can arise, given our assumptions. In this example it is assumed that each month the share price can rise by 4 per cent or fall by 3.846 per cent. Our choice of 3.846 per cent is, of course, deliberate, and is equal to 1/1.04. The effect is that a rise (fall) in one month will be exactly offset if there is a fall (rise) in the following month. For example, starting from $10.00, if the share price rises by 4 per cent in the first month, then falls by 3.846 per cent in the second month, its price after two months is:

$$\$10.00\,(1.04)\,(1 - 0.038\,46)$$
$$= \$10.00\,(1.04)\left(\frac{1}{1.04}\right)$$
$$= \$10.00$$

The benefit of doing it this way is the dramatic reduction in the number of future possible share prices that need to be considered.

In Figure 16.4, the possible future share prices are shown on a lattice diagram in **bold** type. We have labelled each node of the lattice with a capital letter. Today is represented by point A. Points B and C represent the two possible share prices at the end of the first month:
- If the share price increases in the first month: $10.00 × 1.04, then B = $10.40
- If the share price decreases in the first month: $10.00/1.04, then C = $9.6154

Similarly, points D, E and F represent the three possible share prices at the end of the second month:
- If the share price increases in the first month and increases again in the second month: $10.00 × 1.04 × 1.04, then D = $10.816
- If the share price increases (decreases) in the first month and then decreases (increases) in the second month: $10.00 × 1.04/1.04, then E = $10.00
- If the share price decreases in the first month and decreases again in the second month: $10.00/1.04/1.04, then F = $9.2456

Points G, H, I and J represent the four possible share prices at the expiry date of the call and are derived from points D, E and F by multiplying or dividing by 1.04 as appropriate.

*Stage 2: Option payoffs at expiry*

As we know the expiry date share prices from Stage 1, it is a simple matter to calculate the matching call option payoffs. Because the exercise price is $10.25, the call's payoffs are $0.9986 if the expiry share price is $11.25 (point G); $0.15 if the expiry share price is $10.40 (point H); and zero if the expiry share price is $9.6154 (point I) or $8.89 (point J). The call's payoffs are shown on Figure 16.4 in italic type.

*Stage 3: Discounting*

Using the risk-neutral solution method, it is a simple matter to calculate the present value of the call's payoffs. As in the single-period example, we first need to find the probabilities of a rising and falling share price. The risk-neutral probabilities are the same at every node (point). Taking point B as an example, $10.40 must equal the discounted expected value, where the discounting is done at the risk-free interest rate of 1.5 per cent per month:

$$\$10.40 = \frac{(p)(\$10.816) + (1-p)(\$10)}{1.015}$$

where, as before, $p$ is the probability of a rise in price and $1 - p$ is the probability of a fall. This equation solves to give $p = 0.6814$ and $1 - p = 0.3186$.

We can now work back through the lattice from expiry to the present, at each point calculating the present value of the expected payoff. For example, at point D, the call's price is:

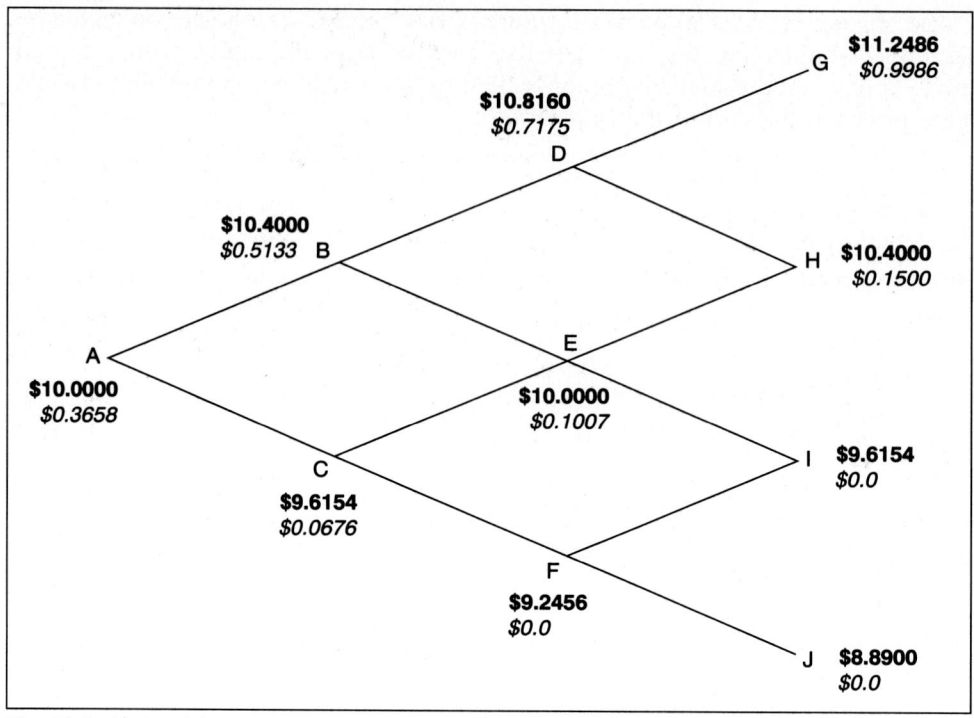

**Fig. 16.4** *Lattice of share prices and call prices*

$$\frac{(0.6814)\,(\$0.9986) + (0.3186)\,(\$0.15)}{1.015}$$
$$= \$0.7175$$

Similarly, at point E, the call's price is:
$$\frac{(0.6814)\,(\$0.15) + (0.3186)\,(\$0)}{1.015}$$
$$= \$0.1007$$

Working back through the lattice to today (Point A) gives the call's price as $0.3658 or about 37 cents.

Example 16.5 is a realistic treatment of a binomial option-pricing problem in all but two respects. First, the number of time periods was set at only three, whereas it should be set at thirty or more to get an accurate answer. However, this is achieved simply by using a computer to perform the calculations. No new issue of principle is involved. Secondly, we made no attempt to justify our choice of 'up' and 'down' factors of 4 per cent per month and 3.846 per cent per month respectively. In practice these factors are selected very carefully. Typically, the model user decides on what is thought to be an accurate estimate of the standard deviation of expiry share prices. In other words, as in the case of the Black–Scholes model, it is necessary to forecast the volatility of share returns during the life of the option. A simple formula then provides the 'up' and 'down' factors that will produce a distribution of expiry share prices that has the desired standard deviation. For example, the 'up' factor is given by $e^{\sigma\sqrt{\Delta t}}$, where $\sigma$ is the standard deviation and $\Delta t$ the length of each time period.[39]

### 16.4.4 Applying the binomial approach to other option problems

So far we have discussed only the case of a call option on a share that does not pay dividends. The Black–Scholes model applies to this case as well. An important difference between the binomial approach and the Black–Scholes approach is that the binomial approach is much easier to adapt to other option-pricing problems.

For example, once the lattice of share prices is laid out, a put option can be priced as easily as a call option. The put option payoffs are calculated and then the same procedure of discounting expected values is undertaken. Moreover, the 'American' feature is easily incorporated just by checking, at each node, whether the calculated option price is less than the payoff from immediate exercise. If it is, the payoff value is substituted for the calculated price. With the kinds of analytical methods used by Black and Scholes, incorporation of the American feature can be an extremely difficult problem.

Similarly, the problem of valuing options on dividend-paying shares is relatively easy to handle using the binomial approach. At the ex-dividend date, all possible share prices are reduced by the amount of the dividend. A practical difficulty here is that the lattice no longer conveniently recombines, with the result that there is a very rapid increase in the number of nodes (possible share prices) that need to be analysed. However, powerful computers can make the method feasible.

## 16.5 Options on foreign currency[40]

In Sections 16.2 and 16.3 we confined the discussion almost entirely to options on shares. However, most of the principles covered in those sections apply to options on other underlying assets. In this section we consider options on foreign currency. Options on futures contracts are considered in Section 16.6.

---

[39] Details are beyond the scope of the book. For an excellent treatment see J. Hull, *Options, Futures, and Other Derivative Securities*, Prentice-Hall, Englewood Cliffs, New Jersey, 1989, pp. 220–33.

[40] For a detailed management-oriented treatment of options on foreign currency, see W. Sutton, *The Currency Options Handbook*, Woodhead-Faulkner, Cambridge, 1988. An application to contingent hedging is discussed in Section 21.6.7.

### 16.5.1 WHAT IS AN OPTION ON FOREIGN CURRENCY?

A call (put) option on foreign currency is a contract that confers the right to buy (sell) an agreed quantity of that foreign currency at a given exchange rate. Options on foreign currency are traded in organised markets such as exist in Philadelphia, as well as in less formal 'over-the-counter' markets and private contracts. Example 16.7 illustrates the nature of options on foreign currency.

*Example 16.7*

Options on several foreign currencies, including UK pounds (sterling), Deutschmarks and Australian dollars, are traded on the Philadelphia Stock Exchange. In that exchange on 5 May 1989 the price of a September put to sell $A50 000 at an exercise price (exchange rate) of $A1 = US$0.81 was US3.57 cents per $A1. To understand what this means, consider the buyer of this put. The cost of the put contract is US3.57 cents per Australian dollar; that is, the cost is US$(0.0357 × 50 000) = US$1785. On payment of this sum, the put buyer obtains the right to sell $A50 000 for US81 cents per Australian dollar; that is, $A50 000 can be sold for US$(0.81 × 50 000) = US$40 500. In short, the put buyer obtains the right to deliver $A50 000 and to receive in return US$40 500. The cost of this right is US$1785. The payoff structure is shown in Table 16.12.

**Table 16.12** *Payoff structure for purchase of a put contract on $A50 000 at an exercise price of $A1 = US$0.81*

| If the spot exchange rate per $A1 on the put's expiration date is | Then the payoff (cash flow) to the put holder is: | |
|---|---|---|
| | in US$ | in $A equivalent |
| US$0.72 | 4500 | 4500/0.72 = 6250 |
| 0.73 | 4000 | 4000/0.73 = 5479 |
| 0.74 | 3500 | 3500/0.74 = 4730 |
| 0.75 | 3000 | 3000/0.75 = 4000 |
| 0.76 | 2500 | 2500/0.76 = 3289 |
| 0.77 | 2000 | 2000/0.77 = 2597 |
| 0.78 | 1500 | 1500/0.78 = 1923 |
| 0.79 | 1000 | 1000/0.79 = 1266 |
| 0.80 | 500 | 500/0.80 = 625 |
| 0.81 | 0 | 0 |
| 0.82 | 0 | 0 |
| 0.83 | 0 | 0 |
| 0.84 | 0 | 0 |
| 0.85 | 0 | 0 |

As can be seen from the payoff structure in Table 16.12, the put provides protection against the effects of a depreciating Australian dollar (equivalently, an appreciating US dollar). This protection begins to take effect when the value of an Australian dollar falls below the exercise price of US81 cents.

If, instead, protection was sought against the effects of an appreciating Australian dollar (equivalently, a depreciating US dollar), a call option to buy Australian dollars is required. The payoff structure for a trader who buys a call option on $A50 000 at an exercise price of $A1 = US$0.84 is shown in Table 16.13.

**Table 16.13** *Payoff structure for purchase of a call contract on $A50 000 at an exercise price of $A1 = US$0.84*

| If the spot exchange rate per $A1 on the call's expiration date is | Then the payoff (cash flow) to the call holder is: | |
|---|---|---|
| | in US$ | in $A equivalent |
| US$0.80 | 0 | 0 |
| 0.81 | 0 | 0 |
| 0.82 | 0 | 0 |
| 0.83 | 0 | 0 |
| 0.84 | 0 | 0 |
| 0.85 | 500 | 500/0.85 = 588 |
| 0.86 | 1000 | 1000/0.86 = 1163 |
| 0.87 | 1500 | 1500/0.87 = 1724 |
| 0.88 | 2000 | 2000/0.88 = 2273 |
| 0.89 | 2500 | 2500/0.89 = 2809 |
| 0.90 | 3000 | 3000/0.90 = 3333 |
| 0.91 | 3500 | 3500/0.91 = 3846 |
| 0.92 | 4000 | 4000/0.92 = 4348 |

### 16.5.2 Combinations of options on foreign currency

Some of the most frequent uses that have been made of options on foreign currency involve combining two or more such options. For example, options can be combined to produce an arrangement sometimes known as a **range forward**.[41] This is shown in Example 16.8.

*Example 16.8*
Conquest Investments Ltd expects to receive a cash inflow of $A50 000 in the next 3 or 4 months and plans to convert this sum to US dollars to invest in an American company. Tim Johns, the manager of Conquest Investments, wants to be guaranteed to receive a minimum of US$40 500 for delivery of the $A50 000. He has considered purchasing a put contract with an exercise price of US81 cents but regards the put price as excessive. However, Johns is also willing to forego some of the benefits of an appreciating Australian dollar. Specifically, Johns is willing to accept a ceiling of receiving no more than US$42 000 in return for delivery of $A50 000. Therefore Johns decides to combine the purchase of a put (with an exercise price of US81 cents) with the sale of a call (with an exercise price of US84 cents). The cash inflow from selling the call can then be used to help pay for the put.[42] The payoff structure is shown in Table 16.14.

---

[41] To simplify the analysis we assume that the options are of the European type. That is, we assume that they can be exercised only on the expiry date. There are numerous examples other than the range forward. These are often accorded eye-catching names such as 'fox', 'scout' and 'break forward'. Several are described in G. Warren, 'Quick Brown Fox Breaks Forward Over Lazy Scout', *Euromoney*, May 1987, pp. 245–64.

[42] In practice it is common for the exercise prices to be selected carefully so that the put price equals the call price. Therefore the inflow from one exactly offsets the cost of the other, making the deal appear 'free'.

**Table 16.14** Payoff structure for Example 16.5, Conquest Investments Ltd

| If the spot exchange rate per $A1 on the expiration date is | On the put[a] | On the call[b] | Purchase of US$ (spot)[c] | Total |
|---|---|---|---|---|
| US$0.76 | +2500 | 0 | +38 000 | +40 500 |
| 0.77 | +2000 | 0 | +38 500 | +40 500 |
| 0.78 | +1500 | 0 | +39 000 | +40 500 |
| 0.79 | +1000 | 0 | +39 500 | +40 500 |
| 0.80 | +500 | 0 | +40 000 | +40 500 |
| 0.81 | 0 | 0 | +40 500 | +40 500 |
| 0.82 | 0 | 0 | +41 000 | +41 000 |
| 0.83 | 0 | 0 | +41 500 | +41 500 |
| 0.84 | 0 | 0 | +42 000 | +42 000 |
| 0.85 | 0 | −500 | +42 500 | +42 000 |
| 0.86 | 0 | −1000 | +43 000 | +42 000 |
| 0.87 | 0 | −1500 | +43 500 | +42 000 |
| 0.88 | 0 | −2000 | +44 000 | +42 000 |
| 0.89 | 0 | −2500 | +44 500 | +42 000 |

[a] Taken from Table 16.12.
[b] Taken from Table 16.13, except that inflows from the purchase of a call (Table 16.13) are now outflows due to the sale of a call in this table.
[c] Calculated using 50 000 × spot exchange rate.

Table 16.14 shows that Conquest Investments Ltd will receive no less than US$40 500, but no more than US$42 000. If the future spot exchange rate is between US81 and 84 cents per $A1, the arrangement requires only a spot transaction.

### 16.5.3 OPTIONS AND FORWARD CONTRACTS

There is a simple relationship between prices of European-type options and forward prices. As forward contracts are most frequently encountered in foreign currency dealings, we have chosen to explain the relationship using options on foreign currency and forward contracts on foreign currency. However, in principle it holds for a much wider range of underlying assets.

*Example 16.9*

Suppose that, in Example 16.8, the exercise price of the call had, like that of the put, been US81 cents. In that case, the payoffs are as shown in Table 16.15.

It can be seen from the final column of Table 16.15 that this combination of transactions is equivalent to a guarantee that $A50 000 can be sold for US$40 500. In effect this is equivalent to having a forward contract to sell $A50 000 at a forward price of US81 cents per $A1.

It is a simple matter to provide an algebraic proof. Given that:

Total cash flow = cash flow from put + cash flow from call
  + cash flow from spot transaction,

**Table 16.15** *Payoffs for put bought and call sold, both with an exercise price of US81 cents*

| If the spot exchange rate per $A1 on the expiration date is | Then the US$ cash flows are: | | | |
|---|---|---|---|---|
| | On the put | On the call | Purchase of US$ (spot) | Total |
| US$0.76 | +2500 | 0 | +38 000 | +40 500 |
| 0.77 | +2000 | 0 | +38 500 | +40 500 |
| 0.78 | +1500 | 0 | +39 000 | +40 500 |
| 0.79 | +1000 | 0 | +39 500 | +40 500 |
| 0.80 | +500 | 0 | +40 000 | +40 500 |
| 0.81 | 0 | 0 | +40 500 | +40 500 |
| 0.82 | 0 | −500 | +41 000 | +40 500 |
| 0.83 | 0 | −1000 | +41 500 | +40 500 |
| 0.84 | 0 | −1500 | +42 000 | +40 500 |
| 0.85 | 0 | −2000 | +42 500 | +40 500 |
| 0.86 | 0 | −2500 | +43 000 | +40 500 |

then if $P < C$, the total cash flow is:
$$(C - P^*) + 0 + P^* = C$$

but if $P \geq C$, the total cash flow is:
$$0 - (P^* - C) + P^* = C$$

Therefore, the future total cash flow is always $C$.

Finally, suppose that the price of the put was equal to the price of the call, and both the put and the call have the same exercise price, term, and so on. In this case, the arrangement illustrated in Table 16.15 requires no net initial cash inflow or outflow and it therefore replicates a forward contract at both initiation and expiry. To prevent arbitrage, the forward price (exchange rate) should therefore equal the exercise price of the options.

In summary, if the prices of a put and its counterpart call are equal, the forward price for the underlying asset should equal the exercise price of the options.

### 16.5.4 Pricing Options on Foreign Currency

The pricing of options on foreign currency is illustrated using the simplest case of a call to buy foreign currency. This problem has been considered in several papers[43] and a suggested solution is as follows:

$$w = Pe^{-iT}N(d_3) - Ce^{-rT}N(d_4) \qquad (16.8)$$

---

[43] For examples, see N. Biger & J. Hull, 'The Valuation of Currency Options', *Financial Management*, Spring 1983, pp. 24–8; and H. C. Yang, 'A Note on Currency Option Pricing Models', *Journal of Business Finance and Accounting*, Autumn 1985, pp. 429–38.

where $d_3 \equiv \dfrac{\ln(P/C) + (r - i + \frac{1}{2}\sigma^2)T}{\sigma\sqrt{T}}$

$d_4 \equiv d_3 - \sigma\sqrt{T}$

The notation in the formula is:

- $w$ = price of the call
- $P$ = spot price of one unit of foreign currency
- $C$ = exercise price (in domestic currency) for one unit of foreign currency
- $T$ = term of the call
- $\sigma^2$ = variance rate of the spot price
- $i$ = foreign currency risk-free interest rate
- $r$ = domestic currency risk-free interest rate

The relationship between Equation 16.8 and the Black–Scholes equation is a simple one. If the foreign currency interest rate $i$ is set equal to zero, then with suitable redefinition of variables the equations are identical. Intuitively, unlike an investment in shares, a sum of foreign currency can earn interest, and this factor has been built into the model. In this context a sum of foreign currency is rather like a share that pays a continuous dividend.[44]

Equation 16.8 can be re-expressed in terms of the forward exchange rate by assuming that the interest rate parity theorem applies. This theorem links the spot rate, the forward rate, and the domestic and foreign interest rates. We discuss it in detail in Section 21.4.2. In its continuous time formulation the theorem states that:

$$\ln(F/P) = (r - i)T$$

where $F$ is the forward exchange rate. This implies that $Fe^{-rT} = Pe^{-iT}$. Substituting into Equation 16.8 gives:

$$w = Fe^{-rT}N(d_5) - Ce^{-rT}N(d_6) \qquad (16.9)$$

$$d_5 \equiv \dfrac{\ln(F/C) + \frac{1}{2}\sigma^2 T}{\sigma\sqrt{T}}$$

$$d_6 \equiv d_5 - \sigma\sqrt{T}$$

Equation 16.9 shows that there should be a connection between forward exchange markets, which set the forward rate $F$, and foreign currency option markets, which set the option price $w$.

Using put–call parity it is a simple matter to convert Equation 16.9 into an equation to value European put options on foreign currency.[45] In addition it is worth mentioning that some put and call options are equivalent. By definition, a sale of US dollars (to receive Australian dollars in return) can equally well be

---

[44] The model is in fact simply a re-interpretation of Merton's continuous dividend case for calls on shares. See R. C. Merton, 'Theory of Rational Option Pricing', *Bell Journal of Economics and Management Science*, Spring 1973, Footnote 62, p. 171. An error in this footnote is corrected in F. Black, 'The Pricing of Commodity Contracts', *Journal of Financial Economics*, January/March 1976, Footnote 10, p. 177. In Merton's equation, $i$ is the dividend yield.

[45] For details, see, for example, Biger & Hull, (Footnote 43), p. 126.

described as a purchase of Australian dollars (paid for by payment of US dollars). In the same way a US dollar put can equally well be described as an Australian dollar call.

Equation 16.9 applies to European-type options. Unfortunately the extension to American-type options is a significant problem. It was explained in Section 16.2.8 that the payment of dividends can cause premature exercise of a call and therefore dividends can make the distinction between American and European calls important. Given that the interest rate on foreign currency is like a continuous dividend payment, it should be no surprise that for calls on foreign currency the American/European distinction can be important. This is especially the case if the foreign interest rate is high relative to the domestic interest rate. Finally, given that a call to buy foreign currency can always be described as a put to sell domestic currency, the distinction must also be important for some puts. However, suggested solutions are beyond the scope of this book.[46]

Empirical evidence on the ability of Equation 16.8 to produce model prices that match the market prices of options on foreign currency suggests that there are inaccuracies in the model. Shastri and Tandon studied 4410 call prices and 2340 put prices taken from the Philadelphia Stock Exchange.[47] They found a systematic tendency for the model to underprice options, relative to market prices. This was particularly true of puts. This poor performance may be due in part to the incorrect assumption of a European-type option and/or may be due to incorrectly assuming that the distribution of exchange rates is lognormal.[48] They conducted trading-strategy tests and concluded that, at least for traders who are not members of the Exchange, the market was efficient. Bodurtha and Courtadon have also studied the efficiency of the Philadelphia market,[49] but their work does not rely on an explicit pricing equation. Instead they test put–call parity and rational restrictions on early exercise and, after taking account of transaction costs, find little evidence of inefficiency.

## 16.6 OPTIONS ON FUTURES
### 16.6.1 WHAT IS AN OPTION ON A FUTURES CONTRACT?

A number of futures exchanges, including the Sydney Futures Exchange, have introduced options on the more heavily traded futures contracts. A call option on futures confers on the buyer of the call the right to enter into a futures contract as a buyer.[50] Similarly a put option on futures confers on the buyer of the put

---

[46] See M. Brenner, G. Courtadon & M. Subrahmanyam, 'Options on the Spot and Options on Futures', *Journal of Finance*, December 1985, pp. 1303–17.

[47] K. Shastri & K. Tandon, 'Valuation of Foreign Currency Options: Some Empirical Tests', *Journal of Financial and Quantitative Analysis*, June 1986, pp. 145–60.

[48] For evidence, see J. W. McFarland, R. R. Pettit & S. K. Sung, 'The Distribution of Foreign Exchange Price Changes: Trading Day Effects and Risk Measurement', *Journal of Finance*, June 1982, pp. 693–715.

[49] J. N. Bodurtha & G. R. Courtadon, 'Efficiency Tests of the Foreign Currency Options Market', *Journal of Finance*, March 1986, pp. 151–62.

[50] In this section it is assumed that the reader is familiar with futures contracts. Futures contracts are explained in detail in Chapter 15.

the right to enter into a futures contract as a seller. Often the expiry date of the option is shortly before the expiry date of the futures contract.

For example, suppose that on 15 February the price of a futures contract on gold, maturing on 20 May, is $500. On 15 February it may also be possible to buy a call option on this futures contract with an exercise price of, say, $520 and an expiry date of 13 May. This call confers the right to assume the role of buyer in the futures contract at a futures price of $520. On 15 February this option may be worth, say, $15. Suppose that the futures price of gold increases and that by 10 May the futures price has reached $550 and the call buyer wishes to take the profit. If the call is an American-type the call buyer could exercise the call on 10 May, thereby becoming registered from that date as a futures buyer at a price of $520. Through operation of the mark-to-market rule the sum of $30 will be credited to the buyer. Alternatively, instead of exercising the call it could simply be sold in the options market. In principle the price obtained should be $30 or more.

### 16.6.2 Uses of options on futures

Options on futures have proved to be popular with traders, particularly in the case of financial futures. Although there are many possible reasons for this, options on futures have three attributes that may have prompted market participants to trade in the option rather than in the underlying futures contract.

First, open futures positions entail very high risks for the speculator, particularly if those positions are held for a long time. For example, if a market participant believed that the share price index (SPI) was likely to rise substantially in the next two months, then without options, and apart from buying the shares themselves, the only way to speculate on this belief is to buy SPI futures. Many speculators would not want to take this risk, simply because they could incur large losses if the SPI should fall. A call option on futures allows the speculator to pay a given sum (the option price) in return for avoiding the possibility of large losses. The ability to profit if the belief proves correct is unimpaired. In short, options on futures can preserve the basic speculative uses of futures, but without the open-ended commitment that futures themselves require.

Secondly, hedgers may not be certain enough of their own circumstances to justify accepting the obligations of a futures contract. Consider the following situation. A small manufacturer has tendered for a particular job and the manager believes that although there is a fair chance of success, it is not certain. If the tender is accepted, there will be an immediate need for short-term funding of approximately $500 000 to buy the necessary raw materials. Of course, if the tender is not accepted, there is no such need. The manager believes that there is a need to hedge, because the financial viability of the project will be threatened if interest rates increase between now and the date on which the name of the successful tenderer will be announced. This risk cannot be hedged using futures contracts because a futures contract is a commitment, but the manufacturer cannot be committed to the project unless and until the tender is accepted. At present the manufacturer's need to hedge is contingent on the future outcome of the tender process.[51] The manufacturer could set up a contingent hedge by buying a put option on a bank bill futures contract. The amount paid for the put can be regarded as an insurance premium. If interest rates rise, bank bill futures prices will fall and the put will be more valuable. The put's increased value will protect the manufacturer, should protection be needed. Of course if interest rates fall, so will the put price. Indeed, the put price may even fall to zero and the manufacturer will then have lost the total price paid for the put. This is like buying fire insurance and not having a fire. No claim is made on the insurance policy and the premium is lost.

Thirdly, the deposit/margin system is simpler for option buyers than for futures traders. (Option sellers still face unlimited risks so there are still complications applicable to them.) Once option buyers have paid the option price they can make no further losses. Consequently there is little or no reason to subject option buyers to a stringent deposit/margin system. For this reason, smaller futures traders may prefer to buy a call instead of buying futures and to buy a put instead of selling futures.

### 16.6.3 PRICING OPTIONS ON FUTURES

One solution to the problem of valuing options on futures contracts is provided by Equation 16.9. Although this equation was presented as a model to price options on foreign currency, with appropriate assumptions it can also be applied to options on futures. As a part of this analysis we first consider the pricing of options on forward contracts.[52] Assume that:
  1. the expiry date of a call on a forward contract coincides with the expiry date of the forward contract;
  2. the call is a European-type.

Equation 16.9 will apply to this case. To see this, consider a European call option to buy US$1 on 28 February at an exercise price of $A1.30. This option cannot be exercised until 28 February and on that date the call buyer will exercise the option if the spot price per US$1 exceeds $A1.30. Otherwise the option will expire unexercised. Compare this contract with a European call (expiring on 28 February) to enter into a forward contract (also expiring on 28 February) to buy US$1 at an exercise price of $A1.30. This option, also, cannot be exercised until 28 February, and on that date the forward contract will be for immediate delivery; that is, the forward contract will have become equivalent to a spot contract. Precisely the same opportunities and decisions will confront the holder of the option on the forward contract as will confront the holder of the option on foreign currency. Therefore Equation 16.9 will apply in this case.

The link to options on futures is provided by the observation that futures contracts are likely to command similar prices to their counterpart forward contracts. In this case, therefore, there should also be little difference between the prices of options on futures contracts and the prices of their counterpart options

---

51 A detailed example of contingent hedging is given in Section 21.6.7. Although that example is set in an international finance context, the principles are the same.
52 Differences between forward contracts and futures contracts are considered in Section 15.2.1.

on forward contracts. Therefore under the conditions assumed here, Equation 16.9 can be used to value European options on futures.

As in the case of options on foreign currency, the extension to American-type options is a significant problem because the ability to exercise prematurely can be valuable in certain circumstances. Suggested solutions to valuing the American-type option on futures are beyond the scope of this book.[53] However, we briefly review some of the empirical evidence on the pricing ability of these models. Whaley studied approximately 15 000 call prices and 13 700 put prices.[54] All options were options on share price index futures contracts traded on the Chicago Mercantile Exchange in 1983. Whaley found that, relative to market prices, the model had a systematic tendency to underprice some types of options and to overprice others. For example, the model tended to overprice out-of-the-money calls, in-the-money puts, and short-term puts and calls. However Bailey, using a more advanced model than Whaley, reported greater accuracy in the pricing of options on gold futures traded on the Commodity Exchange of New York.[55] Both Whaley and Bailey also conducted tests of market efficiency and found that, at least in relation to non-members of the Exchange, the markets were efficient.

## 16.7 CONTINGENT CLAIMS

### 16.7.1 WHAT IS A CONTINGENT CLAIM?

At the most basic level, an option on shares is simply an agreement that allows a choice to be made at a later date. The choice will be exercised if it is in the interests of the option holder to do so and this will depend on the future value of the shares. A 'contingent claim' is an asset whose value depends on the given value of some other asset. A call option is perhaps the simplest type of contingent claim. A large number of financial contracts are contingent claims and this raises the possibility that such contracts might be valued using an option-pricing (that is, contingent-claims) approach. In the following seven sections we provide examples of financial contracts that can be interpreted as options. However, detailed discussion of the pricing formulae is beyond the scope of the book.

### 16.7.2 RIGHTS ISSUES

One of the simplest contingent claims arises when a company raises share capital by way of a rights issue. In this case a shareholder is given the right to purchase new shares in the company at an issue price set by the company. The rights must

---

[53] See M. Brenner, G. Courtadon & M. Subrahmanyam, (Footnote 47), and K. Ramaswamy & S. M. Sundaresan, 'The Valuation of Options on Futures Contracts', *Journal of Finance*, December 1985, pp. 1319–40.

[54] R. E. Whaley, 'Valuation of American Futures Options: Theory and Empirical Tests', *Journal of Finance*, March 1986, pp. 127–50. Broadly similar findings are also reported in K. Shastri & K. Tandon, 'An Empirical Test of a Valuation Model for American Options on Futures Contracts', *Journal of Financial and Quantitative Analysis*, December 1986, pp. 377–92.

[55] W. Bailey, 'An Empirical Investigation of the Market for Comex Gold Futures Options,' *Journal of Finance*, December 1987, pp. 1187–94.

be sold or taken up by a specified date. In fact, a right is simply a call option issued by the company. Unlike listed call options, exercise of the right *does* affect the company's capital structure. Furthermore, in practice the life of a right is usually much shorter than the life of most listed call options. Nevertheless, a right is a call option and therefore can be valued using option-pricing principles.[56]

### 16.7.3 CONVERTIBLE NOTES

A convertible note is a type of debt security that in addition to paying interest, gives the investor the right to convert the security into shares of the company. For example, on the maturity of the convertible note, the investor can take a cash payment in the usual way, or can take a predetermined number of shares instead of the cash payment. The choice is up to the investor. A convertible note is therefore equivalent to ordinary debt plus a call option on the shares of the company.[57]

### 16.7.4 VALUATION OF LEVERED SHARES AND RISKY ZERO-COUPON DEBT

One of the first contracts to be identified as a contingent claim was a share in a company that has debt outstanding. Because companies cannot offer government guarantees, there is some risk of default. Consider, for example, the shareholders in a company that has issued zero-coupon debt.[58] The shareholders must make a choice, which resembles the choice facing the holder of a call option. The shareholders can direct the company to repay the debt on the maturity date or they can allow the company to default. Choosing to repay is equivalent to exercising the call option to reclaim the company's assets from the debtholders, while choosing to default is equivalent to allowing the call to expire unexercised. It is as if the shareholders have transferred the company's assets to the debtholders but have a call option to buy back the assets by repaying the debt. The major variables involved in pricing a call option are reinterpreted as shown in Table 16.16.

In principle, therefore, we could value the shares using an option-pricing approach. Given that the market value of the company is equal to the sum of the market value of the shares and the market value of the debt, once we know the value of the shares we can calculate the value of the debt as well.

---

[56] For a full discussion, see C. W. Smith, 'Alternative Methods for Raising Capital: Rights Versus Underwritten Offerings', *Journal of Financial Economics*, December 1977, pp. 273–307.

[57] For a detailed discussion, see J. Ingersoll, 'A Contingent-claims Valuation of Convertible Securities', *Journal of Financial Economics*, May 1977, pp. 289–322. A brief accessible discussion can also be found in G. R. Courtadon & J. J. Merrick, 'The Option Pricing Model and the Valuation of Corporate Securities', in J. M. Stern & D. H. Chew, Eds, *The Revolution in Corporate Finance*, 2nd edn, Basil Blackwell, 1992, pp. 271–2.

[58] The most important distinguishing feature of zero-coupon debt is that it is repaid by a single lump sum paid on the maturity date. No intermediate (or coupon) interest payments are required. It is also known as 'pure discount' debt.

**Table 16.16** *Interpreting a levered share as a call option*

| Call option interpretation | Levered share interpretation |
|---|---|
| The current (market) value of the share | The current (market) value of the assets |
| The exercise price | The amount due at the debt's maturity (that is, face value) |
| The term to expiry of the option | The term to maturity of the debt |
| The volatility of the share | The volatility of the assets |
| The risk-free interest rate | The risk-free interest rate |

### 16.7.5 VALUATION OF LEVERED SHARES AND RISKY COUPON-PAYING DEBT

The contingent-claims approach can also be applied to the problems of valuing risky coupon-paying debt and valuing the shares of a company which has issued this type of debt. Although this is a more difficult application, it is relatively simple to explain the insight that enables the problem to be solved. In this case shares can be regarded as a sequence of call options. At maturity the lump-sum payment consisting of the face value of the debt and the final coupon payment is a simple call option. This is the case discussed in the previous section. But to have reached this far, the shareholders must have paid the second-last coupon payment. Therefore the second-last coupon is like a call option where the underlying asset is the simple call option represented by the final repayment. In short, the second-last coupon is an option on an option, or, as it is sometimes called, a **compound option**.[59] Thus we can value the shares. The value of the risky debt is given by the value of the assets, less the value of the shares.

### 16.7.6 THE DEFAULT-RISK STRUCTURE OF INTEREST RATES

The term 'default-risk structure of interest rates' refers to the fact that, at any point in time, as the probability of default by a borrower increases, the required yield (or interest rate) on the debt also increases, other things being equal. The default-risk structure is often measured by the difference between a risky debt's required yield and the risk-free interest rate applicable to the same term to maturity. Once we are able to calculate the *price* of risky debt using the approach outlined in the previous two sections, it is a simple matter to calculate the *yield* implied by that price, and we can then analyse the risk structure of interest rates. This approach to the risk structure has been analysed in detail by Merton.[60]

---

[59] See R. Geske, 'The Valuation of Compound Options', *Journal of Financial Economics*, March 1979, pp. 63–81, and 'The Valuation of Corporate Liabilities as Compound Options', *Journal of Financial and Quantitative Analysis*, November 1977, pp. 541–52.

[60] See R. C. Merton, 'On the Pricing of Corporate Debt: The Risk Structure of Interest Rates', *Journal of Finance*, May 1974, pp. 449–70.

## 16.7.7 Capital Budgeting and 'Real' Options

The net present value (NPV) approach to capital budgeting, which we explained in detail in Chapter 5, is based on an analogy between a proposed investment project and a bond. Like a bond, a project produces a set of future cash flows. The NPV approach proposes that, like the cash flows of a bond, the cash flows of a project should be discounted to a present value and summed to find the total value of the project. While the NPV approach has proved to be an extremely valuable tool, this does not mean it is always the best tool to use. Sometimes the bond analogy is *not* the best one available. The problem with the bond analogy is that it assumes that, once a project is started, its cash flows cannot be changed. It assumes that there is no opportunity for the investing company to intervene in the project after it has begun. For example, it ignores the possibility of the project being abandoned. In practice the opportunity to intervene can be extremely important: it is, in fact, an option and hence has a value. Consider, for example, a gold mine that, given the *current* price of gold, has a negative NPV.[61] Does this mean that the mine is worthless? No. Ownership of the mine confers a number of rights that are valuable, including the right to close the mine, and the right to reopen the mine at a later date. Whether and when these rights will be exercised will depend on the cost of exercising the rights and the future price of gold. In short, these rights attached to mine ownership are like options. Mine ownership is, of course, just one example, and many projects involve 'real' options of this general type.

## 16.7.8 Other Contingent Claims

A large number of seemingly diverse and unrelated issues have been studied using the contingent-claims approach. Examples include 'subordinated' (or 'lower ranking') debt, underwriting contracts, insurance,[62] corporate pension funding policy, state-contingent claims, the term structure of interest rates, corporate liquidity management and cancellable operating leases.[63] The common

---

[61] See M. J. Brennan & E. S. Schwartz, 'A New Approach to Evaluating Natural Resource Investments', in Stern & Chew, (Footnote 57), pp. 107–16. The original academic work is M. J. Brennan & E. S. Schwartz, 'Evaluating Natural Resource Investments', *Journal of Business*, 1985, pp. 135–58.

[62] For a review of these three examples and of most of the applications discussed earlier in this section, see C. W. Smith, 'Applications of Option Pricing Analysis', in *Handbook of Financial Economics*, Ed. J. L. Bicksler, North-Holland, Amsterdam, 1979, pp. 79–121.

[63] See W. F. Sharpe, 'Corporate Pension Funding Policy', *Journal of Financial Economics*, June 1976, pp. 183–93; G. L. Willinger, 'A Contingent Claims Model for Pension Costs', *Journal of Accounting Research*, Spring 1985, pp. 351–9; D. T. Breeden & R. H. Litzenberger, 'Prices of State-contingent Claims Implicit in Options Prices', *Journal of Business*, October 1978, pp. 621–51; M. J. Brennan & E. S. Schwartz, 'An Equilibrium Model of Bond Pricing and a Test of Market Efficiency', *Journal of Financial and Quantitative Analysis*, September 1982, pp. 301–29; M. G. Levasseur, 'An Option Model Approach to Firm Liquidity Management', *Journal of Banking and Finance*, June 1977, pp. 13–28; and T. E. Copeland & J. F. Weston, 'A Note on the Evaluation of Cancellable Operating Leases', *Financial Management*, Summer 1982, pp. 60–7. This list is not complete, nor is it intended to be. The only criterion of choice was the apparent diversity of the issues addressed.

link between these (and other) studies is that a choice is to be made in the future and the decision will depend on the exogenous given value of some other asset. Options on shares are but the simplest and most obvious members of the broader class of contingent claims.

## SELECTED REFERENCES

Biger, N. & Hull, J., 'The Valuation of Currency Options', *Financial Management*, Spring 1983, pp. 24-8.
Black, F., 'Fact and Fantasy in the Use of Options', *Financial Analysts Journal*, July–August 1975, pp. 36–41, 61– 72.
Black, F. & Scholes, M., 'The Pricing of Options and Corporate Liabilities', *Journal of Political Economy*, May–June 1973, pp. 637–54.
Cox, J. C. & Rubinstein, M., *Options Markets*, Prentice-Hall, Englewood Cliffs, New Jersey, 1985.
Hull, J., *Options, Futures, and other Derivative Securities*, Prentice-Hall, Englewood Cliffs, New Jersey, 1989.
Merton, R. C., 'Theory of Rational Option Pricing', *Bell Journal of Economics and Management Science*, Spring 1973, pp. 141–83.
Merton, R. C., 'On the Pricing of Corporate Debt: The Risk Structure of Interest Rates', *Journal of Finance*, May 1974, pp. 449–70.
Smith, C. W., 'Option Pricing: A Review', *Journal of Financial Economics*, January–March 1976, pp. 3–51.
Smith, C. W., 'Applications of Option Pricing Analysis', in *Handbook of Financial Economics*, Ed. J. L. Bicksler, North-Holland, Amsterdam, 1979, pp. 79–121.
Stoll, H. R. & Whaley, R. E., *Futures and Options: Theory and Applications*, South-Western Publishing, Cincinnati, 1993.
Whaley, R. E., 'Valuation of American Call Options on Dividend-paying Stocks: Empirical Tests', *Journal of Financial Economics*, March 1982, pp. 29–58.
Whaley, R. E., 'Valuation of American Futures Options: Theory and Empirical Tests', *Journal of Finance*, March 1986, pp. 127–50.

## QUESTIONS

1. Distinguish between the following:
   (a) Put option and call option
   (b) American option and European option
   (c) Option contract and futures contract
   (d) Time value of an option and time value of money.
2. List and explain the factors likely to influence the value of a call option.
3. What is the value of a call option on its expiry date? Why? What is the value of a put option on its expiry date? Why?
4. *Options are so risky that trading in them is really just another form of gambling.* Discuss.
5. What is the minimum value of a call option on a share that does not pay dividends? Why?
6. Explain briefly why it is generally not rational to exercise a call option before its expiry date. Under what circumstances can it be rational? In these cases, what do option holders obtain, and what do they forego?
7. The following is an extract from the *Xanadu Financial Review* of 2 November 1994.

## Call Option Trading

**Company:** Jempip Industries Ltd
**Last sale price:** $3.27

|                | Exercise price ($) | Last sale ($) |
|----------------|--------------------|---------------|
| 1994 December  | 2.75               | 0.51          |
| December       | 3.00               | 0.32          |
| December       | 3.25               | 0.09          |
| December       | 3.50               | 0.04          |
| December       | 4.00               | 0.04          |
| 1995 March     | 2.75               | 0.64          |
| March          | 3.00               | 0.44          |
| March          | 3.25               | 0.18          |
| March          | 3.50               | 0.06          |
| March          | 4.00               | 0.04          |

The risk-free interest rate in Xanadu is 1 per cent per month. Jempip options cover 1000 shares per contract, may be exercised at any time, expire at the end of their expiry month, and are not protected against dividend payments. Jempip pays dividends of 10 cents per share in April and October each year.

Which prices appear to violate option-pricing theory? Give brief reasons.

8. Call options have no maximum value; put options do. Why?
9. Both put and call options are available on the shares of Christopher Toms Ltd (CTL). The options are of the European type. CTL is due to pay its next dividend of 10 cents per share in January 1995. The risk-free interest rate is 1 per cent per month. On 31 August 1994 you observe the following market prices for CTL call options:

**Company:** CTL
**Last sale price:** $2.00

| Expiration date  | Exercise price ($) | Option price ($) |
|------------------|--------------------|------------------|
| 30 November 1994 | 2.25               | 0.10             |
| 30 November 1994 | 5.00               | 0.005            |

Use put–call parity to estimate market prices for the November 2.25 and November 5.00 put options. If these put options had been of the American type, what would their minimum values have been? Does this suggest that, unlike call options, some put options should be exercised prematurely?

10. Calculate the Black–Scholes price for a call option with the following features: share price $3, exercise price $2.75, term to expiry 3 months, risk-free interest rate 10 per cent per annum (continuously compounded), and variance rate 0.16 per annum. Calculate the Black–Scholes price of a put option with the same features.

11. Various authors have described the Black–Scholes model in the following terms: 'path-breaking', 'seminal', 'brilliant', and 'classic'. Why are they so impressed?
12. Use binomial option pricing to price a three-month European call option with an exercise price of $15.00 on a share whose current price is also $15.00. Use three time periods of one month each, a monthly 'up factor' of 1.02, and a monthly 'down factor' of 1/1.02. The risk-free interest rate is 0.5 per cent per month.
13. Use binomial option pricing to calculate the price of the European put option that matches the call option in the previous exercise. Does put–call parity hold?
14. Ozzie Glassworks Ltd of Adelaide has been awarded the contract to supply glass for a giant aquarium to be built in Lancaster, England. However, the contract is conditional on the promoter of the project obtaining a construction approval from the Lancaster City Council. Ozzie Glassworks has quoted a fixed price of 200 000 UK pounds. What advice would you give Ozzie Glassworks?
15. The loan contract described as follows is a simplified version of an actual security: RA Best Constructions International Ltd seeks to borrow from Multi Bank the sum of US$10 million, repayable by a single payment to be made in one year's time. However, this payment is made up of two components:
    1. *Component 1* is a payment of US$2 million, which for convenience may be called 'interest' at the rate of 20 per cent per annum.
    2. *Component 2* is the payment of an amount that depends on the exchange rate between yen and US dollars on the maturity date of the loan. We may call this a repayment R, in full satisfaction of the principal P, which is owed. If the future exchange rate S is 169 (or more) yen per US dollar, then the full principal of US$10 million must be repaid. If the future exchange rate is 84.5 (or fewer) yen per US dollar, then none of the principal needs to be repaid; Best is 'forgiven' all the debt. If the future exchange rate falls between 84.5 and 169 yen per US dollar, the repayment required is related to the principal according to the following formula:

$$R = P\left(1 + \frac{S - 169}{S}\right)$$

    When Multi Bank investigated this proposal, the exchange rate was 185 yen per US dollar. At the same date the interest rate that Best would have paid for a standard 1-year fixed rate US dollar loan was 11 per cent per annum.
    (a) Taking Multi Bank's viewpoint, analyse the loan in terms of its options characteristics.
    (b) Again taking Multi Bank's viewpoint, and assuming that you have a model that can be used to value any option you may define, explain how you would investigate this proposal.
16. Parklands Ltd has issued debentures. Explain how Parklands shares are similar to options.
17. Hi Gear Toys Ltd is facing severe financial difficulties; its cash flows are barely enough to cover its fixed-interest commitments. Hi Gear's share price is very low. Alf Hawke, Hi Gear's Managing Director, decides that

the company should begin manufacturing a new toy called a 'tomato bush doll'. This toy just might prove to be a runaway success (but probably won't). Alf announces the decision at a press conference. Do you think Hi Gear's share price would rise, fall, or stay about the same? Why?

# CHAPTER 17

# THE COST OF CAPITAL

## 17.1 INTRODUCTION

In this chapter we consider the definition, estimation and use of the cost of capital. The cost of capital is important in project evaluation. When a project is evaluated using the net present value (NPV) model it is necessary to have information about two important variables. These are the project's forecast **net cash flows** and its required rate of return, discount rate or **cost of capital**. If a new project is to increase shareholders' wealth, it must generate net cash flows that are sufficient to compensate the suppliers of capital for the resources committed to the project. In other words the project must have a positive net present value when the expected net cash flows are discounted at the project's cost of capital.

In turn, the cost of capital reflects the time value of money and the risk of the project. It follows that the cost of capital for a project depends on the rate of return that investors can obtain on other projects of similar risk. In other words, the cost of capital for a project is an opportunity cost. Therefore, it is not a factor that the management of a company can control; rather it depends on the features of the project in which the capital is to be invested. In particular it depends on the project's risk. These concepts are summarised in an important principle which is fundamental to correct use of the cost of capital concept:

> The cost of capital is an opportunity cost that depends on the risk of the project in which the capital is invested.

The Capital Asset Pricing Model (CAPM) outlined in Chapter 6 can be used as a framework for assessing risk and incorporating its effects in estimates of the cost of capital.

Chapter 18 considers further issues in project evaluation, including the effects of taxes on project cash flows. It is particularly important that taxes be treated consistently in the cash flows and the cost of capital. For example, if after-company tax cash flows are used when evaluating a proposed project, the cost of capital must also be an after-company tax rate. While this principle sounds simple, it can be difficult to apply because there is more than one way to define 'after-company tax' cash flows. Particular care is needed under the imputation tax system because, as discussed in Appendix 17.1, some or all of the tax collected from a company is personal tax, not 'true' company tax. Alternative ways of defining project cash flows and the cost of capital are discussed in Appendix 17.1.

## 17.2 RISK AND THE COST OF CAPITAL

In Chapter 6 it was pointed out that a rational, risk-averse investor will hold a diversified efficient portfolio of assets. It follows that the relevant measure of risk for any asset is its systematic or non-diversifiable risk, because investors will not be compensated for bearing risk that can be eliminated by diversification (that is, they will not be compensated for unsystematic or diversifiable risk). Consistent with this, the CAPM describes an equilibrium relationship between systematic risk and expected returns on risky assets. Before the CAPM was developed, financial managers allowed for risk by using judgement and rules of thumb. For example, projects may have been assigned required rates of return of 15, 20, or 25 per cent, depending on whether their risk was considered to be 'low', 'average', or 'high'. Such an approach is arbitrary and therefore unsatisfactory. In contrast, the CAPM defines a risk–return relationship that can be used when a more precise estimate of the required rate of return is needed. According to the CAPM, the relevant measure of risk is the **systematic risk of the project**, measured by its beta. The definition and estimation of beta is discussed in Sections 6.6.2 and 6.6.3.

### 17.2.1 RISK INDEPENDENCE

It is implicit in the use of a discount rate related to the risk of a project that the cost of capital for a project does not depend on the characteristics of the company considering the project. The decision rule is to accept all projects whose net present values are positive when the expected cash flows are discounted at the project-specific discount rate. Thus the value of a project depends on *what* the project is, not *who* the investor is. Where estimates of the cost of capital are based on the CAPM, all projects whose risk–return coordinates plot on or above the security market line are accepted. Therefore the value of a proposed project does not depend on the correlation of the proposed project's cash flows with the existing cash flows of the company or with other projects being considered by the company. In other words, projects can be evaluated as if they are risk independent. The assumption of risk independence simplifies project evaluation because management can evaluate possible investments on a project-by-project basis, rather than by calculating the net present value for every possible combination of projects.

Myers has shown that risk independence is a necessary consequence of equilibrium in securities markets.[1] The principle of risk independence and its

---

1 S. C. Myers, 'Procedures for Capital Budgeting Under Uncertainty', *Industrial Management Review*, Spring 1968, pp. 1–15.

consequences for project evaluation are explained by considering company diversification. It was explained in Chapter 6 that a rational risk-averse investor will hold a well-diversified portfolio and that the risk of an asset in a large portfolio depends on the covariance of the returns on the individual asset with the returns on the portfolio. It could be argued that companies should also diversify. If so, then companies would take into account the correlation between returns on the proposed project and returns on their existing projects.

Fortunately this argument is incorrect because investors can diversify for themselves simply by investing in the shares of many different companies. Therefore diversification by a company does not create value for investors because it does not provide any new investment opportunity that was not already available to investors. Consequently each project should be evaluated using its *own* cost of capital. This depends on the risk of the particular project. Risk independence comes about because of the effectiveness of the capital market in providing opportunities for investors to diversify.

## 17.3. ALTERNATIVE APPROACHES TO ESTIMATION OF THE COST OF CAPITAL

It is important to recognise that the cost of capital depends on investors' expectations, which cannot be observed. Therefore, in most cases the cost of capital cannot be measured precisely: it must be estimated and the preferred approach will be influenced by the availability of data and by the importance of the investments that will be evaluated using the estimation of cost of capital. The following sections discuss two approaches: direct use of the CAPM, and the use of the weighted average cost of capital (WACC).

### 17.3.1 DIRECT USE OF THE CAPM

According to the CAPM, which is discussed in Section 6.6.2, the cost of capital $k_j$ for project $j$ is:

$$k_j = R_f + \beta_j (E(R_M) - R_f) \tag{17.1}$$

Therefore to use the CAPM directly, it is necessary to estimate the risk-free interest rate $R_f$, the expected rate of return on the market portfolio $E(R_M)$, and the project's systematic risk (beta) $\beta_j$. Estimation of $R_f$ and $E(R_M)$ is discussed in Section 17.5.3 but for now we focus on the problem of estimating the beta of a project.

Techniques for estimating the systematic risk of securities, such as shares, using numbers derived from share price data were explained in Section 6.6.3. The necessary data are readily available where the securities concerned are traded actively on a stock exchange. Proposed investment projects are, of course, not traded on a stock exchange, or on any other market, and therefore the data required to estimate systematic risk directly are not available. This problem could easily be overcome if all of a company's projects had the same systematic risk, and if the company were financed solely by equity. Shareholders would bear all the risk associated with the company's net cash flows. As these cash flows are generated by the company's projects (or assets) the systematic risk of the company's shares would be equal to the systematic risk of its assets.

In practice the vast majority of companies use debt finance as well as equity. This increases the beta of equity because shareholders of levered companies face financial risk as well as business risk. In the absence of taxes, the beta of a company's assets would be equal to a weighted average of the betas of its equity and its debt. While equity betas are routinely estimated using data on sharemarket returns, this is not the case for debt. In Australia, most corporate debt is either non-marketable or, at best, traded irregularly and it is therefore very difficult to estimate the beta of debt. Moreover, in practice the relationship between security betas and asset betas can be more complicated than it is in the no-tax case. This issue arises again in Section 17.6.2 but the approach used in that section relies on the simplifying assumption that corporate debt is risk-free.

In summary, direct use of the CAPM involves two main problems. First, there is the problem of the limited availability of data to estimate betas for debt. Secondly, care is needed to ensure that tax and leverage effects are handled correctly. Because of these problems, direct use of the CAPM is generally not feasible. However, this does not mean that the model should be disregarded. The CAPM can be very useful in estimating some components of the weighted average cost of capital.

## 17.3.2 The Weighted Average Cost of Capital (WACC)

The discussion in the previous sections emphasised the principle that the cost of capital is project-specific. In other words, evaluation of a proposed project should be based on the *project's* cost of capital. However, it can be very difficult to measure a project's cost of capital. The reason is that when a company raises capital there is generally no direct link between the returns to the suppliers of that capital and the returns from individual projects. For example, suppose that a company borrows, using an existing asset as security, to provide the cash needed for a new project. The interest rate paid on the debt is *not* a valid measure of the new project's cost of capital. The reason is simple: the interest rate on the debt depends on the risk of the company and its existing assets, and does *not* depend solely on the risk of the new project. Remember, the borrowed money must be repaid, regardless of whether the new project is a success or a failure. Moreover the lender's return is essentially fixed and will not be increased if the new project turns out to be highly profitable. The situation is similar if a company makes a share issue to raise the cash needed for a new project. Shareholders are exposed to the risk of the whole company. Therefore the cost of equity will depend on the average risk of *all* the company's assets and on its financial leverage, not just the characteristics of the new project. In summary, the rates of return to suppliers of a company's capital do not necessarily reflect the cost of capital specific to any individual project, even if the new capital is raised at the time the project is implemented.

However, there is an important special case that often provides a practical solution to these problems. Suppose that a company's assets are all of similar risk and the risk of a proposed new project is the same as the risk of the company's existing assets. This should be the case if the project is simply an expansion of the company's existing operations. Since there is no change in risk, the cost of capital for the company as a whole should also be a valid measure of the cost of capital for the new project. The overall cost of capital for a company is the discount rate that equates the present value of the company's expected future cash flows to the company's value.

To make this definition useful it is necessary to define both 'cash flows' and 'value'. The **value** of a company is normally defined as the market value of its equity, plus the market value of its debt. However, this definition of value can be combined with several different definitions of **cash flow**, leading to different versions of the cost of capital. For example, cash flows can be measured before tax or after tax. Project cash flows are normally defined as being equal to the project's after-company tax net cash flows, excluding any financing costs associated with the investment and the tax savings on those financing costs. That is, before-tax cash flows are normally converted to after-tax cash flows by multiplying the before-tax cash flows by $(1 - t_c)$, where $t_c$ is the company income tax rate.[2] In Appendix 17.1 we show that when the *classical* tax system applies, and net cash flows are defined in this way, a company's cost of capital $k'$, can be expressed as a weighted average of the costs of equity and debt, given by:

$$k' = k_e \left(\frac{E}{V}\right) + k_d (1 - t_c) \left(\frac{D}{V}\right) \qquad (17.2)$$

where $k_e$ = shareholders' required rate of return (that is, the cost of equity)
$k_d$ = lenders' required rate of return (that is, the cost of debt)
$t_c$ = the company income tax rate
$E$ = the market value of the company's equity capital
$D$ = the market value of the company's debt capital
$V = E + D$ = the total market value of the company

The concept underlying the weighted average cost of capital (WACC) formula is straightforward. Consider a company that has financed its assets using both debt and equity finance. The company's average cost of capital is the minimum rate of return that it needs to earn on its assets in order to meet the cost of debt finance and provide the rate of return that shareholders require. To simplify matters, assume that the company's net operating cash flows remain constant in perpetuity. Then the annual interest cost of the company's debt is:

Interest rate (after-tax) times market value of debt = $k_d(1 - t_c) \times D$.

Similarly, the minimum net cash flow required by shareholders is:

Required rate of return on equity times market value of equity = $k_e \times E$.

Therefore, to meet these required rates of return the company's minimum annual net operating cash flow must be:

$$k_e E + k_d(1 - t_c) D$$

Since we are assuming that cash flows are constant in perpetuity, the company's cost of capital $k'$ is simply the annual net operating cash flow divided by the market value of capital. That is:

---

[2] We refer here to the definitions traditionally used under the classical tax system. Modified definitions that are applicable under the imputation system are outlined in Appendix 17.1.

$$k' = \frac{\text{annual net operating cash flow}}{\text{market value of capital}}$$

$$= \frac{k_e E + k_d (1 - t_c) D}{E + D}$$

$$= k_e \left[\frac{E}{E + D}\right] + k_d (1 - t_c) \left[\frac{D}{E + D}\right]$$

$$= k_e \left[\frac{E}{V}\right] + k_d (1 - t_c) \left[\frac{D}{V}\right]$$

This equation is, of course, the same as Equation 17.2 and shows that the company's cost of capital can be expressed as a weighted average of the costs of equity and debt. Therefore the concept underlying the WACC formula is that, to be acceptable, a new project should generate net cash flows that are sufficient to meet the after-tax cost of debt used to finance the project, as well as providing at least the required rate of return on the equity used to finance the project.

Examination of WACC formulae such as Equation 17.2 shows that all the variables in the equation relate to a company as a whole, which means that the WACC can only be estimated directly for a company. For that reason a company's cost of capital is sometimes viewed as an inherent property of the company *per se*. That interpretation is incorrect. A company's cost of capital depends on the average risk of its assets, not on the identity of the company.

## 17.4 TAX SYSTEMS AND THE COST OF CAPITAL

It should be clear from the discussion in previous sections that the definition and use of the cost of capital involves taxes. Also, we have emphasised the need for consistency in the treatment of taxes when using the cost of capital. Projects are normally evaluated on an after-company-tax basis. Under the imputation system some or perhaps all of the tax paid at the company level can later be recovered by shareholders through tax credits associated with franked dividends. Compared to the previous classical system, the tax burden on equity is lower, and it is necessary to consider the implications of the imputation tax system for the treatment of taxes in evaluating projects and the use of the cost of capital.

Introduction of the imputation tax system for Australian companies raised two issues related to the cost of capital:
1. What effects, if any, did the change in the tax system have on the cost of capital for Australian companies?
2. Is it necessary to change the ways in which after-tax cash flows and/or the cost of capital are defined and measured?

These issues are related, but distinct, and in this section we discuss only the first. The second issue is discussed in detail in Appendix 17.1.

The possible effects of the introduction of imputation on the cost of capital have been discussed by Officer and the following discussion is based largely on his analysis.³ The cost of capital is a price that will reflect conditions in the capital market and will be determined by the demand for, and supply of, capital. In discussing the possible effects of the imputation tax system on the supply of, and demand for, capital, it is useful to contrast a closed economy with an open economy.⁴

## A CLOSED ECONOMY

Assume that the Australian economy is closed, which means that capital cannot flow into or out of the country. Under these circumstances, reducing the tax on equity by the introduction of the imputation system would, other things being equal, increase the supply of funds to companies. The effect of this increased supply of funds on the cost of capital will depend on the demand for funds. To absorb the additional supply of funds, new investments that were previously marginally unattractive will be undertaken. However, if there are few such investments available, the equilibrium cost of capital could fall substantially. If there are many such projects available, the demand for funds will be much more responsive to changes in the cost of capital. In this case the demand for funds is fairly elastic and the change in the cost of capital will be much smaller.

## AN OPEN ECONOMY

Officer points out that in fact the Australian economy is open, in that capital can flow freely into or out of the country. In an open economy, both the supply of and demand for capital will be much more elastic than in a closed economy.⁵ In an open economy, investors are not restricted to holding only local investments and can easily move funds either into or out of the country in response to even small changes in rates of return. Further, the elasticity of demand and supply will depend on the size of the economy relative to world capital markets. Since the Australian economy is in this sense very small, it is unlikely that the cost of capital for Australian companies changed as a result of imputation. The supply of funds available for investment in Australian companies by resident shareholders should have increased, but any resultant downward effect on rates of return should lead overseas investors to withdraw funds. Also, Australian investors, particularly institutions, can readily invest overseas and would be expected to move funds overseas in pursuit of higher returns if the rate of return available in Australia decreased. Consequently, any effect on the cost of capital is likely to have been both minor and transitory.

The argument that the change in the tax system probably had little effect on the cost of capital for Australian companies should not be taken to imply that the tax changes were unimportant. Clearly, the shares of companies paying franked dividends have become more attractive to Australian resident investors

---

3 R. R. Officer, 'The Required Rate of Return and Tax Imputation: Estimating the Effect of the Imputation Tax on Investment Appraisal', *Australian Tax Forum*, No. 3, 1987, pp. 405–17.
4 For a more detailed discussion, see Officer, (Footnote 3), pp. 410–14.
5 See Officer, (Footnote 3), p. 411.

and their prices should have increased. Any such increase may have been substantial, but would be difficult to identify, given the volatility of share prices and the fact that the change is a market-wide effect.

The analysis in Appendix 17.1 shows that the change in the tax system has definite implications for the way that cash flows and the cost of capital should be defined and measured. The adjustments needed can be made to the definition of the cash flows and/or the cost of capital. The simplest approach is to continue using the WACC defined in Equation 17.2 and adjust the cash flows by adding back the value of any tax credits paid out with franked dividends and used by shareholders. These tax credits represent personal tax that, in effect, has been paid by the company on behalf of the shareholders. Therefore, adding back these credits gives cash flows after 'true' company tax. As discussed in Section A17.2.2, true company tax refers to any extra tax that is paid because a business uses a company structure, rather than being unincorporated.

Appendix 17.1 also shows that adjustments are needed where observed market rates of return are used to estimate the cost of equity. Conventionally, the cost of equity $k_e$, is defined and measured on an after-company tax, but before-personal tax, basis. Under the classical tax system this approach is straightforward because observed market rates of return on equity are also after-company tax, but before-personal tax. However, under the imputation system, part of the return to equity consists of tax credits. Because these tax credits are not included in conventional rate-of-return measures, adjustments are required, to obtain true after-company tax rates of return. The adjustment is simple: add back the value of imputation tax credits that represent personal tax that has already been paid. The value of these tax credits can be expressed as a rate of return $\tau$, by dividing the tax credits by the share price. It follows that a similar adjustment is needed when the CAPM is used to estimate the cost of equity. Therefore the CAPM would become:

$$k_e = R_f + \beta_e \left[E\left(R_M + \tau\right) - R_f\right]$$

Adding $\tau$, which can be called a 'franking premium', adjusts the observed return on the market portfolio to an after-company tax rate of return. Estimation of the cost of capital using this approach is illustrated in the next section.

## 17.5 ESTIMATION OF THE COST OF CAPITAL: AN EXTENDED EXAMPLE

Equation 17.2 shows that a company's after-tax cost of capital is equal to the weighted average of the costs of debt and equity, where the cost of each individual source of capital is weighted according to its proportion in the company's capital structure. While the WACC has been explained assuming there are only two classes of capital, namely equity and debt, in reality a company may issue different classes of shares, as well as different classes of debt. These additional classes of capital can be handled by extending Equation 17.2 to include all sources of finance used by the company. Consequently estimation of the WACC requires estimation of each variable in Equation 17.2 or an extended version of it.

To estimate the cost of capital it is necessary to estimate variables of two types: the cost of each source of finance and the proportion of each source of finance in the company's capital structure. Since we are estimating a cost of capital based on investors' expectations of future returns, it is important to use current market rates and current market values, rather than historical rates and book values. Fixed-interest debt will be used as an example to explain why current market rates are relevant, rather than historical rates.

Suppose that a company has, on issue, debentures paying a coupon interest rate of 10 per cent, compared with the current market rate of 15 per cent. When estimating the company's cost of capital, the current rate of 15 per cent should be used. This may appear to ignore the fact that the company is paying an interest rate of only 10 per cent on its existing debentures. Surely there must be some advantage in paying only 10 per cent instead of 15 per cent? There is an advantage, but the company's shareholders have already received the benefit of the old, lower interest rate, because the current share price will take this into account. Investments to be made *now* must be attractive in comparison with the *current* cost of capital, and the old interest rate is irrelevant.

In the next three sections, we discuss estimation of the individual components of the WACC. Each component is illustrated using the information on Xanadu Industries Ltd (XIL). The discussion concludes in Section 17.5.4 with an estimate of the company's WACC using the components calculated in the previous three sections. The sources of finance used by XIL are shown in Table 17.1.

**Table 17.1** *Xanadu Industries Limited. Selected balance sheet data as at 30 June 1994*

| Sources of finance | Book value ($m) |
|---|---|
| Commercial bills | 20.000 |
| Bank overdraft | 7.368 |
| Bonds | 10.000 |
| Preference shares, 13% | 2.000 |
| Ordinary shares: issued and paid up, 12 500 000 at 50 cents | 6.250 |

XIL's financial manager also has the following information:
1. The commercial bills have a current interest rate (yield) of 6.08 per cent per annum. The existing bills mature on 31 August 1994 but will be replaced by a further issue at that date.
2. The interest rate on the bank overdraft is 9.5 per cent per annum, calculated daily and charged to XIL's account twice per year.
3. There are 100 bonds, each with a face value of $100 000 and a coupon interest rate of 10 per cent per annum, payable on 30 April and 31 October each year. The bonds will be redeemed at their face value on 31 October 1997.
4. The preference shares are non-redeemable with a par value of $2 paying a dividend rate of 9 per cent per annum. Dividends are payable on 31 May and

30 November each year. On 30 June 1994 the market price of each preference share was $1.50.
5. XIL pays dividends on its ordinary shares once per year. The latest dividend was 17.5 cents, fully franked, and on 30 June 1994 the market price of each ordinary share was $4.20.
6. The company income tax rate is 33 per cent and the imputation tax system applies.

## 17.5.1 THE COST OF DEBT

Companies can raise debt from a variety of sources. There are short-term and long-term sources of debt and debt may be marketable or non-marketable. The overall cost of debt for a company will therefore be a weighted average of the costs of its individual sources of debt. This weighted average cost will not be accurate if the individual costs are expressed inconsistently. For example, it would be inconsistent to average nominal interest rates that are based on different repayment frequencies. To ensure consistency, all costs of debt for XIL will be expressed as effective annual rates.

The cost of debt can also be expressed in terms of an after-tax cost by multiplying the before-tax cost by $(1 - t_c)$, where $t_c$ is the company income tax rate. For example, if the before-tax cost of debt is 10 per cent per annum, and the company income tax rate is 33 cents in the dollar, the after-tax cost of debt would generally be regarded as 6.7 per cent per annum. This calculation assumes that the company is operating profitably and that there is no time lag involved in the payment of company income tax. The calculation is the same for each item of debt and is reflected in Equation 17.2. Therefore, in the XIL example the annual interest rates applicable to the individual sources of debt finance will be stated as before-tax rates and the conversion to an after-tax cost of debt will be made in the final WACC calculation.

For convenience, debt may be classified as shown in Table 17.2.

**Table 17.2** Types of debt

|  | Short-term debt | Long-term debt |
| --- | --- | --- |
| Marketable | promissory notes<br>commercial bills | bonds<br>debentures<br>unsecured notes |
| Non-marketable | accounts payable<br>bank overdraft<br>intercompany loans | mortgage loans<br>financial leases<br>term loans |

### COST OF SHORT-TERM DEBT

Short-term debt securities such as commercial bills and promissory notes are marketable, and current interest rates are quoted in the financial press. From these quotations the current effective rate of interest on marketable debt can be calculated.[6] In the case of XIL's commercial bills, the quoted interest rate is 6.08 per cent per annum. The market conventions are to quote nominal annual rates and to use simple interest for short-term securities. In calculating the effective annual interest rate on the bills the first step is to convert the nominal rate of 6.08 per cent per annum to the effective rate $i$ for 62 days. Therefore:

$$i = 6.08 \times \frac{62}{365}$$
$$= 1.032767\%$$

The second step is to convert this rate to an annual rate as follows:

$$(1 + i)^{\frac{365}{62}} - 1$$
$$= (1.01032767)^{5.8871} - 1$$
$$= 0.062\ 355$$

Therefore, the rate applicable to bills issued by XIL is approximately 6.24 per cent per annum before tax.

To calculate the WACC it is also necessary to know the market value of debt, which can be found using the nominal interest rate. Therefore, for a commercial bill or promissory note:

$$P = \frac{FV}{\left[1 + \dfrac{jt}{365}\right]} \qquad (17.3)$$

where  $P$ = current market price of the security

$FV$ = face value of the security

$j$ = nominal interest rate per annum

$t$ = the number of days from the date of price calculation to the maturity date

For XIL's commercial bills, the market value at 30 June 1994 is:

$$P = \frac{\$20\ 000\ 000}{\left[1 + 0.0608 \times \dfrac{62}{365}\right]}$$
$$= \$19\ 795\ 558$$

The cost of non-marketable interest-bearing debt such as a bank overdraft will be its current interest rate, converted if necessary to an effective annual rate. The interest rate on XIL's overdraft is 9.5 per cent per annum or 4.75 per cent per half year. Therefore the effective annual rate is:

$$(1.0475)^2 - 1$$
$$= 0.097\ 256$$

---

[6] For a detailed discussion of this topic, see H. G. Stanton & John A. Rickard, 'The True Cost of Borrowing Under a Commercial Bill', *Australian Journal of Management*, December 1983, pp. 95–103.

That is, the rate applicable to the bank overdraft is approximately 9.73 per cent per annum before tax. Other forms of non-marketable short-term debt such as taxes payable, wages payable, and accounts payable, which do not have an explicit interest cost, should be excluded. The reason is not that these forms of debt are 'free', rather their costs are accounted for in other ways. For example, the cost of trade credit (the difference between the price of goods purchased with cash on delivery and the price when purchased on credit) has already been deducted in calculating the cash flows. Therefore, accounts payable do not have to be serviced out of those cash flows; to include accounts payable as a source of finance would be inconsistent.

## COST OF LONG-TERM DEBT

Some forms of long-term debt, such as debentures, unsecured notes, and corporate bonds are marketable. We use the term 'bonds' to refer to these long-term debt securities. Given a current market price $P$, the effective rate of interest $k_d$ on a company's bonds is equal to the discount rate, which equates the market price of the bond with the discounted value of the cash flows promised under the terms of the bond. Most bonds pay interest twice a year, and the price of such a bond is given by:

$$P = \frac{1}{(1+i)^{f/h}} \left\{ R + \frac{R}{i}\left[1 - \frac{1}{(1+i)^n}\right] + \frac{C}{(1+i)^n} \right\} \qquad (17.4)$$

where  $P$ = current market price of the bonds
         $i$ = the effective rate of interest per half year
        $R$ = interest payments = $Fj/2$, where
                  $F$ = face value of the bonds, and
                  $j$ = nominal rate of interest per annum,
       $C$ = redemption price of the bonds
       $n$ = number of future interest payments minus 1
       $f$ = the number of days from the date of price calculation to the next interest payment
      $h$ = the number of days in the half-year ended on the next interest payment date

Equation 17.4 can be used to calculate the effective rate of interest per half-year and it is then a simple matter to calculate the annual rate.

The logic of Equation 17.4 can be explained using XIL bonds as an example. Suppose that on 30 June 1994 an XIL bond was sold for $104 334.53. The terms of the bond were as follows: face value $F$ $100 000; nominal rate of interest $j$, 10 per cent per annum payable on 30 April and 31 October each year; redemption price $C$ $100 000; and maturity date, 31 October 1997. Therefore, each interest payment $R$ is equal to $(\$100\,000)(0.10/2) = \$5000$. The next interest payment is due on 31 October 1994, which is 123 days after the date of purchase (30 June 1994). There are a further six interest payments after 31 October 1994—two in each of the years 1995, 1996, and 1997. If the bond were to be valued as at 31 October 1994, an interest payment of $5000 would be due immediately, the remaining six interest payments would constitute an ordinary annuity,[7] and the redemption price would be a lump sum payable exactly 6 half-years later. At a yield (or required rate of return) of $i$ per half-year, the value of the bond calculated as at 31 October 1994 is given by:

(Immediate payment of $5000) + (present value of the annuity) + (present value of the lump sum)

$$= \$5000 + \frac{\$5000}{i}\left[1 - \frac{1}{(1+i)^6}\right] + \frac{\$100\,000}{(1+i)^6}$$

This calculation corresponds to the term in the braces, { }, in Equation 17.4. However, the valuation required is as at a date 123 days before 31 October 1994. It is therefore necessary to discount the price calculated here to take account of this 123-day period. Because all terms in the equation are based on a half-yearly time period, the 123-day period must also be expressed on a half-yearly basis. The number of days in the half-year ended 31 October 1994 (that is, the period from 30 April to 31 October 1994) is 184. The period involved is 123/184 of a half-year and the discount factor is therefore:

$$\frac{1}{(1+i)^{123/184}}$$

Therefore:

$$\$104\,334.53 = \frac{1}{(1+i)^{123/184}}\left\{\$5000 + \frac{\$5000}{i}\left[1 - \frac{1}{(1+i)^6}\right] + \frac{\$100\,000}{(1+i)^6}\right\}$$

As explained in Section 4.2, equations of this type cannot be solved directly for $i$ but the required value for $i$ can be found by other methods. In this case, $i$ equals 0.0452. This is shown as follows:

$$\frac{1}{(1.0452)^{123/184}}\left\{\$5000 + \frac{\$5000}{0.0452}\left[1 - \frac{1}{(1.0452)^6}\right] + \frac{\$100\,000}{(1.0452)^6}\right\}$$

$$= \frac{1}{(1.0452)^{0.6685}}\left\{\$5000 + (\$5000)(5.154\,6546) + \frac{\$100\,000}{1.303\,756}\right\}$$

$$= \frac{1}{1.029\,993}\left\{\$5000 + \$25\,772.73 + \$76\,701.45\right\}$$

$$= (0.970\,88)(\$107\,474.18)$$

$$= \$104\,334.53$$

The required rate of return on this bond is therefore 4.52 per cent per half-year. Converting this rate to an annual effective rate gives a rate equal to:

$$(1.0452)^2 - 1$$
$$= 0.092\,443$$

Therefore, the rate applicable to XIL bonds is approximately 9.24 per cent per annum before tax.

---

[7] See Chapter 3 for an explanation of the valuation of an ordinary annuity.

Where a fixed-interest debt contract, such as a mortgage, is not marketable, the current cost of the debt cannot be measured in the way described for bonds. The best measure of the current cost in this case is an estimate of the interest rate that the company would now have to pay to raise mortgage funds on conditions that match those of the existing mortgage.

### 17.5.2 THE COST OF PREFERENCE SHARES

Preference shares have attributes of both debt and equity. As explained in Chapter 10 it is usual for non-redeemable preference shares to be cumulative and non-participating. Such preference shares pay a fixed dividend per share, $D_p$, at regular time intervals. Although the payment of a preference dividend is at the discretion of the Board of Directors, it is unusual to omit payment. As a result, preference dividends form a perpetuity, and for a share which pays dividends twice a year the share price is given by:

$$P = \frac{1}{(1 + i)^{f/h}} \left\{ D_p + \frac{D_p}{i} \right\} \tag{17.5}$$

where  $P$  = current market price of preference shares
 $i$  = effective yield per half-year
 $D_p$ = half-yearly preference dividend per share
 $f$  = the number of days from the date of price calculation to the next dividend payment
 $h$  = the number of days in the half-year ended on the next dividend payment date

The logic of Equation 17.5 is analogous to that of Equation 17.4. For XIL's preference shares the market price was $1.50 on 30 June 1994 and the next dividend of 9 cents per share was due on 30 November. Therefore:

$$\$1.50 = \frac{1}{(1 + i)^{153/183}} \left\{ \$0.09 + \frac{\$0.09}{i} \right\}$$

In this case $i = 0.0606$, so the effective annual cost of the preference shares, $k_p$, is:

$$k_p = (1.0606)^2 - 1$$
$$= 0.124\,872$$

Therefore the rate applicable to XIL preference shares is approximately 12.49 per cent per annum after company tax.

If the preference shares are redeemable on a predetermined date, the calculation of the cost of preference shares is the same as the calculation of the effective interest rate on debt. Preference dividends are generally a distribution of profit rather than a tax-deductible expense. However, certain preference shares may carry franked dividends, and their cost can be calculated using the procedures outlined for ordinary shares.

### 17.5.3 THE COST OF ORDINARY SHARES

In contrast to debt, ordinary shares issued by a company do not involve a contractual obligation to provide any specific return. Therefore it is necessary to estimate the rate of return that investors expect the shares to provide in the future. One approach is to focus on the company's expected future dividend stream and estimate the discount rate implied by the current share price. This approach was discussed in Section 4.3 and is summarised in Equation 17.6:

$$P_0 = \sum_{t=1}^{\infty} \frac{E(D_t)}{(1 + k_e)^t} \qquad (17.6)$$

where $P_0$ = current share price
$E(D_t)$ = expected dividend per share in period $t$
$k_e$ = required rate of return (that is, the cost of ordinary shares)

The current share price will be known and, given an estimate of expected future dividends, an estimate of the cost of ordinary shares can be derived. In estimating a company's future dividend stream it is usual to make simplifying assumptions. For example, if it is assumed that the dividend per share will grow at a constant rate $g$ indefinitely, then as shown in Section 4.3.2, Equation 17.6 becomes:

$$P_0 = \frac{D_0(1 + g)}{k_e - g} \qquad (17.7)$$

where $D_0$ is the current period's dividend per share.

The model expressed by Equation 17.7 is usually referred to as the dividend-growth model.

To find $k_e$, Equation 17.7 may be rewritten as:

$$k_e = \frac{D_0(1 + g)}{P_0} + g$$

XIL's share price at 30 June 1994 was $4.20 and its latest annual dividend was 17.5 cents per share, fully franked. Since the dividend is fully franked, the 17.5 cent dividend carries a tax credit of $0.175 \times \left(\frac{t_c}{1 - t_c}\right)$. With a company tax rate of 33 per cent, this tax credit is $0.175 \times 0.33/0.67 = \$0.0862$. This tax credit represents personal tax that has been paid by XIL on behalf of its shareholders and must be added to the cash dividend to give the after-company tax dividend $D_0^*$. Therefore, $D_0^*$ is $0.175 + \$0.0862 = \$0.2612$. If the dividend growth rate is estimated to be 8 per cent per annum, then XIL's cost of equity can be calculated as follows:

$$\begin{aligned} k_e &= \frac{D_0^*(1 + g)}{P_0} + g \\ &= \frac{\$0.2612\,(1.08)}{\$4.20} + 0.08 \\ &= 14.72 \text{ per cent} \end{aligned}$$

It was shown in Section 4.3.2 that estimates of current share price based on the dividend growth model are extremely sensitive to estimates of the future growth rate in dividend per share. The same problem arises when the model is used to estimate the cost of equity. Therefore, while the model is theoretically correct given its assumptions, the practical problems involved in its application mean that the CAPM may be preferred. The CAPM describes the equilibrium relationship between systematic risk and expected returns on risky assets and can therefore be used to estimate the cost of equity. Use of the CAPM requires estimation of the risk-free interest rate $R_f$, the expected rate of return on the market portfolio $E(R_M)$, and the systematic risk of equity, $\beta_e$. Each of these variables is now discussed in turn.

## THE RISK-FREE INTEREST RATE ($R_f$)

There are a large number of risk-free interest rates that could be used. The assets closest to being risk-free are government debt securities. However, unless the term structure of interest rates is flat, the various government securities will offer different interest rates. The appropriate risk-free rate is the current yield on a government security whose term to maturity matches the life of the proposed project. Since major projects typically provide returns over many years, the rate on long-term securities is generally used.

## THE EXPECTED RATE OF RETURN ON THE MARKET PORTFOLIO ($E(R_M)$)

It is necessary to estimate the expected rate of return on the market portfolio to obtain an estimate of the market risk premium $(E(R_M) - R_f)$. As discussed in Chapter 6, in practice it is impossible to calculate the rate of return on the market portfolio. Instead, a share price index is generally used as a proxy. As the rate of return on a share price index is highly variable from year to year, it is usual to calculate the average return on the index over a relatively long period, say 10 years. Suppose that the average rate of return on a share market index such as the All Ordinaries Accumulation Index over the past 10 years was 18.5 per cent per annum. If this rate is used as the estimate of $E(R_M)$ and today's risk-free rate is 8.5 per cent, the market risk premium $(E(R_M) - R_f)$ would be 10 per cent.

A problem with using this approach is that the estimate of $R_f$ reflects the market's current expectations of the future, whereas $E(R_M)$ is an average of the expectations previously held by the market. In other words, the two values may not match, and some unacceptable estimates may result. For example, $(E(R_M) - R_f)$ estimated in this way may be negative if the rate of inflation expected now, which should be reflected in $R_f$, is greater than the realised rate of inflation during the past period used to estimate $E(R_M)$. A better approach is to estimate the market risk premium directly, over a relatively long period. Using this method, Officer found that the premium on the market portfolio in Australia over the 106 years from 1882 to 1987 was approximately 7.9 per cent per annum.[8] Comparable studies in the US, Canada and the UK have also found a long-term average premium of about 7 to 8 per cent per annum.[9]

## THE SHARE'S SYSTEMATIC RISK ($\beta_e$)

The market model, as outlined in Section 6.6.3, is often used to obtain an estimate of ex-post systematic risk. The market model is:

$$R_{it} = \alpha_i + \beta_i R_{Mt} + e_{it} \tag{17.8}$$

where $\beta_i$ = the estimate of systematic risk for asset $i$

To use the market model, it is necessary to obtain time series data on the rates of return on the share and on the market portfolio (that is, a series of observations for both $R_{it}$ and $R_{Mt}$ is needed). It is generally accepted that 60 monthly observations for these variables is suitable.

Fortunately a number of organisations provide estimates of the systematic risk (beta) of the equity of many listed companies. For example, the Risk Measurement Service operated by the AGSM Centre for Research in Finance provides estimates of the betas of the shares of companies listed on the Australian Stock Exchange. Beta values for a selection of companies and industries were presented in Table 6.5.

After estimates of the three variables have been prepared, the cost of equity can be calculated using Equation 17.1. As discussed in Appendix 17.1, if the expected return on the market $E(R_M)$ is based on rates of return observed under the imputation system, the observed rates should be adjusted by adding back a franking premium $\tau$. This adjustment is needed to express the return on the market on an after-company tax basis. Therefore Equation 17.1 becomes:

$$k_e = R_f + \beta_e [E(R_M + \tau) - R_f]$$

If the financial manager of XIL has the following estimates:

$R_f$ = 9% or 0.09
$E(R_M)$ = 15% or 0.15
$\tau$ = 2% or 0.02
$\beta_e$ = 1.2

then:

$k_e$ = 0.09 + 1.2(0.15 + 0.02 − 0.09)
= 18.6 per cent

---

[8] R. R. Officer, 'Rates of Return to Shares, Bond Yields and Inflation Rates: An Historical Perspective' in *Share Markets and Portfolio Theory*, Eds R. Ball, P. Brown, F. J. Finn & R. R. Officer, 2nd edn, University of Queensland Press, St Lucia, 1989. Note that data from a variety of sources were combined to obtain these long-term averages.

[9] See, for example, R. C. Ibbotson & R. A. Sinquefield, *Stocks, Bonds, Bills and Inflation: The Past and the Future*, Financial Analysts Research Foundation, Charlottesville, Virginia, 1982. Over the 1926–1988 period, the average risk premium (return on shares versus Treasury bills) in the US was 8.5 per cent.

## RETAINED EARNINGS COMPARED WITH NEW ISSUES OF ORDINARY SHARES

So far we have discussed the cost of ordinary shares without recognising that ordinary equity capital has two sources: retained earnings and ordinary shares. The earnings retained by a company do not have an explicit cost. However, this does not mean that the cost of retained earnings is zero. If part of a company's profit is retained, shareholders forego the cash dividends that the company could have paid out of that profit. Following the opportunity cost principle, the cost of retained earnings is equal to the rate of return that shareholders could have received, with equal risk, if the retained earnings had been distributed to them. What investment opportunity is foregone by the shareholders? Obviously shareholders would have the opportunity of investing in additional shares of the company and therefore the cost of retained earnings may be viewed as being at least equal to $k_e$. Therefore the cost of retained earnings is the same as the cost of equity calculated earlier.

Issue or flotation costs involved in raising capital by an issue of new shares provide a valid basis for distinguishing between the costs of retained earnings and ordinary share capital. One approach is to adjust $k_e$ as follows:

$$k_n = \frac{k_e}{1 - f} \qquad (17.9)$$

where $f$ = issue costs as a proportion of the current market price of the company's shares
$k_n$ = cost of new ordinary share capital

Alternatively, rather than treating issue costs as an adjustment to the cost of capital, it may be preferable to treat them as an initial cash outflow.[10] Criticisms have been made of both approaches and unless the issue costs are very large it may be preferable simply to ignore them.

### 17.5.4 THE COMPANY'S COST OF CAPITAL

After the explicit cost of each source of funds has been calculated, the company's cost of capital may be calculated by applying the appropriate weights to the cost of each source of funds. The appropriate weights are the proportion that each source represents of the total sources used to finance proposed projects. If the company's capital structure is expected to change, the weights should be based on the proportions of debt and equity in the target capital structure. However, unless there is reason to believe that implementing new projects will alter the company's optimum capital structure, its current capital structure can be used to calculate the weights.

The weights should be calculated using market values of the company's outstanding securities. The current costs of each source of funds have been calculated using current market prices. These prices represent the opportunity costs of investing in any project that has the same risk. Therefore the use of market

---

[10] See J. Ezzell & R. Porter, 'Flotation Costs and the Weighted Average Cost of Capital', *Journal of Financial and Quantitative Analysis*, November 1976, pp. 403–13.

value weights is consistent with decisions that are in the best interests of the ordinary shareholders.

The market value at 30 June 1994 of XIL's commercial bills was calculated previously to be $19 795 558. Each XIL bond had a market value of $104 334.53, so with 100 bonds on issue, their total market value equals $10 433 453. Market value is more than book value in this case, mainly because the market interest rate is less than the coupon interest rate on the bonds. Bank overdraft carries a variable interest rate which is adjusted in accordance with fluctuations in market rates. Therefore, the market value of a bank overdraft will equal its book value which, in this case, is $7 368 000. The data for XIL's debt are summarised in Table 17.3.

**Table 17.3** Calculation of weighted average cost of debt for XIL

| Type of debt | Market value | Proportion | Cost (per cent) | Weighted cost |
|---|---|---|---|---|
| Commercial bills | 19 795 558 | 0.5265 | 6.24 | 3.28536 |
| Bank overdraft | 7 368 000 | 0.1960 | 9.73 | 1.90708 |
| Bonds | 10 433 453 | 0.2775 | 9.24 | 2.56410 |
| | 37 597 011 | | | 7.75654 |

The average cost of debt for XIL is approximately 7.76 per cent before tax.

The $2 preference shares issued by XIL have a book value of $2 million, so it is clear that there are one million shares outstanding. Since the share price at 30 June 1994 was $1.50, the market value totals $1 500 000. There were 12 500 000 ordinary shares issued by XIL and the share price was $4.20, giving a market value of $52 500 000. This represents the value of the ordinary shareholders' interest in the company and does not need to be adjusted to reflect any retained earnings or other items of shareholders' funds that may be shown in the company's balance sheet. The total market value of both types of share is therefore $54 million.

The cost of equity capital for XIL is a weighted average of the costs of preference shares and ordinary shares as follows:

$$k_e = \left(\frac{1.5}{54}\right) 0.1249 + \left(\frac{52.5}{54}\right) 0.186$$
$$= 0.346\,944 + 18.0833$$
$$= 18.43 \text{ per cent}$$

These weighted average costs of debt and equity can then be combined to form a weighted average cost of capital for XIL using Equation 17.2 or one of the alternative formulae shown in Appendix 17.1. The total value of the company is $37.597m + $54.000m = $91.597m. If the 'textbook' formula shown in Equation 17.2 is used, the WACC for XIL is:

$$k' = k_e \left(\frac{E}{V}\right) + k_d (1 - t_c) \left(\frac{D}{V}\right)$$

$$= 0.1843 \left(\frac{\$54}{\$91.597}\right) + 0.0776 (1 - 0.33) \left(\frac{\$37.597}{\$91.597}\right)$$

$$= 0.108\,652 + 0.021\,3407$$

$$= 0.129\,993$$

or approximately 13 per cent after tax.

As shown in Appendix 17.1, other definitions of the after-tax WACC can be used. For example, under the imputation tax system the WACC can be defined as:

$$k_I'' = k_e \left(\frac{E}{V}\right) + k_d [1 - t_c (1 - \gamma)] \left(\frac{D}{V}\right)$$

where $\gamma$ is the proportion of the tax collected from a company that represents personal tax paid by the company. Suppose that, for XIL, $\gamma$ has been estimated as 0.5. This version of the WACC will be:

$$k_I'' = 0.1843 \left(\frac{\$54}{\$91.597}\right) + 0.0776 (1 - 0.33 \times 0.5) \left(\frac{\$37.597}{\$91.597}\right)$$

$$= 0.108\,652 + 0.026\,596$$

$$= 0.135\,25$$

or approximately 13.5 per cent.

The company's cost of capital, as calculated above, should be used as an estimate of the cost of capital for a new project only when certain conditions are met. These conditions follow from the fact that the variables in the WACC formulae apply to the company as a whole. It follows that the company's cost of capital will reflect the risk of its existing projects. Therefore the company's cost of capital should only be applied to projects which are identical, apart from their size, to the company's existing projects. In particular, the risk of the new project should be the same as the average risk of the company's existing projects. Also, the company's cost of capital is based on its existing capital structure. If the debt capacity of a new project differs from that of the existing projects this difference could affect the project's cost of capital. Therefore, another condition is that the new project should not cause the company's optimum or target capital structure to change. The company's cost of capital should therefore be appropriate for evaluating an expansion by a company that operates in only one industry. Where a company's operations are in more than one industry and these industries differ in risk, the company's cost of capital is unlikely to be appropriate for evaluating a new project in any of the individual industries, or in another industry that the company plans to enter. Section 17.6 deals with this issue.

## 17.6 DIVISIONAL COST OF CAPITAL

We have seen that to evaluate a project, management needs to measure the project's cost of capital. One possibility is to estimate the company's cost of capital and use this as an estimate of the project's cost of capital. Suppose, however, that the company is a conglomerate, each division of which operates in a different industry. We pointed out in Section 17.5.4 that the cost of capital for such a company is unlikely to be appropriate for a project being considered by any one of its divisions. The reason is that the systematic risk of such projects is likely to approximate closely to that of the division, and the systematic risk of a division can be significantly different from that of the company as a whole. In the next two sections, we consider:

1. the consequences, for a diversified company, of making the mistake of applying a single discount rate to investment proposals from all divisions;
2. the calculation of the cost of capital for a division of a company.

### 17.6.1 THE IMPLICATIONS OF A SINGLE DISCOUNT RATE

Frequently companies use a single discount rate (which is usually the company's cost of capital) to evaluate all investment proposals. The consequences of using a single discount rate to evaluate all investments where a company has four divisions are illustrated in Figure 17.1.

The broken line represents the cost of capital $k$ for the company as a whole, while the bars (at $k_1$, $k_2$, $k_3$ and $k_4$) represent the cost of capital for each of the

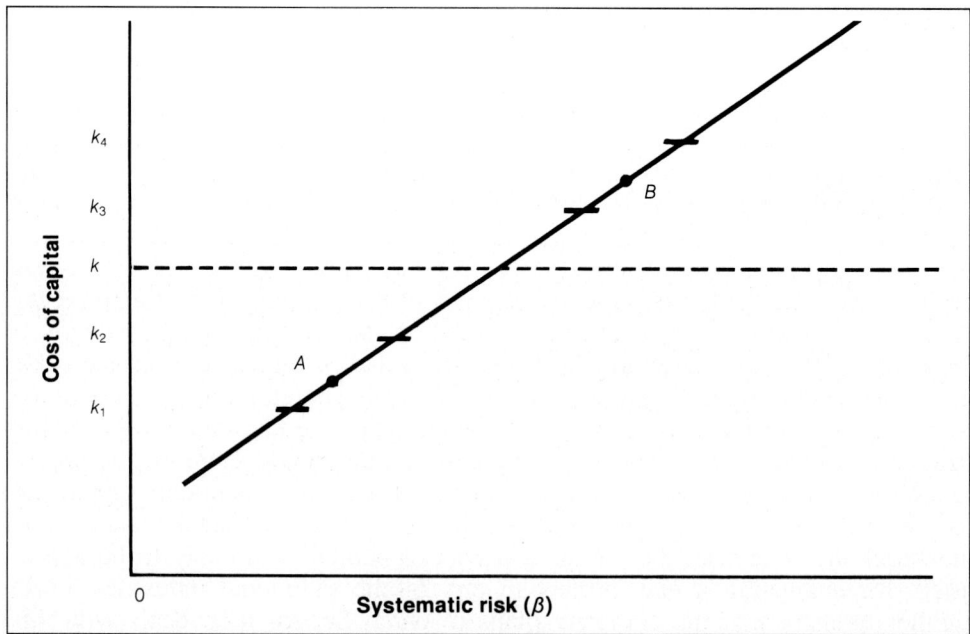

**Fig. 17.1** Applying a single discount rate, $k$, to all projects

four divisions. Assume that Division 1 is considering an investment in project *A* and Division 4 is considering an investment in project *B*. It is also assumed that the systematic risk of each project approximately equals the systematic risk of the division considering the project. The risk–return coordinates for each project are denoted by points *A* and *B* in Figure 17.1, where the vertical axis measures the project's expected rate of return which, in equilibrium, is the cost of capital.

If the company applies a single discount rate *k* to all projects, then project *A* will be rejected, as its expected rate of return is less than *k*, even though it is greater than the cost of capital consistent with Division 1's systematic risk (that is, $\beta_1$). Conversely, project *B* will be accepted because its expected rate of return exceeds *k*, even though it is less than the cost of capital consistent with division 4's systematic risk (that is, $\beta_4$).

Therefore a likely consequence for a diversified company that uses a single discount rate is that it will make incorrect investment decisions (that is, it will accept some projects that have a negative expected net present value and reject some projects that have a positive expected net present value). Moreover, high-systematic-risk divisions will find it comparatively easy to have their proposed projects accepted, while low-systematic-risk divisions will find it difficult to have their proposed projects accepted. As a result, the systematic risk of the company will drift upward over time. The low-systematic-risk divisions are likely to stagnate and may even be closed down.

In principle, each proposed project should be valued using a discount rate appropriate for the risk of that particular project. In practice, provided that the assets in each division are reasonably uniform in terms of risk, it is reasonable that management should calculate a cost of capital for each of the company's divisions. Procedures for making such calculations will now be discussed.

### 17.6.2 CALCULATING THE COST OF CAPITAL FOR DIVISIONS

Finance theory suggests that managers of diversified companies should evaluate projects using discount rates that are adjusted to reflect the systematic risks of individual projects. Many managers also accept this principle, but there has been difficulty in implementing it for two main reasons. First, there are different theories that can be used, and secondly, the most popular theories require the use of data that is difficult, if not impossible, to obtain. The approach that is most commonly recommended relies on identifying other companies that operate only in the same industry as the proposed project.[11] The betas of these companies' shares are estimated and used to estimate an asset beta which can be used in the CAPM to find a cost of capital that reflects the systematic risk of the project. One difficulty is that there may be few if any single-industry companies, often referred to as 'pure plays', that operate in the same industry as the proposed project. The steps for estimating the cost of capital for a project or division using data on a pure-play company are as follows:

---

11 R. J. Fuller & H. S. Kerr, 'Estimating the Divisional Cost of Capital: An Analysis of the Pure-play Technique', *Journal of Finance*, December 1981, pp. 997–1009.

1. Identify a pure-play company with operations similar to the proposed project.
2. Estimate the beta of the pure-play company's equity.
3. Adjust the equity beta for financial leverage to obtain an estimate of the company's asset beta, which is the beta the company would have if it was all-equity financed, that is, the beta of equity has been 'unlevered'.
4. 'Relever' the asset beta, based on the financial leverage of the company that is considering the project, to obtain an estimate of the beta of equity for the project.
5. Use the CAPM to estimate the cost of equity for the project.
6. Calculate the WACC of the project using the target debt–equity ratio of the company that is considering the project.

This procedure is illustrated in Example 17.1.

*Example 17.1*

Perco Parts Ltd has two divisions: one manufactures car parts and the other distributes agricultural machinery. The agriculture division is considering an expansion project. Perco has a target debt–equity ratio of 1:3 which will not be changed by the new project. Perco's financial manager has identified Style Farm Equipment Ltd as a company with the same business risk as the new project. Style Farm Equipment has a debt–equity ratio of 1:1, and its equity has a beta of 1.25. The procedure outlined above requires a relationship between equity betas and asset betas. As discussed in Section 17.3.1, in the absence of taxes the beta of a company's assets is simply a weighted average of the betas of its equity and its debt. That is:

$$\beta_a = \beta_e \left(\frac{E}{D+E}\right) + \beta_d \left(\frac{D}{D+E}\right) \qquad (17.10)$$

where $\beta_a$ = the beta of the company's assets
$\beta_e$ = the beta of the company's equity
$\beta_d$ = the beta of the company's debt
$D$ = the market value of debt
$E$ = the market value of equity

If the company's debt is assumed to be risk free, that is $\beta_d = 0$ then Equation 17.10 can be simplified and rearranged to:[12]

$$\beta_e = \beta_a \left(1 + \frac{D}{E}\right) \qquad (17.11)$$

This equation can be rearranged to:

$$\beta_a = \frac{\beta_e}{1 + D/E} \qquad (17.12)$$

Equations 17.11 and 17.12 will now be used to estimate an asset beta and

---

[12] The conditions under which various relationships between the betas of a company's equity and of its assets apply are discussed by R. Taggart, 'Consistent Valuation and Cost-of-capital Expressions with Corporate and Personal Taxes', *Financial Management*, Autumn 1991, pp. 8–20.

the cost of capital for Perco's farm equipment project. The first step is to use Equation 17.12 to calculate the beta of Style Farm Equipment's assets:

$$\beta_a = \frac{1.25}{1+1}$$
$$= 0.625$$

Next, Equation 17.11 is used to calculate the beta of equity for the project:
$$\beta_e = 0.625\,(1 + 1/3)$$
$$= 0.8333$$

That is, the beta for the equity proportion of Perco's proposed investment is estimated to be approximately 0.833. The cost of equity for the project can now be estimated using the CAPM. If the risk-free interest rate is 9 per cent per annum and the risk premium for the market portfolio is estimated to be 8 per cent per annum, the cost of equity is calculated as follows:

$$k_e = R_f + (E(R_M) - R_f)$$
$$= 0.09 + 0.833\,(0.08)$$
$$= 0.156\,67$$

The project's WACC can now be calculated, assuming that Perco can borrow at the risk-free interest rate of 9 per cent:

$$k' = k_e \left(\frac{E}{V}\right) + k_d\,(1 - t_c) \left(\frac{D}{V}\right)$$
$$= 0.156\,67 \left(\frac{3}{4}\right) + 0.09\,(1 - 0.33) \left(\frac{1}{4}\right)$$
$$= 0.132\,575$$

Therefore, based on the pure-play approach, the appropriate discount rate for Perco Parts' financial manager to use when evaluating the proposed project is 13.26 per cent.

The pure-play approach is used by some companies but it involves conceptual and practical problems. The conceptual problems concern the issue of how best to adjust betas for financial leverage. The adjustments used in Example 17.1 are only approximate because they are based on the simplifying assumption that corporate debt is risk free. Other more complex adjustment models have been suggested, but such models are generally based on a specific theory of capital structure. Also, the appropriate leverage adjustment depends on the company's capital structure policy.[13] The main practical problem is that pure-play companies are rare. Even if some pure plays are available, relying only on data from such

---

13 For example, the relationship between asset betas and equity betas depends on whether the debt associated with a project is assumed to be constant, or whether the debt is adjusted to maintain a constant debt–value ratio over time. See Taggart, (Footnote 12) and T. E. Conine & M. Tamarkin, 'Divisional Cost of Capital Estimation: Adjusting for Leverage', *Financial Management*, Spring 1985, pp. 54–8.

companies means that an enormous amount of information from diversified companies is ignored. A recently developed approach overcomes these problems.[14]

This approach involves estimating, directly, divisional weighted average costs of capital. It is assumed that a diversified company's WACC is itself a weighted average of the WACCs of its divisions, where the weights are the values of the divisions as proportions of the total value of the company. That is:

$$k' = \sum_{j=1}^{n} w_j k'_j \qquad (17.13)$$

where $k'$ = the company cost of capital
$k'_j$ = the cost of capital for the $j$ th division and
$w_j$ = the ratio of the value of the $j$ th division to the total value of the company

Equation 17.13 can be used to estimate divisional costs of capital. The procedure is illustrated in Example 17.2.

*Example 17.2*

Three companies, A, B and C, operate in two industries, 1 and 2. Company A has 40 per cent of its assets invested in Industry 1 and 60 per cent in Industry 2. For companies B and C, the proportions are 30:70 and 80:20 respectively. The costs of capital for companies A, B and C have been estimated to be 15.3 per cent, 15.85 per cent and 13.1 per cent respectively. It is assumed that the risks, and therefore the costs, of capital in a given industry are the same for each company. Equation 17.13 holds for each company, so it can be written as follows:

Company A $\quad 0.153 = 0.4k'_1 + 0.6k'_2$
Company B $\quad 0.1585 = 0.3k'_1 + 0.7k'_2$
Company C $\quad 0.131 = 0.8k'_1 + 0.2k'_2$

Any two of these equations can be solved simultaneously to give $k'_1 = 12$ per cent and $k'_2 = 17.5$ per cent.

Example 17.2 shows that it is possible to infer divisional costs of capital from information on diversified companies, provided that the following information is available:

1. the WACC of each company; and
2. the ratio of the value of each division to total company value for each company.

In practice, these variables will have to be estimated, which means that the estimates will involve some degree of error and it will not be possible to find an exact analytic solution for the divisional costs of capital. This problem can be overcome by using regression to estimate these costs. For this purpose Equation 17.13 is written as:

$$k' = a_1 w_1 + a_2 w_2 + \ldots\ldots + a_n w_n + e$$

where $e$ = an error term with a mean of zero.

---

[14] R. S. Harris, T. J. O'Brien & D. Wakeman, 'Divisional Cost-of-capital Estimation for Multi-industry Firms', *Financial Management*, Spring 1989, pp. 74–84.

In this regression, each company's cost of capital is one observation of the dependent variable $k'$, and each company's division weights are the corresponding measures of the independent variables $w_1$ to $w_n$. The regression coefficients $a_1$ to $a_n$ are estimates of the costs of capital for industries 1 to $n$. The estimate for a given industry can be used as a measure of the divisional cost of capital for all companies that operate in that industry, without any adjustment for financial leverage. This does not mean that differences in leverage are ignored. Rather, if different industries have different debt capacities and these differences affect the cost of capital, then such effects should automatically be reflected in the cost of capital estimates. This is one significant advantage compared to the pure-play approach. Another advantage is flexibility. For example, to estimate the company WACCs there is no need to employ any particular model such as the CAPM. Other models such as the dividend-growth model can be used to estimate the cost of equity as a component of the WACC. On the other hand, the divisional weights $w_j$ must be estimated for each company. In theory these weights should be based on market values, which are typically unknown. Therefore, in practice the weights may be based on book values or, perhaps, divisional sales.

## 17.7 THE WEIGHTED AVERAGE COST OF CAPITAL: ADVANTAGES AND DISADVANTAGES

The weighted average cost of capital (WACC) has important advantages, including flexibility and relative simplicity. It is flexible in that there are different versions of the WACC, each of which is correct, provided that it is used in conjunction with the appropriate definition of net cash flows. The 'textbook' version of the WACC as expressed in Equation 17.2 is the most popular and it is the simplest to use, particularly under the classical tax system where a project can be evaluated using after-tax net cash flows calculated *as if* the project is all-equity financed. That is, the WACC formula takes into account tax effects associated with financing, and there is no need for these effects to be reflected in the cash flows. The WACC is also flexible in that it can be used under different tax systems. For example, we have seen that the textbook formula can still be used under the imputation tax system, but the appropriate definition of cash flows is more complex than it is under the classical tax system.

It has already been emphasised that the WACC has important limitations. In particular it can only be estimated directly for a whole company and a company's cost of capital should only be used to evaluate new projects that are identical to the company's existing operations. Another problem is that the WACC lends itself to misinterpretation because it makes debt appear to be cheaper than equity. For example, in the XIL case, the cost of equity was more than 18 per cent but the cost of debt was less than 8 per cent. An observer could easily jump to the conclusion that a company's cost of capital could be reduced by increasing the proportion of debt in its capital structure. That conclusion is likely to be incorrect because it ignores some important effects of financial leverage. First, if leverage is increased, the risk of the borrower defaulting will increase, and lenders will demand higher interest rates. Secondly, the risk faced by shareholders will also increase and the cost of equity will increase. As a result of these changes the WACC could increase rather than decrease. The WACC is designed to be used as a tool in evaluating investment decisions and it can give misleading results if attempts are made to use it to 'analyse' financing decisions.

## SELECTED REFERENCES

Brennan, M. J., 'A New Look at the Weighted Average Cost of Capital', *Journal of Business Finance*, Winter 1973, pp. 24–30.
Fama, E. F., 'Risk-adjusted Discount Rates and Capital Budgeting Under Uncertainty', *Journal of Financial Economics*, August 1977, pp. 3–24.
Harris, R. S., O'Brien, T. J. & Wakeman, D., 'Divisional Cost-of-capital Estimation for Multi-industry Firms', *Financial Management*, Spring 1989, pp. 74–84.
Miles, J. A. & Ezzell, J. R., 'The Weighted Average Cost of Capital, Perfect Capital Markets, and Project Life: A Clarification', *Journal of Financial and Quantitative Analysis*, September 1980, pp. 719–30.
Myers, S. C., 'Procedures for Capital Budgeting Under Uncertainty', *Industrial Management Review*, Spring 1968, pp. 1–15.
Myers, S. C., 'Interactions of Corporate Financing and Investment Decisions—Implications for Capital Budgeting', *Journal of Finance*, March 1974, pp. 1–25.
Myers, S. C. & Turnbull, S., 'Capital Budgeting and the Capital Asset Pricing Model: Good News and Bad News', *Journal of Finance*, May 1977, pp. 321–33.
Officer, R. R., 'The Measurement of a Firm's Cost of Capital', *Accounting and Finance*, November 1981, pp. 31–63.
Officer R. R., 'The Cost of Capital of a Company Under an Imputation Tax System,' *Accounting and Finance*, May 1994, pp. 1–17.
Rubinstein, M. E., 'A Mean-variance Synthesis of Corporate Financial Theory', *Journal of Finance*, March 1973, pp. 167–81.

## QUESTIONS

1. The Canberra Corporation is considering an investment in a new project which will involve an initial investment of $200 000 and is expected to generate a net cash inflow of $235 000 in one year's time. The risk-free interest rate is 12 per cent and the expected return on the market portfolio is 18 per cent.
   (a) Should the project be accepted if its systematic risk is expected to be 0.75?
   (b) Would your answer to (a) change if the project's systematic risk is expected to be one?
2. Explain the importance of the risk-independence assumption for project appraisal.
3. *When evaluating a new project, management requires an estimate of the project's own cost of capital. The WACC formula only gives a cost of capital applicable to the company as a whole and is therefore inappropriate for this purpose.* Comment on this statement.
4. The cost of capital for a project can be determined using the following equation:

$$k_j = R_f + \beta_j (E(R_M) - R_f)$$

   (a) Justify this statement, and indicate the conditions necessary for it to be correct.
   (b) Discuss the problems associated with estimating $R_f$, $\beta_j$ and $E(R_M)$.

5. Discuss each of the following statements: (a) 'A project's cost of capital reflects the return investors require to finance the project.' (b) 'The cost of capital is project-specific.'
6. *The errors associated with estimating a company's beta are so great that you may as well assume that all betas equal one.* Do you agree? Give reasons.
7. Spares Ltd manufactures car parts and management is considering an expansion of its existing operations at a cost of $600 000. It expects this expansion to generate additional net cash inflows for the next 10 years as follows: $100 000 p.a. in years 1–5 and $130 000 p.a. in years 6–10. The company has made the following estimates:
   (a) The systematic risk of the existing firm is 0.75.
   (b) The risk-free interest rate is 11 per cent.
   (c) The expected rate of return on the market portfolio is 15 per cent. Assuming that there is no company income tax, should the company undertake the expansion?
8. The Ace Clothing Company has decided to diversify its operations by manufacturing and marketing footwear. Management notes that the systematic risk of the shares of a listed footwear company is 0.8. When would it be appropriate to use 0.8 as the estimate of the systematic risk of the equity for the company's new investment?
9. Abco Distributors Ltd wishes to evaluate an investment in a new area of activity—manufacturing paint. Bath Paints (BP) has been identified as a company whose sole activity is to produce paint. The systematic risk of BP's equity is 1.2. However, BP is financed by one part debt to one part equity, whereas Abco Distributors is financed by two parts debt to three parts equity. Further, Abco's management has estimated the risk-free interest rate to be 12 per cent and the expected rate of return on the market portfolio to be 17 per cent. The company income tax rate is 33 cents in the dollar and the before-tax cost of Abco's debt is 14 per cent. Calculate the cost of capital of the proposed new project, specifying the assumptions on which your calculations are based.
10. (a) Use the following information to calculate the cost of capital for SAM Ltd, on the assumption that investors can remove all unsystematic risk by diversification.
    (i) The systematic risk of SAM Ltd's equity is 0.8.
    (ii) The risk-free interest rate is 10 per cent.
    (iii) The expected rate of return on the market portfolio is 15 per cent.
    (iv) The various sources of funds used by SAM Ltd and their respective market values are as follows:

    | Source of funds | Market value ($m) |
    | --- | --- |
    | Debt (par value $100) | 1 |
    | Equity | 3 |

    (v) The interest rate on the debt is 11 per cent paid annually. The debt, which is due to mature in 8 years' time, has a current market price of $111.
    (vi) The company income tax rate is 33 cents in the dollar.
    (b) Under what assumptions is the cost of capital you have calculated for SAM Ltd in (a) appropriate for a proposed project?
11. XYZ Ltd has commenced operations with the following capital structure:

XYZ Ltd
Balance sheet at date of incorporation

| | ($) |
|---|---:|
| **Assets:** | |
| Sundry assets | 1 000 000 |
| **Liabilities and shareholders' funds:** | |
| Debentures, 8% (10 years) | 300 000 |
| Preference shares: 9% | 200 000 |
| Ordinary shares: issued and paid up 500 000 at $1 | 500 000 |
| | 1 000 000 |

The company's prospectus contains estimates that it will earn $100 000 per annum and pay dividends of 10 cents per share. Brokers anticipate that dividends will grow at 5 per cent per annum. The shares are currently selling at $1. The company income tax rate is 33 cents in the dollar. Calculate the cost of capital for XYZ Ltd.

12. The following financial information relates to the operations of Wood Timber Ltd:

Wood Timber Ltd
*Abstract from the statement of income and retained earnings for the year ended 31 December 1994*

| | $ |
|---|---:|
| Net profit after taxes | 200 000 |
| Retained earnings 1.1.94 | 150 000 |
| | 350 000 |
| *less:* Dividends on ordinary shares | 120 000 |
| Dividends on preference shares | 28 000 |
| Retained earnings 31.12.94 | 202 000 |

*Summary balance sheet as at 31 December 1994*

| Assets | $ | $ |
|---|---:|---:|
| Inventory | | 120 000 |
| Accounts payable | | 82 000 |
| Land and buildings | | 1 200 000 |
| Plant and equipment | | 900 000 |
| | | 2 302 000 |
| **Liabilities** | | |
| Accounts payable | 100 000 | |
| Bank overdraft | 200 000 | |
| 12% debentures, $100 par value | 600 000 | 900 000 |
| **Shareholders' funds** | | |
| 14% preference shares, $10 par value | 200 000 | |
| Ordinary shares, $1 par value | 1 000 000 | |
| Retained earnings | 202 000 | 1 402 000 |
| | | 2 302 000 |

*Additional information:*
(a) The nominal interest rate on the bank overdraft is 10 per cent and interest is calculated half-yearly.
(b) The debentures are currently selling at $97 each and mature in 6 years' time.
(c) The preference shares are currently selling at $9.50 each.
(d) The ordinary shares are currently selling at $1.10 each.
(e) The company income tax rate is 33 cents in the dollar and the company is expected to pay fully-franked dividends.

Calculate the cost of capital for Wood Timber Ltd, using the dividend-growth method to calculate the cost of equity. Note any assumptions you make.

13. An aluminium producer is planning to expand by constructing a new rolling mill to produce aluminium sheets used in beverage cans and the building industry. The project's cost of capital has been estimated at 12 per cent, based on a beta of 0.5. Explain the effects, if any, on the project's cost of capital of the following:
    (a) The correlation between the returns from aluminium producers, and the market portfolio, decreases.
    (b) The company reduces its financial leverage.
    (c) The risk-free interest rate increases.
    (d) Owing to a technological breakthrough, the cost of producing sheet steel is reduced. Analysts forecast lower growth in sales of sheet aluminium.

14. Trade credit is a free source of finance. Therefore, when estimating a company's cost of capital, trade credit can be ignored. Comment.

15. In a company that has separate divisions, management should apply different discount rates to projects proposed by its various divisions. Discuss.

16. Discuss the relative merits of the alternative methods of calculating the cost of capital for a division of a company.

17. *If the appropriate cost of debt capital is greater than the coupon rate of a debt security, its price will be less than its face value.* Comment on the validity or otherwise of this statement with the aid of the following example: A 5-year debt security has a face value of $100 and a coupon rate of 10 per cent per annum, with interest paid semi-annually. The appropriate cost of debt capital is 13 per cent per annum (effective).

18. The management of Heavy Clay Ltd wants to know the cost of capital associated with expanding its business. You have been told that funds will be raised for this purpose according to a target capital structure reflected in the market value of its securities. Your task is to calculate the cost of capital for the company. The following information may assist you in your task:
    (a) The 13 per cent debentures have just been rolled over and interest rates have remained stable since the issue. This rate was 1 per cent above the interest rate on government securities.
    (b) The last observed market price of the preference shares was $1.00, whereas it was $3.00 for the ordinary shares.
    (c) The beta of equity of Heavy Clay was recently estimated at 0.5, while the consensus view is that the expected rate of return for the market is 18 per cent, which includes a franking premium of 2 per cent.

(d) An extract of the last balance sheet shows:

| Liabilities and shareholders' funds | ($000) |
|---|---|
| Debentures | 2500 |
| 7% preference shares ($2 par) | 1000 |
| Paid-up capital ($1 par) | 3000 |
| Reserves | 500 |
| | 7000 |

(e) The company income tax rate is 33 cents in the dollar.
(f) The dividends on Heavy Clay's ordinary shares will be fully franked and all the shares are held by Australian residents.

19. Three companies X, Y and Z, operate in industries 1 and 2. The companies' costs of capital and investment in each industry are as follows:

| Company | Cost of capital per cent | Proportion of assets in industry 1 | 2 |
|---|---|---|---|
| X | 14.0 | 0.5 | 0.5 |
| Y | 12.8 | 0.7 | 0.3 |
| Z | 14.6 | 0.4 | 0.6 |

(a) Estimate the divisional cost of capital for each company.
(b) Outline the main assumptions that underlie your model.
(c) Discuss the advantages and disadvantages of the method you used in (a) compared to the 'pure-play' approach.

20. Dribnor Ltd is all equity financed and has a cost of capital of 16 per cent. An observer suggests that Dribnor could easily borrow up to 40 per cent of the value of its assets at an interest rate of 10 per cent and achieve a rating for its debt of A+ or better. He argues that raising new capital by borrowing would lower the company's cost of capital, and increase the net present value of some projects that were recently rejected. Use a numerical example to illustrate the observer's argument. Is his argument correct? Give reasons for your answer.

**APPENDIX 17.1**

# THE COST OF CAPITAL UNDER ALTERNATIVE TAX SYSTEMS[15]

## A17.1 INTRODUCTION

In this appendix we discuss alternative definitions of the cost of capital and derive equations for a company's cost of capital on both a before-tax and an after-tax basis. First, we consider the after-tax cost of capital in the context of the classical tax system. We then examine the imputation tax system and its effects on the definition of the after-tax cost of capital. We show that there is more than one way to define an after-tax cost of capital, and more than one way to make the adjustments needed to reflect the change of tax systems. Finally, we discuss issues that arise when the cost of capital is measured under the imputation system.

One principle that must be stressed is that, whichever approach is adopted, it must be used *consistently*: that is, the definition of the cost of capital must be consistent with the definition of the cash flows that are discounted using that cost of capital. If this consistency is not maintained a biased valuation will result and incorrect investment decisions are more likely.

## A17.2 DERIVING COST OF CAPITAL FORMULAE[16]

To define the cost of capital, we assume that all of a company's cash flows are expected to remain constant in perpetuity. This assumption is necessary for algebraic convenience. The value of a company depends on the net operating cash

---

[15] The discussion in this appendix is largely a simplified version of that provided by Officer R. R., 'The Cost of Capital of a Company Under an Imputation Tax System,' *Accounting and Finance*, May 1994, pp. 1–17. Readers who require further details should consult that source.

[16] The general approach used in this section follows that adopted by Officer R. R., 'The Measurement of a Firm's Cost of Capital', *Accounting and Finance*, November 1981, pp. 31–61.

flows generated by the company's assets, and the cost of capital applicable to those cash flows. For cash flows that remain constant in perpetuity:

$$V = \frac{X_0}{k_0} \tag{A17.1}$$

where $V$ = value of the company (value of equity plus debt)
$X_0$ = annual net operating cash flow before tax
$k_0$ = before-tax cost of capital

From Equation A17.1, the general definition of the before-tax cost of capital is:

$$k_0 = \frac{X_0}{V} \tag{A17.2}$$

Equation A17.2 forms the basis for all the cost-of-capital formulae that we derive. First the classical tax system is considered.

### A17.2.1  THE CLASSICAL TAX SYSTEM

Under the classical tax system, companies are taxed on their income, and dividends are taxed in the hands of shareholders without any credit for the tax paid by the company. To derive formulae for the cost of capital it is necessary to consider only company tax, because we work on a before company tax or after company tax, but always before personal tax, basis. Therefore in this section, unless stated otherwise, 'tax' refers to company income tax. A company's net operating cash flow before tax, $X_0$, is the net cash flow that remains after meeting the costs of all factors of production other than payment of company income tax to the government and providing returns to the suppliers of capital. Therefore $X_0$ can be divided into three components:

$$X_0 = X_e + X_d + X_g \tag{A17.3}$$

where $X_e$ = net cash flow to shareholders
$X_d$ = interest paid to debtholders and
$X_g$ = company income tax

Because interest paid is a tax-deductible expense of the company, the amount of company income tax depends on the interest paid. Therefore:

$$X_g = t_c (X_0 - X_d)$$

where $t_c$ = company income tax rate

Substituting for $X_g$ in Equation A17.3, multiplying out the brackets, and collecting terms, gives:

$$X_0 (1 - t_c) = X_e + X_d (1 - t_c)$$

$$\text{therefore } X_0 = \frac{X_e}{(1 - t_c)} + X_d \tag{A17.4}$$

From Equation A17.2, $X_0 = k_0 V$. Similarly $X_e = k_e E$ and $X_d = k_d D$,

where $k_e$ = cost of equity (after company tax)
$E$ = market value of equity
$k_d$ = cost of debt (before company tax)
$D$ = market value of debt

Substituting for the cash flow terms in Equation A17.4 gives:

$$k_0 V = \frac{k_e E}{(1 - t_c)} + k_d D$$

and dividing by $V$, this becomes:

$$k_0 = \frac{k_e}{(1 - t_c)} \left(\frac{E}{V}\right) + k_d \left(\frac{D}{V}\right) \quad \text{(A17.5)}$$

Equation A17.5 shows that a company's cost of capital is equal to a weighted average of the costs of equity and debt, where the weights are the proportions of equity and debt in the company's capital structure. However, this cost of capital is of limited use because it is a before-tax cost of capital. The returns to investors in a company depend on its after-tax cash flows. The simplest definition of after tax cash flows is:

$$X_0 (1 - t_c)$$

and it follows that the corresponding after-tax cost of capital is obtained by multiplying Equation A17.5 by $(1 - t_c)$, which gives:

$$k' = k_e \left(\frac{E}{V}\right) + k_d (1 - t_c) \left(\frac{D}{V}\right) \quad \text{(A17.6)}$$

where $k'$ = an after-tax cost of capital

The after-tax cost of capital defined by Equation A17.6 is the one that is normally recommended for use in project evaluation and it is commonly known as the 'textbook' formula. The advantage of using this formula is that calculation of the after-tax project cash flows is straightforward. Before-tax cash flows are converted to an after-tax basis by multiplying them by $(1 - t_c)$ which means that there is no need to adjust the cash flows to include tax savings on interest. In other words, calculating after-tax cash flows as $X_0 (1 - t_c)$ assumes that all company income is taxed, and use of the 'textbook' formula enables investment decisions to be evaluated independently of the tax effects of the financing decision. Essentially, after-tax cash flows are understated but the effects of this understatement are offset by adjusting the cost of capital to reflect the fact that interest is tax deductible.

Other definitions of after-tax cash flow are possible. Therefore other definitions of the after-tax cost of capital are also possible. For example, the after-tax cost of capital has also been defined as follows:

$$k'' = \frac{X_0 - X_g}{V} \quad \text{(A17.7)}$$

In this case, the net cash flows are defined as being after the tax that is *actually paid* by the company, which does, of course, take into account any tax that is saved due to deductions for interest on debt. From Equation A17.3 it follows that:

$$X_0 - X_g = X_e + X_d$$
$$\text{therefore, } k'' V = k_e E + k_d D$$
$$\text{and } k'' = k_e \left(\frac{E}{V}\right) + k_d \left(\frac{D}{V}\right) \qquad \text{(A17.8)}$$

The weighted average cost of capital shown in Equation A17.8 may not *look* like an after-tax cost of capital, but it *is* on an after-tax basis because $k_e$ is defined as the after-company tax rate of return required by shareholders. This version of the after-tax cost of capital is not commonly used in evaluating projects but it can be useful in evaluating the overall performance of a company because it is consistent with the concept of profit that is used in a company's profit and loss statement. In other words, profit attributable to shareholders includes tax saved due to the deductibility of interest on debt, as does the measure of after-tax cash flow used to derive Equation A17.8.

## A17.2.2 THE IMPUTATION TAX SYSTEM

The introduction of the imputation tax system reduced the tax burden on the returns to Australian resident shareholders. It also changed the previously clear distinction between company tax and personal tax because resident shareholders can use imputation tax credits to offset their personal tax liabilities. One way to reflect the effects of the change is to adjust the after-tax cash flows generated by a company or project, but other approaches are also possible. One such approach involves adjusting the definition of the cost of capital, and another involves adjusting *both* the cash flows and the cost of capital. These approaches are now discussed.

The introduction of the imputation tax system for Australian companies raised two issues related to the cost of capital:
1. What effects, if any, did the change in the tax system have on the cost of capital for Australian companies?
2. Is it necessary to change the ways in which after-tax cash flows and/or the cost of capital are defined and measured?

These issues are related, but distinct. The first issue was discussed in Section 17.4 where we concluded that the change of tax systems was *unlikely* to have changed the true cost of capital in Australia. Regardless of whether that conclusion is valid, the change in the tax system *does* have implications for the way the cost of capital should be defined and measured. It follows that it also has implications for the way in which net cash flows are defined, since, as noted earlier, it is essential that the respective definitions are consistent.

The changes in the definitions that are needed relate to the fact that, under imputation, the tax collected from companies is a mixture of company tax and personal tax. The tax collected from a company is: $X_g = (X_0 - X_d) t_c$, which is the same as under the classical system. However, under imputation, some, or perhaps all, of this tax can be recovered by shareholders as a consequence of receiving franked dividends. Therefore the tax collected from a company can be divided into two components: implicit personal tax and 'true' company tax.

This concept may require explanation. Suppose that a business is unincorporated. For example, it may be structured as a partnership rather than as a company. A partnership is not taxed as a separate entity; rather its profits will be taxed in the hands of the partners. Therefore, all the tax on its profits is *personal tax*. On the other hand, if a company structure is used, profits paid out as franked dividends are also subject to *personal tax*, but some or all of the tax has already been collected from the company. It is extremely important to understand this point: *under the imputation system, most of the income tax paid on company profits is implicitly personal tax*. Consequently, 'true' company tax is any *extra* income tax incurred due to a business being structured as a company, rather than being unincorporated. The personal tax collected from a company is:

$$t_c (X_0 - X_d) \gamma$$

where $\gamma$ is the proportion of the tax collected from a company that is claimed as a credit by shareholders.

Therefore the true company tax $X_g^*$ is:

$$\begin{aligned} X_g^* &= X_g - t_c (X_0 - X_d) \gamma \\ &= t_c (X_0 - X_d) - t_c (X_0 - X_d) \gamma \\ &= t_c (X_0 - X_d)(1 - \gamma) \end{aligned} \quad \text{(A17.9)}$$

Equation A17.9 illustrates the significance of the variable $\gamma$. If no tax credits can be used, then $\gamma = 0$ and $X_g^* = X_g$. That is, all the tax collected from a company is true company tax and the tax system is effectively a classical system. If all tax credits can be used, then $\gamma = 1$ and $X_g^* = 0$. That is, all the tax collected from a company is really nothing more than a withholding of personal tax.

To determine new definitions of the cost of capital, we begin by rewriting Equation A17.3 as follows:

$$X_0 = X_e^* + X_d + t_c (X_0 - X_d)(1 - \gamma) \quad \text{(A17.10)}$$

where $X_e^* = X_e$ plus tax credits used by shareholders. These tax credits are personal tax that has already been paid, and equal

$$t_c (X_0 - X_d) \gamma$$

Therefore:

$$X_e^* = X_e + t_c (X_0 - X_d) \gamma$$

## THE BEFORE-TAX COST OF CAPITAL

Equation A17.10 can be rearranged as:

$$X_0 = \frac{X_e^*}{(1 - t_c (1 - \gamma))} + X_d$$

Again we can substitute for the cash flow terms using $X_0 = k_I V$, and $X_e^* = k_e E$, and $X_d = k_d D$, where $k_I$ is the before-tax cost of capital under imputation. Thus we obtain:

$$k_I = \frac{k_e}{(1 - t_c (1 - \gamma))} \left(\frac{E}{V}\right) + k_d \left(\frac{D}{V}\right) \quad \text{(A17.11)}$$

This definition of the before-tax cost of capital is the same as it was under the classical system, except that $t_c$ is replaced by a 'true' company tax rate $t_c (1 - \gamma)$.

## THE AFTER-TAX COST OF CAPITAL

Officer shows that under imputation the after-tax cost of capital can be defined in four different ways.[17] We show the derivation of only one of these and then state the other three, together with the corresponding definitions of cash flow.

Consider after-tax cash flow defined as:

$$X_0 (1 - t_c) + t_c (X_0 - X_d) \gamma \qquad (A17.12)$$

This is the same definition that was normally used under the classical system, $X_0 (1 - t_c)$, adjusted by adding back that part of the tax collected from a company which is really personal tax.

We can define an after-tax cost of capital $k'_I$ as follows:

$$k'_I = \frac{X_0 (1 - t_c) + t_c (X_0 - X_d) \gamma}{V}$$

Equation A17.10 can be rearranged to give:

$$X_0 (1 - t_c) + t_c (X_0 - X_d) \gamma = X^*_e + X_d (1 - t_c)$$

Substituting for the cash flow terms gives:

$$k'_I V = k_e E + k_d (1 - t_c) D$$

and dividing by $V$ we find that:

$$k'_I = k_e \left(\frac{E}{V}\right) + k_d (1 - t_c) \left(\frac{D}{V}\right)$$

This is, of course, the familiar 'textbook' version of the after-tax weighted average cost of capital (WACC). The four definitions of after-tax net cash flow and the corresponding versions of the WACC that can be derived from Equation A17.10 are shown in Table A17.1.

---

[17] Officer R. R., 'The Cost of Capital of a Company Under an Imputation Tax System,' (Footnote 15), pp. 6–8.

**Table A17.1** Alternative definitions of net cash flow and WACC under the imputation tax system.

| Version No. | Net cash flow | WACC |
|---|---|---|
| 1. | $X_0(1 - t_c)$ | $k_e \dfrac{(1 - t_c)}{(1 - t_c(1 - \gamma))} \left(\dfrac{E}{V}\right) + k_d(1 - t_c)\left(\dfrac{D}{V}\right)$ |
| 2. | $X_0(1 - t_c(1 - \gamma))$ | $k_e \left(\dfrac{E}{V}\right) + k_d(1 - t_c(1 - \gamma))\left(\dfrac{D}{V}\right)$ |
| 3. | $X_0 - t_c(X_0 - X_d)(1 - \gamma)$ | $k_e \left(\dfrac{E}{V}\right) + k_d \left(\dfrac{D}{V}\right)$ |
| 4. | $X_0(1 - t_c) + t_c(X_0 - X_d)\gamma$ | $k_e \left(\dfrac{E}{V}\right) + k_d(1 - t_c)\left(\dfrac{D}{V}\right)$ |

Version 4 is the one we have derived in this section. Comparing these definitions with those that apply under the classical system, it can be seen that the first uses the traditional definition of net cash flow and all the adjustments needed for the imputation system are made to the WACC. In the second version, the cash flows are adjusted by replacing the statutory company tax rate $t_c$ with a true company tax rate $t_c(1 - \gamma)$, and the WACC is similarly adjusted. For the third version, the cash flows include tax savings on interest and are adjusted for imputation by adding back the imputation credits $t_c(X_0 - X_d)\gamma$. In this case the WACC is the same as in Equation A17.8. Finally, the fourth version uses the traditional definition of the WACC and makes the imputation adjustment *only* to the net cash flows. Officer suggests that this fourth approach is likely to be the easiest to use in practice.[18]

## A17.3 IMPUTATION AND MEASUREMENT OF THE COST OF CAPITAL

Estimation of the cost of capital is discussed in Section 17.5. In this section we focus only on measurement issues that are specific to the effects of the imputation tax system. The tax treatment of debt is the same under both the classical and imputation tax systems; only the tax treatment of equity has changed. Therefore it is only the measurement of the cost of equity that may need to be revised.

### A17.3.1 THE COST OF EQUITY

The cost of equity, $k_e$, is conventionally defined and measured on an after company tax, but before personal tax basis. Under the classical tax system this approach is straightforward because observed market rates of return on equity are also after company tax but before personal tax. However, under the imputation system, part of the return to equity consists of tax credits. Because these tax credits are not included in conventional rate-of-return measures, adjustments are required to obtain after company tax rates of return.

---

[18] See Officer (Footnote 15) p. 8.

To illustrate the nature of these adjustments, consider the measurement of returns under the classical system. The after company tax rate of return, $r_t$, on a share for the period $t - 1$ to $t$ is normally measured as:

$$r_t = \frac{(P_t - P_{t-1} + D_t)}{P_{t-1}} \tag{A17.13}$$

where $P_t$ = share price at time $t$, and

$D_t$ = dividend per share at time $t$

Under imputation, if the dividend is franked it will carry an imputation credit $I_c$, which reflects a pre-payment of personal tax. Therefore the rate of return after company tax but before personal tax under imputation, $r_t^*$, will be:

$$r_t^* = \frac{(P_t - P_{t-1} + D_t + I_c)}{P_{t-1}} \tag{A17.14}$$

where $I_c$ = the tax credit associated with the franked dividend $D_t$

This definition assumes that tax credits are fully valued, that is, one dollar of tax credits is worth one dollar. However, if conventional rate of return measures are used, measured rates will still be based on Equation A17.13.

Comparison of Equations A17.13 and A17.14 shows that:

$$r_t^* = r_t + \frac{I_c}{P_{t-1}}$$
$$= r_t + \tau_t \tag{A17.15}$$

where $\tau$ = the value of tax credits expressed as a proportion of the initial share price

The logic of Equation A17.15 is that under imputation, if rates of return on shares are measured in the conventional way, they then need to be adjusted so that they reflect returns after company tax only, rather than after both company tax and personal tax. This adjustment is illustrated in Example A17.1.

### Example A17.1

During the past year, Nash Ltd shares have increased in price from $4 to $4.50 and shareholders received a final dividend of 20 cents per share, fully franked at the company tax rate of 33 per cent.

Calculate:

(a) The conventional rate of return and dividend yield on Nash shares.
(b) The dividend yield after company tax but before personal tax.
(c) The dividend yield after personal tax for shareholders with personal tax rates of (i) 33 per cent, and (ii) 40 per cent.

### Solution

(a) The conventional measure of the rate of return on Nash shares is:

$$r_t = \frac{\$4.50 - \$4.00 + \$0.20}{\$4.00}$$

= 0.175 or 17.5 per cent, which includes a dividend yield of $0.20/\$4.00 = 0.05$ or 5 per cent.

(b) The dividend yield after company tax, but before personal tax, is based on the cash dividend of $0.20 per share, plus the imputation tax credit which represents personal tax already paid. The imputation credit is:

$$I_c = \frac{D_t \times t_c}{1 - t_c}$$

$$= \frac{\$0.20 \times 0.33}{0.67}$$

$$= \$0.098\,5075$$

The dividend yield after company tax is $\$0.298\,5075/\$4.00 = 0.074\,627$ or 7.4627 per cent.

(c) The shareholder's personal tax will be calculated as follows:
Taxable dividend income = dividend + imputation credit
$$= \$0.20 + \$0.098\,5075$$
Gross personal tax = $\$0.298\,5075 \times t_p$
Net personal tax = $\$0.298\,5075 \times t_p - \$0.098\,5075$

(i) When $t_p = 0.33$
net personal tax = $\$0.298\,5075 \times 0.33 - \$0.098\,5075$
$$= 0$$
The dividend yield after all taxes is $\$0.20/\$4.00 = 5$ per cent, which is exactly equal to the conventional observed yield.

(ii) When $t_p = 0.40$
net personal tax = $\$0.298\,5075 \times 0.4 - \$0.098\,5075$
$$= \$0.020\,8955$$
The dividend after all taxes is $\$(0.20 - 0.020\,8955)$
$$= \$0.179\,1045$$
and the corresponding dividend yield is $\$0.179\,1045/\$4.00 = 0.044\,776$ or 4.4776 per cent.
As a check, this yield can be converted back to a before personal tax yield which is $4.4776/(1 - 0.4) = 7.4627$ per cent: exactly the same as the answer to part (b).

Example A17.1 shows that where dividends are franked, observed rates of return on shares need to be adjusted to obtain after company tax rates of return. The adjustment is simple: add back the value of imputation tax credits, which represent personal tax that has already been paid. The value of these tax credits can be expressed as a rate of return $\tau$ by dividing the tax credits by the share price. It follows that a similar adjustment is needed when the CAPM is used to estimate the cost of equity.

Therefore the CAPM becomes:

$$k_e = R_f + \beta_e \left[E\left(R_M + \tau\right) - R_f\right]$$

Adding $\tau$, which can be called a 'franking premium', adjusts the observed return on the market portfolio to an after company tax rate of return. However, it is important to note that this adjustment should be made only to rates observed under the imputation system. The adjustment will be necessary if rates observed under the imputation system are compared with, or combined with, those observed under the classical system. Until there is a long series of returns observed under the imputation system, a simpler alternative may be to continue to base estimates of expected returns on historical rates of return measured under the classical tax system. For example, it is usual to estimate the expected return on the market portfolio by adding a risk premium to the current risk-free rate. In turn, the risk premium is usually estimated by averaging observed rates of return over a long period. If we found a historical risk premium of $x$ per cent per annum, and if we accept that the change in the tax system should not have changed the true after company tax cost of equity, then we could continue to use the same risk premium, $x$ per cent.

## A17.4 SUMMARY

It is important that projects are evaluated using a cost of capital that is consistent with the projects' cash flows. Traditionally, in project evaluation, both cash flows and the cost of capital have been expressed on an after company tax basis. That approach is easy to use under the classical tax system where there is a clear distinction between company tax and personal tax. However, under the imputation system, some or all of the tax collected from companies is really personal tax. Therefore, to express cash flows on an after company tax basis, adjustments are needed.

Another important factor concerns the tax status of observed market rates of return, which are generally used in measuring the cost of capital. Under the classical tax system, observed market rates of return on equity are after company tax but before personal tax. Therefore these rates are appropriate for discounting after company tax cash flows. Under the imputation system, franked dividends carry tax credits, which represent personal tax that has already been paid, but these tax credits are not included in conventional rate-of-return measures. Consequently, market rates of return observed under imputation will, to some extent, be after personal tax rates rather than after company tax but before personal tax rates. Therefore, adjustments are needed to obtain measures of the cost of capital which are on an after company tax basis.

The required adjustments can be made to the definition of net cash flows only, or to the definitions of both the cash flows and the cost of capital. The simplest approach is generally to continue to use the 'textbook' definition of the cost of capital and adjust the cash flows by adding back the value of tax credits. That is, we recommend and use the definitions of net cash flow and WACC identified as Version 4 in Table A17.1. Where market rates of return observed under imputation, but measured in the conventional way, are used to estimate the cost of equity, they must be adjusted by adding back the value of any tax credits. The adjusted rates will then be expressed on an after company tax basis.

Chapter 18

# THE APPLICATION OF PROJECT EVALUATION METHODS

## 18.1 INTRODUCTION

In Chapter 5, methods of project evaluation were discussed and the reasons for using the net present value method of project evaluation were outlined. However, in Chapter 5 it was assumed that a project's cash flows and the discount rate applicable to those cash flows were both known, and the effects of taxes were not considered. In practice, a project's cash flows and cost of capital are not known with certainty but must be estimated and the effects of taxes must be considered. In other words, practical project evaluation involves important issues concerning the estimation of cash flows, risk, and taxes. These and other issues are the subject of this chapter. In particular, the matters considered in this chapter include:
1. the application of the net present value method, which encompasses estimation of cash flows and the effects of taxes;
2. using the net present value method to solve problems such as comparing projects with different lives and asset-replacement decisions;
3. using the certainty-equivalent method to allow for risk;
4. the application of techniques that allow managers to analyse the risk of projects;
5. the influence of qualitative factors on the selection of investment projects; and
6. the problems associated with using the net present value method where companies are assumed to have only limited access to resources.

## Application of the net present value method

Any application of the net present value method requires estimates of project cash flows, typically on an after-company-tax basis. This section discusses issues that are important in defining the relevant cash flows, and allowing for the effects of taxes under the classical and the imputation tax systems.

### 18.2.1 Estimation of cash flows in project evaluation

A project's net present value is calculated by deducting the initial cash outlay from the present value of future net cash flows. It follows that the estimation of a project's future cash flows is an important step in project evaluation. This involves deciding what cash flow data are relevant for project evaluation, and then estimating those data. While both aspects are important, the mechanics of estimation, which is the job of engineers, market research experts and others, is beyond the scope of this book. We focus on the first aspect, that is, the principles involved in defining and measuring project cash flows.

There are essentially two approaches to measuring a project's net cash flows. The most popular method is to forecast the expected net profit from the project and adjust it for non-cash-flow items, such as depreciation.[1] The second method, and the approach used in this book, is to estimate net cash flows directly. The cash inflows will comprise receipts from the sale of goods and services, receipts from the sale of physical assets, and other cash flows. Cash outflows include expenditures on materials, labour, indirect expenses for manufacturing, selling and administration, inventory, and taxes. While the calculation of net cash flows may seem to be straightforward, there are some aspects of their measurement that warrant further consideration.

#### Financing charges

As noted in Chapter 17, a project's net cash flows should be discounted using a cost of capital that reflects the project's risk. The cost of capital is the return that investors require to finance a project, and it includes the interest cost of debt as well as the cost of equity. Therefore, financing charges such as interest and dividends should not be included in the calculation of a project's net cash flows. The inclusion of financing charges in a project's net cash flows and in the discount rate would result in double counting.

#### Incremental cash flows

In calculating a project's net cash flows, it is the incremental net cash flows that are important. An analyst should include **all** cash flows that change if the project is undertaken. When deciding whether a particular item should be included, the analyst is interested in the answers to two questions: first, Is it a *cash* item? and secondly, Will the amount of the item *change* if the project is undertaken? If the answer to both questions is yes, the item is an incremental cash flow. If the

---

[1] L. D. Schall, G. L. Sundem & W. R. Geijsbeek Jr, 'Survey and Analysis of Capital Budgeting Methods', *Journal of Finance*, March 1978, pp. 283–4.

answer to either question is no, the item is irrelevant to the analysis. For example, assume that a company is receiving $4000 per year from renting a portion of its factory, and that it is considering using that space to manufacture a product that will return net cash flows of $10 000 per year. In this case, $10 000 overstates the net cash flows from the product by an amount of $4000, the cash inflow foregone by using the rented portion of the factory. The incremental net cash flow in this case is $6000 per year. The principle of including only incremental cash flows may seem simple, but it sometimes involves difficulties such as identifying sunk costs and allocated costs.

## SUNK COSTS

Suppose that an oil company has spent $20 million exploring a particular area without success. The geologist who originally identified that area as potentially valuable argues that the company should spend another $5 million to drill an additional well because; 'if we don't, the $20 million that we have already spent will be lost'. The geologist's argument is incorrect because the $20 million is a **sunk cost**. Sunk costs are past outlays and should be ignored in making decisions on whether to continue a project or to terminate it. In this case, the $20 million has already been spent and should not influence the decision to be made now. Allowing sunk costs to influence decisions can lead to 'throwing good money after bad'. Regardless of whether $2 or $20 million has already been spent, decisions on whether to continue a project should be based only on expected *future* costs and benefits.

## ALLOCATED COSTS

Companies often allocate costs such as rent, power, water, research and development, head office costs, travel, and other overhead costs to their divisions. Therefore, when the profitability of a project is estimated, the costs attributed to the project may include a share of these allocated costs. The analyst should remember that when a project is being evaluated, only incremental cash flows should be included. In some cases, implementing an additional project may result in significantly higher overhead costs, but in other cases any increase may be negligible. When estimating project cash flows, any allocated costs should be examined carefully to determine whether they are related to the project. Any that are not should be excluded.

## INVESTMENT OUTLAYS SUBSEQUENT TO THE INITIAL OUTLAY

Investment outlays that occur subsequent to the initial outlay must be deducted from the cash inflows in calculating the net cash flows. This is because it is the amount and timing of the cash flows rather than their nature that is of importance for project evaluation. However, for control purposes, subsequent investment outlays will be recorded separately. In addition, they will generally not qualify as allowable deductions for income tax purposes, but they may affect taxes paid through deductions for depreciation.

## RESIDUAL VALUE

When a project terminates, it is likely that a portion of the initial capital outlay will be recovered. This is often termed the project's **residual value**. A project's residual value will be the disposal value of the project's assets, less any dismantling and removal costs associated with termination of the project.

## TIMING OF THE CASH FLOWS

In some cases, financial calculations are based on the precise timing of the relevant cash flows. For example, such precision is standard practice when calculating the value of marketable debt securities such as bonds and commercial bills. In these cases, both the amount and timing of the cash flows are known. However, when an investment project is evaluated, the cash flows are rarely known but must be estimated, usually with some degree of error. Similarly, the timing of cash flows can rarely be estimated precisely and the simplifying assumption that net cash flows are received at the end of a period is usually adopted. This assumption reduces the complexity of the net present value calculations without causing a marked decrease in their reliability and it is the assumption adopted in the remainder of this chapter.

## EFFECT OF TAX ON NET CASH FLOWS

If there were no taxes, the magnitude and timing of a project's cash inflows and outflows would be the only relevant cash flow information for project evaluation purposes. However, under the provisions of the *Income Tax Assessment Act* 1936, tax is assessed on the taxable income of individuals and companies. Taxable income is the difference between gross income and certain allowable deductions specified in the Act. Income tax payable is generally calculated as a percentage of taxable income. The provisions of the *Income Tax Assessment Act* 1936 affect most firms, except those specifically exempted such as government-owned enterprises and not-for-profit entities. As a result, unless there is a reason for ignoring income tax, its effect should be included in project evaluation. Income tax is a major cash outflow for most companies and its effect on investment projects should be considered, together with other cash inflows and outflows.

The tax relating to a project should be treated as a cash outflow when the tax is paid. For example, if tax is usually paid at the end of the year following the year of income, then a twelve-month lag would be appropriate for calculating after-tax net cash flows. However, this is not what the *Income Tax Assessment Act* 1936 requires and, for ease of calculation, we assume that tax is paid when the associated cash inflow is received.

A project's after-tax net cash flow for each period is calculated by deducting the period's income tax on the project from the period's net cash flows on the project. If it is assumed that for each dollar of net cash flow, a proportion $t_c$ is paid in income tax, then $(1 - t_c)$ remains in the company's hands after income tax is paid. That is:

$$\text{After-tax net cash flow} = \text{net cash flow before tax} \times (1 - t_c) \quad (18.1)$$

where $t_c$ = company income tax rate

However, this equation ignores the effect of the tax deductibility of expenses that do not involve a cash outflow. In particular, depreciation of non-current assets, excluding land and, in some cases, buildings, is an allowable deduction for income tax purposes. Depreciation does not involve an outflow of cash; it represents the allocation of the cost of a depreciable asset over its estimated useful life. However, the tax deductibility of depreciation means that the higher the depreciation charge for tax purposes, the lower will be the income tax payable by the company, and, therefore, the greater will be after-tax net cash flows.[2] The increase in after-tax net cash flows is represented by the tax savings on depreciation which is calculated as follows:

$$\text{Tax savings on depreciation} = \text{depreciation} \times t_c \quad \quad (18.2)$$

Therefore, the after-tax net cash flows generated by an investment project may be calculated by summing Equations 18.1 and 18.2 as follows:

$$\text{After-tax net cash flow} = \text{net cash flow} \times (1 - t_c) + \text{depreciation} \times t_c$$
$$(18.3)$$

Example 18.1 illustrates the application of Equation 18.3.

### Example 18.1

Assume that a project's before-tax net cash flow is expected to be $10 000 per annum; for tax purposes the depreciation charge is $1000 per annum and the company income tax rate is 33 cents in the dollar. The after-tax net cash flow is calculated as follows:

$$\begin{aligned}\text{After-tax net cash flow} &= \$10\,000\,(1 - 0.33) + \$1000\,(0.33) \\ &= \$6700 + \$330 \\ &= \$7030\end{aligned}$$

The effect of depreciation on project cash flows is more complex than Example 18.1 suggests because the Income Tax Assessment Act allows two methods of calculating depreciation: the **straight-line (or prime-cost) method** and the **reducing-balance (or diminishing-value) method**. If the reducing-balance method is used, the allowable depreciation rate is generally 1.5 times the straight-line rate.[3]

It should be noted that the depreciation charge calculated for tax purposes may bear no relationship to that calculated for financial reporting purposes. For example, a company may use the straight-line method for reporting purposes,

---

2 Taxpayers have at times been able to claim an investment allowance which is essentially an additional depreciation deduction. For example, an investment allowance at the rate of 10 per cent applied where eligible assets were acquired under contracts entered into after 8 February 1993 and before 1 July 1994. Assets that qualify for the allowance are basically those that can be depreciated for tax purposes.

3 The exact depreciation rate applicable to an asset depends on the estimated effective life of the asset and on the date the asset was acquired. For assets acquired after 26 February 1992, diminishing value rates are prescribed and the corresponding prime cost rate is two-thirds of the diminishing value rate, rounded to the nearest whole percentage. For example, if the effective life is 3 to 5 years, the diminishing value rate is 60 per cent and the prime cost rate is 40 per cent per annum. If the effective life is 10 to 13 years, the annual rates are 25 per cent and 17 per cent respectively. Special rates apply to certain assets including plant having an effective life shorter than three years and 'eligible motor vehicles'.

and the reducing-balance method for income tax purposes. Straight-line depreciation involves allocating the asset's cost in equal amounts over its estimated useful life.[4] Given the asset's initial cost $C$, and its estimated useful life $n$ years, the straight-line depreciation charge in each year of the asset's life is $\frac{C}{n}$. For example, if an asset costs $10 000 and has a 10-year life, the annual depreciation charge is $\frac{\$10\,000}{10} = \$1000$.

In contrast, reducing-balance depreciation involves charging a fixed percentage of the asset's written down value in each year. The asset's written down value is equal to its cost or other value (such as a revalued amount) less accumulated depreciation, where accumulated depreciation is equal to the sum of the depreciation charges in previous years. In comparison with straight-line depreciation, the reducing-balance method of depreciation results in larger depreciation charges in the early years of an asset's life, and smaller charges in later years. Therefore, reducing-balance depreciation, which increases the depreciation charge in the early years of the asset's life, results in lower taxes and larger after-tax cash flows in those years, compared with the straight-line method. The total income tax paid is not reduced by using the reducing-balance method. However, a portion of the tax payable is postponed in the early years of the project's life. Given that a dollar today is worth more than a dollar in a year's time, it follows that the use of the reducing-balance method is generally advantageous to an asset's owners.

The after-tax cash flows associated with ownership of a depreciable asset also depend on the relationship between the asset's disposal value and its written down value. If the disposal value is equal to the written down value, then sale of the asset has no effect on tax paid by the seller. However, if the two values differ, there are three possibilities:

1. *The asset's disposal value is less than its written down value.* Suppose that an asset is sold for $1000, but its written down value is $2500. The difference of $1500 is regarded as a loss on sale, which is tax deductible. Therefore there is a tax saving on the loss of $1500 × 0.33 = $495. This tax saving is treated as a cash inflow, so the net proceeds are $1495.
2. *The asset's disposal value is more than its written down value but less than its acquisition cost.* Suppose that the asset is sold for $3000 which is $500 more than its written down value. In this case the gain on sale of $500 is regarded as recovery of depreciation deductions that were previously claimed. Therefore the gain is taxable but the tax can be

---

[4] This contrasts with the method of calculating depreciation for financial reporting purposes. In accounting, the straight-line depreciation charge is:

$$\frac{C - S}{n}$$

where $C$ = initial cost, $S$ = estimated residual or scrap value, and $n$ = estimated useful life in years.

deferred by deducting the gain from the written down value of a replacement asset or other depreciable assets.[5] If the gain is taxed immediately, the net sale proceeds are $3000 - $500 × 0.33 = $2835.

3. *The asset's disposal value is more than its acquisition cost.* Suppose that an asset cost $10 000, has a written down value 5 years later of $2500, and is sold at that time for $12 000. In this case the difference of $7500 between the original cost and the written down value is regarded as a recovery of previous depreciation deductions, and is therefore taxable. The capital gain of $2000 may also be taxable if the asset was acquired on or after 20 September 1985. However, any part of the gain that is attributable to inflation will not be taxed. For example, if the Consumer Price Index has increased at 3 per cent per annum during the 5 years since the asset was purchased, the asset's indexed cost base will be $10 000 × $(1.03)^5$ = $11 593. The taxable capital gain is $12 000 - $11 593 = $407. The total tax associated with the sale will be ($7500 + $407) × 0.33 = $2609, leaving net proceeds of $12 000 - $2609 = $9391.

The tax effects of the straight-line and reducing-balance methods are compared in Example 18.2.

## Example 18.2

Table 18.1 shows the calculation of the present value of the tax effects associated with depreciation and disposal of an asset that costs $10 000, has an estimated useful life of 5 years, and a disposal value of $1681 at the end of the fifth year.

Table 18.1 shows that the reducing-balance method should be preferred because it results in a higher present value of tax savings and net sale proceeds.

## INFLATION AND PROJECT EVALUATION

The Australian economy has at times experienced prolonged periods of inflation. During a period of inflation there is an increase in the general level of prices; in other words, there is a fall in the purchasing power of money. There are two approaches to incorporating the effects of inflation into project evaluation. Both approaches, applied consistently, will give the same net present value.

One approach involves making estimates of cash flows that are based on anticipated prices during each year of a project's life, and discounting those cash flows at the nominal cost of capital. In this case, the estimated net cash flows from a project, in say its fourth year of operation, are based on the prices expected in its fourth year of operation. The presence of inflation therefore makes the job of estimating net cash flows more difficult, especially if prices are expected to increase at a rapid rate. The use of the nominal cost of capital means that the discount rate reflects the market's expectations about the rate of inflation. If it is expected that the rate of inflation will increase in the future, market pressure should lead to an increase in the nominal cost of capital on an investment. Therefore, observed nominal rates of return have, built into them, expected

---

[5] Replacement decisions are discussed in Section 18.4.2.

**Table 18.1** Tax effects of depreciation and sale of an asset

| | | Depreciation method | | | | |
|---|---|---|---|---|---|---|
| | | Straight-line(a) | | | Reducing balance(b) | |
| End of year | Present value factor at 10% | Allowable depreciation expense ($) | Tax savings at 33% ($) | Present value of tax savings and proceeds of sale, net of tax ($) | Allowable depreciation expense ($) | Tax savings at 33% ($) | Present value of tax savings and proceeds of sale net of tax ($) |
|---|---|---|---|---|---|---|---|
| 1 | 0.909 09 | 2000 | 660 | 600 | 3000 | 990 | 900 |
| 2 | 0.826 45 | 2000 | 660 | 545 | 2100 | 693 | 573 |
| 3 | 0.751 31 | 2000 | 660 | 496 | 1470 | 485 | 364 |
| 4 | 0.683 01 | 2000 | 660 | 451 | 1029 | 340 | 232 |
| 5 | 0.620 92 | 2000 | 660 | 410 | 720 | 238 | 148 |
| Disposal value | | 1681(b) | | 1044 | 1681 | | 1044 |
| Gain on sale | | 1681 | | | 0 | | |
| Tax on gain | | | (555) | (344) | | 0 | 0 |
| Total | | | | 3202 | | | 3261 |

(a) Straight-line depreciation is charged at a rate of 20 per cent of acquisition cost, and reducing-balance depreciation is charged at a rate of 30 per cent of the written down value.

(b) It is assumed that at the end of Year 5 the asset is sold for $1681. Under the reducing-balance method of depreciation, this is equal to the written down value at the end of Year 5 and there is no gain or loss on sale. Consequently, there is no tax effect on the $1681. The present value of the cash inflow is calculated in the usual way and equals $1681 (0.62092) = $1044. Under the straight-line method of depreciation, as the whole of the asset's acquisition cost has been written off for tax purposes by the end of Year 5, the $1681 received at that time is regarded as a **gain on sale** for tax purposes, and increases tax payable by $555. The present value of this tax payment is $344.

future inflation rates. This approach is consistent, in that net cash flows based on anticipated future price levels are discounted at the nominal cost of capital, which also has built into it expected future inflation rates.

The other approach involves estimating the net cash flows without adjusting them for anticipated changes in prices, and discounting those cash flows at the real cost of capital. In other words, the net cash flows are estimated using existing (constant) prices. To be consistent it is necessary to discount these net cash flows at the real cost of capital, which excludes expected inflation.

The following example illustrates that the two approaches, applied consistently, give the same result.

## Example 18.3

Assume that an investment of $1000 is expected to generate cash flows of $500, at constant prices, at the end of each of 3 years; that prices are expected to increase at the rate of 10 per cent per annum; and that the nominal cost of capital is 15 per cent per annum.

Using the first approach, the net present value of the investment is as follows:

$$-\$1000 + \frac{\$500(1.10)}{1.15} + \frac{\$500(1.10)^2}{(1.15)^2} + \frac{\$500(1.10)^3}{(1.15)^3}$$

$$= -\$1000 + \frac{\$550}{1.15} + \frac{\$605}{1.3225} + \frac{\$665}{1.5209}$$

$$= \$373$$

Using the second approach, the net cash flow of $500 per annum at constant prices is discounted at the real cost of capital. As discussed in Sections 1.6.3 and 3.3.4, the real rate may be expressed in terms of the nominal rate as follows:

$$i^* = \frac{1+i}{1+p} - 1$$

where $i^*$ = the real rate of return per annum;
$i$ = the nominal rate of return per annum and
$p$ = the anticipated rate of inflation per annum

Therefore:
$$i^* = \frac{1.15}{1.10} - 1$$
$$= 4.55\%$$

The net present value is then calculated as follows:

$$-\$1000 + \frac{\$500}{1.0455} + \frac{\$500}{(1.0455)^2} + \frac{\$500}{(1.0455)^3}$$

$$= -\$1000 + \frac{\$500}{1.0455} + \frac{\$500}{1.0931} + \frac{\$500}{1.1428}$$

$$= \$373$$

In subsequent examples, the first approach to incorporating the effect of inflation into project evaluation is generally adopted. Unlike the second approach, it can be readily applied where the analyst wishes to incorporate different rates of change in prices for different components of a project's cash flows. For example, the rate of change in wage rates may be forecast to be different from the rate of change in inventory prices. In addition, the complexity of the relationship between real and nominal rates of return makes the first approach easier to handle in practice.[6]

## 18.2.2 ILLUSTRATION OF CASH-FLOW INFORMATION IN PROJECT EVALUATION

The cash-flow information that should be compiled for project evaluation is illustrated in Example 18.4.

*Example 18.4*

The Frank Stone Company is considering the introduction of a new product. Generally, the company's products have a life of about 5 years, after which they are deleted from the range of products that the company sells.

The new product requires the purchase of new equipment costing $400 000, including freight and installation charges. The useful life of the equipment is 5 years, with an estimated residual value of $157 500 at the end of that period. The equipment will be depreciated for tax purposes by the reducing-balance method at a rate of 15 per cent per annum.

The new product will be manufactured in a factory already owned by the company. The factory originally cost $150 000 to build and has a current resale value of $350 000, which should remain fairly stable over the next 5 years. This factory is currently being rented to another company under a lease agreement that has 5 years to run and provides for an annual rental of $15 000. Under the lease agreement the Frank Stone Company can cancel the lease by paying the lessee compensation equal to 1 year's rental payment. This amount is not deductible for income tax purposes.

It is expected that the product will involve the company in sales promotion expenditures which will amount to $50 000 during the first year the product is on the market. This amount is deductible for income tax purposes in the year in which the expenditure is incurred.

Additions to current assets will require $22 500 at the commencement of the project and are assumed to be fully recoverable at the end of the fifth year.

The new product is expected to generate net operating cash flows (before depreciation and income tax) as follows:

|        |           |
|--------|-----------|
| Year 1 | $200 000  |
| Year 2 | $250 000  |
| Year 3 | $325 000  |
| Year 4 | $300 000  |
| Year 5 | $150 000  |

---

[6] For some empirical evidence on the complexity of the relationship between real and nominal rates of return, see R. R. Officer, 'Valuation Problems in an Inflationary Environment', *Annual Research Lecture*, Australian Society of Accountants, Melbourne, 1982.

It is assumed that all cash flows are received at the end of each year and that income tax is paid at the end of the year in which the inflow occurred.

The company income tax rate is 33 cents in the dollar and the company has a cost of capital of 10 per cent after tax. The solution to this example is set out in Table 18.2.

**Table 18.2** *Cash-flow information for the evaluation of the purchase of new equipment*

| Item | | | | | | After-tax cash flows ($'000s) | | | | | |
|---|---|---|---|---|---|---|---|---|---|---|---|
| | | | | | | Year 0 | Year 1 | Year 2 | Year 3 | Year 4 | Year 5 |
| 1 | **Initial outlay** | | | | | (400) | | | | | |
| 2 | **Depreciation:** | | | | | | | | | | |
| | Year | Written down value ($) | % | Depreciation ($) | Tax savings at 33¢ in $ ($) | | | | | | |
| | 1 | 400 000 | 15 | 60 000 | 19 800 | | 19.8 | | | | |
| | 2 | 340 000 | 15 | 51 000 | 16 830 | | | 16.83 | | | |
| | 3 | 289 000 | 15 | 43 350 | 14 306 | | | | 14.306 | | |
| | 4 | 245 650 | 15 | 36 848 | 12 160 | | | | | 12.16 | |
| | 5 | 208 802 | 15 | 31 320 | 10 336 | | | | | | 10.336 |
| 3 | **Sale of equipment:** | | | | | | | | | | |
| | Sale | | | $157 500 | | | | | | | |
| | Written down value | | | $177 482 | | | | | | | |
| | Loss | | | $19 982 | | | | | | | |
| | Tax savings at 33% | | | $6 594 | | | | | | | |
| | Total proceeds $157 500 + $6 594 | | | | | | | | | | 164.094 |
| 4 | **Factory:** | | | | | | | | | | |
| | The cost and the current resale value of the factory are both irrelevant. | | | | | | | | | | |
| | (a) Cancel lease | | | | | (15) | | | | | |
| | (b) Net cash flow foregone due to rent foregone $15 000 (1 − 0.33) | | | | | | (10.050) | (10.050) | (10.050) | (10.050) | (10.050) |
| 5 | **Market research outlays** | | | | | | | | | | |
| | Outlay | | | $50 000 | | | | | | | |
| | Less net tax savings at 33% | | | $16 500 | | | | | | | |
| | Net outlay | | | $33 500 | | (33.5) | | | | | |
| 6 | **Additions to current assets** | | | | | (22.5) | | | | | 22.5 |
| 7 | **Net cash flows from operations after deducting company income tax:** | | | | | | | | | | |
| | Year 1 | $200 000 | (1 − 0.33) | | | | 134.0 | | | | |
| | Year 2 | $250 000 | (1 − 0.33) | | | | | 167.5 | | | |
| | Year 3 | $325 000 | (1 − 0.33) | | | | | | 217.75 | | |
| | Year 4 | $300 000 | (1 − 0.33) | | | | | | | 201.0 | |
| | Year 5 | $150 000 | (1 − 0.33) | | | | | | | | 100.5 |
| | Total | | | | | (437.50) | 110.25 | 174.28 | 222.01 | 203.11 | 287.38 |
| | Discount factor at 10% | | | | | 1.000 00 | 0.909 09 | 0.826 45 | 0.751 31 | 0.683 01 | 0.620 92 |
| | Present value of net cash flows | | | | | (437.50) | 100.23 | 144.03 | 166.80 | 138.73 | 178.44 |
| | **Net present value   $290.73** | | | | | | | | | | |

On the basis of this quantitative analysis the new product should be manufactured.

### 18.2.3 PROJECT CASH FLOWS AND TAXES UNDER THE IMPUTATION SYSTEM

In the previous sections of the chapter the effect of company tax on net cash flows was based on the classical tax system. Under that system the valuation of a company, or an individual project, can be based on after-company tax cash flows as defined in Equation 18.1. This definition of after-tax cash flows is consistent with the 'textbook' weighted average cost of capital (WACC) as defined in Section 17.3.2 which is as follows:

$$k' = k_e\left(\frac{E}{V}\right) + k_d\,(1 - t_c)\left(\frac{D}{V}\right)$$

This combination of cash flows and cost of capital has normally been used in project evaluation because of its relative simplicity. A project's before-tax cash flows are converted to after-tax cash flows simply by multiplying them by $(1 - t_c)$.

The great advantage of this approach is that investment decisions can be evaluated independently of the tax effects of the financing decision. That is, the effects of the tax deductibility of interest are recognised in the discount rate and therefore tax savings on interest are not included in a project's cash flows. Therefore, when the classical tax system applies, project evaluation can be delegated to divisonal managers, who do not need to have detailed information about the company's tax position. Divisional managers will be able to value projects, provided that they are given a tax rate to apply to before-tax operating cash flows and a value for the company's WACC.

Unfortunately the relative simplicity of valuation under the classical tax system does not extend to the imputation tax system. The reason for the added complexity of the imputation system is that, under imputation, for a given set of before-tax cash flows the company tax paid is affected by the company's financing and dividend decisions in *two* ways:

1. the tax collected from a company will depend on its use of debt finance; and
2. some or all of the tax collected from a company is effectively personal tax and can be recovered by shareholders, who are able to use the tax credits associated with franked dividends.

As discussed in Appendix 17.1, while the textbook WACC can still be used under the imputation system, the company's after-tax cash flows need to be adjusted by adding back the value of tax credits paid out and used by shareholders: $t_c\,(X_o - X_d)\,\gamma$. These tax credits represent personal tax collected from the company and must, therefore, be added back to obtain cash flows which are after company tax, but before personal tax. Therefore, if a company's before-tax cash flow is $X_o$ per year, then under the two tax systems, its after-company tax cash flows would be as follows:

## THE APPLICATION OF PROJECT EVALUATION METHODS

Classical tax system:   $X_o (1 - t_c)$
Imputation tax system:  $X_o (1 - t_c) + t_c (X_o - X_d) \gamma$

The calculation of after-company tax net cash flows for a company is illustrated in Example 18.5.

### Example 18.5

Dribnor Ltd is expected to generate net operating cash flows of $100 000 per annum in perpetuity. Dribnor pays interest of $25 000 per annum and the company income tax rate is 33 per cent. All after-tax profits are paid out as franked dividends. Dribnor's annual profit and loss statement is as follows:

|  | $ per year |
|---|---|
| Profit before interest and tax ($X_o$) | 100 000 |
| Less: interest ($X_d$) | 25 000 |
| Profit before tax ($X_o - X_d$) | 75 000 |
| Less: company income tax ($X_o - X_d)t_c$ | 24 750 |
| Profit after tax ($X_o - X_d)(1 - t_c)$ | 50 250 |

To value Dribnor under the classical tax system, its annual after-tax cash flow would be expressed as:

$$X_o (1 - t_c) = \$100\,000 (1 - 0.33)$$
$$= \$67\,000$$

If the imputation tax system applies, this after-tax cash flow is adjusted by adding back the value of tax credits used by shareholders = $t_c (X_o - X_d)\gamma$. The adjusted cash flows for three possible values of $\gamma$; 0, 0.5, and 1 are as follows:

| $\gamma$ | $X_o (1 - t_c)$ | Value of tax credits | Cash flow after company tax |
|---|---|---|---|
|  | ($) | ($) | ($) |
| 0 | 67 000 | 0 | 67 000 |
| 0.5 | 67 000 | 12 375 | 79 375 |
| 1.0 | 67 000 | 24 750 | 91 750 |

If Dribnor uses a higher proportion of debt in its capital structure so that its interest bill is $40 000 per annum, its profit and loss statement will be as follows:

|  | $ per year |
|---|---|
| Profit before interest and tax ($X_o$) | 100 000 |
| Less: Interest ($X_d$) | 40 000 |
| Profit before tax ($X_o - X_d$) | 60 000 |
| Less: Company income tax ($X_o - X_d)t_c$ | 19 800 |
| Profit after tax ($X_o - X_d)(1 - t_c)$ | 40 200 |

In this case the cash flows for valuation purposes will be as follows:

| $\gamma$ | $X_o(1 - t_c)$ | Value of tax credits | Cash flow after company tax |
|---|---|---|---|
| | ($) | ($) | ($) |
| 0 | 67 000 | 0 | 67 000 |
| 0.5 | 67 000 | 9 900 | 76 900 |
| 1.0 | 67 000 | 19 800 | 86 800 |

Example 18.5 illustrates the point noted earlier that, under the imputation system, the after-company tax cash flows, used for valuation purposes, depend on the company's use of debt finance and on the tax credits that can be used by shareholders. In particular the cash flows decrease as the company uses a higher proportion of debt finance, and increase as the value of $\gamma$ increases. Therefore, because of the complexity of the imputation tax system, it is not possible to value a company independently of its capital structure decisions and its dividend decisions. Similarly it is impossible to value a project that may be implemented by a company, independently of the company's capital structure and dividend decisions.

For project evaluation to be delegated to a company's divisions, the divisional managers will require information on:
1. the proportion of debt used to finance additional projects; and
2. the value to shareholders of the tax credits associated with the company's payment of franked dividends.

The first of these matters is not peculiar to the imputation system. It also arises under the classical system where, as discussed in Section 17.5.4, a company's WACC can only be used to value new projects which are financed using the proportions of debt and equity in the company's capital structure. Similarly, under the imputation system it may be reasonable to assume that new projects are financed using a standard proportion of debt which reflects the company's average use of debt finance.

The effects of dividend decisions are potentially more complex because the value of $\gamma$ may be difficult to estimate. If all of a company's tax credits were used immediately by shareholders, the value of $\gamma$ would be one. However, in practice, its value may be less than one for two reasons:
1. there may be delays in transferring tax credits to shareholders by the payment of franked dividends; and
2. shareholders may be unable to use tax credits because they are tax exempt or non-residents.

Therefore the value of $\gamma$ depends on the company's dividend policy and on the tax class(es) of its shareholders. Even if a company adopts a policy of paying the maximum possible franked dividends, it will be difficult to determine an appropriate value for $\gamma$ in cases where some of the company's shares are held by resident taxpayers (for whom theoretically $\gamma = 1$) and other shares are held by tax exempt or non-resident investors (for whom theoretically $\gamma = 0$).

Theoretically the value of γ should reflect the value of tax credits to the marginal (as distinct from average) shareholder. As Officer[7] points out, if there is a market in tax credits, the market price could be used to estimate the value of γ for the marginal shareholder. However, any market in tax credits is covert, so the 'market price' of tax credits can only be estimated through dividend drop-off ratios, which are discussed in Section 11.4.4. Unfortunately these estimates are subject to a large degree of error. Unless reliable data on the value of tax credits are available, the value of γ will be a matter of judgement by a company's management.

In practice, if a company follows a stable capital structure policy with a known proportion of debt, and management has estimated the value of γ, the adjustment to be made to project cash flows can be specified as an adjustment factor. For instance, consider Example 18.5. With Dribnor's initial capital structure and a value for γ of 0.5, adding the value of tax credits increases the after-company tax cash flows from $67 000 per year to $79 375 per year, an increase of 18.5 per cent. Therefore if the same capital structure is to be maintained, and if 0.5 is considered to be a realistic value of γ, then Dribnor's managers, including divisional managers, could apply the same adjustment factor to the cash flows for proposed new projects, that is, in this case the adjustment is to increase the cash flows by 18.5 per cent.

## 18.3 COMPARING MUTUALLY EXCLUSIVE PROJECTS WITH DIFFERENT LIVES

In practice, management will frequently have to compare mutually exclusive projects which have different economic lives. In some cases this can be done by ranking the projects using their respective net present values. For example, suppose that a company has developed a new type of computer chip, but does not currently have the facilities to produce it. The equipment required to produce the chip is expected to have a useful life of 5 years and the project's NPV is estimated to be $4 million. Alternatively, the right to manufacture the chip can be sold now for $2.5 million. These two alternatives are mutually exclusive and have different lives, but their net present values can be compared directly because they take into account all the relevant cash flows. However, in other cases mutually exclusive projects with different lives cannot be compared directly. Suppose that a furniture manufacturer can buy either Machine A with a life of 3 years, or Machine B with a life of 5 years, to perform the same job. Both machines generate the same cash inflows, so one way to compare them would be to calculate the present value of the cash outflows for each machine. Suppose that the present value of cash outflows is $18 000 for A and $21 000 for B. This does not necessarily mean that Machine A should be preferred. If A is purchased, it will have to be replaced two years earlier than B. The two alternatives are not directly comparable because they involve different future cash flows, which have not been considered. One solution would be to assume that Machine B is sold

---

[7] R. R. Officer, 'The Cost of Capital of a Company Under the Imputation Tax System', *Accounting and Finance*, May 1994, p. 4.

after 3 years. However, the disposal value of the machine may not reflect its value in use, and it is usual to make other assumptions about what will happen at the end of the useful lives of the machines. Consider the following two approaches:

1. It may be assumed that the company will reinvest in a project that is identical to that which is currently being analysed. This is known as the **constant chain of replacement** assumption.
2. Specific assumptions may be made about the reinvestment opportunities that will become available in the future.

The second approach is the most realistic and could be implemented where the future investment opportunities are known. However, in practice this approach would be impossible to implement unless managers have extraordinary foresight. Therefore, the first approach is often used. This approach is illustrated in Example 18.6.

### Example 18.6

Assume that a company is considering the purchase of two different types of equipment, A and B, which will perform the same task and generate the same cash inflows. Therefore, A and B can be compared on the basis of their cash outflows. The information in Table 18.3 relates to A and B.

**Table 18.3** Cash outflows for equipment in Example 18.6

| Equipment | Year 0 | Initial and operating costs ($) | | |
| --- | --- | --- | --- | --- |
| | | Year 1 | Year 2 | Year 3 |
| A (life 1 year) | 15 000 | 6 000 | | |
| B (life 3 years) | 20 000 | 10 000 | 10 000 | 10 000 |

Assuming a cost of capital of 10 per cent per annum for both pieces of equipment, the present values of the costs associated with A and B are as follows:

$$\text{PV of costs for A} = \$15\,000 + \frac{\$6000}{1.1}$$
$$= \$20\,455$$

$$\text{PV of costs for B} = \$20\,000 + \$10\,000 \left[ \frac{1 - \frac{1}{(1.1)^3}}{0.1} \right]$$
$$= \$44\,869$$

If management compares these figures, investment in Equipment A would appear to be the more desirable. However, this comparison is invalid because it ignores the fact that A and B have different lives. To make a valid comparison it is assumed that at the end of both the first and second years Equipment A would be purchased again. If Equipment A is replaced at the end of years 1 and 2 (a chain of replacement) the costs would be as shown in Table 18.4.

**Table 18.4** *Costs for chain of replacement over three years*

| Equipment | Year 0 | Initial and operating costs ($) Year 1 | Year 2 | Year 3 |
|---|---|---|---|---|
| A | 15 000 | 15 000 | 15 000 | |
| A | | 6 000 | 6 000 | 6 000 |
| Total | 15 000 | 21 000 | 21 000 | 6 000 |

In this case, PV of costs for A

$$= \$15\,000 + \frac{\$21\,000}{1.1} + \frac{\$21\,000}{(1.1)^2} + \frac{\$6\,000}{(1.1)^3}$$
$$= \$55\,954$$

Based on this comparison over three years, the present value of costs for A ($55 954) is greater than the present value of costs for B ($44 869) and, therefore, B should be purchased. In the remainder of this section it will be assumed that management adopts this approach; that is, it is assumed that each project is replicated over the years. In this case there are two methods that can be used to compare projects with unequal lives:

1. A valid comparison of two chains of replacement can be made only when both chains are of equal length. For example, if Project A has a life of 6 years and Project B has a life of 9 years, the replacement chains are of equal length after 18 years. At this point, A has been undertaken three times and B twice. The chains will also be equal after 36 years, 54 years, 72 years, and so on. However, it is clearly easier to perform the evaluation over 18 years. In this example, 18 is the lowest common multiple of 6 and 9, so this approach is usually called the **lowest common multiple method**. Although the use of this method correctly ranks mutually exclusive projects with different lives, it can be cumbersome. For example, two projects with lives of 19 and 21 years respectively have a lowest common multiple of 399 years and the cash flows for each of these 399 years would have to be discounted to a present value.
2. A simpler approach, which ranks projects identically to the lowest common multiple method, is to assume that both chains continue indefinitely. In this case the 'lengths' of the chains are 'equal' in the sense that they are both infinite. This method is known as the **constant chain of replacement in perpetuity method**. If the NPV of each replacement project is $N$ dollars, the constant chain of replacement is equivalent to receiving a cash inflow of $N$ dollars at times $0, n, 2n, 3n$, and so on, forever. Therefore the NPV of the chain consists of $N$ dollars at time 0 plus a perpetuity of $N$ dollars payable at $n, 2n, 3n$, and so on. Therefore:

$$\text{NPV} = N + \frac{N}{(1+k)^n} + \frac{N}{(1+k)^{2n}} + \cdots$$

$$= N \left[ 1 + \frac{1}{(1+k)^n} + \frac{1}{(1+k)^{2n}} + \cdots \right]$$

$$= N \left[ \frac{1}{1 - \frac{1}{(1+k)^n}} \right]$$

$$= N \left[ \frac{(1+k)^n}{(1+k)^n - 1} \right]$$

Therefore, the net present value of the infinite chain, $\text{NPV}_\infty$, is:

$$\text{NPV}_\infty = \text{NPV}_0 \frac{(1+k)^n}{(1+k)^n - 1} \qquad (18.4)$$

where $\text{NPV}_0$ is the net present value of each replacement.

A variant of this method is the **equivalent annual value method**. This method involves answering the question: What amount, to be received each year for $n$ years, is equivalent to receiving the net present value of a project whose life is $n$ years? This amount, which is known as the **equivalent annual value (EAV)**, is calculated for each project. The project with the higher EAV is preferred to the project with the lower EAV, provided that both projects have the same risk, and therefore the same cost of capital.

The stream of EAVs over $n$ years is an ordinary annuity and therefore the net present value of the annuity is given by:

$$\text{NPV}_0 = \frac{\text{EAV}}{k} \left[ 1 - \frac{1}{(1+k)^n} \right]$$

or
$$\text{NPV}_0 = (\text{EAV}) \, A_{\overline{n}|i}$$

Therefore
$$\text{EAV} = \frac{\text{NPV}_0}{A_{\overline{n}|i}} \qquad (18.5)$$

The relationship between the constant chain of replacement and EAV methods is straightforward. Assume that a project is replicated indefinitely. The present value of an infinite stream of EAVs is:

$$\text{PV} = \frac{\text{EAV}}{k}$$

$$= \frac{1}{k} \frac{\text{NPV}_0}{A_{\overline{n}|i}}$$

$$= \left(\frac{1}{k}\right) \frac{NPV_o}{\frac{1}{k}\left[1 - \frac{1}{(1+k)^n}\right]}$$

$$= NPV_o \frac{1}{1 - \frac{1}{(1+k)^n}}$$

$$= NPV_o \frac{(1+k)^n}{(1+k)^n - 1}$$

$$= NPV_\infty$$

That is, the present value of an infinite stream of EAVs is, of course, the net present value of the constant chain of replacement in perpetuity. Therefore, if the net present value of the infinite chain $NPV_\infty$ has been calculated, the EAV can be found by multiplying $NPV_\infty$ by the cost of capital. That is, the EAV is given by:

$$EAV = k\,NPV_\infty \qquad (18.6)$$

The constant chain of replacement and equivalent annual value methods are illustrated in Example 18.7. Example 18.8 provides a further illustration of the constant chain of replacement method in a more realistic setting.

### Example 18.7

Suppose that two machines, A and B, are mutually exclusive projects and have the characteristics shown in Table 18.5.

**Table 18.5** *Characteristics of two mutually exclusive projects*

| | | | Net cash flow ($) | | | | |
|---|---|---|---|---|---|---|---|
| Machine | Life (years) | Initial cash outlay ($) | Year 1 | Year 2 | Year 3 | Year 4 | Year 5 |
| A | 3 | 10 000 | 10 000 | 23 000 | 25 000 | — | — |
| B | 5 | 30 000 | 12 000 | 15 000 | 25 000 | 30 000 | 30 000 |

It is also assumed that the cost of capital is 10 per cent per annum for both projects and that there are no taxes.

The net present value of Machine A at time zero is:

$$NPVA_o = -\$10\,000 + \frac{\$10\,000}{1.1} + \frac{\$23\,000}{(1.1)^2} + \frac{\$25\,000}{(1.1)^3}$$

$$= \$36\,882.04$$

The net present value of Machine B at time zero is:

$$NPVB_o = -\$30\,000 + \frac{\$12\,000}{1.1} + \frac{\$15\,000}{(1.1)^2} + \frac{\$25\,000}{(1.1)^3} + \frac{\$30\,000}{(1.1)^4} + \frac{\$30\,000}{(1.1)^5}$$

$$= \$51\,206.70$$

Using Equation 18.4, the net present values of the infinite chains of replacement are:

$$\text{NPVA}_\infty = (\$36\,882.04) \frac{(1.1)^3}{(1.1)^3 - 1}$$
$$= \$148\,308.14$$
$$\text{NPVB}_\infty = (\$51\,206.70) \frac{(1.1)^5}{(1.1)^5 - 1}$$
$$= \$135\,081.98$$

Therefore, Machine A should be accepted, notwithstanding that its net present value (over its 3-year life) is less than the net present value of Machine B (over its 5-year life).

Using Equation 18.5, the equivalent annual value method, it is found that:

$$\text{EAV of A} = \frac{\$36\,882.04}{A_{\overline{3}|0.10}}$$
$$= \$14\,830.81$$

$$\text{EAV of B} = \frac{\$51\,206.70}{A_{\overline{5}|0.10}}$$
$$= \$13\,508.20$$

Therefore Machine A should be chosen because its EAV is greater than that of Machine B.

As proved earlier, the present value of an infinite stream of EAVs is equal to $\text{NPV}_\infty$ for each machine. Therefore:

$$\frac{\$14\,830.81}{0.1} = \$148\,308.10 = \text{NPVA}_\infty$$
$$\frac{\$13\,508.20}{0.1} = \$135\,082.00 = \text{NPVB}_\infty$$

In summary, the results for Machine A show that an investor would be indifferent between receiving payments of $36 882.04 every 3 years, or a single payment of $148 308.14 now, or annual payments of $14 830.81 forever. The corresponding amounts for Machine B are $51 206.70 every 5 years, $135 081.98 now, or $13 508.20 annually forever. Of these three pairs of figures, the second and third pairs adjust for the unequal lives of the machines, and both show that Machine A should be preferred.

### Example 18.8

Assume that Madison Company, which operates a fleet of trucks, is considering replacing them with a new model. The data in Table 18.6 are available on the old and the new trucks:

# THE APPLICATION OF PROJECT EVALUATION METHODS

**Table 18.6** Data on old and new trucks

| Item | | Old truck | New truck |
|---|---|---|---|
| 1 | Net cash flows | $45 000 p.a. | $50 000 p.a. |
| 2 | Estimated life | 2 years | 4 years |
| 3 | Disposal value: | | |
| | (a) at present (assumed to be equal to the truck's written down value); | $10 000 | |
| | (b) in 4 years' time. | nil | $10 000 |
| 4 | Cost of new trucks | | $60 000 |
| 5 | Cost of capital (real) | 10% p.a. | 10% p.a. |
| 6 | It is assumed that there are no taxes. | | |

Management is considering two alternatives:
1. Replace the old trucks now and assume that the new trucks are operated for 4 years and replaced in perpetuity.
2. Replace the old trucks in 2 years' time and assume that the new trucks are operated for 4 years, and replaced in perpetuity.

Obviously there are other alternatives that management could consider, such as replacing the present trucks in 1 year's time or replacing the old trucks now and the new ones in 2 years' time. However, it is assumed that these possibilities have been considered and rejected by management. It is also assumed that there are no expected improvements in truck design that would make the new truck obsolete.

Alternatives 1 and 2 will therefore be evaluated assuming a constant chain of replacement. The alternative with the larger net present value, provided that it is greater than zero, will be accepted, other things being equal. In the following evaluation the net present value for a single truck is calculated. If there are ten trucks in the fleet the net present values of the two alternatives will be multiplied by 10 to find their total net present values.

1. **Replace the old trucks now, operate the new trucks for 4 years and replace them in perpetuity.**

   The net present value of a new truck is:

$$\text{NPV}_o = -\$60\,000 + \$50\,000 \text{ A}_{\overline{4}|0.1} + \frac{\$10\,000}{(1.1)^4}$$
$$= -\$60\,000 + \$158\,493.30 + \$6\,830.13$$
$$= \$105\,323.43$$

The present value of an infinite chain of these trucks is therefore:

$$\text{NPV}_\infty = (\$105\,323.43) \frac{(1.1)^4}{(1.1)^4 - 1}$$
$$= \$332\,265$$

In addition, at the start of this chain Madison Company receives a cash inflow of $10 000 from the disposal value of the old truck. Therefore, the **total** net present value is:

$$332\ 265 + \$10\ 000$$
$$= \$342\ 265$$

2. **Replace the old trucks in 2 years' time, operate the new trucks for 4 years, and replace them in perpetuity.**

   As in the previous calculation, $NPV_\infty = \$332\ 265$. However, the first of the chain of new trucks is now purchased at Year 2 instead of at Year 0 as previously. As a result, $NPV_\infty$ must be discounted to Year 0:

   $$\frac{\$332\ 265}{(1.1)^2}$$
   $$= \$274\ 599.17$$

   In addition, Madison Company obtains the net present value of operating the old trucks for the first 2 years. This is given by:

   $$\frac{\$45\ 000}{1.1} + \frac{\$45\ 000}{(1.1)^2}$$
   $$= \$78\ 099.17$$

   The **total** net present value is therefore:

   $$\$274\ 599.17 + \$78\ 099.17$$
   $$= \$352\ 698.34$$

The net present value of Alternative 2 is greater than the net present value of Alternative 1 and management should replace the old trucks in 2 years' time unless there are qualitative factors that would cause it to favour the first alternative. Qualitative factors are discussed in Section 18.8.

## CHAIN OF REPLACEMENT METHODS AND INFLATION

Chain of replacement methods rely on the assumption that each project will, at the end of its life, be replaced by an identical project. That is, each replacement will cost the same amount, generate the same cash flows, and last for the same time. Clearly, if there is inflation, future costs and cash flows will not be expected to remain the same in nominal terms, but they may remain the same in real terms. To ensure that inflation is treated consistently, all cash flows and the cost of capital should generally be expressed in real terms when a chain of replacement method is used.[8]

## IS THE CHAIN OF REPLACEMENT METHOD REALISTIC?

A possible problem with the constant chain of replacement model is that it employs unrealistic assumptions about the replacement machines in the chain, namely that the machines and the services they provide are identical in every respect. These assumptions are unrealistic. However, the fact that the replacements may be many years in the future, and the fact that their cash flows will be discounted to a present value, reduce the impact of making such unrealistic

---

[8] For a discussion of this issue and presentation of a nominal version of the constant chain of replacement model, see R. Faff & T. Brailsford, 'The Constant Chain of Replacement Model and Inflation', *Pacific Accounting Review*, December 1992, pp. 45–58.

assumptions. It may be even more unrealistic to assume that management has perfect foresight and therefore is able to predict such factors as the capital outlay, net cash flows, life, and residual value, of replacement assets. However, if such information is available, it is not a difficult matter to insert into the analysis the replacement of an existing machine with a machine of improved design.

The methods discussed in this section are very useful but some points should be noted. First, it is not necessary to use these methods in all cases where projects have different lives. For independent projects, the net present value method automatically allows for any such differences. The different lives 'problem' arises only for mutually exclusive projects. Secondly, it is important when using chain of replacement methods, to use the real cost of capital. Thirdly, in many cases mutually exclusive projects will involve the same benefits (cash inflows) but different costs (cash outflows). In these cases the cash inflows can be ignored and the alternatives can be compared on the basis of their cash outflows, as in Example 18.6.

## 18.4 DETERMINING A PROJECT'S OPTIMUM LIFE

Investment projects are not always continued until the end of their estimated physical lives and, as we noted in Chapter 5, the systematic search for new investments should be complemented by a periodic review of the performance of existing projects. Such reviews may result in decisions to terminate activities, or to replace existing equipment.

In this section, a distinction is made between retirement and replacement decisions.

1. **Retirement decisions** involve those situations where equipment is used for some time, and then it is decided not to continue the operation in which the equipment is used. Therefore the equipment is sold and not replaced.
2. **Replacement decisions** involve those situations where a particular type of operation is intended to continue indefinitely. That is, a company's need for the equipment is assumed to continue long after the present equipment has been sold or scrapped. In this case, a company is faced with a decision about when the existing equipment should be replaced.

### 18.4.1 RETIREMENT DECISIONS

The analysis for determining when a project should be discontinued (retired) is outlined in this section. Since the retirement of assets is just another investment decision, the net present value rule is still valid for retirement decisions. Therefore a project should be retired if the net present value of all its future net cash flows is less than zero. Determining the appropriate time of a machine's retirement is illustrated in Example 18.9.

## Example 18.9

Mortlake Ltd owns a machine that is 6 years old and has an estimated remaining physical life of no more than 2 years. Table 18.7 shows the net cash flow and residual value estimates for the machine:

**Table 18.7** *Estimates of net cash flow and residual value for existing machine*

| End of year | Net cash flow ($) | Residual value ($) |
|---|---|---|
| 6 | — | 12 000 |
| 7 | 8 000 | 6 000 |
| 8 | 5 000 | 0 |

The cost of capital is 10 per cent.

The problem is analysed by first calculating the net present value of foregoing the $12 000 current residual value to obtain a net cash flow of $8000, and a residual value of $6000 in 1 year's time. Therefore the net present value of running the machine for 1 more year is:

$$NPV = -\$12\,000 + \frac{(\$8000 + \$6000)}{1.1}$$
$$= -\$12\,000 + \$12\,727$$
$$= \$727$$

Since the net present value is positive, the machine should be retained for at least 1 more year. Secondly, management may be interested in finding out whether, given the current forecasts, the machine should be retained for the remaining 2 years of its life. If the machine is retained for a further 2 years, the company will forego $12 000, the current residual value, and receive instead net cash flows in Years 7 and 8 of $8000 and $5000 respectively. There is no residual value at the end of Year 8. Therefore, the net present value of this alternative is:

$$NPV = -\$12\,000 + \frac{\$8000}{1.1} + \frac{\$5000}{(1.1)^2}$$
$$= -\$12\,000 + \$7273 + \$4132$$
$$= -\$595$$

Unless there is some upward revision in the estimates of cash flows for Year 8, the machine should be retired at the end of the seventh year.

### 18.4.2 REPLACEMENT DECISIONS

In Section 18.3 the use of the constant chain of replacement method to evaluate projects with different lives was discussed. The same approach can be used to evaluate replacement decisions. To discuss these decisions we distinguish between two cases. In the first, the decision is when to replace an existing project with an *identical* project. In the second case the decision is when to replace an existing project with a new one, which involves *different* cash flows.

## IDENTICAL REPLACEMENT

In this case it is assumed that a current project will be replaced by a project identical in every respect. The capital outlay, net cash flows, physical life, and residual value of both projects are the same. Example 18.10 illustrates an analysis of this type.

### Example 18.10

A machine costs $20 000 and has an estimated life of 5 years. The net cash flows are $12 000 in the first year, decreasing by $500 each year as a result of higher maintenance costs. Table 18.8 gives the machine's estimated residual value at the end of each year.

**Table 18.8** Estimated residual values for machine

| Year | Residual value ($) |
|------|--------------------|
| 1    | 16 000             |
| 2    | 14 000             |
| 3    | 12 000             |
| 4    | 6 000              |
| 5    | Nil                |

The cost of capital is assumed to be 10 per cent and there are no taxes. Management wishes to know when the machine should be replaced.

If the machine is used for only 1 year and then sold, the net present value would be as follows:

$$NPV_1 = -\$20\,000 + \frac{\$12\,000}{1.1} + \frac{\$16\,000}{1.1}$$
$$= \$5455$$

If the machine is used for 2 years and then sold, the net present value would be as follows:

$$NPV_2 = -\$20\,000 + \frac{\$12\,000}{1.1} + \frac{\$11\,500}{(1.1)^2} + \frac{\$14\,000}{(1.1)^2}$$
$$= \$11\,983$$

Similarly, net present values can be calculated based on use for three, four, and five years. However, these net present values cannot be compared, because they are based on different lives. As we noted above, this difficulty can be overcome by assuming a constant chain of replacement. If it is assumed that the machine is replaced every year in perpetuity, the net present value will be as follows:

$$NPV_{(1,\infty)} = \$5455 \left[\frac{(1.1)}{(1.1) - 1}\right]$$
$$= \$60\,000$$

If the machine is replaced every second year in perpetuity, the net present value will be as follows:

$$\text{NPV}_{(2,\infty)} = \$11\,983 \left[ \frac{(1.1)^2}{(1.1)^2 - 1} \right]$$
$$= \$68\,500$$

The net present values, assuming the machine is replaced in perpetuity, at the end of the third, fourth, and fifth years respectively, are as follows:

$$\text{NPV}_{(3,\infty)} = \$17\,694 \left[ \frac{(1.1)^3}{(1.1)^3 - 1} \right]$$
$$= \$71\,160$$

$$\text{NPV}_{(4,\infty)} = \$19\,948 \left[ \frac{(1.1)^4}{(1.1)^4 - 1} \right]$$
$$= \$62\,940$$

$$\text{NPV}_{(5,\infty)} = \$20\,060 \left[ \frac{(1.1)^5}{(1.1)^5 - 1} \right]$$
$$= \$52\,920$$

These results show that the machine should be replaced after 3 years. In general the decision rule is to choose the replacement frequency that maximises the project's net present value for a perpetual chain of replacement, or that maximises its equivalent annual value.

### NON-IDENTICAL REPLACEMENT

Suppose that a machine is physically sound but technically obsolete. That is, when the machine is replaced, its replacement will be of a new design, which may have the same capacity but cost less to operate. The question is: When should the old machine be discarded in favour of the new one? The solution involves two steps. First, the optimum replacement frequency for the new machine is determined using the method illustrated in Example 18.10. Secondly, the equivalent annual value of the new machine at its optimum replacement frequency is compared with the net present value of continuing to operate the old machine, as shown in Example 18.9. The decision rule is that the changeover should be made when the net present value of continuing to operate the old machine for one more year is less than the equivalent annual value of the new machine.

## 18.5 USING CERTAINTY EQUIVALENTS TO ALLOW FOR RISK

Up to this point, risk has been incorporated into the evaluation of a project by using a cost of capital that reflects the risk of the project. That is, the project's expected cash flows are discounted using a **risk-adjusted discount rate**. Using this approach, the net present value, NPV, is calculated as follows:

$$\text{NPV} = -C_0 + \sum_{t=1}^{n} \frac{E(C_t)}{(1+k)^t} \qquad (18.7)$$

where $E(C_t)$ = the expected net cash flow in year $t$
$k$ = the cost of capital, appropriate to the risky, expected cash flows $E(C_t)$
$C_0$ = the initial cash outlay
$n$ = the life, in years, of the project

The **certainty-equivalent** approach is an alternative method of incorporating risk into project evaluation.[9] This approach incorporates risk into the analysis by adjusting the *cash flows* rather than the discount rate. That is, each year's expected net cash flow is converted to a certainty equivalent. The certainty-equivalent net cash flow in year $t$, $C_t^*$, is the smallest certain cash flow that the decision maker would be prepared to accept in exchange for the expected risky cash flow, $E(C_t)$. For example, assume that a project's risky net cash flow is $10 000 at the end of the first year. If the decision maker is prepared to exchange the claim to this risky cash flow for a claim to receive, with certainty, $8000 at the end of the first year, then $8000 is the certainty equivalent of the risky $10 000. In this example, $E(C_1)$ is $10 000 and $C_1^* = \$8000$. Therefore the expected net cash flow for any year can be converted to its certainty equivalent as follows:

$$C_t^* = \alpha_t E(C_t) \tag{18.8}$$

where $\alpha_t$ = the certainty-equivalent factor in year $t$

The certainty-equivalent factor in this example can be calculated as follows:

$$\alpha_t = \frac{C_t^*}{E(C_t)} = \frac{\$8\,000}{\$10\,000} = 0.8$$

Using the certainty-equivalent approach, the net present value is calculated by discounting the certainty-equivalent net cash flow for each period at the appropriate risk-free rate:

$$\text{NPV} = C_0 + \sum_{t=1}^{n} \frac{C_t^*}{(1 + R_f)^t} \tag{18.9}$$

If all variables are properly specified, the present value of any future cash flow must be identical in either the risk-adjusted discount rate method or the certainty-equivalent method. Therefore:

$$\frac{E(C_t)}{(1 + k)^t} = \frac{\alpha_t E(C_t)}{(1 + R_f)^t}$$

$$\therefore \alpha_t = \frac{(1 + R_f)^t}{(1 + k)^t} \tag{18.10}$$

In the following examples we illustrate both methods and then discuss their relative merits.

---

[9] For a discussion of the relationship between the certainty-equivalent and risk-adjusted discount rate approaches, see A. Robichek & S. Myers, 'Conceptual Problems in the Use of Risk-adjusted Discount Rates', *Journal of Finance*, December 1966, pp. 727–30.

## Example 18.11

Company A is considering an investment in a new machine. The machine will require an initial outlay of $100 000 and it is expected to generate cash flows of $50 000, $40 000, and $50 000 at the end of Years 1, 2, and 3 respectively. For each year of the machine's life it has been estimated that the project's beta is 0.5, and that the risk-free interest rate and the market premium are both constant at 8 per cent per annum. Therefore, based on the CAPM, the risk-adjusted discount rate is:

$$k = R_f + \beta (E(R_M) - R_f)$$
$$= 0.08 + 0.5 (0.08)$$
$$= 0.12$$

The net present value using the risk-adjusted discount rate method is calculated using Equation 18.7:

$$NPV = -\$100\,000 + \frac{\$50\,000}{1.12} + \frac{\$40\,000}{(1.12)^2} + \frac{\$50\,000}{(1.12)^3}$$
$$= -\$100\,000 + \$44\,643 + \$31\,888 + \$35\,589$$
$$= \$12\,120$$

From Equation 18.10, the certainty-equivalent factor for each year is calculated as follows:

$$\alpha_1 = \frac{1.08}{1.12} = 0.9643$$

$$\alpha_2 = \frac{(1.08)^2}{(1.12)^2} = 0.9298$$

$$\alpha_3 = \frac{(1.08)^3}{(1.12)^3} = 0.8966$$

Using these certainty-equivalent factors, the net present value can be calculated using Equation 18.9:

$$NPV = -\$100\,000 + \frac{0.9643\,(\$50\,000)}{1.08} + \frac{0.9298\,(\$40\,000)}{(1.08)^2}$$
$$+ \frac{0.8966\,(\$50\,000)}{(1.08)^3}$$
$$= -\$100\,000 + \$44\,644 + \$31\,866 + \$35\,588$$
$$= \$12\,118$$

Apart from a difference of $2 due to rounding error, the net present values are the same, and, on the face of it, there seems to be no reason for preferring one method to the other.

However, it should be recognised that in discounting a future cash flow to a present value there are two factors to be taken into account: time and risk. These factors are logically separate but the risk-adjusted discount rate approach requires the effect of both to be incorporated into the discount rate. In particular, use of a constant risk-adjusted discount rate implies that the risk associated with the project increases over time at a constant rate. This was illustrated in Example 18.11 which showed that a constant risk-adjusted discount rate results in the certainty-equivalent factors decreasing at a constant rate in each successive year. In Example 18.11, the rate of decrease is approximately 3.6 per cent per year. The fact that the certainty-equivalent factors decrease at a constant rate over time is shown by Equation 18.10 which can be rewritten as:

$$\alpha_t = \left(\frac{1 + R_f}{1 + k}\right)^t = (\alpha_1)^t$$

The decrease of certainty-equivalent factors at a constant rate indicates that the cumulative risk associated with each successive cash flow increases steadily as we look further into the future. In cases where this risk pattern does *not* apply, a constant risk-adjusted discount rate should not be used, and the certainty-equivalent approach offers practical advantages. This is illustrated in Example 18.12.

## Example 18.12

Teletron Ltd has recently invented a new type of cordless telephone. Further development work is required over the next 2 years and management believes there is a 60 per cent probability of then proceeding to commercial production using a plant costing $2 million. Expected cash inflows are $500 000 per year for 20 years. Alternatively there is a 40 per cent probability that the development work will fail, in which case there will be no cash flows after the first 2 years. The development work will be undertaken by a local university research company in return for an immediate payment of $250 000.

Suppose that, because of the high risk, management evaluates the project using a discount rate of 30 per cent per annum, compared with its normal rate of 15 per cent per annum. The expected cash flows are:

Year 0:
PV of outlays on development work = −$250 000
Year 2:
Construction of plant: $(0.6)(-\$2\,000\,000) + 0.4 \times \$0 = -\$1\,200\,000$
Years 3–23:
Cash inflows: $0.6 \times \$500\,000 + 0.4 \times \$0 = \$300\,000$

$$\therefore \text{NPV} = -\$250\,000 - \frac{\$1\,200\,000}{(1.3)^2} + \$300\,000 \left[\frac{1 - \frac{1}{(1.3)^{20}}}{0.3}\right] \times \frac{1}{(1.3)^2}$$
$$= -\$371\,457$$

Based on this result the project would be rejected now without undertaking the development work. However, much of the risk associated with the project will be resolved after the first 2 years. If the development work is successful, the project may be of normal risk, in which case the future cash flows would be discounted at Teletron's normal rate of 15 per cent per annum. Assuming that the risk-free rate is 8 per cent per annum, the project's NPV can be recalculated using a combination of the two approaches.

If the project goes ahead after the 2 years' development work, the NPV at the end of Year 2 will be:

$$\text{NPV}(2) = -\$2\,000\,000 + \$500\,000 \left[ \frac{1 - \dfrac{1}{(1.15)^{20}}}{0.15} \right]$$
$$= \$1\,129\,666$$

But there is only a 60 per cent probability of this outcome. Assuming a certainty-equivalent factor of 0.6, the project NPV is:

$$\text{NPV} = -\$250\,000 + \frac{0.6 \times \$1\,129\,666}{(1.08)^2}$$
$$= \$331\,104$$

Therefore, the project should proceed, which is the opposite of the decision originally indicated by the constant risk-adjusted discount rate method.

To summarise, discounting risky future cash flows to present values requires adjustments for the effects of two factors: time and risk. In the risk-adjusted discount rate approach the effects of both factors are included in the discount rate. The two factors are logically separate and are treated separately in the certainty-equivalent approach, which is easier to use in cases where the risk per unit of time is *not* constant.

## 18.6 ANALYSING PROJECT RISK

As discussed in Chapter 17, the effect of risk on the value of a project is normally incorporated in the evaluation by using a cost of capital which reflects the risk of the project. However, the calculated net present value is only an estimate that relies on forecasts of the project's cash flows. In practice these forecasts will, almost certainly, turn out to be incorrect, perhaps because the volume of sales turns out to be more or less than expected, the price of the product is higher or lower than expected, or operating costs differ from the forecast. Therefore, in many cases managers will need to analyse proposed projects to answer questions such as: What are the key variables that are likely to determine whether the project is a success or a failure? and: How far can sales fall or costs increase before the project loses money? To answer these and other related questions, managers can use various *project analysis* techniques. The techniques we discuss are sensitivity analysis, break-even analysis, and simulation.

### 18.6.1 SENSITIVITY ANALYSIS[10]

A project's cash flows and cost of capital are usually specified as 'best estimates' or 'expected values' and the resulting net present value, often referred to as the **base-case net present value**, is also a best estimate or expected value. The application of sensitivity analysis to project evaluation involves assessing the impact of changes or errors in the estimated variables on the net present value. This is achieved by calculating net present values based on alternative estimates of the variables. For instance, management may wish to know the effect on net

---

[10] For a more detailed discussion of sensitivity analysis, see A. Rappaport, 'Sensitivity Analysis in Decision-making', *The Accounting Review*, July 1967, pp. 440–7.

present value if a project's net cash flows are either 20 per cent less than, or 20 per cent greater than, those estimated. Knowledge of the sensitivity of net present value to changes or errors in the variables places management in a better position to decide whether a project is too risky to accept. Also, if management knows that the net present value is sensitive to changes in particular variables, it can examine the estimates of these variables more thoroughly, or collect more data in an effort to reduce errors in forecasting.

Assuming that all variables in the analysis are uncertain, a simple example of sensitivity analysis involves the following steps:
1. Pessimistic, optimistic, and expected estimates are made for each variable.
2. Net present value is calculated using the expected estimates for every variable except one, the value for which is, in turn, its optimistic and pessimistic estimate. This procedure is repeated until a net present value has been calculated using an optimistic and pessimistic estimate for each variable, in combination with the expected values of the other variables.
3. The difference between the optimistic and pessimistic net present values is calculated for each variable. A small difference between the net present values suggests that the project's net present value is insensitive to changes or errors in that variable. A large difference between the net present values suggests the opposite. For example, suppose that in a particular project there are only four uncertain variables: sales, fixed operating costs, advertising costs, and the life of the machine. In this case, eight net present value calculations are made, using the data inputs shown in Table 18.9. The symbol O indicates the optimistic value of the variable, P indicates the pessimistic value of the variable, and E indicates the expected value of the variable.

The application of sensitivity analysis to project evaluation in a case such as that shown in Table 18.9 is illustrated in Example 18.13.

**Table 18.9** *Combinations of variable values for sensitivity analysis*

| Estimates | NPV calculation number | | | | | | | |
|---|---|---|---|---|---|---|---|---|
| | (i) | (ii) | (iii) | (iv) | (v) | (vi) | (vii) | (viii) |
| Sales | O | P | E | E | E | E | E | E |
| Fixed operating costs | E | E | O | P | E | E | E | E |
| Advertising costs | E | E | E | E | O | P | E | E |
| Machine life | E | E | E | E | E | E | O | P |

### Example 18.13

Assume that a manager is considering whether to purchase a new machine that costs $500 000. It is assumed that there are only four uncertain variables: sales, fixed operating costs, advertising costs, and the life of the new machine. Sales are expected to be $400 000 per annum, with fixed operating costs and advertising costs of $150 000 and $145 000 per annum respectively, during an expected life of 10 years. All other variables are expected to remain constant during the machine's life. The cost of capital is 10 per cent per annum. The expected annual net cash flows are $400 000 − $150 000 − $145 000 = $105 000, and the base-case net present value is:

$$\text{Base-case NPV} = -\$500\,000 + \$105\,000 \left[ \frac{1 - \frac{1}{(1.1)^{10}}}{0.1} \right]$$
$$= \$145\,180$$

Information needed for the sensitivity analysis is shown in Table 18.10 which presents:
1. for each uncertain variable, expected (column 1), optimistic (column 2) and pessimistic (column 3) estimates;
2. the net present value (column 4) when one of the uncertain variables is set at its optimistic estimate and each of the other variables is set at its expected value;
3. the net present value (column 5) when one of the uncertain variables is set at its pessimistic estimate and each of the other variables is set at its expected value;
4. in column 6, the difference between columns 4 and 5, which is frequently called the 'range of the net present value'.

**Table 18.10** Sensitivity analysis of the purchase of a new machine, based on optimistic and pessimistic estimates of the values of each variable

| Variable | Expected (1) | Optimistic (2) | Pessimistic (3) | NPV: optimistic estimate ($'000s) (a) (4) | | NPV: pessimistic estimate ($'000s) (a) (5) | | Range of the NPV ($'000s) (6) |
|---|---|---|---|---|---|---|---|---|
| Sales ($'000s) | 400 | 420 | 375 | (i) | 268.1 | (ii) | −8.4 | 276.5 |
| Fixed operating costs ($'000s) | 150 | 148 | 152 | (iii) | 157.5 | (iv) | 132.9 | 24.6 |
| Advertising costs ($'000s) | 145 | 115 | 190 | (v) | 329.5 | (vi) | −131.3 | 460.8 |
| Life of machine (years) | 10 | 12 | 9 | (vii) | 215.4 | (viii) | 104.7 | 110.7 |

(a) The figures in lower case Roman numerals in these columns indicate the NPV calculation that corresponds to the input table shown in Table 18.9.

Table 18.10 shows that the estimate of net present value is more sensitive to changes in advertising costs than to changes in the other uncertain variables. In addition it shows that if the pessimistic estimate of either sales or advertising costs occurs, the purchase of the machine will generate a negative net present value.

Before deciding to purchase the new machine, management is therefore likely to gather more information on advertising costs and sales in an effort to minimise forecasting errors. In contrast, the value of additional data about the machine's fixed operating costs and useful life is relatively small. The project is still acceptable, based on the pessimistic values for those variables, and therefore the company is unlikely to lose money on the project even if these variables have been incorrectly estimated.

The use of sensitivity analysis is not without its problems. One is that frequently it is difficult to specify precisely the relationship between a particular variable and net present value. If the assumed relationship is based on past outcomes there is always the possibility that this relationship may not hold in the future. It is further complicated by relationships between the variables. For example, it is inappropriate to examine the effect on net present value of a 20 per cent reduction in sales volume without recognising that lower sales volume may also mean that the selling price is lower than expected. Allowing for these interdependencies will complicate the analysis. Another problem is that the terms 'optimistic' and 'pessimistic' are subject to interpretation, and the results may be somewhat ambiguous. For example, the marketing department's 'optimistic' sales forecasts may be so optimistic that they are virtually unachievable, while 'optimistic' estimates of useful life may be exceeded quite frequently.

## BREAK-EVEN ANALYSIS

Break-even analysis is a form of sensitivity analysis. Sensitivity analysis generally involves finding answers to 'what if' questions such as: What will be the net present value of the project if sales are 10 per cent less than expected? In break-even analysis the question is turned around, in that the manager asks: How poor can sales become before the project loses money? The break-even point is the sales volume at which the present values of the project's cash inflows and outflows are equal, so that its net present value is zero. Break-even analysis is illustrated in Example 18.14.

### Example 18.14

The manager of Alsports Ltd is considering a plan to manufacture aluminium cricket bats. Equipment to manufacture the bats will cost $850 000 and is expected to have a useful life of 3 years. Fixed costs are estimated to be $80 000 per annum and the bats are expected to sell for $40 each, while variable costs will be $28 per bat. About 500 000 cricket bats are sold each year and Alsports' manager expects to capture 10 per cent of the market. Based on sales of 50 000 aluminium bats per year, and a cost of capital of 10 per cent, the project has a net present value of $443 160, but the manager wishes to calculate the break-even point. For this purpose, the present values of the project's cash inflows and outflows are calculated for annual sales of zero, 25 000, and 50 000 bats. To simplify the calculations, taxes and depreciation are ignored. The results are shown in Table 18.11 and plotted in Figure 18.1.

The break-even point corresponds to sales of 35 150 bats per year. Provided that bat sales are more than 35 150 per year, the project has a positive NPV and would proceed if management considers that the sales forecast of 50 000 bats per year is realistic.

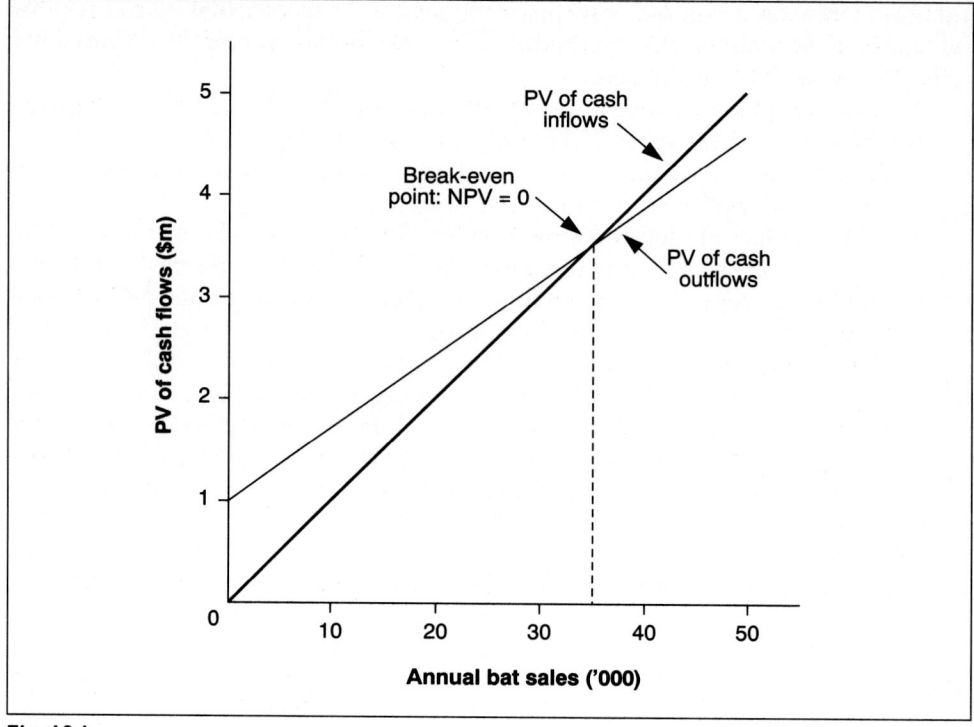

**Fig. 18.1**

**Table 18.11** Break-even analysis of the Alsports aluminium bat project

| Sales (units per year) | Cash inflow ($ per year) | PV of cash inflows ($) | Equipment cost $ | Fixed costs ($ per year) | Variable costs ($ per year) | PV of cash outflows $ | NPV $ |
|---|---|---|---|---|---|---|---|
| | | | Cash outflows | | | | |
| 0 | 0 | 0 | 850 000 | 80 000 | 0 | 1 048 948 | −1 048 948 |
| 25 000 | 1 000 000 | 2 486 852 | 850 000 | 80 000 | 700 000 | 2 789 745 | −302 893 |
| 50 000 | 2 000 000 | 4 973 704 | 850 000 | 80 000 | 1 400 000 | 4 530 541 | +443 163 |

### 18.6.2 SIMULATION

Sensitivity analysis involves changing one variable at a time and examining the effects of the changes on the profitability of a project. On the other hand, simulation allows a manager to consider the effects of changing *all* the relevant variables. The first step in a simulation is to identify the relevant variables and to specify the probability distribution of each variable. For example, in the case of Alsports' aluminium bat project the variables could include selling price, market size, market share, the cost and useful life of the production equipment, and variable operating costs. The second step is to specify any relationships between the variables. For example, a higher sales volume may result in economies of scale in production and distribution, which should be reflected in the variable costs. The third step involves using a computer to calculate a net present value (NPV) or internal rate of return (IRR) distribution for the project. Essentially, the procedure is as follows:

1. The computer selects values randomly from the distribution of each of the specified variables.
2. In the first run of the simulation the computer calculates a value for the NPV or IRR.
3. The result of the first run is stored and a new set of values is chosen and used in the second run of the simulation, which gives a further result that is also stored. This procedure is repeated at least 100 and perhaps thousands of times.
4. The results of all the individual runs are combined to produce a probability distribution for the NPV or IRR of the project.

Simulation is a potentially valuable tool that allows managers to analyse many aspects of the risks associated with a project. While specifying the model can be time consuming, once it has been developed it is relatively easy to examine the effects of changing the probability distribution for one or more variables. Also the availability of suitable computer software has improved, so simulation can now be carried out on a PC using popular spreadsheet programs. Ease of access is likely to be important in making simulation more popular because senior managers are more likely to be confident about the results of a simulation if they have been involved in setting it up and are aware of the assumptions used. However, greater access to simulation could be a mixed blessing because there may be a tendency to rely heavily on the technique without appreciating its limitations. These include the following:

1. Simulation is a technique for processing information and presenting the results of that processing in a particular way. Therefore the results of a simulation cannot be any more reliable than the input data and the model that specifies the relationships between variables.
2. Simulation results can be difficult to interpret. When a project is evaluated by discounting its expected net cash flows at the project's cost of capital, the result is a single NPV figure. This result is an estimate that has some degree of error associated with it. Simulation can provide information about the likely degree of error but it does so by providing a whole distribution of possible outcomes. Managers who are used to assessing projects based on a single NPV, plus a sensitivity analysis, may be unsure how to interpret a distribution which indicates the probabilities associated with a range of NPV values. In contrast to the usual NPV rule, simulation does not provide unambiguous accept/reject decisions for projects.
3. There is a more fundamental problem related to the interpretation of simulation results when the NPV model is used. The simulation calculations must employ a discount rate and this is generally not the project's cost of capital. Instead, the effects of risk are incorporated by allowing the values of all uncertain variables to change according to their specified probability distributions. With risk reflected in the cash flows, discounting is used only to allow for the time value of money, so the NPV values

are calculated by discounting at a risk-free rate. Because the discount rate is a risk-free rate rather than the cost of capital, the resultant NPV values cannot be interpreted in the same way as typical NPV estimates. To avoid this problem, some managers prefer to employ the IRR method, despite its inherent limitations outlined in Section 5.4. The probability distribution of IRR values may be easier to interpret than a distribution of NPV values based on discounting at the risk-free rate.
4. Simulation focuses on the total risk of a project and ignores the possibility that much of this risk might be removed by diversification. As discussed in Section 17.2, it is the systematic or non-diversifiable risk of a project that is important in determining its cost of capital.

In summary, simulation is a potentially valuable technique for analysing the effects of risk, but users should be aware of its limitations.

## 18.7 DECISION-TREE ANALYSIS

Management is sometimes faced with the need to evaluate alternatives involving a sequence of decisions over time. Decision-tree analysis provides a means of evaluating such decisions. The decision-tree approach takes into account the probability of various events occurring and the impact of those events on the expected net present value of a project. Decision-tree analysis uses the concept of 'roll-back' to evaluate alternative decisions. This is illustrated in the following example.[11]

### Example 18.15

The management of a Victorian-based company is considering the proposed construction of a plant to manufacture its products in New South Wales. Initially, management is faced with the choice of constructing either a large plant or a small plant. If it constructs a large plant, the initial outlay will be $2 million, whereas if it constructs a small plant, the initial outlay will be $1 million. If a small plant is chosen, management will reconsider its decision after 2 years. At that time, management may, if it believes that further expansion is warranted, expand the small plant to achieve the same capacity as a large plant. The expansion will cost $1.25 million.

The company has estimated the expected net cash flows to be generated by a large plant, a small plant, and an expanded plant on the basis of a two-way classification of demand: high demand and low demand. These expectations are summarised in Table 18.12.

Management has also estimated the probability of achieving either high demand or low demand during the project's 10-year life. It has estimated the likelihood of high demand throughout the project's life to be 0.6, the probability of achieving high demand for the first 2 years and low demand for the remaining

---

[11] For a simple discussion of decision-tree analysis, see R. I. Levin & C. A. Kirkpatrick, *Quantitative Approaches to Management*, 3rd edn, McGraw Hill, New York, 1975, pp. 160–5.

# THE APPLICATION OF PROJECT EVALUATION METHODS

**Table 18.12** *Expected net cash flows for different plants and levels of demand*

| Possibilities | Expected net cash flow per annum ($m) |
|---|---|
| Large plant, high demand | 0.8 |
| Large plant, low demand | 0.1 |
| Small plant, high demand | 0.4 |
| Small plant, low demand | 0.35 |
| Expanded plant, high demand | 0.5 |
| Expanded plant, low demand | 0.075 |

8 years to be 0.2, and the probability of low demand throughout the project's life to be 0.2. The probabilities and the expected net cash flows are shown in Figure 18.2 in the form of a **decision tree**. The squares represent decision points and the small circles represent chance events that may occur during the life of the project. The base of a decision tree is the beginning Decision point 1. Its branches begin at the first chance event. Each chance event produces two or more possible outcomes, some of which lead to other chance events and/or subsequent decision points.

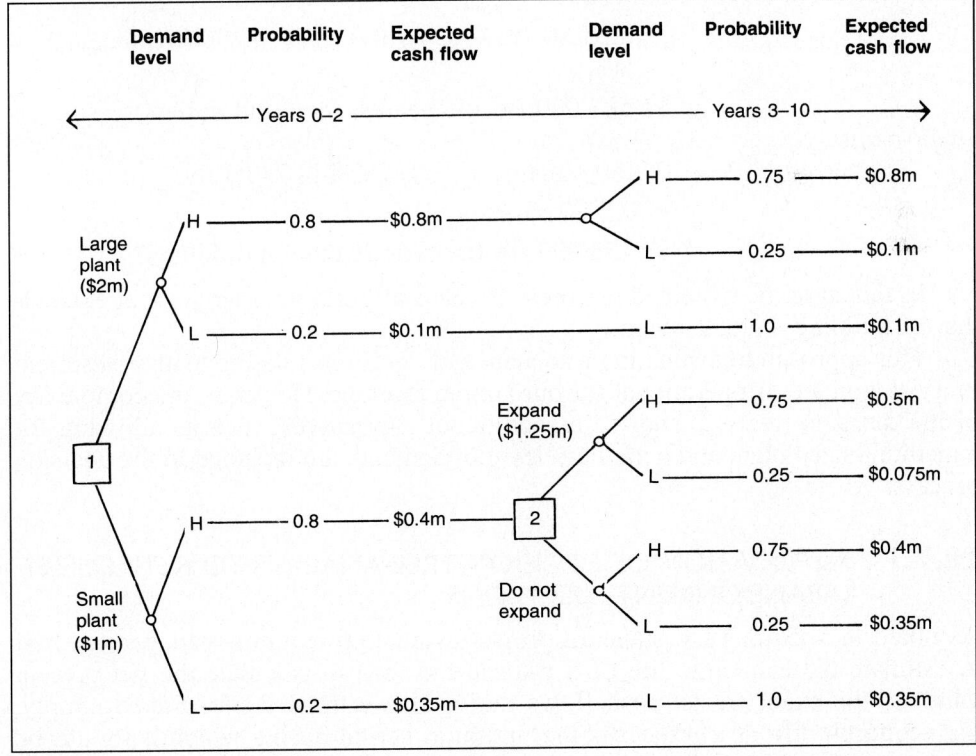

Fig. 18.2

The optimum sequence of decisions is determined using a **roll-back** procedure, which means that the most distant decision—in this case, the decision whether to expand the small plant—is evaluated first. Each alternative is evaluated on the basis of its expected net present value. The cost of capital is assumed to be 9 per cent per annum.

**Decision 2: Whether to expand the small plant**

*Expand:*
$$\text{Expected NPV} = 0.75\,(\$0.5\text{mA}_{\overline{8}|0.09}) + 0.25\,(\$0.075\text{mA}_{\overline{8}|0.09}) - \$1.25\text{m}$$
$$= \$929\,355$$

*Do not expand:*
$$\text{Expected NPV} = 0.75\,(\$0.4\text{mA}_{\overline{8}|0.09}) + 0.25\,(\$0.35\text{mA}_{\overline{8}|0.09})$$
$$= \$2\,144\,743$$

Therefore, the optimum choice is not to expand the small plant at the end of the second year. The roll-back method simplifies the evaluation by eliminating the alternative of building a small plant and then expanding it after 2 years. Once management knows what it ought to do if faced with the expansion decision, it can 'roll back' to today's decision. This decision is whether to build a large plant or a small plant to be operated for 10 years.

**Decision 1: Construct either a large plant or a small plant and operate for 10 years**

*Large plant:*
$$\text{Expected NPV} = 0.8\,(\$0.8\text{mA}_{\overline{2}|0.09}) + 0.8\,[0.75(\$0.8\text{mA}_{\overline{8}|0.09})(1.09)^{-2}$$
$$+ 0.25(\$0.1\text{mA}_{\overline{8}|0.09})(1.09)^{-2}] + 0.20(\$0.1\text{mA}_{\overline{10}|0.09})$$
$$- \$2\text{m}$$
$$= \$1\,583\,000 \text{ (to the nearest thousand dollars)}$$

*Small plant:*
$$\text{Expected NPV} = 0.8(\$0.4\text{mA}_{\overline{2}|0.09}) + 0.8[\$2\,144\,743(1.09)^{-2}]$$
$$+ 0.2(\$0.35\text{mA}_{\overline{10}|0.09}) - \$1\text{m}$$
$$= \$1\,456\,000 \text{ (to the nearest thousand dollars)}$$

In this case the expected net present value of building a large plant exceeds that of building a small plant.

This approach to evaluating a sequence of decisions relating to an investment in a risky project is operational for our simple example. However, the complexity of the decision tree is increased as additional alternatives, such as allowing for a medium-sized plant and a medium level of demand, are included in the decision process.

### 18.7.1 APPLICATION OF DECISION-TREE ANALYSIS TO RETIREMENT (ABANDONMENT) DECISIONS

As noted in Section 18.4, standard project evaluation requires management first to estimate the economic life of a project and then to calculate the net present value of the expected net cash flows during this estimated life. Stated simply, the **economic life** of a project is the optimum period during which it should be operated. Therefore a project should be retired at the end of its economic life, which means that it should be retired when the expected net present value of its continued operation is less than its retirement (or abandonment) value. The retirement value of a project is its disposal value. The method of determining when a project should be retired is seen most clearly if certainty is assumed. This is shown in Example 18.16. A more realistic case, where uncertainty is assumed, is shown in Example 18.17.

## Example 18.16

A project generates net cash flows and has retirement values as shown in Table 18.13.

**Table 18.13** Net cash flows and retirement values for project in Example 18.16

| Item | 0 | 1 | 2 | 3 | 4 | 5 |
|---|---|---|---|---|---|---|
| Net cash flows ($) | −100 000 | 40 000 | 45 000 | 35 000 | 30 000 | 20 000[a] |
| Retirement values ($) | — | 85 000 | 65 000 | 45 000 | 21 000 | 8 000 |

[a] includes the residual value of $8000.

If the cost of capital is 12 per cent per annum, when should the project be retired and what is its net present value? The present values of the net cash flows, together with the progressive total of these present values, are shown in Table 18.14.

**Table 18.14** Present value of the net cash flows in Example 18.16

| Item | 0 | 1 | 2 | 3 | 4 | 5 |
|---|---|---|---|---|---|---|
| Present value of net cash flows ($) | −100 000 | 35 714 | 35 874 | 24 912 | 19 066 | 11 349 |
| Progressive total ($) | −100 000 | −64 286 | −28 412 | −3 500 | 15 566 | 26 915 |

Assuming that the project is operated for 5 years, the net present value is $26 915.

The possibility of retirement is now considered. If the project were to be retired after 1 year, the net present value of operating it would be −$64 286, as shown. However, to this amount must be added the present value of the residual value. The net present value of operating the project for 1 year and then retiring it is therefore:

Retire at the end of year 1:

$$\text{NPV} = -\$64\,286 + \frac{\$85\,000}{1.12}$$
$$= \$11\,607$$

As this is less than $26 915, retirement after 1 year is inferior to operating the project for 5 years. Corresponding calculations assuming retirement in later years are as follows:

*Retire at the end of Year 2:*

$$NPV = \$28\,412 + \frac{\$65\,000}{(1.12)^2}$$
$$= \$23\,406$$

*Retire at the end of Year 3:*

$$NPV = -\$3\,500 + \frac{\$45\,000}{(1.12)^3}$$
$$= \$28\,530$$

*Retire at the end of Year 4:*

$$NPV = \$15\,566 + \frac{\$21\,000}{(1.12)^4}$$
$$= \$28\,912$$

Retiring the project at the end of either Year 3 or Year 4 is preferable to operating it for 5 years. The best alternative is to operate the project for 4 years and then retire it. The net present value of this decision is $28 912.

*Example 18.17*

Consider a company that manufactures and distributes electrical components. It has recently developed a small electronic voice synthesiser, 'Simultalk', which can be built into microcomputers to enable the computer to 'talk'. The company's management forecasts that the cash flows associated with the production and sale of Simultalk will be as shown in Figure 18.3. Management forecasts that the retirement value, that is, the cash inflow from retiring the project, will be $700 000 at the end of the first year, $200 000 at the end of the second year, and $0 at the end of the third year. Assuming a cost of capital of 10 per cent per annum, the effect on expected net present value of retiring the project at the end of Years 1, 2, and 3 can be estimated. Evaluation of retirement involves estimating the expected net present value excluding retirement and comparing it with the expected net present value when the possibility of retirement is included.

**Evaluation excluding retirement alternatives (refer to Table 18.15)**

1. From Figure 18.3 it can be seen that the cost of developing Simultalk is $1 200 000.
2. Three possible net cash flows from operations at the end of Year 1 and their probability of occurrence are specified.
3. Consistent with each net cash flow at the end of Year 1, there is a range of possible net cash flows at the end of Year 2, also with probabilities attached. This process is continued until a range of net cash flows and associated probabilities of occurrence are specified for each year.
4. A net present value is calculated for each of the 23 possible sequences of cash flows from operations. These net present values and associated probabilities of occurrence (from Figure 18.3) are shown in Table 18.15.

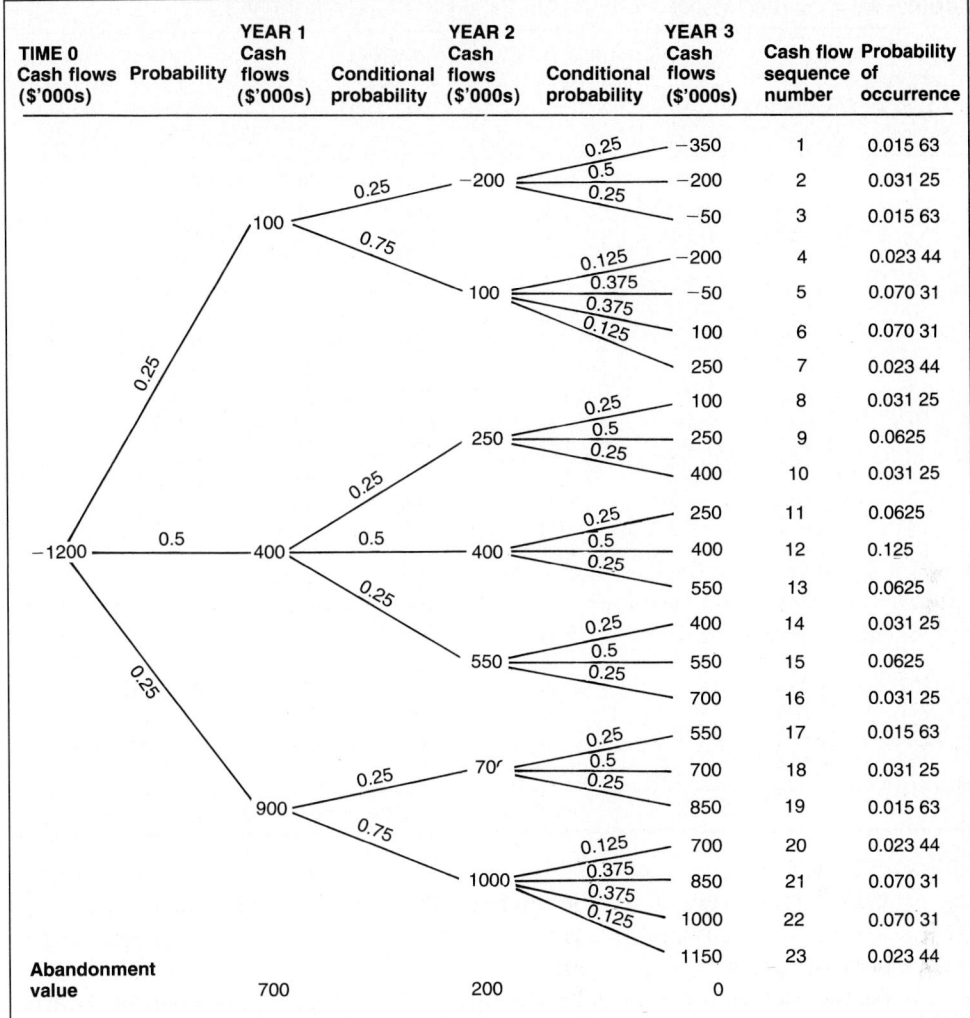

**Fig. 18.3** *Expected future cash flows for 'Simultalk' project*

5. An expected net present value for each sequence of cash flows is calculated by multiplying the probability of occurrence for each sequence by the net present value of that sequence. The sum of the expected values (−$121 700 in Table 18.15) is the expected net present value of the project. The project is therefore unacceptable.

**Evaluation including retirement alternatives (refer to Table 18.16)**
1. When management is evaluating a proposed project it must consider when the project should be retired. In this example the cash flows from retirement are $700 000 at the end of the first year, $200 000 at the end of the second year, and $0 at the end of the third year. If the cash inflow at the end of the first year from operating the project is $900 000, all the available cash flow sequences (17–23) result in a positive net present

**Table 18.15** *Expected net present value without retirement alternatives*

| Cash flow sequence number | Probability of occurrence | Cash flow ($'000s) at end of year: | | | | NPV ($'000s) | Expected value ($'000s) |
|---|---|---|---|---|---|---|---|
| | | 0 | 1 | 2 | 3 | | |
| 1  | 0.01563 | −1 200 | 100 | −200 | −350 | −1 537.3 | −24.0 |
| 2  | 0.03125 | −1 200 | 100 | −200 | −200 | −1 424.6 | −44.5 |
| 3  | 0.01563 | −1 200 | 100 | −200 | −50  | −1 311.9 | −20.5 |
| 4  | 0.02344 | −1 200 | 100 | 100  | −200 | −1 176.7 | −27.6 |
| 5  | 0.07031 | −1 200 | 100 | 100  | −50  | −1 064.0 | −74.8 |
| 6  | 0.07031 | −1 200 | 100 | 100  | 100  | −951.3   | −66.9 |
| 7  | 0.02344 | −1 200 | 100 | 100  | 250  | −836.6   | −19.7 |
| 8  | 0.03125 | −1 200 | 400 | 250  | 100  | −554.6   | −17.3 |
| 9  | 0.0625  | −1 200 | 400 | 250  | 250  | −441.9   | −27.6 |
| 10 | 0.03125 | −1 200 | 400 | 250  | 400  | −329.2   | −10.3 |
| 11 | 0.0625  | −1 200 | 400 | 400  | 250  | −318.0   | −19.9 |
| 12 | 0.125   | −1 200 | 400 | 400  | 400  | −205.3   | −25.7 |
| 13 | 0.0625  | −1 200 | 400 | 400  | 550  | −92.6    | −5.8  |
| 14 | 0.03125 | −1 200 | 400 | 550  | 400  | −81.3    | −2.5  |
| 15 | 0.0625  | −1 200 | 400 | 550  | 550  | 31.4     | 2.0   |
| 16 | 0.03125 | −1 200 | 400 | 550  | 550  | 144.1    | 4.5   |
| 17 | 0.01563 | −1 200 | 900 | 700  | 550  | 609.9    | 9.5   |
| 18 | 0.03125 | −1 200 | 900 | 700  | 700  | 722.6    | 22.6  |
| 19 | 0.01563 | −1 200 | 900 | 700  | 850  | 835.3    | 13.1  |
| 20 | 0.02344 | −1 200 | 900 | 1 000 | 700 | 970.5    | 22.7  |
| 21 | 0.07031 | −1 200 | 900 | 1 000 | 850 | 1 083.2  | 76.2  |
| 22 | 0.07031 | −1 200 | 900 | 1 000 | 1 000 | 1 195.9 | 84.1  |
| 23 | 0.02344 | −1 200 | 900 | 1 000 | 1 150 | 1 308.6 | 30.7  |
| | | | | | Expected net present value: | | −121.7 |

value. However, if at the end of the first year the cash inflow is $100 000, the available cash flow sequences (1–7) result in negative net present values.

2. At the end of the first year the cash inflows from retirement are substituted for those cash flow sequences (1–7) that result from a cash inflow of $100 000. In this case the cash inflows at the end of the first year will be $800 000 (that is, $100 000 from operations and $700 000 from retirement).

3. For each of the revised sequences of cash inflows, a net present value is calculated. The net present values and the probability of occurrence are shown in Table 18.16. It should be noted that the probability of sequences 1–7 occurring is the sum of the individual probabilities of any one of sequences 1–7 occurring.

4. An expected net present value for each sequence is calculated. The sum of the expected values is $38 100. The project is therefore acceptable.

From this example it can be seen that the project that was apparently unacceptable is potentially acceptable if the possibility of retirement is included in the evaluation. Including a retirement alternative in the valuation has resulted in the expected net present value increasing from −$121 700 to $38 100. This

**Table 18.16** Expected net present value with retirement alternative

| Cash flow sequence number | Probability of occurrence | Cash flow ($'000s) at end of year: | | | | NPV ($'000s) | Expected value ($'000s) |
|---|---|---|---|---|---|---|---|
| | | 0 | 1 | 2 | 3 | | |
| 1–7 | 0.25 | −1 200 | 800 | — | — | −472.7 | −118.2 |
| 8 | 0.03125 | −1 200 | 400 | 250 | 100 | −554.6 | −17.3 |
| 9 | 0.0625 | −1 200 | 400 | 250 | 250 | −441.9 | −27.6 |
| 10 | 0.03125 | −1 200 | 400 | 250 | 400 | −329.2 | −10.3 |
| 11 | 0.0625 | −1 200 | 400 | 400 | 250 | −318.0 | −19.9 |
| 12 | 0.125 | −1 200 | 400 | 400 | 400 | −205.3 | −25.7 |
| 13 | 0.0625 | −1 200 | 400 | 400 | 550 | −92.6 | −5.8 |
| 14 | 0.03125 | −1 200 | 400 | 550 | 400 | −81.3 | −2.5 |
| 15 | 0.0625 | −1 200 | 400 | 550 | 550 | 31.4 | 2.0 |
| 16 | 0.03125 | −1 200 | 400 | 550 | 700 | 144.1 | 4.5 |
| 17 | 0.01563 | −1 200 | 900 | 700 | 550 | 609.9 | 9.5 |
| 18 | 0.03125 | −1 200 | 900 | 700 | 700 | 722.6 | 22.6 |
| 19 | 0.01563 | −1 200 | 900 | 700 | 850 | 835.3 | 13.1 |
| 20 | 0.02344 | −1 200 | 900 | 1 000 | 700 | 970.5 | 22.7 |
| 21 | 0.07031 | −1 200 | 900 | 1 000 | 850 | 1 083.2 | 76.2 |
| 22 | 0.07031 | −1 200 | 900 | 1 000 | 1 000 | 1 195.9 | 84.1 |
| 23 | 0.02344 | −1 200 | 900 | 1 000 | 1 150 | 1 308.6 | 30.7 |
| | | | | | Expected net present value: | | 38.1 |

analysis has included a retirement alternative only at the end of the first year where the cash inflow is $100 000. A complete evaluation would require expected net present values to be calculated when a retirement alternative was included at the end of each year as a substitute for all cash flow sequences.

From this example it can be seen that the calculations would become tedious and complex if the number of periods is large, if the number of possible cash flows for each period is large, or if the retirement value is uncertain and is known only by a probability distribution. In such cases the evaluations can be made using a computer simulation model.

## 18.8 QUALITATIVE FACTORS AND THE SELECTION OF PROJECTS

After the quantitative analysis has been completed, management is faced with the problem of selecting the projects to be implemented. In Example 18.8, which involves the decision to replace old trucks with a new model, the net present value of Alternative 2 (replacement in 2 years' time) is slightly greater than that of Alternative 1 (immediate replacement). However, in practice it does not necessarily follow that Alternative 2 would automatically be selected. In making its selection, management should take into account not only the quantitative analysis but also any qualitative factors that may affect those projects.

Essentially, qualitative factors are those that management would like to include in the quantitative analysis but is unable to do because they are difficult, if not impossible, to measure in dollars. For this reason they are assessed separately, after the quantitative analysis of the alternatives has been completed.

It should not be assumed that qualitative factors are less important than the quantitative analysis. A qualitative factor may play a vital role in project selection. For instance, in Example 18.8, management may decide to replace the old trucks now because of qualitative factors such as the desire to maintain a modern image for the company and the improved satisfaction, and consequently the improved productivity, of the drivers, resulting from the comfort of the new trucks.

Some further examples of qualitative factors that may affect management's decisions about projects are:
1. The introduction of labour-saving machinery may be deferred (perhaps indefinitely) because of union opposition, even though on the basis of the quantitative analysis the proposal to introduce the machinery has a net present value greater than zero.
2. Two mutually exclusive investments may have net present values which are almost equal, but one requires much more management supervision, or the use of some other scarce human resource.[12] The use of this scarce resource obviously involves an opportunity cost which is not reflected in the wages paid by the company to its employees. While management may be aware of such an opportunity cost, it is difficult to place a value on this qualitative factor for inclusion in the quantitative analysis. In such cases, therefore, rather than attempting to measure the opportunity cost of using the scarce human resources, management is more likely simply to select the proposal that it believes will use fewer of those resources, other things being equal.

It is essential that such qualitative factors be considered before selecting a project. However, the recognition of qualitative factors is not a general prescription for ignoring or reducing the importance of the quantitative analysis. As all factors cannot be incorporated into the quantitative analysis, a comparison of alternative investment proposals is incomplete without an assessment of the possible effects of the qualitative factors. Indeed, the influence of qualitative factors may be sufficiently important to cause management to select proposals with lower calculated net present values.

## 18.9 PROJECT SELECTION WITH RESOURCE CONSTRAINTS

So far it has been assumed that management is willing and able to accept all independent investment projects that have a net present value greater than zero and, if mutually exclusive projects are being compared, those projects with the highest net present value greater than zero. However, sometimes a company's managers believe that they are prevented from undertaking all acceptable projects because of a 'shortage' of funds. **Capital rationing** is the term used to describe

---

[12] See F. K. Wright, 'Project Evaluation and the Managerial Limit', *Journal of Business*, April 1964, pp. 179–85.

such a situation. It may be classified further into internal (or 'soft') capital rationing and external (or 'hard') capital rationing.

Internal capital rationing occurs when management limits the amount that can be invested in new projects during some specified time period. There are several reasons why management may impose a limit on capital expenditure. One is that management is conservative and has a policy of financing all projects from internally generated cash because it is unwilling to borrow. Similarly management may be unwilling to issue more shares because of possible effects on the control of the company. Alternatively, imposing capital expenditure limits can be a way of maintaining financial control. For example, in a large company, managers may attempt to expand their divisions by proposing many new projects, some of which only *appear* to be profitable because the cash flow forecasts are very optimistic. To avoid this problem, top management may delegate authority for capital expenditure decisions to divisional managers, but retain overall control by giving each division a capital expenditure limit. The aim is to force each divisional manager to decide which of the possible projects really should be adopted.

Another possibility is that it may be desirable to limit the rate at which a company expands because of the organisational difficulties inherent in hiring and training many additional staff. Management may be concerned that rapid expansion will lead to inefficiency and higher costs. To avoid these problems it may limit the number of new projects that are implemented. In this case a capital expenditure limit is used to impose the desired restriction, but it is not *capital* that is the scarce resource. Rather, the scarce resource is management time, and the real concern is that this constraint may result in supervision problems.

External capital rationing occurs when the capital market is unwilling to supply the funds necessary to finance the projects that a company's management wishes to undertake. In this case the company has projects that offer positive net present values but cannot raise, at a cost that management considers acceptable, the funds necessary to finance them. This situation can occur if financial intermediaries are subject to controls such as limits on the volume or growth rate of their lending. However, it is difficult to see why it should occur in deregulated financial markets. Any company that has a project expected to be profitable should be able to obtain the necessary capital, no matter how small its capital budget. For example, suppose that a small company which plans to invest no more than, say, $50 000 in the current year, discovers an inexpensive way of extracting gold from the oceans. Raising capital to build the extraction plant should not be a problem!

Empirical evidence suggests that capital rationing is more likely to result from expenditure limits imposed by management of its own volition than from an unwillingness of the capital market to supply funds.[13] If management's decisions result in the rejection of projects with positive net present values, then management is adopting a policy inconsistent with the objective of maximising the market value of the company's shares. If capital rationing is essentially an

---

13 R. J. Pike, 'The Capital Budgeting Behaviour and Corporate Characteristics of Capital-constrained Firms', *Journal of Business Finance and Accounting*, Winter 1983, pp. 663–7.

internal 'problem', it might appear that the solution should be simple. Management should remove the constraints so that all positive net present value projects can be implemented. In some cases, this does occur. For example, in cases where capital expenditure limits are used to maintain financial control, the limits are likely to be flexible, and additional funds will be provided if a profitable investment opportunity arises unexpectedly.

However, as discussed above, capital expenditure limits may be imposed for valid reasons that do not reflect a shortage of capital. Rather, the real constraint may be a shortage of other resources such as management time. Therefore, capital rationing can be a real phenomenon and managers may need to choose the set of projects that maximises net present value, subject to a resource constraint. On the other hand, if external capital rationing exists, attempts to maximise net present value, subject to a capital expenditure limit, involve an inherent contradiction. The problem is that a project's net present value is calculated using an opportunity cost of capital, but the existence of an external limit on the availability of capital implies that once the limit is reached, the cost of capital is infinite.[14] In the following discussion, therefore, it will be assumed that capital rationing exists only because of internally imposed constraints. A manager attempting to 'maximise' the market value of the company's shares within these self-imposed constraints should calculate the net present value of each project by discounting its cash flows at the cost of capital, and then choose the combination of projects that maximises net present value.

### Example 18.18

Assume that a company is considering the proposals listed in Table 18.17. Assume that it has a capital expenditure limit of $600 000, all projects are independent, the projects are not divisible, and it is not envisaged that an expenditure limit will exist in future years.

**Table 18.17** *Ranking of projects under capital rationing*

| Project | Initial cash outlay $ | Net present value $ |
|---|---|---|
| A | 200 000 | 28 000 |
| B | 200 000 | 20 000 |
| C | 200 000 | 15 000 |
| D | 200 000 | 35 000 |
| E | 400 000 | 45 000 |
| F | 400 000 | 22 000 |

Management must find the combination of projects that maximises net present value, subject to the expenditure limit of $600 000. In this example, examination of all possible outcomes shows that the largest net present value will be achieved

---

[14] For a discussion of the conditions under which capital rationing invalidates the NPV rule, see H. M. Weingartner, 'Capital Rationing: *n* Authors in Search of a Plot', *Journal of Finance*, December 1977, pp. 1403–31.

by the combination of Projects D, A and B. This combination results in a net present value of $83 000, compared with the next best alternative—a combination of Projects D and E, resulting in a net present value of $80 000. As a result of the expenditure limit, even though Projects C, E and F have positive net present values, the company is unable to implement them this year. Without the expenditure limit, all the projects shown in Table 18.17 could have been accepted and the total net present value would have been $165 000 instead of $83 000.

In reality, ranking of investment projects where there is capital rationing is much more complex because of the large number of investment alternatives generally available to a company. To find solutions to such problems, mathematical programming models have been developed.[15]

We now return to the earlier point that the imposition of capital rationing by management can prevent the maximisation of shareholders' wealth. Capital rationing is not in the shareholders' best interests if projects with positive net present values are rejected. In Example 18.18, Projects C, E and F, with positive net present values totalling $82 000, are rejected because of a capital constraint. Unless the company faces a real constraint, such as a shortage of personnel, or rapid expansion involves excessive risk, management should raise the funds necessary to finance these projects by reducing dividends, borrowing, issuing more shares, or some combination of these actions.

## SELECTED REFERENCES

Bierman, H. Jr & Smidt, S., *The Capital Budgeting Decision: Economic Analysis of Investment Projects*, 8th edn, Macmillan Company, New York, 1993.

Finn, F. J., 'Capital Rationing and Market Discount Rates: Some Common Fallacies', *Australian Journal of Management*, October 1976, pp. 37–49.

Hertz, D. B. & Thomas, H., *Risk Analysis and its Applications*, John Wiley & Sons, New York, 1983.

Hespos, R. F. & Strassman, P. A., 'Stochastic Decision Trees for the Analysis of Investment Decisions', *Management Science*, August 1965, pp. 244–59.

Lewellen, W. G. & Long, M. S., 'Simulation vs Single-value Estimates in Capital Expenditure Analysis', *Decision Sciences*, October 1972, pp. 19–33.

Magee, J., 'How to Use Decision Trees in Capital Investment', *Harvard Business Review*, September–October 1964, pp. 79–96.

Officer, R. R., 'The Cost of Capital of a Company Under an Imputation Tax System', *Accounting and Finance*, May 1994, pp. 1–17.

Rappaport, A. & Taggart, R. A., 'Evaluation of Capital Expenditure Under Inflation', *Financial Management*, Spring 1982. pp. 5–13.

Robichek, A. A. & Myers, S. C., 'Conceptual Problems in the Use of Risk-adjusted Discount Rates', *Journal of Finance*, December 1966, pp. 727–30.

Weingartner, H. M., 'Capital Rationing: n Authors in Search of a Plot', *Journal of Finance*, December 1977, pp. 1403–31.

Wright, F. K., 'Project Evaluation and the Managerial Limit', *Journal of Business*, April 1964, pp. 179–85.

---

[15] Detailed discussion of these models is beyond the scope of this book. However, an excellent discussion may be found in H. M. Weingartner, *Mathematical Programming and the Analysis of Capital Budgeting Problems*, Prentice-Hall, Englewood Cliffs, New Jersey, 1963; G. D. Quirin, *The Capital Expenditure Decision*, R. D. Irwin, Homewood, Illinois, 1967, pp. 185–97; and J. C. T. Mao, *Quantitative Analysis of Financial Decisions*, Macmillan, London, 1969, pp. 24–57.

## QUESTIONS

1. A property development company plans to demolish the building on a site that it already owns, and then build a convenience store. Which of the following items should be included as incremental cash flows when the project is evaluated?
   (a) The market value of the property.
   (b) The cost of demolishing the old building.
   (c) The cost of new water and electric power connections installed 3 months ago.
   (d) A portion of the cost of leasing cars used by the company's executives.
   (e) Depreciation of the new building.
   (f) Company tax saved due to depreciation of fittings in the new store.
   (g) Money that has already been spent on architectural concept plans for the new building.

2. Leaving aside the effect of taxes, which of the following items should be considered in the initial outlay on a new machine for project evaluation purposes? Give reasons.
   (a) The disposal value of the old machine, which is $6000.
   (b) The written down value of the old machine, which is $4000.
   (c) The book gain on the sale of the old machine.
   (d) The $400 cost of installing the new machine.
   (e) Additional investment of $10 000 in current assets that will be required.
   (f) Costs of $3000 recently incurred in assessing the suitability of the new machine.

3. *The trouble with discounted cash flow techniques is that they ignore depreciation.* Do you agree? Why?

4. *It doesn't matter whether the straight-line method or reducing-balance method of depreciation is used, since the company's total tax bill over the life of the project is the same.* Comment.

5. The Four and Six Stores Pty Ltd is considering locating another outlet in an eastern suburb of Melbourne. Estimates of sales and operating expenses have been made and an estimated profit and loss statement for the new store drawn up. The profit and loss statement for Year 1 is thought to be representative of each of the 10 years of the expected life of the Four and Six Store. The initial outlay to construct the store is $400 000, while the outlay necessary to stock the store is $20 000.

   The estimated profit and loss statement for the new store for Year 1 is shown in the table on page 591.
   (a) Estimate the project's annual cash flow, assuming that the classical tax system applies.
   (b) Estimate the annual cash flow that would be used to value the project if the textbook WACC is used under the imputation tax system. Assume that all profits are paid out as franked dividends.

| Item | $ | $ |
|---|---|---|
| Revenue | 400 000 | |
| less sales returns, discounts | 40 000 | |
| Net revenue | | 360 000 |
| Operating expenses: | | |
|    Cost of goods sold | 160 000 | |
|    Administration costs | 60 000 | |
|    Depreciation | 36 000 | |
|    Interest | 24 000 | 280 000 |
| Net profit before tax | | 80 000 |
| Tax (33% tax rate) | | 26 400 |
| Net profit after tax | | 53 600 |

6. All-Night Coffee Shops Ltd is a successful profitable company operating several dozen coffee shops throughout the metropolitan area of Melberra. However, the shop in the suburb of Burnaby has not been well patronised, generating a before-tax net cash flow of only $5000 in the past year. The Burnaby shop began trading 2 years ago in premises leased from CBD Ltd. The lease is about to expire and All-Night will not renew it. A competitor, Brazil Coffee Shops Ltd, has offered to buy the fixtures and fittings and the equipment in the Burnaby shop for $40 000. All-Night has agreed to this figure, even though it is $30 000 less than the cost of the fixtures and fittings and the equipment 2 years ago. Assume that:
    (a) for tax purposes the fixtures and fittings and the equipment were depreciated on a straight-line basis at 10 per cent per annum;
    (b) the company tax rate is 39 per cent.
    What is the after-tax net cash flow (for Year 2) attributable to All-Night's Burnaby shop? (Note any assumptions you find it necessary to make, but do not adjust the cash flows for the imputation tax system.)
7. Outline two methods of solving project evaluation problems where the projects under consideration do not have common terminal dates.
8. Define the term 'mutually exclusive projects' and provide a simple example. Outline and justify the basic NPV rule applicable to them. How should this rule be modified when such projects have unequal lives?
9. How should the optimum life of a project be determined?
10. The management of the Teeny Toy Company is considering purchasing a new machine and it has gathered the following data:
    (a) The cash needed to purchase the new machine is $64 000.
    (b) The residual value and annual cash operating expenses for the next 5 years are estimated to be:

| Year | Residual value at end of year ($) | Annual cash operating expenses ($) |
|---|---|---|
| 1 | 50 000 | 11 000 |
| 2 | 40 000 | 13 000 |
| 3 | 30 000 | 18 000 |
| 4 | 23 000 | 24 000 |
| 5 | 3 500 | 28 000 |

(c) No changes in residual values or annual cash operating expenses are expected.
(d) The cost of capital is 15 per cent per annum.
(e) The effects of company income tax may be ignored.

What is the optimum replacement policy for this machine?

11. The furniture division of Playfurn Ltd, a profitable, diversified company, purchased a machine 5 years ago for $7500. When it was purchased the machine had an expected useful life of 15 years and an estimated value of zero at the end of its life. The machine, which is being depreciated on a straight-line basis, currently has a written down value of $5000 and a current market value of $1000. The division manager reports that he can buy a new machine for $10 000 (including installation) which, over its 10-year life, will result in an expansion of sales from $10 000 to $11 000 per annum. In addition, it is estimated that the new machine will reduce annual operating costs from $7000 to $5000.

If the tax rate is 39 cents in the dollar, the classical tax system applies, and the after-tax cost of capital is 10 per cent per annum, should Playfurn buy the new machine?

12. *It doesn't matter whether the straight-line or reducing-balance method of depreciation is used, since the company's total tax bill over the life of the project is the same.* Discuss the validity (or otherwise) of this statement in the context of the following example:

| | |
|---|---|
| Asset cost (now) | $1000 |
| Asset life | 5 years |
| Residual value (in 5 years) | $470 |
| Annual net cash inflow before tax | $600 |
| Straight-line depreciation rate (per annum) | 10% |
| Reducing-balance depreciation rate (per annum) | 15% |
| Company income tax rate | 39% |
| After-tax cost of capital | 10% p.a. |

13. A company must choose between two machines. Machine A costs $50 000 and the annual operating expenses (excluding depreciation) are estimated to be $20 000, while Machine B costs $75 000 and has estimated annual operating expenses (excluding depreciation) of $15 000. Both machines have a 10-year life, zero residual value, and are depreciated on a straight-line basis.
   (a) The company has a tax rate of 39 cents in the dollar and an after-tax cost of capital of 10 per cent per annum. The classical tax system applies. Which machine should it purchase?
   (b) Rework the problem for a 7 per cent cost of capital.

14. A company is considering the purchase of equipment costing $84 000 which will permit it to reduce its existing labour costs by $20 000 a year for 12 years. The company estimates that it will have to spend $2000 every 2 years overhauling the equipment. The equipment may be depreciated for tax purposes by the straight-line method, over a 12-year period. The company tax rate is 39 cents in the dollar, the classical tax system applies, and the after-tax cost of capital is 10 per cent per annum. Assuming all cash flows, including company tax payments, are made at the end of each year, should the company purchase the equipment?

15. The Two-Bit Mining Company has constructed a town at Big Bore, near the site of a rich mineral discovery in a remote part of Australia. The

town will be abandoned when mining operations cease after an estimated 10-year period. The following estimates of investment costs, sales, and operating expenses relate to a project to supply Big Bore with meat and agricultural produce over the 10-year period by developing nearby land.
(a) Investment in land is $1 million, farm buildings $200 000, and farm equipment $400 000. The land is expected to have a realisable value of $500 000 in 10 years' time. The buildings have an estimated useful life of 20 years, at which time their residual value would be zero, and they are to be depreciated on a straight-line basis for tax purposes based on this life. The residual value of the buildings after ten years is expected to be $50 000. The farm equipment has an estimated life of 10 years and a zero residual value. The equipment is to be depreciated on a straight-line basis.
(b) Investment of $250 000 in current assets which will be recovered at the termination of the venture.
(c) Annual cash sales are estimated to be $3 million.
(d) Annual cash operating costs are estimated to be $2.2 million.
(e) Assume tax is paid one year after the year of income.
Is the project profitable, given that the cost of capital after tax is 10 per cent per annum, and that the classical tax system applies, with a company tax rate of 39 cents in the dollar?

16. The management of ABC Transport Ltd, which is engaged in interstate transport, is considering the replacement of its present fleet of ten CB semi-trailers with six AZ Flexivans. A survey has revealed the following estimates of costs, etc. *per vehicle*:

| CB Semi-trailers | Estimates | AZ Flexivans | Estimates |
| --- | --- | --- | --- |
| Remaining life | 3 years | Estimated life | 5 years |
| Residual value: | | | |
| At the present time | $ 5 000 | Cost | $70 000 |
| In 3 years' time | $ 1 000 | Annual net cash flows | $40 000 |
| | | Residual value after 5 years' | |
| Annual net cash flows | $30 000 | operation | $ 5 000 |

Other information is as follows:
(a) Net cash flows are to be regarded as received at the end of each year.
(b) The cost of capital is 10 per cent per annum.
(c) The effects of company income tax may be ignored.
Should management:
(a) retain the CB semi-trailers for 3 years and then replace them with AZ Flexivans? or
(b) replace the CB semi-trailers with the AZ Flexivans now?

17. The management of Harbour Ferries Ltd is considering the replacement of its existing fleet of six steam ferries with three hydrofoils. The following estimates of costs, etc. for each vessel have been calculated:

| Steam ferries | Estimates | Hydrofoils | Estimates |
|---|---|---|---|
| Estimated remaining life | 5 years | Cost | $500 000 |
| Estimated scrap value: | | Estimated life | 10 years |
|   Now | $ 50 000 | Estimated scrap value: | |
|   In 5 years' time | $ 10 000 |   In 5 years' time | $200 000 |
| | |   In 10 years' time | $100 000 |
| Annual net cash flows | $100 000 | Annual net cash flows | $200 000 |

Management is also aware of the development of hovercraft, which the manufacturer estimates will be available in 5 years' time. The following estimates of costs, etc. per hovercraft have been provided by the manufacturer.

| Hovercraft | Estimates |
|---|---|
| Cost | $600 000 |
| Estimated life | 15 years |
| Estimated disposal value: | |
|   After 5 years' operation | $200 000 |
|   After 15 years' operation | $ 50 000 |
| Annual net cash flows | $250 000 |

It is considered that two of the new hovercraft will be adequate to carry the estimated number of passengers.

Other information is as follows:
(i) Management cannot foresee any further developments beyond the hovercraft.
(ii) The annual net cash flows are received at the end of each year.
(iii) The company's after-tax cost of capital is 10 per cent per annum.
(iv) The company's tax rate is 39 cents in the dollar and the classical tax system applies.
(v) The steam ferries are assumed to be fully depreciated.
(vi) Straight-line depreciation may be assumed.

You are required to advise management whether it should:
(a) replace the steam ferries with hydrofoils now, and replace the latter with hovercraft in 5 years' time;
(b) retain the steam ferries for 5 years, and then replace them with hovercraft;
(c) replace the steam ferries with hydrofoils now, and replace the latter with hovercraft in 10 years' time.

Other alternatives are not to be considered.

18. A company is considering the installation of a new machine at a cost of $60 000 to replace a machine purchased 7 years ago for $100 000. The disposal value of the old machine is $15 000 and the accumulated depreciation, which has been allowed for tax purposes, is $70 000. Both machines will have similar outputs and will produce work of identical quality.

The estimated yearly costs of operating each machine are as follows:

|  | Old machine ($) | New machine ($) |
|---|---|---|
| Wages | 15 000 | 5 000 |
| Depreciation | 10 000 | 20 000 |
| Supplies, repairs, power | 5 000 | 3 000 |
| Insurance and miscellaneous | 2 000 | 3 000 |
|  | 32 000 | 31 000 |

Both machines have an estimated remaining life of 3 years, at which time both machines will have an estimated disposal value of $5000. Assume that:
(a) the after-tax cost of capital is 10 per cent per annum;
(b) the operating costs of the old machine and the new machine are incurred at the end of each year;
(c) the company income tax rate is 39 cents in the dollar and the classical tax system applies.
Should the company purchase the new machine, or continue to operate the old one?

19. The management of New World Airlines is considering the replacement of its present fleet of *ten* piston engine planes with *five* turboprops. A survey has revealed the following estimates of costs, etc. per plane:

| Piston engine | Estimates | Turboprop | Estimates |
|---|---|---|---|
| Remaining life | 5 years | Life | 5 years |
| Residual value: |  | Cost | $3 430 000 |
|   At present time | $10 000 | Annual net cash flows | $1 000 000 |
|   In 2 years' time | $5 000 | Residual value: |  |
|   In 5 years' time | nil |   After 2 years' operation | 30% of purchase price |
|  |  |   After 5 years' operation | 5% of purchase price |
| Annual net cash flows | $100 000 |  |  |

(a) Should replacement be undertaken now, or in 5 years' time?
Immediately after the decision has been reached, management is informed of a superjet which will became available in 2 years' time. The estimates for the new plane are:

| Superjet | Estimates |
|---|---|
| Cost | $4 500 000 |
| Annual net cash inflows | $1 200 000 |
| Life | 5 years |
| Residual value after 5 years' operation | 3% of purchase price |

It is considered that *four* of the new superjets will be adequate to cover the estimated passenger load.

Other information is as follows:
(i) Management cannot foresee any further developments beyond the superjet.
(ii) Annual net cash flows are assumed to be received at the end of each year.
(iii) The cost of capital is 10 per cent per annum.

(b) Should management:
(i) retain the piston engine planes for 5 years and replace them with superjets?
(ii) replace them immediately with turboprops, operate them for 5 years, and then replace them with superjets?
(iii) Replace them now with turboprops, operate them for 2 years, and then replace them with superjets?
(iv) Retain the piston engine planes for 2 years and then replace them with superjets?

Other replacement dates are not to be considered.

20. A.B. Pty Ltd is currently operating a suburban taxi-truck business. It is considering the replacement of a 1.5 tonne vehicle with a 2 tonne vehicle. Details of the respective vehicles are as follows:

| 1.5 tonne vehicle | Estimates | 2 tonne vehicle | Estimates |
|---|---|---|---|
| Remaining life | 4 years | Estimated life | 7 years |
| Residual value: | | Cost | $15 000 |
|   Now | $4000 | Residual value after 7 years' | |
|   In four years | $ 0 |   operation | $1 000 |
| Written down value | | Depreciation (allowable for | |
|   (for tax purposes) | $5000 |   tax purposes) | $2 000 p.a. |
| Depreciation (for tax | | Net cash flow | |
|   purposes | $1000 p.a. |   (before taxation) | $10 000 p.a. |
| Net cash flow (before | $6000 p.a. | | |
|   taxation) | | | |

Other information is as follows:
(i) Net cash flows are to be regarded as received at the end of each year.
(ii) The after-tax cost of capital is 10 per cent per annum.
(iii) The company income tax rate is 39 cents in the dollar and the classical tax system applies.

Management is considering the following alternatives:
(a) Replace the 1.5 tonne vehicle with the 2 tonne vehicle now.
(b) Replace the 1.5 tonne vehicle with the 2 tonne vehicle in 4 years' time.

All other alternatives may be ignored.

Advise management as to which alternative it should adopt, and justify your analysis.

21. Explain the theoretical relationship between **nominal** and **real** discount rates. Outline its application to project evaluation in the context of an inflationary economy.

22. Distinguish between **internal** and **external** capital rationing. Give examples of each.

23. (a) Outline possible reasons for the imposition by management of capital rationing. Does the imposition of internal capital rationing imply that management is failing to maximise shareholders' wealth?

    (b) If a company is subject to capital rationing, does this make any difference to project evaluation using the net present value method? Give reasons.

24. Pulp and Paper Ltd has just planted pine trees at a cost of $12 000 per hectare on 500 hectares of land, which it purchased for $400 000. The trees are expected to grow rapidly and the company's estimates of the net future value of the cut timber are:

| Time of harvest<br>End of year: | Net future value<br>($ per hectare) |
|---|---|
| 2 | 17 320 |
| 3 | 20 000 |
| 4 | 22 360 |
| 5 | 24 495 |
| 6 | 26 450 |

The cost of capital is 10 per cent per annum and taxes can be ignored.

(a) Calculate the optimum time to harvest the crop of trees. Assume that the value of the cleared land increases at a rate of 10 per cent per annum.

(b) Estimate the net present value of the project, assuming sale of the land after the trees are harvested. Note any assumptions you make.

25. Hermes Pty Ltd operates a messenger/courier service. A new van is required to meet the increased demand for the company's services. The choice has been narrowed down to three vans A, B and C, each costing $10 000. Net cash flow estimates are as follows:

| | Net cash flow estimates ($) | | |
|---|---|---|---|
| Year | Van A | Van B | Van C |
| 1 | 4600 | 4800 | 4700 |
| 2 | 5000 | 4000 | 4800 |
| 3 | 5000 | 4000 | 4800 |
| 4 | 5800 | 5200 | 5500 |
| 5 | 0 | 4200 | 0 |
| Cost of capital<br>NPV | 20%<br>$3079 | 20%<br>$3288 | 20%<br>$2680 |

By discounting each net cash flow, show that the net present value of Van A has been calculated properly. Which van should be purchased? Give reasons.

26. A videotape manufacturer buys empty cassettes at $55 per hundred and currently uses 2 million cassettes per year. The plant manager believes that it may be cheaper to **make** the cassettes rather than buy them. Direct production costs (labour, materials, fuel) are estimated at 25 cents per cassette. The equipment needed would cost $300 000 and can be depreciated for tax purposes at 20 per cent straight-line. The equipment should last for 15 years, provided it is overhauled every 5 years at a cost of $25 000 each time. The operation will require additional current assets of $40 000. The company tax rate is 39 per cent, the classical tax system applies, and the cost of capital is 12 per cent after tax. Evaluate the manufacturing proposal.

27. A company is considering the replacement of an old machine called 'OLD' with a new machine called 'NEW'. OLD was purchased one year ago for $12 500. Additional information relating to these machines (cash flows are in nominal terms) is as follows:

| | | Estimates | |
| Item | OLD | NEW |
| --- | --- | --- |
| Market value (now) | $7000 | $5000 |
| Depreciation rate per annum (for tax purposes) | 20% (straight-line) | 30% (reducing balance) |
| Service life (when purchased) | 6 years | 5 years |
| Residual value in 5 years' time | $0 | $1000 |
| Cash operating receipts (before tax) | — | $500 per annum in excess of OLD |
| Company income tax rate | 39% | |
| Cost of capital (real, after tax) | 10% per annum | |
| Anticipated inflation rate | 10% per annum | |

(a) Set out the incremental net cash flows (after tax) necessary to evaluate the replacement decision.
(b) Calculate the net present value of replacement, and make the appropriate decision.

28. The Bertie Hamilton Fishing Company (BHF) purchased a trawler 6 years ago for $420 000. It is being depreciated over its 10-year useful life at 10 per cent straight-line for tax purposes. If BHF were to retain this boat it is anticipated that ultrasonic detection equipment would have to be installed in the second-last year of its life at a cost of $40 000. However, the Commercial Trawler Company (CT) has recently launched a faster, computer-assisted trawler that BHF is considering as a replacement. This trawler will cost $600 000 but will need immediate refitting to suit the purchaser's specifications at an additional cost of $15 000. It has an expected useful life of 12 years and may be depreciated by the reducing-balance method at a 20 per cent rate for tax purposes.

If purchased, the new trawler is likely to increase cash operating costs by $10 per tonne of fish which currently sell for $30 per tonne. However, future catches are likely to increase significantly by 6000 tonnes in the first year, and then at a rate of 1000 tonnes per annum, stabilising at 12 000 tonnes from Year 7 onward. Owing to intensive usage, it is expected that towards the end of the fifth year the new trawler will require a minor engine overhaul at a cost of $30 000. Part of the purchase agreement also involves a maintenance contract with CT covering the nets and trawling apparatus, which will cost BHF $12 000, payable at the end of every fourth year.

Any replacements/additions may be written off for tax purposes in the year after acquisition. As a competitive strategy, CT offers an optional financing package for up to 80 per cent of the invoice price on any boat. The rate of interest on this amount is 12 per cent per annum, with the first payment deferred one year. If the financing package is adopted, BHF must undertake to sell the trawler back to CT in 12 years' time for $50 000. BHF estimates that the current second-hand price of its present trawler is only $140 000. It is estimated that the new trawler can be sold for $100 000 at the end of its useful life.

The company income tax rate of 39 per cent is applicable to both capital gains and income. The nominal after-tax cost of capital is 30 per cent.

(a) Estimate the net cash flow (NCF) after tax at the beginning of Year 1.
(b) Estimate the NCF after tax in Year 4.
(c) Management believes that relative to today's prices, the average inflation rate is expected to be 8 per cent per annum over the next 12 years. What is the Year 3 inflation-adjusted NCF after tax?
(d) Estimate the appropriate discount rate to perform an NPV analysis in real terms.

29. *Sensitivity analysis may be used to identify the variables that are most important for a project's success. Discuss.*

30. The management of Ride Ltd is considering the possibility of manufacturing a new motorised golf buggy. The initial outlay for the new plant to manufacture the vehicle is $1 million. The following estimates for the project have been provided by the staff of Ride Ltd:

| Item | Pessimistic | Estimates Most likely | Optimistic |
| --- | --- | --- | --- |
| Sales (units) | 3 000 | 3 500 | 4 000 |
| Selling price ($) | 750 | 800 | 850 |
| Fixed operating costs per annum ($) | 100 000 | 90 000 | 80 000 |
| Variable operating costs per annum per unit of sales ($) | $25 | $24 | $23 |
| Life of the plant (years) | 4 | 5 | 6 |

Assuming a cost of capital of 10 per cent, conduct a sensitivity analysis. What are the major uncertainties if the project is undertaken?

31. Outline the weaknesses of sensitivity analysis.

32. *Simulation is only useful for large-scale investment projects.* Discuss.
33. *Simulation is extremely valuable because it is useful in refining cash flow forecasts and it avoids the need to estimate a project's cost of capital.* Do you agree with these claims? Give reasons for your answer.
34. The project analysis techniques discussed in this chapter focus on the total risk of a project. However, according to the CAPM, it is only systematic risk that is important. Explain this apparent inconsistency.
35. XYZ Ltd is considering producing a new product. It expects that the product will have a life of 10 years, by which time the market for the product will be saturated and the assets necessary to produce it will be sold. The company is uncertain as to whether the product should be manufactured on a large scale in a large plant, or on a small scale in a small plant. If the company chooses a small plant it would consider expanding the plant after 3 years.

    The company estimates that there is a 50 per cent probability that a high level of demand will be attained over the 10 years during which the product will be marketed, a 25 per cent probability that demand will be high during the first 3 years and then drop to a low level over the succeeding 7 years, and a 25 per cent probability that a low level of demand will persist over the entire 10 years.

    The following table indicates the expected annual net cash flows and residual values associated with each scale of production and level of demand:

    | Possibilities | Annual net cash flow ($) | Residual value ($) |
    | --- | --- | --- |
    | Large plant, high demand | 500 000 | 500 000 |
    | Large plant, low demand | 150 000 | 200 000 |
    | Small plant, high demand | 200 000 | 200 000 |
    | Small plant, low demand | 150 000 | 100 000 |
    | Expanded plant, high demand | 300 000 | 400 000 |
    | Expanded plant, low demand | 100 000 | 150 000 |

    The initial cost associated with the construction of a large plant is $2 million, and that associated with a small plant is $1 million. The expected cost of expanding from a small plant to a large plant after 3 years is $1 million. The company's cost of capital of 12 per cent per annum is relevant for all alternatives.
    (a) Which policy should the company pursue?
    (b) Is it likely that the same discount rate will be appropriate for all alternatives? Give reasons.
36. Jupiter Ltd is considering the purchase of a specialised drilling machine from Equipment Ltd. At present Equipment Ltd produces the machine in two sizes, small and large. The small machine costs $680 000 and the large machine costs $1 million. Jupiter Ltd has decided that it must purchase one or other of these two machines now for use in its sprocket-making division. The capacity of the large machine is 410 sprockets per annum; for the small machine the capacity is 270 sprockets per annum. However,

it is known that in 1 year's time, Equipment Ltd will release an upgrading system, expected to cost $325 000, which will enable owners of small drilling machines to increase their capacity to 375 sprockets per annum. The upgrading facility can be purchased at the start of the second or the third year. Thereafter it will be withdrawn from the market. However, there is no known way of converting a large machine either to a small machine or to a small machine which has been upgraded.

Annual costs of running the machines are as follows:

| Machine | Annual running costs ($) | |
|---|---|---|
| | Fixed | Variable |
| Large | 160 000 | 600/sprocket |
| Small (upgraded) | 45 000 | 920/sprocket |
| Small | 20 000 | 1000/sprocket |

Each year, sprockets are sold to only one or two buyers. For this reason the demand for sprockets will, in each year, be either high (400 sprockets) or low (250 sprockets). The selling price of a sprocket is $2000. The life of the project (whether or not the small machine, if purchased, is upgraded) is 8 years. Management has estimated probabilities for future demand in Years 1, 2, and 3 to 8 (inclusive), as follows:

| Sequence | | | Probabilities | | |
|---|---|---|---|---|---|
| H | H | H | 0.6 | 0.7 | 0.8 |
| H | H | L | 0.6 | 0.7 | 0.2 |
| H | L | H | 0.6 | 0.3 | 0.5 |
| H | L | L | 0.6 | 0.3 | 0.5 |
| L | H | H | 0.4 | 0.4 | 0.65 |
| L | H | L | 0.4 | 0.4 | 0.35 |
| L | L | H | 0.4 | 0.6 | 0.2 |
| L | L | L | 0.4 | 0.6 | 0.8 |

For example, consider the sequence HLH. This refers to high demand in the first year, followed by low demand in the second year, and then high demand in Years 3 to 8 (inclusive). The probability of high demand in the first year is 0.6; given this occurrence, the probability of low demand in the second year is 0.3; finally, given these outcomes for the first 2 years, the probability of high demand in the remaining years is 0.5. Each year, output is adjusted so that it equals demand, or capacity, whichever is the lower. Sprockets disintegrate rapidly, so storage is not feasible.

All cash flows occur at year end. Jupiter has a cost of capital of 15 per cent per annum. Ignore the possibility of abandonment.

(a) Determine the net cash flows for each combination of machine and demand level.

(b) Set up a decision tree showing the relevant probabilities, cash flows, and decision points.
(c) Determine the optimum decision for each decision point.
(d) Calculate the NPV of the project and state which machine should be bought.

37. Distinguish between replacement decisions and retirement decisions.

CHAPTER 19

# LEASING AND EQUIPMENT FINANCE

## 19.1 INTRODUCTION

Leasing is distinguished from most other forms of finance by the fact that the financier (**the lessor**) is the legal owner of the leased asset. The asset user (**the lessee**) obtains the right to use the asset in return for periodic payments (lease rentals) to the lessor. In other words, leasing allows a lessee to obtain the *use* of an asset, without also obtaining *ownership* of the asset.

The practice of leasing is by no means new; individuals have been leasing assets such as telephones and motor vehicles for many years. Businesses have also leased real estate such as offices and shops for many years. More recently, the range of assets that can be leased has broadened considerably and is now virtually unlimited. Many motor vehicles, aircraft, computers, photocopiers, items of production equipment, and even whole factories, are leased. Unusual assets to be leased include oil rigs, sewage treatment plants, and communications satellites.[1]

Leases that involve assets other than real estate are one type of equipment finance. The Australian Equipment Lessors Association estimated that in 1993, 24 per cent of all new equipment acquired by Australian businesses was leased. Another important type of equipment finance is commercial hire purchase (CHP). New equipment financing in Australia during 1992/93 totalled an estimated $9700 million, of which 56 per cent was provided by leases and the balance by CHP.[2]

Lease finance is provided on a large scale by banks and finance companies as an alternative to loans. Other sources of lease finance include merchant banks, specialist leasing companies, and vendor leasing companies associated with

---
1 P. Vardigans, 'The Benefits of Leasing', *Banking World*, August 1990, pp. 26–7.
2 Annual Review 1992–93, Australian Equipment Lessors Association, pp. 1, 11.

equipment suppliers. The value of goods leased under new finance lease agreements is presented in Table 19.1.

Table 19.1 Value of goods under new finance lease commitments[a]

| Year to June | $m |
|---|---|
| 1986 | 5592.6 |
| 1987 | 5521.4 |
| 1988 | 6789.3 |
| 1989 | 8801.7 |
| 1990 | 8217.9 |
| 1991 | 5209.4 |
| 1992 | 4476.7 |
| 1993 | 5008.5 |

(a) Excludes leveraged leases
Source: Lease Finance, Australia, Australian Bureau of Statistics, Cat. No. 5644.

## 19.2 TYPES OF LEASE CONTRACTS

Leases can be broadly classified as either **operating leases** or **financial leases**. Within these broad classes, several types of lease contract can also be identified. For our purposes, the importance of distinguishing between operating leases and financial leases is that they have different financial implications for both the lessor and lessee. Therefore, different factors can be important in the evaluation of each type of lease.

The major lease types are discussed in the following sections.

### 19.2.1 OPERATING LEASES

An operating lease is essentially a rental agreement. Assets whose services may be acquired by means of an operating lease include telephones, motor vehicles, construction equipment, computers, and other office equipment. Operating leases are normally offered by the suppliers of those assets, such as computer companies, and by specialist rental companies such as motor vehicle rental companies.

An essential feature of an operating lease is that it is cancellable by the lessee, at little or no cost, provided that the lessee gives the agreed notice (if any) of cancellation to the lessor. As a result, the lessee is usually able to return the asset to the lessor at short notice. An operating lease agreement is normally for a short term and the asset is likely to be leased to a series of users. Therefore, an operating lease enables a company to obtain the use of an asset which is required for only a short period. For example, if a Melbourne-based company needs a car for use by an executive visiting its Adelaide branch for a short period, it is probably preferable to lease the car than to buy it.

Operating leases may also be maintenance leases which means that the lessor is responsible for insuring the asset, maintaining it, and for payment of any government charges. An operating lease enables a lessee to use the asset without directly incurring the risks of ownership such as the risk of obsolescence. Because the lease is cancellable, the risks of ownership are borne by the lessor, and this fact will be reflected in the lease rentals. For the lessor, operating leases are characterised by renting out assets and exposure to the risks of ownership, rather than by the provision of finance. Operating leases are discussed further in Section 19.6.

## 19.2.2 Financial leases

A financial lease is a long-term agreement that generally covers most of the economic life of the asset. The agreement will either be non-cancellable, or cancellable only if the lessee pays a substantial penalty to the lessor. Therefore, a financial lease is effectively non-cancellable and the lessee has an obligation to make all the agreed lease payments. This obligation is essentially the same as a borrower's obligation to repay a loan. Financial lease agreements normally contain restrictive covenants analogous to those in loan agreements and the lessor will be concerned to ensure that a prospective lessee is creditworthy. In this case the role of the lessor is to provide finance, and from the lessor's viewpoint a financial lease is, in effect, a secured loan. While the lessor is the legal owner of the asset, it has no great interest in matters such as the day-to-day use of the asset, and the lessee is responsible for repairs, maintenance, and insurance. Because of these characteristics, particularly the fact that the lease is non-cancellable, there is an effective transfer from the lessor to the lessee of substantially all of the risks and benefits of ownership of the leased asset. In other words, when a company signs a financial lease it is, in effect, entering into an agreement to purchase the asset using funds borrowed from the lessor.

In a typical financial lease the lessor is a financial institution such as a bank or finance company. The role of these institutions is to provide finance rather than to rent assets and they prefer that the lessee should purchase the asset at the end of the lease term. To be treated as a 'genuine lease' for tax purposes, a lease agreement cannot explicitly provide the lessee with an option to purchase the asset. However, under a financial lease the lessee will guarantee that the lessor receives a specified residual value from sale of the asset at the end of the lease term. In practice the lessee normally discharges this obligation by purchasing the asset for the residual value.

There are various types of financial leases, some of which involve the lessor being a partnership of two or more financiers. The main types of such leases are **leveraged leases** and **cross-border leases**. These are discussed in Sections 19.2.4 and 19.2.5. Most leases involve acquisition of new assets but in some cases an existing asset is sold and leased back. Sale and lease-back agreements which are generally financial leases are discussed next.

## 19.2.3 Sale and lease-back agreements

Under a sale and lease-back agreement the owner of an asset sells the asset to a financial institution for an amount usually equal to its current market value and immediately leases it back from the institution. Real estate; such as office buildings, retail stores, hotels and motels, regional shopping centres, warehouses and factories; is often the subject of such transactions. The lessee relinquishes the title to the property in return for cash, and agrees to make periodic lease payments to the lessor. The sale-and-leaseback transaction is an alternative to raising cash by borrowing, using the asset as security. The lessor in most cases is a life insurance company, although some superannuation funds, banks, and specialist leasing companies also offer this form of finance.

The term of such lease agreements will depend on the type of property leased but will generally not exceed 15 years. In addition to the lease payments, the lessee is normally responsible for payment of maintenance costs, insurance, government charges, and any other costs of occupation.

### 19.2.4 LEVERAGED LEASING

**Leveraged leasing**, which is a form of financial leasing, was introduced into the Australian capital market in the mid-1970s.[3] The first leveraged lease was negotiated in 1974, and since then many large and expensive assets have been leased in this way. The structure of a leveraged lease is shown diagrammatically in Figure 19.1.

A leveraged lease differs from an ordinary financial lease in that it involves at least three parties instead of two. The additional party is a lender. In practice there may be many parties involved because the lessor is usually a partnership of two or more equity participants, and there may be two or more lenders. The lenders, or debt participants, lend to the lessor a high proportion, typically between 70 and 80 per cent, of the cost of the asset. The debt participants are usually life insurance companies, superannuation funds, merchant banks, or banks. Typically the loan is a **non-recourse loan** which means that the lessor is not responsible for its repayment. Therefore it is important that the risk of default by the lessee is very low. Security for the lender(s) is provided by an assignment of the lease payments, and in some cases a mortgage over the leased asset. The equity participants are generally banks, merchant banks, or finance companies with sufficient profits to take advantage of the tax deductions associated with ownership of the asset, and the interest payments on the loan. The equity participants provide the funds not already provided by the lender and form a partnership which purchases the asset. As the majority, or in some cases, all, of each lease payment is paid out as interest and principal to the lender, the equity participants receive little, if any, cash inflow from the lease payments. Their investment is levered in that they provide only *part* of the asset's purchase price, but they receive *all* the tax benefits from owning and financing the asset. The equity participants' returns are achieved mainly by deferral of tax payments because the lessor partnership will incur tax losses during the early years of the lease.

---

[3] For more details of leveraged leasing, its legal documentation and taxation requirements, see J. Bennett, 'Equipment Leasing', in *Handbook of Australian Corporate Finance*, Eds R. Bruce et al., 4th edn, Butterworths, Sydney, 1991, pp. 245–50 and pp. 253–64.

# LEASING AND EQUIPMENT FINANCE

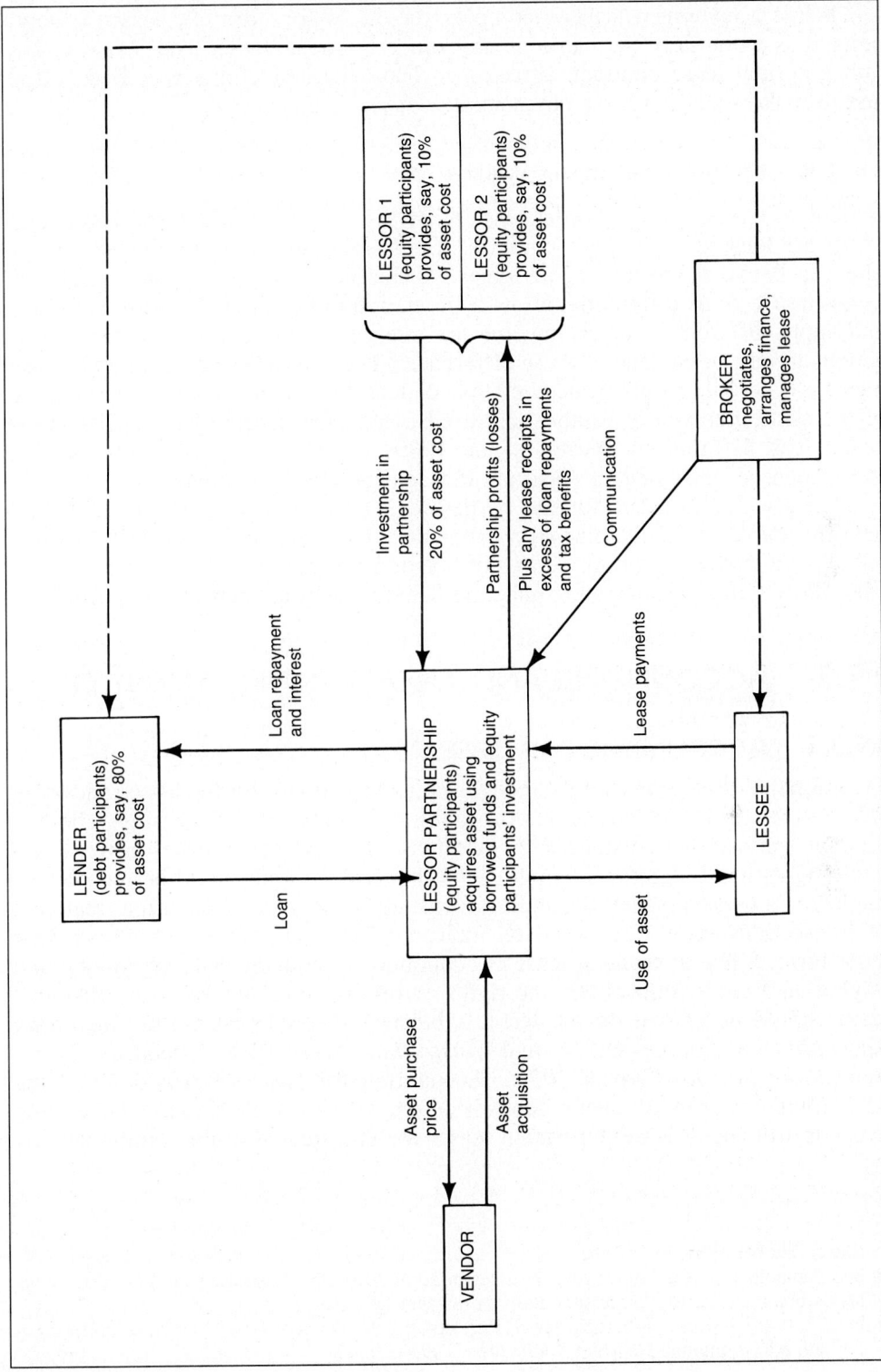

**Fig. 19.1** *The role of participants in a leveraged lease*

While a leveraged lease is complex for the lessor, from the lessee's viewpoint it is essentially the same as any other financial lease. The lessee enters into a normal lease contract, agreeing to lease the asset for a specified period and to make specified lease payments.

### 19.2.5 CROSS-BORDER LEASING[4]

In general terms, a cross-border lease (CBL) is a lease in which the lessee and lessor are located in different countries. Such transactions are motivated by differences between the tax regulations of different countries. Because countries assess transactions differently, allow depreciation to be claimed at different rates, and apply different company income tax rates, it is possible to structure transactions to take advantage of these differences. For example, the lessor and lessee may both be able to claim depreciation deductions on the same asset. Because of the costs involved in establishing a CBL, an asset financed by a CBL must cost at least $20 million. During the late 1980s, assets costing over $2000 million were financed each year in Australia through the CBL technique.[5]

Clearly, the benefits for the parties to a CBL involve a reduction in tax payable and as a result, many governments, including the Australian Government, have moved to curtail the loss of taxation revenue. However, several countries allow CBLs because they generate benefits such as increased exports.

## 19.3 ACCOUNTING AND TAXATION TREATMENT OF LEASES

### 19.3.1 ACCOUNTING FOR LEASES[6]

Traditionally, lease rentals were recognised as an expense for the lessee and there was no recognition of any assets or liabilities associated with leasing. The traditional approach was criticised for two reasons. First, some leases provide valuable rights and obligations which cannot be avoided and should be included in the lessee's balance sheet. Secondly, it was argued that the accounting treatment of transactions should be based on their economic substance rather than their legal form. Since a financial lease is economically equivalent to borrowing and buying an asset it follows that the rights and obligations involved in a financial lease should be shown on the lessee's balance sheet. In Australia, *Australian Accounting Standard AAS17* and *Australian Accounting Standards Board Accounting Standard AASB 1008*: 'Accounting for Leases', provides that the accounting treatment of a lease depends on whether it is classified as an operating lease or a financial lease. Operating leases are still treated in the traditional way

---

[4] See M. Cassino, 'Cross Border Leasing Cuts Upfront Costs', *Decisions*, National Australia Bank, October 1989, pp. 14–16.
[5] See Footnote 4. These figures refer to assets used in Australia. Australia's tax laws discourage leases involving Australian lessors and non-resident lessees.
[6] For a full discussion of this topic see S. Henderson & G. Peirson, *Issues in Financial Accounting*, 6th edn, Longman Cheshire, Melbourne, 1994, Ch. 12.

but financial leases should be recognised as assets and liabilities. AAS17 provides that a lease would normally be classified as a financial lease when the following criteria are satisfied:
1. The lease is non-cancellable; *and*
2. *either* of the following tests is met:
    (a) The lease term is for 75 per cent or more of the useful life of the leased asset; however, if the beginning of the lease term falls within the last 25 per cent of the total useful life of the leased asset, including earlier years of use, this criterion would not be appropriate for purposes of classifying the lease.
    (b) The present value, at the beginning of the lease term, of the minimum lease payments equals or exceeds 90 per cent of the fair value of the leased asset to the lessor at the inception of the lease. The discount rate to be used in calculating the present value is the interest rate implicit in the lease.

These criteria are only guidelines, and the classification of a lease should depend on the economic substance of the transaction. Provided that substantially all of the risks and benefits associated with ownership of the leased asset are effectively transferred to the lessee, the lease is then a financial lease and should be recognised as an asset and a liability. However, some lessees believe that it is advantageous to avoid recognising financial leases as assets and liabilities. Consequently lessors have responded by designing leases which are, in substance, financial leases but can be classified as operating leases under the criteria set out in AAS17. This activity has continued, despite efforts by the standard setters to emphasise that the classification of a lease should depend on its economic substance rather than being based on a literal application of the guidelines in AAS17.

## 19.3.2 TAXATION TREATMENT OF LEASES

The taxation treatment of leases in Australia can be complex and has been subject to many changes through both legislation and taxation rulings.[7] Only a broad outline of the main principles is provided here. If a leased asset is used to generate revenue, the lease rentals paid by the lessee are an allowable tax deduction, provided that the lease is classified as a 'genuine lease' rather than an 'instalment purchase arrangement'. The purpose of this distinction is to prevent taxpayers using leasing as a way of obtaining accelerated tax deductions by claiming, as deductions, outlays which are of a capital nature. Consequently a deduction may not be allowed for lease rentals if the lease agreement gives the lessee an option to purchase the leased asset at the end of the lease term.[8] Similarly, the

---

[7] For more detailed coverage of the taxation effects of leasing see J. Shanahan, *Leasing in Australia*, CCH, North Ryde, 1981 and L. Szekely, 'The Tax Treatment of Leasing', *CCH Journal of Australian Taxation*, August/September 1991, pp. 48–54.

[8] Although the requirements of the Commissioner of Taxation, set out in Taxation Ruling IT28, prevent the lessor from providing the lessee with an option to buy the asset, it is usual for such an option to be implicit in financial lease agreements. In the vast majority of cases the lessee buys the asset by payment of the specified residual value at the end of the initial lease period. In most other cases the lessee renews the lease for an additional period.

Commissioner of Taxation has specified rules concerning acceptable residual values and may disallow a deduction for rentals that have been increased by the use of an unrealistically low residual value.

While lease rentals are deductible, the lessee cannot deduct, for tax purposes, depreciation on the leased asset. Depreciation is deductible by the lessor as the legal owner of the asset,[9] and lease rentals received by the lessor are, of course, taxable. Lessors may attempt to defer tax payments by varying the size or frequency of the rentals during the term of a lease. The tax office may scrutinise such arrangements and is particularly sceptical of lease structures that involve increased rentals over time.[10]

The taxation rules often have an important effect on the choice between leasing and other similar forms of finance. For example, if it is advantageous for depreciation deductions to be claimed by the asset user, a commercial hire purchase agreement may be used, rather than a lease. Commercial hire purchase is discussed in Section 19.8.

## 19.4 Setting Lease Rentals

While the main emphasis in this book is on the viewpoint of the lessee, it is useful to consider the approach used by lessors to set lease rentals. Prospective lessees who understand the factors that influence lease rentals should be in a stronger negotiating position than those who do not. The setting of lease rentals is illustrated in Example 19.1.

### Example 19.1

Monlease has been asked by a group of doctors to quote on a 4-year lease of an item of medical equipment which costs $600 000. The equipment can be depreciated for tax purposes on a straight-line basis over 3 years. Monlease has a tax rate of 40 per cent and requires a rate of return of 8 per cent per annum after tax from leases. There are to be four equal lease payments, payable annually in advance, and a residual value of 20 per cent of the cost of the equipment will apply. The manager of Monlease calculates the lease payments using the following steps.

1. **Calculate the present value of cash flows from asset ownership**. These cash flows are the tax savings on depreciation and the after-tax cash inflow from sale of the asset (at the residual value) at the end of the lease term. The present value of the depreciation tax savings is calculated as follows:

---

[9] Australian businesses buying new plant have, at times, been allowed to claim an additional tax deduction, known as an investment allowance. This allowance is discussed in Section 19.8.
[10] L. Szekely, see Footnote 7, p. 49.

| Year | Depreciation (D) | Tax saving (D × tax rate) | PV factor @ 8% p.a. | Present value |
|---|---|---|---|---|
| 1 | $200 000 | $80 000 | 0.9259 | $74 074 |
| 2 | $200 000 | $80 000 | 0.8573 | $68 587 |
| 3 | $200 000 | $80 000 | 0.7938 | $63 507 |
|   |          |         | Total   | $206 168 |

Monlease will also receive the residual value of $120 000 but will have to pay tax on the resultant profit on the sale of the equipment, which is also $120 000 because the equipment has a written down value for tax purposes of zero. Therefore, the after-tax cash inflow will be $120 000(1 − 0.4) = $72 000, which has a present value of $72 000/1.08^4 = $72 000 × 0.7350 or $52 922. The total cash flows associated with ownership of the equipment have a present value of $206 168 + $52 922 = $259 090.

2. **Calculate the required present value of the lease payments.** The asset costs $600 000, of which Monlease will recover $259 090 from its ownership. Therefore, the required present value of the lease payments is $600 000 − $259 090 = $340 910.

3. **Calculate the minimum after-tax lease payment.** With annual lease payments, $L$, payable in advance:

$$\$340\,910 = L\left\{1 + \left[\frac{1 - \frac{1}{(1.08)^3}}{0.08}\right]\right\}$$

$$= L(1 + 2.5771)$$

$$L = \frac{\$340\,910}{3.5771}$$

$$= \$95\,303$$

4. **Calculate the minimum before-tax lease payment $L'$, given the tax rate $t$.**

$$L' = \frac{L}{1 - t}$$

$$= \frac{\$95\,303}{1 - 0.4}$$

$$= \$158\,839$$

To achieve its required rate of return of 8 per cent after tax, Monlease should quote annual lease payments of $158 839.

From these calculations it should be clear that Monlease would be able to quote *lower* lease rental payments if:

1. There is an investment allowance and/or the depreciation rate for tax purposes is *higher*.
2. The residual value of the equipment is *higher*.
3. The lessor's required rate of return is *lower*.

In practice there are other factors that will also affect lease rental payments. For example, lessors will adjust lease rentals to reflect any transaction costs involved in establishing the lease, and any government charges such as stamp duty. Also they are likely to adjust the required rate of return to reflect differences in credit risk between different lessees, and they may take into account the exact timing of tax effects. Therefore, for some leases, particularly large ones, the calculation of lease rentals is more complex than the procedure illustrated in Example 19.1. On the other hand, the procedure may be less complex. For small leases a lessor may calculate the required lease payments using before-tax cash flows and a before-tax rate of return.

## 19.5 EVALUATION OF FINANCIAL LEASES

A multiplicity of methods has been suggested for evaluating financial leases. One reason for this is that there has been controversy over the question of how to structure the evaluation of leases; some authors suggest that the appropriate comparison is 'leasing versus borrowing', while others suggest that 'leasing versus buying' is the correct approach.

The approach we discuss is presented by Myers, Dill and Bautista (MDB).[11] Essentially, the mechanics of the MDB method of analysing a financial lease are identical to those proposed earlier by other authors.[12] However, the main contribution made by MDB lies in analysing a financial lease in the context of its effect on the lessee's capital structure. In particular, MDB emphasise that entering into a financial lease will use some of the lessee's debt capacity. Therefore it follows that a financial lease should be analysed by comparing it with debt.

MDB show that this conclusion follows even if the comparison is initially viewed as *lease* versus *buy*. They point out that the phrase 'lease versus buy' is virtually meaningless unless the means of financing the purchase is specified. Suppose that the comparison is specified as leasing versus buying, using normal financing—that is, the mixture of debt and equity in the company's normal capital structure. It is then necessary to allow for the fact that lease finance will use some of the company's debt capacity. When this is done it can be seen that, in effect, lease finance must be compared with debt. The effect of lease finance in using debt capacity is illustrated in Example 19.2.

---

[11] S. Myers, D. Dill & A. Bautista, 'Valuation of Financial Lease Contracts', *Journal of Finance*, June 1976, pp. 799–819.
[12] For an analysis of the origins of the MDB method, see G. H. Burrows, 'Evolution of a Lease Solution', *Abacus*, September 1988, pp. 107–119.

## Example 19.2
Heavy Haulage Ltd has assets with a market value of $500 000 financed by a capital structure of $250 000 equity and $250 000 debt. The company needs a new truck, which can either be purchased for $100 000, or leased. If the truck is purchased using the company's normal combination of debt and equity, the balance sheet will be as follows:

**Balance Sheet 1**

| | | | |
|---|---|---|---|
| Assets | $500 000 | Debt | $300 000 |
| Truck | $100 000 | Equity | $300 000 |
| | $600 000 | | $600 000 |

Alternatively, if the truck is leased, the balance sheet will be:

**Balance Sheet 2**

| | | | |
|---|---|---|---|
| Assets | $500 000 | Debt | $250 000 |
| Truck | $100 000 | Lease liability | $100 000 |
| | | Equity | $250 000 |
| | $600 000 | | $600 000 |

Leasing has increased the company's debt–equity ratio because the lease liability is an additional type of debt in the company's capital structure. To restore the original debt–equity ratio, the company should raise another $50 000 of equity and repay debt of $50 000. After these changes the balance sheet will contain equity of $300 000, debt of $200 000, and the lease liability of $100 000. A comparison with Balance Sheet 1 shows that the lease used $100 000 of the company's debt capacity.

Example 19.2 shows that leasing uses a company's debt capacity, which suggests that a financial lease should be evaluated by comparing it with other debt finance. However, this does *not* mean that the alternative to leasing an asset is to borrow an amount equal to the purchase price of the asset. Rather it means that financial lease evaluation must allow for the fact that a company that enters into a financial lease reduces its ability to borrow in other ways. That is, the obligation to make rental payments under a lease uses up some of the debt capacity provided by the company's assets. For leasing to be economically advantageous to a lessee the finance provided by leasing must be greater than the liability incurred by leasing. The MDB method focuses on making that comparison by calculating the liability incurred by leasing. Example 19.3 illustrates the MDB method.

## Example 19.3
Sharemarket Research Ltd (SRL) needs a new computer, which can be purchased for $300 000. The company's financial manager, Elliott Wave, is considering the alternative of leasing the computer from Efficient Finance, which requires six lease rentals of $65 000 each, payable annually in advance. The computer can be depreciated for tax purposes over 3 years on a straight-line basis and its disposal value is expected to be zero at the end of the lease. The company income tax rate is 40 per cent.

The incremental cash flows for leasing the computer, rather than buying it, are shown in Table 19.2.

**Table 19.2** *Cash flows: Lease versus purchase*

| | Cash flows ($) | | | | | |
|---|---|---|---|---|---|---|
| Item | Year 0 | Year 1 | Year 2 | Year 3 | Year 4 | Year 5 |
| 1. Cost of computer | 300 000 | | | | | |
| 2. Lease rentals | −65 000 | −65 000 | −65 000 | −65 000 | −65 000 | −65 000 |
| 3. Tax saving on lease rentals | 26 000 | 26 000 | 26 000 | 26 000 | 26 000 | 26 000 |
| 4. Depreciation tax savings lost | | −40 000 | −40 000 | −40 000 | | |
| Total | 261 000 | −79 000 | −79 000 | −79 000 | −39 000 | −39 000 |

Remembering that the table shows the *incremental* cash flows for leasing versus buying, the explanation for each item is straightforward. First, by leasing the computer, SRL does not need to pay the purchase price of $300 000. Therefore, there is an effective cash inflow of this amount. Secondly, the lease rentals are a cash payment each year, but these payments are tax deductible, generating annual tax savings of $26 000, which are a cash inflow. Finally, by leasing rather than buying, SRL is unable to claim depreciation deductions of $100 000 per annum in years 1, 2 and 3. Therefore, it foregoes tax savings of $40 000 in each of these years. The bottom row of Table 19.2 shows that the lease provides finance of $261 000 to SRL and requires net cash outflows by SRL in years 1 to 5. To determine whether the lease is attractive to SRL the cash outflows in years 1 to 5 can be regarded as after-tax repayments of a loan which is equivalent to the lease. That is, we ask: If SRL had offered this set of repayments to an alternative lender, how much could SRL have borrowed? If the amount is less than $261 000, SRL should accept the lease.

Clearly the amount that could be borrowed from an alternative lender will depend on the interest rate on the hypothetical equivalent loan. The interest rate will, in turn, depend on the security offered to the lender. For the loan to be equivalent to the lease, the security should be the same as that held by the lessor. If the lessor's only security is ownership of the computer, the interest rate on a loan secured by a mortgage or other charge over the computer could be appropriate.[13] Assume that Mr Wave has been quoted a rate of 12.5 per cent per annum on such a loan. Because the cash flows to be discounted are after tax, the discount rate must also be after tax; that is $12.5(1 - 0.4) = 7.5$ per cent per annum.

The present value of the net cash outflows is:

---

[13] The lessor's formal security is generally, but not always, restricted to ownership of the leased asset. A case in which additional security was required is cited by G. H. Burrows, 'Evolution of a Lease Solution', *Abacus*, September 1988, p. 117. For evidence on factors that affect the cost of lease finance, see J. Schallheim, R. Johnson, R. Lease & J. McConnell, 'The Determinants of Yields on Financial Leasing Contracts', *Journal of Financial Economics*, September 1987, pp. 45–67.

$$PV = \$79\,000 \left[ \frac{1 - \frac{1}{(1.075)^3}}{0.075} \right] + \frac{\$39\,000}{1.075^4} + \frac{39\,000}{1.075^5}$$

$$= \$261\,811$$

The lease provides finance of $261 000 and the present value of the liability incurred by leasing is $261 811; so the net present value of the lease relative to the equivalent loan is:

$$\text{NPV} = \$261\,000 - \$261\,811$$
$$= -\$811$$

Based on this analysis the lease is marginally unattractive and should not be accepted by SRL.

### 19.5.1 LEASING DECISIONS AND INVESTMENT DECISIONS

To interpret correctly the result of a lease evaluation such as the one in Example 19.3 it is necessary to understand that this evaluation relates only to the question of whether it is better to lease or buy, *given that the asset is to be acquired*. In other words, the lease evaluation gives a net present value for leasing the asset *relative* to buying it. Suppose that in Example 19.3 the NPV of the lease was $1000. This positive NPV does not necessarily mean that SRL should lease the computer. If buying the computer has a negative NPV, say $-\$5000$, then leasing it would not be attractive because the total NPV for acquiring the computer by leasing is:

| | |
|---|---|
| NPV if purchased | $= -\$5000$ |
| NPV of lease relative to purchase | $= \$1000$ |
| NPV of leasing computer | $= -\$4000$ |

Since the total NPV is negative, the computer should not be leased: leasing is better than purchasing, but both alternatives are unprofitable.

In practice the investment decision would normally be considered first and, if the project is profitable, the alternative of leasing the required assets would then be evaluated. However, the financial manager should not necessarily discard a project if evaluation of the investment decision reveals a negative NPV. The reason is that in some cases the NPV of a lease can be large enough to 'rescue' an otherwise marginally unprofitable project.

### 19.5.2 THE VALUE OF LEASING IN COMPETITIVE CAPITAL MARKETS

Later sections, including Section 19.5.3, discuss some of the conditions that can result in a lease having a positive NPV for the lessee. Lease finance is provided in markets that are highly competitive, and that has important implications for the value of leasing. To examine these implications, suppose that all financiers and asset users operate in a perfect capital market where the following conditions apply:

1. Leasing involves no transaction costs.
2. Information is costless and freely available.

3. All parties are subject to the same tax laws and tax rates.

Under these conditions, the cost of leasing an asset should be exactly the same as the cost of buying it. That is, the lease-or-buy decision should be a matter of indifference. The argument that leads to this conclusion will be explained, using, for illustrative purposes, the data and results of Example 19.3. In that example, the NPV for the lessee of leasing the new computer rather than purchasing it was $-\$811$.

Now consider the position of the lessor, Efficient Finance. From the lessor's viewpoint the decision is whether to lease the computer to SRL, or to lend SRL funds to buy it. If Efficient Finance is to lease the computer to SRL, it must first buy the computer for $300 000. Efficient Finance will receive the lease rentals, be taxed on them, and can claim tax deductions for depreciation of the computer. Therefore, provided that both parties are taxed at the same rate, the lessee's after-tax cash outflows are the lessor's after-tax cash inflows. In other words, Efficient Finance's net cash flows will be those shown in the bottom row of Table 19.2, with the signs reversed. Also the appropriate discount rate will remain unchanged at 7.5 per cent per annum. Therefore the NPV of leasing for the lessor must be $+\$811$.

Under these circumstances the lease alternative is attractive to the lessor but not to the user of the asset. Suppose that Efficient Finance reduces the lease rentals to make the lease attractive to SRL. Because of the symmetry between the positions of the two parties, it is impossible to design a lease which will be *more* attractive to the lessee than borrowing, without simultaneously making the lease *less* attractive to the lessor. Further, in a perfect capital market, lessors should earn only a normal rate of return on their activities. This means that, in equilibrium, the NPV of providing lease finance should be zero. Again, because of the symmetrical positions of the two parties, the NPV of leasing for the lessee must also be zero. Therefore in a perfect capital market all asset users should be indifferent between the alternatives of leasing and buying. This conclusion should not be surprising. The lease or buy decision is a financing decision and, as discussed in Chapter 12, Modigliani and Miller showed that, in a perfect capital market, financing decisions have no effect on shareholders' wealth. In other words, just as there is no magic in financial leverage in a perfect capital market, so there is no magic in leasing.

Calculation of the equilibrium lease rentals that should make an asset user indifferent between leasing and buying is shown in Example 19.4.

## Example 19.4

Western Computer Services Ltd (WCS) is considering the acquisition of a computer that can be purchased for $500 000 or leased. The lease is to involve five equal rental payments, payable annually in advance, with a residual value of $50 000 after 5 years. WCS expects to be paying tax at the company income tax rate of 40 per cent during the term of the lease. The company's financial manager wishes to calculate the maximum lease rentals that should be paid, given that the interest rate on an equivalent loan is 12.5 per cent per annum.

As in Example 19.3, the first step is to determine the incremental cash flows for leasing versus buying. The additional factor to be considered is the treatment of the residual value, which in this case is $50 000. To put the lease and purchase alternatives on the same basis it must be assumed that WCS pays the residual value, and thereby purchases the computer from the lessor. This raises one further complication: if WCS leases the computer, and then purchases it, the company can claim tax deductions, beginning in year 6, for depreciation based on the purchase price of $50 000. If WCS had purchased the computer when it was new, all depreciation deductions would have been claimed during the first 3 years. Therefore the two alternatives involve a difference in allowable tax deductions after the lease term.

To make an unbiased comparison, it will be assumed that in each alternative the computer is sold at the end of year 5. That is, at the end of the lease term, WCS buys the computer by paying the residual value of $50 000, and immediately sells it for its market value, also assumed to be $50 000.

Therefore the sale proceeds will be the same in each case, and do not have to be included, since incremental cash flows are being considered. However, the lease's residual value must be included, as must any tax effects related to the sale of the computer. In this case, the lease alternative does not involve any tax effect, since WCS is assumed to sell the computer for $50 000, which is the same as the price it paid. The alternative of buying the asset involves a profit of $50 000 (since in that case, the written-down value is zero) on which the income tax will be $50 000 × 0.4 = $20 000.

The incremental cash flows for leasing versus buying are shown in Table 19.3, where $L$ represents the annual lease rental.

**Table 19.3** Cash flows: Lease versus purchase

| | Cash flows ($) | | | | | |
|---|---|---|---|---|---|---|
| Item | Year 0 | Year 1 | Year 2 | Year 3 | Year 4 | Year 5 |
| 1. Cost of computer | 500 000 | | | | | |
| 2. Lease rentals | −L | −L | −L | −L | −L | |
| 3. Tax saving on lease rentals | 0.4L | 0.4L | 0.4L | 0.4L | 0.4L | |
| 4. Depreciation tax savings lost | | −66 667 | −66 667 | −66 667 | | |
| 5. Lease residual value | | | | | | −50 000 |
| 6. Tax saved on profit on sale | | | | | | 20 000 |

The after-tax interest rate on an equivalent loan is 12.5(1 − 0.4) = 7.5 per cent per annum, and the equilibrium lease rentals can be found by solving as follows:[14]

---

[14] Since the residual value of $50 000 is specified in the lease agreement, it is of similar risk to the lease rentals and can be discounted at the after-tax cost of debt. However, the tax savings ($20 000) depend in part on the disposal (market) value of the computer and are therefore more risky. Discounting this cash flow at the after-tax cost of debt is an approximation.

$$\text{NPV} = 0 = \$500\,000 - 0.6L\left\{1 + \frac{\left[1 - \frac{1}{(1.075)^4}\right]}{0.075}\right\}$$

$$- \$66\,667\,\frac{\left[1 - \frac{1}{(1.075)^3}\right]}{0.075} - \frac{\$30\,000}{(1.075)^5}$$

$$\therefore 2.6096L = \$500\,000 - \$173\,368 - \$20\,897$$
$$\text{and } L = \$117\,159$$

Therefore the maximum lease rentals that WCS should be prepared to pay are $117 159 per annum. These rentals will also provide a normal rate of return to the lessor.

Does the perfect capital market result, of indifference between leasing and buying, apply in real-world capital markets? The popularity of leasing has varied over time and it is particularly popular for some types of assets. These observations suggest that there are cases where asset users have a systematic preference for leasing or buying. Clearly, for this to be the case there must be tax differences or imperfections that can make leasing advantageous in some cases. Some conditions that may give rise to an overall advantage for leasing are discussed in the next section. The advantages and disadvantages of leasing are also discussed in Section 19.7.

### 19.5.3 Establishing an advantage for leasing

To make leasing attractive to the user of an asset, without simultaneously making leasing unattractive to the lessor, requires some departure from the perfect-market conditions outlined in the previous section. In particular it is necessary to break the symmetry between the positions of the two parties. There are ways in which this can be done. For example, the lessor may be entitled to receive quantity discounts that are not available to the buyer of a single item. Such discounts may be available to specialist lessors of mass-produced assets, such as cars, but are unlikely to apply where the asset is unique, or where the lessor is a general financier. However, an overall advantage associated with leasing can often be established where there is some difference between the tax positions of the lessor and the asset user. This is illustrated in Example 19.5 which uses the same basic information as Example 19.3.

*Example 19.5*

Sharemarket Research Ltd (SRL) is again considering the acquisition of a $300 000 computer, but Elliott Wave has now established that because of past losses that are being carried forward, SRL is unlikely to pay company income tax during the next 5 years.

The revised cash flows for leasing the computer, rather than purchasing it, are shown in Table 19.4. The only relevant cash flows are the cost of the computer and the lease rentals.

**Table 19.4** *Cash Flows: Lease versus purchase*

| | Cash flows ($) | | | | | |
|---|---|---|---|---|---|---|
| Item | Year 0 | Year 1 | Year 2 | Year 3 | Year 4 | Year 5 |
| 1. Cost of computer | 300 000 | | | | | |
| 2. Lease rentals | −65 000 | −65 000 | −65 000 | −65 000 | −65 000 | −65 000 |
| Total | 235 000 | −65 000 | −65 000 | −65 000 | −65 000 | −65 000 |

Because SRL is unlikely to be paying company income tax during the term of the lease, these net cash flows should be discounted at the before tax borrowing rate of 12.5 per cent. The NPV of the lease to SRL is:

$$NPV = + \$235\,000 - \$65\,000 \left[ \frac{1 - \frac{1}{(1.125)^5}}{0.125} \right]$$

$$= \$3563$$

Therefore, because SRL will not be paying company income tax during the term of the lease, the NPV of the lease has increased from −$811 to $3563. Assuming that Efficient Finance will be in a taxpaying position each year, the NPV to it will still be $811. Therefore the lease alternative now has a positive NPV for both parties and there is an overall gain from leasing:

$$\text{Gain from leasing} = \$3563 + \$811 = \$4374$$

This gain is realised at the expense of the government and is achieved because the lessor is utilising tax deductions associated with ownership and financing of the leased asset (in this case, deductions for depreciation and interest on borrowings) as soon as they are available. If SRL purchased the computer using borrowed money, these deductions would be of no immediate value to the company because they would only add to the tax loss being carried forward.

The manner in which the gain of $4374 is shared between the lessor and lessee will depend, in part, on the level of competition in the leasing industry. If there is perfect competition in the industry, the annual lease rentals will be reduced to a level such that the NPV to Efficient Finance is zero and the whole gain will then accrue to SRL.

### 19.5.4 TAXES AND THE SIZE OF LEASING GAINS

Examples 19.3 and 19.5 show that leasing can be less costly than purchasing where the lessor has advantages not available to the potential lessee, and where some of these advantages are passed on to the lessee by way of lower lease payments. However, these examples assumed an extreme case in which the lessee's tax rate was zero and the lessor's tax rate was the full statutory rate, assumed to be 40 per cent. In many cases the difference between the effective tax rates of the two parties may be much smaller, and it may vary over time. For example, the lessee may initially have a tax rate of zero but begin to pay tax during the lease term. Therefore factors such as the timing of the lease rental payments can affect the size of the gain associated with leasing. To identify the factors that can be important, and to illustrate their effects, consider the effects that a lease can have on the present value of the government's tax receipts.

In Examples 19.3 and 19.5 the NPV of the lease involved the present values of three types of cash flows: the cost of the asset, the after-tax lease rentals, and the tax savings on depreciation. The NPV of a lease to the lessee ($NPV_{LES}$) can be expressed as:

$$NPV_{LES} = C - PV(L) - PV(Dep) \qquad (19.1)$$

where  $C$ = cost of the leased asset
$PV(L)$ = present value of lease rentals
$PV(Dep)$ = present value of depreciation tax savings

Similarly, the NPV to the lessor ($NPV_{LOR}$) will be:

$$NPV_{LOR} = -C + PV(L)^* + PV(Dep)^* \qquad (19.2)$$

The asterisks have been added because the present values of the lease rentals and the depreciation tax savings can differ, given that the lessor and lessee have different tax rates. The overall gain from the lease can be found by adding Equations 19.1 and 19.2. The cost of the asset, $C$, will cancel out, leaving only terms involving the lease rentals and the depreciation tax savings. Therefore the lease affects the present value of the government's tax receipts in two ways. First, the government gains, in that it can tax the lease rentals received by the lessor. Secondly, the government loses, in that the lessor is able to claim deductions for depreciation on the leased asset. The net result is that the government can lose through *deferral* of tax receipts and it follows that, other things being equal, the government's net loss will be larger in present value terms if:

1. the difference between the effective tax rates of the lessor and lessee is large;
2. the depreciation rate applicable for tax purposes is high so that depreciation tax savings are received early and/or there is an investment allowance;
3. the term of the lease is long and the lease rentals are concentrated during the later part of the lease term, so that tax payments by the lessor are deferred;
4. interest rates and hence the discount rate applicable to the cash flows are high (if the discount rate is zero, changing the timing of tax payments does not change their present value).

Thus leasing is more likely to be used if there are high company tax rates, high depreciation rates, large investment allowances, and high interest rates. It is not surprising that leasing has grown rapidly at times when these factors have been present.

### 19.5.5 LEASING AND THE IMPUTATION TAX SYSTEM

The discussion in Section 19.5.4 explained that any tax advantages associated with a lease arise from deferral of taxes, usually in the form of company income tax. Moreover it was explained that the potential tax benefits are larger, other things being equal, when there is a large difference between the effective tax rates of the lessor and the lessee. Clearly the potential for there to be large differences between effective tax rates will be greater when tax rates are high. However, as discussed in Appendix 11.1, under the Australian system of full imputation, company income tax is, from the viewpoint of resident shareholders, only a withholding tax. In other words, for many companies the effective rate of *company* income tax (as distinct from tax *collected* at the company level) is extremely low. It follows that for such companies any advantage associated with deferring a company's tax payments will also be very small, and any tax advantage from leasing must also be small.

## 19.6 EVALUATION OF OPERATING LEASES

In Section 19.2.1 it was suggested that a lessee enters into an operating lease because it needs the services provided by an asset, but does not wish to buy the asset. The main reasons for wishing to avoid buying an asset are:
1. uncertainty about the length of time for which the asset is required, which makes attractive the option of leasing the asset under a contract that allows for cancellation; and
2. requiring the asset for only a short period of time relative to its economic life, which makes attractive the option of a short-term lease.

A lease contract with an effective cancellation clause and/or one whose term is substantially less than the economic life of the leased asset, is defined as an operating lease. We discuss separately cancellable long-term operating leases and cancellable short-term operating leases.

### 19.6.1 CANCELLABLE LONG-TERM OPERATING LEASES

If a company owns an asset, there are several reasons why the asset may need to be sold earlier than expected. These include the following:
1. The asset is part of a project which is discontinued.
2. The efficiency of the asset deteriorates at a faster rate than expected.
3. The asset becomes obsolete owing to technological change.
4. The company's requirements outgrow the service potential of the asset.

Cancellable operating leases enable a company to obtain insurance against an unexpectedly large decline in the value of an asset. The risk of an unexpected decline in value can be particularly high for assets such as computers, which can become obsolete very quickly, owing to changes in technology. Where the risk of such a decline is large, a company may prefer to enter a cancellable operating lease rather than buy the asset, as this will mean that the lessor provides insurance against this risk.

Copeland and Weston have shown that the cancellation clause in an operating lease is equivalent to an American put option held by the lessee.[15] A put option enables the holder to sell an asset at a predetermined price, which means that the holder has the opportunity to make a profit if the asset's market price falls below the predetermined price. With a cancellable operating lease the lease payments are calculated after taking into account the expected market price of the asset in future periods. A lessee can benefit from entering into the lease if the market price of the asset falls at a faster rate than that implicit in the lease payments. Therefore a company entering into a cancellable operating lease is not only acquiring the services provided by the leased asset but also a put option over the asset. The value of this option will be taken into account by the lessor when determining the lease payments. The option value will depend on:

1. the degree of uncertainty with respect to the selling price of the leased asset;
2. the expected rate of decrease in the selling price of the asset over its economic life; and
3. the risk-free interest rate.

In practice, the prospective lessee will have to estimate how much the lessor is charging for the option to cancel and assess whether it is worth paying that much for this option. Alternatively an option-pricing model could be used, but such a model is likely to be complex. Therefore it is suggested that an operating lease should first be evaluated as if it were a financial lease. The net present value of the lease relative to the purchase price of the asset will indicate the cost to the lessee of the cancellation option. The financial manager should then assess whether this cost is reasonable, given the risks transferred to the lessor.

### 19.6.2 Cancellable short-term operating leases

The types of leases discussed so far are suitable when an asset's services are needed for an extended period. However, companies frequently need an asset's services for relatively short periods that represent only a small proportion of the asset's economic life. Examples of such assets include cars and trucks.

Consider the case where a company contracts to provide a delivery service for a major retail chain. For most of the year six trucks are sufficient to provide this service. However, there are occasions when, as a result of one or more trucks being out of service, and/or because of peaks in demand for the service, an additional truck is required. Suppose that the additional truck would be required for, say, 6 weeks each year. In this case it is uneconomic for the company to acquire and maintain a seventh truck as the relatively short time for which it is required does not warrant the outlay.

The company may choose to lease the truck for the period it is required. A lessor would be prepared to lease out trucks, provided that there are a number of lessees with a potential short-term need for them, and the demand by those lessees is largely uncorrelated. The trucks may then be leased out for a significant

---

[15] T. Copeland & J. Weston, 'A Note on the Evaluation of Cancellable Operating Leases', *Financial Management*, Summer 1982, pp. 60–7.

proportion of the year, thereby enabling the lessor to earn a return after taking account of the costs of buying and maintaining the trucks. However, the rentals charged can still be attractive to a potential lessee when compared with the alternative of buying the truck.

An alternative to leasing the truck is for the company to buy the truck when it is required, and sell it, possibly to the original vendor, when it is no longer required. This is described as a sale and buy-back arrangement. However, a short-term lease is likely to be preferred to a sale and buy-back arrangement because it is more convenient, and it is likely to involve lower transaction costs.

Therefore when a company requires an asset for a period significantly less than its economic life, a short-term lease will frequently prove to be the most economic means of acquiring the asset's services.

## 19.7 ADVANTAGES AND DISADVANTAGES OF LEASING

The popularity of leasing indicates that there are many cases where users prefer to lease assets rather than to purchase them. It was shown in Section 19.5.3 that leasing may be preferred where:
1. the lessor has an advantage (or advantages) not available to the potential lessee; and
2. the lessor passes on at least some of the advantage(s) to the lessee by way of reduced lease payments.

Alternatively leasing may have advantages such as lower transaction costs. Several of the alleged advantages of leasing are discussed in the following sections. First, we discuss possible advantages of leasing in general. Secondly, we discuss factors that may be important in determining which particular assets should be leased by a company, rather than purchased.

### 19.7.1 POSSIBLE ADVANTAGES OF LEASING

Proponents of leasing often stress taxation advantages, conservation of capital, increased credit availability, and the possibility that leasing may provide capital at a lower cost than other forms of finance. The prevalence of such claims was noted by Scarman who examined promotional literature used by finance companies in their marketing of leases. He found a high incidence of errors, and overstatements which, not surprisingly, were biased in favour of leasing.[16] The possible advantages mentioned above are discussed in turn.

#### COMPANY TAXATION

The tax deductions associated with ownership of an asset are generally the same, regardless of whether the asset is owned by the user or leased. If, as assumed in Examples 19.2 and 19.3, the potential lessee and lessor are taxed at the same rate, there should be no taxation advantage associated with leasing. If this assumption does not hold, then as discussed in Section 19.5.3, leasing may

---

[16] I. Scarman, 'Lease Evaluation: A Survey of Australian Finance Company Approaches', *Accounting and Finance*, November 1982, pp. 33–51.

provide a taxation advantage. Any such advantage arises from the deferral of taxes and can be large in present value terms where a company requires an expensive asset but it is not able to utilise fully the depreciation deductions if the asset is purchased. This problem may be overcome if the asset is acquired by a lessor who can use all the allowable deductions as soon as they are available. In this case the lessor has an advantage over the potential lessee and it would be preferable to lease the asset if the lessor shares some (or all) of this advantage with the lessee. Essentially this advantage arises because the lessor's effective tax rate is higher than the lessee's effective tax rate. Example 19.5 illustrated this advantage in an extreme case where the lessee's effective tax rate was zero.

The inability of some asset users to use immediately all the allowable deductions associated with the acquisition of very expensive assets was a major factor in the growth of leveraged leasing during the 1970s and the early part of the 1980s. While such leases are invariably structured so as to exploit situations where the lessor has a higher effective tax rate than the lessee, it should not be assumed that a profitable lease can be designed in all such cases. Lewellen, Long and McConnell have shown that the existence of a tax advantage for leasing also depends on the term of the lease, the depreciation schedule, the opportunity cost of capital, and the leverage possibilities involved.[17]

Taxation advantages are also the motive for cross-border leases which, as discussed in Section 19.2.5, are structured so as to take advantage of differences between the tax environments of different countries. If there were no differences in tax regulations and tax rates between countries, cross-border leases would probably not exist.

In addition to the factors discussed above, leasing can also have tax advantages where lessors are able to choose between different accounting methods to calculate their taxable income. Naturally, if such a choice is available, lessors will choose the methods that delay payment of company income tax. Traditionally, lessors in Australia have enjoyed such a choice. However, a series of legislative changes, tax rulings, and court decisions has progressively eliminated the tax advantages formerly associated with leasing. These changes, together with the introduction of the imputation tax system, mean that the Australian tax system is now essentially neutral between leasing and other forms of debt finance. However, there can be tax effects that can influence the choice between leasing and buying. These effects are discussed in Section 19.8.

## CONSERVATION OF CAPITAL

It is often suggested that, by leasing, a company can conserve its capital for investment elsewhere. Alternatively, the same argument may be based on the suggestion that leasing provides '100 per cent financing'. In other words it is argued that there is some fundamental difference between leasing and other forms of finance, which allows a lessee to 'borrow' 100 per cent of the purchase price of an asset, compared with perhaps 80 per cent in the case of a secured loan. This argument is flawed. First, where lease rentals are payable in advance, which

---

[17] W. Lewellen, M. Long & J. McConnell, 'Asset Leasing in Competitive Capital Markets', *Journal of Finance*, June 1976, p. 795.

is usual, the finance effectively provided by leasing can be much less than the purchase price of the asset.[18] Secondly, the formal security provided to the lessor is not necessarily restricted to ownership of the leased asset.[19]

This means that to obtain a financial lease, it is necessary to have some equity capital, and the lease will use up some of the debt capacity provided by the company's equity in the same way as other debt. Therefore when only the immediate cash consequences are considered, leasing may give the appearance of 100 per cent financing, but this appearance is misleading. There is no such thing as '100 per cent lease finance', just as there is no such thing as '100 per cent debt finance'.

## CREDIT AVAILABILITY

An argument related to the previous one is that because lessees in the past have not been required to report their lease obligations on the balance sheet, they can use leasing to increase their access to debt. Even if this were true, it is only an advantage if borrowing restrictions imposed by lenders have prevented the potential lessee from attaining the optimal debt–equity ratio. Further, empirical evidence suggests that lease finance is a substitute for debt, with the result that companies may not have been able to use leasing to increase their access to other types of debt.[20] In any event, accounting standards AAS17 and AASB 1008 now require the capitalisation of financial lease obligations, which means that any potential 'off-balance-sheet financing' advantage for leasing should no longer be available.[21]

## COST OF CAPITAL

The analysis outlined earlier is consistent with the principle that, in lease evaluation, the discount rate applicable to a given component of the cash flows must be the same for both the lessee and the lessor. In other words, for a given cash flow, the required rate of return should depend on the risk of the cash flow, not the identity of the recipient.

However, if the lessor's cost of capital is lower (higher) than that of the potential lessee, the existence of competitive capital markets will result in leasing (buying) being preferred to buying (leasing). What circumstances will cause the cost of capital of the lessor and the lessee to differ? The answer to this question will depend on the risks associated with using the asset. Miller and Upton have

---

18 This factor is illustrated by Example 19.3 where the lease provides finance of $261 000, which is much less than the asset cost of $300 000.
19 See Footnote 13.
20 R. Bowman, 'The Debt Equivalence of Leases: An Empirical Investigation', *The Accounting Review*, April 1980, pp. 237–53.
21 There is conflicting evidence on whether the off-balance-sheet aspect of leasing ever provided borrowing opportunities that had a favourable effect on a company's share price. A number of these studies are summarised in B. Lev & J. Ohlson, 'Market-based Empirical Research in Accounting: A Review, Interpretation and Extension', in 'Studies on Current Research Methodologies in Accounting: A Critical Evaluation', *Journal of Accounting Research*, Supplement, 1982, pp. 280–1.

identified two types of relevant risk.[22] One is associated with uncertainty about the asset's economic depreciation, while the other is associated with uncertainty about the net cash flows from using the asset. In the case of a financial lease with a specified residual value, both these risks are borne by the lessee. In the case of an operating lease, both these risks are borne by the lessor. There may be other cases where the risks are shared between the two parties. Although the risks borne by the two parties can differ, competitive capital markets will ensure that the discount rate implicit in the lease agreement will reflect the allocation of risk between the two parties.

Suppose, however, that the lessee can raise capital at a lower cost for a given level of risk than the lessor. If this is so, the prospective lessee should find that it is more profitable to buy than to lease. However, as Miller and Upton point out, the lessee ' . . . would find it even more profitable under those circumstances to enter the leasing business'.[23] Any disequilibrium between the costs of capital for leasing and buying would then be eliminated. In other words, the costs of capital for leasing and buying must be the same, because if they were not, then one of two results would occur. Leasing would either be dominant (all assets would be leased), or leasing would disappear from the market.

## TRANSACTION COSTS

While a financial lease is very similar to other debt, there is a difference that can be important in the event of default. If a lessee defaults, the lessor, as the owner of the asset, can immediately repossess it. However, a secured lender is likely to face considerable delay, and greater costs, because it may be necessary for a defaulting borrower to be liquidated. In this case a liquidator has to be appointed to sell the assets and distribute the proceeds to lenders and other creditors. Therefore there may well be a difference in transaction costs which favours leasing. Similarly, because lessors have the security of ownership of the leased asset, they may be prepared to provide finance without carrying out a full check on the credit standing of the lessee. As a result, leasing can be attractive to small companies that do not have good access to other sources of finance.

In summary, the major reasons for financial leasing appear to involve savings in taxes and transaction costs. There can be significant tax advantages for leasing when there is a large difference between the effective income tax rates of the lessor and lessee. However, under the imputation tax system, any tax advantages of leasing appear to be small. While many of the other claimed advantages of leasing appear to be of dubious validity, it seems that in practice many people do perceive that there are advantages in keeping leases 'off balance sheet'.

Although opportunities to reduce taxes and transaction costs provide the major motive for financial leasing, there are some additional factors that can give rise to advantages for leasing. These are discussed in the next section.

---

[22] M. Miller & C. Upton, 'Leasing, Buying and the Cost of Capital Services', *Journal of Finance*, June 1976, pp. 767–74.
[23] See Footnote 22, p. 767.

## 19.7.2 LEASING POLICY

Smith and Wakeman point out that tax-related factors provide an important, but incomplete, explanation of some aspects of leasing.[24] Differences in effective tax rates are useful in identifying potential lessors and lessees, but provide little explanation of why specific assets are leased, while other similar assets are owned. For example, why is it that leasing of office buildings is more common than leasing of research laboratories? Some of the non-tax reasons that Smith and Wakeman identify are now discussed.

### SENSITIVITY TO USE AND MAINTENANCE DECISIONS

Because a lessee does not have a right to the salvage value of an asset at the end of the lease, there is less incentive to care for and maintain assets that are leased rather than owned. Lessors will recognise this, and will set lease rentals on the basis of expected levels of abuse. Therefore, the more sensitive the value of the asset to the levels of use and maintenance it receives, the more costly it will be to lease rather than purchase the asset. Therefore, it is argued that assets that are very sensitive to use and maintenance decisions will tend to be purchased by the user rather than leased. This argument appears to be more relevant to cancellable operating leases than to financial leases.

### SPECIALISED ASSETS

Smith and Wakeman suggest that there is an incentive to buy, rather than lease, specialised (or company-specific) assets. Such assets are more highly valued within the company than in their best alternative use. They argue that leasing company-specific assets involves negotiation costs and other agency costs that can be significant because of conflicts between the lessor and lessee concerning the division between them of that part of the value of the asset which exceeds its value in alternative uses. For example, the lessor will want to calculate the lease payments using a conservative residual value based on the likely disposal value of the asset. This value is likely to be quite uncertain, and the lessor's estimate will probably be much less than the value placed on the asset by the user. Therefore the lease payments required by the lessor are unlikely to be acceptable to the user.

In contrast, for 'general use' assets such as trucks and forklifts, substitutes are readily available, and the difference between the value-in-use and the value-in-exchange is likely to be small. Moreover, there is an active second-hand market in these assets, so it is relatively easy to forecast likely disposal values and to agree on the terms of a lease. This argument is consistent with the observation that leasing of cars and other motor vehicles is relatively common.

### FLEXIBILITY AND TRANSACTION COSTS

As discussed in Sections 19.2.1 and 19.6.2, an operating lease can have worthwhile advantages when an asset is required for only a short period. It was noted that an operating lease is likely to involve lower costs than purchasing an asset

---

[24] C. W. Smith & L. M. Wakeman, 'Determinants of Corporate Leasing Policy', *Journal of Finance*, July 1985, pp. 895–908.

and then selling it, particularly if the costs of ownership transfer are significant. Leasing rather than buying can also involve differences in search costs and costs of assessing quality.[25] For example, a company that leases a truck will be less concerned about the condition of its engine, transmission, and other mechanical parts than a potential buyer of the same vehicle. Therefore, a less costly inspection will suffice if the truck is to be leased. This advantage for leasing will be offset by the fact that, as discussed above, lessees will tend to be less careful in their use of assets than owners are likely to be. Lessors will recognise this problem and base the rentals on the expected salvage value of the asset, given the normal treatment to which leased assets are subjected. However, there can be an overall advantage for leasing, provided that the cost saving through avoiding frequent ownership transfers is greater than the additional costs associated with deterioration of leased assets.

### COMPARATIVE ADVANTAGE IN ASSET DISPOSAL

If the lessor has a comparative advantage in disposing of an asset, this may cause leasing to be preferred. For example, a lessor may be able to sell an asset at the end of the lease term at a higher price than could a company that had purchased the asset. Smith and Wakeman identify three potential sources of such a comparative advantage.[26]

First, there is the potential for lower search, information, and transaction costs associated with the lessor providing a specialised market for used assets. Such markets make it easier and cheaper for buyers seeking a particular asset to locate potential sellers. Secondly, there may be reduced repair and maintenance costs for current machines from reusing components of previously leased machines. Thirdly, reduced production costs result from reusing components of previously leased machines in the production of new machines. These advantages are likely to exist only where the lessor is also the manufacturer and/or distributor of the asset. However, Smith and Wakeman argue that manufacturers who accept used assets as trade-ins offer the same comparative advantages to asset buyers. Therefore while the cost reductions can be real, they are not peculiar to leasing.

## 19.8 COMMERCIAL HIRE PURCHASE

Commercial hire purchase (CHP) agreements are similar to financial leases and are provided by the same financiers, mainly banks and finance companies. Where an asset is financed by a CHP agreement the purchaser will be required to make a series of payments or instalments to the financier who owns the asset until the last payment is made. The payments may be equal or they can be structured to include a final 'balloon' payment. One essential feature of a CHP agreement is that it will either commit the user to buy the asset or give the user an option to buy it. A lease cannot commit the lessee to buying the asset or explicitly give the lessee an option to do so. This difference is important for tax purposes

---

[25] For a discussion of these and other factors relevant to short-term leasing, see D. Flath, 'The Economics of Short-term Leasing', *Economic Inquiry*, April 1980, pp. 247–59.
[26] Smith & Wakeman, see Footnote 24, p. 902.

because it means that in the case of CHP the user, rather than the financier, will be entitled to claim deductions for depreciation. The user will also be able to claim deductions for the interest component of the CHP payments.

In Australia the popularity of CHP has increased and, as noted in Section 19.1, during 1992/93 it made up an estimated 44 per cent of the equipment finance market. The increased popularity of CHP can be attributed largely to tax-related factors. For example, since June 1992 lessors have not been allowed to use the 'finance' method of accounting for tax purposes. Under the finance method, lease rentals are divided on an actuarial basis into principal and interest components. A lessor would then declare the interest component as taxable income. Lessors are now required to include lease rentals as income, and depreciation as a deduction, in calculating taxable income, which means that they are unable to use the tax deferral opportunities provided by the finance method. This change favoured CHP relative to leasing, in that an advantage that had favoured leasing was removed. The choice between leasing and CHP can also be affected by other taxation rules. In particular, Australian businesses buying new plant have at times been able to claim an additional tax deduction known as the *investment allowance*. This allowance, typically at rates of 10 or 20 per cent of the cost of eligible new plant, has only applied to leased assets when the term of the lease is at least 4 years and the lessor is a 'leasing company' as defined in the *Income Tax Assessment Act*. However these restrictions do not apply to CHP, which can therefore have a tax advantage for agreements with terms of less than 4 years. Similarly, in many States, the cost of leasing is increased by the imposition of stamp duties, currently at rates of up to 1.8 per cent on lease rentals. CHP payments are not subject to stamp duty but may be subject to other financial institutions duties.

## 19.9 CONCLUSIONS

The reasons for leasing differ between the various types of leases. The two basic types are operating leases and financial leases. Operating leases separate the risks of ownership from the use of the leased asset and can provide advantages such as lower transaction costs, convenience, and flexibility, as well as insurance against the risk of obsolescence. In the case of financial leases, the risks of ownership are borne by the user of the asset and leasing is an alternative to other forms of debt finance. Leasing of very expensive assets is driven by tax-related factors. Except where there are significant tax advantages, leasing of specialised assets is much less common than leasing of general use or marketable assets such as motor vehicles and computers. Financial leasing and commercial hire purchase can be attractive for businesses which are small and therefore face relatively high transaction costs in obtaining finance in other ways.

The leasing market is highly competitive and very flexible. Therefore, factors such as changes in tax rules and the level of government charges can have important effects on the popularity of leasing compared to similar forms of finance, particularly commercial hire purchase.

## Selected References

Bennett, J., 'Equipment Leasing', in *Handbook of Australian Corporate Finance*, Eds R. Bruce et al., 4th edn, Butterworths, Sydney, 1991, pp. 235–64.
Bowen R., 'Issues in Lease Financing', *Financial Management*, Winter 1973, pp. 25–33.
Lewellen, W., Long, M. & McConnell, J., 'Asset Leasing in Competitive Capital Markets', *Journal of Finance*, June 1976, pp. 787–98.
Miller, M. & Upton C., 'Leasing, Buying and the Cost of Capital Services', *Journal of Finance*, June 1976, pp. 761–86.
Myers, S., Dill, D. & Bautista, A., 'Valuation of Financial Lease Contracts', *Journal of Finance*, June 1976, pp. 799–819.
Schallheim, J., Johnson, R., Lease, R., & McConnell, J., ' The Determinants of Yields on Financial Leasing Contracts', *Journal of Financial Economics*, September 1987, pp. 45–67.
Smith, C. W. & Wakeman, L. M, 'Determinants of Corporate Leasing Policy', *Journal of Finance*, July 1985, pp. 895–908.
Szekely, L., 'The Tax Treatment of Leasing', *CCH Journal of Australian Taxation*, August/September 1991, pp. 48–54.

## QUESTIONS

1. Distinguish between a 'financial lease' and an 'operating lease'. Why is it important to make this distinction?
2. What are the important characteristics of a financial lease?
3. What are the essential characteristics of a sale and lease-back agreement? Outline the advantages and disadvantages of such an agreement.
4. What distinguishes a leveraged lease from other types of financial leases? What are the roles of the various parties to a leveraged lease?
5. Compare and contrast a 'leveraged lease' and a 'cross-border lease'.
6. *Leasing is a form of tax avoidance that should be outlawed by legislation.* Discuss this statement, indicating why you agree or disagree with it.
7. *Leasing increases a company's access to debt.* Discuss critically.
8. Discuss critically the alleged advantages of leasing.
9. The Hybee Company is evaluating an investment to produce a new product with an expected marketable life of 5 years. The expected annual net cash flow before tax is $120 000. To produce this product the company will have to acquire new plant. The company can either purchase this plant, or lease it. Details of these alternatives are as follows:

*Purchase*

The purchase price of the plant is $250 000, and it is expected that it will have a zero salvage value after 5 years. The allowable annual depreciation charge on the plant is 20 per cent per annum, straight-line.

*Lease*

The lease requires five annual payments, each of $60 000, payable at the beginning of each year. The company tax rate is 40 cents in the dollar. The required rate of return on the investment is 15 per cent annum after tax and the after-tax cost of an equivalent loan is 8 per cent per annum.
    Should the company undertake the investment? If so, should it purchase or lease the plant?

10. The Vision Company is evaluating the acquisition of an asset that it requires for a period of 6 years. The following information relates to the purchase of the asset:
    (a) The purchase price is $1 million.
    (b) It can be depreciated at a rate of 10 per cent per annum, straight-line.
    (c) The estimated disposal value in 6 years' time is $300 000.
    (d) The company income tax rate is 40 cents in the dollar.
    (e) The required rate of return on the investment is 15 per cent per annum after tax.

    Assume that the company has the alternative of leasing the asset from the Ajax Leasing Company. Assume also that the after-tax cost of an equivalent loan is 9 per cent per annum.

    Assuming that the annual lease payments are made at the beginning of each year and that the lease specifies a residual value of $300 000, what lease payments would make Vision indifferent between buying or leasing the asset?

11. Assume that Ajax Leasing Company could acquire the asset required by Vision (see Question 10) for $900 000 and depreciate it at a rate of 15 per cent per annum, straight-line. The other information is the same as that presented in Question 10.
    (a) Calculate the minimum annual lease payment that Ajax Leasing Company would charge.
    (b) Does your answer to (a) necessarily imply that Vision should lease the asset?

12. Carry Ltd is evaluating the possibility of tendering for the licence to operate international flights from Canberra to Queenstown (NZ) for a 5-year period. If its bid is successful, the licence fee has to be paid immediately, and is not tax deductible.

    The company has estimated that the before-tax annual net cash inflow from operating the service would be $2 250 000, and that it would require an after-tax rate of return of 15 per cent per annum on its investment. The company income tax rate is 40 cents in the dollar.

    Carry Ltd has the option of either buying or leasing an aircraft. The following information is relevant to these options:

    *Purchase*

    The purchase price of the aircraft is $6 000 000. It could be depreciated at a rate of 15 per cent per annum, straight-line. The estimated disposal value in 5 years' time is $2 000 000.

    *Lease*

    The annual lease payments would be $1 500 000, payable at the beginning of each year, with a lease residual of $2 000 000. The after-tax interest rate on an equivalent loan is 11 per cent per annum.

    What is the maximum licence fee that Carry Ltd should tender?

13. Ibus Ltd is considering the installation of a new computer. Because of uncertainty as to its future computing requirements and the prospect of advancements in computing technology, it is evaluating the acquisition of the computer by either purchasing it, or leasing it under a contract that

includes a cancellation option. Information relevant to the company's evaluation is as follows:

*Purchase*

The purchase price of the computer is $300 000, and it can be depreciated at a rate of 15 per cent per annum, straight-line. Ibus Ltd plans to operate the computer for a maximum of 5 years. The computer's disposal value at the end of 5 years is estimated to be $50 000.

*Lease*

The annual lease payments on the operating lease would be $90 000, payable at the beginning of each year. The lease can be cancelled by Ibus Ltd at any time without incurring any penalty payment.

The company income tax rate is 40 cents in the dollar, the required return on the investment is 20 per cent per annum and the after-tax cost of an equivalent loan is 10 per cent per annum.

Should the company purchase or lease the asset?

14. Donash Pty Ltd needs a new computer, which it can buy for $440 000, or it can lease from Comlease. The lease requires six annual payments of $100 000 each, in advance. Donash has large tax losses, and does not expect to pay tax for at least 5 years. Comlease pays tax at 40 per cent, and can depreciate the computer on a straight-line basis over 3 years. The computer will have no residual value at the end of 5 years, and the before-tax interest rate on an equivalent loan would be 15 per cent per annum.
    (a) What is the NPV of the lease for Donash?
    (b) What is the NPV for Comlease?
    (c) What is the overall gain to leasing in this transaction?

15. Outline the main factors that are likely to influence the choice between acquiring an asset through a financial lease, or by commercial hire purchase.

16. Which, if any, of the following are genuine advantages of leasing?
    (a) Leasing conserves the lessee's capital.
    (b) Leasing enables needed assets to be acquired even when the Board of Directors will not approve any capital expenditure requests.
    (c) By leasing a computer, the risk of obsolescence can be transferred to the lessor.
    (d) Leasing provides 100 per cent financing.

17. Critically evaluate the following statement. *Many road transport companies are risky businesses which are unable to borrow enough to buy all the trucks they need. For them, leasing makes a lot of sense. Trucks are attractive to lessors because they are durable and there is an active second-hand market.*

18. Connell Finance is determining payments for a 4-year financial lease with a 20 per cent residual on an asset which costs $800 000, and can be depreciated on a straight-line basis over 3 years. The asset qualifies for an investment allowance of 10 per cent. The tax rate for Connell is 40 per cent, and it requires a before-tax rate of return from leases of 12 per cent. Determine the lease payments when the lease payments are made:
    (a) annually in advance;
    (b) quarterly in advance.

**CHAPTER 20**

# ANALYSIS OF TAKEOVERS

## 20.1 INTRODUCTION

Takeovers are important transactions in the **market for corporate control**. A takeover typically involves one company purchasing another company by acquiring a controlling interest in its voting shares. Such an investment is variously described as a 'takeover', an 'acquisition' or a 'merger'. It is possible to distinguish between mergers and takeovers, but in this chapter the term **takeover** will generally be used to refer to all instances where an acquiring company[1] achieves control of another company, referred to as the **target company**.

The market for corporate control is a market in which alternative teams of managers compete for the right to control corporate assets and make top-level management decisions.[2] Essentially, by changes in control, corporate assets can be quickly redeployed in ways expected to bring economic benefits and add value for shareholders. Other transactions in this market include divestitures, spin-offs and buyouts which are defined and discussed in Section 20.7. The main topic of this chapter is takeovers because they are the most important of these transactions in the Australian market for corporate control.

After a takeover, the acquiring company obtains control of all of the target company's assets, so a takeover is an indirect investment in assets. The fact that the investment is made indirectly does not change the basic principle that an investment should proceed if, and only if, it has a positive net present value (NPV). Despite this basic similarity between takeovers and other investments, there are several reasons why takeovers should be treated as a separate topic. These reasons include:

---

[1] When a takeover bid is first announced, the eventual outcome is unknown. Therefore we also use the terms 'bidder' or 'offerer' when a takeover is still in progress.
[2] M. Jensen & R. Ruback, 'The Market for Corporate Control: The Scientific Evidence', *Journal of Financial Economics*, April 1983, pp. 5–50.

1. Takeovers are controversial and at times there has been rather heated public debate about whether takeover activity is beneficial to shareholders and the economy.
2. The NPV of a takeover can be very difficult to estimate, but correct analysis will be easier if it is based on an understanding of why takeovers occur and on knowledge of the evidence on their effects on returns to investors.
3. A takeover may give rise to complex legal, accounting, and tax questions.
4. The acquiring company's plans may be frustrated by defensive tactics employed by the management of the target company, or by the intervention of other potential acquirers.

### 20.1.1 THE IMPORTANCE OF TAKEOVERS IN AUSTRALIA

Takeovers are important in that they involve changes in the ownership and/or control of valuable assets. This is reflected in Table 20.1 which shows that between 1986 and 1992 there were takeover bids for Australian listed companies with a total value of almost $74 billion. This figure includes only the value of the *equity* of the target companies; the value of their assets would be considerably greater.

**Table 20.1** Total value of takeover bids for listed companies ($ billion)

| Year | 1986 | 1987 | 1988 | 1989 | 1990 | 1991 | 1992 |
|---|---|---|---|---|---|---|---|
| All bids | 14.0 | 17.0 | 18.0 | 16.5 | 3.8 | 2.0 | 2.6 |
| Successful bids | 4.8 | 11.1 | 10.3 | 8.9 | 2.8 | 1.2 | 1.5 |

Source: Corporate Adviser

### 20.1.2 FLUCTUATIONS IN TAKEOVER ACTIVITY

Takeover activity fluctuates widely over time. These fluctuations are reflected in the figures in Table 20.2 which show that between 1972 and 1993 the number of bids for listed companies has varied between a high of 289 in 1988 and a low

**Table 20.2** Number of takeover bids for listed companies

| Year | Bids | Year | Bids |
|---|---|---|---|
| 1972 | 198 | 1983 | 94 |
| 1973 | 117 | 1984 | 118 |
| 1974 | 65 | 1985 | 140 |
| 1975 | 74 | 1986 | 142 |
| 1976 | 90 | 1987 | 205 |
| 1977 | 80 | 1988 | 289 |
| 1978 | 107 | 1989 | 179 |
| 1979 | 106 | 1990 | 97 |
| 1980 | 132 | 1991 | 86 |
| 1981 | 126 | 1992 | 55 |
| 1982 | 70 | 1993 | 61 |

Sources: 1972 to 1984, Bishop, Dodd and Officer (1987), (See Footnote 4)
1985 to 1993, Corporate Adviser

of 55 in 1992. Earlier the number of bids had peaked at 198 in 1972 and declined to a low of 70 in 1982.

These fluctuations are often described as takeover 'waves'. Easton notes that there is some agreement that in the US, takeover waves have occurred at the turn of the century, in the 1920s, the 1960s, and most recently during the 1980s.[3] While there is no generally accepted explanation for the existence of takeover waves, there is evidence that takeover activity is positively related to the behaviour of share prices. Using Australian data over the period 1972 to 1984, Bishop, Dodd and Officer reported a close relationship between increases in share prices and the number of takeovers.[4] Positive relationships between takeover activity in Australia and changes in share market indices have also been reported by Argus and Finn who used quarterly data from 1972 to 1990 and by Easton who used annual data from 1946 to 1986.[5] The explanation preferred by Bishop, Dodd and Officer for this relationship is that periods when the prices of shares are increasing rapidly are also periods of optimism for investment. The increase in share prices will reflect increased demand for real goods, which will require companies to increase their productive capacity. While companies will increase their capacity by investing in new plant and equipment (internal investment), managers will also be looking for opportunities to take control of existing assets, particularly assets that are not being used efficiently. When such opportunities are found there will be an increase in takeover activity (external investment). In short, both internal and external investment will respond to the same economic forces. Therefore a relationship between the state of the economy and the level of takeover activity is to be expected. Other factors that may influence the level of takeover activity include changes in legislation controlling takeovers, and controls on foreign investment in Australian companies.

## 20.1.3 TYPES OF TAKEOVERS

Takeovers are usually classified as follows:
1. A **horizontal takeover** is the takeover of a target company operating in the same line of business as the acquiring company. An example is a furniture manufacturer taking over another furniture manufacturer.
2. A **vertical takeover** is the takeover of a target company which is either a supplier of goods to, or a consumer of goods produced by, the acquiring company. Examples are a furniture manufacturer taking over a sawmill or a furniture retail store.
3. A **conglomerate takeover** is the takeover of a target company in an unrelated type of business. An example is a furniture manufacturer taking over a mining company.

---

3 S. Easton, 'Takeover Activity and Share Returns in Australia: A Note', *Applied Economics Letters*, April 1994, pp. 66–8.
4 S. Bishop, P. Dodd & R. R. Officer, 'Australian Takeovers: The Evidence 1972–1985', *Policy Monograph* 12, Centre for Independent Studies, St Leonards, 1987.
5 J. Argus & F. Finn, 'Analysis of the Determinants of Aggregate Takeover Activity', *Proceedings of the Second International Conference on Asian-Pacific Financial Markets*, 1991, pp. 11–20; and S. Easton (Footnote 3).

## 20.2 Reasons for Takeovers

Just as there are different types of takeovers, so there are many different reasons why takeovers occur. We begin by presenting a framework for the evaluation of these reasons and then discuss some of the suggested reasons individually.

As noted above, takeovers are part of the market for corporate control in which alternative management teams compete for the right to manage corporate resources. Competition in this market should ensure that resource control is acquired by those teams who are expected to be the most efficient in utilising the resources. It should also ensure that the interests of management cannot diverge too far from those of shareholders. For example, suppose that a company is poorly managed, resulting in low profits and a low share price. An opportunity then exists for a more efficient management team to take over this company, replace the inefficient managers and reverse the poor performance of the company. However, the market for corporate control should not be viewed only as providing a severe disciplinary measure against incompetent management. Increased profitability through a change of management does not necessarily imply that the previous management was incompetent, only that a more efficient team was available.[6]

Wealth (or value) can be created by combining two companies if the takeover transfers control of assets to managers who can recognise more valuable uses for those assets, either within the combined company or by redeployment of the assets elsewhere. The term **synergy** is often used to describe the value gains that can be associated with combining two entities. In other words, if there are synergistic benefits associated with combining two companies A and T, the combined company will be worth more than the sum of their values as independent entities:

$$V_{AT} > V_A + V_T$$

where $V_{AT}$ = the value of the assets of the combined company
$V_A$ = the value of Company A operating independently
$V_T$ = the value of Company T operating independently

In this chapter the subscripts A and T are used to denote the acquiring and target companies respectively.

To summarise, the main implications of this approach are that takeovers are value-increasing transactions and that the market for corporate control is driven largely by the existence of synergies. It follows that, in evaluating the suggested reasons for takeovers, we need to consider whether the particular reason suggested is consistent with the existence of an economic gain from combining two companies. The suggested reasons for takeovers that we will evaluate are as follows:

1. The target company is managed inefficiently.
2. The acquiring and target companies have assets that are complementary.
3. The target company is undervalued.

---

[6] P. Dodd & R. R. Officer, 'Corporate Control, Economic Efficiency and Shareholder Justice', *Policy Monograph* 9, Centre for Independent Studies, St Leonards, 1986.

4. Cost reductions result from the takeover.
5. Increased market power results from the takeover.
6. Diversification benefits result from the takeover.
7. The target company or the acquiring company has excess liquidity or free cash flow.
8. Tax benefits result from the takeover.
9. There are increased earnings per share and price–earnings ratio effects.

## 20.2.1 Evaluation of the reasons for takeovers
### 1 The target company is managed inefficiently

In this case, the acquiring company's managers may see an opportunity to use the target company's resources more efficiently. The more efficient use of resources may result in an increase in the value of the target company. However, the acquiring company's aspiration to improve the efficiency of the target company's operations may not always be realised. Even if an acquiring company is managed efficiently, this does not necessarily mean that its managers will be able to improve the performance of another company. This is particularly so where the two companies operate in different industries. This suggests that improvements in efficiency are less likely to be achieved with a conglomerate takeover. As a corollary, improvements in efficiency are most likely to be achieved with a horizontal takeover, as the acquiring company's managers are likely to have the expertise needed to manage the target company's operations more efficiently.

However, the market value of a company may be low, not because its managers are inefficient, but rather because they make decisions in their own interests rather than in those of the company's shareholders. The discussion of agency costs in Chapter 1 suggested that managers may attempt to transfer wealth from shareholders to themselves. If the value reduction is large, it is likely that the company will eventually be identified as a takeover target since an acquiring company will be able to eliminate, or at least reduce, the agency costs, thereby providing benefits for its own shareholders.

### 2 The acquiring and target companies have assets that are complementary

A takeover can be attractive if either or both of the companies can provide the other with needed resources at relatively low cost. For example, this can occur when the target company's managers are considered to have valuable skills. The motive for the takeover is to acquire expertise. It may be cheaper to acquire this expertise via a takeover than to hire and train new staff. This is often an argument for taking over small, often unlisted, companies that have failed to realise their full potential because their managers do not have skills in all areas of management. For example, a group of engineers may establish a computer hardware company which does not earn a satisfactory profit because the engineers lack marketing skills. A large company with a strong marketing team may take it over because it is seen as a relatively cheap means of acquiring the technical skills of the target company's staff. Similarly, the complementary skills of the acquiring company's staff may be used to improve the target's profitability.

## 3 THE TARGET COMPANY IS UNDERVALUED

Describing a target company as simply 'undervalued' is not very meaningful, since a takeover always implies that the target is worth more to the acquiring company than it was worth to its previous shareholders. Managers of acquiring companies often refer to their targets as 'presenting wonderful opportunities' or 'too good to pass up', suggesting that they believe in their ability to identify 'bargains'. Chapter 14 presents empirical evidence on market efficiency which suggests that most managers will find it very difficult to identify such opportunities. However, even if managers are able to identify undervalued shares, it is not necessary to buy whole companies, paying premiums for control, to profit from their ability to identify 'bargains'. Instead, they could buy a parcel of the shares at the market price, wait until the market recognises the shares' value, and then sell.

It has never been seriously suggested that share markets are fully efficient in the strong-form sense. It is therefore, possible, that a company's managers may have private information which is not yet reflected in the price of another company's shares. Share acquisition follows, and may extend to acquiring a controlling interest in the target company.

A takeover may also occur when the market value of the target company is less than the sum of the market values of its assets. This does not necessarily mean that the share market is inefficient, as the company's share price may accurately reflect the value of its assets in their current use. However, such a company can become a takeover target because other managers recognise the existence of alternative, better uses for the assets. Investors who focus on searching for takeover opportunities of this type are often referred to as **corporate raiders** or asset strippers. Their activities can be regarded as involving a form of synergy because a crucial factor is the skill of the acquiring company's managers in identifying opportunities to create value by redeploying assets to alternative uses.

## 4 COST REDUCTIONS

Another reason for takeovers is that the total cost of operating the combined company is expected to be less than the cost of operating the two companies separately. These cost savings may be due to various economies of scale, and are therefore more likely to be achieved in the case of a horizontal takeover. For example, two furniture manufacturers, by combining, may be able to reduce their production costs because production runs will be longer, resulting in the fixed costs of a production run being incurred less frequently. Cost savings may also be achieved in a vertical takeover. For example, combining companies where one is a supplier to the other may result in more efficient coordination of the activities of the two companies. One reason is that the costs of communication and various forms of bargaining can be reduced by a vertical takeover.

## 5 INCREASED MARKET POWER

Taking over a company in the same industry may increase the market power of the combined company. The increase in market power may enable the acquiring company to earn monopoly profits if there are significant barriers to entry into the industry. Governments frequently legislate to prevent takeovers that are considered likely to result in an excessive level of concentration in an industry. Section 50 of the *Trade Practices Act* 1974 prohibits a company from acquiring the shares or assets of another company where the acquisition is likely to place the acquiring company in a position to control or dominate a market. However, the Trade Practices Commissioner can invoke section 88 of the Act to permit a takeover which might contravene section 50 if he believes that the takeover is in the public interest.

## 6 DIVERSIFICATION BENEFITS

Portfolio theory shows that investors can reduce their risk by holding a diversified portfolio of assets.[7] A similar reason has been advanced to justify a takeover. The takeover, it is suggested, enables a company to reduce risk via diversification. Assume that a steel manufacturer diversifies its interests by taking over an oil exploration company. The question is: Does the reduced risk brought about by the takeover benefit the steel manufacturer's shareholders? The somewhat surprising answer is generally no. The steel manufacturer's shareholders already had the opportunity to hold shares in oil exploration companies so the takeover does not provide any investment opportunity that did not previously exist. Therefore, when shareholders themselves hold diversified portfolios, diversification by a company is a neutral factor that will neither alter its market value nor benefit its shareholders.[8] Takeovers motivated by diversification can be beneficial to managers. Therefore the occurrence of such takeovers can indicate the existence of agency problems.[9]

A related argument is that combining two companies whose earnings streams are less than perfectly correlated will lower the risk of default on debt so that the debt capacity of the combination is greater than the sum of the debt capacities of the two companies operating separately. This is the result of the **co-insurance effect**, which means that lenders to one company can now be paid out of the combined resources of both companies. While the co-insurance argument is

---

[7] See Section 3.4.
[8] L. Schall, 'Asset Valuation, Firm Investment and Firm Diversification', *Journal of Business*, January 1972, pp. 11–18.
[9] However, there may be cases where company diversification is of value to investors. Shareholdings in a private family company may represent a high proportion of the family's wealth and the family members may wish to reduce their risk by diversifying. To obtain the funds to invest elsewhere, they might have to sell part of their interest in the company, but this would mean diluting their control, and might also cause a large capital gains tax bill. Because of these barriers, diversification by the company will almost certainly be more attractive than diversification by the individual shareholders. Such cases are the exception rather than the rule, and for public companies whose shareholders can diversify cheaply, company diversification will not add value for shareholders.

essentially correct, the problem is that shareholders will not necessarily benefit from the reduction in default risk and interest cost of debt.

Suppose that two companies, each with debt securities outstanding, merge. The default risk of each company's debt will fall and the value of the debt securities will increase. This gain to debtholders is at the expense of shareholders who now have to guarantee the debt of both companies, and the loss to shareholders exactly offsets the gain to debtholders.[10] If two companies combine and *then* borrow, the shareholders will benefit from a lower interest rate, but they are providing the lenders with lower risk, so there is still no net gain. However, shareholders can benefit from the co-insurance effect to the extent that expected bankruptcy costs are reduced, or there are net tax savings.[11] Therefore, while combining companies can yield genuine financing benefits, it is doubtful that their magnitude is sufficient to justify many takeovers.

## 7 EXCESS LIQUIDITY AND FREE CASH FLOW

A company with excess liquidity may be identified as a takeover target by companies seeking access to funds. However, it seems difficult to justify paying a premium to obtain control of a company for this reason alone, because the capital market can provide funds at lower transaction costs. On the other hand, companies with excess liquidity may turn to the acquisition of other companies rather than return more cash to their shareholders. Such takeovers may result from managers pursuing their own interests, rather than maximising the wealth of shareholders. Managers may cause their companies to grow beyond optimum size because larger organisations are often associated with higher salaries and benefits, and more promotion opportunities. Jensen argues that this conflict of interest can be severe in companies that generate substantial free cash flow and can lead to such companies engaging in takeovers that generate very small benefits, or even value reductions.[12] For example, diversification programs achieved through takeover are likely to benefit managers but may reduce shareholders' wealth. Where management persists in this type of activity its own company is likely eventually to become a takeover target. Therefore the free cash flow theory shows how some takeovers are evidence of the conflicts of interest between shareholders and management, while others are a response to the problem.

---

10 The possible benefits of the co-insurance effect were first proposed by W. G. Lewellen, 'A Pure Financial Rationale for the Conglomerate Merger', *Journal of Finance*, May 1971, pp. 521–37. Authors who have explored his failure to allow for wealth transfers from shareholders include R. Higgins & L. Schall, 'Corporate Bankruptcy and Conglomerate Merger', *Journal of Finance*, March 1975, pp. 93–114.

11 W. Lee & H. Barker, 'Bankruptcy Costs and the Firm's Optimal Debt Capacity: A Positive Theory of Capital Structure', *Southern Economic Journal*, April 1977, pp. 1453–65.

12 Free cash flow is defined as cash flow in excess of that required to fund all projects that have positive net present values. See M. Jensen, 'Agency Costs of Free Cash Flow, Corporate Finance, and Takeovers', *American Economic Review*, May 1986, pp. 320–9; and M. Jensen, 'The Takeover Controversy: Analysis and Evidence', in *The Revolution in Corporate Finance*, 2nd edn, J. Stern & D. Chew, Eds., Blackwell, Oxford, 1992.

## 8 TAX BENEFITS

Taking over a company with accumulated tax losses may reduce the total tax payable by the combined company. The Commissioner of Taxation restricts the use of past accumulated tax losses to situations where it can be shown that either the **continuity-of-ownership test** or the **continuity-of-business test** is satisfied.[13] The former test requires that owners of at least 51 per cent of the company's shares when it incurred losses remain as owners when those accumulated losses are offset against taxable income. The continuity-of-business test provides that where the continuity-of-ownership test is not satisfied, the past accumulated losses can still be offset against taxable income where the acquired company continues in the same business after the takeover. For companies with resident shareholders, the incentive to reduce company tax payments in this way is much smaller under the imputation tax system than it was under the classical tax system. This follows from the fact that, as discussed in Appendix 11.1, company tax is essentially a withholding tax against the personal tax liabilities of shareholders. Other things being equal, reduction of company tax will mean that shareholders have to pay *more* personal tax on dividends. Therefore, any advantage associated with lowering company tax payments will be only a timing advantage.

## 9 INCREASED EARNINGS PER SHARE AND PRICE-EARNINGS RATIO EFFECTS

Corporate financial objectives are sometimes expressed in terms of growth in earnings per share (EPS), and this may lead an acquiring company to evaluate the effect of a proposed takeover on its EPS. Unfortunately this approach is unreliable. While a takeover which is economically viable should lead to increased EPS for the acquiring company, it is easy to design a takeover that produces no economic benefits, but which nevertheless produces an immediate increase in EPS. The following example illustrates this situation.

*Example 20.1*

This example refers to the data given in Table 20.3.

**Table 20.3** *Effect of takeover on earnings per share and market value of Company A*

| Item | Company A | Company T | Combined company A + T |
|---|---|---|---|
| No. of shares | 200 000 | 100 000 | 250 000 |
| Earnings ($/year) | 200 000 | 100 000 | 300 000 |
| EPS ($) | 1.00 | 1.00 | 1.20 |
| Share price ($) | 10.00 | 5.00 | 10.00 |
| P/E ratio | 10 | 5 | 8.33 |
| Market value of equity ($m) | 2 | 0.5 | 2.5 |

---

[13] See Section 80 of the *Income Tax Assessment Act* 1936.

Suppose that there are no economic benefits associated with combining companies A and T. Therefore, earnings of the combined company will simply be the sum of the individual companies' earnings, $300 000 per year. Assume that A acquires T by issuing one of its shares, worth $10, for every two T shares, also worth a total of $10. This will mean issuing a further 50 000 A shares, making 250 000 on issue, and the EPS for the combined company will be $300 000/250 000 = $1.20, an immediate increase of 20 per cent. Although the takeover *looks* attractive, it *cannot* be attractive because the takeover generates no economic benefits. The fact that it has no economic benefits is seen in the final row of Table 20.3: the combined company is worth only the sum of the values of the two individual companies. The reason that EPS increases is simply that A was able to acquire a company with earnings of $100 000 per annum by issuing only 50 000 of its shares. This, in turn, was possible because A's P/E ratio of 10 was greater than T's ratio of 5. The effect we have illustrated here has been called **bootstrapping**,[14] and occurs in share-exchange takeovers whenever the acquiring company's P/E ratio exceeds the target company's P/E ratio. Therefore, if EPS is used in takeover evaluation it is important to distinguish between the effects of true growth and the bootstrap effect. To avoid confusion, it might be better simply to ignore EPS in the context of takeovers.

We do not expect everyone to heed our last piece of advice so we will go one step further to highlight another way in which 'analysis' based on EPS can be misleading. An analyst, impressed by the 20 per cent increase in EPS resulting from A's acquisition of T, might be tempted to value the combined company by applying A's P/E ratio of 10 to the new EPS of $1.20, giving a share price of $12 and an equity value of $12 × 250 000 = $3 million. But this must be wrong, because, with no economic benefits, the value of the combined company can only be $2.5 million, so the share price is $10 and the P/E ratio is 8.33 rather than 10. We have more to say about the use of P/E ratios later in the chapter, but the point we wish to emphasise now is that there is no basis for assuming that an acquiring company's pre-takeover P/E ratio will continue to apply to a combined company.

## 20.2.2 THE ROLES OF TAKEOVERS

The valid reasons for takeovers can be classified into two groups, which suggests two main roles for takeovers. First, the threat or potential for takeover can **discipline** management of target companies. To be effective, threats must sometimes be carried out, and in cases where significant inefficiencies or agency problems remain, the managers of target companies can be replaced by takeovers.[15]

---

14 S. Myers, 'A Framework for Evaluating Mergers', in *Modern Developments in Financial Management*, Ed. S. Myers, Praeger, New York, 1976, pp. 633–45.
15 Evidence that the turnover rate for the top executive of target companies increases dramatically following a takeover is provided by K. Martin & J. McConnell, 'Corporate Performance, Corporate Takeovers, and Management Turnover', *Journal of Finance*, June 1991, pp. 671–87. They also found that in cases where the top executive was replaced after a takeover, target companies had been performing poorly relative to other companies in their industry. These results indicate that the takeover market is important in controlling the behaviour of managers.

Secondly, takeovers can take advantage of **synergies** such as economies of scale or complementarity between assets. A basic difference between these two roles is that in the first case the gains are associated with *changes of control*, whereas in the second case, the gains are associated with *combining* previously separate assets or companies. Another difference is that takeovers designed to replace management are more likely to be hostile than those driven by synergies.

In both cases there are usually other ways in which similar benefits can be achieved. Poor management could be replaced by a company's own Board of Directors and synergies associated with combining assets can be achieved through joint ventures. Therefore, takeovers are *one* way in which management can be improved or synergies exploited, but the prevalence of takeovers suggests that they are often the most effective way.

## 20.3 ECONOMIC EVALUATION OF TAKEOVERS

For an acquiring company, takeovers are an investment that should proceed if the net present value (NPV) is positive. This may sound simple, but takeovers are typically complex; the benefits involved may not be obvious, and there are several ways in which NPV analysis could be applied to them. Some of these ways are best avoided because they are particularly prone to the effects of forecast errors. Therefore, it is desirable to use a framework that directs attention to the key issues of identifying and quantifying the benefits of a proposed takeover and comparing benefits with costs.[16]

Assume that you are an investment analyst employed by Company A to evaluate the takeover of Company T. The gain from the takeover can be defined as the difference between the value of the combined company and the sum of their values as independent entities:

$$\text{Gain} = V_{AT} - (V_A + V_T) \qquad (20.1)$$

The logic of Equation 20.1 is that it should prompt the following question: What characteristics of this takeover mean that the two companies should be worth more when combined than when separate? However, the fact that there is a gain from the takeover does not necessarily mean that it should proceed. Management also has to consider the cost of obtaining control of the target. Assuming for the present that cash is used to buy Company T, the net cost is defined as:

$$\text{Net cost} = \text{cash} - V_T \qquad (20.2)$$

The term **net cost** is used to emphasise that we are considering cost in terms of the premium paid over T's value as an independent entity. The takeover will have a positive NPV for Company A's shareholders only if the gain exceeds the net cost:

$$NPV_A = \text{gain} - \text{net cost}$$
$$= \text{gain} - \text{cash} + V_T > 0 \qquad (20.3)$$

If $NPV_A$ is equal to zero, then Equation 20.3 can be used to find the value of

---

[16] The framework suggested here is similar to that set out by Myers (see Footnote 14).

Company T to Company A, $V_{T(A)}$, which is the maximum price A should pay for the target:

$$V_{T(A)} = \text{cash} = \text{gain} + V_T \qquad (20.4)$$

Therefore, the valuation of Company T can be broken into two steps: the first is to estimate $V_T$ and the second is to estimate the gain from the takeover. If the target is a listed company, the evidence on market efficiency shows that the market capitalisation of the company's securities should be an unbiased estimate of $V_T$, so the main emphasis should be on estimating the gain. In other words, it is necessary to focus on the *incremental* cash flow effects of the takeover. There are likely to be effects on both cash inflows and outflows which can be categorised as in the following checklist:

*Incremental inflows*

1. Sales revenue
2. Proceeds from disposal of surplus assets.

*Incremental outflows*

1. Operating costs
2. Taxes paid
3. Capital investment to upgrade existing assets or acquire new assets.

Valuation of a target company based on incremental cash flows is illustrated in Example 20.2.

### Example 20.2

Mayfair Ltd is considering the acquisition of Board Ltd. Mayfair's analyst has identified the following effects of the takeover:

1. Investment of $400 000 will be required immediately to upgrade some of Board's older assets.
2. Asset upgrading, economies of scale, and improved efficiency will increase net operating cash flows by $290 000 per annum in perpetuity.
3. Some of Board's assets which have been producing a cash inflow of $70 000 per annum will be sold. Because the new owners of these assets should be able to use them more profitably, sale proceeds are expected to be $800 000.
4. New plant costing $1 000 000 will be purchased and is expected to generate net operating cash flows of $230 000 per annum in perpetuity.

Board's activities are all of the same risk and the required rate of return is 15 per cent per annum.

Combining these effects, the overall change in net operating cash flows will be $290 000 − $70 000 + $230 000 = $450 000 per annum. This has a present value of $450 000/0.15 = $3 000 000. The gain will be:

$$\text{Gain} = \$3\,000\,000 - \$400\,000 + \$800\,000 - \$1\,000\,000$$
$$= \$2\,400\,000$$

Therefore the maximum price Mayfair should be prepared to pay is the value of Board Ltd as an independent entity, plus the gain of $2 400 000.

Board has 5 million shares on issue which have a market price of $2 each. Assuming that market price equals value as an independent entity:

$$V_T = 5 \text{ million} \times \$2 = \$10 \text{ million}$$

and: $V_{T(A)} = \$2\,400\,000 + \$10\,000\,000 = \$12\,400\,000$

so the maximum price Mayfair should be prepared to pay is:

$$\frac{\$12\,400\,000}{5\,000\,000} = \$2.48 \text{ per share}$$

### 20.3.1 COMMENTS ON ESTIMATION OF TAKEOVER GAINS

The cash flow effects in Example 20.2 were deliberately kept very simple so that complex discounted cash flow calculations would not cloud the central issue of the *incremental* effects of a takeover. In doing so, the impression may have been given that, apart from assessing any immediate cash flow effects associated with sale or purchase of assets, estimating the gain from a takeover only involves estimating the incremental operating cash flows, and discounting these cash flows at the target company's required rate of return. In some cases this may be so, but in other cases there will be a need to divide the incremental cash flows into different risk classes and apply a different discount rate to each class, and there may be cases where discounted cash flow analysis is not the best approach at all. For example, a takeover may open up new growth opportunities, which result in intangible strategic benefits whose values are very uncertain. The immediate cash flow effect of investing in such opportunities is generally negative, but these outlays may be necessary in order to have the opportunity of entering a new development. The outlays can therefore be viewed as the purchase price of an option, and the option-pricing principles discussed in Chapter 16 are likely to be more applicable than discounted cash flow analysis.[17]

### 20.3.2 COMPARING GAINS AND COSTS

In Example 20.2, the gain from Mayfair Ltd acquiring Board Ltd was estimated to be $2.4 million. Before making an offer, Mayfair's management also has to consider the net cost of the takeover. Estimation of the net cost is more complex in a share-exchange takeover, so we will start by assuming that Mayfair pays cash for Board. In Equation 20.2, the net cost of a cash takeover was defined as the amount of cash paid, minus the value of the target as an independent entity. Suppose that Mayfair pays $2.30 per share for Board, giving a total outlay of $11.5 million. The net cost is:

$$\text{Cash} - V_T = \$11.5 \text{ million} - \$10 \text{ million}$$
$$= \$1.5 \text{ million}$$

---

[17] For a detailed discussion of valuation methods see T. Copeland, T. Koller & J. Murrin, *Valuation: Measuring and Managing the Value of Companies*, John Wiley and Sons, New York, 1990.

Therefore, Board's shareholders capture $1.5 million of the gain, and the NPV for Mayfair's shareholders (Equation 20.3) is:

$$\begin{aligned} NPV_A &= \text{gain} - \text{net cost} \\ &= \$2.4 \text{ million} - \$1.5 \text{ million} \\ &= \$0.9 \text{ million} \end{aligned}$$

Note that the amount of the cash consideration determines how the total gain is divided between the two sets of shareholders: every additional dollar paid to Board's shareholders means a dollar less for Mayfair's shareholders.

For a cash takeover, comparing gains and costs is straightforward when, as we have assumed so far, the value of the target as an independent entity is equal to its market value. Suppose, however, that Board Ltd has been regarded by market participants as a likely takeover target and this speculation has increased its share price from $1.70 to $2. In other words, part of the possible gains from a takeover are already impounded in Board's market price and $V_T$ is only $8.5 million, rather than the market value of $10 million. The true value of Board to Mayfair is $8.5 million + $2.4 million = $10.9 million, which means that paying $11.5 million will harm, rather than benefit, Mayfair's shareholders. In terms of our previous calculations, the gain is still $2.4 million, but the true net cost is:

$$\begin{aligned} \text{Net cost} &= \text{cash} - V_T \\ &= \$11.5 \text{ million} - \$8.5 \text{ million} \\ &= \$3.0 \text{ million} \end{aligned}$$

and:

$$\begin{aligned} NPV_A &= \text{gain} - \text{net cost} \\ &= \$2.4 \text{ million} - \$3.0 \text{ million} \\ &= -\$600\,000 \end{aligned}$$

This problem highlights two important lessons for the management of acquiring companies. First, management should check that the share price of a proposed target has not already been increased by takeover rumours. Secondly, management should keep its takeover intentions completely confidential until formally announcing the bid.

Finally, in making a distinction between value and market price, we are not suggesting that there is any market inefficiency, or that there is anything wrong with the market price. In fact the market would be inefficient if it did *not* respond to rumours of a possible takeover. The problem is that if there are rumours that have increased the target's share price, the market price no longer gives a measure of the target's value as an independent entity.

### 20.3.3 ESTIMATING COST FOR A SHARE-EXCHANGE TAKEOVER

Estimating the net cost of a cash takeover offer is straightforward.[18] In the case of the proposed takeover of Board by Mayfair, the net cost was:

---

[18] Fortunately, cash offers are the most common in practice. Of the 1442 takeover bids studied by Bishop, Dodd & Officer (see Footnote 4), 1120 or 77.9 per cent were cash offers.

$$\text{Cash} - V_T = \$11.5 \text{ million} - \$10 \text{ million}$$
$$= \$1.5 \text{ million}$$

Calculation of the cost is more complex when the acquiring company issues shares in exchange for the target's shares. The cost in this case depends on the post-takeover price of the acquiring company's shares. Suppose that Mayfair has 20 million shares on issue with a market price of $4.60 each before the takeover bid for Board is announced. Mayfair offers one of its shares for every two shares in Board and the consideration therefore *appears* to be the same as in the case of the cash offer of $2.30 per share. However, consider what will happen after the takeover offer is announced. The value of the combined company can be found by rearranging Equation 20.1:

$$V_{AT} = V_A + V_T + \text{gain}$$
$$= 20 \text{ million} \times \$4.60 + \$10 \text{ million} + \$2.4 \text{ million}$$
$$= \$104.4 \text{ million}$$

After the takeover, the number of Mayfair shares on issue will be 20 million + 2.5 million and the value of the shares issued to acquire Board is:

$$\frac{2.5}{22.5} \times \$104.4 \text{ million} = \$11.6 \text{ million}$$

Therefore, the net cost of acquiring Board will be:

$$\$11.6 \text{ million} - \$10 \text{ million} = \$1.6 \text{ million}$$

In general the estimated cost of a share exchange takeover is:

$$\text{net cost} = b\, V_{AT} - V_T \qquad (20.5)$$

where $b$ is the fraction of the combined company that will be owned by the former shareholders of the target company. The NPV for Mayfair's shareholders (Equation 20.3) is now:

$$\text{NPV}_A = \text{gain} - \text{net cost}$$
$$= \$2.4 \text{ million} - \$1.6 \text{ million}$$
$$= \$0.8 \text{ million}$$

These calculations show that for the share-exchange offer the true net cost is expected to be $100 000 *more* than it would have been if Mayfair had paid cash for Board. Similarly the NPV to Mayfair's shareholders is $100 000 *less* than it would have been under the cash offer. This difference arises because Mayfair's shares are worth more after the takeover than they were worth previously. If the market agrees with Mayfair's valuations, then once the takeover bid is announced, Mayfair's share price will be $104.4 million ÷ 22 million = $4.64 or 4 cents more than their pre-bid price. Therefore, since Board's shareholders will receive Mayfair shares, rather than cash, they will receive part of the takeover gain.

It should now be clear that there is a basic distinction between cash offers and share-exchange offers: for a cash offer, the net cost is independent of the takeover gain; for a share-exchange offer, the cost depends on the takeover gain, because the cost is a function of the acquiring company's share price *after* the bid is announced. Consequently, the cost of a share-exchange takeover can only be *estimated* when the bid is at the planning stage. Equation 20.5 can be used to make the estimate.

Another important distinction between cash and share-exchange offers is that a share exchange mitigates the effect of valuation errors. For example, suppose that after acquiring Board Ltd, Mayfair's management finds that Board's assets are worth only $5 million. If Mayfair paid $11.5 million cash to Board's former shareholders, then the cash is gone forever and Mayfair's shareholders will bear the full loss of $6.5 million. However, if Mayfair acquired Board by issuing shares, part of the loss will be borne by Board's former shareholders.

## 20.4 ALTERNATIVE VALUATION APPROACHES

The takeover analysis in Section 20.3 has been based on market values and estimates of the present value of incremental cash flows. In some cases, market values may not be available because the target company is unlisted, or they may be considered unreliable, perhaps because the shares are rarely traded. In such cases, there will be a need to use other valuation approaches, the most popular of which are based on earnings and assets.[19]

### 20.4.1 VALUATION BASED ON EARNINGS

In this approach, the bidder values the target by first estimating the future earnings per share (EPS) of the target. The EPS figure is then multiplied by an 'appropriate' price/earnings (P/E) ratio to obtain an implied price (valuation) of the target. This approach can be given a theoretical underpinning by linking it to the present value of a perpetuity. If the appropriate P/E ratio is regarded as $1/r$, the inverse of the discount rate, then, using the perpetuity formula:

$$\begin{aligned} PV &= \frac{EPS}{r} \\ &= EPS \times \frac{1}{r} \\ &= EPS \times \frac{P}{E} \\ &= P \end{aligned}$$

Important assumptions underlying this approach include:
1. The company's future earnings stream can be represented by a single number, typically referred to as 'future maintainable earnings'.
2. Risk differences between companies can be fully captured in the discount rate, $r$.

As Foster points out, when these conditions are not met, the P/E ratio should not be accorded any theoretical significance and is best regarded as a summary indicator of a company's perceived capacity to generate earnings.[20]

---

[19] For a discussion of the valuation methods that are most commonly used, see W. Lonergan, *The Valuation of Businesses, Shares and Other Equity*, Longman Professional, Melbourne, 1992.
[20] G. Foster, *Financial Statement Analysis*, 2nd edn, Prentice-Hall, Englewood Cliffs, 1986, p. 436.

Even where these assumptions hold, *capitalising* earnings using a P/E multiple should *not* be regarded as *discounting* future earnings. The cash flows to investors in shares are dividends, not earnings, part of which are reinvested each year. Therefore we can regard the value of a share as the present value of a stream of dividends, or equivalently, as the present value of a stream of earnings *minus* the present value of the reinvested (retained) earnings stream. Discounting earnings rather than dividends amounts to including all the returns from an investment without allowing for the outlay needed to generate those returns.

### 20.4.2 VALUATION BASED ON ASSETS

A company's equity can be valued by deducting its total liabilities from the sum of the market values of its assets. This approach may be appropriate where the bidder intends to sell many of the target's assets, or where the company has been operating at a loss. Criticisms of this approach include the following:

1. Balance-sheet figures based on historical cost are unlikely to provide a reliable guide to market values.
2. Intangible assets may not be included in the balance sheet.
3. There may be complementarity between assets so that the total market value of the assets may be greater than the sum of their individual market values.

Even where reliable market values can be found for all identifiable assets, the resultant valuation will rarely coincide exactly with the market value of the company's equity.

## 20.5 REGULATION OF TAKEOVERS

Takeover activity and procedures are regulated by Commonwealth and State legislation. The most important legislation is Chapter 6 of the *Corporations Law* which is entitled 'Acquisition of Shares' and regulates takeovers.[21] The Australian Securities Commission (ASC) has a significant role in administering activities covered by the legislation. For example, the ASC can obtain information on the beneficial ownership of shares, and can allow exemptions from compliance with the legislation. Also the ASC can apply to the Corporations and Securities Panel for an acquisition of shares to be declared unacceptable, or for a declaration of unacceptable conduct. These and other powers have been granted to the ASC because it is recognised that takeovers can involve complex legal issues, not all of which can be settled by 'black letter' law. The objectives of this legislation, as stated by the ASC's predecessor the NCSC, are to ensure:[22]

1. that the market for securities is efficient, competitive and informed;

---

[21] For a detailed discussion, see D. D. McDonough, *Annotated Mergers and Acquisitions Law of Australia*, 3rd edn, Law Book Co., Sydney, 1993.

[22] NCSC Policy Statement: *Role of the Commission under the Companies (Acquisition of Shares) Act and Codes*, Release No. 101, Melbourne, July 1981, revised January 1984. The policy statement used the general term 'members' which we have changed to 'shareholders'.

2. that fair dealing and equity exist between all shareholders of a company involved in a takeover bid, and that, as far as practicable, each shareholder has equal access to information, equal opportunity to deal in the market, and equal opportunity to participate in any benefits accruing to shareholders under a bid;
3. that the premium for control of a company is shared by all shareholders;
4. that all shareholders of a company in receipt of a takeover offer are supplied with sufficient information to assess the offer's merits;
5. that the directors of a company whose shareholders are in receipt of a takeover offer do not, by exercising managerial powers, do anything to frustrate the offer before shareholders have had an adequate opportunity to consider it;
6. that actual or potential market manipulation is detected promptly.

The most important aspect of this legislation is that, unless the procedures laid down in Chapter 6 of the *Corporations Law* are followed, the acquisition of additional shares in a company is virtually prohibited if this would:

1. result in a shareholder being entitled to more than 20 per cent of the voting shares; *or*
2. increase the voting shares held by a party that already holds between 20 per cent and 90 per cent of the voting shares of the company.

Any investor is permitted to purchase up to 20 per cent of a company's shares at any time, subject to the requirement that once the holding exceeds 5 per cent, a substantial shareholding notice must be issued within two business days. The takeover threshold has been set at 20 per cent on the basis that anyone who owns less than 20 per cent of a company's shares is unlikely to be able to exercise control. If an investor wishes to exceed the 20 per cent threshold, this can only be done by following one of the three procedures that the legislation permits: a formal offer under a takeover scheme, an on-market takeover announcement, and a 'creeping' takeover.[23]

## I FORMAL TAKEOVER OFFER

Section 616 and Part 6.3 of the *Corporations Law* permit an acquiring company, or an unincorporated offerer, to make an offer (whether by way of a cash offer, a share exchange or a combination of these) to acquire shares in the target company. This offer must remain open for between 1 and 6 months and may be for 100 per cent, or a specified proportion of each holder's shares.

Before making such an offer, the offerer must have a Part A statement registered by the ASC. The statement must include, among other things, the identity of the offerer, particulars of the offerer's intentions regarding the target company if the takeover bid is successful, and other material information which

---

23 Companies may also merge by a Scheme of Arrangement under Part 5.1, sections 411–415 of the *Corporations Law*. However, such schemes are rare and section 411(17) directs the Court not to approve a scheme which is designed to avoid the provisions of Chapter 6 of the *Corporations Law*, unless the Commission has no objection to the scheme. The *Corporations Law* also provides in section 619 that small private companies can be acquired without following the procedures defined in sections 616–18.

may assist the target company's shareholders in deciding whether to accept the offer. If the Part A statement is registered by the ASC, it is then sent to the target company and its shareholders. Within 14 days of the receipt of a Part A statement the target company must furnish to its shareholders and to the Commission a Part B statement. Usually this will include a recommendation on whether the offer should be accepted and other information relevant to the decision facing the target company's shareholders. The Part B statement may also include an independent expert's report which must provide an opinion on whether the offer is 'fair and reasonable'. Under section 648 of the *Corporations Law* such a report is mandatory if the bidder is a director of the target company, or if the bidder owns 30 per cent or more of the target's voting shares, or if the bidder and target have any common directors. In other words, an expert's report is required if the bidder and target are not independent.[24]

Once a formal cash offer has been made, the offerer is allowed to purchase target company shares on the stock exchange, subject to conditions set out in section 620. An offerer can increase its offer price but has to pay this increased amount to all shareholders who accept the offer, including any who have previously accepted a lower price.

## 2 ON-MARKET TAKEOVER ANNOUNCEMENT

This approach, which is applicable only when the target is a listed public company, is permitted by section 617 and Part 6.4 of the *Corporations Law*. It requires an unconditional undertaking by a member firm of the Australian Stock Exchange (ASX), on behalf of the offerer, to stand in the market and acquire, for a period of at least 1 month, all shares offered on the exchange at a specified price. The buyer must pay cash for the shares, and the offer cannot be conditional. The offerer must supply the ASC, the ASX, and the target company's shareholders with a Part C statement which provides information similar to that contained in a Part A statement. The target company must reply by way of a Part D statement, which again contains information similar to that contained in a Part B statement. In this case, if the offer price is increased, there is no need to pay the higher price to target shareholders who sold prior to the increase.

## 3 CREEPING TAKEOVER

This approach is permitted by section 618 of the *Corporations Law*. It allows the acquisition of no more than 3 per cent of the target company's shares every 6 months, provided that the threshold level of 19 per cent has been maintained for at least 6 months. No public statement is necessary. Because of the time required to achieve control, the creeping takeover approach is of little commercial significance.

**Partial takeovers**, where a bidder seeks to gain control by acquiring only 51 per cent, or perhaps less, of the target company's shares, have been the subject of particular regulatory attention. The reasons are, first, that the premium for control may be paid to only a favoured group of shareholders, and secondly, that

---

[24] For a discussion of the role of experts' reports, see G. Hubbard, 'What's in an Expert Report?' *Australian Accountant*, September 1990, pp. 28–40.

there is potential for target shareholders to be coerced into accepting an offer which is not in their best interests.[25]

Suppose that an offer is made for 40 per cent of the shares in a company, and the holders of 80 per cent of the shares accept. Under a pro rata offer, the bidder would then accept half of the shares offered by each of these holders, who would be the only ones to share in the control premium. Pro rata bids have been prohibited in Australia since 1986. The bidder in a partial takeover must specify *at the outset* the proportion of each holder's shares that the bidder will offer to buy. This method is referred to as a **proportional bid**.[26] A disadvantage of proportional bids is greater uncertainty about their outcome from the viewpoint of the bidder, because the bidder must estimate the likely response rate of target shareholders. Partial takeover bids have become extremely rare in Australia.

Other legislation that may influence a bidder's decision to make a takeover offer includes:[27]

1. the *Trade Practices Act* 1974, which was referred to in Section 20.2.1;
2. the *Foreign Acquisitions and Takeovers Act* 1975 which provides the Commonwealth Treasurer with the power to prohibit takeovers that would result in what is regarded as an excessive shareholding by foreign interests;
3. other Commonwealth and State legislation which may inhibit takeovers in specific industries such as the banking and media industries.

In addition to this legislation, some of the listing requirements of the ASX also affect takeovers. These include a requirement that directors maintain secrecy during discussions bearing on a potential takeover offer, and a requirement restricting directors of a target company from making an allotment of shares for a period of 3 months after receiving a takeover offer.

The preceding discussion outlines the major regulations relating to takeovers without addressing their economic consequences. Regulation increases the costs of takeovers, which means that some otherwise profitable takeovers will no longer occur. Therefore, regulation of takeovers will result in a lower level of efficiency. The Australian legislation recognises efficiency as an objective, but it gives greater weight to equity, particularly as it relates to the shareholders of the target company. In other words, the objective of the legislation is not to prevent takeovers from occurring (although the greater costs involved must reduce their number to some extent) but to ensure that those takeovers that do occur are conducted fairly.

---

[25] For a detailed explanation of the problem of coercion, see P. Dodd & R. R. Officer, 'Corporate Control, Economic Efficiency, and Shareholder Justice', *Policy Monograph* 9, Centre for Independent Studies, St Leonards, 1986, pp. 36–9.

[26] For an evaluation of this and other attempts to solve the coercion problem, see J. Coffee, 'Partial Justice: Balancing Fairness and Efficiency in the Context of Partial Takeover Offers', *Company and Securities Law Journal*, November 1985, pp. 216–34.

[27] For more details of this legislation, see M. Irving, B. Beerworth & M. Hodge, 'Mergers, Acquisitions and Takeovers' in *Handbook of Australian Corporate Finance*, Eds R. Bruce et al., 4th edn, Butterworths, Sydney, 1991, pp. 143–72.

## 20.6 TAKEOVER DEFENCES

While most takeover bids that are announced succeed, there are also many cases where management of the target company is successful in preventing a change in control. Defence measures are of two basic types: those that pre-empt or discourage bids, and those implemented after a bid is received.

Pre-emptive measures include arranging interlocking shareholdings and amending the company's Articles of Association in ways that make the company less attractive to a potential bidder. For example, the Articles can contain self-destruct provisions ('poison pills'), or they can simply make life difficult for a bidder by restricting share transfers or by requiring a takeover to be approved by a shareholder plebiscite.

Defence strategies employed after a bid is received are numerous and the more common categories include the following:[28]

### 1  ACQUISITION BY FRIENDLY PARTIES

The management of a target company seeks the assistance of a 'white knight' which generally purchases the target's shares on the open market with the aim of either driving up the share price, or preventing the bidder from achieving its minimum acceptance level.

### 2  DISCLOSURE OF FAVOURABLE INFORMATION

Management of a target company may release information which will, it hopes, convince shareholders that the bid undervalues the company. Such information includes preliminary earnings results, new contracts, and statements of asset market values and profit forecasts.

### 3  CLAIMS AND APPEALS

The management of a target company generally claims that the bid is inadequate and may also appeal to regulatory authorities, criticise the bidding company, or appeal to shareholders for loyalty.

Defensive tactics used during Australian takeover bids were successful in 70 per cent of cases during the 1981–1985 period, indicating that resistance by target directors is a key factor in determining the outcome of a takeover bid.[29] The significance of the target directors' attitude to a takeover bid places the onus on directors to ensure that their recommendation is consistent with their responsibilities to shareholders. Directors of a target company may be faced with a conflict of interest because a takeover bid that they believe to be in the best interests of shareholders may leave them unemployed if it is successful. Therefore directors of a target company may oppose a bid because they place their own interest above their responsibilities to shareholders. On the other hand, resistance to a takeover bid can benefit shareholders if it forces the bidder to increase

---

[28] R. Casey & P. Eddey, 'Defence Strategies of Listed Companies Under the Takeover Code', *Australian Journal of Management*, December 1986, pp. 153–71.
[29] See Footnote 28.

the offer, or attracts a higher offer from another bidder. These competing explanations for the reaction of target management have been termed the **managerial welfare hypothesis** and the **shareholder welfare hypothesis**.[30]

Walkling and Long studied these two hypotheses using US data, and found support for the managerial welfare hypothesis. Eddey and Casey concluded that directors of Australian companies acted in a manner consistent with shareholder's interests in making accept/reject recommendations. In particular, directors recommended rejection of bids that offered relatively low premiums and advised shareholders to accept bids whenever it appeared likely that the bidder would gain control.[31]

The contention that managerial resistance to takeovers may not be in the best interests of shareholders is of concern since the 'market for corporate control' concept sees takeovers as a mechanism for resolving shareholder–manager conflicts by replacing inefficient managers. The effectiveness of this market will be reduced if such managers use defensive tactics to entrench their positions. Of course, it is poorly-performing managers who are likely to have the greatest difficulty in maintaining employment or obtaining other jobs after a takeover. Empirical evidence in the US supports this contention in that companies whose management resisted takeover are characterised by poorer performance prior to the takeover bid.[32] The problem of managers giving predominance to their own interests may be overcome by structuring the compensation of top-level managers so that their own interests will be better aligned with those of shareholders.

Some companies approach this problem by offering top-level managers large termination payments ('golden parachutes') if they lose their jobs due to a takeover. Such payments may be effective in preventing managers from resisting a takeover bid which is in the best interests of shareholders. However, if the payments are too generous, they may cause managers to recommend that shareholders accept an inadequate bid.

## 20.7 Corporate Restructuring

While mergers and takeovers remain the most frequent transactions in the market for corporate control, the 1980s saw an upsurge, particularly in the US, of transactions in which companies or groups are reduced in size by asset disposals, divided into separate entities, or transferred to private ownership. We begin by defining the most frequent of these restructuring transactions:

---

[30] R. Walkling & M. Long, 'Agency Theory, Managerial Welfare, and Takeover Bid Resistance', *Rand Journal of Economics*, Spring 1984, pp. 54–68.

[31] R. Walkling & M. Long, see Footnote 30; and P. Eddey & R. Casey, 'Directors' Recommendations in Response to Takeover Bids: Do They Act in their Own Interests?', *Australian Journal of Management*, June 1989, pp. 1–28.

[32] D. Kummer & J. Hoffmeister, 'Valuation Consequences of Cash Tender Offers', *Journal of Finance*, May 1978, pp. 505–16.

## 1 DIVESTITURES

Assets (often in the form of a whole subsidiary, branch or division) are sold to another company.

## 2 SPIN-OFFS

The operations of a subsidiary are separated from those of its parent by establishing the subsidiary as a separate listed company. However, there is no change in ownership because shares in the former subsidiary are distributed to the shareholders of the parent company.

## 3 BUYOUTS

A company or division is purchased by a small group of investors including, invariably, its senior management. Buyouts are often referred to as **management buyouts**, or, where large amounts of debt finance are employed, as **leveraged buyouts**.

The occurrence of these transactions on a large scale is a relatively recent phenomenon in the US and they are much less frequent in Australia. We therefore have to rely on US evidence, which is much less extensive than the evidence on takeovers. The following subsections briefly summarise the evidence on the wealth effects of restructuring transactions and discuss possible explanations.[33]

### 20.7.1 DIVESTITURES

A **divestiture** or **sell-off** involves assets, which may be a whole subsidiary, being sold for cash, and is therefore essentially a **reverse merger** from the viewpoint of the seller. Just as takeovers increase the wealth of target (seller) shareholders, it has been found that divestitures create value for the shareholders of selling companies. Shareholders of the buying companies receive, on average, positive but statistically insignificant gains.[34] The evidence indicates that the assets transferred must be more valuable to the buyer than the seller. Possible reasons are similar to those for takeovers: the acquisition may yield economies of scale, or other operating synergies for the buyer, perhaps through superior management. In addition, disposal of the assets may benefit the selling company by removing a unit that the selling company was managing poorly, or which had created diseconomies of scale for the selling company.

### 20.7.2 SPIN-OFFS

In this type of transaction, a single organisational structure is replaced by two separate units under essentially the same ownership. For example, in 1987 BHP placed its gold interests into a new company, BHP Gold Mines, with parent shareholders being entitled to take up shares in the gold company on a pro rata

---

[33] The following discussion relies substantially on G. Hite & J. Owers, 'The Restructuring of Corporate America: An Overview', in *The Revolution in Corporate Finance*, 2nd edn, J. Stern & D. Chew, Eds. Blackwell, Oxford, 1992.
[34] P. C. Jain, 'The Effect of Voluntary Sell-off Announcements on Shareholder Wealth', *Journal of Finance*, March 1985, pp. 207–24.

basis. Other spin-offs in Australia have involved companies in the media, paper, and tobacco industries. Research in the US has found a significant positive market reaction to spin-offs and there is evidence that the gains are even larger when the operations of the divested unit are not closely related to those of the parent. Likely explanations focus on expected gains from simplifying a complex conglomerate structure, decentralising decision making and motivating management more effectively.

In a large conglomerate structure it can be extremely difficult to assess the contribution of divisional or subsidiary management to the performance of the group. Spinning-off a subsidiary as a separate listed entity makes it much easier to assess its performance and to design employment contracts which provide performance-related benefits to management. Moreover, in a diversified company, efficiency may be reduced by the need to manage multiple lines of business. For example, funds generated by profitable activities may be siphoned off to subsidise unprofitable activities. Dividing the company into separate entities, each based on a single line of business, reduces the opportunities for such diversion of funds. In general, the argument is that after a spin-off, the individual entities are likely to be better managed separately than as parts of a complex conglomerate.

### 20.7.3 BUYOUTS

A **buyout** or **going-private transaction** can take one of a number of forms, each of which involves a rearrangement of only the financial and ownership structures of a single operating entity. Consequently there is no scope for operating synergies such as economies of scale. Buyouts are initiated by management who presumably expect to gain from the transaction, and there is evidence that the former public shareholders also gain through receiving a substantial premium over the previous share price.[35] It follows that some real gain must be expected to follow from the transfer from public to private ownership. One source of gain is the avoidance of listing fees and shareholder servicing costs, which can be quite substantial for small public companies. Another is the effect on managerial incentives. Managers who also own their company stand to benefit more than salaried employees from their efforts.

In addition to 'pure' going-private transactions where managers use their own resources, possibly supplemented by personal borrowing, to buyout the previous shareholders, there are leveraged buyouts which involve significant corporate borrowing. These buyouts are almost always arranged by a buyout specialist who invests equity capital in the company, arranges the necessary debt finance, and takes an active part in overseeing its performance. The proportion of debt finance can be extremely high: the company may have a debt–equity ratio of the order of 9 to 1 immediately after the buyout. This does not necessarily

---

[35] For example, in a sample of 57 going-private proposals that involved a cash consideration, the premium averaged 56.31 per cent over the market price two months before the announcement. See H. De Angelo, L. De Angelo & E. M. Rice, 'Going Private: Minority Freezeouts and Stockholder Wealth', *Journal of Law and Economics*, October 1984, pp. 367–401.

mean that private companies have an inherently greater debt capacity than their public counterparts. In most leveraged buyouts, early repayment of the debt is a high priority and the initial high level of debt is feasible because most such buyouts involve low-risk businesses with stable cash flows. The debt finance serves mainly to facilitate the transaction and can also serve a positive role by giving the new owners an even greater incentive to improve efficiency.

Finally, the gains associated with transferring some companies to private ownership prompt the following question: Should all companies be privately owned? The answer is no. Public companies have the advantage of access to equity capital on terms that reflect the diversification benefits available to investors in the capital market. The value of such access depends on the growth opportunities available to the company. Therefore public ownership has important advantages for large-scale enterprises that involve significant risks and have an ongoing need to raise capital, but in other cases private ownership can be advantageous. It is also interesting to note that some buyouts have been followed within a few years by a return to public listing. This suggests that the expected benefits of the transfer to private ownership either do not always materialise, or if present, are not necessarily permanent.[36]

## 20.8 EMPIRICAL EVIDENCE ON TAKEOVERS

There has been considerable empirical research into takeovers. For example, many studies have evaluated the wealth effects of takeovers on shareholders of the acquiring and target companies. These studies use share price changes around the time of the first public announcement of a takeover to measure these wealth effects. Abnormal returns on shares in both acquiring and target companies around the time of the takeover announcement are measured by the difference between actual and expected returns. The expected returns take account of the influence of market-wide events on the returns from an individual company's shares. Apart from market-wide events, the only factor assumed to be common to all companies in the studies is their involvement in takeover negotiations. Therefore the abnormal returns are a measure of the wealth effects of the takeover.[37] The empirical evidence on takeovers is voluminous, the results of different studies are sometimes conflicting, and interpretation of some aspects of the results can be controversial. Nevertheless, after surveying the US evidence, Jensen draws several general conclusions, including the following:[38]

1. Takeovers benefit shareholders of target companies. Premiums in hostile offers in the US exceed 30 per cent on average and in the mid-1980s averaged about 50 per cent.

---

[36] Evidence on the performance of buyouts is provided by S. Kaplan, 'The Effects of Management Buyouts on Operating Performance and Value', *Journal of Financial Economics*, October 1989, pp. 217–54.
[37] This 'event study' methodology is commonly employed in tests of the semistrong form of the efficient market hypothesis and is outlined in Chapter 14.
[38] M. Jensen, 'Takeovers: Their Causes and Consequences', *Journal of Economic Perspectives*, Winter 1988, pp. 21–48.

2. Acquiring-company shareholders earn, on average, about 4 per cent in hostile takeovers, and roughly zero in mergers, although these returns seem to have declined from past levels.
3. Takeovers do not waste credit or resources. Instead they generate substantial gains—historically 8 per cent of the total value of both companies. These gains are not merely a redistribution between various parties.
4. Actions by managers that eliminate or prevent offers or mergers are the most likely to be harmful to shareholders.
5. Takeover gains do not result from the creation of monopoly power.

In discussing the empirical evidence in more detail, we make substantial use of a paper by Jarrell, Brickley and Netter, which reviews the results of numerous recent US studies, and a monograph by Bishop, Dodd and Officer who evaluated takeovers in Australia during the period 1972–1985.[39] Bishop, Dodd and Officer's results are consistent with those of Walter who studied Australian takeovers during the 1960s and early 1970s.[40]

## 20.8.1 THE TARGET COMPANY

One result that stands out in all market-based studies is that target company shareholders earn significant positive abnormal returns. For example, Bishop, Dodd and Officer found an average abnormal return of 21 per cent over the 7-month period around the takeover announcement. This result almost certainly understates the total wealth effects of takeovers for target shareholders. Casey, Dodd and Dolan reported significant abnormal returns on target company shares around the time that significant shareholding notices were filed. For their sample this occurred on average 127 days before announcement of a takeover bid.[41] Significant gains to target shareholders are to be expected because the acquiring company must offer more than the previous market price of the shares. The current shareholders are, by definition, parties who prefer to hold rather than sell the shares at the previous market price.

Several of the studies find that, on average, the shares in target companies had performed poorly; that is, on average, shareholders earned negative abnormal returns of up to 15 per cent over periods up to 3 years before the takeover offer. This is consistent with the concept that takeovers transfer control of assets to companies with more efficient managers or more-profitable uses for those assets.

The initial increase in wealth of the target company's shareholders *appears* to be maintained, even where the takeover bid is unsuccessful. This could be because the bid prompted a change in the target company's investment strategy, which is expected to improve performance, or because information released

---

[39] G. Jarrell, J. Brickley & J. Netter, 'The Market for Corporate Control: The Empirical Evidence Since 1980', *Journal of Economic Perspectives*, Winter 1988, pp. 49–68; and S. Bishop, P. Dodd & R. R. Officer, 'Australian Takeovers: The Evidence 1972–1985', *Policy Monograph* 12, Centre for Independent Studies, St Leonards, 1987.
[40] T. Walter, 'Australian Takeovers: Capital Market Efficiency and Shareholder Risk and Return', *Australian Journal of Management*, June 1984, pp. 63–118.
[41] R. Casey, P. Dodd & P. Dolan, 'Takeovers and Corporate Raiders: Empirical Evidence from Extended Event Studies', *Australian Journal of Management*, December 1987, pp. 201–20.

during the bid caused the market to revalue the shares. Another explanation is that the market may expect a further bid for the target company. Research by Bradley, Desai and Kim is consistent with the last explanation.[42] They found that many companies that were the subject of an initial unsuccessful takeover bid received a subsequent successful bid within 5 years of the first. These subsequent bids resulted in further positive abnormal returns for target shareholders. Where no subsequent bid eventuated, the shares of the unsuccessful targets declined, on average, to their (market-adjusted) pre-bid level. Based on this evidence, it appears that the gains associated with takeover bids are permanent only where a change in control occurs. That is, the results do not support the suggestion that gains to target shareholders result from the market's reassessment of previously undervalued shares.

### 20.8.2 THE ACQUIRING COMPANY

On average, the shareholders of acquiring companies earn positive abnormal returns in the years before the takeover bid is made. Bishop, Dodd and Officer found that average abnormal returns accumulated to almost 25 per cent over the 3 years before a takeover bid is made. This suggests that takeover bids are typically made by companies that have been doing well, and have demonstrated an ability to manage assets and growth. In the 7-month period around the announcement of the bid, the average abnormal return for all bidders was 6.0 per cent. While Bishop, Dodd and Officer found positive abnormal returns to bidders over a 7-month period, other studies that have measured returns over shorter periods surrounding the announcement of takeover bids have found that the average abnormal return to shareholders of bidding companies is close to zero, and negative in some cases. Moreover, announcement of a takeover bid is associated with a share price decline in a significant proportion of individual cases.[43] Jarrell and Poulsen identify three general explanations that have been offered for the negligible wealth effects for acquiring company shareholders.[44] These are:

1. Takeovers are profitable, but the wealth effects are disguised.
2. Competition depresses returns to acquirers.
3. Takeovers are neutral or poor investments.

The rationale for each of these proposed explanations is now discussed.

---

[42] M. Bradley, A. Desai & E. Kim, 'The Rationale Behind Interfirm Tender Offers: Information or Synergy?' *Journal of Financial Economics*, April 1983, pp. 183–206.

[43] For example, Dodd notes that results reported in two US studies show that in over 40 per cent of cases, the bidding company's share price fell when a takeover bid was announced. P. Dodd, 'The Market for Corporate Control: A Review of the Evidence', in J. Stern & D. Chew, Eds, *The Revolution in Corporate Finance*, 2nd edn, Blackwell, Oxford, 1992, p. 515.

[44] G. Jarrell & A. Poulsen, 'The Returns to Acquiring Firms in Tender Offers: Evidence from Three Decades', *Financial Management*, Autumn 1989, pp. 12–19.

## 1 THE WEALTH EFFECTS OF TAKEOVERS ARE DISGUISED

Essentially, this explanation suggests that takeovers are profitable but the announcement of an individual takeover has little effect on the acquiring company's share price. One reason is that acquiring companies are typically much larger than their targets, so while there may be a worthwhile dollar gain to shareholders, the gain is small relative to the total value of the acquiring company. A second reason is that many companies have a known strategy of growth by acquisition. Therefore, the expected gains from this strategy may already be reflected in the companies' share prices, and announcement of a particular bid conveys little new information to the market.[45] Thirdly, announcement effects which are small or negative may also reflect market reaction to the financing of the takeover. In particular, a share-exchange offer may signal that the management of the acquiring company considers that its shares are overvalued. Therefore the takeover itself may have a positive announcement effect, but this can be offset by the effects of the information related to the financing of the takeover.[46]

## 2 COMPETITION

The returns to successful bidders are likely to be lower if a takeover is resisted by target management, or contested by multiple bidders. There is evidence that abnormal returns to target shareholders are higher when there are multiple bidders, in which case gains to acquiring company shareholders are insignificantly different from zero. However, when there is only one bidder, acquiring company shareholders earn significant positive returns. The degree of competition in takeovers could be influenced by changes in government regulation, development of innovative financing techniques, and use of defensive strategies by target companies. Therefore, the returns to acquirers may have changed over time.

## 3 TAKEOVERS ARE NEUTRAL OR POOR INVESTMENTS

This explanation is that many takeovers are bad investments and the small or negative returns to acquiring company shareholders correctly reflect this situation. One advocate of this explanation is Roll who argued that many managers of acquiring companies are affected by 'hubris'.[47] That is, they are supremely confident that their ability to value other companies is better than that of the market. Consequently they are likely to pay more for target company shares than they are worth, and Roll argues that the large returns to target company shareholders represent wealth transfers from the shareholders of acquiring companies.

---

[45] For evidence on the prior capitalisation of takeover gains, see K. Schipper & R. Thompson, 'Evidence on the Capitalised Value of Merger Activity of Acquiring Firms', *Journal of Financial Economics*, April 1983, p. 85–119.

[46] For Australian evidence on the effects of the method of payment in takeovers, see D. Bellamy & W. Lewin, 'Corporate Takeovers, Method of Payment and Bidding Firms' Shareholder Returns: Australian Evidence', *Asia Pacific Journal of Management*, October 1992, pp. 137–49.

[47] R. Roll, 'The Hubris Hypothesis of Corporate Takeovers', *Journal of Business*, April 1986, pp. 197–216.

There is also evidence that many acquired companies are later divested, which may indicate that the original takeover turned out to be a failure.[48]

To assess the validity of these explanations, Jarrell and Poulsen examined the returns to acquiring company shareholders in a large sample of successful tender offers over the period 1963 to 1986.[49] They found that returns to acquirers were positively related to the size of the target relative to the bidder, which is consistent with the explanation that returns to acquirers can be disguised when target companies are small. They also found that returns to acquirers were smaller when the bid was opposed by target management, and were lower after changes in regulation which favoured competing bidders. In summary, their results support the first two explanations, but they also note that some other studies have produced evidence that supports the argument that takeovers are not good investments.[50]

## 20.8.3 ARE TAKEOVERS BAD INVESTMENTS?

While there is conclusive evidence that target company shareholders gain significantly from takeovers, the evidence on returns to acquiring company shareholders is much less conclusive. Consequently, whether takeovers generate *net* gains for shareholders has been a contentious issue.

Bradley, Desai and Kim tackled this issue by examining the returns to shareholders of matched pairs of target and acquiring companies in successful tender offers over the period 1963 to 1984.[51] They found an average gain of $117 million, or 7.4 per cent in the combined wealth of shareholders. The total percentage gain remained remarkably constant over time and by far the larger share of the gain went to the target shareholders, although the division of the gain shifted against the acquiring company shareholders over time. In general their results support the hypothesis that takeovers yield real, synergistic gains and do not support Roll's 'wealth transfer' hypothesis. However, they found that for some types of acquisitions there were consistent losses to acquiring company shareholders. In particular the returns were negative on average for acquirers that made late but successful entries to bidding contests. That is, on average these 'white knights' did pay 'too much' for their targets. In summary, the evidence indicates that takeovers yield net gains for shareholders, and that, on average, takeovers do not harm the shareholders of acquiring companies. On the other hand, the returns to acquiring company shareholders are negative in many takeovers and negative on average for at least one type of takeover.

---

[48] However, it has been reported that divestiture of previously acquired companies often yields profits for the selling company. Therefore, subsequent divestiture does not necessarily mean that the original acquisition was a failure. See S. Kaplan & M. Weisbach, 'The Success of Acquisitions: Evidence from Divestitures', *Journal of Finance*, March 1992, pp. 107–38.

[49] Jarrell & Poulsen, see Footnote 44.

[50] For example, there is evidence that some types of takeovers harm the shareholders of acquiring companies. See M. Mitchell & K. Lehn, 'Do Bad Bidders Become Good Targets?', *Journal of Political Economy*, April 1990, pp. 372–98. This evidence is discussed in Section 20.8.4.

[51] M. Bradley, A. Desai & E. Kim, 'Synergistic Gains from Corporate Acquisitions and their Division Between the Shareholders of Target and Acquiring Firms', *Journal of Financial Economics*, May 1988, pp. 3–40.

### 20.8.4 DISTINGUISHING BETWEEN GOOD AND BAD TAKEOVERS

Several studies provide evidence on the characteristics of takeovers that are likely to harm rather than benefit the shareholders of acquiring companies. There are at least three reasons why the managers of acquiring companies might pay more than targets are worth. First, Roll's hubris hypothesis suggests that managers pay too much for target companies because they overestimate their ability to run them. Secondly, managers may pursue their own objectives rather than those of their companies' shareholders. In particular, as discussed in Section 20.2.1, Jensen argues that value-reducing takeovers will be common when the acquiring company has significant free cash flow that gives management the ability to finance unprofitable investments. He also argues that many takeovers are designed to reverse previous unprofitable takeovers. In other words, many companies that have made unprofitable takeovers will, themselves, become targets in takeovers designed to reverse the original value reduction. Therefore, while takeovers can be a 'problem', they can also provide a 'solution'. Thirdly, some managers may make unprofitable takeovers simply because they are poor managers, possibly seeking other fields in which they hope to perform better. Some of the many US studies that provide relevant empirical evidence are now outlined.

Lang, Stulz and Walkling studied successful tender offers and classified the acquiring and target companies using Tobin's $q$ ratio which is the ratio of a company's market value to the replacement cost of its assets.[52] The $q$ ratio was used as a measure of managerial performance on the basis that well-managed companies that make profitable investments should have $q$ ratios greater than one, while poorly-managed companies are likely to have $q$ ratios less than one. The authors found significant relationships between $q$ ratios and the profitability of takeovers to acquiring company shareholders. Takeovers that involved a high-$q$ acquirer and a low-$q$ target produced gains of approximately 10 per cent for shareholders, but when a low-$q$ acquirer announced a bid for a high-$q$ target, acquiring company shareholders lost approximately 4 per cent on average.[53]

Mitchell and Lehn test whether some takeovers are designed to change the control of companies that had previously made value-reducing acquisitions.[54] Two groups of companies that had made takeover bids were identified: (i) those subject to a later takeover bid within the study period ('targets'); and (ii) those not subject to a bid within that period ('non-targets'). Takeover announcements by the 'targets' were associated with significant losses for shareholders, while those by the 'non-targets' were associated with significant gains. Many of the original acquisitions were later reversed, either by voluntary divestiture or by a hostile 'bust-up' takeover. When Mitchell and Lehn examined the market

---

[52] L. Lang, R. Stulz & R. Walking, 'Managerial Performance, Tobin's Q and the Gains from Successful Tender Offers', *Journal of Financial Economics*, September 1989, pp. 137–54.

[53] The results reported by Lang, Stulz & Walking for tender offers have also been supported for mergers, and are not an artefact of the characteristics of the bid itself, such as the method of payment. See H. Servaes, 'Tobin's Q and the Gains from Takeovers', *Journal of Finance*, March 1991, pp. 409–19.

[54] Mitchell & Lehn (see Footnote 50).

response to the initial takeover they found significant differences between the 'divested' and 'not divested' groups. The average market response was positive for those that were not divested, negative for those that were divested, and even more negative for those that were followed by a 'bust-up' takeover. Their results are consistent with the argument that one role of takeovers is to discipline managers who fail to maximise profits, including those who make value-reducing takeovers. Their results also indicate that the stock market is able to distinguish between 'good' and 'bad' bidders.

Morck, Shleifer and Vishny examine the possibility that unprofitable takeovers are driven by managerial objectives.[55] They suggest that takeovers that benefit managers are likely to involve at least one of three characteristics: diversification, rapidly-growing targets, and poor past performance by the acquiring company. Their results show that all three characteristics are associated with losses for shareholders of acquiring companies. That is, acquiring companies do systematically pay too much in takeovers in which the benefits for managers are particularly large.

### 20.8.5 The net effects of takeovers

The evidence seems clear that activity in the market for corporate control has a positive effect on wealth. Bishop, Dodd and Officer estimated that the 1442 bids covered by their study created value of $7200 million for shareholders. Estimates in the US of the total dollar value of the premiums over the pre-announcement price of securities include $US54 000 million paid to the shareholders of target firms in successful tender offers from 1981 to 1986 and $US118 400 million for all change-of-control transactions over the same period.

The evidence discussed above was obtained from market-based studies, that is, studies that used share prices to measure the effects of takeovers. Some researchers have preferred to use accounting data to assess the effects of takeovers on company performance by examining measures of profitability, risk, and growth. For example, McDougall and Round used this approach to study Australian takeovers.[56] In common with other similar studies they were unable to find any evidence of benefits such as improved profitability or reduction of risk. In fact they concluded that 'a strategy of corporate acquisition resulted in a deterioration in the performance of the merging firms relative both to their pre-takeover experience, and also compared with the experience of the matching non-merging firms, measured in accounting terms.'[57]

The accounting-based results are clearly inconsistent with those of the more popular market-based studies. This suggests that at least one of the two approaches is unreliable. Bishop, Dodd and Officer argued that there are serious problems in using accounting data to assess the effects of takeovers.[58] For

---

[55] R. Morck, A. Shleifer & R. Vishny, 'Do Managerial Acquisitions Drive Bad Acquisitions?', *Journal of Finance*, March 1990, pp. 31–48.
[56] F. McDougall & D. Round, *The Effects of Mergers and Takeovers in Australia*, Australian Institute of Management—Victoria, and National Companies and Securities Commission, 1986.
[57] See Footnote 56, p. 182.
[58] S. Bishop, P. Dodd & R. R. Officer, see Footnote 4, pp. 33–4.

example, the benefits of a takeover may take years to be fully reflected in earnings and are likely to show up at different times for different companies. Therefore, the effects may be difficult to detect. Further, profitability ratios are likely to be biased, owing to revaluation of the target company's assets and write-off of takeover-related goodwill.[59]

Market-based studies are also subject to potential measurement problems. Share price changes around the time a takeover is announced will show how investors expected the takeover to work out, but the expected effects may not eventuate. These studies must also rely on some model of the normal returns on shares to estimate the abnormal returns related to takeovers. In summary, while the market-based approach is generally preferred, it is not infallible and it would be desirable to show that the results of market-based studies can be supported by other independent evidence.

This approach was adopted by Healy, Palepu and Ruback who used both accounting data and share price data to examine the effects of the 50 largest mergers in the US between 1979 and mid-1984.[60] To minimise the problems involved in using accounting data, they focused on estimates of operating cash flows before interest and tax, rather than accounting profit which could be influenced both by the method of accounting for the merger and by the financing of the merger. Healy, Palepu and Ruback found that after the mergers performance did improve significantly, on average, relative to the performance of other companies in the same industries. The improvement was greatest in mergers that involved overlapping businesses. Also they found a strong positive relationship between their estimates of merger-related changes in operating cash flows and share price changes of the merging companies at the time that mergers were announced. In summary, they provided further evidence that mergers do result in improved performance and they showed that, when implemented carefully, the accounting-based and market-based approaches can yield consistent results.

### 20.8.6 THE SOURCES OF GAINS FROM TAKEOVERS

Market-based studies are useful in documenting the magnitude of takeover-related wealth changes for shareholders, but they provide no information about the source of the wealth changes. Some critics have suggested that the wealth increases received by shareholders do not represent real economic gains but instead are the result of various redistributive effects. One such hypothesis is based on alleged market myopia. According to this hypothesis, investors are said to be preoccupied with short-term earnings performance and will undervalue companies that undertake long-term developments, making them prime targets for takeover. Other redistributive hypotheses are based on suggestions that takeovers transfer wealth from debtholders to shareholders, or impose losses on

---

[59] For an analysis of these problems, see P. Stanton, 'Accounting Rates of Return, as Measures of Post-merger Performance', *Australian Journal of Management*, December 1987, pp. 293–304.
[60] P. Healy, K. Palepu & R. Ruback, 'Does Corporate Performance Improve after Mergers?', *Journal of Financial Economics*, April 1992, pp. 135–75.

employees of the target company. In addition, there are those hypotheses discussed earlier in the chapter: target undervaluation due to market inefficiency, tax benefits, and monopoly power.

Empirical evidence soundly rejects the 'undervaluation' hypothesis and the 'market myopia' hypothesis. Tax benefits do appear to have at least a minor role in motivating takeover activity, but the evidence is inconsistent with shareholder gains being transferred from debtholders or employees.[61] This is not to suggest that there are no losers in the market for corporate control; managers of target companies are obvious losers in some, possibly many, cases, but there is no evidence of systematic losses that could offset the large gains to shareholders.

Having first identified improvements in post-merger cash flow performance, Healy, Palepu and Ruback proceeded to explore the sources of the changes in cash flow.[62] The changes could have arisen from a variety of sources, including higher operating margins, greater asset productivity, or lower labour costs. The changes might also have been achieved by cutting outlays on capital investment and research and development (R & D). They found that the higher post-merger cash flows were due primarily to increased asset productivity and there was some evidence of lower labour costs. They found no significant changes in capital outlays or in R & D expenditures. Therefore, the improved cash flows were not due to focusing on short-term performance at the expense of long-term viability.

## Selected References

*Corporations Law*, Australian Government Publishing Service, Chapter 6.

Bishop, S., Dodd, P. & Officer, R. R., 'Australian Takeovers: The Evidence 1972–1985', *Policy Monograph* 12, Centre for Independent Studies, St Leonards, 1987.

Irving, M., Beerworth, B. & Hodge, M., 'Mergers, Acquisitions and Takeovers', in *Handbook of Australian Corporate Finance*, Eds R. Bruce et al., 4th edn, Butterworths, Sydney, 1991, pp. 143–72.

Jarrell, G., Brickley, J. & Netter, J., 'The Market for Corporate Control: The Empirical Evidence Since 1980', *Journal of Economic Perspectives*, Winter 1988, pp. 49–68.

Jensen, M. & Ruback, R., 'The Market for Corporate Control: The Scientific Evidence', *Journal of Financial Economics*, April 1983, pp. 5–50.

McDonough, D. D., *Annotated Mergers and Acquisitions Law of Australia*, 3rd edn, Law Book Co., Sydney, 1993.

Myers, S. C., 'A Framework for Evaluating Mergers', in *Modern Developments in Financial Management*, Ed. S. C. Myers, Praeger, New York, 1976, pp. 633–45.

Stern, J. & Chew, D., Eds, *The Modern Revolution in Corporate Finance*, 2nd edn, Blackwell, Oxford, 1992.

## QUESTIONS

1. Takeover activity tends to vary significantly over time. Outline the factors that may explain this variation.
2. There are three types of takeovers: horizontal, vertical, and conglomerate. Give recent Australian examples of each type of takeover.
3. *A company can reduce its risk by taking over another company.* Do you agree with this statement? Is it a justifiable reason for a takeover?
4. *A company with accumulated tax losses is necessarily a valuable takeover proposition.* Discuss.

---

[61] Jarrell, Brickley & Netter, see Footnote 39, p. 58.
[62] P. Healy, K. Palepu & R. Ruback, see Footnote 60.

5. Yam Ltd (Y) has been evaluating the acquisition of Xavier Ltd (X). The annual expected cash flows of Y and X are, respectively, $1.16 million per annum in perpetuity and $0.64 million per annum in perpetuity. These cash flows are expected to be unaffected by the takeover. The systematic risk (beta) of Y is 0.75 and of X is 1.0. The risk-free interest rate is 10 per cent and the expected excess return on the market portfolio is 6 per cent. Calculate the price at which X represents a zero net present value investment. Is it likely that Y's shareholders will benefit from the takeover?

6. Assume the information in Question 5, except that the post-takeover cash flow of the two companies is expected to be $1.95 million per annum in perpetuity. Is the acquisition likely to be of benefit to Y's shareholders?

7. *There is no reason for an acquiring company to prefer a cash bid to a share exchange or vice versa.* Discuss.

8. Bako Ltd (B) has completed an exhaustive evaluation preparatory to the proposed acquisition of 50 per cent of the shares of Cullen Ltd (C). On the basis of this evaluation, B's management has estimated that the value of B's equity will increase from $320 million to $380 million as a result of the partial takeover. The pre-takeover number of shares in the two companies is 80 million in B and 20 million in C. B's management is now considering whether to proceed with the takeover by making one of the following bids:
   (a) a cash offer for C's shares of $5 per share (C's shares are currently selling for $4);
   (b) a share offer of 3 shares in B for every 2 shares in C.
   Should B proceed with the takeover in either case?

9. What are the benefits and costs of an unregulated market for takeovers? In view of the Australian legislation regulating takeovers, evaluate the benefits and costs.

10. *The evidence is clear that takeovers in aggregate in Australia . . . have resulted in substantial increases in the value of the corporate economy.* (Bishop, Dodd & Officer, *Australian Takeovers: The Evidence 1972–1985*, p. 6.) Outline the major points that support this conclusion.

11. Alpha Ltd is considering the acquisition of Beta Ltd. Both companies are wholly equity financed and each has two million shares on issue. The annual net cash flows of Alpha and Beta are $1 million and $0.5 million respectively, and these cash flows are expected to remain constant in perpetuity. Alpha shareholders require a rate of return of 20 per cent per annum, but Beta's operations are of higher risk and its shareholders require a 25 per cent per annum rate of return. After the takeover, Beta's net cash flow is expected to increase to $750 000 per annum in perpetuity with no change in risk.
   (a) Calculate the price per share at which Beta represents a zero net present value investment to Alpha.
   (b) Alpha offers $2.6 million cash for 100 per cent of Beta. Calculate the effect of the takeover on the wealth of each company's shareholders.
   (c) Outline the factors which the management of Alpha should take into account when deciding whether to make a formal bid, or an on-market offer for Beta.

12. Squire Clothing is considering the acquisition of the Skintight Jeans Company. Squire will pay $2 million to buy Skintight's assets and will also assume its liabilities of $900 000. It has been estimated that Skintight's

existing assets will generate pre-tax cash flows of $500 000 per annum for 25 years. The assets can be depreciated for tax purposes at 20 per cent per annum straight-line, with no salvage value. The company tax rate is 33 per cent and Squire estimates that an investment of this level of risk should yield 12 per cent per annum after tax.

Evaluate the proposed takeover.

13. Budget Computers specialises in buying secondhand computers and renting them out. Owing to rapid technological changes and intense competition, Budget has recorded losses in recent years and is now threatened with liquidation. Its major asset is a stock of largely obsolete computers. Fleeting Electrics Ltd is a newly listed company with interests in consumer electrical goods. The Chairman of Fleeting suggests that it should acquire Budget for two reasons. First, it provides diversification, and secondly, he argues that by injecting fresh capital, Budget can be 'rescued' and should appreciate markedly in value.

Critically evaluate the Chairman's arguments.

14. Crocodile Ltd is considering the acquisition of Shark Finance. The values of the two companies as separate entities are $10 million and $5 million respectively. Crocodile estimates that by combining the two companies it will reduce selling and administrative costs by $250 000 per year in perpetuity. Crocodile can either pay $7 million cash for Shark, or offer Shark a 50 per cent holding in Crocodile. If the opportunity cost of capital is 10 per cent per annum:
   (a) what is the gain, in present value terms, from the merger?
   (b) what is the net cost of the cash offer?
   (c) what is the net cost of the share alternative?
   (d) what is the NPV of the acquisition under:
      (i) the cash offer?
      (ii) the share offer?

15. Progressive Ltd is determined to increase its earnings per share from $1 to $1.33, so it acquires Lo-Gear. The following facts are provided:

| Item | Progressive | Lo-Gear | Merged company |
|---|---|---|---|
| Earnings per share ($) | 1.00 | 1.25 | 1.33 |
| Price per share ($) | 20.00 | 12.50 | ? |
| Price–earnings ratio | 20 | 10 | ? |
| Number of shares | 100 000 | 200 000 | ? |
| Total earnings ($) | 100 000 | 250 000 | ? |
| Total market value ($) | 2 000 000 | 2 500 000 | ? |

There are no economic benefits from combining the two companies. In exchange for Lo-Gear shares, Progressive issues just enough of its own shares to ensure its $1.33 earnings per share objective.
   (a) Complete the table for the merged company.
   (b) How many shares of Progressive are exchanged for each share of Lo-Gear?
   (c) What is the net cost of the takeover to Progressive?
   (d) What is the change in the total market value of the Progressive shares that were on issue before the takeover?

(e) Based on these results, comment on the use of earnings-per-share comparisons in assessing the viability of takeovers.

16. The value of Minnow Ltd to Whale Ltd can be determined by:
    (a) discounting Minnow's net cash flows to a present value;
    (b) the present value of Minnow's expected future dividends;
    (c) estimating the present value of the incremental net cash flows directly attributable to the takeover, and adding this to the current market value of Minnow.

    Critically evaluate each of these approaches. Which one would you advise the management of Whale to use? Give reasons.

17. (a) In an efficient market, the price of a company's shares is an unbiased estimate of their 'true' value. How might the 'true' value of a takeover target differ from its value to a potential bidder? What relationship exists between this latter value and the actual offer price?
    (b) *Asset backing is irrelevant as a measure of the worth of a company subject to a takeover bid.* Comment.

18. Farrout Ltd is planning to acquire a small boat builder, Winged Keel Pty Ltd. Three opinions have been obtained on the value of the target. These are as follows:
    (a) Based on the latest earnings of Winged Keel, and applying Farrout's price–earnings ratio, the company is worth $1 200 000.
    (b) Based on total tangible assets, a value of $2 000 000 is indicated.
    (c) Based on the present value of Winged Keel's expected future dividends, it is worth $1 500 000.

    Evaluate each of these approaches and indicate any inherent problems. Which would you select as the most appropriate?

19. Carrion Ltd has announced a takeover bid for Elephant Ltd, one of Australia's largest companies. The Chairman of Carrion argues that the takeover will be economically viable because it will lead to more efficient management of Elephant's assets, there are tax advantages involved, and value can be created by dividing Elephant into three or four separate entities, each based on a single line of business.
    (a) Critically evaluate each of the three reasons for takeover viability suggested by the Chairman.
    (b) Assuming that Carrion already holds 15 per cent of Elephant's shares, briefly outline the legislative requirements that must be met in any bid for control of the target.
    (c) Elephant's shares had a market price of $7.90 prior to any purchases by Carrion. Analysts employed by Carrion have valued the shares at $11.50, based on the present value of future net cash flows. Outline the relationship you would expect between these values and Carrion's bid price.

20. Explain the following terms:
    (a) Market for corporate control
    (b) Synergy
    (c) Disciplinary takeover
    (d) Takeover waves
    (e) Co-insurance effect
    (f) Free cash flow
    (g) Bootstrapping
    (h) Part A offer
    (i) On-market offer
    (j) Proportional bid
    (k) White knight
    (l) Golden parachute
    (m) Spin-off
    (n) Leveraged buyout
    (o) Hubris
    (p) Corporate raider.

21. Maureen Carroll examines the share prices of companies that are the targets of takeover bids. She finds that their share prices rise substantially when the bid is announced and, over the next 12 months, do not drop back to the pre-bid level, even if the takeover is unsuccessful. Advise Maureen of possible explanations for this observation.
22. Duck Ltd, a conglomerate, has a market capitalisation of $400 million. The management of Drake Ltd believes that it can acquire Duck for $500 million and sell its divisions separately for a total of about $800 million. Outline possible reasons for the difference between these values.
23. *Takeovers are important because they provide the only way to exploit synergies, and to ensure that managers of corporations act in the interests of shareholders.* Comment on this statement.
24. Claire McDonald is concerned that market-based evidence on the effects of takeovers may be misleading. She agrees that target company shareholders gain substantially, but argues that these gains could be the result of wealth transfers from employees, and from the shareholders of acquiring companies. Claire says, 'I won't be convinced that takeovers are beneficial until someone can show exactly where the gains come from'. Outline evidence that should convince Claire that takeovers provide real benefits.

**CHAPTER 21**

# INTERNATIONAL FINANCIAL MANAGEMENT

## 21.1 INTRODUCTION

In previous chapters, only passing reference has been made to international financial management. The aim of this chapter is to provide an introduction to some of the major issues in international financial management. Many Australian companies import goods and services, while others export goods and services; similarly, many Australian companies invest funds overseas and/or borrow funds from overseas. Since the floating of the Australian dollar in December 1983, international aspects of finance have become more important for Australian companies. In particular, the value of the Australian dollar has varied considerably during these years, thereby creating problems for financial managers. However, the ability to undertake foreign currency transactions in a deregulated environment has also opened up new opportunities for financial managers. In addition, foreign currency trading and finance has itself become something of an industry, with 72 authorised foreign currency dealers in Australia at May 1992. The Australian dollar is one of the more actively traded currencies in the world.[1]

---

[1] In April 1992 the Australian dollar was the world's ninth most actively traded currency. Turnover in the Australian foreign exchange market at this time was approximately US$30 billion per day, making the Australian market the ninth largest in the world. See 'The Australian Foreign Exchange Market', Reserve Bank of Australia *Bulletin*, May 1993, pp. 4–9.

## 21.2 SOME BACKGROUND STATISTICS

Some idea of the importance of international operations to Australian companies can be obtained from Tables 21.1 to 21.3.

Table 21.1 shows that international trade now represents about 19 per cent of Australia's gross domestic product; this is significantly higher than was the case 20 or 30 years ago.

**Table 21.1** *Value of Australia's exports and imports of goods and services in Australian dollars and as a percentage of gross domestic product*

| Year | Exports of goods and services | | Imports of goods and services | |
|---|---|---|---|---|
| | $A m | % | $A m | % |
| 1962–63 | 2 483 | 14.7 | 2 596 | 15.4 |
| 1972–73 | 7 007 | 15.6 | 5 382 | 12.0 |
| 1982–83 | 25 430 | 14.7 | 28 967 | 16.7 |
| 1988–89 | 54 728 | 16.4 | 61 218 | 18.3 |
| 1989–90 | 60 132 | 16.5 | 67 419 | 18.5 |
| 1990–91 | 65 154 | 17.4 | 65 660 | 17.6 |
| 1991–92 | 68 812 | 17.9 | 67 654 | 17.6 |
| 1992–93 | 74 880 | 18.7 | 76 891 | 19.2 |

Sources: R. A. Foster & S. E. Stewart, 'Australian economic statistics 1949–50 to 1989–90', *Occasional Paper No. 8*, Reserve Bank of Australia, February 1991, Table 5.1a, and Reserve Bank of Australia *Bulletin*, December 1993, Table G.5

Turning from international trade to international capital movements, Tables 21.2 and 21.3 provide information on capital movements between Australia and other countries.

**Table 21.2** *Levels of foreign investment in $A million: non-official sector*

| At 30 June: | Foreign investment in Australia | | | Australian investment abroad | | |
|---|---|---|---|---|---|---|
| | Direct investment | Portfolio and other | Total non-official | Direct investment | Portfolio and other | Total non-official |
| 1979 | 10 039 | 6 617 | 16 656 | 1 522 | 1 738 | 3 260 |
| 1984 | 31 874 | 40 766 | 72 550 | 7 631 | 4 699 | 12 330 |
| 1989 | 83 142 | 119 716 | 202 858 | 37 301 | 28 697 | 65 998 |
| 1990 | 92 410 | 130 933 | 223 343 | 39 984 | 30 746 | 70 730 |
| 1991 | 98 354 | 147 021 | 245 375 | 38 883 | 32 508 | 71 391 |
| 1992 | 104 398 | 154 876 | 259 274 | 42 697 | 36 658 | 79 355 |
| 1993 | 111 778 | 167 685 | 279 463 | 45 774 | 43 503 | 89 277 |

Source: Reserve Bank of Australia *Bulletin*, December 1993, Table H.5

Historically, Australia has been a net importer of capital. Table 21.2 shows recent levels of foreign investment in Australia, and Australian investment abroad. Both have grown strongly through the 1980s and into the 1990s with an average growth rate of around 8 per cent per annum in the 1989–93 period. In

1993, private foreign investment in Australia was estimated at $A280 billion, while Australian investment abroad was estimated at $A90 billion.

The extent of Australia's external indebtedness is indicated in Table 21.3 which shows that Australia's external indebtedness has grown considerably in recent years, with net indebtedness in 1993 standing at more than $A170 billion.

**Table 21.3** *Australia's gross and net external debt in $A million*

| At 30 June: | Gross $A m | Net $A m |
| --- | --- | --- |
| 1980 | 13 498 | 6 863 |
| 1985 | 67 473 | 51 208 |
| 1990 | 162 800 | 131 404 |
| 1991 | 178 200 | 140 798 |
| 1992 | 189 415 | 152 690 |
| 1993 | 210 270 | 171 722 |

Source: Reserve Bank of Australia *Bulletin*, December 1993, Table H.7

As indicated by the data in these tables, Australia has a relatively open economy. It depends significantly on international trade and on foreign sources of capital and, for its size, has significant investments overseas. Moreover, recent government policy and pronouncements have encouraged Australian business to look beyond Australia both for ideas and markets. Not surprisingly, therefore, many companies operating in Australia assign a high priority to decisions on international financial management.

## 21.3 THE FOREIGN EXCHANGE MARKET

### 21.3.1 THE SPOT EXCHANGE RATE

The meaning of the phrase 'spot exchange rate' is most readily understood in the context of international trade. For example, suppose that an Australian company imports goods from the UK. It is likely that the UK supplier will require the Australian company to pay for the goods in UK pounds (often known as pounds sterling). Unless the Australian company has a stock of UK pounds of its own it will need to buy UK pounds in order to pay for the goods. In other words, the Australian company will need to exchange (sell) Australian dollars for UK pounds. The price at which Australian dollars will be converted into UK pounds is known as the **exchange rate** between Australian dollars and UK pounds. However, Australian companies that export goods are also likely to invoice the purchaser in foreign currency rather than in Australian dollars. In this case, the Australian company will wish to sell the foreign currency and receive Australian dollars. Again the exchange rate is used to make the conversion.

In both cases use will be made of the foreign exchange market. This market has no physical marketplace but rather is a communications network linking banks and other dealers in foreign exchange. A company wishing to buy or sell foreign currency may do so through one of the banks or other dealers. Apart from exporting or importing goods and services, reasons for using the foreign exchange market include borrowing foreign currency, lending foreign currency, buying or selling foreign assets, and speculating on exchange rate movements.

An exchange rate is therefore simply the price at which one country's currency can be exchanged for another country's currency in the foreign exchange market. The exchange may be immediate (in practice, two days). In this case the exchange rate is called the **spot rate**, the word *spot* referring to the fact that the delivery of the currency is (almost) immediate. Examples of spot rates for one Australian dollar, as at 23 June 1994, are shown in Table 21.4.

**Table 21.4** *Spot exchange rates for $A1 as at 23 June 1994*

| Currency | (1) Customer sells foreign currency and buys $A1 | (2) Customer sells $A1 and buys foreign currency | (3) Ratio of (2)/(1) % |
|---|---|---|---|
| US dollars (USD) | 0.7362 | 0.7312 | 99.32 |
| UK pounds (GBP) | 0.4823 | 0.4758 | 98.65 |
| Japan yen (JPY) | 74.71 | 73.39 | 98.23 |
| Germany mark (DEM) | 1.1871 | 1.1666 | 98.27 |
| Singapore dollar (SGD) | 1.1302 | 1.1106 | 98.27 |
| Fiji dollar (FJD) | 1.0786 | 1.0482 | 97.18 |
| Indian rupee (INR) | 23.010 | 21.899 | 95.17 |

Source: *Australian Financial Review*, 24 June 1994, p.43. The rates quoted are retail rates; wholesale rates would show lower figures in Column (1) and higher figures in Column (2), and thus ratios in Column (3) would be closer to 100 per cent.

Column (1) provides the exchange rate applicable where a customer has foreign currency and wishes to obtain Australian dollars. Column (2) provides the exchange rate applicable where a customer has Australian dollars and wishes to obtain foreign currency. Using the US dollar spot rate as an example, if a customer (say a company) had US dollars and wanted to buy $A1, it would have needed to deliver (sell) US$0.7362 to obtain the Australian dollar. If, instead, a customer had one Australian dollar and wished to buy US dollars, it would receive US$0.7312 in return for the one Australian dollar.[2] The difference (or spread) between the rates is one source of the foreign exchange dealer's profit. The final column in Table 21.4 shows how the spread varies from currency to currency. The spread for the US dollar is by far the narrowest, followed by the spread on currencies which are heavily traded (such as pounds and yen), with the widest spreads being on those currencies which, from an Australian viewpoint at least, are infrequently required. One reason for this pattern is that the vast majority of trading in Australian dollars is in terms of the US dollar. Therefore, if an Australian company approached its bank to obtain a significant sum in, say, Indian rupees, the bank could obtain the rupees by first selling the Australian dollars for US dollars and then (probably through an overseas foreign exchange market) selling the US dollars for rupees. Thus two transactions would be

---

2 We have used exchange rates in the retail (or small transaction) market. Exchange rates in the wholesale (large transaction) or interdealer market would be more favourable, with a narrower spread between the rates.

required, as there is no direct link between the Australian dollar and the Indian rupee.

Table 21.5 provides data from a survey conducted by the Bank for International Settlements in April 1992. By far the most common transaction in the Australian foreign exchange market involves the Australian dollar–US dollar exchange rate; this accounted for approximately 41 per cent of the value transacted. Recent growth areas have been the Australian dollar against other currencies (now 3 per cent) and cross-currency transactions that involve neither the US dollar nor the Australian dollar (now 5 per cent).

**Table 21.5** *Foreign exchange trading in Australia: market share by currency pair, April 1992*

| Currency pair | Market share (%) |
|---|---|
| Australian dollar—US dollar | 41 |
| US dollar—Deutschmark | 24 |
| US dollar—Japanese yen | 13 |
| US dollar—UK pound | 8 |
| US dollar—other currencies | 6 |
| Australian dollar—other currencies | 3 |
| Cross currency | 5 |
| | 100 |

*Source*: BIS survey reported in 'The Australian foreign exchange market', Reserve Bank of Australia *Bulletin*, May 1993, p. 7

## 21.3.2 THE FORWARD EXCHANGE RATE

In forward exchange trading, the exchange of currencies is not immediate but is at some agreed future date; that is, the exchange rate is determined now, but the currencies are exchanged later. The exchange rate in such a contract is referred to as the **forward rate**. For example, a time period of 1, 3 or 6 months may be specified in a forward exchange contract. Only about 1 per cent of forward contracts are for periods of more than one year.

Forward exchange rates are usually quoted in terms of the difference between the spot rate and the forward rate. This difference is referred to as the **forward margin**.[3] To understand how to interpret forward exchange quotations, suppose that for US dollars (per one Australian dollar) you are told that the spot rate is 0.7460/70 and the 3 months' forward margin is 166/162. This means that the exchange rates are (in US dollars per $A1):

| | | Customer sells US$ and buys $A1 | Customer buys US$ and sells $A1 |
|---|---|---|---|
| less | Spot rate | 0.7470 | 0.7460 |
| | Forward margin | 0.0162 | 0.0166 |
| | Forward rate | 0.7308 | 0.7294 |

---

3 Determinants of the forward margin are discussed in Section 21.4.2.

Therefore, if a company agrees today to sell $A1 in 3 months' time, it will receive US$0.7294 in 3 months' time. If a company agrees to buy $A1 in 3 months' time, it will need to deliver US$0.7308 in 3 months' time. The *spread* between the buying and selling rates for the forward contract is 0.7308 − 0.7294 = 0.0014. This is larger than the spread of 0.0010 for the spot contract. The spread for a forward contract is always greater than the spread for the matching spot contract. The *forward margin* in this example is subtracted from the spot rate, but this is not always the case. For other currencies, or for the same currency at other times, the forward margin has to be added to the spot rate. The reasons why this occurs are explained in Section 21.4.2. However, at this stage, we mention that had the forward margins been added in the example the resulting forward rates would have been 0.7632 and 0.7626, implying a spread of only 0.0006. This would be less than the spread in the spot rates and, therefore, impossible.

### 21.3.3 COMBINED SPOT AND FORWARD TRANSACTIONS

Dealers in foreign exchange markets frequently enter simultaneously into spot and forward transactions. For example, one dealer may agree with another to sell Australian dollars today for, say, US dollars, and simultaneously agree to buy back the Australian dollars on a later date. The exchange rate agreed will, of course, differ between the two 'legs' of the transaction because the first leg is a spot transaction, while the second is a forward transaction. These combined transactions have occurred in foreign exchange markets for many years and are generally known as 'swaps'. However, they should be distinguished from the foreign currency swaps, discussed in Section 21.8.5, which are more complex and whose origin is more recent.

Although calculations using foreign exchange rates are very simple, mistakes are often made. There are only four types of calculation as follows. Each type is illustrated using the UK pound exchange rates given in Table 21.4. These are:

|  | *Customer sells £ and buys $A1* | *Customer buys £ and sells $A1* |
|---|---|---|
| UK pounds (GBP) | 0.4823 | 0.4758 |

#### TYPE 1: TO OBTAIN A GIVEN SUM IN $A USING £

A UK resident may wish to obtain $A10 000. How many pounds are needed? As £0.4823 is needed for every $A1 required, the answer is £(10 000 × 0.4823) = £4823.

#### TYPE 2: TO CONVERT A GIVEN SUM OF £ TO $A

An Australian company has been paid £10 000 and wishes to exchange this for Australian dollars. How many Australian dollars will this buy? As each pound will buy $A(1 ÷ 0.4823), the answer is $A(10 000 ÷ 0.4823) = $A20 733.98.

## TYPE 3: TO OBTAIN A GIVEN SUM IN £ USING $A

An Australian company may wish to obtain £10 000. How many Australian dollars are needed? As $A1 will obtain £0.4758, the answer is $A(10 000 ÷ 0.4758) = $A21 017.23.

## TYPE 4: TO CONVERT A GIVEN SUM OF $A TO £

A UK resident has been paid $A10 000 and wishes to exchange this for pounds. How many pounds will this buy? As each Australian dollar will buy £0.4758, the answer is £(10 000 × 0.4758) = £4758.

To simplify the later discussion we now assume that the spread between exchange rates is zero. We also make no distinction between retail, wholesale or interdealer exchange rates. Therefore there is assumed to be only one spot exchange rate linking two currencies at any given point in time. Similar assumptions are made for the forward rate applicable to any given future time period.

### 21.3.4 TRIANGULAR ARBITRAGE AND CROSS RATES

Suppose that the following spot rates are observed simultaneously: $A1 = US$0.8000 and US$1 = £0.6290. Using only these two spot rates, the spot rate linking Australian dollars and UK pounds must be:

$$\$A1 = £(0.8000 \times 0.6290) = £0.5032$$

If this were not the case, a riskless profit could be made. For example, if the spot rate were instead $A1 = £0.5000, then a foreign exchange dealer could profit from undertaking the following three transactions simultaneously:
 1. Sell $A1 for US$0.8000.
 2. Sell US$0.8000 for £(0.8000 × 0.6290) = £0.5032.
 3. Sell £0.5032 for $A(0.5032 ÷ 0.5000) = $A1.0064.

Obviously, these transactions produce an instantaneous risk-free profit of $A0.0064 for every Australian dollar transacted in Step 1. If, for example, $A1 million were transacted, the profit would be $A6400. Such an arbitrage is called **triangular** as it involves three transactions and three currencies. It is easily shown that if the exchange rate between pounds and Australian dollars had been more than £0.5032, a different triangular arbitrage would have been available. For example, if the rate had been $A1 = £0.5062, one arbitrage would have been to make the following three transactions simultaneously:
 1. Sell $A1 for £0.5062.
 2. Sell £0.5062 for US$(0.5062 ÷ 0.6290) = US$0.804 77.
 3. Sell US$0.804 77 for $A(0.804 77 ÷ 0.8000) = $A1.005 96.

The profit in this case would have been $A5960 on a sale of $A1 million in Step 1.

The practical significance of triangular arbitrage is that, by assuming that competition will eliminate the opportunity for it to occur, exchange rates for any pair of currencies can be calculated from knowledge of other exchange rates involving those currencies. The resulting exchange rates are known as **cross rates**. In the example given, the values of both the Australian dollar and the UK pound were given in terms of US dollars and from those two exchange rates, the cross rate $A1 = £0.5032 was calculated.

# INTERNATIONAL FINANCIAL MANAGEMENT

In the limit, if there are $n$ currencies in the world, the number of distinct pairs of currencies (exchange rates) is $(n)(n-1)/2$. However, if one of those currencies (in practice the US dollar) has a central role, so that the value of the $(n-1)$ other currencies are all known in terms of US dollars, then all exchange rates can be calculated. For example, if $n = 100$, there are $(100 \times 99)/2$, or 4950 exchange rates that may need to be known. This can be achieved indirectly by having markets to determine the exchange rates between each of the ninety-nine currencies and the US dollar.

## 21.3.5 SIZE OF THE FOREIGN EXCHANGE MARKET IN AUSTRALIA

As mentioned earlier, the Australian dollar is one of the more actively traded currencies in the world. Table 21.6 provides data on the average daily turnover in the Australian foreign exchange market (in millions of Australian dollars) from 1990–91 to 1993–94.

**Table 21.6** *Average daily turnover in the Australian foreign exchange market*

| | Transactions by foreign exchange dealers ($A million per day) with: | | | |
|---|---|---|---|---|
| | Other dealers in Australia | Banks overseas | Customers | Total |
| **1990/91** | | | | |
| Spot | 3 808 | 10 936 | 4 116 | 18 860 |
| Forward | 217 | 661 | 1 120 | 1 998 |
| Swap | 4 098 | 12 325 | 3 650 | 20 073 |
| Total | 8 123 | 23 922 | 8 886 | 40 931 |
| **1991/92** | | | | |
| Spot | 3 436 | 10 044 | 3 500 | 16 981 |
| Forward | 139 | 466 | 1 009 | 1 614 |
| Swap | 3 916 | 11 147 | 3 397 | 18 459 |
| Total | 7 491 | 21 657 | 7 906 | 37 054 |
| **1992/93** | | | | |
| Spot | 4 433 | 12 914 | 4 500 | 21 847 |
| Forward | 165 | 766 | 1 319 | 2 250 |
| Swap | 4 660 | 12 598 | 4 940 | 22 198 |
| Total | 9 258 | 26 278 | 10 759 | 46 295 |
| **1993/94** | | | | |
| Spot | 3 976 | 13 354 | 4 917 | 22 247 |
| Forward | 142 | 606 | 1 473 | 2 221 |
| Swap | 5 173 | 14 393 | 5 369 | 24 935 |
| Total | 9 291 | 28 353 | 11 759 | 49 403 |

*Source*: Reserve Bank of Australia *Bulletin*, June 1994, Table F.8. Figures for 1990/91 refer to the period September 1990 to June 1991. Figures for 1993/94 refer to the period July 1993 to April 1994.

From the data in Table 21.6, two important observations can be made. First, by any standards the volume of trading is significant. In the most recent period, average daily turnover is nearly $A50 billion. This figure can be put in perspective by noting that Australian exports plus imports for the *year* 1992–93 amounted to approximately $A119 billion—that is, less than 3 *days* of average foreign exchange turnover. Secondly, just under 60 per cent of the trading volume is between foreign exchange dealers and banks overseas, while approximately twenty per cent is due to trading between foreign exchange dealers. Only about 20 to 25 per cent of trading volume is between foreign exchange dealers and customers.

## 21.4 RELATIONSHIPS BETWEEN INTEREST RATES, INFLATION RATES, SPOT EXCHANGE RATES AND FORWARD EXCHANGE RATES

We now establish links between four important variables: interest rates, inflation rates, spot exchange rates and forward exchange rates. In this analysis it is assumed that market participants are risk neutral and that there are no barriers or frictions (such as taxes or transaction costs) in any market. The analysis applies to any two currencies, but for illustration, we assume that the two currencies are Australian dollars and UK pounds.[4] Similarly the analysis should, in principle, be applicable to any given time period; we will assume that the period involved is 1 year.

### 21.4.1 NOTATION AND STAGES OF ANALYSIS

Throughout Section 21.4, the following notation is used:
- $i$ = interest rate (nominal, per annum)
- $p$ = inflation rate (per annum)
- $s$ = spot exchange rate (expressed as pounds per dollar)
- $f$ = forward exchange rate for 1 year (expressed as pounds per dollar)
- £ = subscript used to indicate that a variable refers to pounds; for example, $i_£$ means the interest rate on pounds
- $ = subscript used to indicate that a variable refers to Australian dollars; for example, $p_\$$ means the inflation rate in Australia
- $E$ = the expectation operator for 1 year; for example, $E(s)$ means the spot exchange rate that today is expected to occur in 1 year's time

The analysis in Sections 21.4.2 to 21.4.4 establishes the following relationships between the four variables:

$$\frac{1 + i_£}{1 + i_\$} = \frac{f}{s} = \frac{E(s)}{s} = \frac{1 + E(p_£)}{1 + E(p_\$)} \qquad (21.1)$$

Equation 21.1 is discussed in three stages:

*Stage 1* links interest rates and exchange rates and is often called **interest rate parity**:

---

[4] As implied in Section 21.3.1, the US dollar–Australian dollar exchange rate is by far the most important for Australian companies. However, we use UK pounds to avoid confusion between the two dollars.

$$\frac{1 + i_£}{1 + i_\$} = \frac{f}{s} \qquad (21.1a)$$

This equation is discussed in Section 21.4.2.

*Stage 2* links forward exchange rates and spot exchange rates and is often called **unbiased forward rates**:

$$\frac{f}{s} = \frac{E(s)}{s} \qquad (21.1b)$$

This equation is discussed in Section 21.4.3.

*Stage 3* links spot exchange rates and expected inflation rates and is often called **purchasing power parity**:

$$\frac{E(s)}{s} = \frac{1 + E(p_£)}{1 + E(p_\$)} \qquad (21.1c)$$

This equation is discussed in Section 21.4.4.

A fourth relationship, known as **uncovered interest parity** or the **international Fisher effect**[5] may be found by combining Equation 21.1a and Equation 21.1b, to give:

$$\frac{E(s)}{s} = \frac{1 + i_£}{1 + i_\$} \qquad (21.1d)$$

This equation is discussed in Section 21.4.5.

## 21.4.2 INTEREST RATE PARITY

Interest rate parity maintains that:

$$\frac{1 + i_£}{1 + i_\$} = \frac{f}{s} \qquad (21.1a)$$

Interest rate parity states that relative interest rates determine the relativity between the forward exchange rate and the spot exchange rate.

Interest rate parity may be proved by considering the choices open to Australian investors who wish to invest $X$ Australian dollars in government securities for a period of 1 year. It is assumed that the investors must choose between an investment in Australian securities and an investment in UK securities. If they choose to invest in Australian securities, they are certain to receive $X(1 + i_\$)$ dollars after 1 year. If they choose to invest in UK securities, they must first convert the Australian dollars to UK pounds. As the spot rate is $s$ pounds per dollar, they will obtain $s$ pounds for each dollar.

Therefore, they have $Xs$ pounds available for investment. After 1 year, they are certain to receive $Xs(1 + i_£)$ pounds. However, to make a valid comparison between the returns offered by the two investments, investors need to be certain of the dollar value of the return from the UK investment. This certainty can be achieved by entering immediately into a forward contract to sell $Xs(1 + i_£)$

---

[5] Where the term 'uncovered interest parity' is used, Equation 21.1a is usually called 'covered interest parity' to distinguish the two equations. The significance of the alternative term 'international Fisher effect' is explained in Section 21.4.5.

pounds in 1 year's time. As the forward rate is $f$ pounds per dollar, they will obtain $1/f$ dollars for each pound, and therefore they can be certain that the UK investment will return $Xs\,(1 + i_£)\dfrac{1}{f}$ dollars after 1 year. The two investments can now be compared because they are expressed in the same currency (Australian dollars) and have identical risk and term. The Australian investment will be chosen if $X\,(1 + i_\$) > Xs\,(1 + i_£)\dfrac{1}{f}$ but the UK investment will be chosen if $X\,(1 + i_\$) < Xs\,(1 + i_£)\dfrac{1}{f}$. However, the difference between the two returns should be very small. Under the assumptions made, the two investments are, in fact, perfect substitutes and in efficient market, perfect substitutes must offer the same return. If this were not so, then arbitrage would be possible. This type of arbitrage is known as **covered interest arbitrage** and would continue to be exploited until the interest rates and/or the exchange rates adjusted so as to eliminate the possibility of further arbitrage. In equilibrium, therefore, the two returns must be equal. That is:

$$X\,(1 + i_\$) = Xs\,(1 + i_£)\dfrac{1}{f}$$

Dividing both sides by $X$ and rearranging:

$$\dfrac{1 + i_£}{1 + i_\$} = \dfrac{f}{s}$$

which is Equation 21.1a.

*Example 21.1*

Suppose that an investor has $A1 million to invest for 1 year in government securities, and that the interest rate on Australian dollars is 14.2 per cent and the interest rate on UK pounds is 11.75 per cent. The spot exchange rate is $A1 = £0.5265 and the forward exchange rate for 1 year is $A1 = £0.5152. The investor wishes to calculate the return on an Australian investment, and the return (in Australian dollars) on an equivalent UK investment.

1. Invest $A1 million in Australian securities for 1 year.
   Cash inflow after 1 year = $A1 000 000 × 1.142
   = $A1 142 000
2. Invest $A1 million in UK securities for 1 year.
   (a) Spot 'conversion' of $A1 million to pounds:
   $A1 000 000 = £(1 000 000 × 0.5265)
   = £526 500
   (b) Cash inflow (in pounds) after 1 year:
   = £526 500 × 1.1175
   = £588 363.75
   (c) 'Reconversion' to Australian dollars at the forward rate:

$$£588\ 363.75 = \$A(588\ 363.75 \div 0.5152)$$
$$= \$A1\ 142\ 010.30$$

The difference between (1) and (2) is only $A10.30.

In Example 21.1 the difference between an Australian dollar investment and a UK pound investment with forward cover is trivial—about $A10 on an investment of $A1 million. This suggests that Equation 21.1a, the interest rate parity equation, should hold in this case. The following calculations confirm that this is indeed the case:

$$\frac{1 + i_£}{1 + i_\$} = \frac{1.1175}{1.1420} = 0.978\ 546$$

or

$$\frac{f}{s} = \frac{0.5152}{0.5265} = 0.978\ 538$$

Equation 21.1a is often rewritten as:

$$f = s\left(\frac{1 + i_£}{1 + i_\$}\right)$$

or $\quad f = s + s(i_£ - i_\$)$ approximately

Interest rate parity is usually seen as a method of calculating the forward rate, given information on the spot rate and on interest rates for the two currencies. Although it can be (and is) used in this way, the theory makes no statement of causality. It simply states that the four variables $f$, $s$, $i_£$, and $i_\$$, must be related as shown in Equation 21.1a and does not necessarily imply that the forward rate is caused by the other three.

The approximate relationship shown makes it very clear that the forward rate can be seen as simply the spot rate plus an adjustment for the difference in interest rates. Where the exchange rate is quoted as a rate per $A1, the forward rate is greater (less) than the spot rate when the pound sterling interest rate is greater (less) than the Australian dollar interest rate.

If the interest rate parity equation is violated, then covered interest arbitrage is possible. Example 21.2 uses US dollar exchange rates to illustrate, in detail, this type of arbitrage.

## Example 21.2

Assuming that the spread is zero and there are no transaction costs, covered interest arbitrage is feasible if the following set of interest rates and exchange rates are observed simultaneously:

Spot rate: $\quad$ $A1 = US$0.7525
Forward rate (1 month): $\quad$ $A1 = US$0.7474
$A interest rate (1 month): $\quad$ 1.25% per month
US$ interest rate (1 month): $\quad$ 0.65% per month

Covered interest arbitrage is possible because Equation 21.1a is violated, as shown in the following:

$$\frac{1 + i_{US}}{1 + i_A} = \frac{1.0065}{1.0123} = 0.994\,074$$

but $\quad \dfrac{f}{s} = \dfrac{0.7474}{0.7525} = 0.993\,223$

Expressing this result in another way, the forward rate indicated by interest rate parity is $(0.994\,074)(0.7525) = 0.7480$, compared with the actual forward rate of 0.7474.

To illustrate covered interest arbitrage, assume that an arbitrageur simultaneously undertakes the following four transactions:

1. Borrows \$A5 million for 1 month at 1.25 per cent per month; this requires a repayment of \$A5 million × 1.0125 = \$A5 062 500.
2. Converts the sum of \$A5 million to US dollars, thereby obtaining US\$(5m × 0.7525) = US\$3 762 500.
3. Lends US\$3 762 500 for 1 month at an interest rate of 0.65 per cent per month, producing a future cash repayment to the arbitrageur of US\$3 762 500 × 1.0065 = US\$3 786 956.25.
4. Sells forward (1 month) the sum of US\$3 786 956.25, thereby ensuring an Australian dollar inflow of \$A(3 786 956.25 ÷ 0.7474) or \$A5 066 840.05 in 1 month's time.

After 1 month, the inflow of \$A5 066 840.05 can be used to make the repayment of \$A5 062 500, thereby giving the arbitrageur a risk-free profit of \$A4340.05 for a net investment of zero.

An alternative mechanism that exploits the same disequilibrium would be for the arbitrageur to keep back the sum of \$A4282.79 between Step 1 and Step 2, thereby producing an immediate profit of this amount.[6] In this case only \$A4 995 717.21 is converted to US dollars, and the assured cash inflow at Step 4 is:

$$\frac{4\,995\,717.21 \times 0.7525 \times 1.0065}{0.7474} \text{ Australian dollars}$$

$= \$A5\,062\,500$

This sum is, of course, just sufficient to meet the repayment required.

Both of the arbitrages described here are **outward covered interest arbitrages**; the term *outward* is used to indicate that, in at least a figurative sense, money is sent out of Australia in the form of an investment in US dollars. Had the forward rate in this example been greater than 0.7480 (which is the rate indicated by interest rate parity, given the spot rate and the two interest rates), the arbitrage would have been of the *inward* type. In this case, US dollars are borrowed, and the funds are converted to Australian dollars to earn interest at the Australian interest rate.

---

[6] In effect, this is the present value of the future profit of \$A4340.05. Note that \$A4340.05 ÷ 1.0125 = \$A4286.47 ≈ \$A4282.79.

### 21.4.3 UNBIASED FORWARD RATES
Equation 21.1b maintains that:
$$\frac{f}{s} = \frac{E(s)}{s}$$

If market participants are risk neutral and there are no transaction costs, the market will set the forward rate $f$ equal to the spot rate which is expected to be observed at the date on which the forward contract matures. If this result did not hold, then risk neutral speculators would trade in foreign currency until the forward rate is equal to the expected spot rate. For example, if the forward rate for 1 year is $\$A1 = £0.5265$, but it is expected that the spot rate in 1 year's time will be $\$A1 = £0.5065$, then a risk neutral speculator would enter into a forward contract to sell Australian dollars in 1 year's time. Under the terms of the forward contract, the speculator must deliver $\$A1$ and in return accept £0.5265. If, as expected, the spot rate at that time is $\$A1 = £0.5065$, the pounds obtained (£0.5265) can then be converted into $\$A(0.5265 \div 0.5065) = \$A1.0395$. The speculator therefore has a profit of nearly 4 cents for every $\$A1$ sold forward.

Of course, there is a good chance that the expectation will not be realised. If the spot rate in 1 year's time is less than £0.5065 per $\$A1$, the profit will be greater than expected; if the spot rate in 1 year's time is between £0.5065 and £0.5265 per $\$A1$, the profit will be smaller than expected. Finally, if the spot rate in 1 year's time is greater than £0.5265 per $\$A1$, a loss will be incurred. A risk-averse speculator may not feel that the expected profit is large enough to warrant bearing the risk, but if speculators are risk neutral, then even a small expected profit will be sufficient to induce them to trade. In this example, the result will be an increased supply of Australian dollars in the forward market, therefore tending to reduce the price $f$ per dollar. The forward rate will continue to decrease until it reaches £0.5065 per dollar. Therefore, in equilibrium:
$$f = E(s)$$

This implies that:
$$\frac{f}{s} = \frac{E(s)}{s}$$

which is Equation 21.1b.

### 21.4.4 PURCHASING POWER PARITY
Purchasing power parity (PPP), maintains (Equation 21.1c) that:
$$\frac{E(s)}{s} = \frac{1 + E(p_£)}{1 + E(p_\$)}$$

In words, PPP holds that the expected change in the exchange rate is due to differences in expected inflation rates in the respective countries.

The simplest derivation of PPP assumes that the **law of one price** is valid. This states that the dollar price of any given commodity should be the same everywhere in the world. If all markets were free and frictionless, and all goods were traded internationally, then the law of one price would hold because, otherwise, an arbitrage could be undertaken. For example, if the price of silver in Australia is $A250/kg, and the exchange rate is $A1 = £0.5000, then the price of silver in the UK ought to be £125/kg. If the price of silver in the UK is anything other than £125/kg, an arbitrage is available. For example, if the UK price is £150/kg, traders would buy silver in Australia at $A250/kg and sell it in the UK at the equivalent of $A300/kg. This would continue until the UK silver price, converted to Australian dollars, is equal to the price of silver in Australia. This equality would be achieved by the price of silver in the UK decreasing and/or the price of silver in Australia increasing and/or the value of the Australian dollar (in pounds) increasing. The eventual equilibrium could be, for example, a UK silver price of £135.20/kg, an Australian silver price of $A260/kg and an exchange rate of $A1 = £0.5200. In this case the UK price of £135.20 is equivalent to an Australian dollar price of $A(135.20 ÷ 0.5200) = $A260, which equals the price in Australia.

Assuming that the law of one price holds at all times, PPP may be proved as follows. If the price of a commodity is currently $A1 in Australia, and the current exchange rate is $A1 = £$s$, then, invoking the law of one price, the UK price of that commodity must be £$s$. If the expected inflation rates are $E(p_\$)$ in Australia and $E(p_£)$ in the UK, then the expected prices are $A[1 + E(p_\$)]$ and £$s[1 + E(p_£)]$. Invoking again the law of one price, the expected exchange rate must equate these two prices. That is:

$$1 + E(p_\$) = \frac{s[1 + E(p_£)]}{E(s)}$$

On rearrangement, this gives:

$$\frac{E(s)}{s} = \frac{1 + E(p_£)}{1 + E(p_\$)}$$

which is Equation 21.1c.

However, for many commodities, the law of one price clearly does not hold. Fortunately, PPP may also be proved by making the weaker assumption that the *ratio* of dollar prices for the same commodity in two countries will stay constant as time passes. In effect, this allows the *levels* of dollar prices to differ at any given time, but holds constant the relative extent of this difference over time. For example, suppose that the spot rate is $A1 = £0.4600 and a particular commodity costs $A2000 in Australia and £1150 in the UK. The dollar equivalent of the UK price is therefore $A(1150 ÷ 0.4600) = $A2500. The ratio of dollar prices is therefore $A2000/$A2500 = 0.80. That is, the Australian price is only 80 per cent of the UK price. The assumption implies that if the ratio of dollar prices is recalculated in, say, 1 year's time, it will again be 0.80, despite differing inflation rates during the year. If the expected inflation rates are, say, 10 per cent in Australia and 4 per cent in the UK, the expected prices are $A2200 in Australia and £1196 in the UK. Invoking the assumption of a constant ratio of dollar prices, the expected spot exchange rate $E(s)$, must be such as to maintain the ratio at 0.80. That is:

$$\frac{2200}{1196 \div E(s)} = 0.80$$

which gives:

$$E(s) = \frac{0.80 \times 1196}{2200}$$

$$\therefore E(s) = 0.4349$$

To apply this approach to derive PPP, suppose that the price of one kilogram of a particular commodity is $X$ dollars in Australia and $K$ pounds in the UK. If the current spot rate is $A1 = £s$, the dollar value of the UK price is $K/s$ dollars. The ratio of the dollar prices is therefore $\frac{X}{K/s}$. If the expected inflation rate in Australia is $E(p_\$)$ per year and the expected inflation rate in the UK is $E(p_£)$ per year, then the expected prices in 1 year are:

$X[1 + E(p_\$)]$ Australian dollars in Australia, and

$K[1 + E(p_£)]$ UK pounds in the UK

The expected dollar value of the UK price is:

$$K[1 + E(p_£)]/E(s)$$

where $E(s)$ is the expected spot exchange rate. Invoking the assumption of a constant ratio of dollar prices, the expected exchange rate must be such that the ratio of dollar prices remains equal to the initial value of $\frac{X}{K/s}$, that is:

$$\frac{X[1 + E(p_\$)]}{K[1 + E(p_£)] / E(s)} = \frac{X}{K/s}$$

Multiplying both sides by $K/X$ and rearranging gives:

$$\frac{E(s)}{s} = \frac{1 + E(p_£)}{1 + E(p_\$)}$$

which is Equation 21.1c.

Although the foundations of PPP are most readily apparent in the case of individual commodities, many practical applications are at a higher level of aggregation.[7] Even if not all goods are traded internationally, and there are transport costs, tariffs and other sources of friction, it is still plausible that an exchange rate between two currencies will (eventually) reflect the relative inflation rates experiences in the two countries. In these circumstances, the inflation rates in the PPP equation are usually specified as price indices which include both traded and non-traded goods. However, the prices of traded and non-traded goods are not independently determined. For example, an imported good may

---

[7] Historically, PPP has often been exclusively presented and interpreted at an aggregated level. However, we prefer to regard PPP as being built up from the micro-foundation of commodity arbitrage. For a historical summary and a contrary view, see L. H. Officer, *Purchasing Power Parity and Exchange Rates: Theory, Evidence and Relevance*, Parts I and II, JAI Press, Greenwich, Connecticut, 1982.

be used to produce a non-traded good, or a non-traded good could be potentially a traded good, should there be a shift in relative prices.

Although PPP has been interpreted in a number of different ways, its central message does not vary: a country with a high inflation rate can expect to have a depreciating exchange rate (a 'weak' currency), whereas a country with a low inflation rate can expect to have an appreciating exchange rate (a 'strong' currency). This tendency is illustrated in Example 21.3.

*Example 21.3*

Suppose that the spot rate is $A1 = £0.4325$. If the inflation rate next year is expected to be 9 per cent in Australia and 4 per cent in the UK, what is next year's spot rate expected to be?

Rearranging Equation 21.1c and solving gives:

$$E(s) = \left[\frac{1 + E(p_£)}{1 + E(p_\$)}\right] s$$

$$= \left[\frac{1.04}{1.09}\right] (0.4325)$$

$$= 0.4127$$

Therefore, it is expected that the Australian dollar will weaken; whereas an Australian dollar is worth £0.4325 at the start of the year, it is expected that by the end of the year an Australian dollar will be worth only £0.4127. This represents a depreciation of approximately 4.6 per cent in the value of the Australian dollar in terms of UK pounds and is approximately equal to the difference between the inflation rates.

### 21.4.5 UNCOVERED INTEREST PARITY OR THE INTERNATIONAL FISHER EFFECT

If interest rate parity (Equation 21.1a) and unbiased forward rates (Equation 21.1b) hold simultaneously, then:

$$\frac{E(s)}{s} = \frac{1 + i_£}{1 + i_\$}$$

which is Equation 21.1d.

Derived in this way, the equation is usually called *uncovered interest parity*. It can also be derived by assuming that purchasing power parity and the Fisher equation are true. The Fisher equation maintains that, for any given currency, the nominal interest rate will be set by the market such that it covers expected inflation and provides a required real return, $i^*$. If the Fisher equation holds for both pounds and dollars, then:

$$1 + i_£ = (1 + i^*)[1 + E(p_£)], \text{ and}$$
$$1 + i_\$ = (1 + i^*)[1 + E(p_\$)].$$

Combining these two equations and purchasing power parity (Equation 21.1c) also gives Equation 21.1d. Derived in this way, Equation 21.1d is usually called **the international Fisher effect**.

Equation 21.1d implies that the spot exchange rate will tend to adjust in the direction indicated by interest rates in the two currencies. In particular, a country's currency will tend to appreciate (depreciate) relative to another currency if its interest rate is lower (higher) than the interest rate on the other currency. This is illustrated in Example 21.4.

## Example 21.4

The current spot exchange rate between Australian dollars and UK pounds is $A1 = £0.4000. Interest rates for one year are 5 per cent for pounds and 15 per cent for dollars. Rearranging Equation 21.1d gives the expected spot exchange rate as:

$$E(s) = \left(\frac{1 + i_£}{1 + i_\$}\right) s$$

$$= \left(\frac{1.05}{1.15}\right) 0.4000$$

$$= £0.3652$$

Thus the Australian dollar, being the higher-interest currency, is expected to depreciate from £0.4000 per dollar to £0.3652 per dollar.

The rationale for this result is that, if it did not hold, then it would be better for investors to lend one of the currencies, but it would be better for borrowers to borrow the other currency. Thus there would be disequilibrium in the markets. This is illustrated in Example 21.5.

## Example 21.5

Suppose, as in Example 21.4, that the spot exchange rate is $A1 = £0.4000 and the one-year interest rates are 5 per cent (in pounds) and 15 per cent (in dollars). However, suppose the expected spot exchange rate is $A1 = £0.3900.

In this case borrowers will wish to borrow pounds, but lenders will want to lend dollars. While the Australian dollar is expected to depreciate in the coming year from £0.40 to £0.39, the extent of this expected depreciation is not sufficient to offset the expected benefit to the borrower of borrowing the lower-interest currency.

Consider a company that wants to borrow $A250 000. This will require a repayment of $A250 000 × 1.15 = $A287 500. Alternatively the company could borrow £100 000 at only 5 per cent interest, thus requiring a repayment £105 000 which, at 39 pence per dollar, is expected to require only 105 000 ÷ 0.39 = $A269 231 to repay the loan. This is clearly better for the borrower than having to pay $A287 500. The expected saving is nearly $A20 000. Of course, if borrowers prefer pounds, lenders must prefer dollars. If the *cost* to borrowers is low in pounds, the *return* to lenders of pounds will also be low. The end result is therefore a disequilibrium in which borrowers want to borrow pounds but lenders want to lend dollars.

## 21.5 EMPIRICAL EVIDENCE ON THE BEHAVIOUR OF EXCHANGE RATES

A number of empirical investigations of the behaviour of exchange rates have been undertaken in recent years. The substantial deregulation of many foreign exchange markets has provided a stimulus for such investigations, as well as the market-based data that such investigations require. Rather than undertake a detailed review, this section outlines some of the major findings, emphasising, wherever possible, evidence concerning the Australian dollar.

### 21.5.1 INTEREST RATE PARITY: EVIDENCE

As mentioned in Section 21.4.2, the interest rate parity theorem is based on the proposition that it should not be possible to undertake successful 'covered interest arbitrage'. Where the interest rate data are collected from unregulated markets (such as the Eurodollar market), the overseas evidence nearly always supports interest rate parity, provided that allowance is also made for transaction costs.[8] In Australia, Bird, Dyer and Tippett[9] found that in the period from the floating of the Australian dollar (in December 1983) to June 1985, there were very few opportunities for covered interest arbitrage if interest rates were measured by rates on government securities and transaction costs were included. However, using other measures of interest rates, there appeared to be some opportunities, most notably in inward arbitrage by foreign exchange dealers. Non-dealers, however, had relatively few opportunities.

### 21.5.2 UNBIASED FORWARD RATES: EVIDENCE

Extensive research has been conducted on the relationship between the forward rate and the spot rate that occurs on the maturity date of the forward contract. As explained in Section 21.4.3, if investors are risk neutral, the market should set the forward rate equal to the expected future spot rate. Therefore, over a sufficiently long period of time, the average observed forward rate should approximately equal the average of the spot rates observed on the maturity dates of the forward contracts.

Although some early tests were consistent with this proposition, most later tests have found that the forward rate is *not* an unbiased estimate of the future spot rate. Tests using many different currencies suggest that the forward premium (or discount) overstates the change that, *on average*, occurs in the spot rate.[10] For example, if today's spot rate is one unit of domestic currency equals

---

[8] See, for example, K. Clinton, 'Transactions Costs and Covered Interest Arbitrage: Theory and Evidence', *Journal of Political Economy*, April 1988, pp. 358–70. For a review, see D. L. Thornton, 'Tests of Covered Interest Parity', Federal Reserve Bank of St Louis *Review*, July/August 1989, pp. 55–66.

[9] R. Bird, A. Dyer & M. Tippett, 'Covered Interest Arbitrage Opportunities: The Australian Experience During a Period of Deregulation', *Proceedings of the Banking and Finance Conference*, Australian Institute of Bankers, Melbourne, 1987, pp. 205–52.

[10] For a representative study, see C. Goodhart, 'The Foreign Exchange Market: A Random Walk with a Dragging Anchor', *Economica*, November 1988, pp. 437–60.

0.71 units of foreign currency (DC1 = FC0.7100), while today's forward rate is DC1 = FC0.7000, then an unbiased prediction of the future spot rate could be, say, DC1 = FC0.7080. This may be compared with the forecast of FC0.7000 that would apply if forward rates were unbiased predictors of future spot rates.[11] Similarly, if today's forward rate had been DC1 = FC0.7200, the unbiased prediction might be, say FC0.7120, rather then the theory's prediction of FC0.7200.

The causes of the bias are unclear. One possibility is that, contrary to the assumption of risk neutrality, participants in the foreign exchange market are risk averse. The extent of the bias might then be explained by the presence of a risk premium. Moreover, the risk premium could vary over time. While, in principle, this could explain the results, many researchers are not optimistic that, in practice, this is likely to provide a satisfactory explanation. Of course, inefficiency in the foreign exchange market is another interpretation.[12]

This evidence prompts another question: if today's *forward* rate is a *biased* predictor of the future spot rate, could it be that today's *spot* rate is an *unbiased* predictor of the future spot rate? Framing this question slightly differently: does the spot rate follow a random walk? The answer is 'yes'—at least to a good first approximation.[13] Consistent with this finding, studies have found that when it comes to predicting the future spot rate, today's spot rate is at least as good a predictor as today's forward rate.[14]

An *unbiased* prediction is not necessarily a very *useful* prediction. Although, all other things being equal, an unbiased prediction is preferable to a biased prediction, an unbiased prediction can still be very inaccurate. An unbiased prediction is simply one which is as likely to be too high as it is to be too low. It should be no surprise to find that it is very difficult—perhaps impossible—to forecast exchange rates with great accuracy. If it were easily achieved, we would have no trouble becoming very rich very quickly by speculating on currency movements. Foreign exchange markets are extremely competitive so we would expect that any easily-discovered rule for profitable forecasting should be quickly exploited until it is no longer profitable. Attempts to forecast exchange rates are considered further in Section 21.5.5.

---

[11] We have perhaps been cautious here. In fact, many studies find that the forward premium or discount does not merely overstate the future change in the spot rate; on average it actually points in the wrong direction. In this case, an unbiased forecast might be, say, FC0.6950, when today's spot rate is FC0.7000 and today's forward rate is FC0.7100.

[12] For a discussion, see Goodhart (Footnote 10) or D. W. R. Gruen & M. C. Gizycki, 'Explaining Forward Discount Bias: Is it Anchoring?', Reserve Bank of Australia *Research Discussion Paper* No. 9307.

[13] For Australian evidence see M. Manzur, 'How Much are Exchange Rate Forecasts Worth?', *Australian Journal of Management*, June 1988, pp. 93–113.

[14] For evidence on the British pound, French franc, German mark and Canadian dollar (all in terms of the US dollar) see T. C. Chiang, 'Empirical Evidence on the Predictors of Future Spot Rates', *Journal of Financial Research*, Summer 1986, pp. 153–62.

### 21.5.3 PURCHASING POWER PARITY: EVIDENCE

The simpler derivation of purchasing power parity (PPP) assumes that the 'law of one price' is valid. In practice, there can be little doubt that this law does not hold for a great many commodities, although it may hold in some fairly special cases. Where a commodity is readily defined, cheaply transportable, and frequently traded in organised markets, it is likely that the law of one price will provide an accurate description of reality. Examples may include precious metals such as gold, and financial 'commodities' such as US government securities or shares in large corporations.

In practice, PPP is most often investigated by way of price indices. Apart from the inclusion (or exclusion) of non-traded goods, another point of difficulty is the need to use a weighting scheme in order to convert a number of different prices into a single index. Different weighting schemes will produce different index values for the same set of prices. As different countries use different weighting schemes in the construction of national price indices, there is an obvious potential for distortion in testing PPP using these indices. Generally, PPP is found to give a poor description of exchange rate behaviour, unless a long time period is used for testing. For example, Edison tested PPP for the US dollar–UK pound exchange rate over the period 1890–1978 and estimated that, on average, about 9 per cent of the deviation from PPP in any given year is eliminated in the following year.[15] Therefore, on average, the exchange rate adjusts in the direction indicated by relative inflation rates, but it may take some years for full adjustment to occur.

Although not all studies support the long-run validity of PPP,[16] it is difficult to imagine that most of the effects of inflation will not eventually show up in the exchange rate. For example, if there were a permanent failure of the exchange rate to reflect inflation, every nation would have a simple route to wealth: inflate the domestic economy and then purchase foreign assets at prices which are artificially low in terms of domestic currency.

### 21.5.4 UNCOVERED INTEREST PARITY: EVIDENCE

As we explained in Section 21.4.5, uncovered interest parity can be seen as a combination of interest rate parity and unbiased forward rates. Given that interest rate parity works extremely well, it is inevitable that uncovered interest parity will have a similar level of accuracy to the hypothesis of unbiased forward rates. This is in fact the case. Like the forward premium or discount, the interest rate difference between currencies typically gives a biased forecast of the future spot rate, and often does not even predict the direction of movement correctly.[17]

---

[15] H. J. Edison, 'Purchasing Power Parity in the Long Run: A Test of the Dollar/pound Exchange Rate (1890–1978)', *Journal of Money, Credit and Banking*, August 1987, pp. 376–87.
[16] See, for example, M. Adler & B. Lehmann, 'Deviations from Purchasing Power Parity in the Long Run', *Journal of Finance*, December 1983, pp. 1471–87, and N. Abuaf & P. Jorion, 'Purchasing Power in the Long Run', *Journal of Finance*, March 1990, pp. 157–74.
[17] For further discussion, see K. A. Froot & R. H. Thaler, 'Anomalies: Foreign Exchange', *Journal of Economic Perspectives*, Summer 1990, pp. 179–92.

## 21.5.5 FORECASTING EXCHANGE RATES

Can exchange rate changes be forecast successfully? A successful forecast is one that a trader could use to make excess profits in the foreign exchange market. At a minimum we would expect a successful forecast to be more accurate than forecasts that can be derived from a simple mechanical rule. For example, to be called 'successful', a forecast should be more accurate than the 'no change' or 'random walk' forecast that the future spot rate will be equal to today's spot rate.

At least in the case of Australia there is little evidence that market participants can forecast successfully the Australian dollar/US dollar exchange rate. Hunt undertook a detailed analysis of short-term forecasts made by sixteen foreign exchange dealers.[18] Every Friday afternoon from February 1985 to April 1987, each dealer was telephoned and asked for a forecast of the exchange rate for 3 p.m. on the following Friday. The accuracy of this extensive set of forecasts was then investigated. Hunt used several statistical techniques to investigate forecast accuracy and employed two benchmarks against which forecast performance was judged. The first benchmark was the 'random walk' prediction that next week's spot rate will be equal to today's spot rate; the second benchmark was the 'average forecast' prediction that next week's spot rate will be equal to the average of the sixteen spot rate forecasts made today. Hunt found very little evidence that the dealers could forecast the spot rate and concluded that:

> The performance of the individual forecasters in predicting future rates was not impressive. No single forecast firm recorded a performance superior to its competitors. Moreover, under most criteria the individual forecasters were surpassed by the performance of the random walk and the average forecast model.[19]

Nor is there much evidence that longer-term exchange rate forecasts are accurate. Easton and Lalor studied 583 forecasts made six or twelve months ahead by a range of business, academic and policy groups.[20] The time period covered was January 1984 to January 1993. Fewer than half of the forecasts correctly predicted the direction of the future movement in the exchange rate. The most accurate predictor of the future level of the spot rate was the 'no change' forecast, the second most accurate was the current forward rate and the least accurate was the average forecast of the 'experts'.

In the literature on capital market efficiency, simulation of a filter-rule investment strategy provides another test of forecasting ability. Essentially, the objective of this test is to determine whether a filter rule can be used to generate risk-adjusted profits after taking into account transaction costs, including any

---

18 B. Hunt, 'Propheteering in the Australian FX Market', Working Paper No. 7/1987, Department of Finance, University of New South Wales. M. Manzur (see Footnote 13) studies the same set of forecasts but only at the level of the average forecast made, whereas Hunt reports separate results for the different forecasters.
19 Hunt (see Footnote 18), p. 12.
20 S. A. Easton & P. A. Lalor, 'The Accuracy and Timeliness of Survey Forecasts of Six-month and Twelve-month Ahead Exchange Rates', Working Paper No. 50, Department of Accounting and Finance, Monash University, Clayton, 1994.

interest foregone. A filter-rule strategy was tested on exchange rate data by Dooley and Shafer.[21] They reported that such a strategy did appear to be profitable, especially if the filter is small (less than 5 per cent). However, they did not take into account transaction costs or interest foregone. Cornell and Dietrich conducted a filter test and found that transaction costs substantially reduced but did not eliminate the apparent profits, especially for small filters.[22] However, a filter-rule strategy clearly involves risk because all filters can generate losses in at least some periods. This suggests that some positive profit rate may be justified. Finally, Sweeney developed a test on the assumption that foreign exchange is a risky investment, but the risk premium does not vary over time.[23] The test explicitly includes interest foregone and Sweeney also uses estimates of other transaction costs. Sweeney's overall finding is that small filters of, say, 1 per cent tend to perform best and the profits generated by such filters are significantly positive, even after taking account of transaction costs. The estimated excess return is typically of the order of 4 or 5 per cent per annum.

There are several possible explanations for these findings, including the following:
1. There exist 'speculative bubbles' in exchange rates.
2. The foreign exchange market may be inefficient. For example, it might be that government intervention in foreign exchange markets produces exchange rate patterns that traders can exploit. Even so, researchers who support this conclusion have observed that 'the risk-return trade-off for a single currency is not very attractive'.[24]
3. The risk premium varies over time, so the risk-adjustment procedure used in the test is flawed.

## 21.6 THE MANAGEMENT OF EXCHANGE RISK
### 21.6.1 WHAT IS EXCHANGE RISK?

A company faces exchange risk when there is the potential for unanticipated changes in an exchange rate to reduce the value of the company. Such a company is said to be **exposed to exchange risk** because it can be adversely affected by an unforeseen movement in an exchange rate. Exchange risk can be illustrated by a simple example.

---

[21] M. P. Dooley & J. R. Shafer, 'Analysis of Short-run Exchange Rate Behavior: March 1973 to September 1975', International Finance Discussion Papers, No. 76, Federal Reserve System, Washington, 1976. Filter rules are described in more detail in Section 14.3.2.
[22] B. Cornell & K. Dietrich, 'The Efficiency of the Market for Foreign Exchange under Floating Exchange Rates', Review of Economics and Statistics, February 1978, pp. 111–20.
[23] R. J. Sweeney, 'Beating the Foreign Exchange Market', Journal of Finance, March 1986, pp. 163–82.
[24] Froot & Thaler (see Footnote 17), p. 189. This comment was made in a slightly different context but is worth repeating here.

*Example 21.6*

Playworld Ltd is an Australian-owned company whose management signs a contract on 31 July to import from the UK 500 000 cricket balls, each costing UK £2.20. The balls are expected to arrive in Australia on 31 October and must be paid for on that date. If the exchange rate on 31 July is $A1 = £0.5000$, the projected cost of the imports, in Australian dollar terms, is 500 000 × 2.20 × (1/0.5000) = $A2.2 million. Therefore, Playworld has a liability to pay for the balls and the amount of this liability is currently estimated to be $A2.2 million. If Playworld expects to sell the balls for $A5.50 each, the projected gross profit per ball is $A5.50 − (2.20 × 1/0.5000) = $A1.10 and the total projected gross profit is therefore 500 000 × $A1.10 = $A550 000. The risk, of course, is that the exchange rate between UK pounds and Australian dollars may change between the purchase date (31 July) and the settlement date (31 October). For example, if the Australian dollar depreciates so that $A1 = £0.4000$, the imports will cost $A2.75 million and if the retail price of $A5.50 cannot be increased, then Playworld's gross profit will be zero.

Similar examples can easily be constructed using export contracts where the price is fixed in foreign currency terms. Contracts to borrow or lend foreign currency also provide ready examples of exposure to exchange risk. The exchange risk arising from trade-related contracts is often termed *transaction risk*, while the exchange risk arising from capital-related contracts is often termed *translation risk*. In each case, the risk derives from the fact that an Australian company can find itself having fewer Australian dollars than it expected to have, given the spot exchange rate at the time of entering into the contract. In economic terms, the point is that an involvement with foreign currencies will increase the riskiness, in Australian dollar terms, of the company's cash flows. In short, there is an exposure to fluctuating exchange rates.

## 21.6.2 WHO FACES EXCHANGE RISK?

Assuming that management makes decisions in the interests of shareholders, exchange risk arises whenever a company needs to deal, now or in the future, in a currency other than the currency that shareholders use to finance their consumption. In Example 21.6, Playworld had a liability denominated in UK pounds, while its shareholders used Australian dollars to finance their consumption. Therefore Playworld faced exchange risk. However, exchange risk can arise even if a company does not itself transact in foreign currency. For example, Australian retail jewellers will generally obtain watches from Australian jewellery wholesalers who, in turn, import watches from several countries including Japan and Switzerland. Retail jewellers may never transact in the foreign exchange market, yet it is clear that changes in the value of the yen and Swiss franc may affect their businesses and therefore affect their shareholders' consumption opportunities. Similarly, companies operating hotels in resort areas will be affected by changes in exchange rates because such changes will, in turn, affect the number of international tourists who are potential patrons of the hotels. While the examples we have provided are trade-related, we reiterate that exchange risk can also be encountered in capital transactions such as borrowing foreign currency, lending foreign currency or purchasing foreign assets.

### 21.6.3 THE HEDGING PRINCIPLE

In the context of exchange risk faced by Australian companies, a *hedge* is usually thought of as a financial strategy that will ensure that the Australian dollar value of a commitment to pay or receive a sum of foreign currency in the future is not affected by changes in the exchange rate. The basic principle of hedging is to undertake another, offsetting, commitment in the same foreign currency. That is, this second commitment is for the same amount as the original commitment but opposite in sign. Therefore, an Australian importer who is committed to making a cash payment in UK pounds can hedge by entering into a commitment to receive UK pounds for the same amount and on the same date. For an Australian importer, this may be achieved by buying the foreign currency in the forward market or by lending the foreign currency. Similarly, an expected sequence of foreign currency receipts, for example from sales made by a foreign subsidiary, may be hedged by entering into a commitment to make an offsetting sequence of foreign currency payments. Such a commitment would be required by a loan repayment schedule. The following two sections provide further details on forward rate hedges and borrowing/lending hedges.

### 21.6.4 FORWARD RATE HEDGING

For a given future commitment, a hedge can be achieved by a transaction in the forward market.[25] For example, suppose that an Australian importer is committed to paying a future sum in UK pounds. In effect, this commitment is a contract to buy UK pounds in the future. By entering into a forward contract to buy UK pounds, the value of the commitment can be fixed in Australian dollar terms. In this case, the future outflow of UK pounds required by the import contract is matched by an inflow of UK pounds required by the forward contract. A similar hedge could be used by an Australian company which has borrowed UK pounds. The commitment to pay interest on the loan and to repay the principal is a commitment to make cash outflows of UK pounds. The hedge is achieved by entering into a commitment to buy UK pounds forward because this will establish an inflow of UK pounds. Similarly, for an exporter whose export price is denominated in foreign currency, or for a lender of foreign currency, the hedge consists of selling the foreign currency in the forward market.

In Example 21.6, Playworld committed itself on 31 July to the payment of £1.1 million on 31 October. If the 3-month forward rate on 31 July was $A1 = £0.4900$, then by entering into a forward contract to buy pounds, Playworld can be certain that the cost of the imported goods would be exactly

---

[25] Alternatively, a position could be taken in a futures contract. However, in practice forward contracts are used much more frequently than futures contracts to hedge exchange risk. Forward and futures contracts are compared in Section 15.2.1.

500 000 × 2.20 × (1/0.4900) = $A2 244 898. Using the current spot rate of $A1 = £0.5000, the cost indicated is $A2.2 million. The extra $A44 898 is sometimes regarded as an 'insurance premium' which must be paid in order to exchange the risky position for a hedged position. This view is discussed further in Section 21.6.6, and for the present we simply assert that it is at best misleading.

## 21.6.5 Hedging by borrowing or lending

The second hedging technique consists of establishing an offsetting cash flow by borrowing or lending the foreign currency. Because the basic principles involved are identical to those in forward rate hedging, this technique will be discussed in less detail. The example of an Australian importer will again be used to illustrate the technique.

In Example 21.6, Playworld committed itself on 31 July to an outflow of £1.1 million on 31 October. To establish a claim to an inflow of £1.1 million in 3 months' time, Playworld can lend UK pounds on 31 July to be repaid on 31 October. If the interest rate on a 3-month loan of UK pounds is 3.25 per cent, then Playworld should lend £1 100 000 ÷ 1.0325 = £1 065 375.30. At the spot rate of $A1 = £0.5000, this is equivalent to a loan in Australian dollar terms of 1 065 375.30 ÷ 0.5000 = $A2 130 750.60. Would Playworld be better off to lend this amount in Australia and simultaneously enter into a forward contract to convert the principal (plus interest) into UK pounds on 31 October? The answer to this question depends on the level of interest rates in Australia. For example, if the Australian interest rate is 5.36 per cent for a 3-month loan, then a loan of Australian dollars will return $A2 130 750.60 × 1.0536 = $A2 244 959 in 3 months' time. Converting this amount to UK pounds at the forward rate of $A1 = £0.4900, Playworld will have a claim to receive £1 100 030. In this example, therefore, it makes almost no difference which procedure is followed.[26] Ignoring the difference of £30, either way Playworld will receive a cash inflow of £1.1 million on 31 October to match its import bill of £1.1 million.

## 21.6.6 Who should hedge exchange risk?

In Section 21.6.2 we pointed out that exchange risk can affect a wide range of companies and individuals. In the present section our aim is to point out that not everyone affected by exchange risk is able to hedge against it and that for those

---

[26] It makes no difference because, using interest rate parity, the interest rates applicable to Playworld imply a forward rate of 0.5000 × 1.0325 ÷ 1.0536 = 0.4900. This is equal to the forward rate that Playworld has been quoted. In practice, forward rates reflect interbank interest rates rather than interest rates applicable to companies such as Playworld. This is one reason why, in practice, companies may have a preference for one type of hedge over the other, notwithstanding that the interest rate parity equation is used by banks and others to set the forward rate.

who have the opportunity to hedge, it does not necessarily follow that such an opportunity should always be taken.[27]

In this discussion, it is useful to distinguish between three broad categories of companies. Category 1 is the basically domestic company that unexpectedly faces a significant foreign exchange involvement. For example, a company may decide to become a 'once-off' exporter when it receives an unanticipated request to supply goods to a foreign buyer at a price denominated in foreign currency. Category 2 is the committed exporter (or importer) who is regularly involved in foreign currency transactions. Category 3 is the multinational company producing and selling in two or more countries. The nature of exchange risk, and the opportunities to hedge against it, differ from category to category.

## CATEGORY 1 (THE ONCE-OFF TRANSACTION)

In this case, the incentive to hedge is obvious. The company has little or no international experience and an unfavourable result from a single large transaction could place a significant strain on the company's finances. A forward contract is likely to be the most suitable means of hedging. However, the once-off transaction is not, in practice, the typical case.[28]

## CATEGORY 2 (THE COMMITTED EXPORTER OR IMPORTER)

A sequence of foreign exchange transactions should not necessarily be treated as merely the equivalent of a once-off transaction repeated many times. It can have quite a different character. For example, repeated or routine forward rate hedging may provide few expected benefits and may, in fact, be harmful. Consider the 'insurance premium' analogy referred to in the discussion of the Playworld example in Section 21.6.4. If the forward rate is $A1 = £0.4900 and the spot rate is $A1 = £0.5000, the 'insurance premium' is 1 penny per $A1. However, from the viewpoint of a UK company importing Australian goods the forward rate is £1 = $A1/0.49 = $A2.0408 and the spot rate is £1 = $A1/0.50 = $A2.0000. Therefore, for the UK company, the 'insurance premium' is *minus* 4.08 cents per £1. In any other area such as general insurance or life insurance a negative insurance premium is unthinkable; insurance companies *charge* insurance premiums, they do not *pay* them. Clearly, something is wrong with the insurance analogy. In fact, as the following discussion shows,[29] the forward rate may provide little, if any, 'insurance'. However, insurance is precisely what the hedger is seeking.

The 'true' cost of a transaction at the forward rate is its opportunity cost. That is, the true cost depends on the foregone alternative. In this case, the foregone alternative is to transact at the spot rate that occurs at the expiration of the forward contract. Suppose that a committed importer does not engage routinely

---

[27] A detailed catalogue of arguments for and against hedging may be found in G. Dufey & S. L. Srinivasulu, 'The Case for Corporate Management of Foreign Exchange Risk', *Financial Management*, Winter 1983, pp. 54–62.

[28] However, an exceptionally large transaction in a sequence of smaller ones might also be included in this category.

[29] This discussion is based on I. H. Giddy, 'Why It Doesn't Pay to Make a Habit of Forward Hedging', *Euromoney*, December 1976, pp. 96–100.

in forward rate hedging but simply pays for the imported goods by transacting at the spot rate on each payment date. Has the importer's exchange risk increased? Exchange risk is really the risk of suffering a greater variability in cash flows and there is no reason to believe that future forward rates will be less variable than future spot rates. That is, a sequence of future transactions to be undertaken at subsequent forward rates (which of course are currently unknown) is no more predictable than a sequence of future transactions to be undertaken at subsequent spot rates (which also are currently unknown).

## CATEGORY 3 (THE MULTINATIONAL COMPANY)

A multinational company is likely to receive net cash flows in a number of currencies on a continuing basis, with no fixed terminal date in contemplation. Long-term debt denominated in the same currencies will commit such a company to foreign currency payments and therefore can act as a 'natural' hedge against exchange rate changes.

Where a company is likely to receive net cash flows in foreign currency for an indefinitely long period, the major risk is a change in the real (as distinct from nominal) exchange rate. To illustrate this point, assume that MNC Ltd is an Australian company that buys a factory in New Zealand at a cost of $NZ1.3 million at a time when this sum is equivalent to $A1.0 million (that is, $A1 = $NZ1.30). If a high rate of inflation in New Zealand subsequently results in a depreciation of the New Zealand dollar to, say, $A1 = $NZ1.56, it does not necessarily follow that MNC has suffered a loss. If the New Zealand inflation rate has simultaneously caused the factory's value to increase to $NZ1.56 million, then MNC has not suffered a loss at all; the depreciation of New Zealand's currency has merely kept pace with inflation,[30] leaving unchanged the value (in Australian dollars) of MNC's New Zealand factory. This is, of course, precisely the result that ultimately can be expected if purchasing power parity holds in the long run.

However, where there is a permanent change in the real value of a currency there is little scope for hedging of a purely financial nature. To cope with changes of this type, management will generally need to change the 'real' aspects of the company by taking such actions as targeting new markets, developing new products, obtaining inputs from new sources, and relocating plants.

Finally, it is wrong to conclude that multinational companies must face high exchange rate risk merely because their activities involve a number of currencies. While it is inevitable that some exchange rate changes will cause losses, others will produce gains. In short, there is likely to be a kind of 'portfolio effect' which will not be experienced by companies that operate in only one or two countries. This aspect of international finance is developed further in Section 21.7.

---

[30] Strictly speaking, it is the New Zealand inflation rate relative to the Australian inflation rate that is relevant.

## 21.6.7 CONTINGENT HEDGING

To this point, it has been assumed that hedging is being considered in the context of a pre-existing fixed commitment involving a foreign currency. For example, we considered the case of Playworld, in which the company was committed to a future payment in UK pounds. A forward contract—that is, an equal but offsetting commitment—is the obvious hedging instrument to consider in these circumstances.

Not all exchange rate risks involve commitments. Consider, for example, the risks facing Thread Power Ltd, an Australian company that has offered to purchase a building from Maine Properties Inc. for US$10 million. The offer is currently being considered by the board of Maine Properties. At this stage, Thread Power does not know whether it will have a future need to buy US dollars; such a need will arise only if Maine Properties accepts the offer. That is, Thread Power's need to buy US dollars is contingent upon Maine's decision.

Thread Power's financial manager has considered whether a forward contract to buy US dollars should be entered into and has reached the correct conclusion that, regardless of whether such a contract is entered into, Thread Power will face exchange risk. Irrespective of the decision, Thread Power will find itself in one of four possible situations:

1. $A appreciates against US$ and Maine accepts the purchase offer.
2. $A appreciates against US$ and Maine rejects the purchase offer.
3. $A depreciates against US$ and Maine accepts the purchase offer.
4. $A depreciates against US$ and Maine rejects the purchase offer.

Thread Power's manager has considered the financial effect on Thread Power of having (and not having) a forward contract to buy US dollars in each of these four situations. The outcomes are shown in Table 21.7.

**Table 21.7** *Possible outcomes for Thread Power Ltd*

| | If $A appreciates: | | If $A depreciates: | |
| --- | --- | --- | --- | --- |
| | If purchase offer is: | | If purchase offer is: | |
| | Accepted (1) | Rejected (2) | Accepted (3) | Rejected (4) |
| If US dollars are bought forward: | nil[a] | loss | nil[a] | gain |
| If US dollars are not bought forward: | gain | nil[b] | loss | nil[b] |

[a] Hedged result—offsetting cash flows
[b] No cash flow

Table 21.7 shows the eight possible outcomes, four of which have no (net) foreign exchange consequences, two of which produce an exchange rate gain, and two of which produce an exchange rate loss. To illustrate the entries in Table 21.7, consider the outcome in the top left corner. In this case, US dollars are bought forward, the Australian dollar appreciates, and the purchase offer is accepted. As a result of the stronger Australian dollar the forward contract produces a loss, but this is offset by the lower price (in Australian dollar terms) of the building to be purchased. The next entry to the right in Table 21.7 shows a loss. In this case, there is the same loss on the forward contract but it is not offset by a gain on the building purchase because the offer to buy the building is rejected. The message of this example is clear: a fixed commitment, like that required by a forward contract, simply does not hedge a contingent exchange risk.

In effect, by offering to buy the building for a fixed price, Thread Power has granted Maine Properties an option to sell its building at an exercise price of US$10 million.[31] Not surprisingly, one suitable way to hedge such a contingency is by purchasing a matching option. For example, Thread Power could buy a put option to sell Australian dollars, receiving on exercise, a given sum of US dollars.[32] Foreign currency options of this type are traded on the Philadelphia Stock Exchange and are available 'over the counter' from banks. If Maine accepts the offer to buy the building, and the Australian dollar has depreciated, the put option will protect Thread Power's position. This occurs because the option will have become more valuable as a result of the depreciation of the Australian dollar. However, if the Australian dollar appreciates, the maximum that Thread Power can lose is the price paid for the option.

## 21.7 INTERNATIONAL DIVERSIFICATION OF INVESTMENTS

In Section 21.6 it was shown that a need to transact in a foreign currency involves an exposure to the risk of fluctuations in the exchange rate. However, it should not be concluded that exposure to exchange rate fluctuations is necessarily unacceptable. This section discusses the potential advantages to be gained from the international diversification of investment portfolios. Such diversification will usually require a conscious decision to adopt a position in a foreign currency which, in turn, implies a conscious decision to be exposed to fluctuations in exchange rates.

When an investor purchases an asset whose returns are measured in foreign currency, the investor's rate of return is the joint result of the rate of return on the investment (in its own currency of denomination) and the rate of return on the exchange rate. Specifically, the rate of return over a single period from an investment in, say, a UK share is, from an Australian investor's viewpoint:

$$r_\$ = (1 + r_£)(1 + r_s) - 1 \qquad (21.2)$$

where $r_\$$ = the rate of return to an Australian investor
$r_£$ = the rate of return to a UK investor
$r_s = \dfrac{s_0}{s_1} - 1$ = the rate of return on the spot exchange rate

where $s_0$ = the spot exchange rate (in pounds per $A1) at the date of investment

---

[31] Options to sell are known as 'put' options. Options are discussed in detail in Chapter 16.
[32] Equivalently, this option can be described as a call option to buy US dollars, requiring a payment, on exercise, of a fixed sum of Australian dollars. Foreign currency options are discussed in Section 16.5. For a more detailed treatment, see W. Sutton, *The Currency Options Handbook*, Woodhead Faulkner, Cambridge, 1988.

$s_1$ = the spot exchange rate (in pounds per $A1) at the date of return measurement

Equation 21.2 is illustrated in Example 21.7.

*Example 21.7*

On 13 February, Harriet, an Australian investor, purchased 1000 shares in the British manufacturer Arrow plc at a price of £8.00 per share. Harriet sold the shares on 26 May at a price of £7.80 per share. On 13 February the exchange rate was $A1 = £0.4816 and on 26 May the exchange rate was $A1 = £0.4608.

Harriet's rate of return may be calculated as follows:

$$\text{Sum invested (in \$A)} = \frac{1000 \times 8.00}{0.4816} = \$A16\,611.30$$

$$\text{Sum returned (in \$A)} = \frac{1000 \times 7.80}{0.4608} = \$A16\,927.08$$

$$\text{Dollar return} = \$A16\,927.08 - \$A16\,611.30$$

$$= \$A315.78$$

$$\text{Dollar rate of return} = \frac{\$A315.78}{\$A16\,611.30}$$

$$= 1.90\%$$

Equivalently, Harriet's rate of return can be calculated using Equation 21.2. The component rates of return are:

$$r_£ = \frac{£7.80 - £8.00}{£8.00} = -0.0250$$

$$\text{and } r_s = \frac{0.4816}{0.4608} - 1 = 0.045\,14$$

Substituting into Equation 21.2 gives:

$$r_\$ = (1 + r_£)(1 + r_s) - 1$$

$$= (1 - 0.0250)(1 + 0.045\,14) - 1$$

$$= (0.9750)(1.04514) - 1$$

$$= 1.90\%$$

In this example Harriet has earned a rate of return of slightly less than 2 per cent, resulting from an exchange rate gain of approximately 4.5 per cent and an investment loss of 2.5 per cent.

As Example 21.7 and Equation 21.2 show, the choice of currency used to calculate returns is not a matter of indifference. The investment in Arrow shares, for example, proved to be profitable for an Australian investor but would not have been profitable for a UK investor over the same period. Of course the opposite situation can also arise.

As explained in Chapter 6, one of the major conclusions of portfolio theory is that there are substantial benefits for investors who diversify their portfolios. By increasing the number of assets in their portfolios, investors can achieve a higher expected return at the same level of risk and/or the same expected return at a lower level of risk. A major determinant of the size of the benefits is the correlation between the returns on the assets in the portfolio. If the correlation is 1, then there is no benefit to be gained, but in other cases the opportunity to benefit exists. Even a correlation of, say, 0.5 can offer worthwhile benefits.

The general presumption in favour of diversification has international as well as domestic application. Consider an investor who is constructing a portfolio consisting of shares issued by various Australian companies listed on the Australian Stock Exchange. After, say, 30 or 40 shares have been selected, the benefit of further diversification is relatively slight; most of the characteristics of the Australian market are already represented in the portfolio and therefore most of the diversifiable risk has already been eliminated. A further source of diversification is to invest in shares listed on foreign stock exchanges. For example, this investor could invest in the shares of companies listed on the London Stock Exchange. The investment opportunities open to a well-diversified Australian investor, who is considering investing in a range of UK shares, can then be inferred by investigating returns on the London share price index and returns on the Australian share price index. In this instance, returns should be measured in Australian dollar terms, and the correlation is then calculated. Provided that the correlation is not 1, international diversification may benefit the investor. Therefore, an indication of the benefits available from diversifying internationally can be obtained by examining estimated correlations between the share price indices of various overseas stock exchanges.

Evidence on the correlation between Australian and overseas share price indices, calculated from the viewpoint of an Australian investor, is provided in Table 21.8. The correlations were calculated using monthly data from December 1981 to December 1986.[33]

Table 21.8 shows that the correlation between the various overseas stock markets is positive, but less than 1, with most falling in the range 0.3 to 0.6. Those involving Australia fall in the range −0.06 to 0.24. This suggests that there are substantial opportunities to benefit from international diversification in share investments. Of course there can be no guarantee that these correlations will not change in the future, but nevertheless it is unlikely that subsequent changes will entirely eliminate all expected benefits. Since the removal of most exchange controls in 1983 and 1984, Australian investors have taken advantage of the opportunity to diversify internationally. As shown in Table 21.2, Australian 'portfolio and other' investment abroad increased nearly tenfold in the period 1984–93.

In Chapter 6 it was shown that there exists an 'efficient frontier' of portfolios. This frontier shows the maximum expected return that can be achieved

---

33 For US-based evidence, covering a longer time period, see B. Solnik, *International Investments*, Addison-Wesley, Reading, Massachusetts, 1988, pp. 40–1.

**Table 21.8** *Inter-country correlation coefficients for share price indices in the period December 1981 to December 1986*

|  | Australia | Canada | France | Germany | Italy | Japan | Netherlands | Switzerland | UK | USA |
|---|---|---|---|---|---|---|---|---|---|---|
| Australia | 1.000 | | | | | | | | | |
| Canada | 0.237 | 1.000 | | | | | | | | |
| France | −0.020 | 0.363 | 1.000 | | | | | | | |
| Germany | −0.036 | 0.341 | 0.625 | 1.000 | | | | | | |
| Italy | −0.054 | 0.346 | 0.686 | 0.497 | 1.000 | | | | | |
| Japan | −0.058 | 0.401 | 0.608 | 0.471 | 0.480 | 1.000 | | | | |
| Netherlands | 0.018 | 0.443 | 0.578 | 0.596 | 0.544 | 0.456 | 1.000 | | | |
| Switzerland | 0.122 | 0.516 | 0.633 | 0.754 | 0.515 | 0.470 | 0.684 | 1.000 | | |
| UK | 0.188 | 0.484 | 0.521 | 0.410 | 0.331 | 0.408 | 0.463 | 0.467 | 1.000 | |
| USA | 0.108 | 0.756 | 0.453 | 0.424 | 0.442 | 0.415 | 0.547 | 0.532 | 0.535 | 1.000 |

Source: Data supplement to J. D. Mitchell, L. B. Wapnah & H. Y. Izan, 'International Diversification; An Australian Perspective', Working Paper No. 88/12, Department of Accounting and Finance, University of Western Australia, 1988

at each level of risk, using the assets available for investment. If new assets become available, the efficient frontier moves outward.

A similar analysis can be performed using various national share indices (portfolios) as the assets available for investment. Mitchell, Wapnah and Izan performed such an analysis from an Australian investor's viewpoint,[34] using data from the share markets of the countries listed in Table 21.8. The Australian index plotted well within the efficient frontier, indicating that substantial benefits from diversification were present. However, such a test is biased because only past data are analysed and, of course, it is always easy to design successful investment strategies with hindsight. Therefore Mitchell, Wapnah and Izan also constructed portfolios using data from one period (December 1981 to June 1984) and then examined the performance of these portfolios over a later period (June 1984 to December 1986). The benefits of diversification were still present. They estimated that, relative to the return on an all-Australian portfolio, an internationally diversified portfolio returned about 1.5 per cent per month more at the same level of risk. On an annual basis, this represents an extra return of around 20 per cent. This is a very large additional return. Moreover, in an extension to this study, it was found that benefits from international diversification were still present in a later time period (1986–89).[35] There can be little doubt that, for investors, the prospect of benefiting from international diversification is real.

---

[34] J. D. Mitchell, L. B. Wapnah & H. Y. Izan, 'International Diversification: An Australian Perspective', Working Paper No. 88/12, Department of Accounting and Finance, University of Western Australia, 1988.

[35] H. Y. Izan, B. R. Jalleh & L. L. Ong, 'International Diverisification and Estimation Risk: Australian Evidence', *Australian Journal of Management*, June 1991, pp. 73–90. This study also controlled for 'estimation risk', which arises because portfolios are constructed using parameter values (variances, covariances and expected returns) that are only *estimated*, rather than known with certainty.

Diversification benefits can also arise in funding decisions as well as in investment decisions. That is, liabilities as well as assets can be diversified to advantage. The extent of the advantage will depend on correlations between exchange rates and between interest rates in different currencies. The evidence suggests that there are diversification benefits available to Australian liability managers.[36]

While international diversification offers substantial advantages, the potential disadvantages should not be overlooked. In particular there could be adverse taxation implications and increased transaction costs due to the need to transact between currencies. Investors may also find it more difficult to obtain reliable information on foreign securities, although this problem is substantially reduced if the security is traded on a developed and active market such as the New York or London Stock Exchanges. Finally, in some countries, foreign investors may face political risks such as sudden limitations being placed on the ability to withdraw capital and/or dividends and, in extreme cases, expropriation of their investment.

## 21.8 Foreign currency borrowing by Australian companies

The data in Table 21.3 show that there has been a significant growth in borrowing overseas by Australian entities. Although some of this growth has been due to borrowing by government and semigovernment bodies, the majority has been due to private sector borrowings. In this section, we consider the possible reasons why Australian companies borrow overseas and we review some of the main forms that these loans can take.

### 21.8.1 Reasons for borrowing overseas

Australian ownership of foreign assets has also shown significant growth in the past decade although it is less spectacular than the growth of debt. As mentioned in Section 21.6.6, foreign currency debt provides a useful hedge for a foreign currency asset holding. If an exchange rate change produces a decrease (increase) in the value of the asset in Australian dollar terms, there will be a simultaneous, matching decrease (increase) in the value of the liability in Australian dollar terms. Some of the overseas borrowing by Australian companies can no doubt be explained by its use as a hedge. However, it is clear that large amounts of foreign currency have been borrowed for other reasons. In short, many Australian companies have borrowed foreign currency, converted the borrowings to Australian dollars, and then used these funds for domestic purposes. If such a borrowing is left unhedged, the borrower faces considerable risk. This is illustrated in Example 21.8.

---

[36] M. Sweeney, 'Measuring the Liability Management Performance of Corporate Treasurers', *Proceedings of the Banking and Finance Conference*, Australian Institute of Bankers, Melbourne, 1993, pp. 554–71.

## Example 21.8

Gippsland Farms Ltd required a loan of $A10 million for 1 year and its bank quoted an interest rate of 14.5 per cent. Instead, Gippsland Farms borrowed 12 million Swiss francs at an interest rate of 5 per cent and, at the then current spot exchange rate of $A1 = 1.2$ Swiss francs, converted the Swiss franc principal to $A10 million. One year later, the spot exchange rate was $A1 = 1.0$ Swiss francs and Gippsland Farms had to repay the sum of:

$$\$A \frac{12 \text{ million} \times 1.05}{1.0}$$
$$= \$A12.6 \text{ million}$$

This represents the equivalent of an Australian dollar interest rate of 26 per cent—nearly double the Australian dollar interest rate originally quoted.

In Example 21.7, Gippsland Farms suffered a loss because of the subsequent depreciation of the Australian dollar. The break-even point was where the Australian dollar equivalent of the required Swiss franc repayment equalled the repayment required on the Australian dollar loan. In Example 21.7 this is where:

$$\$A\ 10\ 000\ 000 \times 1.145 = \$A \frac{12 \text{ million} \times 1.05}{s_1}$$

where $s_1$ is the spot exchange rate on the repayment date. The solution to this equation is $s_1 = 1.100\ 437$. That is, in round terms, break-even was at an exchange rate of $A1 = 1.1$ Swiss francs. Thus the borrower would have benefited if, during the term of the loan, the Australian dollar either appreciated against the Swiss franc or depreciated to a level no lower than $A1 = 1.1$ Swiss francs. Unfortunately for Gippsland Farms the Australian dollar depreciated from 1.2 to 1.0 Swiss francs—well beyond the break-even level of 1.1 Swiss francs.

According to uncovered interest parity (Equation 21.1d) the break-even exchange rate is the result that, on average, should be expected to occur. Rearranging Equation 21.1d, we have:

$$E(s) = \left(\frac{1 + \text{foreign interest rate}}{1 + \text{domestic interest rate}}\right) \text{(current spot rate)}$$
$$= \left(\frac{1.05}{1.145}\right)(1.2)$$
$$= 1.100\ 437$$

As we stated in Section 21.5.4, uncovered interest parity is not strongly supported by the empirical evidence. However, this evidence does not invalidate the main point we wish to make, which is that unhedged foreign currency borrowing entails significant risk. Whether, on average, this risk is rewarded with a small expected cost saving is for many borrowers a much less important issue than the fact that losses will frequently be incurred.

The existence of exchange risk leads many foreign currency borrowers to hedge their borrowings by buying forward the foreign currency needed to repay the loan. The fact that forward rates comply with interest rate parity guarantees that most of the benefits (and also the risks) of a foreign currency borrowing will be eliminated. However, the presence of taxes and other market frictions can still leave, on occasions and for some borrowers, a marginal cost advantage from borrowing overseas, rather than from domestic sources. Such advantages could explain some of the increase in foreign debt.

In many cases cost considerations are only one factor contributing to a decision to borrow overseas. It is likely that overseas funding is often sought in preference to domestic borrowings because of the speed and range of borrowing instruments offered by lenders in foreign markets. This is true of the markets in countries with well-developed financial markets such as the US and is particularly true of the Euromarkets. The following sections discuss some of the overseas financial markets relevant to Australian borrowers, with emphasis on the Euromarkets.

### 21.8.2 OVERSEAS FINANCIAL MARKETS: BACKGROUND

Overseas borrowing can be carried out in many ways. One way is to borrow from an overseas bank with the loan denominated in the bank's domestic currency. Alternatively, a borrower can issue, in a foreign country, marketable securities denominated in the currency of that country. For example, many Australian companies have borrowed by issuing securities denominated in US dollars and sold in the US. If a loan involves a single foreign country and is denominated in that country's currency, it is generally referred to as a foreign loan. Similarly, if an Australian company issued US dollar bonds in the US domestic market, the bonds would be described as foreign bonds.

A third way to raise funds is by transacting in the Euromarkets. The distinguishing feature of Euromarket transactions is that the underlying financial contracts are in terms of a currency other than the currency of the country in which the transaction occurs. Examples of Euromarket transactions include the following: an Arab sheikh deposits US$100 million with a Japanese bank operating in London; in Luxembourg, a Belgian dentist buys a bond which pays interest and principal in deutschmarks; in London, a syndicate of banks lends US$500 million to the Swedish government. Euromarket transactions occur in a number of financial centres throughout the world. In Europe, the main centre is London and in Asia, the main centres are Hong Kong, Singapore and Tokyo. The securities traded in the Euromarkets generally have counterparts in the domestic markets of many countries. For example, most eurobonds are securities which pay a fixed annual coupon interest, plus the repayment of face value at maturity. Therefore they are similar to debentures, but unlike Australian debentures, eurobonds are 'bearer securities'. This is typical of Euromarket securities and means that there is no record of ownership. There is therefore an opportunity to evade tax on the interest income.

Euromarket transactions have experienced considerable growth since the 1950s. Much of this growth has resulted from a desire to avoid regulations and taxes imposed by governments on domestic transactions but not on eurocurrency transactions. We will not review this history[37] but will simply state the end result: today, eurocurrency trading has produced a largely unregulated, highly competitive market in deposits, loans and securities in at least twenty different currencies. The US dollar is the principal currency involved but the importance of other currencies, particularly the yen and deutschmark, is increasing. The major participants in these markets are international banks, who make large loans to high-profile borrowers including governments, semigovernment bodies, large corporations and supranational agencies. The intense competition, together with the relative lack of regulation, means that these banks are often able to respond quickly to new situations and are willing to offer innovative financing methods to meet (and create!) particular needs.[38] From an Australian viewpoint, an important innovation has been the willingness, since about 1985, of Euromarket participants to include Australian dollar securities among those traded.

In the next two sections we discuss the major features of overseas financial markets, with emphasis on eurocurrency loans and securities markets.[39] In the case of securities markets, the Euromarkets have many features in common with some countries' domestic markets. This is particularly so in the case of the US because practices and securities that were already well established in the US market have often been adopted in the Euromarkets. To avoid repetition, we discuss similar markets together, with emphasis on the Euromarkets.

### 21.8.3 EUROCURRENCY LOANS[40]

Eurocurrency loans are provided by banks and have many of the characteristics of domestic bank loans. Two important differences are that the loans are arranged overseas and they are normally denominated in a foreign currency. The main types of eurocurrency loans are short-term bank loans, standby facilities and medium to long-term bank loans.

#### SHORT-TERM EUROCURRENCY BANK LOANS

A short-term eurocurrency bank loan typically involves a principal of at least US$5 million and a lump sum repayment of both principal and interest at the end of the agreed term. The interest rate is set at a margin, typically in the range 0.5 per cent to 3.0 per cent, above an agreed reference rate. Two frequently used reference rates are the London interbank offered rate (LIBOR) and the Singapore interbank offered rate (SIBOR). These rates are an average, calculated every day,

---

[37] For a concise history, see P. Gallant, *The Eurobond Market*, Woodhead-Faulkner, New York, 1988, Ch. 2. For more detail, see I. Kerr, *A History of the Eurobond Market: The First 21 Years*, Euromoney Publications, London, 1984.

[38] For discussion and examples, see 'Innovation in the International Capital Markets', Supplement to *Euromoney*, January 1986; and 'Innovations', Supplement to *Euromoney*, January 1987.

[39] For a detailed review which also emphasises points of particular relevance to Australian borrowers, see G. Mizon & K. Sue, 'Funding from Offshore Sources' in *Handbook of Australian Corporate Finance*, Eds R. Bruce et al., 4th edn, Butterworths, Sydney, 1991, pp. 341–67.

[40] Statistical information provided in Sections 21.8.3 and 21.8.4 has generally been obtained from *International Banking and Financial Market Developments*, Bank for International Settlements, Basle, May 1993 and *Australian Capital Markets Survey 1992*, Ernst & Young Australia, 1993.

of the interest rate at which banks in London and Singapore, respectively, will lend to each other.

Short-term bank loans are sometimes provided under a revolving credit facility where the interest rate can vary at each rollover, which is usually at intervals of 6 months. One feature of these facilities is that the borrower can usually choose a mixture of currencies that can be varied at each rollover.

## EUROCURRENCY STANDBY FACILITIES

A borrower can arrange a standby facility whereby a bank is committed to providing short-term loan funds should the borrower require them. Such facilities are normally arranged for periods of up to two years and are intended to be used only in periods of difficulty or tight liquidity. The bank will charge a commitment fee as well as interest and because of the risk involved, both of these charges are likely to be higher than those that apply to a regular loan.

## EUROCURRENCY TERM LOANS

The typical eurocurrency term loan is for a principal of at least US$5 million, to be repaid over a period of five to 10 years, with interest charged on a floating-rate basis. As is the case for short-term loans, the interest rate is set at a margin above an agreed reference rate such as LIBOR or SIBOR. For example, a loan contract in US dollars may require repayment over 5 years at a margin of 0.5 per cent above LIBOR. The borrower may select the 6-month LIBOR rate for the first period of repayment. Therefore, if LIBOR is, say, 9.5 per cent per annum for 6-month US dollar deposits, the borrower is charged interest at 10.0 per cent per annum for the first 6 months. After 6 months the borrower must select the term (and corresponding LIBOR rate) to apply for the next period. This may be another 6-month period, or it may be some other period, typically from one to 12 months.

The time pattern for the repayment of principal is negotiable between the parties. However, it is usual for some or all of the principal to be repaid steadily throughout the loan. Special requirements, such as an initial period during which no cash payments are required, are also negotiable between the parties.

Large eurocurrency loans of more than, say, US$50 to 100 million will usually require a syndicate of banks to provide the funds. The agreement is negotiated and administered by a lead bank and typically involves a series of fees including establishment fees, participation fees, and annual commitment fees. Many Australian entities have borrowed using the syndicated loan market. For example, in 1992, Qantas borrowed more than US$220 million by this method. The major Australian banks have also often appeared in the lists of syndicate members.

### 21.8.4 EUROCURRENCY AND FOREIGN SECURITIES

Starting around the mid-1970s there has been a trend in the Euromarkets and elsewhere towards borrowers obtaining funds from lenders by selling to them marketable securities, such as bonds and notes, rather than by borrowing from a bank or other intermediary which in turn borrows from depositors. One reason why a borrower may prefer to raise funds by issuing securities, rather than by negotiating a private loan, is that by making this choice, the borrower may qualify for an exemption from the interest withholding tax. Without an exemption, the borrowing cost will usually be higher to compensate the lender for the effect of the tax.[41] Banks may assist in selling the securities, thereby retaining clients and earning fees without having the financial responsibility of making a loan. In addition, banks may buy the securities, which, unlike a normal loan, can later be sold.

Australian borrowers can raise funds by selling securities in the domestic markets of other countries and in the Euromarkets. In the Euromarkets, there is a very wide range of securities from which investors may choose. However, the most popular ways of borrowing from these markets involve issuing euronotes, eurocommercial paper, euromedium-term notes, and eurobonds. While these securities have different names, there are cases where the underlying financial instrument is essentially the same, and the different names reflect differences in the manner in which the instrument is offered to the market. For example, the differences between euronotes and eurocommercial paper are of this type. However, such differences can be very important because they result in significant differences in fees or other costs. Therefore, rather than focus on the financial instruments involved, we discuss the main borrowing methods used in overseas markets.

## EURONOTE ISSUANCE FACILITIES

A note issuance facility (NIF) is a facility under which one or more institutions (generally a syndicate of banks) agree to underwrite a borrower's short-term securities (euronotes). Euronotes are issued for short terms (up to 6 months) but the facility is generally arranged for a much longer period, with terms of three, five and seven years being common. The notes are essentially bearer promissory notes drawn by the borrower, generally with face values of US$100 000 and US$500 000. They do not carry coupon payments and are traded at a discount from face value. The notes are generally issued to banks and other institutions which, as members of a tender panel, are invited to tender for them. Any notes not purchased by the tender panel at the issue date or at a subsequent rollover date will be purchased by the underwriters; that is, the underwriting syndicate guarantees to buy the notes at a predetermined yield if the notes cannot be sold in the market at or below the predetermined yield. The involvement of the underwriters means that the NIF provides a source of funds which is assured but flexible, because the borrower can choose the amount and timing of the notes issued. These facilities are generally arranged for amounts of at least

---

41 Australia's taxation laws generally require that when an Australian taxpayer pays interest to a foreign lender, 10 per cent of the interest must be paid to the government as a tax known as the interest withholding tax (IWT). However, lenders generally require that interest be paid 'free and clear' of withholding taxes. Therefore, for a foreign lender to receive interest of, say, 13.5 per cent free and clear, an Australian borrower must effectively pay 15 per cent, comprising interest of 13.5 per cent and 1.5 per cent IWT. Under s128F of the *Income Tax Assessment Act*, an exemption from IWT may be granted where funds are raised by issuing widely distributed marketable securities.

US$50 million, and while the US dollar is the most popular currency, Australian borrowers have also issued notes denominated in other currencies, including Australian dollars, pounds sterling and deutschmarks.

NIFs involve a range of fees including establishment fees, commitment fees, and take-up fees payable to the arrangers, managers and underwriters. These fees vary in magnitude with the credit rating of the borrower but are likely to increase the interest cost by about 0.5 per cent per annum. These facilities are generally seen as substitutes for bank credit, and grew quickly in the mid-1980s, but have since been replaced to some extent by commercial paper. During 1992, Australian borrowers established new NIFs totalling more than US$2 billion.

## COMMERCIAL PAPER

Commercial paper is the term used for negotiable, short-term, unsecured promissory notes issued in the Euromarkets and in the domestic markets of several countries including the US. A commercial paper facility (CPF) is similar in many respects to a note issuance facility. For example, in both cases the financial instrument involved is a short-term promissory note and in both cases the facility generally involves an amount of at least US$50 million. However, there are some differences, the most important of which is that a CPF is *not* underwritten. Borrowers with high credit ratings are able to obtain attractive interest rates without the assistance of underwriters and the paper is instead issued through a small group of institutional dealers, which is less costly than underwriting. In the absence of underwriters, a borrower can encounter liquidity problems if investors redeem their paper at maturity rather than rolling it over. This potential problem is generally overcome by arranging standby lines of credit, and the existence of such a backup is essential if the paper is to obtain the highest possible credit rating. Commercial paper facilities have grown rapidly because, for many borrowers, they involve lower overall costs than NIFs. At the end of 1992, Eurocommercial paper on issue totalled US$78.7 billion, compared to US$37.0 billion for all other short-term euronotes. During 1992, Australian borrowers established new commercial paper facilities of more than US$6.5 billion, of which more than 60 per cent was in the Euromarkets and the balance in the US market.

## MEDIUM-TERM NOTES

Medium-term notes are unsecured, bearer, coupon securities with terms to maturity ranging from 9 months to 30 years, although most have terms between one and five years. The coupon rate can be fixed or floating, in which case the rate is expressed as a margin above a specified reference rate, typically LIBOR. The size of each facility is typically between US$50 million and US$500 million. A key feature of medium-term notes is the flexibility that they offer the borrower because the notes issued within a given facility are not homogeneous. That is, each facility can include notes with a range of maturities, currencies and fixed or floating coupon interest rates. Also the individual notes can have face values of from US$5000 to US$1 million to suit both retail and institutional investors. Once a facility has been arranged with a syndicate of dealers, notes can be issued continuously or periodically in amounts chosen by the issuer.

Because of its advantages in terms of convenience, flexibility and cost, the euro-medium-term note market has grown rapidly and new facilities totalling US$58.0 and US$93.2 billion were announced in 1991 and 1992 respectively. During 1992, Australian borrowers announced new medium-term note facilities of more than US$2.4 billion. The majority were Euromarket facilities denominated in US dollars. Borrowers included the ANZ Bank, Coles Myer Finance and the AIDC.

## TRANSFERABLE LOAN CERTIFICATES

Euromarket borrowers can obtain a bank term loan with provision for the lender to convert the loan into transferable loan certificates (TLCs). From the viewpoint of the borrower, a TLC facility is very similar to a syndicated loan. That is, an amount typically between US$100 million and US$500 million is borrowed from a syndicate of banks for a term of three to five years. The interest rate is set at a margin over an agreed reference rate such as LIBOR, and the borrower has the right to vary the interest period at each repayment date. As with other loans the credit risk is assessed by, and the funds provided by, the lending banks which will charge a series of fees for their participation and commitment.

The TLC facility gives the lenders the right to convert the loan into transferable certificates with the same term as the original loan. These certificates can be sold to other investors, thus removing the loan from the books of the banks. The certificates differ from most other eurosecurities in that their ownership is registered; that is, they are not bearer securities. A TLC facility is essentially a hybrid of a syndicated loan and a floating rate note. It provides borrowers with a committed source of medium-term funds without the remarketing risk associated with rollover of short-term notes. The TLC market is open to borrowers who may not be sufficiently well known to issue marketable debt securities in their own name. TLC facilities have increased in popularity with Australian borrowers and during 1992 they established facilities totalling about US$2.2 billion.

## EUROBONDS

Eurobonds are medium- to long-term international bearer securities sold in countries other than the country of the currency in which the bond is denominated. The securities traded in international bond markets are of many different types, the main classes being straight fixed-rate bonds, floating-rate notes and equity-related bonds. Of these classes, fixed-rate bonds are the most common and the term 'eurobond' generally refers only to such bonds. That is, eurobonds are securities that pay a fixed annual coupon interest, plus the repayment of face value at maturity. Interest is usually paid annually in arrears via detachable coupons. It is believed that many eurobonds are held by wealthy individuals, although increasingly eurobonds are also held by institutions.[42] A eurobond issue

---

42 One estimate is that institutional investors are now the major buyers and in the late 1980s took up about 70 per cent of new eurobond issues by governments and supranational bodies. See N. Osborn, 'The Unspoken Question: Eurobond Market, Is this Goodbye?', *Euromoney*, September 1989, p. 39.

is usually for a minimum amount of US$50 million (or equivalent in other currencies) but often the amount is much larger. Maturities are usually between three and 12 years. Eurobonds are normally listed on a stock exchange (typically London, Luxembourg or Singapore) but most secondary market trading occurs outside such formalised market structures.

The above details show that eurobonds have many of the features of euro-medium-term notes (EMTNs). In fact the underlying financial instruments are essentially the same and the main difference between them is the manner in which they are issued. For example, EMTNs are issued on a continuous or periodic basis through dealers but a eurobond issue takes place at a specific time (during a public placement period of up to two weeks) and is underwritten by banks and other institutions. A prospectus is required and an issue typically involves fees in the range 1.5 to 2.5 per cent of the amount issued.

At one time, nearly all eurobonds were denominated in US dollars but a trend towards other currencies developed from about 1985 onwards. Eurobonds denominated in Australian dollars began to be issued in large numbers in 1985 and 1986, reaching nearly $A13 billion in 1987.[43] Although the annual volume of issues has since declined, Australian dollar eurobonds on issue in March 1993 totalled US$19.5 billion. Australian borrowers have included state governments, semigovernment bodies such as the AIDC and Telecom, public companies such as CocaCola Amatil and Shell Australia, and banks such as the Commonwealth Bank and St George Bank. Non-Australian borrowers have included governments (Denmark, Austria), semigovernment bodies (Swedish Export Credit Agency), banks (Deutsche Bank), corporations (McDonald's, Toyota and Walt Disney) and supranational bodies (World Bank).

### 21.8.5 SWAPS

Swaps are possibly the most significant financial invention of the 1980s. From a volume of near zero in 1981 the volume by the close of the decade was in the hundreds of billions of dollars annually. Swaps are agreements in which two counterparties undertake to exchange a series of future cash flows. In the early days of the swap market these cash flows were the payments to be made on pre-existing loans. In effect, counterparties agreed to repay each other's pre-existing loans. As the market developed, this was often not *literally* the case, but the swap contracts specified the exchange of a series of future cash flows calculated *as if* pre-existing loan commitments had been swapped.

The two major forms of swap contracts are the **interest rate swap** and the **currency swap**. Under an interest rate swap, future cash flows calculated using future floating interest rates are swapped for future cash flows calculated using

---

[43] Mizon & Sue (see Footnote 39), p. 359. For background information on the early Euro–Australian dollar developments, see P. Beard, 'Why Euro-A$ Bonds are Booming', *Euromoney*, August 1985, pp. 95–8; and R. Jones, 'Aussie Dollar Comes of Age', *Euromoney*, June 1987, pp. 101–5.

a fixed interest rate. Such an agreement mimics the effect of exchanging a floating-rate loan and a fixed-rate loan.[44] Under a currency swap, future cash flows calculated using an interest rate in one currency are swapped for future cash flows calculated using an interest rate in another currency. Such an agreement mimics the effect of exchanging a loan in one currency for a loan in another currency. Interest rate swaps do not necessarily have any 'international' features and were discussed in Section 10.5. In this section we consider only currency swaps. To simplify matters, in the remainder of this section we discuss currency swaps as though they always arise from a swap of pre-existing loans.

In the previous section we mentioned that the Swedish government's Export Credit Agency (SEK) had issued eurobonds denominated in Australian dollars. Why would SEK want to borrow Australian dollars? The short answer is simple: it didn't. The borrowing was part of a currency swap with an Australian bank. The Australian bank was able to borrow US dollars at a floating-interest rate and it then swapped this loan for the fixed-interest rate Australian dollar loan borrowed by SEK. Both parties are said to have reduced their borrowing costs by 0.3 percentage points per annum.[45] This is an example of a fixed-for-floating currency swap. This type of currency swap is complicated by the fact that it has elements of both an interest rate swap and a currency swap because it involves both a change of interest rate type and a change of currency.

The simplest type of currency swap is a swap of a fixed-rate commitment in one currency for a fixed-rate commitment in another currency. The swap consists of an exchange of principal at the outset, followed by exchanges of interest flows on interest payment dates and, at the maturity of the loans, a re-exchange of principals. This type of swap is illustrated in Example 21.9.

### Example 21.9

Yankco wishes to borrow £100 million for 3 years and Britco wishes to borrow US$200 million for 3 years. The current spot exchange rate is US$1 = £0.5000. Both companies wish to repay using the bond cash flow pattern, that is, interest is paid at the end of each year and the principal is repaid in full at the end of the third year. The interest rates (in per cent per annum) applicable to the two borrowers are shown in Table 21.9.

Loosely speaking, while Yankco can borrow more cheaply than Britco in both currencies, it has a 2 percentage points advantage in US dollar borrowings but only a 1 percentage point advantage in UK pound borrowings.

---

[44] This is generally achieved through an intermediary who accepts the credit risk of both borrowers. In fact each borrower may not even be aware of the other's identity. However, the mechanics and motives are easier to understand if it is imagined that the borrowers themselves arrange a swap by direct negotiation.

[45] See 'Survey of the Euromarkets', supplement to *The Economist*, 16 May 1987, p. 14. This is by no means an unusual procedure. Many eurobonds have been issued with the intention to swap.

**Table 21.9** Interest rates payable by Britco and Yanko

| | Interest rates (% p.a.) | |
|---|---|---|
| Company | On US dollar borrowings | On UK pound borrowings |
| Britco | 12.0 | 14.5 |
| Yankco | 10.0 | 13.5 |

The standard funding cost argument for currency swaps is to suggest that Yankco should initially borrow dollars, while Britco should initially borrow pounds, and the two should then swap loan commitments. This is achieved by Yankco and Britco exchanging cash flows on each interest payment date and at the maturity of the loan. Although legally the original loan contracts between Yankco and the dollar lenders, and between Britco and the pound lenders, remain undisturbed, the economic effect is that Britco and Yankco have swapped loan commitments.

However, a straight swap of loan commitments is unlikely. In this example, as in most swaps, one counterparty is financially stronger than the other. In this example, Yankco is the stronger counterparty. In a straight swap, Yankco will simply end up paying the higher interest rate required on a loan to Britco. Thus Yankco will need an inducement to enter into the swap. Such an inducement can be achieved in a number of different ways. For example, Britco could offer Yankco a fee, perhaps in the form of allowing Yankco to retain some of its loan principal, while Britco transfers the whole of its loan principal to Yankco. Alternatively Britco could make swap payments to Yankco at an interest rate higher than the 10 per cent required by Yankco to repay its US dollar creditors. A third approach, which we explain below, involves an intermediary. One solution of this type is shown in Figure 21.1. This figure shows the cash flows that occur after an initial exchange of principals (Yankco borrows US$200 million, which it pays to Britco, while Britco borrows £100 million, which it pays to Yankco).

The originally agreed and post-swap net cash flows are shown in Table 21.10.

**Table 21.10** Originally agreed and post-swap net cash flows

| End of Year | Originally agreed cash flows | | Post-swap net cash flows | | |
|---|---|---|---|---|---|
| | Britco | Yankco | Britco | Yankco | Intermediary |
| 0 | +£100m | +US$200m | +US$200m | +£100m | — |
| 1 | −£14.5m | −US$20m | −US$23.6m | −£13.3m | +US$3.6m − £1.2m |
| 2 | −£14.5m | −US$20m | −US$23.6m | −£13.3m | +US$3.6m − £1.2m |
| 3 | −£14.5m | −US$20m | −US$23.6m | −£13.3m | +US$3.6m − £1.2m |
| 3 | −£100m | −US$200m | −US$200m | −£100m | |

As shown in Figure 21.1, Britco, after the swap, has exactly offsetting inflows and outflows in pounds and is paying 11.8 per cent for US dollars. This is 0.2 per cent better than Britco could have achieved for itself directly.

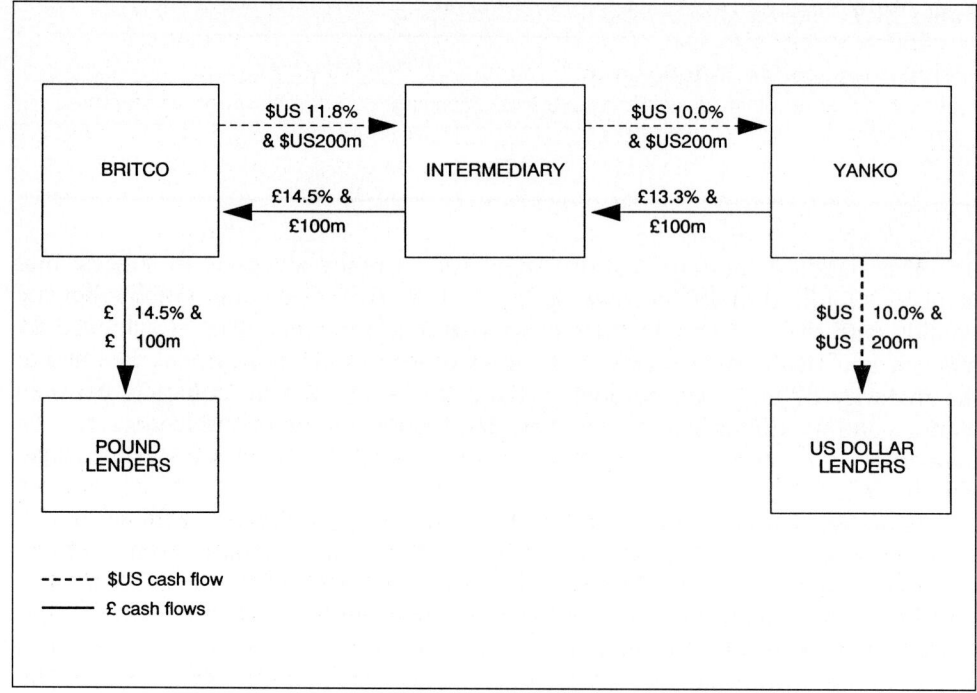

**Fig. 21.1** Post-swap cash flows

Yankco, after the swap, has exactly offsetting inflows and outflows in US dollars, and is paying 13.3 per cent for pounds. This is 0.2 per cent better than Yankco could have achieved for itself directly. The financial intermediary carries an exchange risk in that on each interest payment date, it has a net *dollar inflow* of 0.018 × US$200 million = US$3.6 million, and a net *pound outflow* of 0.012 × £100 million = £1.2 million. The intermediary might seek to hedge this risk by entering into forward contracts, or by entering into other swaps. Alternatively it might choose to carry the risk because its net cash flow will be negative only in the relatively unlikely event that the US dollar depreciates in three years from a value of £0.5000 per dollar to less than £0.3333 per dollar.

The search for interest cost savings are not the only reason for the growth in currency swaps. Market participants have found currency swaps a useful tool in structuring contracts that exploit tax advantages, or that reduce the impact of government regulations. For example, US companies have used currency swaps as part of a method to exploit some tax advantages of borrowing yen.[46]

---

46 For details, see C. W. Smith, C. W. Smithson & D. S. Wilford, *Managing Financial Risk*, Harper Business, New York, 1990, pp. 220–4. For an Australian perspective, see T. Dixon, T. McFadyen & B. Montague, 'Swaps', in Bruce et al., (see Footnote 39), p. 322.

Another theme in the swap literature is the view that currency swaps are exchange rate hedging vehicles which need not have any implications for borrowing costs. Smith, Smithson and Wakeman, for example, emphasise the similarities which exist between currency swaps and forward contracts.[47] Using this approach, the future cash flows in the currency swap between Britco and Yankco could be described as a package of four forward contracts. From Britco's viewpoint, these four contracts are as follows. The first three are, respectively, 1-year, 2-year and 3-year forward contracts to pay US$23.6 million to Yankco and in return receive £14.5 million; that is, they are equivalent to forward contracts to sell US$20 million at an exchange rate of US$1 = £0.6144. The fourth forward contract is implicit in the re-exchange of principals at maturity. In this case, Britco has the equivalent of a forward contract to sell US$200 million at a forward rate which is equal to today's spot rate of US$1 = £0.5000. That is, Britco will pay Yankco US$200 million and in return receive £100 million. Adopting the forward contract approach to currency swaps emphasises their hedging implications. In particular, whereas forward contracts for terms as long as 3 years are still relatively rare, implicitly such contracts are available through the mechanism of currency swaps. With the increased exposure of many companies to exchange rate movements, and the volatility of foreign exchange markets, there is increased demand for a financial instrument that locks in currency exchanges well into the future.

One final, and very important, aspect of currency swaps needs to be mentioned. This is the question of credit risk. The credit risk of a currency swap is usually considerably greater than the credit risk of an interest rate swap. The main reason for the higher risk is that currency swaps require a re-exchange of principals on the maturity date, whereas in interest rate swaps there is no exchange of principals. Obviously, loan principals involve sums that are much greater than associated periodic interest flows. In practice, however, there have been relatively few defaults in currency swaps. There have also been some cases where deposits or guarantees have been used to reduce credit risk when one of the counterparties has been considered financially weak.

## 21.9 CONCLUSION

Australia has always had a relatively open economy and this has been especially the case since the floating of the Australian dollar in 1983. In addition the deregulation of financial markets in Australia and elsewhere has increased both the need and the opportunity for Australian financial managers to become involved in international financial management. For many businesses these issues are no longer optional; they are a part of everyday business.

---

[47] C. W. Smith, C. W. Smithson & L. M. Wakeman, 'The Evolving Market for Swaps', in *The Revolution in Corporate Finance*, 2nd edn, Eds J. M. Stern & D. H. Chew, Basil Blackwell, Oxford, 1992, pp. 355–67.

## SELECTED REFERENCES

Froot, K. A. & Thaler, R. H., 'Anomalies: Foreign Exchange', *Journal of Economic Perspectives*, Summer 1990, pp. 179–92.
Hodrick, R. J., *The Empirical Evidence on the Efficiency of Forward and Futures Foreign Exchange Markets*, Harwood, London, 1987.
Madura, J., *International Financial Management*, 3rd edn, West Publishing, St Paul, 1992.
Mizon, G. & Sue, K., 'Funding from Offshore Sources', in *Handbook of Australian Corporate Finance*, Eds R. Bruce et al., 4th edn, Butterworths, Sydney, 1991, pp. 341–67.
Officer, L. H., *Purchasing Power Parity and Exchange Rates: Theory, Evidence and Relevance*, JAI Press, Greenwich, Connecticut, 1982.
Solnik, B., *International Investments*, Addison-Wesley, Reading, Massachusetts, 1988.
Wilson, L., 'Foreign Exchange', in *Handbook of Australian Corporate Finance*, Eds R. Bruce et al., 4th edn, Butterworths, Sydney, 1991, pp. 390–408.

## QUESTIONS

1. The currency of the nation of Homeland is called the 'home' (symbol H). As in Australia, foreign currency is generally quoted in Homeland as a rate per unit of home currency (that is, per H1). The currency of Foreignland is called the 'foreign' (symbol F).

   You have asked the National Homeland Bank for a quote on the 3-month forward rate for 'foreigns' and have received the following reply:
   Spot rates: 4.6220 and 4.6290
   3 months' forward margin: 227/237

   If you agree to sell F6 500 000 in 3 months' time, how much 'home' currency will you get? Explain briefly how and why you chose the exchange rate you did.

2. The following retail exchange rates (per $A1) are taken from the *Australian Financial Review*:

   Malta, pound 0.2690/0.2606
   Ireland, punt 0.4774/0.4685
   United States, dollar 0.7306/0.7256

   Based on these rates, calculate:
   (a) the minimum value of a punt (in terms of Maltese pounds);
   (b) the minimum value of a Maltese pound (in terms of punts);
   (c) the upper and lower bounds on the exchange rate between these two currencies (on a per Maltese pound basis).

   Why is the spread narrower for the US dollar than for the other currencies?

3. Assume that the buy/sell spread is zero and that you are a currency dealer for Banque Nationale de Paris. Simultaneously you observe the following spot exchange rates:
   FF1 = US$0.1591
   US$1 = DM1.8625
   DM1 = FF3.3492

   The marginal transaction cost is estimated to be one-eighth of one per cent. Explain the arbitrage that is available, and calculate the profit (after transaction costs) that can be made.

4. Suppose that the following spot exchange rates are observed simultaneously:

$C1 = US\$0.8615$
$A1 = US\$0.7475$
$A1 = \$C0.8645$

If the marginal transaction cost is zero, what profit could you make if you began with $A1 million? What proportional transaction cost would eliminate this profit? Assuming that the first two exchange rates above are correct, what should the third exchange rate be? Show your calculations.

5. Assume that the buy/sell spread is zero and there are no transaction costs. You observe the following information on Australia and Xanadu:

   Spot rate: $A1 = \$X1.4715$
   One-month $A interest rate: 0.6% per month
   One-month $X interest rate: 0.5% per month

   Use interest rate parity to calculate the one-month forward rate. Explain. If Xanadu interest rates increased to 0.7% per month (but there was no change in either the spot rate or Australian interest rates), what would the forward rate become? Explain.

6. Suppose that the 90-day bill rate in Australia is 14.16 per cent per annum and in the UK it is 11.35 per cent per annum. The spot exchange rate is $A1 = £0.4143$ and the 90-day forward rate is $A1 = £0.4105$. Show that a disequilibrium exists and construct an example of one type of transaction which would tend to correct this disequilibrium. If all of the required adjustment is reflected in the forward rate, calculate the equilibrium forward rate.

7. Assume that the buy sell spread is zero and there are no transaction costs. You observe the following:

   Spot rate: $A1 = US\$0.7815$
   1-month forward rate: $A1 = US\$0.7765$
   1-month $A interest rate: 1.30% per month
   1-month US$ interest rate: 0.75% per month

   Assuming that you are authorised to borrow or lend up to $A2 million, calculate the cash profit you can make today.

8. Dribnor Ltd is an Australian importer and expects to have to pay £1 million in 180 days' time. Interest rates are as follows: in Australian dollars, 9.25 per cent per annum; in pounds sterling, 6.15 per cent per annum. The spot rate is $A1 = £0.4240$ and the 180-day forward rate is $A1 = £0.4178$. Using this example, show that hedging by borrowing/lending is equivalent (in equilibrium) to forward rate hedging.

9. On the first day of every month, Monpred Ltd releases its forecasts of the exchange rate (in US$ per $A1) for the first day of the subsequent month. Forecasts made during the first 6 months of 19X1 are shown in the following table:

| Date forecast released | Forecast made (US$) |
| --- | --- |
| 1 January | 0.7950 |
| 1 February | 0.7900 |
| 1 March | 0.8350 |
| 1 April | 0.7610 |
| 1 May | 0.7450 |
| 1 June | 0.7560 |

Actual spot exchange rates and 1-month forward exchange rates were observed on the following dates to be:

| Date of observation | Spot rate | 1-month forward rate |
|---|---|---|
| 1 January | 0.7994 | 0.8044 |
| 1 February | 0.7716 | 0.7786 |
| 1 March | 0.8290 | 0.8300 |
| 1 April | 0.7850 | 0.7825 |
| 1 May | 0.7330 | 0.7300 |
| 1 June | 0.7550 | 0.7520 |
| 1 July | 0.7190 | 0.7160 |

Assume that you are an Australian speculator who is willing to act on these forecasts by buying (or selling) $A10 000 forward each month (from January to June, inclusive).

Complete a table showing, for each date, whether you bought or sold Australian dollars, and the resulting profit or loss (in $A).

10. Dora owns a small chain of hairdressing salons in south-west Victoria and is considering expanding into other consumer service retail businesses. She calculates that she will need to borrow approximately $3 million and her bank has approved a loan for this amount at an annual interest rate of 12.5 per cent. Dora had asked about borrowing US dollars instead, because the annual interest rate was only around 9 per cent, but the bank declined her request. Dora feels sure she has missed a great opportunity and seeks your advice. Advise Dora.

11. Suppose that during a given year the Australian dollar appreciates by 8 per cent relative to the UK pound, while in the same year the Australian inflation rate is 6 per cent and the UK inflation rate is 3 per cent. What has happened (in percentage terms) to the real value of the UK pound relative to the Australian dollar?

12. Explain the 'purchasing power parity' theorem. What factors do you think tend to inhibit the achievement of such parity?

13. International Kangaroo Ltd (IKL) is based in Melbourne and has recently taken over three foreign-based manufacturers: Bald Eagle Inc. (of Topeka, Kansas); Maple Leaf Inc. (of Calgary, Alberta) and Thistle plc (of Glasgow, Scotland). All three of these companies export a substantial proportion of their output to various countries in Europe and North America. In addition, Maple Leaf and Thistle import from the US about half of their raw materials. Because of their exposure to international currency fluctuations, management in all four companies is experienced in both spot market and forward market transactions. Advise IKL on what changes it should consider.

14. Carefully evaluate the following proposition: *A cost-conscious manager should never bother with foreign currency options; they cost a lot, whereas banks charge hardly anything for forward contracts.*

15. You are working for an Australian mutual fund. The fund has investments in approximately 100 companies listed on the Australian Stock Exchange. The fund's manager is considering investing in foreign securities. She seeks

your reaction to this idea. Write a brief report, pointing out the possible risks and benefits.

16. Alfred retired from work in March 1986 and received a lump sum superannuation payment. He was advised to invest some of this payment in a fund which invests in a range of US stocks. Basically the fund is structured so that its value follows that of the Dow-Jones industrial average.

    In March 1989, Alfred decides to review his investments and has collected the following data:

    | Date | Dow-Jones industrial average | Australian all-ordinaries index | Exchange rate US$ per $A1 |
    |---|---|---|---|
    | March 1986 | 1818.61 | 1131.0 | 0.7150 |
    | March 1989 | 2293.62 | 1459.6 | 0.8195 |

    Alfred has brought these data to you and asks you to do the following:
    (a) Ignoring tax issues, calculate his rate of return and compare this with his rate of return had he invested in Australian shares.
    (b) Explain whether the advice he received in March 1986 was sound.

17. Crest Services is a successful Australian company that operates both domestically and in Singapore. It is planning to expand into New Zealand. To finance the expansion, it will need to increase its borrowings. Its board is unsure of the currency in which the borrowings should be made.
    *Director A:* 'Singapore has the lowest interest rates, so we should borrow Singapore dollars.'
    *Director B:* 'We're an Australian company, so why take unnecessary risks with foreign borrowings? We should borrow Australian dollars. We know we'll always have Australian dollar inflows to repay debt, but we don't know yet how we'll go in New Zealand.'
    *Director C:* 'We'll be an internationally diversified company, so our debt should be, too. Borrow a mix of all three currencies: Australian, New Zealand and Singaporean, in roughly the same proportions as our assets.'
    Critically appraise all three viewpoints. What advice would you give? Why?

18. Explain the meaning of the terms SIBOR and LIBOR. If you collected daily data on SIBOR and LIBOR for 12 months, what correlation would you expect to find between them? Why? Does this mean you could forecast LIBOR and therefore make money? Give reasons for your answer.

**CHAPTER 22**

# MANAGEMENT OF SHORT-TERM ASSETS: AN INTRODUCTION

## 22.1 INTRODUCTION

Most of the investment decisions considered in previous chapters were concerned with long-term assets such as plant, equipment, buildings and motor vehicles. These assets are regarded as long term because they do not normally need to be replaced for several years. However, most businesses also hold short-term assets such as inventory, liquid assets[1] and accounts receivable. These are 'short term' because any individual item of inventory, or any particular liquid asset, or any single account receivable, will generally be replaced in a matter of days, weeks or months. Both short-term assets and long-term assets require a commitment of resources by the company, and thus both forms of investment deserve careful analysis by the financial manager.

This chapter considers the general area of investment in short-term assets. Chapters 23, 24 and 25 consider, in turn, the three major types of short-term asset: inventory, liquid assets, and accounts receivable.

## 22.2 IMPORTANCE OF SHORT-TERM ASSETS

Compared with multimillion dollar investments in, say, mining ventures, automated factories or space technology, the issues involved in investment in short-term assets may appear trivial. Although such a view is understandable it is nevertheless incorrect from both the theoretical and empirical viewpoints.

---

[1] Liquid assets comprise cash, and assets which can be converted into cash very quickly.

It was made clear in the chapters dealing with long-term investments that funds are invested to earn a competitive return. Short-term investments use resources in exactly the same way as long-term investments: a dollar invested in a short-term asset is a dollar not invested in some other asset. As a result, the wealth-maximising company will want to ensure that all its investments are selected and managed efficiently. The management of short-term assets should not be passive.

Regardless of how important an issue may appear to be in principle, its practical economic significance will generally be limited if there is very little money involved. However, there can be no doubt that a great deal of money is involved in short-term asset holdings in Australia. In June 1986, non-financial companies in Australia had investments in cash, accounts receivable and inventories totalling about $55 billion.[2] To put this figure in perspective it may be noted that, at the time, $55 billion was about the level of three months' Gross Domestic Product, and was equal to approximately 85 per cent of total Commonwealth Government spending for the 1985–86 financial year. Table 22.1 provides some further evidence on the importance of short-term assets. It shows that the typical company holds around 35 per cent of its total assets in short-term assets. This varies between industries, with the media the lowest (at around 12 per cent in 1992), and engineering the highest (at around 50 per cent in 1992), but it is clear that short-term assets are important in all sectors of business.

**Table 22.1**  *Short-term assets as a percentage of total assets, 1985–86 to 1991–92, by industry sector*

| Industry sector | 1986 | 1987 | 1988 | 1989 | 1990 | 1991 | 1992 |
| --- | --- | --- | --- | --- | --- | --- | --- |
| Gold | 23.7 | 30.0 | 16.2 | 19.2 | 19.9 | 21.8 | 25.1 |
| Other metals | 26.4 | 26.3 | 29.2 | 30.6 | 26.3 | 23.2 | 22.7 |
| Solid fuels | 24.9 | 27.9 | 26.4 | 29.9 | 24.7 | 24.0 | 23.8 |
| Oil and gas | 19.7 | 19.0 | 12.6 | 11.8 | 10.0 | 11.4 | 12.5 |
| Diversified resources | 20.5 | 18.6 | 24.6 | 21.5 | 23.9 | 22.3 | 20.6 |
| Developers and contractors | 48.1 | 47.9 | 38.8 | 35.0 | 33.6 | 35.7 | 27.0 |
| Building materials | 43.6 | 40.9 | 37.2 | 35.1 | 31.6 | 29.3 | 31.5 |
| Alcohol and tobacco | 42.5 | 43.8 | 57.3 | 29.3 | 31.8 | 29.7 | 27.8 |
| Food and household | 37.8 | 36.7 | 34.0 | 43.8 | 40.1 | 38.1 | 37.4 |
| Chemicals | 48.4 | 50.4 | 50.4 | 50.9 | 46.2 | 44.3 | 44.0 |
| Engineering | 57.0 | 55.6 | 55.5 | 48.3 | 48.5 | 48.9 | 49.6 |
| Paper and packaging | 37.2 | 36.0 | 28.4 | 28.6 | 33.3 | 25.5 | 26.8 |
| Retail | 45.3 | 42.3 | 38.6 | 37.7 | 36.8 | 39.7 | 44.7 |
| Transport | 34.2 | 35.2 | 35.0 | 33.9 | 32.6 | 34.5 | 31.0 |
| Media | 21.8 | 19.7 | 16.6 | 13.1 | 13.7 | 13.9 | 12.4 |
| Entrepreneurial investor | 31.7 | 29.6 | 23.8 | 30.1 | 30.5 | 30.9 | 27.0 |
| Miscellaneous services | 47.3 | 47.4 | 38.1 | 30.6 | 29.3 | 33.5 | 29.2 |
| Miscellaneous industrials | 51.8 | 47.4 | 50.7 | 42.8 | 39.8 | 38.4 | 40.2 |
| Diversified industrials | 41.1 | 39.4 | 38.4 | 50.9 | 44.0 | 42.5 | 40.2 |

Source: Stock Exchange Financial and Profitability Study, various years.

---

[2] *Bulletin Supplement, Company Finance*, Reserve Bank of Australia, April 1988.

## 22.3 TYPES OF SHORT-TERM ASSET

Three major types of short-term asset will be considered. These are:

### INVENTORY

For the manufacturer, inventory includes raw materials, work in progress, and finished goods not yet sold. For the wholesaler and retailer, inventory consists mostly of merchandise in the warehouse or on the shelves.

### LIQUID ASSETS (CASH AND SHORT-TERM INVESTMENTS)

Obviously, virtually all companies will need to have at least some cash on hand in order to carry on business. For many purposes short-term investments such as commercial bills, overnight deposits with the short-term money market, and very short-term bank deposits, are a good substitute for cash and have the added advantage that they generate interest revenue.

### ACCOUNTS RECEIVABLE (DEBTORS)

Companies often extend short-term credit to their customers. For example, a supplier of goods may not require payment of the amount owed until a period of 30, 60, or even 90 days has passed. During the period from the date of purchase to the date of payment, the supplier has the short-term asset 'account receivable'.

Table 22.2 shows for all non-finance industries, the three main short-term assets as a percentage of total short-term assets for the period 1984–85 to 1991–92.

**Table 22.2** *Specific assets as a percentage of total short-term assets, 1984–85 to 1991–92, all non-finance industries*

| Year ended June | Cash (%) | Accounts receivable (%) | Inventory (%) |
|---|---|---|---|
| 1985 | 16.5 | 30.4 | 42.7 |
| 1986 | 15.5 | 30.7 | 41.5 |
| 1987 | 17.2 | 28.5 | 39.3 |
| 1988 | 14.7 | 22.3 | 33.2 |
| 1989 | 19.0 | 30.3 | 34.0 |
| 1990 | 16.3 | 29.8 | 38.1 |
| 1991 | 18.8 | 29.3 | 37.3 |
| 1992 | 18.8 | 28.8 | 38.6 |

*Source:* Stock Exchange Financial and Profitability Study, various years.

It shows that, quantitatively, inventory is somewhat more important than accounts receivable. By comparison, cash appears to be much less important.

## 22.4 THE NEED FOR SHORT-TERM ASSET MANAGEMENT

In a simple world of frictionless, perfect markets there would be no need for a company to hold short-term assets and consequently issues concerning their management would not arise. For example, if a company required more raw materials it would be able to obtain them instantaneously at the appropriate market price. Under these conditions there would clearly be no need to hold an inventory of raw materials. The same is true of other forms of inventory. Cash holdings are in the same position because any shortage could be instantaneously met at an appropriate market price (interest rate). Similarly, in the case of accounts receivable there would be no need for the company to wait for the customer's payment because the asset could be sold in the market place for its present value. Presumably the buyer would be a company specialising in credit provision.

The point is that, unlike most of the topics studied in finance, the model of the frictionless, perfectly competitive market is usually not a useful starting point for the analysis of short-term asset management. This is not because markets in short-term assets are not competitive. Indeed they are often highly competitive. The problem lies more in the assumption that markets are 'frictionless'. For example, a major reason for holding inventories of raw materials is the fact that there are delays and uncertainties involved in obtaining new supplies. Delays and uncertainties involve costs (both explicit and implicit) and therefore constitute a source of 'friction'. To a lesser extent the same is true of cash. Finally, while it is true that accounts receivable can often be sold ('factored') if desired, most companies choose not to do so.[3] While there will be legal and administrative costs involved in factoring, perhaps of even more significance are the 'information costs'. Many companies know their customers well and can form reliable estimates of the likelihood of receiving payment, but the factoring company (that is, the purchaser of the account) would need to expend resources to obtain the information it needs to form its own estimates. Naturally, the cost of obtaining this information is built into the price offered by the factoring company. The result, of course, is that a company will usually choose to hold rather than sell an account receivable. Again, therefore, a source of friction has proved to be significant. In this case, the friction is the cost of obtaining information.

Because we do not assume frictionless, perfect markets, the analysis of short-term asset management tends to have a different 'feel' to many other topics in finance. Indeed, many of the issues involved are often discussed not only in finance but also in related disciplines such as management accounting and operations research. Nevertheless the management of short-term assets should be of vital concern to the financial manager. As noted previously, short-term assets involve a commitment of the company's resources. Good decisions will mean efficient use of those resources and will result in increased wealth for the shareholders; poor decisions will have the opposite effect.

In principle, determining the optimum level of investment in any particular type of short-term asset can be approached in precisely the same way as decisions concerning long-term assets. For example, an account receivable should be held if its net present value is positive, but should not be held if its net present value is negative. As usual, the appropriate discount rate to apply is the opportunity cost of capital, which in this case is the rate of return required on an asset which has the same risk as the account(s) receivable. Alternatively, the capital asset

---

[3] Factoring is discussed in Section 25.6.1.

pricing model could be applied, given an estimate of the beta of accounts receivable.[4] Unfortunately, such estimates are difficult, if not impossible, to obtain. In most cases, pursuing this line of thought does not provide practical solutions in this area, despite the validity of the principles involved. Although wealth maximisation is still the ultimate objective, different techniques are often needed to estimate and optimise the costs and benefits.

## 22.5 SHORT-TERM ASSETS AND SHORT-TERM LIABILITIES

Although the focus of Chapters 23, 24 and 25 is the management of short-term assets, it should also be remembered that companies must also make decisions about their short-term liabilities. Many companies try to maintain a fairly stable relationship between the maturity structure of their assets and the maturity structure of their liabilities. For example, life insurance companies tend to hold a relatively large proportion of their assets in the form of long-term investments because the average life insurance policy is not expected to mature until a relatively long time has elapsed. This 'matching policy' also applies to shorter maturities, so a company whose short-term assets comprise a relatively large proportion of its total assets will often make greater use of short-term debt than other companies.

The basic ideas underlying the matching policy are easily explained. Assume that a company has only one non-current asset. By borrowing for a period equal to the asset's life, management expects that the asset will generate cash flows sufficient to meet the payments required by the loan. A short-term asset and its matching liability may each involve only one cash flow. The matching policy is seen very clearly in the case of trade bills, which usually require the drawer to pay the face value of the bill on a future date which coincides with the date on which the drawer expects to receive payment for the goods that have been sold.[5] If the maturity of the debt is shorter than the life of the asset, there is a risk that the company either will not have sufficient cash to repay the debt, or will not be able to renew the debt. If the maturity of the debt is longer than the life of the asset, there is a risk that the company will not have sufficient alternative sources of cash at the end of the asset's life to continue meeting the interest payments on the debt.

To illustrate the matching policy, we considered matching a particular asset with a particular liability, but in practice, the matching policy usually does not need to be carried to such an extreme. Instead, management will often focus on broad aggregates relating to different classes of assets and liabilities. For example, management may classify its assets and liabilities into four maturity classes: very short, short, medium, and long. Within each class, management will seek to maintain a balance between assets and liabilities. Alternatively, management may seek to balance the average maturity of assets and liabilities. A more sophisticated approach is to calculate the 'duration' of the company's assets and

---

4 See Section 6.6.2 for a discussion of the capital asset pricing model.
5 See Section 8.3.3 for a more detailed description of bills of exchange.

select a matching liability structure. As discussed in Appendix 4.1, duration is the appropriate measure of maturity where it is sought to immunise a portfolio against changes in interest rates.[6]

## SELECTED REFERENCES

Firth, M. A., *Management of Working Capital*, Macmillan, London, 1976.
Mehta, D. R., *Working Capital Management*, Prentice-Hall, Englewood Cliffs, New Jersey, 1974.
Morris, J. R., 'On Corporate Debt Maturity Strategies', *Journal of Finance*, March 1976, pp. 29–37.
Smith, K. V. & Callinger, G. W., *Readings on Short-Term Financial Management*, 3rd edn, West, St Paul, 1988.

## QUESTIONS

1. Distinguish between the major types of short-term asset.
2. Relative to total assets, businesses in the retail and wholesale sectors invest substantially more in short-term assets than do businesses in the service sector. Suggest reasons for this difference.
3. For the average company, cash represents a much smaller percentage of its total short-term assets than accounts receivable. Suggest reasons for this difference.
4. Should the decision to invest in short-term assets be approached differently to the decision to invest in long-term assets?
5. Explain the 'maturity matching' concept. Why do many companies pursue policies based on this idea?
6. *Uncertainty makes it difficult for a financial manager to predict the company's requirement for short-term funds.* Discuss. What steps can the financial manager take to minimise the resulting risks to the company?

---

[6] It should not be assumed that a matching policy should necessarily be followed rigidly. For an example of circumstances in which a matching policy may not be optimal, see J. R. Morris, 'On Corporate Debt Maturity Strategies', *Journal of Finance*, March 1976, pp. 29–37.

# CHAPTER 23

# INVENTORY MANAGEMENT

## 23.1 INTRODUCTION

In this chapter we consider inventory management. As explained in Chapter 22, inventories form a substantial part of the typical company's investment in short-term assets. As a result, inventory management is needed in every company. Even when compared with total assets, investments in inventories are significant. This is shown in Table 23.1.

Table 23.1 shows that the proportion of total assets held in the form of inventory varies from one industry to another.[1] As would be expected, the percentage is somewhat higher in retailing, and lower in the mining industry.

## 23.2 WHAT IS INVENTORY?

There are three main types of inventory.

- **Raw materials inventory** comprises inventory that will form part of the completed product of a manufacturer, but which has yet to enter the production process. It includes unprocessed inventory, such as iron ore and wheat, and the finished goods of other industries, such as fabricated steel and flour.
- **Work-in-process inventory** comprises partially completed products which require additional processing before they become finished goods.
- **Finished goods inventory** for a manufacturer is completed products not yet sold; for a retailer or wholesaler it is merchandise on hand.

---

[1] These figures include supplies. For example, lubricants, spare parts, and stationery would be included.

**Table 23.1** *Inventory as a percentage of total assets, 1985–86 to 1991–92, by industry sector*

| Industry sector | 1986 | 1987 | 1988 | 1989 | 1990 | 1991 | 1992 |
|---|---|---|---|---|---|---|---|
| Gold | 6.1 | 5.9 | 3.6 | 4.6 | 6.1 | 7.2 | 7.6 |
| Other metals | 11.1 | 10.8 | 11.1 | 10.6 | 10.6 | 10.3 | 9.5 |
| Solid fuels | 8.8 | 9.8 | 7.5 | 4.9 | 6.9 | 9.4 | 10.4 |
| Oil and gas | 1.7 | 1.7 | 1.2 | 0.9 | 0.9 | 1.1 | 1.2 |
| Diversified resources | 8.3 | 7.9 | 6.2 | 8.1 | 9.0 | 8.9 | 8.9 |
| Developers and contractors | 26.5 | 23.6 | 16.1 | 14.3 | 12.6 | 12.0 | 7.0 |
| Building materials | 17.8 | 17.0 | 13.7 | 11.5 | 11.8 | 11.4 | 12.1 |
| Alcohol and tobacco | 25.3 | 24.2 | 31.0 | 7.8 | 5.0 | 6.8 | 7.2 |
| Food and household | 16.4 | 13.2 | 13.5 | 12.4 | 14.5 | 13.5 | 13.1 |
| Chemicals | 24.8 | 23.4 | 23.2 | 28.8 | 26.2 | 23.5 | 23.4 |
| Engineering | 30.5 | 27.0 | 24.4 | 23.1 | 23.0 | 24.3 | 23.6 |
| Paper and packaging | 16.6 | 16.2 | 15.0 | 11.1 | 15.7 | 9.1 | 9.3 |
| Retail | 33.6 | 31.6 | 28.4 | 26.8 | 26.3 | 30.9 | 31.2 |
| Transport | 2.0 | 2.1 | 1.6 | 1.6 | 1.4 | 1.3 | 1.7 |
| Media | 2.0 | 1.9 | 1.8 | 2.0 | 4.9 | 3.5 | 3.2 |
| Entrepreneurial investor | 4.7 | 11.5 | 5.6 | 7.6 | 8.9 | 9.6 | 11.3 |
| Miscellaneous services | 21.6 | 19.8 | 16.9 | 8.9 | 10.4 | 11.3 | 9.1 |
| Miscellaneous industrials | 23.2 | 20.9 | 21.2 | 16.1 | 16.9 | 15.8 | 15.0 |
| Diversified industrials | 16.5 | 15.1 | 12.7 | 17.9 | 18.3 | 17.3 | 16.2 |

*Source:* Stock Exchange Financial and Profitability Study, various years

Many companies also have inventories of consumable supplies and spare parts.

## 23.3 BENEFITS AND COSTS OF HOLDING INVENTORY: OVERVIEW

Before considering in detail the range of costs and benefits of holding inventory, the major issues involved in inventory management will be illustrated by a simple example. Suppose a suburban retail store is considering the level of inventory it should hold. **If too little inventory is held** there will frequently be occasions when customers will arrive at the store, ready and willing to buy a product, only to find that it is unavailable. Sales will be lost and customer goodwill will suffer. In addition, if the inventory level is low the store will need to reorder the products it sells at frequent intervals, thus incurring the costs of ordering more often than would otherwise be the case. **If too much inventory is held** these problems will be avoided, but a different set of problems will arise. High inventory levels tie up large amounts of capital and lead to high storage and insurance costs.

The choice of inventory level therefore involves a balancing of costs and benefits. However, it is convenient to think of the benefits as 'costs avoided'. For example, the benefit of always having inventory on hand can be thought of as avoiding the 'costs' of lost sales and lost customer goodwill. In this way, inventory management becomes a problem of cost minimisation.

The costs of holding inventory are generally classified into three groups: **acquisition costs**, **carrying costs** and **stockout costs**.

## 23.4 INVENTORY COSTS: RETAILING AND WHOLESALING

### 23.4.1 ACQUISITION COSTS

The most obvious cost of acquiring inventory is the price paid for each unit of inventory. However, unless there are quantity discounts available (discussed in Section 23.6.4), the unit price is the same, regardless of the inventory policy, and is therefore not relevant to the choice of policy. Relevant acquisition costs are those which vary with the inventory policy adopted and include:

(a) **ordering costs:** clerical costs are incurred every time an order is placed;
(b) **freight and handling costs:** every order placed will result in freight costs and, when the goods are received, handling costs;
(c) **quantity discounts foregone:** larger orders will often attract a discount in price. If smaller orders are placed, these discounts will not be obtained and consequently an opportunity cost is incurred.

Per unit of inventory, each of these costs will be lower, the larger the order placed. Large orders imply relatively infrequent ordering and high inventory levels.

### 23.4.2 CARRYING COSTS

After inventory has been acquired, it must be held (or 'carried'). The greater the inventory level, the higher will be the total carrying costs. Carrying costs include:

(a) **opportunity cost of investment:** inventory ties up capital which could have been invested elsewhere in the company's activities. The opportunity cost is therefore equal to the company's required rate of return on capital;
(b) **storage costs:** after inventory is received, it must be stored. This will involve the payment of rent, or, if the company owns its storage facilities, the foregoing of rental revenue which could otherwise have been earned;
(c) **insurance premiums:** if the inventory is insured, the premiums will probably vary directly with the value of the inventory held;
(d) **deterioration and obsolescence:** losses attributable to these factors are likely to be higher for higher levels of inventory; and
(e) **price movements:** if there is a decrease in the price of merchandise held in inventory, a loss is incurred. If there is an increase in price, a gain is made, and this element of the carrying costs is negative.

### 23.4.3 STOCKOUT COSTS

Avoidance of stockout costs is the major benefit of holding inventory. If a company's inventory of a particular item is completely exhausted, customers may purchase elsewhere in order to obtain immediate delivery. Sales are lost. Many customers soon lose patience in this situation and may switch all of their business to a competitor, thus causing further sales to be lost.

## 23.5 Inventory Costs: Manufacturing

### 23.5.1 Inventories of Raw Materials

A similar set of costs applies to a manufacturer faced with the problem of choosing an inventory level for raw materials. The major difference relates to stockout costs. A shortage of raw materials inventory will disrupt the production process and impose costs on a manufacturer because machines and labour will be underutilised.

### 23.5.2 Inventories of Finished Goods

As well as holding an inventory of raw materials, most manufacturers hold an inventory of their finished products. In this case, carrying costs and stockout costs are similar to those faced by a retailer or wholesaler, but the set-up cost for a production run is included among the acquisition costs. Set-up costs are incurred each time a new production run is started. High set-up costs call for larger production runs to spread the costs over a greater number of units produced in each run. In turn this implies that a high level of finished products inventory would be carried.

## 23.6 Inventory Management Under Certainty

### 23.6.1 The Basic Economic Order Quantity (EOQ) Model

In this section it is assumed that demand for the product is constant (per unit of time) and known with certainty. It is also assumed that no quantity discounts are available and that orders of new inventory are filled instantly. That is, the lead time between ordering and receiving items to be held in inventory is zero. There is, therefore, no need to order new inventory until the current inventory level reaches zero. This is illustrated in Figure 23.1.

The company places an order for $Q^*$ units at time zero. Since demand is constant, this inventory will then fall steadily over time. At time 1, inventory has reached zero, so a new order for $Q^*$ units is placed and instantly filled, restoring the inventory level to $Q^*$. The second cycle then begins and the process is repeated. This process continues throughout the year.

The problem is to choose an order quantity $Q$ which will minimise the total cost of the inventory policy.[2] The value of $Q$ that achieves this goal is called the **economic order quantity (EOQ)** and is denoted here by $Q^*$. After $Q^*$ has been calculated, the optimum time period between the placement of each order is found by dividing annual demand $D$ by the economic order quantity $Q^*$. For example, if demand is 12 000 units per year, and the economic order quantity is found to be 1000, orders need to be placed 12 times per year, that is, monthly. In calculating EOQ, the notation we use is:

$D$ = demand (in physical units) per period (for example, demand per year)
$a$ = acquisition cost ($) per order placed

---

[2] Note that no stockout cost has been specified. Under conditions of certainty, stockouts need never occur. Similarly, stockouts need never occur if orders are filled instantly.

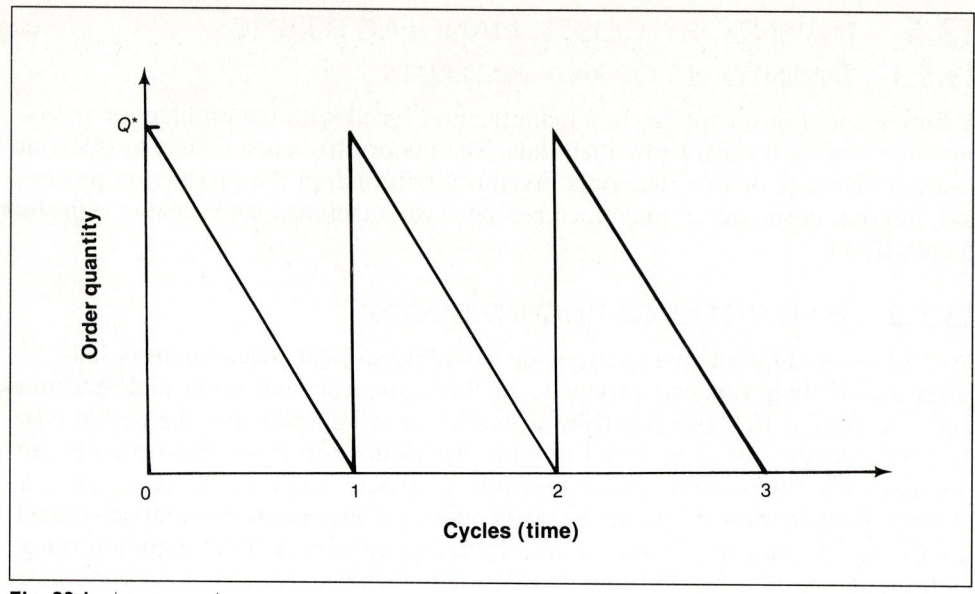

**Fig. 23.1** *Inventory cycles*

$c$ = annual carrying cost ($) per unit of inventory, including the opportunity cost of capital invested in inventory
$Q$ = quantity (in physical units) per order and
$P$ = supply price ($) per unit of inventory

Inventory policy will affect the acquisition costs and carrying costs which are defined as follows:

Acquisition costs per year = acquisition cost per order × number of orders per year
$$= a\frac{D}{Q}$$

Carrying costs per year = annual carrying cost per unit of inventory × average inventory

In each cycle the initial inventory is $Q$ units, and over the cycle the inventory declines steadily to zero. Therefore, the average inventory level is $\frac{Q}{2}$. Therefore:

Carrying costs per year $= c\frac{Q}{2}$

The annual total cost, TC, of the inventory policy is the sum of the acquisition and carrying costs and is given by: 
$$TC = \frac{aD}{Q} + \frac{cQ}{2} \qquad (23.1)$$

The economic order quantity $Q^*$ is the value of $Q$ which minimises TC in Equation 23.1. Note that, as expected, acquisition costs $\frac{aD}{Q}$ fall as $Q$ increases, but carrying costs $\frac{cQ}{2}$ increase as $Q$ increases. To find $Q^*$, differentiate Equation 23.1 with respect to $Q$ and set the derivative equal to zero:

$$\frac{d(TC)}{dQ} = -\frac{aD}{Q^2} + \frac{c}{2} = 0$$

which gives

$$Q^* = \sqrt{\frac{2aD}{c}} \qquad (23.2)$$

The application of this model is illustrated in the following three examples.

### Example 23.1: Retailing

Clarke's Photography Store sells 12 000 rolls of film per year. The wholesale price is $3 per roll. The cost of processing each order is $12.50 and carrying costs are 30 cents per roll per year. Management wants to know the economic order quantity and the optimal time period between orders.

In this example $D = 12\,000$, $a = 12.5$, and $c = 0.3$.
Using Equation 23.2:

$$\begin{aligned} Q^* &= \sqrt{\frac{2aD}{c}} \\ &= \sqrt{\frac{(2)\,(12.5)\,(12\,000)}{(0.3)}} \\ &= \sqrt{\frac{300\,000}{0.3}} \\ &= 1000 \text{ rolls} \end{aligned}$$

The number of orders per year: $= \frac{12\,000}{1000}$
$= 12$

Therefore orders are placed monthly.

### Example 23.2: Manufacturing (raw materials inventory)

Cranfield Manufacturing Ltd uses 4500 metres of wire each year in its production process. Acquisition costs are $250 per order and the wire costs $1 per metre per year to store. Management wants to know the economic order quantity and the optimal time period between orders.

In this example $D = 4500$, $a = 250$, and $c = 1$.
Using Equation 23.2:

$$Q^* = \sqrt{\frac{2aD}{c}}$$

$$= \sqrt{\frac{(2)(250)(4500)}{(1)}}$$

$$= \sqrt{2\,250\,000}$$

$$= 1500 \text{ metres}$$

$$\text{The number of orders per year} = \frac{4500}{1500}$$

$$= 3$$

Therefore orders are placed three times per year, that is, once every 4 months.

### Example 23.3: Manufacturing (finished goods inventory)

Dunbar Fabricating Ltd produces a specialised type of metal sheeting. Demand is 5000 sheets per year. Each production run costs $1750 to set up, and storage costs are $25 per sheet per year. Management wants to know the optimum size of a production run and the number of runs per year.

In this example, $D = 5000$, $a = 1750$, and $c = 25$.
Using Equation 23.2:

$$Q^* = \sqrt{\frac{2aD}{c}}$$

$$= \sqrt{\frac{(2)(1750)(5000)}{25}}$$

$$= \sqrt{700\,000}$$

$$= 837 \text{ sheets}$$

The number of production runs per year is $\frac{5000}{837}$, or approximately six per year. Therefore a production run should be scheduled every 2 months.

## 23.6.2 COST ESTIMATION

The relevant costs in the EOQ model are incremental costs, and may be difficult to estimate in practice. Company accounting systems may not be designed to separate inventory costs from other operating costs, and even where they are, they will generally give average rather than marginal costs. Fortunately both the optimum order quantity and, more importantly, total inventory costs, are likely to be fairly insensitive to errors in estimates of the unit costs. Two factors contribute to this property of the model. First, suppose the acquisition cost $a$ doubles, or the carrying cost $c$ is halved. The optimum order quantity $Q^*$ will then increase by a factor of only $\sqrt{2}$ if all other factors remain unchanged. Secondly, the total cost TC in Equation 23.1 is generally not very sensitive to changes in the size of the order quantity, particularly in the region of $Q^*$. Example 23.4 illustrates the effects of a large error in estimating the acquisition cost.

### Example 23.4: Cost estimation

In Example 23.1, $D = 12\,000$, $a = 12.5$, $c = 0.3$, and it was found that $Q^* = 1000$. Suppose the true value of the acquisition cost $a$ is \$25 per order but management believes it is only \$12.50. The effect of this estimation error on the company's total costs can be assessed by comparing:
1. the cost of the optimum inventory policy that management would adopt if it had the correct information; with
2. the cost of the inventory policy that management believes to be optimum, based on its incorrect estimates.

Using the true value of $a$ and Equation 23.2, the economic order quantity is:

$$Q^* = \sqrt{\frac{2aD}{c}}$$

$$= \sqrt{\frac{(2)(25)(12\,000)}{0.3}}$$

$$= 1414 \text{ rolls}$$

The annual total cost of the optimum inventory policy using Equation 23.1 is:

$$TC = \frac{(25)(12\,000)}{1414} + \frac{(0.3)(1414)}{2}$$

$$= \$424$$

But management, believing that $a$ is \$12.50, will choose an order quantity of 1000 rolls. The annual cost of this policy is:

$$TC = \frac{(25)(12\,000)}{1000} + \frac{(0.3)(1000)}{2}$$

$$= \$450$$

The annual cost of adopting management's estimate of $a$ is only \$26 or 6.1 per cent greater than the annual cost under the 'true' optimum policy. Therefore the EOQ model is fairly robust, and should work well in practice, despite difficulties in making accurate estimates of the input data.

## 23.6.3 THE EOQ MODEL WITH POSITIVE LEAD TIME

In the previous discussion, lead time was assumed to be zero. That is, it was assumed that when an order was placed it was filled instantly. In most cases such an assumption is unrealistic because it will nearly always take time after an order has been placed for the goods to be delivered and placed in inventory. With a positive lead time, a new order must be placed before the current inventory level reaches zero. To minimise carrying costs the reorder point is chosen so that goods from the new order are placed in inventory just as the inventory level reaches zero. Initially, it is assumed that the lead time is less than the time period between orders. This assumption is then relaxed.

*Example 23.5*

Suppose that in Example 23.2 it takes one month for Cranfield's wire orders to be delivered and placed in inventory. Under these circumstances Cranfield simply reorders wire when the current inventory level is equal to one month's usage. The amount used each month is $\frac{1500}{4} = 375$ metres. This is illustrated in Figure 23.2.

*Example 23.6*

Suppose, however, that the wire must be imported, so the lead time is much longer, for example five months. Under certainty, the EOQ model is still appropriate. Referring to Figure 23.2, if a delivery is to arrive at time 4 an order will need to have been placed at time $-1$. However, before this order is delivered, a second order will be placed at time 3, so that the inventory can be replenished at time 8. Similarly, an order will be placed at time 7 for delivery at time 12, and so on. The only difference between this example and the previous one is that there will always be at least one order unfilled. At certain times, for example between times 3 and 4, there will be two orders unfilled.

### 23.6.4 THE EOQ MODEL WITH QUANTITY DISCOUNTS

Where discounts are available on larger quantity orders the supply price of the inventory is relevant to determining the economic order quantity. As the order quantity increases, the inventory holder benefits from the lower price paid for each unit of inventory, and from spreading the other acquisition costs over a

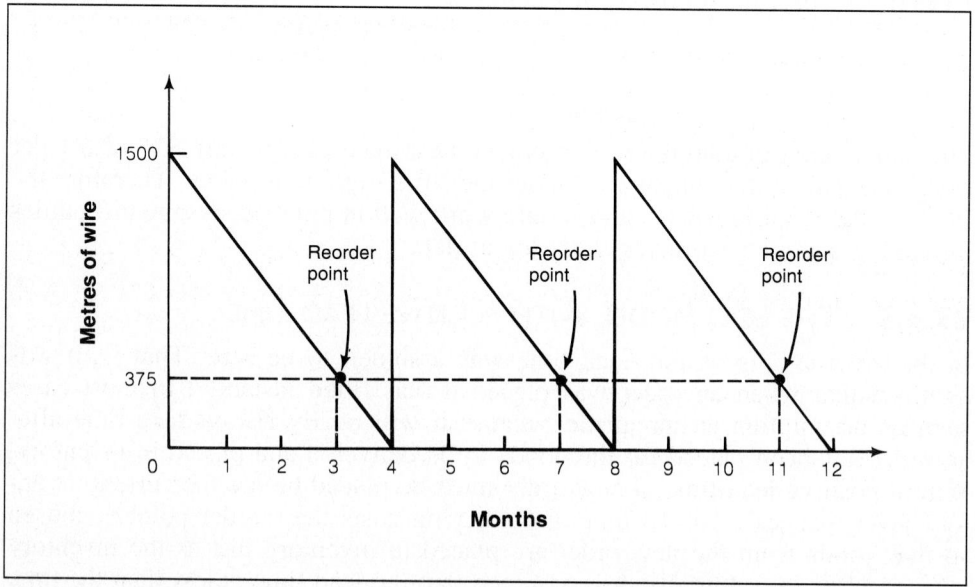

**Fig. 23.2** *Choosing a reorder point*

larger order quantity. However, carrying costs increase as the inventory level increases. The procedures for dealing with quantity discounts are shown in the following example.

### Example 23.7

Consider again the case of Clarke's Photography Store, discussed in Example 23.1. In that example, annual demand $D$ was 12 000 rolls of film; the price $p$ was $3 per roll; acquisition costs $a$ were $12.50 per order; and carrying costs $c$ were $0.30 per roll per year. Suppose, however, that quantity discounts are now available as shown in Table 23.2.

**Table 23.2**

| Purchase quantity, Q | Price per roll, p |
|---|---|
| 1 – 500 | $3.00 |
| 501 – 1 499 | $2.98 |
| 1500 – 2499 | $2.96 |
| 2500 – 4999 | $2.94 |
| 5000 and over | $2.92 |

The annual total cost, TC, to the firm is given by:

$$TC = \text{inventory cost} + \text{acquisition costs} + \text{carrying costs}$$
$$= pD + \frac{aD}{Q} + \frac{cQ}{2}$$
$$= 12\,000p + \frac{150\,000}{Q} + 0.15Q$$

In the absence of quantity discounts, the economic order quantity $Q^*$ was found to be 1000 rolls. It can be shown that with quantity discounts the optimum price–quantity combination must be one of the following combinations:[3]

(1) $p = \$3.00$ and $Q = 500$
(2) $p = \$2.98$ and $Q = 1000$
(3) $p = \$2.96$ and $Q = 1500$
(4) $p = \$2.94$ and $Q = 2500$
(5) $p = \$2.92$ and $Q = 5000$

These combinations are found by the following procedure: First, locate the optimum quantity in the absence of quantity discounts, and the price that would be payable for that quantity if there were quantity discounts. In this case $Q = 1000$ and $p = \$2.98$. This is Combination 2. Next, in each quantity range, select the quantity nearest to the quantity calculated in the first step (in this case 1000). For example, in the quantity range 2500 – 4999, the quantity nearest to 1000 is 2500. The price payable in that case is $2.94 per roll. This is Combination 4. The final step is to calculate the total cost for each of the combinations

---

[3] See B. Goetz, *Quantitative Methods: A Survey and Guide for Managers*, McGraw-Hill, New York, 1965.

of price and quantity, and to select the combination that achieves the lowest total cost. These calculations are as follows:

(1) $(12\,000)(3.00) + \dfrac{150\,000}{500} + (0.15)(500) = \$36\,375$

(2) $(12\,000)(2.98) + \dfrac{150\,000}{1000} + (0.15)(1000) = \$36\,060$

(3) $(12\,000)(2.96) + \dfrac{150\,000}{1500} + (0.15)(1500) = \$35\,845$

(4) $(12\,000)(2.94) + \dfrac{150\,000}{2500} + (0.15)(2500) = \$35\,715$

(5) $(12\,000)(2.92) + \dfrac{150\,000}{5000} + (0.15)(5000) = \$35\,820$

The lowest cost combination is 4, and the economic order quantity is therefore 2500 rolls.

## 23.7 INVENTORY MANAGEMENT UNDER UNCERTAINTY

In Section 23.6, it was assumed that management was perfectly certain about the value of each relevant variable. In particular, it was assumed that retailers and wholesalers knew, with certainty, the level of demand, while manufacturers were assumed to know, with certainty, the rate at which the raw materials inventory would be used in production. Suppose, however, that demand (or usage as the case may be) is uncertain. If the lead time between placement of an order and its delivery is zero, the presence of uncertainty is not a problem. If demand or usage should suddenly increase, management can respond by simply placing an order which is instantly filled and therefore no stockout need occur. However, as explained previously, the lead time for filling orders is usually positive, and therefore stockouts may occur during this time.

Inventory management requires two important decisions. First, management must choose the **quantity** to be ordered. Secondly, management must choose the **reorder point**, that is, the level of inventory that will trigger the placement of a new order. Most of the discussion of inventory decisions under certainty related to the quantity decision. The reorder point decision was simply solved by reordering when the current inventory level would just equal demand (or usage) during the lead time. In Example 23.5, Cranfield's reorder point was 375 metres of wire, because this level was exactly equal to one month's usage, and the lead time was one month. The new order would arrive at Cranfield's factory at precisely the moment when the inventory reached zero. In contrast, when uncertainty is assumed, the quantity decision may be the same as that made under certainty, but the reorder point decision requires a more sophisticated analysis.

A standard approach to inventory management under uncertainty is as follows. First the quantity decision is made by applying the certainty-based EOQ model, using the best estimate of demand (or usage). Secondly, the reorder point decision is made by adding a 'safety stock' to the reorder point which would have been chosen under conditions of certainty. That is, the company deliberately chooses to reorder at a time when the current inventory level exceeds the quantity likely to be required during the lead time. The amount of the excess is called the **safety stock**. For example, if Cranfield is operating under uncertainty, its management may decide on a safety stock of 250 metres of wire. In that case the reorder point is 625 metres instead of 375 metres. An order is placed when 625 metres of wire is still in inventory, even though it is expected that when the new order arrives in one month's time, only 375 metres will have been used so there will still be 250 metres of wire in inventory. Figure 23.3 shows the expected inventory level through time.

The previous discussion illustrates the **notion** of safety stock but does not provide any insight into the factors that **determine its size**. Two approaches to determining safety stock size are discussed. The first approach specifies an acceptable probability of a stockout occurring during the lead time, and the second approach specifies an acceptable expected level of customer service.

Both approaches are explained by using the example of Quintro Electronics Ltd, a wholesale supplier of electronic components. Quintro is open for business for 50 weeks each year. The annual demand for one of Quintro's components is 50 000 units. The lead time for new orders is exactly one week. On a weekly basis, demand is normally distributed with an expected value $E(D)$ of 1000, and a standard deviation $\sigma$ of 250. Acquisition costs are \$200 per order, and carrying costs are 20 cents per component per year. Regardless of the approach taken to calculate safety stock, using Equation 23.2 the economic order quantity $Q^*$ is found to be:

$$Q^* = \sqrt{\frac{(2)(200)(50\ 000)}{0.2}}$$
$$= 10\ 000 \text{ units}$$

The next problem is to determine the reorder point. To what level should inventory be allowed to fall before a new order is placed? Two approaches to answering this question are explained in Sections 23.7.1 and 23.7.2.

### 23.7.1 SPECIFYING AN ACCEPTABLE PROBABILITY OF STOCKOUT

The first approach requires that Quintro's management must determine an acceptable probability of a stockout during the lead time of 1 week. Suppose Quintro's management decides that it is prepared to accept a 2.5 per cent probability of a stockout. The table of areas under the standard normal curve (see Table 5 of Appendix A) shows that there is a 2.5 per cent chance that demand will be more than 1.96 standard deviations above the expected level of demand. The reorder point is therefore:

$$E(D) + 1.96\ \sigma$$
$$= 1000 + (1.96)(250)$$
$$= 1490 \text{ units}$$

The safety stock is therefore 490 units. If a safety stock of 490 units is held, the customers' needs will be less than fully satisfied in 2.5 per cent of all lead times.

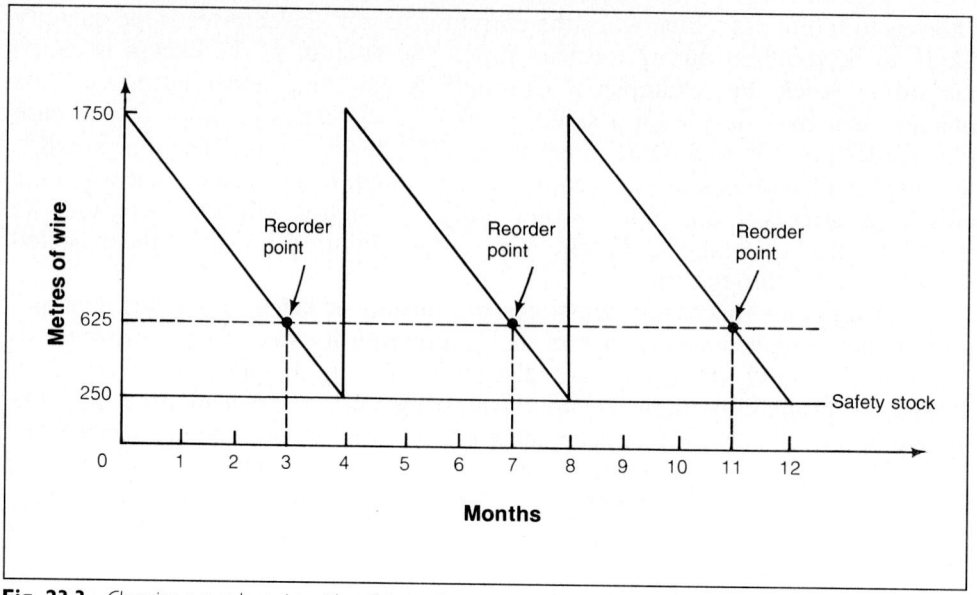

**Fig. 23.3** *Choosing a reorder point with safety stock*

### 23.7.2 SPECIFYING AN ACCEPTABLE EXPECTED CUSTOMER-SERVICE LEVEL

Although the approach based on stockout probability is sometimes recommended in textbooks, it is often unsatisfactory because for most firms it focuses on the wrong measure. Suppose, for example, that during a particular lead time, demand exceeds 1490 units. In this case Quintro cannot meet the demand for electronic components and this is therefore one of those lead times during which a stockout occurs. However, this does not indicate anything about the magnitude of the stockout problem. Knowing that a stockout has occurred does not provide any information on **how many** sales were lost. Given that the cost of a stockout depends directly on the number of lost sales, simply knowing that a stockout has occurred provides very little information about the costs incurred. Likewise knowing the probability of a stockout provides very little information about the likely costs. For example, suppose demand during a particular lead time is 1500 units. In this case only 10 units of sales have been lost, and the stockout cost is quite low.

The same point can be made by referring to the 'customer-service level', which can be quantified by expressing as a percentage the ratio of sales to the level of orders. If the level of demand is 1500 units, the customer service level is $\frac{1490}{1500}$ or 99.33 per cent. This indicates that a high service level, and therefore a low level of stockout costs, has been maintained, notwithstanding the fact that a stockout has occurred. Presumably most companies are more concerned about the impact of a stockout on the customer-service level than they are about the probability of a stockout. This suggests that inventory policy should be based on an expected (target) level of customer service, rather than on a target level of stockout probability. For example, Quintro might specify that its target customer-service level should be 97.5 per cent. In other words, Quintro may decide on a reorder point that will mean that on average, during the lead time, its customers face a 2.5 per cent chance that their demand will not be met. The procedures needed to calculate the inventory level required for this policy are set out in Example 23.9. First, however, we provide a simpler example which illustrates the principles of the customer-service level approach to inventory management.

*Example 23.8*
Sampson Glues Ltd faces an uncertain demand for its product. During the lead time, demand has the probability distribution shown in Table 23.3:

**Table 23.3**

| Probability | Quantity demanded |
|---|---|
| 0.25 | 120 |
| 0.25 | 140 |
| 0.50 | 150 |

The expected demand is therefore:

$$(0.25)(120) + (0.25)(140) + (0.50)(150)$$
$$= 140$$

Sampson Glues has decided on a reorder point of 140 units. What is the probability of a stockout? What is the expected customer-service level?

Clearly the probability of a stockout is 0.50. On 50 per cent of occasions demand during the lead time will be 150 units, and on these occasions a stockout will occur. By this measure Sampson Glues would appear to be understocked. However, when customer-service level is considered, this inventory policy appears much more sensible. On those occasions when demand turns out to be 120 units all customers are satisfied. The service level on these occasions is therefore 100 per cent. The probability of this occurring is 0.25. Similarly, if demand is 140 units the service level is again 100 per cent. The probability of this occurring is also 0.25. Finally, on those occasions when demand is 150 units the customer-service level is $\frac{140}{150}$ or 93.3 per cent, and the probability of this occurring is 0.50. The expected customer-service level is therefore:

$$(0.25)(100) + (0.25)(100) + (0.50)(93.3)$$
$$= 96.7\%$$

In this case, the expected customer-service level is very high, despite the fact that no safety stock is held. It is therefore incorrect to assume that uncertainty necessarily requires that a safety stock should be held. In fact a negative safety stock can be consistent with a high customer-service level. For example, if Sampson Glues' reorder point is 135 units, the expected service level is:

$$(0.25)(100) + (0.25)\left(\frac{135}{140}\right) + (0.50)\left(\frac{135}{150}\right)$$
$$= 94.1\%$$

In this case, the expected customer-service level is still quite high at 94.1 per cent, notwithstanding that a safety stock of $-5$ units is held.

### Example 23.9

Suppose, as in the earlier discussion of Quintro Electronics Ltd, that expected demand during the lead time is 1000 units and the standard deviation of demand is 250 units. Suppose Quintro's management decides that it will accept, on average, a 97.5 per cent expected customer-service level during the lead time. That is, it is Quintro's policy that there should be a probability of 0.025 that any particular customer's demand during the lead time will not be met. What reorder point should be specified? The procedure to solve this problem is as follows. First, calculate $P(Z)$ which is the **partial expectation** of the normal distribution at fractile Z.

$$P(Z) = (1 - s)\frac{E(D)}{\sigma} \qquad (23.3)$$

where $s$ is the required expected service level.
In this example, $s = 0.975$, $E(D) = 1000$ and $\sigma = 250$.

Therefore $P(Z) = (1 - 0.975)\left(\frac{1000}{250}\right)$
$$= 0.10$$

Tables for $P(Z)$ are available.[4] Referring to such a table, the value of $Z$ corresponding to $P(Z) = 0.10$ is found to be 0.9. The reorder point is therefore set at 0.9 standard deviations above the expected demand. That is, the reorder point is:
$$1000 + (0.9)(250)$$
$$= 1225 \text{ units}$$

This result may be compared with a reorder point of 1490 units, which was the solution calculated in Section 23.7.1 when the stockout probability was set at 2.5 per cent. If a new order is placed when the inventory level falls to 1490 units, there is a 2.5 per cent chance that, at the **end** of the lead time, no inventory will remain. Of course at any point **during** the lead time this probability is much smaller. For example, a customer who arrives just after the start of the lead time is almost guaranteed that his order will be met. However, this is not given any weight in the decision to set the inventory level at 1490 units. Instead the focus is on conditions at the end of the lead time. The expected customer-service level associated with a reorder point of 1490 is 99.76 per cent. This is an extremely high level.

---

[4] See, for example, R. Willis, N. Hastings & R. Snyder, 'A Common Misunderstanding in Stock Control', *Australian Society of Operations Research Bulletin*, May 1983, pp. 8–10. For more detailed tables, see R. G. Brown, *Materials Management Systems: A Modular Library*, John Wiley and Sons, New York, 1977.

In contrast, the customer-service level approach takes account of conditions **throughout** the lead time. With the reorder point set at 0.9 standard deviations above expected demand, the probability of a stockout is 0.1841. Therefore customers who arrive right at the end of the lead time face an 18.41 per cent chance that their orders will not be met. However, customers who arrive right at the start of the lead time face an almost zero per cent chance that their orders will not be met. Overall the average chance during the lead time is 2.5 per cent and the expected customer-service level is therefore 97.5 per cent. In general there is no reason why firms should focus only on the end of the lead time, since customers at that point are neither more nor less valuable than customers at any other time. The expected customer-service level approach is therefore preferred.

## 23.8 INVENTORY MANAGEMENT AND THE 'JUST-IN-TIME' SYSTEM

The 'just-in-time' system is a way of organising the manufacture of goods such as motor vehicles, engines, and power tools. It is based on the concept that raw materials, equipment, and labour are each supplied only in the amounts required, and at the times required, to perform the manufacturing task. Therefore a basic element of the system is the coordination of production processes so that raw materials and components are delivered to the location where they are needed at precisely the times they are required. This synchronisation of delivery with demand reduces inventory levels, lead times, and delivery quantities, compared with a traditional system. For example, items which are bulky, expensive, and obtained from local suppliers, may be delivered once per day or even once per shift.

In industries where both customers and suppliers adopt the just-in-time approach, inventories of raw materials, work in process, and finished goods can be reduced substantially. However, the just-in-time system is not simply an inventory management system. Its adoption will reduce inventory, but that is not its major function; rather, it is a system that focuses on the elimination of waste in all forms, and improvements flow from reducing the need to hold inventories. For example, a machine that forms part of a production line may break down several times per day. The traditional solution might be to hold large inventories or safety stock of this machine's inputs and outputs. This ties up capital, requires storage facilities and occupies floor space. Under the just-in-time system the machine would be redesigned so that it operated more reliably, thereby eliminating the need for safety stocks. The result is an improvement in overall efficiency, as well as a reduction in inventory costs.

While many manufacturing operations may be able to reduce work in process by this approach, complete adoption of the just-in-time system involves radical changes in relationships between manufacturers and suppliers, and in materials handling facilities. For example, the requirements for effective just-in-time operation include reliable quality of supplies and transportation, short distances between suppliers and buyers, and frequent delivery of small quantities of goods. Where these requirements cannot be met, an important role remains for inventory management.

## Selected References

Brown, R. G., *Materials Management Systems: A Modular Library*, John Wiley and Sons, New York, 1977.
Kallberg, J. G. & Parkinson, K. L., *Current Asset Management*, John Wiley and Sons, New York, 1984.
Lubben, R. T., *Just-in-time Manufacturing*, McGraw-Hill, New York, 1988.
Mehta, D., *Working Capital Management*, Prentice-Hall, Englewood Cliffs, New Jersey, 1974.
Snyder, R., 'The Safety Stock Syndrome', *Journal of the Operational Research Society*, September 1980, pp. 833–7.
Waters, C. D. J., *Inventory Control and Management*, John Wiley and Sons, Chichester, 1992.
Willis, R., Hastings, N. & Snyder, R., 'A Common Misunderstanding in Stock Control', *Australian Society of Operations Research Bulletin*, May 1983, pp. 8–10.

## QUESTIONS

1. Explain why the proportion of a company's total assets tied up in inventory varies widely from company to company. Give examples.
2. For a retailer, what are the major benefits and costs of holding inventory? What different benefits and costs apply to the raw materials inventory held by a manufacturer?
3. What is 'safety stock'? Explain how it is possible that safety stock might be negative.
4. The Leichhardt Pharmacy sells 5000 bottles of Vitamin C tablets each year. The clerical and related costs of placing and processing an order amount to $25 and the carrying costs are 16 cents per bottle per year. Calculate the economic order quantity and the time period between placement of orders.
5. Drummond Garden Tools Ltd specialises in the manufacture of lawn rakes. Every six months, Drummond buys 1500 rake handles from Kilmarnock Timber Mills at a cost of $1.50 per handle. The clerical and processing cost is $75 per order, and each handle costs $1.80 per year to store. Calculate Drummond's economic order quantity and the annual cost saving that would be achieved using the EOQ.
6. Each year, Palmer Engineering Ltd produces 500 high-quality jet sprockets used in aircraft engines. A production run costs $3000 to set up, and storage costs are $48 per sprocket per year. Calculate the optimum size of a production run, and the number of runs per year.
7. The Vitamin C tablet manufacturer who supplies the Leichhardt Pharmacy (see Question 4) has begun offering quantity discounts to its customers as follows:

| Quantity ordered | Price per bottle |
|---|---|
| 1–999 | $2.00 |
| 1000–1999 | $1.99 |
| 2000–2999 | $1.98 |
| 3000–3999 | $1.97 |
| 4000– | $1.96 |

Calculate the new economic order quantity.

8. Driscoll Magazines Ltd places orders for new stock every month. The new stock arrives one week after placement of the order. Driscoll has estimated that weekly demand follows the probability distribution below.

| Probability | Quantity demanded |
|---|---|
| 0.060 | 100 |
| 0.150 | 120 |
| 0.160 | 140 |
| 0.166 | 160 |
| 0.144 | 180 |
| 0.020 | 200 |

What reorder point will ensure that there is a 2 per cent chance that a stockout will occur during the lead time? What reorder point will ensure that the expected customer service level during the lead time is 98 per cent?

9. David Sheffield operates a large sports store specialising in cricket equipment. Sheffield buys cricket balls from Wombat Sports Ltd. It takes Wombat one month to process and deliver an order. Sheffield estimates that during the cricket season the monthly demand for cricket balls follows the probability distribution below.

| Probability | Quantity demanded |
|---|---|
| 0.10 | 1600 |
| 0.20 | 1800 |
| 0.50 | 2000 |
| 0.15 | 2200 |
| 0.03 | 2400 |
| 0.02 | 2600 |

What reorder point will ensure that there is only a 5 per cent chance that a stockout will occur during the lead time? What reorder point will ensure that the expected customer service level during the lead time is 95 per cent?

10. JLP Stores Ltd orders inventory with a lead time of one month. The monthly demand faced by JLP is normally distributed, with a mean of 4600 and a standard deviation of 1000. Calculate the safety stock level that will ensure that the probability of a stockout during the lead time is 5 per cent. Calculate the safety stock level that will ensure that the expected customer service level during the lead time is 95 per cent. (Note: $P(0.4) = 0.230$ where $P(Z)$ indicates the partial expectation of $Z$.)

11. Because it is impossible to obtain precise measures of the necessary data, theoretical inventory management models are virtually useless. Comment.

12. Using the data on Cranfield Manufacturing Ltd in Example 23.2:
    (a) calculate the total annual cost of the optimal inventory policy;
    (b) demonstrate that any order quantity between 1095 and 2055 metres results in an annual cost within 5% of the minimum. Comment on the implications of this result.

# CHAPTER 24

# LIQUIDITY MANAGEMENT

## 24.1 INTRODUCTION

A company's liquid resources comprise two types of assets: cash and short-term investments. Every company needs to maintain liquidity in order to ensure that its creditors are paid on time. Of course, this objective could easily be met by a company holding a large proportion of its assets in liquid form. However, because cash does not earn interest, and the return on short-term investments is often quite low, such a policy would conflict with the company's ultimate objective of wealth maximisation. In general, therefore, a company will choose to hold a relatively small proportion of its total assets in the form of cash. Table 24.1 shows that, except for the services sector, companies hold a relatively small proportion of their total assets in the form of cash.

## 24.2 OVERVIEW OF LIQUIDITY MANAGEMENT

### 24.2.1 WHAT ARE 'LIQUID' ASSETS?

Liquid assets comprise cash and assets that can be converted into cash in a very short time, and whose cash value can be predicted with a low degree of error. Examples of assets with these features include 'at call' deposits with banks, money market dealers or other financial intermediaries, and various kinds of short-term, marketable securities such as commercial bills and promissory notes. These assets were described in Chapter 8.

### 24.2.2 LIQUIDITY MANAGEMENT AND TREASURY MANAGEMENT

**Liquidity management** refers to the decisions made by the management of a company about the composition and level of the company's liquid resources. In Australia, this typically involves deciding on the mix of liquid assets (such as cash, interest-bearing deposits, and securities) that a company will try to achieve, as well as the level of bank overdraft usage. It is usual for a company in Australia

**Table 24.1** Cash as a percentage of total assets

| Industry sector | 1986 | 1987 | 1988 | 1989 | 1990 | 1991 | 1992 |
|---|---|---|---|---|---|---|---|
| Gold | 9.1 | 9.4 | 3.0 | 5.9 | 5.7 | 7.8 | 8.8 |
| Other metals | 5.6 | 5.3 | 7.5 | 6.0 | 6.5 | 6.0 | 5.9 |
| Solid fuels | 4.5 | 5.4 | 5.7 | 9.3 | 7.7 | 4.3 | 4.6 |
| Oil and gas | 10.8 | 10.7 | 5.7 | 6.0 | 4.0 | 4.9 | 6.3 |
| Diversified resources | 4.4 | 2.9 | 5.5 | 2.9 | 2.7 | 1.9 | 1.5 |
| Developers and contractors | 7.2 | 10.0 | 6.6 | 5.8 | 4.9 | 5.4 | 5.3 |
| Building materials | 4.2 | 5.5 | 6.2 | 4.8 | 4.3 | 3.8 | 4.7 |
| Alcohol and tobacco | 4.4 | 4.0 | 11.6 | 9.9 | 8.0 | 2.5 | 3.0 |
| Food and household | 2.9 | 7.3 | 3.4 | 14.8 | 2.8 | 4.7 | 5.3 |
| Chemicals | 3.6 | 4.8 | 6.0 | 1.4 | 1.6 | 4.3 | 4.1 |
| Engineering | 1.8 | 3.2 | 8.9 | 2.3 | 2.7 | 3.9 | 4.5 |
| Paper and packaging | 4.7 | 3.5 | 0.3 | 4.3 | 3.2 | 5.9 | 6.2 |
| Retail | 2.4 | 2.7 | 2.2 | 1.1 | 1.2 | 1.8 | 5.3 |
| Transport | 9.6 | 8.9 | 12.6 | 11.0 | 10.3 | 12.7 | 8.2 |
| Media | 1.5 | 4.1 | 1.1 | 0.8 | 0.7 | 0.9 | 1.6 |
| Entrepreneurial investor | 11.8 | 6.5 | 5.0 | 8.4 | 10.0 | 12.3 | 5.9 |
| Miscellaneous services | 5.1 | 8.4 | 3.4 | 6.7 | 3.4 | 5.7 | 3.7 |
| Miscellaneous industrials | 4.6 | 4.1 | 6.8 | 9.6 | 4.9 | 6.0 | 8.8 |
| Diversified industrials | 2.9 | 4.4 | 8.5 | 10.2 | 8.2 | 10.4 | 8.8 |

*Source:* Stock Exchange Financial and Profitability Study, various years.

to use an overdraft provided by its bank. Under the terms of such an agreement the company is able to overdraw its bank account up to some agreed limit. This means that the company can borrow any amount up to the agreed limit. In short, an overdraft is a form of short-term finance that, in effect, permits a company to have a negative cash balance. Liquidity management also extends to the management of other sources of short-term finance.

**Treasury management** is a wider concept than liquidity management and includes liquidity management as one of its functions. Many companies have established a separate group or department, under the control of the company treasurer, to manage the company's liquidity, and to oversee its exposure to various kinds of financial risk. Foreign exchange provides one example of exposure to risk. If a company exports, imports, borrows foreign currency, or lends foreign currency, there are risks due to the possibility of exchange rate movements. For example, if the Australian dollar depreciates, the company will face a higher cost of imports in Australian dollar terms. The treasurer will advise on *whether* this risk should be hedged and, if so, *how* it is to be hedged. These issues were discussed in Chapter 21. Another facet of the treasury's role in a company is the management of interest rate risk. For example, suppose that a company has borrowed money on a floating interest rate basis and has lent money on a fixed interest rate basis. If the general level of interest rates increases, the company will find itself in difficulty because while the interest cost of its borrowed funds has increased, the interest received on the funds it has lent remains fixed. Similarly, if a company holds a portfolio of fixed interest securities, or if it has plans to buy or sell (issue) fixed interest securities, there is a risk due to the possibility of changing interest rates. Issues of this type were considered in Appendix 4.1, and Chapters 15 and 16.

### 24.2.3 CENTRALISATION OF LIQUIDITY MANAGEMENT

Many companies centralise the liquidity management function, even if many other functions are not centralised. The main reason is that centralisation allows the matching of inflows and outflows for the whole company, with consequent savings. This principle is clearly seen in the following example.

*Example 24.1*

Megacorp Ltd has a manufacturing division and a customer services division. On a particular day the manufacturing division must meet a net cash outflow of $150 000; on the same day, the customer services division receives a net cash inflow of $50 000. If both divisions are operated independently, the manufacturing division will need to borrow $150 000 and the customer services division will be able to invest $50 000. Clearly, it is easier if, instead, the company simply borrows the net requirement of $100 000, and since the borrowing rate will exceed the lending rate, it is cheaper to do so. For example, if the time period involved is seven days and the annual interest rates are 15 per cent per annum (borrowing) and 12 per cent per annum (lending), the net interest costs are:

1. If liquidity management is centralised:

$$\$100\,000 \times 0.15 \times \frac{7}{365}$$
$$= \$287.67$$

2. If liquidity management is not centralised:

$$\$150\,000 \times 0.15 \times \frac{7}{365} - \left(\$50\,000 \times 0.12 \times \frac{7}{365}\right)$$
$$= \$316.44$$

The centralisation of liquidity management also facilitates the development of specialised staff by having them concentrated in one area of the business. Any economies of scale can also be exploited. Of course it should also be borne in mind that there can be diseconomies of scale. For example, the centralisation of liquidity management is likely to be a failure if there is poor communication between the operating divisions and the group responsible for liquidity management.

### 24.2.4 MOTIVES FOR HOLDING LIQUID ASSETS

Studies of the motives for holding liquid assets have a long history in the literature of economics. The conventional classification of motives, often attributed to Keynes, divides the motives into three groups: the 'transactions motive', the 'precautionary motive', and the 'speculative motive'.[1]

---

[1] In fact, Keynes specified four motives that he termed the 'income motive', the 'business motive', the 'precautionary motive', and the 'speculative motive'. The first relates mainly to transactions by individuals and the second to transactions by enterprises; these two are therefore often combined into a single transactions motive. See J. M. Keynes, *The General Theory of Employment Interest and Money*, Harcourt Brace & World, New York, 1936, Ch. 15.

## TRANSACTIONS MOTIVE

Typically, individuals receive regular inflows of cash in the form of wages or salaries, but make payments, in a more or less continuous stream, for consumption purposes. Therefore, liquid assets are held in order to finance transactions undertaken between cash receipts. Businesses also face a continuous outflow of cash but, unlike most individuals, will often receive a continuous inflow of cash, particularly from sales. If these inflows and outflows were perfectly matched in both timing and amount, then no liquid assets would be required. However, perfect synchronisation is virtually impossible to achieve, with the result that some liquid assets must be held for transaction purposes.

## PRECAUTIONARY MOTIVE

Future cash receipts outflows cannot be predicted with perfect certainty. There is, therefore, always the possibility that extra cash will be needed to meet unexpected costs, or to take advantage of unexpected opportunities. Liquid assets are therefore held as a precaution to cover outflows resulting from these unexpected events. However, the precautionary motive will be weaker if a company can arrange a source of finance that can be called upon in time of need. In Australia, bank overdrafts and commercial bill facilities provide this type of finance.

## SPECULATIVE MOTIVE

When interest rates increase, there is a fall in the market value of income-producing assets such as bonds. Keynes hypothesised that when an individual forecasts an increase in interest rates he or she will sell bonds and, instead, hold cash or bank deposits in order to avoid the resulting capital loss. Therefore liquid asset holdings depend in part on expectations of interest rate changes. Keynes termed this the 'speculative motive'. Speculation may be a potent force for companies in the finance sector. For example, a money market dealer may change the size and/or composition of its portfolio, depending on its expectations of market conditions. However, outside the finance sector it is doubtful whether the speculative motive has much part in liquidity management practices.

Therefore, for most companies, transaction-based motives are probably the dominant influences and are the focus of our discussion of liquidity management.[2]

### 24.2.5 MAJOR ISSUES IN LIQUIDITY MANAGEMENT

All companies have cash receipts and need to make cash payments. Because the cash receipts and payments will not generally be matched in time and amount, the company's cash position must be forecast, monitored, and managed. If this is not done the following situations are likely to arise:

---

[2] For models that focus on the other motives, see, for example, M. G. Levasseur, 'An Option Model Approach to Firm Liquidity Management', *Journal of Banking and Finance*, June 1977, pp. 13–28; and G. W. Emery, 'Optimal Liquidity Policy: A Stochastic Process Approach', *Journal of Financial Research*, Fall 1982, pp. 273–84.

1. If the cash payments exceed the cash receipts, the company will need to borrow money to make the payments, or else postpone payment. If it borrows money, it will need to pay interest and, probably, fees. Alternatively, if payment is postponed, the likely result is disruption to its business and/or damage to its financial reputation.
2. If the cash receipts exceed the cash payments, resulting in a large cash balance, the company is failing to make the best use of its resources. The net funds obtained could be invested to earn interest or used to reduce the company's debt.

In short, the major issues in liquidity management are to ensure that the company has adequate liquid resources to make cash payments as the need arises, without holding such a high level of liquid assets that the company's resources are used inefficiently. This balance is achieved by first forecasting the likely patterns of cash receipts and payments, and then adopting an appropriate mix of cash, liquid assets, and short-term borrowing. As events unfold, the cash position is monitored, new forecasts are made, and a new mix adopted. A basic tool in forecasting cash flows is the cash budget. This is outlined in Section 24.3. Formal models of liquidity management are outlined in Sections 24.4 and 24.5.

## 24.3 CASH BUDGETING

A cash budget provides a forecast of the amount and timing of the cash receipts and payments that will result from the company's operations over a period of time. To assist in day-to-day cash management, forecasts of receipts and payments may be made for each day of the coming week. Alternatively, forecasts may be made on a weekly basis for a number of weeks in advance, or for each month of the coming year. A cash budget on a month-by-month basis is usually prepared as part of the overall master budget for the coming year and it is useful as an indication of the company's short-run debt-paying ability. In addition, monthly forecasts should take into account seasonal and other predictable variations in cash flows. Clearly the cash budget is only as useful for decision making as the accuracy of the estimates used in its preparation. A company whose cash flows are subject to a great deal of uncertainty should provide a safety margin in the form of a minimum cash balance, or have ready access to borrowing, or both, to tide it over periods when cash payments exceed cash receipts. The cash budget therefore assists the treasurer in predicting when such excesses of payments over receipts are likely to occur.

The basic structure of a cash budget is very simple. A forecast of cash receipts and payments is made for each time period. Often this will be done by forecasting separately the major components of the cash flows. For example, separate forecasts may be made for payments for wages, materials, and power. In practice, dozens of separate forecasts may be made. Many of these forecasts will, in turn, depend on the forecast level of sales. Cash receipts are obviously related to the sales level, but so also are many cash payments. For example, in a manufacturing company, high sales means high production, which, in turn, means that more raw materials will need to be purchased. In addition, the corporate treasurer may specify that, for safety reasons, a given minimum required cash balance should be built into the budget. The level at which this minimum is set is often determined on an ad hoc basis. Given forecasts of total receipts, total payments and the minimum required balance, the forecast cash shortage (to be borrowed) or cash surplus (to be invested) is simply:

$$\begin{pmatrix} \text{Total} \\ \text{receipts} \end{pmatrix} \text{less} \begin{pmatrix} \text{Total} \\ \text{payments} \end{pmatrix} \text{less} \begin{pmatrix} \text{Minimum} \\ \text{required} \\ \text{balance} \end{pmatrix}$$

### 24.3.1 FORECASTING RECEIPTS

The sales forecast is probably the most important factor affecting the accuracy of the cash budget. An error in the forecast of sales will be reflected in an error in the expected collections from customers. Such an error will also affect budgeted cash payments, as the company's level of operations will usually be adjusted in response to expected changes in the level of sales.

The preparation of a sales forecast usually involves the following steps. First, a thorough analysis of past sales performance is made for each product. Any relationship or trend observed can then be taken into account in making the sales forecast. For example, a seasonal pattern of sales may be observed and then built into the forecast. Secondly, some factors external to the company will have an important effect on the sales forecast. For example, the forecasters will probably be provided with projections of likely business and economic conditions that should be taken into account.

After the sales forecast has been made, the next step is to estimate the cash receipts from sales. Cash sales present no problem because the cash is received immediately. However, credit sales require estimation of the timing of cash receipts. This will be influenced by the company's credit terms, the type of customer, and the general credit and collection policies of the company.[3] Experience will usually indicate the proportion of total sales that are cash sales; the remainder will be credit sales. The rate of collection may be estimated from an analysis of past records, taking into account any special factors.

### 24.3.2 FORECASTING PAYMENTS

In the case of a manufacturing company, after the sales forecast has been prepared, a production schedule consistent with this forecast is established for each product.[4] On the basis of the production schedule, management can estimate the

---

[3] The management of accounts receivable is discussed in Chapter 25.
[4] A company's management may either allow production to follow sales closely, or produce at a relatively constant rate. Where the former strategy is employed, inventory carrying costs are generally lower, but production costs are higher than where the latter strategy is employed. If sales fluctuate, then with constant production, finished goods inventories build up during certain months and will have to be stored. Because storage is uneven throughout the year, inventory carrying costs are generally greater than they would be if production closely followed sales. On the other hand, where production is at a relatively constant rate, it is generally more efficient. The strategy to be employed will depend on a cost–benefit analysis of the alternatives.

expected payments for materials and labour. A company will also incur overheads, which include supplies, insurance, light and power, and repairs and maintenance. In some cases the goods and services may be obtained on credit and therefore there will be a lag between the date of purchase and the date of the cash payment. For example, if suppliers of materials sell on 30 days' credit, and do not post invoices until the end of the month of purchase, the purchaser may have a period of up to two months between the date of purchase and the date of cash payment. Other regular cash payments may include administrative expenses, marketing expenses, and interest payments. Payments that typically are made less frequently, but are nevertheless relatively predictable, include income tax payments, capital expenditures, and dividend payments.

The preparation of a simple cash budget is illustrated in Example 24.2.

*Example 24.2*

Lancaster Manufacturing Ltd has forecast its monthly sales for the next 6 months as shown in Table 24.2:

**Table 24.2** *Monthly sales forecast*

| Month | Sales ($'000) |
|---|---|
| January | 1600 |
| February | 1750 |
| March | 1750 |
| April | 1800 |
| May | 1900 |
| June | 1900 |

It is expected that in each month, 20 per cent of sales will be cash sales and 80 per cent of sales will be credit sales. It is forecast that the collection pattern for credit sales will be as follows:

5 per cent in the month of sale;
80 per cent in the month following sale;
10 per cent in the second month following sale;
2.5 per cent in the third month following sale; and
2.5 per cent uncollectable (bad debts).

Management can then use this information to forecast cash collections (receipts) from Lancaster's customers in April, May and June.

The first step is to divide total sales into cash sales (20 per cent) and credit sales (80 per cent) as shown in Table 24.3:

**Table 24.3** Cash sales and credit sales

| Month | Total sales ($'000) | Cash sales ($'000) | Credit sales ($'000) |
|---|---|---|---|
| January | 1600 | 320 | 1280 |
| February | 1750 | 350 | 1400 |
| March | 1750 | 350 | 1400 |
| April | 1800 | 360 | 1440 |
| May | 1900 | 380 | 1520 |
| June | 1900 | 380 | 1520 |

Credit sales then generate cash receipts according to the pattern of collections, as shown in Table 24.4.

**Table 24.4** Cash receipts

| | Are collected as cash receipts ($'000) in: | | | | | |
|---|---|---|---|---|---|---|
| Credit sales made in: | Jan | Feb | Mar | April | May | June |
| Jan (1280) | 64 | 1024 | 128 | 32 | | |
| Feb (1400) | | 70 | 1120 | 140 | 35 | |
| Mar (1400) | | | 70 | 1120 | 140 | 35 |
| Apr (1440) | | | | 72 | 1152 | 144 |
| May (1520) | | | | | 76 | 1216 |
| Jun (1520) | | | | | | 76 |
| Credit sales collected | | | | 1364 | 1403 | 1471 |
| Cash sales | 320 | 350 | 350 | 360 | 380 | 380 |
| Cash receipts ($'000) | | | | 1724 | 1783 | 1851 |

The cash flows for January, February and March are incomplete because not enough information has been provided. For example, January will see a cash receipt from the credit sales made in December. Presumably, Lancaster will already have actual (rather than forecast) figures for December's credit sales, and for the cash already collected from these sales. These figures would then be used in forecasting the collections for January and subsequent months. In practice, Lancaster Manufacturing would then have to forecast other cash receipts, as well as cash payments and the minimum required cash balance to complete its cash budget. The resulting forecasts for the June quarter might be those shown in Table 24.5.

**Table 24.5** *Lancaster Manufacturing Ltd—Forecast cash receipts and payments for June quarter, by month*

|  | April $'000 | May $'000 | June $'000 |
|---|---|---|---|
| Cash balance at beginning of month | 740 | 565 | 547 |
| *Add* Cash receipts | | | |
|    Collections from customers | 1724 | 1783 | 1851 |
|    Dividends on investments in other companies | — | 310 | — |
|    Sale of equipment | 300 | — | — |
|    Other | 50 | 50 | 140 |
| Total cash receipts | 2074 | 2113 | 1991 |
| Total cash available | 2814 | 2113 | 2538 |
| *Less* Cash payments | | | |
|    Payments to creditors | 1400 | 1600 | 1300 |
|    Wages and salaries | 500 | 525 | 510 |
|    Dividends | — | — | 500 |
|    Income tax | — | — | — |
|    Purchase of land | 300 | — | — |
|    Other | 50 | 25 | 30 |
| Total cash payments | 2250 | 2150 | 2340 |
| Cash balance at end of month | 564 | 547 | 198 |
| Required minimum cash balance | 300 | 300 | 300 |
| Cash available for investment (or required) | 264 | 247 | (102) |

Finally, actual results should be compared with forecast results on an ongoing basis. Factors influencing the cash position of the company that were not foreseen when the cash forecast was prepared may be disclosed by the comparisons. For example, customers may not be paying their accounts as promptly as was expected and, as a result, cash receipts may be less than forecast. In the event of large deviations from the cash budget, the budget should be revised immediately. Comparisons between the budgeted and actual figures may also indicate ways in which the forecasting procedure can be improved.

## 24.4 CASH MANAGEMENT MODELS ASSUMING CERTAINTY

To facilitate the management of cash, a number of models have been developed. One of the most influential of these has been Baumol's model of cash management which treats a company's cash holding as a type of inventory.[5] Accordingly, the problem of cash management is analogous to determining an inventory level that balances the costs and benefits of holding inventory. Baumol assumes that

---

[5] W. J. Baumol, 'The Transactions Demand for Cash: An Inventory Theoretic Approach', *Quarterly Journal of Economics*, November 1952, pp. 545–56.

a company receives a cash receipt of a known amount at regular intervals, but must finance a steady flow of cash payments between each receipt. On receipt of an inflow, the company retains a proportion in the form of cash, and invests the remainder in interest-bearing liquid assets. When this initial cash holding is exhausted by the stream of cash payments, the company withdraws some of its interest-bearing liquid assets and converts them to cash.[6] When, in turn, this cash holding is exhausted, a further withdrawal is made. This process is repeated until the company's holdings of cash and interest-bearing liquid assets reach zero, at which time a new cash receipt is due to be received. The cycle is then repeated indefinitely. Baumol's model also assumes that each act of investment and subsequent withdrawal generates transaction costs which consist of a fixed and a variable component. In addition, cash holdings incur an opportunity cost in the form of interest foregone. Given these assumptions, Baumol's model provides a means for calculating the optimum division of each cash receipt into cash balances and interest-bearing liquid assets, as well as the optimum amount for each subsequent withdrawal. A numerical example of the situation envisaged by Baumol's model is described in Example 24.3.

## Example 24.3

Suppose that a company receives a cash receipt of $20 000 every 8 weeks. Its current cash-management practices have been determined without the benefit of Baumol's model, and consist of the following. Of each $20 000 inflow, $15 000 is retained in cash, and the remaining $5000 is invested in interest-bearing liquid assets. The company then spends cash steadily until its cash balance is zero. Since it will take 8 weeks to spend the $20 000, it will take $\left(\frac{\$15\ 000}{\$20\ 000}\right) \times 8 = 6$ weeks to spend the $15 000. After the 6 weeks have passed, it withdraws $1000 from its investments, in order to replenish its cash balance. When the cash balance again reaches zero, it withdraws a further $1000. This process is continued until the 8-week period is over. At this time the original fund of $20 000 is exhausted and a new inflow of $20 000 is received. The whole process is then repeated. Each investment and withdrawal entails a fixed cost of $8 and a variable cost of $0.002 per dollar invested (or withdrawn, as the case may be). The interest rate is 2 per cent per 8-week period. The treasury group wishes to calculate the total cost of the present cash management policy so that it may be compared with the total cost of an alternative policy. The total cost of the present policy can be calculated as follows.

### I  INITIAL INVESTMENT

The transaction cost of the initial investment is $8 + (0.002 \times \$5000) = \$18$. The initial cash balance is $15 000. Over the next 6 weeks this balance declines steadily until it reaches zero, so the average cash balance in this period is

---

[6] Note the use of the term 'withdraws'. For example, a company may have funds deposited 'at call' with a money-market dealer or a bank. It will withdraw these funds when cash is required. Alternatively, a company may invest in short-term assets, in which case these assets will be sold (rather than withdrawn) when cash is required. The model applies to both situations.

$\dfrac{\$15\,000}{2} = \$7500$. Using simple interest, the interest rate for the 6-week period is $0.02 \times \dfrac{6}{8} = 0.015$. Therefore, interest foregone by holding cash in this period is $\$7500 \times 0.015 = \$112.50$. The total cost of the initial investment is therefore $\$18.00 + \$112.50 = \$130.50$.

## 2 SUBSEQUENT WITHDRAWALS

There are five subsequent withdrawals, each of $1000. The transaction cost of each withdrawal is therefore $\$8 + (0.002 \times \$1000) = \$10$. The total transaction costs for the five withdrawals amount to $50. The average cash balance during the 2-week period when these withdrawals are being spent is $\dfrac{\$1000}{2} = \$500$. The interest rate for a 2-week period is $0.02 \times \dfrac{2}{8} = 0.005$. The interest foregone is $\$500 \times 0.005 = \$2.50$. The total cost during this period is therefore $\$50.00 + \$2.50 = \$52.50$.

## 3 TOTAL COST

During the 8-week period, the total cost is therefore $\$130.50 + \$52.50 = \$183$.

Given the interest rate and the transaction costs involved, the treasury group needs to consider whether a lower total cost could be achieved by some other choice of initial cash balance, initial investment level, and the amount of each subsequent withdrawal.

Baumol's model is used to answer this question. To derive Baumol's solution it is necessary to reformulate the problem using algebra, and then to use calculus to minimise the resulting expression for total cost. The notation is set out here and to assist the reader, the value of each variable in Example 24.3 is given in brackets.

Let $T$ = the initial total transaction balance ($20 000)
$\quad\ \ I$ = the amount of the initial investment ($5000)
$\quad\ C = T - I$ = the amount of the initial transaction balance held in the form of cash ($15 000)
$\quad W$ = the amount of each subsequent withdrawal ($1000)
$\quad\ \ a$ = the fixed cost of an investment or withdrawal ($8)
$\quad\ \ b$ = the variable cost per dollar of an investment or withdrawal ($0.002)
$\quad\ \ i$ = the interest rate (0.02)

Total cost comprises the following items:

### 1 INITIAL INVESTMENT

Transaction costs equal $a + bI$. The initial transaction balance of $C$ (equals $T - I$) will reach zero after the fraction $\dfrac{T - I}{T}$ of the total period has elapsed.

The average balance during this period is $\frac{T-I}{2}$ and the interest rate is $i$. Therefore, interest foregone is $\left(\frac{T-I}{2}\right)(i)\left(\frac{T-I}{T}\right)$. The total cost of the initial investment is, therefore:

$$a + bI + \left(\frac{T-I}{2}\right)(i)\left(\frac{T-I}{T}\right)$$

## 2 SUBSEQUENT WITHDRAWALS

There are $\frac{I}{W}$ withdrawals, each of $W$ dollars. The transaction cost of each withdrawal is $a + bW$, so the total transaction costs of the withdrawals amount to $(a + bW)\left(\frac{I}{W}\right)$. The average cash balance is $\frac{W}{2}$, the interest rate is $i$ and the fraction of the total time period represented by the expenditure of the initial investment is $\frac{I}{T}$. Therefore, the interest foregone is $\left(\frac{W}{2}\right)(i)\left(\frac{I}{T}\right)$.

The total cost of the subsequent withdrawals is therefore:

$$\left(a + bW\right)\left(\frac{I}{W}\right) + \left(\frac{W}{2}\right)(i)\left(\frac{I}{T}\right)$$

**Total cost** $Z$ is the sum of the costs during the two sub-periods. That is:

$$Z = a + bI + \left(\frac{T-I}{2}\right)(i)\left(\frac{T-I}{T}\right) +$$

$$(a + bW)\left(\frac{I}{W}\right) + \left(\frac{W}{2}\right)(i)\left(\frac{I}{T}\right) \quad (24.1)$$

The problem facing the company is to choose $I$ and $W$ so as to minimise $Z$. One first-order condition is:

$$\frac{\partial Z}{\partial I} = b - \frac{i}{T}(T - I) + \frac{a}{W} + b + \frac{Wi}{2T} = 0$$

This implies that:

$$T - I + \frac{2bT}{i} + \frac{aT}{Wi} + \frac{W}{2} = 0 \quad (24.2)$$

The other first-order condition is:

$$\frac{\partial Z}{\partial W} = -\frac{aI}{W^2} + \frac{Ii}{2T} = 0$$

This implies that:

$$\frac{a}{W^2} = \frac{i}{2T}$$

and, therefore, the optimum amount, $W^*$, of each withdrawal is:

$$W^* = \sqrt{\frac{2aT}{i}} \qquad (24.3)$$

Substituting Equation 24.3 in Equation 24.2 gives:

$$T - I = \frac{2bT}{i} + \frac{aT}{i\sqrt{\frac{2aT}{i}}} + \frac{1}{2}\sqrt{\frac{2aT}{i}}$$

$$= \frac{2bT}{i} + \frac{aT + \frac{1}{2}i\,(2aT/i)}{i\sqrt{2aT/i}}$$

$$= \frac{2bT}{i} + \frac{2aT}{\sqrt{i}\sqrt{2aT}}$$

$$= \frac{2bT}{i} + \sqrt{\frac{2aT}{i}}$$

and therefore the optimum amount $I^*$ of the initial investment is:

$$I^* = T - \frac{2bT}{i} - \sqrt{\frac{2aT}{i}} \qquad (24.4)$$

Returning to Example 24.3, the optimum values may be found. Using Equation 24.3, the optimum amount of each withdrawal is:

$$W^* = \sqrt{\frac{2aT}{i}}$$

$$= \sqrt{\frac{2 \times \$8 \times \$20\,000}{0.02}}$$

$$= \$4000$$

Using Equation 24.4, the optimum amount of the initial investment is:

$$I^* = T - \frac{2bT}{i} - \sqrt{\frac{2aT}{i}}$$

$$= \$20\,000 - \frac{2 \times 0.002 \times \$20\,000}{0.02} - \sqrt{\frac{2 \times \$8 \times \$20\,000}{0.02}}$$

$$= \$20\,000 - \$4000 - \$4000$$

$$= \$12\,000$$

This indicates that the company's initial investment should be $12 000 instead of $5000 and that it should make three subsequent withdrawals of $4000 each, instead of five withdrawals of $1000 each. The initial cash balance $C$ equals $20 000 − $12 000 = $8000. Using Equation 24.1, the total cost of this policy is:

$$Z = \$8 + (0.002)(\$12\,000) + \left(\frac{\$8000}{2}\right)(0.02)\left(\frac{\$8000}{\$20\,000}\right)$$

$$+ \left[\$8 + (0.002)(\$4000)\right]\left(\frac{\$12\,000}{\$4000}\right) + \left(\frac{\$4000}{2}\right)(0.02)\left(\frac{\$12\,000}{\$20\,000}\right)$$

$$= \$8 + \$24 + \$32 + \$48 + \$24$$

$$= \$136$$

The company's current policy costs $183. Therefore the implementation of the optimal policy will achieve a cost reduction of $47, or approximately 26 per cent.

For many purposes a simplified version of Baumol's model is sufficient. One simplification is to assume that the dollar cost of making an investment or withdrawal is fixed at an amount $a$, and has no variable component. In other words it is assumed that $b = 0$. In this case the amount of each withdrawal is unaffected and is still given by Equation 24.3. However, substituting $b = 0$ in Equation 24.4 gives:

$$I^* = T - \sqrt{\frac{2aT}{i}}$$

$$= T - W^*$$

and therefore:

$$C^* = T - I^* = W^*$$

Expressed in words, this says that the optimum initial cash balance $C^*$ is $W^*$. Therefore if $b = 0$, the initial amount held in cash is $W^*$, and each later withdrawal is also of an amount $W^*$. The first period is the same as subsequent periods.

Therefore, using Baumol's model, cash management involves minimising the cost of holding an inventory of cash. The model is deficient in a number of respects, including the following. First, under Baumol's assumptions the company is unable to have a negative cash balance. However, as explained in Section 24.2.2, many companies in Australia have overdrafts, and this in effect means that they can have a negative cash balance. Baumol's model has been extended to cover this possibility by Sastry[7] and McHugh.[8] Secondly, Baumol's model assumes that the pattern of future cash flows is known with certainty. This is a serious shortcoming. Two models that assume uncertainty are considered in the next section.

---

[7] Rama A. S. Sastry, 'The Effects of Credit on Transactions Demand for Cash', *Journal of Finance*, September 1970, pp. 777–81.
[8] A. McHugh, 'Cash Management Using Inventory Models', *Accounting Education*, November 1976, pp. 56–70.

## 24.5 CASH MANAGEMENT MODELS ASSUMING UNCERTAINTY

### 24.5.1 MILLER AND ORR MODEL[9]

Miller and Orr assume that, if left unmanaged, the company's cash balance would follow a random walk with zero drift. What does this assumption mean? Suppose that a company has numerous sources of cash receipts and cash payments, but no single source is very significant, relative to the total cash flow. However, over a very long period of time, total cash receipts are expected to equal total cash payments. This assumption implies that, over any given time period (such as a day), the most likely result is that the cash receipts and payments will exactly offset each other, with the result that the cash balance is left unchanged. Although this is the most likely result, it will probably still be quite rare. Usually, the cash receipts and payments will not balance perfectly and hence some small increase or decrease will result. However, an increase is just as likely as a decrease, so it is still true that today's cash balance is the best prediction of tomorrow's cash balance.[10]

Of course, the company's cash balance cannot be allowed to wander freely for an indefinite length of time. If it did, the company's cash balance would, sooner or later, impose heavy costs on the company by becoming either very high or very low. The Miller and Orr model proposes that management should intervene in the process by withdrawing cash if the balance becomes too high, and by injecting cash if the balance becomes too low. Miller and Orr also assume that the company has a target cash balance. When management intervenes in the process, it restores the company's cash balance to the target level. The company's cash balance is then again allowed to wander freely until the next occasion on which it becomes either too high or too low.

Therefore, the problem of cash management is reduced to determining values for the upper limit $U$, the lower limit $L$, and the target level $T$. The Miller and Orr model does not actually determine the lower limit; rather, given some exogenously determined value for $L$, it then determines the values of $U$ and $T$ in terms of $L$. For example, if a company is unable to obtain an overdraft, then $L$ may be set at zero.[11] In this case, the model determines the following optimum values:

$$L^* = 0 \qquad (24.5)$$

---

[9] M. H. Miller & D. Orr, 'A Model of the Demand for Money by Firms', *Quarterly Journal of Economics*, August 1966, pp. 413–35.

[10] In this respect, the Miller & Orr assumption is as extreme as Baumol's assumption, but in the opposite direction. Whereas Baumol assumed perfect certainty (and therefore perfect predictability), Miller & Orr assume that not even the direction of change can be predicted. For an attempt to steer a middle course, see B. K. Stone, 'The Use of Forecasts and Smoothing in Control-limit Models for Cash Management', *Financial Management*, Spring 1972, pp. 72–84.

[11] However, in practice, $L$ would need to be set at above zero in order to reduce the probability of the cash balance becoming negative before management became aware of this fact.

$$T^* = \sqrt[3]{\frac{3a\sigma^2}{4i}} \text{ above } L^* \qquad (24.6)$$

$$U^* = 3\sqrt[3]{\frac{3a\sigma^2}{4i}} = 3T^* \text{ above } L^* \qquad (24.7)$$

where $a$ = the fixed cost of each intervention (that is, of each withdrawal or injection)
$\sigma^2$ = the variance of the daily changes in cash balance;
$i$ = the daily rate of return foregone, (that is, the company's marginal yield on its investments).

Therefore, according to the model, the upper limit should be set at three times the target level which, in turn, depends on the fixed cost, the variance and the interest rate. This is illustrated in Figure 24.1.

At point A, cash holdings have reached the upper limit $U^*$ so management intervenes by withdrawing $U^* - T^*$ dollars to return the cash balance to the target level $T^*$. At point B, the cash balance has reached the lower limit of zero, and management intervenes by injecting $T^*$ dollars to return the cash balance to the target level $T^*$.

### Example 24.4

Nui Ltd has no overdraft and therefore sets the lower cash limit at zero. Nui's treasurer estimates that the standard deviation of the company's daily change in cash balance is $20 000, the fixed cost of each withdrawal and injection of cash is $10, and the daily marginal yield on the company's investments is 0.0005. What is the optimum target level and the upper limit?

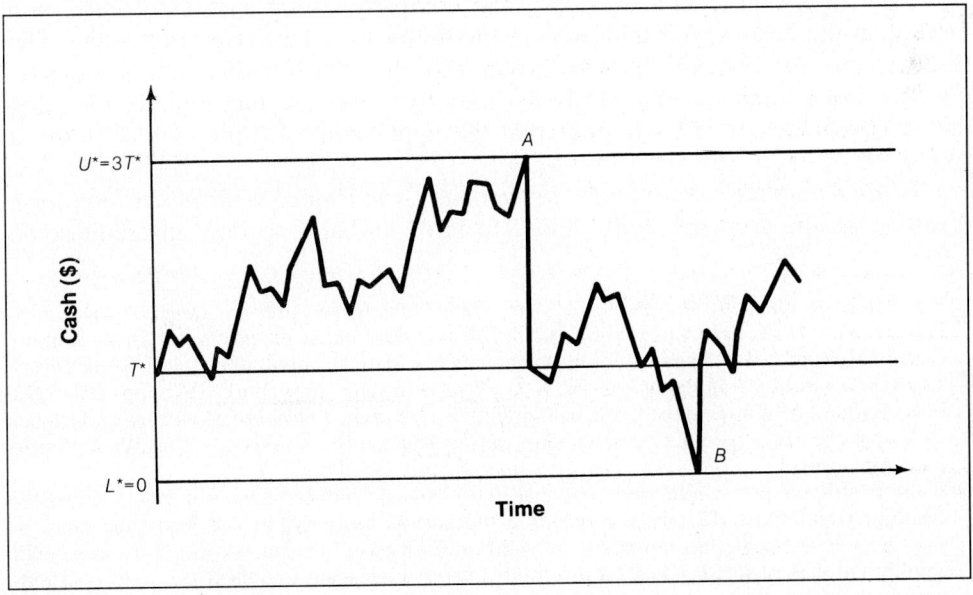

Fig. 24.1

In this example, $L = 0$, $\sigma = 20\,000$, $a = 10$, and $i = 0.0005$. Using Equation 24.6, the optimum target level is:

$$T^* = \sqrt[3]{\frac{3 \times 10 \times (20\,000)^2}{4 \times 0.005}} \text{ above zero}$$

$$= \$18\,171$$

Using Equation 24.7, the optimum upper limit is therefore:

$$U^* = 3T^* = \$54\,513$$

The Miller and Orr model has been found to result in cost savings when it has been tested against the cash-management practices of companies.[12] However, from an Australian viewpoint it has the defect that it does not allow for the use of overdrafts. As noted earlier, overdrafts play an important role in the cash-management policies of many Australian companies.

### 24.5.2 Miller and Orr Model with Overdrafts

Wright has adjusted the Miller and Orr model to incorporate the availability of overdrafts.[13] At the outset it is important to distinguish between cases where the company's marginal yield on its long-term investments exceeds the overdraft interest rate and cases where the opposite is true.

If *the company's marginal yield on its long-term investments exceeds the overdraft rate* (which, in turn, will nearly always exceed the yield on short-term investments),[14] then the company's optimum policy will be never to allow its bank account to be in credit. That is, the company should meet all its liquidity needs through the use of its overdraft. At the margin, a dollar invested in short-term assets will earn less than the costs saved by applying that dollar to reduce overdraft usage. Therefore, the company invests nothing in short-term assets. However, the same dollar invested in the company's long-term assets will earn more than the costs saved by applying the dollar to reduce overdraft usage. The result is that the company invests nothing in short-term assets and as much as possible in long-term assets, while its liquidity needs are met entirely by using the overdraft facility. This implies that the upper control limit should be set at zero.

If *the overdraft rate exceeds the company's marginal yield on its long-term investments*, the company will choose to have its bank account in credit some

---

[12] For details on two case studies, see D. Orr, *Cash Management and the Demand for Money*, Praeger, New York, 1970, pp. 158–67. For a critical review and an extension, see D. W. Mullins & R. B. V. Homonoff, 'Applications of Inventory Cash Management Models', in *Modern Developments in Financial Management*, Ed. S. C. Myers, Praeger, New York, 1976, pp. 494–527.

[13] F. K. Wright, 'Minimizing the Costs of Liquidity', *Australian Journal of Management*, October 1978, pp. 203–24. A simplified discussion can be found in F. K. Wright, 'Can We Optimize Cash Management?', *The Australian Accountant*, April 1980, pp. 157–65.

[14] If the overdraft interest rate were less than the yield on short-term investments, a profitable arbitrage would exist. That is, a company could borrow on overdraft and invest the funds in short-term investments. By doing so, the yield on short-term investments would decrease until equilibrium was restored, when the overdraft interest rate again exceeded the yield on short-term investments.

of the time. When the account is in credit the company suffers the opportunity cost of not having this amount invested in short-term assets. However, unlike the previous case, there is not the same incentive to invest in the company's long-term assets because the company's yield is less than the overdraft rate. This indicates that the target level for the cash balance should be set at zero.

Of these two cases the former is the more important, since virtually all companies would aim to earn at a higher rate than the overdraft interest rate. If a company's rate of return persistently failed to match the overdraft interest rate, it could almost certainly reduce its risk, and at least maintain its rate of return by discontinuing its activities and investing the proceeds in risk-free bonds. It is therefore assumed that the company's marginal yield exceeds the overdraft interest rate. In the earlier discussion of the Miller and Orr model, the lower control limit was exogenously set at zero and the upper limit was found to be three times the target level. However, in the present case it is the upper limit which has been exogenously determined at zero. Wright has shown that the optimum solution in this case is:[15]

$$U^* = 0 \qquad (24.8)$$

$$T^* = \sqrt[3]{\frac{3 \, a' \, \sigma^2}{4 \, (i - d)}} \text{ above } L^* \qquad (24.9)$$

$$L^* = 3\sqrt[3]{\frac{3a' \, \sigma^2}{4 \, (i - d)}} = 3T^* \text{ below } U^* \qquad (24.10)$$

where  $U^*$ = the upper control limit
$T^*$ = the target level
$L^*$ = the lower control limit
$a'$ = the fixed cost of each intervention (that is, of each act of investment or disinvestment in long-term assets)
$\sigma^2$ = the variance of the daily changes in its cash balance (that is, overdraft)
$i$ = the company's daily marginal yield
$d$ = the daily overdraft rate

The application of this model is shown in Example 24.5.

### Example 24.5

Assume that the standard deviation of the daily change in a company's cash balance is $20 000, the daily marginal yield on its investments is 0.0005, the fixed cost per transaction in long-term assets is $800, and the daily overdraft rate is 0.0004. Using Equation 24.9, the target level will be $T^*$ dollars above the lower limit, where:

---

[15] An unused limit fee $u$ may also be incorporated into the model. In Equations 24.9 and 24.10, the term $(i - d)$ is replaced by $(i - d + u)$. See Wright, *Australian Journal of Management*, (Footnote 13).

$$T^* = \sqrt[3]{\frac{3a'\,\sigma^2}{4(i-d)}}$$

$$= \sqrt[3]{\frac{3 \times \$800 \times (\$20\,000)^2}{4(0.0005 - 0.0004)}}$$

$$= \$133\,886.57$$

Using Equation 24.10, the lower limit will be $L^*$ dollars below the upper limit (of zero) where:

$$L^* = 3T^*$$
$$= 3 \times \$133\,886.57$$
$$= \$401\,659.71$$

Rounding these numbers to convenient figures, the lower limit is set at an overdraft limit of $400 000 and the target level is set at $134 000 above this level. That is, the target level is an account which is $266 000 overdrawn. As noted previously, the upper limit is set at zero.

The major advantage of models of the Miller and Orr variety is the explicit recognition of uncertainty. Models based on certainty may well capture important elements of cash-management decisions, but the omission of uncertainty is clearly a major drawback. This, of course, does not imply that the Miller and Orr model is free of deficiencies. These include:

1. The basic model does not recognise the possibility of borrowing. However, the discussion of overdrafts shows that this deficiency can be remedied.
2. It is assumed in the models presented that action can be taken as soon as the control limit is reached. In practice this is most unlikely. For example, suppose that a company adopts a lower control limit of $400 000 overdraft and its balance at the close of business on a particular day is $399 900 overdrawn. It is quite possible that the next day's net cash flow will be a net outflow greater than $100 and, as a consequence, the company's overdraft will exceed the agreed limit before management becomes aware of the fact and is able to intervene. To overcome this problem, management will need to include a further safety margin in its decision rules.
3. The model assumes fixed transaction costs, whereas, in practice, many transaction costs are variable. For example, both the bank accounts debits tax and the financial institutions duty vary according to the amount transacted. Similarly, brokerage fees are nearly always related to the amount transacted.
4. The model assumes that the cash balance follows a random walk. The basic model assumes that the random walk exhibits no drift, although Miller and Orr also discuss cases where drift is present.[16] However, even with a drift term the model is likely to understate the ability of management to forecast changes in cash flows. Many cash flows such as the

---

[16] Miller & Orr, see Footnote 9, pp. 427–9.

payment of wages and the regular receipts associated with sales under long-term contracts recur at regular, predictable intervals. However, the model makes no use of these predictable elements.
5. The model assumes that the company can invest in only one type of short-term financial asset. In fact there is a variety of short-term investments available, with different assets offering different risks, terms, and rates of return. In practice, investments must be selected from the range available, and none of the models discussed provides any direct guidance for this decision.

In the remainder of the chapter we discuss the types of short-term investments available in Australia and how a manager may choose to spread investments between them.

## 24.6 THE CHOICE OF SHORT-TERM SECURITIES

The previous discussion has outlined models for determining the amount of cash a company should hold, the amount of credit it should have available, and the level of investment in short-term securities (particularly the policy for converting short-term securities into cash). However, these models are not concerned with the way in which the company can achieve the best possible mix of investments in short-term securities. In this section, we outline the alternative investments available and suggest how a company's portfolio of short-term securities may be determined.

If a company decides to invest a temporarily idle cash balance, it must choose an investment that can be converted easily into cash. Therefore it is essential that the investment either be marketable or mature within a short period of time. At the same time as the treasurer determines the amount of funds available for investment, an estimate must also be made of the length of time for which these funds can be invested. This is important because of the advantages to be gained by selecting investments whose maturity dates match the cash needs of the company. If the funds are available for only a short time, they should be invested in a marketable security or an investment that matures in a suitably short time. However, if the funds are expected to be available for a longer period, the company may benefit from investing in longer-term fixed-period investments. An advantage of such a policy is that the company can usually obtain a higher interest rate on longer-term investments. A further advantage is that the company avoids the higher transaction costs incurred by a policy of continual reinvestment in short-term securities. A problem with a policy of investing in longer-term fixed-period investments arises when the company encounters an unforeseen cash shortage. If the company has investments that are neither marketable nor approaching maturity, the conversion into cash may involve a penalty such as the loss of accrued interest.

There are many types of investments in which a company can invest temporarily idle cash. These investments offer a wide range of risk and return. The treasurer has the opportunity to invest in higher-yielding securities, provided that he is prepared to accept the greater risk of such investments. The greater risk may refer not only to the risk that rates of return may change (*interest rate risk*), but also to the possibility of default (*default risk*) and to the risk associated with the liquidity of the investment (*liquidity risk*). For example, an investment in a call deposit with a merchant bank is uncertain to the extent that the merchant bank may be unable to meet its debt commitments. However, for most merchant banks, most of the time, the probability of default is quite low and therefore the default risk is very small. A risk of greater consequence relates to the liquidity of the investment. The more difficult it is to convert a security into cash, the greater is the liquidity risk of that security. For example, a 3-month fixed deposit with a bank is more risky than a call deposit with the same bank, as the company may unexpectedly need the cash before the 3 months have elapsed. Therefore, the treasurer should take into account interest rate risk, default risk, and liquidity risk when considering the investment of temporarily idle cash.

## 24.7 TYPES OF SHORT-TERM INVESTMENTS

The following discussion does not attempt to compile a complete list of possible investments, but does examine some of the avenues available for investing a company's temporarily idle cash. For each investment we highlight the characteristics that are important to a treasurer who must choose the most appropriate forms of investment, given the company's circumstances. Table 24.6 provides some short-term interest rates and yields.

**Table 24.6** *Examples of short-term interest rates and yields*

| Type of investment | Interest rates and yields (% p.a.) |
|---|---|
| Treasury notes — 71–105 days | 4.65 |
| Government bonds — 3 years | 5.63 |
| Bank term deposits — 3 months | 5.00 |
| Bank certificates of deposit | 3.72 |
| Official call, average rate | 4.75 |
| Unofficial overnight, average rate | 4.75 |
| Commercial bills — 90-day bank bills | 4.77 |
| — 180-day bank bills | 4.77 |
| Cash management trusts — Macquarie Cash Trust | 3.61 |

Source: *Australian Financial Review*, 1 February 1994.

### 24.7.1 PURCHASE OF GOVERNMENT SECURITIES

The most suitable form of government security for short-term investment is Treasury notes. They are issued by the Commonwealth Government, with a term of either 13 or 26 weeks. However, this does not necessarily mean that a company should restrict its investment in Treasury notes to those idle balances which are available only for a minimum of 13 weeks. Treasury notes are marketable and can be readily converted into cash. They are a secure investment and consequently their yield is lower than that offered by many other investments. The Reserve Bank sells Treasury notes through competitive tenders, with the result that the yields always reflect current market conditions.

Government bonds are another form of investment that may be suitable. Although the term of a newly issued government bond is usually measured in years, a company may purchase a previously issued bond, either as the bond approaches maturity, or with the intention of selling it in the future. Again, the treasurer who invests company funds in bonds must consider whether it can hold the bonds for a length of time sufficient to ensure a worthwhile return. The treasurer should be aware that there may be adverse changes in interest rates during the investment period and these changes can cause capital gains or losses on bonds.

## 24.7.2 Deposits of funds with financial institutions

Several types of financial institution accept deposits.[17] The basic terms of the deposit will differ from one kind of institution to another and a treasurer's choice will depend upon:
1. the period that the funds are available for investment;
2. the risk that the company is prepared to accept; and
3. the required rate of return.

### Banks

A company can invest funds in interest-bearing fixed deposits with a bank, or purchase certificates of deposit from a bank. Terms to maturity for fixed deposits and certificates of deposit are negotiable. Certificates of deposit are more liquid than fixed deposits as they are marketable. Funds can also be invested for very short terms; for example, funds may be placed on 24-hour call. The default risk associated with depositing funds with a bank is negligible[18] and consequently the interest rates offered tend to be less than those for most alternative investments.

### Authorised dealers

A company can deposit funds, either at call or for a fixed period of time, with authorised dealers in the short-term money market. However, the majority of the funds invested with the dealers are at call. This form of investment is suitable for a company with cash available for investment for a very limited period of time—frequently, a period as short as 1 day.[19] Funds invested with authorised dealers for a fixed term are usually invested for a period significantly less than 3 months and are usually secured by bank-accepted bills of exchange held by the dealers. As a result, such an investment is virtually risk-free. The interest rates offered on these deposits vary considerably, both between dealers and over

---

[17] These were discussed in Chapter 7.
[18] However, private banks in Australia do not have government guarantees. Nor do all private banks have the same credit rating.
[19] It is common practice for 'call' funds deposited with authorised dealers to be recalled before 11 a.m. for repayment on the same day. Similar investments with other institutions are normally placed at '11 a.m. same-day call', '24-hour call', '7-day call', or as otherwise negotiated between borrower and lender. In practice, 24-hour call means that notice may be given up to the close of business on the previous business day for repayment of funds the following day.

time. The interest rate depends on the immediate liquidity position of the dealer, the amount of funds available in the market, the amount of funds offered for deposit, and the length of time for which funds will be deposited.

**MERCHANT BANKS**[20]

Merchant banks also accept funds at call, usually on an unsecured basis. The interest rate offered on these deposits depends on factors similar to those that influence the interest rates offered by the authorised dealers.

**CASH MANAGEMENT TRUSTS**

Cash management trusts act as intermediaries between small investors and the money markets. Many companies are large enough to enter the money markets directly, but smaller companies may find indirect access via the trusts to be an attractive outlet for funds available for investment for periods as short as a few days.

### 24.7.3 DISCOUNTING OF COMMERCIAL BILLS

The commercial bills market is discussed in Chapter 8. A company can invest its idle cash balances in this market in one of two ways. First, a company can be the original discounter of a commercial bill and, as a result, supply funds to the drawer of the bill. Secondly, a company can 'rediscount' a bill which has previously been discounted by another party. This simply means that the bill is purchased from another investor in the bills market. Such purchases are easily arranged as there is an active market in bills. The marketability of commercial bills is one of the major advantages of this form of investment. There are two distinct types of bills: bank and non-bank. A bank bill is bank-guaranteed, virtually risk free, and marketable. A non-bank bill does not have a bank guarantee and consequently has a greater risk, the extent of which depends on the financial standing of the drawer and acceptor of the bill. As a result, a non-bank bill offers a higher return than a bank bill. If interest rates increase, the investor may sustain a loss if forced to sell (that is, rediscount) a bill before it matures.

## 24.8 PORTFOLIO THEORY AND CASH MANAGEMENT

The cash-management models discussed earlier have, at best, indicated how much cash to hold and how much to invest in short-term securities. However, each model has assumed that there is only one short-term security and consequently the models cannot help a treasurer to decide how much to invest in each of the available short-term securities. In principle, portfolio theory might provide a solution to this problem.[21] By treating cash as the risk-free asset, and estimating the rate of return on each short-term security, the variance of the returns on each

---

20 Many of the larger stockbroking firms offer facilities similar to those offered by merchant banks. For a discussion of the functions common to each, see Chapter 7.
21 For a discussion of the basics of portfolio theory, see Chapter 6.

security, and the covariance of the returns on each security with all other securities, it is possible to determine the optimum balance between cash and an investment in each short-term security for given risk–return preferences.

However, an important disadvantage of the portfolio theory approach is that it assumes that all short-term securities will be held until the end of the planning period. This denies one of the more important options available to the treasurer, namely the ability to convert short-term securities into cash at short notice. In fact the portfolio theory approach assumes that the variance of a portfolio's return is the only type of risk that matters to the portfolio holder. Application of this approach implicitly assumes that liquidity risk is zero. As is evident from the discussion in Section 24.7, liquidity risk is not zero for many short-term securities.

Chen, Jen and Zionts have attempted to develop a portfolio approach that incorporates liquidity risk.[22] By their own admission the implementation of their model is 'much too cumbersome' and 'further research is therefore needed'.[23] However, they examine some of the implications of their analysis for the demand for cash and conclude, among other things, that the demand for cash will increase as the liquidity risk of other assets increases.[24]

From what we have said, it would seem that a company would benefit from holding more than one short-term security in its portfolio, if only because there is an advantage in having different maturity dates. Therefore, the portfolio decision is still one that has to be made and is of some importance, as there are notable differences in the features of the various short-term investments. The treasurer should try to forecast the company's future cash needs so as to determine the period(s) for which idle cash balances can be invested. For example, the treasurer may forecast that some cash may be required in a few days, a further amount in a few weeks, and a still further amount in a few months. An obvious possibility is to invest in three different short-term securities in the determined proportions. The next step is to decide which short-term securities satisfy the firm's liquidity requirements and then to choose between them on the basis of their rate of return and risk.

## 24.9 THE TREASURER AND LIQUIDITY MANAGEMENT

In this chapter we have concentrated on how liquidity can be managed. The task of the treasurer includes the preparation of cash budgets, the determination of the optimum cash balance, the investment of idle cash in short-term investments and the arrangement of credit facilities to see the company through periods of cash shortage.

---

22 A. H. Y. Chen, F. C. Jen & S. Zionts, 'The Joint Determination of Portfolio and Transaction Demands for Money', *Journal of Finance*, March 1974, pp. 175–86. Also see A. H. Y. Chen, E. H. Kim & S. J. Koh, 'Cash Demand, Liquidation Costs and Capital Market Equilibrium under Uncertainty', *Journal of Financial Economics*, 1975, pp. 293–308.
23 Chen, Jen & Zionts, see Footnote 22, p. 185.
24 For a discussion of all their theorems, see Chen, Jen & Zionts, Footnote 22, pp. 181–3.

The demand for liquidity stems from transactions that result in cash receipts and payments which are not synchronised in either timing or amount. One means of reducing the necessary cash balance is to smooth the pattern of cash flows. For example, the company may be able to negotiate credit terms with suppliers so that payment is not required until the goods are sold. Similarly, the dates on which employees' wages are paid could be altered to bring these dates more into line with times when the company has a cash surplus. In fact, there are opportunities for reducing a company's cash requirements wherever the pattern of cash payments can be brought more into line with the pattern of cash receipts. Usually this will require delaying cash payments for as long as possible, in order to bring them closer to the time when the goods and services acquired can be converted into cash receipts through sales.

Acceleration of the flow of cash receipts will also have a desirable effect on liquidity. In this case the aim is to reduce the time that elapses between the date of sale and the date of the cash receipt. These issues fall into the category of 'credit and collection policy' and are discussed in Chapter 25.

## SELECTED REFERENCES

Baumol, W. J., 'The Transactions Demand for Cash: An Inventory Theoretic Approach', *Quarterly Journal of Economics*, November 1952, pp. 545–56.
Beehler, P. J., *Contemporary Cash Management: Principles, Practices, Perspectives*, 2nd edn, John Wiley and Sons, New York, 1983.
Carew, E., *Fast Money 3: The Financial Markets in Australia*, Allen & Unwin, North Sydney, 1991.
Chen, A. H. Y., Jen, F. C. & Zionts, S., 'The Joint Determination of Portfolio and Transaction Demands for Money', *Journal of Finance*, pp. 175–86, March 1974.
Elton, E. J. & Gruber, M. J., 'Cash Management' in Bicksler, J. L. (Ed.), *Handbook of Financial Economics*, North-Holland, Amsterdam, 1979, pp. 205–28.
Eppen, G. D. & Fama, E. F., 'Three-asset Cash Balance and Dynamic Portfolio Problems', *Management Science*, January 1971, pp. 311–19.
Kelly, J. M., *Cash Management*, Franklin Watts, New York, 1986.
Miller, M. H. & Orr, D., 'A Model of the Demand for Money by Firms', *Quarterly Journal of Economics*, August 1966, pp. 413–35.
Orr, D., *Cash Management and the Demand for Money*, Praeger, New York, 1970.
Wright, F. K., 'Minimizing the Costs of Liquidity', *Australian Journal of Management*, October 1978, pp. 203–24.

## QUESTIONS

1. *For most Australian companies, cash is a very small proportion of total assets, and therefore cash management is unimportant.* Discuss.
2. Explain the costs and benefits of holding liquid assets.
3. In late June of each year, Keating Clocks Ltd prepares a cash budget for the next six months. The company has a policy of maintaining a cash balance at the beginning of each month equal to the difference between the estimated cash receipts and payments for the month, plus a safety margin of $4000.

    Actual sales for May and estimated sales for June and for the next seven months are as follows:

| | | | |
|---|---|---|---|
| May | $20 000 | October | $94 000 |
| June | $28 000 | November | $74 000 |
| July | $24 000 | December | $52 000 |
| August | $26 000 | January | $40 000 |
| September | $50 000 | | |

Approximately 25 per cent of the sales are for cash and 75 per cent are on credit. Experience has shown that two-thirds of all credit sales are collected in the month following sale, and the remaining one-third is collected in the second month following sale. No discounts are given.

Keating Clocks follows a policy of basing its purchases on estimated sales. Purchases are equal to 70 per cent of the following month's estimated sales. The policy of the company is to ensure that the goods needed in each month are acquired in the preceding month. Keating's suppliers permit it to take a 2 per cent discount if the goods are paid for within the first ten days of the month following purchase. All goods must be paid for by the end of the month following purchase.

Other payments are expected to be:

| | | | |
|---|---|---|---|
| July | $7400 | October | $11 000 |
| August | $7450 | November | $7800 |
| September | $9100 | December | $7150 |

At the beginning of July, the company is expected to have $8400 in its bank account.

Prepare a monthly cash budget for Keating Clocks Ltd for the six months ended 31 December. Will any outside funds be required? If so, how much?

4. Discuss the relative merits of the cash management models of Baumol and Miller and Orr.
5. Under the terms of a government contract, Frank Supplies Ltd receives a cheque for $100 000 every twenty weeks. These funds are then spent in a steady stream until the next cheque is received. At present, Frank's policy is to hold $20 000 in cash and to deposit the remaining $80 000. Every few weeks, a further $20 000 is withdrawn and spent. The interest rate is 0.4 per cent per week (or 8 per cent per 20-week period using simple interest). Each transaction costs $10, plus 1 per cent of the amount transacted.

   Using Baumol's model, design an alternative cash-management policy and calculate the cost savings that the alternative policy would achieve.
6. Wilson Products Ltd estimates that the standard deviation of its daily change in cash balance is $30 000. The fixed cost of each withdrawal and injection of cash is $10 and the daily marginal yield on its investments is 0.0006. Wilson does not operate on an overdraft.

   Calculate the target level and upper limit for a cash-management approach that uses the Miller–Orr model. What problems do you foresee if this approach is implemented?
7. A company has $1 million in idle funds and it is estimated that these will be available for investment for approximately two months. The treasurer is considering the following investments:
   (a) purchasing Treasury notes;
   (b) purchasing a one-month bank certificate of deposit;
   (c) lodging a fixed deposit with a bank; and
   (d) purchasing commercial bills.

Discuss the advantages and disadvantages of each investment.
8. *Liquidity risk is more important than return risk in the choice between alternative short-term investments.* Discuss.
9. You are the treasurer of a company which has $1 million in idle funds to invest for a period of ninety days. List the available short-term investments and obtain current interest rates from the financial press. Prepare a report and recommended action for consideration by the Board of Directors, pointing out the return(s) and risk(s) involved.

**CHAPTER 25**

# ACCOUNTS RECEIVABLE MANAGEMENT

## 25.1 INTRODUCTION

Many companies sell on credit. That is, instead of a company exchanging its products for cash, it will agree to deliver the products immediately, in return for the customer's promise to pay at a later date. For example, payment may not be required until a period of 30 days has elapsed. During this period the selling company holds an asset 'accounts receivable'. As with any other short-term asset, accounts receivable should be managed efficiently, with the ultimate goal of maximising shareholders' wealth.

The importance of accounts receivable is indicated in Table 25.1 which shows accounts receivable as a percentage of total assets in various industrial sectors.

Table 25.1 shows that in the non-finance industries as a whole, accounts receivable represent about 10 per cent of total assets. Variations between industries are apparent, with mining showing the lowest percentage, and engineering the highest percentage. Clearly, accounts receivable are a significant asset for many companies, and therefore an important investment.

The purpose of this chapter is to identify the variables that can be influenced by the manager responsible for accounts receivable, and to discuss techniques and procedures that may be employed in choosing the optimum values for these variables. Collectively, these decisions are often referred to as the company's **credit and collection policies**. Establishment of a **credit policy** involves four elements:

1. Is the company prepared to offer credit?
2. Assuming that credit is to be offered, what standards will be applied in the decision to grant credit to a customer?
3. How much credit should a customer be granted?
4. What credit terms will be offered?

**Table 25.1** *Accounts receivable as a percentage of total assets*

| Industry sector | 1986 | 1987 | 1988 | 1989 | 1990 | 1991 | 1992 |
|---|---|---|---|---|---|---|---|
| Gold | 6.0 | 5.7 | 1.7 | 2.1 | 3.2 | 2.1 | 4.5 |
| Other metals | 6.0 | 6.6 | 7.5 | 8.1 | 5.8 | 5.3 | 4.8 |
| Solid fuels | 8.0 | 8.3 | 8.5 | 3.9 | 3.7 | 4.8 | 2.6 |
| Oil and gas | 2.0 | 2.2 | 2.1 | 1.8 | 2.3 | 3.0 | 2.7 |
| Diversified resources | 5.7 | 5.4 | 5.3 | 7.5 | 7.3 | 7.6 | 6.5 |
| Developers and contractors | 8.8 | 7.7 | 10.6 | 9.5 | 10.0 | 6.8 | 5.5 |
| Building materials | 17.0 | 14.7 | 14.1 | 14.1 | 12.2 | 10.6 | 11.9 |
| Alcohol and tobacco | 10.7 | 12.4 | 11.8 | 7.1 | 5.2 | 8.8 | 9.4 |
| Food and household | 15.7 | 13.4 | 11.7 | 10.9 | 14.6 | 13.8 | 13.4 |
| Chemicals | 16.9 | 17.8 | 17.2 | 17.3 | 15.5 | 13.2 | 13.3 |
| Engineering | 21.0 | 21.0 | 19.1 | 17.4 | 16.7 | 16.8 | 18.0 |
| Paper and packaging | 12.5 | 13.6 | 11.3 | 11.5 | 10.4 | 8.8 | 9.7 |
| Retail | 3.1 | 3.3 | 1.9 | 2.7 | 2.4 | 3.0 | 3.5 |
| Transport | 16.2 | 13.9 | 13.7 | 15.1 | 14.4 | 14.2 | 12.3 |
| Media | 10.2 | 7.3 | 7.0 | 6.1 | 6.1 | 6.9 | 6.9 |
| Entrepreneurial investor | 6.4 | 4.5 | 5.3 | 8.0 | 8.8 | 4.6 | 2.8 |
| Miscellaneous services | 14.5 | 13.3 | 13.0 | 9.8 | 9.8 | 10.5 | 9.9 |
| Miscellaneous industrials | 16.3 | 14.8 | 16.2 | 13.1 | 12.9 | 12.4 | 12.1 |
| Diversified industrials | 15.8 | 13.2 | 11.2 | 14.5 | 14.0 | 11.6 | 10.7 |

*Source:* Stock Exchange Financial and Profitability Study, various years.

When credit has been offered and accepted, the company must then seek to ensure that the promised amount is paid. Inevitably, some accounts will prove difficult to collect and the company will need to take steps to try to recover the amount owing; that is, the company will adopt a **collection policy**. This requires the manager to determine which procedures will be used to encourage payment, and for how long these procedures should be followed. In practice, credit and collection policies will be interrelated, but it is convenient in the first instance to consider them separately.

Before further discussion of credit and collection policies, we first describe the characteristics of accounts receivable in more detail and indicate the benefits and costs of holding accounts receivable.

## 25.2 WHAT ARE ACCOUNTS RECEIVABLE?

Accounts receivable may be defined as money owed to a company from the sale, on credit, of goods or services in the normal course of business. **Trade credit** refers to credit sales made to other businesses, whereas **consumer credit** refers to credit sales made to individuals. Trade credit terms may provide a discount for prompt payment, whereas consumer credit terms are unlikely to have this feature. Consumer credit may also require the customer to pay a service fee, but this is unusual in the case of trade credit.

An individual purchasing goods on credit from a retailer may either charge the amount to a credit account, or enter into a longer-term consumer credit agreement which is likely to require regular repayment of an agreed amount. A business purchasing goods on credit may be offered trade credit 'on open account', or, if the amount involved is substantial, it may be required to negotiate a trade bill.[1] Trade credit on open account is the more usual method. For example, a timber yard is likely to provide trade credit on open account to builders who obtain their supplies regularly from the yard. This requires little or no formal documentation and the selling company sends regular statements to notify its customers of their current indebtedness.

In the remainder of this chapter, decisions relating to trade credit on open account will be considered. However, much of the material presented is applicable to other forms of trade credit and to consumer credit.

### 25.2.1 BENEFITS AND COSTS OF HOLDING ACCOUNTS RECEIVABLE

The major benefits and costs of holding accounts receivable can be illustrated by a simple example. Suppose that the manager of a suburban timber yard is reviewing its accounts receivable policy. A lenient policy would be to provide credit to nearly all customers who request it, to allow these customers a long credit period, and to delay taking steps to collect overdue accounts. Such a policy would almost certainly attract new customers and perhaps win more business from existing customers. However, a lenient policy would also increase costs substantially. The long credit period would tie up resources that could otherwise be invested elsewhere. Further, the costs of administering the accounts would rise, and the lower credit standard required of customers would lead to increased costs of collection and a higher incidence of unpaid accounts. Conversely, a very strict policy would keep these costs at very low levels, but would also lead to lost sales as customers turned to competing timber yards whose policies were more lenient. The aim of the manager is to choose that set of policies which will maximise the net benefit to his timber yard.

The benefits and costs are now explained in more detail.

#### BENEFIT OF INCREASED SALES

A company will offer credit terms to its customers only if its management believes that there will be an increase in sales. The benefit is therefore the net increase in sales revenue directly attributable to the credit terms offered. This net increase in sales revenue is calculated by deducting from the gross increase in sales revenue the cost of the goods sold and other associated costs, such as delivery costs.

#### OPPORTUNITY COST OF INVESTMENT

Accounts receivable tie up funds that could otherwise be invested in some other way. There is therefore an opportunity cost which is equal to the return that these funds could otherwise have earned.

---

[1] See Section 8.3.5 for a description of trade bills.

## COST OF BAD DEBTS AND DELINQUENT ACCOUNTS

Some customers may delay unduly the payment of their accounts (called **delinquent accounts**) and others may not pay their accounts at all (called **bad debts**). A delinquent account means that the supplier must wait a longer time before it receives payment, and therefore the opportunity cost is greater. A bad debt means that the supplier incurs the cost of a credit sale without obtaining any benefit.

## COST OF ADMINISTRATION

Each credit account must be administered. At a minimum, these costs will generally include staff costs, the costs of checking the creditworthiness of customers, and office expenses such as stationery, postage, and telephone charges. Delinquent accounts impose further expenses because of the collection costs they involve. Collection costs may include further staff costs and office expenses, and, as a final step, the costs of legal action. Such action may be justified if the amount involved is substantial and there is a reasonable probability that the debtor has the ability to pay.

## COST OF ADDITIONAL INVESTMENT

Increased sales will, of themselves, generally involve further costs. For example, a higher inventory level may be required.[2] In the case of a manufacturer, new investment in plant and equipment may be needed to meet the increased demand.

## 25.3 CREDIT POLICY

In Section 25.1, four elements of credit policy were mentioned. These elements are now considered further.

### 25.3.1 THE DECISION TO OFFER CREDIT

In principle a company must decide whether it will sell on a strictly 'cash only' basis or whether some credit will be extended. In practice an individual company will often have little choice but to extend credit. If competitors provide credit to customers, it is likely that the company will also have to extend credit if it is to retain its customers' business. The reason is simple: an offer of credit is equivalent to a price reduction, and naturally a lower price tends to increase demand. It was noted earlier that from the seller's viewpoint the need to wait for payment involves an opportunity cost. Equally, from the buyer's viewpoint, the ability to defer payment is equivalent to a price reduction. For example, if a customer has a required rate of return of 1 per cent per month, and buys an item for $101 on 1 month's credit, the effective cost in today's terms is only $100.[3]

---

[2] The costs associated with investments in inventory are discussed in Chapter 23.
[3] More formally, from the buyer's viewpoint, the present value of $101 payable in one month's time is $\frac{\$101}{1.01}$ or $100.

## 25.3.2 SELECTION OF CREDITWORTHY CUSTOMERS

A company will usually offer similar terms to all its creditworthy customers but it must first decide which of its customers will be granted credit and which will be refused credit. In reaching this decision one of the best guides is often the company's own experience with the customer. One technique which is a useful aid in deciding whether to grant credit is the 'decision tree'. This technique was discussed in Chapter 18 and is illustrated in the context of the selection of creditworthy customers by the following example.

*Example 25.1*

Suppose that Company A has a large number of credit customers and it receives from Company B a request for credit for the purchase of 100 units of Company A's product at $10 per unit. In the first instance, Company A has three choices: it may grant the request immediately, it may refuse the request immediately, or it may postpone the decision pending investigation. At a minimum, this investigation will usually involve checking its own records to see if Company B has received credit from Company A in the past.[4] Such an investigation will show whether Company B is a low credit risk, a high credit risk, or is a new customer about whom no information is available from the company's records. Company A wishes to choose the course of action that has the lowest expected cost. The possible actions confronting Company A are shown in the form of a decision tree in Figure 25.1.

To employ this approach, it is necessary to estimate the cost associated with each end point on the tree. In turn, this requires information on the following items:[5]

1. the marginal cost of producing each unit, the sales revenue generated by each unit, and the marginal net benefit of each unit sold; in this example, the marginal cost of each unit is assumed to be $7, and since the associated sales revenue is $10, the marginal net benefit is $10 − $7 = $3. Therefore, for this order the marginal cost is $700 and the marginal net benefit is $300;
2. the cost of investigation, assumed in this example to be $2 per investigation;[6]
3. the probability that Company B is low risk, high risk or is a new customer; in this example, Company A's experience suggests that these probabilities are 0.80, 0.15 and 0.05 respectively;
4. the cost of capital assumed in this example to be 2 per cent per month;[7] and

---

[4] Other forms of investigation, such as checking with a credit bureau, are discussed later in this section.
[5] To simplify the example it is assumed that there are no costs of additional investment in non-current assets or inventory.
[6] For companies with well-maintained computerised records, this cost may well be negligible. A non-zero cost is used in this example in order to show how such a cost is handled.
[7] To simplify the discussion, we use simple interest. That is, 2 per cent for one month, 4 per cent for two months, and so on.

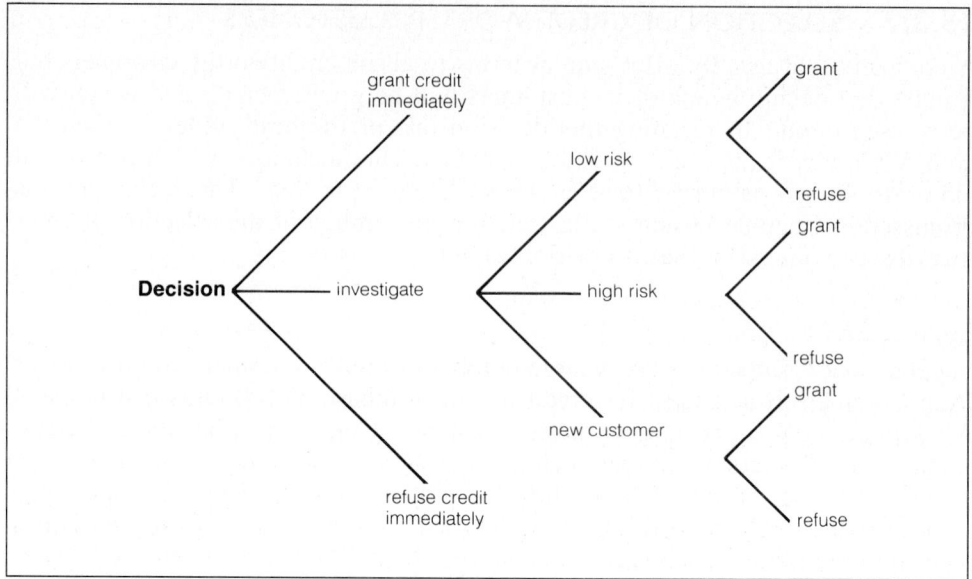

**Fig. 25.1** Decision tree showing possible courses of action for Company A

5. data for each category on the probability of payment, the probability of a bad debt occurring (which is simply 1 minus the probability of payment), the average waiting period from the date of sale to the date of payment, and the average collection cost. This is shown in Table 25.2.

**Table 25.2** Data relating to Example 25.1

| Decision | Probability of payment | Probability of bad debt | Average waiting period (months) | Average collection cost ($) |
|---|---|---|---|---|
| No investigation | 0.93 | 0.07 | 2 | 5 |
| Finding of investigation: | | | | |
|   Low risk | 1.00 | 0 | 1 | 2 |
|   High risk | 0.60 | 0.40 | 7 | 20 |
|   New customer | 0.80 | 0.20 | 3 | 8 |

To determine whether a customer should be granted credit immediately, refused credit immediately, or investigated, the manager needs to compare the costs of these alternatives. The cost of **granting** credit is given by:

Expected bad debt cost + investment opportunity cost + collection cost

$$= \left(\begin{array}{c}\text{probability}\\ \text{of bad debt}\end{array}\right)(\$700) + (0.02 \times \$700)\left(\begin{array}{c}\text{waiting}\\ \text{period}\end{array}\right) + \text{collection cost.}$$

The cost of **refusing** credit is given by:

Expected value of marginal net benefit foregone
= (probability of payment) ($300)

Using these equations, the cost at each end point on the decision tree can be calculated as shown below.

**Grant credit immediately**
$$\text{Cost} = (0.07 \times \$700) + (0.02 \times \$700 \times 2) + \$5 = \$82$$

**Investigate, with the following findings and decisions**
Low risk/grant: Cost = $(0 \times \$700) + (0.02 \times \$700 \times 1) + \$2 = \$16$
Low risk/refuse: Cost = $(1 \times \$300) = \$300$
High risk/grant: Cost = $(0.4 \times \$700) + (0.02 \times \$700 \times 7) + \$20 = \$398$
High risk/refuse: Cost = $(0.6 \times \$300) = \$180$
New customer/grant: Cost = $(0.2 \times \$700) + (0.02 \times \$700 \times 3) + \$8 = \$190$
New customer/refuse: Cost = $(0.8 \times \$300) = \$240$

**Refuse credit immediately**
$$\text{Cost} = (0.93)(\$300) = \$279$$

In Figure 25.2 these amounts are shown on the decision tree.

If an investigation is undertaken, there is a probability of 0.80 that Company B will be found to be in the low-risk category. In that case, the lower cost decision is to grant credit (since $16 is less than $300). If Company B is found to be in the high-risk category (probability 0.15), the request will be refused (cost $180). If Company B is found to be a new customer (probability 0.05), the request will be granted (cost $190). The investigation itself will cost $2. Therefore, the total expected cost of investigating the request is:

$$\$2 + (0.8 \times \$16) + (0.15 \times \$180) + (0.05 \times \$190) = \$51.30$$

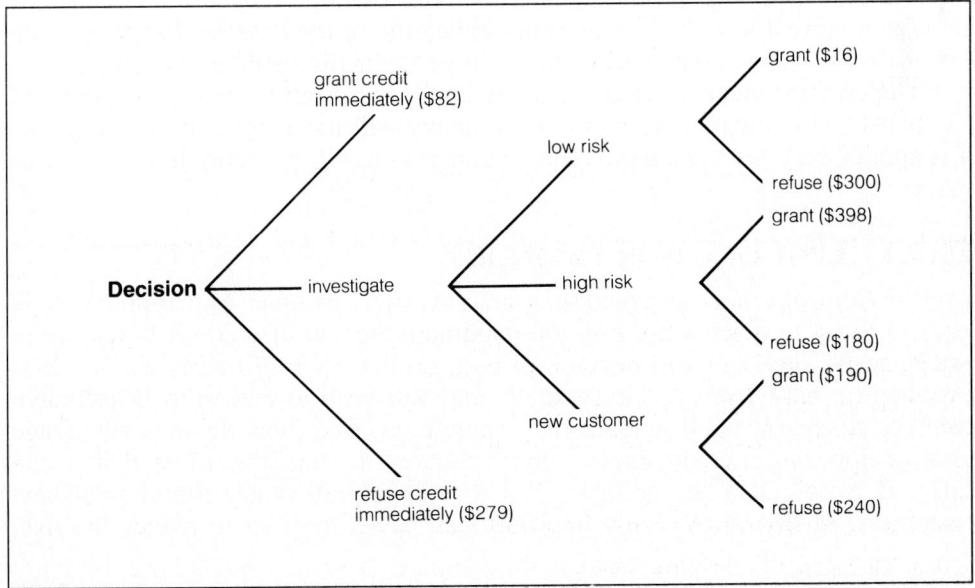

**Fig. 25.2** *Decision tree showing costs of alternative actions for Company A*

Finally, comparing the three decisions—grant immediately, refuse immediately, or investigate—it is found that the lowest cost choice is to investigate this request. The expected cost of investigating the request is $51.30, as against $82 for an immediate granting of credit, and $279 for an immediate refusal of credit. If the investigation shows that Company B is either an existing customer in the low-risk category or is a new customer, the request will be granted. However, if Company B is an existing customer in the high-risk category, the request will be refused.

The decision-tree approach discussed in Example 25.1 is appropriate for a company that relies to a large extent on information obtained from experience with its own customers. Undoubtedly, this is a convenient and very useful source of information. Frequently, however, companies look to other sources as well. For example, Company A may require Company B to complete a credit application form. Generally this form will require the applicant to provide the names of both trade and bank referees who can be contacted to provide information on the applicant's creditworthiness. Larger companies may have a credit rating assigned by a credit rating agency such as S & P–Australian Ratings, a member of the Standard & Poor's Rating Group.[8] Other major sources of information are credit bureaus such as Dun and Bradstreet. These bureaus maintain records of companies' financial details, including their record in paying trade debts, and provide this information to interested parties for a fee. Other information on the creditworthiness of Company B may be obtained from other businesses with whom it has an account. These businesses will have first-hand knowledge of Company B's payment record. Company A may also require information on the financial condition of Company B. This is usually obtained from the company's financial statements and from the completed application form. Company A's main concern is the short-term liquidity position of Company B as this provides a measure of its ability to pay. In addition, the value of Company B's unencumbered non-current assets provides some indication of the degree of security. The use of financial statement analysis in credit policy is discussed in Appendix 25.1.

The credit standards that a company applies will influence the incidence of bad debts and delinquent accounts. A company will incur virtually no bad debts if it applies very high standards, but in doing so it will probably have to forego sales.

### 25.3.3 LIMIT OF CREDIT EXTENDED

Even if Company B is accepted as a creditworthy customer by Company A, it is usual for A to place a limit on the maximum amount of credit it is willing to extend to B. The limit will depend, in part, on the value of purchases that B is expected to make from A. However, A may not wish to extend to B sufficient credit to finance the full amount of its purchases. The most obvious advantage to A of imposing a credit limit is that it reduces the maximum loss that A can suffer if B defaults. The ability to set a limit is particularly useful with new customers. At first, a relatively low limit can be set in order to reduce the risk,

---

[8] See Section 4.7 for a description and examples of such ratings.

but, as time passes, and the account is satisfactorily maintained, higher limits can be established. In this way, business is not lost through refusal of credit, but the risk exposure is not excessive.

### 25.3.4 CREDIT TERMS

A company's credit terms specify a credit period and may also specify a discount period(s) and a discount rate(s). The **credit period** is the period that elapses between the date when the purchasing company is invoiced and the date when payment is due.[9] The **discount period** is the period that elapses between the date when the purchasing company is invoiced and the date when the discount is foregone. The **discount rate** expresses, in effect, the price reduction that the purchasing company will receive if it pays within the discount period.

Typical examples of credit terms are as follows:
1. n/30: There is no discount and the credit period is 30 days.
2. 2/10, n/30: The discount rate is 2 per cent, the discount period is 10 days and the credit period is 30 days. Therefore, if Company B purchases, on credit, goods worth $100 from Company A, and the purchase is included in its statement of account dated 31 March, then Company B would have to pay only $98 if the account is paid by 10 April. If it foregoes the discount, Company B is required to pay $100 by the end of April.
3. $3\frac{1}{2}$/10, $2\frac{1}{2}$/30: There are two discount periods. A higher discount of $3\frac{1}{2}$ per cent is allowed if payment is made within 10 days of being invoiced, while a discount of $2\frac{1}{2}$ per cent is received if payment is made within 30 days. The credit period is also set at 30 days. Therefore, a company will receive a discount for paying within the credit period.

A company offers a discount to accelerate its cash inflow and/or to improve its competitive position. If we consider the credit terms 2/10, n/30, the purchasing company obtains an effective reduction in price by paying within 10 days. Therefore a company may obtain a larger share of the market for its product by offering higher discounts than its competitors. Also the discount will encourage the company's credit customers to pay earlier. In percentage terms, the financial inducement to pay earlier can be quite large. Referring again to the credit terms 2/10, n/30, consider the position of Company B on 10 April. To find a better use for its $98, Company B would need to find an investment that, with zero risk, can turn $98 into $100 within 20 days. The annual effective rate of return required is therefore:

$$\left(1 + \frac{2}{98}\right)^{\frac{365}{20}} - 1$$
$$= 44.6\%$$

---

[9] The statement of account is the regular notification that the selling company sends to its debtors to indicate their current indebtedness. These statements are normally sent out monthly, often at the end of the month. This practice is important because the credit period does not commence from the date of sale but rather from the date on the monthly statement. A debtor can use this to his advantage by purchasing at the beginning of the month and stretching a 30-day credit period into an almost 60-day credit period.

Earlier payments by customers will reduce the amount that Company A has tied up in receivables, and will also reduce the incidence of bad debts and delinquent accounts. In turn, this will reduce its collection costs.

## 25.4 COLLECTION POLICY

A company that never has a bad debt almost certainly has a suboptimal credit policy. That is, if a more lenient policy were adopted, the increase in sales would more than offset the losses imposed by a few bad debts. For most companies, some bad debts are inevitable. Notwithstanding this fact, it is also true that in most cases some attempt to collect overdue debts is worth while. These efforts are referred to as the company's **collection policy**.

The critical problem in collection policy is the need to recognise when an account warrants special attention. Obviously it is not sensible to institute legal action on a $10 account which is 2 days overdue. But what if the account were for $10 million, rather than $10? Is action warranted if a $100 account is 30 days overdue? If so, what action should be taken? There are no hard and fast answers to these questions. However, most businesses adopt a set of procedures. Generally, attempts to collect an account which is overdue begin with a standard reminder notice, followed by personal letters and telephone calls. Eventually visits may be made in person. The final resort is legal action, but this can be very expensive and may involve long delays. An alternative is to employ a debt collection agency, but this too can be expensive. It may also sometimes pay a business to accept a partial payment, rather than continue with attempts to collect the full amount owed.

As the amount spent on collection activities increases, it is to be expected that bad debt losses will be reduced and the average collection period will be shorter. However, these relationships are unlikely to be linear. For example, an initial small level of expenditure is unlikely to have any marked effect in reducing bad debts, or in shortening the average collection period, while additional expenditures are likely to have a much greater effect. However, beyond a certain level of collection expenditure the benefits will diminish until eventually a saturation point is reached. The relationship between the average collection period and the level of collection expenditures is likely to be similar.[10]

Collection policy is a trade-off between the costs of collection, and the benefits of lower bad debt losses and a shorter average collection period, which in turn will result in a reduction in the company's investment in accounts receivable. Therefore a collection policy can be evaluated with respect to these associated costs and benefits and an optimum policy determined. However, in seeking this optimum policy, it is advisable to take account of the effect of the collection policy on sales, as a more forceful collection procedure may adversely affect sales. For example, if collection procedures are begun too early, customers may be offended and switch to alternative suppliers.

---

[10] J. C. Van Horne, *Financial Management and Policy*, 4th edn, Prentice-Hall, Englewood Cliffs, New Jersey, 1977, pp. 379–82.

## 25.5 NET PRESENT VALUE AND ACCOUNTS RECEIVABLE MANAGEMENT

The net present value (NPV) method of evaluating investment projects was discussed in Chapters 5 and 18. The investment projects analysed in those chapters related to investments in non-current assets such as vehicles and machinery. However, in principle the NPV method is appropriate for other types of investment, including investment in accounts receivable. In this section, we consider the application of the NPV method to a company's credit and collection policies.

The benefits associated with a change in credit policy can be measured by the net increase in sales revenue, while the costs will include manufacturing, selling, collection and administration expenses, and bad debts. In addition, by discounting the net cash flows generated by the credit policy at the required rate of return, the analysis will incorporate the cost to the company of having funds tied up in receivables.[11] Therefore, if all the benefits and costs associated with a particular credit policy are quantified and expressed in present value terms, the particular credit policy under consideration will be profitable if the net present value is positive. The company's optimum credit policy is the one that results in the largest net present value.

The application of NPV analysis to the evaluation of alternative policies is outlined in the following examples. We begin with a highly simplified example, and introduce additional factors relevant to the decision in subsequent examples.

*Example 25.2*
Zippo Ltd, which currently does not offer credit, is considering extending credit to its customers for a period of 60 days. This is assumed to result in an increase in sales revenue of $20 000. The additional cost associated with these sales is $16 000. Initially, it is assumed that Zippo's existing cash customers will not seek credit if the proposed credit policy is introduced. It is also assumed that there are no bad debts, administration costs, or collection costs and that all credit customers will take full advantage of the credit terms by delaying payment until the sixtieth day.[12] Zippo's required rate of return on all accounts receivable is 2 per cent per month.[13]

---

[11] The appropriate required rate of return depends on the risk class of credit customers. In addition, the analysis should take into account the costs of financing any additional inventory or non-current assets that the company requires to support a higher level of operations. In the subsequent examples it will be assumed that these costs have been included in the costs associated with the sale. However, in practice, these costs will only include accounting costs, such as the cost of the goods sold and delivery charges. Therefore, it is usually necessary to impute a figure so as to include the cost of the additional funds invested in inventory and non-current assets.

[12] In this and subsequent examples, it is assumed for simplicity that the credit period and the discount period extend from the date of purchase, rather than from the date on the monthly statement.

[13] In accordance with business practice, the length of the credit period is referred to in terms of days. However, to make the present value calculations less cumbersome, monthly discounting is used. It is assumed that 1 month equals 30 days and to ease the exposition, the phrase 'at the end of the month' will be stated more simply as 'at month' since all cash flows in these examples are assumed to occur at the end of the month.

Given these assumptions, the investment opportunity being considered by Zippo consists of an initial outlay of $16 000 at time zero, and a cash inflow of $20 000 at the end of month 2. With a required rate of return of 2 per cent per month, the NPV of the proposed policy is:

$$\text{NPV} = \frac{\$20\,000}{(1.02)^2} - \$16\,000$$
$$= \$3223.37$$

Since the NPV is positive, the proposed credit policy is profitable.

The credit policy proposed in Example 25.2 did not offer discounts for payments received before the expiration of the credit period. This possibility is shown in Example 25.3.

*Example 25.3*

Suppose that the assumptions made in Example 25.2 are retained, except that Zippo now offers a discount of $2\frac{1}{2}$ per cent for payments received within 30 days. That is, the proposed credit terms are $2\frac{1}{2}/30$, n/60. It is estimated that 75 per cent of credit customers will take advantage of the discount.

As in Example 25.2, the initial outlay is $16 000. The cash inflow at month 1 is $(1 - 0.025) \times 0.75 \times \$20\,000 = \$14\,625$ and the cash inflow at month 2 is $0.25 \times \$20\,000 = \$5000$. The NPV of the proposed policy is therefore:

$$\text{NPV} = \frac{\$14\,625}{1.02} + \frac{\$5000}{(1.02)^2} - \$16\,000$$
$$= \$3144.08$$

The NPV of this policy is positive and it is therefore preferred to the current policy of not offering credit at all. However, the NPV of this policy is less than the NPV of a credit policy that offers no discount for early payment. This indicates that Zippo should not offer the discount assumed in the example.

Example 25.3 did not allow for the possibility that the offer of a discount could well attract even more new customers to Zippo. Because a discount amounts to a reduction in price, it is possible that demand would increase. The increased demand could be sufficient to justify offering the discount. This is shown in Example 25.4.

*Example 25.4*

It is now assumed that, as well as the additional sales of $20 000 assumed in Examples 25.2 and 25.3, further sales of $4000 (at a cost of $3200) are made to customers, all of whom take advantage of the $2\frac{1}{2}$ per cent discount.

The initial outlay is now $\$16\,000 + \$3200 = \$19\,200$. The cash inflow at month 1 is $\$14\,625 + ((1 - 0.025) \times \$4000) = \$18\,525$ and the cash inflow at month 2 remains at $5000. The NPV of the proposed policy is therefore:

$$\text{NPV} = \frac{\$18\,525}{1.02} + \frac{\$5000}{(1.02)^2} - \$19\,200$$
$$= \$3767.61$$

Since the NPV is positive, and exceeds the NPV calculated in Example 25.2, the proposed policy that offers a $2\frac{1}{2}$ per cent discount for payment received within 30 days is preferable to a policy that offers no discount for early payment.

To summarise the position so far, the initial outlay is $19 200, the cash inflow at month 1 is $18 525 and the cash inflow at month 2 is $5000. Bad debts and delinquent accounts have so far been ignored. The impact of these factors is illustrated in Example 25.5.

*Example 25.5*
To illustrate the treatment of bad debts and delinquent accounts, it is now assumed that the offer of a discount will still result in a cash inflow of $18 525 at month 1, but of the remaining $5000 owing, $3000 will be paid on time (at month 2), $1000 will be paid late (at month 3), $400 will be paid still later (at month 4) and $600 will never be paid. That is, bad debts will amount to unpaid accounts of $600.

The NPV is therefore:

$$\text{NPV} = \frac{\$18\,525}{1.02} + \frac{\$3000}{(1.02)^2} + \frac{\$1000}{(1.02)^3} + \frac{\$400}{(1.02)^4} - \$19\,200$$
$$= \$3157.13$$

Since the NPV is positive, the proposed credit policy is still an acceptable investment.

The costs of administration and collection still have to be included in the analysis. A large proportion of these costs do not depend on the value of the account. For example, the clerical cost of producing and posting an invoice for a customer who owes $200 is not likely to be different from the cost incurred for a customer who owes $10 000. At the level of the individual account, the total amount spent in an effort to collect the amount owing will increase, the longer the account remains unpaid. However, taking the company's monthly spending on collection procedures for all accounts which have been granted credit at a given point in time, the amount spent each month on collection is likely to decrease as time passes. For example, suppose that ten accounts are overdue and the company spends $2 per account to send a first reminder notice. Expenditure on collection procedures for that month is therefore $20. If, in the next month, seven of these accounts have been paid, there are three remaining unpaid accounts to be sent a second reminder notice at a total cost of $6. Expenditure on collection has therefore fallen from $20 to $6. The extent of this decrease may be lessened by the fact that later stages of the collection procedure may be more expensive on a 'per account' basis. For example, a personal letter uses more staff time and therefore imposes more costs than sending a standard reminder notice. Administration and collection costs are illustrated in Example 25.6.

*Example 25.6*
Zippo estimates administration costs to be $200 at month 0, $100 at month 1 and $150 at month 2. Collection costs are estimated to be $70 at month 3 and $40 at month 4. The initial outlay is therefore $19 200 + $200 = $19 400, and

the net cash flows in the following months are $18\,525 - \$100 = \$18\,425$; $\$3000 - \$150 = \$2850$; $\$1000 - \$70 = \$930$ and $\$400 - \$40 = \$360$.

The NPV is therefore:

$$\text{NPV} = \frac{\$18\,425}{1.02} + \frac{\$2850}{(1.02)^2} + \frac{\$930}{(1.02)^3} + \frac{\$360}{(1.02)^4} - \$19\,400$$
$$= \$2612.00$$

Since the NPV is positive, the proposed credit policy is still an acceptable investment.

So far it has been assumed that Zippo's existing customers, all of whom pay cash, will not also demand that they be granted credit. While many existing customers would no doubt continue to pay cash, it is inevitable that some would now seek to obtain credit. If these customers are creditworthy, a refusal of credit could well be offensive and may therefore result in lost sales. Some existing cash-paying customers would therefore become credit customers and this would impose further costs on Zippo. This is illustrated in Example 25.7.

### Example 25.7

It is now assumed that existing customers switch $15\,000 worth of business from a cash basis to a credit basis. Table 25.3 shows the estimated changes to Zippo's cash flows.[14]

**Table 25.3** *Cash flow effects of existing cash customers switching to credit*

| Month | Accounts paid ($) | Discount ($) | Admin. costs ($) | Collection costs ($) | Total ($) |
|---|---|---|---|---|---|
| 0 | | | − 140 | | − 140 |
| 1 | 10 000 | − 250 | − 50 | | 9 700 |
| 2 | 4 000 | | − 150 | | 3 850 |
| 3 | 500 | | | − 30 | 470 |
| 4 | 200 | | | − 30 | 170 |

The present value of these cash flows is as follows:

$$\text{PV} = -\$140 + \frac{\$9700}{1.02} + \frac{\$3850}{(1.02)^2} + \frac{\$470}{(1.02)^3} + \frac{\$170}{(1.02)^4}$$
$$= \$13\,670.25$$

In present value terms, the increased costs imposed by the need to grant credit to customers who currently pay cash is $\$15\,000 - \$13\,670.25 = \$1329.75$. The NPV of the proposed credit policy is reduced by this amount. The final estimate of the NPV is therefore $\$2612.00 - \$1329.75 = \$1282.25$.

We have now examined a number of components of credit and collection policies and decided that each should be set with the aim of maximising the net present value resulting from the company's investment in accounts receivable.

---

[14] Note that there is no entry in Table 25.3 to show the costs of manufacturing the goods. Such costs are not incremental, since they are incurred regardless of whether the sale is for credit or cash.

Any company may use this approach to determine if there is a more effective policy available to it. However, management must consider competitors' reactions to a change in its policy because it is usual for competing firms to adopt similar policies. Therefore, if a company benefits from a change in its policy, its competitors are likely to change their own policies to try to neutralise this advantage.

This does not mean that a company can never benefit from a change in its credit policy because it is possible for all competing companies to benefit from a change in credit policy. For example, this can occur if the usual credit terms within the industry are too lenient, and companies can sell more goods and services if they offer them at a lower price, but on stricter credit terms. In addition there are components of credit policy that a company may alter without any immediate response from its competitors. For example, a company may benefit from a change in its collection procedures or credit standards, neither of which is likely to be noticed immediately by its competitors. Consequently, the company may enjoy an advantage over its competitors for a limited time.

## 25.6 Factoring and Accounts Receivable Financing

Accounts receivable are a valuable asset and, as with other such assets, accounts receivable can be sold (known as **factoring**) or used as security for debt finance. These financial services are discussed separately.

### 25.6.1 Factoring

The act of selling a company's accounts receivable is known as **factoring**. Both the selling company and the factoring company can benefit because the factoring company specialises in the administration and collection of accounts receivable and therefore may be able to provide these services at a lower cost than the selling company would be able to achieve through its own efforts. From the seller's viewpoint, factoring also assists in maintaining liquidity because it substitutes cash for accounts receivable.

Factoring agreements can take many different forms. However, the basic distinctions to be drawn are between **notification** agreements and **non-notification** agreements, and between **recourse** agreements and **non-recourse** agreements.

#### Notification agreements

This is the more usual form of agreement and is given this name because the selling company's customers are notified that the agreement exists. The invoices sent to the selling company's customers will bear the name of the factoring company and payment is made direct to the factoring company. The accounts receivable or debtor's ledger is maintained by the factoring company. Some notification agreements also require the factoring company to assume the bad-debt risk and these agreements are known as **credit-risk agreements** or **non-recourse factoring**.

## NON-NOTIFICATION AGREEMENTS

In this form of agreement, which is also known as **discounting** or **confidential factoring**, the selling company's customers are not notified about the agreement. This type of factoring agreement is only available with **recourse**. The invoices sent to the selling company's customers bear the name of the selling company, and customers either pay the selling company, which then passes on the proceeds to the factoring company, or send payments to a post office box rented by the factoring company. The debtors' ledger may be maintained by the selling company or, for a higher fee, the factoring company may agree to perform this function. This type of agreement has the advantage that the selling company's customers are not informed that the selling company has factored its accounts. This is thought to be an advantage because it is sometimes believed that a company that uses factoring must be financially weak. This belief is based on the misconception that the cost of factoring is much higher than the cost of alternative sources of finance and would therefore be used only as a last resort. However, as we show later, the cost of factoring may be competitive with the cost of other sources of short-term finance.

## COSTS AND BENEFITS OF FACTORING

For its services, the factoring company usually charges a flat percentage of the value of the accounts factored, which may range from 2.5 per cent to 4 per cent, and covers administration and interest charges.[15] If a selling company is charged 3 per cent, this means that it will receive $97 for every $100 of credit sales. The fee charged by the factoring company will vary with the selling company's average turnover of debtors and the number of accounts involved, and will include an allowance for any discounts offered, and an amount to cover government charges such as stamp duty.

A company considering factoring its accounts receivable should try to ensure that the costs saved by factoring exceed the factoring fee. It is a common misconception to believe that, for example, a fee of 3 per cent on 30-day accounts is equivalent to borrowing at a simple interest rate of 36 per cent per annum. As this is an interest rate that no financially sound company would be prepared to pay, it is claimed that factoring is too costly. However, as indicated earlier, a company will often need to wait for payment for a much longer time than the length of the credit period. If the average waiting time is, say, 60 days, then the equivalent simple interest rate is 18 per cent per annum, which is much closer to the rate payable on other sources of short-term finance. Furthermore there are cost reductions obtained by the selling company; it can avoid the costs of operating a credit department and some of the costs of checking the creditworthiness of customers. The company should estimate these cost savings and deduct them from the equivalent interest cost in order to obtain the net cost of the funds

---

[15] These percentages are appropriate to cases where the factoring company makes an immediate payment for the accounts purchased. A smaller percentage (around 1–2 per cent) is charged if the factoring company delays payment. For example, payment may be delayed until 30 days after the invoice date. This type of factoring is known as 'maturity factoring'.

provided by factoring accounts receivable. This net cost is not necessarily prohibitive and factoring may provide an economic source of finance for some companies.

Factoring is particularly well suited to the needs of relatively small companies that have limited access to traditional sources of finance, and whose credit facilities prove costly to operate because they provide credit to a relatively small number of customers. Factoring is used in Australia by companies in a wide range of manufacturing and service industries. Factoring is not well suited to companies providing consumer credit as this involves offering small amounts of credit to a large number of customers and would involve the company in the payment of a high factoring charge.[16]

When a factoring company is approached by a potential client it will investigate the business' sales, past balance sheets, and particularly the quality of its debtors. An 'age' analysis of debtors, which analyses debtors' accounts by reference to the period of time they have been outstanding, will be required. On the basis of this analysis, the factoring company will decide which accounts it is prepared to purchase. A factoring charge will be determined and, if both parties are satisfied, a factoring agreement will be drawn up and signed.

The selling company will generally receive immediate payment for only a specified percentage of the accounts sold. This percentage will usually be between 60 per cent and 80 per cent. The larger this percentage, the larger will be the factoring fee in return for the larger amount of funds provided by the factoring company. For example, if the percentage is 60 per cent, then for every $10 000 of accounts factored, $6000 is paid immediately to the selling company and the fee may be 2.5 per cent; if the percentage is 80 per cent, then $8000 is paid immediately and the fee may be 3 per cent. The residual (say 20 per cent if 80 per cent is paid immediately) is paid when the debts are paid. The selling company will therefore eventually receive $10 000, less the 3 per cent factoring fee, when all accounts have been paid. Under a factoring agreement, finance is supplied on a continuing basis. Consequently the selling company will receive funds amounting to 80 per cent of its initial acceptable accounts, and the accounts receivable from all subsequent credit sales to acceptable clients will be sold to the factoring company, which will also pay the selling company 80 per cent of those accounts. Where the company wishes to sell to a new client on credit, it will either have to obtain approval from the factoring company or finance the account itself. In the event of any of the factored debts proving to be 'bad' (this may be determined as debts outstanding for more than a specified period of time, say 6 months), the selling company has to repurchase them by paying 80 per cent of the amount of the debt.

---

[16] Credit card services such as Bankcard have made a form of factoring available to retailers. Credit card purchases provide almost immediate cash to the retailer because when the retailer deposits the credit card dockets at the bank, the amount is credited to the retailer's account by the card issuer. Retailers pay a turnover-related fee and the card issuer accepts the risk of bad debts. Credit cards therefore provide retailers with a service similar to that provided under non-recourse factoring.

### 25.6.2 Accounts Receivable Financing

As an alternative to factoring, the financial manager of a company may choose to obtain finance by means of **accounts receivable financing**. In this case the company borrows funds and pledges its accounts receivable as security for the loan. The suppliers of this type of finance will usually be finance companies and they are generally prepared to lend up to 70 per cent of the total value of all acceptable accounts receivable. Accounts receivable would be considered to be unacceptable by the lender if they have been outstanding for a lengthy period, say, 90 days where the credit period is 30 days.

Suppose that a company approaches a finance company to raise funds on the security of its accounts receivable which total $110 000. The finance company, after evaluating the debtors, may reject a number of accounts on the grounds that they are a bad risk, and accept only $100 000 of the company's accounts receivable. As a result the finance company may be prepared to lend $70 000 to the company, secured by a registered equitable charge over its accounts receivable. The finance company will keep a close check on these accounts to ensure that the security is maintained. In the event that the value of the company's accounts receivable declines significantly, it will be required to repay a portion of the loan. Accounts receivable financing is well suited to a company in need of short-term seasonal funds. Compared with accounts receivable financing, factoring is better suited to a long-term arrangement and also permits the company to raise more funds. In addition, the amount financed by a factoring agreement will increase automatically with an increase in the company's credit sales. Further, accounts receivable financing provides none of the additional services a company receives as a result of factoring its accounts receivable.

## 25.7 Credit Insurance

A company may obtain protection against bad debt losses by taking out a credit insurance policy.[17] There are several forms of credit insurance cover including **specific account** and **whole turnover** policies. A specific account policy insures the company against a particular account or accounts of a specified type proving to be bad, while a whole turnover policy can cover the occurrence of bad debts on any of the company's accounts.[18] The annual premium on whole turnover credit insurance usually ranges from 0.2 per cent to 0.6 per cent of the total value of the accounts covered. When any account covered by credit insurance is proved to be bad, generally through insolvency of the debtor, the insurance company pays a specified proportion, normally 80 per cent, of the loss. The

---

[17] See F. Chong, 'More Businesses go for Credit Cover', *Business Review Weekly*, 5 May 1989, pp. 89–90. In a maturity factoring agreement, the factor offers the selling company 100 per cent credit cover, which is rarely the case with a credit insurance policy, see R. Bruce et al., *Handbook of Australian Corporate Finance*, 4th edn, Butterworths, Sydney, 1991, p. 270.

[18] For example, a 'specific account' policy may be used to cover all accounts that fall into a specified range of dollar values. Similarly a 'whole turnover' policy can apply to all accounts related to a particular product line, rather than to turnover in all of a company's products.

insurance company does not provide a complete coverage against bad debt losses. This is to ensure that the insured company has an incentive to recover the bad debt before making a claim. Insurance cover can also be obtained against losses arising from **protracted default**. Under this form of cover, the insurance company will pay claims, once an account has been overdue for 6 months, despite efforts to locate and collect from the debtor.

## SELECTED REFERENCES

Emery, G., 'A Pure Financial Explanation for Trade Credit', *Journal of Financial and Quantitative Analysis*, September 1984, pp. 271–85.
Giancotto, C., 'Accounts Receivable Policy under Stochastic Inflation', *Journal of Accounting Auditing and Finance*, Summer 1992, pp. 291–312.
Kim, Y. H. & Atkins, J. C., 'Evaluating Investments in Accounts Receivable: A Maximizing Framework', *Journal of Finance*, May 1978, pp. 403–12.
Kim, Y. H. & Chung, K. H., 'An Integrated Evaluation of Investment in Inventory and Credit: A Cash Flow Approach', *Journal of Business Finance and Accounting*, Summer 1990, pp. 381–90.
Melare, B. & Willoughby, R., 'Finance Company Finance', in *Handbook of Australian Corporate Finance*, Eds R. Bruce, et al., 4th edn, Butterworths, Sydney, 1991, Ch. 11.
Mian, S. L. & Smith Jr., C. W., 'Accounts Receivable Management Policy: Theory and Evidence', *Journal of Finance*, March 1992, pp. 169–200.
Oh, J. S., 'Opportunity Cost in the Evaluation of Investment in Accounts Receivable', *Financial Management*, Summer 1976, pp. 32–6.
Schwartz, R. A., 'An Economic Model of Trade Credit', *Journal of Financial and Quantitative Analysis*, September 1974, pp. 643–7.
Smith, J. K., 'Trade Credit and Information Asymmetry', *Journal of Finance*, September 1987, pp. 863–72.
Woolford, J., 'Equity Raisings through Existing Assets', *The Australian Accountant*, December 1979, pp. 774–9.

## QUESTIONS

1. Discuss the reasons for a company offering credit terms to its customers.
2. Hayworth Ltd uses a decision-tree approach for screening credit applicants. Gables Ltd has sought credit for the purchase of 1000 units priced at $16 each. The marginal cost of producing each unit is $12. Based on its past experience, Hayworth estimates that there is a 70 per cent chance that Gables falls into the low-risk category, a 20 per cent chance that it is high risk and a 10 per cent chance that it is a new customer. The following table summarises other data estimated by Hayworth's credit department.

| Decision | Probability of payment | Probability of bad debt | Average waiting period (months) | Average collection cost ($) |
|---|---|---|---|---|
| No investigation | 0.92 | 0.08 | 2 | 93 |
| Finding of investigation: | | | | |
| Low risk | 1.00 | 0 | 1 | 10 |
| High risk | 0.70 | 0.30 | 5 | 400 |
| New customer | 0.80 | 0.20 | 3 | 60 |

The cost of conducting an investigation is $2. Hayworth estimates the opportunity cost of capital to be 2 per cent per month. What decision should Hayworth make?
3. A company offers credit terms of 1/7, n/30. Explain the meaning of these terms. What effective annual rate of return is implicit in this offer?
4. What are the advantages and disadvantages of offering a discount for early payment?
5. What are the advantages and disadvantages of an aggressive collection policy?
6. Company A at present sells only on a cash basis and it averages $50 000 of sales per month, with associated expenses of $40 000. It is thought that all customers would accept an offer of 90-day free credit terms and that the company's monthly sales would increase to $55 000 and its associated expenses to $44 000. Company A's required rate is 1 per cent per month.
   (a) Assuming that there are no costs associated with providing credit, will Company A benefit from offering such credit terms?
   (b) If expenses remain at 80 per cent of sales, what would the increase in sales need to be in order to justify the provision of these credit terms?
7. Each month, Jumbo Pty Ltd sells 10 000 units at $25 per unit. The marginal cost of producing each unit is $15. At present all Jumbo's sales are made on a strict 'cash only' basis. Jumbo's manager believes that the 'cash only' policy has led to many sales being lost as there have been a number of inquiries concerning the possibility of credit sales. Jumbo's manager estimates that a credit policy of 1/30, n/60 could increase sales by 1000 units per month, of which 500 would be paid for at the end of month 1 and 400 would be paid for at the end of month 2. Of the remaining 100 units, 70 are expected to be paid for a month late and 30 are expected to be bad debts. Administration and collection costs are estimated to be $250 (month 0), $100 (month 1), $100 (month 2), and $150 (month 3). However, it is expected that some existing customers will also seek credit in order to obtain the discount offered. This is likely to affect the sale of 600 units. Buyers of the remaining 9400 units are expected to continue to pay cash. Administration costs are estimated to be $150 (month 0) and $60 (month 1). Jumbo's required rate of return is 1.5 per cent per month. Should Jumbo adopt the proposed credit arrangements?
8. Distinguish between 'notification' and 'non-notification' factoring agreements, and discuss their relative merits.
9. In what ways do credit card services, such as Bankcard, resemble a factoring service for retailers? How do they differ?

# APPENDIX 25.1

# FINANCIAL STATEMENT ANALYSIS

In the chapters on short-term asset management, no specific reference has been made to the analysis of financial statements, which is frequently used by the financial manager in short-term asset management. Analysis of financial statements involves the calculation of financial ratios using the financial data in the profit and loss statement and balance sheet. In this appendix, some of the more frequently used financial ratios are defined, their application examined, and their usefulness for short-term asset management discussed.[19]

## MEASUREMENT AND INTERPRETATION OF SEVERAL FINANCIAL RATIOS

First we define and calculate a number of financial ratios, using the financial statements of Pacific Dunlop Limited, shown in Tables A25.1.1 and A25.1.2.

**Table A25.1.1** *Pacific Dunlop Limited—Profit and loss account for the year ended 30 June 1992*

| 1991 ($'000) | | 1992 ($'000) | ($'000) |
|---|---|---|---|
| 4 921 605 | Sales | | 5 806 156 |
| (a)294 953 | Operating profit before tax | (b)309 695 | |
| 75 071 | *less* income tax | 91 967 | |
| 219 882 | Operating profit | 217 728 | |

(a) Includes interest expense of $175 661 000.
(b) Includes interest expense of $183 737 000.

---

19 For a more detailed discussion of the usefulness of financial ratios for short-term asset management, see K. V. Smith, *Guide to Working Capital Management*, McGraw-Hill, New York, 1979, Ch. 9; and G. W. Gallinger & P. B. Healey, *Liquidity Analysis and Management*, Addison-Wesley, Reading, Massachusetts, 1987, Ch. 3.

**Table A25.1.2** *Pacific Dunlop Ltd—Balance sheet as at 30 June 1992*

| 1991 ($'000s) | | 1992 ($'000s) | ($'000s) |
|---:|---|---:|---:|
| | Assets | | |
| | Current assets: | | |
| 964 509 | Cash | 1 003 310 | |
| 713 315 | Receivables | 953 014 | |
| 889 726 | Inventories | 1 065 807 | |
| 50 073 | Prepayments | 51 992 | |
| 2 617 623 | Total current assets | | 3 074 123 |
| | Non-current assets: | | |
| 42 539 | Receivables | 46 768 | |
| 156 362 | Investments | 289 534 | |
| 1 062 262 | Property, plant and equipment | 1 348 739 | |
| 575 351 | Intangibles | 877 669 | |
| 190 402 | Future income tax benefit | 305 068 | |
| 2 026 916 | Total non-current assets | | 2 867 778 |
| 4 644 539 | TOTAL ASSETS | | 5 941 901 |
| | Liabilities: | | |
| | Current liabilities: | | |
| 37 394 | Bank overdrafts | 75 016 | |
| 785 810 | Bank loans and other loans | 736 682 | |
| 11 | Amounts owing to South Pacific Tyres P'ship | 9 | |
| 467 764 | Trade creditors | 482 697 | |
| 493 771 | Bills payable | 617 705 | |
| 94 440 | Other creditors | 169 705 | |
| 31 361 | Lease liabilities | 94 269 | |
| 82 596 | Provision for tax | 68 562 | |
| 236 501 | Other provisions | 449 842 | |
| 74 673 | Other liabilities | 74 538 | |
| 2 304 321 | Total current liabilities | | 2 768 438 |
| | Non-current liabilities: | | |
| 839 079 | Creditors and borrowings | 1 021 602 | |
| 66 711 | Provision for deferred income tax | 85 486 | |
| 49 866 | Other | 14 549 | |
| 955 667 | Total non-current liabilities | | 1 121 637 |
| 3 259 988 | TOTAL LIABILITIES | | 3 890 075 |
| 1 384 551 | NET ASSETS | | 2 051 826 |
| | Shareholders' equity | | |
| 366 771 | Share capital | 451 174 | |
| 907 959 | Reserves | 1 488 007 | |
| 89 691 | Retained profits | 85 892 | |
| | Shareholders' equity attributable to Pacific | | |
| 1 364 421 | Dunlop Ltd shareholders | 2 025 073 | |
| 20 130 | Outside equity interest in controlled entities | 26 753 | |
| 1 384 551 | TOTAL SHAREHOLDERS' EQUITY | | 2 051 826 |

There are four broad categories of financial ratios. They are liquidity ratios, activity ratios, leverage ratios, and profitability ratios.

## LIQUIDITY RATIOS

Liquidity ratios are a measure of a company's ability to meet its maturing short-term financial obligations. The following ratios are classified as liquidity ratios.

### Current ratio

Traditionally the current ratio has been used to measure a company's liquidity. It is calculated by dividing total current assets by total current liabilities. Its use dates from the nineteenth century and it is still widely used as an important measure of a company's ability to pay its short-term debts when they are due.[20] Using the data for Pacific Dunlop, the current ratio is as follows:[21]

$$\text{Current ratio} = \frac{\text{total current assets}}{\text{total current liabilities}}$$
$$= \frac{\$3\,074\,123\,000}{\$2\,768\,438\,000}$$
$$= 1.11\,(1.14)$$

The higher the current ratio, the greater will be the company's ability to meet its immediate financial obligations. However, the higher this ratio, the greater will be the proportion of the company's resources tied up in relatively unproductive assets. This may have an adverse effect on profitability. Management therefore has to decide on the appropriate balance between profitability and liquidity.

### 'Quick' ratio

The quick ratio is calculated by dividing total current assets minus inventories and prepayments, by total current liabilities minus bank overdraft. Prepayments are deducted because they represent amounts paid for services yet to be provided and therefore are not easily converted into cash. Similarly inventory is the least liquid current asset and could be difficult to sell at short notice. Bank overdraft is deducted from current liabilities because it is unlikely to be withdrawn at short notice.[22] The quick ratio is more useful than the current ratio as a measure of the company's ability to meet its financial obligations should they become payable almost immediately.

---

[20] George Foster, *Financial Statement Analysis*, 2nd edn, Prentice-Hall, Englewood Cliffs, New Jersey, 1986, p. 61.
[21] The value for each ratio, based on the figures in the 1990–91 financial statements, is included in parentheses.
[22] See Chapter 8.

$$\text{Quick ratio} = \frac{\text{total current assets} - \text{inventories} - \text{prepayments}}{\text{total current liabilities} - \text{bank overdraft}}$$

$$= \frac{\$3\,074\,123\,000 - \$1\,065\,807\,000 - \$51\,992\,000}{\$2\,768\,438\,000 - \$75\,016\,000}$$

$$= 0.73\ (0.74)$$

As with the current ratio, the higher the quick ratio, the greater is the company's ability to meet its immediate financial obligations.

## ACTIVITY RATIOS

Activity ratios measure the effectiveness of a company's use of its assets. These ratios generally relate the amount of a particular group of assets (such as inventory, accounts receivable, or total assets) to the activity generated by that group (such as sales, cost of goods sold, and operating profit). We consider three such ratios.

### Inventory turnover

Inventory turnover is a measure of the number of times a company turns over its inventory during the year, and is usually calculated by dividing annual sales by the average inventory for the year.

$$\text{Inventory turnover} = \frac{\text{annual sales}}{\text{average inventory for the year}}$$

$$= \frac{\$5\,806\,156\,000}{\$1\,065\,807\,000}$$

$$= 5.45\ (5.53)$$

A problem in calculating inventory turnover is that it requires calculation of the average inventory for the year. This is usually an average of the opening and closing annual inventory figures. In this example we have used year-end inventories as a proxy for average inventory. This could distort the computed ratio. In addition, this ratio is distorted by comparing sales with inventory valued at historical cost. Ideally the numerator (sales) used in the equation should be replaced by 'cost of goods sold' if the figure is available. Before this ratio can be used effectively it is necessary for an 'ideal' or benchmark ratio to be specified.

The higher a company's inventory turnover, the lower will be the amount that the company has tied up in inventory at a particular time. However, as a consequence, the company will have to place orders for goods more frequently. We discussed possible solutions to this problem in Section 23.6. However, it is unlikely that an ideal inventory turnover can be estimated for use in determining an optimum policy. The reverse is more likely to be true; that is, an optimum policy for each inventory item or group of items will result in an optimum turnover ratio.

## Average collection period

The average collection period is calculated by dividing the average accounts receivable balance by the average daily credit sales. The average collection period is a measure of the average number of days a company must wait after making a credit sale before it receives payment, and indicates whether accounts receivable are being collected within a reasonable period of time. Assuming that all of Pacific Dunlop's sales were on credit in both the 1990–91 and 1991–92 financial years, the average collection period is calculated as follows:

$$\text{Average collection period} = \frac{\text{average receivables}}{\text{average daily credit sales}}$$
$$= \frac{\$953\,014\,000}{\$5\,806\,156\,000/365}$$
$$= 59.9 \text{ days } (52.9)$$

The average receivables figure is usually calculated as the average of opening and closing accounts receivable balances. However, in this calculation we have assumed that the year-end accounts receivable balance is typical of the average balance during the year.

The ratio is calculated because management is interested in the average number of days resources are tied up in accounts receivable. However, in Section 25.4, it was shown that reducing the collection period involves various costs. We suggested that there is an optimum collection period that balances benefits and costs.

## Total asset turnover

Total asset turnover measures the turnover of the company's assets and is calculated by dividing sales by total tangible assets.

$$\text{Total asset turnover} = \frac{\text{sales}}{\text{total tangible assets}}$$
$$= \frac{\$5\,806\,156\,000}{\$5\,941\,901\,000}$$
$$= 0.98 \ (1.06)$$

This ratio is a measure of a company's efficiency in the use of its assets to generate sales. An efficient company will generate a higher level of sales with a given level of assets than its less efficient competitors. A weakness in the method of calculation is that it is based on the book value of assets, which may seriously distort the total asset turnover ratio. For example, it is conceivable that management may continue to operate an asset that is no longer efficient and that has been almost fully depreciated because its use will have a favourable effect on the total asset turnover ratio.[23]

---

[23] J. C. Van Horne, *Financial Management and Policy*, 4th edn, Prentice-Hall, Englewood Cliffs, New Jersey, 1977, p. 686.

## LEVERAGE RATIOS

Leverage ratios show the extent to which a company uses debt in its capital structure and provide evidence of a company's ability to pay lenders in the long run. There are many measures of leverage but we will consider only two ratios.

### Debt to total assets

This is calculated by dividing total liabilities by total assets.

$$\text{Debt to total assets (Leverage ratio)} = \frac{\text{total liabilities}}{\text{total assets}}$$
$$= \frac{\$3\,890\,075\,000}{\$5\,941\,901\,000}$$
$$= 65.47\% \ (70.19\%)$$

The higher this percentage, the greater is the company's reliance on debt in its capital structure. The effects that changes in leverage have on a company's cost of capital were considered in Chapter 12.

### Earnings coverage ratio

The earnings coverage ratio is calculated by dividing a company's earnings before interest and taxes (EBIT) by the interest expense. It is a measure of a company's ability to meet the interest charges on its debt.

$$\text{Earnings coverage ratio} = \frac{\text{EBIT}}{\text{interest expense}}$$
$$= \frac{\$493\,432\,000}{\$183\,737\,000}$$
$$= 2.69 \ (2.68)$$

In many ways this ratio is superior to the leverage ratio as a measure of financial risk because it attempts to measure the company's ability to pay the interest on its debt and so avoid future financial difficulties. The higher this ratio, the greater will be the reduction in the company's earnings that can occur before it will default on its interest payments.

Donaldson has suggested an approach suitable for determining a company's ability to meet its long-term obligations that improves upon this ratio in two ways.[24] First he emphasised that it is cash flow and not earnings that is important for debt-servicing purposes. Secondly, he stressed that in addition to interest payments there are other financial obligations that have to be met. These include dividends on preference shares, lease payments, repayment of debt at maturity, and other unavoidable expenditures. He suggested that a company's ability to service its debt depends on its cash flow coverage of these fixed charges. He then developed a method to determine the probability of cash insolvency and cash inadequacy in a period of recession.

---

[24] G. Donaldson, 'New Framework for Corporate Debt Policy', *Harvard Business Review*, March–April, 1962, pp. 117–31.

## PROFITABILITY RATIOS

The aim of profitability ratios is to measure the effectiveness of management in using a company's resources to generate returns for shareholders.

### Profit margin on sales

This ratio is calculated by dividing operating profit after taxes by total annual sales. It shows the amount of profit generated by the company from each dollar of sales.

$$\text{Profit margin} = \frac{\text{operating profit after tax}}{\text{sales}}$$
$$= \frac{\$217\,728\,000}{\$5\,806\,156\,000}$$
$$= 3.75\% \ (4.47\%)$$

This is a measure of relative efficiency, as it reflects management's efforts to generate sales and control costs. Success in reducing costs will increase the profit margin.

### Return on shareholders' equity

This ratio is calculated by dividing operating profit after tax by the book value of shareholders' equity. It is a measure of the earning power of the shareholders' investment.

$$\text{Return on shareholder's equity} = \frac{\text{operating profit after tax}}{\text{shareholders' equity}}$$
$$= \frac{\$217\,728\,000}{\$2\,051\,826\,000}$$
$$= 10.61\% \ (15.88\%)$$

## USEFULNESS OF FINANCIAL RATIOS

So far we have discussed the measurement of a number of financial ratios, with only passing reference to their usefulness. To assess the usefulness of financial ratios we must distinguish between 'insiders', or managers, and 'outsiders', or investors and creditors. Management needs information of direct assistance to it in making decisions. When this criterion is applied to financial ratios it is questionable whether they provide management with information that is of direct use for decision making. For example, the current ratio of Pacific Dunlop is 1.11. What information would this figure convey to management? We suggested that a very high ratio indicates that the company has too many of its resources tied up in relatively unproductive short-term assets. Alternatively, if the current ratio is very low, it may indicate that there is a liquidity problem. Between these two extremes there is an optimum current ratio that management needs to know if it is to decide whether any action is necessary.

A ratio of 2 was frequently quoted as a current ratio at which to aim.[25] However, the basis for such a benchmark is not apparent. It seems most unlikely

---

[25] K. W. Lemke, 'The Measurement of Working Capital Adequacy', *Society Bulletin No. 3*, Accountants' Publishing Co., Melbourne, 1968, p. 6.

that one figure will prove to be optimum for all companies. The current ratio will be affected by all decisions made with respect to short-term assets and short-term liabilities. We have already suggested, in relation to the management of short-term assets, that it is likely that different companies will have different policies. It seems likely, therefore, that different policies will result in different current ratios.[26]

Alternatively, management may obtain useful information by comparing the company's ratio with those of other companies in the same industry. Companies in the same industry operate in a similar environment, and therefore most factors that could cause differences in their optimum ratios are eliminated. As a result, a company could consider the average ratio of the other companies in the industry as a guide to the optimum ratio. If, in our example, the average current ratio of Pacific Dunlop's competitors was, say, 2.11, does this mean that Pacific Dunlop's current ratio of 1.11 is too low? The answer to this question is not obvious. It may be that its competitors have too high a proportion of their resources invested in short-term assets. Nevertheless, intercompany comparisons may provide a reason to re-examine policies on the management of short-term assets.

It is frequently suggested that useful information may also be obtained by studying the trend in the ratios over time. However, knowledge of the optimum ratio will enhance the use of trend analysis for decision-making purposes. For example, although there may be an improvement in the profit margin from one year to the next, this may still be below its optimum value. This method of evaluation is further complicated by the fact that the optimum values of financial ratios are likely to change over time. Under these circumstances, maintaining a stable ratio from one year to the next is not necessarily desirable. For example, the techniques used to determine inventory policy suggest that a company's inventory should increase at a much slower rate than sales. Therefore, a company's optimum inventory turnover ratio will increase as the company's sales grow. Similarly, a company's cash balance should also increase at a much slower rate than sales. This implies that the current ratio should decline as a company's operations grow.[27]

The discussion of the usefulness of financial ratios has concentrated on the current ratio. It was suggested that management must know the optimum current ratio before it can make decisions about the present level of a company's current ratio. This applies equally to each of the other ratios.

So far we have only considered the usefulness of financial ratios to the managers of a company. However, many of these ratios are of value to interested outsiders who have only limited information on which to base their decisions. Outsiders include financial analysts, creditors, and investors. Since outsiders use financial ratios to assess companies' financial performance, management generally takes account of the impact of its decisions on financial ratios. If investors use financial ratios to assess the composition of their portfolios it could be foolhardy for management to ignore the impact of its decisions on financial ratios. In Chapter 5 this explanation was considered as a possible reason why managers

---

[26] See Footnote 25, pp. 11–14.
[27] See Footnote 25, p. 17.

tend to use both the accounting rate of return and discounted cash flow methods to determine the acceptability of investment projects.

Banks and other lending institutions also frequently use financial ratios as a means of assessing the creditworthiness of applicants for loans. For example, a bank may be prepared to lend funds to a company only if the company has a current ratio of 2 or higher. Therefore, even if it is optimum for a company to maintain a current ratio of 1.10, the bank's policy is likely to mean that the company maintains a ratio greater than the optimum ratio. In addition, a company's decisions may be influenced by debt covenants, some of which are based on allowable limits for certain financial ratios. The nature of such covenants, and their impact upon capital structure decisions, were discussed in Chapter 12.

## FINANCIAL RATIOS AND SHORT-TERM ASSET MANAGEMENT

We now consider in more detail those ratios considered to be useful for short-term asset management.

### Current ratio and 'quick' ratio

The current ratio and the 'quick' ratio serve as a measure of a company's liquidity position and consequently have particular application to liquidity management. The usefulness of these ratios for decision making by management has already been questioned, although empirical studies have produced evidence that these and other ratios may be used to assist outsiders in predicting the failure of companies.[28]

These ratios provide an indication of a company's ability to meet its immediate financial obligations. The current ratio is calculated by dividing the book value of current assets by the book value of current liabilities. However, this does not take into account either the relative liquidity of the various assets or the relative urgency for repayment of the current liabilities. It is not useful to know that the company has a current ratio of 2 if all the liabilities are due to be paid within a week, and most of the short-term assets cannot be realised within 2 months. A further limitation of the current ratio is that it includes inventory, which is usually valued at historical cost. As it is assumed that inventory can generate cash to meet financial obligations, it may be argued that inventory should be valued at net selling price, which is a better indication of the asset's ability to generate cash. Finally, it is possible for management to 'window dress' the financial statements to improve these ratios. This may be achieved either by delaying purchases, or by paying off a larger amount of the company's current liabilities just before the end of the financial year.

### Inventory turnover

Inventory turnover is a measure of the number of times a company turns over its inventory during the year. This ratio is related to inventory management because inventory turnover will be a direct result of the company's inventory management policy defined in terms of economic order quantities and reorder

---

[28] For a review of the work in this area, see George Foster, *Financial Statement Analysis*, 2nd edn, Prentice-Hall, Englewood Cliffs, New Jersey, 1986, Ch. 15.

points. An increase in inventory turnover is frequently regarded as desirable since profit is generated as inventory is sold (that is, turned over). However, an increase in inventory turnover is not necessarily desirable, because it may have been achieved by reducing the quantity of inventory to such a low level that purchasing costs and stockout costs have become excessive. The techniques available for determining the optimum inventory holding and, consequently, the optimum turnover, were discussed in Chapter 23. It is important to note that the turnover ratio, which uses balance sheet data, measures only the average turnover for all inventory items, whereas it is desirable to ascertain the optimum inventory policy for each individual inventory item or group of items.

### Average collection period

This ratio provides useful information for accounts receivable management since there are benefits that can result from a reduction in the collection period. However, it needs to be recognised that a continual reduction in the collection period is not necessarily a sign of increasing efficiency. To show this, it is assumed that there are two types of account. The first pays at the end of the credit period (assuming no cash discount). Provided that the credit terms remain unchanged, there will be no reduction in the collection period for such accounts. The second type of account is a delinquent account, which does not pay within the collection period. In Section 25.4, we suggested that a company will incur collection expenditures in order to encourage payment of a delinquent account. There will be an optimum policy for collection procedures, which usually means that the company has to accept a certain number of late collections (that is, delinquent accounts) and non-collections (that is, bad debts). Therefore, there is a lower limit to the average collection period, which depends on the company's credit terms. The optimum average collection period will usually be above this lower limit. It may be concluded that the optimum average collection period depends on the optimum credit policy, with the collection policy having the greatest direct effect. If an optimum average collection period exists, then it is not in the company's interest to reduce its average collection period below this optimum.

The average collection period provides management with information about the quality of the company's accounts receivable and the efficiency of its credit control. Valuable information can also be obtained from an 'age' analysis of accounts. This analysis lists debtors' accounts with reference to the period of time they have been outstanding, and highlights the incidence of delinquent accounts. It therefore directs management's attention to those accounts on which its collection efforts should be concentrated.

## SELECTED REFERENCES

Beaver, W. H., 'Financial Ratios as Predictors of Failure', *Empirical Research in Accounting: Selected studies*, 1966, pp. 71–111.
Donaldson, G., 'New Framework for Corporate Debt Policy', *Harvard Business Review*, March–April 1962, pp. 117–31.
Foster, George, *Financial Statement Analysis*, 2nd edn, Prentice-Hall, Englewood Cliffs, New Jersey, 1986.
Horngren, C. T. & Foster, G., *Cost Accounting: A Managerial Emphasis*, 7th edn, Prentice-Hall, Englewood Cliffs, 1991.
Horrigan, J. O., 'A Short History of Financial Ratio Analysis', *The Accounting Review*, April 1968, pp. 284–94.
Lemke, K. W., 'The Measurement of Working Capital Adequacy', *Society Bulletin No. 3*, Accountants' Publishing Co., Melbourne, 1968.
Lemke, K. W., 'The Evaluation of Liquidity: An Analytical Study', *Journal of Accounting Research*, Spring 1970, pp. 47–77.
Lev, Baruch, *Financial Statement Analysis: A New Approach*, Prentice-Hall, Englewood Cliffs, New Jersey, 1974.
Smith, K. V., *Guide to Working Capital Management*, McGraw-Hill, New York, 1979, Ch. 9.

**APPENDIX A**

# NUMERICAL TABLES

**Table 1**  *Accumulated value of a present sum* ..........................................803

**Table 2**  *Present value of a future sum* ....................................................805

**Table 3**  *Accumulated value of an ordinary annuity* ...............................807

**Table 4**  *Present value of an ordinary annuity* ........................................809

**Table 5**  *Areas under the standard normal curve* ....................................811

**Table 1** Accumulated value of $1
$(1+i)^n$

| n | 0.25% | 0.5% | 0.66% | 0.75% | 1.0% | 1.5% | 1.75% | 2.0% | 2.5% | 3.0% | 3.5% | n |
|---|---|---|---|---|---|---|---|---|---|---|---|---|
| 1 | 1.00250 | 1.00500 | 1.00667 | 1.00750 | 1.01000 | 1.01500 | 1.01750 | 1.02000 | 1.02500 | 1.03000 | 1.03500 | 1 |
| 2 | 1.00501 | 1.01003 | 1.01338 | 1.01506 | 1.02010 | 1.03023 | 1.03531 | 1.04040 | 1.05063 | 1.06090 | 1.07123 | 2 |
| 3 | 1.00752 | 1.01508 | 1.02013 | 1.02267 | 1.03030 | 1.04568 | 1.05342 | 1.06121 | 1.07689 | 1.09273 | 1.10872 | 3 |
| 4 | 1.01004 | 1.02015 | 1.02693 | 1.03034 | 1.04060 | 1.06136 | 1.07186 | 1.08243 | 1.10381 | 1.12551 | 1.14752 | 4 |
| 5 | 1.01256 | 1.02525 | 1.03378 | 1.03807 | 1.05101 | 1.07728 | 1.09062 | 1.10408 | 1.13141 | 1.15927 | 1.18769 | 5 |
| 6 | 1.01509 | 1.03038 | 1.04067 | 1.04585 | 1.06152 | 1.09344 | 1.10970 | 1.12616 | 1.15969 | 1.19405 | 1.22926 | 6 |
| 7 | 1.01763 | 1.03553 | 1.04761 | 1.05370 | 1.07214 | 1.10984 | 1.12912 | 1.14869 | 1.18869 | 1.22987 | 1.27228 | 7 |
| 8 | 1.02018 | 1.04071 | 1.05459 | 1.06160 | 1.08286 | 1.12649 | 1.14888 | 1.17166 | 1.21840 | 1.26677 | 1.31681 | 8 |
| 9 | 1.02273 | 1.04591 | 1.06163 | 1.06956 | 1.09369 | 1.14339 | 1.16899 | 1.19509 | 1.24886 | 1.30477 | 1.36290 | 9 |
| 10 | 1.02528 | 1.05114 | 1.06870 | 1.07758 | 1.10462 | 1.16054 | 1.18944 | 1.21899 | 1.28008 | 1.34392 | 1.41060 | 10 |
| 11 | 1.02785 | 1.05640 | 1.07583 | 1.08566 | 1.11567 | 1.17795 | 1.21026 | 1.24337 | 1.31209 | 1.38423 | 1.45997 | 11 |
| 12 | 1.03042 | 1.06168 | 1.08300 | 1.09381 | 1.12683 | 1.19562 | 1.23144 | 1.26824 | 1.34489 | 1.42576 | 1.51107 | 12 |
| 13 | 1.03299 | 1.06699 | 1.09022 | 1.10201 | 1.13809 | 1.21355 | 1.25299 | 1.29361 | 1.37851 | 1.46853 | 1.56396 | 13 |
| 14 | 1.03557 | 1.07232 | 1.09749 | 1.11028 | 1.14947 | 1.23176 | 1.27492 | 1.31948 | 1.41297 | 1.51259 | 1.61869 | 14 |
| 15 | 1.03816 | 1.07768 | 1.10480 | 1.11860 | 1.16097 | 1.25023 | 1.29723 | 1.34587 | 1.44830 | 1.55797 | 1.67535 | 15 |
| 16 | 1.04076 | 1.08307 | 1.11217 | 1.12699 | 1.17258 | 1.26899 | 1.31993 | 1.37279 | 1.48451 | 1.60471 | 1.73399 | 16 |
| 17 | 1.04336 | 1.08849 | 1.11958 | 1.13544 | 1.18430 | 1.28802 | 1.34303 | 1.40024 | 1.52162 | 1.65285 | 1.79468 | 17 |
| 18 | 1.04597 | 1.09393 | 1.12705 | 1.14396 | 1.19615 | 1.30734 | 1.36653 | 1.42825 | 1.55966 | 1.70243 | 1.85749 | 18 |
| 19 | 1.04858 | 1.09940 | 1.13456 | 1.15254 | 1.20811 | 1.32695 | 1.39045 | 1.45681 | 1.59865 | 1.75351 | 1.92250 | 19 |
| 20 | 1.05121 | 1.10490 | 1.14213 | 1.16118 | 1.22019 | 1.34686 | 1.41478 | 1.48595 | 1.63862 | 1.80611 | 1.98979 | 20 |
| 21 | 1.05383 | 1.11042 | 1.14974 | 1.16989 | 1.23239 | 1.36706 | 1.43454 | 1.51567 | 1.67958 | 1.86029 | 2.05943 | 21 |
| 22 | 1.05647 | 1.11597 | 1.15740 | 1.17867 | 1.24472 | 1.38756 | 1.46473 | 1.54598 | 1.72157 | 1.91610 | 2.13151 | 22 |
| 23 | 1.05911 | 1.12155 | 1.16512 | 1.18751 | 1.25716 | 1.40838 | 1.49036 | 1.57690 | 1.76461 | 1.97359 | 2.20611 | 23 |
| 24 | 1.06176 | 1.12716 | 1.17289 | 1.19641 | 1.26973 | 1.42950 | 1.51644 | 1.60844 | 1.80873 | 2.03279 | 2.28333 | 24 |
| 25 | 1.06441 | 1.13280 | 1.18071 | 1.20539 | 1.28243 | 1.45095 | 1.54298 | 1.64061 | 1.85394 | 2.09378 | 2.36324 | 25 |
| 30 | 1.07778 | 1.16140 | 1.22059 | 1.25127 | 1.34785 | 1.56308 | 1.68280 | 1.81136 | 2.09729 | 2.42726 | 2.80679 | 30 |
| 35 | 1.09132 | 1.19073 | 1.26182 | 1.29890 | 1.41660 | 1.68388 | 1.83529 | 1.99989 | 2.37321 | 2.81386 | 3.33359 | 35 |
| 40 | 1.10503 | 1.22079 | 1.30445 | 1.34835 | 1.48886 | 1.81402 | 2.00160 | 2.20804 | 2.68506 | 3.26204 | 3.95926 | 40 |
| 45 | 1.11892 | 1.25162 | 1.34852 | 1.39968 | 1.56481 | 1.95421 | 2.18298 | 2.43785 | 3.03790 | 3.78160 | 4.70236 | 45 |
| 50 | 1.13297 | 1.28323 | 1.39407 | 1.45296 | 1.64463 | 2.10524 | 2.38079 | 2.69159 | 3.43711 | 4.38391 | 5.58493 | 50 |
| 60 | 1.16162 | 1.34885 | 1.48985 | 1.56568 | 1.81670 | 2.43220 | 2.83182 | 3.28103 | 4.39979 | 5.89160 | 7.87809 | 60 |

| n | 4.0% | 4.5% | 5.0% | 6.0% | 7.0% | 8.0% | 10.0% | 12.0% | 15.0% | 20.0% | n |
|---|---|---|---|---|---|---|---|---|---|---|---|
| 1 | 1.040 00 | 1.045 00 | 1.050 00 | 1.060 00 | 1.070 00 | 1.080 00 | 1.100 00 | 1.120 0 | 1.150 | 1.200 | 1 |
| 2 | 1.081 60 | 1.092 03 | 1.102 50 | 1.123 60 | 1.144 90 | 1.166 40 | 1.210 00 | 1.254 4 | 1.322 | 1.440 | 2 |
| 3 | 1.124 86 | 1.141 17 | 1.157 63 | 1.191 01 | 1.225 04 | 1.259 71 | 1.331 00 | 1.404 9 | 1.521 | 1.728 | 3 |
| 4 | 1.169 86 | 1.192 52 | 1.215 51 | 1.262 47 | 1.310 79 | 1.360 48 | 1.464 10 | 1.573 5 | 1.749 | 2.074 | 4 |
| 5 | 1.216 65 | 1.246 18 | 1.276 28 | 1.338 22 | 1.402 55 | 1.469 32 | 1.610 51 | 1.762 0 | 2.011 | 2.488 | 5 |
| 6 | 1.265 32 | 1.302 26 | 1.340 10 | 1.418 51 | 1.500 73 | 1.586 87 | 1.771 56 | 1.973 8 | 2.313 | 2.938 | 6 |
| 7 | 1.315 93 | 1.360 86 | 1.407 10 | 1.503 63 | 1.605 78 | 1.713 82 | 1.948 72 | 2.210 7 | 2.660 | 3.583 | 7 |
| 8 | 1.368 57 | 1.422 10 | 1.477 46 | 1.593 84 | 1.718 18 | 1.850 93 | 2.143 59 | 2.476 0 | 3.059 | 4.300 | 8 |
| 9 | 1.423 31 | 1.486 10 | 1.551 33 | 1.689 47 | 1.838 45 | 1.999 00 | 2.357 95 | 2.773 1 | 3.518 | 5.160 | 9 |
| 10 | 1.480 24 | 1.552 97 | 1.628 89 | 1.790 84 | 1.967 15 | 2.158 92 | 2.593 74 | 3.105 8 | 4.046 | 6.192 | 10 |
| 11 | 1.539 45 | 1.622 85 | 1.710 34 | 1.898 29 | 2.104 85 | 2.331 63 | 2.853 12 | 3.478 5 | 4.652 | 7.430 | 11 |
| 12 | 1.601 03 | 1.695 88 | 1.795 86 | 2.012 19 | 2.252 19 | 2.518 17 | 3.138 43 | 3.896 0 | 5.350 | 8.916 | 12 |
| 13 | 1.665 07 | 1.772 20 | 1.885 65 | 2.132 92 | 2.409 84 | 2.719 62 | 3.452 27 | 4.363 5 | 6.153 | 10.699 | 13 |
| 14 | 1.731 68 | 1.851 94 | 1.979 93 | 2.260 90 | 2.578 53 | 2.937 19 | 3.797 50 | 4.887 1 | 7.076 | 12.839 | 14 |
| 15 | 1.800 94 | 1.935 28 | 2.078 93 | 2.396 55 | 2.759 03 | 3.172 16 | 4.177 25 | 5.473 6 | 8.137 | 15.407 | 15 |
| 16 | 1.872 98 | 2.022 37 | 2.182 87 | 2.540 35 | 2.952 16 | 3.425 94 | 4.594 97 | 6.130 3 | 9.358 | 18.488 | 16 |
| 17 | 1.947 90 | 2.113 38 | 2.292 02 | 2.692 77 | 3.158 81 | 3.700 01 | 5.054 47 | 6.866 1 | 10.761 | 22.186 | 17 |
| 18 | 2.025 82 | 2.208 48 | 2.406 62 | 2.854 33 | 3.379 93 | 3.996 01 | 5.559 92 | 7.690 0 | 12.375 | 26.623 | 18 |
| 19 | 2.106 85 | 2.307 86 | 2.526 95 | 3.025 59 | 3.616 52 | 4.315 70 | 6.115 91 | 8.612 8 | 14.232 | 31.945 | 19 |
| 20 | 2.191 12 | 2.411 71 | 2.653 30 | 3.207 13 | 3.869 68 | 4.660 95 | 6.727 50 | 9.646 3 | 16.367 | 38.338 | 20 |
| 21 | 2.278 77 | 2.520 24 | 2.785 96 | 3.399 56 | 4.140 56 | 5.033 83 | 7.400 25 | 10.803 8 | 18.821 | 46.005 | 21 |
| 22 | 2.369 92 | 2.633 65 | 2.925 26 | 3.603 53 | 4.430 40 | 5.436 54 | 8.140 27 | 12.100 3 | 21.645 | 55.206 | 22 |
| 23 | 2.464 72 | 2.752 17 | 3.071 52 | 3.819 74 | 4.740 52 | 5.871 46 | 8.954 30 | 13.552 3 | 24.891 | 66.247 | 23 |
| 24 | 2.563 30 | 2.876 01 | 3.225 10 | 4.048 93 | 5.072 36 | 6.341 18 | 9.849 73 | 15.178 6 | 28.625 | 79.497 | 24 |
| 25 | 2.665 84 | 3.005 43 | 3.386 35 | 4.291 87 | 5.427 43 | 6.848 47 | 10.834 71 | 17.000 1 | 32.919 | 95.396 | 25 |
| 30 | 3.243 40 | 3.745 32 | 4.321 94 | 5.743 49 | 7.612 25 | 10.062 65 | 17.449 40 | 29.960 0 | 66.212 | 237.376 | 30 |
| 35 | 3.946 09 | 4.667 35 | 5.516 02 | 7.686 08 | 10.676 58 | 14.785 34 | 28.102 44 | 52.800 0 | 133.175 | 590.668 | 35 |
| 40 | 4.801 02 | 5.816 36 | 7.039 99 | 10.285 71 | 14.974 45 | 21.724 52 | 45.259 26 | 93.051 0 | 267.862 | 1469.771 | 40 |
| 45 | 5.841 18 | 7.248 25 | 8.985 01 | 13.764 61 | 21.002 45 | 31.920 44 | 72.890 48 | 163.987 6 | 538.767 | 3657.258 | 45 |
| 50 | 7.106 68 | 9.032 64 | 11.477 40 | 18.420 15 | 29.457 02 | 46.901 61 | 117.390 85 | 289.002 1 | 1083.652 | 9100.427 | 50 |
| 60 | 10.519 63 | 14.027 41 | 18.679 19 | 32.987 69 | 57.946 43 | 101.257 06 | 304.481 64 | 897.596 9 | 4383.999 | 56347.514 | 60 |

**Table 2** Present value of $1

$$\frac{1}{(1+i)^n} = (1+i)^{-n}$$

| n | 0.25% | 0.50% | 0.66% | 0.75% | 1.0% | 1.5% | 2.0% | 2.5% | 3.0% | 3.5% | n |
|---|---|---|---|---|---|---|---|---|---|---|---|
| 1 | 0.99751 | 0.99502 | 0.99338 | 0.99256 | 0.99009 | 0.98522 | 0.98039 | 0.97560 | 0.97087 | 0.96618 | 1 |
| 2 | 0.99502 | 0.99007 | 0.98680 | 0.98517 | 0.98029 | 0.97066 | 0.96116 | 0.95181 | 0.94259 | 0.93351 | 2 |
| 3 | 0.99254 | 0.98515 | 0.98026 | 0.97783 | 0.97059 | 0.95631 | 0.94232 | 0.92859 | 0.91514 | 0.90194 | 3 |
| 4 | 0.99006 | 0.98025 | 0.97377 | 0.97055 | 0.96098 | 0.94218 | 0.92384 | 0.90595 | 0.88848 | 0.87144 | 4 |
| 5 | 0.98759 | 0.97537 | 0.96732 | 0.96333 | 0.95146 | 0.92826 | 0.90573 | 0.88385 | 0.86260 | 0.84197 | 5 |
| 6 | 0.98513 | 0.97052 | 0.96092 | 0.95616 | 0.94204 | 0.91454 | 0.88797 | 0.86229 | 0.83748 | 0.81350 | 6 |
| 7 | 0.98267 | 0.96569 | 0.95455 | 0.94094 | 0.93271 | 0.90102 | 0.87056 | 0.84126 | 0.81309 | 0.78599 | 7 |
| 8 | 0.98022 | 0.96089 | 0.94823 | 0.94198 | 0.92348 | 0.88771 | 0.85349 | 0.82074 | 0.78940 | 0.75941 | 8 |
| 9 | 0.97778 | 0.95610 | 0.94195 | 0.93496 | 0.91433 | 0.87459 | 0.83675 | 0.80072 | 0.76641 | 0.73373 | 9 |
| 10 | 0.97534 | 0.95135 | 0.93571 | 0.92800 | 0.90528 | 0.86166 | 0.82034 | 0.78119 | 0.74409 | 0.70891 | 10 |
| 11 | 0.97291 | 0.94661 | 0.92952 | 0.92109 | 0.89632 | 0.84893 | 0.80426 | 0.76214 | 0.72242 | 0.68494 | 11 |
| 12 | 0.97048 | 0.94191 | 0.92336 | 0.91424 | 0.88744 | 0.83638 | 0.78849 | 0.74355 | 0.70137 | 0.66178 | 12 |
| 13 | 0.96806 | 0.93722 | 0.91725 | 0.90743 | 0.87866 | 0.82402 | 0.77303 | 0.72542 | 0.68095 | 0.63940 | 13 |
| 14 | 0.96565 | 0.93256 | 0.91117 | 0.90068 | 0.86996 | 0.81184 | 0.75787 | 0.70772 | 0.66111 | 0.61778 | 14 |
| 15 | 0.96324 | 0.92792 | 0.90514 | 0.89397 | 0.86134 | 0.79985 | 0.74301 | 0.69046 | 0.64186 | 0.59689 | 15 |
| 16 | 0.96084 | 0.92330 | 0.89914 | 0.88732 | 0.85282 | 0.78803 | 0.72844 | 0.67362 | 0.62316 | 0.57670 | 16 |
| 17 | 0.95844 | 0.91871 | 0.89319 | 0.88071 | 0.84437 | 0.77638 | 0.71416 | 0.65719 | 0.60501 | 0.55720 | 17 |
| 18 | 0.95605 | 0.91414 | 0.88727 | 0.87416 | 0.83601 | 0.76491 | 0.70015 | 0.64116 | 0.58739 | 0.53836 | 18 |
| 19 | 0.95367 | 0.90959 | 0.88140 | 0.86765 | 0.82773 | 0.75360 | 0.68643 | 0.62552 | 0.57028 | 0.52015 | 19 |
| 20 | 0.95129 | 0.90506 | 0.87556 | 0.86119 | 0.81954 | 0.74247 | 0.67297 | 0.61027 | 0.55367 | 0.50256 | 20 |
| 21 | 0.94892 | 0.90056 | 0.86976 | 0.85478 | 0.81143 | 0.73149 | 0.65977 | 0.59538 | 0.53754 | 0.48557 | 21 |
| 22 | 0.94655 | 0.89608 | 0.86400 | 0.84810 | 0.80339 | 0.72068 | 0.64683 | 0.58086 | 0.52189 | 0.46915 | 22 |
| 23 | 0.94419 | 0.89162 | 0.85828 | 0.84210 | 0.79544 | 0.71003 | 0.63415 | 0.56669 | 0.50669 | 0.45328 | 23 |
| 24 | 0.94184 | 0.88719 | 0.85260 | 0.83583 | 0.78756 | 0.69954 | 0.62172 | 0.55287 | 0.49193 | 0.43795 | 24 |
| 25 | 0.93949 | 0.88277 | 0.84695 | 0.82961 | 0.77976 | 0.68920 | 0.60953 | 0.53939 | 0.47760 | 0.42314 | 25 |
| 30 | 0.92783 | 0.86103 | 0.81927 | 0.79919 | 0.74192 | 0.63976 | 0.55207 | 0.47674 | 0.41198 | 0.35627 | 30 |
| 35 | 0.91632 | 0.83982 | 0.79250 | 0.76988 | 0.70591 | 0.59386 | 0.50002 | 0.42137 | 0.35538 | 0.29997 | 35 |
| 40 | 0.90495 | 0.81914 | 0.76661 | 0.74165 | 0.67165 | 0.55126 | 0.45289 | 0.37243 | 0.30655 | 0.25257 | 40 |
| 45 | 0.89372 | 0.79896 | 0.74156 | 0.71445 | 0.63905 | 0.51171 | 0.41019 | 0.32917 | 0.26443 | 0.21265 | 45 |
| 50 | 0.88263 | 0.77929 | 0.71732 | 0.68825 | 0.60803 | 0.47500 | 0.37152 | 0.29094 | 0.22810 | 0.17905 | 50 |
| 60 | 0.86087 | 0.74137 | 0.67121 | 0.63870 | 0.55045 | 0.40930 | 0.30478 | 0.22728 | 0.16973 | 0.12693 | 60 |

| n | 4.0% | 4.5% | 5.0% | 6.0% | 7.0% | 8.0% | 10.0% | 12.0% | 15.0% | 20.0% | n |
|---|------|------|------|------|------|------|-------|-------|-------|-------|---|
| 1 | 0.96153 | 0.95693 | 0.95238 | 0.94339 | 0.93457 | 0.92592 | 0.90909 | 0.89286 | 0.86957 | 0.83333 | 1 |
| 2 | 0.92455 | 0.91572 | 0.90702 | 0.88999 | 0.87343 | 0.85733 | 0.82645 | 0.79719 | 0.75614 | 0.69444 | 2 |
| 3 | 0.88899 | 0.87629 | 0.86383 | 0.83961 | 0.81629 | 0.79383 | 0.75131 | 0.71178 | 0.65752 | 0.57870 | 3 |
| 4 | 0.85480 | 0.83856 | 0.82270 | 0.79209 | 0.76289 | 0.73502 | 0.68301 | 0.63552 | 0.57175 | 0.48225 | 4 |
| 5 | 0.82192 | 0.80245 | 0.78352 | 0.74725 | 0.71298 | 0.68058 | 0.62092 | 0.56743 | 0.49718 | 0.40188 | 5 |
| 6 | 0.79031 | 0.76789 | 0.74621 | 0.70496 | 0.66634 | 0.63016 | 0.56447 | 0.50663 | 0.43233 | 0.33490 | 6 |
| 7 | 0.75991 | 0.73482 | 0.71068 | 0.66505 | 0.62274 | 0.58349 | 0.51316 | 0.45235 | 0.37594 | 0.27908 | 7 |
| 8 | 0.73069 | 0.70318 | 0.67683 | 0.62741 | 0.58200 | 0.54026 | 0.46651 | 0.40388 | 0.32690 | 0.23257 | 8 |
| 9 | 0.70258 | 0.67290 | 0.64460 | 0.59189 | 0.54393 | 0.50024 | 0.42410 | 0.36061 | 0.28426 | 0.19381 | 9 |
| 10 | 0.67556 | 0.64392 | 0.61390 | 0.55839 | 0.50834 | 0.46319 | 0.38554 | 0.32197 | 0.24718 | 0.16151 | 10 |
| 11 | 0.64958 | 0.61619 | 0.58467 | 0.52678 | 0.47509 | 0.42888 | 0.35049 | 0.28748 | 0.21494 | 0.13459 | 11 |
| 12 | 0.62459 | 0.58966 | 0.55683 | 0.49696 | 0.44401 | 0.39711 | 0.31863 | 0.25667 | 0.18691 | 0.11216 | 12 |
| 13 | 0.60057 | 0.56427 | 0.53032 | 0.46883 | 0.41496 | 0.36769 | 0.28966 | 0.22917 | 0.16253 | 0.09346 | 13 |
| 14 | 0.57747 | 0.53997 | 0.50506 | 0.44230 | 0.38781 | 0.34046 | 0.26333 | 0.20462 | 0.14133 | 0.07789 | 14 |
| 15 | 0.55526 | 0.51672 | 0.48101 | 0.41726 | 0.36244 | 0.31524 | 0.23939 | 0.18270 | 0.12289 | 0.06491 | 15 |
| 16 | 0.53390 | 0.49446 | 0.45811 | 0.39364 | 0.33873 | 0.29189 | 0.21763 | 0.16312 | 0.10686 | 0.05409 | 16 |
| 17 | 0.51337 | 0.47317 | 0.43629 | 0.37136 | 0.31657 | 0.27026 | 0.19784 | 0.14564 | 0.09293 | 0.04507 | 17 |
| 18 | 0.49362 | 0.45280 | 0.41552 | 0.35034 | 0.29586 | 0.25024 | 0.17986 | 0.13004 | 0.08080 | 0.03756 | 18 |
| 19 | 0.47464 | 0.43330 | 0.39573 | 0.33051 | 0.27650 | 0.23171 | 0.16351 | 0.11611 | 0.07026 | 0.03130 | 19 |
| 20 | 0.45638 | 0.41464 | 0.37688 | 0.31180 | 0.25841 | 0.21454 | 0.14864 | 0.10367 | 0.06110 | 0.02608 | 20 |
| 21 | 0.43883 | 0.39678 | 0.35894 | 0.29415 | 0.24151 | 0.19865 | 0.13513 | 0.09256 | 0.05313 | 0.02174 | 21 |
| 22 | 0.42195 | 0.37970 | 0.34184 | 0.27750 | 0.22571 | 0.18394 | 0.12285 | 0.08264 | 0.04620 | 0.01811 | 22 |
| 23 | 0.40572 | 0.36335 | 0.32557 | 0.26179 | 0.21094 | 0.17031 | 0.11168 | 0.07379 | 0.04017 | 0.01509 | 23 |
| 24 | 0.39012 | 0.34770 | 0.31006 | 0.24697 | 0.19714 | 0.15769 | 0.10153 | 0.06588 | 0.03493 | 0.01258 | 24 |
| 25 | 0.37511 | 0.33273 | 0.29530 | 0.23299 | 0.18424 | 0.14601 | 0.09230 | 0.05882 | 0.03038 | 0.01048 | 25 |
| 30 | 0.30831 | 0.26700 | 0.23137 | 0.17411 | 0.13136 | 0.09937 | 0.05731 | 0.03338 | 0.01510 | 0.00421 | 30 |
| 35 | 0.25341 | 0.21425 | 0.18129 | 0.13010 | 0.09366 | 0.06763 | 0.03558 | 0.01894 | 0.00751 | 0.00169 | 35 |
| 40 | 0.20828 | 0.17192 | 0.14204 | 0.09722 | 0.06678 | 0.04603 | 0.02209 | 0.01074 | 0.00373 | 0.00068 | 40 |
| 45 | 0.17119 | 0.13796 | 0.11129 | 0.07265 | 0.04761 | 0.03132 | 0.01372 | 0.00610 | 0.00186 | 0.00027 | 45 |
| 50 | 0.14071 | 0.11070 | 0.08720 | 0.05428 | 0.03394 | 0.02132 | 0.00852 | 0.00346 | 0.00092 | 0.00011 | 50 |
| 60 | 0.09506 | 0.07129 | 0.05354 | 0.03031 | 0.01726 | 0.00988 | 0.00328 | 0.00111 | 0.00023 | 0.00002 | 60 |

**Table 3** Accumulated value of $1 per period

$$s_{\overline{n}|i} = \frac{(1+i)^n - 1}{i}$$

| n | 0.25% | 0.5% | 0.66% | 0.75% | 1.0% | 1.5% | 2.0% | 2.5% | 3.0% | 3.5% | n |
|---|---|---|---|---|---|---|---|---|---|---|---|
| 1 | 1.00000 | 1.00000 | 1.00000 | 1.00000 | 1.00000 | 1.00000 | 1.00000 | 1.0000 | 1.0000 | 1.0000 | 1 |
| 2 | 2.00250 | 2.00500 | 2.00667 | 2.00750 | 2.01000 | 2.01500 | 2.02000 | 2.0250 | 2.0300 | 2.0350 | 2 |
| 3 | 3.00751 | 3.01503 | 3.02004 | 3.02256 | 3.03010 | 3.04523 | 3.06040 | 3.0756 | 3.0909 | 3.1062 | 3 |
| 4 | 4.01503 | 4.03010 | 4.04018 | 4.04523 | 4.06040 | 4.09090 | 4.12161 | 4.1525 | 4.1836 | 4.2149 | 4 |
| 5 | 5.02506 | 5.05025 | 5.06711 | 5.07556 | 5.10101 | 5.15227 | 5.20404 | 5.2563 | 5.3091 | 5.3625 | 5 |
| 6 | 6.03763 | 6.07550 | 6.10089 | 6.11363 | 6.15202 | 6.22955 | 6.30812 | 6.3877 | 6.4684 | 6.5502 | 6 |
| 7 | 7.05272 | 7.10588 | 7.14157 | 7.15948 | 7.21354 | 7.32299 | 7.43428 | 7.5474 | 7.6625 | 7.7794 | 7 |
| 8 | 8.07035 | 8.14141 | 8.18918 | 8.21318 | 8.28567 | 8.43284 | 8.58297 | 8.7361 | 8.8923 | 9.0517 | 8 |
| 9 | 9.09053 | 9.18212 | 9.24377 | 9.27478 | 9.36853 | 9.55933 | 9.75463 | 9.9545 | 10.1591 | 10.3685 | 9 |
| 10 | 10.11325 | 10.22803 | 10.30540 | 10.34434 | 10.46221 | 10.70272 | 10.94972 | 11.2034 | 11.4639 | 11.7314 | 10 |
| 11 | 11.13854 | 11.27917 | 11.37410 | 11.42192 | 11.56683 | 11.86326 | 12.16872 | 12.4835 | 12.8078 | 13.1420 | 11 |
| 12 | 12.16638 | 12.33556 | 12.44993 | 12.50759 | 12.68250 | 13.04121 | 13.41209 | 13.7956 | 14.1920 | 14.6020 | 12 |
| 13 | 13.19680 | 13.39724 | 13.53293 | 13.60139 | 13.80933 | 14.23683 | 14.68033 | 15.1404 | 15.6178 | 16.1130 | 13 |
| 14 | 14.22979 | 14.46423 | 14.62315 | 14.70340 | 14.94742 | 15.45038 | 15.97394 | 16.5190 | 17.0863 | 17.6770 | 14 |
| 15 | 15.26537 | 15.53655 | 15.72063 | 15.81368 | 16.09690 | 16.53343 | 16.68214 | 17.9319 | 18.5989 | 19.2957 | 15 |
| 16 | 16.30353 | 16.61423 | 16.82554 | 16.93228 | 17.25786 | 17.93237 | 18.63929 | 19.3802 | 20.1569 | 20.9710 | 16 |
| 17 | 17.34429 | 17.69730 | 17.93761 | 18.05927 | 18.43044 | 19.20136 | 20.01207 | 20.8647 | 21.7616 | 22.7050 | 17 |
| 18 | 18.38765 | 18.78579 | 19.05719 | 19.19472 | 19.61475 | 20.48938 | 21.41231 | 22.3863 | 23.4144 | 24.4997 | 18 |
| 19 | 19.43362 | 19.87972 | 20.18424 | 20.33868 | 20.81090 | 21.79672 | 22.84056 | 23.9460 | 25.1169 | 26.3572 | 19 |
| 20 | 20.48220 | 20.97912 | 21.31880 | 21.49122 | 22.01900 | 23.12367 | 24.29737 | 25.5447 | 26.8704 | 28.2797 | 20 |
| 21 | 21.53341 | 22.08401 | 22.46093 | 22.65240 | 23.23919 | 24.47052 | 25.78332 | 27.1833 | 28.6765 | 30.2695 | 21 |
| 22 | 22.58724 | 23.19443 | 23.61066 | 23.82230 | 24.47159 | 25.83758 | 27.29898 | 28.8629 | 30.5368 | 32.3289 | 22 |
| 23 | 23.64371 | 24.31040 | 24.76807 | 25.00096 | 25.71630 | 27.22514 | 28.84496 | 30.5844 | 32.4529 | 34.4604 | 23 |
| 24 | 24.70282 | 25.43196 | 25.93319 | 26.18847 | 26.97346 | 28.63352 | 30.42186 | 32.3490 | 34.4265 | 36.6665 | 24 |
| 25 | 25.76457 | 26.55912 | 27.10608 | 27.38488 | 28.24320 | 30.06302 | 32.03030 | 34.1578 | 36.4593 | 38.9499 | 25 |
| 30 | 31.11331 | 32.28002 | 33.08885 | 33.50290 | 34.78489 | 37.53868 | 40.56808 | 43.9027 | 47.5754 | 51.6227 | 30 |
| 35 | 36.52924 | 38.14538 | 39.27373 | 39.85381 | 41.66028 | 45.59209 | 49.99448 | 54.9282 | 60.4621 | 66.6740 | 35 |
| 40 | 42.01320 | 44.15885 | 45.66754 | 46.44648 | 48.88637 | 54.26789 | 60.40198 | 67.4026 | 75.4013 | 84.5503 | 40 |
| 45 | 47.56606 | 50.32416 | 52.27734 | 53.29011 | 56.48107 | 63.61420 | 71.89271 | 81.5161 | 92.7199 | 105.7817 | 45 |
| 50 | 53.18868 | 56.64516 | 59.11042 | 60.39426 | 64.46318 | 73.68283 | 84.57940 | 97.4843 | 112.7969 | 130.9979 | 50 |
| 60 | 64.64671 | 69.77003 | 73.47686 | 76.42414 | 81.66967 | 96.21465 | 114.05154 | 135.9916 | 163.0534 | 196.5169 | 60 |

APPENDIX A 807

# 808 BUSINESS FINANCE

| n | 4.0% | 4.5% | 5.0% | 6.0% | 7.0% | 8.0% | 10.0% | | 15.0% | 20.0% | n |
|---|---|---|---|---|---|---|---|---|---|---|---|
| 1 | 1.0000 | 1.0000 | 1.0000 | 1.0000 | 1.0000 | 1.0000 | 1.0000 | | 1.000 | 1.00 | 1 |
| 2 | 2.0400 | 2.0450 | 2.0500 | 2.0600 | 2.0700 | 2.0800 | 2.1000 | | 2.150 | 2.20 | 2 |
| 3 | 3.1216 | 3.1370 | 3.1525 | 3.1836 | 3.2149 | 3.2464 | 3.3100 | | 3.472 | 3.64 | 3 |
| 4 | 4.2465 | 4.2782 | 4.3101 | 4.3746 | 4.4399 | 4.5061 | 4.6410 | | 4.993 | 5.36 | 4 |
| 5 | 5.4163 | 5.4707 | 5.5256 | 5.6371 | 5.7507 | 5.8666 | 6.1051 | | 6.742 | 7.44 | 5 |
| 6 | 6.6330 | 6.7169 | 6.8019 | 6.9753 | 7.1533 | 7.3359 | 7.7156 | | 8.754 | 9.93 | 6 |
| 7 | 7.8983 | 8.0192 | 8.1420 | 8.3938 | 8.6540 | 8.9228 | 9.4872 | | 11.067 | 12.92 | 7 |
| 8 | 9.2142 | 9.3800 | 9.5491 | 9.8975 | 10.2598 | 10.6366 | 11.4359 | | 13.727 | 16.50 | 8 |
| 9 | 10.5828 | 10.8021 | 11.0266 | 11.4913 | 11.9780 | 12.4876 | 13.5795 | | 16.786 | 20.80 | 9 |
| 10 | 12.0061 | 12.2882 | 12.5779 |  | 13.8164 | 14.4866 | 15.9374 | | 20.304 | 25.96 | 10 |
| 11 | 13.4864 | 13.8412 | 14.2068 |  | 15.7836 | 16.6455 | 18.5312 | | 24.349 | 32.15 | 11 |
| 12 | 15.0258 | 15.4640 | 15.9171 |  | 17.8885 | 18.9771 | 21.3843 | | 29.002 | 39.58 | 12 |
| 13 | 16.6268 | 17.1599 | 17.7130 | 18.  | 20.1406 | 21.4953 | 24.5227 | | 34.352 | 48.50 | 13 |
| 14 | 18.2919 | 18.9321 | 19.5986 | 21.0 | 22.5505 | 24.2149 | 27.9750 | | 40.505 | 59.20 | 14 |
| 15 | 20.0236 | 20.7841 | 21.5786 | 23.276 | 25.1290 | 27.1521 | 31.7725 | | 47.580 | 72.04 | 15 |
| 16 | 21.8245 | 22.7193 | 23.6575 | 25.6725 |  | 30.3243 | 35.9497 | | 55.717 | 87.44 | 16 |
| 17 | 23.6975 | 24.7417 | 25.8404 | 28.2129 |  | 33.7502 | 40.5447 | | 65.075 | 105.93 | 17 |
| 18 | 25.6454 | 26.8551 | 28.1324 | 30.9057 |  | 37.4502 | 45.5992 | | 75.836 | 128.12 | 18 |
| 19 | 27.6712 | 29.0636 | 30.5390 | 33.7600 |  | 41.4463 | 51.1591 | | 88.212 | 154.74 | 19 |
| 20 | 29.7781 | 31.3714 | 33.0660 | 36.7856 |  | 45.7620 | 57.2750 | | 102.443 | 186.69 | 20 |
| 21 | 31.9692 | 33.7831 | 35.7193 | 39.9927 | 44. | 50.4229 | 64.0025 | 81.699 | 118.810 | 225.03 | 21 |
| 22 | 34.2480 | 36.3034 | 38.5052 | 43.3923 | 49. | 55.4568 | 71.4028 | 92.502 | 137.631 | 271.03 | 22 |
| 23 | 36.6179 | 38.9370 | 41.4305 | 46.9958 | 53.4 | 60.8933 | 79.5430 | 104.603 | 159.276 | 326.24 | 23 |
| 24 | 39.0826 | 41.6892 | 44.5020 | 50.8156 | 58.17 | 66.7648 | 88.4973 | 118.155 | 184.167 | 392.48 | 24 |
| 25 | 41.6459 | 44.5652 | 47.7271 | 54.8645 | 63.2490 | 73.1059 | 98.3471 | 133.334 | 212.793 | 471.98 | 25 |
| 30 | 56.0849 | 61.5706 | 66.4388 | 79.0582 | 74.4608 | .2832 | 164.4940 | 241.532 | 434.744 | 1181.88 | 30 |
| 35 | 73.6522 | 81.4966 | 90.3203 | 111.4348 | 138.2369 | 68 | 271.0244 | 431.663 | 881.168 | 2948.34 | 35 |
| 40 | 95.0255 | 107.0303 | 120.7998 | 154.7620 | 199.6351 | .0565 | 442.5926 | 767.088 | 1779.090 | 7343.95 | 40 |
| 45 | 121.0294 | 138.8500 | 159.7002 | 212.7435 | 285.7493 | 386.5056 | 718.9048 | 1358.224 | 3585.128 | 18281.31 | 45 |
| 50 | 152.6671 | 178.5030 | 209.3480 | 290.3359 | 406.5289 | 573.7702 | 1163.9085 | 2400.008 | 7217.716 | 45497.19 | 50 |
| 60 | 237.9907 | 289.4980 | 353.5837 | 533.1281 | 813.5204 | 1253.2133 | 3034.8164 | 7471.641 | 29219.992 | 281732.57 | 60 |

**Table 4** Present value of $1 per period

$$A_{\overline{n}|i} = \frac{1-(1+i)^{-n}}{i}$$

| n | 0.25% | 0.5% | 0.66% | 0.75% | 1.0% | 1.5% | 2.0% | 2.5% | 3.0% | 3.5% | n |
|---|---|---|---|---|---|---|---|---|---|---|---|
| 1 | 0.99751 | 0.99502 | 0.99338 | 0.99256 | 0.99010 | 0.98522 | 0.98039 | 0.97561 | 0.97087 | 0.96618 | 1 |
| 2 | 1.99252 | 1.98510 | 1.98018 | 1.97772 | 1.97040 | 1.95588 | 1.94156 | 1.92742 | 1.91347 | 1.89969 | 2 |
| 3 | 2.98506 | 2.97025 | 2.96044 | 2.95556 | 2.94099 | 2.91220 | 2.88388 | 2.85602 | 2.82861 | 2.80164 | 3 |
| 4 | 3.97512 | 3.95050 | 3.93421 | 3.92611 | 3.90197 | 3.85438 | 3.80773 | 3.76197 | 3.71710 | 3.67308 | 4 |
| 5 | 4.96272 | 4.92587 | 4.90154 | 4.88944 | 4.85343 | 4.78265 | 4.71346 | 4.64583 | 4.57971 | 4.51505 | 5 |
| 6 | 5.94785 | 5.89638 | 5.86245 | 5.84560 | 5.79548 | 5.69719 | 5.60143 | 5.50813 | 5.41719 | 5.32855 | 6 |
| 7 | 6.93052 | 6.86207 | 6.81701 | 6.79464 | 6.72819 | 6.59821 | 6.47199 | 6.34939 | 6.23028 | 6.11454 | 7 |
| 8 | 7.91074 | 7.82296 | 7.76524 | 7.73661 | 7.65168 | 7.48593 | 7.32548 | 7.17014 | 7.01969 | 6.87396 | 8 |
| 9 | 8.88852 | 8.77906 | 8.70719 | 8.67158 | 8.56602 | 8.36052 | 8.16224 | 7.97087 | 7.78611 | 7.60769 | 9 |
| 10 | 9.86386 | 9.73041 | 9.64290 | 9.59958 | 9.47130 | 9.22219 | 8.98254 | 8.75206 | 8.53020 | 8.31661 | 10 |
| 11 | 10.83677 | 10.67703 | 10.57242 | 10.52067 | 10.36763 | 10.07112 | 9.78685 | 9.51421 | 9.25262 | 9.00155 | 11 |
| 12 | 11.80725 | 11.61893 | 11.49578 | 11.43491 | 11.25508 | 10.90751 | 10.57534 | 10.25778 | 9.95400 | 9.66333 | 12 |
| 13 | 12.77532 | 12.55615 | 12.41303 | 12.34235 | 12.13374 | 11.73153 | 11.34837 | 10.98318 | 10.63496 | 10.30274 | 13 |
| 14 | 13.74096 | 13.48871 | 13.32420 | 13.24302 | 13.00370 | 12.54338 | 12.10625 | 11.69091 | 11.29607 | 10.92052 | 14 |
| 15 | 14.70420 | 14.41662 | 14.22934 | 14.13699 | 13.86505 | 13.34323 | 12.84926 | 12.38138 | 11.93794 | 11.51741 | 15 |
| 16 | 15.66504 | 15.33993 | 15.12848 | 15.02431 | 14.71787 | 14.13126 | 13.57771 | 13.05500 | 12.56110 | 12.09412 | 16 |
| 17 | 16.62348 | 16.25863 | 16.02167 | 15.90502 | 15.56225 | 14.90765 | 14.29187 | 13.71220 | 13.16612 | 12.65132 | 17 |
| 18 | 17.57953 | 17.17277 | 16.90894 | 16.77918 | 16.39827 | 15.67256 | 14.99203 | 14.35336 | 13.75351 | 13.18968 | 18 |
| 19 | 18.53320 | 18.08236 | 17.79034 | 17.64683 | 17.22601 | 16.42617 | 15.67846 | 14.97889 | 14.32380 | 13.70984 | 19 |
| 20 | 19.48449 | 18.98742 | 18.66590 | 18.50802 | 18.04555 | 17.16864 | 16.35143 | 15.58916 | 14.87747 | 14.21240 | 20 |
| 21 | 20.43340 | 19.88798 | 19.53566 | 19.36280 | 18.85698 | 17.90014 | 17.01121 | 16.18455 | 15.41502 | 14.69797 | 21 |
| 22 | 21.37995 | 20.78406 | 20.39967 | 20.21121 | 19.66038 | 18.62083 | 17.65805 | 16.76541 | 15.93692 | 15.16712 | 22 |
| 23 | 22.32414 | 21.67568 | 21.25795 | 21.05331 | 20.45582 | 19.33086 | 18.29220 | 17.33211 | 16.44361 | 15.62041 | 23 |
| 24 | 23.26598 | 22.56287 | 22.11054 | 21.88915 | 21.24339 | 20.03041 | 18.91393 | 17.88499 | 16.93554 | 16.05837 | 24 |
| 25 | 24.20547 | 23.44564 | 22.95749 | 22.71876 | 22.02316 | 20.71961 | 19.52346 | 18.42438 | 17.41315 | 16.48151 | 25 |
| 30 | 28.86787 | 27.79405 | 27.10885 | 26.77508 | 25.80771 | 24.01584 | 22.39646 | 20.93030 | 19.60044 | 18.39205 | 30 |
| 35 | 33.47243 | 32.03537 | 31.12455 | 30.68266 | 29.40858 | 27.07560 | 24.99862 | 23.14516 | 21.48722 | 20.00066 | 35 |
| 40 | 38.01986 | 36.17223 | 35.00903 | 34.44694 | 32.83469 | 29.91585 | 27.35548 | 25.10278 | 23.11477 | 21.35507 | 40 |
| 45 | 42.51088 | 40.20720 | 38.76658 | 38.07318 | 36.09451 | 32.55234 | 29.49016 | 26.83302 | 24.51871 | 22.49545 | 45 |
| 50 | 46.94617 | 44.14279 | 42.40134 | 41.56645 | 39.19612 | 34.99969 | 31.42361 | 28.36231 | 25.72976 | 23.45562 | 50 |
| 60 | 55.65236 | 51.72556 | 49.31843 | 48.17337 | 44.95504 | 39.38027 | 34.76089 | 30.90866 | 27.67556 | 24.94473 | 60 |

| n | 4.0% | 4.5% | 5.0% | 6.0% | 7.0% | 8.0% | 10.0% | 12.0% | 15.0% | 20.0% | n |
|---|---|---|---|---|---|---|---|---|---|---|---|
| 1 | 0.9615 | 0.9569 | 0.9524 | 0.9433 | 0.9345 | 0.9259 | 0.9091 | 0.8929 | 0.8695 | 0.8333 | 1 |
| 2 | 1.8861 | 1.8727 | 1.8594 | 1.8333 | 1.8080 | 1.7832 | 1.7355 | 1.6901 | 1.6257 | 1.5278 | 2 |
| 3 | 2.7751 | 2.7490 | 2.7232 | 2.6730 | 2.6243 | 2.5770 | 2.4868 | 2.4018 | 2.2832 | 2.1065 | 3 |
| 4 | 3.6299 | 3.5875 | 3.5460 | 3.4651 | 3.3872 | 3.3121 | 3.1698 | 3.0373 | 2.8549 | 2.5887 | 4 |
| 5 | 4.4518 | 4.3900 | 4.3295 | 4.2123 | 4.1001 | 3.9927 | 3.7907 | 3.6048 | 3.3521 | 2.9906 | 5 |
| 6 | 5.2421 | 5.1579 | 5.0757 | 4.9173 | 4.7665 | 4.6228 | 4.3552 | 4.1114 | 3.7844 | 3.3255 | 6 |
| 7 | 6.0021 | 5.8927 | 5.7864 | 5.5823 | 5.3892 | 5.2063 | 4.8684 | 4.5638 | 4.1604 | 3.6046 | 7 |
| 8 | 6.7327 | 6.5959 | 6.4632 | 6.2097 | 5.9712 | 5.7466 | 5.3349 | 4.9676 | 4.4873 | 3.8372 | 8 |
| 9 | 7.4353 | 7.2688 | 7.1078 | 6.8016 | 6.5152 | 6.2468 | 5.7590 | 5.3282 | 4.7715 | 4.0310 | 9 |
| 10 | 8.1109 | 7.9127 | 7.7217 | 7.3600 | 7.0235 | 6.7100 | 6.1445 | 5.6502 | 5.0187 | 4.1925 | 10 |
| 11 | 8.7605 | 8.5289 | 8.3064 | 7.8868 | 7.4986 | 7.1389 | 6.4950 | 5.9377 | 5.2337 | 4.3271 | 11 |
| 12 | 9.3851 | 9.1186 | 8.8633 | 8.3838 | 7.9426 | 7.5360 | 6.8136 | 6.1944 | 5.4206 | 4.4392 | 12 |
| 13 | 9.9856 | 9.6829 | 9.3936 | 8.8526 | 8.3576 | 7.9037 | 7.1033 | 6.4235 | 5.5831 | 4.5327 | 13 |
| 14 | 10.5631 | 10.2228 | 9.8986 | 9.2949 | 8.7454 | 8.2442 | 7.3666 | 6.6282 | 5.7244 | 4.6106 | 14 |
| 15 | 11.1184 | 10.7395 | 10.3797 | 9.7122 | 9.1079 | 8.5594 | 7.6060 | 6.8109 | 5.8473 | 4.6755 | 15 |
| 16 | 11.6523 | 11.2340 | 10.8378 | 10.1058 | 9.4466 | 8.8513 | 7.8237 | 6.9740 | 5.9542 | 4.7296 | 16 |
| 17 | 12.1657 | 11.7072 | 11.2741 | 10.4772 | 9.7632 | 9.1216 | 8.0215 | 7.1196 | 6.0471 | 4.7746 | 17 |
| 18 | 12.6593 | 12.1600 | 11.6896 | 10.8276 | 10.0590 | 9.3718 | 8.2014 | 7.2497 | 6.1279 | 4.8122 | 18 |
| 19 | 13.1339 | 12.5933 | 12.0853 | 11.1581 | 10.3355 | 9.6035 | 8.3649 | 7.3658 | 6.1982 | 4.8435 | 19 |
| 20 | 13.5903 | 13.0079 | 12.4622 | 11.4699 | 10.5940 | 9.8181 | 8.5135 | 7.4694 | 6.2593 | 4.8696 | 20 |
| 21 | 14.0292 | 13.4047 | 12.8212 | 11.7640 | 10.8355 | 10.0168 | 8.6486 | 7.5620 | 6.3124 | 4.8913 | 21 |
| 22 | 14.4511 | 13.7844 | 13.1630 | 12.0415 | 11.0612 | 10.2007 | 8.7715 | 7.6446 | 6.3586 | 4.9094 | 22 |
| 23 | 14.8568 | 14.1478 | 13.4886 | 12.3033 | 11.2721 | 10.3710 | 8.8832 | 7.7184 | 6.3988 | 4.9245 | 23 |
| 24 | 15.2470 | 14.4955 | 13.7986 | 12.5503 | 11.4693 | 10.5287 | 8.9847 | 7.7843 | 6.4337 | 4.9371 | 24 |
| 25 | 15.6221 | 14.8282 | 14.0939 | 12.7833 | 11.6535 | 10.6747 | 9.0770 | 7.8431 | 6.4641 | 4.9476 | 25 |
| 30 | 17.2920 | 16.2889 | 15.3725 | 13.7648 | 12.4090 | 11.2577 | 9.4269 | 8.0552 | 6.5659 | 4.9789 | 30 |
| 35 | 18.6646 | 17.4610 | 16.3742 | 14.4982 | 12.9476 | 11.6545 | 9.6441 | 8.1755 | 6.6166 | 4.9915 | 35 |
| 40 | 19.7928 | 18.4016 | 17.1591 | 15.0462 | 13.3317 | 11.9246 | 9.7790 | 8.2438 | 6.6417 | 4.9966 | 40 |
| 45 | 20.7200 | 19.1563 | 17.7741 | 15.4558 | 13.6055 | 12.1084 | 9.8628 | 8.2825 | 6.6542 | 4.9986 | 45 |
| 50 | 21.4822 | 19.7620 | 18.2559 | 15.7618 | 13.8007 | 12.2334 | 9.9148 | 8.3045 | 6.6605 | 4.9995 | 50 |
| 60 | 22.6235 | 20.6380 | 18.9293 | 16.1614 | 14.0392 | 12.3766 | 9.9672 | 8.3240 | 6.6651 | 4.9999 | 60 |

APPENDIX A  811

**Table 5** Areas under the normal curve measured from the mean to values $z = \frac{x}{\sigma}$
An entry in the table is the proportion under the entire curve which is between $z = 0$ and a positive value of $z$. Areas for negative value of $z$ are obtained by symmetry.

| $z = \frac{x}{\sigma}$ | 0.00 | 0.01 | 0.02 | 0.03 | 0.04 | 0.05 | 0.06 | 0.07 | 0.08 | 0.09 |
|---|---|---|---|---|---|---|---|---|---|---|
| 0.0 | 0.0000 | 0.0040 | 0.0080 | 0.0120 | 0.0159 | 0.0199 | 0.0239 | 0.0279 | 0.0319 | 0.0359 |
| 0.1 | 0.0398 | 0.0438 | 0.0478 | 0.0517 | 0.0557 | 0.0596 | 0.0636 | 0.0675 | 0.0714 | 0.0753 |
| 0.2 | 0.0793 | 0.0832 | 0.0871 | 0.0910 | 0.0948 | 0.0987 | 0.1026 | 0.1064 | 0.1103 | 0.1141 |
| 0.3 | 0.1179 | 0.1217 | 0.1255 | 0.1293 | 0.1331 | 0.1368 | 0.1406 | 0.1443 | 0.1480 | 0.1517 |
| 0.4 | 0.1554 | 0.1591 | 0.1628 | 0.1664 | 0.1700 | 0.1736 | 0.1772 | 0.1808 | 0.1844 | 0.1879 |
| 0.5 | 0.1915 | 0.1950 | 0.1985 | 0.2019 | 0.2054 | 0.2088 | 0.2123 | 0.2157 | 0.2190 | 0.2224 |
| 0.6 | 0.2257 | 0.2291 | 0.2324 | 0.2357 | 0.2389 | 0.2422 | 0.2454 | 0.2486 | 0.2518 | 0.2549 |
| 0.7 | 0.2580 | 0.2612 | 0.2642 | 0.2673 | 0.2704 | 0.2734 | 0.2764 | 0.2794 | 0.2823 | 0.2852 |
| 0.8 | 0.2881 | 0.2910 | 0.2939 | 0.2967 | 0.2995 | 0.3023 | 0.3051 | 0.3078 | 0.3106 | 0.3133 |
| 0.9 | 0.3159 | 0.3186 | 0.3212 | 0.3238 | 0.3264 | 0.3289 | 0.3315 | 0.3340 | 0.3365 | 0.3389 |
| 1.0 | 0.3413 | 0.3438 | 0.3461 | 0.3485 | 0.3508 | 0.3531 | 0.3554 | 0.3577 | 0.3599 | 0.3621 |
| 1.1 | 0.3643 | 0.3665 | 0.3686 | 0.3708 | 0.3729 | 0.3749 | 0.3770 | 0.3790 | 0.3810 | 0.3830 |
| 1.2 | 0.3849 | 0.3869 | 0.3888 | 0.3907 | 0.3925 | 0.3944 | 0.3962 | 0.3980 | 0.3997 | 0.4015 |
| 1.3 | 0.4032 | 0.4049 | 0.4066 | 0.4083 | 0.4099 | 0.4115 | 0.4131 | 0.4147 | 0.4162 | 0.4177 |
| 1.4 | 0.4192 | 0.4207 | 0.4222 | 0.4236 | 0.4251 | 0.4265 | 0.4279 | 0.4292 | 0.4306 | 0.4319 |
| 1.5 | 0.4332 | 0.4345 | 0.4357 | 0.4370 | 0.4382 | 0.4394 | 0.4406 | 0.4418 | 0.4430 | 0.4441 |
| 1.6 | 0.4452 | 0.4463 | 0.4474 | 0.4485 | 0.4495 | 0.4505 | 0.4515 | 0.4525 | 0.4535 | 0.4545 |
| 1.7 | 0.4554 | 0.4564 | 0.4573 | 0.4582 | 0.4591 | 0.4599 | 0.4608 | 0.4616 | 0.4625 | 0.4633 |
| 1.8 | 0.4641 | 0.4649 | 0.4656 | 0.4664 | 0.4671 | 0.4678 | 0.4686 | 0.4693 | 0.4699 | 0.4706 |
| 1.9 | 0.4713 | 0.4719 | 0.4726 | 0.4732 | 0.4738 | 0.4744 | 0.4750 | 0.4758 | 0.4762 | 0.4767 |
| 2.0 | 0.4773 | 0.4778 | 0.4783 | 0.4788 | 0.4793 | 0.4798 | 0.4803 | 0.4808 | 0.4812 | 0.4817 |
| 2.1 | 0.4821 | 0.4826 | 0.4830 | 0.4834 | 0.4838 | 0.4842 | 0.4846 | 0.4850 | 0.4854 | 0.4857 |
| 2.2 | 0.4861 | 0.4865 | 0.4868 | 0.4871 | 0.4875 | 0.4878 | 0.4881 | 0.4884 | 0.4887 | 0.4890 |
| 2.3 | 0.4893 | 0.4896 | 0.4898 | 0.4901 | 0.4904 | 0.4906 | 0.4909 | 0.4911 | 0.4913 | 0.4916 |
| 2.4 | 0.4918 | 0.4920 | 0.4922 | 0.4925 | 0.4927 | 0.4929 | 0.4931 | 0.4932 | 0.4934 | 0.4936 |
| 2.5 | 0.4938 | 0.4940 | 0.4941 | 0.4943 | 0.4945 | 0.4946 | 0.4948 | 0.4949 | 0.4951 | 0.4952 |
| 2.6 | 0.4953 | 0.4955 | 0.4956 | 0.4957 | 0.4959 | 0.4960 | 0.4961 | 0.4962 | 0.4963 | 0.4964 |
| 2.7 | 0.4965 | 0.4966 | 0.4967 | 0.4968 | 0.4969 | 0.4970 | 0.4971 | 0.4972 | 0.4973 | 0.4974 |
| 2.8 | 0.4974 | 0.4975 | 0.4976 | 0.4977 | 0.4977 | 0.4978 | 0.4979 | 0.4980 | 0.4980 | 0.4981 |
| 2.9 | 0.4981 | 0.4982 | 0.4983 | 0.4984 | 0.4984 | 0.4984 | 0.4985 | 0.4985 | 0.4986 | 0.4986 |
| 3.0 | 0.4987 | 0.4987 | 0.4987 | 0.4988 | 0.4988 | 0.4988 | 0.4989 | 0.4989 | 0.4989 | 0.4990 |

*Note:* Mean $\pm 1\sigma$ contains 68.26% of the cases: 0.3413 $\times$ 2 = 68.26%
Mean $\pm 2\sigma$ contains 95.46% of the cases: 0.4773 $\times$ 2 = 95.46%
Mean $\pm 3\sigma$ contains 99.74% of the cases: 0.4987 $\times$ 2 = 99.74%

# GLOSSARY

**ASC**: Australian Securities Commission. An independent statutory body that replaced the National Companies and Securities Commission. Its main functions and powers are conferred by the Corporations Law which covers the regulation of companies, and the securities and futures markets in Australia.

**ASX**: Australian Stock Exchange.

**abandonment decision**: A decision where the net present value of continuing to operate a project is compared with the net cash flows if the project is terminated.

**abnormal return**: A realised return in excess of the return expected for a given level of risk.

**accounting rate of return (AROR)**: The average after-tax accounting profit (earnings) expressed as a percentage of either the average investment, the initial investment, or the average book value. It is used as a method of project evaluation.

**acid test ratio**: *See* quick ratio.

**agency costs**: Costs that arise due to a conflict of interest between principals and agents (for example between shareholders and managers). These costs include monitoring costs borne by principals in an attempt to ensure that agents act in the principals' best interests.

**American option**: An option contract that may be exercised at any time up to and including the expiry date. *See* European option.

**annuity**: A cash flow stream of equal amounts, paid at equal time intervals for a specified number of periods.

**annuity due**: An annuity where the first payment is to occur immediately.

**arbitrage**: Buying an asset in one market and simultaneously selling it for a higher price in another market, so as to make a risk-free profit.

**arbitrage pricing theory**: A theory of asset pricing that describes the expected return on a risky asset as a linear combination of various factors. The theory is based on the principle that markets should price assets so that arbitrage is not possible.

**arbitrageur**: A person engaged in arbitrage. *See* arbitrage.

**at-the-money-option**: A put or call option where the current price of the underlying asset is approximately equal to the exercise price.

**Australian Stock Exchange**: The national stock exchange formed in April 1987 by amalgamation of the six state stock exchanges. This created one body to govern share market trading in Australia. The exchange sets uniform trading rules, listing requirements, and ethical standards.

**autocorrelation**: *See* serial correlation.

**average collection period**: The average period required by a firm to collect a credit account. It is calculated from accounts receivable divided by (annual credit sales/365).

**bank accepted bill**: A negotiable bill where a bank guarantees payment of the bill's face value at maturity. This guarantee is made at the inception of the bill.

**bank endorsed bill**: A bill purchased by a bank, and which when sold carries a guarantee that, if necessary, the bank will pay the face value at maturity.

**bankruptcy**: In Australia, a legal status applying to individuals unable to pay their debts. American usage, which has been followed in this book, extends this concept to cover corporations. *See* liquidation.

**basis point**: The unit measure when describing changes in interest rates in financial markets. If an interest rate changes from 10 per cent to 10.01 per cent, the rate has increased one basis point. Thus a basis point is one-hundredth of a per cent.

**basis risk**: The risk faced by a hedger as a result of futures prices and spot prices changing by different amounts.

**beta**: A measure of a security's systematic risk, describing the amount of risk contributed by the security to the market portfolio. It is calculated as the covariance between the security's returns and returns on the market portfolio, divided by the variance of returns on the market portfolio.

**bid–ask spread**: The difference between the price buyers are prepared to pay for an asset and the price at which sellers are offering to sell the asset.

**binomial option pricing model**: An option pricing model based on the assumption that there are only two possible returns on the underlying asset in each period.

**bird-in-the-hand dividend theory**: The theory that investors prefer dividend income to capital gains because current dividends are more certain than future capital gains.

**Black–Scholes option pricing model**: An exact formula for pricing a European call option. The formula describes the price as a function of five variables: the current price of the underlying asset, the exercise price, the risk-free interest rate, the volatility of the underlying asset, and the term to expiration.

**bond**: A long-term debt security.

**bonus issue**: A free issue of shares to existing shareholders in proportion to their current shareholding.

**book value**: The depreciated amount of a firm's assets (acquisition cost or revalued amount less accumulated depreciation).

**book value weights**: The relative proportion of financing provided by various sources, based on the book value of the respective contributions recorded in the firm's balance sheet.

**business risk**: The variability of future net cash flows attributed to the nature of the firm's operations. It is the risk shareholders face if the firm is financed only by equity.

**call option**: An option in which the buyer has the right, but not the obligation, to buy an asset (such as shares) at a specified exercise price within a specified time period.

**capital asset pricing model (CAPM)**: A one-period asset pricing model that describes the equilibrium risk–return relationship of single risky assets and portfolios in equilibrium. It specifies that the expected rate of return on an asset is a function of the risk-free interest rate, the asset's beta, and the expected market risk premium.

**capital gain or loss**: The difference between the acquisition cost of an asset and its disposal price; the gain or loss that arises from the sale of an asset.

**capital market**: A market in which medium- and long-term financial securities are traded.

**capital market line (CML)**: The efficient set of all portfolios that provides the investor with the best possible investment opportunities when a risk-free asset is available. It describes the equilibrium risk–return relationship for efficient portfolios, where the expected return is a function of the risk-free interest rate, the expected market risk premium, and the proportionate risk of the efficient portfolio to the risk of the market portfolio.

**capital rationing**: A condition where a firm has limited resources available for capital investment.

**capital structure**: The mix of debt and equity finance used by a firm.

**CAPM**: Capital asset pricing model.

**CAR**: Cumulative average abnormal return.

**carrying costs**: Costs that increase as the level of investment in current assets increases.

**certainty equivalent**: The certain amount of cash a person would be willing to exchange for a larger but uncertain amount of cash.

**characteristic line**: The line that describes the relationship between the returns on a particular security and the returns on the market portfolio. Its slope is a measure of the security's *beta*.

**classical taxation system**: The taxation system that operated in Australia until 30 June 1987. It was replaced by the *imputation taxation system*. Under the classical taxation system, company profits, and dividends paid from those profits, were taxed separately. That is, profit paid as a dividend was effectively taxed twice.

**clientele effect**: The effect of investors choosing to invest in firms that have policies meeting their particular requirements. For example, investors who require high current income may choose to invest in firms that have high dividend payouts.

**commercial paper**: *See* promissory note.

**compound interest**: Interest calculated each period on the principal amount and on any interest earned on the investment up to that point. The interest earned in one period effectively becomes part of the principal in the succeeding period.

**consol**: A bond that does not have a maturity date, that is, its periodic interest payments are expected to continue forever.

**constant chain of replacement**: In order to evaluate projects of unequal lives, the projects are assumed to be replaced to a common point in time by projects which are identical in terms of cash flow stream, technology, life span, and so on.

**convertible note**: A debt security which, at the option of the investor, may be converted into a specified number of ordinary shares at maturity.

**correlation coefficient**: A statistical measure describing the degree of relationship between two variables.

**cost of capital**: The rate of return necessary to compensate the providers of finance for investing in the firm.

**coupon rate**: The amount of interest payable on a bond or debenture, expressed as a percentage of the par value.

**covariance**: A statistical measure describing the relationship between the returns of two assets.

**credit risk**: The possibility of loss because of default by the counterparty to a transaction.

**cross rates**: The exchange rate between two currencies, derived from the exchange rates between the currencies and a third currency.

**cum-dividend period**: The time period during which the purchaser of a share qualifies for receipt of a previously announced dividend. The cum-dividend period ends on the *ex-dividend date*.

**cum-rights period**: The time period during which the purchaser of a share qualifies for receipt of a previously announced rights issue. The cum-rights period ends on the *ex-rights date*.

**cumulative average abnormal return (CAR)**: A measure of the average response of security prices to a specified event and cumulated over a period of time.

**current ratio**: A liquidity ratio measured by current assets divided by current liabilities.

**discounted cash flow (DCF)**: The process of discounting a series of cash flows due in future periods to their present values.

**debenture**: A long-term debt security issued by a company.

**debt**: The obligation of an entity to pay a specific amount of money to another entity.

**default risk**: The chance that a firm will not meet obligations to pay interest and principal as promised.

**defeasance**: A debt restructuring technique that allows a company to remove debt from its balance sheet through the creation of a trust that will service the debt.

**deferred annuity**: An annuity where the first payment is to be made at a stated time in the future.

**delta**: The change in the market value of an option position in response to a change in the market value of the underlying security.

**depreciation**: The process of allocating the cost (or other value) less estimated disposal value of a non-current asset over its expected useful life. The two main methods of calculating depreciation are the straight-line and reducing-balance methods.

**derivative security**: A security whose value depends on the value of an underlying security.

**direct quote**: The local currency price of a unit of foreign currency.

**diversifiable risk**: That element of total risk unique to the firm and which may be eliminated by diversification.

**dividend**: The periodic payment of cash by a company to its shareholders. In Australia dividends are usually paid half-yearly.

**dividend growth model**: A mathematical model describing the present value of a share as the sum of the discounted future dividends, where the dividends are assumed to increase each period.

**dividend payout ratio**: The percentage of profit paid to ordinary shareholders as cash dividends.

**dividend yield**: The dividend per share, divided by the current price of the share.

**earnings per share (EPS)**: A company's profit, divided by the number of ordinary shares on issue.

**EBIT**: Earnings before interest and taxes.

**economic order quantity (EOQ)**: The optimum quantity of inventory ordered that minimises the cost of purchasing and holding the inventory.

**effective rate of interest**: The interest rate earned per annum that builds in the effect of compounding.

**efficient market hypothesis (EMH)**: The hypothesis that asset prices fully reflect all available information about the asset. This implies that prices adjust instantaneously and in an unbiased way to new information about the asset. Therefore investors cannot consistently earn abnormal returns.

**efficient portfolio**: A portfolio that maximises the expected return for a given level of risk.

**equipment finance**: A loan or lease used to finance an item of equipment where that equipment is used as security for the finance.

**equity**: The ownership interest in the firm. In the case of a company it is represented by shareholders' funds.

**equivalent annual cost (EAC)**: The annual cash flow of an annuity that has the same life as a project and whose present value equals the present value of the cash outflows associated with the project. It can be used to evaluate public sector projects where costs, but not benefits, can be quantified.

**equivalent annual value (EAV)**: The annual cash flow of an annuity that has the same life as a project and whose present value equals the net present value of the project. It can be used to compare mutually exclusive projects with different lives.

**eurobond**: A medium- to long-term international bearer security sold in countries other than the country of the currency in which the bond is denominated.

**European option**: An option that can be exercised only on the expiration date. *See* American option.

**event study**: A statistical study that examines how an event such as the release of profit figures affects security prices.

**exchange rate**: The price of one country's currency expressed in terms of another country's currency.

**ex-dividend date**: The date on which a share begins trading ex-dividend. A share purchased ex-dividend does not have a right to the forthcoming dividend payment.

**exercise price**: The price at which an option holder can buy (if it is a call option) or sell (if it is a put option) the underlying security; also called *strike price*.

**exercise value**: The value to an option holder of exercising an option; also called *intrinsic value*.

**expectations hypothesis**: An hypothesis that attempts to explain the term structure of interest rates. It suggests that investors' expectations for future interest rates determine the current term structure of interest rates, and states that, in a perfect capital market, the implicit forward interest rate is an unbiased estimate of the future interest rate.

**expected rate of return**: The expected return, divided by the sum invested.

**expected return**: The mean value of the probability distribution of possible outcomes for returns of a security.

**ex-rights date**: The date on which a share begins trading ex-rights. After the ex-rights date a share does not have attached to it the right to purchase any additional share(s) on the subscription date.


**factoring**: The sale of a firm's accounts receivable at a discount to a financial institution (the factor).

**feasible set**: The available combinations of risk and expected return.

**financial asset**: A claim on the cash flows generated by assets.

**financial distress**: A situation where a firm's financial obligations cannot be met, or can be met only with difficulty.

**financial distress costs**: Direct costs (such as legal and administrative costs) and indirect costs (such as an impaired ability to conduct business) associated with financial distress.

**financial intermediary**: An institution that accepts funds from depositors and lends them to borrowers.

**financial lease**: A long-term non-cancellable lease that effectively transfers the risks and benefits of ownership of an asset from the lessor to the lessee.

**financial risk**: The risk attributable to the use of debt as a source of finance. The total risk of a firm includes both *business risk* and financial risk.

**fixed charge**: A form of security which, if the borrower defaults on the loan contract, gives the lender the right to take control of the specific asset (or assets) pledged.

**floating charge**: A form of security which, if the borrower defaults on the loan contract, gives the lender the right to take control of any of the borrower's assets other than those specifically pledged to another lender.

**foreign bond**: A bond issued outside the borrower's country and denominated in the currency of the country in which it is issued.

**foreign exchange market**: A market in which the world's currencies are bought and sold.

**forward contract**: A contract in which a seller agrees to deliver to a buyer an asset (for example a commodity, an amount of foreign currency, or a bank bill) on an agreed future date at an agreed price.

**forward price**: The price of an asset purchased for delivery at a given time in the future. Examples include *exchange rates* and *interest rates*.

**forward rate agreement**: An agreement to pay or receive a sum of money representing an interest differential, such that the interest rate applicable to a specific period is fixed.

**franked dividend**: A dividend that carries a credit for income tax paid by the company.

**fundamental analysis**: The analysis of securities based on estimates of variables such as earnings, dividends, and the risk of the security.

**future value**: A future sum equivalent to a specified amount today, or to a specified cash flow. A future value is calculated by compounding at a given interest rate.

**futures contract**: An agreement between two parties to buy and sell an asset at a specified price on a specified future date. It differs from a forward contract in that futures contracts are traded on a futures market.

**gearing**: Financial leverage.

**goodwill**: The future benefits from unidentifiable assets. It is calculated as the excess of purchase consideration over the fair market value of the identifiable net assets acquired.

**hedge**: A risk reduction technique involving the creation of a cash flow to offset an existing cash flow. For example, the cash flow created by a forward contract can be used to offset an operating cash flow.

**holding period return**: The rate of return earned over the period of time an investor holds a security.

**home-made leverage**: The duplication of the effects of corporate leverage by investors borrowing on their own account.

**horizontal merger**: The merger of two companies that produce similar goods or services.

**hurdle rate**: The cost of capital, or required rate of return, in the evaluation of an investment project.

**imputation tax system**: A system under which share investors can use tax credits associated with *franked dividends* to offset their personal tax. The system eliminates the double taxation inherent in the *classical tax system*.

**independent project**: A project that may be accepted or rejected without affecting the acceptability of another project.

**indirect quote**: The foreign currency price of a single unit of the local currency.

**information asymmetry**: A situation where all relevant information is not known by all interested parties.

**inside information**: Information about a firm that is not known to the general public.

**interest rate**: The rate paid for borrowing or lending money.

**interest rate parity**: A theory that states that a forward exchange rate is given by relative interest rates in the two currencies.

**interest rate risk**: The chance that the interest rate will change in the future, thereby changing the value of an asset.

**intermediation**: The process whereby funds are borrowed or invested through *financial intermediaries*. Financial intermediaries do this by taking deposits and lending to borrowers.

**internal equity**: The portion of a firm's net profit that is retained by the firm.

**internal rate of return (IRR)**: The discount rate that equates the *present value* of a project's net cash flows to the initial outlay on that project; it is the discount rate at which the *net present value* is equal to zero.

**internally generated funds**: Funds available for investment that are generated from the firm's operations.

**in-the-money-option**: An option where exercise would produce a positive cash flow.

**inventory turnover ratio**: The ratio of cost of goods sold to inventory. It measures the number of times a firm's inventories are sold and replaced during the year, reflecting the relative liquidity of inventories.

**investment allowance**: A provision of the tax system that allows a business to reduce its taxable income by an amount equal to specified percentages of the cost of eligible new plant. This provision has been introduced periodically to stimulate investment.


**law of one price**: A principle maintaining that an asset's price in a given currency will be the same regardless of the currency in which the price is quoted.

**lease**: An agreement where one party (the *lessee*) is granted the right to use the property of the *lessor* for a specified period of time at an agreed rental.

**lessee**: In a lease contract, the party using the asset.

**lessor**: In a lease contract, the party that owns the asset.

**leveraged buyout (LBO)**: Takeover of a firm whereby existing shareholders sell their shares to a small group of investors (usually including management) involving a high proportion of borrowed funds.

**leveraged lease**: A financial lease where the *lessor* borrows most of the funds to acquire the asset.

**liquidation**: The process of selling a firm's assets, either individually or as a whole. It is frequently undertaken when a company is no longer able to meet its financial obligations. The company is wound up and the proceeds of the sale of its assets are distributed to creditors and shareholders as specified in the Corporations Law.

**liquidity**: The speed and ease with which assets can be converted to cash.

**liquidity premium theory**: A theory that attempts to explain the term structure of interest rates by stating that although future interest rates are determined by investors' expectations, investors require some reward (liquidity premium) to assume the increased risk of investing long term.

**lognormal probability distribution**: A probability distribution where the logarithm of the random variable follows a normal probability distribution.

**London interbank offered rate (LIBOR)**: A commonly used reference rate, derived daily from the interest rates at which major international banks in London will lend to each other.

**long hedge**: The purchase of a futures contract, to reduce risk.

**margin call**: The requirement to lodge additional funds when adverse movements in the price of a contract erode the initial deposit to a level below the specified minimum level.

**marginal cost of capital**: The cost of capital on an incremental project.

**market model**: A time series regression of an asset's returns on returns on the market index.

**market portfolio**: The portfolio of all risky assets, weighted according to their market capitalisation.

**market risk**: Systematic or non-diversifiable risk. That component of return variability due to economy-wide factors.

**market risk premium**: The difference between the expected return on the market portfolio and the risk-free interest rate.

**market segmentation theory**: A theory of the term structure of interest rates in which it is assumed that the capital market is segmented into different maturity ranges, and within each range the interest rate is determined solely by the interaction of demand and supply for loanable funds of that maturity range.

**market value weights**: The relative proportion of financing sources in the capital structure, where the proportions are based on current market values.

**marking to market**: The process of adjusting frequently (sometimes daily) the recorded value of a contract or asset to its market price. For example, in futures markets this process results in daily adjustments to traders' accounts.

**merger**: A combination of businesses into a single entity.

**minimum variance portfolio**: The portfolio of risky assets with the lowest possible variance.

**money market**: The market in which short-term debt securities are traded.

**monitoring costs**: Costs incurred by principals in monitoring the behaviour of their agents.

**mortgage**: A form of security where the lender (mortgagee) has the right to take possession of and sell property if the borrower (mortgagor) defaults.

**mutually exclusive projects**: Alternative investment projects, only one of which can be accepted.

**net present value (NPV)**: The difference between the present value of the net cash flows from an investment, discounted at the cost of capital and the initial outlay on the investment.

**net profit margin**: Net profit as a percentage of sales.
**non-diversifiable risk**: *See* market risk.
**nominal cash flow**: Cash flows that include the effects of inflation.
**nominal interest rate**: The quoted or advertised rate of interest. Also, an interest rate unadjusted for the effects of inflation.
**normal distribution**: A symmetric, bell-shaped distribution which is completely characterised by two parameters, the mean (or expected value) and the *standard deviation*.

**off-balance-sheet finance**: Liabilities that are not required to be reported on a firm's balance sheet.
**opportunity cost**: The return on the next best alternative foregone as a result of undertaking an investment.
**opportunity set**: The set of all feasible portfolios that can be constructed from a given set of assets.
**optimum capital structure**: The capital structure that maximises the value of a company.
**option contract**: A contract that confers the right, but not the obligation, to buy or sell underlying assets at a fixed price for a specified period.
**option writer**: The seller of an option contract.
**ordinary annuity**: An annuity where the first cash flow will occur at the end of the first time period.
**ordinary share**: A share in the equity of a company that entitles the holder to a proportion of distributed profits after any lenders and preference shareholders have been paid.
**out-of-the-money option**: An option where exercise would not produce a positive cash flow.
**overdraft**: A bank loan that permits borrowing up to a specified limit at the option of the borrower. Thus the amount owing increases or decreases, according to the borrower's requirements.

**par value**: The nominal or face value of a share or bond.
**payback period**: The time it takes to recover the initial outlay on an investment.
**perfect capital market**: A frictionless market in which there are no taxes, no transaction costs, all relevant information is costlessly available to all participants, and all participants are price takers.
**perpetuity**: An annuity with an infinite life.
**preference share**: A security that provides the holder with priority over ordinary shareholders in the receipt of dividends.
**present value**: The cash equivalent today of an amount to be paid or received at some future time. It is typically calculated by discounting future cash flows at a required rate of return.
**price earnings ratio**: Share price divided by *earnings per share*.
**price taker**: A market participant who is unable to influence the trading price.
**primary market**: The market for new issues of securities where the sale proceeds go to the issuer of the securities.

**prime asset ratio (PAR)**: A prudential requirement of the Reserve Bank of Australia, whereby banks must maintain a minimum level of specified assets, which include liquid assets.

**prime rate**: The interest rate at which banks lend to their most creditworthy customers.

**private placement**: Issue of securities direct to chosen investors, rather than to the general public.

**profitability index**: An index used in investment evaluation, calculated by dividing the *present value* of the future cash flows by the initial investment.

**promissory note**: A security usually issued for a term of 90, 120 or 180 days where the issuer unconditionally promises to pay to the bearer a specified sum at a fixed future time.

**prospectus**: A document required by the Australian Securities Commission (ASC) when a company offers its securities for sale.

**purchasing power parity**: A theory that the exchange rate between two currencies adjusts to reflect the relative inflation rates in the two currencies.

**put–call parity**: The relationship between the market value of puts and calls on the same underlying asset, and with the same exercise price and term to maturity.

**put option**: An option giving the holder the right to sell a specified asset at a specified exercise price within a specified time period.

**quick ratio**: Current assets minus inventories, divided by current liabilities.

**random walk**: A time series where the probability distribution of changes is constant and unrelated to past changes.

**real cash flow**: A cash flow adjusted to remove the effects of inflation.

**real interest rate**: The interest rate, excluding the effect of inflation.

**required rate of return**: The minimum rate of return necessary to justify undertaking an investment, also the *cost of capital*.

**residual value**: Under a lease agreement, an amount guaranteed to the lessor at the end of the lease period.

**restrictive covenant**: A provision in a loan agreement that restricts the actions of the borrower.

**retained earnings**: Earnings not distributed to shareholders as dividends.

**return on assets**: *Earnings before interest and tax*, as a percentage of average assets invested.

**return on equity**: Earnings after interest and tax, as a percentage of shareholders' funds.

**right**: An option to purchase an additional share in a company by paying the *subscription price*.

**rights issue**: An issue by a company of new shares to existing shareholders in proportion to their current shareholding at a price less than the current market price. Usually the right to take up new shares can be transferred or sold.

**risk**: The uncertainty of future cash flows. It is typically measured by the variance or standard deviation of the distribution of possible cash flows.

**risk-adjusted discount rate**: A required rate of return, adjusted for the risk associated with the project under consideration.
**risk aversion**: Dislike of risk on the part of investors. As a consequence, investors require compensation in the form of a higher expected rate of return.
**risk-free interest rate**: An interest rate that is certain to be paid. In practice, the interest rate on assets such as government securities that are regarded as having no risk of default is often used as a proxy for the risk-free interest rate.
**risk premium**: The difference between the expected return on a risky asset and the risk-free interest rate.

**sale and leaseback agreement**: An agreement in which a company sells an asset and then leases it back.
**secondary market**: A market where previously issued securities are traded.
**security market line (SML)**: The graphical representation of the *capital asset pricing model*.
**semistrong-form efficient market**: A market that is efficient in impounding into security prices all publicly available information.
**sensitivity analysis**: Analysis of the effect of changing one or more input variables to observe the effects on the results.
**serial correlation**: The correlation of a variable with itself over successive time periods.
**short hedge**: The sale of a futures contract, to reduce risk.
**short selling**: The act of selling an asset not owned by the seller.
**signalling**: The process of revealing information through actions.
**spot rate**: The rate for transactions for immediate delivery. In the case of foreign exchange, the spot rate is for settlement in two days.
**standard deviation**: The square root of the *variance*.
**strike price**: *See* exercise price.
**strong-form efficient market**: A market that is efficient in impounding all information into security prices.
**subscription price**: The price that must be paid to obtain a new share.
**sunk cost**: A cost that has been incurred and cannot be recovered, and therefore is not relevant to future decision making.
**swap**: An agreement to exchange one set of future cash flows for another. For example, in an interest-rate swap, a set of cash flows calculated using a fixed interest rate is exchanged for a set of cash flows calculated using a floating interest rate.
**synergy**: In takeovers, the situation where the value of a combined entity exceeds the value of the individual companies as independent entities.
**systematic risk**: Market-related or non-diversifiable risk. *See* market risk.

**takeover**: Acquisition of control of one company by another.
**target firm**: The object of a takeover bid.
**technical analysis**: Analysis of securities, based on their historical price/volume relationships, for example, charting.

**term loan**: A loan requiring a schedule of repayments over a fixed period. Typically each repayment comprises principal and interest components.
**term structure of interest rates**: The relationship between the interest rate and the term to maturity for securities in the same risk class.
**trade credit**: Short-term credit provided by suppliers of goods.

**underwriting agreement**: In a primary issue of a security, an agreement by an underwriting institution to purchase any securities not taken up by the public at the close of the issue.
**unsystematic risk**: *See* diversifiable risk.
**utility**: The amount of satisfaction that a consumer derives from consuming goods or services.

**value additivity principle**: The principle that present values can be summed. One application of this principle is taking the value of an entity to be equal to the sum of the values of its components.
**variance**: A measure of variability; the mean squared deviations from the mean or expected value.
**vertical takeover**: A takeover where the bidding company acquires a supplier or customer.

**weak-form efficient market**: A market that is efficient in impounding only information about that security's historical price series.
**weighted average cost of capital (WACC)**: The average cost of capital for a company, calculated as a weighted average of the costs of the individual sources of finance.
**working capital**: Current assets, less current liabilities.

**yield curve**: A graph of yield to maturity against bond term at a given point in time.
**yield to maturity**: The *internal rate of return* on a bond.

**zero coupon bond**: A bond that provides only one cash flow, the payment at maturity.

# AUTHOR INDEX

Page numbers followed by $n$ indicate footnote references

Abuaf, N., 690$n$
Adler, M., 690$n$
Aldersley, J., 250$n$
Alexander, G. J., 82$n$
Allen, D. E., 349, 349$n$, 352$n$, 357, 358$n$
Altman, E., 276$n$, 346, 346$n$
Anderson, D., 396$n$
Argus, J., 635, 635$n$
Ariel, R. A., 393, 393$n$
Asquith, P., 269, 269$n$
Australian Options Market, 455$n$

Bailey, W., 494, 494$n$
Balakrishnan, S., 342, 342$n$, 343
Ball, R., 94, 161$n$, 226$n$, 273, 273$n$, 365$n$, 369, 369$n$, 380$n$, 388$n$, 390$n$, 395$n$, 396, 396$n$, 399, 399$n$, 518$n$
Banz, R. W., 394$n$
Barclay, M., 275, 275$n$
Barker, H., 640$n$
Barnea, A., 314$n$
Baskin, J., 349, 349$n$
Basu, S., 393, 393$n$, 395, 395$n$
Baumol, W. J., 752$n$
Bautista, A., 612, 612$n$
Beard, P., 711$n$
Beedles, W., 394, 394$n$, 752–3, 754, 757, 758$n$
Beerworth, B., 652$n$
Bellamy, D., 660$n$
Benington, G., 369$n$
Bennett, J., 606$n$
Bernstein, L., 402$n$
Bhaskar, K., 10$n$
Bhattacharya, S., 265$n$, 272
Bicksler, J. L., 497$n$
Bierman, H., Jr, 115$n$
Biger, N., 489$n$, 490$n$
Bird, R., 160$n$, 381$n$, 688, 688$n$
Bishop, S., 380$n$, 635, 635$n$, 658, 658$n$, 659, 663, 663$n$
Black, F., 161$n$, 263, 263$n$, 273, 273$n$, 396$n$, 471–9, 471$n$, 475$n$, 477$n$, 478$n$, 490$n$
Blanchard, O. J., 386$n$
Bloch, F., 90, 90$n$
Blomeyer, E. C., 476$n$, 478$n$, 479$n$
Blume, M., 369, 369$n$, 395$n$, 398$n$
Bodurtha, J. N., 491, 491$n$
Bosons, J., 266$n$

Bower, D., 163$n$
Bower, R., 163$n$
Bowers, J., 390$n$, 399, 399$n$
Bowman, R., 625$n$
Bradley, M., 340, 340$n$, 341, 343, 659, 659$n$, 661, 661$n$
Brailsford, T. J., 155$n$, 386$n$, 392$n$, 564$n$
Brealey, R., 91$n$, 353$n$, 362, 362$n$
Breeden, D. T., 497$n$
Brennan, M. J., 261$n$, 361$n$, 497$n$
Brenner, M., 478$n$, 479$n$, 491$n$, 494$n$
Brickley, J., 269, 269$n$, 658, 658$n$, 665$n$
Brooks, L. D., 405$n$
Brown, P., 161$n$, 226$n$, 270, 270$n$, 271, 273, 273$n$, 275, 275$n$, 374–5, 374$n$, 375$n$, 376–8, 376$n$, 380$n$, 382, 382$n$, 392$n$, 393, 394, 394$n$, 395$n$, 396, 396$n$, 398$n$, 518$n$
Brown, R. G., 740$n$
Brown, R. L., 264$n$, 384$n$, 471$n$, 478, 478$n$
Brown, S. J., 371$n$
Bruce, R., 175$n$, 210$n$, 223$n$, 241$n$, 244$n$, 606$n$, 706$n$, 714$n$, 788$n$
Bureau of Industry Economics, 291$n$
Burrows, G. H., 612$n$

Cadsby, C., 391, 391$n$, 393$n$
Campbell, J. K., 174$n$
Carew, E., 414$n$
Casey, R., 654, 654$n$, 658, 658$n$
Cassino, M., 608$n$
Castagna, A. D., 479, 479$n$
Chan, K., 280$n$
Chang, R. P., 342$n$
Chen, A. H. Y., 767, 767$n$
Chen, N. F., 167, 167$n$, 168$n$
Cheung, J. K., 361$n$
Chew, D. H., 163$n$, 318$n$, 353$n$, 403$n$, 495$n$, 497$n$, 640$n$, 655$n$, 659$n$, 715$n$
Chiarella, T., 342$n$
Chin, H., 381$n$
Chiras, D., 479$n$
Chiu, J., 10, 10$n$
Cho, D. C., 167$n$
Chong, F., 788$n$
Chow, D., 345, 345$n$, 346, 346$n$
Clarke, A., 275, 275$n$
Clinton, K., 688$n$
Cochrane, J. H., 383$n$, 388$n$
Coffee, J., 652$n$

Committee of Inquiry into the Australian Financial System, 174$n$
Condoyanni, L., 391$n$
Conine, T. E., 525$n$
Connor, G., 399, 399$n$
Cooley, D., 10, 10$n$
Copeland, T., 274$n$, 323$n$, 396$n$, 497$n$, 622$n$, 645$n$
Cordes, J., 311$n$
Cornell, B., 410$n$, 692$n$
Cornett, M., 347, 347$n$
Courtadon, G., 491, 491$n$, 494$n$, 495$n$
Cox, J. C., 88$n$, 106, 410$n$, 469$n$, 478$n$, 479, 479$n$
Crockett, J., 266$n$, 274$n$
Crutchley, C., 271, 271$n$
Culbertson, J., 91$n$

Davies, P., 175$n$, 223$n$
De Angelo, H., 310–11, 311$n$, 339, 344, 656$n$
De Bondt, W., 385–6, 386$n$
Desai, A., 659, 659$n$, 661, 661$n$
Dietrich, K., 692$n$
Dill, D., 612, 612$n$
Dimson, E., 383$n$, 390$n$, 391$n$, 393$n$, 395$n$
Dixon, T., 244$n$, 714$n$
Dodd, P., 364$n$, 380$n$, 394, 394$n$, 635, 635$n$, 636$n$, 652$n$, 658, 658$n$, 659, 659$n$, 663, 663$n$
Dodds, J., 92$n$
Dolan, P., 658, 658$n$
Donaldson, G., 348, 348$n$, 352$n$, 796
Dooley, M. P., 692, 692$n$
Dorfman, R., 116$n$
Dornbusch, R., 266$n$
Dufey, G., 696$n$
Dyer, A., 688, 688$n$

Easterbrook, F., 262$n$, 266$n$
Easton, S., 271, 271$n$, 379–80, 379$n$, 380$n$, 384$n$, 389, 389$n$, 390$n$, 391$n$, 392$n$, 635, 635$n$, 691, 691$n$
Eddey, P., 654, 654$n$
Edison, H. J., 690, 690$n$
Elton, E., 78$n$, 160$n$, 167, 167$n$, 274$n$
Emery, G. W., 747$n$
Ezzell, J., 519$n$

Fabozzi, F. J., 181$n$
Faff, R., 155$n$, 161$n$, 167, 167$n$, 383$n$, 390$n$, 393$n$, 564$n$

Fama, E. F., 24n, 26n, 91, 91n, 149, 152n, 161n, 362, 362n, 364, 364n, 365n, 369, 369n, 370n, 380, 380n, 381n, 383n, 384, 384n, 385, 385n
Ferguson, R., 401n
Figlewski, S., 443n
Finn, F., 216n, 226n, 270, 270n, 271, 273, 273n, 376–8, 376n, 380n, 382, 382n, 391n, 395n, 396, 396n, 518n, 635, 635n
Fischer, S., 266n
Fisher, I., 14, 14n
Fisher, L., 105
Flath, D., 628n
Flood, R. P., 387n
Ford, J., 92n
Foster, G., 389, 389n, 648, 648n, 793n, 799n
Fox, I., 342, 342n, 343
French, K., 384n, 385, 385n, 390, 390n, 410n
Friedman, B. J., 91n, 341n
Friend, I., 266n, 274n
Froot, K. A., 690n, 692n
Fuller, R. J., 523n

Galai, D., 478n, 479n
Gallant, P., 706n
Gallinger, G. W., 791n
Garber, P. M., 386n
Gatward, P., 343, 343n
Geijsbeek, W. R., Jr, 544n
Geske, R., 476n, 478n, 496n
Ghosh, C., 270, 270n
Gibbons, M. R., 162n
Giddy, I. H., 696n
Gizycki, M. C., 689n
Glassman, D., M., 403n
Goetz, B., 735n
Goodhart, C., 688n, 689n
Gordon, M., 261–2, 261n
Goss, B. A., 419n, 422n, 423n
Granger, C., 367n
Gruber, M., 78n, 160n, 167, 167n, 274n
Gruen, D. W. R., 689n
Gultekin, B., 392n
Gultekin, M., 392n

Haley, C. W., 113n
Hamson, D., 264n
Hancock, P., 270, 270n, 271, 376–8, 376n
Hansen, R., 271, 271n
Harris, L., 391, 391n
Harris, R. S., 526n
Hastings, N., 740n
Hathaway, N., 274n, 275–6, 275n
Haugen, R., 314n, 393n
Healy, P., 269, 269n, 403n, 664, 664n, 665, 665n, 791, 791n
Henderson, S., 608n
Herzberg, A., 213n, 214n, 256n
Hicks, J., 89
Higgins, R., 261n, 640n
Higham, R., 216n
Hirshleifer, J., 14n, 123n
Hite, G., 655n
Hodge, M., 652n
Hodrick, R. J., 387n
Hoffmeister, J., 654n

Hogan, W. P., 190n
Homonoff, R. B. V., 760n
Howard, L., 412n
Howard, P., 264n
Hubbard, G., 651n
Hull, J., 485n, 489n, 490n
Hunt, B., 244n, 691, 691n

Ibbotson, R. C., 518n
Ingersoll, J., 88n, 106, 410n, 495n
Irving, R., 652n
Irwin, R. D., 261n, 364n, 589n
Izan, H. Y., 702, 702n

Jaffe, J., 381, 381n, 391n, 393n
Jain, P. C., 655n
Jalleh, B. R., 702n
Jameson, K., 412n
Jarrell, G., 340, 340n, 658, 658n, 659, 659n, 661, 661n, 665n
Jen, F. C., 767, 767n
Jensen, G., 271, 271n, 277, 277n
Jensen, M., 161n, 266n, 314n, 320, 320n, 321, 321n, 350, 350n, 403n, 633n, 640, 640n, 657n, 662, 369n
Johnson, H., 476n
Johnson, R., 614n
Jones, C. P., 375n, 389, 389n
Jones, D. S., 91n
Jones, R., 711n
Jorion, P., 690n
Jubb, P., 376n
Juttner, D. J., 90, 90n

Kalay, A., 274, 274n
Kamphuis, R., 387n
Kaplan, S., 657n, 661n
Karmel, P. H., 117n
Keane, S. M., 403n
Keim, D. B., 383n, 392n, 395n
Kerr, H. S., 523n
Kerr, I., 706n
Keynes, J. M., 746n, 747
Khoury, N., 276, 276n
Kim, E. H., 340, 340n, 659, 659n, 661, 661n, 767n
Kimpton, M. H., 364n
Kinney, W., 392, 392n
Kirkpatrick, C. A., 578n
Kleidon, A., 392n, 394n
Klemkosky, R. C., 469, 469n, 478n, 479n
Knox, D., 186n
Koh, S. S., 767n
Kolb, R. W., 419n, 423n
Koller, T., 645n
Kon, S., 443n
Korajczyk, R., 399, 399n
Kummer, D., 654n

Lakonishok, J., 225n, 390, 390n, 391, 391n, 393n
Lalor, P. A., 691, 691n
Lang, L., 662, 662n
Larner, R., 10, 10n
Latane, H. A., 389, 389n
Latham, M., 362n
Lease, R., 273, 273n
LeBaron, B., 384n
Lee, W., 640n

Lehmann, B. N., 362n, 690n
Lehn, K., 661n, 662–3, 662n
Lemke, K. W., 797n
LeRoy, S. F., 383n, 387, 387n, 388n
Lev, B., 625n
Levasseur, M. G., 497n, 747n
Levi, M., 390, 390n
Levin, R. L., 578n
Levy, R.,155n, 369n
Lewellen, W., 273, 273n, 624, 624n, 640n
Lewin, W., 660n
Lewis, M. K., 174n
Lilleyman, P. G., 109n
Lintner, J., 152, 152n, 257–8, 257n, 265n
Lipton, P., 213n, 214n, 256n
Litzenberger, R., 375n, 497n
Logue, D., 163n
Lonergan, W., 648n
Long, J., 273n
Long, M., 341, 341n, 624, 624n, 654n
Lorie, J., 123n, 362, 362n, 364n, 381, 381n
Loudon, G. F., 469, 469n
Lowe, P., 36–7, 336n, 343, 343n, 345, 345n
Lusztig, P., 125n
Lutz, F., 88n
Lynch, A., 391n, 396n


Ma, R., 396n
Macaulay, F., 80n, 99–100, 105
MacBeth, J., 161n
MacKie-Mason, G., 344, 344n, 345
Madden, G., 90n
Majluf, N., 324, 324n, 325, 348, 348n, 349, 351, 351n, 352
Malitz, I., 341, 341n
Manaster, S., 479n
Manuel, T. A., 405n
Manzur, M., 691n
Mao, J. C. T., 589n
Markham, J. W., 408n
Markovic, M., 410n
Markowitz, H. M., 143, 143n, 152
Marsh, T., 257n, 392n, 394n
Marshman, P., 175n, 223n
Martin, K., 642n
Martin, V., 174n
Masulis, R., 310–11, 311n, 339, 344, 347, 347n
Mathiou, N., 396n
Matolcsy, Z. P., 479, 479n
Mayers, D., 396n
McColough, D., 280n
McConnell, J., 614n, 624, 624n, 642n
McCrae, M., 381n
McDonough, D. D., 649n
McDougall, F., 663, 663n
McFadyen, T., 244n, 714n
McFarland, J. W., 491n
McHugh, A., 757, 757n
McKern, B., 223n
McNamee, P., 10n
Meckling, W., 314n, 320, 320n
Mellare, B., 210n
Merrett, A. J., 116n
Merrick, J. J., 495n

# INDEX

Merton, R. C., 257*n*, 463*n*, 466*n*, 490*n*, 496, 496*n*
Miller, M., 14*n*, 258–61, 258*n*, 262, 263, 263*n*, 265*n*, 266*n*, 267, 268, 272, 274*n*, 276, 276*n*, 277, 277*n*, 296–303, 296*n*, 304*n*, 306*n*, 307–10, 307*n*, 309*n*, 311, 313–14, 322, 331, 331*n*, 333, 335, 356, 616, 625–26*n*, 758–63, 758*n*, 762*n*
Mills, K., 337*n*
Mitchell, J. D., 702
Mitchell, M., 661*n*, 662–3, 662*n*, 702*n*
Mizon, G., 241*n*, 706*n*, 711*n*
Modigliani, F., 181*n*, 258*n*, 258–61, 262, 263, 265*n*, 267, 268, 272, 273, 273*n*, 296–303, 296*n*, 304–6, 304*n*, 335, 616
Monsen, R., 10, 10*n*
Montague, B., 244*n*, 714*n*
Moore, S., 391*n*
Morck, R., 663, 663*n*
Morgenstern, O., 367*n*
Morris, J. R., 724*n*
Morling, S., 337*n*, 343, 343*n*, 345, 345*n*
Mossin, J., 152*n*
Mullins, D., 269, 269*n*, 760*n*
Murrin, J., 645*n*
Myers, S., 316*n*, 324, 324*n*, 325, 325*n*, 338, 338*n*, 348, 348*n*, 349, 351, 351*n*, 352, 352*n*, 353*n*, 503, 503*n*, 569*n*, 612, 612*n*, 642*n*, 643*n*

NCSC, 649–50, 649*n*
Netter, J., 658, 658*n*, 665*n*
Nicol, R., 265, 276*n*, 279, 279*n*, 280, 280*n*
Niederhoffer, V., 381, 381*n*

O'Brien, K. P., 174*n*
O'Brien, T. J., 526*n*
Ofer, A., 270, 270*n*
Officer, L. H., 685*n*
Officer, R. R., 94*n*, 161*n*, 273, 273*n*, 274*n*, 275–6, 275*n*, 365*n*, 368, 368*n*, 380*n*, 391, 391*n*, 394, 394*n*, 395*n*, 398, 398*n*, 507–8, 508*n*, 517–18, 518*n*, 533*n*, 538, 538*n*, 539, 539*n*, 635, 635*n*, 636*n*, 652*n*, 658, 658*n*, 659, 663, 663*n*
O'Hanlon, J., 391*n*
Ohlson, J., 625*n*
Olsen, C., 389, 389*n*
Ong, L. L., 702*n*
Orr, D., 758–63, 758*n*, 760*n*, 762*n*
Osborn, N., 710*n*
Owers, J., 655*n*

Palepu, K., 269, 269*n*, 403*n*, 664, 664*n*, 665, 665*n*
Patell, J. M., 384, 384*n*
Peirson, G., 608*n*
Peters, R. W., 199*n*
Pettit, R. R., 272, 272*n*, 491*n*
Pham, T., 342*n*, 345, 345*n*, 346, 346*n*
Pike, R. J., 587*n*
Pilotte, E., 350, 350*n*
Pollard, I., 223*n*
Porter, G., 369*n*
Porter, R., 519*n*
Porter, R. D., 388*n*

Poterba, J., 276, 276*n*
Poulsen, A., 659, 659*n*, 661, 661*n*
Praetz, P., 367*n*, 368, 368*n*, 381*n*

Quirin, G. D., 589*n*

Rachlin, R., 109*n*
Rainbow, K. A., 471*n*
Ramaswamy, K., 494*n*
Rappaport, A., 572*n*
Ratner, M., 391, 391*n*, 393*n*
Reinganum, M., 394*n*, 395, 395*n*, 410*n*
Remolona, E., 337–8, 337*n*, 352, 352*n*
Rendleman, R. J., 389, 389*n*
Reserve Bank of Australia, 180*n*, 182*n*
Resnick, B. G., 469, 469*n*
Rhee, S. G., 342*n*
Rice, E. M., 656*n*
Richardson, G., 269, 269*n*, 273, 273*n*
Rickard, J. A., 512*n*
Ritchken, P., 478*n*
Robichek, A., 569*n*
Robson, G. N., 381*n*
Rock, K., 216*n*, 265*n*
Roley, V. V., 91*n*
Roll, R., 161, 161*n*, 162, 162*n*, 167, 167*n*, 168, 168*n*, 384*n*, 478*n*, 660, 660*n*, 661, 662
Ross, S. A., 88*n*, 106, 163, 167, 167*n*, 168, 168*n*, 324, 324*n*, 410*n*, 479, 479*n*
Round, D., 663, 663*n*
Rozeff, M., 266*n*, 271, 271*n*, 276, 276*n*, 392, 392*n*
Ruback, R., 633*n*, 664, 664*n*, 665, 665*n*
Rubinstein, M., 469*n*, 478*n*, 479, 479*n*

Sarnat, M., 155*n*
Sastry, R. A. S., 757, 757*n*
Savage, L. J., 123*n*
Scarman, I., 623*n*
Schadler, F. P., 405*n*
Schaefer, S., 91*n*
Schall, L. D., 113*n*, 544*n*, 639*n*, 640*n*
Schallheim, R., 614*n*
Scheinkman, J. A., 384*n*
Schipper, K., 660*n*
Schlarbaum, G., 273, 273*n*
Schleifer, A., 383*n*
Scholes, M., 161*n*, 263, 263*n*, 273, 273*n*, 277, 277*n*, 398*n*, 471–9, 471*n*, 478*n*
Schwab, B., 125*n*
Schwartz, E. S., 361*n*, 497*n*
Schwert, G. W., 393*n*
Scott, J., 321*n*
Seelenfreund, A., 369*n*
Sefcik, S., 269, 269*n*, 273, 273*n*
Senbet, L., 314*n*
Servaes, H., 662*n*
Shafer, J. R., 692, 692*n*
Shanahan, J., 609*n*
Shapiro, A. C., 318, 318*n*, 353, 353*n*
Sharpe, S., 343, 343*n*
Sharpe, W. F., 82*n*, 152, 152*n*, 190*n*, 479, 497*n*
Shastri, K., 478*n*, 491, 491*n*, 494*n*
Sheffrin, S., 311*n*
Shevlin, T. J., 371*n*, 380*n*, 389, 389*n*, 478, 478*n*
Shiller, R. J., 388*n*, 400*n*

Shleifer, A., 663, 663*n*
Shuetrim, G., 336–7, 336*n*, 343, 343*n*, 345, 345*n*
Siegel, D., 270, 270*n*
Sim, A., 342*n*
Sinclair, N., 167, 167*n*, 271, 271*n*, 379–80, 379*n*, 389, 389*n*
Singh, R. A., 380*n*
Sinquefield, R. A., 518*n*
Sloan, R. G., 225*n*
Smidt, S., 115*n*, 390, 390*n*, 391, 391*n*, 393*n*
Smith, C. W., Jr, 222*n*, 272, 272*n*, 316*n*, 317*n*, 346–-7, 346*n*, 350, 350*n*, 403*n*, 478*n*, 495*n*, 497*n*, 627*n*, 628, 628*n*, 714*n*, 715, 715*n*
Smith, K., 276, 276*n*
Smith, K. V., 791*n*
Smithson, C. W., 715, 715*n*
Snyder, R., 740*n*
Solberg, D., 271, 271*n*, 277, 277*n*
Solnik, B., 701*n*
Solomons, D., 13, 13*n*
Srinivasulu, S. L., 696*n*
Stambaugh, R. F., 398*n*
Stanley, K., 273, 273*n*
Stanton, H. G., 512*n*
Stanton, P., 664*n*
Stern, J. M., 163*n*, 318*n*, 353*n*, 403*n*, 495*n*, 497*n*, 640*n*, 655*n*, 659*n*, 715*n*
Steward, G. B., 403*n*
Stoll, H. R., 454*n*, 466*n*
Stone, B. K., 758*n*
Stulz, R., 662, 662*n*
Subrahmanyam, M., 276*n*, 491*n*, 494*n*
Sue, K., 241*n*, 706*n*, 711*n*
Summers, L. H., 276, 276*n*, 383*n*, 385, 385*n*
Sundaresan, S. M., 494*n*
Sundem, G. L., 544*n*
Sung, S. K., 491*n*
Sutton, W., 485*n*, 699*n*
Sweeney, H. W. A., 109*n*
Sweeney, R. J., 692, 692*n*, 703*n*
Sykes, A., 116*n*
Szekely, L., 610*n*

Taggart, R., 524*n*, 525*n*
Tamarkin, M., 525*n*
Tan, M., 342*n*
Tandon, K., 491, 491*n*, 494*n*
Taylor, S., 368*n*, 397*n*
Tease, W. J., 91*n*, 337*n*
Terry, C., 244*n*
Thaler, R., 385–6, 386*n*, 690*n*, 692
Theil, H., 405*n*
Thompson, R., 269, 269*n*, 273, 273*n*, 660*n*
Thornton, D. L., 688*n*
Tilley, L., 376*n*
Tippett, M., 160*n*, 688, 688*n*
Titman, S., 318–19, 318*n*, 342, 342*n*, 343
Travlos, N., 347, 347*n*
Treynor, J. L., 401*n*
Tuckwell, R., 91*n*

Upton, C., 625–6, 626*n*

Van Horne, J., 369$n$, 780$n$, 795$n$
Vardigans, P., 603$n$
Vermaelen, T., 225$n$
Vishny, R., 663, 663$n$

Wakeman, D., 526$n$
Wakeman, L. M., 627$n$, 628, 628$n$, 715, 715$n$
Walkling, R., 654$n$, 662, 662$n$
Wallace, R. H., 174$n$
Walter, T., 275, 275$n$, 382, 382$n$, 393$n$, 398$n$, 658, 658$n$
Wapnah, L. B., 702, 702$n$
Ward, C. W. R., 391$n$
Warner, J., 316$n$, 317$n$, 322$n$, 345, 345$n$, 346, 371$n$

Warren, G., 487$n$
Watts, R., 272, 272$n$
Weil, R. L., 105
Weingartner, H. M., 125$n$, 588$n$, 589$n$
Weisbach, M., 661$n$
Wessels, R., 342, 342$n$, 343
Westerfield, R., 391$n$, 393$n$
Weston, J. F., 274$n$, 323$n$, 497$n$, 622$n$
Whaley, R. E., 361$n$, 454$n$, 478, 478$n$, 479$n$, 494, 494$n$
Whittred, G. P., 380$n$, 396$n$
Wilford, D. S., 714$n$
Williams, J., 398$n$
Willinger, G. L., 497$n$
Willoughby, R., 210$n$
Wills, A., 279$n$

Wills, R., 740$n$
Wolfson, M. A., 384, 384$n$
Wonnacott, R. J., 405$n$
Wonnacott, T. H., 405$n$
Wood, J., 161$n$
Woolridge, J., 270, 270$n$
Wright, F. K., 586$n$, 760, 760$n$, 761, 761$n$

Yamey, B. S., 419$n$, 422$n$, 423$n$
Yang, H. C., 489$n$

Ziegler, P., 264$n$
Zionts, S., 767, 767$n$
Zorn, T., 271, 271$n$, 277, 277$n$

# SUBJECT INDEX

Page numbers followed by *n* indicate footnote references

abandonment decisions, 110, 346, 347, 565–6, 580–5
accommodation bills, *see* commercial bills
accounting rate of return, 111, 125–8, 781, 781*n*, 799
accounts payable
   as a source of short-term finance, 195–6
   characteristics of, 197–206
   importance to companies of, 195–6
   stretching payment of, 196–7
accounts receivable
   administration costs of, 774, 783–4
   bad debts and, 774, 776, 778, 780, 787*n*, 800
   benefits and costs of, 773–4
   collection policy and, 771, 772, 780
   credit insurance and, 788–9
   credit policy and, 774–80
   defined, 195, 722, 772–4
   delinquent accounts and, 774, 778, 800
   discounting and, 779, 786
   factoring of, 210, 785–8
   management of, 771–90
   net present value and, 781–5
   *see also* financial statement analysis
accounts receivable financing, 788
activity ratios, 794–5
agency theory, 9–10, 11, 266, 266*n*, 271–2, 277, 314–21, 326, 340, 358
All-Ordinaries, *see* share price index
American type options, 45, 464–5, 466, 468–9, 470, 471, 476*n*, 485, 492, 494
annuities
   defined, 51
   future value of, 58–60
   types of, 51
   *see also* deferred annuities; general annuities; ordinary annuities; ordinary perpetuities
annuities due, 52, 54–5, 59
arbitrage
   capital structure and, 296–9
   covered interest, 680–2
   triangular, cross rates and, 676–7
arbitrage pricing theory, 9, 80, 163–8
   identity of factors, 168
   performance of factors, 167
asset pricing and portfolio theory, 134–71

assets and asset management
   characteristics of, 356
   company-specific, 343, 355, 356
   comparative advantage in disposal of, 628
   financing of, 2
   importance of, 720–1
   nominal price of, 7
   short-term, 720–800
   specialised, 627
   substitution of, 317
   *see also* accounts receivable; cash; depreciation; financial statement analysis; intangible assets; inventory; leasing and equipment finance; liquidity finance; takeovers; tangible assets
audits, post-completion, 110
Aussie Macs, 181, 181*n*
Austraclear, 202*n*
Australian Associated Stock Exchanges, *see* Australian Stock Exchange
Australian Industry Development Corporation, 186, 239, 240–1
Australian Options Market, 455, 457, 458
Australian Resources Development Bank, 240
Australian Securities Commission, 217, 649, 651
Australian Stock Exchange, 3, 176–7, 214, 214*n*, 237, 248, 256, 441, 651, 652
Australian United Corporation, 178
authorised dealers, 183–4, 183*n*, 194, 198, 200, 202, 765–6

bad debts, 774, 776, 778, 780, 787*n*, 800
balloon payments, 243, 628
bank bills
   explanation of, 202, 203, 205, 766
   futures contracts on, 414–15, 419, 429–37, 445–7
   *see also* commercial bills
Bank for International Settlements, 674
*Banking Act* 1959, 183*n*, 191
*Banking Legislation Amendment Act* 1989, 191
Bank of Melbourne, 183
bank overdrafts, *see* overdrafts
bankruptcy costs, 314, 314*n*, 315–16, 318, 319, 322, 326, 340, 344, 345–6, 355, 640

banks
   bills of exchange and, 209
   borrowing from, 206–9
   deposits of funds with, 765
   finance leases and, 209, 603, 606
   forward-rate agreements and, 449–50
   fully drawn advances from, 208–9
   futures contracts and, 415
   interest in financial institutions of, 178, 179, 182, 185, 187
   introduction to, 182–3
   list of licensed, 189–90
   regulation of, 191–3
   short-term loans and, 195, 198, 706–7
   term loans and, 239–40
   variable interest rate loans and, 232
   *see also* capital adequacy of banks; deregulation; foreign banks; merchant banks; overdrafts; Reserve Bank of Australia
*Banks (Shareholding) Act* 1972, 191
Baumol's model of cash management, 752–7
benefit–cost ratio, *see* investment evaluation
beta factor
   asset, 156–8, 161, 164*n*, 166, 393, 394, 399, 505, 518, 523, 524–5, 525*n*
   debt, 505
   equity, 505, 524, 525, 525*n*
   project, 503, 504
bill acceptance companies, 202
bills of exchange, 209
   *see also* commercial bills
binominal option pricing, 479–85
bird-in-the-hand argument, 261, 262
Black–Scholes model, 471–9, 485, 490
bond duration, 99–106
   *see also* debt-security immunisation
bonds, *see under type of bond eg* debentures
bonus shares, *see* ordinary shares
bootstrapping, 642
break-even analysis, 575–6
bridging finance, 210–11
Broken Hill Proprietary Company Ltd, 3–5, 206
broking houses
   banks and, 182
   brokers and, 177
   business funding and, 175
   described, 175–6

**829**

funds on call and, 766
merchant banks and, 178
public issue of ordinary shares and, 216, 218–19
*see also* stock exchange/market
building societies, 174, 415,
business risk, 293–6, 301, 302, 315, 339, 355, 358, 505

call options, 415, 454–6, 458–64, 466, 469–81, 496, 699*n*
*see also* put-call parity
Campbell Committee Report, 173–4, 174*n*
capital adequacy of banks, 179, 184, 185, 192–3, 200
capital asset pricing model
  arbitrage pricing model and, 166–7
  cost of capital and, 502, 503, 504–5, 509, 517, 523, 541
  dividends, rate of return and, 273–4
  empirical evidence for, 161–2
  market efficiency and, 8–9
  portfolio theory and, 155–8
  problems with, 398–400, 405
  risk and, 89, 80, 160–1
  security market line and, 155–8
capital budgeting, *see* investment evaluation
capital-expenditure process
  approval and control of, 109–10, 587
  background to, 108
  evaluation and selection of investments and, 109
  generation of proposals for, 108
  post-completion audit and, 110
capital gains, 255, 266, 274, 275, 276, 277, 288, 311, 330*n*
capital gains tax, 262, 263, 264, 266, 273, 274, 277, 281, 286, 290*n*, 307, 330*n*, 332, 333, 334
capital loss, 84
capital market line, 153–5, 161
capital markets
  consumption, investment and, 16–19
  deregulation, 173–4, 179, 180, 185, 207, 219*n*, 343, 344, 688
  financial agency institutions in, 175–81
  financial intermediaries in, 182–7
  inefficiency/efficiency in, 385, 400
  introduction to, 172–5
capital rationing, 586–8
capital structure
  Australian/overseas companies, of, 336–8, 343, 346, 349
  bankruptcy and, 314, 314*n*, 315–16, 318, 319, 322, 340, 344, 345–6, 355
  company value and, 322–3, 330–4, 335, 345
  defined, 292
  determinants of, 340–5, 354–9
  empirical research on, 338–53
  exchange offers/recapitalisations and, 346–8, 351
  factors influencing decisions on, 293, 336, 350–3
  financial distress costs and, 314–21, 339, 343, 344, 345–6, 351, 353

financial leverage and, 293–6, 303, 309, 311, 318, 330–4, 335*n*, 336–8, 339, 340, 341, 343–4, 345, 348, 351, 352–3, 527
information asymmetry and 307–10, 323–5, 336, 349, 357–8
Modigliani/Miller theories of, 296–303, 307–10, 336
optimal, 311, 321–3, 339, 345, 351, 355
pecking-order theory and, 325, 326, 335–6, 340, 341, 348–50, 351, 352
reserve borrowing capacity. 357–8
taxes and, 313–14, 322–3, 330–4, 340, 344–5, 346, 351, 356–7
trade-off theory and, 321–3, 325, 326, 335, 335*n*, 338, 339, 340, 341–2, 345, 347, 351, 352
cash
  financial asset benefit, as, 76–7
  motives for holding, 108, 747
  *see also* liquidity management
cash budgeting, 748–53
cash management models
  assuming certainty under, 752–7
  assuming uncertainty under, 758–63
cash management trusts, 766
certainty
  cash management models assuming, 752–7
  financial asset valuation under, 76–8
  inventory management under, 729–36
  *see also* perfect certainty; uncertainty
certainty-equivalents and risk, 568–72
chain of replacement, 558–65, 566, 567, 568
classical income tax system
  cost of capital and, 507, 534–6
  gain from leverage and, 331–3
  policy and, 263, 276, 277, 278, 356
  shareholders and, 289, 290, 303–4
  *see also* imputation tax system
commercial bills
  acceptance fee and, 205
  authorised dealers and, 200, 202
  banks and, 200, 202, 204
  cost of, 34, 201, 204–5
  creation of, 200–2
  discounting of, 198, 200–1, 202, 204, 205, 766
  finance companies and, 199, 200, 202, 210
  merchant banks and, 179, 200, 202, 204, 211
  short-term money market and, 198, 199–205
  trading banks and, 200
  *see also* bank bills; non-bank bills
commercial hire purchase, 293, 603, 610, 628–9
commercial paper, 709
Commonwealth Bank of Australia, 183, 183*n*, 187, 217, 219, 241
Commonwealth Development Bank, 187, 241
company tax, 304–6, 310, 311, 313, 335*n*, 339, 347, 351, 356, 357, 509, 517, 5345, 5367, 539, 541, 623–4

*see also* classical tax system; imputation tax system; income tax
compound interest
  accumulated value at, 36
  continuous interest rates and, 42–6
  defined, 34–5
  formula development for, 35–7
  geometric rate of return and, 44–6
  nominal and effective interest rates and, 37–40
  present value at, 37
  real interest rates and, 40–2
compound options, 496
conglomerate takeovers, 635, 637
constant chain of replacement, 558–60, 561–5, 566, 567, 568
constant payout policy, 257
consumer credit, 772
contingent claims, 454, 494–8
continuity-of-business test, 641
continuity-of-ownership test, 641
continuous compounding, 42–6
contracts
  defined, 29*n*
  mortgage loan, 180–1
  principal-and-interest loan, 60–6
  types of lease, 604–8
  *see also* futures contracts; loan contracts
convergence, *see* imperfect convergence
convertible securities, 175, 249–53, 495
corporate bonds, 168, 238–9
corporate raiders, 638
corporate restructuring, 654–7
  buyouts, 321, 655, 656–7
  divestitures, 655, 663
*Corporations Law*, 3, 227, 228, 237, 248, 649–51, 650*n*
cost of capital
  capital structure effects on, 299–301, 299*n*, 521, 525
  CAPM and, 502, 503, 504–5, 509, 517, 523, 541
  company's, 519–21
  debt funds and, 511–15
  defined, 502, 533–4, 536
  divisions and, 522–7
  equity and, 539–42
  leasing and, 625–6
  ordinary shares and, 516–19
  preference shares and, 515
  retained earnings, new share issue and, 519
  return rate and, 13*n*, 120, 502, 517–18
  risk and, 503–4, 521
  systematic risk and, 518, 522
  tax systems and, 502–3, 507–9, 527, 533–42
  weighted average, 505–7, 509–10, 427–8
coupon-paying debt, 496
coupons, 98–9, 100, 438
covered interest arbitrage, 680–2
credit
  administration costs of, 774
  benefits and costs of providing, 773–4
  customer selection and, 775–6
  limits of, 778–9
  reasons for providing, 774
  terms of, 779–80

# INDEX

*see also* accounts payable; accounts receivable; consumer credit; credit insurance
credit assessments, 247–8
credit bureaus, 778
credit card services, 787n
credit enhancement, 180
credit foncier loans, *see* principal-and-interest-loans
credit insurance, 788–9
credit periods, 779, 779n, 781n
credit policy, 771–2, 774–80
credit ratings, 173, 180, 196, 778
credit risk, 715
creeping takeovers, 651–2
cross-border leases, 605, 608, 624
currency exposure, 247
currency swaps, *see* swap transactions
current assets, *see* accounts receivable; assets and asset management; inventory; liquidity management
current ratio, 793, 797–8, 799

debentures and unsecured notes, 83, 232, 235–9
debt
 defined, 30–1
 interest cost of, 233–4, 304
 subordinated, 233
 unsubordinated, 233
 *see also* bad debts; collection policy; delinquent accounts
debt finance
 adverse incentive effects of, 318–19
 cost of, 511–15
 foreign currency, 703–15
 hybrids of equity finance and, 248–53, 293, 295–6, 309, 310, 311, 315, 316, 317, 319, 323, 348, 357
 types of marketable, 232, 233–4, 235–9, 511–12, 513
 types of non-marketable, 232–3, 239–43, 511, 512–13, 515
 value created by, 293
 *see also* long-term finance; short-term finance; swap transactions
debt markets, 173
debt securities
 duration, immunisation and, 98–106
 ownership of, 83, 309
 ratings on, 93–4
 realisation of, 176
 time value of money and, 76–106
 types of long-term, 235–9
 valuation of, 83–4
 *see also under type of security eg* ordinary shares
debt-security immunisation, 98–9
debtholders, 233, 234, 236, 296, 309, 314, 316, 317, 319, 321
decision-tree analysis, 578–85, 775–7, 778
default risk, 85, 92–4, 175, 301, 315–16, 315n, 318–19, 326, 715, 764, 765
deferred annuities, 52, 55–7
deferred perpetuity annuities, 52n
deferred shares, 228
depreciation
 accounting rate of return and, 126
 as a source of funds, 229–30

funds from operation and, 229
lease rentals and, 610, 620
reducing-balance method of, 547, 548, 550
straight-line method of, 547, 548, 550
taxation and, 311, 547–9, 547n
derivative securities, 178, 178n
Descartes' rule of signs, 116n
discounted cash flow methods, *see* investment evaluation
discounted value, *see* present value
diversifiable risk, *see* unsystematic risk
diversification benefits/gains, 147–50, 152, 639–40, 639n, 657, 663, 701, 703
dividend-clientele effect, 263, 264, 267–8, 272–3, 275–6
dividend decisions, 2, 245, 255–85
dividend drop-off ratio, 274–5, 275n, 557
dividend election schemes, 280–1, 281n
dividend growth model, 516–17
dividend imputation tax system, *see* imputation tax system
dividend payout ratios, 257, 271, 276, 277, 279, 312, 317, 348, 349
dividend reinvestment plans, 230, 280–1, 282, 282n
dividends
 agency costs and, 266, 266n, 271–2, 277, 321
 declaration procedures for, 256
 empirical studies of, 268–77
 growth in, 266, 270
 importance to shareholders of, 257–62
 information effects of, 265–6, 268–71, 277, 350
 internal equity finance and, 229
 issue and transaction costs of, 267, 268
 legal considerations and, 256
 managers and, 257–8
 options and, 463–4, 466, 477, 478, 491
 par value and, 215
 policy
  alternative types of, 257
  company attributes and, 276–7
  defined, 255
  establishment of, 277–82
  irrelevance of, 258–61
  pure residual, 257
  relevance of, 262–8
  under imputation, 281–2
 preference shares and, 248
 resolution of uncertainty and, 261–2
 retained earnings and, 230
 shareholders and, 255, 260, 262, 267, 269, 272,
 shares and 7, 78, 80–2, 83, 265, 273, 274–5, 276
 signalling and, 265–6
 taxation and, 262–4, 267, 273–6, 277, 278–9, 282, 286–91
 types of, 256
 *see also* income tax; ordinary shares
Dunn and Bradstreet, 778

earnings coverage ratio, 796

earnings per share
 profit announcement prices and, 374–5
 takeovers and, 641–2, 648
economic order quantity model, 729–36
effective interest rates, 37–40, 511–12, 513
efficient frontier, 150–2, 153, 701–2
efficient market hypothesis, 361–5, 382–96
 implications of, 400–6
employee options, 227
equipment finance, *see* leasing and equipment finance
equity finance
 cost of, 539–42
 deferred shares source of, 228
 hybrid debt and, 248–53, 293, 295–6, 309, 310, 311, 315, 316, 317, 319, 323, 348, 357
 internal/external, 228–30, 325n
 ordinary shares source of, 213–26
 private issue of, 223–4
 public company floats and, 215–16
 *see also* ordinary shares
equity leasing, 606
eurobonds, 239, 241, 705, 708, 710–11, 710n, 712n
eurocurrency loans, 187, 706–11
Euromarkets, 705–6, 709
euronotes, 708–9, 711
European type options, 455, 464n, 465n, 466–8, 469, 470, 471, 476n, 480, 490, 491, 493–4
event studies, methodology of, 346–7, 370–3
excess present value index, *see* benefit-cost ratio
excess price volatility debate, 387–8
exchange offers and recapitalisation, 338, 346–8, 351
exchange rates, forecasting of, 691–2
exchange risk, 692–9
expectations theory of term structure, 85–90, 91, 92n

factoring, 185, 210, 722, 785–8
 confidential, 786
 maturity, 786n
 non-notification agreements, 785, 786
 non-recourse agreements, 785
 notification agreements, 785
family issue, *see* debentures and unsecured notes
Federal National Mortgage Association, 181
filter rule, 368–9
finance companies
 banks interest in, 182, 185
 commercial bills market and, 199, 200, 202
 described, 185
 factoring by, 210
 flow of funds through, 173
 futures contracts and, 415
 instalment credit and, 198, 211
 intercompany loans and, 199
 inventory loans by, 210
 lease finance by, 603
 short-term debt and, 195
 short-term mortgages and, 210–11
 short-term money market and, 198, 210

financial agency institutions, 175–81
*Financial Corporations Act 1974*, 177
financial futures, *see* futures contracts
financial institutions, 92, 172, 175–81, 182, 198, 216, 765–6
financial intermediaries
  authorised dealers as, 183–4
  broking houses as, 175
  business funding and, 175
  finance companies as, 185
  flow of funds through, 173
  investment companies as, 186
  life insurance companies as, 185–6
  merchant banks as, 178–80
  superannuation companies as, 185–6
  unit trusts as, 186
financial leases, 198, 209, 211, 293, 603–4, 609, 612–21, 626
financial leverage, *see* capital structure; leverage ratios
financial ratios, 791–800
financial statement analysis, 778, 791–801
financing decisions
  defined, 2
  determination of, 354–9
  finished goods inventory and, 727, 729, 732
  Fisher's analysis implications and, 24
  marketing problems and, 353–4
  tax position and, 356–7
  *see also* investment decisions
First Australian National Mortgage Corporation Limited, 181
Fisher effect, international, *see* uncovered interest parity
Fisher's Separation Theorem, 14, 20–1, 225, 114
fixed-charge debentures, 235
floating charge debentures, 235
floor-plan finance, 210
flotation of a company, 215–16, 519
*Foreign Acquisitions and Takeovers Act 1975*, 652
foreign banks, 174, 178, 179, 182$n$, 183
  *see also* deregulation
foreign currency options, 485–91, 699
foreign exchange market, 178, 179, 182, 193, 672, 719
foreign securities, 707–15
forward contracts, 409–10, 488–9, 698
forward rate agreements, 182, 447–50, 674–7, 678–87, 688–9 *see also* hedging
franked dividends, 264, 276, 278, 279, 280, 281, 282, 287, 291, 304, 357, 507, 509, 515, 536, 537, 540, 541, 542, 555
fully drawn advances, 208–9
fully drawn bill facility, 204
  *see also* revolving credit bill facility
futures contracts
  background to, 408–14
  bank bills and, 429–37
  basis risk, 423–4, 435
  defined, 408
  deposits, margins, the mark-to-market rule and, 413–14, 415
  determinants of prices of, 416–18

forward contracts compared with, 409–10
  imperfect convergence, 422
  options contracts compared with, 458
  options on, 491–4
  present value of, 414
  share price index and, 441–4
  ten-year Treasury bonds and, 415, 437–41
  valuation of financial, 445–7
  volume traded, 412
  *see also* hedging; merchant banks; speculating
futures exchanges, 408

gearing, *see* capital structure; forward rate agreements; leverage
general annuities, 66–8
geometric rates of return, 44–6
government securities, 76, 85, 90, 184, 192, 307–10, 307$n$, 517, 764–5
Government Insurance Office, 217

hedging
  foreign currency and, 182, 694–9, 703, 745
  futures and, 409, 418, 421–9, 432–6, 440–1, 443–4, 492–3
  risk-free portfolios and, 472–4
hire purchase contracts, *see* commercial hire purchase
horizontal takeovers, 635
housing loans, 174, 180

immunisation, 98–9
imputation tax system
  bonus share issues and, 226
  capital structure and, 311–14, 322, 330–1, 333–4, 335$n$, 356–7
  cost of capital and, 503, 507–9, 536–9
  dividend decisions and, 263–4, 275, 276, 277, 278–9, 281–2, 286–91, 303–4
  internal equity finance and, 229
  leasing and, 621, 624, 626
  overview of, 286–91
  project cash flows and taxes and, 554–7
  *see also* classical income tax system
income tax
  accounting rate of return and, 126
  capital structure decisions and, 303–14, 322–3, 330–4, 340, 344–5, 346, 351, 356–7
  commercial hire purchase and, 628–9
  cost of capital and, 506, 5079, 527, 533–42
  dividends and, 262–4, 267, 272, 304, 541
  hybrid securities and, 252–3
  investment evaluation and, 546–9, 550
  lease financing and, 608–10, 619–21, 623–4, 626, 627
  net cash flows and, 546–9, 554–7
  takeovers and, 641
  *see also* classical income tax system; company tax; dividends; imputation tax system; interest withholding tax

*Income Tax Assessment Act* 1936, 252, 253, 264, 288, 546, 629, 708
independent investment proposals, 111, 118, 130
indifference curves, 15–16, 17, 19
inflation
  chain of replacement methods and, 564
  expected rates of, 31$n$
  interest rates and, 358, 678, 684–6
  investment evaluation and, 549, 551–2, 564
  term structure of interest and, 91
  value of money and, 7–8
information efficiency, 364–5, 370, 379
instalment credit, 211
insurance, credit, *see* credit insurance
Insurance and Superannuation Commission, 185
insurance companies, 182, 185–6, 199, 242–3, 264
intangible assets, 339, 341, 342, 343, 356
intercompany loans, 198–9, 208,
'interest only' loans, 37
interest rate parity, 678–82, 688
interest rate swaps, *see* swap transactions
interest rates
  changing on loan contracts, 65–6
  commercial bill, 204
  concept of, 30–1
  convertible note, 250
  debentures, unsecured notes and, 235, 235$n$, 2367, 236$n$, 237$n$
  debt and, 83, 233–4, 309
  default risk structure of, 85, 92–4, 496
  elasticity bond duration and, 101–2
  eurocurrency loans and, 706–7
  financial leases and, 614
  fixed terms of, 233, 240, 245, 246
  floating rates of, 232, 233, 241, 246
  forward-rate agreements and, 449–50
  fully drawn advance, 209
  function of, 77
  inflation and, 358, 678, 684–6
  intercompany loans and, 199
  inventory loan and, 210
  market determination of, 89$n$
  monetary policy and, 184
  nominal/real terms of, 8
  options and, 463
  overdrafts and, 19, 207, 760, 760$n$
  risk and, 83, 84–5, 89–90, 92–4, 134, 233
  risk-free, *see* risk-free interest rates
  short-term deposits and, 765–6
  term loan, 240
  term structure of, 85–92, 517
  *see also* compound interest; deregulation; immunisation; international financial management; market interest rates; simple interest; swaps
interest-withholding tax, 708$n$
intermediated funding, 173, 175
internal equity finance, 228–30
internal rate of return
  compared to net present value, 117, 120–3, 130
  incremental, 123–4
  indeterminate, 116–18

# INDEX 833

investment evaluation and, 111, 112,
    114–18, 119, 120, 125
  multiple, 116–18
  mutually exclusive investments and,
    123–4
  simulation analysis and, 577
international financial management
  background to, 187, 671–2
  empirical evidence on behaviour of
    exchange rates and, 688–92
  exchange management risk and,
    692–9, 745
  foreign currency borrowing and,
    703–15
  foreign exchange market and, 672–8
  hedging and, 694–9
  introduction to, 670
  investment diversification and, 699–
    703
  rates of inflation, spot exchange,
    forward exchange and, 678–87
international Fisher effect, *see* uncovered
  interest parity
International Swap Dealers Association,
  244
intrinsic value, 461
inventory
  benefits and costs of holding, 727–9
  certainty and management of, 729–36
  defined, 722, 727
  economic order quantity model and,
    729–32
  expected customer-service level and,
    738–41
  just-in-time system and, 741
  loans on, 210
  management of stockout and, 728, 737
  reorder point, 736–7
  stockouts, 728, 729, 737–41
  types of, 727
  uncertainty and management of,
    736–41
inventory turnover, 736–7, 741, 794,
  799–800
investment allowance, 610n, 629
investment analysts, 382
investment companies, 186
investment decisions, 1, 2, 24, 77, 615
investment evaluation
  accounting rate of return method of,
    111, 125–8, 799
  benefit-cost ratio and, 124–5
  discounted cash flow methods of,
    111, 112, 113–25, 302, 502, 503,
    799
  equivalent annual value method, 560–2
  *see also* risk-adjusted discount rate
  internal rate of return method of, 111,
    112, 114–18, 119, 120, 121
  multiple and indeterminate internal rate
    of return and, 116–18
  net present value method of, 111, 112,
    113–14, 121, 497, 544–57
  net terminal value method of, 112n
  pay-back method of, 111, 126, 128–30
  principles and methods of, 107–33,
    543–602
  'real' options and, 497, 543–602
  *see also* abandonment decisions;
    replacement decisions

investors
  attitude to risk of, 138–42, 143, 147,
    151
  conflicts of interest between, 316–18,
    319–20
  diversification by, 147–52, 320, 504
  liability of, 214
  managers decisions and, 25, 266,
    319–20, 347
  professional types of, 381–2
  tax exempt, 308, 309
  utility function and, 138–42
  *see also* debtholders; dividends;
    income tax; shareholders

January effect, 391–2, 394, 396, 399
just-in-time system, 741

law of conservation of value, 298–9
law of one price, 683–4
lease-back agreements, sale and, 605–6
leasing and equipment finance
  accounting for, 608–10
  advantages of possible, 623–6
  cross-border, 605, 608, 642
  establishing advantage for, 618–19
  introduction to, 603–4
  investment decisions and, 615
  leveraged, 605, 606–8
  operating, 604–5, 608, 609, 621–3
  policy of, 627–8
  sale and lease-back, 605–6, 623
  setting rentals of, 610–12
  tax and, 608–10, 619–21, 623–4, 626,
    627
  types of, 604–8
  *see also* commercial hire purchase;
    financial leases
leverage effect, 235, 249
leverage ratios, 353, 796
  *see also* capital structure
leveraged leases, 605, 606–8
liabilities
  companies and, 2, 3, 213, 214–15
  debentures and, 237
  lenders and, 92
  secondary markets and, 173
  short-term assets and, 724
  trade credit, 195–6
LIBOR, 706–7, 709, 710
life insurance companies, 92, 94, 183,
  185–6, 242–3, 606
liquid assets
  defined, 720n, 722, 744
  motives for holding, 746–7
Liquid Assets and Government
  Securities, 179, 192n
liquidation, *see* bankruptcy costs
liquidity management
  authorised dealers and, 184
  cash budgets and, 746, 748–52
  cash management models of, 752–63
  defined, 744–5
  major issues in, 747–8
  overview of, 744–8
  pay-back period and, 129–30
  portfolio theory and, 766–7
  secondary markets and, 173
  short-term securities and, 763–6
  takeovers and, 640

treasurers and, 767–8
treasury management and, 744–5
liquidity premium theory, 89–90, 91
liquidity ratios, 793–4
liquidity risk, 764
loan contracts
  changing interest rates on, 65–6
  covenants in, 317–18
  principal-and-interest, 60–6
  terms required for, 63–5
loan security, *see* secured loans
long-term finance
  balance between short-term and, 2
  cost of, 513–15
  sources of, 213–54

Macquarie Bank, 183
margin calls, 413–14
mark-to-market rule, 413
market interest rates, 78, 83–5
market model, 158, 518
market portfolio, 154, 161–2, 166
market risk, *see* systematic risk
market segmentation, 91–2
marketability of securities, 94, 206, 763,
  766
marketable debt, 232, 233–4, 235–9,
  511–12, 513
Martin Report, 174, 174n
merchant banks
  banks interest in, 182
  broking houses interest of, 219n
  business funding and, 175
  deposits with, 766
  described, 177–80
  functions of, 178
  futures contracts and, 415
  intercompany loans and, 199
  issue of ordinary shares and, 216, 218,
    219
  lease finance and, 603, 606
  short-term money market and, 198,
    200, 202, 204, 206, 211
  syndicated loans and, 241
  term loans and, 241
  trends in, 178–80
  *see also* deregulation
mergers, *see* takeovers
Miller and Orr model of cash
  management, 758–60
Modigliani and Miller analysis of capital
  structure, 296–303, 304–10, 313,
  323, 335, 336, 338, 354
money, value of, 7–8
  *see also* deregulation; time value
money market, 173n, 178, 194
Moody's Investors Service, 93, 94n
Mortgage Guaranteed Insurance
  Corporation of Australia Ltd, 181
mortgage loans
  long-term, 242–3
  short-term, 210–11
  *see also* First Australian National
    Mortgage Corporation; National
    Mortgage Market Corporation;
    secondary mortgage markets
motor vehicle finance, 185, 210, 603,
  604
mutually exclusive investments, 118–24,
  557–65

National Mortgage Market Corporation, 181, 181n
natural logarithms, 64n
negative pledge lending, 243
net cash flows, 502, 539, 542, 544–5, 546–9, 554–7
net operating cash flows, 292, 292n, 293, 296, 533–4
net present value
 abandonment decisions and, 565, 566
 accounts receivable management and, 781–85
 application of, 113–14
 capital rationing and, 587–8, 589
 decision-tree analysis and, 580, 581–5
 defined, 22–3, 544
 Fisher's Separation Theorem and, 23, 24, 114
 internal rate of return and, 120–4
 leases and, 620, 622
 mutually exclusive projects and, 557, 561–2, 563–4, 565
 project evaluation and, 111, 112, 112n, 119, 120, 123, 125, 130, 497, 544–57, 568–9, 570, 571–2
 sensitivity analysis and, 572–6
 simulation analysis and, 576–8
 takeovers and, 634, 643–4
net terminal value, 112n
nominal interest rates, 37–40
non-bank bills, 202–3, 766
non-callable deposits, 191, 191n, 200
non-discounted cash flow methods, see investment evaluation
non-diversifiable risk, see systematic risk
non-marketable debt, 232–3, 239–43, 505, 511, 512–13, 515
note issuance facility, 708–9

objectives
 of investment and financing decisions, 2
 of firms, 3, 6, 13–14, 113, 114, 115, 361, 744
 of managers, 10–11, 587
 of shareholders, see shareholders
on-market takeover announcements, 651, 660
operating leases, 604–5, 608, 609, 621–3, 627–8
optimum capital structure, see capital structure
options
 capital budgeting and 'real', 497
 contingent claims, as, 494–8
 exercise price of, 455, 461, 464, 465, 470, 471, 487n
 foreign currency, 485–91, 699
 forward contracts and, 488–9
 hedge ratios, 481
 intrinsic value, 461
 market efficiency and, 479
 merchant banks and, 178, 179
 nature of, 454–6
 on futures, 415, 415n, 458, 491–4
 prices of, 455, 457, 458–85
 placement, see private issue
 rights issue of, 223
 see also binomial approach; Black–Scholes model; call options on futures; contingent claims; put options on futures; share options
ordinary annuities, 51–4, 57–8, 514
ordinary perpetuities, 52, 57–8
ordinary shares
 alternative issues of, 224–8
 bond yields and required rate of return on, 94
 bonus issues of, 224–6, 281–2, 281n
 broker to issues of, 218–19
 buy-backs/repurchases of, 228
 cost of, 516–19
 deferred, 228
 dividends on, 76, 78, 80–2, 83, 94, 173, 234, 248, 265, 273, 274–5, 276, 325, 376–7, 379–80, 394–5, 397, 516
 financial leverage and, 294–6
 general characteristics of, 213–15
 historical price of, 401, 401n
 information asymmetry and signalling and, 324–5
 maximising market value of, 6, 10, 13–14
 options on, 226–8
 par value of, 213–14, 215
 portfolios of, 143, 368, 369, 402–3, 701
 pre-marketing of, 217, 218
 price-earnings ratio of, 82–3, 216
 price movements of, see capital market efficiency
 pricing new, 216–18, 404
 private issues of, 215–16, 223–4
 public issues of, 1, 216–19, 352, 404
 response to new financing of, 350
 rights issue of, 219–23
 takeovers and, 635, 641–2, 646–8, 657–61
 underwriting issues of, 216, 218
 valuation of, 78–83, 94, 273–6
 voting rights and, 214, 214n
 see also Australian Stock Exchange; capital market efficiency; exchange offers and recapitalisations; options
overdrafts, 198, 199, 206–8, 512–13, 520, 744–5, 760–3, 760n
 security for, 207–8
overnight loans, 199
overseas borrowing, see international financial management

'par value' concept for shares, 213–14, 215
partial takeovers, 651–2
 proportional bidding, 652
partnerships, 2–3, 537
pay-back method of project evaluation, 111, 126, 128–30
pecking order theory, 325, 326, 335–6, 340, 341, 348–50, 351, 352
perfect certainty, 26, 78–9, 83
perpetuity-due annuities, 52n
personal taxes, see capital structure; income tax
placement, see private issue
political risk, 358
portfolio theory
 asset pricing and, 134–71

cash management and, 766–7
 see also Capital Asset Pricing Model
Potter Partners, 178, 396
preference shares, 248–9, 251–3, 293, 347, 357, 515
present value
 of annuities, 58
 of annuities due, 54–5, 59
 at compound interest, 37
 of deferred annuities, 52, 55–7
 of financial assets, 77
 of futures contracts, 414
 of ordinary annuities, 52–4, 57–8
 of perpetuities, 52
 at simple interest, 33
price bubbles, 386
price-earnings ratio, 82–3, 395, 641–2
price effect, 84
price elasticity, 101
primary markets, 173
principal-and-interest loan contracts, 60–6, 243
principal repayment, 83
production possibilities curve, 14–15
profit maximisation, 6, 13
profitability index for investment evaluation, see benefit-cost ratio
profitability ratios, 797
project analysis techniques, 572–8
project evaluation
 applying methods of, 543–602
 cost of capital and, 502
 principles and methods of, 107–33
project managers, 109
project selection, 403, 585–9
promissory notes, 180, 181, 198, 205–6, 709
prospectuses, 217–18, 217n, 218n, 223, 238
public issue
 of debentures, 185, 236
 of ordinary shares, 1, 216–18, 352, 404
purchasing power parity, 679, 683–6, 685n, 690
pure residual dividend policy, 257
put-call parity, 466–9, 490
put options, 415, 454–6, 458–60, 464–6, 699n

quick ratio, 793–4, 799

random-walk hypothesis, 365–6, 365n, 384, 401, 691, 758, 762
rate of interest, see interest rates
rates of return
 after tax, 113
 arbitrage pricing model and, 164, 165
 compensation and higher, 79–80
 cost of capital and, 505, 517–18
 internal, see internal rate of return
 measurement of, 49–51
 required, 300, 354, 781
 risk and, 134–8, 143, 148, 234
 see also accounting rate of return; cost of capital; geometric rates of return
ratings, Australian corporate and government, 93–4, 95
real interest rates, 40–2

# INDEX

real value of money, 7–8, 30
recapitalisation, *see* exchange offers and recapitalisation
reducing balance depreciation, 547, 548, 550
reinvestment effect, 84
rental agreements, *see* operating leases
replacement decisions, 558–65, 566–8
Reserve Bank of Australia,
  authorised dealers and, 183–4, 183$n$
  banks and, 182–3, 183$n$, 192–3, 192$n$
  bonds and, 91
  commercial bills market and, 199–200, 764
  monetary policy and 184, 190
  open-market operations of, 191
  overdraft interest rates and, 207
  powers of, 191
residual value
  lease agreements and, 609–10
  project life and, 546, 566, 567, 581
retained profits, 230, 349, 519
retirement decisions, *see* abandonment decisions
revolving credit bill facility, 204
rights issues, 219–23, 398, 494–5
risk
  asset pricing and, 152–61
  beta factor, 393
  CAPM and, 160–1, 502
  cash flow variables and, 358
  certainty equivalents and, 568–72
  currency swaps and, 715
  debentures, unsecured notes and, 236
  debt securities and, 79–80, 82–3, 84–5, 92–4, 205
  decision-tree approach to, 777
  dividend decisions and, 261–2
  effect of debt on, 234, 249, 317
  financial leverage and, 293–6
  futures contracts and, 416, 418, 426, 427–8
  interest rates and, 84–5, 89–90, 233
  intermediation and, 175
  investment decisions and, 26–7, 302–3, 315
  investor utility function and, 138–43
  leases and, 626
  measures for, 135–6
  options and, 463, 481–2, 492
  ordinary shares and, 94
  project evaluation and, 109, 502, 544, 572–8
  return and, 134–8
  saving-deficit unit and, 173
  sensitivity analysis and, 572–3
  simulation and, 577–8
  standard deviation as measure of, 142–3
  treasury management and, 745
  uncertainty compared with, 135$n$
  *see also* basis risk; business risk; default risk; efficient frontier; exchange risk; inflation risk; political risk; systematic risk; time and uncertainty; uncertainty; unsystematic risk
risk-adjusted discount rate, 113$n$, 568–72
risk-averse investors, 138, 139, 140, 141–2, 143, 147, 151, 154, 261, 301

risk-free interest rates, 113$n$, 152, 153, 154, 463, 517, 525
risk independence, 503–4
risk neutral investors, 138, 139, 140
risk seeking investors, 138, 139, 140
risk-weighted assets, 192–3

S and P–Australian Ratings, 93–4, 95, 778
safety stock, 737
sale and lease-back agreements, 605–6, 623
sales forecasting, 749
savings banks, 200$n$
savings-deficit units, 172, 173, 174, 175
savings-surplus units, 172, 173, 174, 175
second board markets, 176
secondary markets, 173, 175, 202, 219
secondary mortgage market, 181–2
secondary options markets, 457
secured debt, 235–9, 241–3
Securities and Exchange Commission, 381
securitisation, 180–1
security market line, 155–8, 161
semi-strong-form efficiency, 364, 370–80, 402
sensitivity analysis, 572–6
share options, 226–8
share price index, 415, 441–4, 446–7, 492, 517
share splits, 226
shareholders
  capital market and, 173
  capital structure decisions and, 300, 301, 309, 319–20, 321, 347
  definition of, 3
  Fisher's analysis and, 15, 21
  imputation tax system and, 286, 287–90
  interest cost of debt and, 233
  liability of, 214–15
  objectives of, 10, 113, 114, 115
  required rate of return on, 300
  takeovers and, 639, 658–9
  *see also* investors; ordinary shares; voting rights
shares, *see* ordinary shares; preference shares
short-term assets, *see* accounts receivable; assets and asset management; inventory; liquidity management
short-term finance
  balance between long-term and, 2
  bank overdrafts as, 198, 206–8
  bills of exchange as, 209
  commercial bills as, 199–205
  cost of, 511–13
  definition of, 195
  factoring as a source of, 210
  finance leases as, 209, 211
  fully drawn advances as, 208–9
  instalment credit as, 211
  intercompany loans as, 198–9
  inventory loans as, 210
  money-market source of, 197–206
  mortgages as, 210–11
  promissory notes as, 205–6
  sources of, 511

stockbrokers and, 177
  terms of, 196
  trade credit and, 195–7
  *see also* banks
short-term money market, 177, 183–4, 194, 197–206
short-term mortgages, 210–11
short-term security management, *see* liquidity management
SIBOR, 706–7
simple interest, 31–4
simulation, 576–8
sole proprietorship, 2
specialised assets, 627
specific account credit insurance, 788, 788$n$
speculating, 409, 418, 419–20, 432, 434, 439–40, 442–3
spin-offs, 655–6
spot exchange rates, 672–4, 675–6, 677, 678, 680, 681, 685, 686, 688–9
spot prices, 416–17, 418, 421, 422, 423, 427
stable dividend policy, 257
Standard and Poor's Rating Group, 93–4, 95, 778
standard deviation, 136–7, 140, 142–3, 144, 146–7, 146$n$, 147, 148, 149
Statutory Reserve Deposits, 179, 191$n$, 200
stock exchange/market
  anomalies of, 396–400, 405
  brokers and, 177, 183
  broking houses and, 175–7
  crash of 1987 and, 387
  efficient market hypothesis and, 382–96
  financial managers and, 403
  listing on, 215, 218
  *see also* Sydney Stock Exchange
Stock Exchange Automated Trading System, 176
stockouts, 728, 729, 737–41
straight-line depreciation, 547, 548, 550
strong-form market efficiency, 364, 381–2
subordinated debt, 192, 192$n$, 233, 497
subscription price, 220, 222, 223, 235
superannuation funds, 185–6, 242, 275, 278, 280, 281, 282, 286, 381, 606
swap transactions
  currency, 675, 677, 711, 712–15
  interest rate, 232, 2448, 711–12
Sydney Computerised Overnight Market, 415–16
Sydney Futures Exchange, 408, 414–16, 429–37, 441–4, 458, 491
syndicated loans, 241
systematic risk, 8, 159–60, 320, 503, 504, 517, 518, 522, 523

10-Year Treasury Bonds, 415, 437–41
takeovers
  agency problems and, 321, 637
  alternative valuation approaches to, 648–9
  cost of, 643–8
  defences against, 653–4
  definition of, 633–4
  economic evaluation of, 643–8

empirical evidence on, 657–65
formal offer, 650–1
importance of, 634
reasons for, 636–43
regulation of, 649–52
roles of, 642–3
synergy in, 643
types of, 635
waves under, 635
*see also* corporate restructuring; partial takeovers
tangible assets, 339, 341, 342, 344, 356
tax loss selling, 392
taxation, *see* capital gains tax; classical income tax system; company tax; imputation tax system; income tax
Term Loan Fund, 240
term loans, 232, 239–41, 240$n$, 707
term of securities, 84–5
term structure of interest rates
explanation of, 85
market segmentation theory of, 91–2
premium theory of, 85–90
thin trading problem, 397, 398
time and uncertainty, 7
time value
of money, 7, 29–106, 502
of options, 462, 463
Tobin's $q$ ratio, 662
trade, *see* international financial management
trade bills, *see* commercial bills
trade credit, *see* accounts payable; accounts receivable
trade-off theory of capital structure, 321–3, 325, 326, 335, 335$n$, 338, 339, 340, 341–2, 345, 347, 351, 352

*Trade Practices Act* 1974, 639, 652
transferable loan certificates, 710
Treasury bonds, 168, 415, 437–41, 437$n$
treasury management, 745
Treasury Notes, 85, 152, 199, 764
triangular arbitrage, 676–7
trust deeds, 237, 238
*see also* unit trusts
trustees, 237, 238
turn-of the month effects, 392–3, 397

unbiased forward rates, 679, 683, 688–9
uncertainty
cash management models assuming, 758–63
dividend policy and resolution of, 261–2, 266
inventory management under, 736–41
risk compared with, 135$n$
securities and, 79–82, 89, 92–4
*see also* risk
uncovered interest parity, 679, 679$n$, 686–7, 690–1
underwriting, 172, 177, 178, 186, 206, 216, 218, 218$n$, 219, 223, 224, 497, 708
unique risk, *see* unsystematic risk
unit trusts, 186, 381
unsecured loans, 235, 241, 242
unsecured notes, *see* debentures and unsecured notes
unsubordinated debt, 233
unsystematic risk, 8, 159–60, 161, 320, 503

valuation
of cash flows, 46–51, 555–6
of debt securities, 76–106

of financial futures, 445–7
of levered shares and risky zero-coupon debt, 495–6
of risky assets, 163
of shares, 82–3
and takeovers, 636, 637, 638, 643–9
value
company defined, of, 506
concept of, 6–7
financial leverage and company, 330–4
law of conservation of, 298–9
*see also* capital structure
value additivity principle, 46–8
Value Line, 396
vertical takeovers, 635, 638

weak-form efficiency, 364
runs tests, 367–8
serial correlation tests, 366, 368, 384, 385
weighted average cost of capital, 505–7, 509–10, 519–21, 526–8, 536, 538–9, 554, 556
whole turnover policies, 788
wholesale finance, 210
Woolworths, 217, 219
work-in-process inventory, 727
working capital, *see* assets and asset management

yield curves, 85–6, 88, 89, 90, 92, 99, 105
yield-to-maturity, 51$n$, 438

zero-coupon bonds, 76$n$, 86, 98, 100, 239
zero-coupon debt, 495, 495$n$